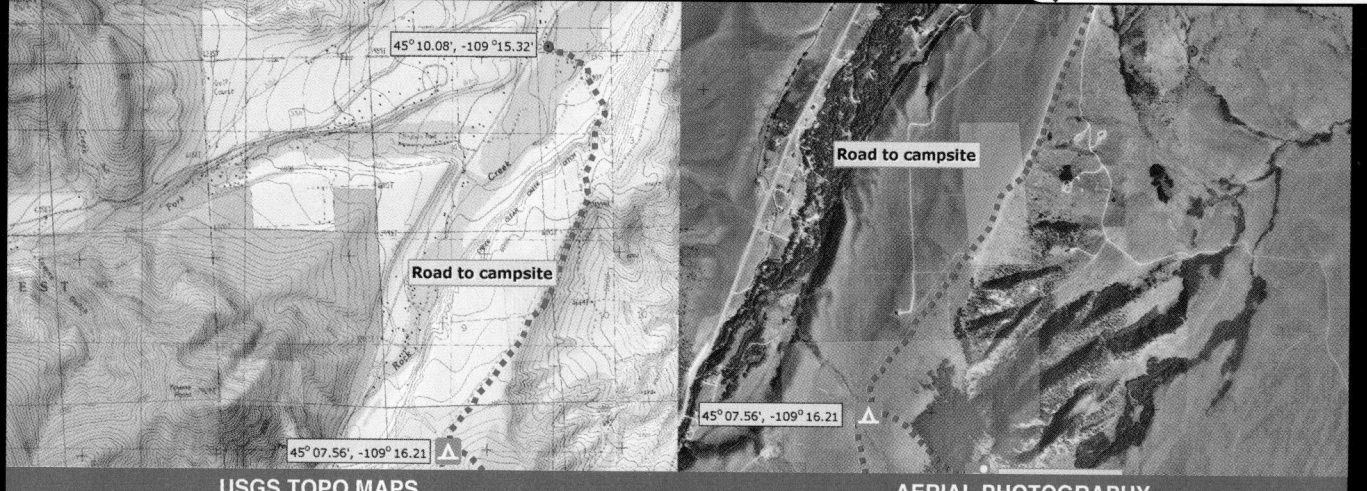

# Stoeger Publishing ®
## Great Outdoor Books & More Since 1924

For over 80 years, Stoeger Publishing has been dedicated to publishing the best outdoor titles available. Currently our catalog of books includes more than 80 titles on hunting, shooting, firearms, reloading, collecting, cooking game and fish, motorcycles, trucks and more.

## GUN TRADER'S GUIDE
*Twenty-seventh Edition*
For more than half a century, millions of gun buffs have chosen Gun Trader's Guide as their main reference guide for firearms identification and pricing. The Gun Trader's Guide features annually updated specifications, dates of manufacture, and up to date market values for more than 6,000 domestic and foreign handguns, rifles, and shotguns.

## ARCHER'S BIBLE 2005
*Edited by Keith Sutton*
Archer's Bible is an annually updated, comprehensive guide to archery equipment, accessories and related gear, showcasing thousands of items ranging from the latest high-tech bows to tree stands and accessories. Feature articles by experts in the field provide fascinating insights into the world of archery and bowhunting.

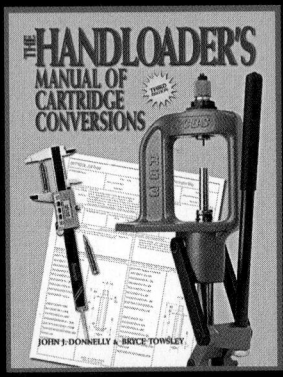

## THE HANDLOADER'S MANUAL of CARTRIDGE CONVERSIONS
*John J. Donnelley and Bryce M. Towsley*
Stoeger's classic guide has been revised and updated with a new format and additional cartridge data. The Handloader's Manual provides the data and drawings needed to convert modern materials into more than 900 rifle and pistol cartridge cases.

Archer's Bible Presents
## The BOWHUNTING GUIDE
*Dwight Schuh*
Expert archer Dwight Schuh explores every aspect of the challenging sport of bowhunting. Step-by-step he explains the skills of hunting with a bow: how to shoot a hunting bow, choosing equipment, how to stalk game, aiming skills and a wealth of other information.

## WILD ABOUT SEAFOOD
*Edited by Jay Langston*
Stoeger presents the fifth title in our "Wild About" series of game cookbooks. Wild About Seafood offers original and meticulously crafted recipes filled with fresh new ways to prepare a wide variety of popular seafood from Maine Lobster to bluefin tuna.

# Shooter's Bible

No. 95 2005 Edition

Stoeger Publishing Company, Accokeek, Maryland

**Stoeger Publishing**
*Great Outdoor Books & More Since 1924*

## STOEGER PUBLISHING COMPANY
is a division of Benelli U.S.A.

### Benelli U.S.A.
*Vice President and General Manager:* Stephen Otway
*Vice President of Marketing and Communications:*
  Stephen McKelvain

### Stoeger Publishing Company
*President:* Jeffrey K. Reh
*Publisher:* Jay T. Langston
*Managing Editor:* Harris J. Andrews
*Design and Production Director:* Cynthia T. Richardson
*Photography Director:* Alex Bowers
*Imaging Specialist:* Williams Graves
*National Sales Manager:* Jennifer Thomas
*Sales Manager Assistant:* Julie Brownlee
*Publishing Assistant:* Christine Lawton
*Administrative Assistant:* Shannon McWilliams
*Proofreader:* Celia Beattie

*Published by:*
Stoeger Publishing Company
17603 Indian Head HIghway, Suite 200
Accokeek, Maryland 20607-2501

ISBN:0-88317-286-0                      BK0401
Library of Congress Control Number: 2003116080

Manufactured in the United States of America
*Distributed to the book trade and the sporting goods trade by:*
Stoeger Industries, Stoeger Publishing Company
17603 Indian Head HIghway, Suite 200
Accokeek, Maryland 20607-2501
301 283-6300    *Fax:* 301 283-6986

*Note:* Every effort has been made to record specifications and descriptions of guns, ammunition and accessories accurately, but the Publisher
can take no responsibility for errors or omissions. The prices shown for
guns, ammunition and accessories are manufacturers' suggested retail
prices (unless otherwise noted) and are furnished for information only.
These were in effect at press time and are subject to change without
notice. Purchasers of the book have complete freedom of choice in pricing for resale.

*Front Cover:* This year's cover exhibits just a few of the broad
array of firearms manufactured by the Beretta Holdings family of
companies. From top to bottom, they are:

| | |
|---|---|
| Sako 75 Deluxe Rifle | Beretta AL391Teknys Gold |
| Tika T3 Lite Rifle | Benelli Super Black Eagle II |
| Uberti 1866 "Yellowboy" | Franchi Alcione SX |
| Sporting Rifle | Benelli Nova Pump |
| Beretta EELL Diamond Pigeon | Stoeger Silverado Coach Gun |
| Beretta White Onyx | Beretta Model 92/96 |
| Beretta A391 Xtrema 3.5 | Semiautomatic Pistol |

---

## OTHER PUBLICATIONS:

**Gun Trader's Guide**
  "Complete Fully Illustrated Guide
    to Modern Firearms
    with Current Market Values"

**Hunting & Shooting**
  Trailing the Hunter's Moon
  Shotgunning for Deer
  Advanced Black Powder Hunting
  Archer's Bible
  Hounds of the World
  Hunting Whitetails East & West
  Hunt Club Management Guide
  The Turkey Hunter's Tool Kit:
    Shooting Savvy
  Elk Hunter's Bible
  Complete Book of
    Whitetail Hunting
  Hunting and Shooting with
    the Modern Bow
  The Ultimate in Rifle Accuracy
  Labrador Retrievers
  Hunting America's Wild Turkey
  Taxidermy Guide
  The Truth About Turkey Hunting
    According to "Cuz"
  The Whole Truth About Turkey
    Hunting According to "Cuz"

**Collecting Books**
  Sporting Collectibles
  The Working Folding Knife
  The Lore of Spices

**Firearms**
  Antique Guns
  P-38 Automatic Pistol
  The Walther Handgun Story
  Complete Guide to
    Compact Handguns
  Complete Guide to
    Service Handguns
  America's Great Gunmakers
  Firearms Disassembly with
    Exploded Views
  Rifle Guide
  Gunsmithing at Home
  The Book of the Twenty-Two
  Complete Guide to Modern Rifles
  Complete Guide to Classic Rifles
  Legendary Sporting Rifles
  FN Browning Armorer to
    the World
  Modern Beretta Firearms
  How to Buy & Sell Used Guns
  Heckler & Koch: Armorers of
    the Free World
  Spanish Handguns

**Reloading**
  The Handloader's Manual of
    Cartridge Conversions -
    3rd Edition
  Modern Sporting Rifle Cartridges
  Complete Reloading Guide

**Fishing**
  Fishing Online:
    1,000 Best Web Sites
  Fishing Made Easy
  Flyfishing for Trout A to Z
  Ultimate Bass Boats
  Bassing Bible
  The Flytier's Companion
  Deceiving Trout
  The Complete Book of
    Trout Fishing
  The Complete Book of Flyfishing
  The Flytier's Manual
  Flytier's Master Class
  Handbook of Fly Tying
  The Fly Fisherman's
    Entomological Pattern Book
  Fiberglass Rod Making

**Motorcycles & Trucks**
  The Legend of Harley-Davidson
  The Legend of Indian
  Great Trucks
  4X4 Vehicles

**Cooking Game**
  Fish & Shellfish Care & Cookery
  Game Cookbook
  Dress 'Em Out
  Wild About Venison
  Wild About Game Birds
  Wild About Fresh Water Fish
  Wild About Waterfowl
  Wild About Seafood
  World's Best Catfish Cookbook

**Fiction**
  Wounded Moon

# CONTENTS

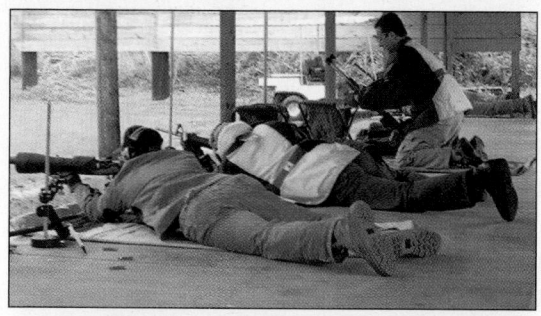

# INTRODUCTION

Four years ago the magnum craze caught fire again as firearms and ammunition manufacturers raced to tout their hottest and fastest performers. New to the magnum mania were the short magnums, and today the super short magnums are getting their fair share of press about the heavy hitters.

Going in the opposite direction, the .17 HMR has been welcomed by shooters and sales for guns and ammo alike have skyrocketed. This year, the new .17 Mach2 hopes to duplicate sales enjoyed by its bigger brother. Spanning the gap between the new .17s and always-popular .22 centerfires, Sturm Ruger is teaming up with Hornady Manufacturing once again to introduce a scorcher labeled as the .204 Ruger. Initial testing puts this cartridge above the mystical 4,000 fps threshold. Ruger is offering their No. 1 and M77 bolt actions in .204, and Thompson/Center is already tooled up to offer carbine-length barrels to fit their single-shot actions. See more about the .204 Ruger on page 99.

Among the hand cannons, the .375 JDJ is big news in the Thompson/Center Contender G2. During a hunt in western Kentucky I found the T/C rifle version of the .375 JDJ is a handy woods carbine that performs like a sledgehammer on whitetails. The .375 JDJ is based on the .444 Marlin case and sends 300 grain bullets down range at better than 1,900 fps.

In this new edition of Shooter's Bible, we're offering up yet again a thorough selection of shooting gear, accompanied with articles that range from historical celebrations of the gun making legends like Beretta and the many companies beneath the Beretta Holdings umbrella. Several more features share how-to knowledge on subjects from shotguns and slug loads, to recoil reduction, and brand new research on high-performance muzzleloaders.

Special thanks go to Specifications Editor, Wayne van Zwoll and Stoeger's staff of editors and designers who teamed up to put this book in your hands. We hope you enjoy The Shooter's Bible as much as we have delighted in bringing together, this, the finest of firearms reference guides.

*Special thanks to the National Rifle Association, for access to their image archives.*

Good shooting!
Jay Langston, Editor & Publisher

# FEATURE ARTICLES

# The World of Beretta

by Harris Andrews

For nearly five centuries, the Beretta family of Gardonne Val Trompia in Italy's Alpine north has remained dedicated to the craft of producing fine firearms and holds the distinction of being the world's oldest industrial enterprise. Records show that in 1526 Bartolomeo Beretta of Gardonne received 296 ducats for the manufacture of 185 harquebus barrels for the Grand Arsenal in Venice, the beginning of a long relationship between the Berettas and the powerful Venetian Republic.

By the 19th century, despite the upheavals of the Napoleonic Wars and the struggle for Italian Reunification, Pietro Antonio Beretta extended his market throughout Italy and his son, Giuseppe, moved Beretta into the international arena. At the beginning of the 20th century, Pietro Beretta modernized manufacturing methods, turning Beretta's Val Trompia factory into one of the most modern firearms production facilities in the world. Fabbrica d'Armi Pietro Beretta provided weapons to

**Completed in 1925, Villa Beretta overlooks formal gardens on the grounds of the Beretta factory in Gardonne.**

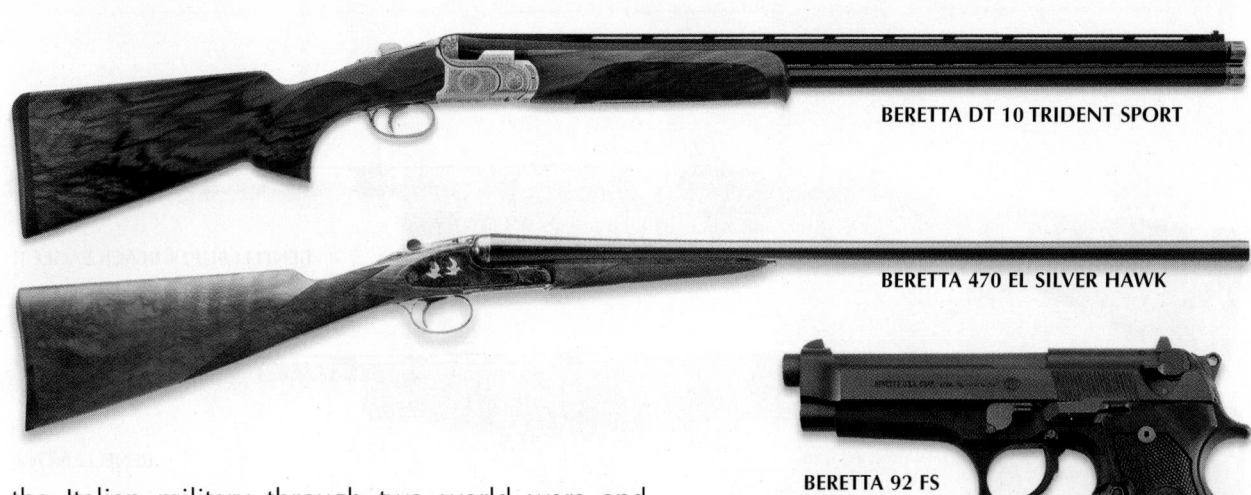

BERETTA DT 10 TRIDENT SPORT

BERETTA 470 EL SILVER HAWK

BERETTA 92 FS

BERETTA 8000 F COUGAR

the Italian military through two world wars and moved into the international arena in the post-war years creating successful ventures in the military, law enforcement and private sectors.

Today, under the leadership of Ugo Gussalli Beretta and his sons, Franco and Pietro, Beretta continues nearly five centuries of manufacturing excellence and fine craftsmanship, combined with investments in technology, organization and growing product lines, to make Beretta one of the world's premier industrial concerns. Beretta offers an exceptional array of fine firearms including the Onyx, Pigeon, and Ultralight series of over/under field shotguns and the 391, Teknys, Urika and Xtrema line of autoloaders. Beretta's also offers classic Silver Hawk 12- and 20-gauge doubles and produces the DT 10 Trident, 682 Gold and 687 Pigeon lines of world-class competition shotguns. Fine craftsmanship is displayed in some models with the choice of select wood and the option of hand engraving and inlay. Sporting arms comprise about 75 percent of Beretta's production and are exported to more than a hundred countries.

Stacks of walnut stock blanks await fitting and hand finishing. Stocks and fore-ends are manufactured by a Beretta subsidiary in Trento.

A gunsmith works on shotgun barrels at the Beretta main factory in Gardonne.

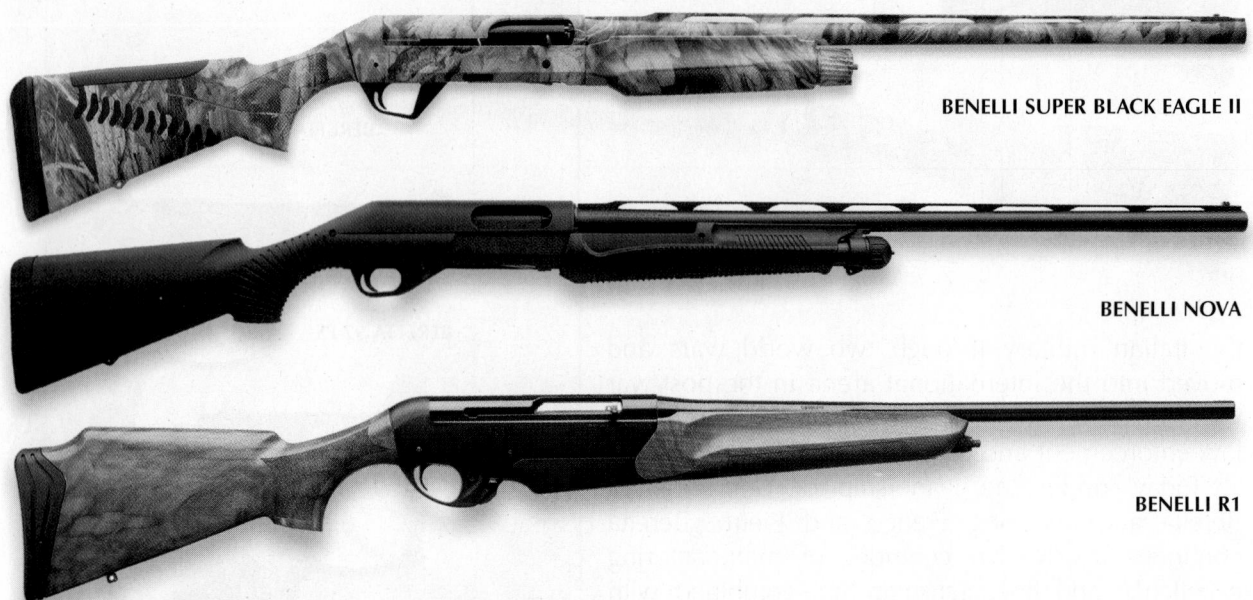

BENELLI SUPER BLACK EAGLE II

BENELLI NOVA

BENELLI R1

A computer-controlled robotic arm inserts shotgun receivers into a CNC machine at the Benelli factory in Urbino. The use of precision automation guarantees accurate machining of precision parts.

In 1985 the United States Department of Defense selected the 9mm Beretta Model 92SB-F pistol to replace the venerable 1911 Colt. By 1989 Beretta USA began production of the Model 92—designated the M9—in modern facilities at Accokeek, Maryland. Beretta produces and licenses manufacture of the Model 92 and other handguns for military and law enforcement authorities around the world. Beretta handguns for sport and home protection range from the .22 caliber Neos target pistol and civilian version of the Model 92/96 to the compact Cheetah, Bobcat and Tomcat lines.

In recent years the family of corporations under the umbrella of Beretta Holdings has expanded to include several innovative and dynamic arms manufacturers and distributors and a key publishing concern dedicated to the outdoor sporting industry.

In 1989 Beretta added Benelli, a manufacturer of innovative self-loading shotguns, to its holdings. Benelli is located in the historic Renaissance city of Urbino in the province of Pesaro. Situated on a hill between the valleys of the Metaurus and Foglia Rivers, the city became a leading manufacturer of precision devices including clocks, compasses, scientific instruments and firearms under the rule of Duke Federico of Montefeltro in the 1500s.

In 1911, the Benelli family opened a factory in nearby Pesaro to manufacture bicycles, motorbikes and trucks. In 1920, Giovanni

A Franchi craftsman hand polishes the components of a shotgun lock in the factory in Brescia. Hand finishing guarantees flawless operation.

Benelli, pursuing a personal dream, built his first side-by-side shotgun using English Greener locks and German Krupp steel barrels and continued his experimentation over the next two decades designing his own 12-gauge autoloader with a lightweight aluminum alloy receiver. Benelli's desire to produce fine arms was finally realized in the mid-1960s, with the opening of a modern factory in Urbino—Benelli Armi — to produce shotguns featuring a revolutionary, super-fast inertia action.

Under Beretta, the Benelli plant was modernized in 1995 with space-age computer-controlled machinery and state-of-the-art systems for heat-treating and assembly. Benelli is recognized the world over for its

FRANCHI 612

FRANCHI ALCIONE T

BENELLI M4 1014
LIMITED EDITION

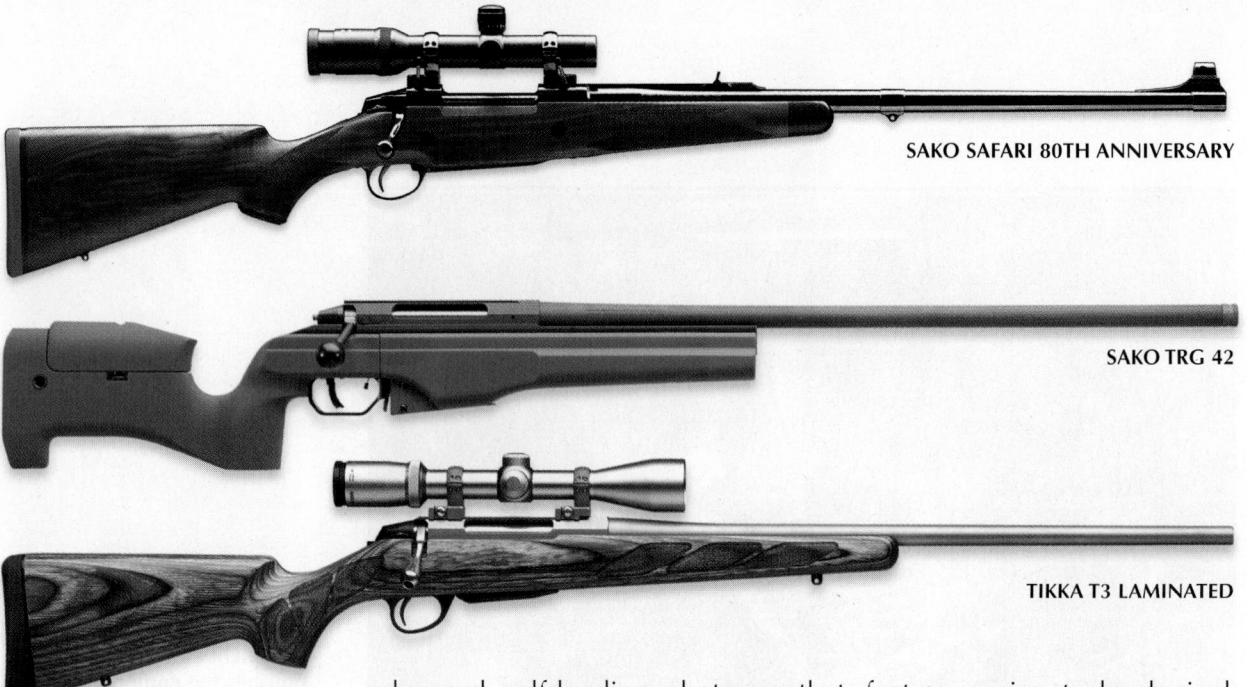

SAKO SAFARI 80TH ANNIVERSARY

SAKO TRG 42

TIKKA T3 LAMINATED

advanced self-loading shotguns that feature major technological advances ranging from the world's fastest inertia action to cryogenically treated barrels and sophisticated recoil management systems. Benelli produces a full line of autoloading shotguns including the Super Black Eagle, M1 Field and Sport II and one of the world's most advanced pump guns—the Nova. Recently Benelli has entered the world of hunting rifles with the pioneering R1 Rifle design, an autoloader that features a self-regulating gas-operated system and sleek modern design. In addition to its sporting arms, Benelli also holds the contract for the U.S. armed forces M4 combat shotgun.

In 1996, the Luigi Franchi Company was added to Beretta Holdings. Located in Brescia, about ten miles southwest of Gardonne, the venerable firm's association with shotguns dates back to its founding in 1868. Franchi has always prided itself on the quality of their barrels and the first Franchi shotgun to gain international renown was the Aquila side-by-side followed in later years by the hammerless Imperiale Montecarlo and the external hammer Diana. Restructured and modernized by Beretta, Franchi has remained in the forefront of technology and has pioneered in the use of light alloys. As a division of Benelli, Franchi lines include the Alcione and lightweight Veloce over/unders and several models—612, 620, 712, 720, 912 and 48 AL—of light-receiver autoloaders. Franchi contributed toward reinventing the combat shotgun with the SPAS 12, and SPAS 15, magazine-fed double-action weapons used by police and military forces.

Finnish arms manufacturer Sako Ltd. was purchased by Beretta Holdings in 1999. Formed by the merger of three companies, Sako, Tikkakosi and Valmet in 1921, shortly after Finland gained its independence from Russia, Sako became known in the United States for well-crafted, accurate hunting rifles shortly after World War II. The acquisition of Sako furnished Beretta with a source of quality, bolt-action hunting and competition rifles and ammunition. A significant product

The *Gun Trader's Guide,* published annually by Stoeger Publishing since 1953, is one of the world's premier guides to firearms values.

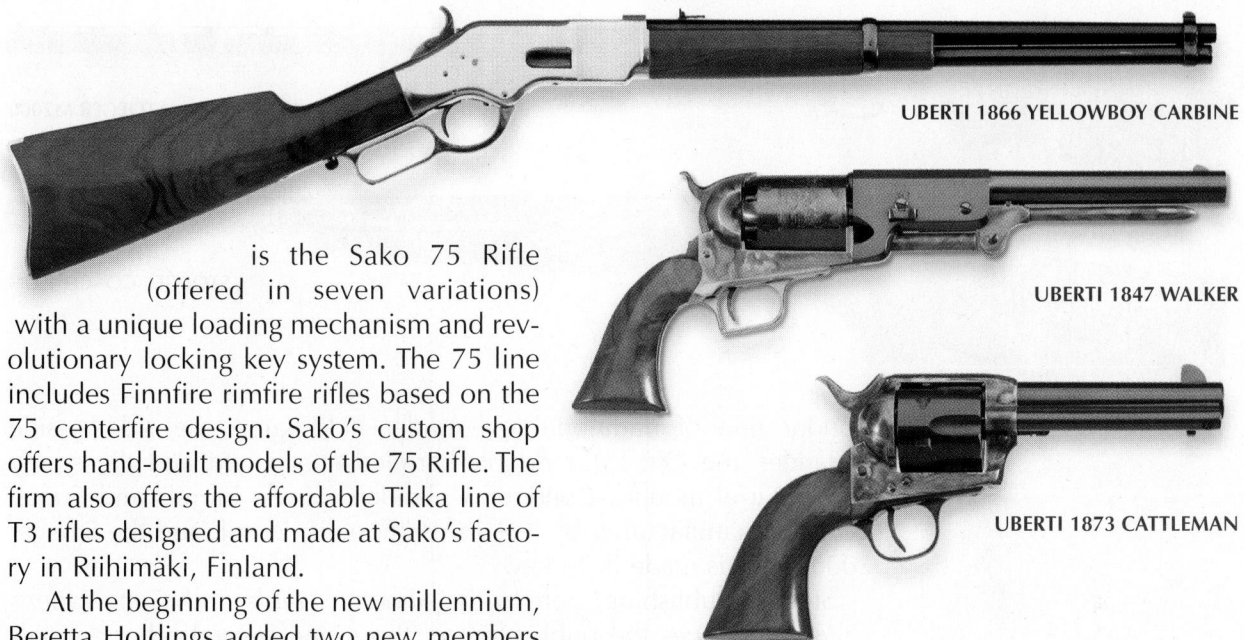

UBERTI 1866 YELLOWBOY CARBINE

UBERTI 1847 WALKER

UBERTI 1873 CATTLEMAN

is the Sako 75 Rifle (offered in seven variations) with a unique loading mechanism and revolutionary locking key system. The 75 line includes Finnfire rimfire rifles based on the 75 centerfire design. Sako's custom shop offers hand-built models of the 75 Rifle. The firm also offers the affordable Tikka line of T3 rifles designed and made at Sako's factory in Riihimäki, Finland.

At the beginning of the new millennium, Beretta Holdings added two new members to its family of corporations, Uberti and the American Stoeger Industries, both organized under Benelli USA Corp. A. Uberti Srl. was founded in 1959 by Aldo Uberti, a native of Inzino, a mountain village near Gardonne Val Trompia who had learned the craft of gunmaker at Beretta. Uberti initially specialized in quality reproductions of cap-and-ball revolvers—re-creations of the famous handguns of the Civil War era. Over the past 44 years its product line has expanded to include cartridge revolvers, single-shot and lever-action rifles, and even miniature arms. Uberti handguns range from the formidable four-pound 1847 Colt Walker revolver to the classic 1873 Cattleman, a re-creation of the famous Colt Single Action Army. Longarms include the 1860 Henry, Winchester 1866 "Yellowboy" and 1873 rifles and carbines and powerful 1885 high-wall single-shot rifles.

The other recent addition was firearms importer and distributor Stoeger Industries and its publishing house. In 1924 Austrian-born A. F. Stoeger, who held the exclusive importation agreement for Luger pistols, opened a store in the "Hells Kitchen" area of New York City. Stoeger's innovative catalog offered imported German and Austrian firearms in addition to those of famous American manufacturers. Stoeger moved uptown to Fifth Avenue in 1928 and by 1946 the *Stoeger Catalog and Handbook* had become recognized as a major source for shooters and changed its name to *Shooter's Bible*. By the 1950s Stoeger added the *Gun Trader's Guide* to its list of flagship publications.

Today, Stoeger Industries distributes the Model 2000 autoloading shotgun, the only shotgun licensed to use the Benelli inertia operating system. Other products include the

By the 1950s Stoeger's *Shooter's Bible* contained feature articles, technical data and offered hundreds of items—firearms, accessories and sporting goods—for sale.

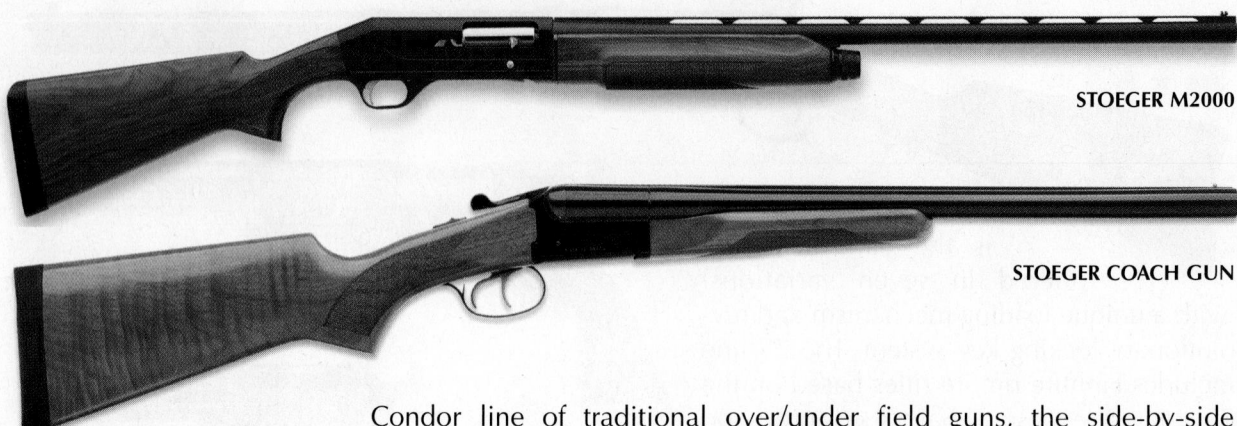

**STOEGER M2000**

**STOEGER COACH GUN**

Condor line of traditional over/under field guns, the side-by-side Uplander, the Old West double-barreled coach gun and the sturdy Single Barrel models. Condors, Uplanders, Single Barrels and Coach guns are manufactured by IGA in Veranopolis, Brazil, and the Stoeger 2000 series is made in Turkey.

Stoeger Publishing, heir to the *Shooter's Bible* and *Gun Trader's Guide*, continues the publication of those and several other annuals including Archer's and Bassing Bibles. The Stoeger list includes over seventy-five active titles on firearms, hunting, fishing, cooking and outdoor sports.

In 2003 Beretta Holdings acquired Burris Optics, a firm that has produced quality optical products such as sights and binoculars for over twenty five years. Burris continues its legacy of meticulous engineering and the use of ultrapure grades of optical glass to manufacture close to 200 different rifle and handgun scopes configurations including Euro Diamond, Black Diamond, Signature, Fullfield and other lines. Other Burris products include scope-mounting systems, binoculars, range finders, image stabilizers and spotting scopes.

At the beginning of the third millennium, the world of Beretta Holdings represents a balanced family of companies with a truly worldwide reach, offering firearms and related products to a broad spectrum of customers and interests. Beretta, Benelli, Franchi, Sako and Stoeger, the pillars of Beretta Holdings, share a heritage of innovation, craftsmanship and entrepreneurial spirit that makes them a truly important force in the world of firearms and shooting sports.

**BURRIS EURO DIAMOND
3X 10X40**

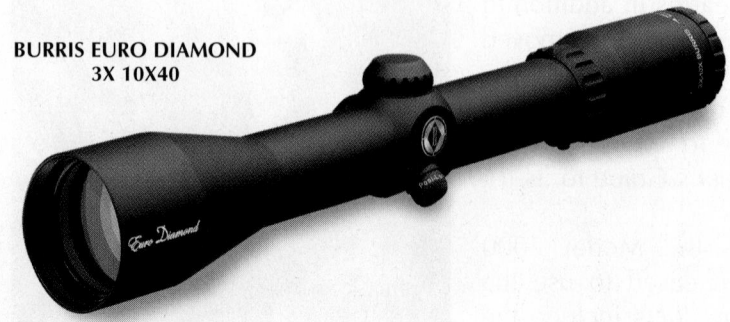

# Guns of the 101st Airborne—Iraq 2003
by Philip Schreier

The Screaming Eagles of the 101st Airborne Division (Air Assault) have had another "Rendezvous with Destiny" and continued to add chapters to their campaign history on a daily basis while in Iraq. As one of the contingency divisions of XVIII Airborne Corps, the 101st left "jump status" in 1969 while in Vietnam, trading in parachutes for helicopters. While a blow to tradition, the added maneuverability of Air Assault makes the 101st the fastest moving division in military history. Always prepared to answer the country's call for defense, the entire division mobilized for possible war with Iraq in February 2003. With record-setting speed, hundreds of trains, ships and cargo planes were packed sending the Screaming Eagles on deployment to Kuwait and becoming a lead element in Gulf War II.

On March 22, 2003, the division moved across the sand berm that separated Kuwait from Iraq, beginning an aerial and land based drive on Baghdad that took only 21 days. Over a year later, having moved from all-out war to uneasy peace, the division rotated back home to Ft. Campbell, Kentucky. They had made the longest air assault in history, moving 310 miles in one night, and used their aerial mobility to cover more territory than any other U.S. division. (Their sector stretched from Kuwait to Turkey and from Jordan to Iran.) This did not come without

**A Squad Automatic Weapon (SAW) mounted on the roof of a "Humm-V," gets a wipedown before its next mission. The fine, talc-like dust encountered in Iraq was a threat to both men and equipment.**

cost, as the 101st suffered higher combat losses than any other American unit.
Fifty-eight Eagles were killed, and 384
were wounded.

This was all done with the most
sophisticated infantry equipment that
the United States has ever fielded. Long
gone are the days where a soldier was
a draftee, worth the sum total of his
uniform, web gear and M1 Garand.
Today's infantryman is a modern mar-
vel of high-tech equipment worth
thousands of dollars and even more
thousands spent in training him to be
proficient in their use. Behind each soldier stands a variety of equipment from
trucks and howitzers to the flying-bat-
tleship AH-64D Apache Longbow helicopters; however, it is the rifleman that
remains the prime focus. As an Air
Assault unit, the arms and equipment
of the 101st are often different than
some of the other, heavier units that
were involved in the move on
Baghdad. This article will examine the
various firearms used by the division
during the yearlong campaign, especially the 101st's close-in cutting edge,
her nine infantry battalions.

## Small Arms

The primary service weapon for the
division is the M-4 carbine. At six pounds, it's a full pound and a half
lighter and significantly shorter (29 inches) than the 39-inch M16A2
rifle, the M4 allows the soldier a greater amount of maneuverability
while the flattop Picatinny rail and the Rail Interface System, purchased
separately from Knight's Armament, allow the best in accessories and
optics. M4-equipped 101st troopers often jokingly refer to the 1980's
vintage M16A2s of the rear echelon support units as "muskets." The M4
fires the NATO-standard 62-grain 5.56mm (.223) round, recognized by
its green painted tip. With a maximum effective range of 500 meters, it
is capable of firing semi-automatic or in 3-round bursts. The division's
infantrymen are carefully schooled in semiautomatic fire, often in an
urban warfare environment. Heavy cross training with their Fort
Campbell neighbors, the 5th Special Forces Group (Airborne), in pre-
deployment allowed the division's 327th, 502nd, and 187th Infantry
Regiments an advantage in the close fight.

**Flanked by friendly townspeo-
ple and a young admirer, a
member of the 101st provides
perimeter security for his
company armed with a
Beretta Model 12 SMG.**

The M4 is just the foundation for the integrated weapons system that gives the troopers their edge. The 101st infantry battalions are generously equipped with targeting equipment superior to what Special Forces units had a decade ago. Most obvious on almost every weapon are the M68 "close combat optics," the Aimpoint CompM2 red dot sight familiar to civilian shooters. These replaced the earlier CompMs the division had fielded for several years both in stateside training and in the Balkans and Afghanistan.

**Shown here with its slide locked back, the 9mm Beretta M9 pistol was the most common side arm carried by soldiers of the 101st.**

Trijicon's ACOG (Advanced Combat Optical Gunsight) series of 4x scopes are also popular with soldiers who desire an advanced sighting system. Issued to some units later in the campaign, and in the hands of some soldiers who purchased their own equipment, this scope gave fire teams the ability to discriminate between innocent civilians and insurgents at greater range.

**A trooper displays his well-equipped M4 carbine with attached PAQ-4C laser, iron sights and red dot day scope. Beneath the barrel is an M203 40mm grenade launcher.**

The night fight is where the 101st reigns supreme, and with every infantryman generally possessing night vision goggles, either PVS-14 monoculars or the older PVS-7s, it is an advantage undreamed of in even the first Gulf War. Infrared aiming lasers, either the standby PAQ-4C or the PEQ2A (with infrared spotlight) from New Hampshire's Insight

Technologies creates a glowing green dot in the night vision goggles at point of impact. Infantrymen also use them to mark targets for each other or for helicopters, and sometimes just signal each other silently.

For those times, like the close-quarters chaos of a room clearing or searching for prisoners, the blinding SureFire tactical light was the rifleman's new friend. The division procured several thousand just before the war. While darkness and careful use of night vision equipment is the preferred method for the infantry, sometimes nothing beats a good bright light and the SureFires provided that. A "Rakkasan," the nick-name adopted by members of the 187th Infantry in Japan shortly after World War II, told me how he had cut small strips of black electrician's tape and applied them to the SureFire lens in a "Happy Face" pattern. He informed me that, "It was the last smile that more than one combatant ever saw."

Another common add-on is the "gangster grip." Usually it was the vertical handgrip included with the Knight rail system; however, sometimes other add-ons were used. One soldier that I encountered in the 502nd Infantry mounted a metal spring clamp to his M4 forend and held it in place with duct tape as a field expedient "gangster grip." Not only does it improve the weapon's handling in rapid fire in the classic Thompson submachine gun style, it allows a convenient place to Velcro the pressure switches that control the SureFire or IR laser.

In the northern Iraqi town of Talafar, I saw one scout platoon sniper section from the 187th that had been provided with a variety of weapons including an M4 decked out with a Gemtech sound suppressor. Suppressor "cans" were often seen elsewhere in the 187th with one or two per platoon by October 2003. It proved to be a very useful combination employed from the rooftops of the often-hostile city, making it easier for the units to take shots from concealment.

The M4 was also host to the "old reliable" late Vietnam-era M203 grenade launcher. This single-shot breechloader fires a 40mm high explosive projectile 300 to 350 meters with devastating accuracy and was employed frequently during the war to dislodge enemy combatants from behind walls. It also lofted illumination rounds when called for, and some soldiers prayed aloud for a supply of the Vietnam-era 40mm buckshot loading.

The most common side arm in the 101st was the Army standard Beretta M9, 9mm semiauto pistol. It was adopted in 1987 to replace the venerable Colt

"Rakkasan" Sergeant Yeater outfitted his M4 with an infrared laser, red dot scope and Gemtech sound suppressor. His carbine also features a Knight pattern handgrip.

In the course of the fighting, many troopers of the 101st acquired Iraqi Tariq 9mm pistols. The Tariq, manufactured at the Al Qadissiya plant north of Baghdad, was a licensed copy of the Beretta Model 951.

Sergeant Covington fits a SAW to one of the newly manufactured "Dohuk" mounts. The Dohuk swivel-mounts were designed and manufactured in Iraq to allow the SAWs to be mounted atop the division's Humm-Vs.

.45ACP 1911A1 and to equip the American soldier with a common caliber to our NATO allies. Not unlike any precision-made instrument, care and cleaning are important to function and dependability. Most of the complaints about the M9 stemmed from worn out or filthy magazines. Fellow NRA staffer and USMC Sergeant Eric Poole served during the war and had this to say about the M9: "The magazines were the largest problem with the M9, however, when they came to us to replace them we would find compressed springs where they had stored 15 rounds for months without ever removing the ammunition. Most springs in any pistol will suffer metal fatigue when placed under the stress of 15 rounds. When troops would give us magazines, we would disassemble them, CLEAN them, and stretch the springs. When reassembled, they functioned like new. As we would give them back, they would thank us for giving them new magazines ... ittle did they know." It is also important to note that unauthorized use of nonfactory/nonmilitary issue magazines also contributed to function problems.

As it often is with armies on the march, captured weapons get soaked up and assimilated by those with needs greater than their current equipment capabilities. Rarely has the United States soldier gone into battle where the enemy has had better firepower available for the taking. Iraq was a rare exception as numerous examples—albeit non-regulation examples—were spotted of 101st soldiers carrying captured firearms. Soldiers armed with rifles who desired a handgun for close-in work and vehicle security searched for an alternative to augment their weaponry. Browning Hi-Powers, leftovers from the British influence on the region, were the side arm of choice by those who could get their hands on one and a supply of magazines. Not only were the Hi-Powers rugged and effective, they fit reasonably well in US holsters and tac-

tical vests. One old GI 1911A1 was spotted in the 502nd Infantry at one point, and a Colt Series 70 was picked up on the battlefield, but the .45s were greatly outnumbered by 9x18mm Makarovs and Iraqi-made Beretta 1951 copies called "Tariqs." These varied in quality from very nice to abysmal.

The compact 9mm Beretta Model 12 provided swift and maneuverable performance in the cramped cab of an HMMWV.

Some HMMWV (High Mobility Multipurpose Wheeled Vehicle) drivers, plus other truck-driving types, sought a sub-machine gun that could be hung around their neck to allow hands-free driving and quick access to a short-barreled gun. The M4, even at 29 inches overall length, was considered too long for the task and more than a few guys acquired captured British Sterlings and highly prized Beretta Model 12s. Rarer were Egyptian copies of the Swedish K45 9mm submachine gun, and one mint H&K MP-5 that was picked up and carried by the 3/502 Infantry's Sergeant Major for a while.

Also making an appearance in the 101st's weapons inventory was the Mossberg 590 12-gauge pump action shotgun. The 8-shot "room broom" proved to be dev-

Sergeant Vaughn, of 101st MP carries a 12-gauge Mossberg 590 combat shotgun fitted with a Picatinny rail for accessories and a SureFire tactical light.

astatingly effective during house-to-house searches for Fedyaheen combatants, as well as lock busting during door breaches.

## Sniper Weapons

The arms and equipment of scout/snipers have always been popular, watched and admired from afar by combat arms afficionados. The 101st's sniper teams, two per battalion in the headquarters scout platoon, use the Army standard M-24 sniper rifles. These are McMillan-stocked Remington Model 700s in 7.62x51mm NATO, using M118 Ball Ammo. The example I was allowed to examine was equipped with a Northrop-Grumman PVS-10, SNS (Sniper Night Sight). This sight allows use during day and night operations with 800 meters maximum effective viewing range during the day and 600 meters at night. Without the sight, the gun is a manageable 14.5 pounds.

The legendary USMC sniper Carlos Hathcock popularized the .50

**Scout/snipers of the 502nd Battalion pose with the author** *(center)*. **The marksman at right holds an M24 fitted with a 10x M3A scope and folding bipod.**

caliber sniper rifle in Vietnam by installing his 10x Unertl scope to a Browning M2 "Ma Deuce" heavy machine gun and firing it in the rarely used single-shot mode. His effective and powerful rifle was not exactly a new idea on the battlefield. The German Army and Mauser developed a similar bolt-action 13mm single-shot rifle in 1916 to shoot clean through Allied tanks on the muddy battlefields of the Great War. Taking a page from the Mauser rifle and the field modifications Gunny Hathcock made to

This M24 sniper rifle is outfitted with a PVS-10 Sniper Night Sight. The sight is intended for both day and night operations using a light intensifying night vision tube that can be easily switched to regular optics during daylight.

the M2, Ronnie Barrett of Tennessee proved the impossible possible by designing the "Light Fifty," a semiauto .50BMG rifle he dubbed the M82. The Marines bought some, then Special Forces, and it has been type-classified by the Army as the XM107. The 30-pound, short-recoil semiautomatic rifle has a 10-round detachable box magazine. With an issue 10x Leupold scope, the XM107 was scoring aimed hits on enemy targets at 2,000 meters.

## The Belt-Feds

The 101st has four different belt-fed weapons in its current inventory. The most prolific is the SAW (Squad Automatic Weapon), the Americanized variant of the FN 5.56mm Minimi, officially known as the M249. There are two per squad, each the centerpiece of the squad's two four-man fire teams. Feeding from a disintegrating belt of 200 rounds or from standard M4 (M16) 20- or 30-round magazines in a pinch, it weighs 15 pounds and has a cyclic rate of 750 rounds per minute. Right before deployment, Elcan 3.4x scopes were fitted along with Knight's Armament rail forends. This allowed SAW gunners to accessorize in much the same manner as their rifle-carrying squad mates.

As the normally walking 101st moved to more mounted operations, the SAWs were mounted atop HMMWVs. Ending the mounting difficulties this caused was a division innovation, a new pintle mount called the "Dohuk" mount. Named after the Kurdish town in northern Iraq where they were fabricated, the Dohuk mount provided an iron basket to hold and secure the ammo can to the gun while it bounced around as well as a cradle mount for the weapon. Designed and manufactured in the field, this mount is a testament to the continuing ingenuity of "Joe," the nameless riflemen who can adapt to and overcome any obstacle.

The M240B is the Army's replacement for the venerable M60. Joining the 30 other nations, from Britain to Israel, who use the Belgiandesigned MAG-58, the 26-pound gun feeds 7.62x51mm rounds and spits them back out at 600 to 900 rounds per minute. Two M240's form the cornerstone of every rifle platoon, and in time it will replace the division's remaining M60s.

My personal favorite is the MK19, 40mm grenade machine gun. This General Dynamics-produced behemoth, originally intended for Navy gunboats in Vietnam, can launch a 40mm HEDP (High Explosive Dual Purpose) grenade to ranges exceeding 2,000 meters and is most effective at ranges up to 1,500 meters. It fires at a rate of 350 rounds per minute, only slightly slower than the old M3 Grease Gun. Many of the HMMWVs that I saw in the 101st AOR (Area of Responsibility) were equipped with both the MK19 and the M240B or an M249 on a revolving turret. It has a distinctive firing sound as well as a signature slow rate of fire, bringing a smile and a sense of comfort to those nearby when it begins to engage the enemy.

The old lady of the battlefield is, of course, the M2 Browning .50 heavy machine gun, also affectionately known as "Ma Deuce." The Browning .50 has been around since 1923, making it the most venerable weapon in the inventory of the 101st. Having seen service in World War II, Korea,

A "Humm-V" convoy moves toward Baghdad. The lead vehicle is armed with an M19 grenade launcher as well as a side-mounted SAW.

Vietnam, Granada, Panama, Haiti, Somalia, Afghanistan, Gulf War I and now Gulf War II, the old Ma Deuce still holds her own on the battlefield. Capable of firing as many as 450 to 1,250 rounds per minute, depending on the particular version, the M2 can be employed in every battlefield circumstance from anti-personnel to shooting down aircraft.

It's comforting to know that our fighting warriors have the best equipment and firepower on any field of battle and that in the hands of trained professional soldiers such as those of the 101st Airborne, few stand anything more than a fighting chance against our beloved Screaming Eagles.

(Editor's note: Philip Schreier, for the past 15 years, has been a Curator at the NRA's National Firearms Museum in Fairfax, Virginia. He ventured into Iraq as an embedded reporter last August-September, becoming the first NRA War Correspondent since WWII.)

Thanks to Division Commander MG David H. Petraeus, Division Master Gunner, MSGT J.C. Reich as well as SFC L. Covington and SGT D. Kemp.

The queen of the desert—the MK19 belt-fed 40mm grenade machine gun. The MK19 can deliver accurate, direct or indirect fire against enemy personnel and lightly armored vehicles.

"Ma Deuce"—a .50 caliber Browning M2 machine gun mounted onthe roof of a "Humm-V."

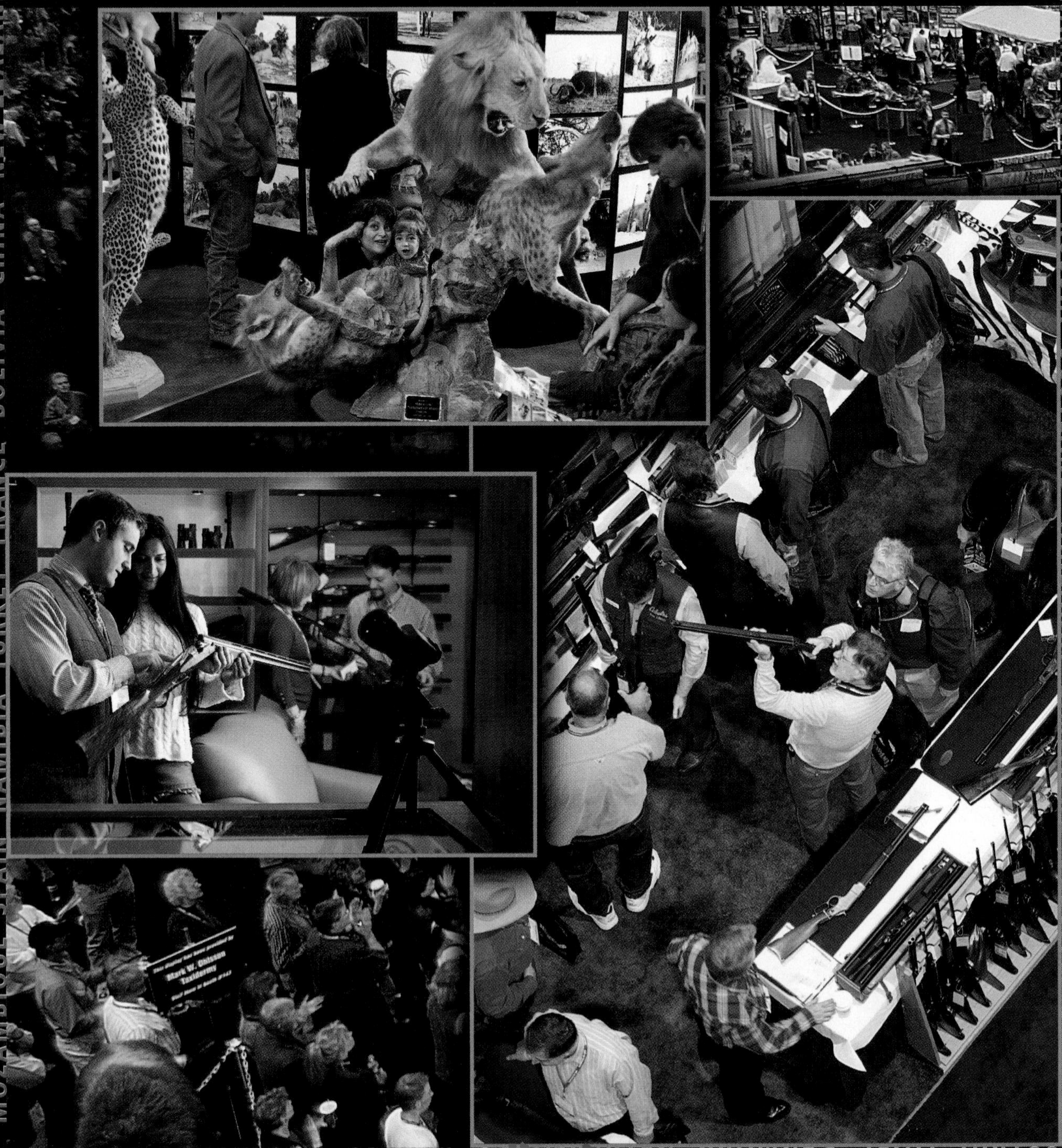

# Ballistic Plex™

## The Original • The Easiest • The Most Versatile • The Most Effective

close-up at 400 yards (standard trajectory)

**Standard Trajectories**

| | |
|---|---|
| 100 | |
| 200 | |
| 300 | |
| 400 | |
| 500 | |

Example Cartridges that calibrate for 100 to 500 yards.

| | |
|---|---|
| .223 | 55grain |
| .243 | 100grain |
| .270 | 150grain |
| 7mm-08 | 140grain |
| 7mm Mags | 175grain |
| 30-06 | 150grain |
| 30-06 | 165grain |
| 338 Mag | 225grain |

**Magnum Trajectories**

| | |
|---|---|
| 200 | |
| 300 | |
| 400 | |
| 500 | |
| 600 | |

Example Cartridges that calibrate for 200 to 600 yards.

| | |
|---|---|
| .243 WSSM | 100grain |
| .25-06 | 100grain |
| .270 | 130grain |
| .270 WSM | 150grain |
| 7mm Mags | 140grain |
| 7mm Shrt Mg | 160grain |
| 300 Mag | 150grain |
| 300 Ultra | 180grain |

**Ballistic Plex™.** The simplest, most confidence-building trajectory-compensating reticle for connecting at long range. Will work for almost any cartridge 30 calibration labels come with each scope. Ballistic Plex is fast, simple and accurate. Add an accurate rifle, a laser range finder, some long range practice, and you have the ingredients to create capable and successful marksmen. Available in the Fullfield II, Signature Select, Compact and Handgun scopes.

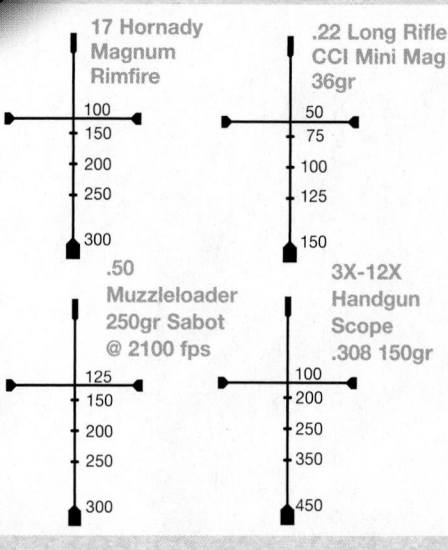

**17 Hornady Magnum Rimfire**

| |
|---|
| 100 |
| 150 |
| 200 |
| 250 |
| 300 |

**.22 Long Rifle CCI Mini Mag 36gr**

| |
|---|
| 50 |
| 75 |
| 100 |
| 125 |
| 150 |

**.50 Muzzleloader 250gr Sabot @ 2100 fps**

| |
|---|
| 125 |
| 150 |
| 200 |
| 250 |
| 300 |

**3X-12X Handgun Scope .308 150gr**

| |
|---|
| 100 |
| 200 |
| 250 |
| 350 |
| 450 |

**BURRIS®**

All riflescopes are warranted forever.
Burris Company
331 E. 8th Street, Greeley, CO 80631
(970) 356-1670
**www.burriscompany.com**

# Selecting the Right Slugs, Buckshot Loads

## by Dave Henderson

I f you use a shotgun for deer hunting, it's probably because you don't have a choice in the matter.

State and municipal governments, after all, have jurisdiction over the playing fields for our pastime and thus dictate the rules, including allowable equipment. We grudgingly must admit that it makes sense that, as humanity continues its encroachment into deer habitat, more and more municipalities are opting for short-range shotguns over the potential "beyond-the-horizon" lethality of the modern rifle.

Most of us do, however, have a choice of loads and guns. And since slug shooting is the fastest-emerging technology in the shooting industry, there are plenty of interesting options.

Which one is right for you? Let's take a look.

The basic choice—again, if regulations allow—is between slugs and buckshot. Granted, buckshot is a devastatingly effective close-range load, but in terms of overall performance, slugs are absolutely the most effective load you can put into a shotgun.

Any slug, full-bore or sabot, 20, 16, 10 or 12 gauge, has a much, much more extensive effective range than buckshot in the same gauge. And, although the margin for error is slightly less, slugs are every bit as deadly in close quarters.

**The modern shotgun is a very effective short-range deer hunting implement.**

Besides, of the nearly 3 million whitetail hunters who are not allowed to use rifles, only 3 percent are forced to or opt to use buckshot.

Yes, given the choice, the vast majority of American shotgunners will go with slugs every time.

## Today's Slugs

Among slugs, the sabot style is the state of the art—a bullet-like projectile encased in a hard polymer bore-diameter sleeve designed to grip the barrel's rifling and impart the spin that stabilizes the slug at far longer ranges than conventional full-bore slugs.

But the sabot slug also costs upward of five times as much as the conventional slugs and requires a (rifled) barrel that dedicates the gun to slug shooting—it's not going to pattern your duck or pheasant loads. Thus, despite all of the hype about saboted ammunition that you read, the conventional full-bore slug still represents more than 60 percent of the retail sales to slug hunters.

It's true that saboted ammunition has a longer effective range. And sabot slugs are definitely more accurate when fired from a rifled bore than full-bore slugs are from a smoothbore. But the fact remains that about 95 percent of all deer killed with shotguns are taken at ranges less than 100 yards—and the vast majority of those are actually taken inside of 75 yards. Foster-type full-bore slugs such as those loaded by Winchester, Federal and Remington and the various non-saboted Brenneke-style designs are very effective at that range. If you shoot a smoothbore shotgun and take typical shots within these parameters, you are not at a disadvantage with these slugs.

Nearly 3 million of the nation's 10 million whitetail deer hunters go afield with shotguns.

At least before the advent of the new high-velocity loads, saboted ammunition offered no advantage over full-bore slugs at traditional deer woods ranges (40-80 yards). The high-tech stuff didn't really show its stuff until it had a chance to stretch out and run at longer distances. At that point the superior aerodynamics and ballistic coefficient and the stabilizing effect of the spin generated by the rifling helped the projectile maintain its velocity, trajectory and energy far longer than the bulky full-bore slug.

## What About Barrels??

What about choke for slug shooting? Odds are that your smoothbore will shoot slugs more accurately with a relatively open choke. The industry, in fact, used to suggest improved cylinder for slug shooting. But shotgun bores vary in dimension, bore to bore, even in the same brand and model.

A slug that has been squeezed tightly throughout its journey down the barrel will react differently when it

**The Foster-style slug, so called because it was developed by ballistician Karl Foster in the 1930s, is still the best-selling slug load on the market.**

**Hunters who use shotguns for deer hunting usually do so because they don't have a choice.**

hits the choke—regardless of the constriction of that choke—than one that fit loosely and tipped slightly as it traversed the same distance.

A little advice here: Saboted ammunition will actually be less effective in a smoothbore than conventional slugs since if the slug is not spinning the sabot sleeves will have difficulty separating from the slug and it will actually destabilize the projectile.

Sabot slugs are designed for rifled barrels—the sabot sleeves grip the rifling and impart spin on the projectile, which it needs to maintain stability in flight. Full-bore slugs rely on their nose-heavy design to stay stable for their relatively short flight.

If you shoot a smoothbore but would like to take advantage of the high-tech loads, your best bet is to add a rifled choke tube. All major shotgun manufacturers offer rifled tubes and they are improving all the time. You can also look into aftermarket tubes from Hastings, Colonial, Cation, Kicks, Rhino and others.

Be advised that the length of the choke tube is a factor in how well it stabilizes slugs. After all, asking 2 to 3 inches of spiraled grooves to impart a rotation of up to 37,000 rpm on a projectile that has already reached terminal velocity is asking a lot. Regardless, there are some rifled tubes that shoot far more accurately, particularly inside of 100 yards, than the laws of physics should allow.

The fact remains, however, if you want to take advantage of the latest innovations and vast ballistic superiority of today's high-tech slugs, you'll need a rifled slug barrel. As noted previously, however, a rifled barrel dedicates the gun to slug-shooting only —it will not effectively pattern shot.

It will, however, stabilize any slugs—sabot or full-bore Foster or some Brenneke-style slugs—farther and extend their effective range. Full-bore slugs actually skid a bit in the rifling and will leave copious amounts of lead fouling in the grooves in a very short period of time, but they will generally shoot well in a rifled bore.

Like rifled choke tubes, all major shotgun manufacturers offer at least one model with a rifled barrel and most offer optional rifled barrels that can replace your conventional barrel for the deer season. Hastings and Ithaca Gun also have a wide variety of aftermarket rifled barrels.

With a stiff barrel, good trigger and solidly mounted scope—use steel rings and a good-quality scope—your rifled barrel slug gun should be able to consistently put three conventional-velocity saboted slugs through the same hole at 50 yards from a solid rest. Accuracy at 100 yards will vary with the wind conditions, trigger pull, load and the shooter's ability.

**Today's high-tech slug loads are capable of outstanding accuracy when coupled with the right gun, shooter and conditions.**

## Debunking Slug Myths

Thanks to advancing technology, and the ever-expanding retail market that drives that technology, slug shooting has taken a quantum leap forward since the 1980s. But don't believe those articles promising "200-yard slug guns" or "rifle-like ballistics." Such claims are based loosely

**Hunters using smoothbore shotguns should use full-bore slugs like these.**

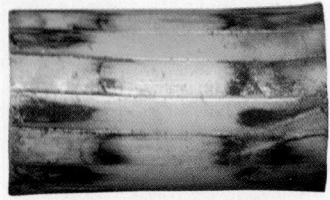

The sleeves on sabot slugs are designed to grip the rifling and impart a spin on the slug before being discarded.

on the truth, but application is problematical at best.

Yes, today's high-velocity, controlled-expansion, bullet-style slugs—the Winchester Partition Gold and Platinum Tip, Hornady H2K Heavy Mag, Federal's high-velocity Barnes EXpander and Remington's Core-Lokt-Ultra—do retain lethal energy out to 200 yards and their ballistics do eclipse the venerable .45-70, .300 Savage, .30-30 and other elderly centerfire calibers.

But the truth is that trajectory, lack of downrange stability, vulnerability to barrel vibration and wind make the slugs extremely difficult, if not impossible, to shoot with much consistent accuracy at 200 yards. You must understand that these are essentially pistol bullets being fired under low chamber pressures from long barrels—they lack the ballistic coefficient of true "deer caliber" centerfire bullets.

Consider that a conventional shotgun slug has a maximum range of less than 900 yards, and that's when it's fired from a barrel elevated 30 degrees. Your .30-06 will carry more than three miles from the same position. A 10 m.p.h. crosswind will move a conventional shotgun slug 6-8 inches off target at 100 yards. A 130-grain bullet from a .270 fired from the same bench under the same conditions will move about an eighth of an inch.

Shotguns and slugs are short-range ordnance, period. Modern high-velocity shotgun slugs are effective, under the right conditions, with the right shooter, out to 125 yards. An expert might stretch it to 150 or 160 under the right conditions but once you get much beyond 125 luck has far more influence on the results than do ballistics.

Regardless, the new stuff may not threaten rifle performance but it's virtually light-years ahead of yesterday's slugs.

If you're shooting a smoothbore, certainly today's Foster-style and other full-bore slugs will perform well for you at ranges out to 75-90 yards, after which their velocity is subsonic and they are apt to lose stability in flight. If you add a rifled choke tube to that smoothbore, a conventional velocity (1,200-1,450 fps) sabot slug will increase your effective range comfortably past 100 yards. A fully rifled barrel will stabilize

The state of the art in shotgun slugs are the jacketed, controlled-expansion, high-velocity bullets like the Hornady H2K *(left)* and the Winchester Partition Gold *(right)*.

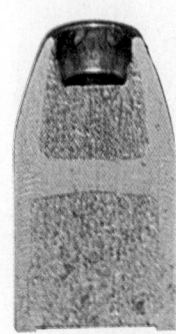

any saboted slug and open the door for you to use the high-velocity (1,600-2,000 fps), high-performance slugs.

## What About Buckshot?

As noted previously, buckshot is a time-honored and effective load for deer. That is, it's effective provided you understand and operate within its limits. While a single 00 pellet will pierce human skin at 400 yards, the load's true effectiveness is based on the cumulative effect of the entire pattern—and with most loads and guns beyond 30-40 yards that pattern deteriorates to the point that you're relying far more on a lucky hit than ballistics.

In fact, U.S. Army specs note 40 yards as the absolute effective range for 00 buck used on humans. The same could be said for 00 as a deer load – in most contexts. The newest kid on the buckshot block, Hevi-Shot (tungsten—rather than lead-based pellets) is an exception, the effectiveness of which is still being examined.

Buckshot has been a popular and effective load since black powder days and is still the load mandated for deer hunting in specific areas of at least 10 states. It's legal in 29 states, although five of them don't have any whitetails.

**Virtually all shotgun slugs incorporate some sort of a hollow nose to accentuate expansion upon impact.**

Like all shotgun loads, buckshot has improved markedly in the last couple of decades. Development of the shot cup, copper plating, improved lead-antimony or tungsten mixes and granulated plastic buffering have turned the once willy-nilly patterning characteristics of buckshot into an even more devastating tool.

At one time, users of No. 00 (double-aught) buckshot found patterns extremely ragged at close range—to the point where a deer-sized target might be missed altogether at 40 yards.

**Modern sabot slugs are often jacketed or all-copper bullets.**

Plated buckshot patterns tighter than conventional lead in many chokes, but doesn't expand as readily.

Like any shotgun scatter load, the problem is that the bigger the pellet (00 pellets are .33 caliber; 000 are .36) the less room it has to negotiate in the crowded confines of a shotgun bore.

Be advised that, despite industry claims, backbored barrels no longer give demonstrably better patterning performance than conventional diameter barrels. That may have been the case years ago when the majority of the soft, unplated pellets were damaged or worn by the barrel walls as they sorted themselves out en route to the muzzle, but no more.

Major manufacturers are offering copper-plated buckshot designed to enhance penetration, and Remington now markets 12- and 10-gauge Hevi-Shot buckshot loads that penetrate even farther.

Not everyone wants that "blow-through" effect, however. Many veteran buckshot users resist the hard stuff, including copper-plated and tungsten-based buckshot, for that very reason—they want the pellets deforming and dumping their energy in the animal instead of using it to blow exit holes.

Another school of thought, however, is that Hevi-Shot's extreme density and remarkable patterning capabilities extend the effective range of buckshot into heretofore uncharted territory. In fact, it patterned tighter at much longer ranges and carried its energy much, much farther than anything I've ever shot.

## Using Buckshot

Because patterning conventional buckshot is often seen as difficult, many buckshot hunters opted for smaller shot such as No. 4 (.24 caliber), which patterned much denser than the larger shot. The lethality of No. 4 shot, however, is questionable beyond 20-30 yards.

If you talked to old-time buckshot hunters full choke was the only logical choice. But with today's improved choke systems, and with the plastic sleeves and buffer keeping the shot from being deformed in the

The advent of the rifled barrel paved the way for sabot slugs and a new era in shotgun slug performance.

A rifled choke tube will transform a smoothbore shotgun into one capable of shooting high-tech sabot slugs.

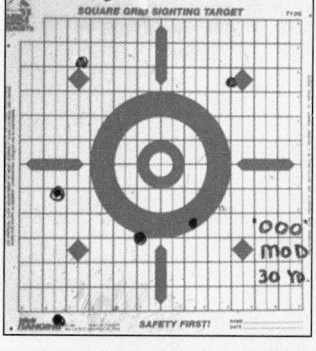

Shotgunners should shoot a variety of slug or buckshot loads through their guns to determine which one performs best for them.

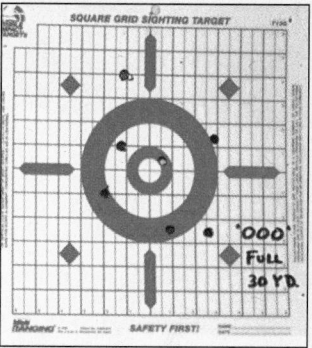

These targets show the effect of different chokes on the same buckshot load.

barrel, good patterns can be obtained with modified or even improved cylinder choking.

New loads, including the relatively new No. 000 (.36 caliber pellets), are more effective than ever in open-choke guns, too.

With today's loads, effective patterning ranges have lengthened appreciably. For instance, No. 00 plated lead today, fired through a full-choke 12-gauge barrel, would probably average 50 percent (six of 12 pellets) in the traditional patterning target of a 30-inch circle at 70 yards. Just 20 years ago a 50 percent pattern could be achieved at no longer than 40 yards.

But please note that I'm talking about "effective patterning ranges." This is not an endorsement of or suggestion that one take 70-yard shots with buckshot, although the effective range is appreciably longer with Hevi-Shot.

Back to patterning. While a 30-inch pattern is a fine criteria for wing shooting birds, but we're aiming at 12- to 16-inch vital area in a deer, which can fit its cardio-pulmonary system inside a basketball.

This being the case, a 10-inch pie plate is a realistic buckshot target. You must pattern a variety of loads to determine which is most effective in your particular gun and choke. All are different.

To sum it up, what you need from a deer-hunting shotgun depends entirely on how you are going to use it. There's nothing wrong with buckshot or smoothbore shotguns and full-bore slugs for the relatively short-range shooting found in most deer woods. But if you're looking for long-range performance, that option is there in the rifled barrel shotguns and high-tech sabot ammunition.

(Dave Henderson is the author of *Shotgunning for Deer*. He can be contacted through his website, www.HendersonOutdoors.com)

Hevi-Shot's tungsten base makes it pattern tighter and carry its energy farther down-range, but resists pellet expansion on impact.

# Bonded Bullet Bonanza!

by Wayne van Zwoll

**W**hen the elk thundered into view, I was rethinking a stalk gone awry just hours earlier. Half the morning I'd committed to a pair of bulls that had eventually slipped onto the timbered crest of a ridge. I'd wound up tip-toeing into the shadows, then spotting the younger animal in bed at 30 steps. I backed out, came in again looking for his companion—and caught a glimpse as he sneaked out the back door into heavier cover in the canyon below.

Now, suddenly, I was ripping the rifle from my shoulder to swing on a bull that had dashed out of the gulf to my right, a tan rocket hurtling through aspens too dense for shooting. I scrambled uphill and knelt where I could command a narrow shot alley. Inexplicably, the bull stopped just short of it. I waited. An instant later, his nose and antlers appeared. I pulled the trigger. The bullet took him high behind the shoulder, dropping him right away.

Probably I could have killed that elk with any bullet—or, for that matter, any deer cartridge. My rifle this day was a Model 70 Featherweight in .300 WSM, shooting Nosler's new AccuBond, a bullet Winchester is loading in its Combined Technology ammunition. It's one of a plethora of big game bullets that feature chemical bonding of core to jacket, to improve penetration and weight retention and minimize fragmentation.

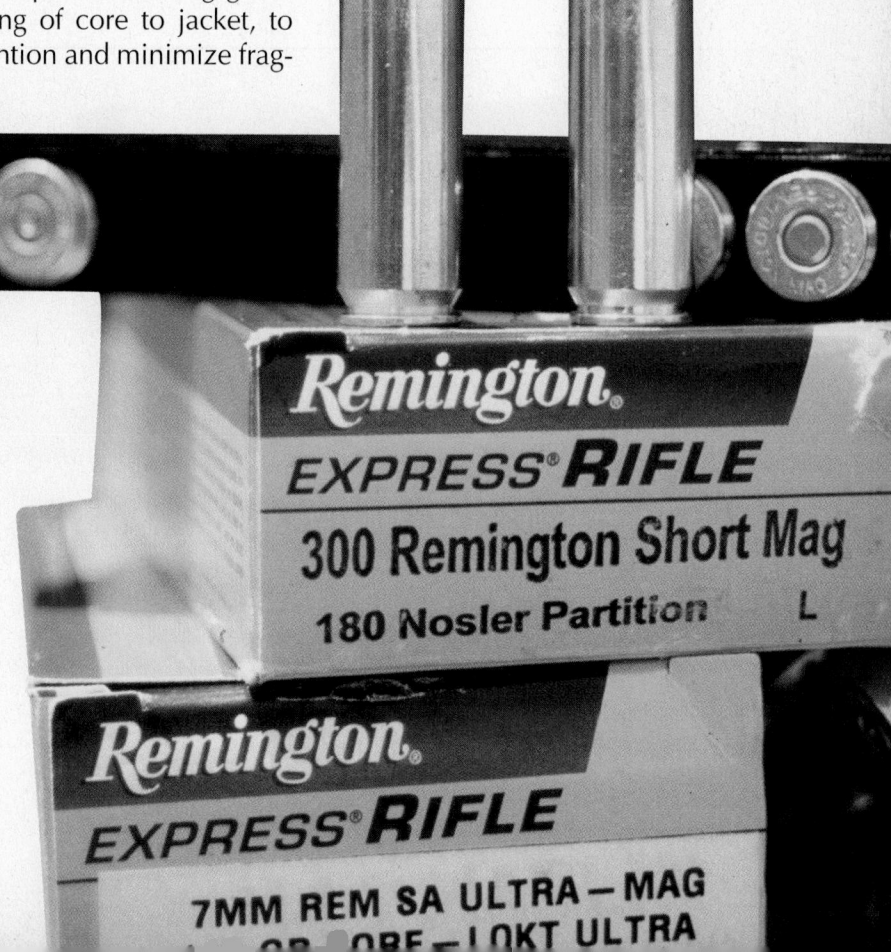

**Short Magnums and bonded bullets are taking center stage as ammo makers announce new products.**

Remington

EXPRESS RIFLE

300 Remington Short Mag

180 Nosler Partition    L

Remington

EXPRESS RIFLE

7MM REM SA ULTRA — MAG

Big-bore bullets like these .45s from Northern Precision are meant for relatively low impact speeds.

Broad choices in bullet design add even more versatility to versatile cartridges like the .30-06.

Over the last century, internal bullet design has changed in response to increasing velocity. The first jacketed softpoint bullets were round-nosed, with lots of lead exposed in front so they'd open readily because their great weight limited velocity to between 2,000 and 2,400 fps. When Charles Newton developed his line of potent cartridges before World War I, he found traditional bullets went to pieces when driven into heavy game at velocities exceeding 2,700 fps. Pointed softnose bullets sometimes zipped through an animal without opening. In 1914 Newton was marketing a spitzer bullet with a wire nose insert to control expansion. He wrote: "A copper wire is embedded in the center of the bullet point, and ... protects the point against every deformation except upsetting, and the jacket is sufficiently long to prevent this." Newton's bullets also featured paper insulation between jacket and core to keep cores from melting from barrel friction. Newton found evidence of core melt by drilling holes in bullet jackets and firing into white cardboard at 20 feet. A smear of melted lead on the cardboard resulted. Wrapping cores in thin paper eliminated the smears but also increased the cost of bullet manufacture.

Controlling the terminal performance of bullets became a priority as traditional designs proved to be increasingly unreliable. Winchester's early Precision Point had a cone of jacket material covering the bullet tip and inserted at three points under the jacket proper. Three windows of lead exposed at the juncture of cone and jacket initiated expansion.

For the Peters label, Remington developed the Protected Point. A cone point capped a flat-topped lead core whose front third was wrapped in a "driving band" under the jacket. On impact, the front of the bullet pushed back as it expanded, forcing the driving band down. The band controlled the core's expansion. The manufacture of one Protected Point bullet required three hours and 51 operations. Winchester's Silvertip was similar but far less expensive. It lacked the driving band.

Among the most popular deer bullets in my youth was the Remington Bronze Point, essentially a hollowpoint with a peg in the hole. The peg had a bronze cone that formed the bullet tip. Impact forced the peg back into the bullet core, making it mushroom. My limited experience with Bronze Points has shown them to open violently at high impact speeds. The long, pointed nose ensures a high ballistic coefficient. That hard tip is less easily damaged than exposed lead —a factor of greater importance in the catalog than in the field. Remington's current best-seller, the Core-Lokt, is a more versatile bullet than the Bronze Point. Its "inner belt" is really a thickening of the jacket that serves to limit expansion and inhibit core-jacket separation. The Core-Lokt has an enviable reputation among big game hunters.

**Early softpoints were heavy for the bore, clocked well under 3,000 fps and often had round noses.**

Hollowpoint bullets are less commonly used on tough game. But before World War II the Western Tool and Copper Works made a hollowpoint with a tiny cavity that worked well on elk-size animals, even when driven at high speed by cartridges like the .30 Newton and .300 H&H Magnum. DWM offered a "strong-jacket" bullet with a long, narrow nose cavity lined with copper tubing. This hollowpoint was capped. Behavior of hollowpoint bullets depends on cavity dimensions and the design and materials of jacket and core. Sierra GameKing hollowpoints I've used on deer kill like lightning bolts. They also shoot very accurately. On big-boned animals, however, they don't penetrate as well as many traditional softpoints of the same profile.

**Roy Weatherby's magnum cartridges, introduced beginning in 1943, required stronger bullets.**

Perhaps the most popular of bullet designs these days is the polymer-tipped spitzer. The sleek form delivers flat flight, and accuracy is typically better than hunters have come to expect from ordinary softpoints. Nosler's Ballistic Tip has a lot of fans. Hornady's SST and the new Remington AccuTip are similar in shape and performance. For deer-size game, these bullets in traditional deer cartridges are good picks. They're not noted for deep penetration, but through-the-slats hits almost invariably mean sudden death. Incidentally, the sharp nose is less significant than you

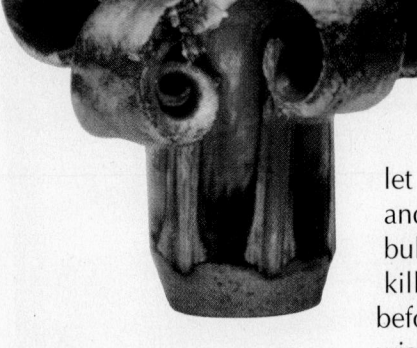

Bonding minimizes petal loss and ensures that lead core and alloy jacket remain intact during upset.

The necessity of making fast shots at quartering bulls in Idaho elk country is cause enough to choose bonded bullets, even from an '06.

might expect in the bullet's battle with drag. The ogive (radius between nose and shank) has more to do with air resistance and bullet drop than does the first .1 inch of nose.

Bonding the jacket to the core has a lot to do with how the bullet will behave when it hits an animal. Big game like elk have bones and muscles that will stop or shred a fragile bullet. But deer don't test bullets as severely, and with side-to shots you'll generally get quicker kills with bullets that open violently and expend most of their energy before reaching the off shoulder. Once in a while, though, you may wish to take a quartering shot, or hit the shoulder of a buck so close that a high-speed bullet of ordinary design will come apart on impact. The best bullets for these situations open without fragmenting, then drive deep while plowing a wide wound channel.

Peters' Inner-Belted and its successor, the Remington Core-Lokt, were among the first bullets whose names challenged cores to stay in their jackets during upset. Now there are many bullets claiming inseparable unions between jacket and core. Trophy Bonded, designed by the late Jack Carter, then bought by Federal Cartridge, followed the thick-jacketed Bitterroot Bonded Core bullet that first served elk hunters in northern Idaho. A bevy of bonded-core bullets came on the heels of Swift's A-Frame, whose internal dam of jacket material and two-piece core mirrored the European H-Mantle and the Partition bullet developed by John Nosler in 1947. Swift soon came up with another bonded bullet, the Scirocco, which combined the sleek profile of the popular polymer-tipped Nosler Ballistic Tip with the integrity to penetrate deep in tough game. Similar bullets from Hornady (InterBond) and Nosler (AccuBond) followed. Remington came through with the Core-Lokt Ultra, a bonded version of its flagship big game bullet. Small shops like Lost River Technologies, and overseas firms like Woodleigh (Australian) and Norma (Swedish) market other versions. All bonded bullets cost more than ordinary softpoints. Few shoot more accurately. Nosler's Partition and Partition Gold, with the Barnes Traditional and X-Bullets, penetrate deep without bonding, and give adequate precision for big game hunting.

Controlled-expansion bullets can be very accurate. The author shot this group with Winchester Fail Safes.

Manufacturers of bonded bullets are reluctant to tell you how they do it. Speer does say its Hot-Core process ensures a flaw-free union because the lead snuggles up tighter to the jacket than is the case with cold-forming; but the company is careful not to claim bonding. Corbin, a leading manufacturer of bullet-making equipment for hobbyists, points out that with its gear you can make your own chemically-bonded bullets—also partitioned bullets and bullets with telescoping jackets. Corbin's swaging machinery has apparently helped launch more than 200 bullet businesses. That might be why you see many more brands of big game bullets advertised now than a decade ago.

Internal design largely determines how a bullet will behave in the target. But shape and weight matter too, and they're much more important to the bullet's flight. Besides aiding penetration, the high sectional density of a long bullet contributes to a high ballistic coefficient, which flattens the bullet's trajectory. There are practical limits to bullet length, however. Long bullets require a fast rifling twist for the best accuracy. Even if you find one that shoots well, it may not fit your gun. If a bullet in your magazine box touches the box fore and aft, or if you see rifling marks on a bullet

Deep penetration is the hallmark of the Barnes X-Bullet. With no lead core, the X-Bullet is long for its weight.

## The Changing Shape of Bullets

Many big game animals have fallen to patched round balls driven from muzzleloaders. After the Civil War, hunters preferred conical bullets because they "carried up" better at long range and penetrated better at all ranges. The ratio of bullet weight to diameter (sectional density) was highest with long bullets. But long bullets, because they were heavy and generated lots of friction as they spun down the bore, could not be driven as fast as shorter, lighter bullets.

Sharps catalogs of the late 1870s listed bullet weights of 293 to 550 grains for the .45-70. When smokeless rounds supplanted black-powder cartridges in military service a couple of decades later, the hunting and military rounds were given long bullets, heavy for the bore. Popular weights: 162 grains in 6.5x52 Carcano, 173 grains in 7x57 Mauser, 215 grains in .303 British. These bullets poked along at less than 2,300 fps but were considered fast in their day.

Germany's 7.9x57 cartridge, designed for the Gewehr 88 infantry rifle, arrived two years after the French had made the first official move to smokeless powder with their 8mm Lebel. Like the military rounds that followed it, the 7.9x57 used a heavy round-nose bullet. In 1898 the modified Mannlicher action of the 1888 rifle was replaced by a new, much stronger mechanism: Paul Mauser's Model 1898. The cartridge remained unaltered until 1905, when German engineers came up with a lighter bullet at higher velocity. They changed bore diameter from .318 to .323 (8mm) and replaced the blunt 226-grain bullet with a pointed 154-grain spitzer. Muzzle velocity jumped from 2,090 to 2,880 fps.

Because both the 7.9x57 and later 8x57 have been called 8mm Mauser cartridges, letter designations were added to distinguish them. The early .318 round carries a "J" suffix for "infanterie" (J and I are similar in old German type). The .323 ammunition with spitzer bullets has an "S" suffix.

American ordnance officers, who'd picked a 220-grain round-nose bullet at 2,300 fps in the 1903 Springfield responded to Germany's lighter, faster bullet with a new cartridge. Its case was .07 inch shorter than the 1903's and featured a 150-grain bullet loaded to 2,700 fps. It became known as the .30-06. The '06 was revamped in 1926 to launch a 172-grain boat-tail bullet at 2,640 fps. This sleek missile offered a higher ballistic coefficient, thus greater energy and flatter trajectory down-range. Machine-gunners loved it. In 1940 the Army reinstated the 150-grain flat-base bullet, mainly because the Garand rifle didn't function as well with long boat-tails.

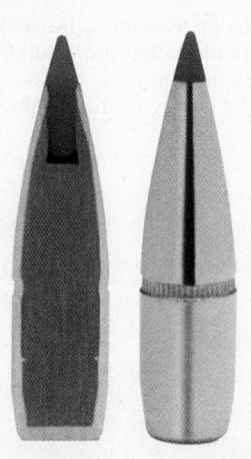

The Hornady SST features the popular polymer tip; the InterBond is a bonded version for tough game.

Most big game can be taken handily with accurate, inexpensive bullets like these.

SIERRA

7 MM .284 DIA

SPEER

7 mm
.284" MAG-T

that's been chambered, you must seat that bullet deeper in the case. But deep seating may compromise the ballistic potential of your cartridge by limiting powder choices or kicking up pressures. You can go shorter without going lighter if you pick a blunt bullet—though in doing so you'll whack ballistic coefficient (by as much as 30 percent!).

One common-sense way to choose a deer bullet is to start near the midpoint in bullet weights for the bore and consider only spitzer or semi-spitzer bullets designed for big game. Match your bullet to your case. That is, if you have a .25-06, try 100-grain bullets. I'd pick 130s in a .270, 140s in 7mms. If you shoot a .308 Winchester, try 150- and 165-grain bullets. A 200-grain spitzer will give better penetration, all things equal, and its high ballistic coefficient will help it catch and pass lighter bullets at long range. But bullets heavier than 165 grains aren't needed for deer, and the extra velocity between 100 and 250 yards will probably prove more useful (because it means flatter trajectory) than additional bullet weight. Should you favor the 6mms, mid-weight bullets can be too light and fragile for big deer. Look to the 95-grain Nosler Partition, and various 100-grain softpoints.

For elk and heavier game, bullets in the same weight ranges will suffice, but you may wish to bump up to a slightly heavier bullet. While you could defend almost any bullet weight as minimum for elk, I prefer bullets no lighter than 130 grains. That leaves out the .24s and .25s, though a friend routinely kills elk with 100-grain bullets from his .25-06. Sometimes you aren't able to see the forward slats on a bull, and if you must penetrate even soft tissue to reach the vitals, it's best to have a bullet of substance. Controlled-expansion bullets—bonded and otherwise built to retain weight and drive deep—give you more options. A bullet too light for elk in traditional softpoint form might be deadly, even on quartering shots, if its internal construction guarantees penetration.

Here's an overview of rifle bullets popular with deer hunters.

*Federal Hi-Shok Softpoint:* The standard bullet for Federal's Classic line, Hi-Shok is available in round-nose, flat-nose and spitzer form, in diameters .224 to .375. Unremarkable in design, it is a bargain in loaded ammo.

## Jackets to Stand the Heat

Sporting ammunition has always borrowed heavily from military prototypes. The first softnose hunting bullets were long and blunt, just like the bullets that bloodied French battlefields in WWI. Hunters got speedy spitzers only after armies had proven them. In those days, the most vexing result of high velocity was heat generated by high-energy fuel and increased bore friction. Pure lead would melt into the rifling if driven at speeds much over 1,200 fps. Alloying it with up to 10 percent tin increased hardness and reduced leading. An alloy of 90 percent lead, 5 percent tin and 5 percent antimony would stand even more heat, but velocities still had to be kept under 1,500 fps for acceptable accuracy.

By 1900 English shooters were using gas checks to protect bullet bases from hot powder gas. Introduced in the United States. five years later by the Ideal Manufacturing Company, gas checks are brass or copper cups crimped onto the base of the bullet. Half-jackets are similar but extend most of the way up the bullet's sides to keep lead from touching the rifling. A gas check lets you wring 2,000 fps from most bullets without compromising accuracy. Half-jackets are good for 2,200 fps or so. At higher speeds, jacketed bullets are necessary. The first of these came along in the 1890s. They were of steel, coated with cupronickel. Though they kept bullet cores from melting and leading bores at .30-40 Krag velocities, they produced metal fouling in .30-06 barrels. Plating the bullets with tin seemed to help, but tin was dropped when shooters found that, over time, it "cold-soldered" to case mouths and occasionally sent pressures through the roof.

Incorporating tin in the jacket proved a better idea. Western Cartridge Company soon announced its "Lubaloy" bullet, with a jacket of 90 percent copper, 8 percent zinc and 2 percent tin. Later, the tin was dropped from most jacket alloys altogether. Now most bullet jackets are of gilding metal, commonly 95 percent copper, 5 percent zinc. Nosler's Partition bullets originally had a 90-10 jacket composition.

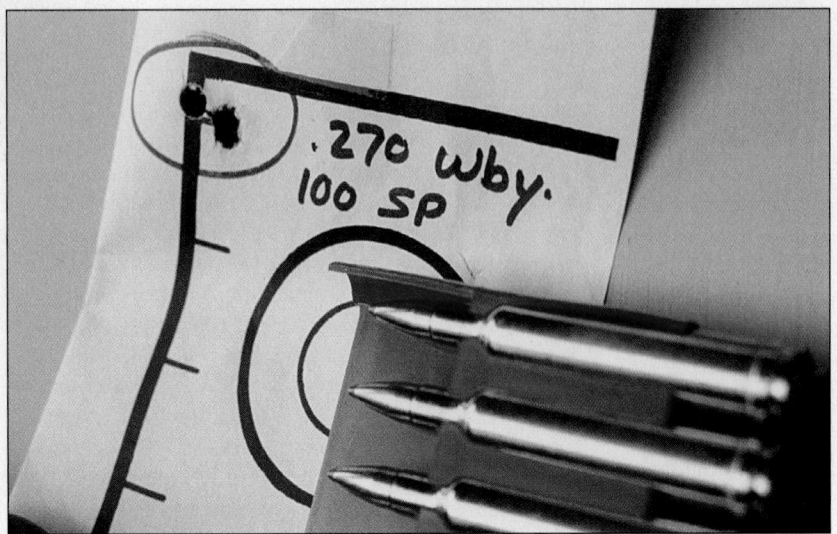

The best accuracy often comes from traditional soft-points like these Hornadys.

The Swift Scirocco *(right)* and Remington Core-Lokt Ultra are two flat-shooting bonded bullets.

***Hornady Interlock:*** Derived from the company's flagship Spire Point, the Interlock features inner jacket belting to hold the core in place during upset. Don't neglect the accurate round-nose versions for modest ranges.

***Hornady SST:*** It's the answer to Nosler's Ballistic Tip. The red-nosed polymer-tipped bullet has become more prominent in the Hornady line than traditional soft-nose spitzers. Very accurate.

***Remington AccuTip:*** Designed to compete with other polymer-tipped bullets, this new offering is built to Remington specs under contract. It's available in Remington loaded ammo from .243 to .300 Winchester Magnum.

***Remington Core-Lokt:*** In both round-nose and pointed form, this veteran may have killed more big game animals than any other soft-point. It has an internal lip to hold the core in place and is available in many weights.

***Sierra GameKing:*** Long renowned for superior accuracy and flat flight, Sierra boat-tail bullets are quick openers. Expect lightning-like kills on deer. The 250-grain .338 and 300-grain .375s have extra-thick jackets.

***Speer Hot-Cor:*** Traditional softnose construction and a sleek profile make Speer Hot-Cors ideal for long shooting at deer-size game. You'll find weights not available elsewhere, even .366 spitzers for that 9.3mm rifle.

***Winchester Power Point:*** This 40-year-old softpoint is an archetype. It has no special features, save nose notches on its tapered jacket. They ensure violent but predictable upset, with more than adequate penetration.

***Winchester Silvertip:*** For years the company's heavy-game bullet, Silvertip got a more fragile nose cap in the 1960s. This bullet now opens more quickly—sometimes even quicker than the Power Point.

... and a list of bullets built specifically for tough game:

***Alaska Kodiak:*** This bonded-core bullet delivers double-diameter upset, superior weight retention. Jackets are of drawn gilding metal, not pure copper.

***Barnes X:*** A solid copper hollowpoint, this bullet is long for its weight. Weight retention of 95 percent or more means you can get penetration with lighter weights and higher starting speeds.

***Hornady InterBond:*** This bonded, polymer-tipped bullet has an inner-belted jacket to help control upset, which is relatively violent. A sleek ogive gives it a flat trajectory.

*Lapua Mega:* The copper jacket of this bullet has a wide inner belt to hold core to jacket. Mega is available in Lapua ammunition. Its round nose profile is consistent with European tradition.

*Norma Oryx:* I used this bullet in Norway. It typically expands to double diameter before peeling back, the bonded core preventing separation and yielding a retained weight higher than 90 percent.

*Norma TXP:* A partitioned core of pure lead is Nosler-like in cross section. The front end is cold-soldered to the jacket. Like Oryx, it has a "protected point" meplat. It's really a Swift A-Frame renamed for Norma sales.

*Nosler AccuBond:* To stay competitive in a market enamored of polymer-tipped bullets that Nosler itself popularized, the company now offers a bonded version of its Ballistic Tip.

*Nosler Partition:* Developed in 1947 by John Nosler, this classic bullet with two-piece core has a dam that stops expansion, guarantee-

**Jack Carter's Trophy Bonded bullet is now being manufactured and loaded by Federal. It's a dandy!**

**Nosler's AccuBond, loaded by Winchester, delivers Partition-like performance with a polymer tip.**

ing penetration by the heel. Loss of the nose is common in tough game.

**Remington Core-Lokt Ultra:** The Ultra has a bonded core to withstand close-range impact from Ultra Mag rounds. Jacket is 20 percent heavier than Core-Lokt's, belt 50 percent thicker. Weight retention: 80 to 90 percent.

**Speer Grand Slam:** A flat meplat atop a long, sleek ogive and a cannelure groove distinguish this bullet. The thick rear jacket arrests expansion. I've had it come apart in elk shoulders.

**Swift A-Frame:** Developed by Lee Reed on the Nosler Partition design, this bullet has a bonded front end that gives it better weight retention. Expect a wide, deep wound channel and picture-book upset.

**Swift Scirocco:** This sleek polymer-tipped bullet has great flight characteristics. But the bonded core and thick jacket hold it together in tough game. I've shot it through 6-inch spruce trees.

When antlers like these are at stake, don't pick the cheapest ammo.

**Trophy Bonded Bear Claw:** Developed by Jack Carter and now loaded by Federal, this bonded softpoint is among my favorites because it mushrooms broadly but doesn't fragment. Not streamlined.

**Winchester Fail Safe:** This black-oxide-coated bullet has a lead core capped by a steel insert in the heel, a solid-copper front with a hollow nose. It flies flat, penetrates deep. Weight retention typically exceeds 95 percent.

**Winchester Partition Gold:** Based on the Nosler Partition, this bullet has a longer shank section to boost weight retention, and a steel cap at the rear of the dam to control bulging there at impact.

**Woodleigh Weldcore:** Made in Australia and distributed by Huntington's in Oroville, California, Weldcores are made in many diameters, and in extra-heavy weights. Expect 90 percent weight retention or better.

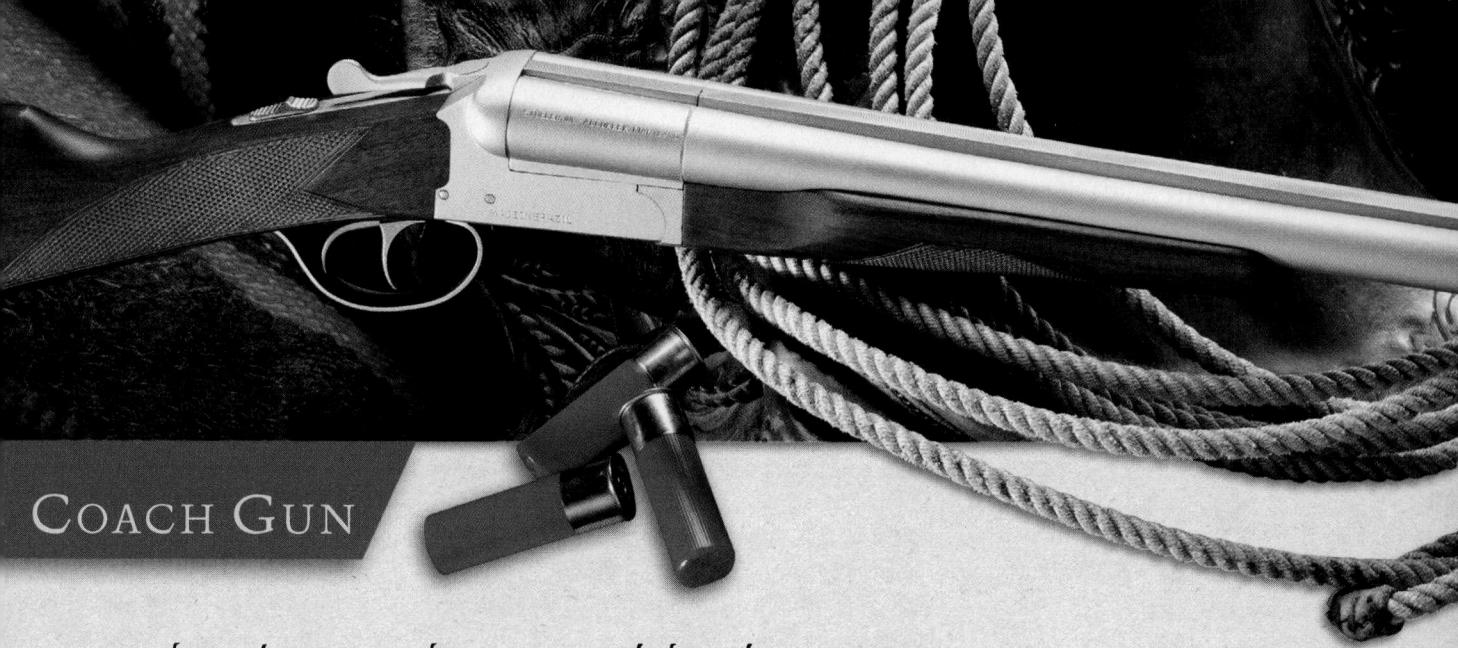

# COACH GUN

## *It's a showdown at the Dry Gulch Saloon.*

*Your hogleg's run dry and you're the only one between the outlaws and the open prairie. It's Stoeger Coach Gun time.*

Cowboy shooting has grown like jimson weed in the last few years, and top competitors count on the Stoeger Coach Gun to pile up points in those crucial shotgun matches. All versions have traditional double triggers for lightning-fast barrel selection in any scenario and conventional barrels with fixed improved cylinder and modified chokes.

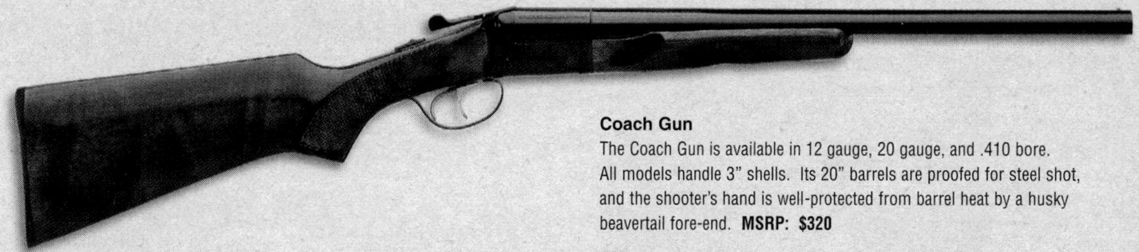

**Coach Gun**
The Coach Gun is available in 12 gauge, 20 gauge, and .410 bore. All models handle 3" shells. Its 20" barrels are proofed for steel shot, and the shooter's hand is well-protected from barrel heat by a husky beavertail fore-end. **MSRP: $320**

SINGLE ACTION SHOOTING SOCIETY
SASS

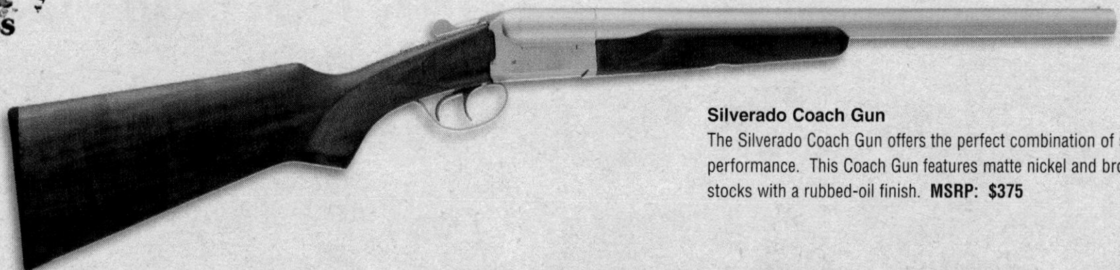

**Silverado Coach Gun**
The Silverado Coach Gun offers the perfect combination of style and performance. This Coach Gun features matte nickel and brown hardwood stocks with a rubbed-oil finish. **MSRP: $375**

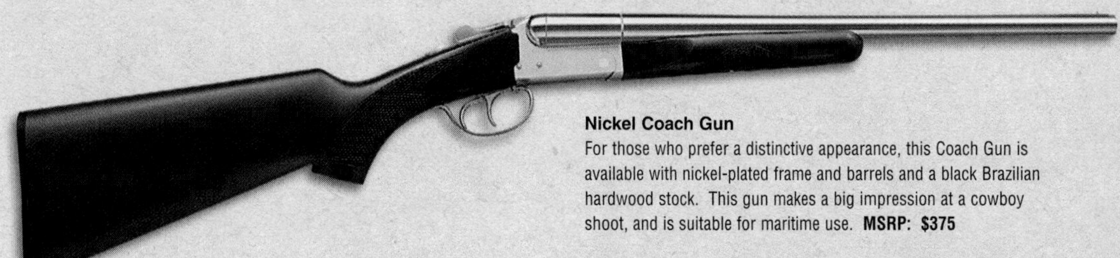

**Nickel Coach Gun**
For those who prefer a distinctive appearance, this Coach Gun is available with nickel-plated frame and barrels and a black Brazilian hardwood stock. This gun makes a big impression at a cowboy shoot, and is suitable for maritime use. **MSRP: $375**

**Stoeger®**
*Serving America's Sportsmen* *Since 1924*

Stoeger Industries • 17603 Indian Head Highway, Suite 200, Accokeek, MD 20607 • (301) 283-6300 • www.StoegerIndustries.com
Part of the Benelli USA® family

# Mule Deer: America's Most Wanted

by Wayne van Zwoll

Not long after World War II, deer hunters entering private land on the Utah/Wyoming border northwest of Evanston were assessed a $5 access fee. That was $5 more than hunters paid during the previous 10,000 autumns mule deer are suspected to have roamed the skirts of the Rockies. It may have been 70,000. The Bering-Chukchi Platform, a land bridge linking Siberia to Alaska, was last exposed in the Wisconsin glacial stage of the late Pleistocene, and back then nobody recorded either dates or fees.

We're better at numbers now, so though we're unsure of just when deer came to North America, we do know that hunting them is getting more expensive. The ranch that charged a $5 access fee when I was a lad now bleeds you for more than $5,000 if you want to chase mule deer. A hundred-fold increase during what, in glacial terms, is the blink of an eye.

The rate hike reflects a growing demand for big mule deer bucks. When *Odocoileus hemionus* was plodding across the Platform, you couldn't find videos on Monster Mule Deer, or hunters to watch them. There was no blaze orange requirement, no Boone & Crockett score sheet. Mercifully, the hairy men wielding spears did not have to pass through TSA screenings on their way to the field.

Largely because of a post-WWII boom in western deer populations,

Client and guide collaborate, using spotting scopes to search mountainsides at long range. Choosing a stand high on saddles or canyon walls is one method of covering slopes traversed by bucks.

hunters during my youth came to expect wide four-point antlers with every Colorado dawn. Livestock management practices in the '30s and '40s, with aggressive predator control and the timing of range regeneration after fire, helped boost deer herds already robust after decades of protection and a wartime hiatus of hunting pressure. My home in Washington State lies at the foot of the Okanogan River, as fabled for big mule deer as Colorado's west slope and the Paunsugunt corner in southwestern Utah. But huge bucks came from all parts of the Rocky Mountains, and from the plain stretching to the Cascades and Sierras. Some states allowed two bucks per hunter. Draw for a license? No one would have taken you seriously.

Fast-forward that eye blink.

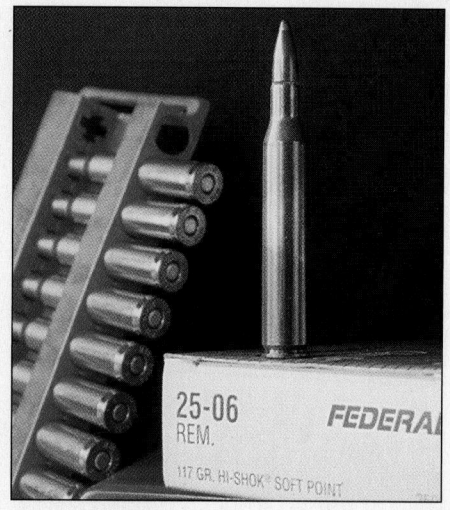

You can't beat the .25-06 for open-country deer. The .270 and .280 are top picks too.

These days, mule deer hunting is by permit only in eastern Oregon, where I shot my first buck on a frigid hill three decades ago. In most places that deliver even a remote chance at big antlers, you'll need preference points to draw a tag. Records-book deer still ghost above Wyoming's Greys River, where my High Country Adventures summer camp teaches outdoors skills to women. But come fall, only a handful of hunters will be allowed to carry rifles on those trails.

Hunters have themselves to thank. Heavy pressure on public land has diminished hunting quality there and boosted demand for areas with limited access. State wildlife agencies have responded with road closures and special "trophy" units with modest deer tag allocations. Ranchers who once regarded deer as pests are finding that hunters will pay to shoot not only exceptional bucks but any bucks. Access once free for the asking now comes with a price tag. And in places that deliver big bucks, sticker shock awaits.

A hunt on the Paunsugunt now costs well into five figures. "A truly impressive mule deer buck is worth more than a Boone & Crockett bull elk," observed one rancher with top-drawer hunting. Ranches like Utah's 210,000-acre Deseret, heir to the $5 access fee, had no trouble drawing hunters even after the brutal winter of 1992-93 knocked their mule deer herd for a loop. And while some handsome bucks fall to Deseret hunters each year, the odds are still stacked mightily against your seeing a candidate for the books.

The books. They've certainly had something to do with the surge in demand for big bucks. When C.J. MacElroy founded Safari Club International in the 1970s, he astutely reasoned that men of means and accomplishment would shell out lots of money to be told that in their silver years they were still vigorous, able men. What better way than an awards program that delivered peer recognition for hunting exploits? A new records book evolved, with less stringent minimum scores than those listed in

Weatherby's Mark V is the quintessential long-range deer rifle. Keep your scope power manageable.

**Big bucks often bed in aspen stands. If the going is noisy, find an alley and a trail and wait.**

**Climb above deer before the sun gets to the valleys. Here a hunter watches bucks ascend.**

Boone & Crockett's. Young, fit sportsmen followed their elders onto a trophy treadmill. No longer was the hunting paramount; what mattered was what you brought back, conveniently reduced to inches of score. And while you might call an animal a trophy, there was also the trophy you received from SCI acknowledging that you'd shot it. And another trophy if you collected several animals of a type. The Grand Slam of wild sheep was only a start.

Lest you sense sarcasm, I'll point out that Safari Club International has been of incalculable value to both wildlife and hunters. By establishing a market for big trophies among people flush enough to keep it buoyed well above reason, SCI priced wildlife into the management of vast private holdings, especially in mule deer country. Ranchers began to think about bolstering deer populations by manipulating habitat and riding herd on poachers. Instead of shooting young bucks with promising antlers, they developed, in conjunction with state biologists, programs that would ensure cohort survival sufficient to maintain old deer on the property. Selective shooting spared deer that showed the best antler potential. Meanwhile, agencies that had once sold as many hunting licenses as possible replaced mass cropping of juvenile deer with more conservative harvest strategies that included doe shooting to maintain higher buck/doe ratios. Antler point minimums added bucks. Reducing quotas in response to dips in herd cycles protected mature bucks.

But assessing value can bolster supply only when Mother Nature goes along. For a variety of interdependent reasons, mule deer numbers Westwide are still in the slide that began alarming biologists in the early 1970s. Mild winters and hunting strictures have delivered revivals locally; however, the big view remains troubling.

You wouldn't think mule deer would have a problem. After all, whitetail numbers are at nuisance levels throughout much of the Midwest, South and Northeast. And they're pioneering in mule deer habitat that historically had no whitetails. Why can't the mule deer make it?

It isn't that they're fussy about habitat. Mule deer have occupied all but a handful of the 60-odd climax vegetation types west of the Mississippi, plus others in Mexico and Canada. They've been known to eat 788 plant species, including forbs, grasses, shrubs, trees, even lichens and mosses. They adjust their diets seasonally to take advantage of highly palatable and nutritious growth stages in plants. Mobile and in many areas migratory, mule deer can move to where the groceries are better and easier to reach. They're comfortable around cattle and elk (less so around domestic sheep), and can benefit from certain livestock grazing rotations. They're adept at finding forage even where we don't see it, and they relish fresh burns.

## Tips for Ambushing Mule Deer

Some hunters post themselves for mule deer, typically on saddles or on canyon walls that afford a view of slopes traveled by bucks. Long-range rifles make stand-hunting for mule deer effective. I prefer to still-hunt, moving slowly along deer trails within rifle-shot of ridgetops, stopping often to glass. No matter your chosen method, remember to:

Keep the wind to your front as much as you can. Mule deer have keen eyes and ears, but their nose is as sensitive as a whitetail's. In the mountains, thermal drag runs uphill most days, so I climb in the dark to get high before the thermals reverse. Cold or rainy weather can scotch thermals, and a prevailing wind can override them. A crosswind is as good as a breeze in your face, but you'll find in alpine terrain that wind commonly fishtails and changes direction as you round a peak.

Carry high-quality binoculars and use them frequently, preferably with the sun behind you. That way, the deer will be most visible, and you'll be hard to see in the glare of the sun. Look near as well as far; bucks often lie tight and can hide handily in a shallow ravine or clump of brush.

Arrive early and hunt late, and bring enough supplies and clothing to stay comfortable all day. Reaching remote country burns lots of time and energy, so you'll want to make your effort worthwhile. Big bucks typically stay in bed most of the day; you'll want to be glassing likely areas (in shadows) early and late. Remember, too, that deer seek warm places in cold weather. An east-facing ridge, sheltered from the wind, is a good bet on a cold October dawn.

You won't always find more deer where hunters are scarce, but you'll probably find bigger deer.

**Three Forks Ranch in north-western Colorado offers spectacular scenery and fine hunting.**

Vulnerable to coyotes when young, and always to cougars, mule deer are prolific enough to counter the effects of normal predation. Yearling does typically breed, though they often bear singlets. Healthy does 2½ to 9½ years of age can be expected to twin.

One reason mule deer aren't coping is that they're not skulkers. Whitetails can live comfortably near humans. Mule deer seek safety in remote country. With subdivisions and agricultural projects eating more and more of prime mule deer habitat, the big-eared animals are moving away—and running out of places to go. In addition, mule deer are particularly vulnerable to the kind of hardware hunters are toting now. A whitetail bursting from underfoot in a weed patch or streaking through the swamp is in no greater danger from a scoped .270 WSM than from an iron-sighted .30-30. Bring the Short Magnum to a mule deer hunt, though, and it will soon demonstrate its superiority in open country. Deer that depend on distance for security have no defense against flat-shooting bullets and powerful optics.

Another tool that ratchets up the pressure on mule deer is the ATV. Three-wheelers, then four-wheelers, replaced the surplus Willys Jeep that post-war sportsmen used to reach remote campsites. Men in no condition to reach deer hideouts on foot can get there easily with four-wheel-drive, a thumb throttle and a scabbard. Increasingly, you see pickups ferrying ATVs across deer country, and sometimes pulling trailers stacked with them. Quicker to use than horses, these machines don't require barns or pastures or hay deliveries. They incur no veterinary charges. They don't run off in the night. And they can go almost anywhere a horse can go.

Motor vehicle restrictions keep ATVs at bay on National Forest and BLM ground—as long as they're enforced. They often are not. A couple of years ago, after climbing two hours in the dark, I came upon an old man watching the eastern sky brighten from a promontory overlooking a remote canyon. I asked him how he'd reached the place, given the motor ban in effect. "Got up real early," he replied, not looking at me. He appeared about 20 pounds overweight. I'd been training for marathons and had come up the hill at full throttle. The snow had shown me no boot tracks. "Where'd you start?" I queried. Just then his two-way radio squawked, and the other party was obviously distressed when the old man indicated I was on the ridge. I left, then, and in short order found the tracks of two four-wheelers. I followed them to a copse of stunted pines. Somehow, I refrained from cutting the fuel lines.

If you can get away from pressured places, you'll find hunting more enjoyable but not necessarily more productive. Mule deer generally live where the living is easy, and areas that have yielded bucks in the past are top bets for hunters. So lots of deer are taken where hunters congregate. And no matter how difficult an adjacent ridge or canyon, you may not find the big buck you think should be hiding there. On the other hand, out-of-the-way places remain my pick when I'm hunting mule deer. Here's why.

I like to hunt where the outcome depends on my own skills, not on the movements of other hunters and the subsequent reactions of the deer. Sometimes other hunters bring you opportunity; sometimes they deny you a shot you deserve. Either way, I prefer to make my own luck. Secondly, I want to look for deer where they're undisturbed. If I know the area is untouched, I hunt more carefully, more thoroughly and with

Use your binocular up close as well as far away, to spot bucks holding tight.

Bowhunting mule deer on South Dakota prairie demands graduate-level hunting skills.

Long shots across sagebrush are less common among veteran hunters, who work to get close.

The world is awash in good deer cartridges. The author likes some obscure calibers, such as these .338-06s.

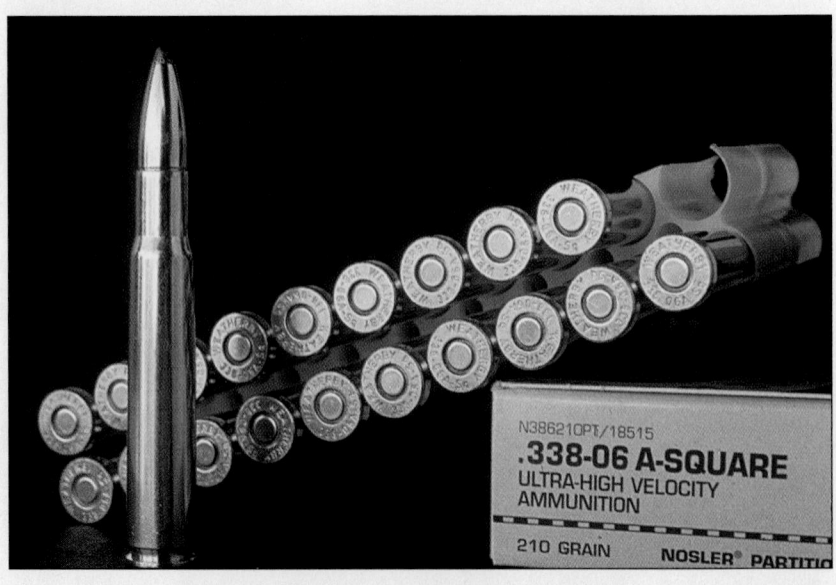

N386210PT/18515
**.338-06 A-SQUARE**
ULTRA-HIGH VELOCITY
AMMUNITION

210 GRAIN      NOSLER® PARTITIO

more anticipation. In sum, I hunt better, and because all hunting is practice, minding the fundamentals is making me a more accomplished hunter. When I observe deer or read deer sign, I'm learning about the animal, not about its response to pressure.

Sure, it's good to know how mule deer behave under the gun, but more valuable to me is tutoring in deer habit. Predicting where deer will be and what they'll do when pressured is relatively easy, if you know the country. Big bucks can lie tight, just like whitetails, and let you walk by. I've shot bucks after having hunted past them, which is why I look frequently to the side and behind me in cover. When hunters push bucks, they often move some distance—into another drainage or across a substantial stretch of prairie.

In the mountains, keep an eye on saddles, but remember that savvy deer know hunters post these places. Once I tracked a big buck just above timberline all afternoon. He didn't drop into canyon timber until my final sighting just at dusk. But he refused to expose himself on a trail to a saddle. On a different hunt, a buck split from a group of deer that hurtled off a ridge to the security of forest. They passed me at slingshot range. He stayed in the rocks above a small copse of trees, reluctant to skyline himself or move across the open slope with his companions.

Finding big deer isn't as easy as finding deer, partly because in most deer herds, few bucks get old enough to grow big antlers. Also, mature bucks have different priorities than other deer. Security is at the top of the list. They like easy living, but they'll settle in places a little less comfortable than attract other deer. They move less (except during rut), and mostly at night. The bigger the buck, the more likely he is to be alone during October, when most riflemen are chasing mule deer. It's easier for a single buck to escape detection than for a herd to hide.

Experienced mule deer hunters look for big deer high in the mountains, above the

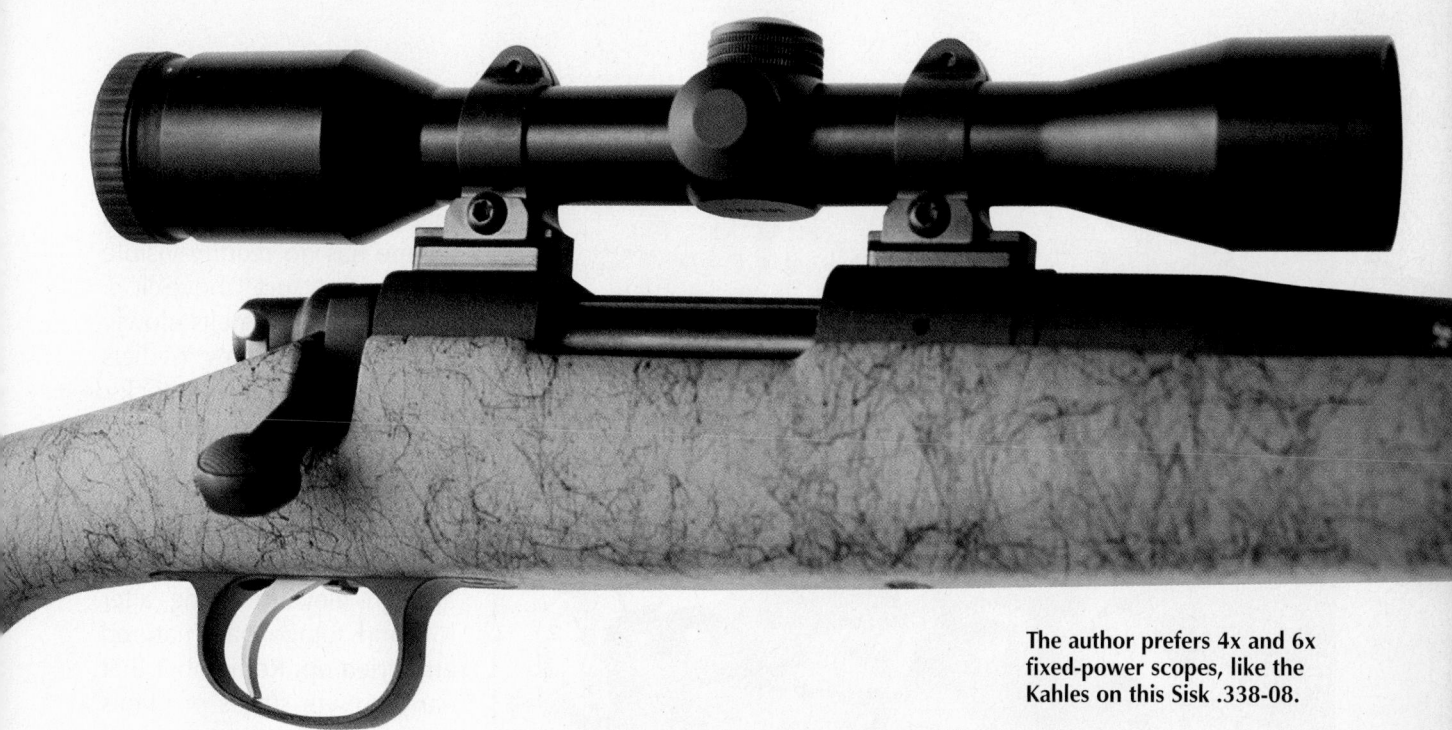

The author prefers 4x and 6x fixed-power scopes, like the Kahles on this Sisk .338-08.

## Rifles, Optics and Ammunition for Mule Deer

You don't need high-priced, sophisticated equipment for hunting mule deer. The most important item is a binocular, because finding deer is a lot harder than shooting them, and it always comes first. My pick in binoculars: a lightweight 8x32 glass. The 4mm exit pupil delivers enough light at dawn and dusk, and 8x is plenty of magnification most of the time. Swarovski's new EL binocular is a lovely instrument, so too are the top-end Zeiss glasses and Leica's Ultravids. My Nikon SE shows me an equally sharp, bright image at less cost, and features the Porro prism design I prefer. These four companies also offer spotting scopes designed for hunters, with 62 to 65mm front lenses. Variable power is useful in a spotting scope, to accommodate different light and wind conditions. You'll find 40x as much power as you can use, and 15x handy for locating game quickly, especially in dim light.

Bolt-action rifles are far and away the most popular among western hunters. Reliable, inexpensive and intrinsically accurate, they come in many guises. Pick one with an adjustable trigger, or install an aftermarket trigger from Timney. You'll want a crisp, consistent pull no heavier than 4 pounds. I like my triggers to break at 2. Good mule deer cartridges abound. My favorite is the .270. Zeroed at 200 yards, it will plant 130-grain spitzers only 6 or 7 inches low at 300. The .25-06, .280 and .30-06 deliver equally flat flight and deadly results. In short-action rifles, the .260, 7mm-08 and .308 excel. Polymer-tipped bullets like Nosler's Ballistic Tip, Hornady's SST and Remington's AccuTip combine precision with the terminal performance that kills deer like lightning. If elk season is on, you might want a controlled-expansion bullet like a Nosler Partition, Remington Core-Lokt Ultra or Winchester Fail Safe. Some hunters favor Barnes's X-Bullet, others the Swift Scirocco for long reach with high weight retention.

Keep scope power reasonable. Many hunters over-scope their rifles with optics too powerful for accurate shooting at common shot distances. I like a straight 4x or 6x scope. In variables, the Leupold 2.5-8x36 Vari-X III is hard to beat. Oversize objective lenses and 30mm tubes add unnecessary weight and bulk. Mount the scope as low as you can for fast aim.

**This last-day buck for Wayne van Zwoll made a Colorado trip worth all the effort.**

**Remington and Winchester Short Magnums flank the .300 Winchester Magnum. All are great choices where deer and elk seasons overlap.**

green places novice sportsmen identify as deer cafeterias. One rocky north slope that's produced several bucks for me has no readily visible forage. But just above it a pocket of snow melts slowly all summer, sending rivulets of water between the rocks. Forbs and grasses spring up there and draw deer, whose slender noses reach into the crevices easily. Palatable, nutritious vegetation remains at high elevation long after lowland forage has matured and dried up. Remember that early growth stages of plants are most appealing to deer, and that during summer and fall these animals are selective feeders.

You'll find good mule deer hunting on both public and private land. For big bucks, it only makes sense to go where buck/doe ratios are high and pressure limited. Last fall, I visited such a place: Three Forks Ranch north of Steamboat Springs, Colorado. A first-class lodge and guide service were bonuses, but the most attractive part of this trip was access to thousands of acres of rolling aspen stands and high prairie, with enough conifer slopes and steep ridges to give shy bucks seclusion. I hunted five days, spending most of my time on ridgelines and in places that would have discouraged other hunters. I saw fewer deer than people hunting the easy spots, but several of the animals I found were mature bucks. Keen to shoot an exceptional specimen, I declined them all until the last morning.

My guide, Paul Brown, had become a hunting companion—a chum who enjoyed spotting and stalking deer and who didn't fret when I refused to shoot. He and I were beating the sun to a barren knob on that final chilly morning, when Paul spied a lone deer about 300 yards away. We sneaked closer, and I bellied onto a talus outcrop. The antlers were high, though of average width. As the first tangerine rays of sun shot into the aspens below us and fired the skyline above the deer, I felt this was the moment to shoot. Sling tight, I settled the crosswire on a forward rib and squeezed the trigger. A 140-grain Core-Lokt Ultra landed with a "thwuck." The deer staggered backward. In a few seconds it was over, a successful hunt made memorable with good companionship, stunning country and nearly a full week of lessons in mule deer behavior.

Shooting early in a hunt may bring you the biggest buck, and it's certainly the most efficient plan if you're after meat. But the most knowledgeable hunters I know make the most of the time they've set aside to hunt. Some set the bar high, shooting only if there's an exceptional buck in their sights. Others explore new territory, leaving honey-holes for last. Saving shots till the end can mean unpunched tags, but you'll learn a great deal when you're hunting.

We can't know if conservative license quotas and an assist from easy winters will brake the slide of mule deer numbers in the Rockies, or if habitat protection and restoration will improve the fortunes of deer whose range has dwindled or deteriorated. But right now, big mule deer still lure enterprising hunters across the West. If to you the hunt is more important than antlers, mule deer season remains as promising and compelling as when you could access the best private coverts for $5.

This old, heavy Montana buck fell to a last-day still-hunting effort in heavy cover.

The author killed this Wyoming mule deer with a Dakota 97 rifle in .300 Dakota.

FEDERAL
PREMIUM
AMMUNITION

*For a few weeks each year, the leading cause of high blood pressure isn't cholesterol.*

Boil a year's worth of dreaming down to that four-second moment of truth and you'll be no stranger to inner turmoil. There's the adrenaline. The knots in your stomach. That shaking in your knees you hope won't find its way to your trigger finger. When your moment comes, be prepared with new Vital-Shok™ from the world leader in premium ammunition. It's available in the world's finest big game bullets including Nosler, Sierra, Barnes, and the unrivaled Speer Trophy Bonded Bear Claw® that features 95% bullet retention. Simply put, there's nothing better for taking trophy animals. We know, because at Federal we search the world over for the highest performing components, and load them with a prescription that can relieve a season's worth of blood pressure in a way no diet <u>ever could</u>.

To find your nearest premium ammunition dealer, visit www.federalpremium.com.

*Every shot counts*™

FEDERAL
PREMIUM®
AMMUNITION

VITAL-SHOK™

20
CENTERFIRE
RIFLE CARTRIDGES
CARTOUCHES

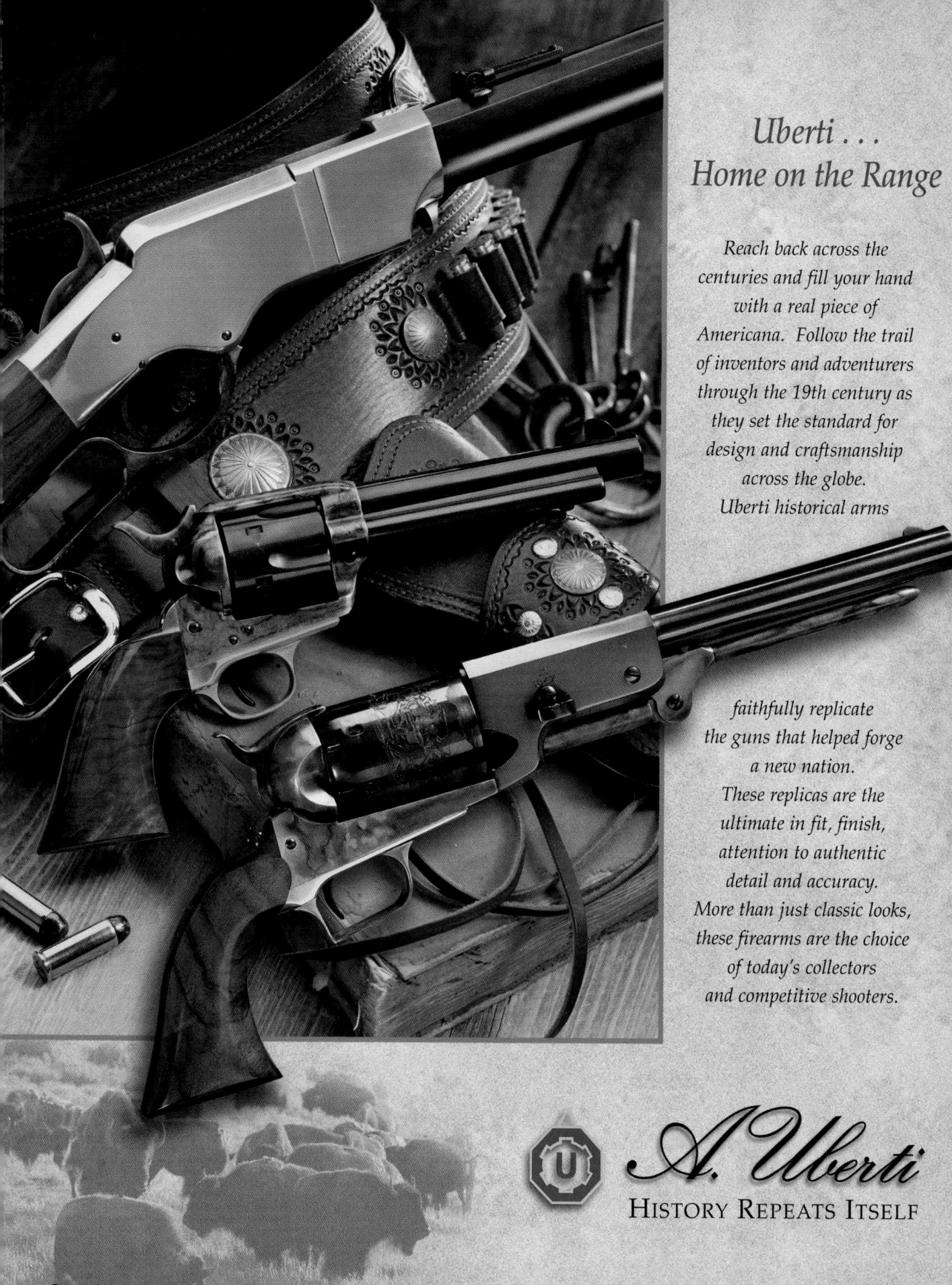

## Uberti . . .
## Home on the Range

Reach back across the
centuries and fill your hand
with a real piece of
Americana. Follow the trail
of inventors and adventurers
through the 19th century as
they set the standard for
design and craftsmanship
across the globe.
Uberti historical arms

faithfully replicate
the guns that helped forge
a new nation.
These replicas are the
ultimate in fit, finish,
attention to authentic
detail and accuracy.
More than just classic looks,
these firearms are the choice
of today's collectors
and competitive shooters.

## A. Uberti
### HISTORY REPEATS ITSELF

# CMP Competitions

## By Ken Horowitz

"Is the line ready?... The line is ready.... Ready on the left.... Ready on the right.... All ready on the firing line.... Fire!"

A barrage unlike any that had ever been experienced by some shooters on the line followed the command of "Fire!" In a minute, it was all over. For those who may have been involved with such rapid fire events under less pleasant circumstances, the range officer's "Cease Fire!" command was a welcome end. For prior combatants and non-veterans alike, this first rapid fire drill of a CMP competition was equally rewarding. Exhilarating is a more appropriate term, for regardless of background, the thrill of this military-style drill has a mysterious draw for everyone involved.

The Civilian Marksmanship Program (CMP) is the current "privatized" incarnation of the DCM (Director of Civilian Marksmanship) programs that had been conducted under the auspices of the United States Army. For most of us, this differentiation of form is about as transparent as that of our Postal Service. How the program is managed, funded and soforth has little to do with its mission or our attraction to it. Although we all know that it is properly the CMP, many of us still fondly refer to our local competitions as DCM.

The DCM was originally formed as a result of the frustrating and time-consuming training of green troops required during the Spanish-American War. While our romantic memories of Teddy Roosevelt and his Rough Riders "storming" San Juan Hill (whatever the historical accuracy of the event may have been) will long outlive trivial concerns such as Doughboy training, the problematical logistics of getting a "soft" America into

A competitor takes aim with his bolt-action Model 1903-A3 Springfield. While most shooters keep their spotting scopes on their offhand side, this particular rifleman keeps his on the strong side.

fighting shape is the spark that ignited the formation of the DCM.

Contrary to our perceptions that our late 19th-century forebears were rugged folks adept at shooting disciplines, for the most part, the general population was not so skilled. Being the first and second generations following the hostilities of the Civil War, the gentrification of America began to insulate its children from the art of weaponry. While many of the recruits of the Civil War period had some basic skill in wielding firearms (many, particularly in the South, had to bring their own into service during the first year of the war), for many Spanish-American War recruits, that rifle issued during the first boot camp drill may well have been the first one they ever touched.

It was apparent that the citizenry at large did not represent the ever ready militia contemplated by our founding fathers. For national security, it was necessary to jump-start a program encouraging the public to develop and maintain skills at arms, especially civilians and youth who were expected to join the armed forces. Thus, in 1903, Congress passed an Act establishing the National Board for the Promotion of Rifle Practice which led to the subsequent formation of the DCM, and later the CMP.

From its inception, the CMP (for simplicity, we'll just refer to all progenitors by the current name) promoted excellence in marksmanship through the conduct of Annual National Matches, originally conducted at Sea Girt, New Jersey, but soon moved to the present Camp Perry, Ohio, site. However, while the Camp Perry matches are very well attended, as a practical matter, most sanctioned CMP competitions take place at local affiliated clubs throughout the country. According to the CMP's most recent Annual Report available at the time of this writing, its safety and training programs reached an estimated 300,000 youth and likely an estimated total of one million people per year.

Soon after I joined Falls Township Rifle and Pistol Association (Falls Township, Pennsylvania), I decided to give CMP competition a try. As an affiliated CMP club, there are club M-1 Garands available for use by members. Additionally, club ammunition, acquired surplus through the CMP, is available at a modest cost. Never having held one of Patton's greatest battle rifles, I attended a short training session the day before the match where I was shown the safety, loading and firing features peculiar to the M-1 Garand. Admittedly, I was a bolt-action guy up to that point, never having been attracted to semiautomatic actions in general. On the other hand, I am a target shooter, not a hunter, sometimes shooting more rounds off a bench in a day than a casual annual deer permit hunter fires in a lifetime. I was well aware of the recoil dampening benefits of a gas-operated action. I was so

An open class shooter's well-equipped gear cart supports a high-tech target version of the FN-FAL military rifle. Such customized rifles do not compete against service grade rifles but are permitted in open competitions.

Competitors also work the range. These shooters are setting targets for the upcoming match. There are no guns on the line during this setup process.

impressed with the performance of the Garand at the next day's match that I immediately began the paperwork process to acquire one through the CMP's Sales Program (more on that later).

## The Game

At the local level, the CMP sanctions several types of competitions, pistol as well as rifle, which are outlined in its CMP Competition Rules booklet. In rifle, while the basic rules are designed for 200 yards and farther, there are appropriate modifications allowed for conversion of the courses of fire to 100 yards, thus enabling many more ranges to participate in CMP competitions. Essentially, at 100 yards, the official targets are half the size at half the distance, with the resultant same sight picture. Additionally, local match directors are allowed some latitude to make modifications to the course of fire that do not interfere with the overall match objectives. For example, while the published rules the CMP's official course of fire "As-issued Military Rifle Match, Course B" calls for a string of 20 slow-fire shots for score, plus up to 5 sighting shots in 25 minutes, at the competitions I've attended, this is broken into two strings of 10 shots in 10 minutes each starting after all sighting shots have already been made. A complete list of all of the official CMP courses of fire can be found in the previously mentioned CMP Competition Rules booklet available from the CMP.

At Falls Township Rifle and Pistol Association, a shooter may fire the 100-yard course or the 200-yard course, as follows:

- **First relay**–10 shots in 10 minutes from a prone position, loaded singly.
- **Second relay**–10 shots in 10 minutes from a prone position, loaded singly.
- **Third relay**–10 shots in 70 seconds from a prone position. For this relay, the shooter starts in the standing position with 2 rounds. The time starts with the command of "Fire!" and includes getting into position and changing to a second magazine loaded with 8 rounds.
- **Fourth relay**–10 shots in 60 seconds from a sitting or kneeling position (shooter's choice). Again, the shooter starts in the standing position with 2 rounds. The time starts with the command of "Fire!" and includes getting into position and changing to a second magazine loaded with 8 rounds.
- **Fifth relay**–10 shots in 10 minutes from a standing position, loaded singly. For this relay, the sling may not be used.

Each relay is shot at a black bullseye target, officially sized in accordance with rules relating to each relay. Another competitor does the scoring of your target and hits range from 5 points to 10 points; thus, a perfect score would be 500. An even "more perfect" score would have the 10-point hits in the smaller X-ring within the 10-ring.

The competition is as friendly as it can get and there is no award other than your own satisfaction and perhaps, admiration by your peers.

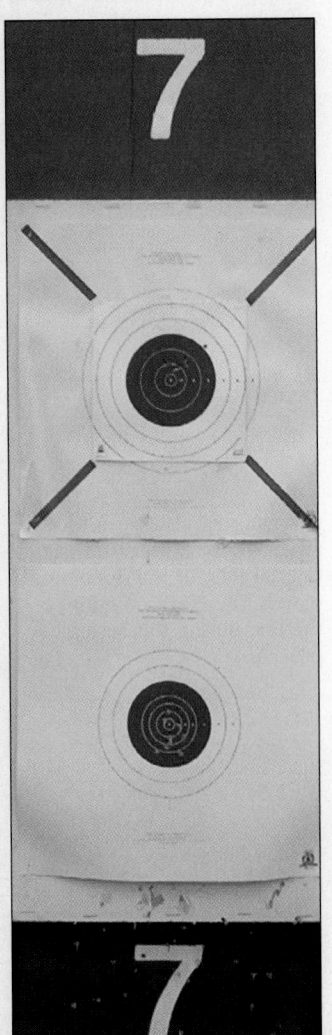

This is a typical CMP target board for a 100-yard slow fire relay. The upper target is for sighting-in only. The lower target is for score.

Regardless of shooter skill, you're really shooting against yourself. In fact, the less skilled shooter gains even more from these matches than the top shooters. Everyone wants to help and I can say that more of my improvement over the years has come from competitor advice than any other source. Whether shooting technique, load data, accouterments, I'm always learning from the better shooters, allegedly competitors, but not really. They're more like mentors. Interestingly, after the post-match range cleanup, more time is frequently spent at the range with informal after-sessions, than the time it actually takes to run through the course of fire.

While target setters are downrange, shooters remain behind the yellow safety line until the range officer gives the command allowing them to cross the line and handle their equipment.

## The Guns

While certain matches are specific as to gun type, as, for example, an "all Garand" match, there is a lot of flexibility in most local matches as long as the rifle is capable of being reloaded during the rapid-fire drills. Obviously, so-called "space guns" that have been tricked-out with a lot of features are in a different class than standard issue military arms, but as a competitor, your interest should be on what you are shooting and how you fare against shooters using like-kind arms. More important, in keeping with the spirit of the original Congressional Act, shooters should strive to constantly improve, thus competing with themselves over long periods of time.

Commonly, a current match will have a variety of weaponry, ranging from bolt-action 1903 Springfields through M-1 Garands and civilian versions of M-14 and M-16 rifles (since the M-14 and M-16 are current government issue, they are not available as military surplus; further, even if they become available in the future, any full-automatic features would have to be eliminated before public sale).

Once the range is clear, competitors are allowed to approach their equipment, and can begin to ready themselves for the upcoming round of competition.

When I started shooting CMP matches, M-1 Garands dominated the scene. At that point, it was the latest of military surplus rifles to be available to the public (still the case as this is written) and ammunition requirements were .30 caliber. At the inception of the CMP, the 30-40 Krag was in general issue and the later military version of the 30-06 Springfield was the ammunition for both the 1903 Springfield and M-1 Garand. The M-14 uses the military version of the 308

After each relay, targets are pulled and a fresh target is stapled in place for the next relay.

This target shows an excellent result. Any shots on a line are given the higher score. This score of 100 includes 5 shots that are in the X-ring.

Winchester. For a long time after the issue of the M-16 with its military version of the .223 Remington, CMP rules continued to specify .30 caliber.

Then one day the scene changed dramatically. With more M-16s being issued to our military personnel than any other rifle in history, with the intent of the CMP to get civilians adequately trained in the use of arms, it only made sense to allow the use of the smaller .223 caliber ammunition and the civilian AR-15 types of rifles associated with it. This put the general public on the same footing as the team shooters of the military.

As a result, the "black guns" with their straight-through stocks, pistol grips, high sights and diminutive cartridges now dominate the scene. M-1 Garands continue to hold a respectable second place in quantity of rifles at the matches I've attended and there are still regulars who shoot a 1903 Springfield or other suitable rifle. Whatever you choose, it's not as important as choosing something and getting out to a match. If there are any doubts as to the eligibility of your outfit, the match director will gladly help you. Typically, CMP affiliated clubs have a number of M-1 Garands or other rifles available for use by club members.

I started shooting CMP competitions with a club M-1 Garand inasmuch as I owned no rifle at that time that would have qualified for a match and subsequently I acquired my own through the CMP Sales Program. Years later, I also acquired an AR-15 type rifle (Bushmaster Competition rifle) through the CMP Sales Program. Currently, I use both, depending on my whim at the moment. In evaluating my progress, I keep tabs on my scores separately. The M-1 Garand is an as-issued battle rifle whose groups are not intended to do what the Bushmaster competition-style rifle is designed to do.

## CMP Sales Program

An additional benefit of shooting in a CMP competition is the qualification to participate in the CMP Sales Program to acquire a rifle. At one time, the CMP Sales Program offered only direct sales of surplus firearms consistent with its mission of encouraging citizens to become more proficient shooters, ostensibly in the event an emergency call-up of our citizen army were necessary. While many shooters don't envision the likelihood of such a call-up, there is no shortage of those who take advantage of the opportunity to own a piece of history at a reasonable price. In order to qualify, a purchaser must be a member of a CMP affiliated club, comply with all state and local laws, provide proof of U.S. citizenship, age and complete a marksmanship participation requirement. Of course, there are further requirements, such as an FBI NICS check, but due to the possibility of change, these are best gotten directly from your club program director or from the CMP.

While certain lots of surplus rifles include special grade or collector value items, the vast majority of them are service grade, just like the M-1 Garand I purchased and now regularly use in local competitions. Other than a good cleaning, I left all the wood dings and dents of history occasionally wondering their pedigree. Pointing a piece of history downrange lends an aura that cannot be matched by any modern factory firearm. Additionally, being somewhat recoil shy, this is the only rifle in .30-06 that I shoot comfortably. The heavyweight and gas-operated recoil dampening effect are features that I am sure went a long way in rapidly readying troops.

**These shooters are firing a slow fire relay at 200 yards. The targets at different ranges (100 and 200 yards) are sized so that the sight picture remains the same regardless of which range you shoot.**

At CMP matches each scorer must carefully record and compile a competitor's score.

While some prefer traditional military arms such as the M-1 Garand or 1903 Springfield, others, such as this shooter, opt for an AR-15 type rifle for CMP open competitions.

As previously mentioned, to a point not so long ago, service rifle competition demanded that CMP competitors use .30 caliber rifles capable of shooting the rapid fire drill with a reload during the drill. Surplus M-1 Garands as well as a decreasingly limited Springfield 1903s could be purchased directly from the CMP for this purpose or a shooter could acquire an M-1A type rifle or other qualified firearm from a commercial source.

Inevitably, someone woke up to the fact that standard service issue has been using 5.56mm ammunition à la the M-16 for close to four decades now. As a result, the .30 caliber requirement was changed. Since that time, dominance in high-power rifle shooting in CMP competitions has changed dramatically to M-16 type and AR-15 type rifles with fast twist barrels designed to stabilize heavy 5.56mm (military) or .223 Remington (commercial version) bullets that have higher ballistic coefficients.

Promotion of civilian marksmanship along the lines it was originally intended required getting quality rifles available to nonmilitary personnel. However, since the M-16 is still standard military issue, it cannot qualify as surplus; even if it were, such features as selective fire would preclude its general use, even if legal to possess; further, the M-16 retains too many "military" features which would ban the rifle in certain states (mine, for example).

The CMP developed a unique solution whereby it heavily subsidizes the purchase price of a target rifle when purchased through a CMP affiliated club or state association that has both a high-power rifle program and a junior rifle program. This is a brand-new match grade rifle available through Bushmaster or Compass Lake. In addition to the normal CMP purchase eligibility requirements, due to the nature of the subsidy, there are more stringent restrictions to ensure that these rifles are not purchased for profiteering. Resale is strictly regulated since the intent is that these rifles be used for competition, not otherwise.

There are lots of target goodies on these rifles, the details of which can be gotten from the CMP website, but some of the more salient features are worth noting. As for the Bushmaster Competition Rifle that I acquired through the CMP's Sales Program, it has a free-floated extra heavy competition

barrel, a full 1 inch under the hand guard. The chrome-moly vanadium steel barrel, nicely crowned at the muzzle, has a 1 inch in 8 inch right-hand twist for heavy bullet stabilization. While not necessary for local 100- or 200-yard courses of fire, the fast twist allows for the use of heavyweight bullets at long distances, as for example, an 80-grain bullet at 600 yards.

The trigger is a finely honed competition trigger factory set at a CMP compliant 3.5-pound first stage with a 1.0-pound second stage let-off. For me, this is about the crispest trigger I have. I'm somewhat lax when it comes to accepting triggers as they are, with perhaps a minor adjustment here or there, but just a few pulls on the Bushmaster have spoiled me. Believe me, I still love my M-1 Garand, but it takes such a love to overlook the lousy trigger!

The rear sight of the Bushmaster is specially modified to accept interchangeable micro-aperture peeps. It is adjustable for windage and elevation with very noticeable clicks. The mate is a front sight specially ground for clarity.

To offset the front heavy rifle, largely attributed to the massive barrel, and also to give the rifle the weight that has become associated with target performance, there is a lead insert in the buttstock, which brings the total weight of the package to just under 13 pounds; yet, despite its weight, the rifle is very comfortable to hold. There are even more features and options available on the Compass Lake rifles.

**The offhand standing position is often the downfall of many shooters. Some, however, fare better in this relay than in the others. Note that the use of a sling is not permitted in this relay.**

## Getting Started

It's easier to get started in this exciting target sport than many shooters think. Check with your local shooting club to see if CMP competitions are offered there. If not, someone at the club should be able to tell you where to go. Your local sporting goods shop, the place where you buy your guns and ammunition, usually has a pretty good idea of what's happening in the area. You can contact the CMP directly by phone, fax, mail or e-mail or check out its website.

Between relays, competitors go downrange to score each other's targets. After the scorer enters the results on the shooter's record card, the shooter has an opportunity to review it. If there is any disagreement, it is settled by the range officer.

The next step is to start playing. I've talked to many would-be club members who watch our local competitions and I frequently get the same reply when I ask why they are watching instead of shooting. Usually they don't think they are good enough. That's nonsense. If you know the safe handling and operation of the rifle, you're good enough. just like I was the first time and everyone else on the line. No one cares what your score is except you and if you enjoy the shoot and the camaraderie associated with it, you can always come back the next time and try to improve it. In fact, that's what we keep doing, coming back and trying to improve our marksmanship. I guess that 1903 Congressional Act had some vision!

For more information on CMP programs contact:
Civilian Marksmanship Program
PO Box 576
Port Clinton, OH 43452
419-635-2141
888-267-0786    Fax: 419-636-2802 or 419-635-2573
www.civilianmarksmanshipprogram.com
E-mail: clubs3@odcmp.com or custserve@odcmp.cpm

# High Performance Muzzleloading
## by Toby Bridges

**The smokeless powder loads shot out of the Savage Model 10ML II produce tremendous knockdown power, putting game down clean and fast.**

hink about the title of this article for just a few seconds. Now, whoever would have thought that the term "high performance" would ever be used in conjunction with "muzzleloading"? But that's exactly what's happening with this centuries-old sport. And as more and more big game hunters turn to rifles of front-loaded design to take full advantage of special "muzzleloader" big game seasons, they are now demanding performance that, until now, muzzle-loaded firearms had been incapable of delivering.

Let's face it, the muzzleloading guns … the powders now loaded … the technology of modern saboted bullets … the sighting systems now preferred … and the performance expectations of the modern-day muzzleloading hunter have all changed dramatically over the past two

Through the late 1980s and early 1990s, in-line muzzle-loading hunters went after big game with saboted jacketed hollow-point pistol bullets, like the .45-inch Nosler shown here.

The light spire-pointed Knight/Barnes all-copper "Red Hot" bullets for the .50 caliber in-line rifles can be loaded with hot charges of Pyrodex or Triple Seven to produce some of the highest velocities possible from a modern "non-smokeless" in-line muzzleloader.

Outdoor writer Tom Fegely used his .50 caliber Knight MK-85 to cleanly drop this mulie buck at just over 150 yards.

decades. Back when William "Tony" Knight introduced the first Knight MK-85, in 1985, a "hot" load for one of the .50 caliber modern in-line rifles consisted of 100 grains of Pyrodex "RS" behind a saboted 240- to 260-grain jacketed hollow-point bullet. Such loads would produce a muzzle velocity of around 1,600 f.p.s., with just a little over 1,400 f.p.e. Today, it would be safe to claim that every modern in-line ignition .50 caliber muzzle-loaded rifle on the market is easily capable of getting a saboted bullet out of the muzzle at well over 2,000 f.p.s., and the manufacturers of several so-called "Super .45" caliber in-line rifles are claiming, or rather boasting, sabot bullet velocities of 2,500+ f.p.s.

While vast improvements in the rifles themselves can be partially credited with the significantly greater performance capabilities of today's ultramodern in-line percussion hunting rifles, just as much, if not more, credit goes to what these rifles are now being loaded with. Without the new powders, better source of fire for ignition, improved sabots and projectiles that have been designed to be driven at higher speeds, muzzleloading hunters would still be faced with the same performance possible nearly 20 years ago.

When it comes to optimum .50 caliber muzzleloader performance, the new "King of the Hill" is unquestionably the No. 209 primer ignited Savage Model 10ML II. And what this rifle can be loaded with is definitely just as important as the rifle itself when it comes to living up to such claims. You see, this is the only production muzzleloader on the market that can be safely loaded and shot with modern nitrocellulose-based smokeless powders. And with some of the hotter loads, this .50 caliber is capable of getting a 250-grain bullet out of the muzzle at better than 2,400 f.p.s.

Big jacketed hollow-point bullets, like the 300-grain .452-inch Hornady XTP, are often exceptionally accurate at 100 yards, but can lack the aerodynamics to maintain velocity and energy well out at 200 yards.

The polymer-tipped Precision Rifle bullets offer exceptionally high ballistic coefficients for improved downrange performance. The 300-grain belted "QT" bullet shown here has a .270 b.c.

The author used a prototype Knight DISC Rifle to take this bull elk, the first ever for the new muzzleloader. The DISC Rifle was among the first to be loaded with a 150-grain charge of Pyrodex Pellets.

Thanks to the cleanliness of smokeless powders like IMR-SR4759, Accurate Arms XMP5744 and VihtaVuori N110, I have truly enjoyed shooting and hunting with the Savage muzzleloader. I can shoot all afternoon, or hunt all week, and not have to worry about rushing home or back to camp to tear down a rifle that has had one or fifty shots fired through it. Cleaning can be put off for a week, or a month without worrying about corrosive powder fouling ruining the bore. With 45 grains of VihtaVuori N110, the stainless Model 10ML II I hunt with will spit a saboted 250-grain .45 caliber bullet out of the muzzle at 2,405 f.p.s. That's an amazing 3,200 foot-pounds of muzzle energy from a muzzleloader!

New sleek bullet designs like the .452 inch diameter Hornady SST (Super Shock Tip) really turn this rifle into a potent muzzle-loaded big game rifle. With 45 grains of N110 pushing the aerodynamic polymertipped 250-grain SST out of the muzzle, this .240 ballistic coefficient projectile will maintain velocity and energy exceptionally well downrange. In fact, all the way out at 200 yards, this load is still good for around 1,750 f.p.s., and will hit a whitetail with right at 1,700 foot-pounds of wallop. That's 300 foot-pounds more energy than the popular 100-grain Pyrodex loads shot during the late 1980s generated at the muzzle! (Thompson/Center Arms also

Early in-line rifles and loads were excellent performers out to about 150 yards, often making it difficult to get shots at open country game like pronghorns.

Early Knight in-line rifle models, like the BK-92 Black Knight, left, and MK-85 Predator, right, proved to be excellent performers with 100-grain charges of Pyrodex.

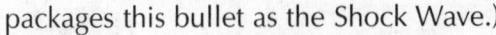

packages this bullet as the Shock Wave.)

Thanks to Hodgdon Powder Company's new black powder substitute known as Triple Seven, many of the new non-smokeless hi-tech in-line rifles are also now producing muzzle velocities that were basically unheard of just five years ago. Like earlier Pyrodex, which is still also produced by Hodgdon, Triple Seven is offered in both loose grain and pellet form. However, the new powder is significantly hotter, producing noticeably higher velocities than equal charges of either loose powder or pelletized Pyrodex.

By actual weight, one of the so-called 50-grain Pyrodex Pellets weighs in at around 38 grains, while a Triple Seven Pellet weighs just 31 grains. Yet, both are supposed to be the equivalent of a 50-grain black powder charge. During the late 1990s, both Knight Rifles, of Centerville, Iowa and Thompson/Center Arms, of Rochester, New Hampshire, popularized shooting magnum 150-grain (3-pellet) Pyrodex Pellet charges to get saboted 240- or 250-grain bullets out of the muzzle at velocities approaching 2,000 f.p.s. To ensure positive ignition and complete burn of the compressed pellet charges, rifles like the Knight DISC Rifle and T/C Encore 209x50 Magnum relied on the hotter fire from No. 209 shotshell primers. Today, just about every top -selling in-line rifle model utilizes similar primer ignition systems.

Since those days, both Knight and T/C have slightly revamped their "magnum" muzzleloaders, and with three of the new Triple Seven Pellets, both of these rifles are now capable of topping 2,000 f.p.s. with a 250-grain bullet. And to compete with the higher velocities possible with the new smokeless powder Savage Model 10ML II, both of these companies have more recently promoted the use of lighter saboted projectiles.

During the late 1990s, Knight Rifles introduced a new line of all-copper spire-point hollow-point saboted bullets for their .50 caliber DISC Rifle. Produced by Barnes Bullets, the lightweight .451-inch diameter projectiles have been offered in 180-, 200- and 220-grain weights. Ahead of hefty charges of Pyrodex or Triple Seven, loose powder or pellets, these bullets are capable of developing some pretty impressive velocities out of 24- and 26-inch barrels.

With a 150-grain charge of Pyrodex Pellets, the 180-grain bullet leaves the muzzle at around 2,175 f.p.s. Due to the light weight, the load generates right at 1,890 f.p.e. at the muzzle, but thanks to a near .210 ballistic coefficient, this light and aerodynamic spire point still maintains around 900 f.p.e. at 200 yards, which is sufficient for taking deer-sized game. The slightly heavier 200 grain .451 inch Knight "Red Hot" has a slightly higher .220 b.c., and pushed from the muzzle of a 24-inch Knight DISC Extreme barrel at 2,104 f.p.s. by three 50-grain Pyrodex Pellets, the bullet generates 1,962 f.p.e. Because of the slightly better b.c., out at 200 yards the 200-grain bullet hits with around 935 f.p.e. And even with the "magnum" charges of Pyrodex Pellets, recoil with either of these two bullets is very tolerable.

Hodgdon Powder Company does not recommend loading either Pyrodex or Triple Seven (loose powder or pellet) in any quantities greater than 100 grains. Still, just about every modern primer ignited in-line muzzleloading rifle maker now recommends 3-pellet loads for optimum velocities and range. As already stated, Triple Seven is hotter than Pyrodex, and that's why a Triple Seven Pellet by actual weight is around 7 grains lighter than a Pyrodex Pellet. A 2-pellet load of each will give about the same velocities, around 1,675 f.p.s. with a saboted 250-grain bullet. Likewise, a 100-grain charge of Pyrodex "RS" will give close to 1,625 f.p.s. with the same weight bullet. However, a 100-grain charge of FFFg Triple Seven will push the velocity of a saboted 250-grain bullet to around 1,950 f.p.s. This powder is noticeably hotter.

Precision Rifle of Manitoba, Canada, has earned a reputation for producing outstanding cold swaged lead muzzleloader hunting bullets. Of particular interest to the performance-minded muzzleloading hunter has been the company's line of "QT" and "Dead Center" bullets. Both feature a sharp polymer tip to give these bullets tremendous-

The Savage Model 10ML II rifle has significantly raised the bar for in-line muzzle-loader performance. This muzzle-loaded big game rifle has been designed to digest loads of modern smokeless powder.

ly high ballistic coefficients. In fact, even the hefty 300-grain saboted .45 caliber "Dead Center" (for shooting out of a .50 caliber bore) has a b.c. of .336. Loaded with a 110-grain charge of FFFg Triple Seven, the bullet is pushed from the muzzle of a 24-inch barrel at 1,880 f.p.s., with 2,354 f.p.e. At 200 yards, the big polymer-tipped spire point will still drive home with 1,487 f.p.e.

Easily the most unusual sabot bullet in the Precision Rifle lineup is a long cylindrical spire-point .375 b.c. bullet of 195 grains that measures just .357 inch in diameter. The bullet can be loaded into either a .45 caliber rifle, using a sabot designed for the small diameter, or it can be loaded into a .50 caliber bore using a unique double sabot arrangement. With a 110-grain charge of FFFg Triple Seven, Precision Rifle data shows the duplex-saboted bullet leaving the muzzle of a .50 caliber at 2,180 f.p.s., with 2,057 f.p.e. Thanks to the extremely high ballistic coefficient, the load still hits with 1,365 f.p.e. at 200 yards.

A couple of years ago, Thompson/Center Arms introduced their new Omega "drop-action" muzzleloader. The gun has become extremely popular largely due to the ease of cleaning a rifle design that allows the action to drop down completely out of the way. Another reason for the Omega's popularity has been that with such a short action, this rifle features a full 28-inch barrel, yet is shorter overall than just about any other in-line muzzleloader with a 24-inch barrel (due to the receiver length). An added benefit of the longer barrel has been slightly higher velocities with the same amounts of Pyrodex or Triple Seven than from shorter 24-inch barreled in-line muzzleloaders.

Shooting a 200-grain .400-inch diameter Hornady SST, loaded with a .40x.50 Muzzleload Magnum Pro-

**The Savage Model 10ML II is a stellar performer with hot loads of FFFg Triple Seven. This 1¼-inch, 100-yard group was produced by a 130-grain charge of the powder behind the 250-grain Hornady SST bullet.**

**Never before have muzzle-loading hunters been more interested in the long-range performance of the rifles and loads they shoot.**

ducts sabot, ahead of a 100-grain charge of FFFg Triple Seven, I have found that I can get right at 2,204 f.p.s. at the muzzle of the T/C Omega's 28-inch barrel. The same load shot out of the Savage Model 10ML II 24-inch barrel has recorded 2,166 f.p.s. Thompson/Center does not address shooting heavier loads of loose grain FFFg Triple Seven, so I didn't increase the powder charge. However, since the Savage muzzleloader has

been designed for far greater pressures, I worked on up to 130 grains of the powder in that rifle, to get the spire-pointed .225 b.c. bullet out of the muzzle at around 2,320 f.p.s., with 2,390 f.p.e. And with a 43-grain charge of VihtaVuori N110, the Savage muzzleloader recorded 2,488 f.p.s. with the 200-grain .40 caliber SST. At 200 yards, the bullet would retain 958 f.p.e. with the hot charge of Triple Seven, and just over 1,350 f.p.e. with the N110 smokeless load out of the Savage 10ML II.

As this was being written, Knight Rifles was preparing to unveil a new "drop action" in-line muzzleloader of their own, to be dubbed the "Revolution." This 209 primer ignited .50 caliber muzzleloader will feature a 27-inch barrel for optimum velocities with hefty loads of Pyrodex and Triple Seven. If the company does endorse the use of as much as 130 grains of the FFFg granulation, this long barreled modernistic frontloader would get the saboted 180-grain Knight "Red Hot" out of the bore at around 2,375 f.p.s. At the muzzle, the load would generate 2,500 f.p.e., and the .220 b.c. all-copper spire point would still hit with more than 1,200 f.p.e. downrange at 200 yards.

The outstanding performance on deer and similarly sized big game

**Smokeless powders like IMR-SR4759 perform exceptionally well out of the Savage Model 10ML II, but produce pressures that can destroy just about any other muzzleloader.**

**Just about any of today's newer in-line rifle models are capable of delivering exceptional accuracy. Muzzleloading hunter Ted Hatfield checks out a great sub 1½ inch, 100-yard group shot with an Austin & Halleck Model 420.**

Although lighter in actual weight, each Triple Seven Pellet is pretty much equivalent to the performance of a Pyrodex Pellet.

Hodgdon Powder Company's new Triple Seven in powder form is producing higher velocities than possible with any other "black powder substitute" that has been available to the modern muzzleloading hunter.

Aerodynamic new bullet designs, like the Hornady SST, shown here with the company's own "Lock-N-Load" Speed Sabot, are proving capable of delivering outstanding accuracy and game-taking performance.

with the hyper speed (for a muzzleloader anyway) "Super Magnum" .45 caliber in-line muzzleloaders promised by rifle makers simply hasn't been realized by many who have switched to the smaller bore. I've shot a few, and haven't been impressed with the accuracy of the hotter loads. Unfortunately, my most accurate loads were generally with 100 grain charges of Pyrodex Pellets and not the hot 150-grain loads that are required to deliver the speed, range and knockdown power so many muzzleloader manufacturers claim. And with just 100-grain charges, most of these rifles and the light bullets shot with them simply become 100- to 150-yard effective hunting rifles. Many of those who went to the .45 for flat shooting to 200 yards are already coming back to the .50 caliber in-lines, once again looking for the punch needed to ensure a clean kill on big game.

A number of .45 caliber in-line rifle makers have openly bragged about 2,400 to 2,500 f.p.s. velocities with 150-grain Pyrodex Pellet charges behind light saboted bullets. In its recent catalog, Thompson/Center touts that their new Super Encore 209x45 Magnum is capable of getting a saboted 155-grain .40 caliber Hornady XTP out of the 26-inch barrel at over 2,600 f.p.s. with a 150-grain charge of Pyrodex Pellets. And that is very possible. However, the 155-grain .40 caliber XTP has a b.c. of just .138. Even with a 2,600 f.p.s. muzzle velocity, this bullet will slow to 1,500 f.p.s. at 200 yards, and retain just 775 f.p.e.

One of T/C's Encore 209x50 Magnum in-line rifles is capable of getting a saboted 250-grain Shock Wave (SST) out of the muzzle at around 1,990 f.p.s. (thanks to the 26-inch barrel), generating 2,200 f.p.e. at the muzzle. Now, this bullet has a .240 b.c., and by the time it gets to the 200-yard mark, velocity has decreased to around 1,425 f.p.s., but the bullet retains 1,125 f.p.e. The heavier 250-grain Shock Wave may start off more than 600 f.p.s. slower than the light 155-grain XTP, but at the finish line, it retains nearly one-third more energy. And it is the lackluster energy levels down-range which is causing hunters to put less and less emphasis on the .45 caliber in-line big game rifles.

Today's muzzleloading hunter is more in tune to muzzle-loader ballistics than at anytime in history. Not only do they want to know what kind of muzzle velocity and energy a rifle

Outside temperatures were near 100 degrees when the author took this South Texas wild pig with a Savage muzzleloader. When temperatures get this hot, getting top performance from hot loads can get tough.

and load develops, they also want to know what kind of energy the load retains at the outer limits of muzzleloader effectiveness—out at 200 to 250 yards. And they want to know what kind of bullet drop to expect from 100 to 200 yards. To get the velocities needed to turn any of today's hot high performance muzzleloading big game rifles into effective 200-yard hunting rifles, these shooters are also now ready and willing to employ specialized loading techniques to tap the accuracy possible with many of the modern rifles and equally modern loads. In short, they are looking for consistent one-shot kill performance, whether at 50 yards or 200 yards.

Today's sabots are the best we've ever had. When I first began shooting the Savage Model 10ML II with smokeless powder loads about five years ago, a 41-grain charge of VihtaVuori N110 was about the hottest charge I could hold back with the plastic cup. The powder charge would give me around 2,250 f.p.s. with a 250-grain bullet riding in the plastic sabot. Any more of the powder would blow the sabot just about every time. I'm now loading a full 45 grains of the same powder behind the Muzzleload Magnum Products standard length high-pressure sabot and 250-grain Hornady .452 inch SST. The load gets the bullet out of the rifle at 2,405 f.p.s. with exceptional sub 1½-inch, 100-yard accuracy.

Many shooters have discovered that by loading a simple "sub-base" between the powder charge and saboted bullet, the accuracy with many hotter loads improves dramatically. This is especially true in hot weather when the heat retained by the barrel can soften the sabot and make it less resilient. This is true whether you're working with hot loads of loose grain Triple Seven in any of today's top-performing in-line rifles or smokeless loads in the Savage muzzleloader. These sub-bases have been made from everything ranging from the gas seal cut from the rear

**Thompson/Center Arms media relations manager Larry Weishuhn shows one of the company's 28-inch barreled "Omega" drop-action in-line muzzleloaders. The long barrel is capable of producing high muzzle velocities with maximum loads.**

of a 28-gauge wad (for the .50 caliber) to plastic discs to several stacked felt cushion wads. Muzzleload Magnum Products, of Harrison, Arkansas, is now even marketing a Ballistic Bridge Sub-Base, with a dome-shaped top that will fit right up into the rear of the sabot that holds the bullet.

Muzzleloading has definitely gone hi-tech, and shooters are enjoying the effort it takes to actually build a load for a specific rifle. And when one does take the time to seek the optimum combination of powder charge, bullet and loading technique, the majority of today's high performance muzzleloading big game rifles are capable of delivering the accuracy and knockdown power once only possible with a center-fire hunting rifle. These days, the challenge of muzzleloading is refining that load at the range, then duplicating the performance in the field.

(Toby Bridges is the author of more than a dozen books, including a brand-new title for Stoeger Publishing Company—*High Performance Muzzleloading Big Game Rifles*. He is also the host of the *High Performance Muzzleloading* website, at www.hpmuzzleloading.com)

**Muzzleloading hunter Steve Puppe relied on a magnum 150-grain charge of Pyrodex Pellets and a light saboted 150-grain .40 caliber bullet to take this fine Iowa buck with one of the .45 caliber Knight DISC Extreme in-line rifles.**

# Tools and Tactics of the Anti-Terror Professional
by Robert K. Campbell

I n America we face an ever-increasing threat from terror activity. I have studied terror action long before the problem was brought brutally home to us by the events of September 11. Terrorism is by definition the use of violent acts and murder to achieve political ends. The terrorist is a murderer not a freedom fighter. He uses his own freedom of movement to take away the liberty and lives of others. Civilian casualties are his goal. If casualties are caused by reprisals from the authorities, that is all to the better since it will make the authorities appear brutal and repressive. As former Prime Minister Netanyahu of Israel has stated, the hardest thing to do is not let go with everything you have immediately upon confronting the enemy.

In order to combat these groups, most governments require counter-agencies. In Europe, the first wave of terrorism caught police agencies unprepared. Most European police authorities issued .32 caliber automatics such as the Walther PPK. Practically overnight, these agencies rushed to upgrade to 9mm, .38 and .357 Magnum caliber revolvers and appropriate long arms. As an example, in Italy shortly after the death of Aldo Moro, former premier and leader of the Christian Democratic Party, I observed numerous officers armed with submachine guns. The once common .32 ACP Beretta pistol had been replaced with .38 caliber revolvers and American-style police holsters.

The incredible MP5K briefcase gun does exist. Note the trigger mechanism that reaches from the SMG to the carrying handle. This is quite an asset for skilled operators.

This Olympic Arms CAR-97M4 carbine in .223 caliber is a civilian version of what the military M4 used by special operations units. The carbine is both lightweight and accurate.

The Heckler & Koch MP5 SD3 has an integral aluminum sound suppressor and ported barrel. The SD3 does not require the use of subsonic ammunition to reduce noise.

Years later, while visiting Paris, I observed not only the French paras but various peace officers armed with the Mitra Mat submachine gun. Ruger revolvers, the 9mm M 50 and even old M 35s were in evidence in police holsters. In Britain, the SAS was in place to deal with the ongoing threat from Irish Republican Army operatives. When the first wave of Soviet-sponsored Arab nationalist terrorists appeared, Britain was better prepared than other nations. In America, the police have quietly upgraded their arms due not only to the threat posed by terrorists, but also because of the appearance of heavily armed robbers and gangsters.

There has been little confusion during this move. There were weapons available proven in military and civil operations in Europe, most of which were adaptable to police use. Anti-terror agencies are able to choose weapons appropriate for any scenario. The North Hollywood gun battle in Los Angeles showed the need for carbines in police hands. The AK 47 and the AR 15 clashed once again in this battle, on the side of wrong and right.

Handguns have seen considerable development as well. Prior to 1975, a German police commission looked at the needs of anti-terror operations and several standards were set for police handguns. The first

was reliability—the weapon would have to be reliable in operation above all else. In addition, the caliber would have to be up to the requirements of personal defense and combat, which to the Europeans meant the 9mm Parabellum or Luger cartridge. Any weapon would also have to be accurate enough for a successful hostage rescue shot. Finally, since special team members were to rely primarily upon long guns, the handgun was a backup. This was the opposite of normal police doctrine, where the handgun was the primary weapon and the shotgun or long gun a backup. The backup status of the handgun demanded that an action be as simple as possible, with resulting ease of manipulation. The absence of a manual safety was seen as an advantage. The SIG P series and the Heckler & Koch P7M8 solved this problem in different ways, but each faced stringent requirements.

The other side was armed with a variety of Soviet and Arab weapons. The Tokegypt, a 9mm Tokarev, was a favorite of the German Bader Meinhoff gang. Carlos the Jackal, as Venezuelan-born leftist Illich Ramirez Sanchez was known, used a variety of weapons. These included the Beretta submachine gun, the Czech Skorpion, and the Soviet Makarovs Carlos used in pairs during the attack on the OPEC Headquarters in Vienna in 1975. However, his favorite was the Czech CZ 52 pistol. This weapon fired a hot 1,500 fps+ load based on the 7.62mm Tokarev cartridge. Its roller cam locking action could absorb the energy of this potent round. Carlos killed two Sûreté officers in his apartment in Paris with such a pistol. In London, his attempt to kill a "Zionist" was thwarted when the 9mm slug

A stock Beretta 92 is a good weapon in trained hands.

This H&K USP underwent an extensive test, firing thousands of rounds of .40 S&W ammunition without any malfunction.

stopped in the man's strong front teeth. Carlos adopted the CZ 52.

The IRA often used Astra .357 Magnum revolvers, referring to them as "artillery," to provide cover for escaping men during special operations. For long guns, the IRA preferred the Armalite AR 180.

Against this backdrop of heavily armed terrorists, police agencies had to follow suit and adopt suitable answers in the form of increasingly effective weapons. Professionals adopt weapons that are suited to the task at hand. This means that dynamic entry and overwhelming firepower become watchwords. Perimeter defense and anti-terror interdiction, concerns once not considered a problem in police work, were included in threat assessment. The main defenses against terror come in two areas: static and active defense. Active defense is the collection of evidence, surveillance, and active pursuit of terror groups. Static defense is hardening buildings and defending important sites as well as establishing an armed presence.

There are many weapons available for both types of defense. The

## Heckler & Koch MP 5 Variations

| WEAPON | CALIBER | RPM | CAPACITY | WEIGHT | OVERALL LENGTH |
|---|---|---|---|---|---|
| MP 5 A2 | 9mm | 800 | 15/30 | 5.59 lbs | 26.77 inches |
| MP 5 KA4 | 9mm | 900 | 15/30 | 4.4 lbs | 12.28 inches |

(RPM is round per minute

handgun will always be in heavy use because it is handy and portable. It is the ideal on-the-spot, always-on-hand defensive tool. The level of success with a handgun has not always been high but it is there when needed. Security forces in Europe have traditionally used the .30 caliber Luger —or 7.65mm Parabellum as it is known in Europe—largely due to restrictive legislation, but they primarily depend upon handguns using the 9mm Parabellum. In addition, the .357 Magnum revolver is especially popular in France. The magnum is seen as capable of penetrating any vehicles that terrorists might use to escape after an attack.

The side arm can be an entry weapon or a hostage rescue weapon. These guns are often heavily modified. The FBI has made excellent use of the single-action 9mm High Power and recently adopted the .45 caliber Springfield as a SWAT issue weapon. The NYPD Emergency Service district has used the Beretta 9mm with good results. LAPD's SWAT units used various Colt .45 pistols and recently adopted the Kimber Custom II. A heavy caliber round is suited to close-range encounters and the .45 ACP has been thoroughly proven in close-range combat. In nearly a century of use, it has cleared rooms, bunkers, trenches, tunnels and the occasional fort. The FBI set a standard of 1.25 inches for a five-shot group at 25 yards in their pistol, a very difficult standard indeed. The French perfected their hostage rescue handgun in the form of an 8-inch barrel,

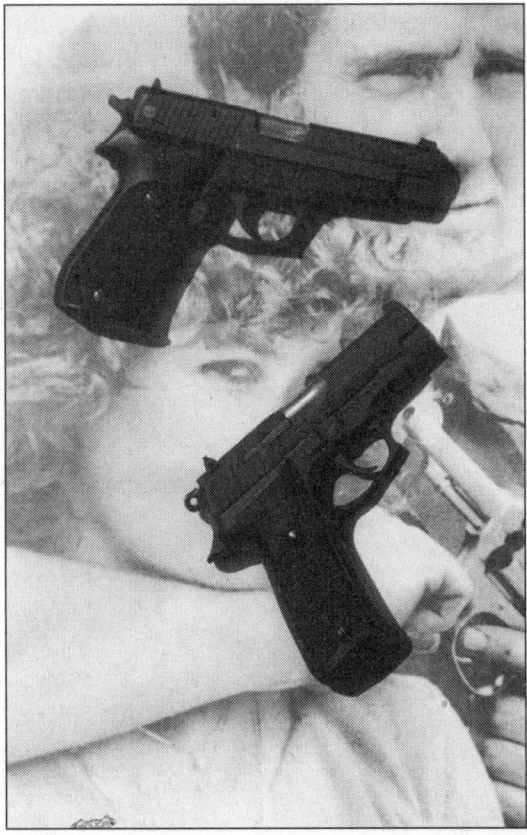

This is what a hostage rescue target should look like—one hit to the right place. No other standard is acceptable.

The SIG P 220, top, is used by many agencies, especially in Germany. The Astra A 100 was once used by Spanish units.

## Ammunition Performance in Suppressed Weapons

**MP 5 FIRING 9MM LUGER**

| | |
|---|---|
| Winchester 115-grain Silvertip | 1,225 fps (supersonic crack) |
| Winchester 147-grain Subsonic | 1,010 fps |

**MP 5 FIRING .40 CALIBER SMITH AND WESSON**

| | |
|---|---|
| Winchester 155-grain Silvertip | 1,205 fps |
| Winchester 180-grain SXT | 990 fps |

**MP 5 FIRING 10MM AS USED BY THE FBI**

| | |
|---|---|
| 10mm 170-grain Normal JHP | 1,473 fps |

scope-mounted Magnum revolver. Useful in tight spots with a minimum of cover, this weapon was deployed by gendarmes of the elite Groupe de Sécurité et d'Intervention de la Gendarmerie Nationale (GIGN) during the 1994 storming of a hijacked Air France passenger jet at Marseilles airport. With over 1,100 rounds fired by the French gendarmes, all of the terrorists, members of the Algerian Armed Islamic Group, were killed and no civilians were wounded.

In long guns, the widespread intermediate weapon is the Heckler & Koch MP 5 9mm submachine gun. This weapon is in use by over 50 nations including virtually every anti-terror unit in the free world. Our own FBI and the Navy SEALs have used this weapon operationally. The MP 5 uses the proven roller cam blowback operated system, the same system used in the H&K 63 rifle. Generally excellent in overall performance, reliability and accuracy are this weapon's strong points. The MP 5 differs from most SMGs in that it fires from a closed bolt. Most SMGs have a fixed firing pin on the bolt and the gun fires when the bolt slams forward. This controls the rate of fire and prevents "cookoffs" in overheated guns. Unlike many SMGs the MP 5 is accurate enough for hostage rescue work in the semi-auto mode. The MP 5 boasts an excellent set of high-visibility adjustable sights and the weapon is a pleasure to fire, even in the full auto mode. To offer a weapon more advanced than the HK series would require considerable expense and research.

In 1977 Grenzschutzgruppe 9 (GSG-9), an elite counter-terrorist unit of the German Border Police, used H&K MP 5s when they stormed Lufthansa Flight 181 in Mogadishu Airport in Somalia. Flight 181 had been seized by hijackers led by "Captain Mahmoud" (Zohair Youssef Akache) acting in sympathy with the German terrorist Red Army Faction. Assisted by two members of the British SAS hurling "flash-bang"

**Understanding how bullets perform when they penetrate auto glass is an important part of the operator's training.**

grenades, the GSG-9 assault team killed three of the terrorists and severely wounded the fourth. Flight 181's five crew and 86 passengers were rescued without injury.

A weapon that has served long, honorably and well is the Israeli Uzi. The Uzi is of an earlier generation than the MP 5 and it shows, but the Uzi remains quite a weapon. I have extensive experience with a semi-auto closed bolt version in .45 ACP, made especially for the American police market. It is far more robust and reliable than the various commercial semi-auto carbines often used by police. True military designs always are. Avoid the imitations—they are scrap and little more. The Uzi handles well—simply place the hands together and they meet—and reloads quite handily as well. For lightness and ease of handling the SMG has many advantages. For police use the full power carbine is a better choice in true anti-terror work—bursting into a room with guns blazing—and the Uzi seems to be the right tool.

The author takes a long shot with an Uzi carbine.

The lightweight AR 15, 5.56mm carbine is one of the most versatile weapons in any team's arsenal. The 5.56mm cartridge is not as effective as the 9mm Luger in urban penetration but far more destructive in wound potential. Tactical penetration is good, however. The short AR

## Accuracy Tests – 5-Shot Groups at 25 Yards from a Solid Benchrest

I tested some of the popular anti-terror handguns at 25-yard range. As you can see, the SIG P series performs as designed. But the other pistols are almost as accurate, and the Beretta in particular is very easy to handle well, with little muzzle flip and slight recoil.

| WEAPON | AMMUNITION | 5-SHOT GROUP |
|---|---|---|
| SIG P 225 | Winchester 147-grain SXT | 2.0 inches |
| SIG P 226 | Winchester 147-grain SXT | 2.25 inches |
| H&K P7M8 | Winchester 124-grain Partition | 2.4 inches |
| Beretta 92 | Winchester 147-grain SXT | 3.0 inches |
| Beretta Elite | Winchester 147-grain SXT | 2.0 inches |
| SIG P 220 (.45 ACP) | Winchester 230-grain SXT | 1.5 inches |
| H&K USP (.45 ACP) | Winchester 230-grain SXT | 2.1 inches |

15 is a triumph of human engineering. The controls are well placed and positive in action. The AR 15 is among a few battle rifles that allows a true rapid reload. Variants range from sniper versions to short barrel entry weapons. The 5.56mm weapon is a must-have for any anti-terror unit, with short versions replacing submachine guns in many units.

# WEAPONS OF INTERNATIONAL ANTI-TERROR FORCES

## FRANCE
Groupe de Sécurité et d'Intervention de la Gendarmerie Nationale (GIGN)
Le Groupe de Combat en Milieu Clos (GCMC)
SMG
H&K MP5
PISTOLS
Various 9mm pistols; .357 cal revolvers

## GERMANY
Grenzschutzgruppe 9 (GSG-9)
Kommando Spezialkraefte (KSK)
RIFLES
H&K G36
SMG
H&K MP5, MP5 SD3 (silenced), MP5K, MP5A2
SNIPER RIFLES
PSG-1; H&K G3; G22 Sniper Weapon System (Accuracy Int. AW w/folding stock German Optics in .300 Win mag).
PISTOLS
P7, P8, P9; PII underwater pistol; .357 magnums.

## GREAT BRITAIN
Special Air Service (SAS)
RIFLES
M16A2; H&K G3; HK53
SMG
H&K MP5, MP5K
SNIPER RIFLES
L96A1 Rifle (Accuracy International PM); Barrett Model 82A1
PISTOLS
SIG-Sauer P226; Walther PPK

## INDIA
National Security Guards ("Black Cats")
Special Protection Group
RIFLES
M-16A2
SMG
Uzi, H&K MP5-A2/A3
SNIPER RIFLES
PSG-1; MSG-90; SSG-2000

## IRELAND
Army Ranger Wing (Sciathan Fhiannoglaigh an Airm )
SMG
H&K MP5A3
SNIPER RIFLES
H&K 33/SG1 Semiautomatic Sniper Rifle, AI96 .308 Accuracy International
PISTOLS
Sig-Sauer P226
SHOTGUNS
Remington 870 Combat Shotgun

## ISRAEL
Sayeret MATKAL
S'13
Unit YAMAM, Special Police Unit ("Yechida Mishtartit Meyuchedet")
Unit YAMAS ("Mistaravim Unit")
RIFLES
Colt Commando
SMG
IMI Mini and Micro Uzi
SNIPER RIFLES
Mauser 86SR (SWS); M24 SWS; IMI Galil SWS (Galat'z)
PISTOLS
Glock 17 9; IMI Jericho 941; Sig Sauer P226; FN Browning High Power
SHOTGUNS
Remington 870 (short barrel)

## REPUBLIC OF KOREA
707th Special Mission Unit
RIFLES
Daewoo K1 and K2 assault rifles
SMG
H&K MP5
SNIPER RIFLES
H&K PSG-1 M-24, M-40 .50; RAI .50
PISTOLS
Colt 1911; Daewoo 9mm; Berretta M9
SHOTGUNS
Benelli Super-90

## RUSSIA
Group A (Spetsgruppa "Alfa")
OMON "Special Operations State Militia"
Spetsnaz (Spetsialnoye nazranie)
RIFLES
5.45mm AKS
PISTOLS
5.45mm PRI automatic
SHOTGUNS
Saiga

The SIG P 220 is shown with
a German police holster.

The Tokarev is rugged and reliable
and often used by terrorists.

## Suppressed Weapons

Surreptitious firing is sometimes needed in anti-terror work, but not
always for the obvious reasons. There may be times when a sentry
must be neutralized, and there is no other way than with the use of a
firearm. Just as often, a suppressed weapon may be used to take out
elements such as guard animals and vehicle
tires or lights, in order to give a team the
edge in dynamic entry. During a raid, a suppressed weapon can also protect the users
hearing and make the relay of commands
and warnings possible. Of course, the
weapon is not truly silenced but the sound is
greatly reduced. This requires subsonic-
velocity ammunition, or ammunition that
does not create a sonic boom as it breaks the
sound barrier.

In America, handguns have often been
used in immediate defense. Among the most
incredible examples is of Sergeant A. P.
Brown. When a madman began firing a rifle
inside a military compound, Sgt Brown
responded with his Beretta pistol. He stopped
the assailant, saving many innocent lives.
The range was a long 80 yards, well out of
normal handgun range. A good man who
knows his weapon can connect at longer
ranges than we would commonly expect.

In the final analysis, it is the person
behind the gun that counts. But some guns
are better than others to be behind. The
weapons in use by anti-terror units are
among the best available.

At 50 yards the author signals
a small group. Note that his
Magnum revolver, carried in
a crossdraw holster, is out of
the way when handling the
carbine.

This SIG P 225 showed outstanding accuracy.

## Tactics

Tactics used by anti-terror units include rapid entry and explosive demolition of walls. But perhaps the most daunting tactic is the simplest. In Malta, the SAS used a standard tactic to neutralize IRA terrorists. They ran at the terrorists while firing their Browning High Power 9mm pistols. This tactic is carefully thought out and boldly executed. When the terrorist realizes he is the center of attention he will not shoot hostages, he will attempt to fire at his enemy before he is killed. While this tactic places the operator in harm's way, it is "part of the job." At Malta, it worked. In Marseilles, the French Commandos who stormed an airliner used a similar tactic. The first five of six Commandos who entered the plane were shot, although all survived. The last man finally neutralized the immediate threat. Dynamic entry and incredible marksmanship are expected and delivered.

The author evaluates the Uzi carbine from kneeling position.

# Living with Recoil

## by Stan Warren

Coping with recoil, excessive or otherwise, is a chore that requires both physical and mental adjustments. To get the most in terms of accuracy from either a rifle or shotgun, the smart shooter does what it necessary.

Back in a long-ago time when most shotguns were 12 gauge, single shot and sported full chokes, at least those encountered on farms near ours, there was a firm belief that the harder a shotgun kicked, the harder it shot. A ridiculous notion I now readily admit but a fair number of those old cannons had stocks with far too much drop in them, butts so skinny that the old hard plastic (remember Bakelite?) buttplates could really thump an unwary collarbone or shoulder, and generally kicked, as my uncle once put it, "like a striped-legged mule." These were not potent 3-inch jobs either. They were wicked even with the standard 3¼-dram equivalent loads of the day. Sitting in my gun case and fully retired these days is an old Nitro Hunter that could wring tears from the eyes of a stone figure of a hunter.

Reposing only one space away is a modern 3½-inch 12-bore autoloader that delivers a payload that would probably reduce the ancient Hunter into fragments even if the chamber was long enough to handle the shotshell. I do not even want to think of what the kick would be like in any event.

Given these two comparisons, perhaps it is reasonably obvious that the terms "kick" and "recoil" are not interchangeable. If the weight of two guns is the same and shotshells of the same loading are used, the recoil (speed at which the shooting iron is forced backwards—remember the old "equal and opposite reaction" from high-school science?) will be the same. Old Gun A and New Gun B start for the shooter's shoulder with equal intensity. What they do when they get there is a different story altogether.

Since stock design is a critical factor in recoil and its management, let me point out that a stock that is too short does not point well while it can put the shooter's snout in danger of his own thumb. I have seen it happen, and many military marksmen learned to shoot the 1903 Springfield with their thumb laid down beside the stock for that reason. Also, you are so far out over and around the butt that there is precious little way to flex or give with

This elk hunter is carrying a .300 Winchester Magnum. In practice the rifle's weight and stock design will keep perceived recoil from being a problem in actual hunting situations.

Gunstock design has changed considerably over the past century. This replica Sharps mimics the original's thin, curved buttplate that made the kick from even a modestly loaded .45-70 round something to reckon with if you mounted the rifle wrong.

each shot, so you really soak up the punches. This is kick, not recoil per se.

A stock that is too long is annoying since it will tend to catch in your shirt, coat or vest when you shoulder it in a hurry. It will also cause the force delivered by the recoiling butt to be placed too far out on your shoulder, usually on or near a major bone and joint complex. My daughter worked up a real dread of recoil after shooting her older brother's 20-gauge shotgun which had a full-sized stock that was too much for her 10-year-old frame. The gun hurt her shoulder bone so it took some time before she could be pried away from her beloved .22 rimfire that did not hurt at all.

Too much drop will whack your shoulder and your cheekbone if the latter protrudes as do mine. I have actually had to walk away from registered trapshoots in mid-match when my pet smoothbore, shooting light loads only, pounded my cheekbone sufficiently to produce a headache that would have given a concussion a run for its money. It was bad enough to finally cause me to give up on my favorite sport, so trust me when I say that I know something about recoil and stock design.

The most telling example of how much a factor the shape of a gun's stock can make took place when my Nebraska buddy Joe Arterburn and I became the proud owners of a couple of .45-70 replica rifles. Mine was a snazzy copy of the Sharps falling block while his was patterned after the Remington rolling block. The ersatz Sharps had a lot of curve at the rear and was fairly narrow although the amount of drop was not excessive for iron sight use. Joe's rolling block had a wide, shotgun-style butt and much less curvature. Using identical ammunition ranging from timid factory fodder up through some 570-grain handloads I could count on using colorful cowboy-type language at least once out of every shooting session when using my rifle. With his, neither of us complained because it did a better job of dispersing the recoil and allowing us to avoid or absorb it.

### The Noise Factor

At one time a major U.S. sporting arms dealer promoted a Mannlicher-stocked rifle in 7mm Remington magnum. It was a cute rig, built if I recall correctly on a Mark X Yugoslavian Mauser action. However, with its 18-inch barrel it barely allowed the belted magnum round to get up to .280 Remington ballistics if it managed that. What it did provide was a muzzle flash that could have barbe-cued a buffalo in about six shots and light an auditorium on a dark night, and make enough noise to drown out a double shift at the local foundry.

A taxidermist buddy of mine acquired one on a trade and could not wait to get it out to the range. He figured that he was the owner of one of the neatest mountain rifles ever conceived since the rig weighed in scope and all at about 8½ pounds and the 7mm was known as a round that shot flat and hit hard. His first session on the

bench had him thinking otherwise. The first three shots were not that bad in terms of grouping and after that things came apart. He could not have put three more in a syrup bucket.

While listening to his tale of woe, I casually asked if he had been wearing the protective earmuffs that are a normal part of our gear on sighting-in runs. Nope. It seems that he had been too excited with his new toy to swing by his home and grab a pair. We checked the rings, mounts, stock screws and anything else that might conceivably have had an unfavorable impact on his rifle and found nothing amiss.

Being the sneaky sort, I recommended trying it again the next day with some handloads that I would brew up. What I actually did was to substitute 10 rounds of the same factory stuff that he had used into an unmarked box. A good set of shooting muffs protected his ears and a midday trip minimized the flamethrower muzzle flash that his late afternoon excursion had shown so clearly.

My buddy was quite happy with the 2-inch groups turned out by the stubby little magnum, although it was easy to see that it would always be more sow's ear than silk purse. When I confessed my trickery and explained that he had been shooting the same ammunition on both trips to the range, he became an instant convert to adequate hearing protection. Noise is a very real part of perceived recoil, a combination of factors that gives the body and brain a sometimes-false reading on how much punishment is being dealt out by a shooting iron. Although hearing protection is not something that you might want to carry along on a high country elk or sheep hunt, in a situation like that you should hopefully have enough adrenaline flowing to ignore the few shots that will (hopefully) be fired from a rifle that you are not already afraid of.

**One of the easiest ways of dealing with recoil is to use a gun and load combination that handles the job without overdoing it. Light loads of #6 shot from this autoloader were all that the author needed for a crow-hunting outing.**

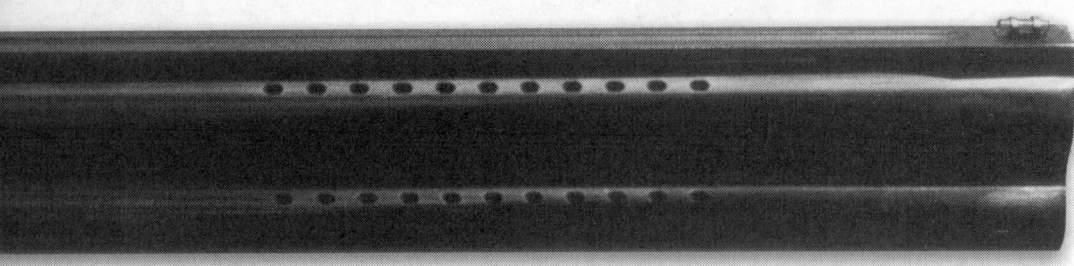

A ported barrel, such as this aftermarket version by Magna-Port, is an effective way of managing recoil and muzzle jump. While popular with competitive shooters, the increased noise level might not be welcome in a water-fowl blind.

Stock design and weight are critical factors in hard-kicking magnum rifles like this .470 Capstick. Mental discipline and good shooting techniques are equally important when it comes to placing a bullet exactly where you want it.

## Pads and Shoulder Protection

What? Show up for a hunt with a rifle whose kick you fear? Yes my friends, it happens all of the time. When a couple of buddies were getting ready for their first Rocky Mountain big game trip, one of the two brothers acquired a garden variety .30-06 bolt action and was convinced that it was the kickingest thing ever. He had potted a few whitetails with a .30-30 but did not think he could ever come to terms with his new '06 even after I made sure that he had decent hearing protection. At that time the best strap-on shoulder protection available was the PAST Recoil Shield, a couple of which I still have and still use. I got my friend to use one every time he went to the range and it was not long before he was concentrating on what he saw through his scope and not what the rifle was going to do to his shoulder. For long bench sessions with anything more potent that a .243 you can bet that I will be wearing something of the sort. If nothing else, it lets the shooter relax and worry about one less variable.

There are more types of shoulder pads available these days, all filled with some sort of space-age foam or gel, that absorb and disperse the force generated when a rifle or shotgun shoves violently to the rear. Most are very good, and even the worst is far better than nothing. The pads come in vests, shirts and strap-on units so take your pick.

## Gun Modifications

Whenever the subject of recoil control comes up, somebody is going to leap ahead of the field and mention muzzle brakes, or porting if you prefer the term. For a time I had a .411 KDF with what I believe they called the Recoil Arrestor. You will see similar versions around today, the kind that you supposedly screw on when shooting targets and remove when going after game. Then there are the kind that are actually made into the barrel by one of several methods on both rifles and shotguns. Those of us who have spent a fair amount of time around such creations tend to have very specific feelings about them.

For one, there is usually no problem using a ported firearm when you are popping targets and your companions have enough sense to stay well back from the muzzle. The same is true in competitive shooting situations. Late in my trapshooting days I had a lovely Lanber over/under given the full treatment by the folks at Magna-Port and still regret ever having parted with that shotgun. Like all Lanber guns it pointed sweetly and smoothly, and the porting job worked like a charm. If I had only found it a few decades earlier, things would have probably been very different.

Where the chief problem arises with ported guns, primarily shotguns, is when they are used in close proximity to other shooters who may have little, if any, hearing protection. Porting sends a tremendous amount of racket out to the rear and sides. When I was guiding waterfowl hunters in Canada, we made it a rule that ported guns could not be used in a blind of any sort. If the owner insisted on shooting his wunderkind, he was told that he had to do it on

Comparing this modern over/under *(left)* to a double gun of the mid-1800s *(right)* shows how the amount of drop in a shotgun stock has changed. The old "smoke-poles" were intended for a "high-head" type of gunning rather than the current line of sight down the barrel.

his own because the rest of us were already deaf enough. In my mind's eye it is still possible to see the willow branches used for camouflage bending backwards in the proximity of a ported muzzle.

The competitive shotgunning industry has come up with numerous add-ons over the years designed for recoil reduction. The Edwards Recoil Reducer was around three decades ago I know for certain because I still have one in the stock of a Remington 870 waterfowl gun and a friend had a pair of them installed in his Krieghoff trap rig. They worked just fine and the K-80 is a real pussycat to shoot thanks to the reducers. There are mercury reducers and heaven knows what all.

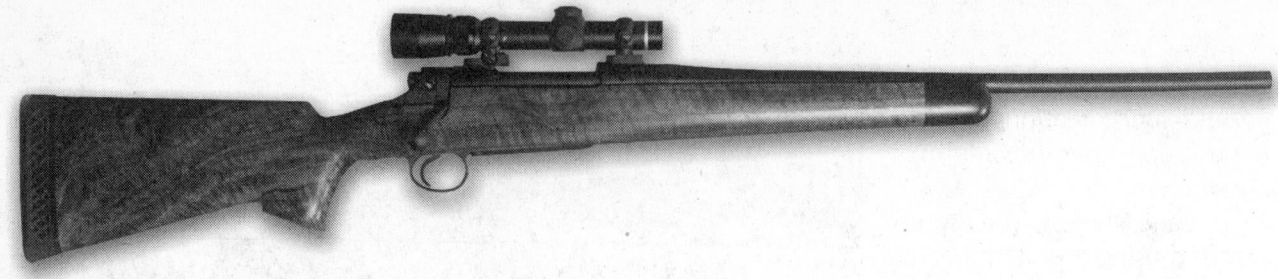

An excellent example of a modern firearm meant to handle substantial recoil is this A-Square Hannibal in .470 Capstick. The stock has a broad, properly padded butt, high straight comb, and a grip that positions the trigger hand to help soak up the recoil forces.

The hard-hitting .458 Winchester Magnum on the left has a wide and well-padded butt while the milder 7x75 Mauser beside it needs precious little to protect the shooter.

Some have been designed to go into magazine tubes, some into stocks, and at least one oddball was to be used in whichever barrel of your over/under was not in use at the time. Some are straightforward while others are weird, but if they work I like them. Reduced recoil and no increase in noise suit most of us quite nicely.

## Doing Your Part

For a lot of folks, getting kicked by a rifle or shotgun starts when they put the gun to their shoulder. My stepfather was a wonderful rifle shot but just never connected when it came to shotguns. His ancient 12-gauge beat him unmercifully after just a few shots in a dove field so I picked up a bargain 16-bore autoloader. I shot the same gauge most of the time and usually had plenty of light stuff for my double gun so I could do him two favors at the same time. The shotgun would kick less and he could have free ammo. The next opening day when the gray darters became legal I happily watched him blaze away only to find when we arrived back at the homestead that his right arm looked like a bad cut of steak. He could not break the habit of letting the buttstock get out onto the bicep muscle where he got pounded. I shot substan-

tially more than he, using a fixed-breech gun and barely had a red mark to show for it. Holding a shotgun wrong or "crawling" the stock on a rifle so that recoil can smack the eyepiece of your scope back into an eyebrow will make you appreciate recoil in an unfavorable way. Unfortunately, there is no aftermarket add-on that will correct poor shooting habits.

Sometimes it is the littlest of things that add to the effects of recoil and thus enhance the "kick" aspect. For instance, it you are shooting clay targets one at a time as in trap and using an over/under, load the bottom barrel. Its lower positioning causes the smoothbore to rotate back rather than moving in a straight line punching manner. If you are heading for a hot dove field, leave the fixed breech stuff at home and take an autoloader that is gas-operated if there is a chance that long bouts of shooting could ruin you day. An acquaintance once laid down a bundle to go on a combo birdshooting trip in South America and spent the last two of his five days on the sidelines simply because he took a new, elegant, $3,000 double gun instead of his prosaic self-loader. He looked good, though. At least until he took off his shirt and the bruises became visible.

Ditto for the guy who took a bargain 10-gauge single shot on a

The author leans into a .458 Winchester. His left hand is tucked under the rifle butt rather than holding the fore-arm in an attempt to restrain the rifle during recoil.

Recoil-sensitive shooters should start light and move up gradually. From left to right are the 7mm JDJ, 7x57 Mauser and the 7mm Remington Magnum.

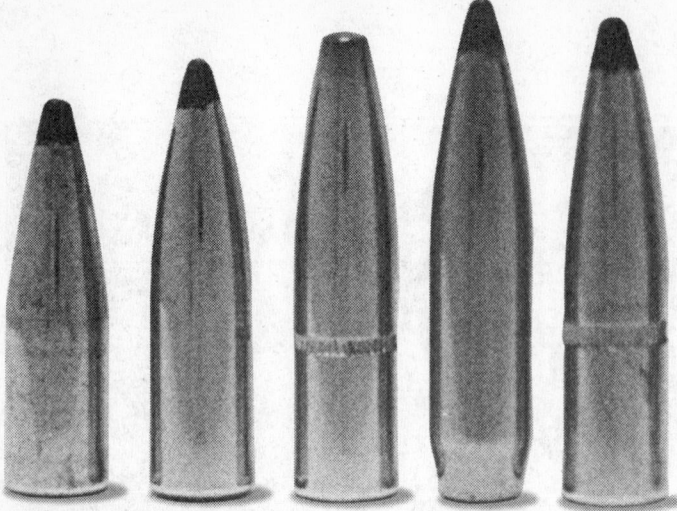

Bullet weight is a factor in recoil. These .284 caliber bullets range from 120 to 175 grains.

This shooter has just burst a jug of water with a .458 Winchester. His feet are spread for good balance and he has allowed the rifle's natural motion to carry it up rather than straight back.

turkey hunt and used a maximum dose of shot on the first gobbler to come along. Unfortunately, he was sitting with his back firmly against a big oak tree at the time and could not roll with the punch so he came to understand that recoil + stupidity = one heck of a kick.

Then there are the little things that can add to discomfort and possibly even poor performance with a good gun. Who would think that the mounting of a scope on a new rifle could have a tangible impact on its usefulness or that a noticeable increase in perceived recoil would be the result? One of my nuttier gun nut friends decided, upon obtaining a new Marlin lever gun in .45-70, that this could be the close-range gun of which dreams are made. Because this is a very sturdy rig he handloaded some .405-grain projectiles until he had enough horsepower to swat elephants in his garden if we had such in Tennessee. For some obscure reason he decided not to mount his scope low over the bore as usual but slapped on a set of those peek-a-boo things that some folks imagine will allow them to go from scope to iron sights at will. If I hear the line, "This way I can get on a running deer quicker …" one more time I very well may scream.

As it turned out, my friend did not much care for the groups he was getting, plus the recoil was stiffer than he had expected. The guy is a reasonably experienced shooter so I was a bit puzzled until he and I wound up on the range together. A casual examination showed that having the scope mounted roughly an inch high-

er than usual meant that his cheek had less contact with the stock and thus less support. He could not "lock down" on his target with the scope and the stock's comb was a tad too high to let him get down to view the iron sights without making a conscious effort. When he did that, the comb of the stock thumped his cheekbone more than he liked. We pulled his do-it-all mount off and replaced it with low mounts and a low-powered scope placed as low as it would go without hitting the barrel after removing the rear iron sight. At last account his .45-70 is the "hoss" that he had expected it to be and there have been no more comments concerning running deer.

Shown here are the basic tools for building confidence with recoil. Ear protection shuts out noise while the PAST Recoil Shield absorbs the kick allowing the shooter to concentrate.

## Stating the Obvious
In all honesty, most hunters run into recoil problems when they try to use more gun than they need for a given job. I love my various belted magnums and when the job justifies their use they get dragged out and carried along, but for general use I leave them in the rack. When deer hunting here in the Southeast, I carry a light Ruger Number One International in 7 x 57 caliber unless I am going into really nasty country, usually a swamp, when the Marlin lever action in .356 Winchester comes out. Neither is going to put me in need of a chiropractor. In the event that I am hunting over a large field or anywhere that a lengthy shot might be needed, the nod usually goes to a .25-06 or even a battle-scarred .280. How many deer I have taken over the past 30-plus years I

Popular American sporting cartridges range widely in case size, bullet weight and powder charge. Select the one that suits your needs and learn to handle its recoil.

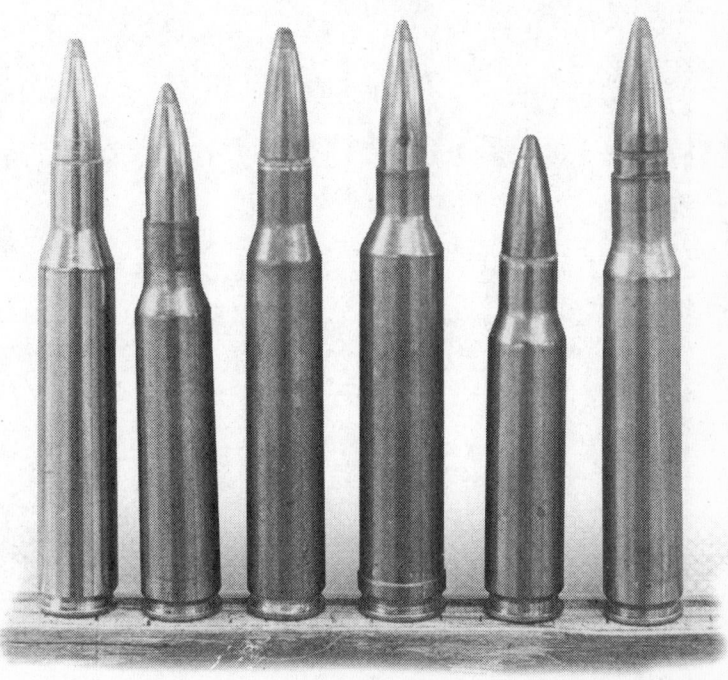

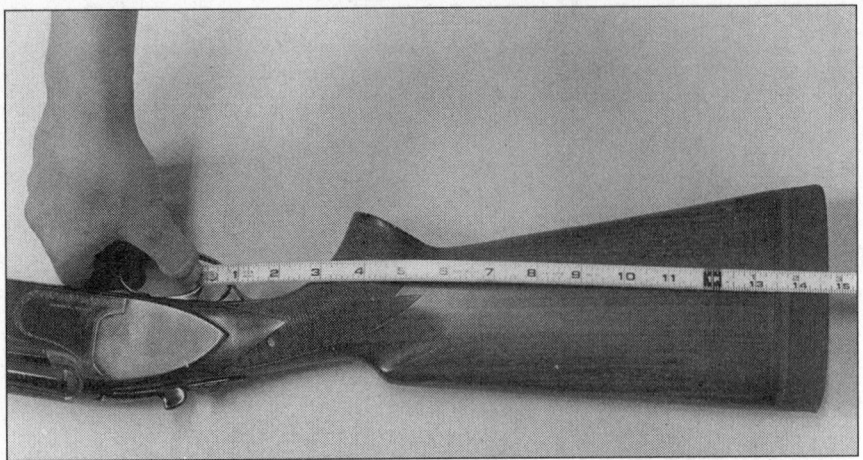

Stock length is critical to recoil control. If the stock is too long, recoil will strike the shooter's bicep—too short, and you could get a thumb in the nose.

Try starting tour target session with a fairly mild firearm. Here, the author begins with a gentle .44-40 lever gun.

have no idea, but most of them have been within 100 yards of the muzzle so why carry a cannon when an accurate light rifle will do the job?

The same holds true with shotguns. Many clients in Canada showed up carrying 3½-inch pumps and auto-loaders to use on birds that usually decoyed to 25 to 35 yards. They would have been as well served using 3-inch ammunition, and I punched a bunch of birds with a muzzleloader double choked cylinder/modified and an ounce and one-half of Bismuth #2 shot.

Forget the idea that bigger and faster is always better and get what works best for you. If you're driving at Daytona you might need some sort of souped-up car, but most of us spend more time driving to the market and sporting goods store than around the track. Use the same logic when picking a rifle or shotgun.

# .204 Ruger Breaks New Barrier

by Jay Langston

**S**ince its introduction in 1935, the .220 Swift has reigned supreme as the fastest factory loaded cartridge at a blazing 4,140 fps. That mark was surpassed when Sturm Ruger & Company announced the release of the .204 Ruger in Las Vegas, Nevada, at the 2004 Shooting, Hunting and Outdoor Trade (SHOT) Show in February. A joint venture between Ruger and Hornady Manufacturing, the .204 Ruger clocks speeds up to 4,225 fps from factory test barrels. Hornady is initially offering two bullet weights in the new cartridge: a 32-grain Hornady V-Max at 4,225 fps and a 40-grain Hornady V-Max at 3,900 fps.

Ruger is chambering the .204 in three M77 Mark II rifles and two No. 1 Single Shots. The M77 is offered with a standard weight blued barrel and wood stock, a black synthetic/stainless and a target gray varmint-weight and brown laminated stock. The No. 1's offerings are: standard weight barrel with walnut stock and stainless varmint-weight with laminated stock.

At the close of the SHOT Show, Ruger's Press Liaison Margaret Sheldon and Press Relations Manager Ken Jorgensen packed up a couple of the company's hottest new rifles and sent them to the Stoeger Publishing office for testing and evaluation. Once the eagerly awaited rifles arrived I waited until Hornady Manufacturing could cook up some test loads and then headed to the range.

Test loads were in short supply, so I dialed in the scopes' adjustments and started punching paper for groups. Test firing was conducted under adverse conditions with cross-range gusts up to 18 mph. During lulls in the wind I fired several three-shot groups with both the 32- and 40-grain Hornady loads. Predictably, the heavier bullets bucked the wind slightly better than the 32-grain pills. The first few groups from each rifle produced groups that averaged between 1 and 1⅛ inches. As evening approached and the wind dissipated, groups shrank. The 40-grain loads from the Ruger No. 1 with a Nikon tactical scope produced the best three-shot group of the day at just a hair under 7/16 inch. Both

The new .204 Ruger cartridge *(below)* is a small, fast, and efficient cartridge, with an extremely efficient ballistic coefficient and high muzzle velocity. The five-shot target groups above were fired from a rest at 100 yards.

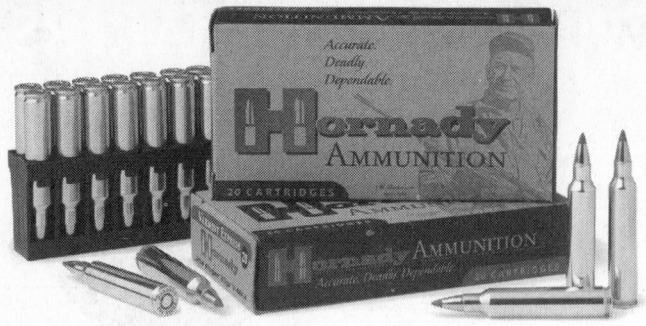

**Despite their blazing muscle velocity, Hornady's .204, 32- and 40-grain loads are low-recoil cartridges well suited to long-range varmint shooting.**

| CARTRIDGE: .204 Ruger | | |
|---|---|---|
| OTHER NAMES: | DIA: .204 | |
| | BALLISTEK NO: | |
| | NAI NO: | |
| DATA SOURCE: Hornady | | |
| HISTORICAL DATA: Created jointly with Hornady and Ruger in 2003. Based on the .222 Magnum case. | | |
| NOTES: Developed to provide a long range, flat shooting alternative to .22 centerfire cartridges for varmint hunting. Highest muzzle velocity of any current factory loaded hunting cartridge. | | |
| **LOADING DATA:** | | |
| BULLET WT./TYPE: .32 Hornady V-Max | POWDER WT./TYPE: 4225i | VELOCITY (FBE): SOURCE: Factory Load |
| CASE PREPARATION: | SHELLHOLDER (RCBS): 10 | |
| MAKE FROM: Can be made by necking down .222 Magnum and fire forming. Then ream neck. Trim to length. | | |

| PHYSICAL DATA (INCHES): | DIMENSIONAL DRAWING: |
|---|---|
| CASE TYPE: Rimless Bottleneck | |
| CASE LENGTH: A = 1.8500 | |
| HEAD DIAMETER: B = .3763 | |
| RIM DIAMETER: D = .3780 | |
| NECK DIAMETER: F = .231 | |
| NECK LENGTH: H = .200 | |
| SHOULDER LENGTH: K = .1116 | |
| BODY ANGLE (DEG'S/SIDE): | |
| CASE CAPACITY CC'S = | |
| LOADED LENGTH: 2.260 | |
| BELT DIAMETER: C = N/A | |
| RIM THICKNESS: E = .0450 | |
| SHOULDER DIAMETER: G = .3599 | |
| LENGTH TO SHOULDER: J = 1.5380 | |
| SHOULDER ANGLE (DEG'S/SIDE): 30.0 | |
| PRIMER: S/R | |
| CASE CAPACITY (GR'S WATER): 32 | |

-NOT ACTUAL SIZE-
-DO NOT SCALE-

rifles tended to prefer the 40-grain loads, with groups averaging between ¾ and 1 inch.

The trigger on the No. 1 broke cleanly at 3¼ pounds and had absolutely no creep. On the other hand, the M77 had an appreciable amount of creep but broke at a lighter 2¼ pounds. Even though the trigger pull on the No. 1 was heavier, it was more predictable and was easier to control under range conditions.

The design of the .204 Ruger cartridge is a close cousin of an earlier wildcat that was named the .20/222 Remington Magnum. Both the wildcat and the new factory cartridge are based on the .222 Remington Magnum that fell from popularity at the advent of the .223 Remington. Even the .222 Remington has suffered from the popularity of the .223 chambering, owing to the ample availability of surplus ammo and brass.

In benchrest competition circles the .222 has earned many fans with its accuracy potential.

The early .20/222 Remington Magnum wildcat more closely resembles the .222 Remington with a longer neck, while the .204 Ruger carries its shoulder farther forward with a correspondingly shorter neck.

This hot new rifle and load combination is sure to create the same swell of attention as the .17 HMR did only a few months ago. In the race to create new cartridges, Ruger has once again stepped up the competition to lead the velocity race.

**Reloading specifications for the .204 Ruger from** *Handloaders Guide to Cartridge Conversion* **by Stoeger Publishing.**

**A Ruger MK 77 Target Gray .204 is locked into a rifle rest ready for test firing. This model has a brown laminated stock and 26-inch Target Gray finish barrel.**

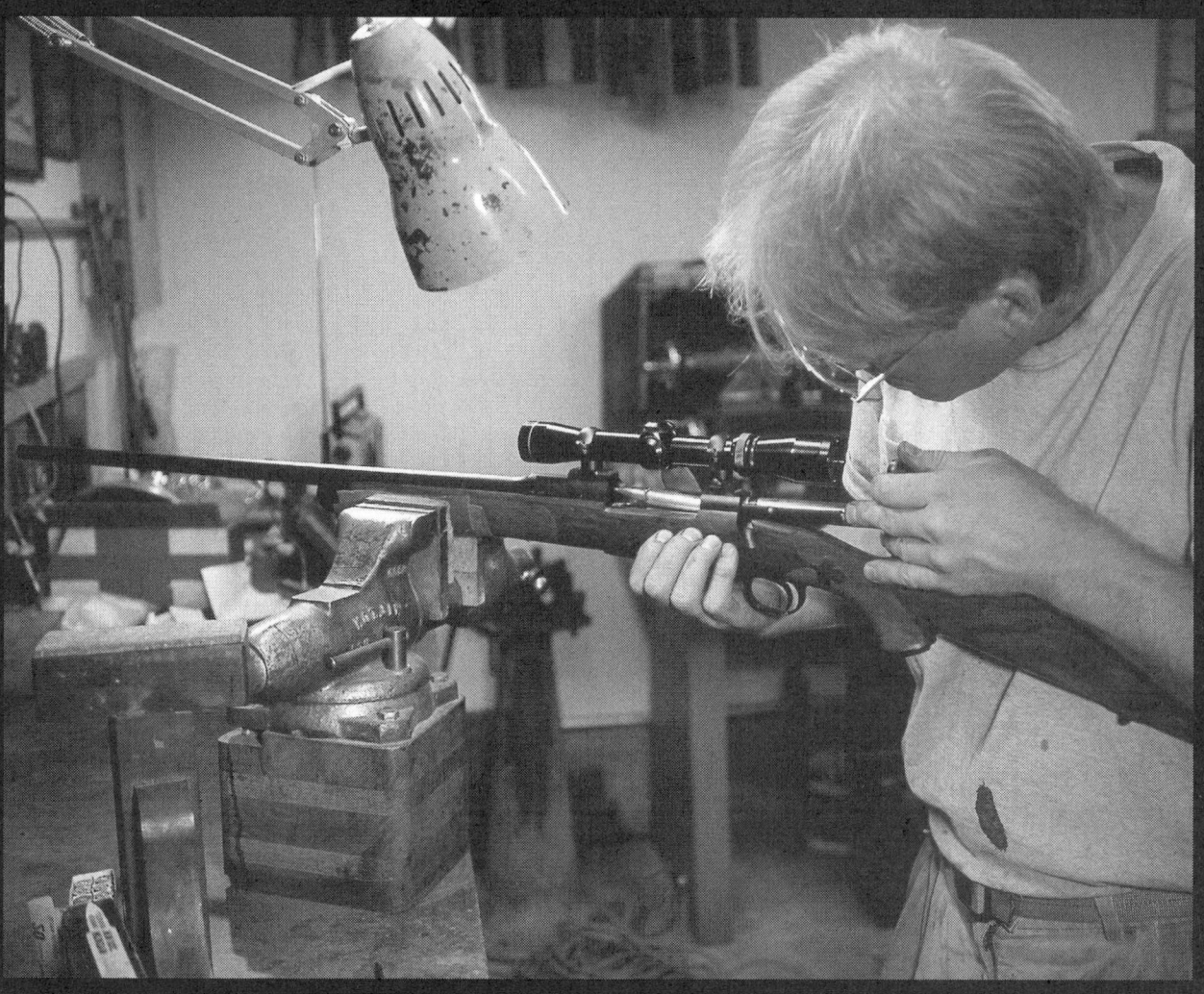

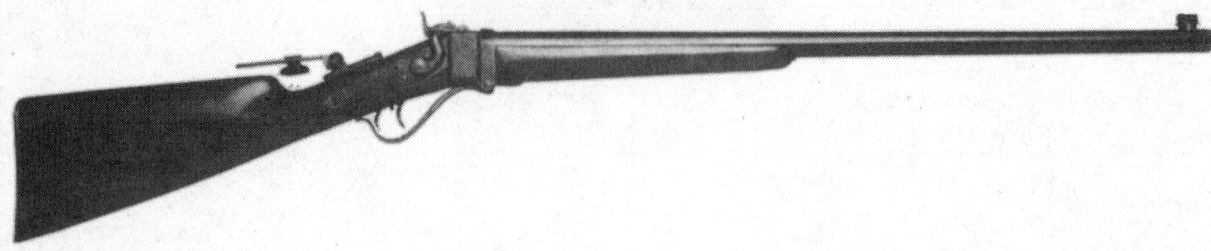

# Axtell Rifle Company
## Sheridan, Montana

In 1973, Riflesmith, Inc. began manufacturing replicas of the late 19th-century sights traditionally installed on Sharps and other long-range rifles. In 1989 the Axtell Rifle Company began manufacture of a New Model 1877 Sharps.

Casual gun enthusiasts are more familiar with the 1874 Sharps "buffalo guns" of book and film. The Model 1877 is nonetheless better. It evolved from calls for a more accurate long-range target rifle following a match at the Creedmoor Rifle Range on Long Island between American and Irish shooters. The 1874 Sharps had proven itself there but even the winners wanted faster lock time and a heavier barrel.

Of the new 1877 Sharps, explains Carmen Axtell, "It's not a cheap rifle to build. Our prices reflect cost more than profit. And you'll never be disappointed." The rifles are remarkably true to the line, balance and mechanism of the originals. Also noticeable is the meticulous fitting and finishing of parts. The case coloring is exquisite and the wood and metal finish are even better than on the original!

Axtell Rifle Company makes several variations of the 1877 Sharps: Custom Express, No. 1 Creedmoor, No. 2 Long Range, Lower Sporter, Lower Business, and Overbaugh Scheutzen. All 10 chamberings are original Sharps rounds, from the .45-70, .45-90 and .45-100 Express to the various 40- and 45-caliber cartridges popular during the late 1800s.

# Les Baer Custom
## Hillsdale, Illinois

Well known among pistol shooters seeking superior M1911 .45 target guns, Les Baer is equally talented in turning out street-worthy hardware. His Hillsdale, Illinois shop has served law enforcement officers and consumers wanting best-quality pistols for home protection. Les offers compact Comanche and Stinger 1911s, as well as standard-size pistols. You can buy frames in steel, stainless steel and alloy to build your own .45. Slides and barrels are available too. Other components include safeties, triggers, bushings, sights, magazines. Les has earned the loyalty of many national pistol champions as well as people like Clint Smith, who runs a training facility for police and civilian shooters

The shop also deals in autoloading "AR" series rifles (like the M-16) for tactical shooters and service rifle competitors. Components too: from hand-stops and stocks to barrels, bolts and upper and lower receivers. His NRA Match rifle has a 30-inch, hand-lapped fast-twist barrel, floating handguard, titanium striker and two-stage Jewell trigger, plus many other refinements. The Picatinny rail, available on other Baer .223s, accommodates scope rings and a receiver sight.

Les, incidentally, established quite a reputation racing automobiles. His guns show the fine machine work and close tolerances of track-worthy V-8 engines; and Les goes about gun-building with the same intensity he brought to racing.

# Mark Bansner
## Adamstown, Pennsylvania

Mark Bansner started a gunshop with a concept for improving shot patterns for turkey hunters. Now his focus is on bolt-action hunting rifles. He furnishes his own synthetic stocks of graphite, epoxy and fiberglass cloth and his stocks are hand-bedded to cradle the receiver without stress points. Mark has formed a separate company, High Tech, to produce these lightweight stocks for sale to the trade.

At Bansner's shop, match-grade, hand-lapped Lilja barrels are fitted to actions trued from centerline to ensure concentric chambering. Mark and his craftsmen tune or replace triggers to ensure a crisp, consistent pull. Bansner rifles are guaranteed to deliver fine accuracy. "We sell mainly to discriminating hunters who expect a high level of field performance."

Stacks of proof targets from the Bansner files should impress the most critical rifleman. One-hole groups are common. Trim but functional lines give Bansner's rifles an elegant look. Stock finish and color options include speckling and spider-webbing and their stock-to-steel fit is skintight except on the barrel, which Mark offers in both fluted and conventional form. He even makes his own muzzle brakes, which reduce recoil by up to 45 percent.

Mark ships about 120 custom rifles each year from his Adamstown, Pennsylvania shop. While his brochure shows standard rifle configurations and options, each customer can personalize his rifle. Prices range from $2200 to $3700.

# The Biesens
## Spokane, Washington

Now 87, Alvin Biesen isn't turning out the number of rifles he did while Jack O'Connor was toting – and touting – his Biesen-stocked .270s all over the world. But son Roger and grand-daughter Paula carry on the tradition. For decades Biesen's modest Spokane, Washington basement shop was a sanctuary for people who dreamed of fine rifles.

"Dad didn't force me into this," says Paula, who has become an accomplished engraver. "I got plenty of encouragement but no push. I began by etching into steel what I painted in school – mostly animals." Refining her talent on gold and German silver name plates, Paula started cutting grip caps and bottom metal. Her work has appeared on rifles commissioned for auction by the National Rifle Association, the Rocky Mountain Elk Foundation and Safari Club International.

Strikingly evident in Paula's work is her clean detail, the mark of a careful and confident artist. The animals she scribes appear lifelike. "You learn tricks," she shrugs. "Like never setting an animal face-on so you have to duplicate details right and left. Engraving game scenes is much harder than painting with a brush because you can't just sweep over them and try again."

Roger, whose stocks show the bold comb and traditional lines that Al established as his trademark decades earlier, is as proud of his daughter as of his own work. "It isn't often you see three generations of gunmakers working at the same time in the same place," he said. But Al, who more than once expressed pride in raising four children as an independent gunmaker, might have had it in mind.

# Kent Bowerly
## Redmond, Oregon

In 1958 Winchester announced its .338 Magnum and Roy Weatherby came up with the Mark V rifle. Young Kent Bowerly mated a Springfield 03-A3 to a Roberts semi-inletted stock.

All three events were of lasting significance. Friends admired Kent's craftsmanship, and they offered to pay him for stockwork on their rifles. Eagerly, he obliged. During the 1960s, Bowerly studied the work of Al Biesen and Earl Milliron, both masters of the trade and both living close by in the Pacific Northwest. He practiced their techniques on hunting rifle stocks he shaped, fitted and finished, mostly for Winchester Model 70s.

"In those days, you could still get the early 70s for a reasonable price, and a lot of hunters preferred them." He still likes those Winchester bolt guns, but he's also fitted walnut to Mausers and the occasional Dakota 76. He has fashioned stocks for Ruger Number Ones, a rifle that adds variety to his workbench in Redmond, Oregon. Kent says that his stocks are meant to be used, though they feature the lines and detailing that sophisticated gun enthusiasts admire. "If a rifle won't shoot well in your hands, if it's not responsive, if it lacks the fine balance to point itself and put your eye behind the sight automatically, it's not stocked properly." Wood and detail work, he insists, are of no value on a rifle that doesn't point naturally.

Since his early retirement from the boat-building industry in 1985, Bowerly has worked full-time as a stockmaker, applying his artistry on occasion to shotgun stocks.

# David Christman
## Delhi, Louisiana

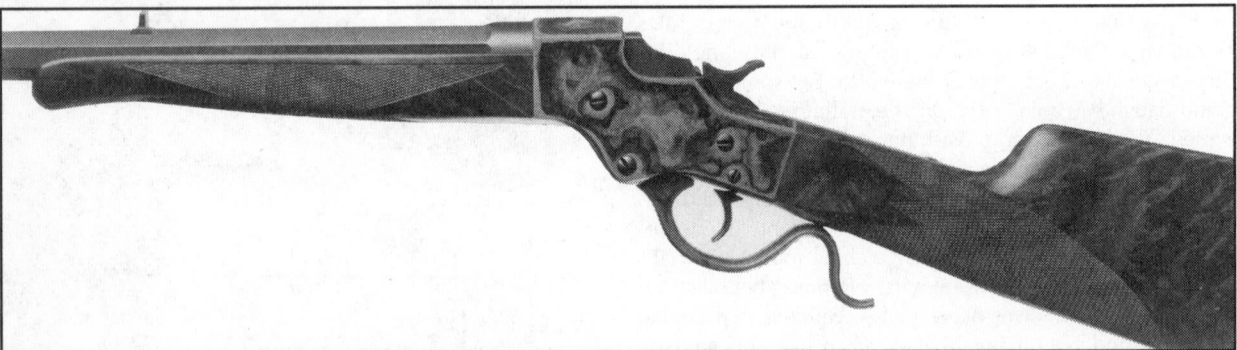

Colville, Washington was David Christman's home for 20 years, until a downsizing at U.S. West freed him to return to his native Louisiana. There David has revved up his gun work, restocking Parker double shotguns and Stevens single-shot rifles, besides building the bolt-action rifles so popular with custom makers. David shows a rare versatility; he fashions both wood and metal work. Only the engraving gets outsourced. David offers a full suite of restocking and refinishing services, including rust bluing, in the same shop that turns out complete custom shotguns and rifles.

His favorite project? "Probably still a bolt rifle on a Mauser 98 or Winchester 70 action," he says. "A classic hunting rifle deserves a stock of fine English walnut, but Don Cantwell sells some very nice high-grade Claro." He'd not too fussy on action types. "Given the right parts and a little metal work, the Remington 700 can become a handsome custom rifle.

# Melissa Dibbens
## Harrisonville, Missouri

Melissa Dibben, an engraver from Harrisonville, Missouri, started sculpting gunmetal in 1982. "My grandfather built a local jewelry business during the 1940s, and my parents bought it in 1976. Engraving allowed me to live at home and put my imagination to work," she says. Melissa trained on the pneumatic Gravermeister tool in Little Rock, Arkansas, then put her bench in front of the jewelry store. A Remington Model 11-48 shotgun was her first project. Then she scrimshawed roses on revolver grips. "One of the store's customers saw me working and told me yellow roses had no place on a gun. That hurt a little, but not for long."

Since 1988, when her parents closed the jewelry store and moved to Corpus Christi, Melissa has worked mostly on guns. Active in Safari Club International, she has engraved three rifles for the Kansas City chapter.

Melissa, Dave and son Ben live on 20 acres with six dogs, two cats and two horses. The Dibbens also own 90 acres in northern Missouri, where they hunt deer and turkeys. Melissa also spends a good deal of time in Wyoming. Does she have a favorite canvas? "No. I don't want to do the same thing all the time. I'm easily bored. Variety and new challenge bring me back to the bench."

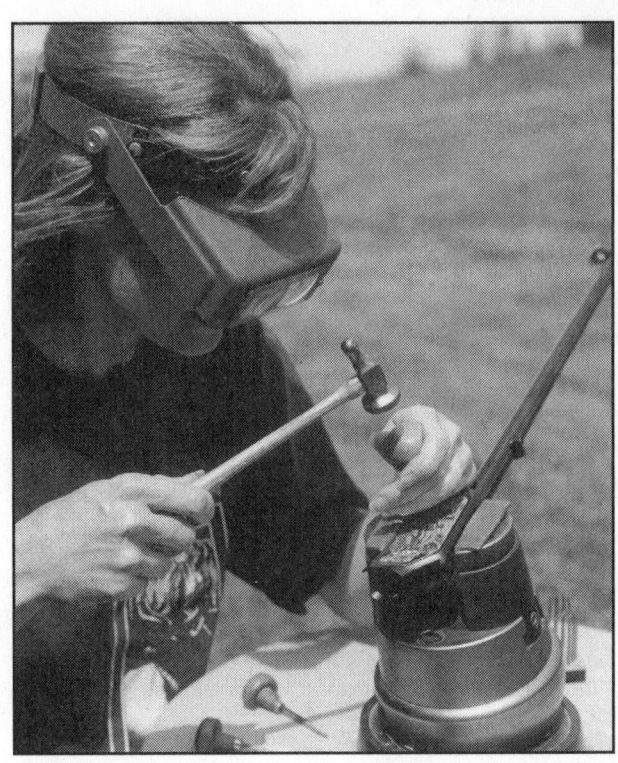

# D'Arcy Echols
## Providence, Utah

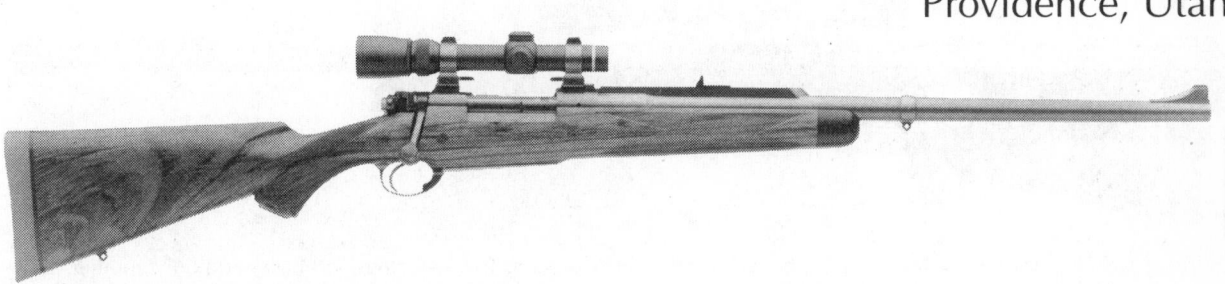

"I like to build rifles you'd hunt with," says gunmaker D'Arcy Echols. "The profile of a great rifle must serve a purpose, not just attract attention on a rack." Echols achieves superiority with straight lines and a mating of wood to metal that looks impossibly tight. His symetrical checkering adorns a grip and forend that all but grab your hands. Cast-off is standard, and D'Arcy's pantograph is adjustable to deliver cast-off (a slight angling of the butt away from the shooter's cheek).

To speed up production (in 1997 Echols was turning out about four a year) he introduced the "Legend" rifle with a synthetic stock. Built on new Winchester 70 Classic actions, the Legend wears a McMillan stock that D'Arcy designed. He overhauls the action, modifying the magazine box to hold an extra round. Then he lengthens the loading port and bores out scope base holes to accept 8-40 screws. D'Arcy remachines and laps the lug seats and lugs, and squares up the receiver and bolt face. "I use Krieger cut-rifled barrels," he says. "And I make sure they're fitted on-axis with the receiver. He repins the trigger and bolt stop and grinds the sear surface for a consistent 3-pound pull.

After matte-bluing the metal and hand-bedding it in the stock, D'Arcy shoots each rifle at least 40 times to break in the barrel and make sure the rifle meets his accuracy standards. D'Arcy also builds a Dangerous Game Rifle with a barrel-mounted sling swivel and action work to accommodate round-nose bullets.

# Kent "Buzz" Fletcher
## Alamosa, Colorado

The youngest of 10 children, Buzz Fletcher had an early interest in guns, and he longed to accompany his six brothers in the field. One of them pointed out that some hunters had money enough to buy custom rifles and books by those who built them. "The notion that I could build fine rifles suddenly had never occurred to me," Buzz would say later. "But when the idea struck, I latched onto it!"

Buzz read ace stockmaker Monte Kennedy, gunsmithing guru Roy Dunlap and Francis Sell, a master hunter and rifleman. Enrolled in gunsmithing school at Trinidad State Junior College, Buzz studying with the likes of Maurice Ottmar, Chuck Grace, Jim Turtin and others who later would establish themselves as premier gunmakers. He graduated in 1972, then worked in an Austrian gunshop for a year. Returning to Colorado, he set up shop in Alamosa to build classic bolt-action sporting rifles.

But Kent is also an accomplished shotgun stocker. "British bird guns point like magic because the Brits know how to build stocks," he says. The stocks he builds are as trim. Their cast, pitch and drop, and the spartan lines of butt and forend, result from painstaking study of the British game gun. Buzz also builds rifles after British patterns. Whatever the style, he strives to make a firearm handle like an extension of the shooter's body. As with his rifle stocks, shotgun wood in Buzz's shop is typically checkered 22 lines per inch, though he does cut some patterns at 24 lpi. He uses various fillers to get the stock surface he wants, but finishes only with Tung Oil.

# Rick Freudenberg
## Everett, Washington

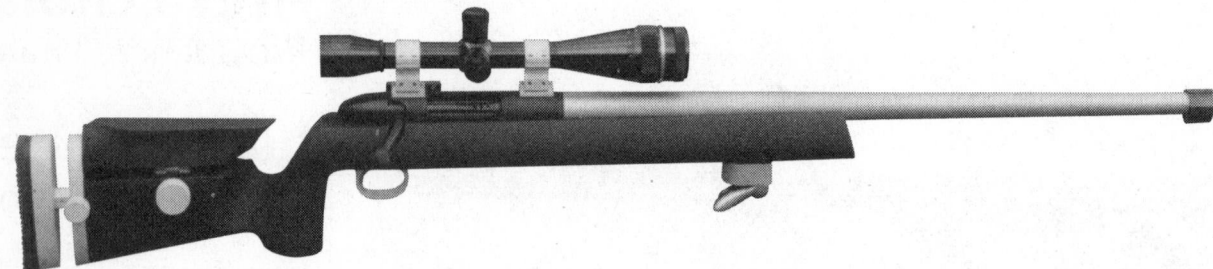

Hunting is still a passion for Rick Freudenberg. Big antlers adorn the walls of his well-equipped machine shop but once there you'll find that Rick is focused on building rifles. His match and hunting rifles are as accurate as he can make them, which means he prefers synthetic stocks. Rick also offers wood stocks but says that, properly fitted, a walnut-stocked rifle won't shoot as well as a synthetic.

Rick prefers Winchester 70 actions, pre-64s first and current Classics next. He's also built rifles on the Remington 700 action. He favors a three-groove Lilja barrel with a 1-11 twist for the .30-06, and commonly gets it to deliver sub-half-minute groups with Nosler Ballistic Tip bullets.

Rick's latest project is a lightweight hunting rifle with a #4 fluted barrel 23½ inches long. He trims a Remington 700 receiver and flutes the bolt, outfitting it with a Sako-type extractor. The S&K rings and bases add only another ounce, and with a 3-9x36 Swarovski scope, the rifle tips the scales at just 6½ pounds.

Jim Spradlin, in Colorado, finishes metal parts for Rick, using a Teflon-like material that comes in 11 colors and protect the metal as no bluing can.

Rick Freudenberg builds accurate hunting rifles because he assembles and uses super-accurate match rifles, shooting at ranges to 1000 yards. He'll chamber to just about any cartridge but prefers those "with legs" – like the 6.5/284 and the .300 Winchester. Many elk hunters have ordered a Freudenberg rifle in .330 Dakota. Rick's personal .300 Dakota will launch 180-grain Sciroccos at 3360 fps from its 26-inch barrel. A rifle of this type, including a pre-64 M70 action, starts at about $3500.

# Gary Goudy
## Dayton, Washington

Semi-retired after 37 years fashioning elegant rifle stocks, Gary Goudy is still known in the trade as one of the most talented and productive of his fraternity. He's not shutting the shop door anytime soon, though, because "hunting's expensive. I can't afford to quit!"

Gary's work bespeaks a perfectionist's obsession, and a genuine affinity for fine guns and the best walnut. "I work mainly with California English," he says. "Or Bastogne. I've not had good luck with European blanks." Unlike many of his colleagues, Gary buys most of his wood green, preferring to dry it himself. "Most blanks need a couple of years, but I like to give them four seasons before inletting." Gary is renowned for skin-tight wood-to-metal fit and impossibly detailed checkering that leaves ribbons the width of a pencil line and even as a lightbeam.

His favorite action? The Model 70 Winchester, "because it makes such a good hunting rifle." But he says that a 98 Mauser worked over by Hermann Waldron or Tom Burgess is every bit as desirable. He's stocked shotguns from time to time, almost all of them side-by-sides. The two most recent are Dakotas, a

12 and a 20. "They took a very long time to finish, the they're true exhibition-grade guns." Gary is also working on a Dakota take-down rifle for his own use.

Among relatively few rifle-makers who are also keen hunters, Gary spends much of the fall afield, some of it in the Blue Mountains within hiking distance of his Dayton, Washington shop. But he travels out-of-state too, and last year killed a bull elk that scored over 330 points. He isn't saying where. Gary often hunts with an ordinary Winchester Model 70 Featherweight. "It doesn't have one of my stocks," he laughs. "It shoots just fine in the factory wood, and I've been too busy to change it."

# Chuck Grace
## Trinidad, Colorado

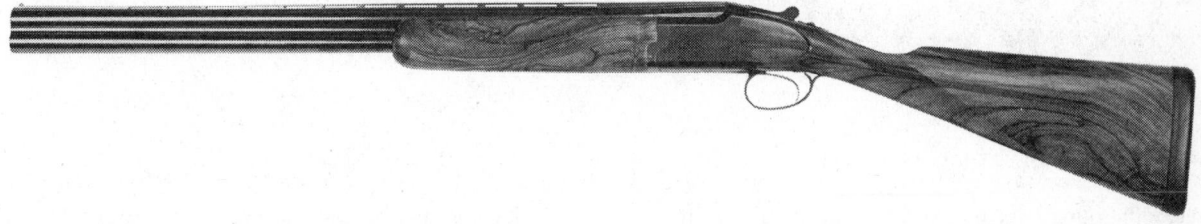

In 1971 Chuck Grace left his Michigan home for gunsmithing school in Colorado. He stayed there to hone his skills and in 1980 became a full-time stockmaker. Three years later he joined the American Custom Gunmakers Guild as a charter member. His considerable talent was evident on the ACGG's 16th annual fundraising project: a Winchester Model 70 rifle in 7x57. His rifles, built on clean, classic lines, have open grips

that make for fast handling.

Best known as a stockmaker, Chuck also takes on rifle restoration and custom metal work in his Trinidad shop. His perfect execution of "the simple things, like a straight line" have earned him widespread respect among gun enthusiasts. The rifles he stocks seem to point themselves, a mark of a master.

# Darwin Hensley
## Brightwood, Oregon

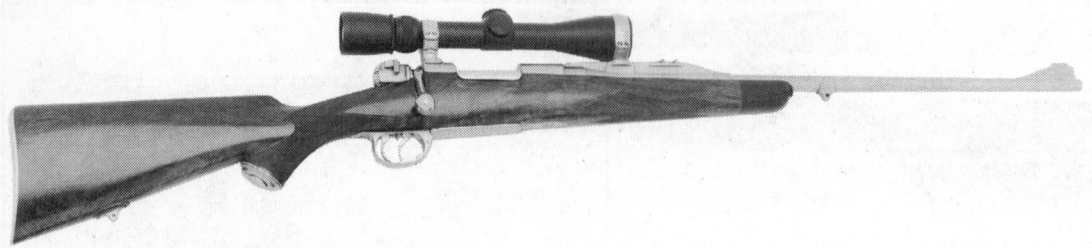

A childhood spent whittling might have given Darwin Hensley's parents a clue as to this talented stock-maker's future. Growing up on an Iowa farm in the 1940s allowed Darwin the time to do a lot of whittling. In 1952, when he was 10, the Hensleys moved into town, but Darwin still spent summers on the farm, where he entertained himself with an 1890 Winchester .22 pump.

Darwin taught art for two years after earning his B.A. and B.S. degrees. He left to earn more money in marketing. He stayed with that for 25 years, and raised a family. Always on the prowl for fine guns, he bought and sold many for profit. All the while he continued to whittle, but now on gunstocks. In 1985 he gave up "real work" and became a full-time stockmaker.

Darwin says "I've been blessed with wonderful clients. I wake up every day eager to go to work. It's not the life for everyone, but there's nothing I'd rather do." Darwin's commitment to superior craftsmanship is evident in his rifles, which show an artist's eye for line, and are notable for their trim profiling. "It's important that a rifle shoot and handle well; beyond that, its design should show a harmony of parts. Profile, components, engraving, checkering, fit and finish – all must work together to achieve the best effect. It's wrong for one part to draw attention from the whole."

Carefully fitting each rifle stock to its owner, Darwin ncludes detailing so subtle that it's often visible only upon close inspection. The single-shot rifles shown here – a miniature Gibbs Farquharson in .17 Hornet, a miniature Jeffery Farquharson in 2R Lovell and a miniature Alex Henry in .218 Bee – have the sleek, spare profiles that under Hensley's hand become elegant. Metalwork on the first two (and on the featured bolt rifles) is by Steve Heilmann.

# Hill Country Rifle Company
## New Braunfels, Texas

Every Hill Country rifle is built with a single purpose in mind: to instill confidence every time the rifle is used. HCR specializes in high-quality bolt-action rifles built to order on commercial actions. Synthetic and wood-stocked rifles are available in configurations to meet individual needs. All rifles are pillar-bedded, all barrels free-floated to shoot 1/2-inch three-shot groups at 100 yards with factory ammunition.

Following the success of Winchester Short Magnum catridges, HCR stockmaker J. Earl Bridges designed a Hill Country Classic synthetic stock, built exclusively for the company by McMillan Fiberglass Stocks. The Classic is sleek and trim, with an open grip and 18-lpi checkering with a mull border and shadow-line cheekpiece. Its slim profile makes it both quick in hand, and very well balanced.

# Bob Hisserich
## Mesa, Arizona

"Accuracy is mainly installing a good barrel on an action that's square with it," says Bob Hisserich, shrugging. "Naturally, the bolt face must be true and the lugs made to bear evenly. And of course, the stock can't be allowed to interfere." It all sounds so simple. But pin him down, and Bob Hisserich admits that building an accurate rifle takes care as well as know-how. Building one "that looks as good as it shoots," he says, is a real challenge.

Now 18 years into his career as a gunmaker, Bob lives in Mesa, Arizona, where he uses a Honig/Rodman stock duplicator (pantograph) capable of .0001 precision. His rifle stocks -- both laminated and traditional walnut versions – are all on classic patterns, though Bob will fashion a crossover stock if you have an off-side dominant eye. You'll find his stock work on shotguns as well as on rifles. Conservative lines and painstaking attention to detail make him a popular pick among shooters who covet fine guns.

# Patrick Holehan
## Tucson, Arizona

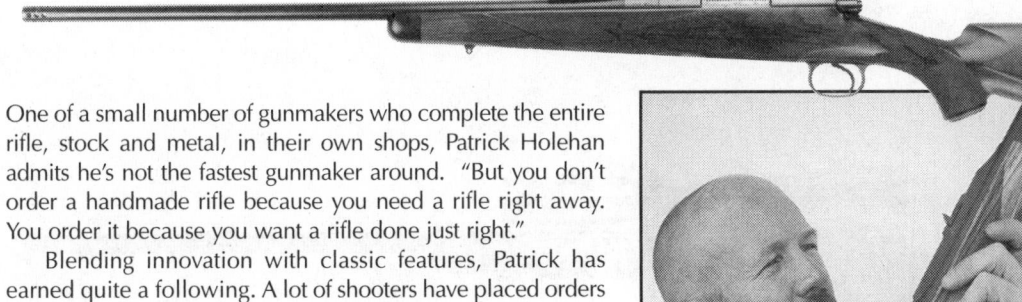

One of a small number of gunmakers who complete the entire rifle, stock and metal, in their own shops, Patrick Holehan admits he's not the fastest gunmaker around. "But you don't order a handmade rifle because you need a rifle right away. You order it because you want a rifle done just right."

Blending innovation with classic features, Patrick has earned quite a following. A lot of shooters have placed orders after seeing what Patrick calls his Arizona square bridge actions. "I start with Model 70 Winchester metal, then add scope mount blocks, making them integral and contouring them into the receiver. They're machined on top to accept quick-detachable rings." This Holehan touch is just one of many that make his rifles unique.

Patrick's M70 bolt rifles include Long Range, Lightweight and Safari versions. Together they comprise the "Hunter" series, with walnut or high-quality synthetic stocks pillar-bedded to the actions. Patrick trues barrel seating surfaces, laps the locking lugs and hones and polishes the feed ramp and bolt face. His stocks fit skin-tight except where customers want barrels to float. A long list of options includes wildcat chamberings in cryogenically treated barrels.

# Steven Dodd Hughes
## Livingston, Montana

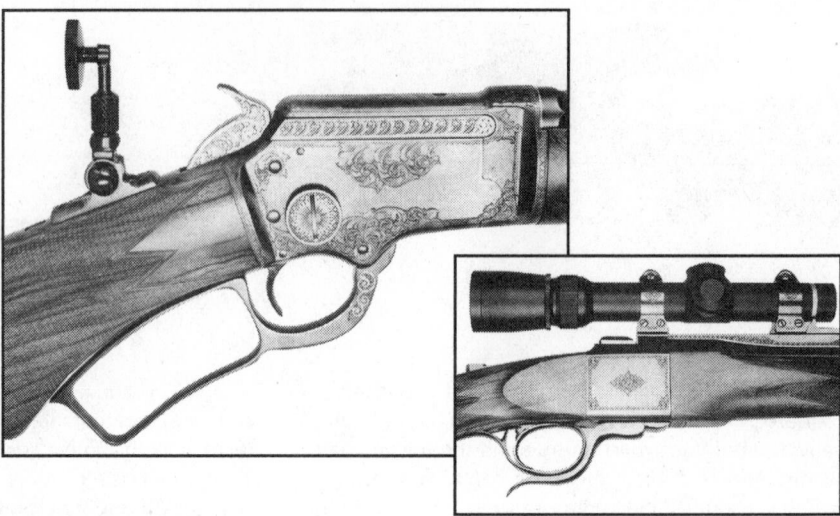

For a decade after starting his career in 1978, Steven Hughes focused on muzzleloading firearms faithful to 18th and 19th century patterns. Now he works almost exclusively on cartridge guns, like the Marlin Model 39 lever rifle shown here with a 1920s-pattern Winchester High Wall.

"Bolt rifles don't interest me much anymore," says Steven. "I leave those to the masses." He adds that there are a dozen craftsmen building custom turnbolt guns for every one keen to tackle a single-shot. "I also like old lever-actions. One of my favorite projects was an original Winchester 1873. I stocked it like one of the original 1-of-1,000 rifles after refitting the action with new parts."

Hughes also builds first-class double shotguns, which he appreciates as much as the classic American hunting rifles that demand much of his time. Steven writes a column for *Shooting Sportsman* magazine and has authored a couple books as well, but this multi-talented resident of Livingston, Montana considers himself primarily a gunmaker.

# David Miller
## Tucson, Arizona

"It's not a cheap rifle," David Miller says without apology. "We don't build cheap rifles. We build very accurate rifles that look good, for people who want the best there is."

He's been doing that for decades now, from a Tucson shop that's also the workplace for Curt Crum, an equally talented gunmaker. Miller and Crum produce true custom rifles built to the highest standards. Miller Classic rifles have earned the spotlight at several SCI conventions.

Some years ago, David assembled a rifle for his own use, a .300 Weatherby on a Model 70 Winchester action, with a long, fluted barrel and a laminated stock. The rifle wore a Leupold 6.5-20x scope in David's own bomb-proof mount. This outfit had the same clean lines as David's Classic rifle, but not the hand-checkering and expensive wood. As soon as other hunters heard of the project, Miller's phone started ringing. Now David and Curt offer their Marksman rifle as an affordable alternative to the Classic. It's still not cheap, but it shoots extremely well. After killing a Coues deer with one, I fired a three-shot group that measured an inch and a half – at 400 yards!

**CUSTOM GUNMAKERS**

"Strictly defined, a custom firearm is one built for an individual," insists Steve Nelson. "The rifle or shotgun has a stock fitted specifically for its owner, who also decides chambering, barrel dimensions, choke, sights, trigger and all the options that might make the product perform better or give the customer the look he or she wants.

Steve should know about custom rifles. The first one he owned, he built. "That was back in 1974. The result wasn't what I had in mind, but the process taught me a great deal. Before I bungled again, I signed up for one of Jerry Fisher's NRA summer seminars at Trinidad, Colorado. Then I attended the annual meeting of the American Custom Gunmakers Guild. What an eye-opener! I determined to come as close

as I could to the unbelievable craftsmanship I saw there." A decade later, after much hard work, he was accepted as a member of ACGG.

"I like to think I'm a consultant as well as a gunbuilder," he says. "My aim is to deliver a rifle that meets the client's needs specifically. The firearm must satisfy me as regards craftmanship. If it fails that test, or if it won't shoot well, it doesn't go out the door."

# Dave Norin
## Waukegan, Illinois

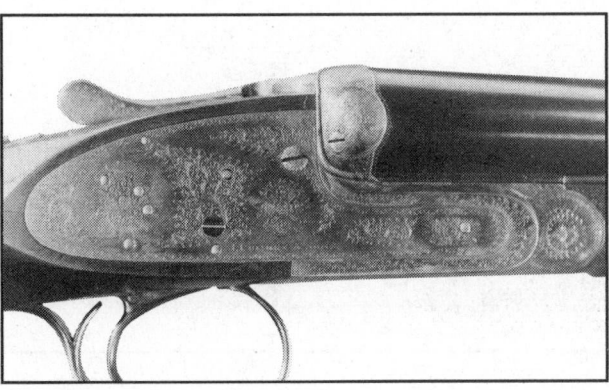

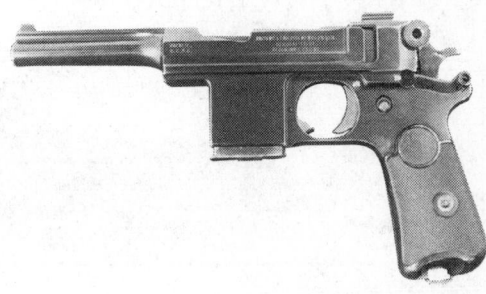

In early interest in firearms led Dave Norin to Trinidad State College in Colorado, there to study gunmaking. He graduated in 1972, joining a huge fraternity of custom gun-builders with that alma mater. But he has since distinguished himself from other craftsmen by steering toward unusual projects. "I have a broad range of interests," he says. "Obscure old guns fascinate me."

Dave's specialty these days is restoration of collector-quality firearms. Not long ago he was rebuilding a German 8x46R take-down target rifle and bringing an ultra-rare Farrow rifle back to life. He has restored Luger, Mauser and Mannlicher pistols and lever-action Winchester rifles. He

admits to producing a few classic bolt rifles – "the kind everybody works on." But few other custom shops boast the suite of services available from Norin: rust bluing, Niter bluing, color case hardening, stocking from blanks and vintage wood finishes. Dave's work shows an artist's attention to detail, and a faithfulness to original color and form.

Dave Norin lives and works in Waukegan, Illinois. He and his wife have four children and a grandchild. "Even without the shop and my whitetail hunting, I'd be busy!" he says. In his spare time, Dave collects pre-1945 self-loading pistols, Winchesters and "any nice double I can afford.

# Ray Riganian
## Glendale, California

In another life, Ray Riganian was a machinist in the aerospace industry, and he brings a machinist's eye for tight tolerances to his gun-building. Ray specializes in elegant and distinctive bolt-action hunting rifles, marrying such unlikely features as red-and-black laminated stocks with a classic stock profile and austere matte-finished steel. He does "almost all the work" himself. "I machine my own sight and scope bases from bar stock, my own swivel bands too," he explains. Some components come from other sources: Ted Blackburn bottom metal, for instance. He uses Talley scope rings. "Everything is carefully matched to the other components, and to the use the customer expects to make of his rifle."

Ray likes the Model 70 Winchester for hunting rifles, because of its beefy extractor – "also the 98 Mauser, but it requires a lot of work to finish." If the customer wants a Mauser, Ray recommends Searcy and Johannsen magnum actions. His varmint rifles are built on 700 Remingtons. Long-range target and bench rifles typically get Stolle or Nisika actions and Riganian uses Krieger barrels for big game rifles and Hart barrels on target guns. He sends the metal out for cold rust-bluing or a "special treatment that's more durable than Teflon and sticks better to the steel."

Ray pillar-beds the actions to stocks that show the same attention to detail he lavishes on metal. "I prefer to work on California English, but Circassian walnut makes a lovely stock. I buy dry blanks and will not shape any until it's down to 8 percent moisture. Though on high-quality wood I sometimes cut checkering as fine as 28 lines per inch, most of my checkering is 22 or 24 lpi, because hunters find it easier to grip. Rifles must be functional to be truly beautiful."

# Tony Schuelke
## Glencoe, Minnesota

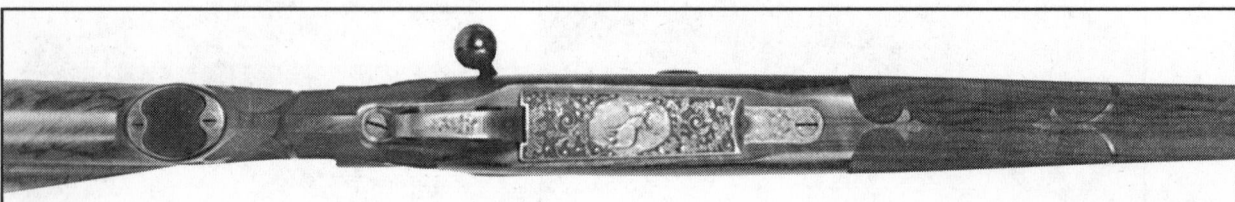

At 16 Tony Schuelke bought a shotgun and tried to refinish the wood. It was a start. But not until many years and countless amateur projects later did Tony start building guns. That was after stints in auto repair, life insurance, banking and real estate.

Tony says he's a machinist, but that label is inadequate. Tony has artistic talent, obvious when you look at what he's wrought with a file. Checkering not only stocks but bolt handles, and fabricating skeleton grip caps, he doesn't imitate anyone. He's constantly innovating. "If you're not a creative kind of a guy, there's not much interesting about building guns," he says, adding that the customer's ideas are very important. He'd rather respond to them than recommend his own design.

"Custom guns are more art than implements," he explains. "Customers have their own tastes, and they're paying the freight. So I listen." He adds that individuality can be important to gun people, and little details that have no bearing on performance often matter a great deal. He admits that untested ideas intrigue him. "But in this industry it's hard to find an idea that hasn't popped up sometime in wood or steel." Tony Schuelke's shop is in Glencoe, Minnesota, where he can hunt grouse with the double shotguns that get a lot of his attention, and where he says winters "are just right for working on guns."

# Gene Simillion
## Gunnison, Colorado

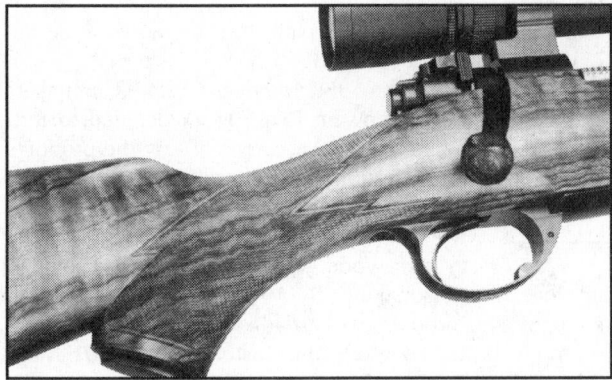
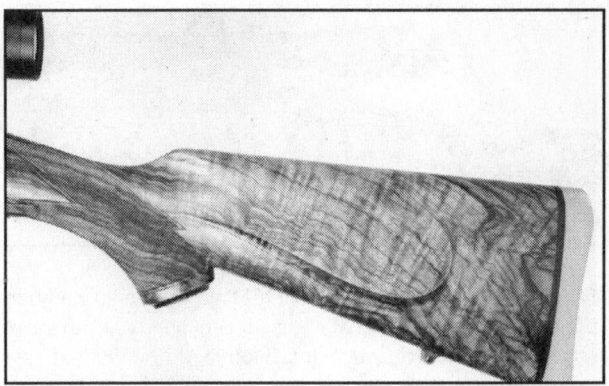

Gene Simillion's gun-building career started in Kalispell, Montana, where he worked under the tutelage of crack stockmaker Jerry Fisher. "Not far down the road was Tom Burgess," grins Gene. "He's forgotten more about metalsmithing than most gunmakers will ever learn." Gene also credits D'Arcy Echols, Monte Mandarino and Don Klein for giving him " the best education a young fellow could hope for."

Over the last couple of decades, Gene has earned a reputation for building some of the classiest-looking rifles available. The classic bolt rifle is still his favorite project. Gene's aim is to produce a rifle with "fine accuracy, flawless function and elegant beauty."

Gene's best rifle he calls the "Premier." Each is built to customer's specifications, usually on a new Winchester Model 70 Classic action because that's what Gene prefers. But he's willing to substitute early Model 70s, Mauser 98s and Remington 700s. Stocks, sleek and spartan of line, are exquisitely checkered and fitted skin-tight to the metal. Magnums get a second recoil lug and a crossbolt in front of the magazine well. Quarter ribs and drop-box magazines are two of many options. Gene fashions his own scope mounts. His less costly Classic Hunter comes only on the new M70 action. It has fewer options and less detailing, but its cut-rifled barrel, hand-bedded to a checkered walnut stock, delivers the same level of performance.

# Charlie Sisk
## Dayton, Texas

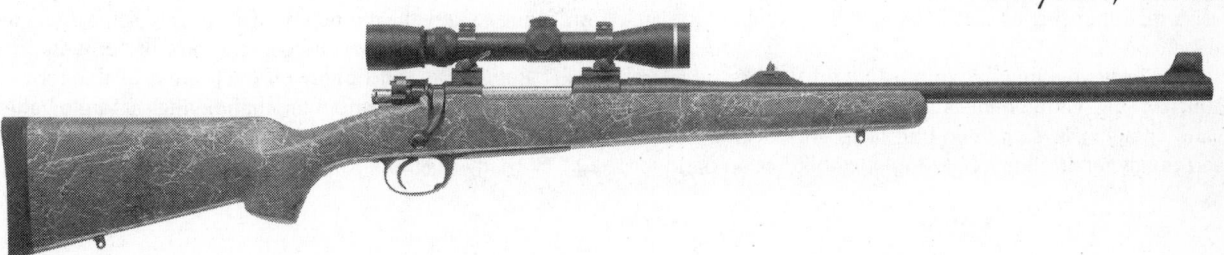

Texas is home to several well-known gunmakers and shooters who appreciate accurate rifles. Charlie Sisk is right at home there, assembling synthetic-stocked bolt guns for hunters and tackling "other projects I find interesting."

Charlie's rifles don't wear handsome wood or engraving. They're meant to be shot. "Beauty is as beauty does." In bolt rifles, Charlie prefers Model 700 Remingtons but says Winchester 70s come in a close second. He uses barrels from several top-brand suppliers but air-gauges them to cull those that vary more than .0001. He inspects each barrel with a bore-scope. Chambering is done with match-grade live-pilot reamers to ensure concentricity.

Charlie's standard rifle jobs include "blueprinting" the action to square up the bolt with the bore. He thinks most rifles will shoot about as well as they can shoot if the forend tip puts some pressure on the barrel. However, he will free-float barrels on request. Charlie installs and adjusts aftermarket triggers, mainly Timneys, and he takes care that his synthetic stocks fit each client perfectly. He makes his own muzzle brakes and works up loads for customers who request that service. Still in his thirties, Charlie enjoys hunting near his Dayton shop, where he also has a target range for testing his work.

# Mark Stratton
Lynnwood, Washington

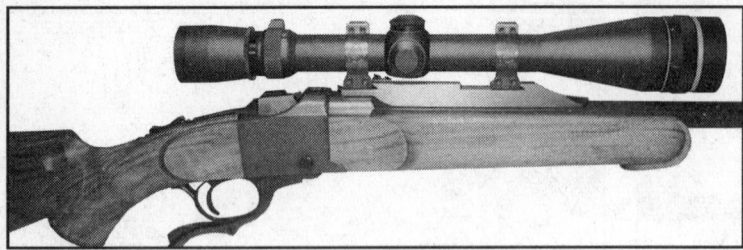

Early on, Mark Stratton found that his training as a gunsmith in Trinidad, Colorado, good as it was, did not guarantee financial security in his native southern California. So he worked as a machinist for an electronics firm, building rifles as a hobby during off-hours. He peddled his first rifle in 1974 to a friend for the cost of the parts; then he moved to Seattle and another job.

At the 1988 American Custom Gunmakers Guild show in Reno, Mark decided to turn his hobby into a career. "I saw the products of the country's finest craftsmen and wanted to become one. I was pretty good at metal work, but these fellows were way beyond me in the wood." Inspired, Mark set out to improve his stockmaking. By 1994, Mark was confident enough in his products to start advertising his work, which promptly brought kudos from customers. In 2001 Mark joined the ACGG and became one of its more accomplished members.

# Virgin Valley Guns
Hurricane, Utah

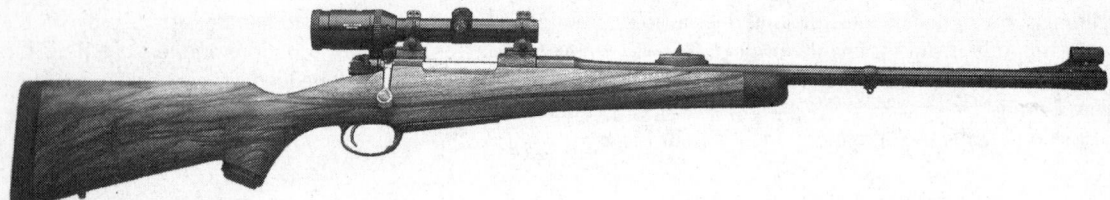

Virgin Valley's craftsmen turn out custom rifles on actions ranging from Martinis to the Nisika Bay. "We've built something of a reputation with the T/Cs," gunmaker Steve Stratton tells me. Other single-shots like the Ruger Number One are also favored.

The overwhelming majority of Virgin Valley's rifles are built for big game hunters and varmint shooters. Virgin Valley machinists square up bolt faces and locking lugs as part of any rebarreling job. Complete tooling is on hand for "blue-printing" the popular Remington 700 action and a few others. A custom rifle normally includes a Shilen match-grade barrel, though Steve says "select" barrels are available on request, and the company also installs some Douglas barrels. "We prefer Jewell triggers for most of our work," he adds. But Canjar and Timney products are available too.

Currently the most popular chamberings at Virgin Valley are the new short magnums, especially in T/C Encores. The .17 Hornady Magnum Rimfire is another hot number.

# Z-Hat Custom
Casper, Wyoming

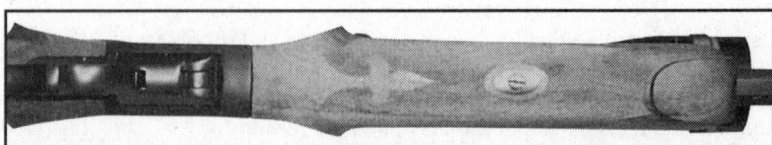

Z-Hat Custom specializes in barrel work and the building of accurate hunting rifles. Proprietor Fred Zeglin offers a variety of options on those rifles. "True custom guns include features that no factory delivers," says Fred. "We listen to our clients and make suggestions based on our experience with hunting rifles."

Most custom rifles at Z-Hat are built on client-supplied actions with either a synthetic or laminated stock. Prices start at around $2500. You can also get Fred to build you a take-down lever rifle on the Model 1895 Winchester and replica Browning frames. The price is $1990 with two barrels. A take-down Model 70 is in the works.

Recently, Fred has developed an in-line seating die similar to the old Vickerman. He has taught a class in wildcatting at the NRA Gunsmithing School held at Murray State College.

# NEW PRODUCTS

# NEW Products: **Blaser Rifles**

**BLASER S2 SAFARI**
*Action:* tilting block, double-barrel
*Stock:* select Turkish walnut,
checkered
*Barrels:* 24 inches, gas-nitrated,
sand-blasted, independent
*Sights:* open rear, blade front
on solid rib

*Weight:* 10.1 to 11.2,
depending on caliber.
*Caliber:* .375 H&H, .500/.416 NE,
.470 NE, .500 NE
*Magazine:* none
*Features:* selective ejectors, Pachmayr
Decelerator pad, snap caps, leather
sling, Americase wheeled travel case,

scope mount of choice
**Price: (standard grade)** . . . . . . **$8500**
**(extra barrel set):** . . . . . . . . . . **$5300**

*Also available:* S2 double rifle in
standard chamberings, from .222
to 9.3x74R, 7.7 pounds.

NEW PRODUCTS

# NEW Products: **Charles Daly Rifles**

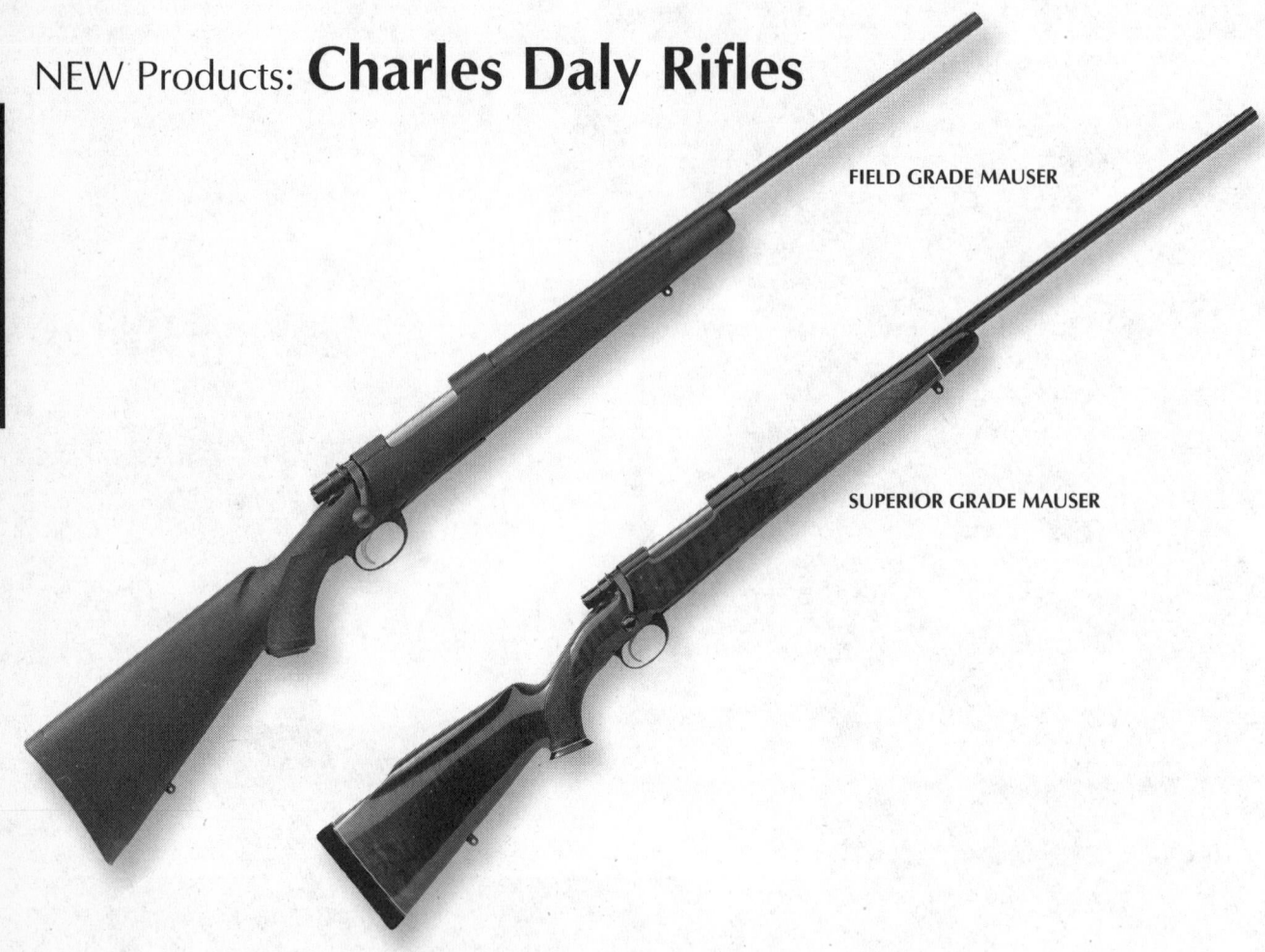

**FIELD GRADE MAUSER**

**SUPERIOR GRADE MAUSER**

**CHARLES DALY FIELD GRADE
MAUSER RIFLE**

*Action:* bolt, Zastava Mauser
*Stock:* molded black polymer,
classic style with cheekpiece,
reverse checkering
*Barrel:* hammer-forged, chrome

vanadium (also stainless), 22 inches
(standard) and 24 inches (magnum).
*Sights:* none (drilled and tapped for
scope mounts)
*Weight:* 7.5 and 7.8
*Caliber:* .22-250, .243, .25-06, .270,
.308, .30-06, 7mm Rem. Mag, .300
Win. Mag.

*Magazine:* box, capacity 5+1
(standard), 3+1 (magnum)
*Features:* fully adjustable trigger,
long Mauser claw extractor
**Price: (blue, standard)** . . . . . . . **$489**
**(blue, magnum)** . . . . . . . . . . . **$524**
**(stainless, standard)** . . . . . . . . **$549**
**(stainless, magnum)** . . . . . . . . **$579**

**SPORTSTER SL**

### H&R 1871 NEF Sportster

*Action:* blowback autoloading
*Stock:* hardwood
*Barrels:* 19 inches, button rifled
*Sights:* adjustable open rear, blade front on ramp

*Weight:* 5.5
*Caliber:* .22 Long Rifle
*Magazine:* 10-shot detachable box
*Features:* grooved for scope mounts; manually operated hold-open bolt
*Price:* . . . . . . . . . . . . . . . . . . . . $144

## NEW Products: **Marlin Rifles**

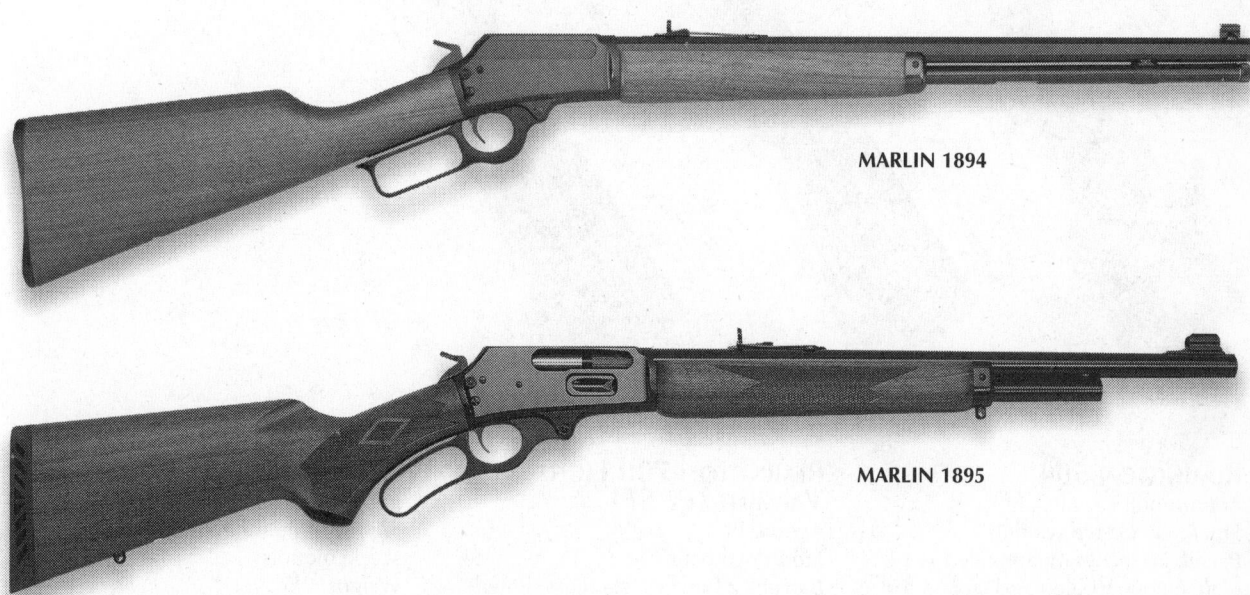

**MARLIN 1894**

**MARLIN 1895**

### Marlin 1895RL

*Action:* exposed-hammer lever-action
*Stock:* checkered American walnut with pistol grip, ventilated black recoil pad
*Barrel:* 18½ inches
*Sights:* adjustable folding semi-buckhorn rear, brass bead front (drilled and

tapped for scope mounts)
*Weight:* 7.0
*Caliber:* .480 Ruger, .475 Linebaugh
*Magazine:* 6-shot (.480) or 5-shot (.475) under-barrel tube,
*Features:* swivel studs, steel forend cap, offset hammer spur for scope use
*Price:* . . . . . . . . . . . . . . . . . . . . $695

# NEW Products: **Remington Rifles**

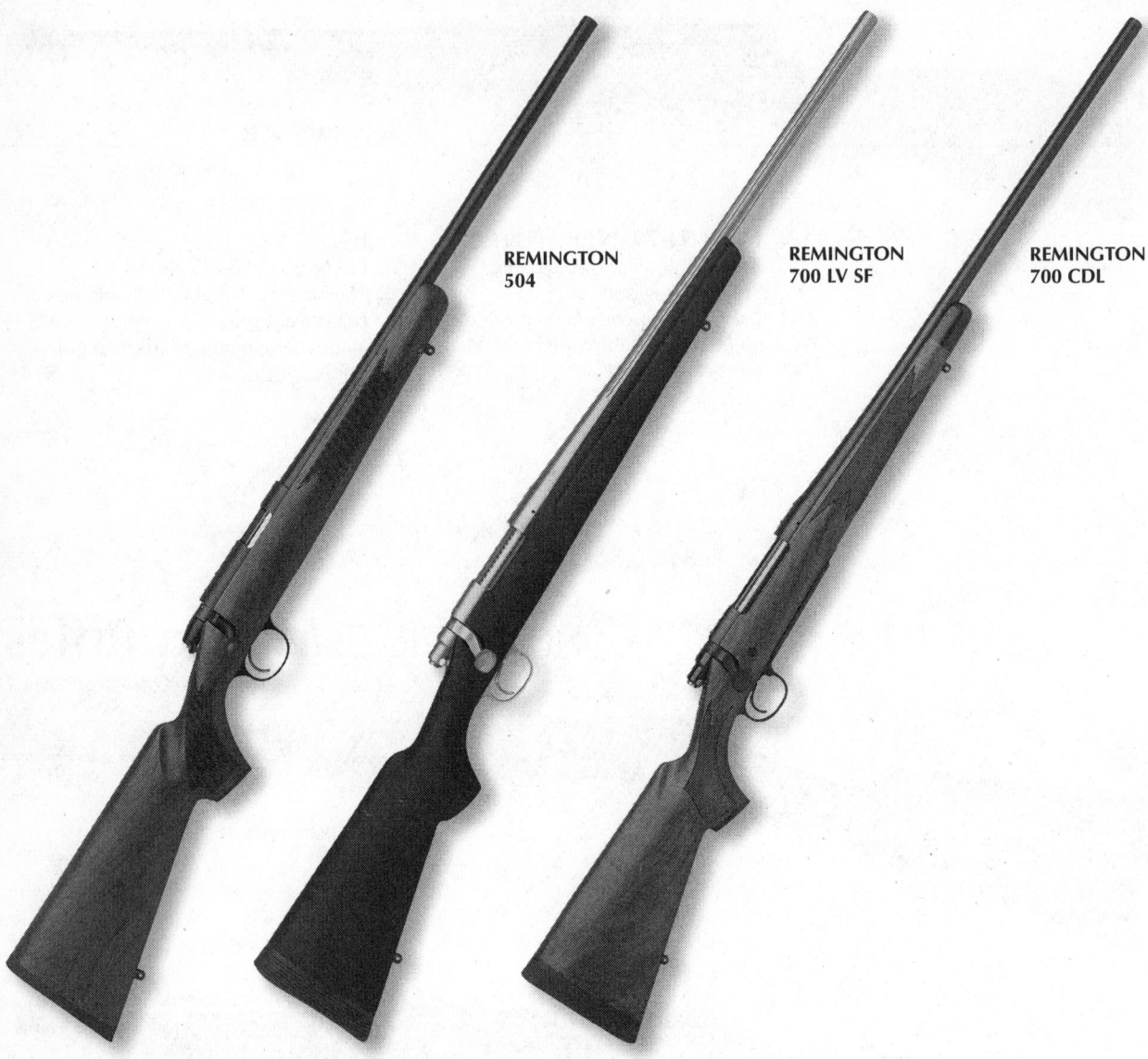

REMINGTON
504

REMINGTON
700 LV SF

REMINGTON
700 CDL

## REMINGTON 504

*Action:* bolt
*Stock:* checkered walnut
*Barrel:* 20 inches, button-rifled 1: 14 ½
*Sights:* none (drilled and tapped for scope mounts)
*Weight:* 6.0
*Caliber:* .22 Long Rifle
*Magazine:* 6-round detachable box
*Features:* fully adjustable trigger, nickel-plated bolt, removable barrel with "match" chamber,
*Price:* . . . . . . . . . . . . . . . . . . . $710

## REMINGTON 700 LIGHT VARMINT (LV SF)

*Action:* bolt
*Stock:* synthetic
*Barrel:* 22 inches, stainless, fluted
Sights: none (drilled and tapped for scope mounts)
*Weight:* 6.7
*Caliber:* .220 Swift, .22-250, .223
*Magazine:* 4-round box (5 in .223)
*Features:* fully adjustable trigger
*Price:* . . . . . . . . . . . . . . . . . . . $919

## REMINGTON 700 CDL

*Action:* bolt
*Stock:* walnut

*Barrel:* 24 inches (standard) and 26 inches (magnum, Ultra Mag)
*Sights:* none (drilled and tapped for scope mounts)
*Weight:* 7.5
*Caliber:* .243, .270, 7mm-08, 7mm Rem. Mag., 7mm Ultra Mag, .30-06, .300 Win. Mag. .300 Ultra Mag
*Magazine:* 4-round box (3 in magnums, Ultra Mags)
*Features:* fully adjustable trigger
*Price: (standard)* . . . . . . . . . . . . $710
*(belted magnum)* . . . . . . . . . . . $736
*(Ultra Mag)* . . . . . . . . . . . . . . . $749

# NEW Products: **Ruger Rifles**

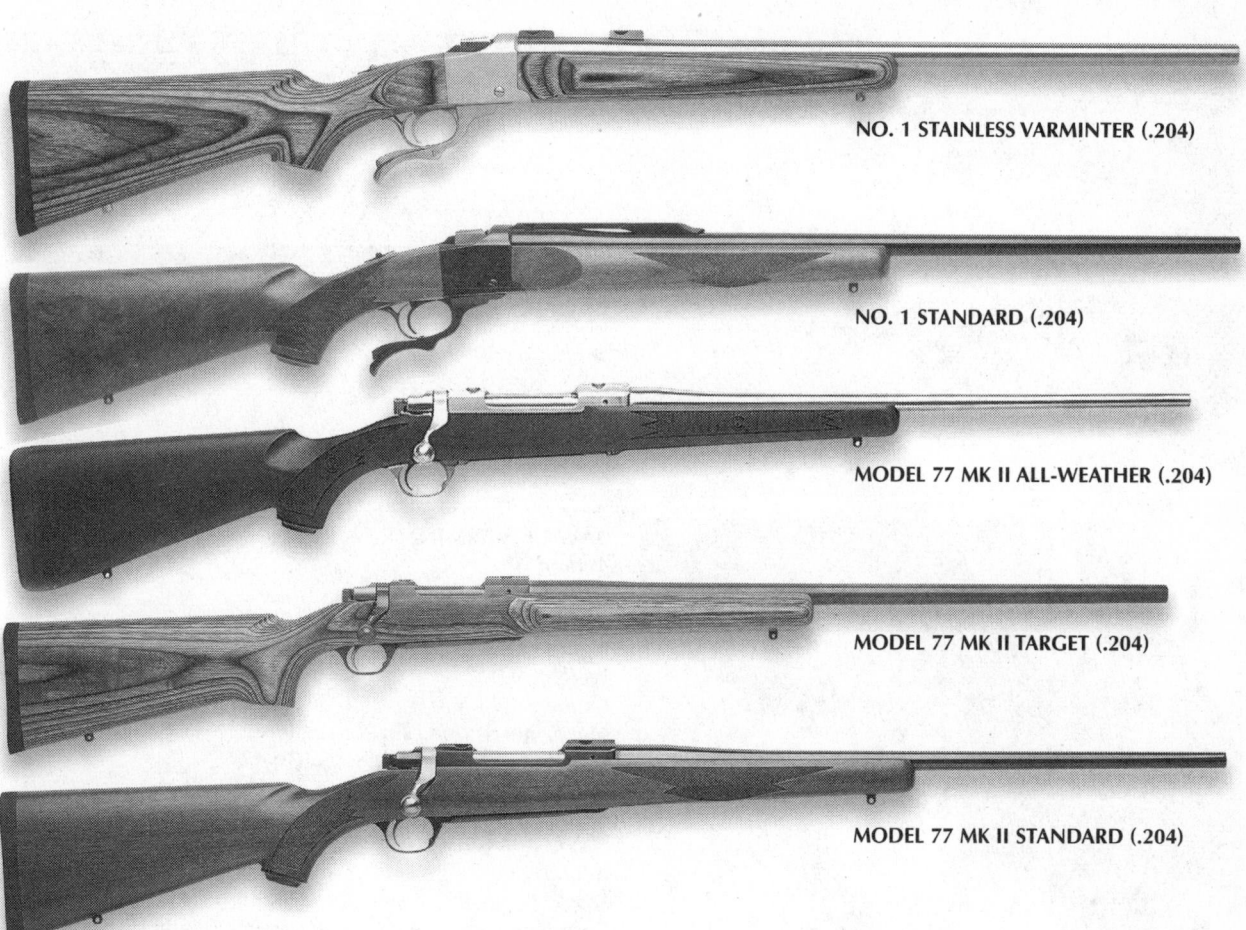

NO. 1 STAINLESS VARMINTER (.204)

NO. 1 STANDARD (.204)

MODEL 77 MK II ALL-WEATHER (.204)

MODEL 77 MK II TARGET (.204)

MODEL 77 MK II STANDARD (.204)

## MODEL 77 MKII STANDARD - 204 RUGER

*Action:* Bolt
*Stock:* Walnut
*Barrel:* 24 in.
*Sights:* None
*Weight:* 7 lbs.
*Caliber:* .204 Ruger
*Magazine:* 4
*Features:* Blued alloy steel action and barrel with stainless bolt, 3-position safety, medium height 1in. scope rings, and gun lock,
*Price* . . . . . . . . . . . . . . . . . . . $695

## MODEL 77 MKII TARGET GREY® - 204 RUGER

*Action:* Bolt
*Stock:* Brown Laminate
*Barrel:* 26 in.
*Sights:* None
*Weight:* 93/4 lbs.
*Caliber:* .204 Ruger
*Magazine:* 4
*Features:* Low glare stainless finish,

stainless steel barrel and action with stainless bolt, 3-position safety, medium height 1in. scope rings, and gun lock.
*Price* . . . . . . . . . . . . . . . . . . . $845

## MODEL 77 MKII ALL-WEATHER ULTRALIGHT - 204 RUGER

*Action:* Bolt
*Stock:* Synthetic
*Barrel:* 20 in.
*Sights:* None
*Weight:* 61/4 lbs.
*Caliber:* .204 Ruger
*Magazine:* 4
*Features:* Stainless action with stainless bolt, stainless steel barrel, 3-position safety, medium height 1" scope rings, and gun lock.
*Price* . . . . . . . . . . . . . . . . . . . $695

## NO.1 STANDARD - 204 RUGER

*Action:* Falling Block
*Stock:* American Walnut
*Barrel:* 26" Alloy Steel
*Sights:* None; quarter rib accepts

Ruger scope rin
*Weight:* 8 lbs.
*Caliber:* .204 Ruger
*Magazine:* N/ A
*Features:* Lever-operated falling block, stainless breech block, 2-position tang mounted safety, medium height 1-in. scope rings, and gun lock
*Price* . . . . . . . . . . . . . . . . . . . $920

## NO.1 STAINLESS VARMINTER - 204 RUGER

*Action:* Falling Block
*Stock:* Black Laminate
*Barrel:* 26in. Stainless Steel
*Sights:* None; drilled and tapped for target bloc
*Weight:* 9 lbs.
*Caliber:* .204 Ruger
*Magazine:* N/A
*Features:* Lever-operated Falling Block Stainless Steel Construction Satin Stainless Finish, medium height 1" scope rings, and gun lock
*Price* . . . . . . . . . . . . . . . . . . . $950

NEW PRODUCTS

# NEW Products: **Savage Rifles**

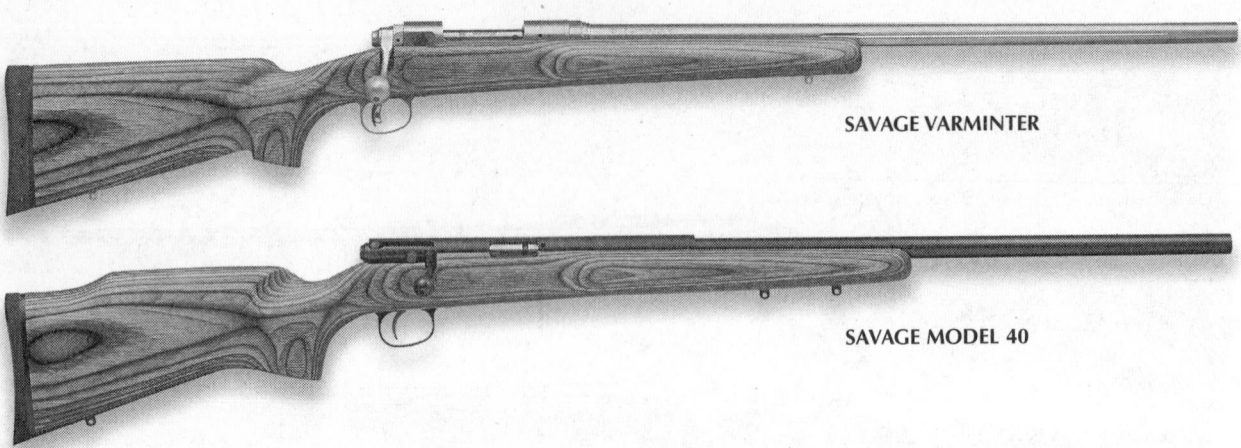

SAVAGE VARMINTER

SAVAGE MODEL 40

**ACCU TRIGGER**

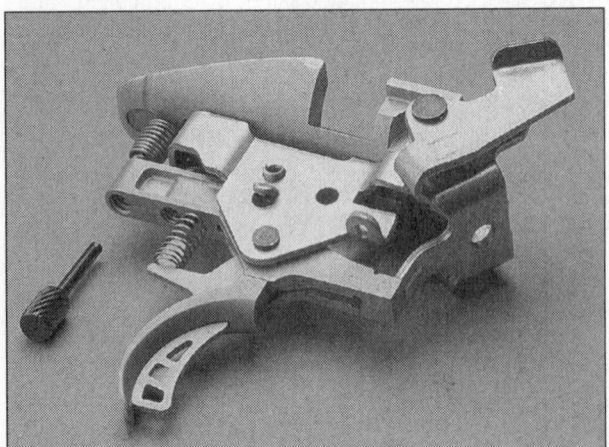

**ACCU TRIGGER**

## SAVAGE VARMINTER
*Action:* bolt
*Stock:* laminated
*Barrel:* heavy fluted stainless, button-rifled
*Sights:* none (drilled and tapped for scope mounts)
*Weight:* 9.0
*Caliber:* .223 and .22-250
*Magazine:* 4-round box or single-shot
*Features:* fully adjustable AccuTrigger
Price:. . . . . . . . . . . . . . . . . . . **$752**

## SAVAGE MODEL 40
*Action:* bolt
*Stock:* laminated, beavertail, with third swivel stud
*Barrel:* 24 inches, heavy, sleeved, free-floating
*Sights:* none (drilled and tapped for scope mounts)
*Weight:* 8.5
*Caliber:* .22 Hornet, .223 Rem.
*Magazine:* none
Price: (Hornet). . . . . . . . . . . . **$374**
(.223). . . . . . . . . . . . . . . . . . **$408**

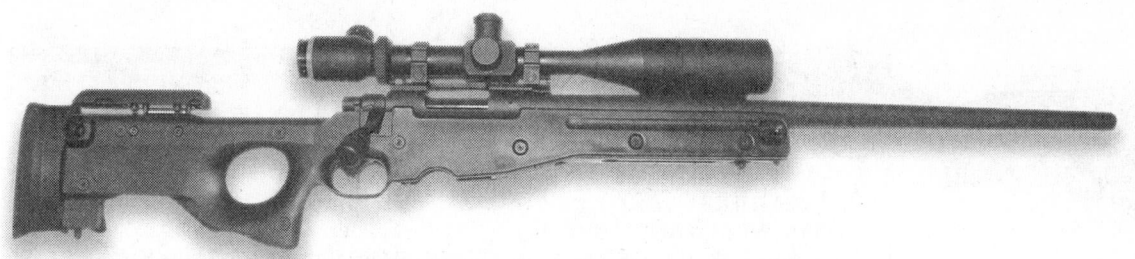

## TACTICAL L.R.

**Action:** bolt, M700 Remington
**Stock:** thumbhole aluminum, with resin panels, optional adjustable cheekpiece
**Barrel:** heavy, match-grade, 26 inches

**Sights:** none (drilled and tapped for scope, supplied with Picatinny rail)
**Weight:** 13.4
**Caliber:** 7.62 NATO (Magnum version available, in .300 WSM)
**Magazine:** 5-shot detachable box

(10-round boxes available)
**Features:** adjustable trigger, soft rubber recoil pad, swivel studs; options include stainless fluted barrel.
**Price:**................... $2450

## NEW Products: **Tikka Rifles**

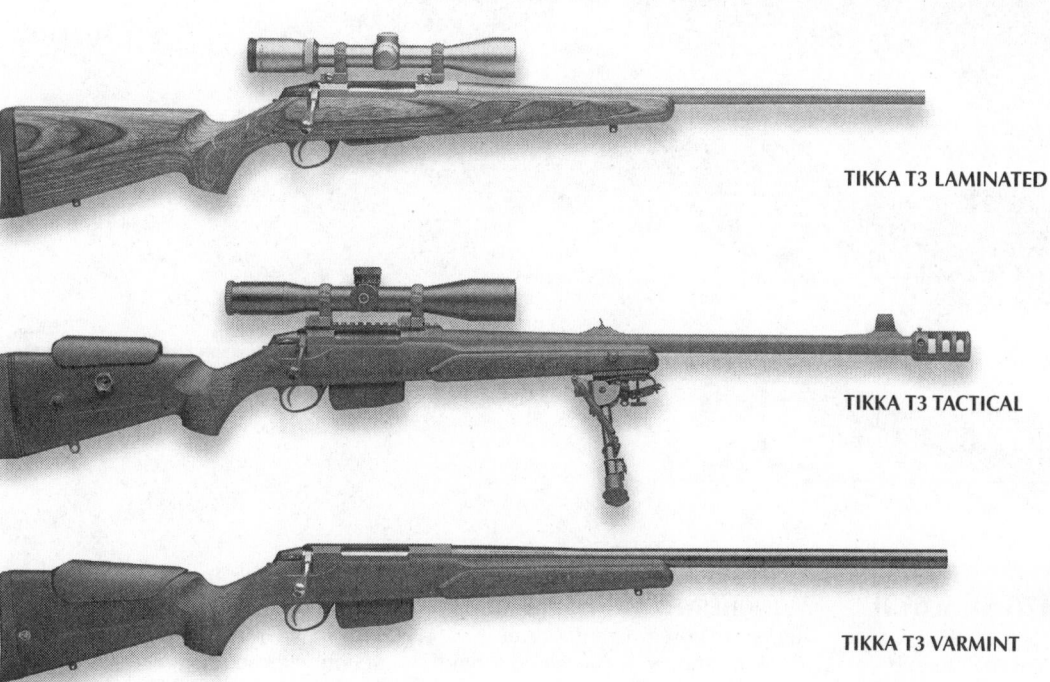

TIKKA T3 LAMINATED

TIKKA T3 TACTICAL

TIKKA T3 VARMINT

## TIKKA T3 LAMINATED STAINLESS

**Action:** two-lug bolt
**Stock:** laminated
**Barrel:** free-floating, hammer-forged, 22 inches (standard) and 24 inches (magnum)
**Sights:** none (drilled and tapped for scope mounts)
**Weight:** 7.0
**Caliber:** .243, .308, .25-06, .270, .30-06, .270 WSM, .300 WSM, 7mm Rem. Mag., .300 Win. Mag., .338

Win. Mag.
**Magazine:** 3-round detachable box
**Features:** fully adjustable trigger
**Price: (standard)**........... $752
**(magnum)** ............... $780

## TIKKA T3 VARMINT AND TACTICAL

**Action:** two-lug bolt
**Stock:** synthetic
**Barrel:** heavy, 23 inches (Varmint) and 20 inches (Tactical), free-floating,

hammer-forged
**Sights:** none (drilled and tapped for scope mounts)
**Weight:** 9.0 (Varmint), 8.5 (Tactical)
**Caliber:** .223, .22-250, .308 (Varmint), .223, .308 (Tactical)
**Magazine:** 5-round detachable box
**Features:** fully adjustable trigger
**Price:**................... $697
**(Varmint, chrome-moly and stainless)**.............. $752
**(Tactical)** ............... $1311

NEW PRODUCTS

# NEW Products: **Weatherby Rifle**

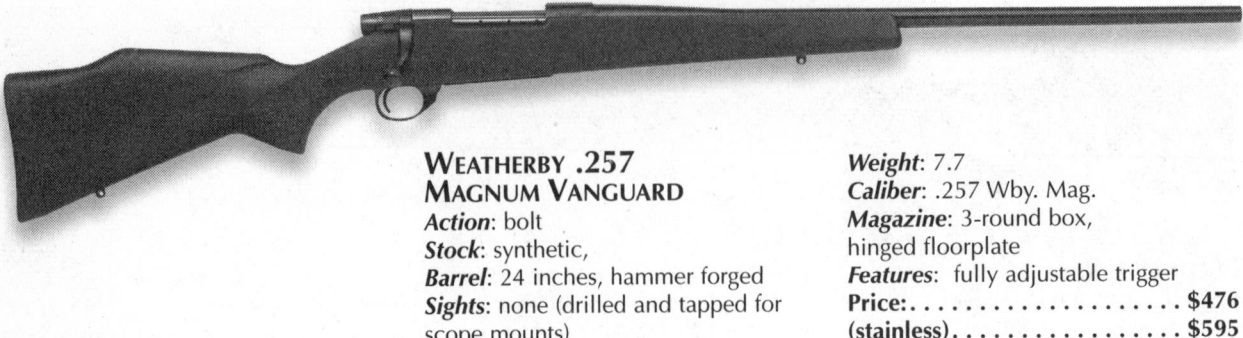

**WEATHERBY .257 MAGNUM VANGUARD**
*Action*: bolt
*Stock*: synthetic,
*Barrel*: 24 inches, hammer forged
*Sights*: none (drilled and tapped for scope mounts)

*Weight*: 7.7
*Caliber*: .257 Wby. Mag.
*Magazine*: 3-round box, hinged floorplate
*Features*: fully adjustable trigger
Price:................... $476
(stainless)................ $595

# NEW Products: **Winchester Rifles**

NEW PRODUCTS

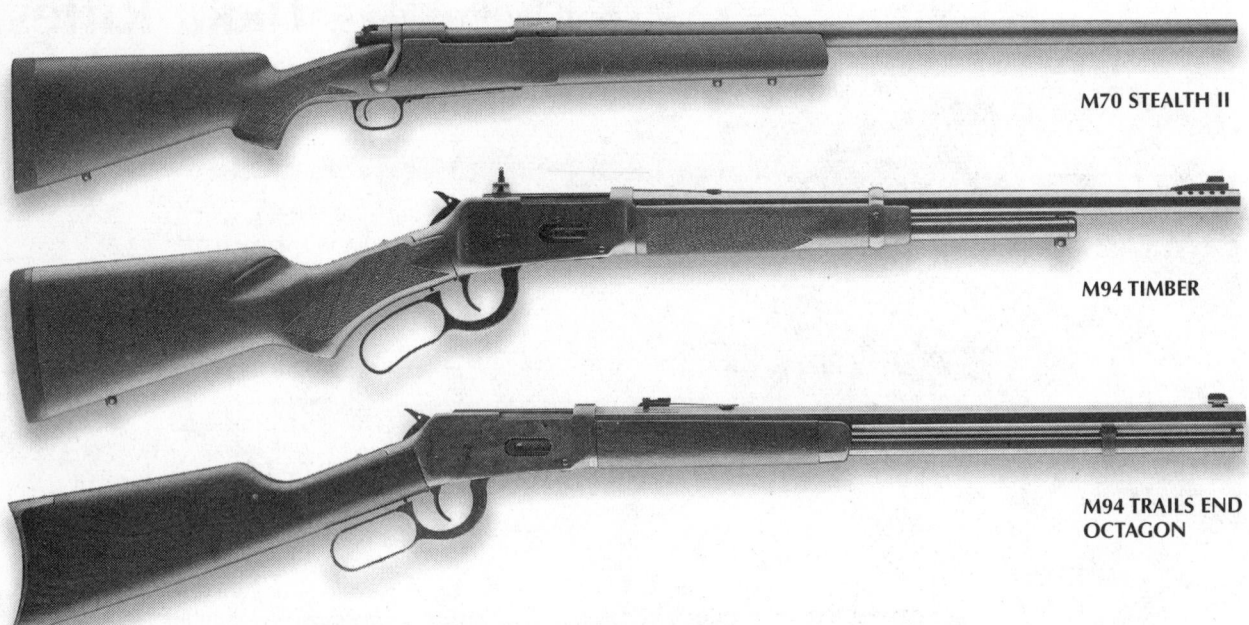

M70 STEALTH II

M94 TIMBER

M94 TRAILS END OCTAGON

### WINCHESTER M70 STEALTH II
*Action:* bolt
*Stock:* synthetic, beavertail forend with third stud, checkered pistol grip
*Barrel:* heavy, 26 inches
*Sights:* none (drilled and tapped for scope mounts)
*Weight:* 10
*Caliber:* .22-250, .308, .223 WSSM, .243 WSSM, .25 WSSM
*Magazine:* 3-round box with hinged floorplate
*Features:* three-position safety, pillar bedding, matte black finish
Price: (.22-250 and .308) ..... $832
(WSSMs) ................ $885

### WINCHESTER M94 TIMBER
*Action:* exposed-hammer lever
*Stock:* walnut with checkered forend and pistol grip
*Barrel:* 18-inch, ported
*Sights:* XS Ghost Ring rear and ramp front with bead
*Weight:* 6.0
*Caliber:* .450 Marlin
*Magazine:* under-barrel $^2/_3$-length tube, 4-shot
*Features:* Pachmayr recoil pad, crossbolt safety, receiver drilled and tapped for scope
Price: ................... $610

### WINCHESTER M94 TRAILS END OCTAGON
*Action:* exposed-hammer lever
*Stock:* walnut, uncheckered, with straight grip, forend cap
*Barrel:* 20 inches, octagonal
*Sights:* step-adjustable semi-buckhorn rear, bead front
*Weight:* 6.8
*Caliber:* .357 Magnum, .44 Magnum, .45 Colt
*Magazine:* full-length under-barrel tube, 11-shot
*Features:* Case colored receiver and furniture on TECC version
Price: (Octagon)........... $757
(Octagon Case Colored) ...... $815

M2

SUPER BLACK EAGLE II

SUPER BLACK EAGLE II MAX-4

SPORT II

SUPER SPORT

**NEW PRODUCTS**

## SPORT II

**Action:** recoil-operated autoloading
**Stock:** walnut, with spacers to adjust pitch, cast, length of pull
**Barrel:** hammer-forged, cryogenically treated, 28 or 30 inches
**Sights:** red bar on tapered stepped rib
**Chokes:** extra-long screw-in tubes (four provided)
**Weight:** 7.8 or 8.0
**Bore/Gauge:** 12
**Magazine:** four-shot tube (2¾-inch shells); two-shot with plug
**Features:** fires 2¾- and 3-inch shells, light and heavy loads interchangeably without adjustment; easily disassmbled
**List price:**. . . . . . . . . . . . . . . **$1400**

## M2 FIELD

**Action:** autoloader
**Stock:** synthetic or satin walnut
**Barrel:** 21, 24, 26 or 28 in.
**Chokes:** screw-in tube
**Weight:** 6.9 to 7.1 lbs.
**Bore/Gauge:** 12
**Magazine:** 3
**Features:** Comfor tech recoil reduction system, Crio barrel, inertia-recoil system, 3-in. chamber, rotating bolt

with dual lugs, Advantage Timber HD, Advantage –MAX-4 camo or black synthetic stock
**Walnut**. . . . . . . . . . . . . . . . . **$1035**
**Synthetic** . . . . . . . . . . . . . . . **$1065**
**Camo**. . . . . . . . . . . . . . . . . . **$1165**

## SPORT II

**Action:** autoloader
**Stock:** satin walnut
**Barrel:** 28 or 30 in.
**Chokes:** screw-in tubes
**Weight:** 7.85 lbs.
**Bore/Gauge:** 12
**Magazine:** 4
**Features:** Comfor tech recoil reduction system, Crio barrel, inertia-recoil system, 3-in. chamber
**Price** . . . . . . . . . . . . . . . . . **$1465**

## SUPER SPORT

**Action:** autoloader
**Stock:** synthetic
**Barrel:** 24 or 26 in.
**Chokes:** screw-in tubes
**Weight:** 7.2 lbs.
**Bore/Gauge:** 12
**Magazine:** 3
**Features:** Comfor tech recoil reduction

system, Crio barrel, inertia-recoil system, 31/2-in. chamber, rotating bolt with dual lugs, Advantage HD camo or black synthetic stock
**Price** . . . . . . . . . . . . . . . . . **$1465**

## SUPER BLACK EAGLE II

**Action:** autoloader
**Stock:** synthetic
**Barrel:** 24 or 26 in.
**Chokes:** screw-in tubes
**Weight:** 7.2 lbs.
**Bore/Gauge:** 12
**Magazine:** 3
**Features:** Comfor tech recoil reduction system, Crio barrel, inertia-recoil system, 3½-in. chamber, rotating bolt with dual lugs, Advantage Timber HD, Advantage –MAX-4 camo or black synthetic stock, Super Black Eagle II Flyway comes with walnut stock and choice of three scroll engraved receivers.
**Walnut**. . . . . . . . . . . . . . . . . **$1335**
**Synthetic** . . . . . . . . . . . . . . . **$1365**
**MAX-4 & HD Timber** . . . . . . . **$1465**
**Flyway Editions**. . . . . . . . . . . **$2130**

## NEW Products: **Beretta Shotgun**

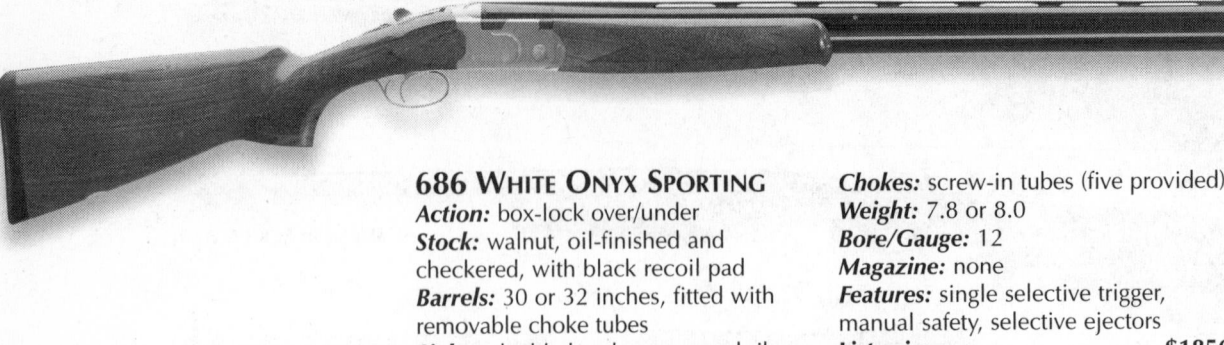

### 686 White Onyx Sporting
*Action:* box-lock over/under
*Stock:* walnut, oil-finished and checkered, with black recoil pad
*Barrels:* 30 or 32 inches, fitted with removable choke tubes
*Sights:* double beads on tapered rib

*Chokes:* screw-in tubes (five provided)
*Weight:* 7.8 or 8.0
*Bore/Gauge:* 12
*Magazine:* none
*Features:* single selective trigger, manual safety, selective ejectors
**List price:** . . . . . . . . . . . . . . . $1856

## NEW Products: **Browning Shotgun**

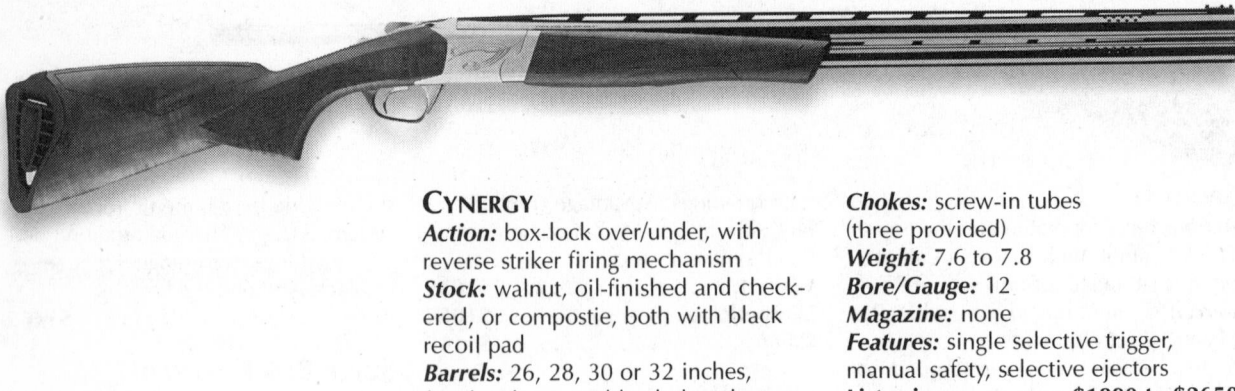

### Cynergy
*Action:* box-lock over/under, with reverse striker firing mechanism
*Stock:* walnut, oil-finished and checkered, or compostie, both with black recoil pad
*Barrels:* 26, 28, 30 or 32 inches, fitted with removable choke tubes
*Sights:* double beads on tapered rib

*Chokes:* screw-in tubes (three provided)
*Weight:* 7.6 to 7.8
*Bore/Gauge:* 12
*Magazine:* none
*Features:* single selective trigger, manual safety, selective ejectors
**List price:** . . . . . . . . **$1890 to $2650**

## NEW Products: **CZ Shotgun**

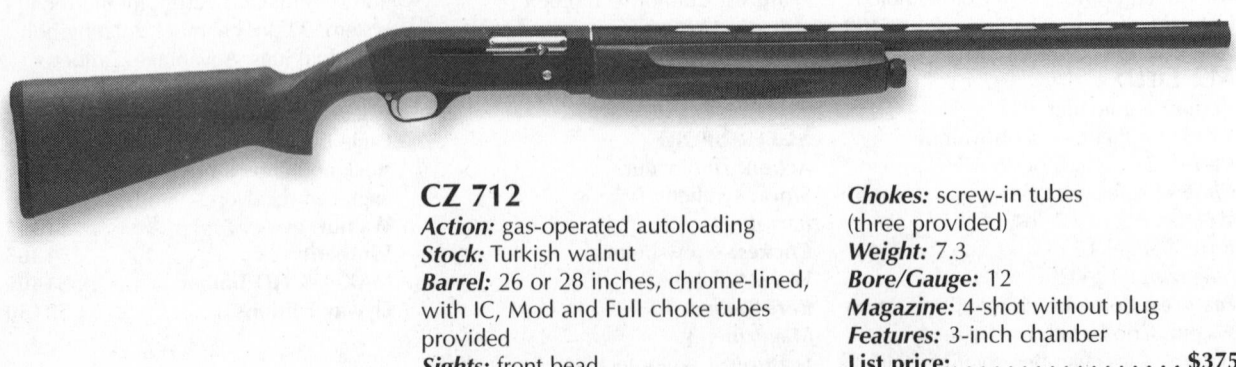

### CZ 712
*Action:* gas-operated autoloading
*Stock:* Turkish walnut
*Barrel:* 26 or 28 inches, chrome-lined, with IC, Mod and Full choke tubes provided
*Sights:* front bead

*Chokes:* screw-in tubes (three provided)
*Weight:* 7.3
*Bore/Gauge:* 12
*Magazine:* 4-shot without plug
*Features:* 3-inch chamber
**List price:** . . . . . . . . . . . . . . . $375

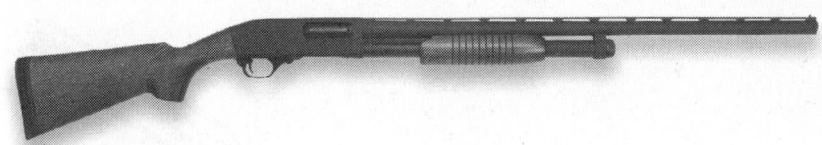

## 1871 PARDNER PUMP SHOTGUN

**Action:** hammerless pump
**Stock:** walnut with black recoil pad
**Barrel:** 28 inches, with vent rib, screw-in choke tube

**Sights:** gold bead front
**Chokes:** screw-in Browning/Winchester/Mossberg tubes (one provided)
**Weight:** 7.5
**Bore/Gauge:** 12

**Magazine:** 5-shot tube, with 2-shot plug provided
**Features:** twin action bars, easy take-down
**Price:**..................... $223

NEW Products: **Stoeger Shotguns**

COACH SUPREME BLUE

CONDOR COMBO

MODEL 2000
SYNTHETIC ADVANTAGE MAX-4

SINGLE BARREL SPECIAL

## MODEL 2000 SYNTHETIC ADVANTAGE MAX-4

**Action:** autoloader
**Stock:** synthetic
**Barrel:** 26 or 28 in.
**Chokes:** screw-in tubes
**Weight:** 6.8 lbs.
**Bore/Gauge:** 12
**Magazine:** 4
**Features:** inertia-recoil system; ventilated rib; Advantage MAX-4 camo stock; fires 33/4- and 3-in. ammunition
**Price**................... $495

## CONDOR COMBO

**Action:** over/under
**Stock:** hardwood
**Barrel:** 28 or 26 in.
**Chokes:** improved cylinder, modified

**Weight:** 7.4 to 6.8 lbs.
**Bore/Gauge:** 12, 20
**Magazine:** none
**Features:** boxlock; single trigger, 2 barrel sets (12- and 20-gauge)
**Price: Field**.............. $500
**Special**.................. $550
**Supreme**................ $600

## SINGLE BARREL SPECIAL

**Action:** hinged single-shot
**Stock:** hardwood
**Barrel:** 24 to 26 in.
**Chokes:** screw-in tubes or fixed
**Weight:** 5 lbs.
**Bore/Gauge:** 20, .410
**Magazine:** none
**Features:** transfer bar mechanism, crossbolt safety, .410 has fixed choke
**Price**.................... $125

## COACH GUN

**Action:** side-by-side
**Stock:** hardwood
**Barrel:** 20 or 24 in.
**Chokes:** screw-in, .410 fixed
**Weight:** 6.4 to 6.5 lbs.
**Bore/Gauge:** 12, 20, .410
**Magazine:** none
**Features:** boxlock, double triggers, automatic safety, improved cylinder and modified screw-in chokes for 20-gauge, available with stainless receiver and blued or polished nickel finish
**Price: Supreme Blue**......... $380
**Stainless Receiver**........... $390
**Polished Nickel** ............ $410

NEW PRODUCTS

# NEW Products: **Winchester Shotgun**

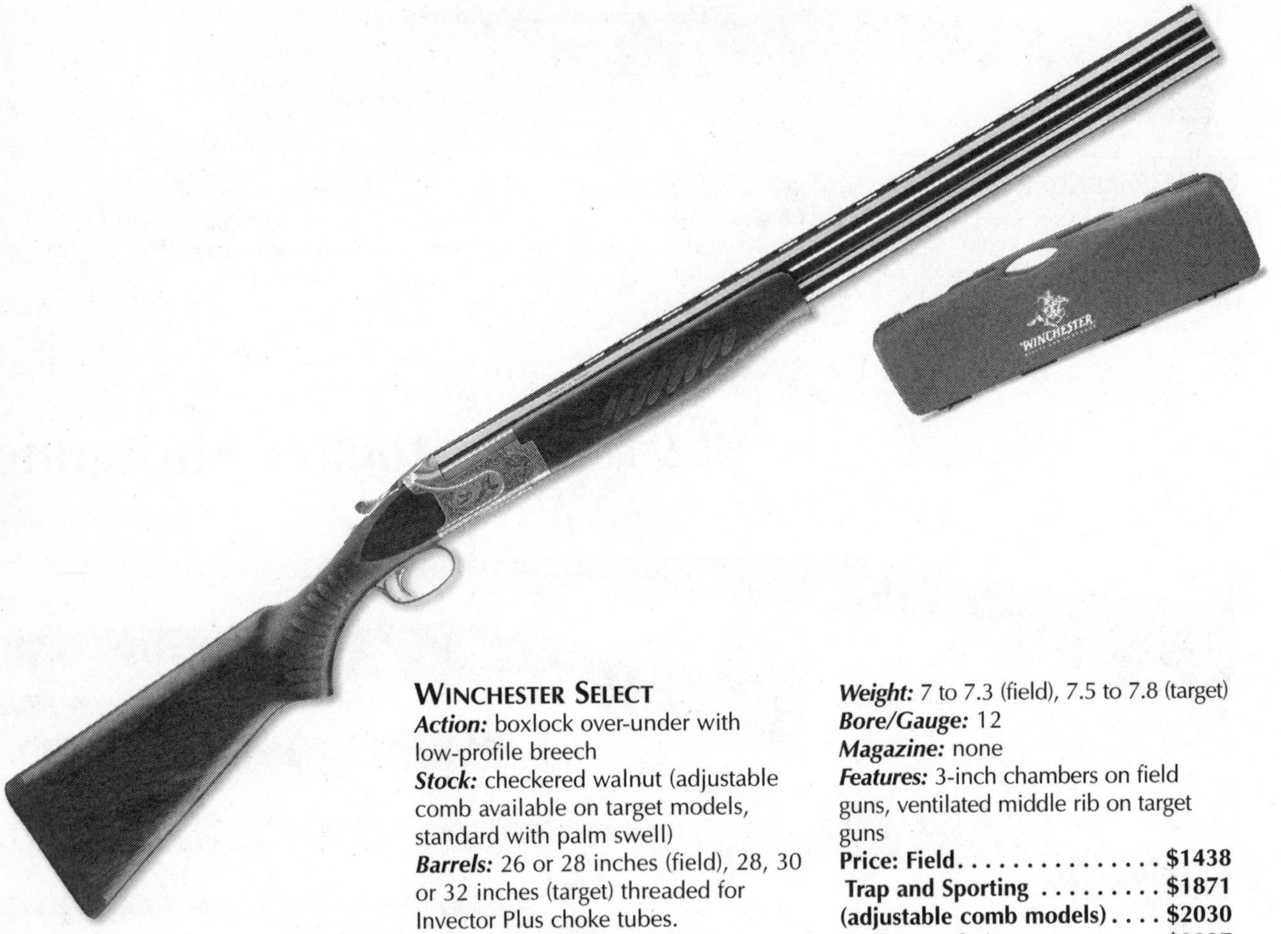




### WINCHESTER SELECT

***Action:*** boxlock over-under with low-profile breech
***Stock:*** checkered walnut (adjustable comb available on target models, standard with palm swell)
***Barrels:*** 26 or 28 inches (field), 28, 30 or 32 inches (target) threaded for Invector Plus choke tubes.
***Sights:*** bead front (TruGlo on target versions)
***Weight:*** 7 to 7.3 (field), 7.5 to 7.8 (target)
***Bore/Gauge:*** 12
***Magazine:*** none
***Features:*** 3-inch chambers on field guns, ventilated middle rib on target guns

**Price: Field . . . . . . . . . . . . . . . $1438**
**Trap and Sporting . . . . . . . . . $1871**
**(adjustable comb models) . . . . $2030**
**(higher grades) . . . . . . . . . . . . $2227**

*A quick fit test for length of pull: Rest the shotgun butt in the crook of your arm. If your finger rests comfortably on the trigger, the buttstock is about the right length*

# NEW Products: **Beretta Handguns**

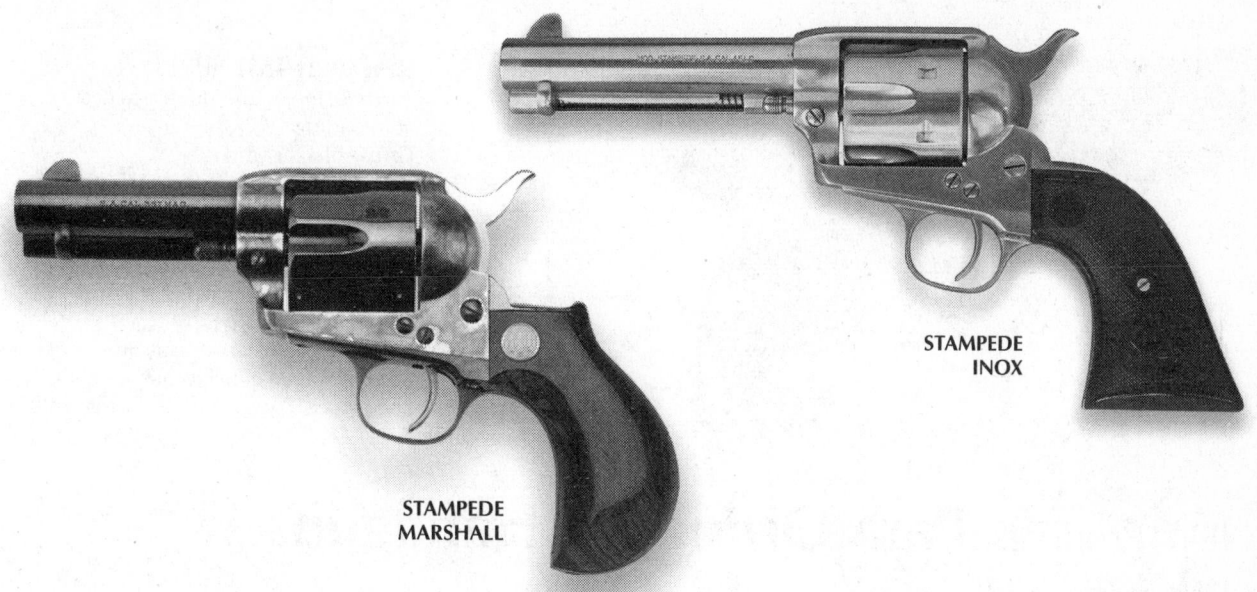

STAMPEDE
INOX

STAMPEDE
MARSHALL

## Beretta Stampede Inox and Marshall

**Action:** single-action revolver
**Grips:** black composite (Inox)
and walnut (Marshall)
**Barrel:** 3½ (Marshall), 4¾, 5½ or 7½
inches (Inox)

**Sights:** blade front, strap groove in rear
**Weight:** 37 ounces (4¾-inch barrel)
**Caliber:** 357 Magnum, .45 Long Colt
**Capacity:** 6
**Features:** various finishes available
on Stampede metal, including nickel,
charcoal blue

List price: Inox . . . . . . . . . . . . . $644
Marshall. . . . . . . . . . . . . . . . . $522
others from . . . . . . . . . . . . . . . $493

# NEW Products: **CZ Handguns**

## CZ 2075

**Action:** single- and double-action
autoloading
**Grips:** lack composite
**Barrel:** 3 inches
**Sights:** blade front, shrouded rear
**Weight:** 25 ounces

**Caliber:** 9mm Luger, .40 S&W
**Magazine Capacity:** 10 (9mm),
8 (.40 S&W)
**Features:** firing pin block, manual
safety, double-stack magazine
**Price:** . . . . . . . . . . . . . . . . . . . $559

# NEW Products: **Magnum Research Handguns**

**MAGNUM RESEARCH/IMI SP-21**
*Action:* single- and double-action autoloading
*Grips:* black composite
*Barrel:* 3.9 inches, polygonal rifling
*Sights:* blade front, adjustable or fixed tritium rear
*Weight:* 26 ounces (27 in .45 ACP)
*Caliber:* 9x19, .40 S&W, .45 ACP
*Magazine Capacity:* 10
*Features:* decocker, ambidextrous safety, no-snag hammer, rail for night sights
**List price:. . . . . . . . . . . . . . . . . $495**

# NEW Products: **Para Ordnance Handguns**

**PARA ORDNANCE PXT 1911 PISTOLS**
*Action:* single-action autoloading
*Grips:* cocobolo with gold medallion and beavertail extension
*Barrel:* 4.25 and 5 inches
*Sights:* blade front, white three-dot rear
*Weight:* 37 ounces and 39 ounces
*Caliber:* .45 ACP
*Magazine Capacity:* 7+1
*Features:* match trigger, extended slide lock, Para Kote Regal finish, stainless competition hammer
**List price: . . . . . . . . . . . . . . . . $739**

# NEW Products: **Smith and Wesson Handguns**

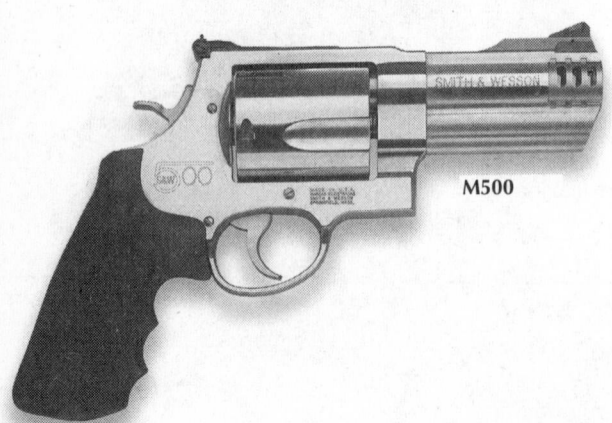

M500

**S&W .500 "SHORT BARREL"**
*Action:* double-action revolver
*Grips:* rubber
*Barrel:* 4 inches, sleeved, with brake
*Sights:* adjustable rear, red ramp front
*Weight:* 56 ounces
*Caliber:* .500 S&W
*Capacity:* 5
**Price:. . . . . . . . . . . . . . . . . . . $1150**

# NEW Products: **Smith and Wesson Handguns**

325 PD

351 PD

**NEW PRODUCTS**

## S&W MODELS 325 PD AND 351 PD REVOLVER

*Action:* double-action revolver
*Grips:* wood (.45), rubber (.22)
*Barrel:* 2¾ inches (.45), 1⅞ inches (.22)
*Sights:* adjustable rear, HiViz front (.45), fixed rear, red ramp front (.22)

*Weight:* 21.5 ounces (.45), 10.6 ounces (.22)
*Caliber:* .45 ACP (Model 325), .22 WMR (Model 351)
*Capacity:* 6 (.45), 7 (.22)
**Price: (.45)**................$907
**(.22)**....................$627

# NEW Products: **Springfield Armory Handguns**

1911 A1

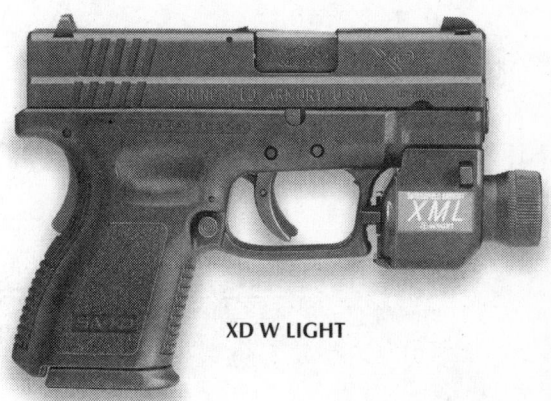

XD W LIGHT

## SPRINGFIELD ARMORY XD SUB-COMPACT

*Action:* self-loading, short-recoil, locked-breech
*Grips:* black composite
*Barrel:* 3.1 inches, cold hammer forged
*Sights:* 3-dot, fixed rear and front
*Weight:* 20.5 ounces
*Caliber:* 9x19mm and .40 S&W

*Magazine capacity:* 10+1
*Features:* Polymer frame with heat-treated steel slide and rails, dual recoil springs, three safeties, cocking indicator, light rail (Mini Light optional)
**Price:**....................$498

## SPRINGFIELD ARMORY 1911-A1

*Action:* autoloading, M1911 design
*Grips:* double-diamond walnut

*Barrel:* 5 inches
*Sights:* early service-style, fixed
*Weight:* 36 ounces
*Caliber:* .45 ACP
*Capacity:* 7+1
*Features:* forged frame, barrel, slide; titanium firing pin; standard ejection port; vertical slats; lanyard loop
**Price:**....................$482

# NEW Products: **Springfield Armory Handguns**

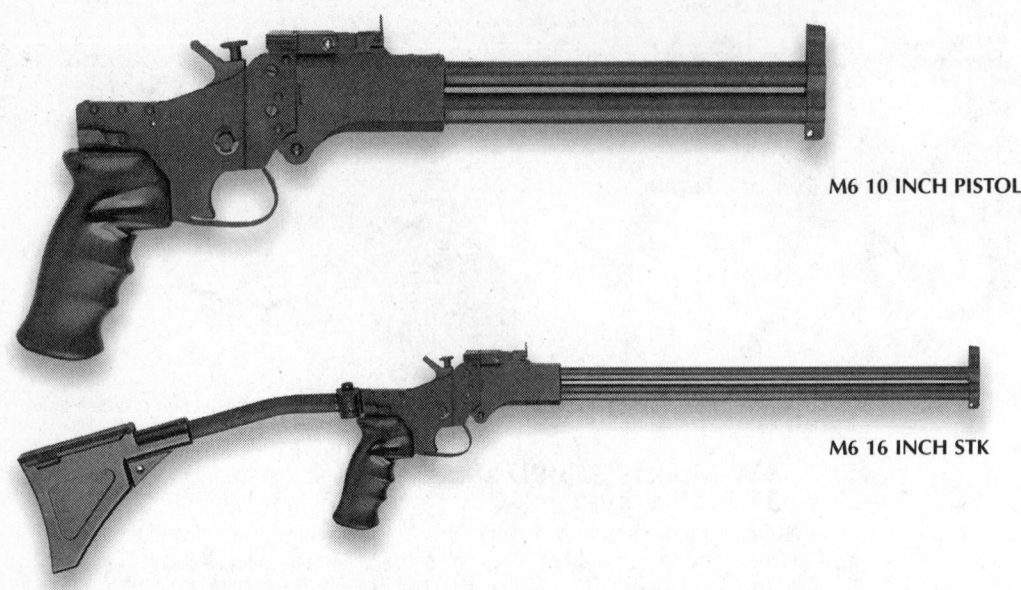

**M6 10 INCH PISTOL**

**M6 16 INCH STK**

**SPRINGFIELD M6 SCOUT**
*Action*: hinged breech
*Grips*: synthetic
*Barrel*: 10 inch
*Sights*: open
*Caliber*: .22LR, .22 Hornet (upper barrel)

and .45 LC or .410 (lower barrel)
*Magazine Capacity:* none
*Features*: over/under combination gun, stainless or parkerized finish.
**Price: Parkerized . . . . . . . . . . . $199**
**Stainless. . . . . . . . . . . . . . . . . $223**

# NEW Products: **Thompson/Center Handguns**

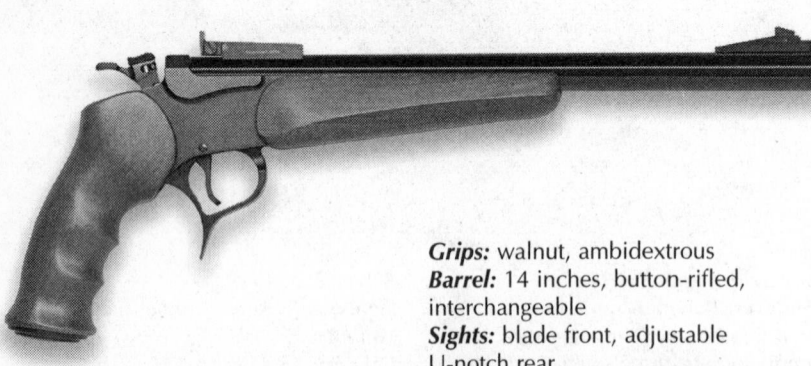

**CONTENDER G2 PISTOL**

**THOMPSON/CENTER CONTENDER G2 .375 JDJ**
*Action:* single-shot, under-lever, hinged-breech

*Grips:* walnut, ambidextrous
*Barrel:* 14 inches, button-rifled, interchangeable
*Sights:* blade front, adjustable U-notch rear
*Weight:* 56 oz. (12-inch pistol)
*Caliber:* 17 HMR, .22 LR Match, .204 Ruger, .22 Hornet, .223 Remington, 7-30 Waters, .30-30 Winchester, .375 JDJ, .44 Remington Magnum, .45-70 Government, .45 Colt/.410 shotshell.

(These are available in 14-inch pistol barrels; fewer are offered in 12-inch barrels and rifle barrels. T/C's custom shop chambers for more than 100 cartridges).
*Capacity:* 1
*Features:* centerfire and rimfire capability with hammer selector and interchangeable barrels; drilled and tapped for scope mounts.
**List price: (12-inch pistol). . . from $556**

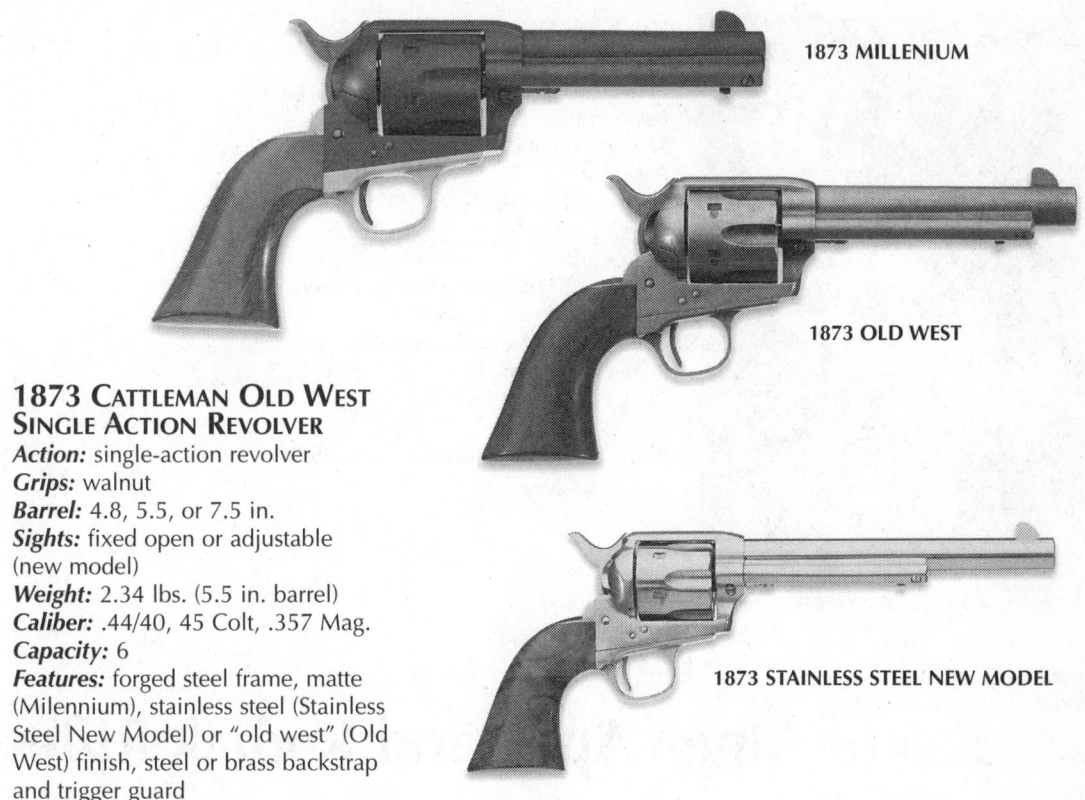

**1873 MILLENIUM**

**1873 OLD WEST**

**1873 STAINLESS STEEL NEW MODEL**

## 1873 CATTLEMAN OLD WEST SINGLE ACTION REVOLVER

*Action:* single-action revolver
*Grips:* walnut
*Barrel:* 4.8, 5.5, or 7.5 in.
*Sights:* fixed open or adjustable (new model)
*Weight:* 2.34 lbs. (5.5 in. barrel)
*Caliber:* .44/40, 45 Colt, .357 Mag.
*Capacity:* 6
*Features:* forged steel frame, matte (Milennium), stainless steel (Stainless Steel New Model) or "old west" (Old West) finish, steel or brass backstrap and trigger guard
**Price: SS New Model** . . . . . . . . **$475**
**Old West** . . . . . . . . . . . . . . . . **$470**
**Millennium** . . . . . . . . . . . . . . . **$260**

# NEW Products: **Black Powder**

## CVA BLACKPOWDER

### KODIAK™ 209 MAGNUM

*Lock:* in-line  *Stock:* synthetic
*Barrel:* 28 in.  *Sights:* fiber optic
*Weight:* 7.5 lbs.

*Bore/Caliber:* .45 or .50
*Features:* ambidextrous solid stock in black or Mossy Oak Camo, stainless steel 209 breech plug
**Mossy Oak Camo/**
  **Nickel Barrel:** . . . . . . . . .**$329.95**

**Mossy Oak Camo/**
  **Blue Barrel:** . . . . . . . . . .**$309.95**
**Black FiberGrip/**
  **Nickel Barrel:** . . . . . . . . .**$289.95**
**Black FiberGrip/**
  **Blue Barrel:** . . . . . . . . . .**$259.95**

NEW PRODUCTS

# NEW Products: **Black Powder**

### KNIGHT BLACKPOWDER REVOLUTION

*Lock:* in-line
*Stock:* synthetic
*Barrel:* 27 in.
*Sights:* fiber optic
*Weight:* 7.14 lbs.
*Bore/Caliber:* .50
*Features:* 209 full plastic jacket ignition system, sling swivel studs.
Options: Stainless w/ laminate, Realtree, or Black Blued w/ Mossy Oak, Walnut or black

**Black Stock/Blue Barrel: . . . $605.32**

# NEW Products: **Alpen Apex and Kodiak Riflescopes**

ALPEN APEX 3.5-10X50

KODIAK 4-12X40

Familiar to many outdoorsmen as a purveyor of binoculars and spotting scopes, Alpen Optics has announced two lines of riflescopes, comprising 11 models. Three Apex variables feature fully multi-coated lens systems, plus resettable finger-adjustable windage and elevation adjustments with 1/4-minute clicks.

Three models are available: 3-9x42, 3.5-10x50 and 6-24x50. All have fast-focus eye-pieces and the Alpen AccuPlex reticle, plus a lifetime warranty.

The companion line to the Apex is called Kodiak. Its scopes are also fully waterproof, fog-proof and warranteed.

They feature multi-coated lenses, but apparently not all lenses are treated. A 4x32 is the only fixed-power scope. The others range in magnification from the 1.5-4.5x32 to the 6-24x50. As with the Apex, eye relief is about 3 inches on all models save the 1.5-4x, which offers 4 inches of ER.

# NEW Products: **Browning/Bushnell Optics**

**SCOPE 3-9X50**

New for 2004 is a line of riflescopes with the Browning name but Bushnell lineage. Browning's line consists of 4 scopes — 2-7x32, 3-9x40, 3-9x50 and 5-15x40. Claiming 94 percent light transmission people at Browning point out also the fast-focus eyepiece, finger-friendly, quarter-minute click adjustments and a one-piece tube guaranteed waterproof and fog-proof. Eye relief is a generous 3½ inches. The lenses are all multi-coated.
**Bushnell/**
**Browning scopes:. . . . . $352 to $490**

# NEW Products: **Burris Optics**

**EURO DIAMOND 3X-10X40**

The Burris Euro Diamond line, new for 2004, includes four 30mm riflescopes: 1.5-6x40, 3-10x40, 2.5-10x44, 3-12x50. All come in matte black finish, with fully multi-coated lenses and ¼-minute clicks on re-settable dials. Eye relief is 3½ to 4 inches. The eyepiece and power ring are integrated and the scopes have a helical rear ocular ring. reticle focus. A German 3P#4 reticle is standard.
**Euro Diamond Scopes:. $728 to $983**

# NEW Products: **Bushnell Optics**

**TASCO 8-32X44 TARGET**

**TASCO GA 2.5X32 CB**

**TASCO RGD PRO POINT**

This year Bushnell adds a 2-7x32 scope to the Legend line, and the Firefly reticle will be installed on more Elite models. The Firefly operates on the principle of a luminous watch dial, "storing" illumination. Another red dot sight, under the Tasco label, is the ProPoint, with a red and green 5-minute dot. There's also a new Tasco target/varmint scope, an 8-32x44 with 1/4-minute dot and three new Golden Antler scopes, including a 2.5x32 for crossbows.

**LEGEND 2-7X32**

# NEW Products: **Kahles Optics**

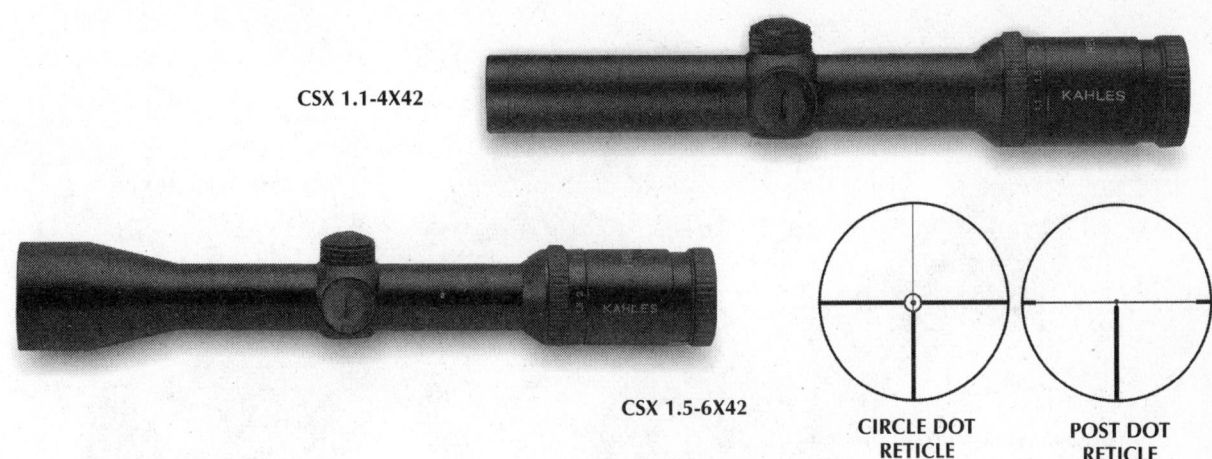

**CSX 1.1-4X42**

**CSX 1.5-6X42**

**CIRCLE DOT RETICLE**

**POST DOT RETICLE**

For 2004 Kahles has announced the Helia CSX daylight illumination reticles for the compact 1.1-4x24 and 1.5-6x42 scopes in its 30mm line. Two such reticles are available: an illuminated circle dot and an illuminated dot on top of a post. A red bulb indicates when the illumination is activated, and a safety switch prevents accidental operation. Fully multi-coated optics are standard.

They weigh 14.6 and 16.4 ounces, deliver 3.5 inches of eye relief.

**Helia CSX Scopes:**
1.1-4x24 . . . . . . . . . . . . . . . $1443
1.5-6x42 . . . . . . . . . . . . . . . $1666

# NEW Products: **Leupold Optics**

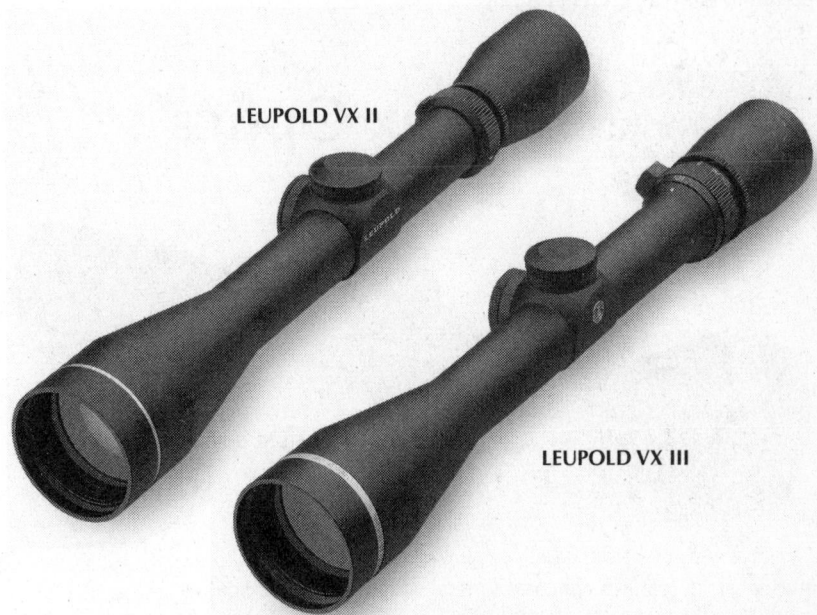

**LEUPOLD VX II**

**LEUPOLD VX III**

The new VX-III scopes, which replace the Vari-X III line, feature new lens coatings and the Index Matched Lens System (IMLS). The IMLS matches coatings to the different types of glass used in a scope's lens system. Other refinements include finger-adjustable dials with re-settable pointers to indicate zero, a fast-focus, lockable eyepiece and a 30mm main tube for scopes with side-mounted focus (parallax correction) dials. Thirteen models of VX-III scopes are available, from 1.5-5x20 to 8.5-25x50.

Leupold's VX-II scope now comes with Multicoat 4 lens coatings. The power ring on the VX-II has been given a bump that you can feel. The lockable, fast-focus eyepiece of the VX-III has been added to the VX-II.

All 2005 VX-I scopes – the 2-7x33, 3-9x40 and 4-12x40 – now come in matte black as well as gloss finish, with new Micro-friction windage and elevation dials, and the availability of the Wide Duplex reticle.

**VX-I Scopes**
2-7x33 . . . . . . . . . . . . . . . . . . . $250
3-9x40 . . . . . . . . . . . . . . . . . . . $275
4-12x40 . . . . . . . . . . . . . . . . . . $340
**VX-II Scopes** . . . . . . . $325 to $615
**VX-III Scopes** . . . . . . . $500 to $1115

# NEW Products: **Nikon Optics**

BUCKMASTER 6-18X40

BUCKMASTER 4-12X50

Nikon's newest addition is a 6-8x40AO in the Buckmaster series. Multi-coated optics deliver up to 92 percent light transmission. The ⅛-minute adjustments are on tall target stems with caps; the scope has a traditional parallax correction ring on the objective bell. Also new to the Buckmasters category is a 4-12x50, again with a front-mounted parallax ring.
**Buckmaster Scopes
6-18x40 and 4-12x50** . . . . . . . **$330**

# NEW Products: **Pentax Optics**

LIGHTSEEKER-XL 3-9X50

Lightseeker XL features centered turrets for additional ring space. "PentaBright" technology, plus internal lenses "up to 40% larger than the competition," deliver extraordinarily bright images.

**Lightseeker-XL Scopes
XL 2.5-10x50,
3-9x43,
3-9x50 and
4-16x44:** . . . . . . . . . . **$495 to $682**

# NEW Products: **Schmidt & Bender**

**SCHMIDT-BENDER 1.5-6X42**

The Schmidt-Bender 1.5-6x42 Zenith FD scope has been fitted with the Flash Dot, S&B's luminous reticle. Battery powered, the Flash Dot is controlled by a knob on the left-hand side of the turret. Turn the knob from stops 1 through 6, and you get an increasingly bright dot to use against a dark target or when light levels are low. A neutral click between stop 6 and 7 alerts you to a change in dot intensity. From stops 7 through 11, the dot is noticeably brighter, for use on well-illuminated targets. You can turn the dot off and use the standard black crosswire by itself, of course. The 1.5-6x42 weighs 21 ounces with a 30mm tube.

**1.5-6x42 Zenith FD** . . . . . . . . $1699

# NEW Products: **Sightron Optics**

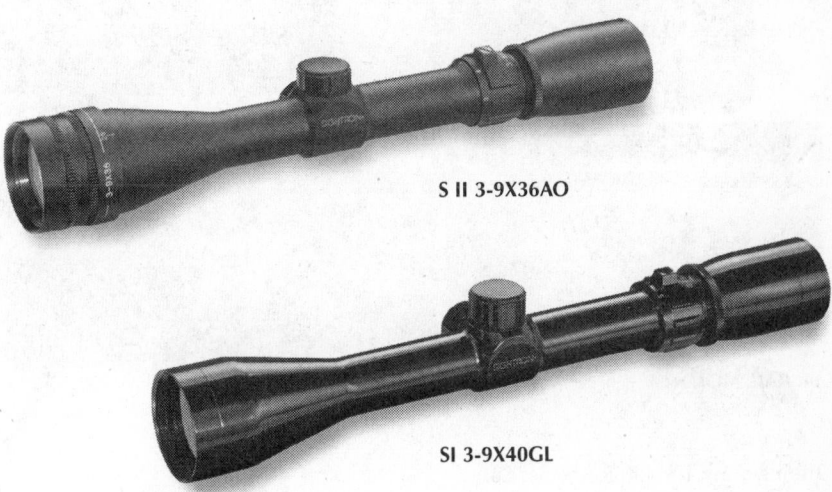

**S II 3-9X36AO**

**SI 3-9X40GL**

The Sightron SII family of scopes has a new member, a 3-9x36AO model with the parallax ring up front. Its compact profile and close-up focus distance of 30 feet make this 3-9 an ideal mate for a .22 rimfire rifle or an air gun. Also new: an SII 3-9x32RF, specifically designed for rimfire shooting with zero parallax at 50 yards. Another introduction at Sightron in 2004: the SI 3-9x40GL in high gloss finish.

**Sightron SII Scopes**

| | |
|---|---|
| **3-9x36AO** . . . . . . . . . . . . . . . | $356 |
| **3-9x32RF** . . . . . . . . . . . . . . . . | $156 |
| **SI 3-9x40GL** . . . . . . . . . . . . . . | $205 |

# NEW Products: **Springfield Armory Optics**

**6-20X50**

After significant redesign, Springfield Armory scopes feature range-finding reticles, ballistic drop compensators, illuminated crosswires and mil dots, only the 3-9x42 and the 3.5-10x50 are "hunting-style" sights, with plex reticles. Only four of the 15 scopes in Springfield's line have 1-inch tubes; the others are all 30mm. All have an internal bubble level at the bottom of the scope field to tell you if you're canting. Target knobs are standard on 4-16x50 models, BDC knobs on 6-20x50 scopes.
**Springfield Armory Scopes 6x40 to 6-20x50: . . . . . $419 to $899**

# NEW Products: **Swarovsky Optics**

**SR RAIL MOUNT**

The new Swarovski SR line uses an integral toothed rail on PH 1.25x24, PH 1-6x42 and PH 3-12x50 scopes that makes the tube stronger while eliminating the ring/tube juncture that can fail during heavy recoil.
**Swarovski SR Scopes: . . . over $1000**

For 2004, there's a new T-10 target model (no AO) with quarter-minute click adjustments and a $\frac{1}{8}$-minute dot reticle. It weighs just one pound, has a 40mm objective lens and comes in black satin finish – a fine choice for a light varmint rifle or a dual-purpose coyote/pronghorn rifle. The other new offering of note is T-24, also with a 40mm front end.  The parallax (AO) adjustment is the traditional forward ring. At 17 ounces, it is very light for its magnification. Choose a $\frac{1}{8}$-minute dot or a $\frac{1}{2}$-minute dot.

**T-10 Target Scope:** . . . . . . . . . . **$420**
**T-24 Scope:** . . . . . . . . . . . . . . **$450**

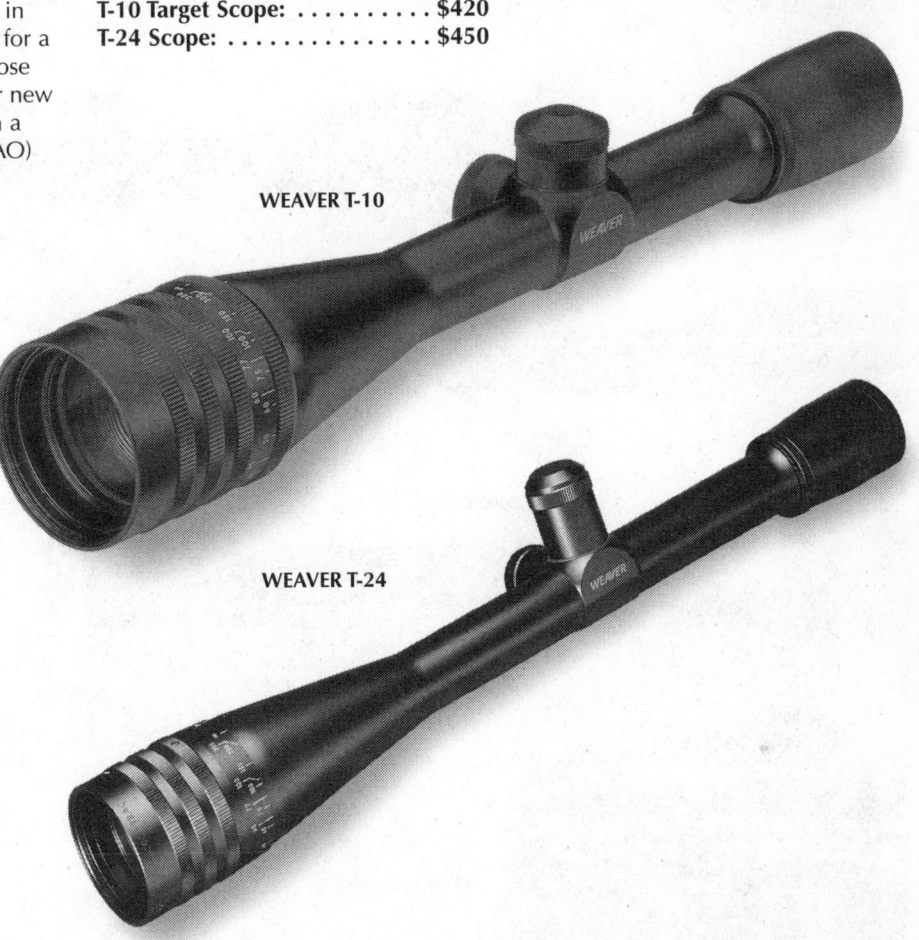

**WEAVER T-10**

**WEAVER T-24**

*A smooth, perfectly aligned bearing surface is critical to holding power in scope rings. Accomplish this by using a lapping tool and rubbing compound. This removes high spots and produces a vice-like grip. Check out Gunsmithing at Home, by Stoeger Publishing.*

# NEW Products: **Zeiss Optics**

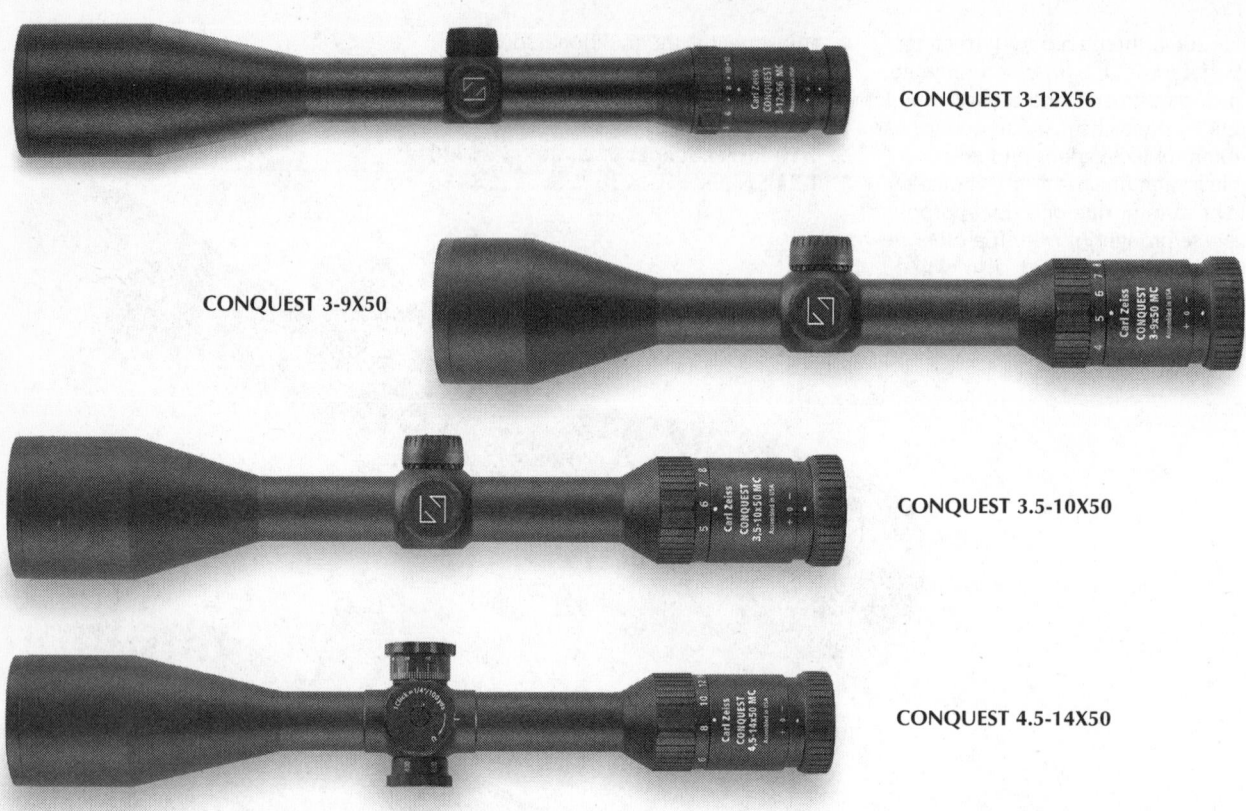

CONQUEST 3-12X56

CONQUEST 3-9X50

CONQUEST 3.5-10X50

CONQUEST 4.5-14X50

ZEISS Z-POINT

Zeiss introduces a new trio of Conquest scopes with super-size 50mm objectives for enhanced light transmission at dawn and dusk. The 3-9x50, 3.5-10x50 and 4.5-14x50 weigh 17, 18 and 20 ounces and feature 1-inch alloy tubes and reticles in the second focal plane. All Conquest scopes have Zeiss MC multi-coating. These scopes are waterproof and fog-proof and come with a plex reticle and quarter-minute click adjustments. Eye relief is 3.3 inches.

Zeiss also offers the new 3-12x56 high-powered scope, with a huge objective on a 30mm alloy tube. It has 3.2 inches of eye relief and more than 30 inches of windage and elevation adjustment. Field of view: 9.9 to 27.6 feet at 100 yards. The scope weighs 25.8 ounces.

The new VM/V 6-24x56 has 57.6 inches of elevation with a 5.2-foot field at 24x and an 18.6-foot field at 6x. A quick-focus eyepiece and turret-mounted parallax adjustment (55 yards to infinity) deliver a perfect sight picture almost instantly. The VM/V 6-24x56 features the "Advanced Optical System" lenses and Zeiss T* coatings. Eye relief is 3.1 inches.

The new Zeiss Z-Point is a red-dot sight designed to mount on a 1913 Picatinny rail. This compact unit weighs only 3.5 ounces. The dot operates on a 3-volt Lithium battery but also has a solar cell to provide extended illumination.

**Conquest Scopes**

| | |
|---|---|
| **3-9x50:** | **$550** |
| **3.5-10x50:** | **$700** |
| **4.5-14x50:** | **$800** |
| **3-12x56 High-Powered Scope:** | **$1050** |
| **(stainless anodized):** | **$1080** |

**VM/V Scopes**

| | |
|---|---|
| **6-24x56** | **$1500** |
| **6-24x56** | |
| **with illuminated reticle:** | **$1900** |
| **Z-Point Scope:** | **$450** |

# NEW Products: **Brenneke Ammunition**

For 2004, Brenneke has introduced the SuperSabot, a 1 1/8-ounce lead-free projectile with a soft brass jacket that folds back like the petals on a mushrooming rifle bullet. The center resembles a peg, exposed by the upset. Available in 2 3/4-inch and 3-inch 12 gauge hulls only, the SuperSabot produces up to 2536 ft-lbs of muzzle energy

# NEW Products: **Federal Ammunition**

In 2004, Federal Cartridge added 74 new centerfire rifle loadings under revised category headings. The Premium label covers Federal's best big game loads, featuring bullets, including Nosler Partition and AccuBond, Solid Base, Ballistic Tip, Trophy Bonded, and Sierra GameKing. The Barnes Triple-Shock X-Bullet are offered under the Vital Shok lable. The Cape Shok list includes loads for the .375 H&H, .416 Rigby, .416 Remington Magnum, .458 Winchester and .470 Nitro Express. Choose a Partition, Bear Claw or Woodleigh Weldcore softpoint, or a Woodleigh or Trophy Bonded solid. V Shok ammunition features Ballistic Tip, Sierra Varminter and others.

Federal's Classic line has been replaced in name by Power Shok featuring hunting loads from the .222 to the .375 Holland and .45-70 Government. New loads include the .308 and .30-06 with low recoil loads Also on the Power Shok list now: the .270 and 7mm Winchester Short Magnums, with 130- and 150-grain loads at 3250 and 3200 fps.

Federal has added a .45 G.A.P (Glock Automatic Pistol) 185-grain load to its American Eagle handgun offerings and a high-performance 3-inch 20-gauge listing that kicks a ⅝-ounce Barnes slug out the muzzle at 1900 fps.

# NEW Products: **Hornaday Ammunition**

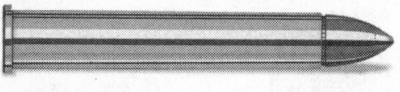

**405W IN 300GR**

**500 S&W**

**204 RUGER**

**17HMR**

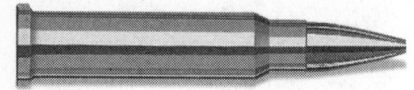

**17HMR 20 GR XTP**

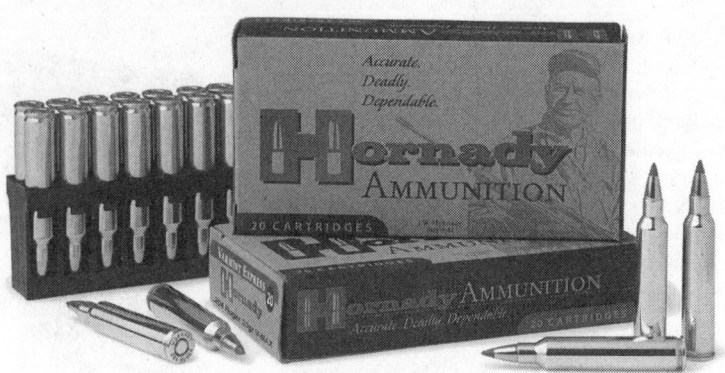

**.204 RUGER**

**.17 MACH 2**

Hornady has unveiled a new .17 rimfire round, the .17 Mach 2, with a bottleneck hull. Based on the high-performance .22 Stinger case. At .975, cartridge length matches that of Long Rifles and Stingers and fits the mechanisms of ordinary .22s. It functions in self-loaders, and the tiny 17-grain V-Max bullet flies flatter than bullets from any .22 rimfire ammunition

Hornady's new .204 Ruger derives from the .222 Magnum, with its slightly greater capacity and longer neck. A 32-grain polymer-tipped, V-Max bullet, .204 in diameter, clocks 4200 fps. Hornady has cataloged a 40-grain load at 3900 fps. Ruger is chambering both its 77 bolt rifle and Number One dropping-block single-shot for the .204. An endearing quality of the .204 is its mild recoil.

Hornady's also offers a .500 Smith & Wesson handgun cartridge with a 350-grain XTP bullet that clocks 1900 fps at the muzzle of a 7½-inch barrel. The other muscle round introduced this year is a .405 Winchester with a 300-grain Interlock spitzer at 2200 fps. You get 3224 ft-lbs of punch up close. More importantly, there's 1250 ft-lbs remaining at the 300-yard mark.

**.17 Mach 2:** . . . . . . . . . . . . . . . . . **$8**
**.204 Ruger:** . . . . . . . . . . . . . . **$17.95**
**.500 S&W (box of 20)** . . . . . . **$53.34**
**.405** . . . . . . . . . . . . . . . . . . . . **$39.50**

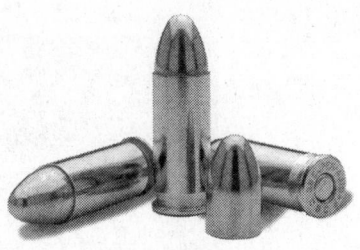

**.38 SUPER**

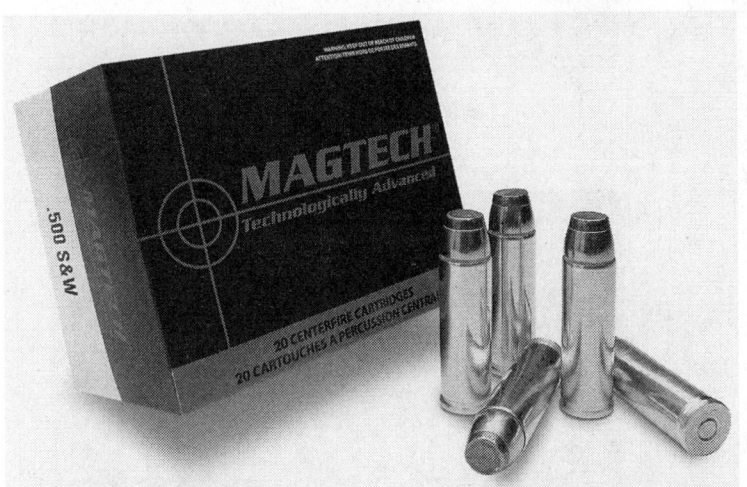

The Magtech line of pistol and revolver cartridges boasts 22 new loadings for 2004. The most potent is the .500 Smith & Wesson, with a 400-grain semi-jacketed softpoint at 1608 fps. Almost as crushing: a 260-grain FMJ.454 Casull bullet that gets going a little faster (1800 fps). Magtech also offers new .357 and .44 Magnum rounds. A First Defense line of ammo for autoloading pistols is new this year, with three entries: 9mm Luger, .40 S&W and .45 ACP +P. There's a new .357 load in the Cowboy Action clan, and a new .45 ACP non-toxic offering. The .38 Super, dear to many pistoleros, has a home at Magtech, which lists a +P load with a 130-grain bullet at 1215 fps. Muzzle energy: 563 ft-lbs, more than half again as much as available from a 9mm.

# NEW Products: **PMC Ammunition**

PMC is expanding its shotshell line to include Gold Line Ultimate High Velocity shotshell. Available in 2³⁄₄-inch 12-, 20- and 28-gauge offerings and 3-inch .410, the new shells feature shot sizes ranging from 4 to 9. The 12-bore 1¹⁄₄-ounce load chronographs 1400 fps. A 1-ounce 20-gauge charge leaves the muzzle at 1300, the ⁷⁄₈-ounce 28 at 1250 and the ¹¹⁄₁₆-ounce .410 at 1135. Also new this year: extra heavy Silver Line shotshells, 12-gauge only, with 1³⁄₈ ounces of shot at 1320 fps. Choose 4, 5, 6 or 7¹⁄₂ shot size. PMC has included new target loads for the .410 and 28 gauge both with a velocity of 1220 fps. To round out its shotgun ammo list, the firm has also introduced a 12-gauge deer load with a ⁷⁄₈-ounce slug in a sabot sleeve.

In centerfire ammunition, there's a "PMC Green" line with non-toxic frangible loads for the .223, .308 and 7.62x39 (bullet weights 40, 120 and 100 grains). Seven pistol rounds, from .38 Special to .357 Sig and .45 ACP, are included.

New PMC Gold, Silver and Bronze hunting loads range from .223 to .375 H&H, The Gold Line features Barnes XLC-HP bullets, the Silver Line Sierra BlitzKing and Match bullets, with softpoint boattails. The Bronze Line has softpoint and pointed softpoint bullets. New this year are .45-90 and .40-65 rifle cartridges for the Cowboy Action shooter, and Predator .22 WMR ammo with a 40-grain full-jacket bullet at 1910 fps.

# NEW Products: **Remington Ammunition**

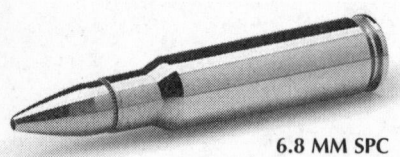

**6.8 MM SPC**

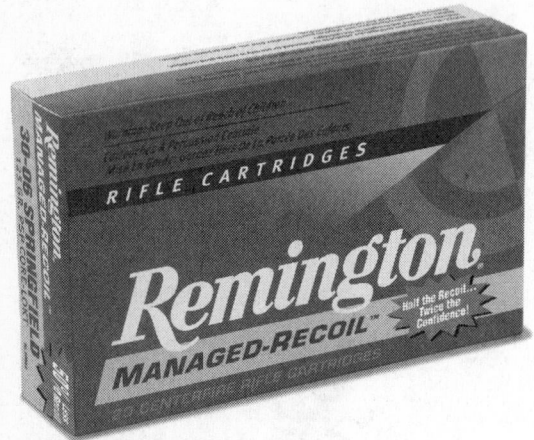

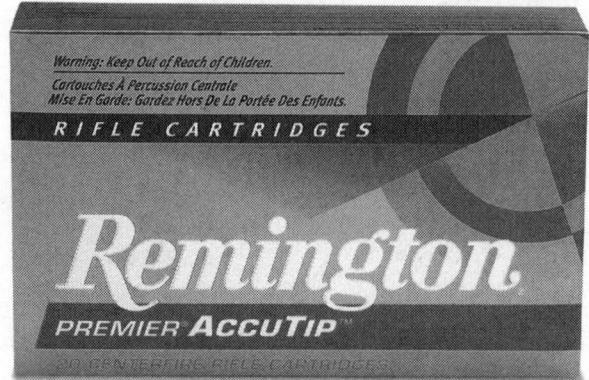

Remington is offering a Nitro Steel high-velocity shotshell with a ⅛-ounce payload of 2s and 4s at 1390 fps. Also available in 3½-inch options: a 1 3/8-ounce charge at 1450 fps. Available for 12-, 20-, 28-gauge and .410. Remington is now offering Sportsman steel shot in a 10-gauge 3½-inch load (1⅜ ounces of BBs or 2s at 1500 fps) and a 12-gauge 3-inch load (1¼, BB, 1, 2, 3, 4).

The Buckhammer shotgun slug, is available 12-gauge 2¾-inch loads and 3-inch 12 and 2¾-inch 20-gage hulls. The new loads feature 1⅜- and 1-ounce slugs respectively, at 1500 fps. Muzzle energy: 3232 and 2236 ft-lbs.

Remington is also offering new Managed Recoil loads that generate half the kick of ordinary ammunition. The bullets are designed for 2x expansion and 75-percent weight retention between 50 and 200 yards. Managed Recoil loads are available in .270 (115-grain bullet), .30-06 (125-grain) and 7mm Rem. Mag. (140-grain). Muzzle velocities are 2710, 2660 and 2710 fps, respectively. All deliver more than 1100 ft-lbs of energy to 200 yards. Also new is the Remington: Premier Match line which includes the 6.8mm Remington SPC, .223, .308, .300 Winchester Magnum and .300 Remington Short Ultra Mag.

**Managed Recoil Ammunition**
.270 and .30-06 (box of20)..... $14
7mm Rem. Mag. (box of 20).... $18
12-gauge (box of 5)........... $3

# NEW Products: **Winchester Ammunition**

NEW PRODUCTS

The new .223 and .224 Super Short Magnums are fashioned from the .300 Winchester Short Magnum case and are 1.67 inches from base to mouth. They fit rifles designed for the .308 Winchester and squeeze into the shorter mechanisms of the WSSM family. The newest WSSM is a 25-caliber round designed to duplicate or exceed the performance of the .25-06. Two other loads are available in the Supreme line: an 85-grain Ballistic Silvertip at 3470 fps, and a 115 Balllistic Silvertip at 3060. Winchester now offers CT (Combined Technology) AccuBond bullets in their centerfire line — .270 Win. (140-gr.), .270 WSM, (140-gr.), 7mm Rem. Mag., (160-gr.), 7mm WSM, (160-gr.), .30-06, (180-gr.), .300 Win. Mag. (180-gr.), .300 WSM, (180-gr.), .338 Win. Mag., (225-gr.). Also new is the .45 Glock Automatic Pistol Winchester's new Super-Target shotshell line in 12 and 20 gauge, are inexpensive but effective on clays. Choose 7½ or 8 shot. The 12-bore 1⅛-ounce charge can be had with 2¾- or 3-dram equivalent thrust – 1145 fps or 1200. The 2½-dram 20-bore shells kick ⅞-ounce shot columns down-range at 1200. Winchester is also fielding a 3-inch 12-gauge slug load featuring the 385-grain Partition Gold slug in a sabot.

**Super-Target shotshell per case . . $57**
**Partition Gold slug**
  **box of five rounds . . . . . . . $19.40**

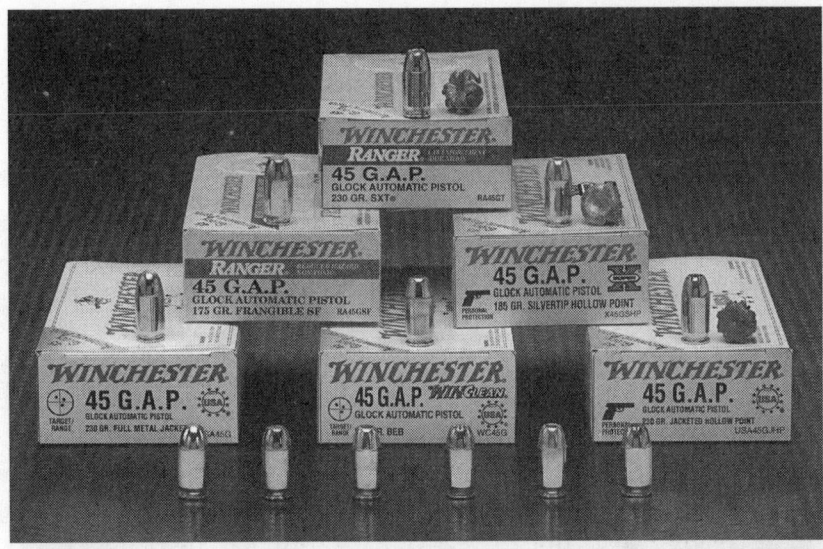

# NEW Products: **Barnes Ammunition**

The new Barnes hollowpoint, solid-copper Spit-Fire MZ, is offered in 245- and 285-grain weights for 50-caliber rifles and sabot sleeves. Its ballistically efficient tapered heel makes it easy to seat. The dry, blue coating on Barnes VLC bullets reduces barrel friction and copper fouling.

# NEW Products: **RCBS Handloading**

The Mini-Grand shotgun press, a seven-station single-stage press, loads 12- and 20-gauge hulls, from 2¾ to 3½ inches in length. It utilizes RCBS, Hornady and Ponsness Warren powder and shot bushings.  A ½-pound capacity powder hopper and 12½-pound capacity shot  hopper help you attain the advertised loading rate of 200 shells an hour.  The machine will load both lead and steel shot, though steel requires optional accessories. Compound leverage ensures easy handle manipulation.

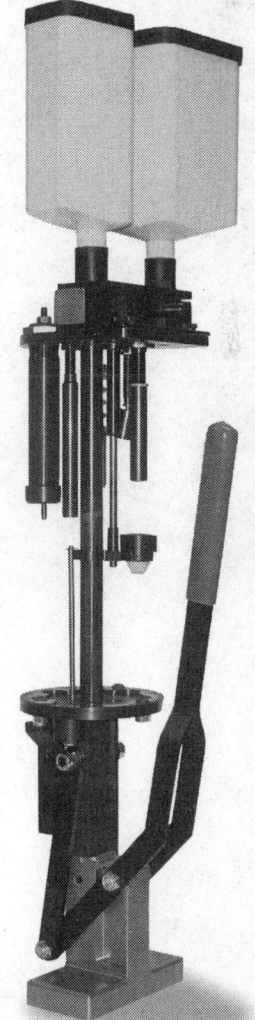

*Try shooting lighter loads in your turkey gun. Many times a high-velocity one-and-three-quarter ounce load will put more pellets where they count than heavier two-ounce loads. Find more tips like this in Turkey Hunter's Tool Kit, by Stoeger Publishing.*

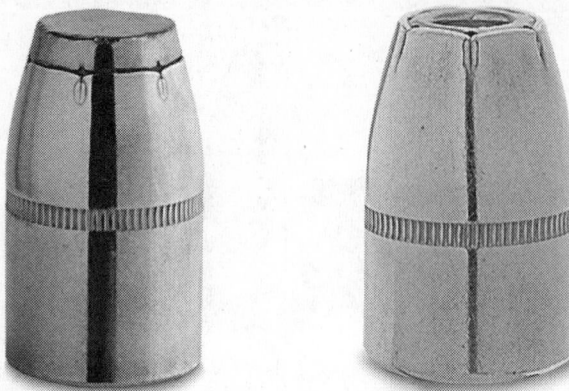

For 2004, Sierra has announced two new jacketed bullets for the .500 Smith & Wesson cartridge. The 350-grain jacketed hollowpoint and 400-grain jacketed softpoint are constructed with heavy jackets for deep penetration in game, and a cannelure for crimping to prevent bullet creep during recoil. Hunters who favor .22 centerfire rifles for deer can now load up with 65-grain Sierra GameKings. The boattail bullet has a very high ballistic coefficient and is recommended for rifling twists at least as sharp as 1-in-10.

**.500 Smith & Wesson:**
  (box of 50) . . . . . . . . . . . . . . . **$18**
**Sierra Game Kings:**
  (box of 100) . . . . . . . . . . . . . . **$14**

RIFLES

# Anschutz Rifles

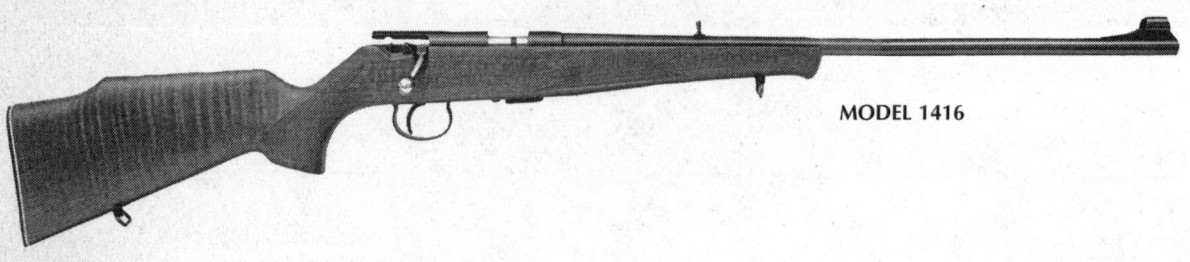

MODEL 1416

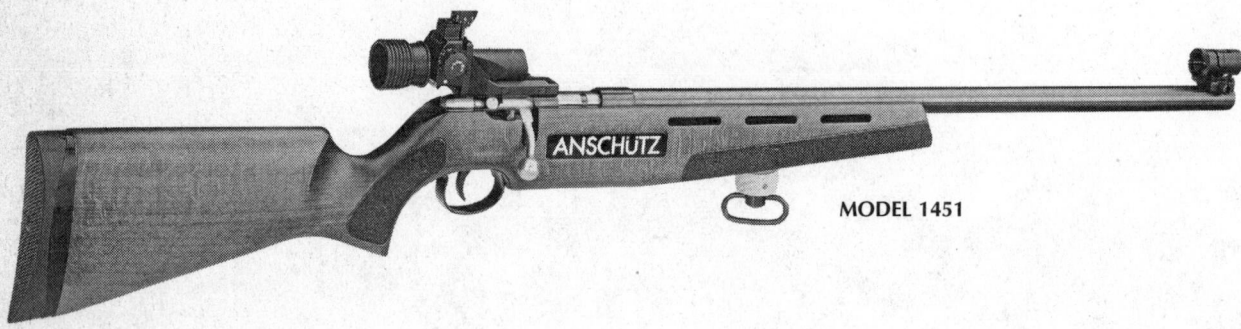

MODEL 1451

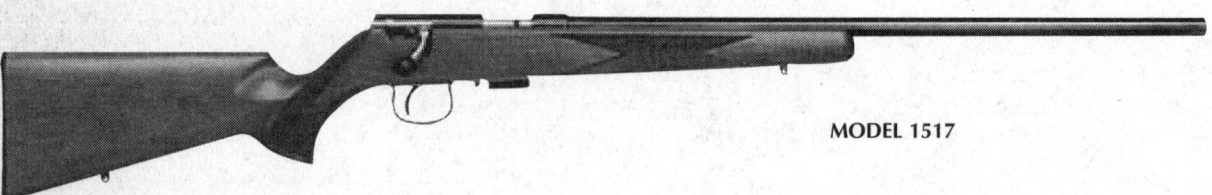

MODEL 1517

## MODEL 1416
*Action:* bolt
*Stock:* checkered walnut
*Barrel:* 22 in.
*Sights:* open
*Weight:* 5.5
*Caliber:* .22LR, .22 WMR
*Magazine:* detachable box, 5-round
.22 LR, 4-round .22 WMR
*Features:* M64 action; 2-stage match
trigger; stock available in classic or
Monte Carlo
Classic: . . . . . . . . . . . . . . . . . $718
Monte Carlo: . . . . . . . . . . . . . $766

## MODEL 1451
*Action:* bolt
*Stock:* Sporter Target, hardwood
*Barrel:* heavy 22 in.

*Sights:* open
*Weight:* 6.3
*Caliber:* .22 LR
*Magazine:* detachable box, 10-round
*Features:* M64 action
1451: . . . . . . . . . . . . . . . . . . . $515

## MODEL 1517
*Action:* bolt
*Stock:* walnut
*Barrel:* target-grade sporter, 22 in.
*Sights:* none
*Weight:* 6.0lbs.
*Caliber:* .17 HMR
*Magazine:* 4
*Features:* M64 action, heavy and
sporter barrels, Monte Carlo and
Classic stocks available; target-grade
barrel, adjustable trigger (2.5 lbs.)

Classic . . . . . . . . . . . . . . . . . . $781
Monte Carlo. . . . . . . . . . . . . . $801

## MODEL 1730 AND 1740 CLASSIC SPORTER
*Action:* bolt
*Stock:* sporter, walnut
*Barrel:* 23 in.
*Sights:* none
*Weight:* 7.3
*Caliber:* .22 Hornet and .222
*Magazine:* detachable box, 5-round
*Features:* M54 action; Meister grade
about $250 additional
1730 .22 Hornet, Monte Carlo. . $1598
1730 .22 Hornet
  with heavy barrel . . . . . . . . $1500
1740 .222 with heavy barrel . . $1500
1740 .222, Monte Carlo . . . . . $1598

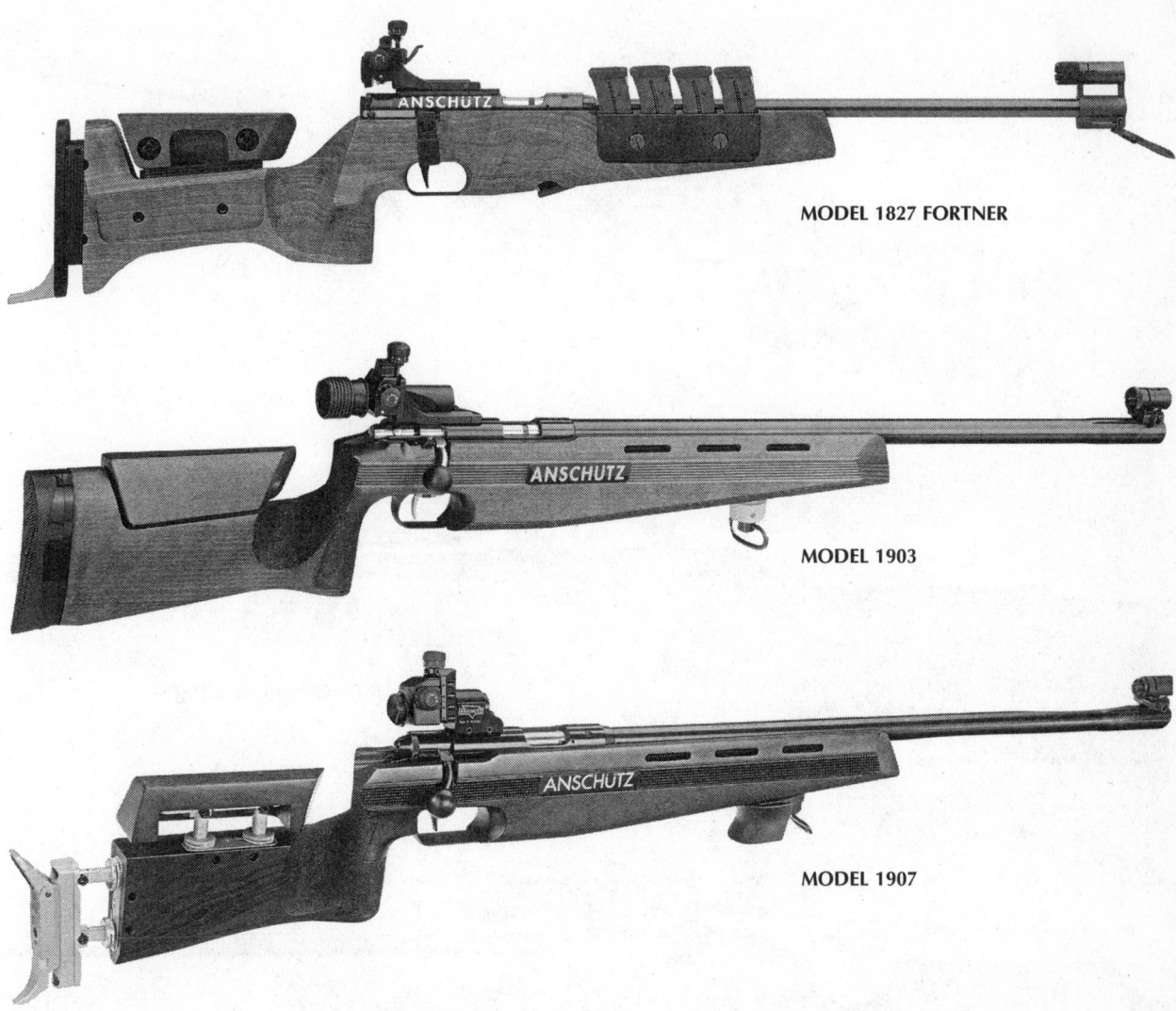

MODEL 1827 FORTNER

MODEL 1903

MODEL 1907

## MODEL 1710

*Action:* bolt
*Stock:* walnut
*Barrel:* target-grade sporter, 22 in.
*Sights:* none
*Weight:* 6.7lbs.
*Caliber:* .22 LR
*Magazine:* 5
*Features:* M54 action; two-stage trigger, Monte Carlo stock; silhouette stock available
Model 1710 . . . . . . . . . . . . . . $1358
with fancy wood. . . . . . . . . . $1612
Silhouette Model 1712 . . . . . . $1438

## MODEL 1827 FORTNER

*Action:* bolt
*Stock:* Biathlon, walnut

*Barrel:* medium 22 in.
*Sights:* none
*Weight:* 8.8
*Caliber:* .22 LR
*Magazine:* detachable box, 5 rounds
*Features:* M54 action, stock has holder for four magazines
1827:. . . . . . . . . . . . . . . . . . . $1850
with thumbhole stock: . . . . . . $1940

## MODEL 1903

*Action:* bolt
*Stock:* Standard Rifle, hardwood
*Barrel:* heavy 26 in.
*Sights:* none
*Weight:* 10.5
*Caliber:* .22 LR
*Magazine:* none

*Features:* M64 action, adjustable cheekpiece, forend rail
1903:. . . . . . . . . . . . . . . . . . . $690
left-hand:. . . . . . . . . . . . . . . $730

## MODEL 1907

*Action:* bolt
*Stock:* Standard Rifle, walnut
*Barrel:* heavy 26 in.
*Sights:* none
*Weight:* 10.5
*Caliber:* .22 LR
*Magazine:* none
*Features:* M54 action, adjustable cheekpiece and butt, forend rail
1907:. . . . . . . . . . . . . . . . . . . $1375
left-hand:. . . . . . . . . . . . . . . $1475

RIFLES

# Anschutz Rifles

MODEL 1912 SPORT

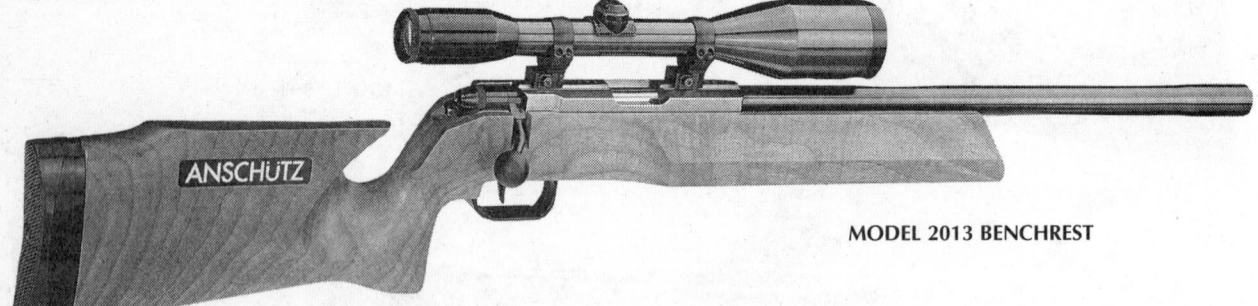

MODEL 2013 BENCHREST

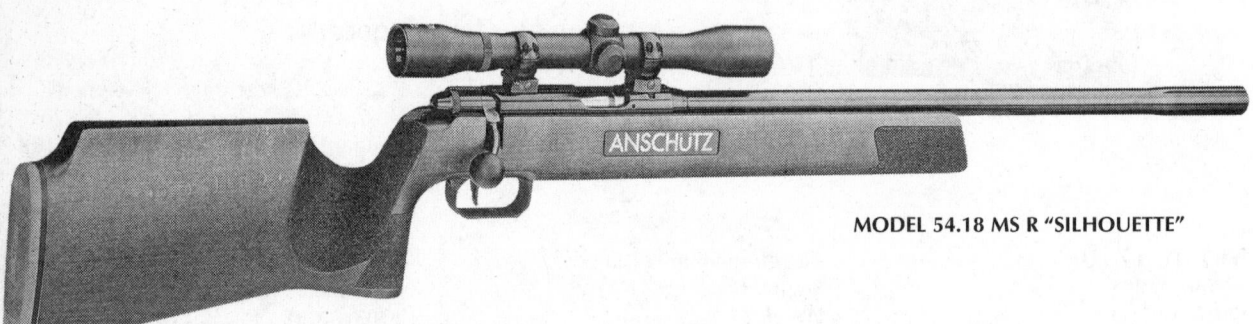

MODEL 54.18 MS R "SILHOUETTE"

## MODEL 1912 SPORT
*Action:* bolt
*Stock:* International, laminated
*Barrel:* heavy 26 in.
*Sights:* none
*Weight:* 11.4
*Caliber:* .22 LR
*Magazine:* none
*Features:* M54 action, adjustable cheekpiece and butt, forend rail
1912:. . . . . . . . . . . . . . . . . .$1690
left-hand:. . . . . . . . . . . . . . .$1785

## MODEL 2013 BENCHREST
*Action:* bolt
*Stock:* Benchrest (BR-50) walnut
*Barrel:* heavy 20 in.
*Sights:* none
*Weight:* 10.3
*Caliber:* .22 LR
*Magazine:* none
*Features:* M54 action
2013:. . . . . . . . . . . . . . . . . .$1575

## MODEL 54.18 MS
*Action:* bolt
*Stock:* Silhouette, walnut
*Barrel:* heavy 22 in.
*Sights:* none
*Weight:* 8.1
*Caliber:* .22 LR
*Magazine:* none
*Features:* M54 action
54.18: . . . . . . . . . . . . . . . . . .$1225
with thumbhole stock: . . . . . .$1350

# Auto-Ordnance Rifles

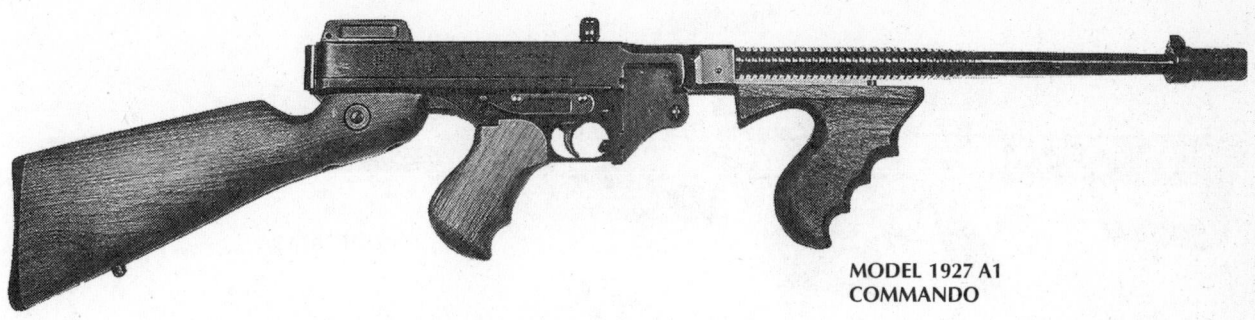

MODEL 1927 A1
COMMANDO

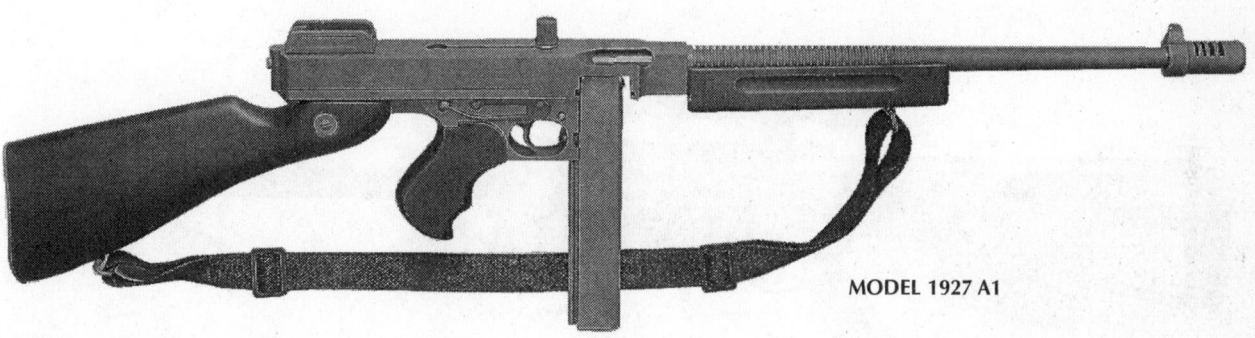

MODEL 1927 A1

## AUTO-ORDNANCE RIFLES
This veteran design, the Thompson Submachine Gun, became famous during the "Roaring Twenties" and World War II. These replicas are legal autoloaders, not machine guns.

## MODEL 1927 A1 COMMANDO
*Action:* autoloading
*Stock:* walnut, horizontal fore-grip
*Barrel:* 16 in.
*Sights:* open
*Weight:* 13.0

*Caliber:* .45 ACP
*Magazine:* detachable box 20-round
*Features:* Top-cocking, autoloading blowback; carbine version with side-cocking lever, 11.5 lbs.
1927:. . . . . . . . . . . . . . . . . . $1088
carbine: . . . . . . . . . . . . . . . . $1041

## MODEL 1927A1
*Action:* autoloading
*Stock:* walnut, vertical foregrip
*Barrel:* 16 in.
*Sights:* open

*Weight:* 13.0
*Caliber:* .45 ACP
*Magazine:* detachable box, 20-round
*Features:* top-cocking, autoloading blowback; lightweight version 9.5 lbs.
standard: . . . . . . . . . . . . . . . $1109
lightweight: . . . . . . . . . . . . . $1088

 *Heavy barrels are not intrinsically more accurate than lightweight barrels. But they are typically more consistent when shooting long strings because they don't "walk" as readily when they heat.*

# Barrett Rifles

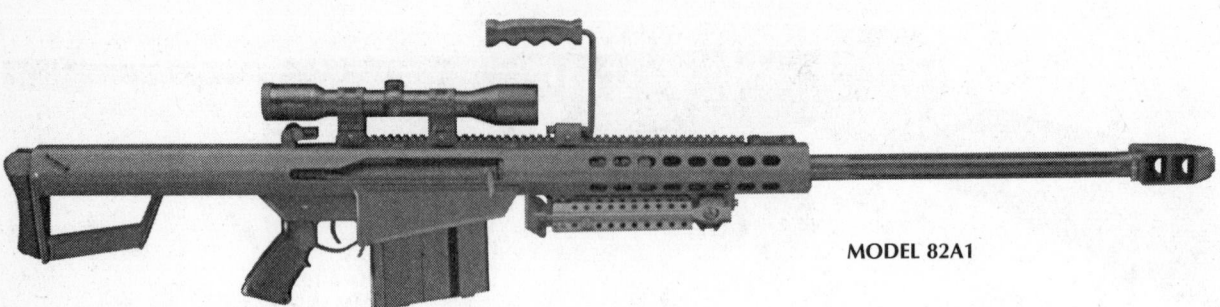

MODEL 82A1

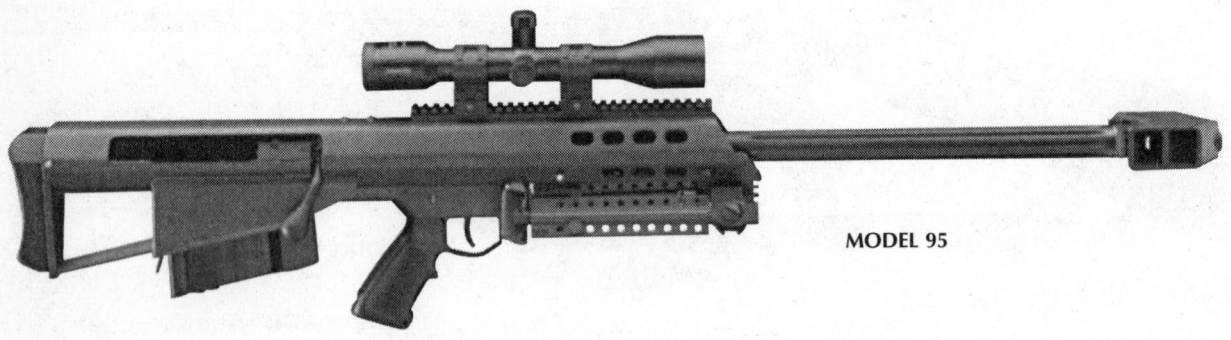

MODEL 95

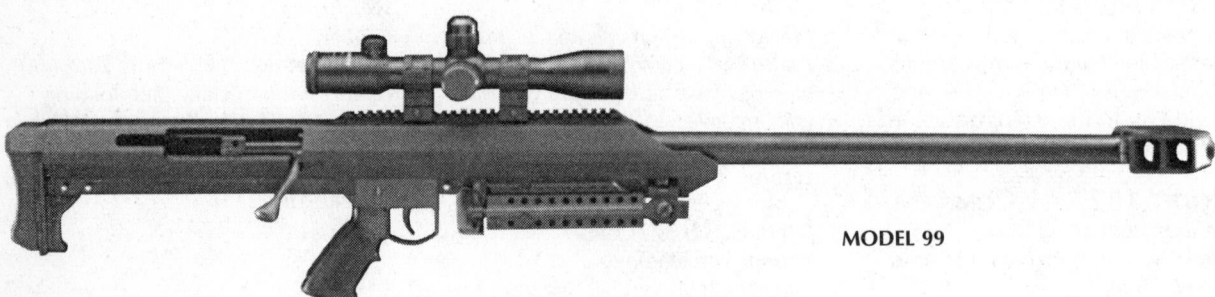

MODEL 99

## MODEL 82A1

*Action:* autoloading
*Stock:* synthetic
*Barrel:* 29 in.
*Sights:* target
*Weight:* 28.5lbs.
*Caliber:* .50 BMG
*Magazine:* 10
*Features:* Picatinny rail and scope mount, fluted barrel, detachable bipod and carrying case

**82A1:** . . . . . . . . . . **price on request**

## MODEL 95, MODEL 99

*Action:* bolt
*Stock:* synthetic
*Barrel:* 29 in. or 33 in. (M99)
*Sights:* none
*Weight:* 25.0lbs.
*Caliber:* .50 BMG
*Magazine:* 5 (M95) or none (M99)
*Features:* Picatinny rail, detachable bipod, M95 has fluted barrel and weighs 22 lbs.

**M95, M99** . . . . . . . . **price on request**

RIFLES

# Benelli Rifles

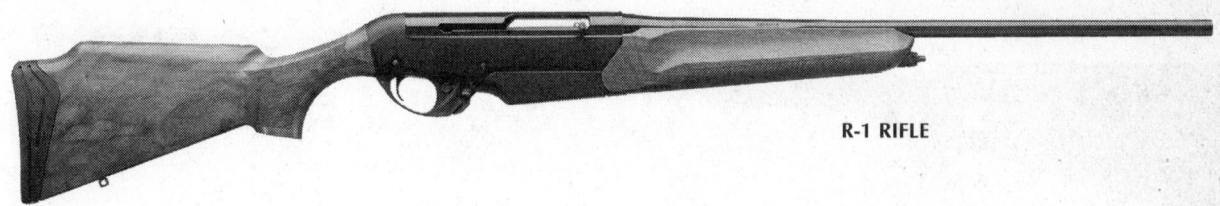

R-1 RIFLE

## R-1 RIFLE

**Action:** autoloading
**Stock:** walnut
**Barrel:** 22 in. (Standard Rifle); 20 in. (Standard Carbine); 24 in. (Magnum Rifle), 20 in. (Magnum Carbine)
**Sights:** none

**Weight:** 7.1 lbs. (Standard Rifle); 7.0 lbs. (Standard Carbine); 7.2 lbs. (Magnum Rifle), 7.0 lbs. (Magnum Carbine)
**Caliber:** Standard 30-06; Magnum .300 Win. Mag.
**Magazine:** 3-4 shot detachable box
**Features:** auto-regulating gas-operated system; three lugged rotary bolt; select satin walnut stock; receiver drilled and tapped for scope mount; base included
**Standard Rifle & Carbine . . . . $1065**
**Magnum Rifle & Carbine . . . . $1080**

# Blaser Rifles

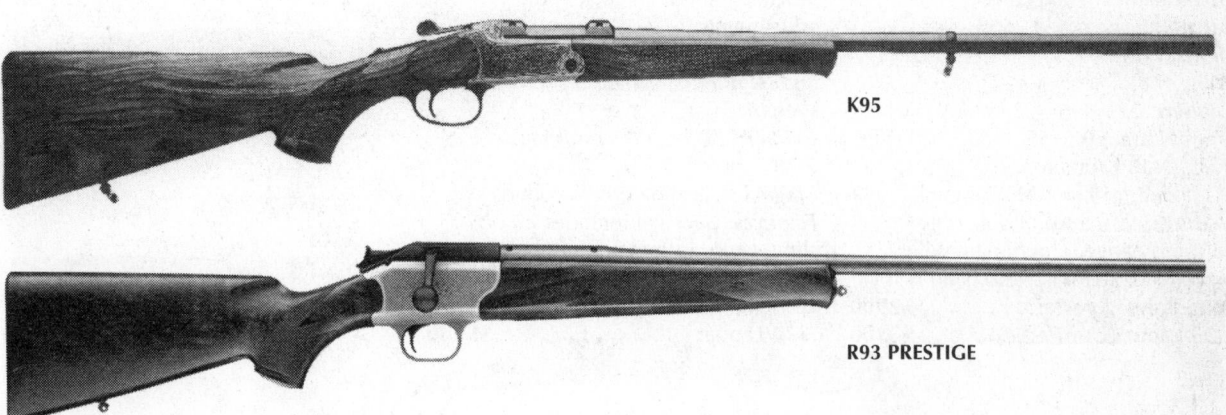

K95

R93 PRESTIGE

## MODEL K95

**Action:** hinged breech
**Stock:** walnut
**Barrel:** 24 in. and 26 in. (magnum)
**Sights:** none
**Weight:** 5.5
**Caliber:** .222, .22 Hornet, .25-06, .243, .270, .308, .30-06; magnum: 7mm Rem., .300 Win., .300 Wby.
**Magazine:** none
**Features:** easy takedown with no loss of zero; magnum calibers weigh 5.8 lbs.; Luxus has hand engraving on receiver
**Prestige:. . . . . . . . . . . . . . . . $3300**
**Luxus: . . . . . . . . . . . . . . . . $3800**

## MODEL R93

**Action:** bolt
**Stock:** walnut or synthetic
**Barrel:** 22 in.
**Sights:** none
**Weight:** 6.5
**Caliber:** .22-250, .243, .25-06, 6.5x55, .270, 7x57, 7mm/08, .308, .30-06; Magnums: .257 Wby. Mag., 7mm Rem. Mag., .300 Win. Mag., .300 Wby. Mag., .300 Rem UM, .338 Win. Mag., .375 H&H, .416 Rem. Mag.
**Magazine:** in-line box, 5 rounds
**Features:** straight-pull bolt with expanding collar lockup; higher grades available; magnums weigh 7 lbs.; left-hand versions available, add $141
**Prestige:. . . . . . . . . . . . . . . . $2600**
**Synthetic:. . . . . . . . . . . . . . . $2000**
**Luxus: . . . . . . . . . . . . . . . . $3400**
**Attache . . . . . . . . . . . . . . . . $4800**

RIFLES

# Blaser Rifles

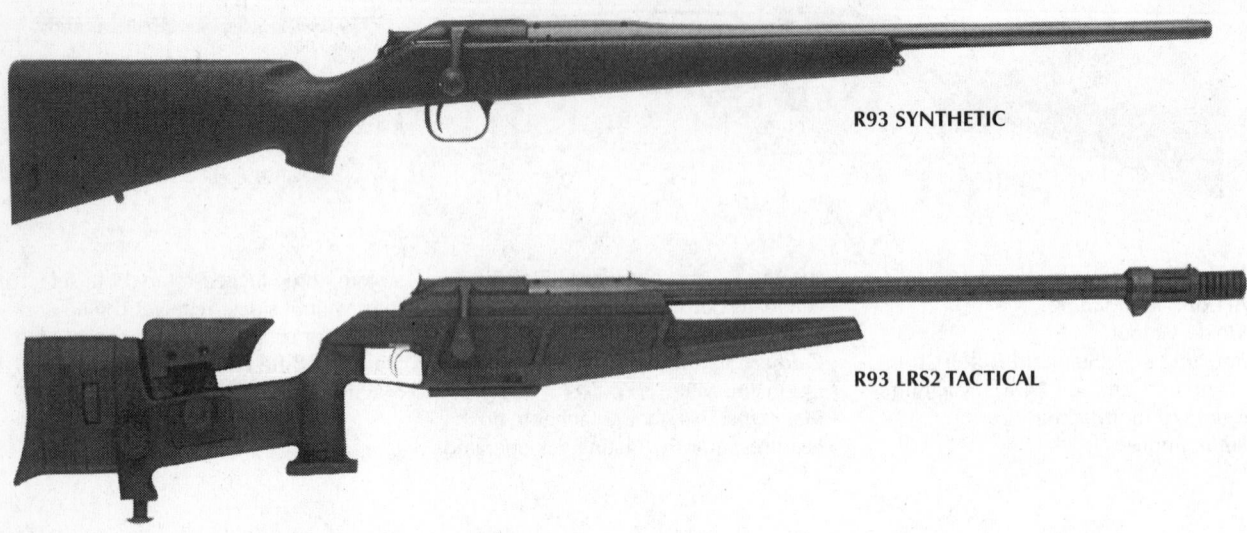

R93 SYNTHETIC

R93 LRS2 TACTICAL

## MODEL R93
### LONG RANGE SPORTER 2
*Action:* bolt
*Stock:* tactical composite
*Barrel:* heavy, fluted 26 in.
*Sights:* none
*Weight:* 8.0
*Caliber:* .223 Rem., .243, .22-250, 6mm Norma, 6.5x55, .308, .300 Win. Mag., .338 Lapua Mag.
*Magazine:* in-line box, 5 rounds
*Features:* straight-pull bolt; fully adjustable trigger; optional folding bipod, muzzle brake and hand rest
**Long Range Sporter:** . . . . . . . **$2900**
**.338 Lapua:** . . . . . . . . . . . . . **$3300**

## MODEL R93
### LRS2 TACTICAL RIFLE PACKAGE
*Action:* bolt
*Stock:* synthetic tactical with adjustments
*Barrel:* heavy, fluted 26 in.
*Sights:* none
*Weight:* 10
*Caliber:* .308, .300 Win. Mag., .338 Lapua
*Magazine:* in-line box, 5 rounds
*Features:* package includes bipod, sling, Leupold Tactical scope, mirage band, muzzle brake
**Long Range Tactical:** . . . . . . . **$4200**
**.338 Lapua:** . . . . . . . . . . . . . **$5000**

*Practice fast reloading during the off-season. Smooth bolt operation comes with repetition; so does loading the magazine quickly from your pouch.*

RIFLES

# Brown Precision Rifles

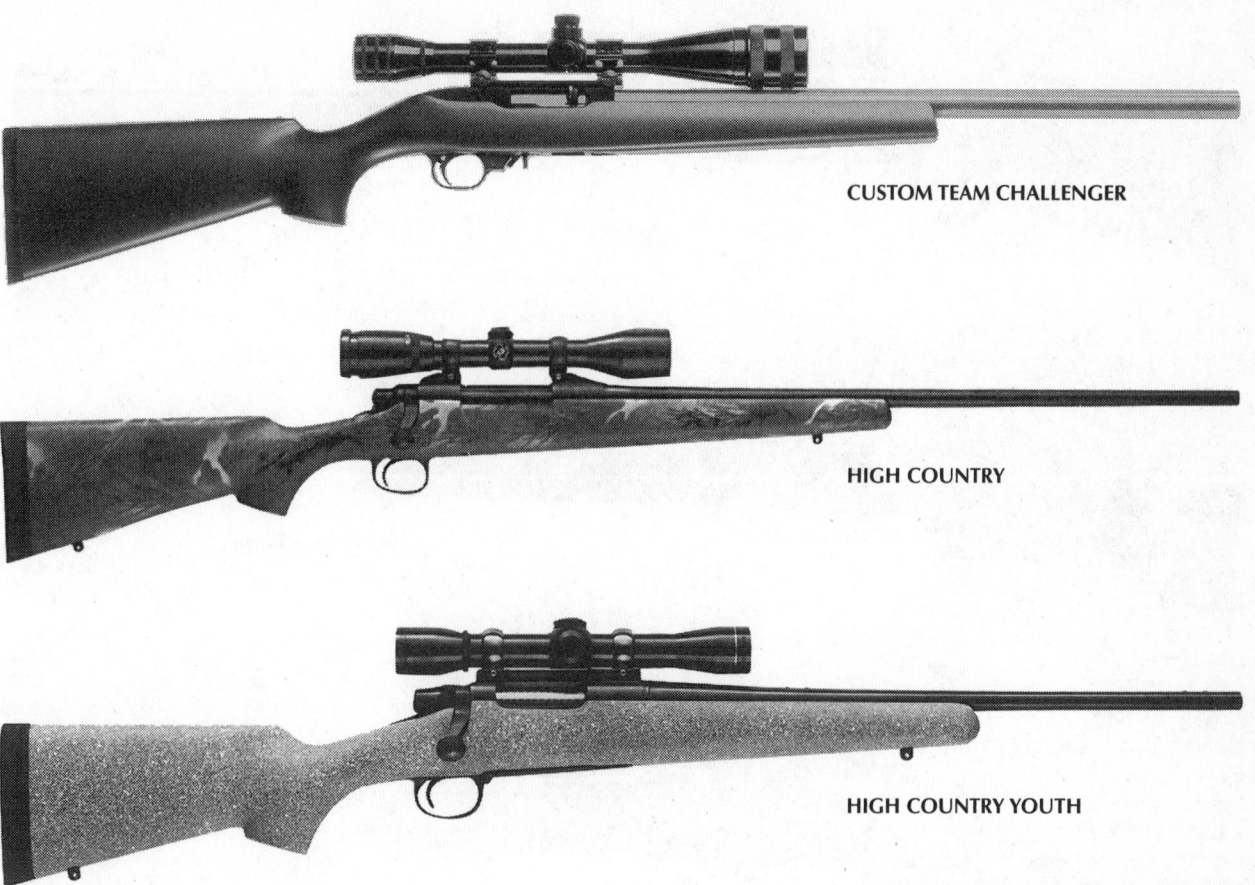

CUSTOM TEAM CHALLENGER

HIGH COUNTRY

HIGH COUNTRY YOUTH

**CHET BROWN,** and now son Mark, have produced the Pro-Hunter rifle for discriminating big game hunters. It begins life as a Winchester Model 700 Super Grade action with controlled feed claw extractor, the trigger tuned to a crisp let-off at a customer-specified weight. A Shilen Match-Grade stainless-steel barrel is custom crowned and hand fitted to the action. The Pro-Hunter Elite features choice of Express rear sight or Talley removable peep sight. The banded front ramp sight comes with European dovetail and replaceable brass bead. A flip-up white night sight is available. So tooTalley detachable TNT scope mount rings and bases installed with Brown's Magnum Duty 8X40 screws.

All metal parts on the Pro-Hunter are finished in either matte electroless nickel or black Teflon. The barreled action is neatly glass bedded to a Brown Precision Alaskan-configuration fiberglass stock, painted as the cus-tomer desires and fitted with a high-quality 1-inch buttpad and a Talley trapdoor grip cap. Finished weight ranges from 7 to 15 pounds, depending on chambering, barrel length and contour and options.

## CUSTOM TEAM CHALLENGER
*Action:* autoloading
*Stock:* composite
*Barrel:* heavy Shilen match grade 18 in.
*Sights:* open
*Weight:* 7.0
*Caliber:* .22 LR
*Magazine:* rotary, 10 rounds
*Features:* also available with stainless barrel
**Team Challenger:** . . . . . . . . . . $1395
**stainless:** . . . . . . . . . . . . . . . $1495

## HIGH COUNTRY
*Action:* bolt
*Stock:* composite classic stock
*Barrel:* choice of contours, lengths
*Sights:* none

*Weight:* 6.0
*Caliber:* any popular standard caliber
*Magazine:* box, 5 rounds
*Features:* Remington 700 barreled action; tuned trigger; choice of stock colors and dimensions
**High Country:** . . . . . . . . . . . . $2795

## HIGH COUNTRY YOUTH
*Action:* bolt
*Stock:* composite sporter, scaled for youth
*Barrel:* length and contour to order
*Sights:* none
*Weight:* 5.0
*Caliber:* any popular standard short action
*Magazine:* box, 5 rounds
*Features:* Remington Model 700 or Model 7 barreled action; optional muzzle brake, scopes, stock colors and dimensions; included: package of shooting, reloading, and hunting accessories
**Youth:** . . . . . . . . . . . . . . . . . $1435

# Brown Precision Rifles

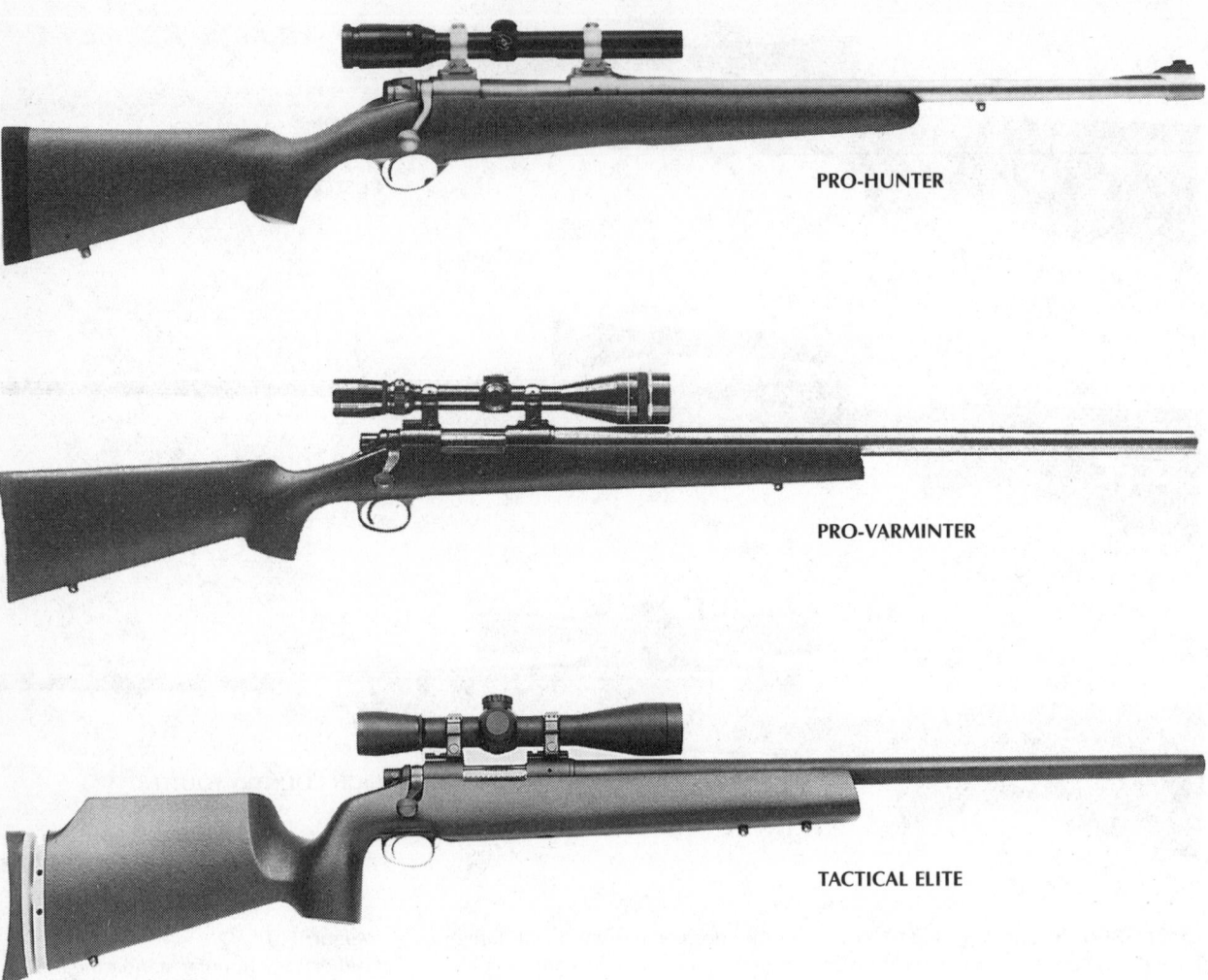

**PRO-HUNTER**

**PRO-VARMINTER**

**TACTICAL ELITE**

### PRO HUNTER
*Action:* bolt
*Stock:* composite sporter
*Barrel:* Shilen match grade stainless
*Sights:* none
*Weight:* 8.0
*Caliber:* any standard and belted magnum caliber up to .375 H&H
*Magazine:* box, 3 to 5 rounds
*Features:* Model 70 action with Mauser extractor; tuned trigger; optional Talley peep sight and banded ramp front sight or Talley mounts with 8-40 screws; optional muzzle brake, Mag-Na-Porting, Americase aluminum hard case
**Pro Hunter:** . . . . . . . . . . . . . $3495
**in left-hand:** . . . . . . . . . . . . . $3695

### PRO VARMINTER
*Action:* bolt
*Stock:* composite, varmint or bench rest
*Barrel:* heavy stainless match grade 26 in.
*Sights:* none
*Weight:* 9.0
*Caliber:* all popular calibers
*Magazine:* box (or single shot)
*Features:* Remington 40X or 700 action (right or left-hand); bright or bead-blasted finish; optional muzzle brake; after-market trigger; scope and mounts optional
**Model 700, right-hand:** . . . . . . $2495
**Model 700, left-hand:** . . . . . . . $2695
**Rem. 40X**
    **(with target trigger):** . . . . . . $3195

### TACTICAL ELITE
*Action:* bolt
*Stock:* composite tactical
*Barrel:* Shilen match-grade, heavy stainless
*Sights:* none
*Weight:* 9.0
*Caliber:* .223, .308, .300 Win. Mag., (others on special order)
*Magazine:* box, 3 or 5 rounds
*Features:* Remington 700 action, Teflon metal finish; adjustable butt plate; tuned trigger; optional muzzle brakes, scopes
**Elite:** . . . . . . . . . . . . . . . . . . . $3195

# Browning Rifles

**.22 SEMI-AUTOMATIC**

**JONATHAN BROWNING** was among the persecuted Mormon people who made their way west from Nauvoo, Illinois in 1846. A talented gun designer, he came up with a "slide rifle" featuring multiple chambers in a mouth-organ-type bar that serviced a fixed barrel. The gun proved serviceable, and when the U.S. government asked for Mormon conscripts to fight Mexico, Brigham Young kept Jonathan in his shop. Neither did Jonathan join the vanguard of emigrants to the Salt Lake valley. His task was to supply them with guns.

Settling in Ogden in 1852, five years after the Young party arrived, Jonathan set up a gunshop and built a home with $600 he'd hidden in the floor of his wagon. His first wife and surviving 11 children were soon to be joined by two more wives and 11 more youngsters, including John Moses Browning.

John, a prodigy, left school at age 15 to work in his father's shop. By then he had already designed and built his first gun. In 1869 John M. Browning and his brother Matt established their own gunshop in Ogden, 50 miles from Promontory Point. Its crossroads location brought plenty of business. In 1878 at age 23, John Browning designed a breech-loading mechanism, then, with no blueprints or milling machines, fashioned a working prototype. On October 7, 1879, Browning received his first patent for a single-shot rifle, an immensely strong gun with big, simple parts that were easy to make and hard to break.

By 1879 John and his brother Ed had bought a 30-foot lot at the edge of Ogden's business district. Within two years the brothers had formed a partnership, and John had designed another dropping-block rifle — this one with a fixed trigger guard and forward-mounted operating lever. By

1882 he'd patented a repeating rifle with a tubular magazine and immediately set to work on a second repeating mechanism. John received patents for both rifles, but shelved the designs until he could improve upon them.

In 1883 Winchester salesman Andrew McAusland sent a used Browning rifle to company president Thomas G. Bennett in New Haven, Connecticut. While Winchester had a firm grip on the market for lever-action repeaters, it had no guns stout enough to handle heavy cartridges like the Army's .45-70. Rights to Browning's rifle would give Winchester a competitive gun. In 1883, Bennett bought the rights for Browning breech-loader for $8,000.

John, no longer permitted to build his single-shot rifle, quickly resurrected his lever-action designs. In 1884 he and brother Matt visited Winchester's headquarters with a new repeater, the Winchester Model 1886. The following year John designed the Model 1887 lever-action shotgun — widely considered to be the first practical repeating shotgun.

After a two-year hiatus as a Mormon missionary John was back at his bench by 1889, setting a blistering pace, netting 20 patents in less than four years. During the next 17 years Winchester bought 44 designs from the Browning shop. Among John Browning's most famous designs was the Model 1897 pump shotgun, which immediately smothered all competition and stayed in production for 60 years. When Bennett turned to Browning to replace Winchester's outdated Model 1873, a prototype of the Model 1892 arrived within 30 days.

Ironically, John Browning's next achievement scuttled his relationship with Bennett. John had long been intrigued by automatic guns; but un-like R.J. Gatling who had used multiple barrels and a hand-operated

mechanism, he sought to use the firing force of one round to manipulate the action to fire another round.

In 1890 John offered Colt, the manufacturer of the Army's Gatling guns, an "Automatic Machine Gun" that could be built "as cheaply as a common sporting rifle." In tests John fired 200 .45-70 rounds without a hitch.

In 1893 tests Browning demonstrated an action which vented gas through a port in the barrel to operate the spring-loaded bolt. The bolt ejected the spent case on its rearward stroke, then chambered and fired another round as it slammed home. Colt started production for the Navy in 1895.

John adapted his autoloading principle to shotguns. When Thomas Bennett refused Browning's terms for a long-recoil shotgun, the productive relationship dissolved. Browning marketed his design, the Auto 5, in Belgium and through Remington, in the U.S. Even more famous was Browning's military pistol, the powerful Colt Model 1911.

John continued to work on military designs, completing a water-cooled machine gun in 1910 and, soon after, developing an infantry weapon called the Browning Automatic Rifle, or BAR.

Rumblings of war in Europe revived interest in John Browning's machine gun. In tests at Springfield Armory he triggered 20,000 rounds without malfunction and, in a second demonstration, fired another 20,000 cartridges! In the fall of l9l7, ordnance officers tendered $750,000 for manufacturing rights for the Model 19l17 machine gun, the BAR and Colt's Model 1911 pistol. It was about $12 million less than he could have received from private royalties, but he accepted. "Had I been 20 years younger," he stated, "I might have been ducking German bullets in French mud, wishing for a better gun."

# Browning Rifles

**A-BOLT HUNTER**

**A-BOLT ECLIPSE**

**A-BOLT HUNTER MEDALLION BOSS**

**A-BOLT WSSM MEDALLION**

In l926, on a trip to the F.N. plant in Belgium, John felt chest pains and retired to the office. A couple of minutes later his heart stopped beating. John Browning was 71.

No gun designer in American history has contributed as much to firearms development. In nearly 50 years at the bench he was issued 128 patents on 80 distinct mechanisms, from single-shots to selfloaders.

## .22 SEMI-AUTOMATIC
*Action:* autoloading
*Stock:* walnut
*Barrel:* 19 in.
*Sights:* open
*Weight:* 5.2
*Caliber:* .22 LR
*Magazine:* tube in stock, 11 rounds
*Features:* Grade VI has high grade walnut, finer checkering, engraved receiver
**Grade I:** . . . . . . . . . . . . . . . . . . $519
**Grade VI:** . . . . . . . . . . . . . . . $1112

## A-BOLT HUNTER
*Action:* bolt
*Stock:* walnut
*Barrel:* 20 to 26 in.
*Sights:* none
*Weight:* 7.0
*Caliber:* all popular cartridges from .22 Hornet to .30-06, including WSM's and WSSM's.
*Magazine:* detachable box, 4 to 6 rounds
*Features:* BOSS (ballistic optimizing shooting system) available; Micro Hunters weigh 6.3 lbs. with 20 in. barrel and shorter stock. Left-hand Medallion available. Eclipse thumbhole stock available with light or heavy barrel (9.8 lbs.) and BOSS.
**Hunter:** . . . . . . . . . . . . . . . . . $672
**Medallion:** . . . . . . . . . . . . . . . $782
**Medallion BOSS:** . . . . . . . . . . $862
**Medallion, white gold:** . . $1121-1149
**Medallion, white gold BOSS:**
. . . . . . . . . . . . . . . . $1201-1229

**Micro Hunter:** . . . . . . . . . $664-693
**Eclipse Hunter:** . . . . . . . . . . . $1101

## A-BOLT HUNTER MAGNUM
*Action:* bolt
*Stock:* walnut
*Barrel:* 23 and 26 in.
*Sights:* none
*Weight:* 7.5
*Caliber:* popular magnums from 7mm Rem. to .375 H&H, including .270, 7mm and .300 WSM plus .25, .223 and .243 WSSMs.
*Magazine:* detachable box, 3 rounds
*Features:* rifles in WSM calibers have 23 in. barrels and weigh 6.5 lbs.; BOSS (Ballistic Optimizing Shooting System) available; left-hand available.
**Magnum:** . . . . . . . . . . . . . . $698-719
**Medallion Magnum:** . . . . . . . . . $811
**Medallion Magnum BOSS:** . . . . $911
**Eclipse Magnum:** . . . . . . . . . . $1134

# Browning Rifles

A-BOLT STALKER

BAR

BAR SAFARI, BOSS, WALNUT

BLR LIGHTWEIGHT 81

## A-BOLT STALKER

*Action:* bolt
*Stock:* synthetic
*Barrel:* 22, 23 and 26 in.
*Sights:* none
*Weight:* 7.5
*Caliber:* most popular calibers and magnums, including .270, 7mm and .300 WSMs; and .25, .223 and .243 WSSMs.
*Magazine:* detachable box, 3 to 6 rounds
*Features:* BOSS (Ballistic Optimizing Shooting System) available; stainless option. Rifles in WSM calibers have 23 in. barrels and weigh 6.5 lbs.

Stalker: . . . . . . . . . . . . . . . $684-733
BOSS: . . . . . . . . . . . . . . . . $764-813
Stainless : . . . . . . . . . . . . . $871-899
Stainless, BOSS: . . . . . . . . . $951-999
Stainless, left-hand: . . . . . . $898-926
Stainless, left-hand, Boss: . . $978-1006
Varmint Stalker: . . . . . . . . . $811-860

## BAR

*Action:* autoloading
*Stock:* walnut or synthetic
*Barrel:* 20, 23, and 24 in.
*Sights:* open
*Weight:* 7.5
*Caliber:* .243, .25-06, .270, .308, .30-06, 7mm Rem. Mag., .300 Win. Mag., .270 WSM, 7mm WSM, .300 WSM, .338 Win. Mag.
*Magazine:* detachable box, 3 to 5 rounds
*Features:* gas operated; lightweight model with alloy receiver and 20 in. barrel weighs 7.2 lbs.; magnum with 24 in. barrel weighs 8.6 lbs. \BOSS (Ballistic Optimizing Shooting System) available; higher grades also available.

Lightweight Stalker: . . . . . . . . $825
  WSM's: . . . . . . . . . . . . . . . . $901
  Magnums: . . . . . . . . . . . . . . $901
Safari (no sights): . . . . . . . . . $831

Magnums: . . . . . . . . . . . . . $908
Safari, BOSS: . . . . . . . . . . . . $930
  WSM & Mag.: . . . . . . . . . . $1007

## MODEL BLR LIGHTWEIGHT 81

*Action:* lever
*Stock:* straight-grip walnut
*Barrel:* 20, 22 or 24 in.
*Sights:* open
*Weight:* 6.5 or 7.3 lbs.
*Caliber:* .22-250, .243, 7mm-08, .308, .358, .450 Marlin, .270, .30-06 (22 in.), 7mm Rem. Mag., .300 Win. Mag. (24 in.)
*Magazine:* 5 and 4 (magnums)
*Features:* short action, alloy receiver, front-locking bolt, rack-and-pinion action

BLR Lightweight . . . . . . . . . . . $710
BLR Long Action . . . . . . . . . . . $752
WSMs . . . . . . . . . . . . . . . . . . $779

RIFLES

# Browning Rifles

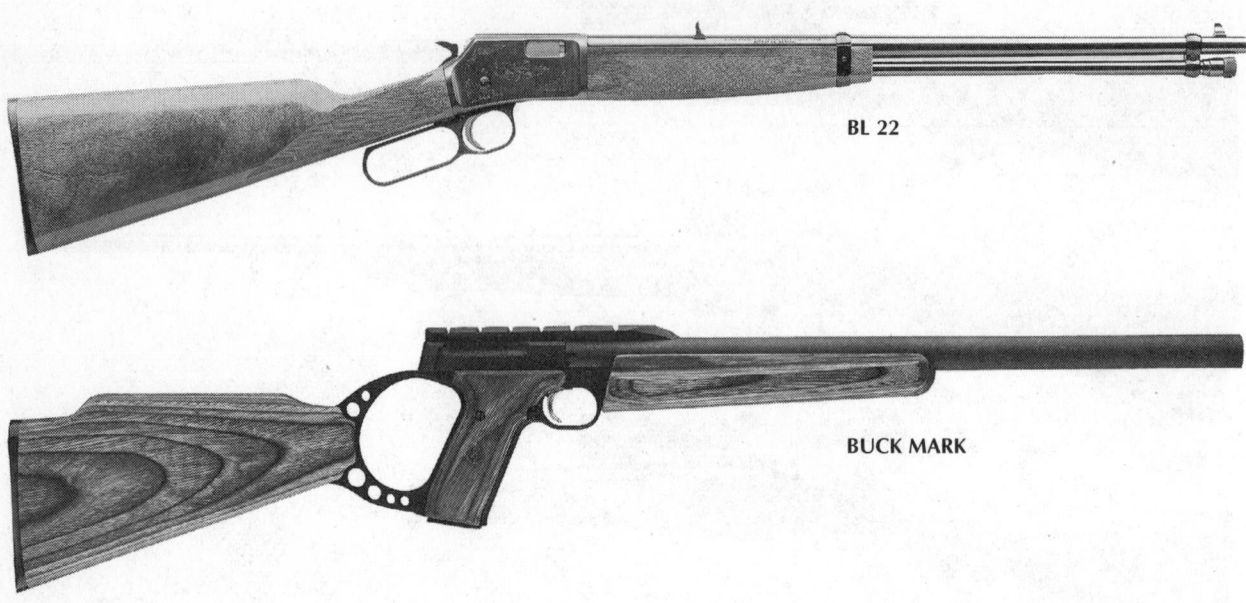

BL 22

BUCK MARK

## BL 22

**Action:** lever
**Stock:** walnut
**Barrel:** 20 in.
**Sights:** open
**Weight:** 5.0
**Caliber:** .22 LR
**Magazine:** under-barrel tube,
15 rounds
**Features:** short stroke, exposed
hammer, lever action; straight grip;
also available in Grade II with fine
checkered walnut.
Grade I: . . . . . . . . . . . . . . . . . $449
Grade II: . . . . . . . . . . . . . . . . $509
With 24" octagon bbl.: . . . . . . $705

## BUCK MARK

**Action:** autoloading
**Stock:** laminate
**Barrel:** 18 in.
**Sights:** open
**Weight:** 5.2
**Caliber:** .22 LR
**Magazine:** detachable box, 10 rounds
**Features:** also in target model with
heavy barrel
Sporter: . . . . . . . . . . . . . . . . . $555
Target, heavy barrel: . . . . . . . . $572
Classic Carbon (3.6 lbs.): . . . . . $633

*After you shoot at game, reload and keep your eye
to the scope. Your best chance for a follow-up shot is
almost always from where you are. Move, and you
can miss it.*

# Charles Daly Rifles

FIELD GRADE MAUSER SS

SUPERIOR GRADE MINI-MAUSER

SUPERIOR GRADE SAFARI MAUSER

RIFLES

### FIELD GRADE MAUSER
**Action:** bolt
**Stock:** synthetic
**Barrel:** 22 or 24 in.
**Sights:** none
**Weight:** 7.0
**Caliber:** .22-250, .243, .25-06, .270, 7mm Rem. Mag., .308, .30-06, .300 Win. Mag.

**Magazine:** box, 3 or 5 rounds
**Features:** Mauser 98 action; stainless barrel available; also Superior grade with walnut stock and high-polish blue and Superior grade Mini Mauser in .22 Hornet, .223, 7.62x39 with 20 in. barrel; superior grade Safari available in .375 H&H and .458 Win.
**field grade:**. . . . . . . . . . . . . . . $489

stainless: . . . . . . . . . . . . . . . . $549
magnum: . . . . . . . . . . . . . . . . $524
magnum stainless: . . . . . . . . . . $579
**Superior grade**
    **and superior mini:** . . . . . . . . $599
**Superior magnum:** . . . . . . . . . . $629
**Superior safari:**. . . . . . . . . . . . $789

# Christensen Arms Rifles

**CARBON CHALLENGER THUMBHOLE**

**CARBON ONE CUSTOM**

**CARBON ONE HUNTER**

**CARBON RANGER**

**CARBON TACTICAL**

### CARBON CHALLENGER THUMBHOLE
**Action:** autoloading
**Stock:** synthetic or wood thumbhole
**Barrel:** graphite sleeved 20 in.
**Sights:** none
**Weight:** 4.0
**Caliber:** .22 LR
**Magazine:** rotary, 10 rounds
**Features:** 10/22 Ruger action; custom trigger and bedding
**Challenger:** . . . . . . . . . . . . . $1150

### CARBON ONE CUSTOM
**Action:** bolt
**Stock:** synthetic or wood sporter
**Barrel:** graphite sleeved 26 in.
**Sights:** none
**Weight:** 6.0
**Caliber:** all popular magnums
**Magazine:** box, 3 rounds

**Features:** Remington 700 action; optional custom trigger
**Custom:** . . . . . . . . . . . . . . . $2950

### CARBON ONE HUNTER
**Action:** bolt
**Stock:** synthetic
**Barrel:** graphite sleeved 26 in.
**Sights:** none
**Weight:** 7.0
**Caliber:** any popular
**Magazine:** box, 3 or 5 rounds
**Features:** Remington 700 action
**Hunter:** . . . . . . . . . . . . . . . $1499

### CARBON RANGER
**Action:** bolt
**Stock:** retractable tactical skeleton
**Barrel:** graphite sleeved, up to 36 in.
**Sights:** none
**Weight:** 18.0

**Caliber:** .50 BMG
**Magazine:** box, 5 rounds
**Features:** Omni Wind Runner action; custom trigger; guaranteed 5 shots in 8 in. at 1000 yds.
**Ranger:** . . . . . . . . . . . . . . . $4999

### CARBON TACTICAL
**Action:** bolt
**Stock:** synthetic
**Barrel:** graphite sleeved, 26 in.
**Sights:** none
**Weight:** 7.0
**Caliber:** most popular calibers
**Magazine:** box, 3 or 5 rounds
**Features:** guaranteed accuracy ½ in. at 100 yards; optional custom trigger, muzzle brake
**Tactical:** . . . . . . . . price on request

# Cimarron Rifles

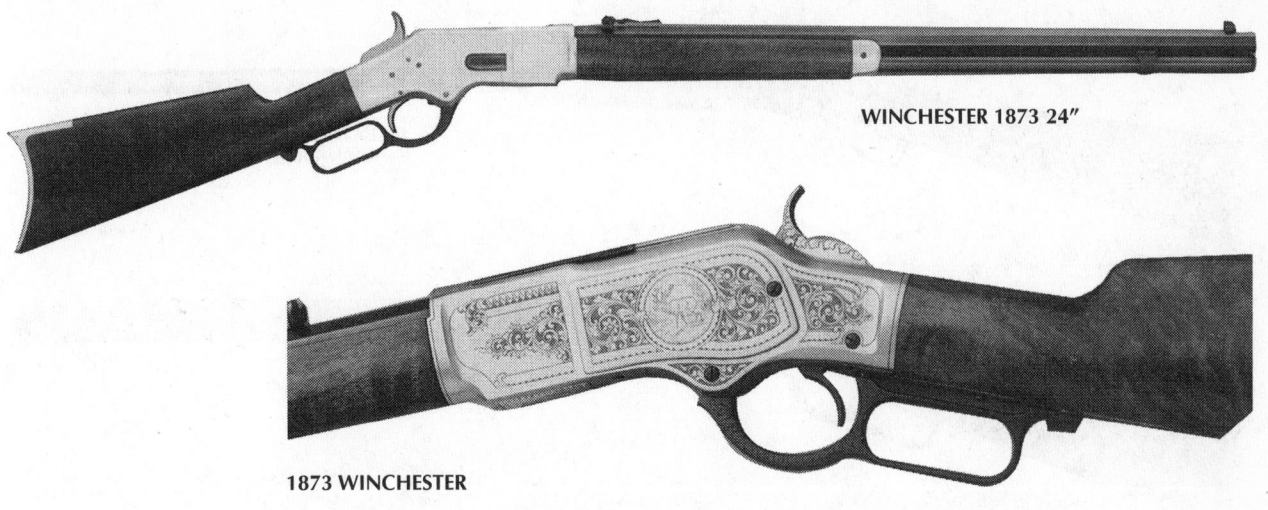

**WINCHESTER 1873 24"**

**1873 WINCHESTER**

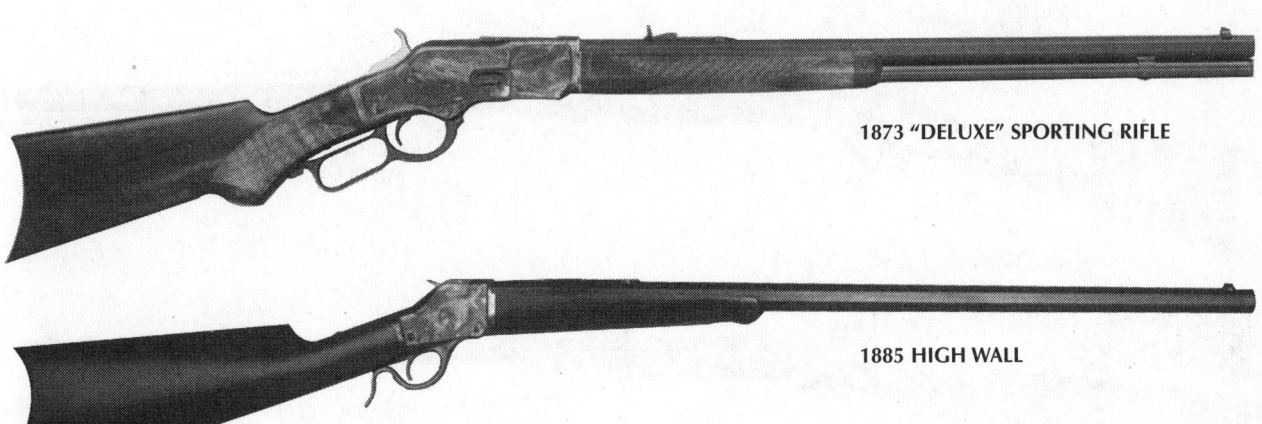

**1873 "DELUXE" SPORTING RIFLE**

**1885 HIGH WALL**

**RIFLES**

## 1873 WINCHESTER

*Action:* lever
*Stock:* walnut, straight grip
*Barrel:* 24 in.
*Sights:* open
*Weight:* 7.5
*Caliber:* .45 Colt, .44 WCF, .357-38 Special, .32-20, .44 Special, .38-40
*Magazine:* under-barrel tube, 11 rounds
*Features:* Available: "Sporting" model, "Deluxe" model, "Long Range" model (30 in. barrel), and carbine (19 in. barrel); Deluxe model has pistol grip

| | |
|---|---|
| Sporting: | $1049 |
| Deluxe: | $1149 |
| Long Range: | $1049 |
| Long Range Deluxe: | $1199 |
| Carbine: | $999 |

## 1885 HIGH WALL

*Action:* dropping block
*Stock:* walnut, straight grip
*Barrel:* octagon 30 in.
*Sights:* open
*Weight:* 9.5
*Caliber:* .45-70, .45-90, .40-65, .38-55
*Magazine:* none
*Features:* reproduction of the Winchester single shot hunting rifle popular in the 1880s

| | |
|---|---|
| 1885 Sporting: | $995 |
| 1885 Deluxe: | $1175 |

*Bench technique is critical to accurate shooting. Sandbags won't guarantee a tight group if your body position and pressure on the rifle is not identical with each shot.*

# Cimarron Rifles

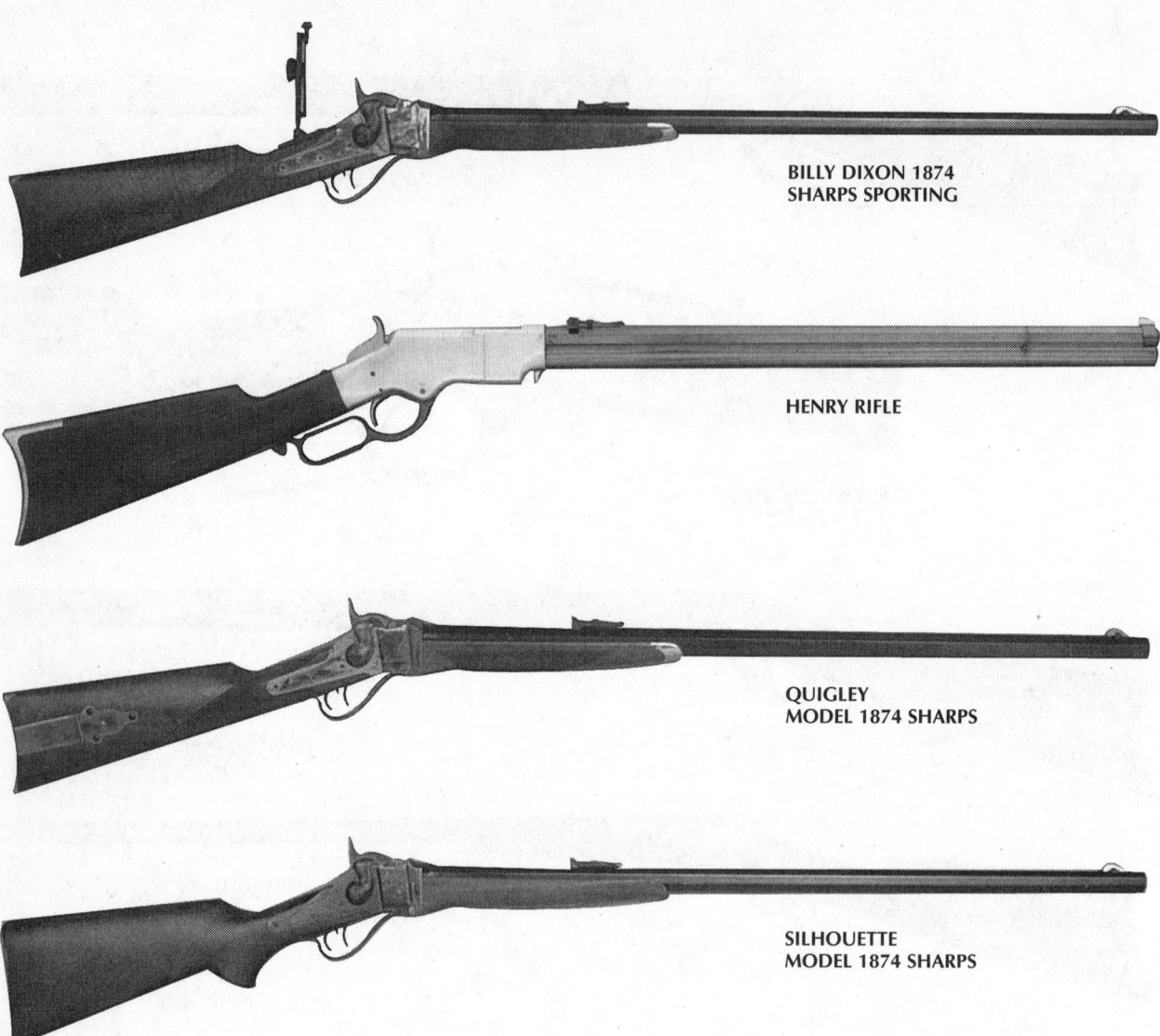

BILLY DIXON 1874
SHARPS SPORTING

HENRY RIFLE

QUIGLEY
MODEL 1874 SHARPS

SILHOUETTE
MODEL 1874 SHARPS

### BILLY DIXON 1874 SHARPS SPORTING
*Action:* dropping block
*Stock:* walnut, straight grip
*Barrel:* octagon 32 in.
*Sights:* open
*Weight:* 10.5
*Caliber:* .45-70, .45-90, .45-110, .50-90
*Magazine:* none
*Features:* Single-shot reproduction
**Billy Dixon:** . . . . . . . . . . . . . **$1295**

### HENRY RIFLE
*Action:* lever
*Stock:* walnut, straight grip
*Barrel:* 24 in.
*Sights:* open
*Weight:* 7.5
*Caliber:* .44 WCF, .45 LC
*Magazine:* under-barrel tube, 11 rounds
*Features:* replica of the most famous American rifle of the Old West
**Henry:** . . . . . . . . . . . . . . . . . **$1149**

### QUIGLEY MODEL 1874 SHARPS
*Action:* dropping block
*Stock:* walnut, straight grip
*Barrel:* octagon 34 in.
*Sights:* open
*Weight:* 10.5
*Caliber:* .45-70, .45-90, .45-120
*Magazine:* none
*Features:* single-shot reproduction
**Quigley:** . . . . . . . . . . . . . . . . **$1350**

### SILHOUETTE MODEL 1874 SHARPS
*Action:* dropping block
*Stock:* walnut, pistol grip
*Barrel:* 32 in. octagon
*Sights:* open
*Weight:* 10.5
*Caliber:* .45-70, .50-70
*Magazine:* none
*Features:* single-shot reproduction; shotgun style buttplate; barrel features cut rifling, lapped and polished
**Silhouette:** . . . . . . . . . . . . . . **$1299**

# Colt Rifles

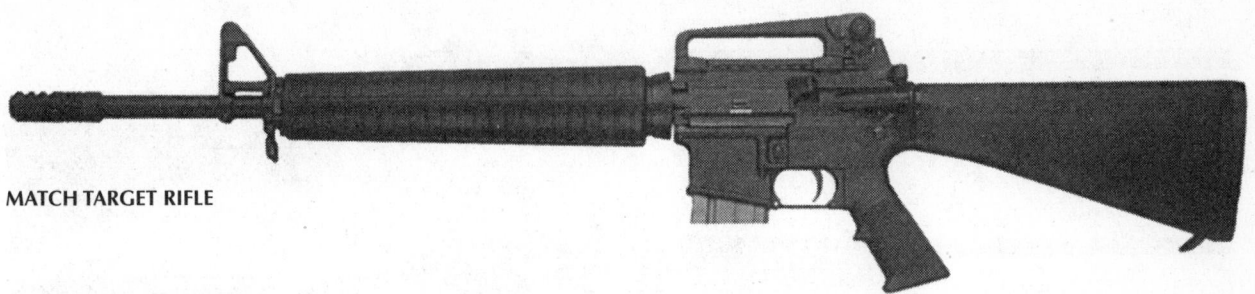

**MATCH TARGET RIFLE**

### MATCH TARGET RIFLE
*Action:* autoloading
*Stock:* combat-style, synthetic
*Barrel:* 16 or 20 in.

*Sights:* open
*Weight:* 8.0
*Caliber:* .223
*Magazine:* detachable box, 9 rounds

*Features:* suppressed recoil; accepts optics; 2-position safety; available with heavy barrel, compensator
**Target:** . . . . . . . . . . . . . . . . . $1194

# Cooper Arms Rifles

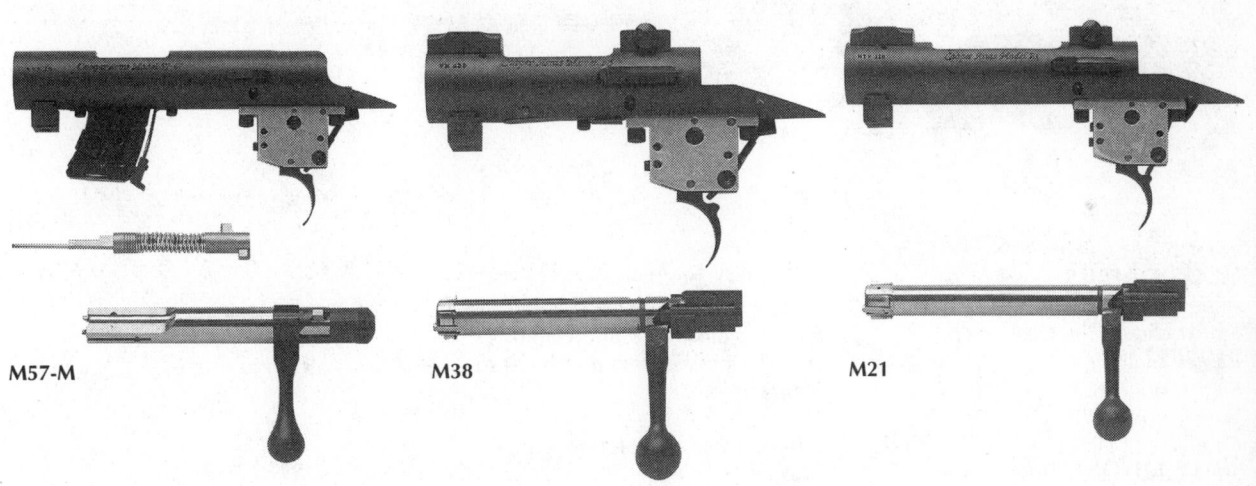

M57-M       M38       M21

DAN COOPER worked for Kimber during the founding of that company in western Oregon. Clean, conservative lines characterize both rifles. Cooper Arms came about in 1990, after Dan had walked from Mexico to Canada "because I wanted to." His can-do attitude put Cooper on the map in Montana's Bitterroot Valley, where Cooper Arms employs 27 artisans. They produce a line of bolt-action single-shot centerfire and repeating rimfire rifles famous for their fine fit and finish. And their tack-driving accuracy. Four action sizes are available in any of six stock configurations. Cooper Arms offers varmint and traditional models. Barreled actions are hand fitted to the stocks, then glass bedded behind the recoil lug and 1" forward of the breech. The barrels are free-floated. Cooper guarantees ½-minute accuracy.

### M57-M CALIBERS:
22LR, 22WMR, 17HMR

### M38 CALIBERS:
.17 Ackley Hornet, .22 Hornet, .22 K-Hornet, .218 Bee, .218 Mashburn Bee

### M21 CALIBERS:
.17 Rem, .17 Mach IV, Tactical 29, .221 Fireball, .222 Rem Mag, .223, .223 AI, .22 PPC, 6 PPC, .204 Ruger

### M22 CALIBERS:
.22-250 Rem, .22-250 AI, .25-06 AI, .243 Win, .243 Win, .243 AI, 220 Swift, .257 Roberts, .257 AI, 7-08, 6mm Rem, 6x284, .22 BR, 6 BR, .308 Win, .20 Rem

### M15 CALIBERS:
.223 WSSM, .243 WSSM

# Cooper Arms Rifles

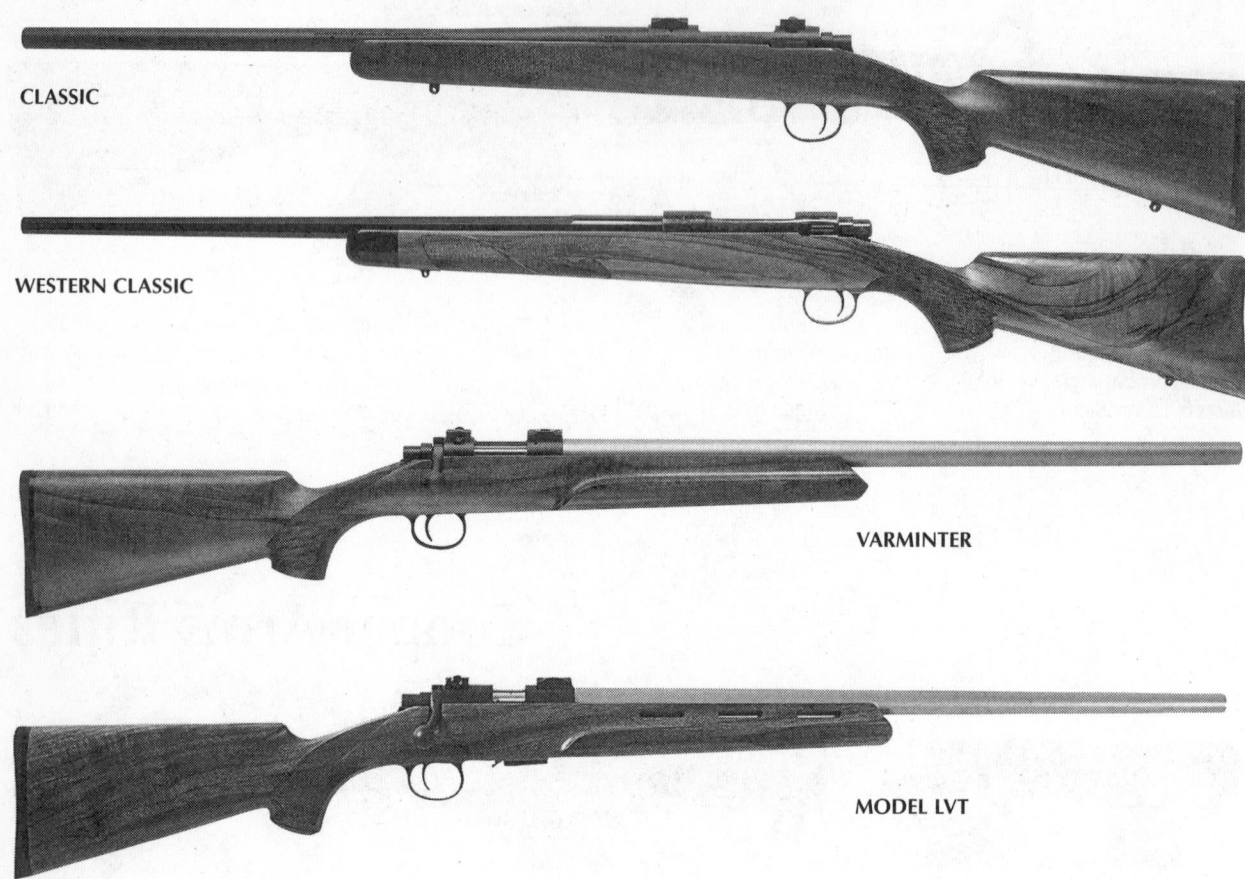

CLASSIC

WESTERN CLASSIC

VARMINTER

MODEL LVT

## CLASSIC SERIES
**Action:** bolt
**Stock:** checkered, Claro walnut
**Barrel:** match grade 22 in.
**Sights:** none
**Weight:** 6.5
**Caliber:** .22 LR, .22 WMR, .17 HMR, .38 Hornet, .223, .308
**Magazine:** none
**Features:** single shot; 3-lug bolt; also available in: Custom Classic and Western Classic with upgraded wood
Classic: . . . . . . . . . . . . . $1100-1295
Custom Classic: . . . . . . . $1895-2195
Western Classic: . . . . . . $2495-2795

## VARMINT SERIES
**Action:** bolt
**Stock:** checkered, Claro walnut
**Barrel:** stainless steel match, 24 in.
**Sights:** none
**Weight:** 7.5
**Caliber:** .223, .38 Hornet, .308
**Magazine:** none
**Features:** 3-lug action in 4 sizes; also available: Montana Varminter, Varminter Extreme and Lightweight LVT
Varminter: . . . . . . . . . . . $995-1250
Montana Varminter: . . . . $1395-1495
Varminter Extreme: . . . . $1795-1995
LVT (.22 LR): . . . . . . . . . . . . $1295
LVT (.22 WMR, .17 HMR): . . . $1395

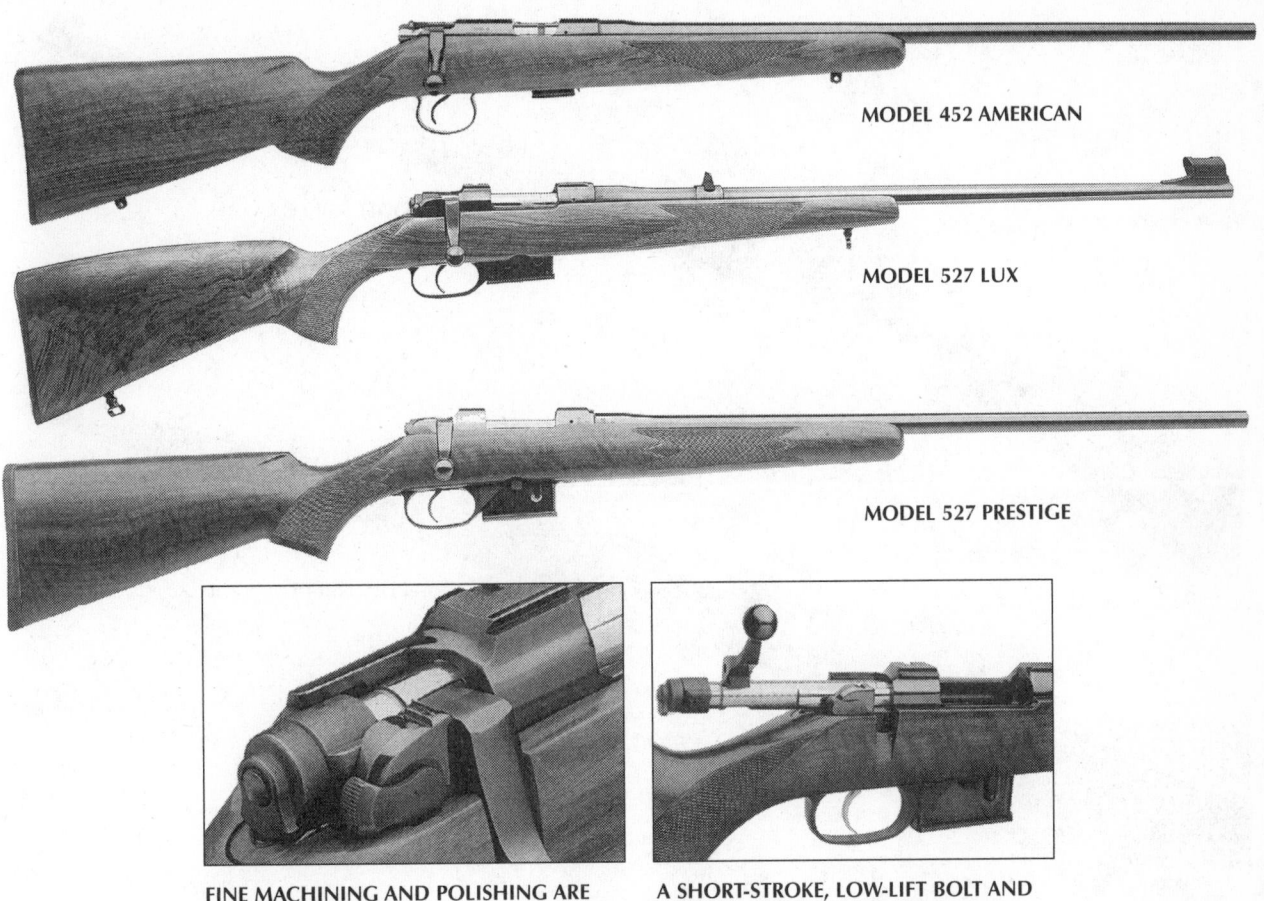

MODEL 452 AMERICAN

MODEL 527 LUX

MODEL 527 PRESTIGE

FINE MACHINING AND POLISHING ARE
CZ TRADEMARKS

A SHORT-STROKE, LOW-LIFT BOLT AND
DETACHABLE BOX MAGAZINE ARE
DESIGNED FOR SMOOTH FEEDING.

**CESKA ZBROJOVKA UHERSKY BROD** – a mouthful. Easier to say that CZ rifles rank among the best of their kind. CZ 452 rimfire rifles offer a compact design with a robust Mauser-type action and five-shot magazine. The rifles feature a tangent rear sight adjustable for elevation and windage on a receiver factory milled for telescopic sight mounts.

The CZ 550 is a line of elegant centerfire bolt guns with two-lug bolts and long claw extractors, an adjustable single-stage trigger and two-position thumb safety.

The CZ 527, with its small centerfire action, features a single set trigger adjustable for pull and trigger travel. The safety is a two-position rotary lever, which locks the trigger mechanism, while simultaneously locking the bolt closed.

## MODEL 452 AMERICAN
*Action:* bolt
*Stock:* checkered walnut sporter
*Barrel:* 22 in.
*Sights:* none
*Weight:* 6.0
*Caliber:* .22 LR, .17 HMR, .22 WMR
*Magazine:* detachable box, 5 rounds
*Features:* adjustable trigger; Model 452 Lux has European-style stock and open sights on 24 in. barrel; Varmint version has heavy 22 in. barrel, both weigh 7 lbs. Youth Scout rifle has shortened stock, 16 in. barrel, single loading device and weighs 4 lbs..
**American and Lux, .22 LR:** . . . . $378
**.22 WMR** . . . . . . . . . . . . . . . $407
**.17 HMR** . . . . . . . . . . . . . . . $420

## MODEL 527 LUX
*Action:* bolt
*Stock:* checkered, walnut sporter
*Barrel:* 24 in.
*Sights:* open
*Weight:* 6.2
*Caliber:* .22 Hornet, .222, .223
*Magazine:* detachable box, 5 rounds
*Features:* single-set, adjustable trigger; also available: CZ 527 Carbine in .223, CZ 527 full stock (FS) in .22 Hornet, .222 and .223 with 20 in. barrel and 527 Prestige in .22 Hornet and .223 with 22 in. barrel
**Lux :** . . . . . . . . . . . . . . . . . . $582
**carbine:** . . . . . . . . . . . . . . . . $588
**FS:** . . . . . . . . . . . . . . . . . . . $670
**Prestige:** . . . . . . . . . . . . . . . . $854

# CZ Rifles

MODEL 550 LUX

MODEL 550 FS

## MODEL 550 LUX

**Action:** bolt
**Stock:** checkered walnut sporter
**Barrel:** 24 in.
**Sights:** open
**Weight:** 7.3
**Caliber:** .243, 6.5x55, .270, 7x57, 7x64, .308, .30-06, 9.3x62
**Magazine:** box, 5 rounds
**Features:** adjustable single set trigger; detachable magazine optional; full-stocked model (FS) available; CZ 550

Safari Magnum has magnum length action, express sights in calibers: .375 H&H, .416 Rigby, .458 Win.

**Lux:**. . . . . . . . . . . . . . . . . . . . . $588
**FS:**. . . . . . . . . . . . . . . . . . . . . $684
**Safari magnum:** . . . . . . . . . . . $833

## MODEL 550 VARMINT

**Action:** bolt
**Stock:** walnut
**Barrel:** heavy varmint 24 in.
**Sights:** open

**Weight:** 8.5
**Caliber:** .308 Win., 22-250
**Magazine:** box, 5 rounds
**Features:** adjustable single set trigger, laminated stock optional; detachable magazine optional; also available: CZ 550 medium magnum in .7mm Rem. Mag. and .300 Win. Mag.
**Varmint:**. . . . . . . . . . . . . . . . . $633
**Varmint Laminate:** . . . . . . . . . . $727
**Medium Magnum:** . . . . . . . . . . $670

# Dakota Arms Rifles

MODEL 10 SINGLE SHOT

MODEL 76

MODEL 97 HUNTER

### MODEL 10 SINGLE SHOT

*Action:* dropping block
*Stock:* select walnut
*Barrel:* 23 in.
*Sights:* none
*Weight:* 5.5
*Caliber:* from .22 LR to .375 H&H: magnum: .338 Win. to .416 Dakota
*Magazine:* none
*Features:* receiver and rear of breech block are solid steel; removable trigger plate

| | |
|---|---|
| standard or magnum: | $3995 |
| barreled actions: | $2150 |
| action only: | $1675 |

### MODEL 76

*Action:* bolt
*Stock:* select walnut
*Barrel:* 23 to 24 in.
*Sights:* none
*Weight:* 6.5
*Caliber:* Safari: from .257 Roberts to .458 Win. Mag. Classic: from ..22-250 through .458 Win. Mag.(inc. WSM). African: .404 Jeffery, .416 Dakota, .416 Rigby, .450 Dakota
*Magazine:* box, 3 to 5 rounds
*Features:* three-position striker-blocking safety allows bolt operation with safety on; stock in oil-finished English, Bastogne or Claro walnut; African model weighs 9.5 lbs. and the Safari is 8.5 lbs.

| | |
|---|---|
| Classic: | $3995 |
| Safari: | $4995 |
| African: | $5795 |

### MODEL 97 HUNTER

*Action:* bolt
*Stock:* walnut or composite
*Barrel:* 24 in.
*Sights:* open
*Weight:* 7.0
*Caliber:* Hunter; .25-06 through .375 Dakota; Lightweight Hunter: .22-250 through .330; Varmint hunter: .17 Rem. through .22-250
*Magazine:* blind box, 3 to 5 rounds
*Features:* 1 in. black recoil pad, 2 sling swivel studs; Varmint model has #4 chrome-moly barrel, adjustable trigger, ½ in. black pad and weighs 8 lbs.

| | |
|---|---|
| Hunter: | $2195 |
| 97 with semi-fancy wood stock: | $2495 |
| action only: | $1000 |
| barreled action: | $1300 |

RIFLES

*If you drop .22 cartridges on the ground or even on a shooting mat or the floor, wipe them off thoroughly before loading. Bullet lubricant picks up grit that can scour your bore.*

# Dakota Arms Rifles

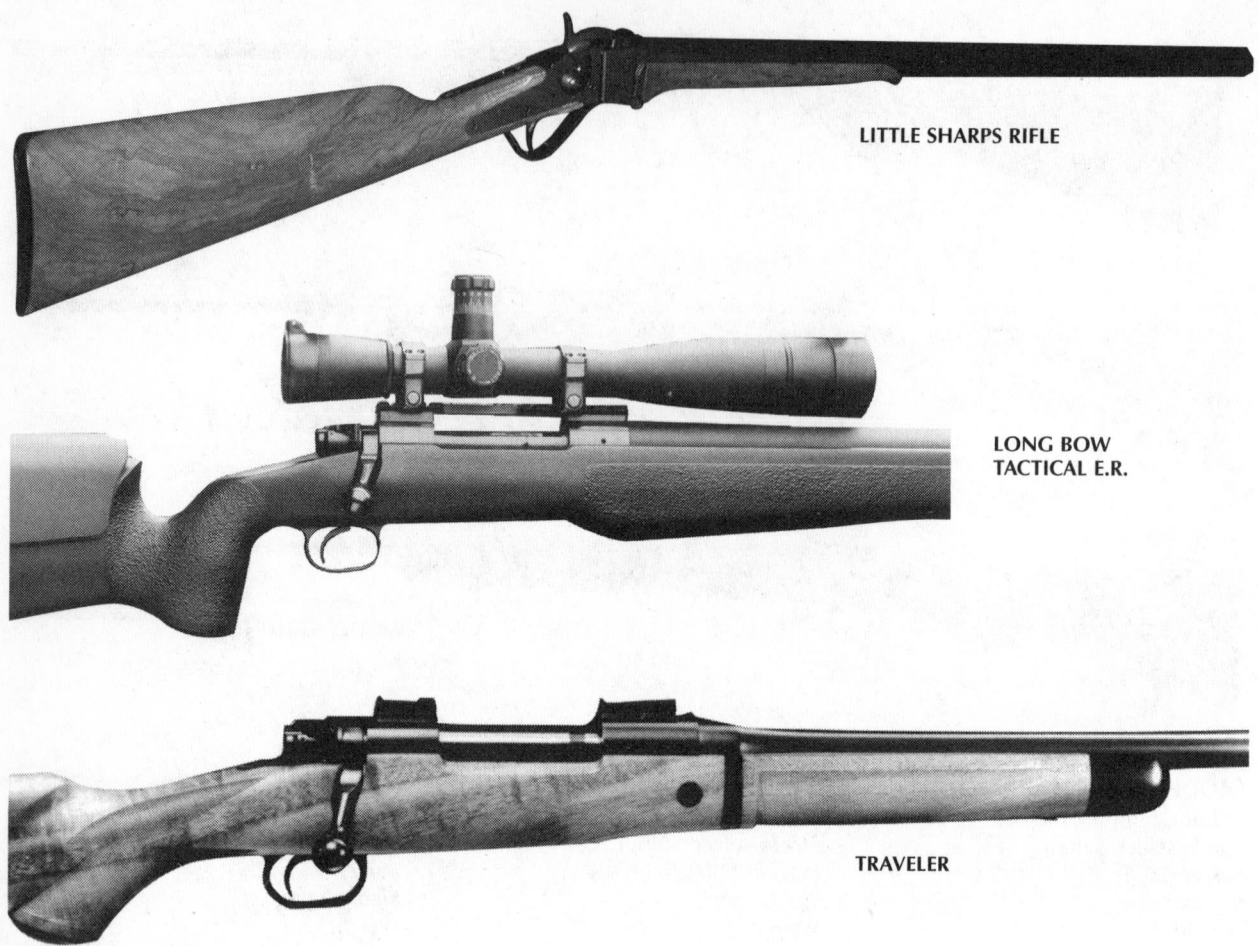

LITTLE SHARPS RIFLE

LONG BOW
TACTICAL E.R.

TRAVELER

### DOUBLE RIFLE
*Action:* hinged breech
*Stock:* exhibition walnut, pistol grip
*Barrel:* 25 in.
*Sights:* open
*Weight:* 9.5
*Caliber:* most common calibers
*Magazine:* none
*Features:* round action, elective
ejectors, recoil pad, Americase
**Double Rifle:** . . . . . . . . . . . **$27,500**

### LITTLE SHARPS RIFLE
*Action:* dropping block
*Stock:* walnut, straight grip
*Barrel:* octagon 26 in.
*Sights:* open
*Weight:* 8.0
*Caliber:* .17 HRM to .30-40 Krag
*Magazine:* none
*Features:* small frame version of
1874 Sharps
**Little Sharps:** . . . . . . . . . . . . **$3100**

### LONG BOW TACTICAL E.R.
*Action:* bolt
*Stock:* McMillan fiberglass, matte finish
*Barrel:* stainless, 28 in.
*Sights:* open
*Weight:* 13.7
*Caliber:* .338 Lapua, .300 Dakota and
.330 Dakota
*Magazine:* blind, 3 rounds
*Features:* Adjustable cheekpiece;
3 sling swivel studs; bipod spike in
forend; controlled round feeding;
one-piece optical rail; 3-position firing
pin block safety; deployment kit;
muzzle brake
**Tactical E.R.:** . . . . . . . . . . . . . **$4500**
**Action only:** . . . . . . . . . . . . . **$2400**

### TRAVELER
*Action:* bolt
*Stock:* take-down, checkered walnut
*Barrel:* choice of contours, lengths
*Sights:* none
*Weight:* 8.5
*Caliber:* all popular cartridges
*Magazine:* box, 3 to 5 rounds
*Features:* The Dakota Traveler is based
on the Dakota 76 design. It features
threadless disassembly. Weight and
barrel length depend on caliber and
version.
**Classic:** . . . . . . . . . . . . . . . . **$4995**
**Safari:** . . . . . . . . . . . . . . . . . **$5995**
**African:** . . . . . . . . . . . . . . . . **$6795**

# Dixie Rifles

1873 TRAPDOOR CARBINE

1873 TRAPDOOR SPRINGFIELD

1874 SHARPS SILHOUETTE MODEL

1874 SHARPS LIGHTWEIGHT
HUNTER RIFLE

KODIAK MARK IV
.45-.70 DOUBLE BARREL RIFLE

## 1873 SPRINGFIELD "TRAPDOOR"

**Action:** hinged breech
**Stock:** walnut
**Barrel:** 26 or 32 in. (22 in carbine)
**Sights:** adjustable
**Weight:** 8.0lbs.
**Caliber:** .45-70
**Magazine:** none
**Features:** single shot rifle, first cartridge rifle of U.S. Army; Officer's Model (26 in.) has checkered stock; weight with 32 in. barrel: 8.5 lbs. and 7.5 lbs. for carbine
**1873 Springfield "Trapdoor"** . . . $895
**Officer's Model** . . . . . . . . . . . $1050

## 1874 SHARPS LIGHTWEIGHT HUNTER

**Action:** dropping block
**Stock:** walnut
**Barrel:** 30 in.
**Sights:** ajustable
**Weight:** 10.0lbs.
**Caliber:** .45-70
**Magazine:** none
**Features:** case-colored receiver, drilled for tang sights; also 1874 Sharps Silhouette Hunter in .40-65 or .45-70
**Hunter** . . . . . . . . . . . . . . . . . $925
**Silhouette** . . . . . . . . . . . . . . . $1025

## KODIAK DOUBLE RIFLE

**Action:** hinged breech
**Stock:** walnut
**Barrel:** 24 in.
**Sights:** open, folding leaf
**Weight:** 10.0lbs.
**Caliber:** .45-70
**Magazine:** none
**Features:** double-barrel rifle with exposed hammers
**Kodiak Double Rifle** . . . . . . . . $2500

# Ed Brown Rifles

BUSHVELD

DENALI

M40A2 MARINE SNIPER

DAMARA

## BUSHVELD
**Action:** bolt
**Stock:** McMillan composite
**Barrel:** medium to heavy 24 in.
**Sights:** open
**Weight:** 8.5
**Caliber:** .338 Win., .375 H&H, .416 Rem., .458 Win. Mag.
**Magazine:** deep box, 4 rounds
**Features:** lapped barrel, 3 position safety, steel bottom metal, Talley scope mounts with 8-40 screws; optional QD scope rights, barrel-mounted swivel
**Bushveld:** . . . . . . . . . . . . . . . $2995

## DENALI
**Action:** bolt
**Stock:** McMillan composite
**Barrel:** 22 or 23 in.
**Sights:** none
**Weight:** 6.8
**Caliber:** .22-250, .243, 6mm, .260, .270 WSM, 7mm WSM, 7mm/08, .308, .300 WSM
**Magazine:** box, 3 or 4 rounds
**Features:** Short action; lapped barrel, 3 position safety, steel bottom metal, Talley scope mounts with 8-40 screws. Also available: Long-action version in .25-06, .270, .280, .30-06, 7mm Rem. Mag.
**Denali:** . . . . . . . . . . . . . . . . . $2895

## MODEL 40A2 MARINE SNIPER
**Action:** bolt
**Stock:** McMillan composite tactical
**Barrel:** heavy match 24 in.
**Sights:** none
**Weight:** 9.3
**Caliber:** .308, .30-06
**Magazine:** box, 5 rounds
**Features:** lapped barrel, 3 position safety, steel bottom metal; available in left-hand
**Marine Sniper:** . . . . . . . . . . . $2995

## DAMARA
**Action:** bolt
**Stock:** McMillan composite
**Barrel:** #1.5, 22 in.
**Sights:** none
**Weight:** 6.1
**Caliber:** .22-250, .243, 6mm, .260, 7mm/08, .308, 270 WSM, 7mm WSM, .300 WSM
**Magazine:** box, 5 rounds (WSM: 3)
**Features:** lapped barrel, 3 position safety, steel bottom metal; Talley scope mounts with 8-40 screws
**Damara:** . . . . . . . . . . . . . . . $3100

# Ed Brown Rifles

SAVANNA

TARGET

LIGHT TARGET

VARMINT

## SAVANNAH
**Action:** bolt
**Stock:** McMillan composite
**Barrel:** #3 lightweight 24 in.
**Sights:** open
**Weight:** 8.0
**Caliber:** .223, .22-250, .243, 6mm, .260, .270 WSM, 7mm/08, 7mm WSM, .308, .300 WSM
**Magazine:** box, 3 or 5 rounds
**Features:** short action; lapped barrel, 3 position safety, steel bottom metal; long-action model in .25-06, .270, .280, 7mm Rem. Mag., 7STW, .30-06, .300 Win. Mag., .300 Wby. Mag., .338 Win. Mag. with 26 in. #4 barrel in magnums, 8.5 lbs.
**Savannah:** . . . . . . . . . . . . . . . . $2895

## TARGET
**Action:** bolt
**Stock:** McMillan composite tactical
**Barrel:** heavy 26 in.
**Sights:** none
**Weight:** 11.3
**Caliber:** .308, .300 Win. Mag., .338 Lapua
**Magazine:** box, 3 or 5 rounds
**Features:** Jewell trigger; Talley scope mounts with 8-40 screws. Also available: Lightweight Tactical with sporter stock, 21 in. medium barrel, 8.8 lbs., in .223 and .308
**Target:** . . . . . . . . . . . . . . . . $2995
**Light Target:** . . . . . . . . . . . . . $2895

## VARMINT
**Action:** bolt
**Stock:** McMillan composite varmint
**Barrel:** medium 24 in. or heavy 24 in.
**Sights:** none
**Weight:** 9.0
**Caliber:** .223, .22-250, .220 Swift, .243, 6mm, .308
**Magazine:** none
**Features:** lapped barrel, 3 position safety, steel bottom metal; optional 2 oz. trigger
**Varmint:** . . . . . . . . . . . . . . . $2895

RIFLES

# EMF Replica Rifles

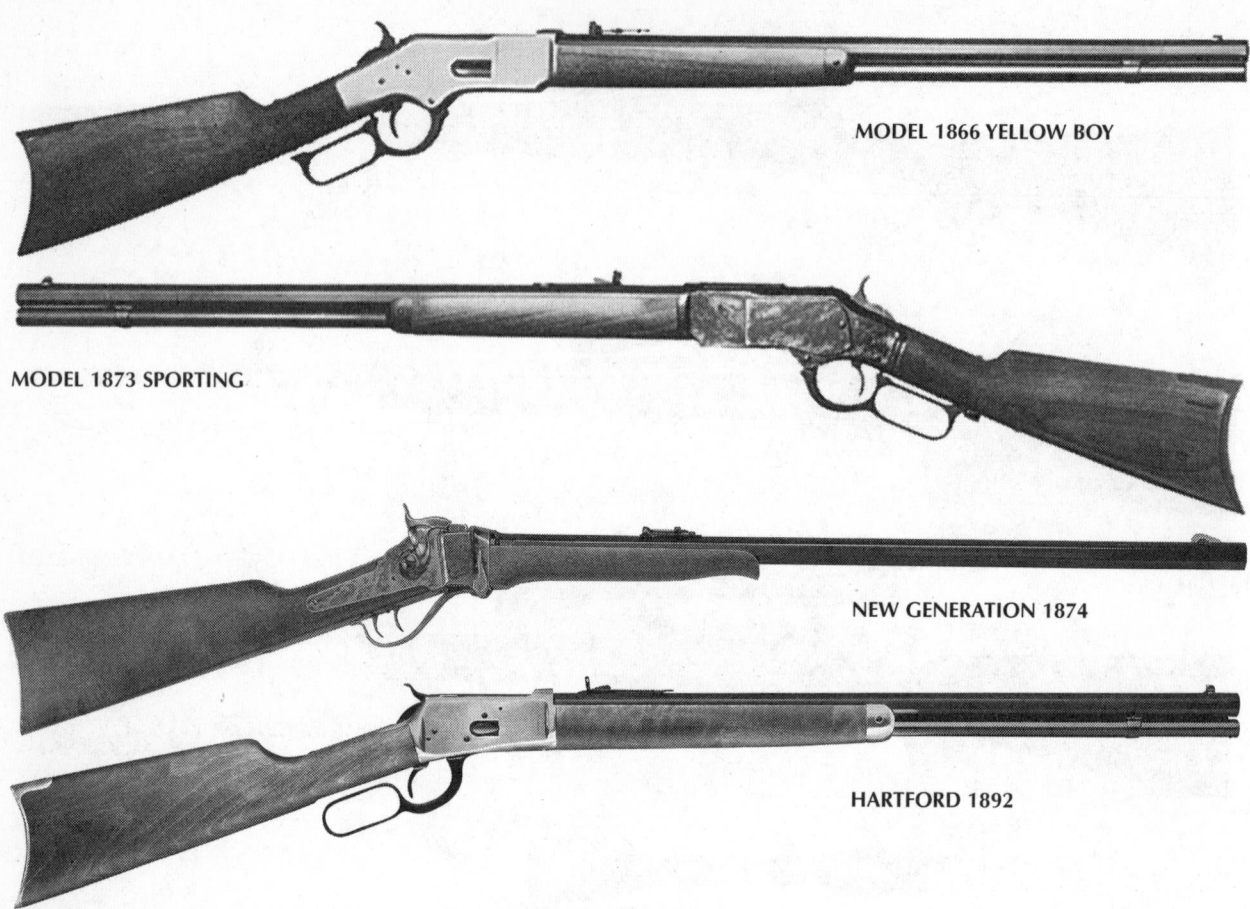

MODEL 1866 YELLOW BOY

MODEL 1873 SPORTING

NEW GENERATION 1874

HARTFORD 1892

## MODEL 1860 HENRY
*Action:* lever
*Stock:* walnut
*Barrel:* 24 in.
*Sights:* open
*Weight:* 9.3
*Caliber:* .44-40 and .45 LC
*Magazine:* under-barrel tube, 11 rounds
*Features:* blued barrel, brass frame
1860 Henry:. . . . . . . . . . . . . $1045

## MODEL 1866 YELLOW BOY
*Action:* lever
*Stock:* walnut
*Barrel:* 24 in.
*Sights:* open
*Weight:* 8.0
*Caliber:* .45 LC, .38 Special and .44-40
*Magazine:* under-barrel tube, 11 rounds
*Features:* blued barrel, brass frame
Yellow Boy: . . . . . . . . . . . . . . $850
carbine:. . . . . . . . . . . . . . . . . $850
white barrel: . . . . . . . . . . . . . $875

## MODEL 1873 SPORTING
*Action:* lever
*Stock:* walnut
*Barrel:* octagon 24 in.
*Sights:* open
*Weight:* 8.1
*Caliber:* .32-20, .357, .38-40, .44-40, .45 LC; carbine: .32-30, .357, .45LC
*Magazine:* under-barrel tube, 11 rounds
*Features:* Magazine tube in blued steel; frame is casehardened; carbine has 20 in. barrel
standard: . . . . . . . . . . . . . . . . $985
carbine:. . . . . . . . . . . . . . . . . $985

## HARTFORD 1892
*Action:* lever
*Stock:* walnut
*Barrel:* octagon or round 24 in.
*Sights:* open
*Weight:* 7.5
*Caliber:* .357 and .45 LC
*Magazine:* under-barrel tube, 11 rounds
*Features:* blued, casehardened or stainless steel; carine has 20 in. barrel
blued: . . . . . . . . . . . . . . . . . . $440

case-hardened:. . . . . . . . . . . . $430
stainless: . . . . . . . . . . . . . . . . $465
Carbine, blued, round barrel: . . $370
Carbine, case-hardened, round barrel: . . . . . . . . . . . . $370
Carbine, stainless, round barrel:. . $400

## NEW GENERATION 1874 SHARPS
*Action:* dropping block
*Stock:* walnut
*Barrel:* octagon 28 in.
*Sights:* open
*Weight:* 9.0
*Caliber:* .45-70
*Magazine:* none
*Features:* Created by Christian Sharps, this rifle played a major role in the Civil War. Single shot, double-set triggers, Schnabel forearm, barrel in blue, white or brown patina.
1874 Sharps: . . . . . . . . . . . . . $875
  with brown patina: . . . . . . . $900
  with white patina:. . . . . . . . $960
Carbine model: . . . . . . . . . . . $750

RIFLES

# European American Armory Rifles

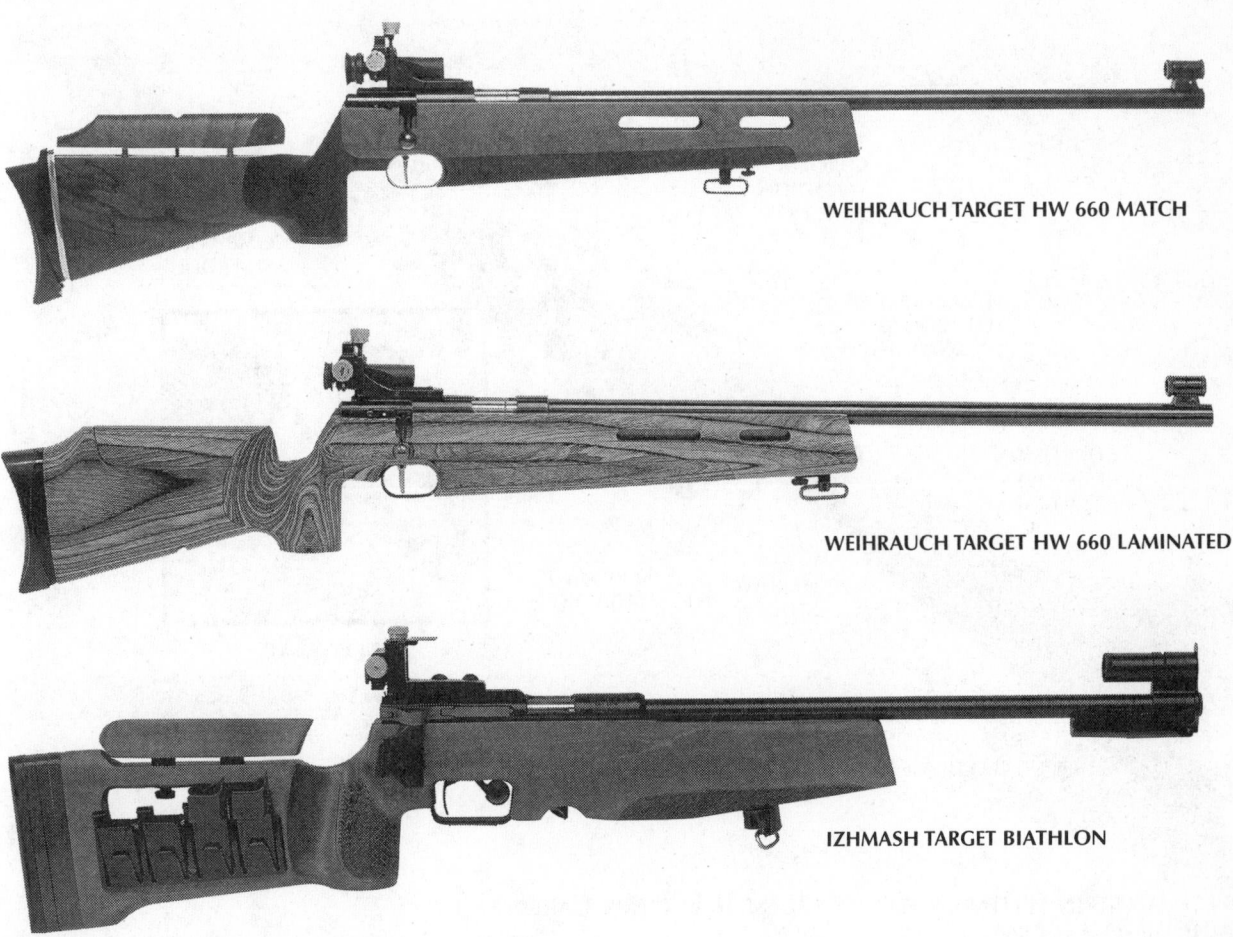

WEIHRAUCH TARGET HW 660 MATCH

WEIHRAUCH TARGET HW 660 LAMINATED

IZHMASH TARGET BIATHLON

## WEIHRAUCH HW660 TARGET
*Action:* bolt
*Stock:* walnut or laminated
*Barrel:* target-weight 26 in.
*Sights:* Anschutz
*Weight:* 10.7 lbs..
*Caliber:* .22 LR
*Magazine:* none
*Features:* match-grade barrel, stock with adjustable butt, comb; front rail with accessories
HW 660. . . . . . . . . . . . . . . . .$999
laminated. . . . . . . . . . . . . . .$1159

## IZHMASH BIATHLON
*Action:* bolt
*Stock:* walnut
*Barrel:* Target-weight, 19.5 in.
*Sights:* adjustable
*Weight:* 8.5 lbs.
*Caliber:* .22 LR
*Magazine:* none
*Features:* Match-grade barrel, adjustable butt, comb, front rail with accessories
Price:. . . . . . . . . . . . . . . . . .$999

RIFLES

# Gibbs Rifle Company

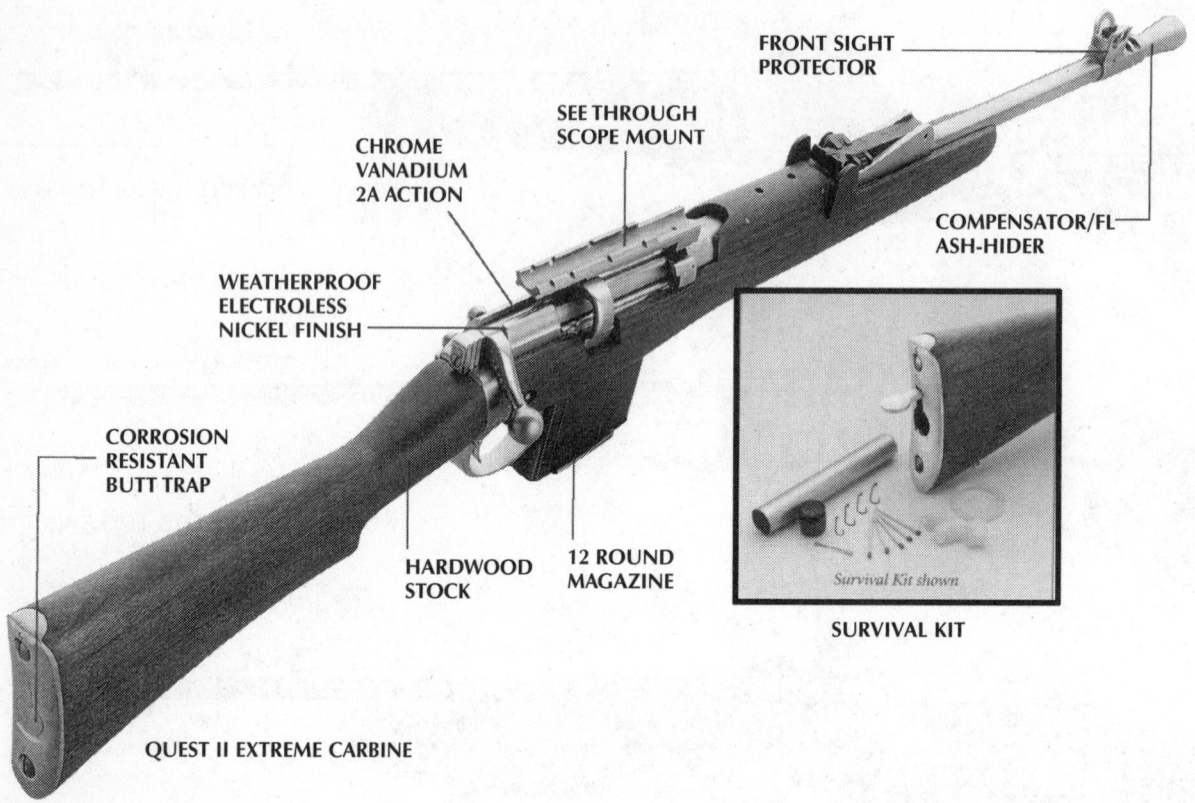

FRONT SIGHT
PROTECTOR

SEE THROUGH
SCOPE MOUNT

CHROME
VANADIUM
2A ACTION

COMPENSATOR/FL-
ASH-HIDER

WEATHERPROOF
ELECTROLESS
NICKEL FINISH

CORROSION
RESISTANT
BUTT TRAP

HARDWOOD
STOCK

12 ROUND
MAGAZINE

*Survival Kit shown*

SURVIVAL KIT

**QUEST II EXTREME CARBINE**

**SPECIALIZING IN MILITARY RIFLES**
reconfigured for sporting use, the
Gibbs Rifle Company offers the Quest
II Extreme Carbine. The Quest II is
built around on a modern barreled
action of Chrome Vanadium steel,
chambered for the popular, powerful
.308 Winchester. An electroless nickel
finish protects against the elements.
The barrel is fitted with a compen-
sator/flash-hider that tames recoil and
reduces muzzle jump. See-through
scope mount allows open sights to be
used and accepts Weaver-based optics
and accessories. The butt trap houses a
waterproof survival kit with Brunton
liquid-filled compass.

## QUEST II EXTREME CARBINE

**Action:** bolt
**Stock:** walnut
**Barrel:** 19 in. with flash-hider
**Sights:** open
**Weight:** 7.0
**Caliber:** .308
**Magazine:** detachable box, 10 rounds
**Features:** British SMLE design; pre-fitted
scope mount for Weaver rings; trap
buttplate with survival kit
**Quest II:** . . . . . . . . . . . . . . . . . $280
**Quest (.303 British)** . . . . . . . . $250

*Before taking a shot, inhale deeply, then let your
lungs relax. A surge of oxygen improves your vision
and sight picture; but if you hold your breath, you
tense up and pulse becomes a problem.*

RIFLES

# Harrington & Richardson Rifles

BUFFALO CLASSIC

ULTRA HUNTER

## BUFFALO CLASSIC
*Action:* hinged breech
*Stock:* checkered walnut
*Barrel:* 28 and 32 in.
*Sights:* target
*Weight:* 8.0
*Caliber:* .45-70 and .38-55 Target
*Magazine:* none
*Features:* single-shot, break-open
action; steel buttplate; Williams
receiver sight; Lyman target front sight;
antique color case-hardened frame
**standard or target:** . . . . . . . . . **$425**

## ULTRA
*Action:* hinged breech
*Stock:* hand-checkered, laminate
*Barrel:* 22, 24, and 26 in.
*Sights:* none
*Weight:* 7.0
*Caliber:* .22 WMR, .223 Rem. and
.243 (Varmint), .25-06, .30-06, .270,
.308 Win., .450 Marlin
*Magazine:* none
*Features:* Single-shot with break-open
action and side lever release. Monte
Carlo stock with sling swivels on stock

and forend; scope mount included.
Weight varies to 8 lbs. with bull bar-
rel. Also available: Ultra Comp with
camo stock in .30-06 and .270
**Ultra:** . . . . . . . . . . . . . . . . . . . **$338**
**Ultra in .22 WMR:** . . . . . . . . . **$197**

# Heckler & Koch Rifles

SL8-1 RIFLE

## MODEL SL8-1
## .223 RIFLE
*Action:* autoloading
*Stock:* polycarbonate, combat-style
*Barrel:* 21 in.

*Sights:* open
*Weight:* 8.5
*Caliber:* .223
*Magazine:* detachable box, 10 rounds
*Features:* Picatinny rail for scope

mounts; ambidextrous safety and bolt
cocking lever; clear polymer magazine; gas operated
**SL8-1:** . . . . . . . . . . . . . . . . . . **$1249**

RIFLES

# Heckler & Koch Rifles

SLB 2000

USC CARBINE

## SLB 2000
**Action:** autoloading
**Stock:** polycarbonate sporter-style
**Barrel:** 22 in.
**Sights:** open
**Weight:** 8.0
**Caliber:** .308, .30-06,
**Magazine:** detachable box, 5 rounds

*Features:* gas operated
**SLB 2000:** . . . . . . . . . . . . . . . $1299

## USC .45 ACP CARBINE
**Action:** autoloading
**Stock:** polycarbonate, combat-style
**Barrel:** 16 in. hammer-forged
**Sights:** open

**Weight:** 6.0
**Caliber:** .45 ACP
**Magazine:** detachable box, 10 rounds
**Features:** Picatinny rail for scope mounting; ambidextrous safety; oversized trigger guard; blow-back action
**Carbine:**. . . . . . . . . . . . . . . . $1249

# Henry Repeating Arms Rifles

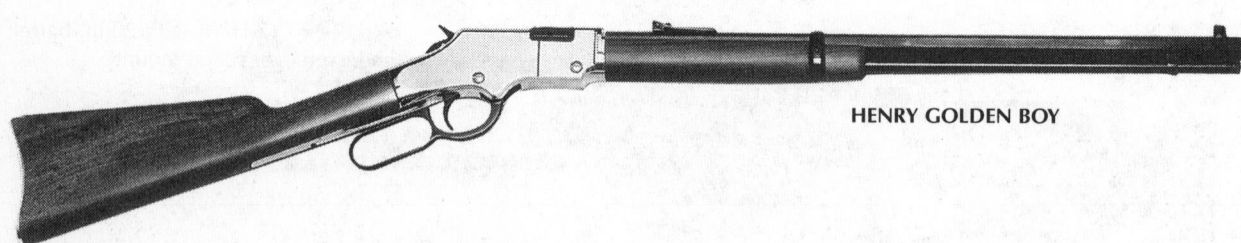

HENRY GOLDEN BOY

## HENRY GOLDEN BOY
**Action:** lever
**Stock:** walnut, straight-grip
**Barrel:** octagon 20 in.
**Sights:** open
**Weight:** 6.8
**Caliber:** .22 S, .22 L, .22 LR, .22 WMR, .17 HMR

**Magazine:** under-barrel tube, 16 to 22 rounds
**Features:** brass receiver and buttplate per Winchester 66
**Golden Boy:**. . . . . . . . . . . . . . $400

RIFLES

# Henry Repeating Arms Rifles

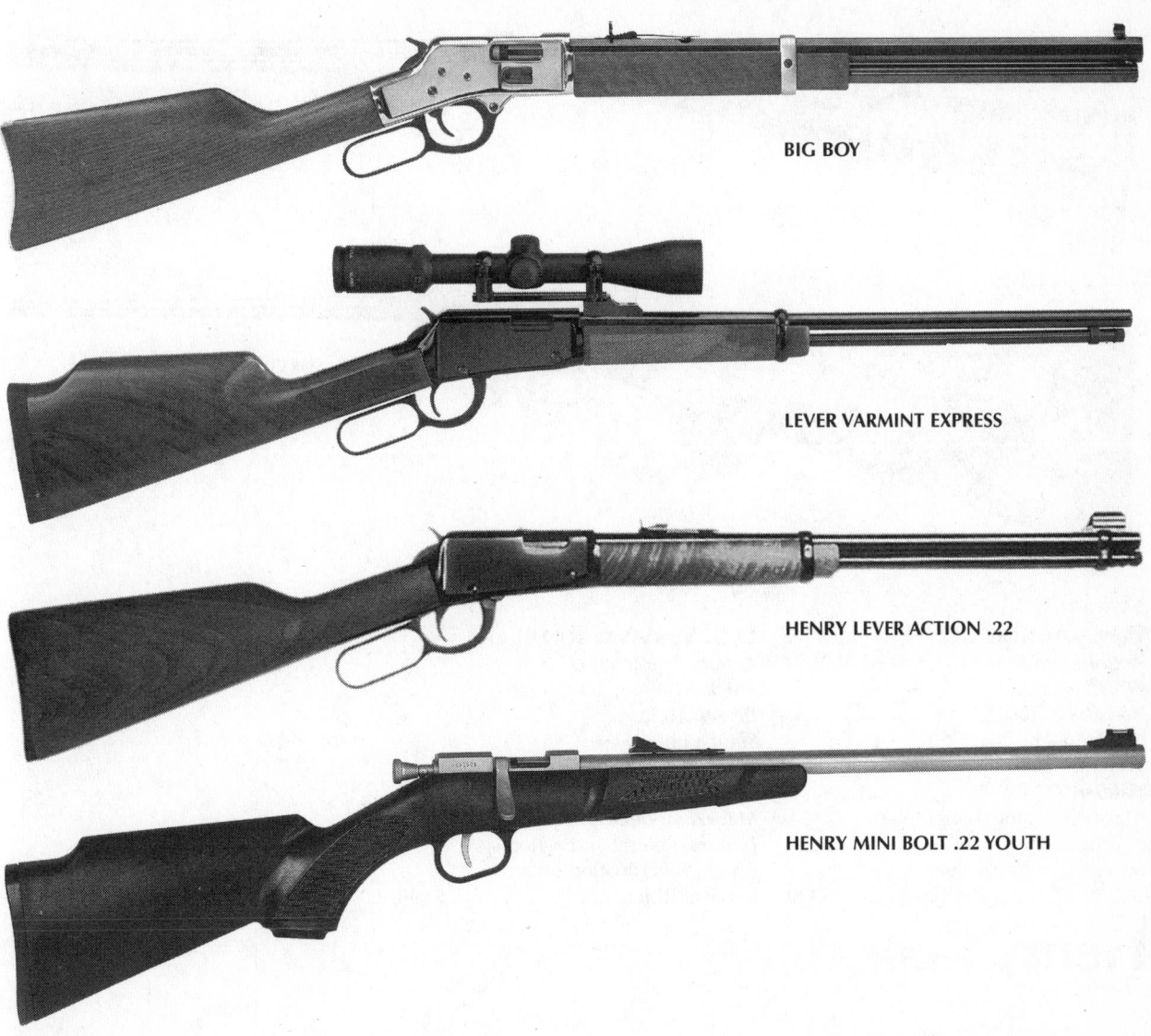

BIG BOY

LEVER VARMINT EXPRESS

HENRY LEVER ACTION .22

HENRY MINI BOLT .22 YOUTH

## MODEL BIG BOY
*Action:* lever
*Stock:* walnut
*Barrel:* 20 in. octagon
*Sights:* open
*Weight:* 8.7lbs.
*Caliber:* .44 Magnum, .45 LC
*Magazine:* 10
*Features:* brass receiver, barrel band, buttplate
**Big Boy** . . . . . . . . . . . . . . . . . **$750**

## MODEL LEVER VARMINT EXPRESS
*Action:* lever
*Stock:* walnut
*Barrel:* 20 in.
*Sights:* none
*Weight:* 5.8lbs.

*Caliber:* .17 HMR
*Magazine:* 11
*Features:* Monte Carlo stock; scope mount included
**Varmint Express** . . . . . . . . . . . **$460**

## HENRY LEVER ACTION .22
*Action:* lever
*Stock:* American walnut
*Barrel:* 18 in.
*Sights:* open
*Weight:* 5.5
*Caliber:* .22 S, .22 L, .22 LR
*Magazine:* under-barrel tube, 15 to 21 rounds
*Features:* also available: carbine and youth model, .22 WMR with checkered stock, 19 in. barrel; Varmint

Express in .17 HMR with 20 in. barrel and cantilever scope mount
**rifle, carbine or youth:** . . . . . . . **$260**
**magnum:** . . . . . . . . . . . . . . . . **$380**
**Varmint Express:** . . . . . . . . . . . **$475**

## MINI BOLT .22 YOUTH
*Action:* bolt
*Stock:* synthetic
*Barrel:* stainless 16 in.
*Sights:* illuminated
*Weight:* 3.3
*Caliber:* .22 S, .22 L, .22 LR
*Magazine:* none
*Features:* single-shot; designed for beginners
**Mini Bolt:** . . . . . . . . . . . . . . . . **$200**

# Henry Repeating Arms Rifles

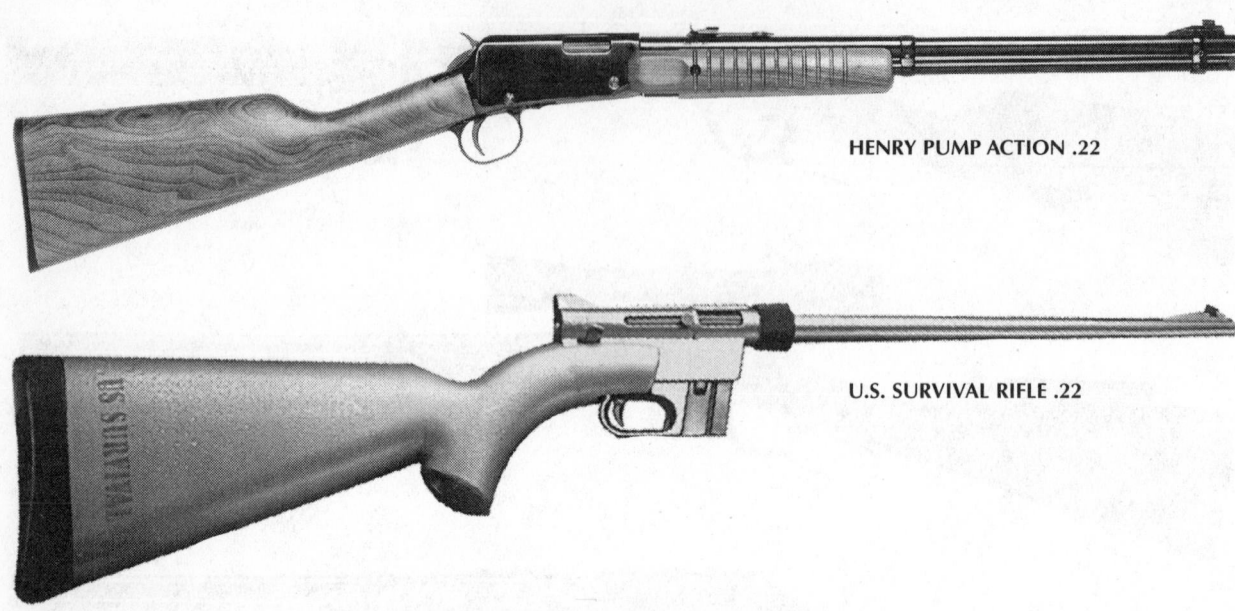

HENRY PUMP ACTION .22

U.S. SURVIVAL RIFLE .22

## PUMP-ACTION .22
*Action:* pump
*Stock:* walnut
*Barrel:* 18 in.
*Sights:* open
*Weight:* 5.5
*Caliber:* .22 LR
*Magazine:* under-barrel tube, 15 rounds
*Features:* alloy receiver
.22: . . . . . . . . . . . . . . . . . . . . . $300

## U.S. SURVIVAL RIFLE
*Action:* Autoloading
*Stock:* synthetic butt stock
*Barrel:* 16 in.
*Sights:* open
*Weight:* 4.5
*Caliber:* .22 LR
*Magazine:* detachable box, 8 rounds
*Features:* barrel and action stow in water-proof, floating stock
Survival Rifle:. . . . . . . . . . . . . $190

# HOWA Rifles

HOWA M-1500 LIGHTNING-BLUE FINISH

## MODEL 1500 LIGHTNING
*Action:* bolt
*Stock:* Black Polymer with cheekpiece
*Barrel:* 22 in.
*Sights:* none
*Weight:* 7.6 lbs.

*Caliber:* Popular standard and magnum calibers from .223 Rem. to.300 WSM
*Magazine:* box, 5 rounds
*Features:* choice of blue or stainless; 22 in. (standard) or 24 in. (magnum) barrels; checkered grips and foreend;

barreled actions are available
blue finish standard: . . . . . . . . $488
   magnum: . . . . . . . . . . . . . . . $511
stainless standard: . . . . . . . . . . $595
   magnum: . . . . . . . . . . . . . . . $625

# HOWA Rifles

HOWA M-1500 HUNTER-STAINLESS STEEL

HOWA 1500 SUPREME JRS CLASSIC

HOWA 1500 THUMBHOLE VARMINTER

HOWA M-1500 ULTRALIGHT

## HOWA M-1500 SUPREME SERIES
*Action:* bolt
*Stock:* laminated or black matte
*Barrel:* 22 or 24 in.
*Sights:* none
*Weight:* 7.6lbs.
*Caliber:* .223, .25-06, .22-250, .243, 6.5x55, .270, .308, .30-06, 7mm Rem. Mag., .300 Win. Mag., .338 Win. Mag., .270 WSM, 7mm WSM, .300 WSM
*Magazine:* 5 or 3
*Features:* stainless or blue, nutmeg or pepper stock; also: Hunter rifles with walnut stock
**Blue, JRS stock . . . . . . . . . . . . $625**
**Stainless, JRS stock . . . . . . . . . $730**
**Magnum, blue, JRS stock . . . . . $655**
**Magnum, stainless, JRS stock . . $760**
**Also available in thumbhole stock:**
**. . . . . . . . . . . . . . . . . . . add $50**

## HOWA 1500 THUMBHOLE VARMINTER
*Action:* bolt
*Stock:* laminated
*Barrel:* heavy 22 in.
*Sights:* none
*Weight:* 9.9lbs.
*Caliber:* .223, .22-250, .308
*Magazine:* 5
*Features:* nutmeg, pepper or black

stock color, blued or stainless; also: new Sporter thumbhole version (7.6 lbs.) in 13 calibers including WSMs
**blue . . . . . . . . . . . . . . . . . . . . . $710**
**stainless . . . . . . . . . . . . . . . . . $805**
**blued sporter . . . . . . . . . . . . . $690**
**stainless Sporter . . . . . . . . . . . $790**

## MODEL 1500 HUNTER
*Action:* bolt
*Stock:* American black walnut with cheekpiece
*Barrel:* 22 in.
*Sights:* none
*Weight:* 7.6 lbs.
*Caliber:* popular standard and magnum calibers from .223 Rem. to.300 WSM
*Magazine:* box, 5 rounds
*Features:* choice of blue or stainless; 22 in. (standard) or 24 in. (magnum) barrels; varmint model in .223, .22-50 and .308; checkered grips and foreend.
**blue finish standard: . . . . . . . . $548**
**     magnum: . . . . . . . . . . . . . . $571**
**stainless: standard: . . . . . . . . . $595**
**     magnum: . . . . . . . . . . . . . . $676**

## MODEL 1500 VARMINT
*Action:* bolt
*Stock:* Black Polymer or American walnut

*Barrel:* 22 in.
*Sights:* none
*Weight:* 9.3 lbs.
*Caliber:* .223, .22-50 and .308
*Magazine:* box, 5 rounds
*Features:* choice of blue or stainless; 24 in. barrels; wood stocks with weather-resistant finish and laser-stippled grip and forearm panels
**blue finish black polymer:. . . . . $525**
**     walnut:. . . . . . . . . . . . . . . . $585**
**stainless black polymer: . . . . . . $640**
**     walnut:. . . . . . . . . . . . . . . . $690**

## MODEL 1500 ULTRALIGHT
*Action:* bolt
*Stock:* Black texture wood
*Barrel:* 20 inches
*Sights:* none
*Weight:* 6.4 lbs.
*Caliber:* .243 Win., .308, 7mm-08
*Magazine:* box, 5 rounds
*Features:* mill-cut lightweight receiver; wood stock with textured flat black finish, blue finish; Youth model available
**Ultralight "Mountain Rifle": . . . $520**
**Stainless (.308 only): . . . . . . . . $634**

*All Howa Rifles imported by Legacy Sports International, Alexandria VA*

RIFLES

# H-S Precision Rifles

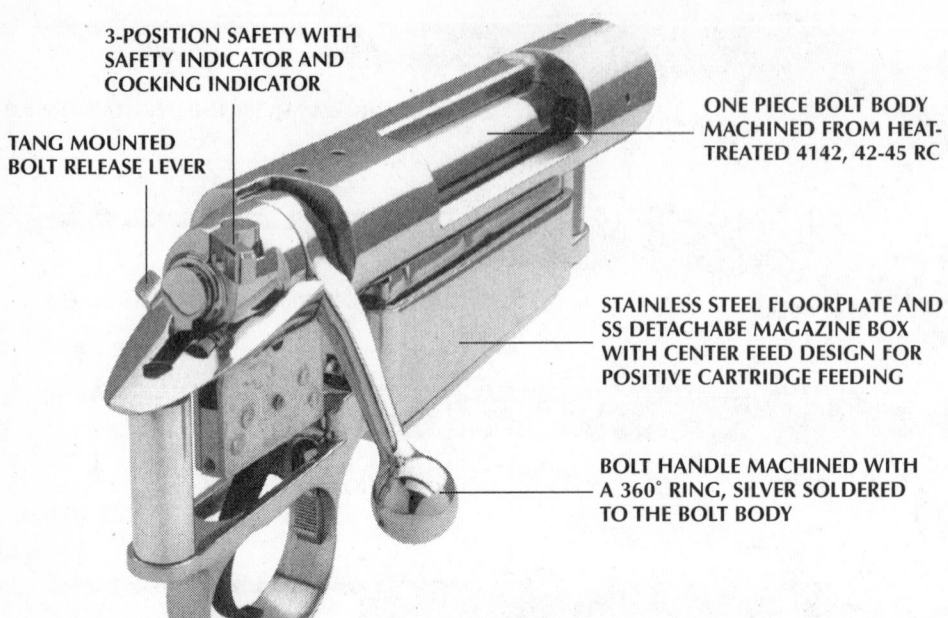

**3-POSITION SAFETY WITH SAFETY INDICATOR AND COCKING INDICATOR**

**TANG MOUNTED BOLT RELEASE LEVER**

**ONE PIECE BOLT BODY MACHINED FROM HEAT-TREATED 4142, 42-45 RC**

**STAINLESS STEEL FLOORPLATE AND SS DETACHABE MAGAZINE BOX WITH CENTER FEED DESIGN FOR POSITIVE CARTRIDGE FEEDING**

**BOLT HANDLE MACHINED WITH A 360° RING, SILVER SOLDERED TO THE BOLT BODY**

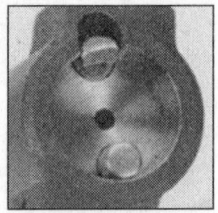

**HARDENED STEEL-TIPPED FIRING PIN WITH SPEED LOCK SPRING**

**RATHER THAN GET A JOB** in 1978, Tom Houghton started a gun company. His degree in chemistry wasn't much help, but Tom had vision. "I hoped a few shooters would pay a premium for exceptionally accurate rifles." H-S tapped quickly into the tactical and varmint-shooting market and now manufactures big game rifles as well. H-S offers a broad array of synthetic gunstocks, and barrels that have won the allegiance not only of competitive shooters, but ballistics laboratories. "We're the world's leading supplier of pressure, velocity and accuracy test barrels," says Tom proudly. H-S Precision also offers ballistic test equipment, including universal receivers, return-to-battery assemblies, and a laser aiming system. You can get an H-S muzzle brake and scope rings, and after-market bottom metal for your Remington 700.

H-S Precision's plant in Rapid City, South Dakota is a showplace of cleanliness and efficiency. The focus: quality and attention to tolerances. H-S barrels are all cut rifled in 416R stainless steel and so accurate that all Pro-Series 2000 rifles up to 30-caliber come with a half-minute accuracy guarantee. Most other firms cringe at the thought of any accuracy pledge. It means using the best barrels and ensuring close-tolerance, on-axis assembly of bolt, receiver and barrel. It means bedding the stock securely in a channel that won't shift. "In short, it means doing what we do to give the customer superior accuracy," says Tom's daughter, Tricia Hoeke.

The Pro Series 2000, chambered in .223 (1-in-12 twist) routinely drills out dime-size groups. It is built around a stainless action with a two-lug bolt. The bolt handle is silver-soldered to a one-piece bolt body. Its semi-cone head incorporates a face-mounted extractor. A barrel with .0002 uniformity from breech to muzzle is part of the accuracy formula (H-S 10x barrels are given a slight radius at the juncture of land and groove as an additional gas seal). Another ingredient is a rigid H-S fiberglass, Kevlar and carbon fiber stock. "H-S is not really a custom shop," Tricia says, "and we're leaning more and more to producing stock rifles, including those for military and government use." She adds that H-S still accommodates special orders.

RIFLES

# H-S Precision Rifles

PHR (PROFESSIONAL HUNTER RIFLE)

VTD (VARMINT TAKE-DOWN SYSTEM)

VAR (VARMINT RIFLE)

## PHR
### (PROFESSIONAL HUNTER RIFLE)
*Action:* bolt
*Stock:* composite
*Barrel:* 24 to 26 in.
*Sights:* none
*Weight:* 8.0
*Caliber:* all popular magnum calibers up to .375 H&H and .338 Lapua
*Magazine:* detachable box, 3 rounds
*Features:* Pro series 2000 action: full-length bedding block, optional 10x Model with match-grade stainless, fluted barrel, muzzle brake, built-in recoil reducer; Lightweight SPR rifle is chambered in standard calibers
**PHR:** . . . . . . . . . . . . . . . . . . .$2200
**SPR:**. . . . . . . . . . . . . . . . . . . .$1950

## TAKE-DOWN RIFLES
*Action:* bolt
*Stock:* 2-piece composite
*Barrel:* any contour and weight 22 to 26 in.
*Sights:* none
*Weight:* 8.0
*Caliber:* any popular standard or magnum chambering
*Magazine:* detachable box, 3 or 4 rounds
*Features:* rifle disassembles in front of action and reassembles to deliver identical point of impact; price includes carrying case, TD versions with sporter or tactical stocks; customer's choice of barrels and chambering; left-hand model: add $200
**Take-Down:** . . . . . . . . . . . . . .$3600

## VAR (VARMINT )
*Action:* bolt
*Stock:* composite
*Barrel:* heavy 24 in.
*Sights:* none
*Weight:* 11.0
*Caliber:* all popular varmint calibers
*Magazine:* detachable box, 4 rounds
*Features:* Pro-series 2000 action; full-length bedding block; also 10x version with fluted, stainless barrel, optional muzzle
**VAR:** . . . . . . . . . . . . . . . . . . . .$1975
**HTR (heavy tactical):** . . . . . . .$2100

# Jarrett Custom Rifles

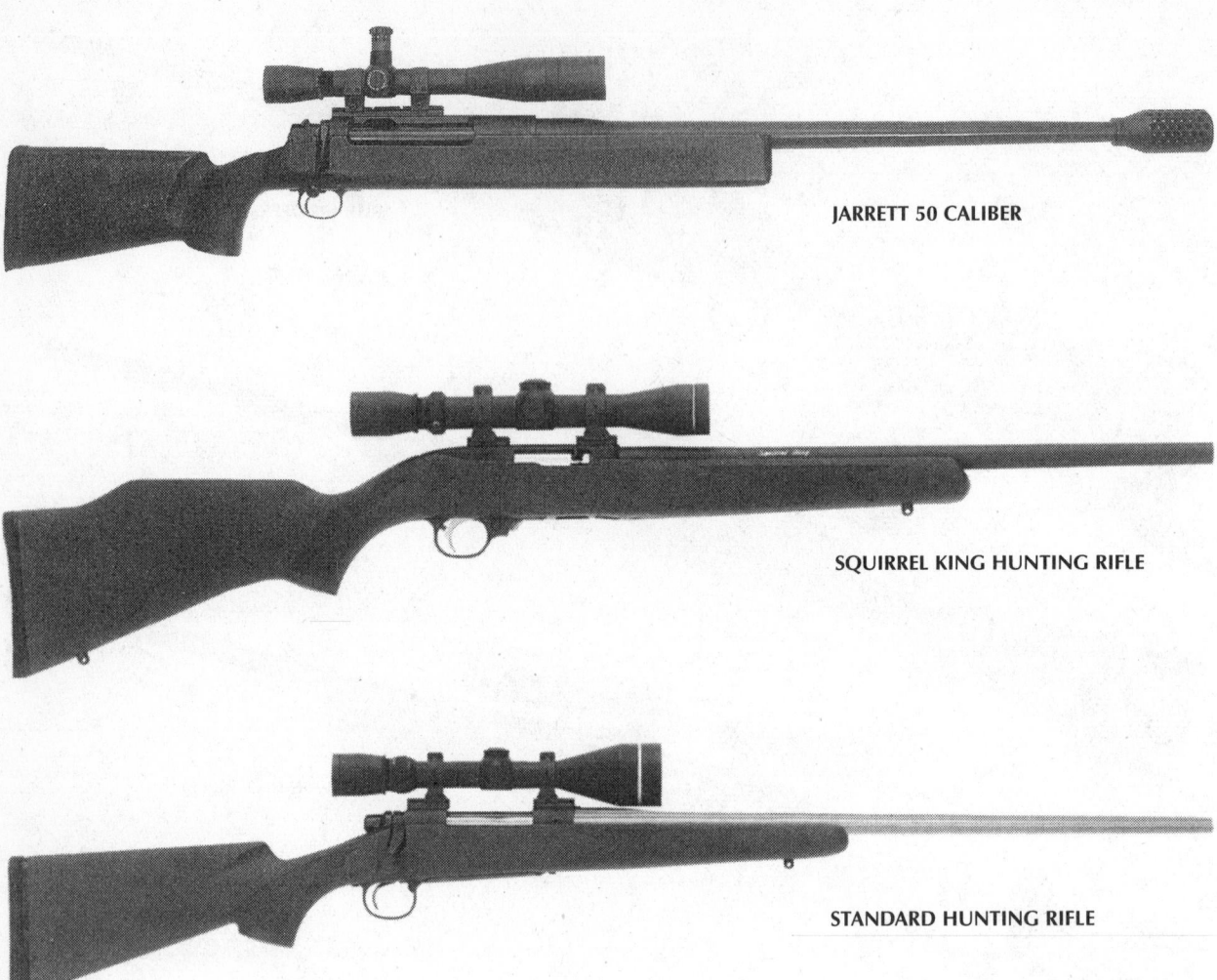

JARRETT 50 CALIBER

SQUIRREL KING HUNTING RIFLE

STANDARD HUNTING RIFLE

### .50 CALIBER
*Action:* bolt
*Stock:* McMillan composite
*Barrel:* 30 to 34 in.
*Sights:* none
*Weight:* 35.0
*Caliber:* .50 BMG
*Magazine:* none
*Features:* single-shot; choice of barrel length and contours; rifle comes with load data and 20 rounds of ammunition, military scope mounts and muzzle brake; repeater available
**Single shot:** . . . . . . . . . . . . . $8050
**Repeater:** . . . . . . . . . . . . . . . $8350

### SQUIRREL KING
*Action:* autoloading
*Stock:* Brown Precision composite
*Barrel:* match grade 18 in.
*Sights:* none
*Weight:* 6.0
*Caliber:* .22 LR
*Magazine:* rotary, 10 rounds
*Features:* built on Ruger 10/22 action; target and hunting configurations available; Talley rings and bases included; guaranteed ½" groups at 50 yards
**Hunting model:** . . . . . . . . . . . $2150
**Target model:** . . . . . . . . . . . . $2400

### STANDARD HUNTING RIFLE
*Action:* bolt
*Stock:* McMillan synthetic
*Barrel:* #4 match grade, 24 in.
*Sights:* none
*Weight:* 8.5
*Caliber:* any popular standard or magnum
*Magazine:* box, 3 or 5 rounds
*Features:* Shilen trigger; Remington 700 or Winchester 70 action; Talley scope mounts, case, sling, load data and 20 rounds of ammunition; Wind Walker has skeletonized 700 action (7.3 lbs.), muzzle brake. Professional Hunter rifle has additional options
**Standard:** . . . . . . . . . . . . . . . $4625
**Wind Walker:** . . . . . . . . . . . . . $5300
**Professional Hunter:** . . . . . . . . $5300

# Jarrett Custom Rifles

**WALKABOUT**

**PROFESSIONAL HUNTER**

**SERIES RIFLE**

### WALK ABOUT
*Action:* bolt
*Stock:* synthetic
*Barrel:* 20 in.
*Sights:* none
*Weight:* 7.5
*Caliber:* any popular short-action
*Magazine:* box, 3 or 5 rounds
*Features:* Remington Model 700 short action; includes Talley scope mounts, choice of scope plus case, sling, load data and 20 rounds of ammunition
**Walk About:** . . . . . . . . . . . . . $4625

### PROFESSIONAL HUNTER
*Action:* bolt
*Stock:* synthetic
*Barrel:* 24 in.
*Sights:* open
*Weight:* 9.0lbs.
*Caliber:* any popular standard or wildcat chambering
*Magazine:* 5 or 3
*Features:* muzzle brake, also, two Leupold 1.5-5x scopes zeroed in Talley QD rings
**Professional Hunter:** . . . . . . . $8040

### SERIES RIFLE
*Action:* bolt
*Stock:* synthetic
*Barrel:* 24 in.
*Sights:* none
*Weight:* 9.0
*Caliber:* any popular standard or wildcat chambering
*Magazine:* 5 or 3
*Features:* muzzle brake, phenolic metal finish in color of your choice, Swarovski or similar scope included; all features most often specified on orders
**Series Rifle:** . . . . . . . . . . . . . $5025

# Johannsen Express Rifles

**TRADITION**

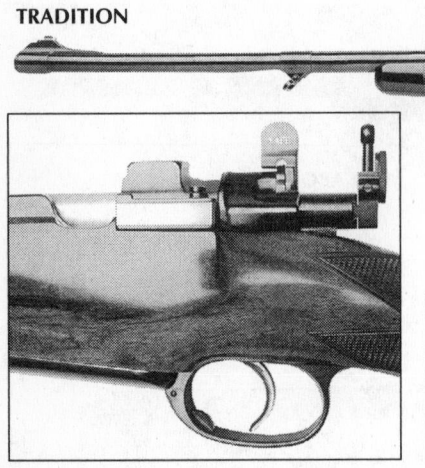

### WING SAFETY

The "Classic Safari" features a wing safety with "safe" and "fire" clearly indicated in gold.

### PEEP SIGHT

For precision sighting with open sights - or to compensate for less than perfect vision - the peep sight mounted on the cocking piece can be raised into position.

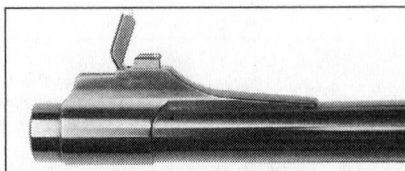

### HOLLAND & HOLLAND-TYPE NIGHT SIGHT

The "Classic Safari" and "Safari" models come with a 4-mm ivory bead that can be flipped up to cover the 2-mm silver bead under poor light conditions.

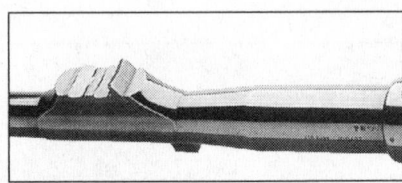

### EXPRESS SIGHT

The rear sight with its two leaves fits into a special ring base. The rear sight base extends around the barrel and has the second recoil shoulder on the underside, which is important for large-bore rifles.

| SAFARI MAGAZINE CAPACITIES, MAXIMUM: | NORMAL Caliber | RIGBY Floorplate | Floorplate |
|---|---|---|---|
| | .300 Weatherby Magnum | 4 | 5 |
| | .338-378 Weatherby Magnum | 3 | 4 |
| | .375 H & H Magnum | 4 | 5 |
| | .416 Rigby | 3 | 4 |
| | .450 Dakota | 3 | 4 |
| | .500 Jeffery | 3 | 4 |
| | Other calibers upon request. | | |

**THREE MODELS** of this rifle are available - the "Classic Safari", the "Safari" and the "Tradition". The "Classic Safari", is the choice of hunters after African big game. The "Safari" is designed for scope use as well. The "Tradition" is ideal for the globe-trotting big-game hunter. All models are available in several chamberings with standard and custom features, and each rifle is produced individually. A Johannsen Express Rifle represents true custom work.

### SAFARI

Double square bridge action without thumbcut. 4-lb. double-pull trigger. Three-position safety with horizontal lever. Bolt handle close to side of action. Especially suitable for EXPERT scope mount. 2-mm silver bead combined with fold-away 4-mm Holland & Holland-type ivory bead. Express sight with two leaves. Safari-style stock with 1¾"/2½" drop. Oil finish. 26" barrel. Length overall 47". Weight from approx. 8 lbs. 6 oz. depending upon caliber. Standard calibers: .375 H & H Magnum, 4-shot, or .416 Rigby, 3-shot.
**Price:** . . . . . . . . . . . . . . . . $10,250

### CLASSIC SAFARI

Single square bridge action with thumbcut. 4-lb. double-pull trigger. Three-position wing safety. Traditional bolt handle. 2-mm silver bead combined with a fold-away 4-mm Holland & Holland-type ivory bead. Express sight with two leaves. Safari-style stock with 1¾"/2½" drop. Oil finish. 24" barrel. Length overall 45". Weight from approx. 8 lbs. 3 oz. depending upon caliber. Standard calibers: .375 H & H Magnum, 4-shot, or .416 Rigby. 3-shot.
**Price:** . . . . . . . . . . . . . . . . 9,500

### TRADITION

Double square bridge action without thumbcut. Adjustable-pull single-set trigger. Three-position safety with horizontal lever. Low bolt handle. Especially suitable for EXPERT scope mount. "Masterpiece" front sight base with 2.5-mm fluorescent bead. Express sight with two leaves. Stock with straight comb and 1¾"/2" drop. Oil finish. 26" barrel. Length overall 47". Weight from approx. 8 lbs. depending upon caliber. Standard calibers: .300 Weatherby Magnum, 4-shot, .375 H & H Magnum, 4-shot.
**Price:** . . . . . . . . . . . . . . . . 10,550

RIFLES

# Kimber Rifles

MODEL 84M CLASSIC

**CONCEIVED IN OREGON** by Jack Warne in 1979, Kimber is a relative late-comer to firearms manufacture. This company introduced the high-quality Model 82 rimfire sporting rifle in the 1980s. Nearly as petite was a follow-up rifle: the Model 84, designed for the .17 Rem. and the .222s and .223. The Model 89, a Winchester M70 in profile, chambered standard hunting cartridges like the .30-06. When bankruptcy in 1989 left Kimber's future in doubt, original owners Jack and Gregg Warne bought some of the machinery and retained use of the Kimber name (from Jack's native Australia). By 1992 a revamped .22, the 82C, had appeared.

Les Edelman emerged from the bankruptcy proceedings as majority stakeholder in a new gun company. In 1995, handgun sports were becoming more popular, and many people were concerned with the effect of stricter regulations on the availability of handguns. Les Edelman thought there'd be a market for high-quality pistols based on the 1911 Colt. He enlisted both the reputation and expertise of ace pistol shooter Chip McCormick, bought a factory in Yonkers and began turning out pistols, projecting a run of 5000. His projection proved conservative; now the Kimber plant makes 44,000 Model 1911-style pistols annually, more than its closest seven competitors combined.

It's no wonder that some shooters think of pistols when the Kimber name comes up. But Les and his company, now assisted by Montana rifle enthusiasts Dwight Van Brunt and Ryan Busse, diversified in 1998, introducing a svelte .22 caliber rifle designed by Nehemiah Sirkis. The new rifle, called the Kimber 22, looked like the 82 but has a side-swing safety like the Winchester Model 70. At about the same time, Kimber got a centerfire rifle design to the prototype stage. The Model 770, designed by Jack Warne and Pete Grisel, never made it to market, but now there's an 84M, also designed by Sirkis. Initially bored for the .243, .260, 7mm-08 and .308 (as well as the .22-250), it weighs 5½ pounds with a 22-inch barrel and classic-style walnut stock designed by Darwin Hensley. The stock is trim, with conservative lines. It is glassed and pillar-bedded to the action. The barrel floats and a 1-inch Pachmayr decelerator pad is standard.

This Kimber lightweight has an adjustable match-grade trigger and match-grade barrel. There's a Mauser-style extractor, steel bottom metal (a floorplate with release button in the guard) and a steel grip cap – refinements you see on best-quality custom rifles. It is to Kimber's credit that it retained these features in a rifle scaling 5½ pounds. The three-position wing safety looks like a Model 70's. Kimber offers its own steel scope bases for the rifle. They're satin-blued to match and can be used on the Kimber 22, because hole spacings and receiver diameters are the same.

The latest Kimber big game rifle, the 8400, carries the lines of the 84M into magnum territory. Chambered for Winchester Short Magnum cartridges, it has the refinements of its forebears with more muscle. The magazine box holds three, but the third fits tightly, so closing the bolt without chambering that top round is problematic. One of the most elegant and portable short magnum rifles around, the 8400 comes in three configurations.

## MODEL 84M CLASSIC

**Action:** bolt
**Stock:** checkered, Claro walnut
**Barrel:** light sporter, 22 in.
**Sights:** none
**Weight:** 5.6
**Caliber:** .243, .260, 7mm-08, .308
**Magazine:** box, 5 rounds
**Features:** also Varmint model (7.4 lbs.) in .22-250 with 26 in. stainless, fluted barrel; Long Master Classic (7.4 lbs) in .308 with 24 in. stainless, fluted barrel and Long Master VT (10 lbs.) in .22-250 with stainless, bull barrel, laminated target stock

| | |
|---|---|
| Classic: | $917 |
| Varmint : | $1001 |
| Long Master Classic: | $1001 |
| Long Master VT: | $1122 |

RIFLES

# Kimber Rifles

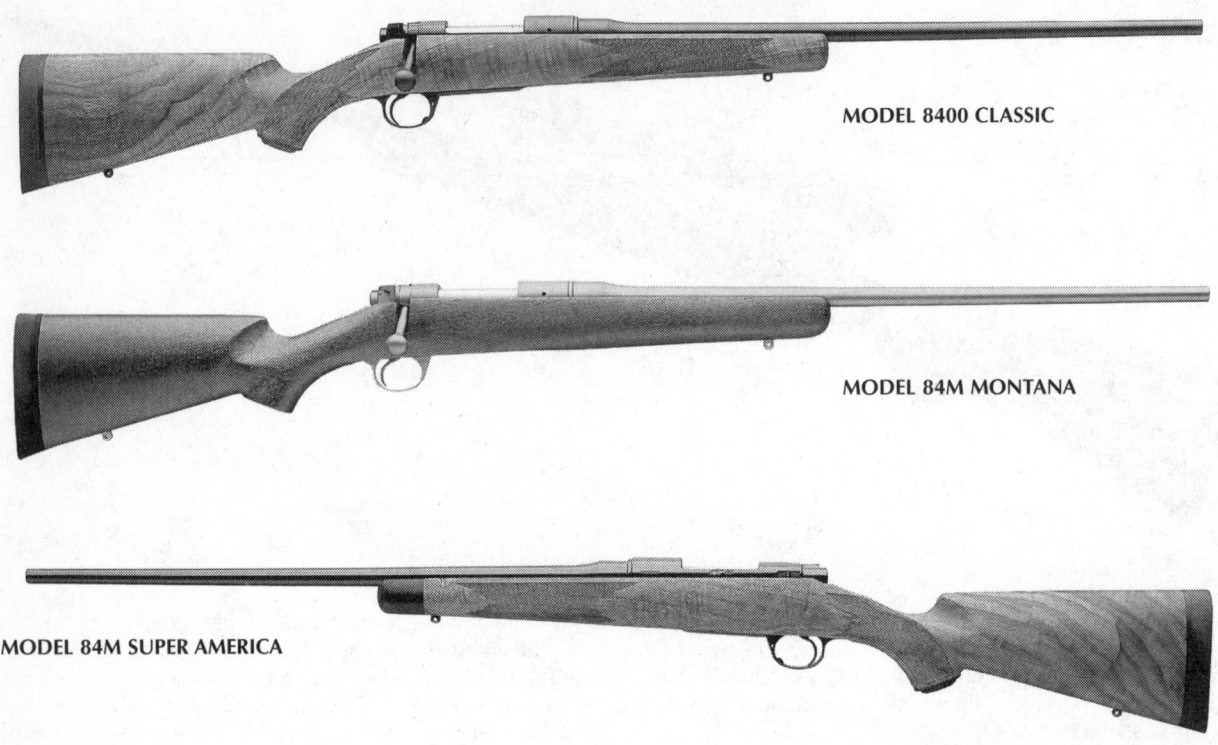

MODEL 8400 CLASSIC

MODEL 84M MONTANA

MODEL 84M SUPER AMERICA

### MODEL 8400 CLASSIC
**Action:** bolt
**Stock:** walnut
**Barrel:** 24 in.
**Sights:** none
**Weight:** 6.6lbs.
**Caliber:** .270, 7mm and .300 WSM
**Magazine:** 3
**Features:** 3-position safety
8400 Classic. . . . . . . . . . . . . $1030
8400 Montana, WSMs . . . . . . $1178
8400 Super America. . . . . . . . $1952

### MODEL 84M MONTANA
**Action:** bolt
**Stock:** synthetic
**Barrel:** 22 in.
**Sights:** none
**Weight:** 5.3 lbs..
**Caliber:** .308, .243, .260, 7mm-08
**Magazine:** 5
**Features:** stainless steel
84M Montana, standard calibers
. . . . . . . . . . . . . . . . . . . . . $1086

### MODEL 84M SUPER AMERICA
**Action:** bolt
**Stock:** AAA walnut
**Barrel:** 22 in.
**Sights:** none
**Weight:** 5.3 lbs.
**Caliber:** .308, .243, .260, 7mm-08
**Magazine:** 5
**Features:** wrap checkering on select wood
84M Super America . . . . . . . . $1764

*When shooting, keep your head erect, and the buttplate high on your shoulder so that you look directly into the sight. You see best when looking straight ahead, not from the corner of your eye.*

RIFLES

# Kimber Rifles

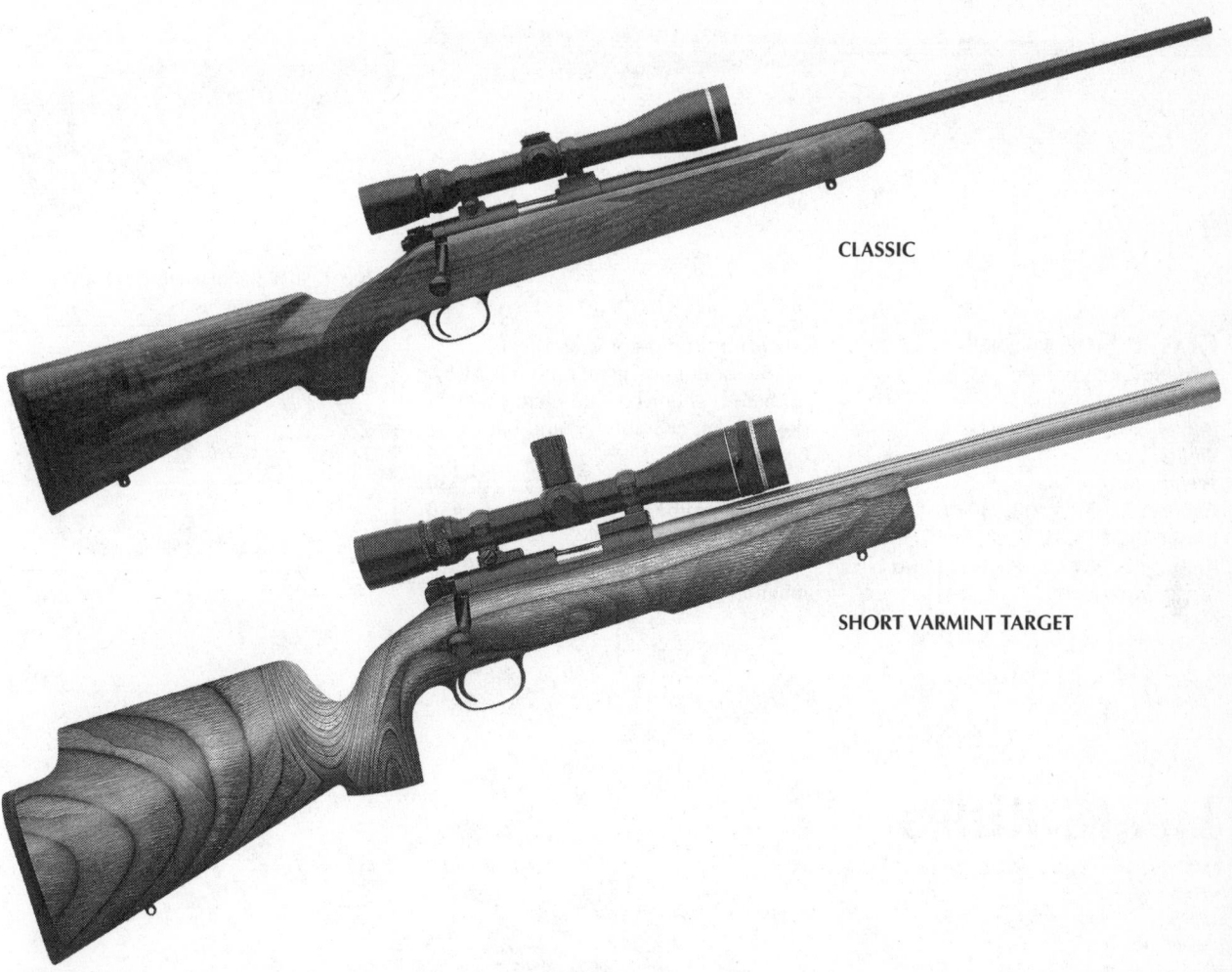

CLASSIC

SHORT VARMINT TARGET

## CLASSIC
**Action:** bolt
**Stock:** checkered, AA walnut
**Barrel:** 22 in. match grade
**Sights:** none
**Weight:** 6.5
**Caliber:** .22 LR
**Magazine:** detachable box, 5 rounds
**Features:** Model 70-type safety; bead blasted finish; deluxe checkering, hand-rubbed finish; 50-yard groups less than .4 in.; also available: no-frills Hunter model; Super America with fancy AA walnut stock with wrap-around checkering
**Classic:** . . . . . . . . . . . . . . . . $1107
**Hunter:** . . . . . . . . . . . . . . . . . $788
**Super America:** . . . . . . . . . . $1800

## HS (HUNTER SILHOUETTE)
**Action:** bolt
**Stock:** high-comb walnut
**Barrel:** medium-heavy, half-fluted 24 in.
**Sights:** none
**Weight:** 7.0
**Caliber:** .22 LR
**Magazine:** detachable box, 5 rounds
**Features:** designed for NRA rimfire silhouette competition
**HS:** . . . . . . . . . . . . . . . . . . . . $883

## SVT (SHORT VARMINT TARGET)
**Action:** bolt
**Stock:** heavy, competition style Laminate
**Barrel:** extra heavy, fluted, stainless 18.25 in.
**Sights:** none
**Weight:** 7.5
**Caliber:** .22 LR
**Magazine:** detachable box, 5 rounds
**Features:** bead-blasted blue; gray laminated stock
**SVT:** . . . . . . . . . . . . . . . . . . . . $949

RIFLES

# Krieghoff Rifles

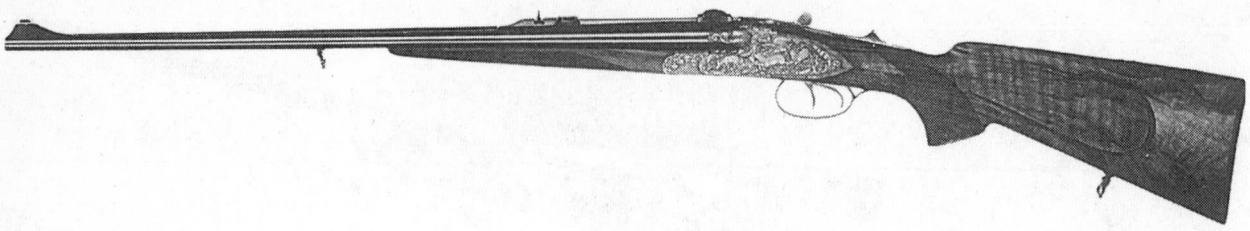

CLASSIC SIDE-BY-SIDE DOUBLE RIFLE

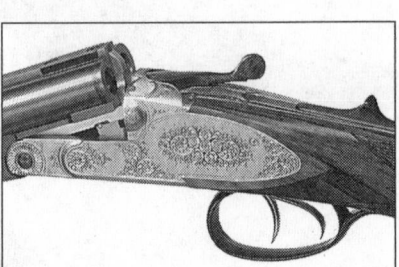

## CLASSIC SIDE-BY-SIDE
**Action:** hinged breech
**Stock:** select walnut
**Barrel:** 23.5 in.
**Sights:** open
**Weight:** 8.0
**Caliber:** 7x65R, .308, .30-06, .30R Blaser, 8x57, 9.3x74, .375 H&H, .416 Rigby, .458 Win., .470 N.E., .500 N.E.
**Magazine:** none

**Features:** thumb-cocking, break-action; double triggers; optional 21.5 in. barrel; engraved side plates; weight depends on chambering and barrel contour

standard calibers:. . . . . . . . . . $7850
magnum calibers:. . . . . . . . . . $9450
extra barrels with
   forearm (fitted): . . . . . . . . . $4500
magnum barrels:. . . . . . . . . . $5500

# L.A.R. Rifles

GRIZZLY BIG BOAR

## GRIZZLY BIG BOAR
**Action:** bolt
**Stock:** all steel sleeve with rubber butt pad
**Barrel:** 36 in.
**Sights:** none
**Weight:** 30.4
**Caliber:** .50 BMG

**Magazine:** none
**Features:** Bull Pup single-shot; descending pistol grip; bi-pod; finish options

Grizzly: . . . . . . . . . . . . . . . . $2195
Parkerized:. . . . . . . . . . . . . . $2395
nickel-frame: . . . . . . . . . . . . $2445
full nickel: . . . . . . . . . . . . . . $2545

RIFLES

# Lazzeroni Rifles

MODEL L2000DG

MODEL L2000SA

MODEL L2000SP

MODEL L2000ST

## MODEL L2000DG

*Action:* bolt
*Stock:* composite
*Barrel:* 24 in.
*Sights:* none
*Weight:* 8.0
*Caliber:* 10.57 (.416) Meteor
*Magazine:* box, 4 rounds
*Features:* matchgrade, stainless steel barrel; fully adjustable trigger, aluminum pillar block bedding; barrel mounted swivel stud
**L2000DG:** . . . . . . . . . . . . . . . $5500

## MODEL L2000SA

*Action:* bolt
*Stock:* composite
*Barrel:* 24 in.
*Sights:* none
*Weight:* 6.8
*Caliber:* 6.17 (.243) Spitfire, 6.71 (.264) Phantom, 7.21 (.284) Tomahawk, 7.82 (.308) Patriot, 8.59 (.338) Galaxy
*Magazine:* box, 4 rounds
*Features:* match-grade, stainless steel barrel, fully adjustable trigger; aluminum pillar block bedding; left-hand available.
**L2000SA:** . . . . . . . . . . . . . . . $5500

## MODEL L2000SP

*Action:* bolt
*Stock:* thumbhole (right hand only), composite
*Barrel:* 25 in.
*Sights:* none
*Weight:* 7.8
*Caliber:* 6.53 (.257) Scramjet, 7.21 (.284) Firebird, 7.82 (.308) Warbird, 8.59 (.338) Titan
*Magazine:* box, 4 round

*Features:* matchgrade, stainless steel barrel; fully adjustable trigger; aluminum pillar block bedding
**L2000SP:** . . . . . . . . . . . . . . . $5500

## MODEL L2000ST

*Action:* bolt
*Stock:* composite
*Barrel:* 27 in.
*Sights:* none
*Weight:* 8.1
*Caliber:* 6.53 (.257) Scramjet, 7.21(.284) Firebird, (.308) 7.82 Warbird, (.338) 8.59 Titan
*Magazine:* box, 4 rounds
*Features:* stainless steel matchgrade barrel; fully adjustable trigger; aluminum pillar block bedding; left-hand stock available
**L2000ST:** . . . . . . . . . . . . . . . $5499

RIFLES

# Lone Star Rifles

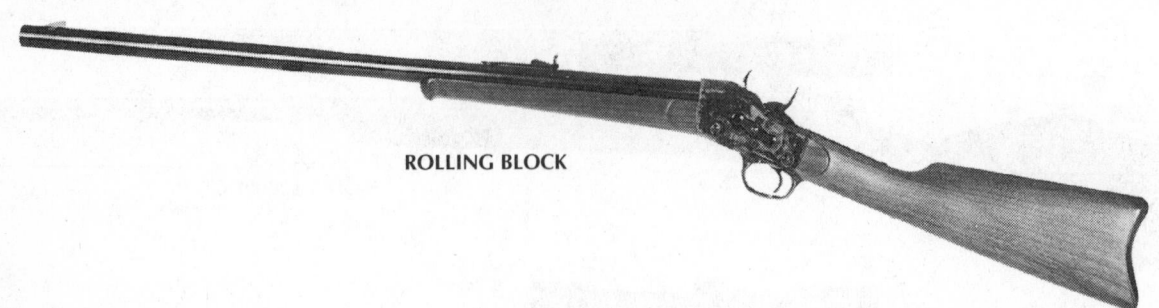

ROLLING BLOCK

## ROLLING BLOCK

**Action:** single shot
**Stock:** walnut
**Barrel:** 28 – 34 in.
**Sights:** many options
**Weight:** 6.0 to 16 lbs.
**Caliber:** .25, .20 WCF, .25-35, .30-30, .30-40, .32-20, .32-40, .38-50, .38-55, .40-50SS, .40-50SBN, .40-70SMB, .40-70SS, .40-82, .40-90SS, .45-70, .45-90, .45-100, .45-110, .45-120, .44-60, .44-77SBN, .44-90SBN, .44-100 Rem. Sp., .50-70, .50-90, .50-140
**Magazine:** none
**Features:** true-to-form replicas of post-Civil War Remington rolling blocks; single set or double set triggers, case-colored actions on Silhouette, Creedmoor, Sporting, Deluxe Sporting, Buffalo, Custer Commemorative, #5, #7
**standard:** . . . . . . . . . . . . . . . . $1595
**custom:** . . . . . . . . . . . . . . . . . $1995
**#7:** . . . . . . . . . . . . . . . . . . . . . $3500

# Magnum Research Rifles

BARRACUDA STOCK MAGNUM LITE

MOUNTAIN EAGLE SPORT BARREL

TACTICAL RIFLE

## MAGNUM LITE RIMFIRE

**Action:** autoloading
**Stock:** Hogue composite or Turner laminated
**Barrel:** graphite sleeved, 16.75 in.
**Sights:** none
**Weight:** 5.2
**Caliber:** .22LR and .22 WMR
**Magazine:** rotary, 9 rounds
**Features:** Ruger 10/22 action; carbon-fiber barrel with steel liner (75% lighter than steel); muzzle porting
**with composite stock:** . . . . . . . $599
**with laminated stock:** . . . . . . . . $799
**magnum with composite:** . . . . . $799
**magnum with laminated:** . . . . . $999

## MOUNTAIN EAGLE

**Action:** bolt
**Stock:** composite
**Barrel:** graphite, sleeved 24 or 26 in.
**Sights:** none
**Weight:** 7.8
**Caliber:** .280, .30-06, 7mm Rem. Mag., .300 Win. Mag., 7 WSM, .300 WSM
**Magazine:** box, 3 or 4 rounds
**Features:** adjustable trigger, free-floating match-grade barrel; platform bedding system; steel bottom metal; left-hand available
**Mountain Eagle:** . . . . . . . . . . . $2295
**Varmint model:** . . . . . . . . . . . $2295

## TACTICAL RIFLE

**Action:** bolt
**Stock:** H-S Precision, synthetic tactical
**Barrel:** graphite sleeved 26 in.
**Sights:** none
**Weight:** 8.3
**Caliber:** .223, .22-250, .300 WSM, .308, .300 Win. Mag.
**Magazine:** box, 3 or 5 rounds
**Features:** accurized Rem. 700 action; adjustable comb; adjustable trigger and length of pull
**Tactical:** . . . . . . . . . . . . . . . . $2400

# Marlin Rifles

MODEL 60

MODEL 70PSS "PAPOOSE"

MODEL 7000

MODEL 925M



RIFLES

## MODEL 60

*Action:* autoloading
*Stock:* hardwood
*Barrel:* 19 in.
*Sights:* open
*Weight:* 5.5lbs.
*Caliber:* .22 LR
*Magazine:* under-barrel tube, 14 rounds
*Features:* last shot hold-open device;
stainless, synthetic and laminated
stocked versions available; also avail-
able with camo-finished stock

standard. . . . . . . . . . . . . . . . . . $189
camo . . . . . . . . . . . . . . . . . . . . $224
stainless . . . . . . . . . . . . . . . . . . $240
stainless, synthetic . . . . . . . . . . $263
stainless, laminated two-tone . . $302

## MODEL 70 PSS PAPOOSE

*Action:* autoloading

*Stock:* synthetic
*Barrel:* 16 in.
*Sights:* open
*Weight:* 3.3lbs.
*Caliber:* .22 LR
*Magazine:* detachable box, 7 rounds
*Features:* take-down rifle; nickel-plated
swivel studs; floatable, padded carrying
case included

Papoose . . . . . . . . . . . . . . . . . $309

## MODEL 7000

*Action:* autoloading
*Stock:* synthetic
*Barrel:* target weight, 28 in.
*Sights:* none
*Weight:* 5.3lbs.
*Caliber:* .22 LR
*Magazine:* detachable box, 10 rounds
*Features:* also available as Model 795

and 795 SS, with sights and lighter
barrel (*Weight:* 4.5 lbs.)

7000 . . . . . . . . . . . . . . . . . . . . $255
795 . . . . . . . . . . . . . . . . . . . . . $163
795 SS . . . . . . . . . . . . . . . . . . . $240

## MODEL 925M

*Action:* bolt
*Stock:* hardwood
*Barrel:* 22 in.
*Sights:* open
*Weight:* 6.0lbs.
*Caliber:* .22 WMR
*Magazine:* detachable box, 7 rounds
*Features:* T-900 Fire Control System,
Micro-Groove barrel; also available
with Mossy Oak camo-finish stock

925M. . . . . . . . . . . . . . . . . . . . $247
925MC (camo) . . . . . . . . . . . . . $284

# Marlin Rifles

MODEL 925C CAMO

MODEL 981T

MODEL 983TS

MODEL 917VS

LITTLE BUCKAROO

## MODEL 925

*Action:* bolt
*Stock:* hardwood
*Barrel:* 22 in.
*Sights:* open
*Weight:* 5.5lbs.
*Caliber:* .22 LR
*Magazine:* detachable box, 7 rounds
*Features:* T-900 Fire Control System,
Micro-Groove rifling; can be ordered
with scope; also available with Mossy
Oak camo stock finish

925 . . . . . . . . . . . . . . . . . . . . . $216
925 with scope. . . . . . . . . . . . $224
925C (camo) . . . . . . . . . . . . . $253

## MODEL 981T

*Action:* bolt
*Stock:* synthetic
*Barrel:* 22 in.
*Sights:* open
*Weight:* 6.0lbs.
*Caliber:* .22 L, S, or LR
*Magazine:* under-barrel tube, 17 rounds

*Features:* Micro-Groove rifling, T-900
Fire Control System
918T . . . . . . . . . . . . . . . . . . $217

## MODEL 983T

*Action:* bolt
*Stock:* synthetic
*Barrel:* 22 in.
*Sights:* open
*Weight:* 6.0lbs.
*Caliber:* .22 WMR
*Magazine:* under-barrel tube, 12 rounds
*Features:* T-900 Fire Control System,
Micro-Groove rifling; available as
Model 983 with walnut stock or lami-
nated stock and stainless barrel

983T . . . . . . . . . . . . . . . . . . . $264
Model 983 . . . . . . . . . . . . . . . $344
Model 983TS . . . . . . . . . . . . . $365

## MODEL 917V

*Action:* bolt
*Stock:* hardwood
*Barrel:* heavy 22 in.

*Sights:* none
*Weight:* 6.0lbs.
*Caliber:* .17 HMR
*Magazine:* detachable box, 7 rounds
*Features:* T-900 Fire Control System,
1-in. scope mounts provided; also
available: 917VS stainless steel with
laminated hardwood stock (7 lbs.)

917V . . . . . . . . . . . . . . . . . . . $274
917VS . . . . . . . . . . . . . . . . . . $410

## LITTLE BUCKAROO

*Action:* bolt
*Stock:* hardwood
*Barrel:* 16 in.
*Sights:* open
*Weight:* 4.3lbs.
*Caliber:* .22 S, L or LR
*Magazine:* none
*Features:* T-900 Fire Control System;
stainless version available

Little Buckaroo (Model 915Y) . . $213
Stainless (Model 915YS) . . . . . . $239

RIFLES

# Marlin Rifles

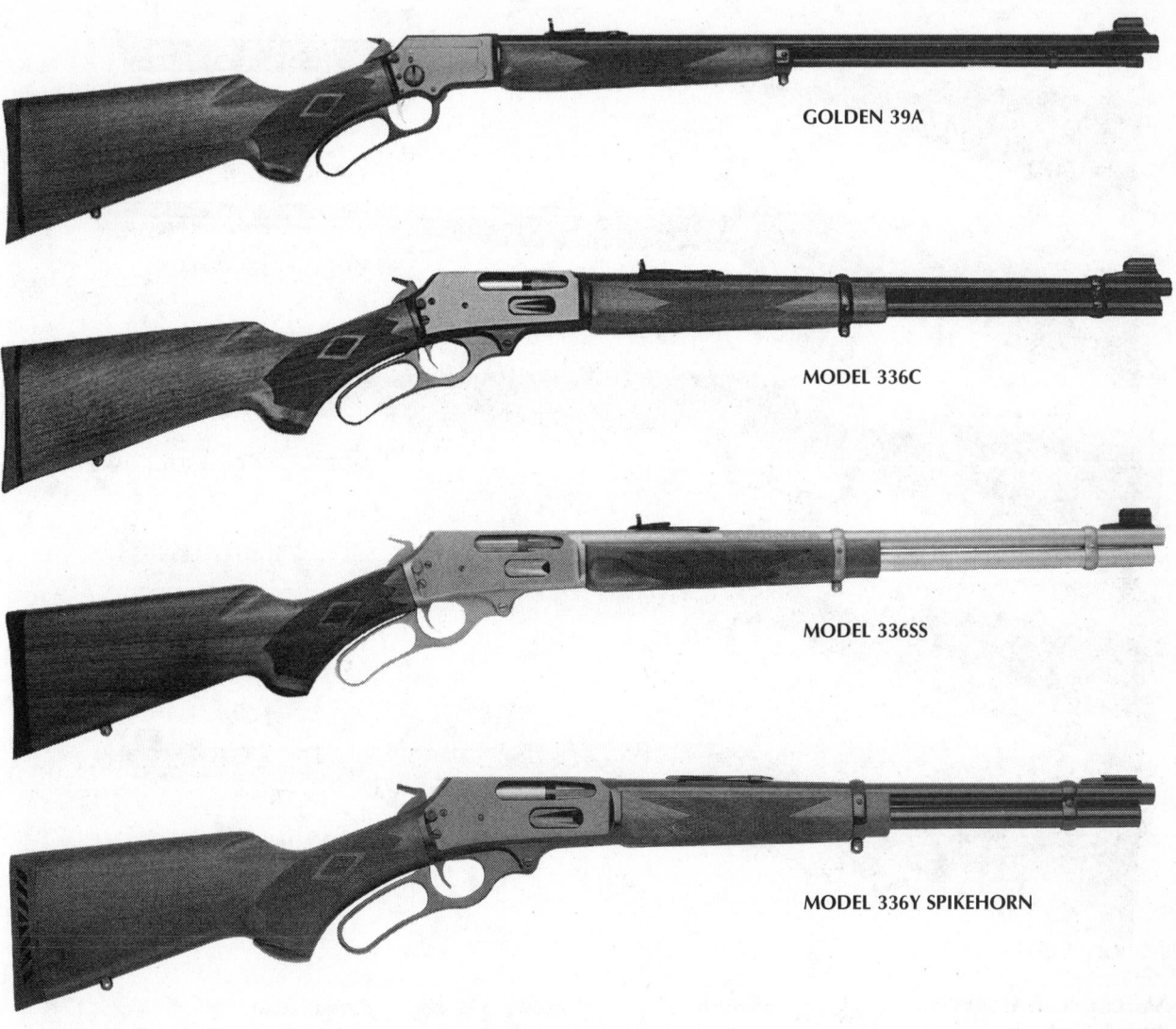

GOLDEN 39A

MODEL 336C

MODEL 336SS

MODEL 336Y SPIKEHORN

## GOLDEN 39A
**Action:** lever
**Stock:** checkered walnut, pistol grip
**Barrel:** 24 in.
**Sights:** open
**Weight:** 6.5lbs.
**Caliber:** .22 LR
**Magazine:** under-barrel tube, 19 rounds
**Features:** Micro-Groove rifling, single-screw take-down; swivel studs
**Golden 39A** . . . . . . . . . . . . . . **$563**

## MODEL 336C
**Action:** lever
**Stock:** checkered walnut, pistol grip
**Barrel:** 20 in.
**Sights:** open
**Weight:** 7.0lbs.

**Caliber:** .30-30 Win., and .35 Rem.
**Magazine:** tube, 6 rounds
**Features:** blued, hammer-block safety, offset hammer spur for scope use
**Model 336C** . . . . . . . . . . . . . . **$539**
**Model 336A, .30-30 only, birch stock** . . . . . . . . . . . . . . **$461**
**Model 336, .30-30 only, camo stock** . . . . . . . . . . . . . . **$503**
**Model 336W, .30-30 only, gold-plated** . . . . . . . . . . . . . . **$466**

## MODEL 336SS
**Action:** lever
**Stock:** checkered walnut, pistol grip
**Barrel:** 20 in.
**Sights:** open
**Weight:** 7.0lbs.
**Caliber:** .30-30

**Magazine:** under-barrel tube, 6 rounds
**Features:** offset hammer spur for scope use; Micro-Groove rifling
**336SS** . . . . . . . . . . . . . . . . . . **$654**

## MODEL 336Y SPIKEHORN
**Action:** lever
**Stock:** walnut
**Barrel:** 16.5 in.
**Sights:** open
**Weight:** 6.5lbs.
**Caliber:** .30-30
**Magazine:** 5
**Features:** pistol grip stock; 12.5-inch pull for small shooters
**336Y Spikehorn** . . . . . . . . . . . **$547**

# Marlin Rifles

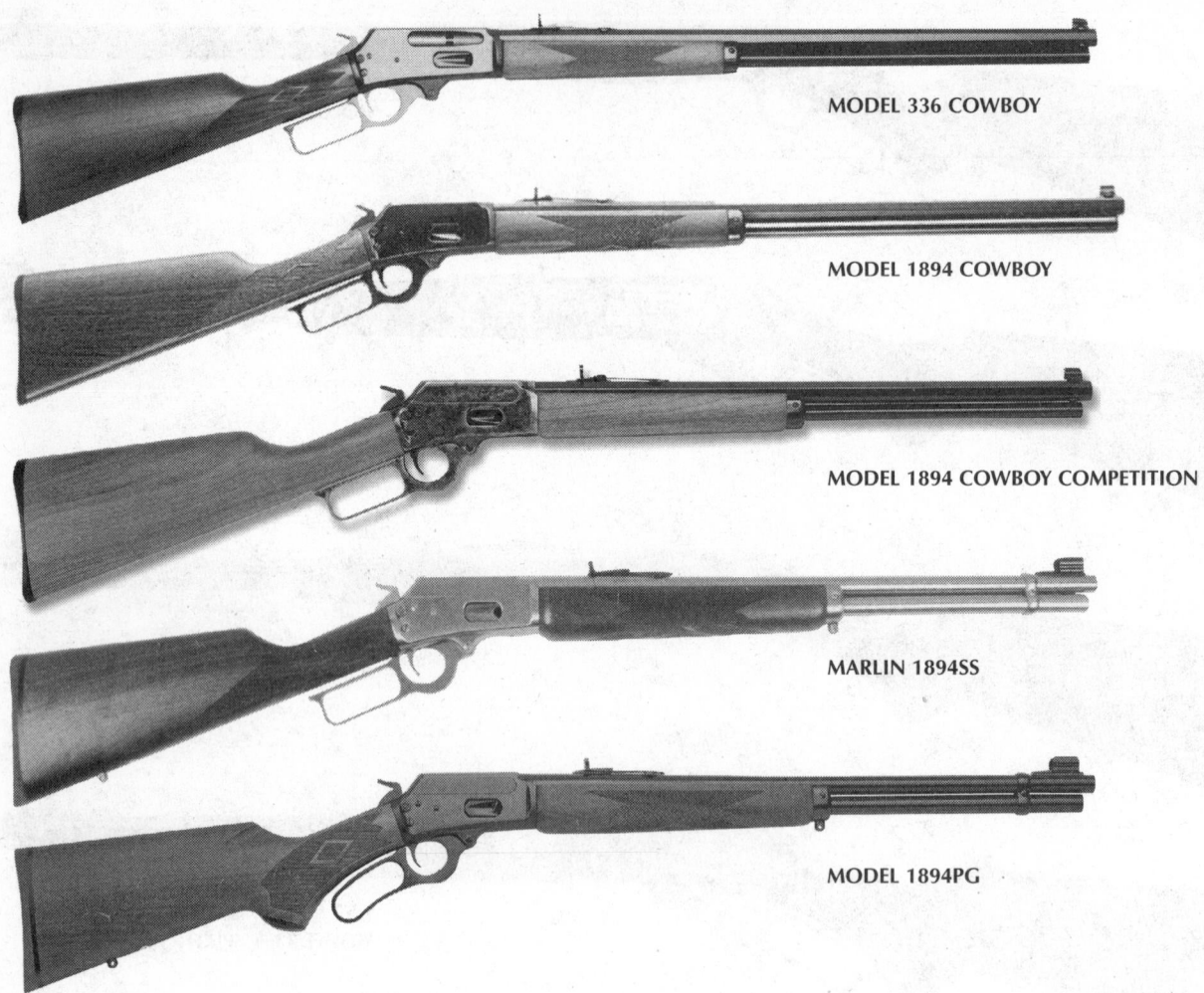

MODEL 336 COWBOY

MODEL 1894 COWBOY

MODEL 1894 COWBOY COMPETITION

MARLIN 1894SS

MODEL 1894PG

## MODEL 336 COWBOY

**Action:** lever
**Stock:** walnut, straight grip
**Barrel:** octagon 24 in.
**Sights:** open
**Weight:** 7.5lbs.
**Caliber:** .38-55
**Magazine:** under-barrel tube, 8 1/12 rounds
**Features:** Ballard-style rifling
Cowboy . . . . . . . . . . . . . . . . . . $735

## MODEL 1894 COWBOY

**Action:** lever
**Stock:** walnut, straight grip, checkered
**Barrel:** tapered octagon 24 in.
**Sights:** open
**Weight:** 6.5lbs.
**Caliber:** .357 Mag./38 Special, .44 mag./.44 Special and .45 Colt
**Magazine:** tube, 10 rounds
**Features:** blued finish, hammer-block safety, hard rubber buttplate; Competition model available in .38 Special or .45 Colt with 20 in. barrel
1894 Cowboy . . . . . . . . . . . . . . $36
Cowboy in .32 H&R Mag . . . . . $849

## MODEL 1894 COWBOY COMPETITION

**Action:** lever
**Stock:** walnut
**Barrel:** 20 in.
**Sights:** open
**Weight:** 7.0lbs.
**Caliber:** .38 Spl., .45 Long Colt
**Magazine:** 10
**Features:** case-colored receiver
1994 Cowboy . . . . . . . . . . . . . $836
1894 Cowboy(32 H&R Mag.) . . $936

## MODEL 1894 SS

**Action:** lever
**Stock:** checkered walnut, straight grip
**Barrel:** 20 in.
**Sights:** open
**Weight:** 6.0lbs.
**Caliber:** .44 Rem. Mag.
**Magazine:** under-barrel tube, 10 rounds
**Features:** Micro-groove rifling
1894 SS . . . . . . . . . . . . . . . . $680
1894C (blued) . . . . . . . . . . . . $567

## MODEL 1894PG

**Action:** lever
**Stock:** checkered walnut, straight grip
**Barrel:** 20 in.
**Sights:** open
**Weight:** 6.5lbs.
**Caliber:** .44 Rem. Mag./.44 Special
**Magazine:** tube, 10 rounds
**Features:** solid-top receiver tapped for scope mount
Model 1894PG . . . . . . . . . . . . $622
Model 1894FG
   in .41 Rem. Mag. . . . . . . . . . $622

# Marlin Rifles

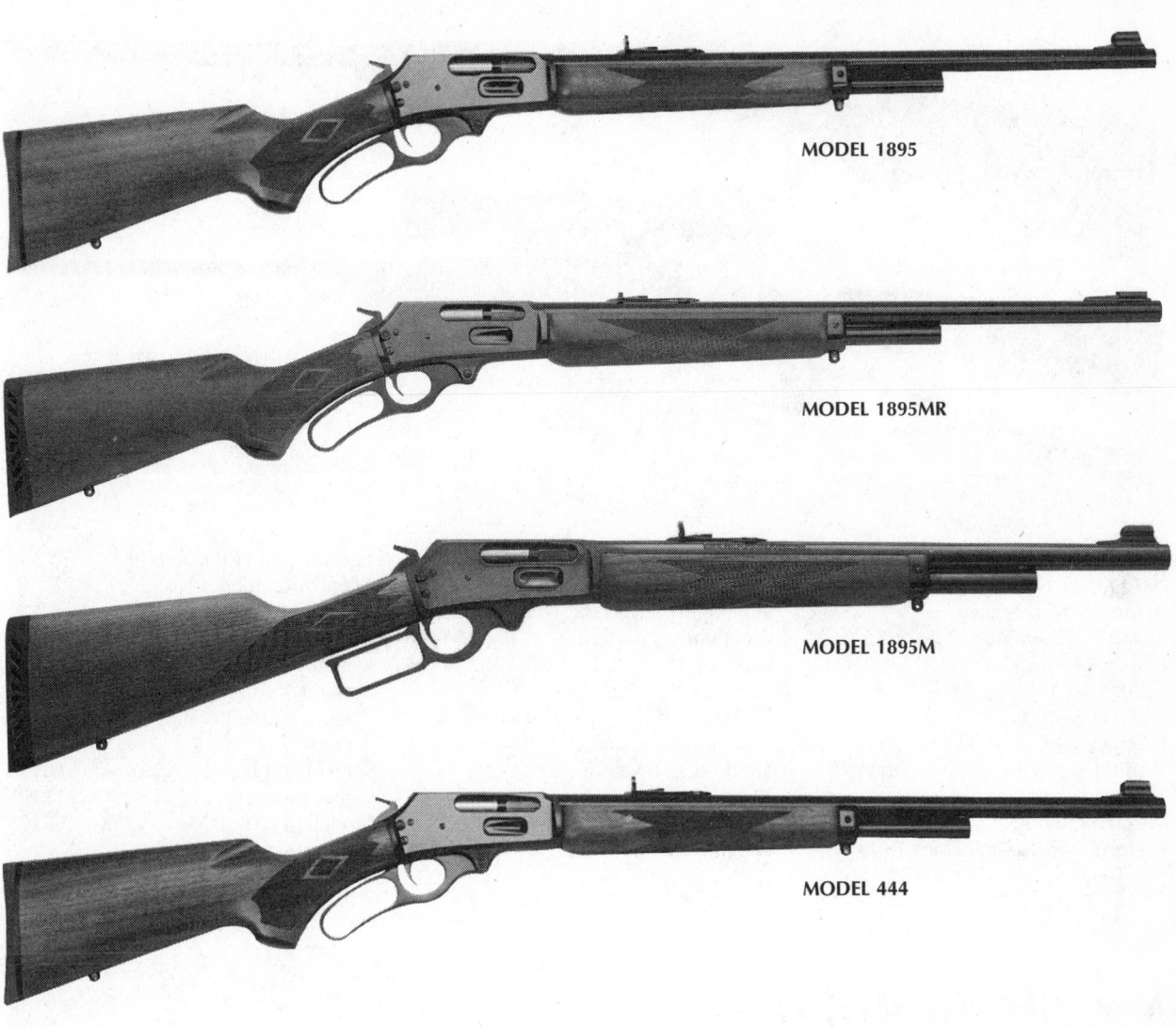

MODEL 1895

MODEL 1895MR

MODEL 1895M

MODEL 444

## MODEL 1895

*Action:* lever
*Stock:* checkered walnut, pistol grip
*Barrel:* 22 in.
*Sights:* open
*Weight:* 7.5lbs.
*Caliber:* .45-70 Govt.
*Magazine:* tube, 4 rounds
*Features:* blued, hammer-block safety, offset hammer spur for scope use; Model 1895G has 18.5 in. barrel and straight grip.

1895 . . . . . . . . . . . . . . . . . . . $631
1895G . . . . . . . . . . . . . . . . . . $646
1895GS in stainless steel . . . . . $760
1895 Cowboy (26" octagon
   barrel) . . . . . . . . . . . . . . . . $820

## MODEL 1895MR

*Action:* lever
*Stock:* walnut
*Barrel:* 22 in.
*Sights:* open
*Weight:* 7.5lbs.
*Caliber:* .450 Marlin
*Magazine:* 4
*Features:* pistol-grip stock
1895 . . . . . . . . . . . . . . . . . . . $761

## MODEL 1895M

*Action:* lever
*Stock:* checkered walnut, straight grip
*Barrel:* Ballard rifled, 18.5 in.
*Sights:* open
*Weight:* 7.0lbs.
*Caliber:* .450

*Magazine:* tube, 4 rounds
*Features:* blued finish, hammer-block safety, offset hammer spur for scope use.
1895M . . . . . . . . . . . . . . . . . . $695
1895 MR with 22 in. bbl. . . . . . $761

## MODEL 444

*Action:* lever
*Stock:* walnut, pistol grip, fluted comb, checkering
*Barrel:* 22 in.
*Sights:* open
*Weight:* 7.5lbs.
*Caliber:* .444 Marlin
*Magazine:* tube, 5 rounds
*Features:* blued, hammer-block safety, offset hammer spur for scope use.
444 . . . . . . . . . . . . . . . . . . . . . $631

# Merkel Rifles

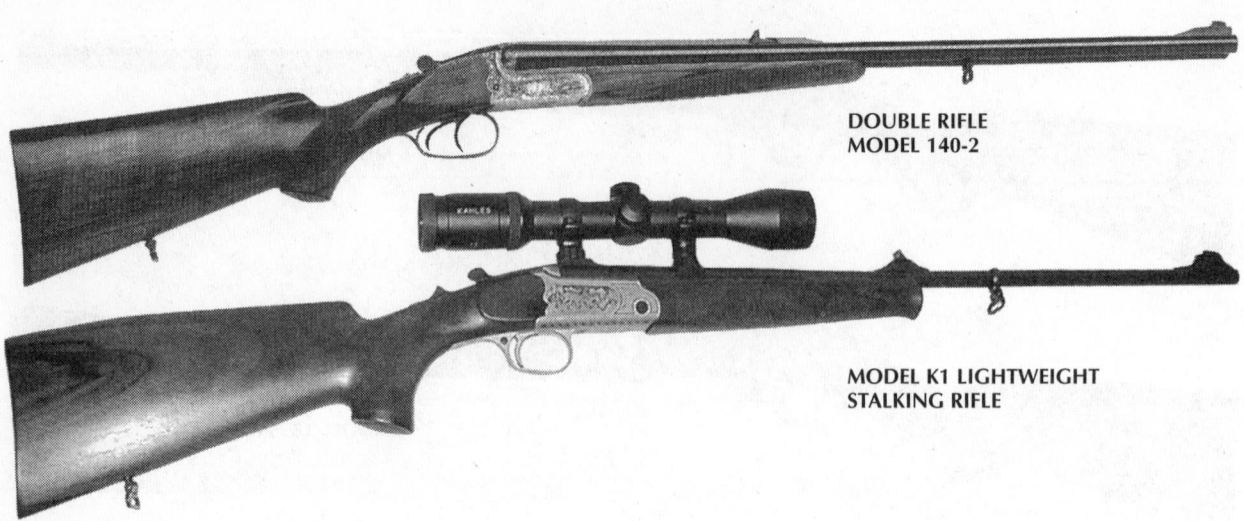

DOUBLE RIFLE
MODEL 140-2

MODEL K1 LIGHTWEIGHT
STALKING RIFLE

## MODEL K1 LIGHTWEIGHT STALKING RIFLE

**Action:** hinged breech
**Stock:** select walnut
**Barrel:** 24 in.
**Sights:** open
**Weight:** 5.6
**Caliber:** .243, .270, 7x57R, 7mm Rem. Mag., .308, .30-06, .300 Win. Mag., 9.3x74R
**Magazine:** none
**Features:** single-shot; Franz Jager action; also available: Premium and Jagd grades

Stalking Rifle:............ $3395
Premium:................ $4395
Jagd: ................... $4695

## DOUBLE RIFLE MODEL 140-2

**Action:** hinged breech
**Stock:** select walnut
**Barrel:** length and contour to order
**Sights:** open
**Weight:** 9.0

**Caliber:** .375 H&H, .416 Rigby, .470 N.E.
**Magazine:** none
**Features:** Anson & Deely box-lock; double triggers; includes oak and leather luggage case; higher grade available; also Model 141.1, lightweight double in .308, .30-06, 9.3x74R

Safari Double: ........... $10195
higher grade: ............ $11395
Model 141.1: ............. $7195

# Mossberg Rifles

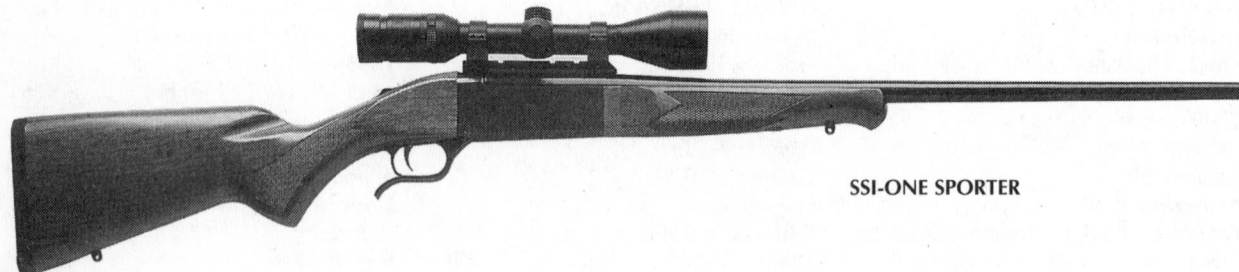

SSI-ONE SPORTER

## MODEL SSI-1

**Action:** hinged breech
**Stock:** walnut
**Barrel:** interchangeable 24 in.
**Sights:** none
**Weight:** 8.0

**Caliber:** .223, .22-250, .243, .270, .308, .30-06, 12 ga., 3.5 in. chamber)
**Magazine:** none
**Features:** barrel drilled and tapped for scope; hammerless with top tang safety, selected ejector; also available:

SSI-1 Varmint in .223, .22-250 with bull barrel (10 lbs.)
SSI-1:.................... $483
Varmint .................. $505

RIFLES

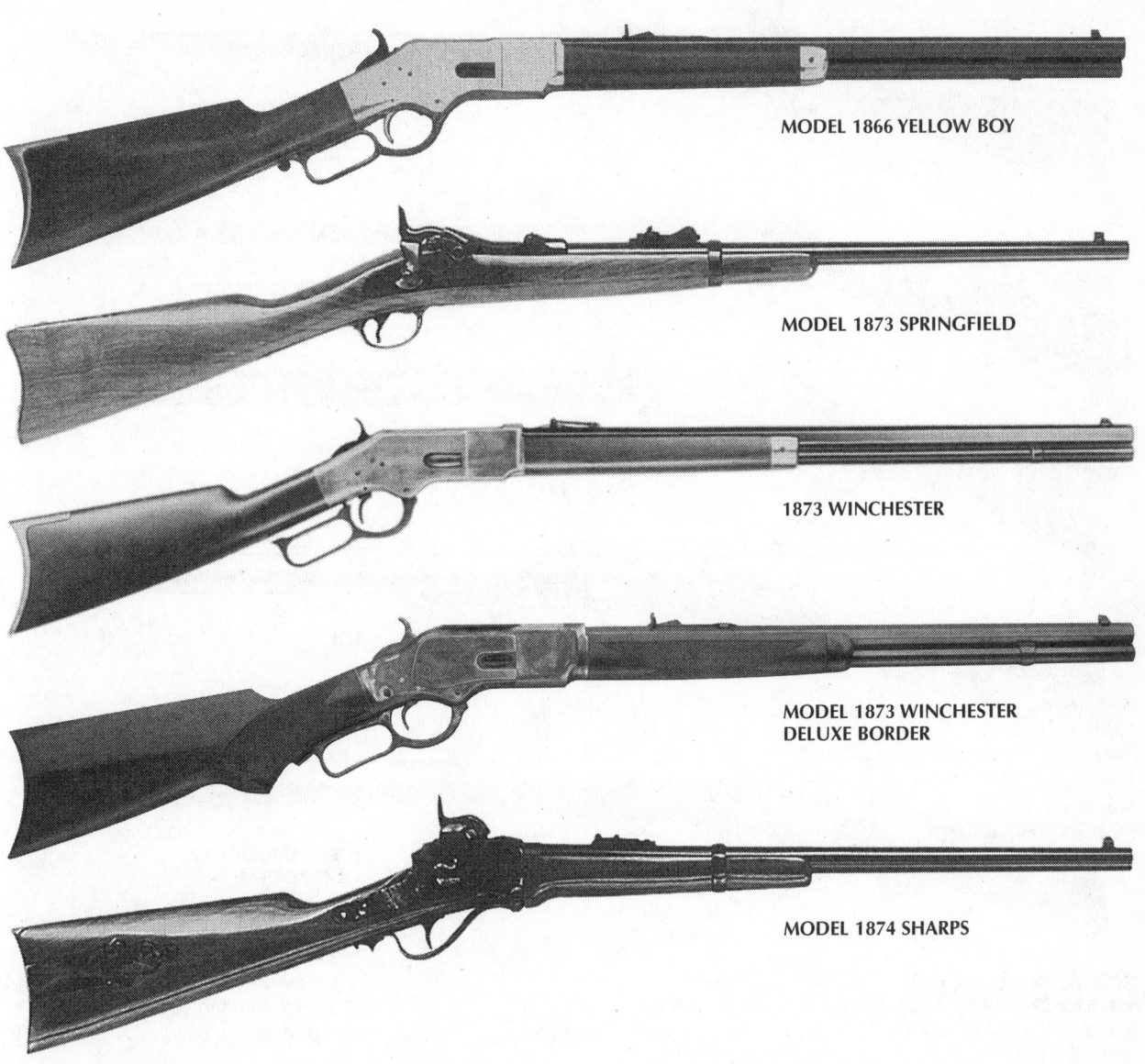

MODEL 1866 YELLOW BOY

MODEL 1873 SPRINGFIELD

1873 WINCHESTER

MODEL 1873 WINCHESTER
DELUXE BORDER

MODEL 1874 SHARPS

## MODEL 1866 YELLOW BOY

*Action:* lever
*Stock:* walnut, straight grip
*Barrel:* octagon 20 in.
*Sights:* open
*Weight:* 7.5
*Caliber:* .38 Special, .44-40, .45 Colt
*Magazine:* under-barrel tube, 10 rounds
*Features:* also available: Yellow Boy
with 24 in. barrel (8.3 lbs.)
**1866 Yellow Boy:** . . . . . . . . . . . **$914**

## MODEL 1873 SPRINGFIELD

*Action:* dropping block
*Stock:* walnut
*Barrel:* 22 in.

*Sights:* open
*Weight:* 7.0
*Caliber:* .45-70
*Magazine:* none
*Features:* "Trapdoor" replica, saddle
bar with ring
**1873 Springfield:** . . . . . . . . . **$1474**

## MODEL 1873 WINCHESTER

*Action:* lever
*Stock:* walnut, straight grip
*Barrel:* 24 in.
*Sights:* open
*Weight:* 8.3
*Caliber:* .357 Mag., .44-40, .45 Colt
*Magazine:* under-barrel tube, 13 rounds

*Features:* case-colored receiver; also:
Carbine, Border, Deluxe (checkered)
Border and Sporting models
**1873 Winchester:** . . . . . . . . . . **$1047**
**Carbine:** . . . . . . . . . . . . . . . **$1024**
**Border Model:** . . . . . . . . . . . . **$1047**
**Deluxe Border Model:** . . . . . . **$1182**
**Sporting Rifle:** . . . . . . . . . . . . **$1182**

## MODEL 1874 SHARPS

*Action:* dropping block
*Stock:* walnut
*Barrel:* 22 in.
*Sights:* open
*Weight:* 7.8
*Caliber:* .45-70

RIFLES

# Navy Arms Rifles

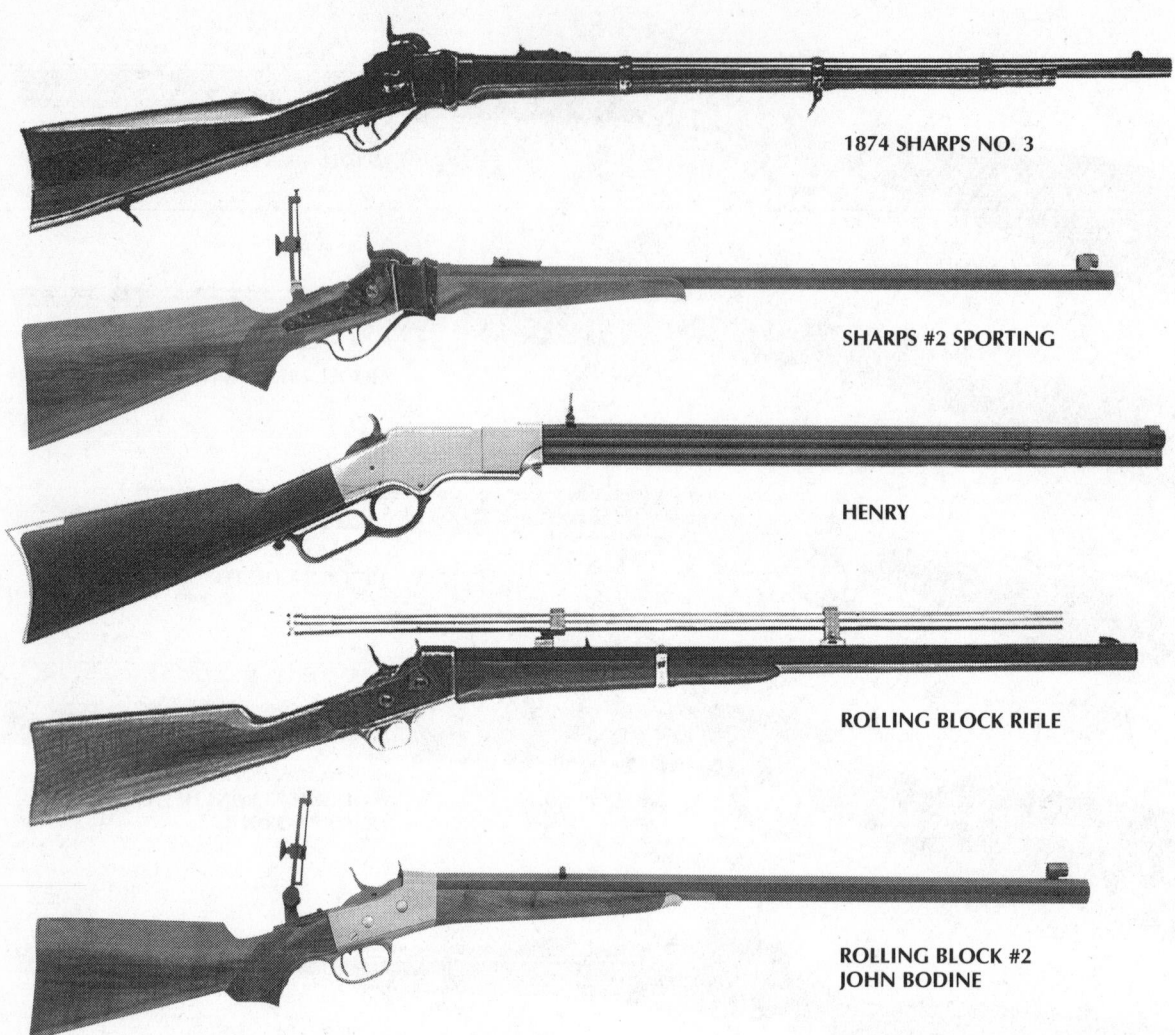

1874 SHARPS NO. 3

SHARPS #2 SPORTING

HENRY

ROLLING BLOCK RIFLE

ROLLING BLOCK #2
JOHN BODINE

*Magazine:* none
*Features:* also: No. 3 Long Range Sharps with double set triggers, 34 in. barrel (10.9 lbs.) and Buffalo Rifle with double set triggers, 28 in. octagon barrel (10.6 lbs.)
Carbine:. . . . . . . . . . . . . . . . $1185
No. 3: . . . . . . . . . . . . . . . . . $2205

## MODEL SHARPS #2 SPORTING
*Action:* dropping block
*Stock:* walnut
*Barrel:* 30 in.
*Sights:* target
*Weight:* 10.0lbs.
*Caliber:* .45-70
*Magazine:* none
*Features:* also #2 Silhouette Creedmoor and Quigley (with 34 in. barrel)
Sporting and Creedmoor. . . . . $1603
Silhouette. . . . . . . . . . . . . . . $1638
Quigley . . . . . . . . . . . . . . . . $1702

## HENRY
*Action:* lever
*Stock:* walnut, straight grip
*Barrel:* 24 in.
*Sights:* open
*Weight:* 9.0
*Caliber:* .44-40, .45 Colt
*Magazine:* under-barrel tube, 13 rounds
*Features:* blued or case-colored receiver
Henry:. . . . . . . . . . . . . . . . . $1221
Military Henry . . . . . . . . . . . $1164

## ROLLING BLOCK RIFLE
*Action:* dropping block
*Stock:* walnut
*Barrel:* 26 or 30 in.
*Sights:* open
*Weight:* 9.0
*Caliber:* .45-70
*Magazine:* none
*Features:* case-colored receiver; optional brass telescopic sight; drilled for Creedmoor sight; also; checkered #2 model with tang and globe sights
John Bodine . . . . . . . . . . . . . $1640

## MODEL ROLLING BLOCK #2 JOHN BODINE
*Action:* dropping block
*Stock:* walnut
*Barrel:* 30 in.
*Sights:* adjustable tang
*Weight:* 12.0lbs.
*Caliber:* .45-70
*Magazine:* none
*Features:* double set triggers, nickel-finish breech
John Bodine . . . . . . . . . . . . . $1640

# New England Firearms Rifles

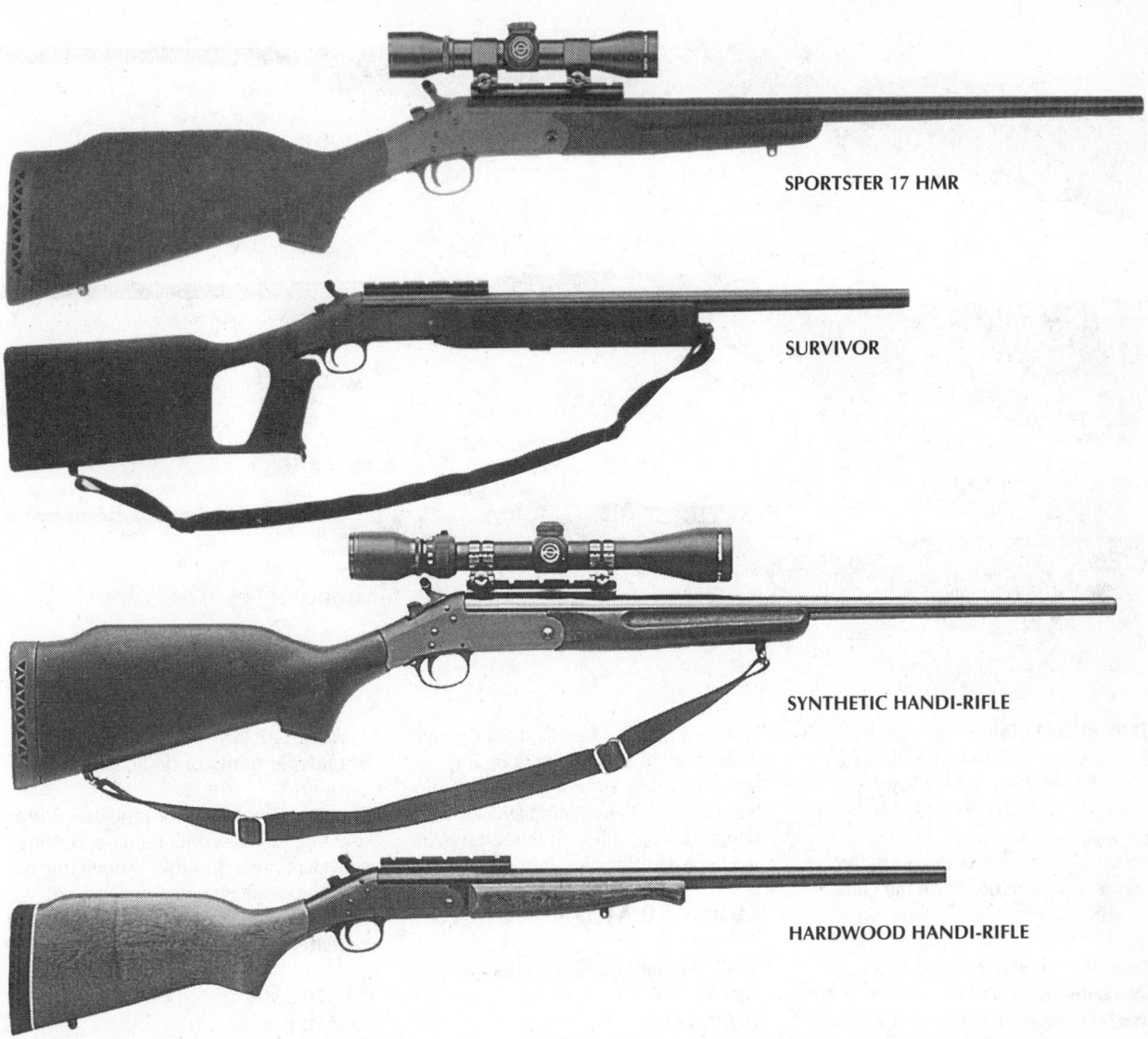

SPORTSTER 17 HMR

SURVIVOR

SYNTHETIC HANDI-RIFLE

HARDWOOD HANDI-RIFLE

## SPORTSTER 17 HMR
*Action:* hinged breech
*Stock:* synthetic
*Barrel:* heavy varmint 22 in.
*Sights:* none
*Weight:* 6.0
*Caliber:* .17 Hornady Magnum Rimfire
*Magazine:* none
*Features:* Monte Carlo stock; sling swivel, recoil pad; Sportster Youth available with 20 in. barrel (5.5 lbs.), in .22 LR or .22 WMR.
Sportster:. . . . . . . . . . . . . . . . $183
Youth: . . . . . . . . . . . . . . . . . $153

## SURVIVOR
*Action:* hinged breech
*Stock:* lightweight synthetic
*Barrel:* light sporter, 20 in.
*Sights:* open
*Weight:* 5.5
*Caliber:* .22 Hornet, .223, .243
*Magazine:* none
*Features:* single-shot; recoil pad; also: Survivor in .223 and .308 with 22 in. bull barrel, hollow synthetic stock, thumbscrew take down
Superlight:. . . . . . . . . . . . . . . $286
Survivor: . . . . . . . . . . . . . . . . $288

## HARDWOOD HANDI-RIFLE
*Action:* hinged breech
*Stock:* Monte Carlo synthetic
*Barrel:* 22 or 26 in.
*Sights:* none
*Weight:* 7.0
*Caliber:* .223, .22-250, .243, .270, .30-06
*Magazine:* none
*Features:* offset hammer; open-sight version of Handi-Rifle in .22 Hornet, .30-30, .357 Mag., .44 Mag., .45-70 Govt. Youth models in .223, .243 and 7mm-08.
Handi-Rifle:. . . . . . . . . . . . . . $286
with hardwwod stock: . . . . . . $276
Synthetic stainless: . . . . . . . . $345
Youth Synthetic:. . . . . . . . . . . $276

# New Ultra Light Arms

MODEL 20 MOUNTAIN RIFLE

MODEL 20 RF

MODEL 28

**THIS BREED** of super-light rifles dates to 1984, when Melvin Forbes designed, from the ground up, his Model 20 Ultra Light. This bolt-action looks like a Remington 700. But close up you'll notice a lot of differences. First, the bolt and receiver diameters on the Ultra Light rifle are smaller. To keep weight down, Melvin made efficient use of steel. The receiver has standard wall thickness, but a slimmer bolt made for less receiver wall. The Model 20 wasn't conceived as a universal mechanism, for cartridges of all sizes. It was made for relatively short cartridges. In a fit of brilliance, Melvin chose to make the magazine box 3.00 inches long, not the 2.85 inches common in short-action rifles, to accommodate the 7x57 Mauser and its derivatives, and the .284 Winchester. He didn't skeletonize anything or shorten the barrel to shave ounces. So after configuring the action, Melvin chose synthetic material to further reduce weight. Walnut was too heavy. Besides, it could warp, and he wanted this rifle to be fly-speck accurate. The resulting stock scaled less than a pound. Other rifles followed, with action lengths suited to different cartridges. There was even a .22 rimfire. Manufacturing agreements with Colt left

ULA in a pickle when Colt fell on hard times. Melvin bought the company back, honoring all orders and renaming his enterprise New Ultra Light Arms. The rifles today are made in the same pain-staking way they were in the 1980s.

## MODEL 20 MOUNTAIN RIFLE
*Action:* bolt
*Stock:* Kevlar/graphite composite
*Barrel:* 22 in.
*Sights:* none
*Weight:* 4.75
*Caliber:* short action: 6mm, .17, .22 Hornet, .222, .222 Rem. Mag., .22-250, .223, .243, .250-3000 Savage, .257, .257 Ackley, 7x57, 7x57 Ackley, 7mm-08, .284, .300 Savage, .308, .358
*Magazine:* box, 4, 5 or 6 rounds
*Features:* two-position safety; choice of 7 or more stock colors; available in left-hand
Mountain Rifle: . . . . . . . . . . $2700
left-hand:. . . . . . . . . . . . . . $2800

## MODEL 20 RF
*Action:* bolt
*Stock:* composite
*Barrel:* Douglas Premium #1 Contour 22 in.
*Sights:* none
*Weight:* 5.25

*Caliber:* .22 LR
*Magazine:* none (or detachable box, 5 rounds)
*Features:* single shot or repeater; drilled and tapped for scope; recoil pad, sling swivels; fully adjustable Timney trigger; 3-position safety; color options
single-shot:. . . . . . . . . . . . . $1150
repeater: . . . . . . . . . . . . . . . $1200

## MODEL 24
*Action:* bolt
*Stock:* Kevlar composite
*Barrel:* 22 in.
*Sights:* none
*Weight:* 5.25
*Caliber:* long action: .270, .30-06, .25-06, .280, .280 Ackley, .338-06, .35 Whelen; Magnum (Model 28): .264, 7mm, .300, .338, .300 WSM, .270 WSM, 7mm WSM; Model 40: (magnum) .300 Wby. and .416 Rigby
*Magazine:* box, 4 rounds
*Features:* Model 28 has 24 in. bbl. and weighs 5.5 lbs.; Model 40 has 24 in. bbl. (6.5 lbs.) All available in left-hand versions.
Model 24: . . . . . . . . . . . . . . $2800
Model 24, left-hand:. . . . . . . $2900
Model 28 or Model 40:. . . . . $3100
Model 28 or
    Model 40, left-hand:. . . . . . $3200

# Pedersoli Replica Rifles

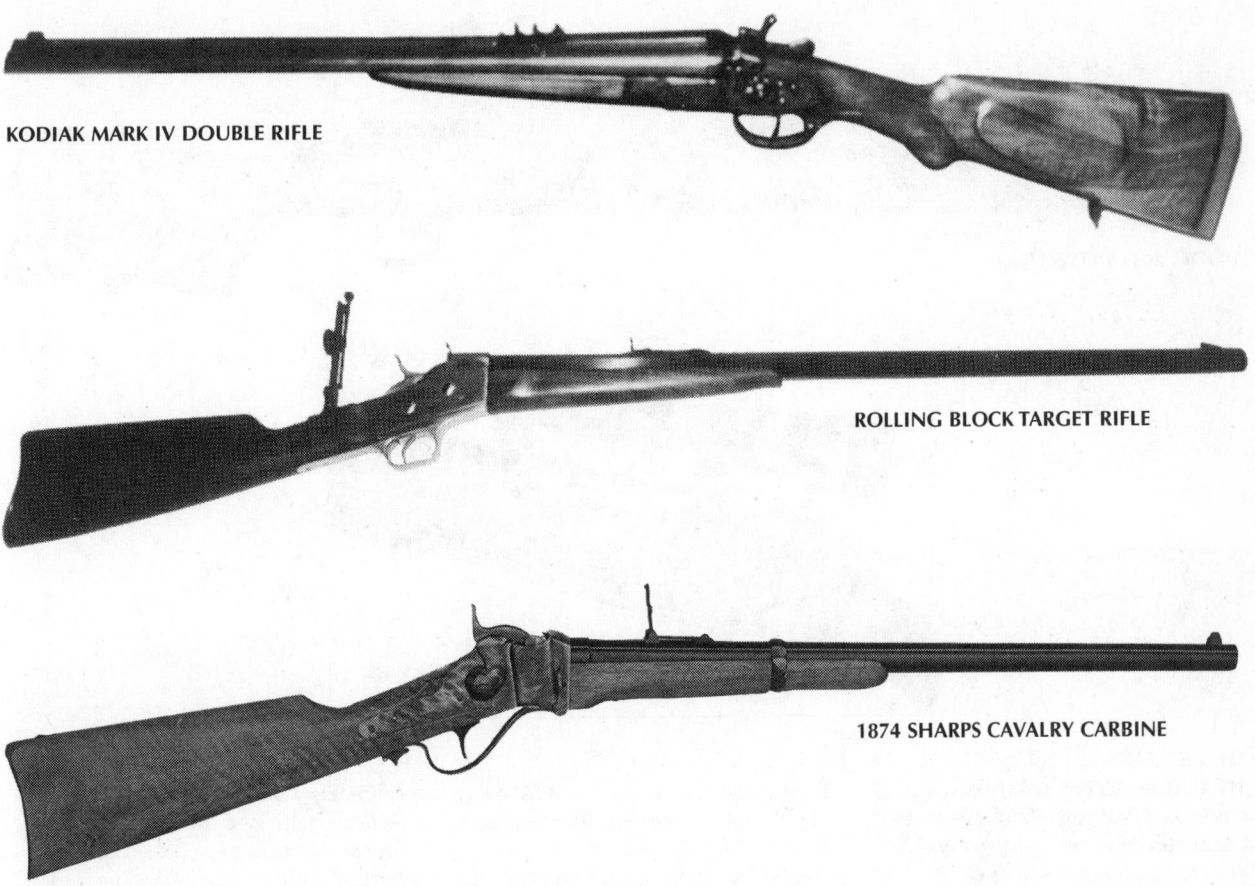

KODIAK MARK IV DOUBLE RIFLE

ROLLING BLOCK TARGET RIFLE

1874 SHARPS CAVALRY CARBINE

## KODIAK MARK IV DOUBLE
*Action:* hinged breech
*Stock:* walnut
*Barrel:* 22 and 24 in.
*Sights:* open
*Weight:* 8.2
*Caliber:* .45-70, 9.3x74R, 8x57JSR
*Magazine:* none
*Features:* .45-70 weighs 8.2 lbs.;
also available: Kodiak Mark IV with
interchangeable 20-gauge barrel
**45-70:** . . . . . . . . . . . . . . . . . . **$3250**
**8x57, 9.3x74:** . . . . . . . . . . . . . **$3250**
**Kodiak Mark IV:** . . . . . . . . . . **$4925**

## ROLLING BLOCK TARGET
*Action:* dropping block
*Stock:* walnut
*Barrel:* octagon 30 in.
*Sights:* target
*Weight:* 9.5
*Caliber:* .45-70 and .357 (10 lbs.)
*Magazine:* none
*Features:* Creedmoor sights; Also
available: Buffalo, Big Game, Sporting,
Baby Carbine, Custer, Long Range
Creedmoor
**Rolling Block Target, brass:** . . . . **$875**
    **Steel:** . . . . . . . . . . . . . . . . . **$995**

## SHARPS 1874 CAVALRY MODEL
*Action:* dropping block
*Stock:* walnut
*Barrel:* 22 in.
*Sights:* open
*Weight:* 8.4
*Caliber:* .45-70
*Magazine:* none
*Features:* also available: 1874 Infantry
(set trigger, 30 in. bbl.), 1874 Sporting
(.40-65 or .45-70, set trigger, 32 in.
oct. bbl.), 1874 Long Range (.45-70
and .45-90, .45-120, 34 in. half oct.
bbl., target sights)
**Cavalry:** . . . . . . . . . . . . . . . . **$1050**
**Infantry (one trigger):** . . . . . . **$1250**
**Infantry (two triggers):** . . . . . . **$1325**
**Sporting:** . . . . . . . . . . . . . . . **$1195**
**Long Range:** . . . . . . . . . . . . . **$1595**
**Long Range Big Bore:** . . . . . . . **$1685**

# Prairie Gun Works Rifles

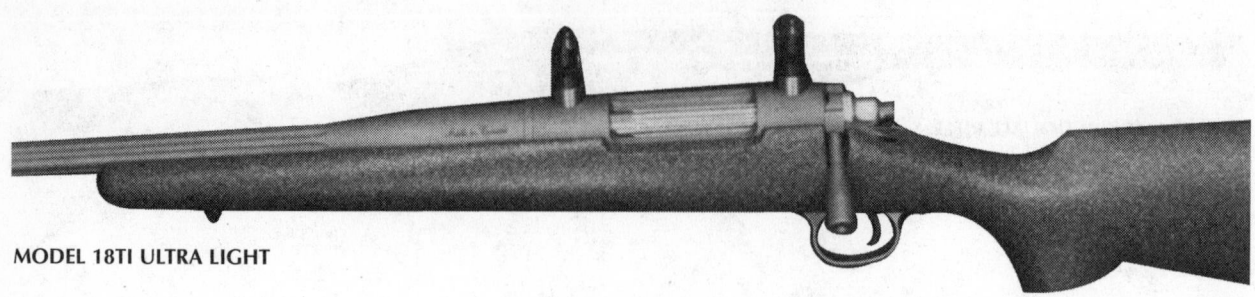

MODEL 18TI ULTRA LIGHT

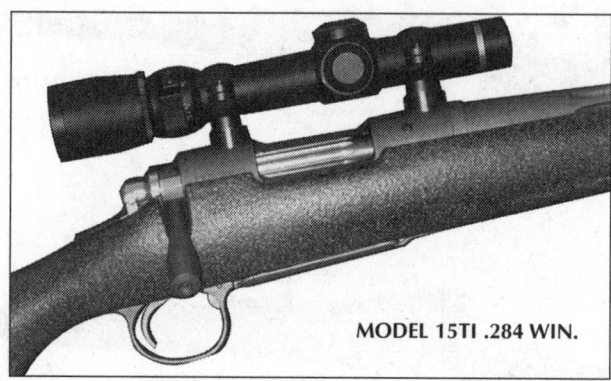

MODEL 15TI .284 WIN.

**TITANIUM RIFLES** weigh less, and that's how Prairie Gun Works keeps the accuracy in while paring ounces. These rifles feature match grade stainless barrels, kevlar/glass stocks, Titanium scope bases, fully adjustable triggers. Customers can specify stock dimensions, barrel length, rifling twist. The M15Ti rifle (short) is suitable for cartridges up to the size of the .284 Winchester. The M18Ti rifle (long) is suitable for rounds as big as

Remington Ultramags. Depending on action size, a finished rifle weighs from 4.25 lbs. to 6.25 lbs.

Some of the unique features found on the Ti series rifles: cone breech, EDM-cut lugways, one-piece bolt, double plunger ejectors, Sako type extractor, left- or right-hand bolt/port configuration, aluminum pillar bedding, removable muzzle brake with cap, barrel flutes.

## MODEL 15TI ULTRA LIGHT

**Action:** bolt
**Stock:** composite
**Barrel:** 22 in.
**Sights:** none
**Weight:** 5.0
**Caliber:** most short-action calibers
**Magazine:** box, 5 rounds
**Features:** Rem. 700 short action, custom alloy scope mounts, new firing pin and bolt shroud tuned; also: Model 18Ti with long 700 action

Model 15Ti: . . . . . . . . . . . . . $2800
Model 18Ti: . . . . . . . . . . . . . $2800

*"Swamping" was done by old-time gunmakers to give muzzle-loader barrels slightly greater diameter at the front end than in the middle, for a pendulum effect that steadied the rifle quickly.*

# Purdey

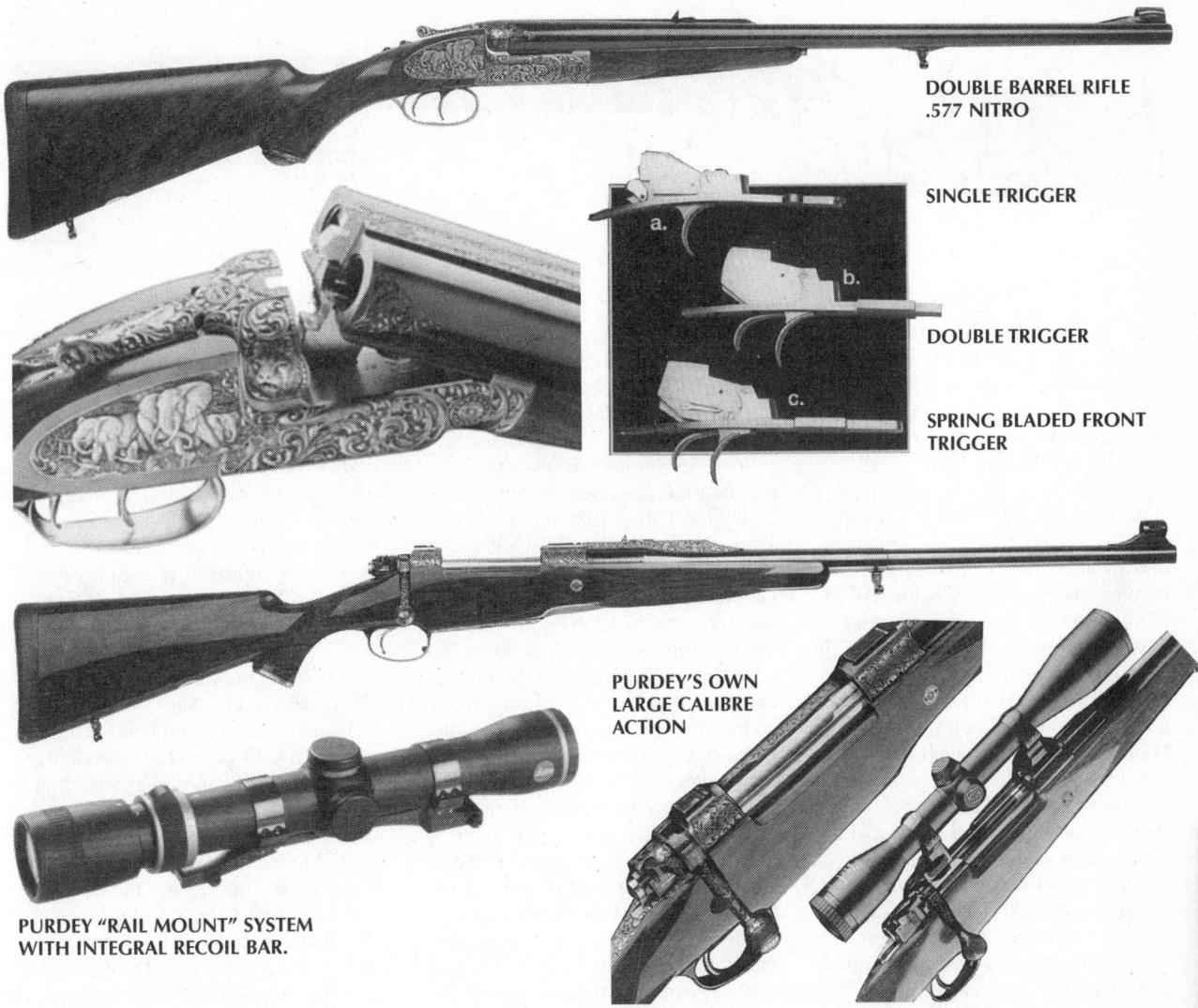

**DOUBLE BARREL RIFLE .577 NITRO**

**SINGLE TRIGGER**

**DOUBLE TRIGGER**

**SPRING BLADED FRONT TRIGGER**

**PURDEY'S OWN LARGE CALIBRE ACTION**

PURDEY "RAIL MOUNT" SYSTEM WITH INTEGRAL RECOIL BAR.

## DOUBLE BARREL RIFLE .577 NITRO

The word "Express" was coined by James Purdey the younger to publicize his rifles. He likened their performance to a railway or "Express" train, which was heavy, travelled with great velocity and had a flat trajectory.

Purdey's double-barrel Express rifles are built to customer specifications on actions sized to each particular cartridge. Standard chamberings include .375 H&H Magnum and .470, .577 and .600 Nitro Express. The Purdey side-by-side action patented in 1880 is still made now with only very minor changes. The action mechanism, designed by Frederick Beesley, retains a portion of the energy in the mainsprings to facilitate the opening of the gun.

The over-under is derived from the Woodward, patented in 1913. The action blocks for all guns are cut from certified forgings, for consistency of grain throughout, and are so fitted to the barrels as to give an absolute joint. The actioner then fits the fore-part, the locks, the strikers and the safety work before finally detonating the action.

## A – SINGLE TRIGGER

The Purdey single trigger works both by inertia and mechanically. It is simple, effective and fast. The firing sequence is fixed, therefore no barrel selection is possible.

## B & C – DOUBLE TRIGGERS

The standard double triggers (B) can be augmented with an articulated front trigger (C). This device alleviates damage to the back of the trigger finger on discharge.

Purdey makes its own dedicated actions for bolt rifles in the following calibers: .375 H&H, .416/450 Rigby or other, .500 and .505 Gibbs.

The action length is suited to cartridge length in each caliber. Mauser Square Bridge and Mauser '98 actions are available.

## RAIL MOUNT SYSTEM

This is Purdey's own system for big bolt rifles. It is very secure and facilitates fast on/off. Rings and mounts are all made with an integral recoil bar from a single piece of steel. This system is recommended for Purdey actions and Mauser Square Bridge actions.

# Remington Arms Rifles

**MODEL 40-XB TACTICAL**

**OUR OLDEST GUNMAKER,**
Remington got its start on a hand-operated forge in up-state New York in 1816. That rifle, was, of course, a muzzleloader. But as the company grew, it manufactured rifles of all types, then shotguns and pistols.

In 1908, John D. Peterson began working on a pump-action centerfire rifle, which would become the Remington Model 14. Chambered in .30 and .32 Remington, the Model 14was introduced in August 1912. The .35 Remington was added soon thereafter. Standard-grade rifles initially sold for $20. The 14R Carbine, with an 18-inch barrel and straight-grip stock listed for $18.

During this period, Remington designed and marketed the Model 8 autoloading rifle. Initially called simply the Remington Autoloading Repeating Rifle, the Model 8 was bored for the .25, .30, .32 and .35 Remington. It had a box magazine that could be clip-charged. The barrel recoiled within a fixed jacket.

In 1922 Remington's Crawford Loomis began working on a small-frame centerfire that became the Model 25 a year later. Loomis' pump gun was really an adaptation of the Model 12 rimfire rifle, rather than a redesign of the Model 14. It came in .25-20 and .32-20; the tube magazine held 10 shots. A six-shot carbine followed. The 25 remained in production until it was replaced in 1936, by the Model 141 Gamemaster. Bored for the .30, .32 and .35 Remington, the Gamemaster proved a popular deer gun in both rifle and carbine version. A more powerful pump rifle, the

Remington 760, supplanted it in 1950. Meanwhile, Remington's Model 8 autoloader had been replaced (in 1936) by the Model 81, essentially a beefy version of the Model 8.

In 1955 Remington introduced a fixed-barrel, gas-operated autoloader called the 740. It shared the 760's sleek profile and the buttstock, receiver and trigger group were, in fact, essentially the same. The Woodsmaster was replaced in 1960 by an improved version, the 742. Both it and the 760 Gamemaster remained in the line for another 20 years. In 1981 Remington changed them, internally and cosmetically. The new Model Four and 7400 autoloaders and Model Six and 7600 pumps featured fewer locking lugs than their predecessors, improved magazines, one-piece barrel extensions, rivetless extractors and a counterbore at the rear of the chamber to further enhance feeding. Chambered for such high-power rounds as the .30-06, .270, and .280, as well as for the .243 and .308 short-action rounds, the 7400 and 7600 remain favorites of many hunters today. The Models Four and Six were dropped in 1988.

Remington's first bolt-action rifle pre-dated its first centerfire pump, but not by much. In 1898, Roswell F. Cook patented a change to the Lee bolt-action rifle, moving the locking lugs from the bolt body to the head. The upshot: a Remington-Lee Small Bore Magazine Rifle. Chambered in 7X57, 7.65 Mauser, .236 Remington, .30-30 Winchester and .30-40 Krag, which stayed in the Remington line for a decade. The military rifles and carbines, in .30-40 Krag, armed Cuba

as well as U.S. National Guard units. The next Remington bolt-action centerfire was conceived by Crawford C. Loomis and C.H. Barnes. Announced in 1921, the Model 30 had been several years in the making, the result of efforts to use surplus 1917 Enfield receivers. It was, predictably, a heavy rifle. It was also expensive and sold poorly. An improved version appeared in 1926. The 30 Express was chambered in .30-06, also in 25, .30, .32 and .35 Remington.

A more economical rifle came along after World War II. The Models 721 and 722 (long and short actions) were designed from scratch to deliver power, accuracy and reliability at an affordable price. Available in .270, .30-06 and .264 Winchester and .300 H&H Magnums, the 721 became a hit in the West. The 722 in .300 Savage was a popular deer gun. It was also chambered in .257 Roberts and .244 Remington, .308 and .243 Winchester, plus the diminutive .222 Remington. A dressier Model 700 upstaged the 721-722 in 1963. It is still Remington's flagship bolt rifle.

## MODEL 40-XR CUSTOM SPORTER AND 40-XB TACTICAL

**Action:** bolt
**Stock:** walnut (Tactical, black with green fiberglass)
**Barrel:** 24 or 26 in.
**Sights:** none
**Weight:** 6.5lbs. (Tactical: 10.25 lbs.)
**Caliber:** .22 LR or .22 WMR
**Magazine:** 5 shot, detachable box
**Features:** built to order
**.22 XR Sporter** . . . . . . . . . . . $3383
**.308 XB Tactical** . . . . . . . . . . $2108

MODEL 40-XB

MODEL 552 SPEEDMASTER

MODEL 572 FIELDMASTER

MODEL 597

## MODEL 40-X TARGET RIFLE

*Action:* bolt
*Stock:* target, benchrest or tactical
*Barrel:* heavy 24 in. or 27" XB
*Sights:* none
*Weight:* 10.25 –11.75 lbs.
*Caliber:* 16 popular standard and magnum calibers
*Magazine:* box, 3 or 5 rounds
*Features:* rimfire and single-shot versions available; walnut, laminated and composite stocks; forend rail, match trigger
40-X:. . . . . . . . . . . . . $1636 - 2108
Left-hand. . . . . . . . . . $1636 - 1970

## MODEL 552 BDL DELUXE SPEEDMASTER

*Action:* autoloading
*Stock:* walnut
*Barrel:* 21 in.
*Sights:* Big Game
*Weight:* 5.8
*Caliber:* .22 S, .22 L, .22 LR
*Magazine:* under-barrel tube, 15 rounds (LR), 17 (L) and 20 (S)
*Features:* classic autoloader made 1966 to date
552:. . . . . . . . . . . . . . . . . . . $393

## MODEL 572 BDL DELUXE FIELDMASTER

*Action:* pump
*Stock:* walnut
*Barrel:* 21 in.
*Sights:* Big Game
*Weight:* 5.5
*Caliber:* .22 S, .22 L, .22 LR
*Magazine:* under-barrel tube, 15-20 rounds
*Features:* grooved receiver for scope mounts
Fieldmaster:. . . . . . . . . . . . . . $407

## MODEL 597

*Action:* autoloading
*Stock:* synthetic or laminated
*Barrel:* 20 in.
*Sights:* Big Game
*Weight:* 5.5 to 6
*Caliber:* .22 LR, .22 WMR, .17 HMR
*Magazine:* detachable box, 10 rounds (8 in magnums)
*Features:* magnum version in .22 WMR and .17 HMR (both 6 lbs.); also: heavy-barrel model
597:. . . . . . . . . . . . . . . . . . . . $169
stainless: . . . . . . . . . . . . . . . . $224
stainless laminated: . . . . . . . . $279
22 WMR . . . . . . . . . . . . . . . . $335
magnum: . . . . . . . . . . . . . . . . $361
heavy-barrel: . . . . . . . . . . . . . $265
heavy-barrel magnum: . . . . . . . $399

RIFLES

# Remington Arms Rifles

MODEL 673

MODEL 700 ADL

MODEL 700 CUSTOM C GRADE

MODEL 700 AFRICAN BIG GAME

## MODEL 597 .17 HMR
**Action:** autoloading
**Stock:** synthetic
**Barrel:** 20 in.
**Sights:** Big Game
**Weight:** 6.0lbs.
**Caliber:** .17 HMR
**Magazine:** 8
**Features:** detachable box magazine
**Model 597 .17 HMR.** . . . . . . . . **$361**

## MODEL 673
**Action:** bolt
**Stock:** laminated
**Barrel:** 22 in.
**Sights:** open
**Weight:** 7.5lbs.
**Caliber:** .350 Rem. Mag., .308 Win.,
6.5 Rem. Mag., 300 SAUM
**Magazine:** 3 + 1
**Features:** vent rib, Model Seven action
**Model 673** . . . . . . . . . . . . . . . **$825**

## MODEL 700 ADL
**Action:** bolt
**Stock:** synthetic or walnut
**Barrel:** 22 in. (Youth 20")
**Sights:** Big Game
**Weight:** 6.75 – 7.5
**Caliber:** .223, .22-250, .243, .270,
7mm Rem. Mag., .308, .30-06, .300
Win. Mag.
**Magazine:** Internal box, 3 or 5 rounds
**Features:** walnut in .270 and .30-06
only; magnums with 24 in. barrels;
youth model available with 20" barrel
(6.8 lbs.) or Magnum, 22" (7.25 lbs.)
**ADL synthetic:** . . . . . . . . . . . . . **$500**
**synthetic magnum:** . . . . . . . . . **$527**
**Youth (.270 and .30-06):** . . . . . . **$500**
**walnut:** . . . . . . . . . . . . . . . . . **$580**

## MODEL 700 CUSTOM C GRADE
**Action:** bolt
**Stock:** fancy American walnut
**Barrel:** 24 in.
**Sights:** none
**Weight:** 7.5lbs.
**Caliber:** any popular standard or
magnum chambering
**Magazine:** 3 to 5
**Features:** some custom-shop options
available
**Model 700 Custom C Grade** . . **$1733**

## MODEL 700 AFRICAN BIG GAME
**Action:** bolt
**Stock:** laminated
**Barrel:** 26 in.
**Sights:** open
**Weight:** 9.5
**Caliber:** .375 H&H, .375 RUM, .458
Win, .416 Rem.
**Magazine:** box, 3 rounds
**Features:** barrel-mounted front swivel
**African Big Game:** . . . . . . . . . **$1726**

RIFLES

MODEL 700 AFRICAN
PLAINS RIFLE (APR)

MODEL 700 CLASSIC

MODEL 700 BDL DM

MODEL 700 KS MOUNTAIN RIFLE

## MODEL 700 AFRICAN PLAINS RIFLE

*Action:* bolt
*Stock:* laminated
*Barrel:* 26 in.
*Sights:* none
*Weight:* 7.75
*Caliber:* 9 offerings from 7mm Rem. Mag. to .385 RUM
*Magazine:* box, 3 rounds in magazine
*Features:* barrel-mounted front swivel, epoxy bedded action, machined steel trigger and floor plate.
**African Plains Rifle:** . . . . . . . . **$1716**

## MODEL 700 CLASSIC

*Action:* bolt
*Stock:* walnut
*Barrel:* 24 in.
*Sights:* none
*Weight:* 7.3
*Caliber:* 8mm Mauser

*Magazine:* box, 5 rounds
*Features:* one-year run per caliber
**700 Classic:** . . . . . . . . . . . . . . **$683**

## MODEL 700 BDL CUSTOM DELUXE

*Action:* bolt
*Stock:* walnut
*Barrel:* 22 – 26 in.
*Sights:* open
*Weight:* 7.5
*Caliber:* popular standard calibers from .17 Rem. to .338 RUM
*Magazine:* box, 5 rounds
*Features:* magnums have 24 in. barrels; DM version features detachable magazine; left-hand bolt available on many 700s for $25 premium
**BDL:** . . . . . . . . . . . . . . . . . . . **$683**
**BDL Magnum:** . . . . . . . . . . . . **$709**
**BDL Ultra-Mags:** . . . . . . . . . . **$723**
**BDL Stainless:** . . . . . . . . . . . . **$735**

**BDL Stainless Magnum:** . . . . . . **$761**
**BDL Stainless Ultra-Mags:** . . . . **$775**
**BDL Stainless DM:** . . . . . . . . . **$801**
**BDL Stainless DM Magnum:** . . . **$828**
**BDL DM** . . . . . . . . . . . . **$749 - 776**

## MODEL 700 CUSTOM KS MOUNTAIN RIFLE

*Action:* bolt
*Stock:* lightweight composite
*Barrel:* 24 or 26 in., blued or stainless
*Sights:* none
*Weight:* 6.5
*Caliber:* 15 choices from .270 to .375 RUM
*Magazine:* box, 3 or 5 rounds
*Features:* stainless or chrome-moly steel; also: magnum model with 26 in. barrel
**standard:** . . . . . . . . . . . . . . . . **$1314**
**stainless:** . . . . . . . . . . . . . . . . **$1500**
**Left-hand:** . . . . . . . . . . **$1393 - 1580**

# Remington Arms Rifles

MODEL 700 SENDERO

MODEL 700 SENDERO SF
(STAINLESS FLUTED)

MODEL 700 VLS
(VARMINT LAMINATED STOCK)

MODEL 710

## MODEL 700 MOUNTAIN RIFLE DM

*Action:* bolt
*Stock:* walnut
*Barrel:* 22 in.
*Sights:* none
*Weight:* 6.5
*Caliber:* .260, .270, 7mm-08, .280, .30-06
*Magazine:* detachable box, 4 rounds
*Features:* also; LSS with laminated stock, stainless steel
Mountain DM: . . . . . . . . . . . . $749
LSS: . . . . . . . . . . . . . . . . . . . $800

## MODEL 700 SENDERO SF

*Action:* bolt
*Stock:* composite
*Barrel:* 26 in. heavy stainless
*Sights:* none
*Weight:* 8.5
*Caliber:* 7mm Rem. Mag., .300 Ultra Mag., 7 mm Rem Ultra Mag., 7mm & 300 Rem SA Ultra Mag. and .300 Win. Mag.

*Magazine:* box, 3 or 5 rounds
*Features:* full-length bedding block; fluted barrel
Sendero: . . . . . . . . . . . . . . . . $1003
Ultra Magnum calibers: . . . . . $1016

## MODEL 700 TITANIUM

*Action:* bolt
*Stock:* synthetic
*Barrel:* stainless 22 in.
*Sights:* none
*Weight:* 5.5
*Caliber:* .260, .270, 7mm-08, .308, .306, 7mm SAUM, .300 SAUM
*Magazine:* box, 5 rounds
*Features:* Titanium receiver; fluted bolt, skeleton handle, RC recoil pad
Titanium: . . . . . . . . . . . . . . . $1239
Magnums: . . . . . . . . . . . . . . $1279

## MODEL 700 VS

*Action:* bolt
*Stock:* synthetic
*Barrel:* 26 in.
*Sights:* none

*Weight:* 9.5
*Caliber:* .223, .220 Swift, .22-250, 6mm Rem., .243, .308
*Magazine:* box, 5 rounds
*Features:* SF has fluted barrel; also in .220 Swift (8.5 lbs.); VLS has laminated stock, also in .243, 6mm
VS: . . . . . . . . . . . . . . . . . . . . $811
VSSF: . . . . . . . . . . . . . . . . . . $976
VLS: . . . . . . . . . . . . . . . . . . . $725
Left hand: . . . . . . . . . . . . . . . $837

## MODEL 710

*Action:* bolt
*Stock:* synthetic
*Barrel:* 22 in.
*Sights:* none
*Weight:* 7.3
*Caliber:* .270, .30-06, 7mm Rem. Mag., .300 Win. Mag.
*Magazine:* detachable box, 4 rounds
*Features:* self-lubing nylon receiver insert; 60° bolt throw; includes mounted 3-9x40 Bushnell scope
710 with scope: . . . . . . . . . . . $426

RIFLES

# Remington Arms Rifles

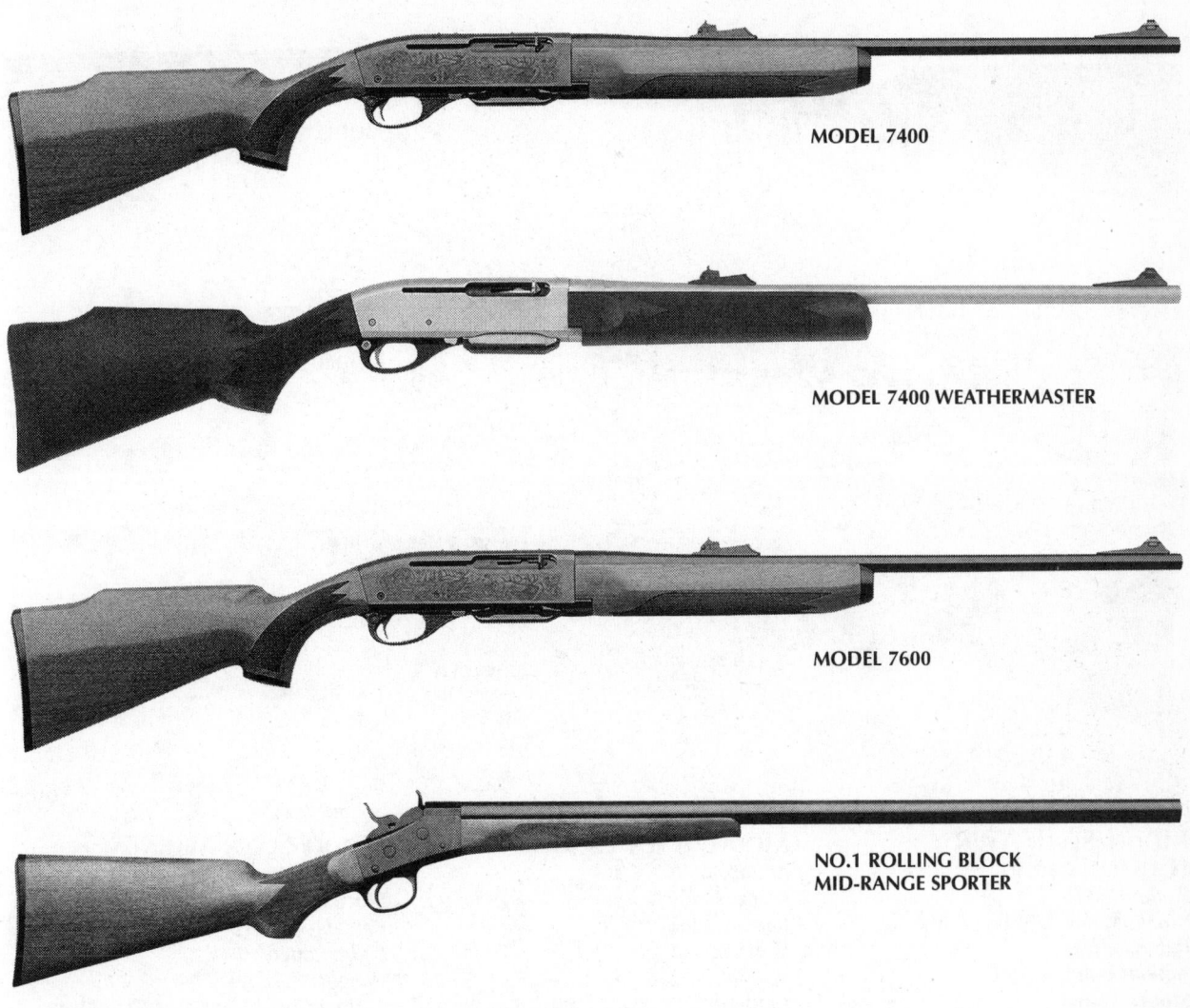

MODEL 7400

MODEL 7400 WEATHERMASTER

MODEL 7600

NO.1 ROLLING BLOCK
MID-RANGE SPORTER

## MODEL 7400

*Action:* autoloading
*Stock:* walnut or synthetic
*Barrel:* 22 in.
*Sights:* open
*Weight:* 7.5
*Caliber:* .243, .270, .308, .30-06
*Magazine:* detachable box, 4 rounds
*Features:* also; 7400 carbine with 18 in. barrel (7.3 lbs.)
walnut: . . . . . . . . . . . . . . . . . $624
synthetic:. . . . . . . . . . . . . . . . $520

## MODEL 7400 WEATHERMASTER

*Action:* autoloading
*Stock:* synthetic
*Barrel:* 22 in.
*Sights:* open
*Weight:* 7.5lbs.
*Caliber:* .270, .30-06
*Magazine:* 4
*Features:* nickel plated, weather resistant receiver and barrel
Weathermaster. . . . . . . . . . . . $624

## MODEL 7600

*Action:* pump
*Stock:* walnut or synthetic
*Barrel:* 22 in.
*Sights:* open
*Weight:* 7.5
*Caliber:* .243, .270, .308, .30-06
*Magazine:* detachable box, 4 rounds
*Features:* also: 7600 carbine with 18 in. barrel (7.3 lbs.)
walnut: . . . . . . . . . . . . . . . . . $588
synthetic:. . . . . . . . . . . . . . . . $484

## ROLLING BLOCK MID-RANGE SPORTER RIFLE

*Action:* dropping block
*Stock:* walnut
*Barrel:* heavy 30 in. Round barrel
*Sights:* Buckhorn rear, blade front
*Weight:* 9.0
*Caliber:* .45-70
*Magazine:* none
*Features:* single set trigger
Mid-Range Sporter: . . . . . . . . $1450
Rolling Block Silhouette:. . . . . $1560

# Remington Arms Rifles

MODEL SEVEN AWR

MODEL SEVEN LS

MODEL SEVEN MAGNUM

## MODEL SEVEN AWR (CUSTOM SHOP)
*Action:* bolt
*Stock:* lightweight composite or laminated
*Barrel:* stainless 22 in.
*Sights:* open
*Weight:* 6.5
*Caliber:* 7mm SAUM, .300 SAUM
*Magazine:* box, 3 rounds
*Features:* Alaska Wilderness Rifle has lightweight composite stock; also: MS laminated, full-length stock (7.3 lbs.); Model Seven KS in standard short-action calibers has 20 in. barrel
**Model Seven AWR:** . . . . . . . . **$1546**
**MS:** . . . . . . . . . . . . . . . . . . . **$1332**
**KS:** . . . . . . . . . . . . . . . . . . . **$1314**

## MODEL SEVEN LS (LAMINATED)
*Action:* bolt
*Stock:* synthetic
*Barrel:* 20 in.
*Sights:* open
*Weight:* 6.5
*Caliber:* .223, .243, .260, 7mm-08, .308
*Magazine:* box, 5 rounds
*Features:* choice of chrome-moly and stainless steel; synthetic and laminated stocks; also: youth model with short hardwood stock
**LS:** . . . . . . . . . . . . . . . . . . . . **$701**
**Youth (.260 Rem. only):** . . . . . . **$547**
**Stainless synthetic:** . . . . . . . . . **$729**
**Also available:**
**Model Seven Youth (synthetic in .223, .243, 7mm-08)** . . . . . . . **$547**

## MODEL SEVEN MAGNUM
*Action:* bolt
*Stock:* synthetic
*Barrel:* stainless or blued 22 in.
*Sights:* open
*Weight:* 7.3
*Caliber:* 7mm SAUM, .300 SAUM
*Magazine:* box, 3 rounds
*Features:* also: laminated stock versions with chrome-moly steel
**LS laminated:** . . . . . . . . . . . . . **$741**
**SS synthetic:** . . . . . . . . . . . . . . **$769**

# Rifles, Inc.

CLASSIC

LIGHTWEIGHT STRATA
STAINLESS MODEL

MASTER SERIES

SAFARI MODEL

## CLASSIC

*Action:* bolt
*Stock:* laminated fiberglass
*Barrel:* stainless steel,
match grade 24 to 26 in.
*Sights:* none
*Weight:* 6.5
*Caliber:* all popular chamberings
up to .375 H&H
*Magazine:* box, 3 or 5 rounds
*Features:* Winchester 70 stainless steel,
controlled-round feed action; lapped
bolt; pillar glass bedded stock;
adjustable trigger; hinged floor-plate;
also: Signature Series, stainless Rem.
700 action, 27 in. fluted barrel,
synthetic stock in .300 Rem. UM
**Classic:** . . . . . . . . . . . . . . . . $2500
**Classic, left-hand:** . . . . . . . . . $2600
**Signature :** . . . . . . . . . . . . . . $2800
**Signature, left-hand:** . . . . . . . $2950

## LIGHTWEIGHT STRATA STAINLESS

*Action:* bolt
*Stock:* laminated with textured epoxy

*Barrel:* stainless match grade 22 to
25 in.
*Sights:* none
*Weight:* 4.75
*Caliber:* all popular chamberings up to
.375 H&H
*Magazine:* box, 3 or 5 rounds
*Features:* Stainless Rem. action, fluted
bolt and hollowed-handle;
pillar glass bedded stock; stainless
metal finish; blind or hinged
floorplate; custom Protektor pad; also:
Lightweight 70 (5.75 lbs.); Lightweight
Titanium Strata
**Lightweight Strata:** . . . . . . . . $2850
**Strata, left-hand:** . . . . . . . . . . $2950
**Lightweight 70:** . . . . . . . . . . . $2750
**70, left-hand:** . . . . . . . . . . . . $2850
**Titanium Strata:** . . . . . . . . . . . $3850

## MASTER SERIES

*Action:* bolt
*Stock:* laminated fiberglass
*Barrel:* match grade 24 to 27 in.
*Sights:* none

*Weight:* 7.75
*Caliber:* all popular chamberings up to
.300 Rem. Ultra Mag.
*Magazine:* box, 3 rounds
*Features:* Remington 700 action
**Master Series:** . . . . . . . . . . . $2950

## SAFARI MODEL

*Action:* bolt
*Stock:* laminated fiberglass
*Barrel:* stainless match grade 23 to
25 in.
*Sights:* optional Express
*Weight:* 9.0
*Caliber:* all popular chamberings
*Magazine:* box, 3 or 5 rounds, optional
drop box
*Features:* Win. Model 70 action;
drilled and tapped for 8-40 screws;
Stainless Quiet Slimbrake; stainless or
black Teflon finish; adjustable trigger;
hinged floor-plate; barrel band optional
**Safari:** . . . . . . . . . . . . . . . . . $3000
**with options:** . . . . . . . . . . . . $4100

# Rogue Rifle Company

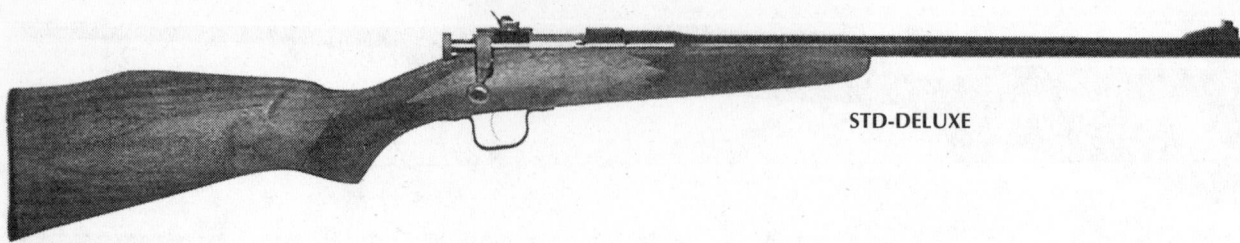

**STD-DELUXE**

**CHIPMUNK**
*Action:* bolt
*Stock:* walnut, laminated black, brown or camo
*Barrel:* 16 in.
*Sights:* target
*Weight:* 2.5

*Caliber:* Sporting rifle in .17 HMR; Target model in .22, .22 LR, .22 WMR
*Magazine:* none
*Features:* single-shot; manual-cocking action; receiver-mounted rear sights; Target model weighs 5 lbs. and comes with competition-style receiver sight

and globe front and adjustable trigger, extendable buttplate and front rail.
Also: .22 WMR
**standard:** . . . . . . . . . . . . . . . . . **$164**
**Target with options:** . . . . . . . . . **$349**

# Rossi Rifles

**MATCHED PAIR**

**MATCHED PAIR**
*Action:* hinged breech
*Stock:* hardwood
*Barrel:* 18.5 in (rifle), 22 in. (shotgun)
*Sights:* open
*Weight:* 4.0
*Caliber:* .22 LR and .410 bore
*Magazine:* none
*Features:* single shot; stainless steel; single-stage trigger; also; Centerfire Rifle/Shotgun Matched Pair, full size 12 or 20 gauge with .223 or .243
**blued:** . . . . . . . . . . . . . . . . . . . **$144**
**.410 and .17 HMR, blue:** . . . . . **$180**

RIFLES

# Rossi Rifles

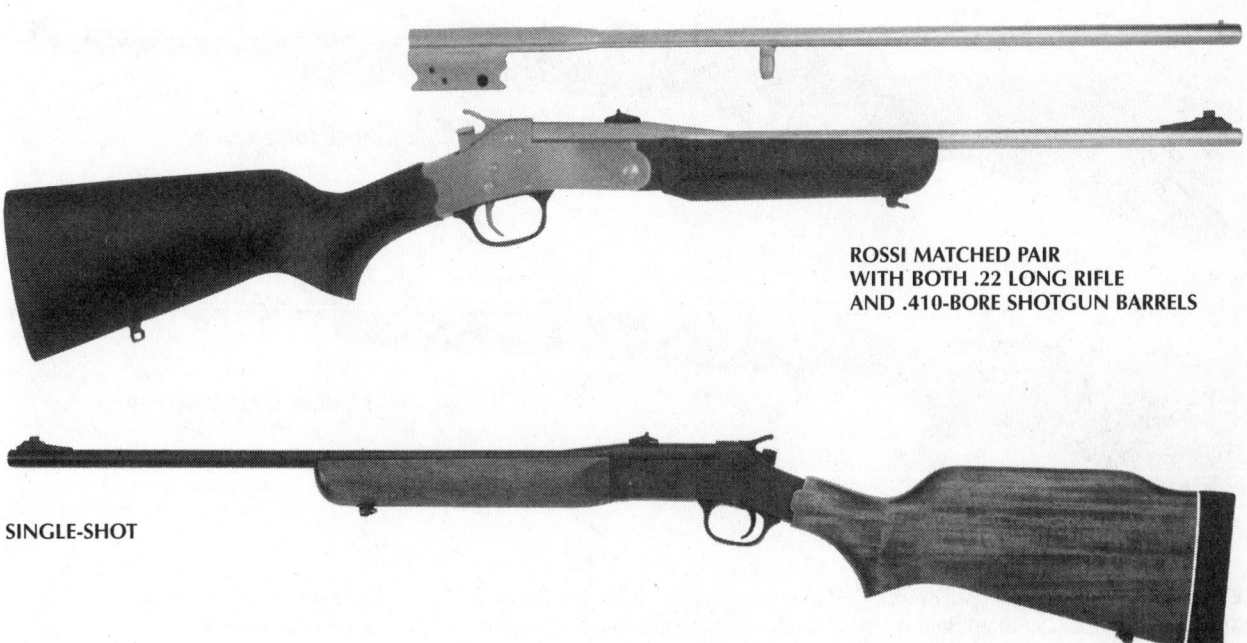

**ROSSI MATCHED PAIR
WITH BOTH .22 LONG RIFLE
AND .410-BORE SHOTGUN BARRELS**

SINGLE-SHOT

## CENTERFIRE MATCHED PAIR

*Action:* hinged breech
*Stock:* hardwood
*Barrel:* 23 in.
*Sights:* open
*Weight:* 6.3lbs.
*Caliber:* .17 HMR, .270 WSM, .50
muzzleloader
*Magazine:* none
*Features:* carry case and sling included;
adjustable sights
**Matched Pair** . . . . . . . . . . . . . **$325**

## SINGLE SHOT

*Action:* hinged breech
*Stock:* hardwood
*Barrel:* 24 in.
*Sights:* open
*Weight:* 5.5
*Caliber:* .17 HMR, .22 LR, .22 Mag.,
.357 Mag., .44 Rem Mag., 223, 243,
.45/410, .308, .30-06, .270, .270 WSM
*Magazine:* none
*Features:* single shot; recoil pad;
sling swivels; extra-wide positive-
action extractor; good rifle for first
time shooters

.17 HMR or .22 LR, .22 Mag.
  blue: . . . . . . . . . . . . . . . . . $159
.17 HMR or .22 LR, .22 Mag.
  stainless,/black: . . . . . . . . . $202
.357 or .44 Rem. Mag., blue: . . $173
.357 or .44 Rem. Mag.,
  stainless/black: . . . . . . . . . . $216
.223, .243, .308, .30-06, .270,
  .270 WSM, blue: . . . . . . . . . $202
.410/.45 Colt, blue: . . . . . . . . $188
.410/.45 Colt, stainless: . . . . . . $231
Youth w/Monte Carlo stock: . . . $202

RIFLES

*Synthetic stocks are sturdier than walnut, but not
always lighter in weight. Choose one of carbon fiber
and Kevlar, not injection-molded material.*

# Ruger Rifles

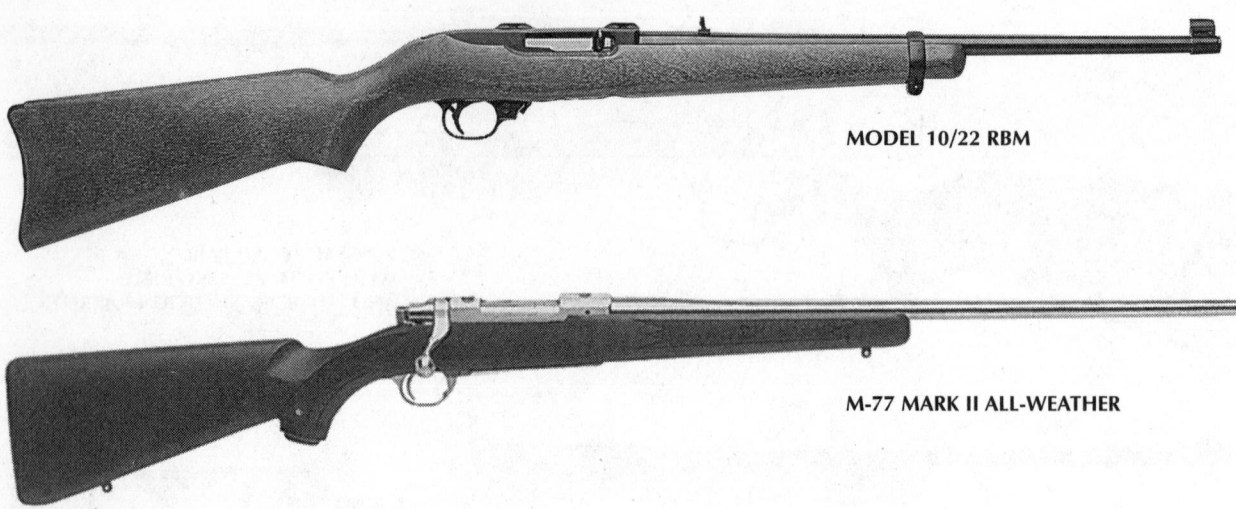

**MODEL 10/22 RBM**

**M-77 MARK II ALL-WEATHER**

**CAR COLLECTOR,** art connoisseur and philanthropist, William Batterman Ruger, founder of Sturm, Ruger & Company, was also the most prominent gun designer in the U.S. during the last half of the 20th century. Born June 21, 1916 in Brooklyn, New York, Ruger discovered a passion for guns when he received a rifle from his father at age 12. As a student at the University of North Carolina, he converted an empty room into a machine shop, and, 1938 came up with initial designs for what eventually became a light machine gun for the Army. Ruger executed the drawings on his in-laws' dining room table. Ordnance officials liked the gun, which launched Ruger to become a full-time gun designer. Over the next 53 years he helped invent and patent dozens of models of sporting firearms.

In 1949, Ruger teamed with Alexander McCormick Sturm to establish Sturm, Ruger & Company. After Sturm's death in 1951, Ruger took full control of the Company, whose first firearm, a stylish .22 caliber target pistol, is still one of the most popular target pistols in the U.S. Bill Ruger had a hand in the original design and styling of every firearm his company produced, and continued to work on new products up until his death in 2002. When not involved with his firearms company, Ruger collected antique firearms and early Western American art. His garages housed more than 30 antique vehicles, included Bentleys, Rolls-Royces, Bugattis, Stutzes, and a 1913 Mercer Raceabout. In 1970, Ruger commissioned the design and construction of a sports tourer automobile. Called the Ruger Special, it was based on the 1929 Bentley 4½ liter. Bill Ruger's philanthropy helped fund several charities, and the Buffalo Bill Historical Center in Cody, Wyoming, where he served as a member of the Board of Trustees for over 15 years. His son, William B. Ruger, Jr., is currently Chairman of the company.

Sturm, Ruger & Company, is the largest firearms manufacturer in the U.S., and has produced more than 20 million firearms for hunting, target shooting, collecting, self-defense, law enforcement and military use. Plants are located in Newport, New Hampshire, and Prescott, Arizona, with corporate headquarters in Southport, Connecticut. Sturm, Ruger precision investment castings are made for a wide variety of applications, including aero-space, automotive, general manufacturing and the golf market.

## Model 10/22

*Action:* autoloading
*Stock:* walnut, birch, synthetic or laminated
*Barrel:* 18 in.
*Sights:* open
*Weight:* 5.0
*Caliber:* .22 LR
*Magazine:* rotary, 10 rounds
*Features:* blowback action; also: International with full-stock, heavy-barreled Target and stainless steel versions; Magnum with 9-shot magazine

| | |
|---|---|
| 10/22: | $250 |
| walnut: | $315 |
| stainless: | $295 |
| International: | $250 |
| stainless International: | $295 |
| Target: | $445 |
| Target stainless, laminated: | $495 |
| magnum: | $510 |
| .17 HMR | $510 |

## Model 77 RFP Mark II

*Action:* bolt
*Stock:* synthetic
*Barrel:* 22 in.
*Sights:* none
*Weight:* 7.0
*Caliber:* most popular standard and magnum calibers
*Magazine:* box, 5 rounds
*Features:* stainless steel barrel and action, (magnums with 24 in. barrel); scope rings included; also: RSFP with sights

| | |
|---|---|
| RFP: | $695 |
| RSFP: | $780 |

# Ruger Rifles

M77RSM MKII

MODEL 77VT MARK II HEAVY BARREL TARGET

MODEL 77/17 BOLT ACTION RIFLE

MODEL 96/17

## MODEL 77 RSM MAGNUM
**Action:** bolt
**Stock:** Circassian walnut
**Barrel:** 23 in. with quarter rib
**Sights:** open
**Weight:** 9.3
**Caliber:** .375 H&H, .416 Rigby (10.3 lbs.), .458 Lott
**Magazine:** box, 3 or 4 rounds
**Features:** barrel-mounted front swivel; also: Express rifle in popular standard and magnum long-action calibers
**Price:**...................$1795

## MODEL 77 VT MARK II
**Action:** bolt
**Stock:** laminated
**Barrel:** heavy stainless 26 in.

**Sights:** none
**Weight:** 9.8
**Caliber:** .223, .22-250, .220 Swift, .243, .25-06, .308
**Magazine:** box, 5 rounds
**77 VT:**...................$845

## MODEL 77/17
**Action:** bolt
**Stock:** walnut, synthetic or laminated
**Barrel:** 22 in.
**Sights:** none
**Weight:** 6.5
**Caliber:** .17 HMR
**Magazine:** 9 rounds
**Features:** also: stainless (P) and stainless varmint with laminated stock (VMBBZ), 24 in. barrel (6.9 lbs.)

77/17 RM:................$595
77/17 RMP:..............$595
K77/17 VMBBZ:...........$665

## MODEL 96 LEVER ACTION RIFLE
**Action:** Lever
**Stock:** Hardwood
**Barrel:** 18½ inches blued
**Sights:** Adjustable rear sight
**Weight:** 5.25 lbs.
**Caliber:** .17 HMR, .22 WMR, .44 Mag.
**Magazine:** 9 round rotary magazine
**Features:** Enclosed short-throw lever action; cross bolt safety; standard tip-off scope-mount base.
**Price:**...................$ 375
**.44 Mag.**................$525

RIFLES

# Ruger Rifles

MODEL 77/22VBZ VARMINT

MODEL 77/44 RS

MODEL M-77R MKII

MODEL M-77RL MKII ULTRA LIGHT

## MODEL 77/22 RIMFIRE RIFLE
**Action:** bolt
**Stock:** walnut
**Barrel:** 20 in.
**Sights:** none
**Weight:** 6.0
**Caliber:** .22 LR, .22 Mag.
**Magazine:** rotary, 10 rounds
**Features:** also: Magnum (M) and stainless synthetic (P) versions; scope rings included for all; sights on S versions. VBZ has 24 in. medium stainless barrel (6.9 lbs.)

77/22R: . . . . . . . . . . . . . . . . . . $595
77/22RM: . . . . . . . . . . . . . . . . $595
K77/22RP: . . . . . . . . . . . . . . . . $595
K77/22 RMP: . . . . . . . . . . . . . . $595
K77/22RSP: . . . . . . . . . . . . . . . $620
K77/RSMP:. . . . . . . . . . . . . . . . $620
K77/22VBZ:. . . . . . . . . . . . . . . . $665
K77/22VMBZ:. . . . . . . . . . . . . . $665
77/22RH (.22 Hornet):. . . . . . . $630
K77/22VHZ (.22 Hornet):. . . . . $665

## MODEL 77/44RS
**Action:** bolt
**Stock:** walnut
**Barrel:** 18 in.
**Sights:** open
**Weight:** 6.0
**Caliber:** .44 Magnum
**Magazine:** rotary, 6 rounds
**Features:** also: stainless synthetic (P) version

77/44RS: . . . . . . . . . . . . . . . . . $635
K77/44 RSP:. . . . . . . . . . . . . . . $635

## MODEL 77R MARK II
**Action:** bolt
**Stock:** walnut
**Barrel:** 22 in.
**Sights:** none
**Weight:** 7.0
**Caliber:** most popular standard and magnum calibers
**Magazine:** box, 5 rounds
**Features:** scope rings included; RS

Model has open sights; RBZ has stainless steel, laminated stock; RSBZ with sights

77R:. . . . . . . . . . . . . . . . . . . . $695
RS:. . . . . . . . . . . . . . . . . . . . . $780
RBZ: . . . . . . . . . . . . . . . . . . . $750
RSBZ:. . . . . . . . . . . . . . . . . . . $825

## MODEL 77RL MARK II ULTRA LIGHT
**Action:** bolt
**Stock:** walnut
**Barrel:** 20 in.
**Sights:** none
**Weight:** 6.0
**Caliber:** .223, .243, .257, .270, .308, .30-06
**Magazine:** box, 5 rounds
**Features:** RSI International Model has full-length stock, 18 in. barrel

77RL Ultra Light: . . . . . . . . . . . $750
International Model:. . . . . . . . . $795

# Ruger Rifles

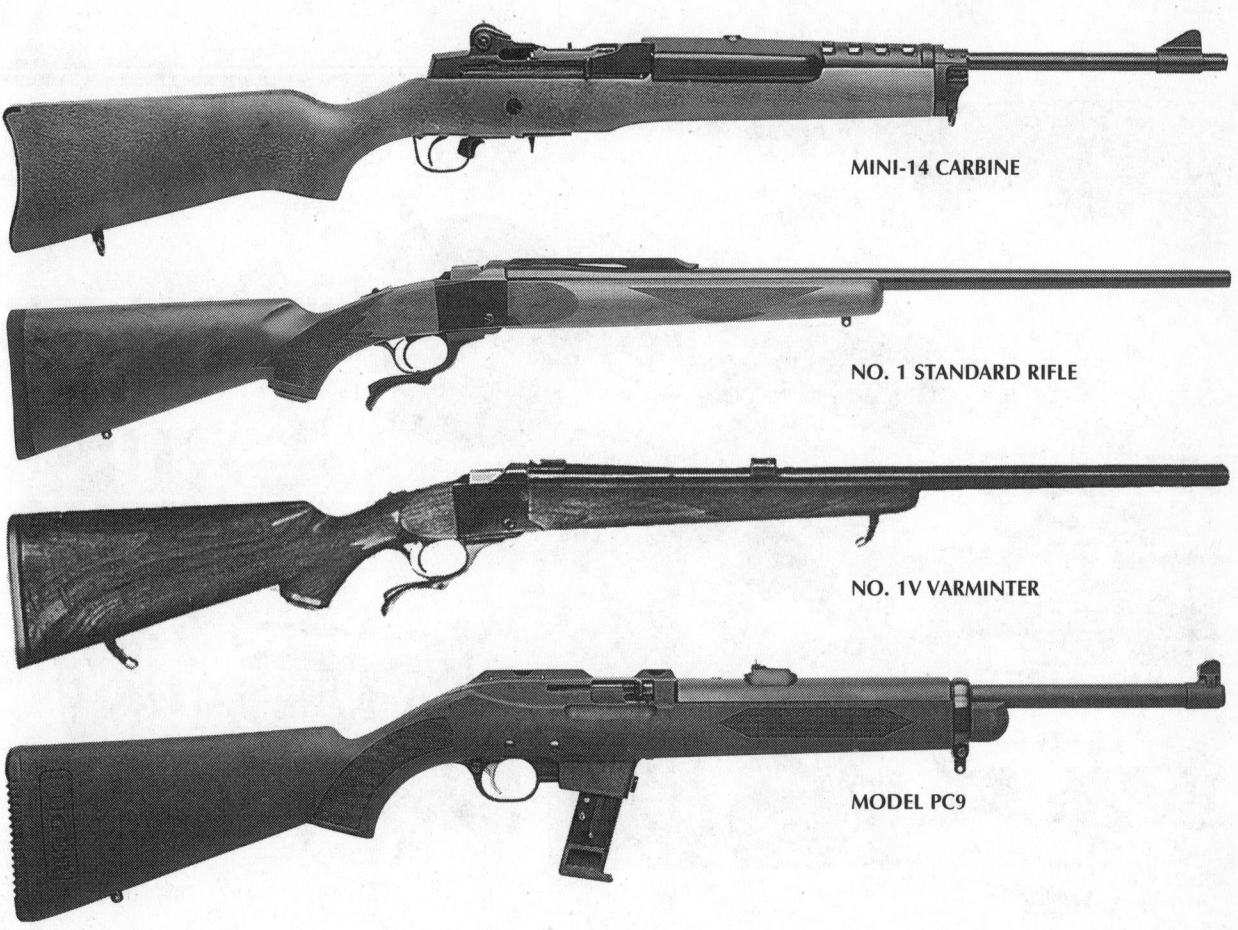

MINI-14 CARBINE

NO. 1 STANDARD RIFLE

NO. 1V VARMINTER

MODEL PC9

## MINI-14 CARBINE
*Action:* autoloading
*Stock:* hardwood
*Barrel:* 18 in.
*Sights:* target
*Weight:* 6.5
*Caliber:* .223
*Magazine:* detachable box, 5 rounds
*Features:* also: stainless, stainless synthetic versions of Mini-14/5; Ranch Rifle (with scope mounts) and Mini-thirty (in 7.62x39)
Mini 14:. . . . . . . . . . . . . . . . . $655
stainless Mini 14: . . . . . . . . . . $715
stainless synthetic Mini 14:. . . . $715
Ranch Rifle: . . . . . . . . . . . . . . $695
Ranch rifle, stainless: . . . . . . . . $770
Ranch rifle, stainless synthetic: . $770
Mini-Thirty: . . . . . . . . . . . . . . $695
Mini-thirty, stainless: . . . . . . . . $770
Mini-Thirty, stainless synthetic:. $770
Deerfield Carbine .44 Mag.. . . . $675

## NO. 1 SINGLE-SHOT
*Action:* dropping block

*Stock:* select checkered walnut
*Barrel:* 22, 24, or 26 in.
*Sights:* open
*Weight:* 7.25
*Caliber:* all popular chamberings in Light Sporter, Medium Sporter, Standard Rifle
*Magazine:* none
*Features:* pistol grip; all rifles come with Ruger 1" scope rings; Medium Sporter weighs 8 lbs. and 45-70 is available in stainless; Standard Rifle weighs 8 lbs. No. 1 Stainless comes in .243, .25-06, 7mm Rem. Mag., 7mm STW, .30-06, .308
No. 1: . . . . . . . . . . . . . . . . . . $920
Stainless steel: . . . . . . . . . . . . $950

## NO. 1V (VARMINTER)
*Action:* dropping block
*Stock:* select checkered walnut
*Barrel:* heavy 24 or 26 in. (.220 Swift)
*Sights:* open
*Weight:* 9.0
*Caliber:* .22-250, .220 Swift, .223,

.25-06, 6mm
*Magazine:* box, 5 rounds
*Features:* Ruger target scope block, stainless available in .22-250; also: No. 1H Tropical (heavy 24 in. bbl.) in .375 H&H, .416 Rigby, .45 Lott, .405; No.1 RSI International (20 in. light bbl. and full-length stock) in .243, .270, .30-06, 7x57
Varmint:. . . . . . . . . . . . . . . . . $950
Tropical: . . . . . . . . . . . . . . . . $950
International: . . . . . . . . . . . . . $950

## MODEL PC9 CARBINE
*Action:* autoloading
*Stock:* synthetic
*Barrel:* 16
*Sights:* open
*Weight:* 6.3
*Caliber:* 9mm, .40 auto
*Magazine:* detachable, 10 rounds
*Features:* delayed blowback action; optional ghost ring sight
Carbine:. . . . . . . . . . . . . . . . . $605
with ghost ring sights:. . . . . . . $628

# Sako Rifles

**SAKO 75 HUNTER**

**KEY**

**SAKO ACTIONS**

**LOCKED**     **READY**

**THUMB SAFETY, DOVETAILED RECEIVER**

**THE FINNISH RIFLE-MAKER SAKO** has long been known for producing smooth, finely fitted bolt actions – sized to accommodate specific cartridge families. The Sako 75 is the first to offer a bolt with three locking lugs and a mechanical ejector while maintaining a bolt lift of only 70°. Five guiding surfaces prevent the bolt from binding and provide ultra smooth-operation. The two-position thumb safety is located conveniently behind the bolt handle. A separate button in front of the safety allows the bolt to be opened while the safety is on. The detachable magazine can be loaded through the ejection port. Both carbon steel and stainless steel actions are available.

The three largest Sako actions now feature "key concept," a mechanism on the cocking piece that locks or unlocks the striker. You can thus disable the 75 with a turn of the key. Three keys are provided with each

rifle; others can be ordered by rifle serial number from 7500 patterns. All Sako Model 75 rifles except those built on the smallest actions come standard with the key concept lock.

"The key blends into the rifle contours when the lock is open and the gun is operational," explained Paul-Erik Tolvo, former president of Sako Ltd. "When the key is removed, the the hunting rifle is completely safe." More to the point for most hunters, the 75 is an accurate, well-balanced rifle that's available in a wide range of chamberings and in both sytethic and wood stocks. You can specify a stainless steel or chrome-moly barrel, even a left-hand bolt.

## MODEL 75 HUNTER
**Action:** bolt
**Stock:** walnut or synthetic
**Barrel:** hammer-forged 22, 24 or 26 in.
**Sights:** none
**Weight:** 7.0

**Caliber:** most popular standard and magnum calibers from .222 Rem. to .375 H&H and .300 and .270 WSM
**Magazine:** detachable box, 4 to 6 rounds
**Features:** barrel length depends on caliber; 4 action lengths; also: stainless synthetic and short-barreled Finnlight versions, Deluxe Grade with fancy walnut stock

Hunter: . . . . . . . . . . . . . . . . . . . $1173
.375 H&H: . . . . . . . . . . . . . . . $1242
Stainless synthetic: . . . . . . . . . . $1242
Left-hand (.25-06, .270, .30-06): . $1173
Finnlight: . . . . . . . . . . . . . . . . . $1311
Deluxe: . . . . . . . . . . . . . . . . . . $1691
.416 Rem: . . . . . . . . . . . . . . . . $2001
.375 Hunt Mag. with iron sights. $1691

# Sako Rifles

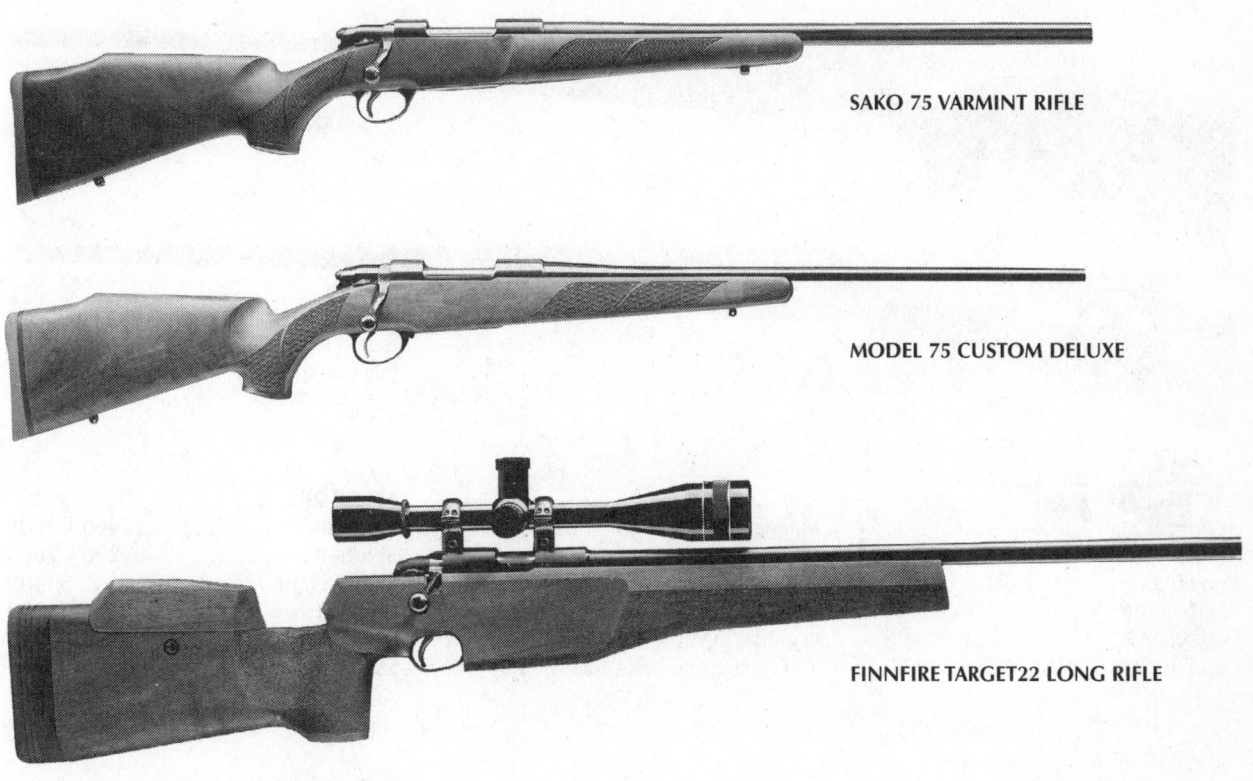

**SAKO 75 VARMINT RIFLE**

**MODEL 75 CUSTOM DELUXE**

**FINNFIRE TARGET22 LONG RIFLE**

## MODEL 75 VARMINT
*Action:* bolt
*Stock:* varmint-style walnut
*Barrel:* heavy 24 in.
*Sights:* none
*Weight:* 9.0
*Caliber:* most popular standard and magnum calibers from .17 Rem. to .375 H&H
*Magazine:* detachable box, 4 to 6 rounds
*Features:* also: 75 Varmint Laminated Stainless in .222, .223, 6PPC, .22-250, .243, 7mm-08, .308
**Varmint:. . . . . . . . . . . . . . . . $1346**
**Varmint LS: . . . . . . . . . . . . . $1484**

## MODEL 75 CUSTOM DELUXE
*Action:* bolt
*Stock:* walnut
*Barrel:* 23 in.
*Sights:* none
*Weight:* 7.8lbs.
*Caliber:* .270, .30-06
*Magazine:* 5
*Features:* select walnut stock, oil-finished; engraved metal
**Custom Deluxe. . . . . . . . . . . $3588**
**Single Shot (.308) . . . . . . . . . $2850**
**80th Anniversary Edition**
    **(.375 H&H) . . . . . . . . . . $16,560**

## FINNFIRE TARGET 22
*Action:* bolt
*Stock:* walnut
*Barrel:* 22 in.
*Sights:* none
*Weight:* 5.3
*Caliber:* .22 LR
*Magazine:* detachable box, 5 or 10 rounds
*Features:* adjustable trigger; 2-lug, 50-degree bolt; available with open sights; also: varmint (heavy) and Sporter (adjustable target) versions
**Hunter: . . . . . . . . . . . . . . . . $863**
**Varmint:. . . . . . . . . . . . . . . . $897**
**Target: . . . . . . . . . . . . . . . . . $966**

## MODEL TRG-22
*Action:* bolt
*Stock:* synthetic
*Barrel:* 26 in.
*Sights:* none
*Weight:* 10.3
*Caliber:* .308
*Magazine:* detachable box, 10 rounds
*Features:* 3-lug bolt; fully adjustable trigger; optional bipod, brake; also: TRG 42 in .300 Win. Mag. and .338 Lapua (5-round magazine, 27 in. barrel, 11.3 lbs.)
**TRG-22:. . . . . . . . . . . . . . . . $2967**
**TRG-42:. . . . . . . . . . . . . . . . $3312**

# Sauer Rifles

**202 STANDARD**

**202 VARMINT**

## MODEL 202

**Action:** bolt
**Stock:** Claro walnut
**Barrel:** 24 in.
**Sights:** none
**Weight:** 7.7
**Caliber:** .243, .25-06, 6.5x55, .270, .308, .30-06
**Magazine:** detachable box, 5 rounds
**Features:** adjustable trigger; quick-change barrel; also: Supreme Magnum with 26 in. barrel in 7mm Rem., .300 Win., .300 Wby., .375 H&H; Varmint and Tactical versions too

| | |
|---|---|
| Model 202: | . . . . . . . . . . . . . $2200 |
| Magnum: | . . . . . . . . . . $2400 - 2600 |
| Synthetic: | . . . . . . . . . . $2200 - 2600 |
| Lightweight: | . . . . . . . . . . . . . $3400 |
| Varmint: | . . . . . . . . . . . . . . . $3400 |
| Left-hand (.30-06, walnut): | . . . $3700 |
| SSG 3000 Tactical: | . . . . $2900 - 5000 |

# Savage Rifles

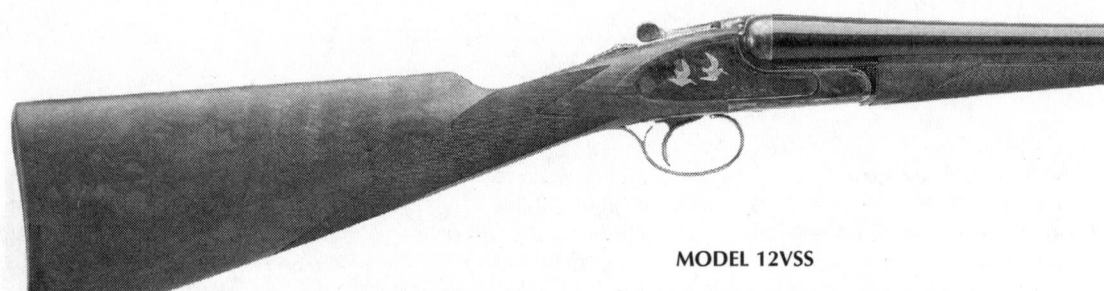

**MODEL 12VSS**

**THE MOST PROLIFIC AGE** in gun design was surely the last half of the 19th century, when flintlocks gave way to caplocks, which evolved into cartridge guns that quickly became repeaters. Smokeless powder replaced black, and in short decades the jacketed rifle bullet had supplanted the lead ball. Beginning in 1849 with Christian Sharps's dropping-block rifle and the Hunt Volitional Repeater, manufacturers found ways to marry mass production with powerful cartridges and rapid-fire guns that worked every time. Among the most brilliant rifle designs appearing at the end of this era was

one by Arthur William Savage.

Born June 13, 1857 in Kingston, Jamaica, Arthur Savage was schooled in England and the United States. His father served as England's Special Commissioner to the British West Indies. Young Savage had an adventurous streak and immediately after college sailed for Australia, where he found work on a cattle ranch. Arthur also found a wife (Annie Bryant) and started a family. One of his sons was born in a wagon on a wilderness trek. Eventually the Savages would have four sons and four daughters. An astute businessman, Arthur quickly built himself a stake in

cattle. After an 11-year stay, he was said to own the biggest ranch in Australia.

The Outback had provided fortune and thrills (Aborigines once captured him and held him for several months), but Savage itched for new frontiers. He sold his ranch, moved back to Jamaica and bought a coffee plantation. There he tinkered with machinery and pursued an interest in firearms and explosives. With another inventor, he developed the Savage-Halpine torpedo. It got good reviews from the U.S. Navy, but no contract came. Later the design was sold to the Brazilian government. Savage also worked on plans for recoilless rifles.

# Savage Rifles

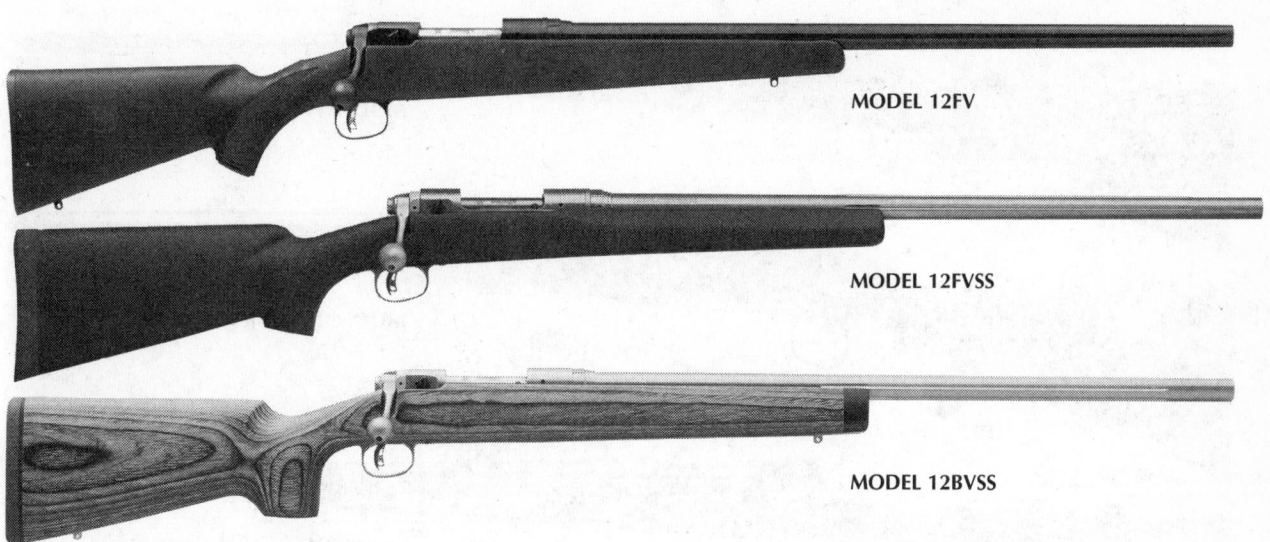

MODEL 12FV

MODEL 12FVSS

MODEL 12BVSS

In l892, when Savage was just 35 years old, he finished the blueprint for a new lever-action repeating rifle – a hammerless gun with a rotary magazine. It was a daring design in the wake of analyses that blamed the failure of the similar Model l878 Sharps-Borchardt on its lack of a visible hammer. By this time Savage was living in the U.S. and he submitted his rifle for testing at the l892 ordnance trials on Governor's Island, New York. It was beaten by the Krag-Jorgensen, and Savage turned to sportsmen. Arthur Savage redesigning his gun, paring magazine capacity to five and altering the lever to accommodate three fingers. He also developed a new cartridge for the rifle and in l894 formed the Savage Arms Company in Utica, New York.

Savage's first commercial rifle was called the Model l895. Its rear-locking bolt abutted a steel web machined into the tail of a streamlined receiver milled from a forging. There were no openings rearward to allow the escape of gas from a ruptured case. Side ejection kept cases out of the line of sight and would later permit low scope mounting.

Savage's action was less vulnerable to water and debris than were the exposed-hammer lever guns of the day. It had a coil mainspring (the first of its kind on a commercial lever action) and a through-bolt to join butt-stock and receiver. The through-bolt made for a stronger union than tiny wood screws in a tang extension. But the most exciting part of the Savage

gun was its magazine, a spring-loaded brass spool with a visible cartridge counter that showed how many rounds remained.

Savage's spool magazine design was better protected than an under-barrel tube, and it didn't affect rifle balance, because, full or empty, the weight stayed between your hands. The Savage magazine didn't affect barrel vibrations as tubular magazines did, so accuracy was enhanced. Most importantly, pointed bullets were safe to use in the Model 95 because the cartridges did not rest primer-to-bullet tip. A hunter thus could use more powerful ammunition with greater reach.

The Model 1892 Savage lost out to the Krag-Jorgensen in military trials, but its potential as a sporting rifle was clear. Refined, it became the 1895, then the 1899. The 99 Savage survived for nearly a century, a favorite of big game hunters. The Krag rifle had a brief stint as our infantry rifle before its replacement by the Springfield in 1903. While the 99 is too expensive to manufacture these days, Savage's gun company has prospered, with sturdy, affordable bolt-action centerfire rifles, a plethora of rimfire rifles, and now high-performance handguns. Shotguns, from doubles to autoloaders and combination guns, have played a part in the company's fortunes, especially with the acquisition of the Fox and Stevens names.

Until his death in 1914 at age 84, Arthur William Savage continued to indulge the curiosity that made him one

of our great gun designers. He invested in oil exploration, a citrus plantation, a tire company. The firearms firm he established has become one of the most recognized and best loved in America.

## Model 12, 112 10FP Series
**Action:** bolt
**Stock:** synthetic or laminated
**Barrel:** 20 or 26 in.
**Sights:** none
**Weight:** 8.3lbs.
**Caliber:** .223, .22-250, .243, .25-06, 7mm Rem. Mag., .308, .30-06, .300 WSM, .300 Win. Mag.
**Magazine:** 3 or 4
**Features:** single-shot or box magazine; new in these rifles for 2003 is the Savage AccuTrigger
**12 youth** . . . . . . . . . . . . . . . . . $532
**12 VSS Stainless single-shot.** . . . $934

## Model 12FV (Short Action)
**Action:** bolt
**Stock:** synthetic
**Barrel:** varmint 26 in.
**Sights:** none
**Weight:** 9.0lbs.
**Caliber:** .223, .22-250, .243, .308, .300 WSM
**Magazine:** box, 5 rounds
**Features:** also: 12VSS with fluted stainless barrel, Choate adjustable stock (11.3 lbs.) and V2BVSS with stainless fluted barrel, laminated or synthetic stock (9.5 lbs.)
**FV** . . . . . . . . . . . . . . . . . . . . . $515
**FVSS** . . . . . . . . . . . . . . . . . . . . $645
**BVSS laminated** . . . . . . . . . . . . $696

RIFLES

# Savage Rifles

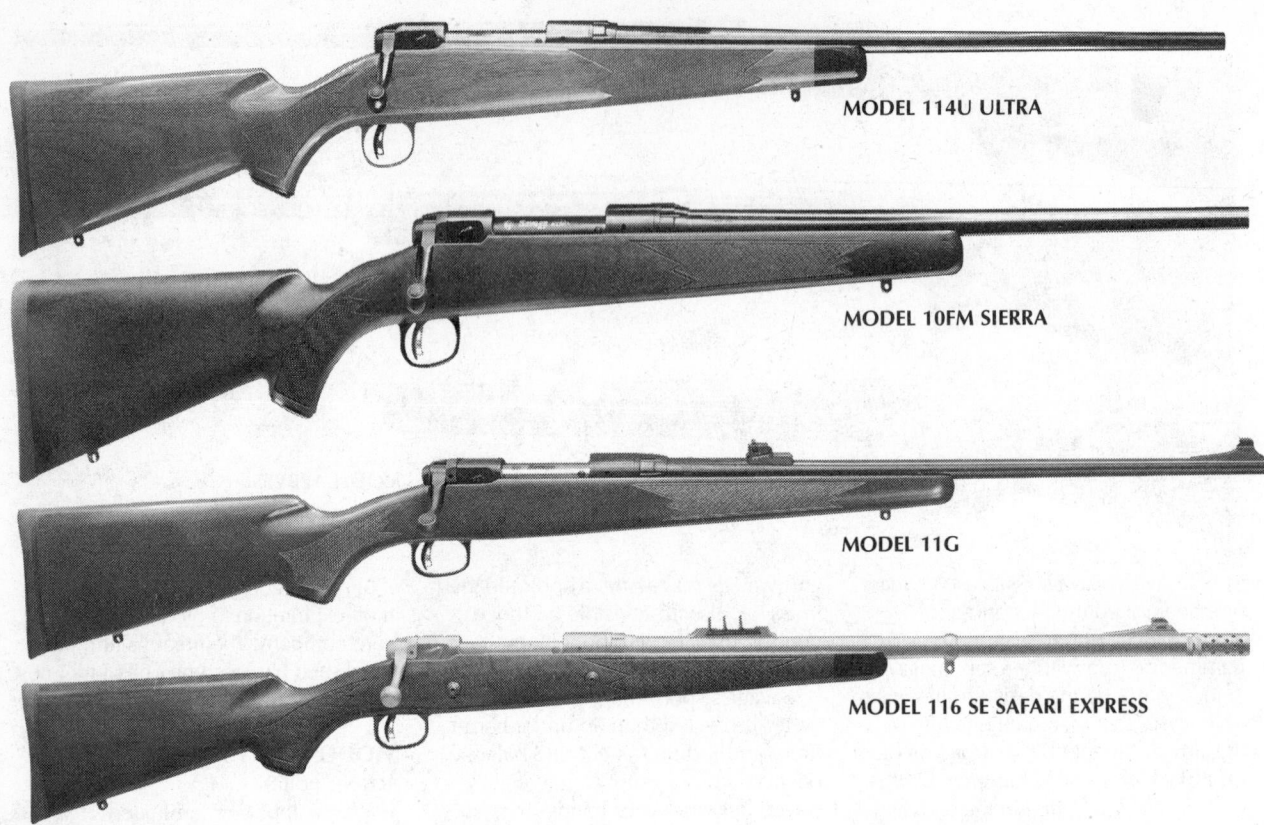

MODEL 114U ULTRA

MODEL 10FM SIERRA

MODEL 11G

MODEL 116 SE SAFARI EXPRESS

RIFLES

## MODEL 112 BVSS (LONG-ACTION)
**Action:** bolt
**Stock:** lightweight composite
**Barrel:** fluted stainless 26 in.
**Sights:** none
**Weight:** 10.3lbs.
**Caliber:** .25-06, 7mm Rem. Mag., .30-06, .300 Win. Mag.
**Magazine:** box, 4 rounds
**Features:** also: 112BVSS with laminated stock
BVSS . . . . . . . . . . . . . . . . . . . $696

## MODEL 114U
**Action:** bolt
**Stock:** walnut
**Barrel:** 22 in.
**Sights:** none
**Weight:** 7.0lbs.
**Caliber:** .270, .30-06
**Magazine:** box, 5 rounds
**Features:** also Magnum in 7mm Rem., .300 Win. (3-round magazine)
114U . . . . . . . . . . . . . . . . . . . $569

## MODEL 10FM SIERRA
**Action:** bolt
**Stock:** lightweight composite

**Barrel:** 20 in.
**Sights:** none
**Weight:** 6.3lbs.
**Caliber:** .243, .270 WSM, 7mm-08, .308, .300 WSM
**Magazine:** box, 5 rounds
**Features:** open sights available; LE (Law Enforcement) version with heavy 20 or 26 in. barrel; FCM Scout with ghost ring sight, detachable box magazine and forward scope mount
FM. . . . . . . . . . . . . . . . . . . . . $511

## MODEL 11F
**Action:** bolt
**Stock:** synthetic
**Barrel:** 22 in.
**Sights:** none
**Weight:** 6.8lbs.
**Caliber:** .223, .22-250, .243, 7mm-08, .308, .270 WSM, 7mm WSM, .300 WSM,
**Magazine:** box, 5 rounds
**Features:** open sights available; also 11G with walnut stock, 10 GY Youth with short stock in .223, .243, and .308
11F . . . . . . . . . . . . . . . . . . . . . $473
11G. . . . . . . . . . . . . . . . . . . . . $476

## MODEL 11/111
**Action:** bolt
**Stock:** hardwood or synthetic
**Barrel:** 24 in.
**Sights:** none
**Weight:** 7.0lbs.
**Caliber:** .270 WSM, 7mm WSM, .300 WSM, 7mm SUM, .300 SUM (all new for 2003 in various configurations)
**Magazine:** 3
**Features:** top tang safety; adjustable sights available
from . . . . . . . . . . . . . . . . . . . . . $473

## MODEL 116 SE SAFARI EXPRESS
**Action:** bolt
**Stock:** walnut with cut checkering, ebony tip
**Barrel:** stainless 24 in.
**Sights:** open
**Weight:** 8.5lbs.
**Caliber:** .458 Win. Mag.
**Magazine:** box, 4 rounds
**Features:** Classic-style stock with select-grade wood, stainless-steel crossbolts, internally vented recoil pad
Safari Express. . . . . . . . . . . . . $1045

# Savage Rifles

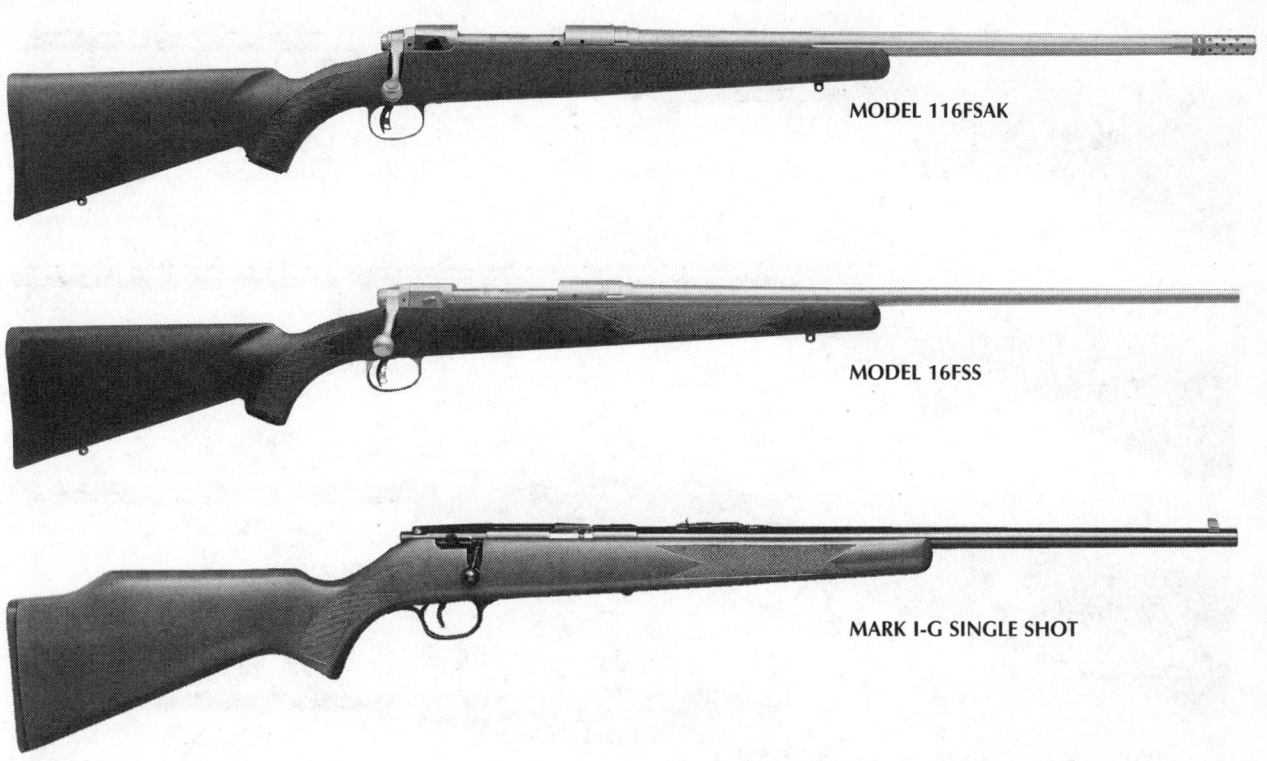

MODEL 116FSAK

MODEL 16FSS

MARK I-G SINGLE SHOT

## Model 116FSAK

*Action:* bolt
*Stock:* synthetic
*Barrel:* stainless, fluted 22, 24, and 26 in.
*Sights:* none
*Weight:* 6.8lbs.
*Caliber:* .270, .30-06 (22 in.), 7mm Rem. Mag., .300 Win. Mag. (24 in.), .300 RUM (26 in.), .338 Win. Mag.
*Magazine:* box, 4 rounds
*Features:* included: adjustable muzzle brake
**116 FSAK . . . . . . . . . . . . . . . $619**

## Model 116FSS (Long Action)

*Action:* bolt
*Stock:* synthetic
*Barrel:* stainless 22, 24, or 26 in.
*Sights:* none
*Weight:* 6.5lbs.
*Caliber:* .270, .30-06 (22 in.), 7mm Rem. Mag., .300 Win. Mag., .338 Win. Mag., .300 RUM (26 in.)
*Magazine:* box, 3 or 4 rounds
*Features:* also: 116BSS with checkered laminated stock
**116FSS. . . . . . . . . . . . . . . . . $536**

## Model 10/110

*Action:* bolt
*Stock:* checkered synthetic
*Barrel:* 24 in. with recessed target-style muzzle
*Sights:* none
*Weight:* 8.5lbs.
*Caliber:* .223, .308.
*Magazine:* box, 5 rounds
*Features:* Black matte finish on metal; black graphite stock; drilled and tapped for scope mount, bases included. Left-hand available.
**Model 10/110 . . . . . . . . . . . . $572**

## Model 110 Long Range

*Action:* bolt
*Stock:* lightweight composite
*Barrel:* heavy 24 in.
*Sights:* none
*Weight:* 8.5lbs.
*Caliber:* .25-06, 7mm Rem. Mag., .30-06, .300 Win. Mag.
*Magazine:* box, 4 rounds
*Features:* also short-action Model 10 LR in .223, .308
**110 . . . . . . . . . . . . . . . . . . . . $572**
**10 . . . . . . . . . . . . . . . . . . . . . $572**

## Model 16FSS (Short Action)

*Action:* bolt
*Stock:* synthetic
*Barrel:* stainless 22 in.
*Sights:* none
*Weight:* 6.0lbs.
*Caliber:* .223, .243, 7mm WSM, .22-250 REM, 7-08, 7 SUM, .308, .270 WSM, .300 WSM
*Magazine:* box, 3 or 4 rounds
*Features:* also: 16BSS with checkered laminated stock in .300 WSM only
**16FSS. . . . . . . . . . . . . . . . . . $536**

## Mark I

*Action:* bolt
*Stock:* hardwood
*Barrel:* 21 in.
*Sights:* open
*Weight:* 5.5lbs.
*Caliber:* .22 S, .22 L, .22 LR
*Magazine:* none
*Features:* also: MkIG Youth (19 in. barrel), MkILY Youth laminated stock, MIY Youth camo stock
**Mark I G . . . . . . . . . . . . . . . . $147**
**G Youth . . . . . . . . . . . . . . . . . $147**
**LY . . . . . . . . . . . . . . . . . . . . . $180**
**Y Camo . . . . . . . . . . . . . . . . . $178**

RIFLES

# Savage Rifles

MARK II-FSS

MARK II-FV HEAVY BARREL REPEATER

MODEL 30GM

MODEL 30G

### MARK II F
*Action:* bolt
*Stock:* synthetic
*Barrel:* 21 in.
*Sights:* open
*Weight:* 5.0lbs.
*Caliber:* .22 LR
*Magazine:* detachable box, 5 rounds
*Features:* also: MkIIG with hardwood stock, MkIIFSS stainless, MkIIGY with short stock and 19 in. barrel

| | |
|---|---|
| F | $144 |
| G | $156 |
| FSS | $205 |
| GY | $156 |
| GXP (with scope) | $164 |
| camo | $174 |

### MARK II FV
Heavy-Barrel
*Action:* bolt
*Stock:* synthetic
*Barrel:* heavy 21 in.
*Sights:* none
*Weight:* 6.0lbs.
*Caliber:* .22 LR
*Magazine:* detachable box, 5 or 10 rounds
*Features:* Weaver scope bases included; also: MkII LV with laminated stock (6.5 lbs.)

| | |
|---|---|
| FV | $253 |
| BV | $248 |
| FVXP (with scope) | $254 |

### MODEL 30
*Action:* dropping block
*Stock:* walnut
*Barrel:* octagon 21 in.
*Sights:* open
*Weight:* 4.3lbs.
*Caliber:* .22 LR, .22 WMR, .17 HMR
*Magazine:* none
*Features:* re-creation of Steven's Favorite

| | |
|---|---|
| 30G | $221 |
| 30GM | $258 |
| 30R17 | $284 |
| Take-down .22 | $242 |
| Take-down .17 | $305 |

# Savage Rifles

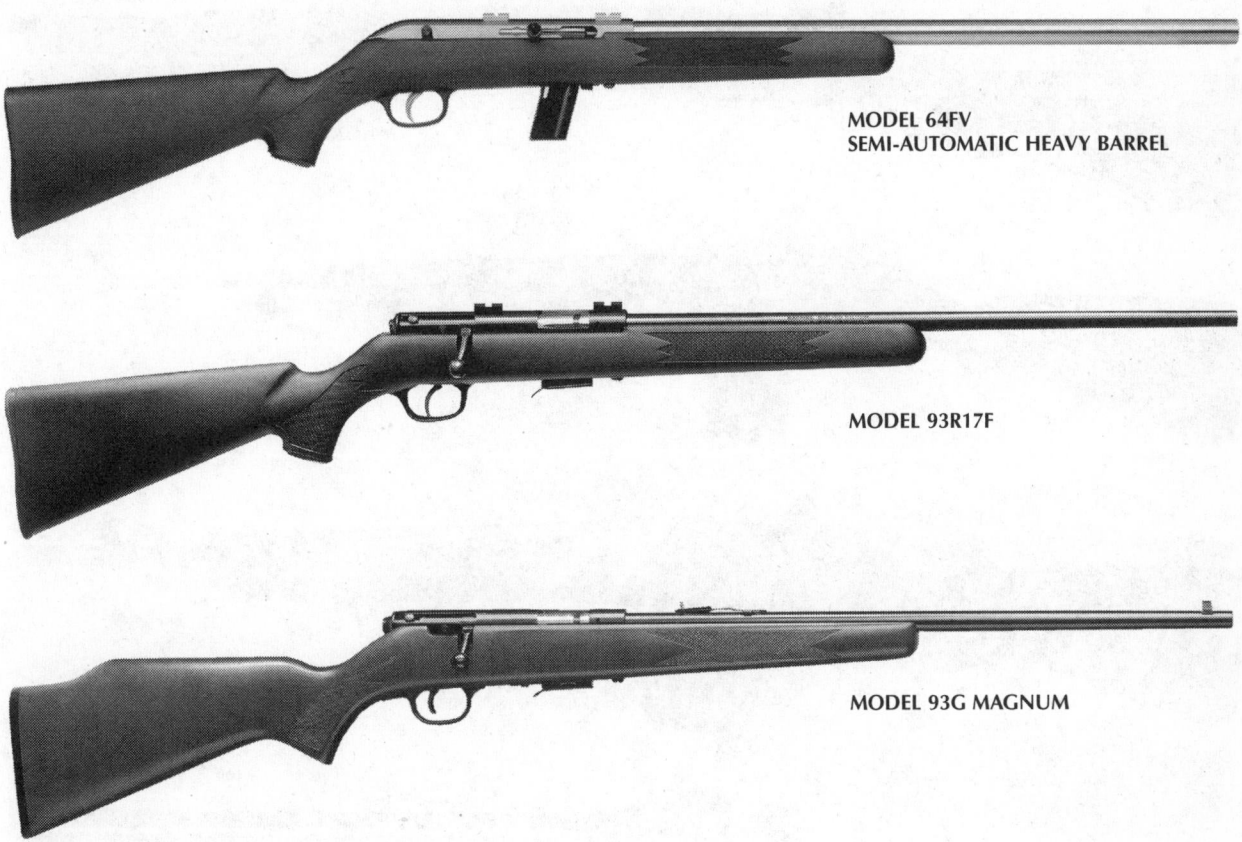

**MODEL 64FV**
**SEMI-AUTOMATIC HEAVY BARREL**

**MODEL 93R17F**

**MODEL 93G MAGNUM**

## MODEL 64F

*Action:* autoloading
*Stock:* synthetic
*Barrel:* 21 in.
*Sights:* open
*Weight:* 5.5lbs.
*Caliber:* .22 LR
*Magazine:* detachable box, 10 rounds
*Features:* also; 64 FSS stainless, 64FV and FVSS heavy barrel, 64G hardwood stock

| | |
|---|---|
| 64F | $139 |
| 64FV | $187 |
| 64FVSS | $240 |
| 64G | $158 |

## MODEL 93

*Action:* bolt
*Stock:* synthetic, hardwood or laminated
*Barrel:* 21 in.
*Sights:* none
*Weight:* 5.0lbs.
*Caliber:* .17 HMR
*Magazine:* 5
*Features:* scope bases included; eight versions with stainless or C-M steel, different stocks; varmint models weigh 6.0 lbs.

| | |
|---|---|
| synthetic F | $180 |
| camo | $211 |
| hardwood GV or GLV | $226 |
| laminated stainless BVSS | $313 |

## MODEL 93G

*Action:* bolt
*Stock:* synthetic
*Barrel:* 21 in.
*Sights:* open
*Weight:* 5.8lbs.
*Caliber:* .22 WMR, .17 HMR
*Magazine:* detachable box, 5 rounds
*Features:* 93G with hardwood stock; 93 FSS stainless, 93FVSS with heavy barrel, 93G with hardwood stock

| | |
|---|---|
| G | $188 |
| GV in .17 HMR | $226 |

**RIFLES**

# Springfield Rifles

M1 GARAND

M1A STANDARD

M1A-A1 SCOUT RIFLE

MODEL M-6 SCOUT RIFLE/SHOTGUN
COMBO FOLDING SURVIVAL GUN

## M1 GARAND
*Action:* autoloading
*Stock:* walnut
*Barrel:* 24 in.
*Sights:* target
*Weight:* 9.5
*Caliber:* .30-06
*Magazine:* clip-fed, 8 rounds
*Features:* gas-operated; new stock,
receiver, barrel; other parts mil-spec
**M1 Garand .308:** . . . . . . . . . . $1378
**M1 Garand .30-06:** . . . . . . . . $1348

## M1A
*Action:* autoloading
*Stock:* walnut
*Barrel:* 22 in.
*Sights:* target
*Weight:* 9.2
*Caliber:* .308
*Magazine:* detachable box,
5 or 10 rounds
*Features:* also with fiberglass stock
and M1A/Scout with 18 in. barrel and
scope mount (9.0 lbs.)
**M1A:** . . . . . . . . . . . . . . . . . . . $1586
**M1A fiberglass:** . . . . . . . . . . . $1498
**M1A Camo:** . . . . . . . . . . . . . $1507
**M1A Scout Rifle:** . . . . . . . . . $1727
**M1A Scout Rifle, fiberglass:** . . $1610

## MODEL M-6 SCOUT
*Action:* hinged breech
*Stock:* synthetic
*Barrel:* 16 in.
*Sights:* open
*Weight:* 4.0
*Caliber:* .22LR and .410 or .22 Hornet
and .410
*Magazine:* none
*Features:* over/under combination gun;
lockable plastic case; also:
stainless M-6
**M-6:** . . . . . . . . . . . . . . . . . . . $215
**M-6 stainless:** . . . . . . . . . . . . $249

# Szecsei & Fuchs Rifles

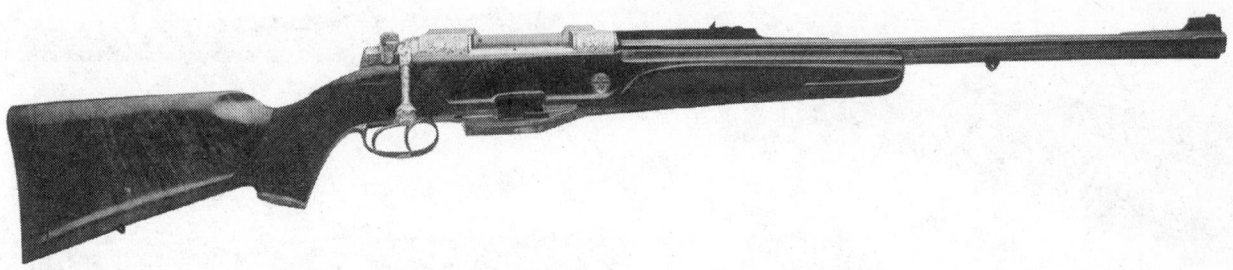

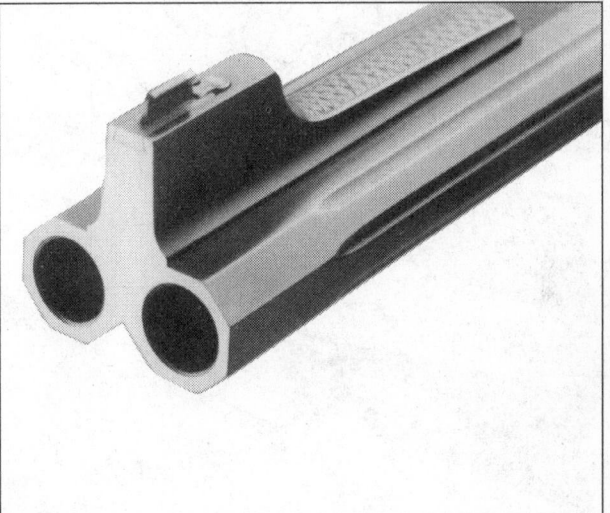

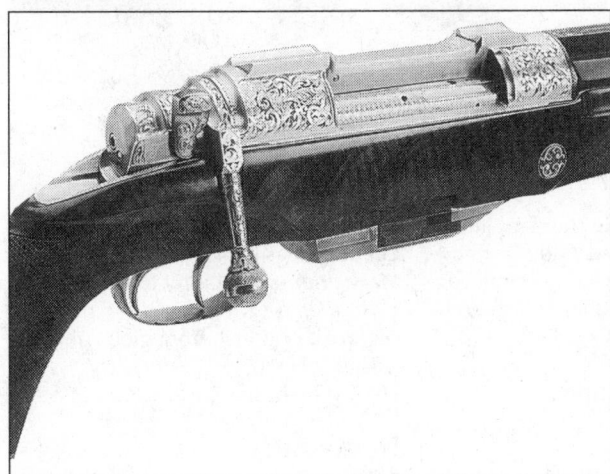

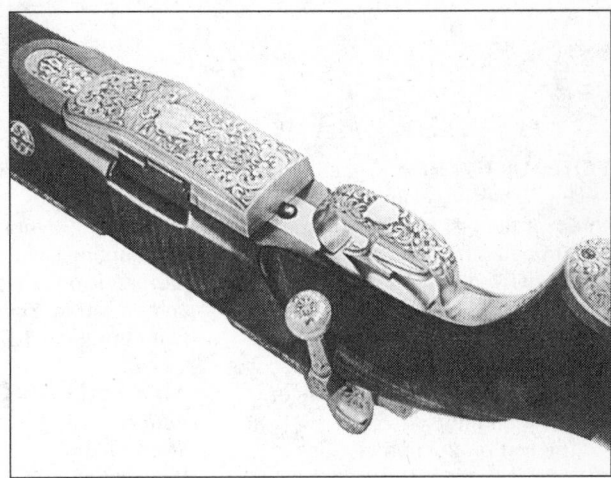

**THE SZECSEI & FUCHS** double-barrel bolt action rifle may be the only one of its kind. Built with great care and much handwork from the finest materials, it follows a design remarkable for its cleverness. And while the rifle is not light-weight, it can be aimed quickly and offers more large-caliber firepower than any competitor. The six-shot magazine feeds two rounds simultaneously, both of which can then be fired by two quick pulls of the trigger.

**SPECIFICATIONS**
**Chamberings:** .300 Win, 9.3 x 64, .358 Norma, .375 H&H, .404 Jeff, .416 Rem., .458 Win., .416 Rigby, .450 Rigby, .460 Short A-Square, .470 Capstick, .495 A-Square, .500 Jeffery
**Weight:** 14 lbs. with round barrels, 16 with octagon barrels.
**Price:** . . . . . . . . **Available on request**

# Taylor's Rifles

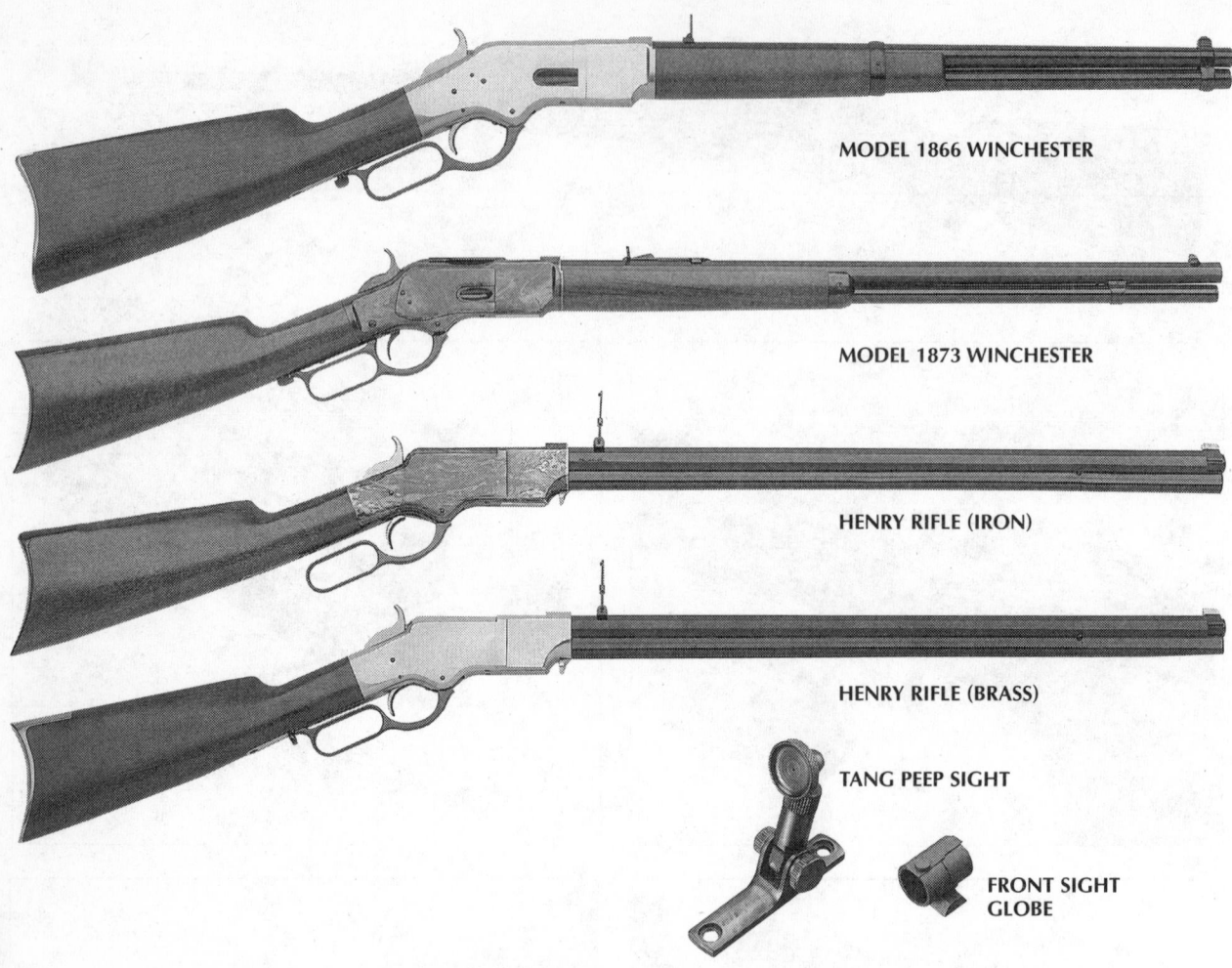

**MODEL 1866 WINCHESTER**

**MODEL 1873 WINCHESTER**

**HENRY RIFLE (IRON)**

**HENRY RIFLE (BRASS)**

**TANG PEEP SIGHT**

**FRONT SIGHT GLOBE**

**FAITHFUL TO THE** original, the Taylor "Henry", has the features that made its forebear the first lever-action repeating rifle to be both practical and reliable. It was derived from the Volcanic carbines of Walter Hunt, and was named after B. Tyler Henry, who refined the rifle. The Henry design would become the cornerstone of the Winchester lever-action line.

The first production versions of the Henry Rifles had steel frames and butt plates with a total production of around 400 rifles. These first models also lacked the lever latch. Only a few specimens are available now and they are highly prized by collectors around the world.

The original Winchester 73 had a long life, from 1873-1927. Its steel frame enabled the use of .44/40 ammunition, a more powerful round than the .44 Henry. Demand quickly

pushed production into the hundreds of thousands.

This tang sight is the standard target and hunting sight of the Old West and has precision adjustment for windage and elevation. Sight is blue finish and will fit original 1873 Winchester Rifles.

## MODEL 1866 CARBINE
*Action:* lever
*Stock:* walnut
*Barrel:* 19 in.
*Sights:* open
*Weight:* 6.5
*Caliber:* .44-40, .45 Long Colt
*Magazine:* under-barrel tube, 9 rounds
*Features:* brass frame
**Carbine:**. . . . . . . . . . . . . . . . . $780

## MODEL 1873 WINCHESTER RIFLE
*Action:* lever
*Stock:* walnut

*Barrel:* 24 in.
*Sights:* open
*Weight:* 7.5
*Caliber:* .44-40, .45 Long Colt
*Magazine:* under-barrel tube, 13 rounds
*Features:* optional: front globe and rear tang sights
**1873 Winchester:**. . . . . . . . . . $925

## HENRY RIFLE
*Action:* lever
*Stock:* walnut
*Barrel:* 24 in.
*Sights:* open
*Weight:* 7.5
*Caliber:* .44-40, .45 Long Colt
*Magazine:* under-barrel tube, 13 rounds
*Features:* brass frame; also: original-type steel-frame in .44-40 only
**Henry:**. . . . . . . . . . . . . . . . . . $960
**.44-40 Steel frame:**. . . . . . . . $1025

RIFLES

# Thompson & Campbell Rifles

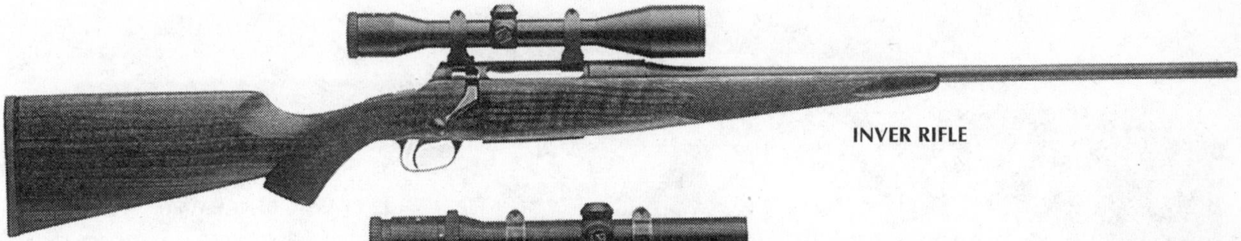

**INVER RIFLE**

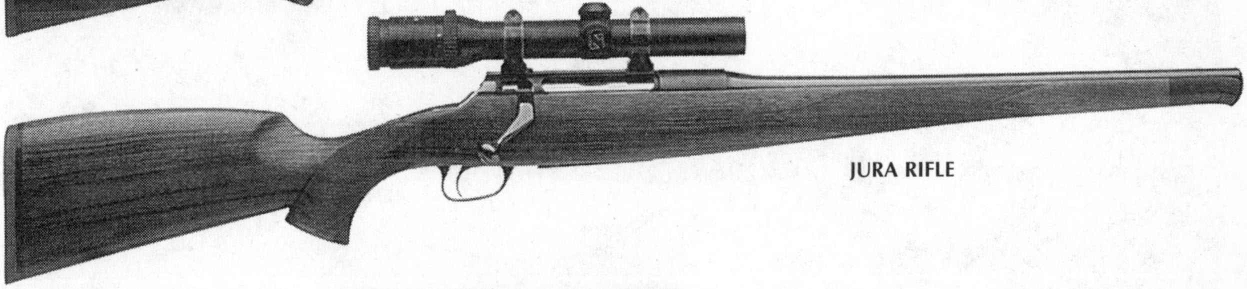

**JURA RIFLE**

**CHROMIE RIFLE**

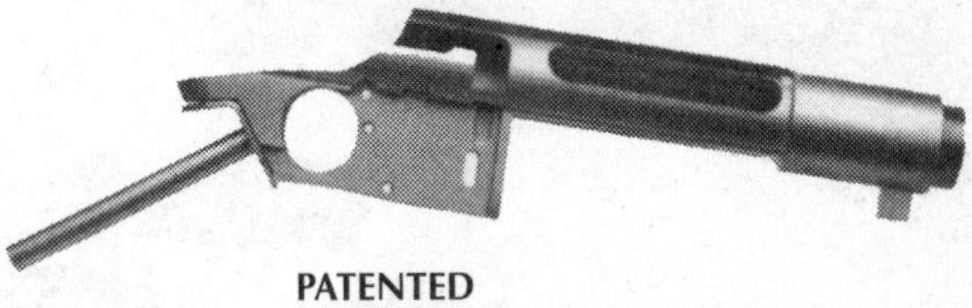

**PATENTED INVER ACTION SHOWING BEDDING PLATE.**

**INVER**
*Action:* bolt
*Stock:* select walnut
*Barrel:* 22 in.
*Sights:* none
*Weight:* 8.0
*Caliber:* all popular standard calibers
*Magazine:* detachable box, 4 rounds

*Features:* takedown barrels; optional removable sights and two-stage trigger; also: Chromie deluxe version
**Inver:** . . . . . . . . . . . **price on request**

**JURA**
*Action:* bolt
*Stock:* full length walnut

*Barrel:* 17 in.
*Sights:* none
*Weight:* 7.5
*Caliber:* all popular standard calibers
*Magazine:* detachable box, 4 rounds
*Features:* optional removable sights, two-stage trigger
**Jura:** . . . . . . . . . . . **price on request**

# Thompson/Center Rifles

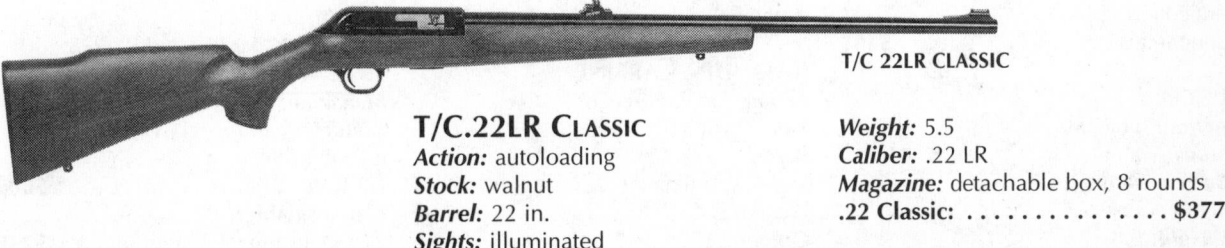

**T/C 22LR CLASSIC**

**T/C .22LR CLASSIC**
*Action:* autoloading
*Stock:* walnut
*Barrel:* 22 in.
*Sights:* illuminated

*Weight:* 5.5
*Caliber:* .22 LR
*Magazine:* detachable box, 8 rounds
**.22 Classic:** . . . . . . . . . . . . . . . **$377**

# Thompson/Center Rifles

**22 CLASSIC BENCHMARK**

**ENCORE RIFLE**

**ENCORE KATAHDIN**

**CONTENDER G2**

## MODEL 22 CLASSIC BENCHMARK
**Action:** autoloading
**Stock:** laminated
**Barrel:** 18 in., heavy
**Sights:** none
**Weight:** 6.8lbs.
**Caliber:** .22 LR
**Magazine:** 10
**Features:** target rifle for bench shooting; drilled for scope
benchmark. . . . . . . . . . . . . . . $481

## ENCORE
**Action:** hinged breech
**Stock:** walnut
**Barrel:** 24 and 26 in.
**Sights:** open
**Weight:** 6.8

**Caliber:** most popular calibers, from .22 Hornet to .300 Win. Mag. and .45-70
**Magazine:** none
**Features:** also: synthetic and stainless versions; Hunter package with .308 or .300 includes 3-9x40 T/C scope and hard case
walnut: . . . . . . . . . . . . . . . . . $635
synthetic: . . . . . . . . . . . . . . . . $602
stainless: . . . . . . . . . . . . . . . . $674

## KATAHDIN CARBINE
**Action:** hinged breech
**Stock:** synthetic
**Barrel:** 18 in.
**Sights:** illuminated
**Weight:** 6.6
**Caliber:** .450, .45-70

**Magazine:** none
**Features:** integral muzzle brake
Carbine: . . . . . . . . . . . . . . . . $617

## CONTENDER G2
**Action:** hinged breech
**Stock:** walnut
**Barrel:** 23 in.
**Sights:** none
**Weight:** 5.4 lbs.
**Caliber:** .17 HMR, .22 LR, .223, .30-30, .204 Ruger, .45/70, .375 JDJ
**Magazine:** 1
**Features:** can recock without opening rifle
G2 Rifle . . . . . . . . . . . . . . . . $600
**Also available:**
209 x .45 muzzleloader . . . . . . $246

**RIFLES**

# Uberti Rifles

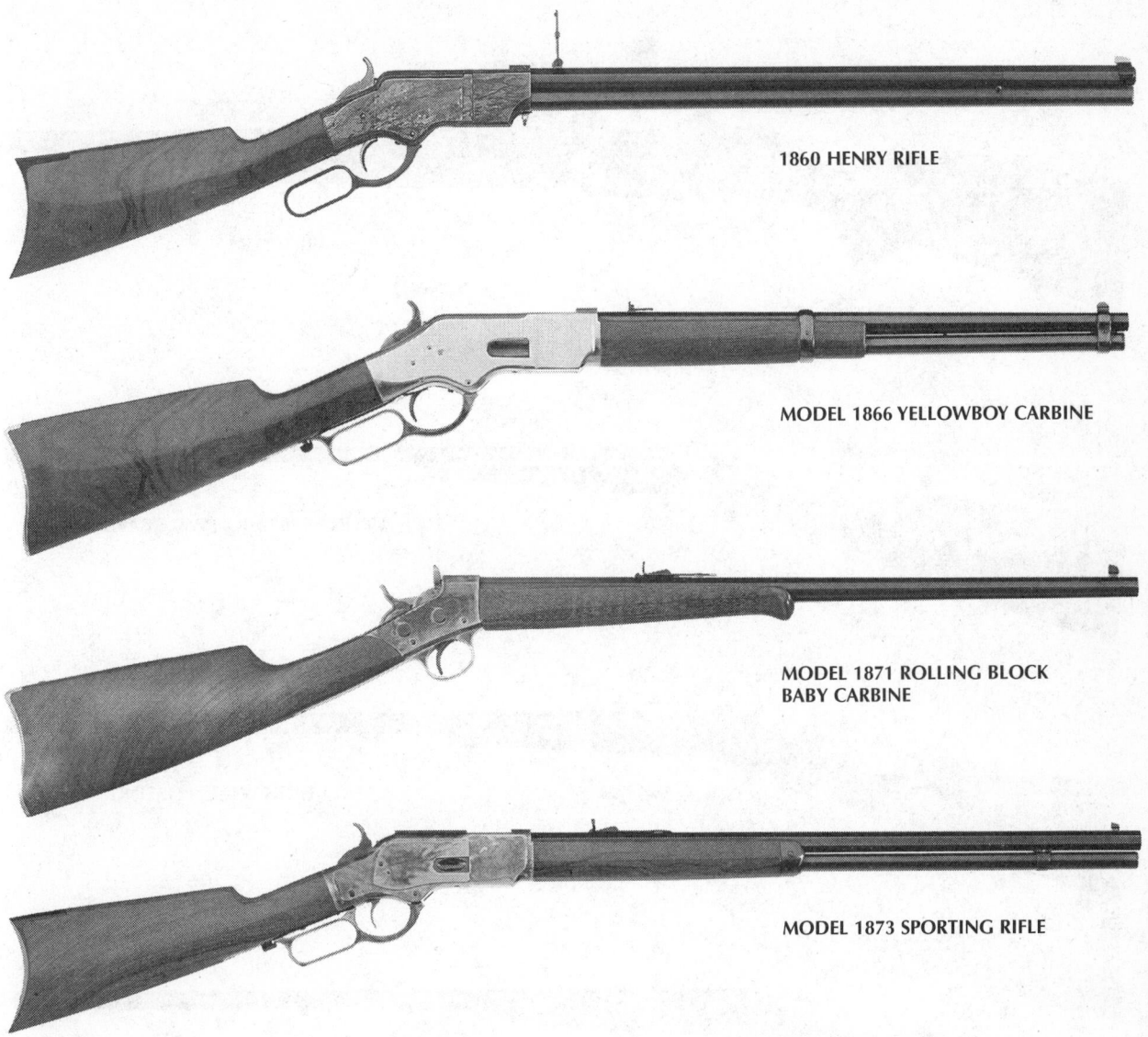

1860 HENRY RIFLE

MODEL 1866 YELLOWBOY CARBINE

MODEL 1871 ROLLING BLOCK BABY CARBINE

MODEL 1873 SPORTING RIFLE

**RIFLES**

## 1860 HENRY RIFLE
*Action:* lever
*Stock:* walnut, straight grip
*Barrel:* octagon 18, 22 and 24 in.
*Sights:* open
*Weight:* 7.9
*Caliber:* .44-40, .45 Colt
*Magazine:* under-barrel tube, 13 rounds
*Features:* brass or steel frame
brass frame: . . . . . . . . . . . . . . $995
steel frame: . . . . . . . . . . . . . . $1085

## MODEL 1866 WINCHESTER CARBINE "YELLOWBOY"
*Action:* lever
*Stock:* walnut, straight grip
*Barrel:* 19 in.

*Sights:* open
*Weight:* 7.4
*Caliber:* .38 Spl., .44-40, .45 Colt
*Magazine:* under-barrel tube
*Features:* brass frame
1866 Yellowboy Carbine: . . . . . $755
1866 Rifle (24" BBL): . . . . . . . . $775

## MODEL 1871 ROLLING BLOCK BABY CARBINE
*Action:* rolling block
*Stock:* walnut, straight grip
*Barrel:* 22 in.
*Sights:* open
*Weight:* 4.9
*Caliber:* .22 LR, .22 WMR, .22 Hornet
*Magazine:* none

*Features:* case-colored receiver
Baby Carbine: . . . . . . . . . . . . . $515
1871 Rifle (26" BBL): . . . . . . . . $580

## MODEL 1873 WINCHESTER SPORTING RIFLE
*Action:* lever
*Stock:* walnut, straight grip
*Barrel:* octagon 20, 24 in.
*Sights:* open
*Weight:* 7.5
*Caliber:* .357 Mag., .44-40, .45 Colt
*Magazine:* under-barrel tube, 13 rounds
*Features:* optional pistol grip
straight grip (20" BBL): . . . . . . . $930
(24" BBL): . . . . . . . . . . . . . . . . $930
pistol grip: . . . . . . . . . . . . . . . $1015

# Weatherby Rifles

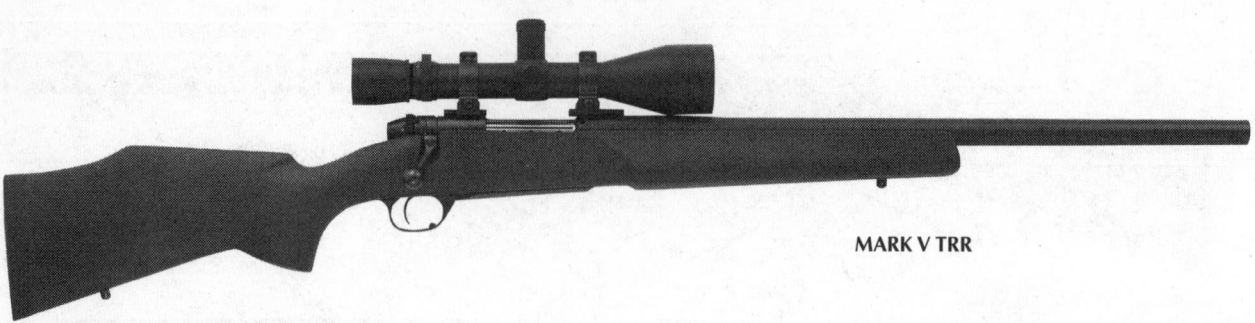

MARK V TRR

UBERT1 1885 HIGH WALL CARBINE

UBERT1 HIGH WALL SPORTING

UBERT1 LOW WALL SPORTING

## MARK V THREAT RESPONSE RIFLE
**Action:** bolt
**Stock:** composite
**Barrel:** heavy 22 in.
**Sights:** none
**Weight:** 8.5
**Caliber:** .223, .308
**Magazine:** box, 5 + 1 rounds

**Features:** magnum custom has adjustable stock, 26 or 28 in. barrel
TRR:. . . . . . . . . . . . . . . . . . . $1737
magnum custom 26" bbl.:. . . . $2888
magnum custom 28" bbl.:. . . . $3061

## MODEL SVR
**Action:** bolt
**Stock:** composite
**Barrel:** 22 in.
**Sights:** none
**Weight:** 7.3lbs.
**Caliber:** .223, .22-250
**Magazine:** 5 and 4
**Features:** 6-lug action, made in USA; barrel #3 contour, lapped, fluted, floated; 1½-inch factory guarantee for 3-shot group
SVR . . . . . . . . . . . . . . . . . . $1176

ACCUMARK

MARK V DANGEROUS GAME RIFLE

MARK V DELUXE

MARK V FIBERMARK STAINLESS

## MARK V ACCUMARK

*Action:* bolt
*Stock:* composite
*Barrel:* 24, 26 and 28 in. barrels
*Sights:* none
*Weight:* 7.0
*Caliber:* .223, .22-250, .243, .25-06, .270, .280, 7-08, 7mm Rem. Mag., .240 Wby., 7mm STW, 30-06, .308, .300 Win. Mag., Wby. Magnums: .257, .270, 7mm, .300, .340, .30-378, .338-378
*Magazine:* box, 3 or 5 rounds
*Features:* lightweight and standard MK V actions; weight depends on caliber

Accumark: . . . . . . . . . . . . . . . **$1666**
magnums: . . . . . . . . . . . . . . . **$1726**
.30-378, .338-378: . . . . . . . . **$1974**

## MARK V DANGEROUS GAME RIFLE

*Action:* bolt
*Stock:* composite
*Barrel:* 24 or 26 in.
*Sights:* open

*Weight:* 9.0
*Caliber:* .300 Wby., .340 Wby., .375 H&H, .375 Wby., .416 Rem., .458 Win., .458 Lott; also: .378, .416, .460 Wby.
*Magazine:* box, 3 rounds
*Features:* express sights, barrel band swivel

Dangerous Game Rifle: . . . . . . **$3095**
.378, .416: . . . . . . . . . . . . . . **$3266**
.460: . . . . . . . . . . . . . . . . . . **$3360**

## MARK V DELUXE

*Action:* bolt
*Stock:* Claro walnut
*Barrel:* 24, 26 and 28 in.
*Sights:* none
*Weight:* 8.5
*Caliber:* .22-250, .243, .240 Wby., .25-06, .270, .280, 7-08, .30-06, .308; Wby. Magnums: .257, .270, 7mm, .300, .340, .378, .416, .460
*Magazine:* box, 3 or 5 rounds
*Features:* 26 in. barrels for most magnum calibers; 28 in. barrel for .378,

.416, .460 (with brake)
standard: . . . . . . . . . . . . . . . **$1963**
magnum: . . . . . . . . . . . . . . . **$2023**
.378, .416: . . . . . . . . . . . . . . **$2380**
.460: . . . . . . . . . . . . . . . . . . **$2797**

## MARK V FIBERMARK

*Action:* bolt
*Stock:* composite
*Barrel:* 24 and 26 in.
*Sights:* none
*Weight:* 8.0
*Caliber:* popular standard and magnum chamberings from .22-250 to .30-378 Wby.
*Magazine:* box, 3 to 5 rounds
*Features:* stainless versions available

Price: . . . . . . . . . . . . . . . . . . **$1225**
magnum: . . . . . . . . . . . . . . . **$1285**
.30-378: . . . . . . . . . . . . . . . . **$1542**
stainless: . . . . . . . . . . . . . . . **$1334**
magnum, stainless: . . . . . . . . **$1432**
.30-378 stainless: . . . . . . . . . **$1635**

# Weatherby Rifles

MARK V LAZERMARK

MARK V SPORTER

MARK V SBGM

MARK V SUPER
PREDATORMASTER

## MARK V LAZERMARK
*Action:* bolt
*Stock:* walnut
*Barrel:* 26 in.
*Sights:* none
*Weight:* 8.5
*Caliber:* Wby. Magnums from .257
to .340
*Magazine:* box, 3 rounds
*Features:* laser-carved stock, button
rifled Krieger barrel
**Lazermark:**. . . . . . . . . . . . . . **$2202**

## MARK V SPORTER
*Action:* bolt
*Stock:* walnut
*Barrel:* 24 and 26 in.
*Sights:* none
*Weight:* 8.0
*Caliber:* popular standard and
magnum chamberings from .22-250
to .340 Wby.

*Magazine:* box, 3 or 5 rounds
*Features:* checkered grip and forend
**Mark V Sporter:** . . . . . . . . . . **$1249**
**magnums:** . . . . . . . . . . . . . . **$1309**

## MARK V SUPER BIG
GAMEMASTER
*Action:* bolt
*Stock:* composite
*Barrel:* 24 and 26 in.
*Sights:* none
*Weight:* 6.8
*Caliber:* .240 Wby., .25-06, .270,
.280, 7mm Rem. Mag., .30-06, .300
Win. Mag., Wby. Magnums: .257,
.270, 7mm, .300
*Magazine:* box, 3 or 5 rounds
*Features:* button rifled Krieger barrel
**Super Big Game Master:**. . . . . **$1670**
**magnums:** . . . . . . . . . . . . . . **$1736**

## MARK V SUPER
PREDATORMASTER
*Action:* bolt
*Stock:* composite
*Barrel:* 24 in.
*Sights:* none
*Weight:* 6.3
*Caliber:* .223, .22-250, .243,
7-08, .308
*Magazine:* box, 5 rounds
*Features:* Super VarmintMaster has
heavy 26 in., fluted stainless barrel,
flat-bottomed stock (8.5 lbs.)
**SPM:** . . . . . . . . . . . . . . . . . . **$1670**
**SVM:** . . . . . . . . . . . . . . . . . . **$1737**

# Weatherby Rifles

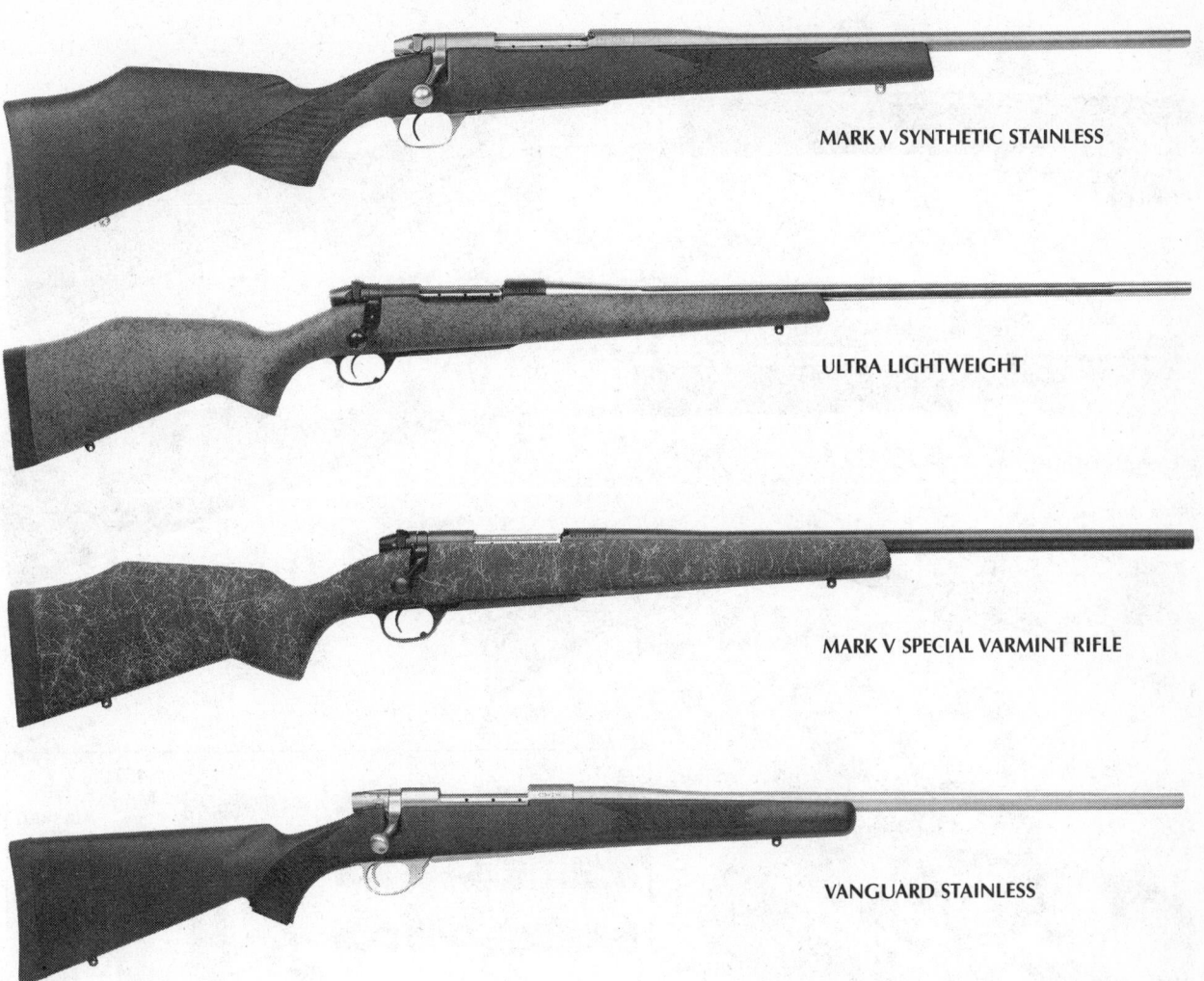

MARK V SYNTHETIC STAINLESS

ULTRA LIGHTWEIGHT

MARK V SPECIAL VARMINT RIFLE

VANGUARD STAINLESS

## MARK V SYNTHETIC
*Action:* bolt
*Stock:* synthetic
*Barrel:* 24, 26 and 28 in.
*Sights:* none
*Weight:* 8.5
*Caliber:* popular standard and magnum calibers from .22-250 to .338-378 Wby.
*Magazine:* box, 3 or 5 rounds
*Features:* also: stainless version.
Mark V Synthetic: . . . . . . . . . $1057
magnum: . . . . . . . . . . . . . . . . $1116
.30-378, .338-378: . . . . . . . . . $1318
stainless: . . . . . . . . . . . . . . . $1166
magnum, stainless: . . . . . . . . $1282
.30-378, .338-378 stainless: . . $1482

## ULTRA LIGHTWEIGHT
*Action:* bolt
*Stock:* composite
*Barrel:* 24 and 26 in.
*Sights:* none
*Weight:* 6.0
*Caliber:* .243, .240 Wby., .25-06, .270, 7-08, .280, 7mm Rem. Mag., .308, .30-06, .300 Win. Mag., Wby. Magnums: .257, .270, 7mm, .300
*Magazine:* box, 3 or 5 rounds
*Features:* lightweight action; 6-lug bolt
Ultra Lightweight: . . . . . . . . $1670
magnums: . . . . . . . . . . . . . . $1752

## MARK V SPECIAL VARMINT RIFLE
*Action:* bolt
*Stock:* composite
*Barrel:* 22 in.
*Sights:* none
*Weight:* 7.3lbs.
*Caliber:* .223, .22-250
*Magazine:* 5 and 4
*Features:* 6-lug action, made in USA; barrel #3 contour, lapped, fluted, floated; 1½-inch factory guarantee for 3-shot group
SVR . . . . . . . . . . . . . . . . . . . $1176

## VANGUARD
*Action:* bolt
*Stock:* composite
*Barrel:* 24 in.
*Sights:* none
*Weight:* 7.8lbs.
*Caliber:* .223, .22-250, .243, .270, .308, .30-06, 7mm Rem. Mag., .300 Win. Mag., .300 WSM, .270 WSM, .257 Wby.,.300 Wby. Mag., .338 Win. Mag.
*Magazine:* 5 to 3
*Features:* 2-lug action, made in Japan, 1½-inch factory guarantee for 3-shot group
synthetic . . . . . . . . . . . . . . . . $476
stainless . . . . . . . . . . . . . . . . . $595

# Wild West Guns

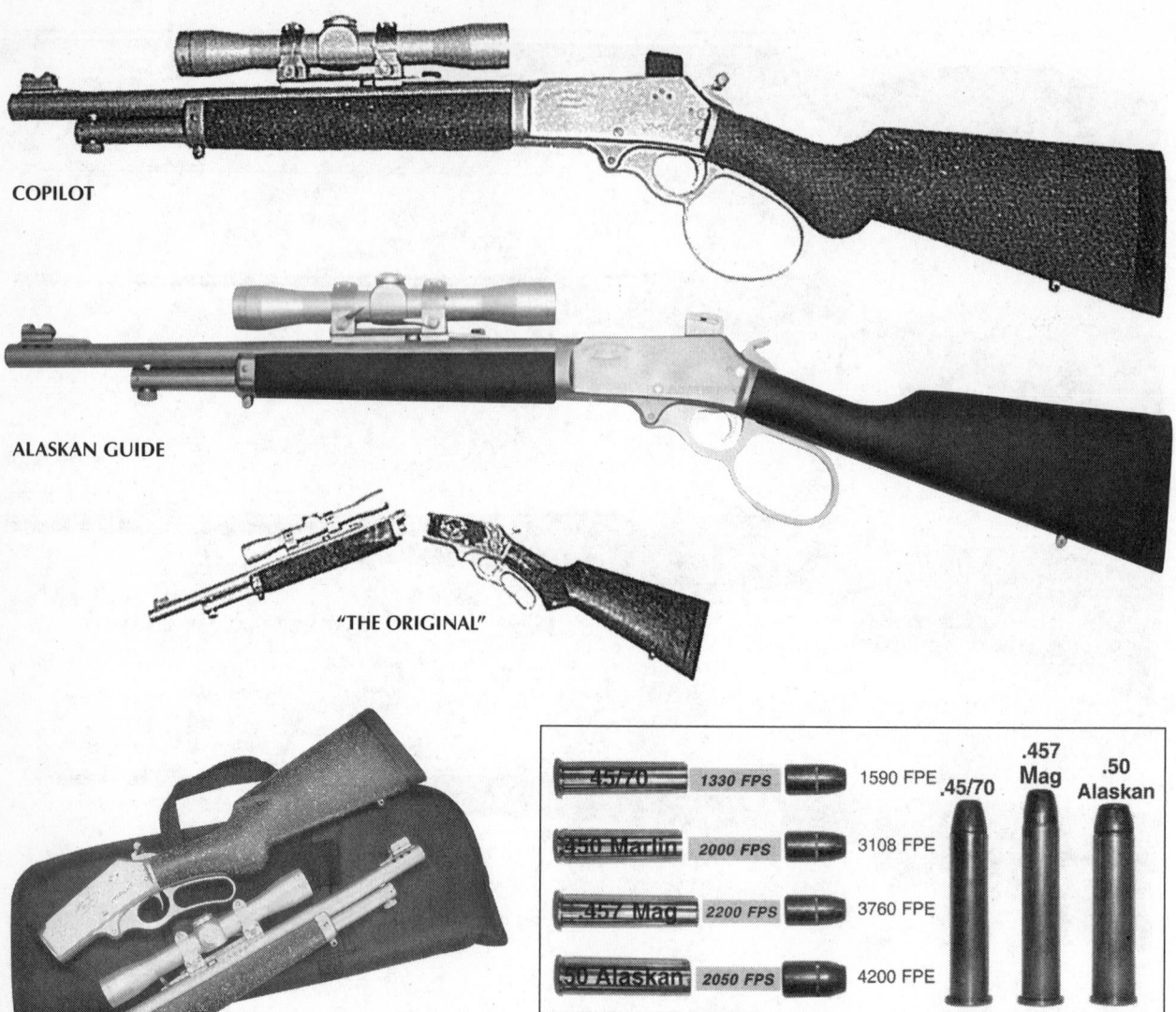

COPILOT

ALASKAN GUIDE

"THE ORIGINAL"

| | | | .45/70 | .457 Mag | .50 Alaskan |
|---|---|---|---|---|---|
| .45/70 | 1330 FPS | 1590 FPE | | | |
| .450 Marlin | 2000 FPS | 3108 FPE | | | |
| .457 Mag | 2200 FPS | 3760 FPE | | | |
| .50 Alaskan | 2050 FPS | 4200 FPE | | | |

BIG GUNS FOR BIG STUFF

## CO-PILOT

**Action:** lever
**Stock:** walnut
**Barrel:** 16, 18 or 20 inch
**Sights:** illuminated
**Weight:** 7.0
**Caliber:** .45-70, .457 Magnum, .50 Alaskan

*Magazine:* under-barrel tube
*Features:* 1895 Marlin action; ported barrels; take-down feature; Alaskan Guide similar, not take-down
Co-Pilot: . . . . . . . . . . . . . . . $1980
on supplied 1895 Marlin: . . . . $1595
.50 Alaskan conversion: . . . . . . $250
Alaskan Guide:. . . . . . . . . . . $1320

Alaskan on supplied
   1895 Marlin: . . . . . . . . . . . . $935
.50 Alaskan conversion: . . . . . . $250
Master Guide Take-Down:. . . . $1865
Take-Down
   on supplied 1895G: . . . . . . $1485

RIFLES

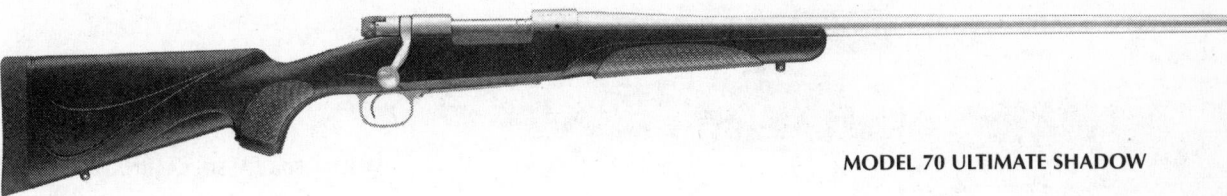

**MODEL 70 ULTIMATE SHADOW**

**IN THE EARLY 1850S,** Oliver Winchester was selling shirts. Walter Hunt was failing in his attempts to perfect a rifle. Called the "Volition Repeater," the Hunt rifle used a 54-caliber conical "rocket ball." The base of the bullet was hollow and a charge of fulminate nearly filled the cavity. The cavity was covered by a cork cap whose central hole was sealed by paper. Priming pellets were fed under the hammer by a pill-lock mechanism as the rocket balls advanced from a tube magazine.

Beset by numerous defects, Hunt sold his design to George Arrowsmith of New York. Arrowsmith hired Lewis Jennings to improve the Volitional rifle, which he did by combining two operating levers and installing a rack-and-pinion gear. Arrowsmith then sold the rifle to New York financier Courtland Palmer who contracted with Robbins and Lawrence of Windsor, Vermont, for 5000 Jennings rifles. The mechanism proved hard to make and unreliable and early guns were marketed as single-shots.

Horace Smith and Benjamin Tyler Henry added improvements and in 1855, a group of 40 New York and New Haven businessmen formed the Volcanic Repeating Arms Company and bought out Smith, Wesson and Palmer. Among the group was Oliver F. Winchester, a 45-year-old shirt-maker, who soon became the company director. Winchester moved Volcanic Repeating Arms from Norwich to New Haven. Daniel Wesson stayed on as shop superintendent until 1856, when he joined Horace Smith to start another firm. Sales of Volcanic guns slumped, however, and early in 1857, creditors forced receivership. Winchester purchased all assets for $40,000. In April, 1857, he reorgan-

ized Volcanic Repeating Arms into the New Haven Arms Company. Benjamin Tyler Henry, then 36, became shop foreman. From his work with the Volitional Repeater emerged a lever-action rimfire rifle with a l5-round, under-barrel magazine and a two-pronged firing pin. Some of the early Henrys had iron frames, but brass soon became standard. The $40 Henry used 26 grains of black powder to push 44-caliber 216-grain bullets to 1025 fps. Anemic by modern standards, the .44 Henry developed 10 times the energy of Volcanic bullets! The rifle's main fault was a slotted magazine. Dents rendered the follower unreliable, and debris clogged the slot. But the rifle had advantages over the Spencer (which the U.S. Army proclaimed sturdier): It held l5 rounds to the Spencer's seven, and one motion of the lever would load and cock the gun.

By mid 1860s, Winchester Repeating Arms Company had swallowed New Haven Arms, and B. Tyler Henry had left the company. In 1866 shop foreman Nelson King redesigned the Henry's magazine, adding a spring-loaded port in the receiver. These changes, along with with a forend, resulted in the Winchester 1866. This rifle became an immediate hit.

In 1870 Thomas G. Bennett began work for Winchester. He became company secretary the following year and, later, Oliver Winchester's son-in-law. Bennett helped design of the Winchester Model 1873, the firm's first centerfire rifle. Its .44 WCF (.44-40) cartridge struck with nearly nearly 30 percent more energy than the .44 Henry – over 12 times the payload of the old Volcanic bullet. The brass frame of the l866 became forged iron on the 73 and iron was replaced with steel in l884.

The next Winchester lever gun, the Model l876, was just a big Model l873. The .45-75 Winchester, with its 350-grain bullet, doubled the energy of the .44 WCF. Later Winchester added the .50-95 Express, .45-60 WCF and .40-60 WCF. The 1876 became the official rifle of Canada's Royal Canadian Mounted Police.

One day in 1883 Bennett was shown a used dropping-block rifle picked up by a Winchester salesman. He traced the barrel stamping to a Utah gunshop – and booked train passage there. He found a handful of young Mormon men, barely out of their teens, building rifles. From John Moses Browning, Bennett secured manufacturing rights to two rifles John had designed. One would become the Model 1885 single-shot, the other the Model 1886 lever-action. John Browning would later sell Winchester the plans for more than 40 mechanisms, ensuring that Winchester would remain the dominant name in gnn manufacture for the next 50 years.

## MODEL 70 ULTIMATE SHADOW

*Action:* bolt
*Stock:* composite
*Barrel:* 22 and 24 in.
*Sights:* none
*Weight:* 6.5
*Caliber:* .223 WSSM, .243 WSSM, .25 WSSM, .270 WSM, 7mm WSM, .300 WSM
*Magazine:* box, 3 rounds
*Features:* push-feed; Ultimate Shadow has integrated, rubberized, oval gripping surfaces on the stock pistol grip and forend.

**WSM's:** . . . . . . . . . . . . . . . . . . **$816**
**WSSM's:**. . . . . . . . . . . . . . . . . **$838**
**Stainless:** . . . . . . . . . . . . . **$861 - 882**
**Camo:** . . . . . . . . . . . . . . . **$913 - 936**
**Super Shadow:** . . . . . . . . **$554 - 576**

**RIFLES**

# Winchester Rifles

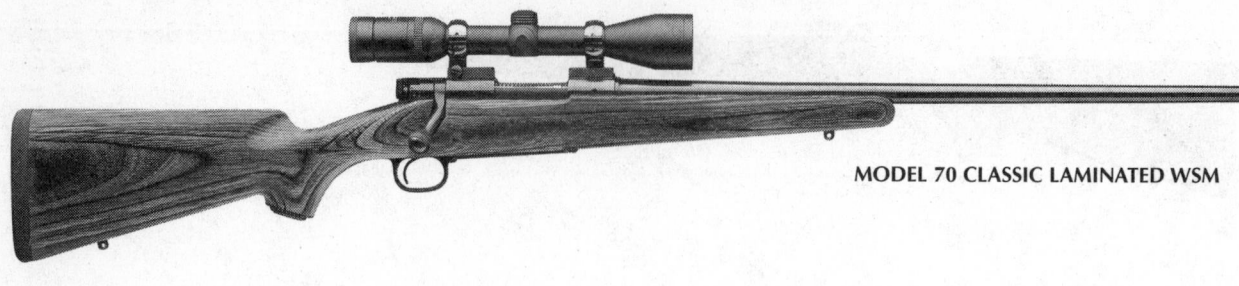

**MODEL 70 CLASSIC LAMINATED WSM**

**MODEL 70 CLASSIC FEATHERWEIGHT**

**MODEL 70 WSSM FEATHERWEIGHT**

RIFLES

## MODEL 70 CLASSIC COMPACT
*Action:* bolt
*Stock:* walnut
*Barrel:* 20 in.
*Sights:* none
*Weight:* 6.0
*Caliber:* .243, .308
*Magazine:* box, 4 rounds
*Features:* features 13-in. pull for small-frame people
**Compact:** . . . . . . . . . . . . . . . . **$762**

## MODEL 70 CLASSIC FEATHERWEIGHT
*Action:* bolt
*Stock:* walnut
*Barrel:* 22 and 24 in.
*Sights:* none
*Weight:* 7.0
*Caliber:* .22-250, .243, 6.5x55, .270,

.270 WSM, 7-08, 7mm WSM, .308, .30-06, .300 WSM, .223 WSSM, .243 WSSM, .25 WSSM
*Magazine:* box, 3 or 5 rounds
*Features:* stainless available in .22-250, .243, .270, .308, .30-06
**Classic Featherweight:** . . . . . . . **$762**
**WSM's:** . . . . . . . . . . . . . . . . . **$792**
**WSSM's:** . . . . . . . . . . . . . . . . . **$813**

## MODEL 70 CLASSIC SPORTER LT
*Action:* bolt
*Stock:* walnut
*Barrel:* 24 and 26 in.
*Sights:* none
*Weight:* 7.8
*Caliber:* .25-06, .270, 7mm Rem. Mag., .30-06, .300 Win. Mag., .338 Win. Mag., .270 WSM, 7mm WSM, .300 WSM
*Magazine:* box, 3 or 5 rounds

*Features:* also in .270, 7mm and .300 WSM with laminated stock; left-hand models available.
**Classic Sporter:** . . . . . . . . . . . . **$741**
**magnum:** . . . . . . . . . . . . . . . . **$772**
**WSM:** . . . . . . . . . . . . . . . . . . **$772**
**Classic laminated WSM:** . . . . . . **$809**

## MODEL 70 CLASSIC STAINLESS
*Action:* bolt
*Stock:* synthetic
*Barrel:* 24 and 26 in.
*Sights:* none
*Weight:* 7.3
*Caliber:* .270, .30-06, .300 Win. Mag., .338 Win. Mag., .375 H&H
*Magazine:* box, 3 or 5 rounds
*Features:* open sights on .375 H&H
**Classic Stainless:** . . . . . . . . . . **$816**
**magnum:** . . . . . . . . . . . . **$829 - 846**
**.375:** . . . . . . . . . . . . . . . . . . . **$943**

# Winchester Rifles

MODEL 70 CLASSIC SUPER GRADE

MODEL 70 COYOTE

MODEL 94 TRADITIONAL

## MODEL 70 CLASSIC SUPER GRADE

*Action:* bolt
*Stock:* walnut
*Barrel:* 24 and 26 in.
*Sights:* none
*Weight:* 7.8
*Caliber:* .25-06, .30-06, .338 Win. Mag., .270 WSM, 7mm WSM, .300 WSM
*Magazine:* box, 3 or 5 rounds
*Features:* also; Safari Express in .375 H&H (8.5 lbs.), .416 Rem. Mag. and .458 Win. with open sights
**Classic Super Grade:** . . . . . . . **$1035**
**magnum:** . . . . . . . . . . . . . . . . **$1065**
**Safari express:** . . . . . . . . . . . **$1147**

## MODEL 70 COYOTE

*Action:* bolt
*Stock:* laminated
*Barrel:* 24 in.
*Sights:* none
*Weight:* 9.0
*Caliber:* .22-250, .308; also .270 WSM, 7mm WSM, .300 WSM, .223 WSSM, .243 WSSM, .25 WSSM
*Magazine:* box, 3 to 5 rounds
*Features:* push-feed action
**Coyote:** . . . . . . . . . . . . . . . . . **$705**
**magnum:** . . . . . . . . . . . **$763 - 786**

## MODEL 70 WSSM

*Action:* bolt
*Stock:* walnut, synthetic or laminated
*Barrel:* 24 in.
*Sights:* none
*Weight:* 6.0lbs.
*Caliber:* .223 WSSM, .243 WSSM
*Magazine:* 3
*Features:* shortened M70 action, new synthetic shadow stock with grip inserts; laminated Coyote weighs 9 lbs.
**Shadow** . . . . . . . . . . . . . . . . . **$543**
**Featherweight** . . . . . . . . . . . . **$769**
**Coyote** . . . . . . . . . . . . . . . . . . **$734**

## MODEL 94 TRADITIONAL

*Action:* lever
*Stock:* walnut, straight grip
*Barrel:* 20 in.
*Sights:* open
*Weight:* 6.25
*Caliber:* .30-30, .480 Ruger
*Magazine:* under-barrel tube, 6, 10 or 11 rounds
*Features:* also available: TraditionalCW in .30-30, .44 Rem. Mag.; Ranger with hardwood stock; Trails End with large-loop option in .357, .44 Mag., .45 Long Colt
**Traditional in .30-30:** . . . . . . . . **$435**
**Traditional-CW in .30-30:** . . . . . **$469**
**Traditional-CW in .44 Rem.**
   **Mag.:** . . . . . . . . . . . . . . . . . . **$492**
**Ranger:** . . . . . . . . . . . . . . . . . . **$379**
**Ranger Compact (16" bbl.):** . . . **$402**
**Trails End:** . . . . . . . . . . . . . . . **$474**

RIFLES

# Winchester Rifles

**MODEL 94 TRAPPER**

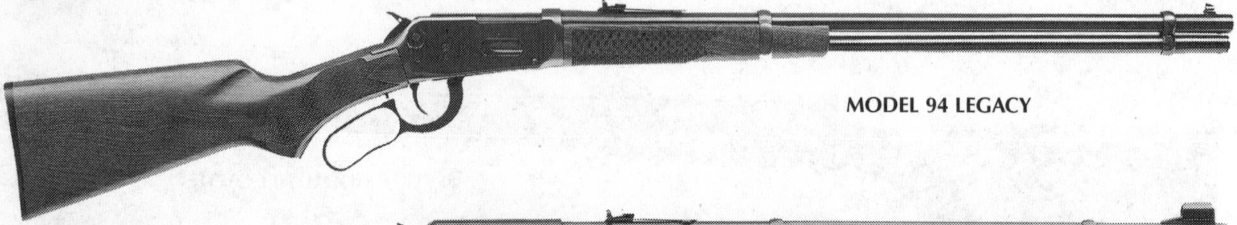

**MODEL 94 LEGACY**

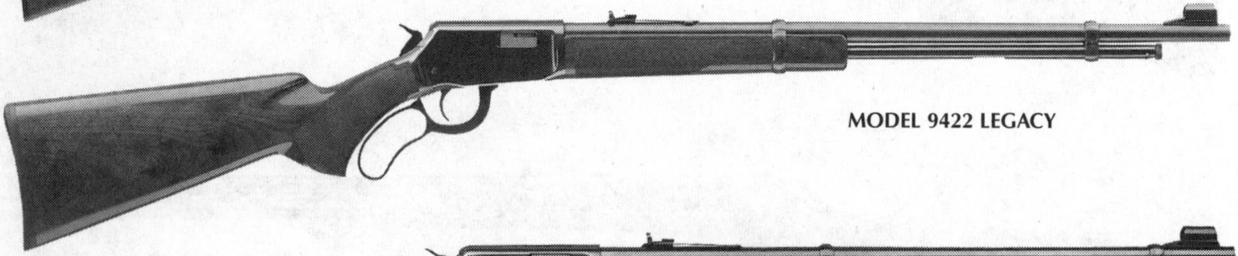

**MODEL 9422 LEGACY**

**MODEL 9422 TRADITIONAL**

## MODEL 94 TRAPPER

*Action:* lever
*Stock:* walnut
*Barrel:* 16 in.
*Sights:* open
*Weight:* 6.0
*Caliber:* .30-30, .357 Mag., .44 Mag., .45 Long Colt
*Magazine:* under-barrel tube, 5 or 9 rounds
*Features:* saddle ring; 8rounds only in .357, .44, .45
**Trapper:**................**$459**

## MODEL 94 LEGACY

*Action:* lever
*Stock:* checkered walnut, pistol grip
*Barrel:* 20 or 24 in.
*Sights:* open
*Weight:* 6.8
*Caliber:* .30-30, .357 Mag., .44 Mag., .45 Long Colt
*Magazine:* under-barrel tube, 6 rounds
*Features:* deluxe version of 94; 11 rounds only in .357, .44, .45
**Legacy:**.................**$487**

## MODEL 9422 RIFLES

*Action:* lever
*Stock:* checkered walnut, straight grip
*Barrel:* 20 in.
*Sights:* open
*Weight:* 6.0
*Caliber:* .22 LR or .22 WMR
*Magazine:* under-barrel tube, 15 round (11 in WMR)
*Features:* also available: legacy with pistol grip, 22 in. barrel
**9422:**....................**$479**
**Magnum:**.................**$501**
**Legacy:**..................**$512**
**Legacy, magnum:**..........**$537**
**9417 (.17 HMR)**...........**$515**
**Legacy**...................**$551**

*Bonding a bullet's core to its jacket helps reduce core/jacket separation during upset, increasing penetration. Bonded bullets make sense for tough game, but generally aren't needed for deer.*

**RIFLES**

SHOTGUNS

# Armsco Shotguns

MODEL 201

## Model 103
**Action:** over/under
**Stock:** walnut pistol grip
**Barrel:** 26, 28 or 30 in.
**Chokes:** improved cylinder/modified, screw-in tubes
**Weight:** 7.0lbs.
**Bore/Gauge:** 12, 16, 20, 28, 410
**Magazine:** none
**Features:** boxlock over/under, single trigger, silver, black or case-finished breech
base model . . . . . . . . . . . . . . . $799
mid-grade . . . . . . . . . . . . . . . . $949
high-grade . . . . . . . . . . . . . . . $1299

## Model 201
**Action:** side-by-side
**Stock:** walnut, straight or pistol grip
**Barrel:** 26 in.
**Chokes:** improved cylinder/modified, screw-in tubes
**Weight:** 6.3lbs.
**Bore/Gauge:** 12, 16, 20, 28, 410
**Magazine:** none
**Features:** boxlock double, single trigger, silver, black or case-finished breech; IC/M in 16 ga. and .410
silver or black . . . . . . . . . . . . . $899
case-colored . . . . . . . . . . . . . . $999

## Model 601
**Action:** autoloader
**Stock:** walnut
**Barrel:** 24, 26 or 28 in.
**Chokes:** screw-in tubes
**Weight:** 7.0lbs.
**Bore/Gauge** 12
**Magazine:** 4
**Features:** matte or polished metal; also 20 gauge 701
601 . . . . . . . . . . . . . . . . . . . . . $549

# AYA Shotguns

MODEL 4/53

COUNTRYMAN

## Model 4/53
**Action:** side-by-side
**Stock:** walnut, straight grip
**Barrel:** 26, 27 or 28 in.
**Chokes:** improved cylinder, modified, full
**Weight:** 7.0lbs.
**Bore/Gauge:** 12, 16, 20, 28, .410
**Magazine:** none
**Features:** boxlock; chopper lump barrels, bushed firing pins, automatic safety and ejectors
Model 4/53 . . . . . . . . . . . . . . $2595

## Countryman
**Action:** side-by-side
**Stock:** walnut, straight grip
**Barrel:** 26, 27, 28, 29 or 32 in.
**Chokes:** improved cylinder, modified, full
**Weight:** 7.0lbs.
**Bore/Gauge:** 12, 16, 20
**Magazine:** none
**Features:** Holland sidelock design, chopper lump barrels, bushed firing pins, automatic safety and ejectors, replaceable hinge pin; deluxe wood on order
Countryman . . . . . . . . . . . . . $3695

SHOTGUNS

# Benelli Shotguns

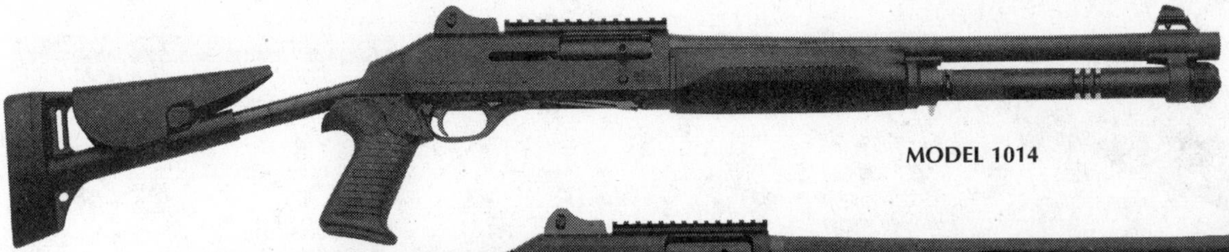

**MODEL 1014**

**M4 STANDARD OR PISTOL GRIP**

**M1 FIELD GRIP**

**NOVA H2O PUMP**

## MODEL 1014 AND M4

*Action:* autoloader
*Stock:* synthetic
*Barrel:* 18.5 in.
*Chokes:* improved cylinder, modified, full
*Weight:* 8.0lbs.
*Bore/Gauge:* 12
*Magazine:* 4 + 1
*Features:* M4 has pistol grip; gas operated, ghost-ring sight, modular buttstocks
**M1014**. . . . . . . . . . . . . . . . . **$1600**
**M4.**. . . . . . . . . . . . . . . . . . . . **$1530**

## M1 FIELD STEADY GRIP, SUPER BLACK EAGLE STEADY GRIP

*Action:* autoloader
*Stock:* synthetic with vertical pistol grip
*Barrel:* 24 in.
*Chokes:* screw-in tubes
*Weight:* 7.3lbs.
*Bore/Gauge:* 12
*Magazine:* 3
*Features:* Benelli inertia-system mechanism; Super Black Eagle also handles 3 1/2-inch shells
**M1 Field** . . . . . . . . . . . . . . . . **$1175**
**Super Black Eagle**. . . . . . . . . **$1465**

## NOVA H20 PUMP

*Action:* pump
*Stock:* synthetic
*Barrel:* 18.5 in.
*Chokes:* cylinder, fixed
*Weight:* 7.2 lbs.
*Bore/Gauge:* 12
*Magazine:* 4 + 1
*Features:* matte nickel finish, open rifle sights
**synthetic** . . . . . . . . . . . . . . . . **$480**

*When shopping for an autoloader, mind its mechanism. Some accept loads of various lengths and recoil without adjustment. An asset if you change ammo often.*

SHOTGUNS

# Benelli Shotguns

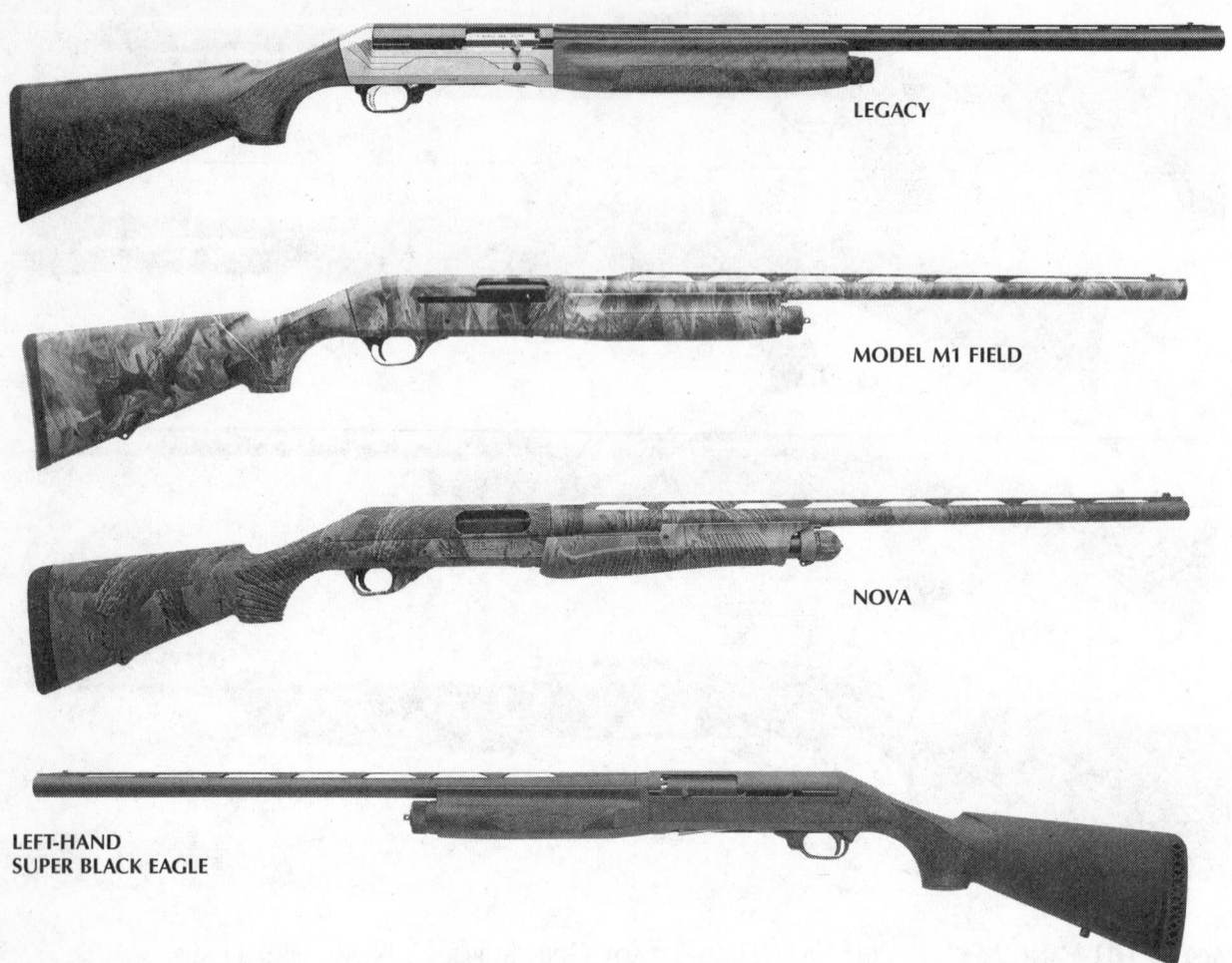

LEGACY

MODEL M1 FIELD

NOVA

LEFT-HAND
SUPER BLACK EAGLE

## LEGACY
**Action:** autoloader
**Stock:** walnut
**Barrel:** 24, 26 or 28 in.
**Chokes:** screw-in tubes
**Weight:** 7.5lbs.
**Bore/Gauge:** 12, 20
**Magazine:** 3
**Features:** 3-inch chambers, inertia recoil system, rotating bolt with dual lugs; Executive series, Grades I, II and III at extra cost
**Legacy** . . . . . . . . . . . . . . . . . $1435

## MODEL M1 FIELD
**Action:** autoloader
**Stock:** walnut, synthetic or camo
**Barrel:** 21, 24, 26, 28 or 30 in.
**Chokes:** screw-in tubes
**Weight:** 7.3lbs.
**Bore/Gauge:** 12, 20
**Magazine:** 3

**Features:** 3-inch chambers, inertial recoil system, rotating bolt with dual lugs, rifled slug (12-gauge) about $80 more; Sport: 8 pounds, walnut, 12 ga.; Montefeltro: walnut, 5.3 to 7.1 pounds.
synthetic . . . . . . . . . . . . . . . $1000
wood . . . . . . . . . . . . . . . . . . $1015
camo . . . . . . . . . . . . . . . . . . $1100
tactical . . . . . . . . . . . . . . . . . $1040
Sport . . . . . . . . . . . . . . . . . . $1430
Montefeltro . . . . . . . . . . . . . . $1035

## NOVA
**Action:** pump
**Stock:** synthetic
**Barrel:** 24, 26 or 28 in.
**Chokes:** screw-in tubes
**Weight:** 8.1lbs.
**Bore/Gauge** 12, 20
**Magazine:** 4
**Features:** molded polymer (steel rein-

forced) replaces traditional stock and receiver; bolt locks into barrel
**Nova synthetic** . . . . . . . . . . . . $340
camo . . . . . . . . . . . . . . . . . . $405
rifled slug . . . . . . . . . . . . . . . $505
rifled slug, camo . . . . . . . . . . $580

## SUPER BLACK EAGLE
**Action:** autoloader
**Stock:** walnut or synthetic
**Barrel:** 24, 26 or 28 in.
**Chokes:** screw-in tubes
**Weight:** 7.3lbs.
**Bore/Gauge:** 12
**Magazine:** 3
**Features:** 3½" chamber, inertial recoil system; rotating bolt with dual lugs; rifles slug and left-hand versions about $50 extra
synthetic . . . . . . . . . . . . . . . $1305
walnut . . . . . . . . . . . . . . . . . $1315
camo . . . . . . . . . . . . . . . . . . $1400

SHOTGUNS

# Beretta Shotguns

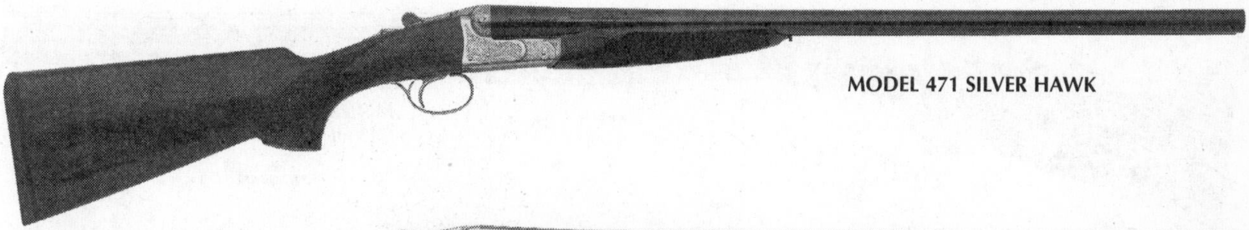

**MODEL 471 SILVER HAWK**

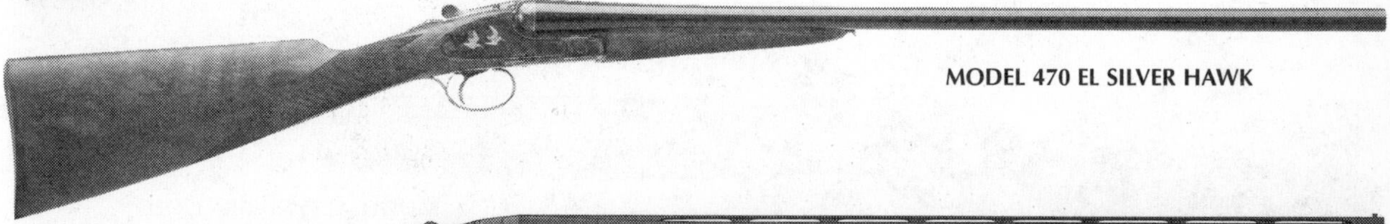

**MODEL 470 EL SILVER HAWK**

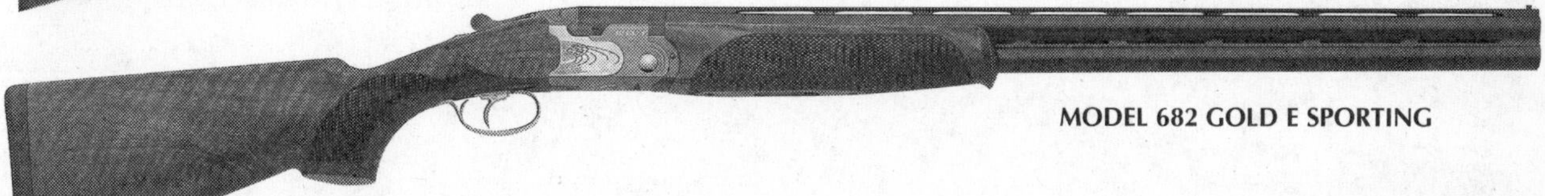

**MODEL 682 GOLD E SPORTING**

**MODEL 682 GOLD E COMPETITION SKEET**

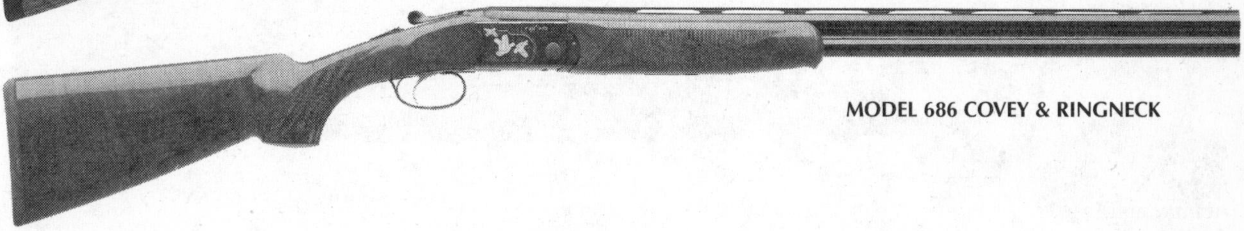

**MODEL 686 COVEY & RINGNECK**

## SILVER HAWK
*Action:* side-by-side
*Stock:* walnut
*Barrel:* 26 or 28 in.
*Chokes:* 12 Gauge Optima-Chokes, 20 Gauge Mobile Chokes
*Weight:* 6.5lbs.
*Bore/Gauge:* 12, 20
*Magazine:* none
*Features:* boxlock; satin chromed receiver, single selective trigger, automatic ejectors; EL has case-colored receiver, gold inlay, straight or pistol grips.
Model 471: . . . . . . . . . . . . . . $3098
Model 470 EL . . . . . . . . . . . . $6134

## MODEL 682 GOLD E
*Action:* over/under
*Stock:* walnut
*Barrel:* 28, 30 or 32 in.
*Chokes:* screw-in tubes
*Weight:* 6.8lbs.
*Bore/Gauge:* 12
*Magazine:* none
*Features:* boxlock; single selective adjustable trigger; automatic ejectors
Skeet . . . . . . . . . . . . . . . . . . $3933
Trap . . . . . . . . . . . . . . . . . . . $3933
Combo Trap . . . . . . . . . . . . . $5003
Sporting . . . . . . . . . . . . . . . . $3485

## MODEL 686 AND ONYX SERIES
*Action:* over/under
*Stock:* walnut
*Barrel:* 26, 28, 30 or 32 in.
*Chokes:* screw-in tubes
*Weight:* 6.8-7.7lbs.
*Bore/Gauge:* 12, 20, 28
*Magazine:* none
*Features:* boxlock; 3-inch chambers; single selective trigger; automatic ejectors; 3.5 has 3½-inch chambers
Onyx Pro: . . . . . . . . . . . . . . .$1856
Onyx Pro 3.5 . . . . . . . . . . . . .$1929
686 Covey and Ringneck . . . .$2027
686 E Sporting . . . . . . . . . . .$1856

*Short shotgun barrels make for easy carry and fast shooting. Long ones offer little or no ballistic advantage but add weight for a smooth swing and move the blast farther from your face.*

# Beretta Shotguns

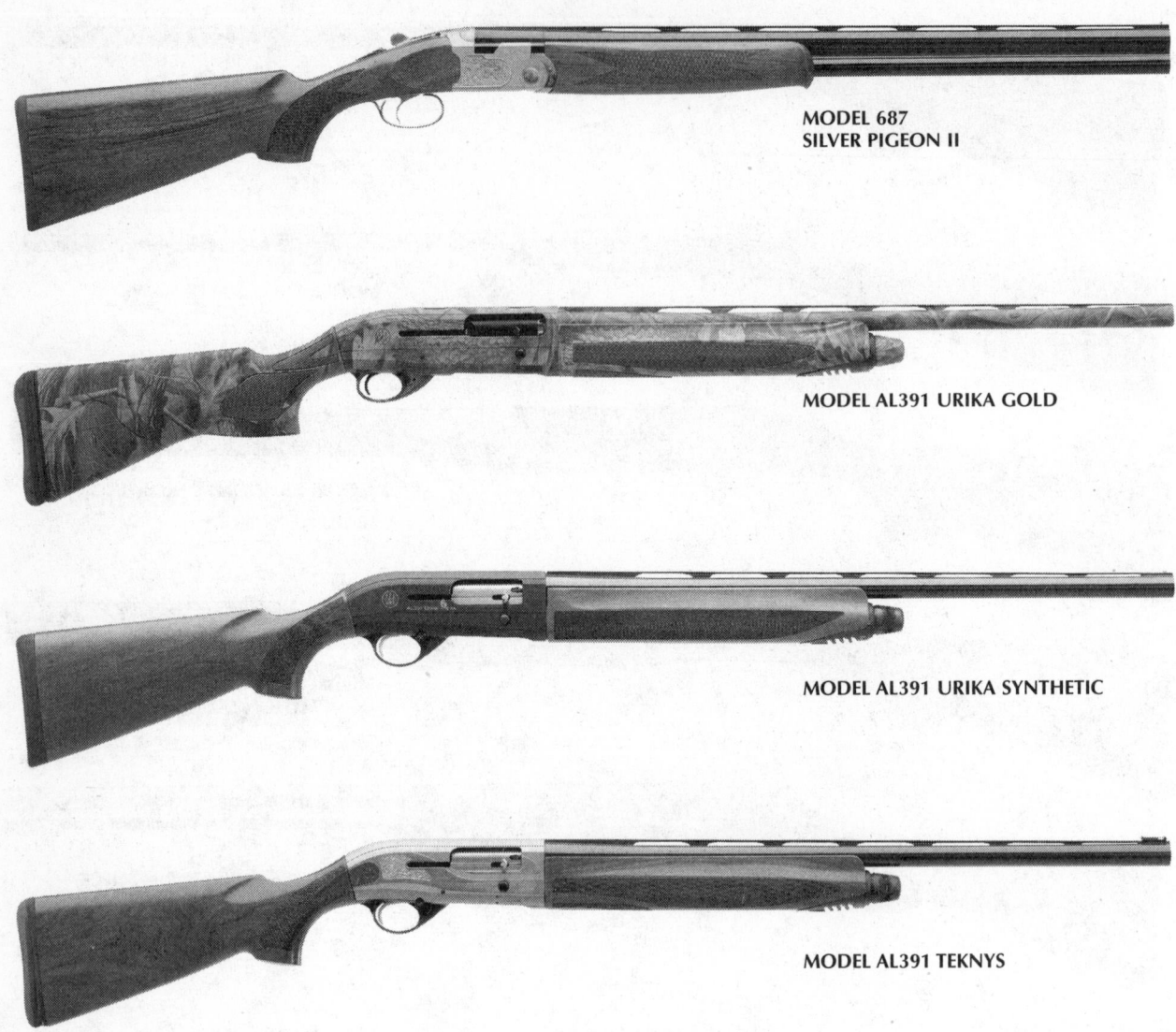

MODEL 687
SILVER PIGEON II

MODEL AL391 URIKA GOLD

MODEL AL391 URIKA SYNTHETIC

MODEL AL391 TEKNYS

## MODEL 687 SILVER PIGEON SERIES

**Action:** over/under
**Stock:** walnut
**Barrel:** 26 or 28 in.
**Chokes:** screw-in tubes
**Weight:** 6.8lbs.
**Bore/Gauge:** 12, 20, 28/20 Combo
**Magazine:** none
**Features:** boxlock; 3-inch chambers; single selective trigger; automatic ejectors; Ultralight (12 ga. only)

| | |
|---|---|
| Silver Pigeon S | $1994 |
| Silver Pigeon II | $2270 |
| Silver Pigeon IV | $2684 |
| EL Gold Pigeon II | $4616 |
| EELL Diamond Pigeon | $5931 |

## AL391 TEKNYS

**Action:** autoloader
**Stock:** walnut
**Barrel:** 26, 28, 30 or 32 in.
**Chokes:** screw-in tubes
**Weight:** 7.3 lbs. (12 ga.), 5.9 lbs. (20 ga.)
**Bore/Gauge:** 12, 20
**Magazine:** 3
**Features:** Self-compensating gas system, Gel-Tek recoil pad, reversible cross-bolt, Optima-Bore overbored barrels (12-gauge), Optima-Choke flush tubes, Tru-Glo front sight

| | |
|---|---|
| AL391 Teknys | $1,194 |
| AL391 Teknys Gold | $1,515 |
| AL391 Teknys Gold Sporting | $1,653 |
| AL391 Teknys Gold Trap | $1,791 |

## MODEL AL391 URIKA

**Action:** autoloader
**Stock:** walnut or synthetic
**Barrel:** 24, 26, 28 or 30 in.
**Chokes:** screw-in tubes
**Weight:** 7.4 lbs.
**Bore/Gauge:** 12, 20
**Magazine:** 3
**Features:** gas-operated action; alloy receiver; stock adjust-ment shims; high-grade "Gold" versions available

| | |
|---|---|
| wood or synthetic | $1035 |
| camo | $1139 |
| Youth | $1035 |
| Trap | $1101 |
| Sporting | $1101 |
| Gold | $1377 |

SHOTGUNS

# Beretta Shotguns

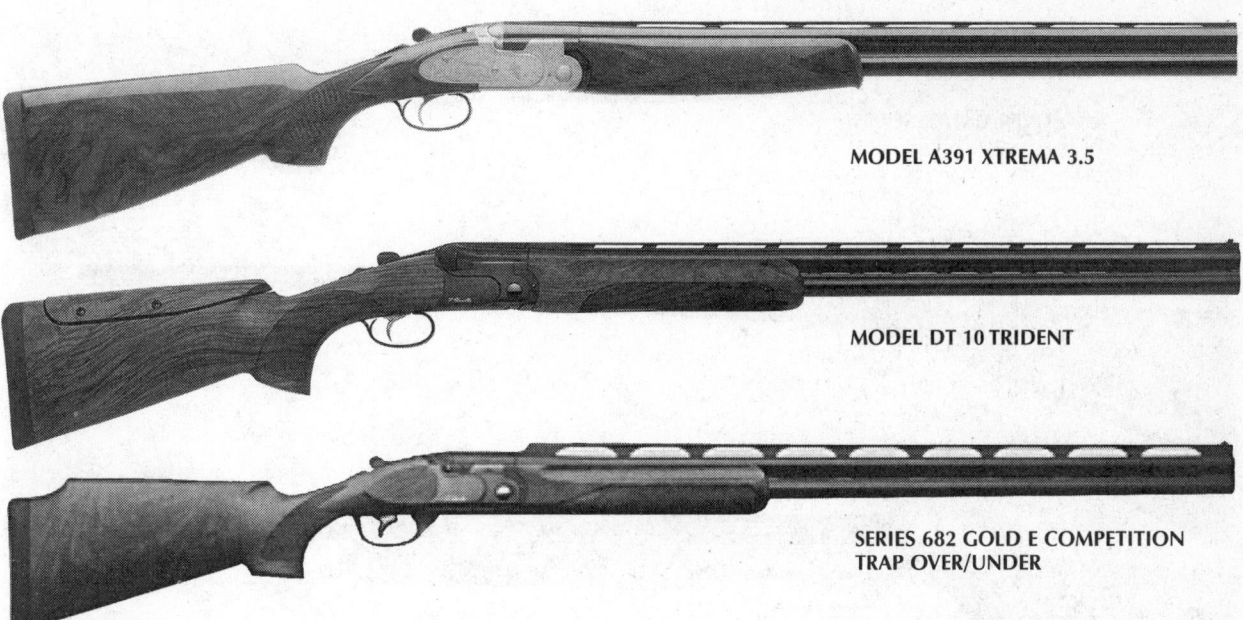

**MODEL A391 XTREMA 3.5**

**MODEL DT 10 TRIDENT**

**SERIES 682 GOLD E COMPETITION TRAP OVER/UNDER**

## MODEL A391 XTREMA
*Action:* autoloader
*Stock:* synthetic
*Barrel:* 28 in.
*Chokes:* screw-in tubes
*Weight:* 7.8lbs.
*Bore/Gauge:* 12
*Magazine:* 3
*Features:* 31/2-inch chambers
synthetic . . . . . . . . . . . . . . . . . $1173
camo . . . . . . . . . . . . . . . . . . . . $1311

## DT 10 TRIDENT
*Action:* over/under
*Stock:* walnut
*Barrel:* 28, 30, 32 or 34 in.
*Chokes:* screw-in tubes
*Weight:* 7.5lbs.
*Bore/Gauge:* 12
*Magazine:* none
Features: boxlock; single selective trigger, automatic ejectors; Skeet, Trap and Sporting models are Beretta's best competition guns. Combo with top single or bottom single; Trap versions available
**Sporting** . . . . . . . . . . . . . . . . $6383
**Trap** . . . . . . . . . . . . . . . . . . . $6866
**Trap, Bottom Single** . . . . . . . $7418
**Trap, Combo Top Single** . . . . . $9005

## MODEL 682 GOLD E
*Action:* over/under
*Stock:* walnut
*Barrel:* 28, 30 or 32 inches
*Chokes:* screw-in tubes
*Weight:* 8.8lbs.
*Bore/Gauge:* 12
*Magazine:* none
*Features:* Skeet, Trap, Sporting, Combo and adjustable-stock models available
**Sporting:** . . . . . . . . . . . . . . . $3485
**Skeet, Trap:** . . . . . . . . . . . . . $3933
**Combo:** . . . . . . . . . . . . . . . . $5003

# Bernardelli Shotguns

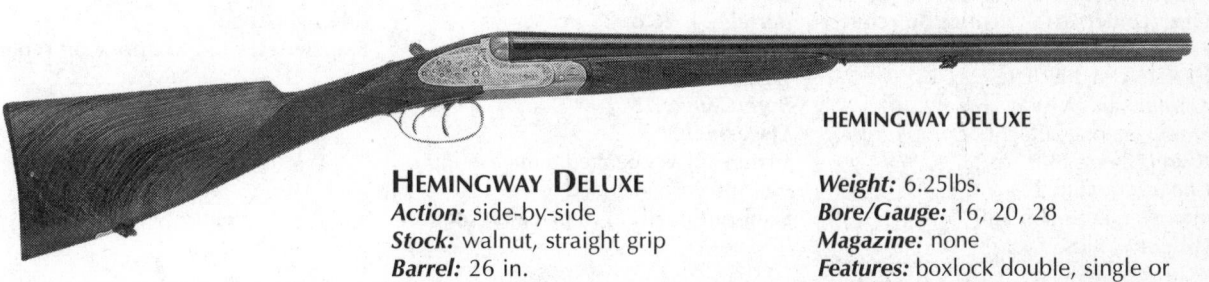

**HEMINGWAY DELUXE**

## HEMINGWAY DELUXE
*Action:* side-by-side
*Stock:* walnut, straight grip
*Barrel:* 26 in.
*Chokes:* modified, improved modified, full

*Weight:* 6.25lbs.
*Bore/Gauge:* 16, 20, 28
*Magazine:* none
*Features:* boxlock double, single or double trigger, automatic ejectors
**Hemingway Deluxe . . price on request**

# Bernardelli Shotguns

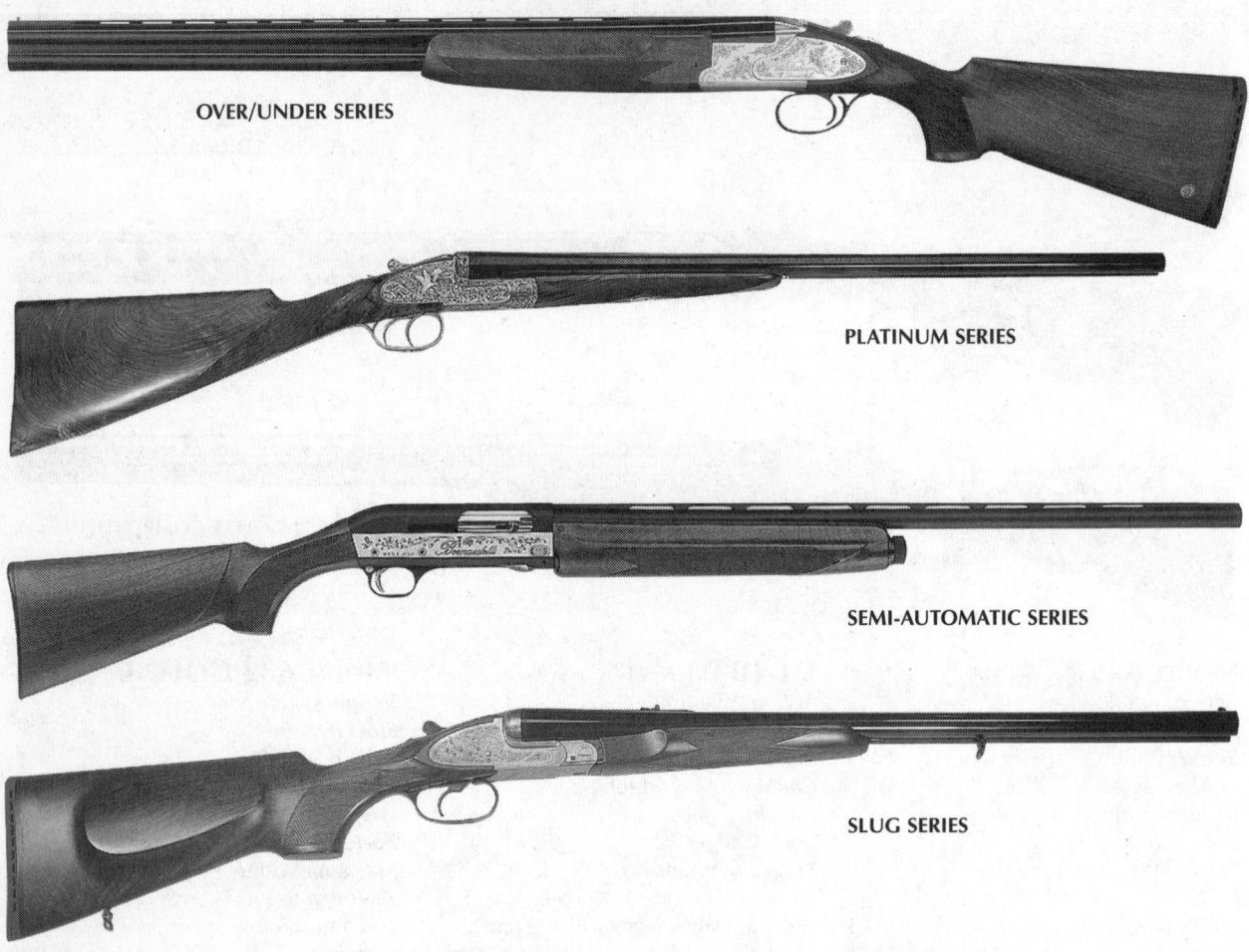

OVER/UNDER SERIES

PLATINUM SERIES

SEMI-AUTOMATIC SERIES

SLUG SERIES

### OVER/UNDER SERIES

*Action:* over/under
*Stock:* walnut, pistol grip
*Barrel:* 26 or 28 in.
*Chokes:* modified, improved modified, full, screw-in tubes
*Weight:* 7.2lbs.
*Bore/Gauge:* 12, 20
*Magazine:* none
*Features*: boxlock over/under, single or double triggers, vent rib, various grades
**Over/Under** . . . . . .price on request

### PLATINUM SERIES

*Action:* side-by-side
*Stock:* walnut, straight or pistol grip
*Barrel:* 26 or 28 in.
*Chokes*: modified, improved modified, full
*Weight:* 6.5lbs.

*Bore/Gauge:* 12
*Magazine:* none
*Features:* sidelock double; articulated single selective or double trigger, triple-lug Purdey breeching automatic ejectors, various grades
**Platinum Series . . . . price on request**

### SEMI-AUTOMATIC SERIES

*Action:* autoloader
*Stock:* walnut, synthetic or camo
*Barrel:* 24, 26 or 28 in.
*Chokes:* screw-in tubes
*Weight:* 6.7lbs.
*Bore/Gauge:* 12
*Magazine:* 5
*Features:* gas-operated, concave top rib, ABS case included
**Semi-Automatic. . . . price on request**

### SLUG SERIES

*Action:* side-by-side
*Stock:* walnut, pistol grip
*Barrel:* 24 in.
*Chokes:* modified, improved modified, full
*Weight:* 7.0lbs.
*Bore/Gauge:* 12
*Magazine:* none
*Features*: boxlock double, single or double trigger, automatic ejectors, rifle sights
**Slug Series. . . . . . . . price on request**

SHOTGUNS

# Browning Shotguns

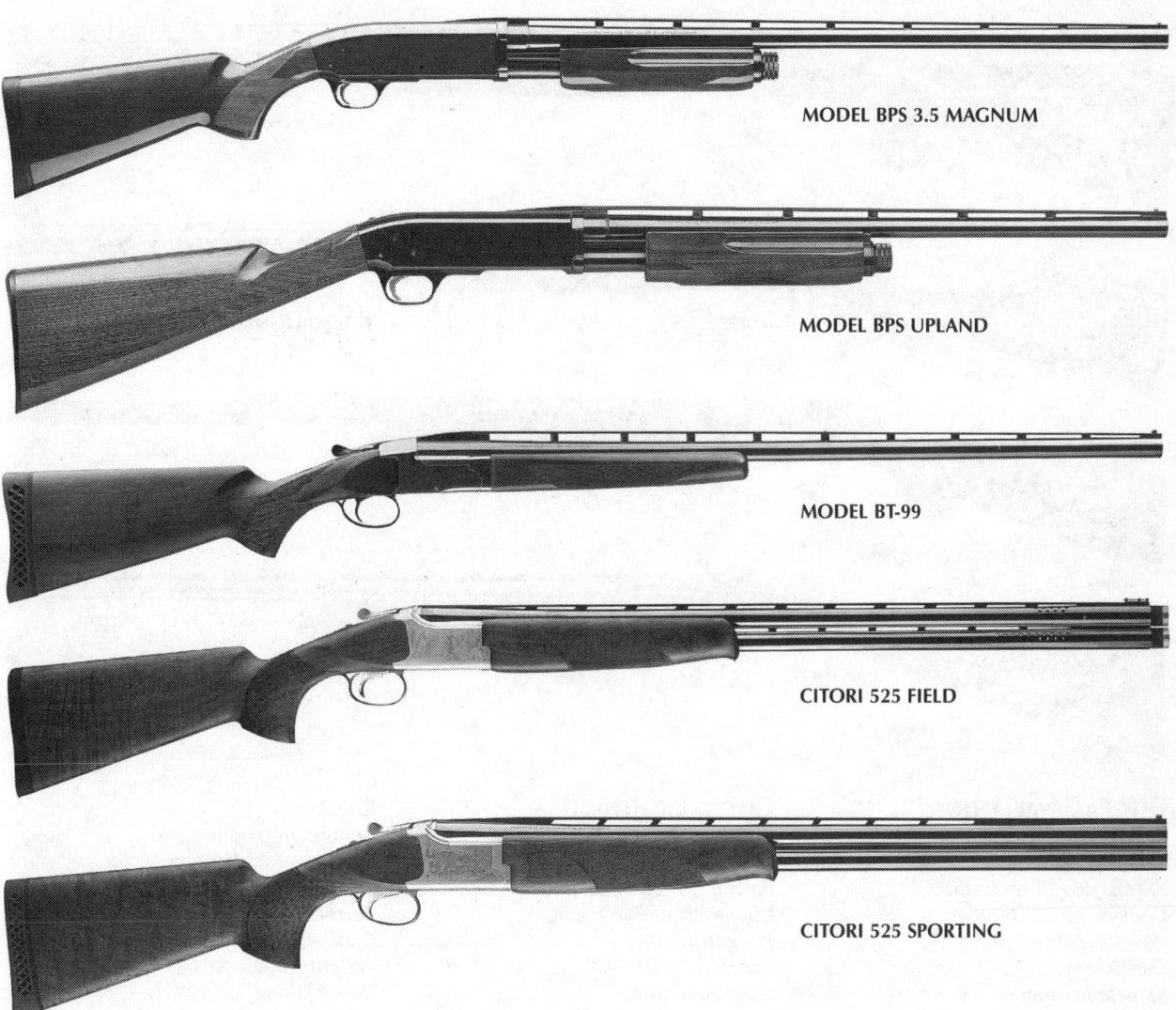

MODEL BPS 3.5 MAGNUM

MODEL BPS UPLAND

MODEL BT-99

CITORI 525 FIELD

CITORI 525 SPORTING

## MODEL BPS
*Action:* pump
*Stock:* walnut or synthetic
*Barrel:* 20, 22, 24, 26, 28 or 30 in.
*Chokes:* screw-in tubes
*Weight:* 8.0lbs.
*Bore/Gauge:* 10, 12, 20, 28, .410
*Magazine:* 4
*Features:* Both 10 and 12 gauge available with 3.5-inch chambers; Upland Special has short barrel, straight grip; Deer Special has rifled barrel; Micro BPS has short barrel, stock

| | |
|---|---|
| **Hunter (walnut)** | **$494** |
| **Stalker (synthetic)** | **$478** |
| **Camo synthetic** | **$587** |
| **28 or .410** | **$528** |
| **Magnum (3.5-inch)** | **$562** |
| **Magnum Camo** | **$668** |

| | |
|---|---|
| **Upland (12, 20)** | **$494** |
| **Micro (20)** | **$494** |
| **Rifled Deer (12)** | **$606** |

## MODEL BT-99
*Action:* hinged single-shot
*Stock:* walnut, trap-style
*Barrel:* 30, 32 or 34 in.
*Chokes:* screw-in tubes
*Weight:* 8.0lbs.
*Bore/Gauge:* 12
*Magazine:* none
*Features:* boxlock single-shot competition gun with high-post rib

| | |
|---|---|
| **BT-99** | **$1290** |
| **with adjustable comb** | **$1538** |
| **Micro** | **$1290** |
| **Golden Clays** | **$3407** |

## CITORI 525
*Action:* over/under
*Stock:* walnut
*Barrel:* 26, 28, 30 or 32 in.
*Chokes:* screw-in tubes
*Weight:* 7.3lbs.
*Bore/Gauge:* 12, 20, 28, .410
*Magazine:* none
*Features:* boxlock; European-style stock, pronounced pistol grip, floating top and side ribs; Golden Clays has gold inlays

| | |
|---|---|
| **Field** | **$1885** |
| **Sporting** | **$2645** |
| **Golden Clays** | **$4236** |
| **Field (28 or .410)** | **$1914** |
| **Sporting (28 or .410)** | **$2652** |
| **Golden Clays (28 or .410)** | **$4429** |

# Browning Shotguns

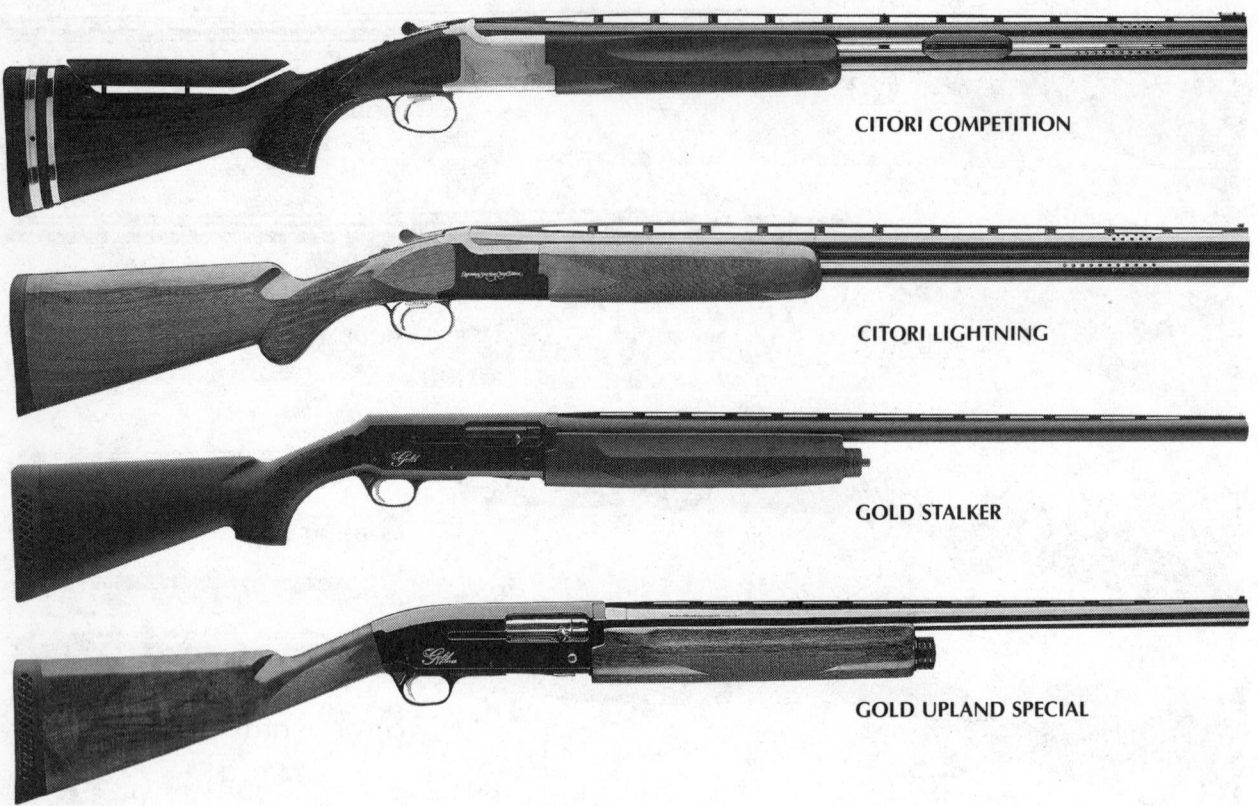

CITORI COMPETITION

CITORI LIGHTNING

GOLD STALKER

GOLD UPLAND SPECIAL

## CITORI COMPETITION
**Action:** over/under
**Stock:** walnut
**Barrel:** 26, 28 or 30 in.
**Chokes:** screw-in tubes
**Weight:** 8.0lbs.
**Bore/Gauge:** 12
**Magazine:** none
**Features:** boxlock; XS Pro-Comp has ported barrels, adjustable stock comb, GraCoil recoil reducer; Trap and Skeet Models are stocked and barreled accordingly

XS Pro-Comp . . . . . . . . . . . . $4027
XT Trap . . . . . . . . . . . . . . . . $2209
XT Trap with adjustable comb . $2475
XS Skeet . . . . . . . . . . . . . . . $2363
XS Skeet with adjustable comb $2629

## CITORI LIGHTNING
**Action:** over/under
**Stock:** walnut
**Barrel:** 26, 28 or 30 in.
**Chokes:** screw-in tubes
**Weight:** 6.0lbs.
**Bore/Gauge:** 12, 20, 28, .410
**Magazine:** none
**Features:** boxlock; single selective trigger, automatic ejectors; higher grades available; ported barrels optional

Grade I Sporting . . . . . . . . . . $1878
Grade III 12 or 20 . . . . . . . . $2464
Grade III 28 or .410 . . . . . . . $2754
Grade VI 12 or 20 . . . . . . . . $3797
Grade VI 28 or .410 . . . . . . . $4090

## GOLD
**Action:** autoloader
**Stock:** walnut (Hunter) or synthetic (Stalker)
**Barrel:** 24, 26, 28 or 30 in.
**Chokes:** screw-in tubes
**Weight:** 8.0lbs.
**Bore/Gauge:** 10, 12, 20
**Magazine:** 3
**Features:** gas-operated, 31/2-inch chambers on 10 and one 12 gauge version; Youth and Ladies versions available

Stalker . . . . . . . . . . . . . . . . . . $917
Hunter . . . . . . . . . . . . . . . . . . $958
Sporting Clays . . . . . . . $1033 - 1596
Upland Special . . . . . . . . . . . . $958
Rifled Deer Stalker . . . . . . . . $1015
Rifled Deer Hunter . . . . . . . . $1057
3¹/₂-inch Hunter . . . . . $1073 – 1112
Gold Fusion . . . . . . . . . . . . . $1055
Camo . . . . . . . . . . . . . $1053 - 1245
Classic HighGrade . . . . . . . . . $1838
Micro . . . . . . . . . . . . . . . . . . $958

*Slug-shooting shotguns with rifle-like groups with sabot ammunition but are not suitable for the bore-sized soft-lead Foster slugs developed for smooth bores.*

SHOTGUNS

# Charles Daly Shotguns

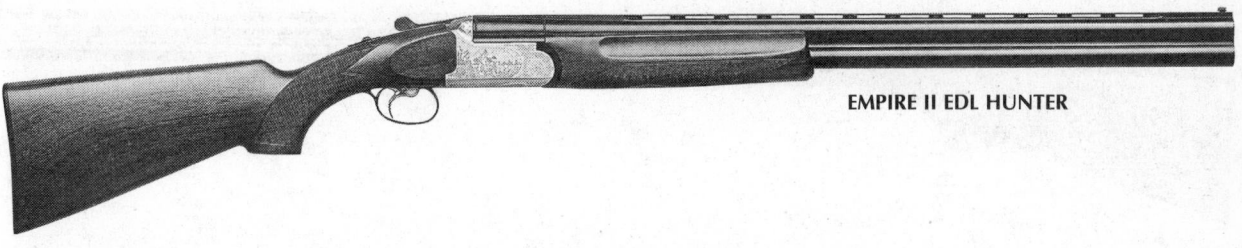

EMPIRE II EDL HUNTER

FIELD HUNTER PUMP

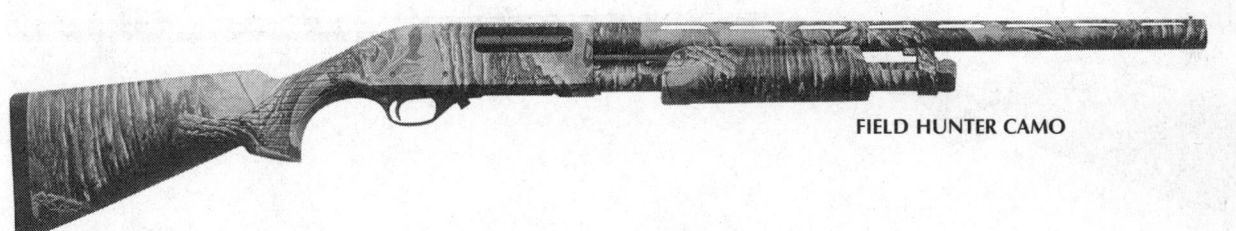

FIELD HUNTER CAMO

## EMPIRE II EDL HUNTER

*Action:* over/under
*Stock:* walnut
*Barrel:* 26 or 28 in.
*Chokes:* screw-in tubes
*Weight:* 7.2lbs.
*Bore/Gauge:* 12, 20, 28, .410
*Magazine:* none
*Features:* boxlock; single selective trigger, automatic safety, automatic ejectors
12 or 20 ga.. . . . . . . . . . . . . . .$1899
28 ga.. . . . . . . . . . . . . . . . . . .$1889
.410. . . . . . . . . . . . . . . . . . . .$1889
Trap. . . . . . . . . . . . . . . . . . . .$1999

## FIELD HUNTER AUTOLOADER

*Action:* autoloader
*Stock:* synthetic
*Barrel:* 22, 24, 26, 28 or 30 in.
*Chokes:* screw-in tubes
*Weight:* 7.5lbs.
*Bore/Gauge:* 12, 20, 28
*Magazine:* 4
*Features:* ventilated rib; Superior II Grade has walnut stock, ported barrel
12 or 20 ga.. . . . . . . . . . . . . . .$409
28 ga.. . . . . . . . . . . . . . . . . . .$465
camo . . . . . . . . . . . . . . . . . . .$499
3.5-in. magnum synthetic . . . . .$499
3.5-in. magnum camo. . . . . . . .$599
Superior Field. . . . . . . . . . . . . .$559
Superior Trap . . . . . . . . . . . . . .$610

## FIELD HUNTER PUMP

*Action:* pump
*Stock:* synthetic
*Barrel:* 26 or 28 in.
*Chokes:* screw-in tubes
*Weight:* 7.0lbs.
*Bore/Gauge:* 12, 20
*Magazine:* 4
*Features:* ventilated rib
Field Hunter. . . . . . . . . . . . . .$239
camo . . . . . . . . . . . . . . . . . . .$319
3.5-in. magnum synthetic . . . . .$269
3.5-in. magnum camo. . . . . . . .$349

 *Pattern your shotgun not only to determine pellet-strike percentages in 30-inch circles at 40 yards but to find the center of impact relative to your sightline. The gun must shoot where you look!*

SHOTGUNS

# Charles Daly Shotguns

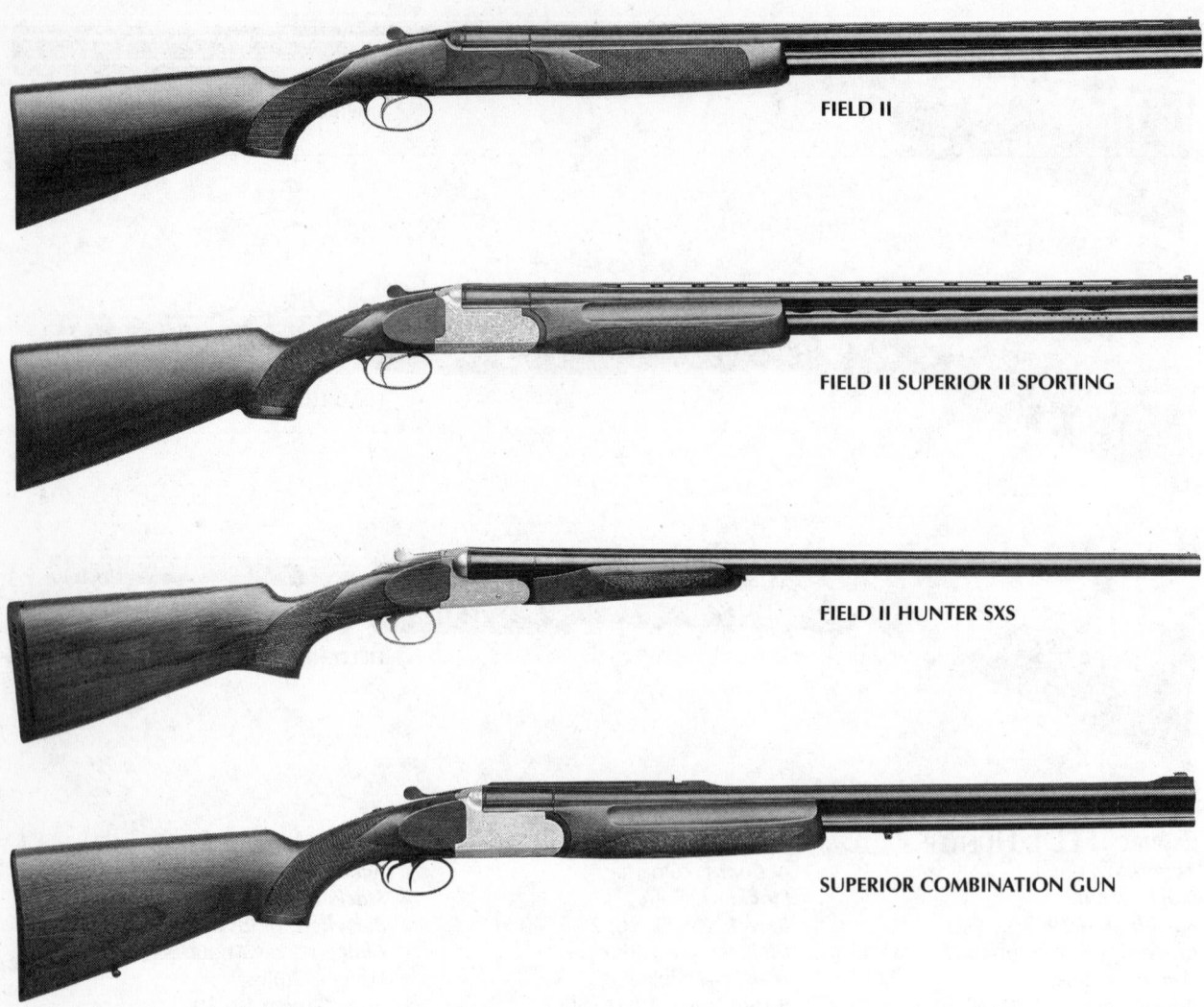

FIELD II

FIELD II SUPERIOR II SPORTING

FIELD II HUNTER SXS

SUPERIOR COMBINATION GUN

## FIELD II

*Action:* over/under
*Stock:* walnut
*Barrel:* 26 or 28 in.
*Chokes:* mod/full (28 in.), imp.cyl/mod (26 in.), full/full (.410)
*Weight:* 7.2lbs.
*Bore/Gauge:* 12, 16, 20, 28, .410
*Magazine:* none
*Features:* boxlock; single selective trigger, automatic safety

| | |
|---|---|
| Field II | $959 |
| 28-gauge | $1059 |
| .410 | $1059 |
| Ultra-Light (12, 20) | $1149 |
| Superior II | $1449 |
| Superior II Trap | $1629 |

## FIELD II HUNTER SXS

*Action:* side-by-side
*Stock:* walnut
*Barrel:* 26, 28 or 30 in.
*Chokes:* imp.cyl/mod (26 in.), mod/full (28, 30 in.), full/full (.410)
*Weight:* 10.0lbs.
*Bore/Gauge:* 12, 20, 28, .410
*Magazine:* none
*Features:* boxlock; single selective trigger, automatic safety

| | |
|---|---|
| 12 or 20 ga. | $919 |
| 28 ga. or .410 | $839 |
| Superior Grade | $1599 |

## SUPERIOR COMBINATION GUN

*Action:* side-by-side
*Stock:* walnut
*Barrel:* 24 in.
*Chokes:* improved cylinder
*Weight:* 7.5lbs.
*Bore/Gauge:* 12
*Magazine:* none
*Features:* boxlock drilling; 12 gauge over .22 Hornet, .223 or .30-06 rifle; double triggers, sling swivels

| | |
|---|---|
| Superior | $1369 |
| Empire Grade | $2759 |

SHOTGUNS

# European American Armory Shotguns

IZH43 BOUNTY HUNTER

SAIGA

# Flodman Shotguns

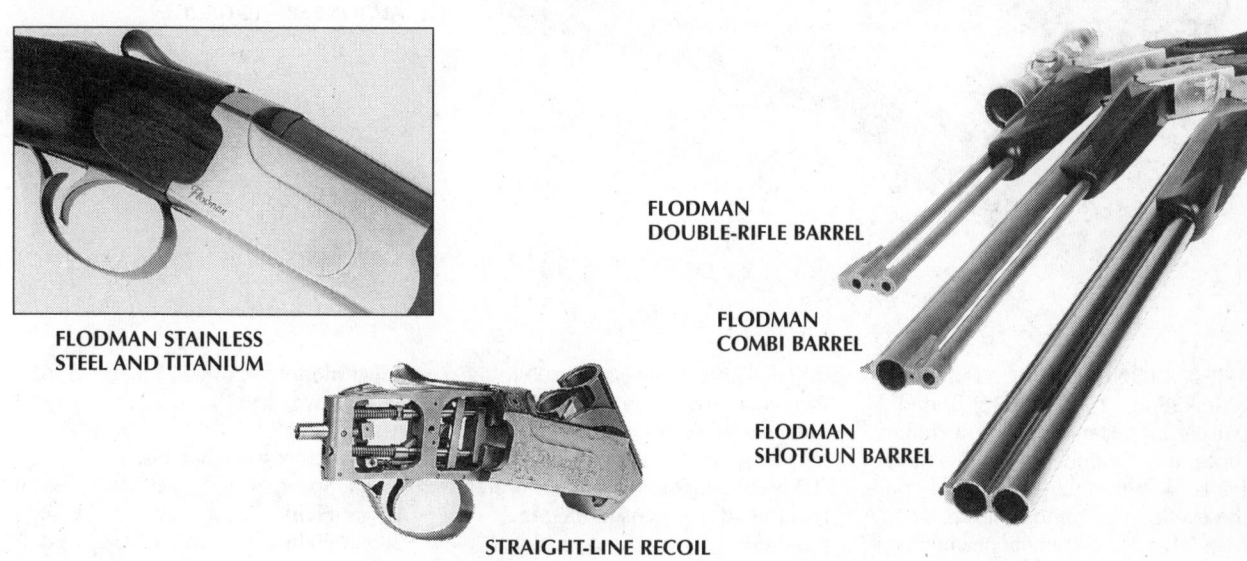

FLODMAN STAINLESS
STEEL AND TITANIUM

FLODMAN
DOUBLE-RIFLE BARREL

FLODMAN
COMBI BARREL

FLODMAN
SHOTGUN BARREL

STRAIGHT-LINE RECOIL

## BOUNTY HUNTER
*Action:* side-by-side
*Stock:* walnut
*Barrel:* 24, 26 or 28 in.
*Chokes:* screw-in tubes
*Weight:* 6.8lbs.
*Bore/Gauge:* 12, 16, 20, 28, 410
*Magazine:* none
*Features:* hinged breech boxlock; ejectors, single selective trigger, automatic safety, chrome-lined, hammer forged barrels, choked .410 IM/F and 28 ga. IC/M; also, exposed-hammer "Cowboy" model, 12-gauge rifle barrel inserts available
12 ga. . . . . . . . . . . . . . . . . . . $389
other gauges . . . . . . . . . . . . . $439

English stock in .410 . . . . . . . . $439
20 and 28 ga. two-barrel set . . . $630
rifle barrel inserts .45/70 . . . . . $159

## SAIGA
*Action:* autoloader
*Stock:* synthetic
*Barrel:* 19, 21, 22 or 24 in.
*Chokes:* screw-in tubes
*Weight:* 7.4lbs.
*Bore/Gauge:* 12, 20, 410
*Magazine:* 5 + 1 (4 + 1 .410)
*Features:* AK-47 mechanism, detachable box magazine
12 ga. . . . . . . . . . . . . . . . . . . $439
20 ga. . . . . . . . . . . . . . . . . . . $389
.410 . . . . . . . . . . . . . . . . . . . . $299

## FLODMAN SHOTGUN
*Action:* over/under
*Stock:* walnut, fitted to customer
*Barrel:* any standard length
*Chokes:* improved cylinder, modified, full
*Weight:* 7.0lbs.
*Bore/Gauge:* 12, 20
*Magazine:* none
*Features:* boxlock offered in any standard gauge or rifle/shotgun combination; true hammerless firing mechanism, single selective trigger, automatic ejector
Flodman shotgun . . . . . . . . $13,600

SHOTGUNS

# Franchi Shotguns

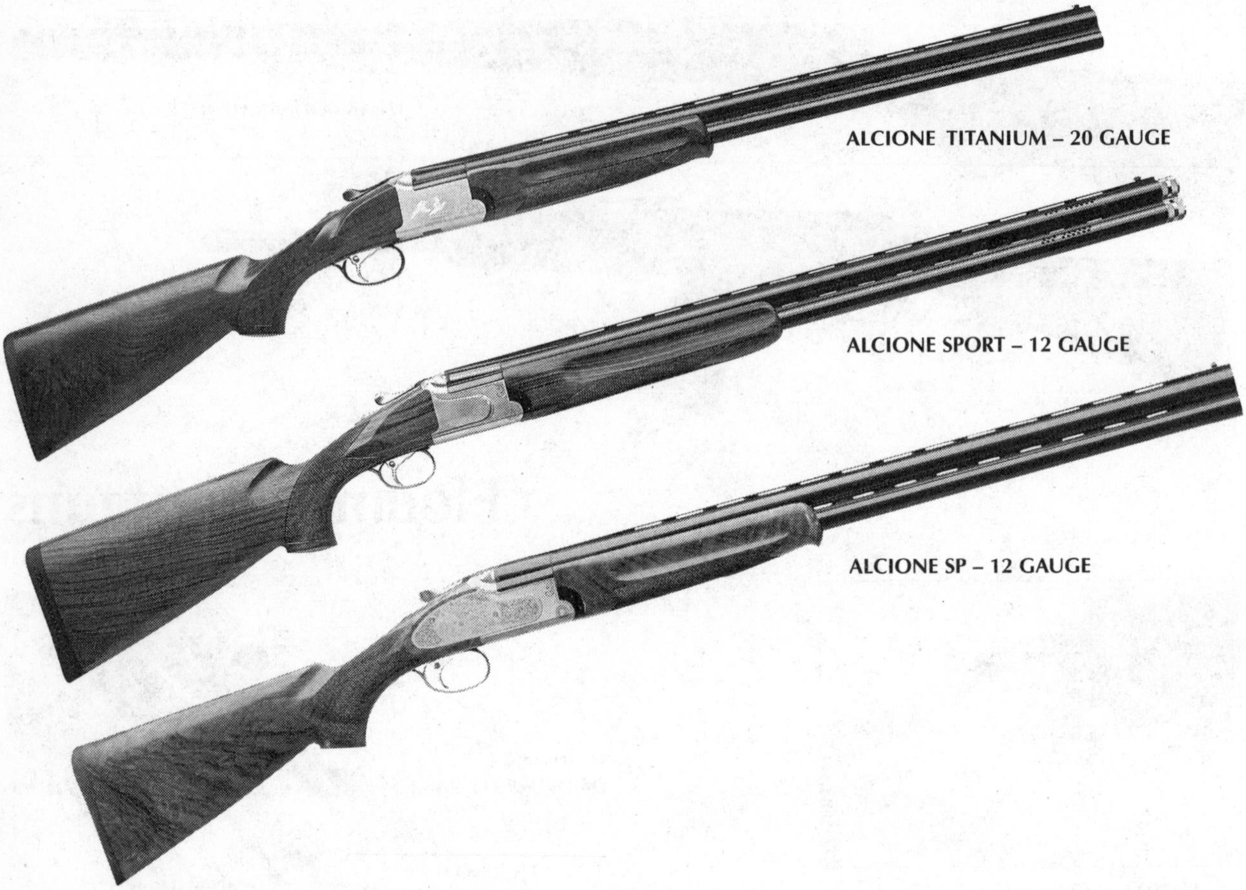

**ALCIONE TITANIUM – 20 GAUGE**

**ALCIONE SPORT – 12 GAUGE**

**ALCIONE SP – 12 GAUGE**

**THE ALCIONE SPORT** over-under is available in 12 ga. with 30" ported barrels and extended knurled choke tubes. It is chambered for 2¾" target loads. A 10mm-wide rib quickly pulls the eye to targets and builds scores. A manual safety complements mechanical triggers, which do not require recoil from the first barrel to fire the second barrel.

The Alcione Sport and SX have removable receiver sideplates. The stock and forend are shaped from high-grade walnut and have special dimensions for the serious competitor. The Alcione Sport and Field offer left-handed stock dimensions.

The Alcione SX has a high-grade walnut stock with fine checkering. The receivers are highly polished and fea-ture delicate etchings. Unique to the Alcione product line is the ability to interchange barrels without the need for fitting. Simply swap any barrel set (12 or 20 gauge) onto any other frames and forend. No gunsmithing is required.

## ALCIONE
*Action:* over/under
*Stock:* walnut
*Barrel:* 26 or 28 in.
*Chokes:* screw-in tubes
*Weight:* 5.4lbs.
*Bore/Gauge:* 12, 20
*Magazine:* none
*Features:* boxlock; mechanical single selective trigger
Alcione . . . . . . . . . . . . . . . . . $1275
titanium . . . . . . . . . . . . . . . . $1425

Sport model . . . . . . . . . . . . . $1650
SX Lightweight . . . . . . . . . . . $1800
**Also available:**
**Alcione accessory barrels:**
12 ga. Sport . . . . . . . . . . . . . $550
12 ga. Field . . . . . . . . . . . . . $475
20 ga. Field . . . . . . . . . . . . . $475

## ALCIONE SP
*Action:* over/under
*Stock:* walnut
*Barrel:* 28 in.
*Chokes:* improved cylinder, modified, full
*Weight:* 7.5lbs.
*Bore/Gauge:* 12
*Magazine:* none
*Features:* boxlock, engraved, coin-finish sideplates, fitted hard case
Alcione SP . . . . . . . . . . . . . . $2700

*Remington's "Hevi-Shot" isn't round or even uniform in size, but it's 10 percent denser than lead and delivers tight patterns, even from open chokes. Use it only in barrels that handle steel shot.*

**SHOTGUNS**

# Franchi Shotguns

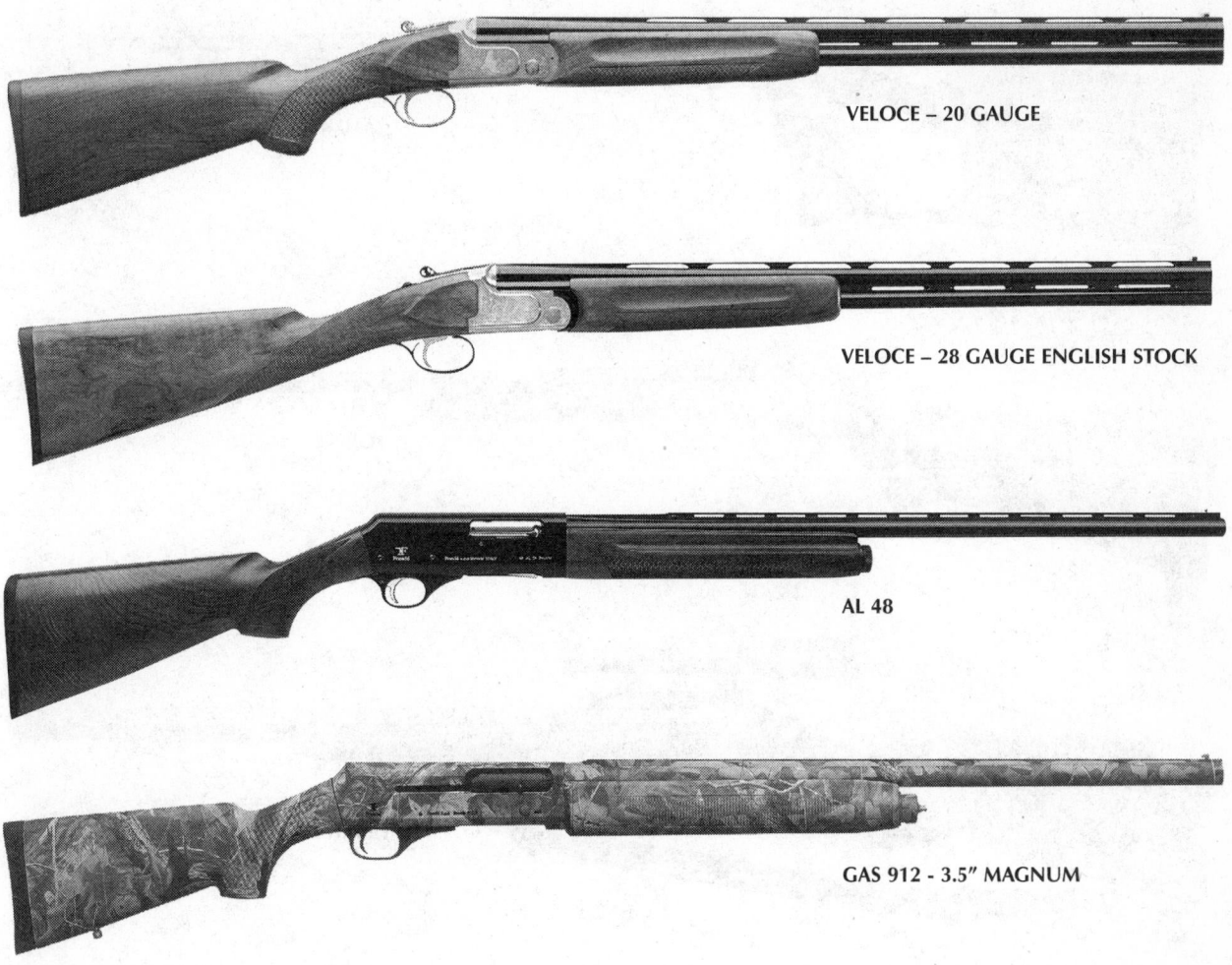

VELOCE – 20 GAUGE

VELOCE – 28 GAUGE ENGLISH STOCK

AL 48

GAS 912 - 3.5" MAGNUM

## VELOCE
*Action:* over/under
*Stock:* walnut, straight English or pistol grip
*Barrel:* 26 or 28 in.
*Chokes:* screw-in tubes
*Weight:* 5.5lbs.
*Bore/Gauge:* 20, 28
*Magazine:* none
*Features:* boxlock; alloy frame, steel breech insert, mechanical single selective trigger, engraved inside plate, 3-inch chambers (12 gauge), 2¾-inch chambers (28-gauge), aluminum alloy frame.
20 ga. . . . . . . . . . . . . . . . . $1425
28 ga. . . . . . . . . . . . . . . . . $1500

## MODEL AL 48
*Action:* autoloader
*Stock:* walnut pistol grip or English
*Barrel:* 24, 26 or 28 in.
*Chokes:* screw-in tubes
*Weight:* 5.6lbs.
*Bore/Gauge:* 20, 28
*Magazine:* 4
*Features:* long recoil action
20 ga. . . . . . . . . . . . . . . . . . $715
28 ga. . . . . . . . . . . . . . . . . . $825
Deluxe 20 . . . . . . . . . . . . . . $940
Deluxe 28 . . . . . . . . . . . . . . $990

## MODEL 612, 620, 912
*Action:* autoloader
*Stock:* walnut or synthetic camo
*Barrel:* 18, 24, 26, 28, or 30 in.
*Chokes:* screw-in tubes
*Weight:* 7.7 to 9.0lbs.
*Bore/Gauge:* 12, 20
*Magazine:* 4
*Features:* gas-operated, rotary bolt; Model 912 chambered for 3.5-inch shells
walnut . . . . . . . . . . . . . . . . . . $675
synthetic . . . . . . . . . . . . . . . . $660
camo . . . . . . . . . . . . . . . . . . . $765
defense (18 in.) . . . . . . . . . . . $635
Sporting. . . . . . . . . . . . . . . . . $975
Model 912 3.5-inch, walnut . . . $825
Model 912, synthetic . . . . . . . $765
Model 912, camo . . . . . . . . . . $885

SHOTGUNS

# Harrington & Richardson Shotguns

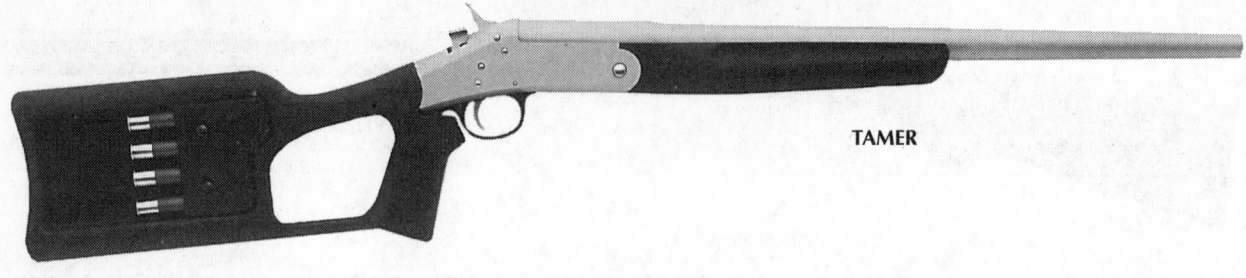

**TAMER**

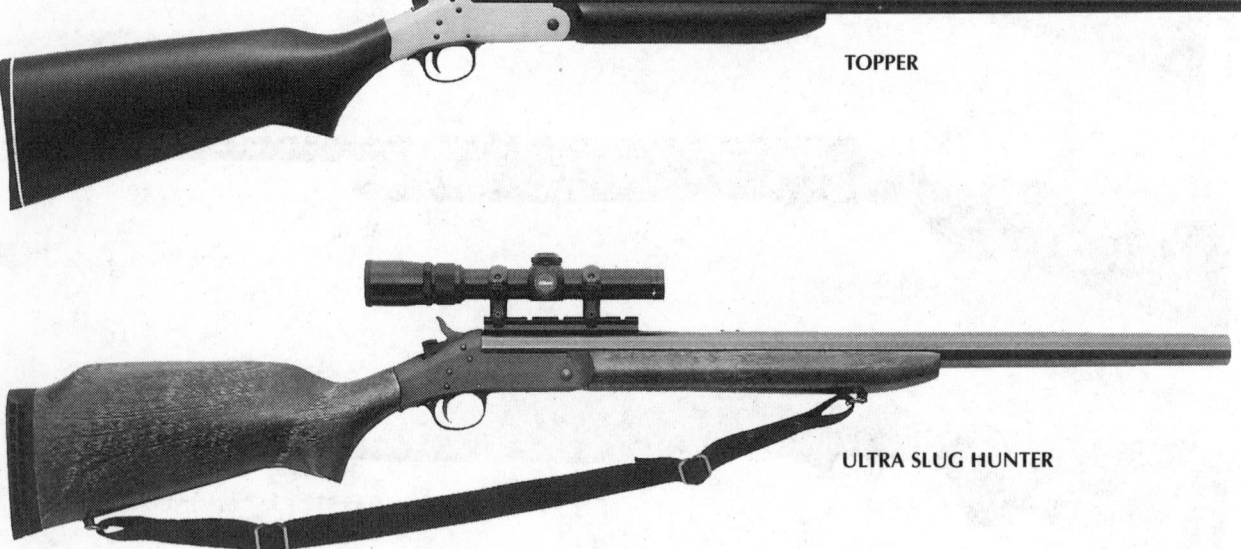

**TOPPER**

**ULTRA SLUG HUNTER**

### TAMER
*Action:* hinged single-shot
*Stock:* synthetic
*Barrel:* 19 in.
*Chokes:* full
*Weight:* 6 lbs..
*Bore/Gauge:* .410
*Magazine:* none
*Features:* thumbhole stock with recessed cavity for ammo storage
Tamer . . . . . . . . . . . . . . . . . . $164

### TOPPER
*Action:* hinged single-shot
*Stock:* hardwood
*Barrel:* 26 or 28 in.
*Chokes:* screw-in tubes
*Weight:* 6.0lbs.
*Bore/Gauge:* 12, 20, 28, .410
*Magazine:* none
*Features:* hinged-breech with side lever release, automatic ejection
Topper . . . . . . . . . . . . . . . . . . . $145
12 gauge 3.5-inch. . . . . . . . . . $169
Junior with walnut stock. . . . . . $188
Deluxe Classic . . . . . . . . . . . . . $213

### ULTRA SLUG HUNTER
*Action:* hinged single-shot
*Stock:* hardwood
*Barrel:* 24 in., rifled
*Chokes:* none
*Weight:* 7.5lbs.
*Bore/Gauge:* 12, 20
*Magazine:* none
*Features:* factory-mounted Weaver scope base, swivels and sling
Ultra Slug Hunter. . . . . . . . . . . $259
Youth. . . . . . . . . . . . . . . . . . . $259
with checkered laminated wood $318

*Turkey and heavy waterfowl loads extend your reach but batter your gums. More power doesn't always add birds to the bag. Standard loads in lighter guns can help you shoot sooner.*

SHOTGUNS

# H&K Fabarm Shotguns

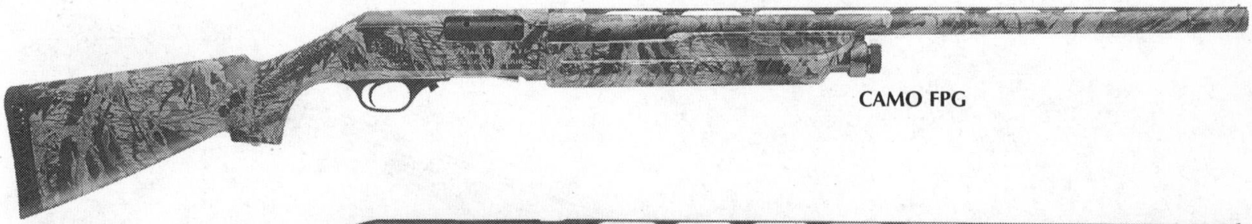

**CAMO FPG**

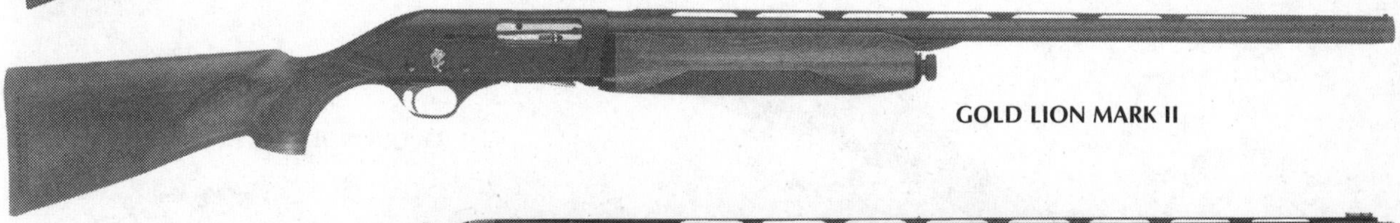

**GOLD LION MARK II**

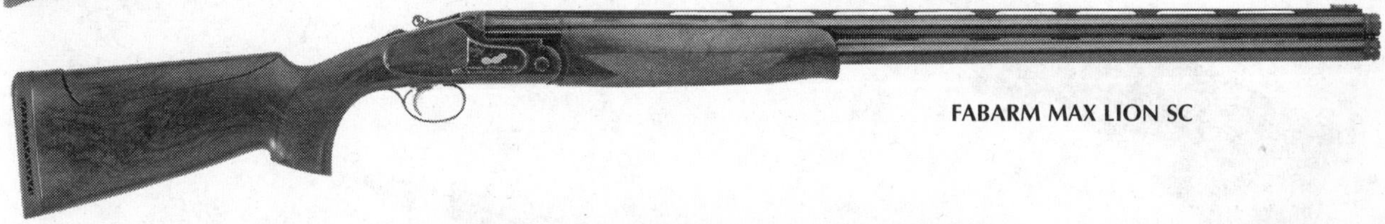

**FABARM MAX LION SC**

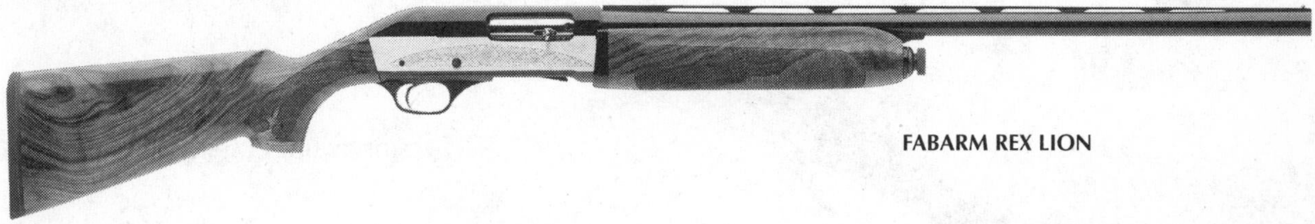

**FABARM REX LION**

## MODEL FP6
*Action:* pump
*Stock:* walnut
*Barrel:* 26 or 28 in.
*Chokes:* screw-in tubes
*Weight:* 7.0lbs.
*Bore/Gauge:* 12
*Magazine:* 4
*Features:* back-bored barrel
FP6 . . . . . . . . . . . . . . . . . . . . $549
camo . . . . . . . . . . . . . . . . . . . $469

## GOLDEN LION MARK II
*Action:* autoloader
*Stock:* walnut or synthetic
*Barrel:* 24, 26 or 28 in.
*Chokes:* screw-in tubes
*Weight:* 7.0lbs.
*Bore/Gauge:* 12
*Magazine:* 4

*Features:* gas-operated actions, shim-adjustable buttstock
Golden Lion Mark II . . . . . . . . $939
Sporting Clays . . . . . . . . . . . $1249

## PARADOX LION
*Action:* over/under
*Stock:* walnut
*Barrel:* 24 in.
*Chokes:* screw-in tubes
*Weight:* 7.6lbs.
*Bore/Gauge:* 12, 20
*Magazine:* none
*Features:* boxlock; choke tube on top barrel and rifled below; case-colored receiver; 6.6 lbs for 20 gauge; also, new Max Lion Sporting Clays with adjustable stock and 32 in. tube-choked barrels (7.9 lbs.)
Paradox Lion . . . . . . . . . . . . . $1129
Max Lion SC . . . . . . . . . . . . . $1799

## REX LION AND GOLD LION
*Action:* autoloader
*Stock:* walnut
*Barrel:* 26 or 28 in.
*Chokes:* screw-in tubes
*Weight:* 7.7lbs.
*Bore/Gauge:* 12
*Magazine:* 2
*Features:* gas operated, Turkish walnut stock, chrome-lined barrel
Rex Lion. . . . . . . . . . . . . . . . . $1049
Gold Lion. . . . . . . . . . . . . . . . $939

*Try shooting lighter loads in your turkey gun. Many times a high-velocity one-and-three-quarter ounce load will put more pellets where they count than heavier two-ounce loads. Find more tips like this in Turkey Hunter's Tool Kit, by Stoeger Publishing.*

# H&K Fabarm Shotguns

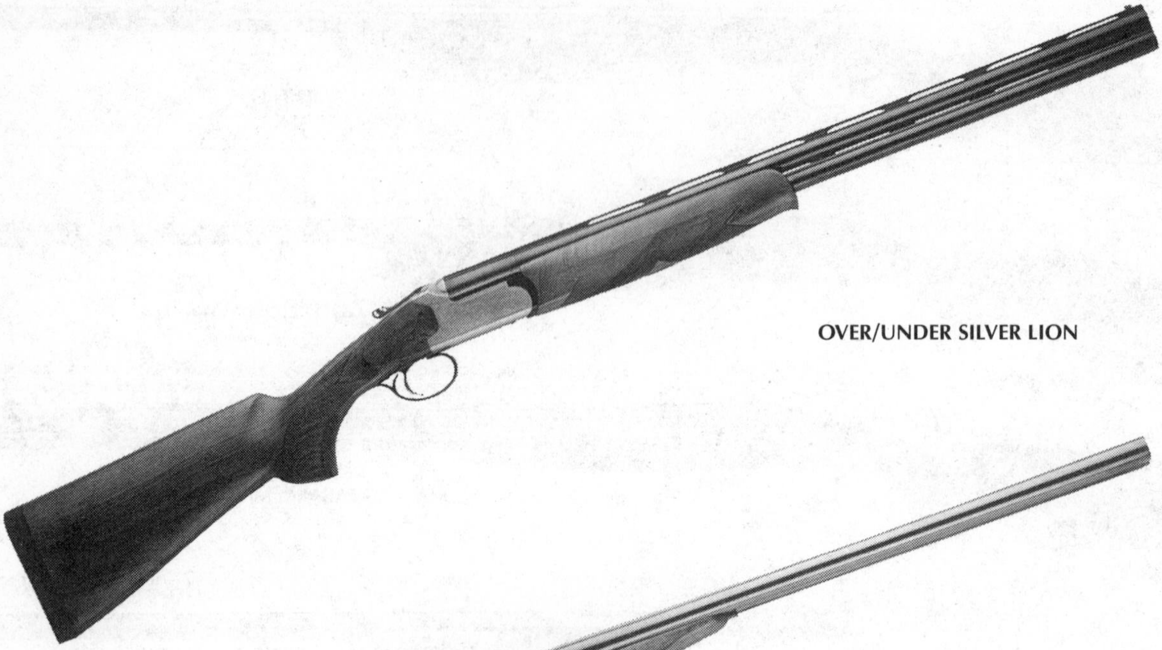

**OVER/UNDER SILVER LION**

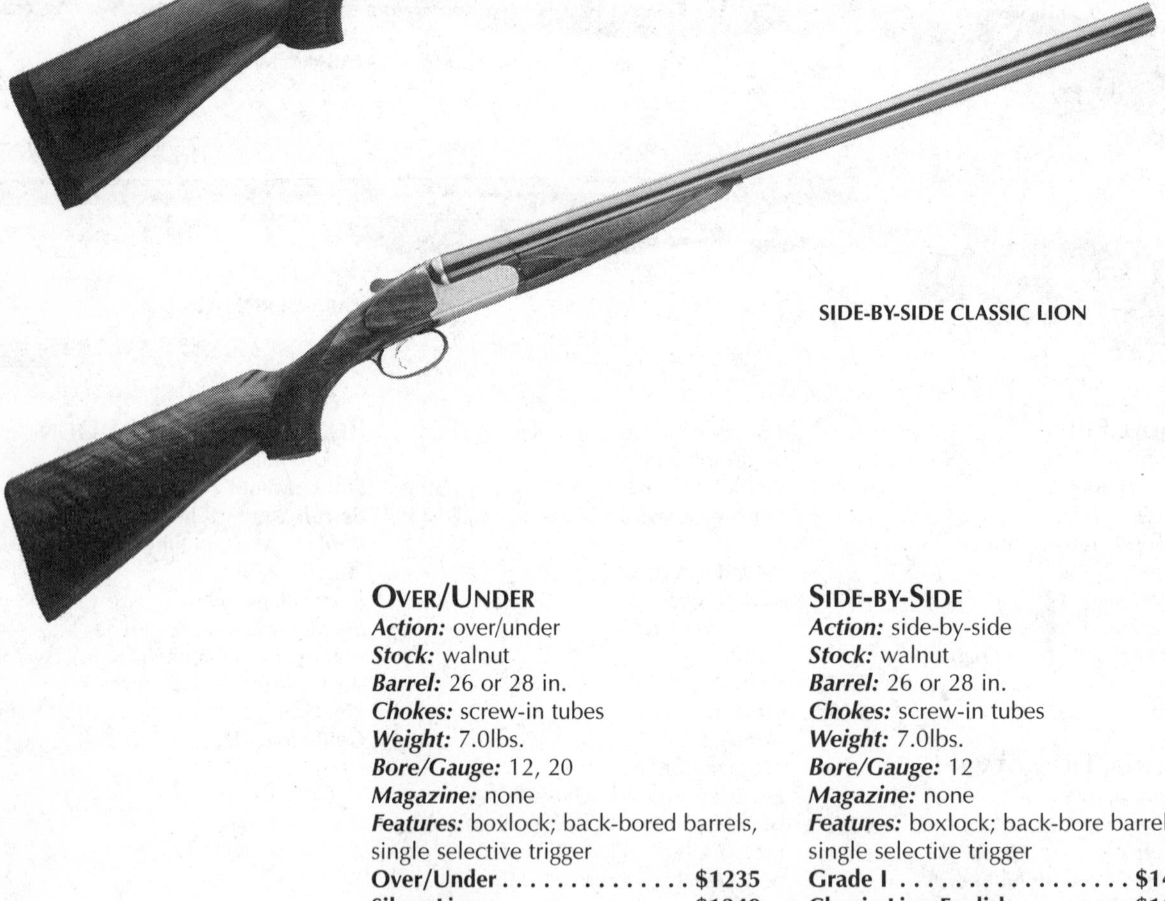

**SIDE-BY-SIDE CLASSIC LION**

## OVER/UNDER
*Action:* over/under
*Stock:* walnut
*Barrel:* 26 or 28 in.
*Chokes:* screw-in tubes
*Weight:* 7.0lbs.
*Bore/Gauge:* 12, 20
*Magazine:* none
*Features:* boxlock; back-bored barrels, single selective trigger
Over/Under . . . . . . . . . . . . . . $1235
Silver Lion . . . . . . . . . . . . . . . $1349
Sporting Clays . . . . . . . . . . . . $1925
UltraMag Camo . . . . . . . . . . . $1349

## SIDE-BY-SIDE
*Action:* side-by-side
*Stock:* walnut
*Barrel:* 26 or 28 in.
*Chokes:* screw-in tubes
*Weight:* 7.0lbs.
*Bore/Gauge:* 12
*Magazine:* none
*Features:* boxlock; back-bore barrels, single selective trigger
Grade I . . . . . . . . . . . . . . . . $1499
Classic Lion English . . . . . . . . $1649
Classic Lion Grade II . . . . . . . $2325

*Recoil – or anticipation of it – can cause flinching and missing. There are several ways to cut the kick in Turkey Hunter's Tool Kit and Shotgunning for Deer both by Stoeger Publishing.*

# Ithaca Shotguns

MODEL 37

MODEL 37 ENGLISH VERSION

STORM DEERSLAYER II

STORM WATERFOWLER

DEERSLAYER III

MODEL 37 DEERSLAYER II 12 GA.

## MODEL 37

*Action:* pump
*Stock:* walnut or synthetic
*Barrel:* 20, 22, 24, 26 or 28 in.
*Chokes:* screw-in tubes
*Weight:* 7.0lbs.
*Bore/Gauge:* 12, 16, 20
*Magazine:* 4
*Features:* bottom ejection
**Model 37** . . . . . . . . . . . . . . . . . **$618**
**Ultralight 20 ga.** . . . . . . . . . . . . **$649**
**English straight-grip** . . . . . . . . . **$803**
**Trap or Sporting Clays** . . . . . . . . . . .
**with Briley tubes** . . . . . . . . . **$1495**

## MODEL 37 DEERSLAYER II

*Action:* pump
*Stock:* walnut
*Barrel:* 20 or 25 in. rifled or
smoothbore
*Chokes:*
*Weight:* 7.0lbs.
*Bore/Gauge:* 12, 16, 20
*Magazine:* 4
*Features:* open sights; receiver fitted
with Weaver-style scope base; also
available: Deerslayer III with 26-in.
heavy rifled barrel and Turkeyslayer
(12 or 20) with 22 in. barrel,
extra-full tube
**Deerslayer II** . . . . . . . . . . . . . . **$633**
**Deerslayer III** . . . . . . . . . . . . . . **$900**

## STORM SERIES

*Action:* pump
*Stock:* solid synthetic
*Barrel:* 24 or 28 in.
*Chokes:* screw-in tubes
*Weight:* 5.5lbs.
*Bore/Gauge:* 12, 20
*Magazine:* 4
*Features:* parkerized steel finish; port-
ed 24 in. Turkey barrel with Tru-Glo
sights, rifled 24 in. Deerslayer II barrel
with Tru-Glo sights, or 28 in.
Waterfowler barrel; camo available
**Deerslayer** . . . . . . . . . . . . . . . . **$399**
**Waterfowl/Upland Storm** . . . . . **$499**
**Turkeyslayer Storm** . . . . . . . . . . **$459**

# Kimber Shotguns

AUGUSTA FIELD

## AUGUSTA FIELD
**Action:** over/under
**Stock:** walnut
**Barrel:** 26, 27.5 in.
**Chokes:** screw-in tubes

**Weight:** 7.1lbs.
**Bore/Gauge:** 12
**Magazine:** none
**Features:** boxlock; backbored barrel with long forcing cones; adjustable

single trigger, automatic ejectors, Hi-Viz sights (Sporting, Field, Trap and Skeet models available)
**Augusta** . . . . . . . . . . . . . . . . . $4500

# Krieghoff Shotguns

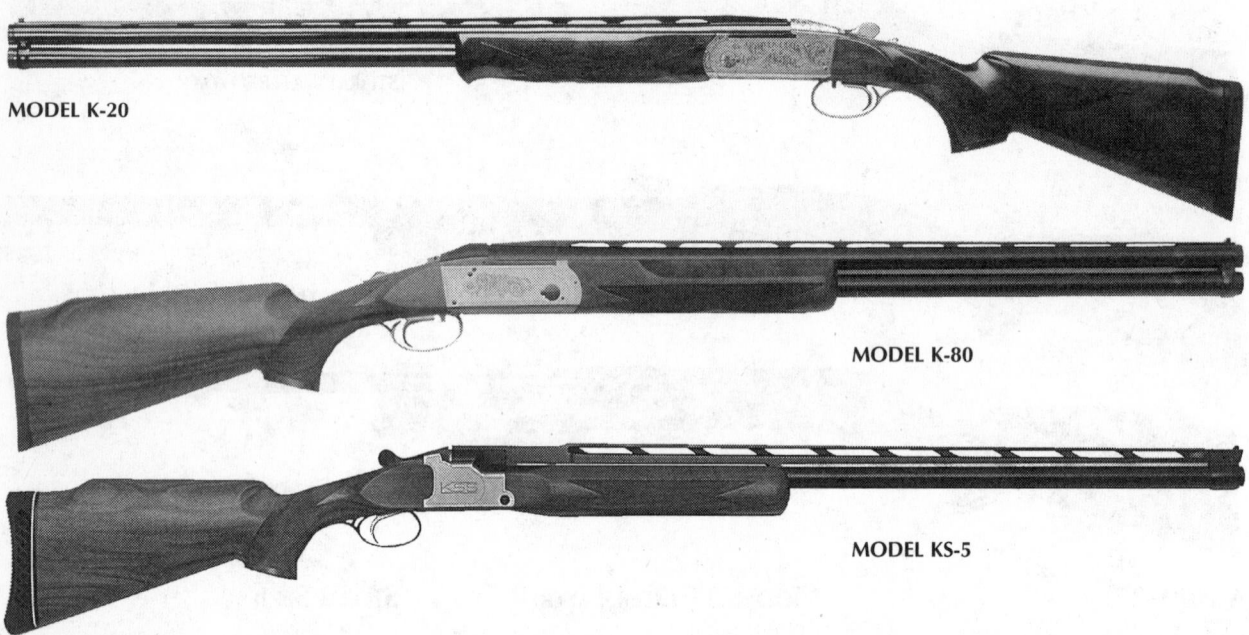

MODEL K-20

MODEL K-80

MODEL KS-5

## MODEL K-20
**Action:** over/under
**Stock:** walnut
**Barrel:** 28 or 30 in.
**Chokes:** screw-in tubes
**Weight:** 7.2lbs.
**Bore/Gauge:** 20, 28, .410
**Magazine:** none
**Features:** boxlock; single selective trigger, automatic ejectors, tapered rib, choice of receiver finish; fitted aluminum case
**K-20** . . . . . . . . . . . **price on request**

## MODEL K-80
**Action:** over/under
**Stock:** walnut
**Barrel:** 28 or 30 in.
**Chokes:** screw-in tubes
**Weight:** 8.0lbs.
**Bore/Gauge:** 12
**Magazine:** none
**Features:** boxlock; single selective trigger, automatic ejectors, tapered rib, choice of receiver finish; (Sporting Clays, Live Bird, Trap and Skeet models available)
**K-80** . . . . . . . . . . . **price on request**

## MODEL KS-5
**Action:** hinged single-shot
**Stock:** walnut
**Barrel:** 30 in. or length to order
**Chokes:** screw-in tubes
**Weight:** 8.0lbs.
**Bore/Gauge:** 12
**Magazine:** none
**Features:** boxlock; adjustable trigger (release trigger available), step rib, case-colored receiver, optional fronthangers to adjust point of impact, optional adjustable comb
**KS-5** . . . . . . . . . . . **price on request**

SHOTGUNS

# Legacy Sports Shotguns

ESCORT FIELD, CAMO

COMBO, AIM-GUARD

## ESCORT PUMP-ACTION SHOTGUN

*Action:* pump
*Stock:* Black or chrome polymer
*Barrel:* 28 in. (Field Hunter 24 in.)
*Sights:* Hi Viz
*Chokes:* IC, M, F
*Weight:* 6.4 lbs.
*Bore/Gauge:* 12
*Magazine:* 5-shot with cut-off button
*Features:* Alloy receiver with 3/8" milled dovetail for sight mounting. Black chrome or camp finish; black chrome bolt. Trigger guard safety. 5-shot magazine with cut-off button. Two stock adjustment shims. Three choke tubes; IC, M, F (except AimGuard). 24" Bbl comes with extra turkey choke tube and HI Viz TriViz sight combo.

**Field Hunter, black . . . . . . . . . $224**
**Aim Guard, 20" bbl. . . . . . . . . $199**
**Field Hunter Camo . . . . . . . . $271**
**Camo, 24", TriViz sights, turkey choke**
**. . . . . . . . . . . . . . . . . . . . . $444**

## ESCORT SEMI-AUTOMATIC SHOTGUN

*Action:* autoloader
*Stock:* polymer or walnut
*Barrel:* 28 in.
*Sights:*
*Weight:* 7 lbs.
*Bore/Gauge:* 12
*Magazine:*
*Features:* gas operated and chambered for 3" or 23/4-inch shells. Barrels are nickel-chromium-molybdenum steel with additional chrome plating internally and a ventilated anti-glare checkered rib. Bolts are chrome plated. Extras include three chokes, a migratory plug, and two spacers to adjust the slope of the stock. Camo waterfowl and turkey combo available with Hi Viz sights, 28" barrel, hard case.

**Escort AS polymer: . . . . . . . . . $363**
**Escort PS walnut: . . . . . . . . . . $386**
**Waterfowl & turkey: . . . . . . . . $519**
**Combo AimGuard (20" bbl, black stock, cyl. bore) . . . . . . . . . . . $363**

*Many savvy hunters add a pistol-grip stock to their favorite shotgun. Benelli's Steady Grip turkey guns are the first production models to offer the new grip option. Check out the benefits of adding a pistol grip stock to your shotgun in Turkey Hunter's Tool Kit, by Stoeger Publishing.*

# Marlin Shotguns

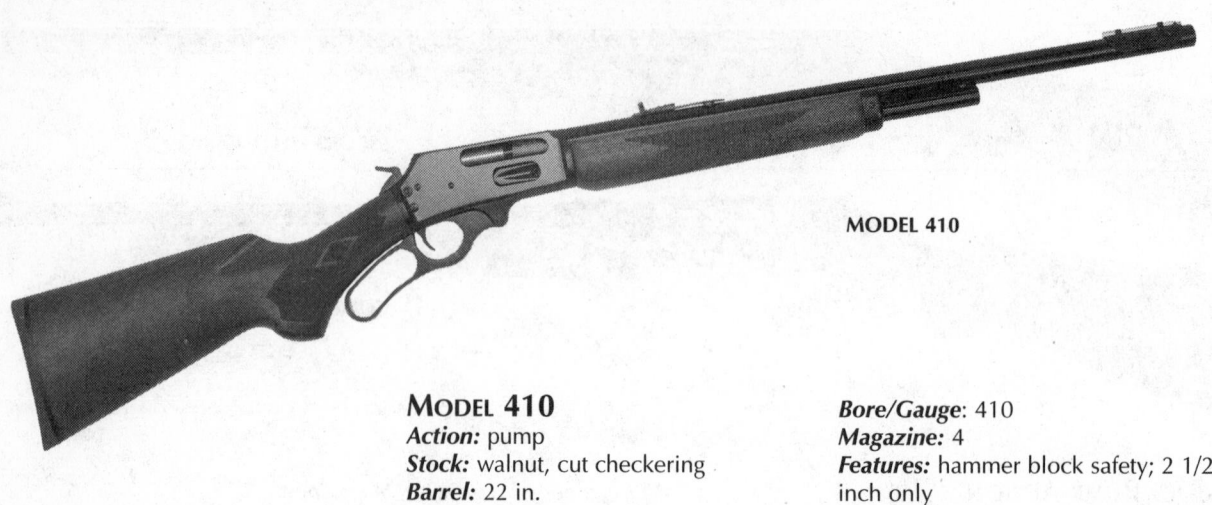

**MODEL 410**

## MODEL 410
**Action:** pump
**Stock:** walnut, cut checkering
**Barrel:** 22 in.
**Chokes:** none
**Weight:** 7.3lbs.

**Bore/Gauge:** 410
**Magazine:** 4
**Features:** hammer block safety; 2 1/2-inch only
**Model 410** . . . . . . . . . . . . . . . **$614**

# Marocchi Shotguns

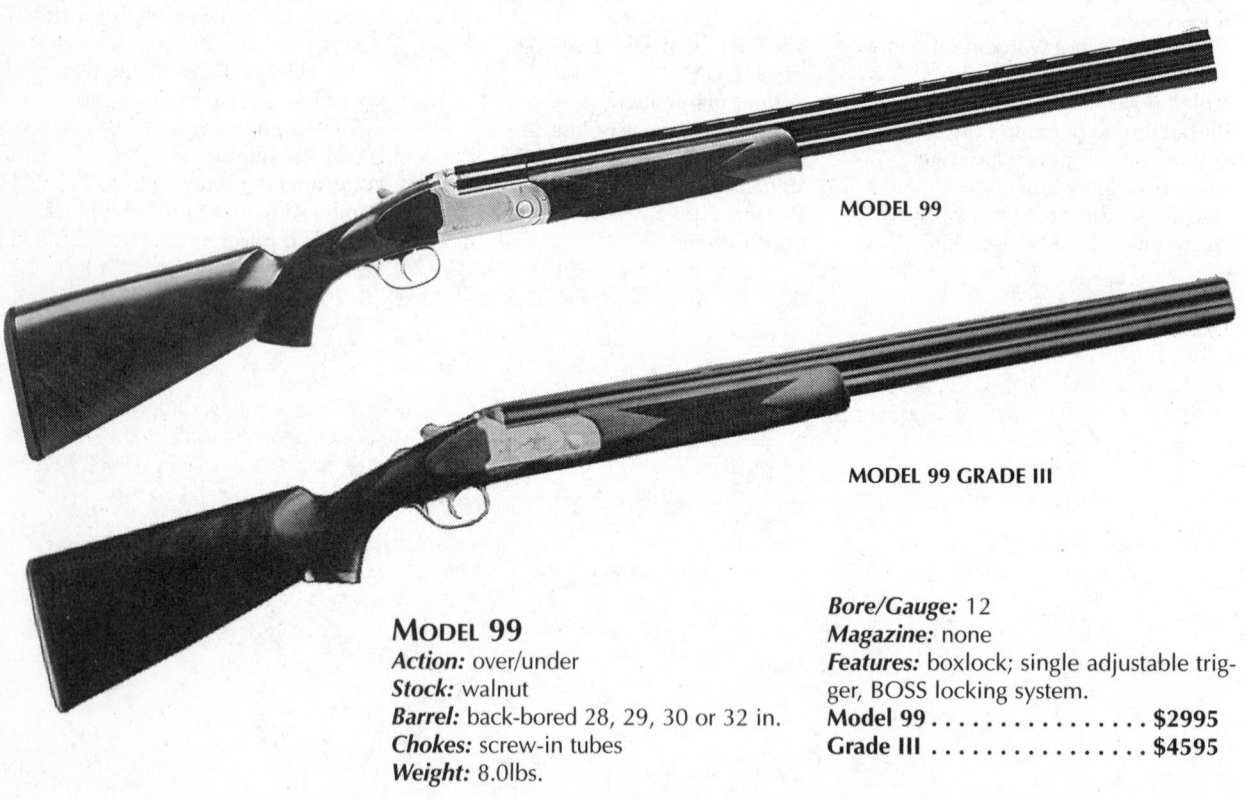

**MODEL 99**

**MODEL 99 GRADE III**

## MODEL 99
**Action:** over/under
**Stock:** walnut
**Barrel:** back-bored 28, 29, 30 or 32 in.
**Chokes:** screw-in tubes
**Weight:** 8.0lbs.

**Bore/Gauge:** 12
**Magazine:** none
**Features:** boxlock; single adjustable trigger, BOSS locking system.
**Model 99** . . . . . . . . . . . . . . . **$2995**
**Grade III** . . . . . . . . . . . . . . . **$4595**

*Most standard shotgun stocks are too low to get your eye properly aligned with a scope. Get lined up by adding a raised cheek piece. Find it in Turkey Hunter's Tool Kit, by Stoeger Publishing.*

SHOTGUNS

# Merkel Shotguns

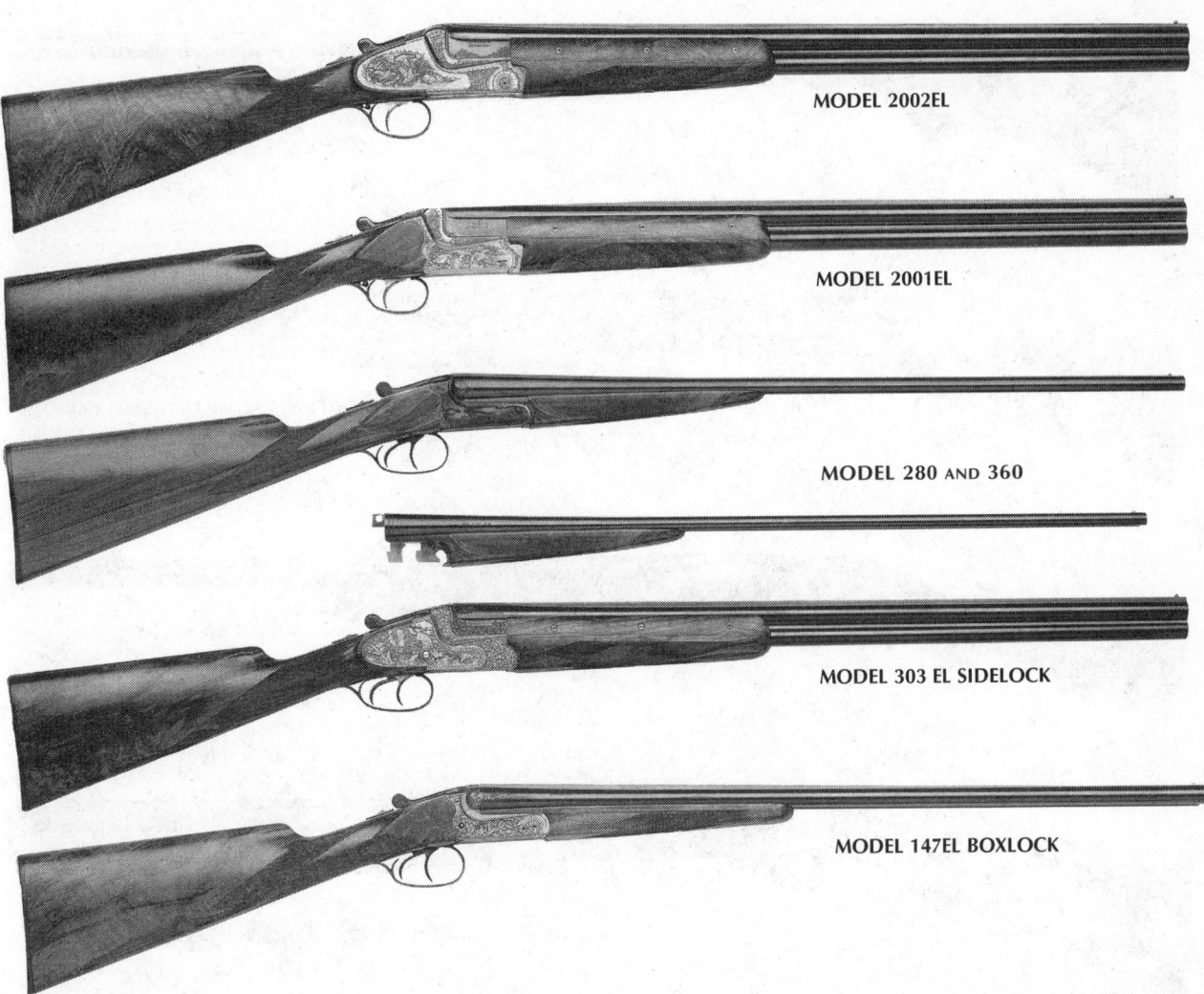

MODEL 2002EL

MODEL 2001EL

MODEL 280 AND 360

MODEL 303 EL SIDELOCK

MODEL 147EL BOXLOCK

## MODEL 2000 EL

*Action:* over/under
*Stock:* walnut, straight or pistol grip
*Barrel:* 27 or 28 in.
*Chokes:* improved cylinder, modified, full
*Weight:* 7.3lbs.
*Bore/Gauge:* 12, 20, 28
*Magazine:* none
*Features:* boxlock; single selective or double trigger; three-piece forend, automatic ejectors

2000 EL . . . . . . . . . . . . . . . . . $6495
2001 EL (deluxe) . . . . . . . . . . $8295
2016 EL (16 ga.) . . . . . . . . . . . $6496
2002 EL (with sideplates) . . . . P.O.R.

## MODEL 280 AND 360

*Action:* side-by-side
*Stock:* walnut, straight grip
*Barrel:* 28 in.

*Chokes:* imp.cyl/mod (28 ga.), mod/full (.410)
*Weight:* 6.0lbs.
*Bore/Gauge:* 28, .410
*Magazine:* none
*Features:* boxlock; double triggers, automatic ejectors; fitted luggage case (Model 280: 28 gauge and Model 360: .410)

Model 280 or Model 360 . . . . $4195
two-barrel sets . . . . . . . . . . . $6495
S models with sidelocks . . . . . $9395

## MODEL 303 EL

*Action:* over/under
*Stock:* walnut, straight or pistol grip
*Barrel:* 27 or 28 in.
*Chokes:* improved cylinder, modified, full
*Weight:* 7.3lbs.
*Bore/Gauge:* 16, 20, 28

*Magazine:* none
*Features:* sidelock; automatic ejectors, special-order features

303 EL . . . . . . . . . . . . . . . . $22,995

## MODEL 147E

*Action:* side-by-side
*Stock:* walnut, straight or pistol grip
*Barrel:* 27 or 28 in.
*Chokes:* imp.cyl/mod or mod/full
*Weight:* 7.2lbs.
*Bore/Gauge:* 12, 20
*Magazine:* none
*Features:* boxlock; single selective or double triggers; automatic ejectors; fitted luggage case

47E . . . . . . . . . . . . . . . . . . . $3795
147E (deluxe) . . . . . . . . . . . . . $4495
147EL (super deluxe) . . . . . . . $5695

# Mossberg Shotguns

**MODEL 500 SPORTING**

**MODEL 835 PUMP ULTI-MAG CAMO**

**MODEL 835 ULTI-MAG**

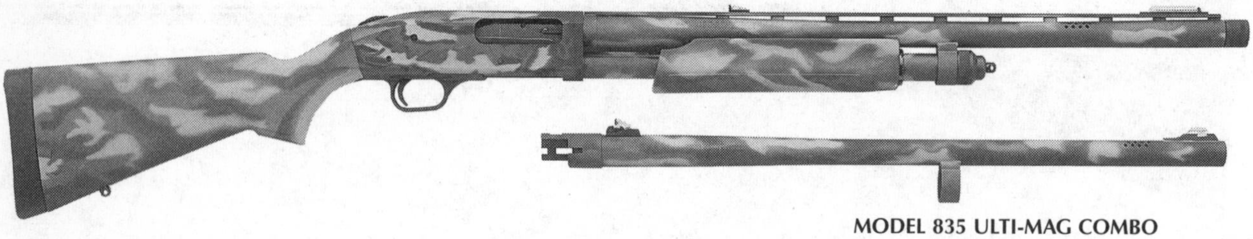

**MODEL 835 ULTI-MAG COMBO**

### MODEL 500
*Action:* pump
*Stock:* wood or synthetic
*Barrel:* 18, 22, 24, 26 or 28 in.
*Chokes:* screw-in tubes
*Weight:* 7.5lbs.
*Bore/Gauge:* 12, 20, .410
*Magazine:* 5
*Features:* barrels mostly vent rib, some ported; top tang safety; camouflage stock finish options; 10-year warranty
Model 500 . . . . . . . . . . . . . . . $316
Slugster Ported 24" bbl: . . . . . . $361
two-barrel combo set . . . . . . . . $376

### MODEL 500 MARINER
*Action:* pump
*Stock:* synthetic
*Barrel:* 18 or 20 in.
*Chokes:* cylinder
*Weight:* 7.0lbs.
*Bore/Gauge:* 12
*Magazine:* 5
*Features:* top tang safety; 12-gauge has "Marinecote" metal and 10-year warranty; 20 gauge and .410 variations available in blued finish
Mariner . . . . . . . . . . . . . . . . . . $497
20 gauge and .410 . . . . . . . . . . $513

### MODEL 835 ULTI-MAG
*Action:* pump
*Stock:* synthetic or camo
*Barrel:* 24 or 28 in.
*Chokes:* full
*Weight:* 7.0lbs.
*Bore/Gauge:* 12
*Magazine:* 4
*Features:* barrel ported, back-bored with vent rib; 3.5-inch chamber; top tang safety; rifled slug barrel and combination sets available; 10-year warranty
Model 835 . . . . . . . . . . . . . . . . $394
Model 835, camo . . . . . . . . . . . $438
Combo: . . . . . . . . . . . . . . . . . . $556

*Good shooting starts with your feet. If your torso is twisted uncomfortably, it will unwind as you release muscle tension at the shot. Practice pointing your feet quickly where the shot will come.*

SHOTGUNS

# New England Arms/FAIR Shotguns

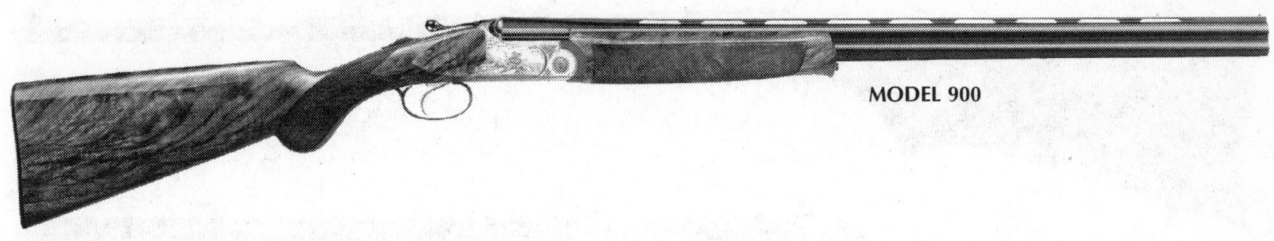

**MODEL 900**

## MODEL 900
**Action:** over/under
**Stock:** walnut, straight or pistol grip
**Barrel:** all standard lengths
**Chokes:** screw-in tubes
**Weight:** 7.5lbs.

**Bore/Gauge:** 12, 16, 20, 28, .410
**Magazine:** none
**Features:** boxlock; single selective trigger, automatic safety, automatic ejector; .410 has fixed choke
Model 900 . . . . . . . . . . . . . . $3995

# New England Firearms Shotguns

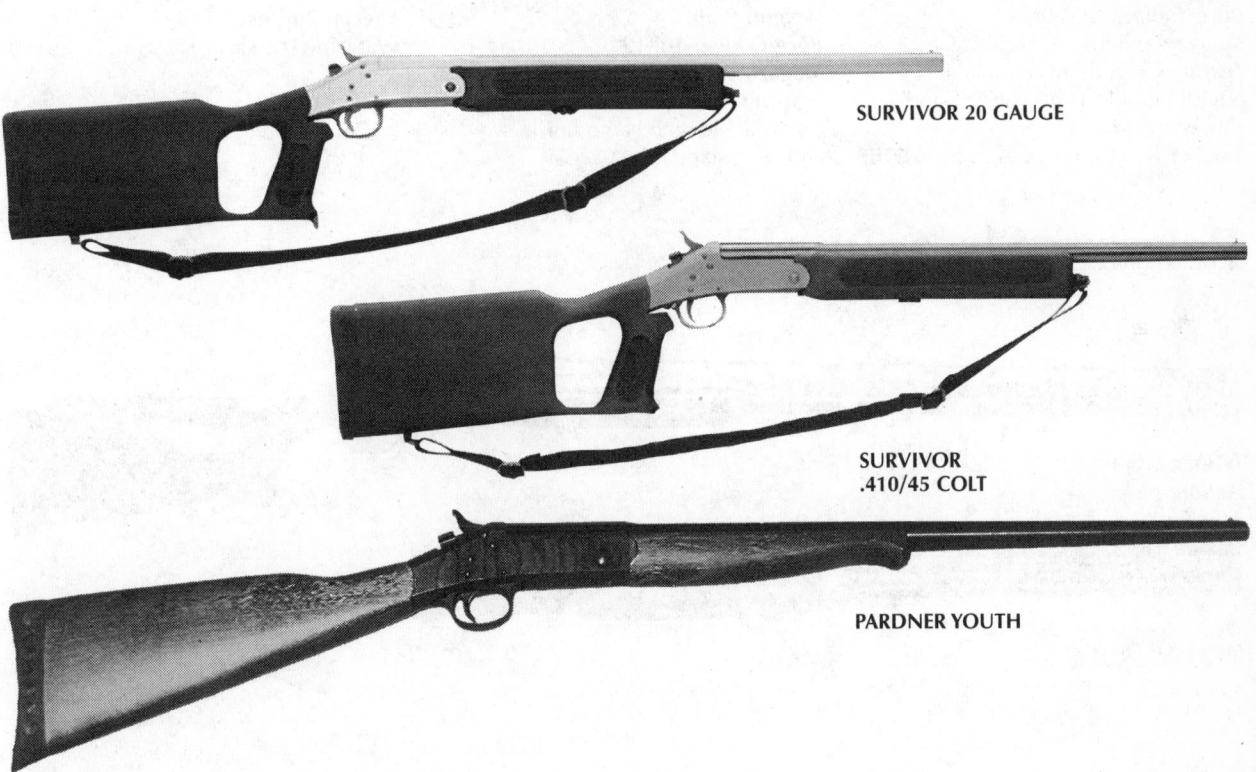

**SURVIVOR 20 GAUGE**

**SURVIVOR .410/45 COLT**

**PARDNER YOUTH**

## SURVIVOR AND PARDNER
**Action:** hinged single-shot
**Stock:** synthetic
**Barrel:** 22, 26, 28 or 32 in.
**Chokes:** modified, full
**Weight:** 6.0lbs.
**Bore/Gauge:** 12, 16, 20, 28, .410

**Magazine:** none
**Features:** Youth and camo-finish Turkey models available; Survivor has hollow pistol-grip buttstock for storage, chambers .41 and .45 Colt
Survivor . . . . . . . . . . . . . . . . . $161
Pardner . . . . . . . . . . . . . . . . . $133

Pardner Turkey
(3½", 10 and 12ga.) . . . . . . $189-278
Pardner Youth. . . . . . . . . . . . . $141
Pardner Turkey Camo Youth . . . $189

SHOTGUNS

# New England Firearms Shotguns

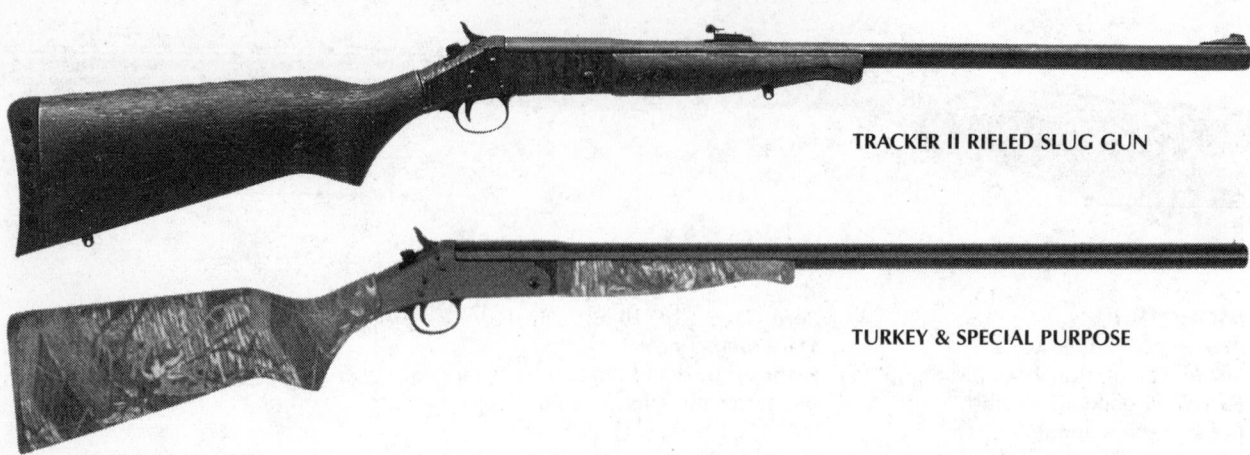

**TRACKER II RIFLED SLUG GUN**

**TURKEY & SPECIAL PURPOSE**

### TRACKER II RIFLED SLUG GUN
*Action:* hinged single-shot
*Stock:* hardwood
*Barrel:* rifled 24 in.
*Chokes:* none
*Weight:* 6.0lbs.
*Bore/Gauge:* 12, 20
*Magazine:* none
*Features:* camo finish available, adjustable rifle sights, swivels and sling standard
**Tracker II** . . . . . . . . . . . . . . . **$187**

### TURKEY & SPECIAL PURPOSE
*Action:* hinged single-shot
*Stock:* hardwood
*Barrel:* 24 in. (Turkey) or 28 in. (Waterfowl)
*Chokes:* full, screw-in tubes
*Weight:* 9.5lbs.
*Bore/Gauge:* 10, 12
*Magazine:* none
*Features:* Turkey and Waterfowl models available with camo finish, swivels and sling standard

**Turkey Gun**
**(camo, full choke)** . . . . . . **$189 - 278**
**Turkey Gun (black, tubes) $180 - 251**
**Special Purpose**
**Waterfowl 10 ga.** . . . . . . . . . . . **$272**
**with 28 in. barrel, walnut** . . . . . **$215**
**Special Purpose**
**Waterfowl12 ga.** . . . . . . . . . . . **$168**

# Perazzi Shotguns

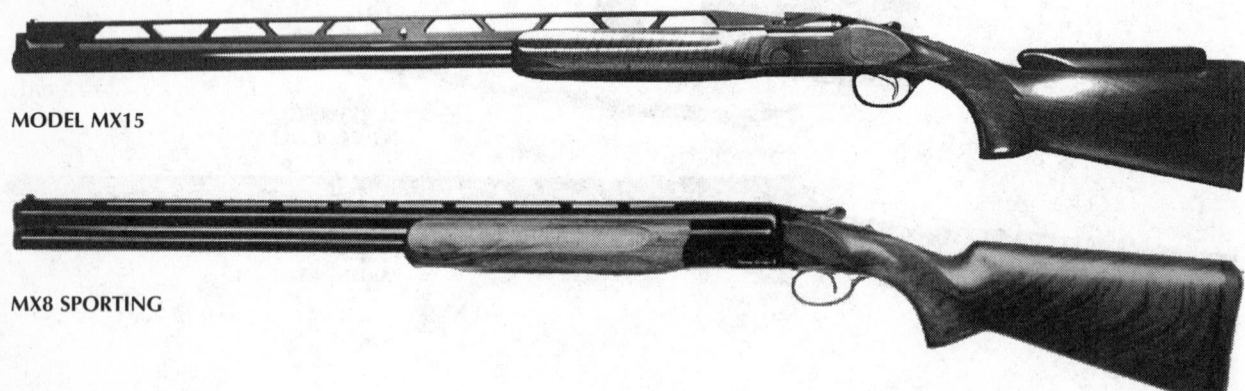

**MODEL MX15**

**MX8 SPORTING**

### MODEL MX15
*Action:* hinged single-shot
*Stock:* walnut, adjustable comb
*Barrel:* 32 or 34 in.
*Chokes:* full
*Weight:* 8.4lbs.
*Bore/Gauge:* 12
*Magazine:* none

*Features:* high trap rib
**MX15** . . . . . . . . . . . . . . . . . **$8140**

### MODEL MX8
*Action:* over/under
*Stock:* walnut
*Barrel:* 26 or 28 in.
*Chokes:* screw-in tubes

*Weight:* 7.3lbs.
*Bore/Gauge:* 12, 20, 28, .410
*Magazine:* none
*Features:* hinged-breech action; double triggers or single selective or non-selective trigger; Sporting, Skeet and Trap models available
**MX8** . . . . . . . . . . . . . . . . . **$9560**

# Purdey Shotguns

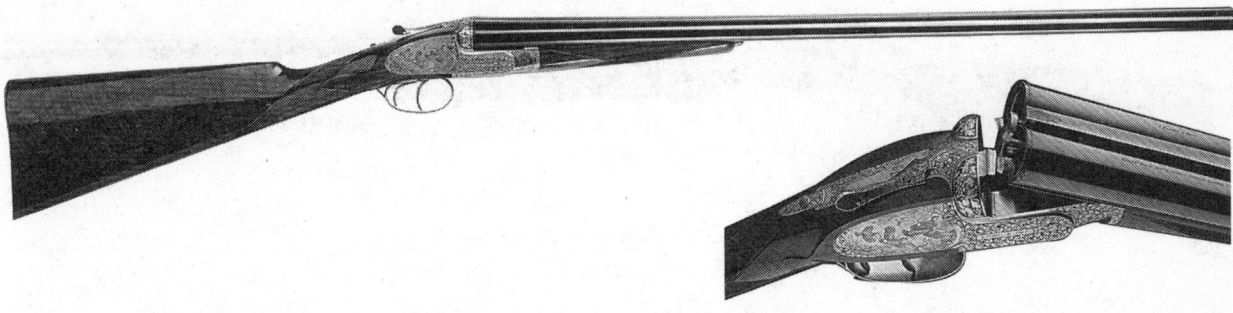

## SIDE-BY-SIDE GAME GUN
**Purdey easy opening action:**
All side-by-side guns are built on the easy opening system invented by Frederick Beesley. This system is incorporated in guns built from 1880 onwards.

Purdey offers dedicated action sizes for each of the bores 10, 12, 20, 28 & .410 cores. An extra pair of barrels can be ordered, even if you want a barrel set one gauge smaller. For example, you can have fitted 28 gauge barrels on a 20 gauge, and .410 on a 28 gauge. These guns are made with a single forend for both bores.

All Purdey barrels, both SxS and O/U, are of chopper lump construction. Each individual tube is hand filled and then "struck up" using striking files. This gives the tube the correct Purdey profile.

Once polished, the individual tubes are joined at the breech using silver solder. The loop iron is similarly fixed. Once together, the rough chokes can be cut and the internal bores finished using a traditional lead lapping technique.

Ribs are hand-filed to suit the barrel contour exactly, and then soft-soldered in place, using pine resin as the fluxing agent. Pine resin provides extra water resistance to the surfaces enclosed by the ribs.

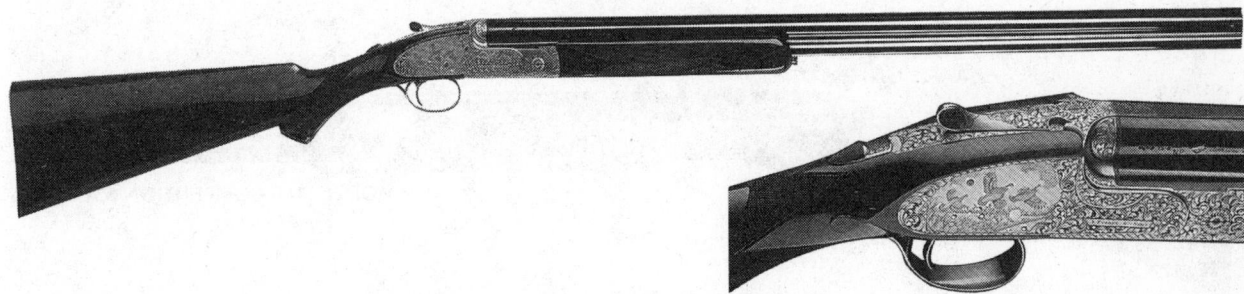

## OVER/UNDER GUN
The Over-Under gun is available in 12, 16, 20, 28 and .410, with each bore made on a dedicated action size. As with Side-by-Side, the shape of the action has an effect on the weight of the gun.

Conventionally, the Purdey over-under will shoot the lower barrel first, but can be made to shoot the top barrel first if required. All prices on request.

The standard for regulating and patterning the shooting of a gun is the percentage of the shot charge, which is evenly concentrated in a circle of 30" diameter at a range of 40 yards. (Purdey choke restrictions 1/1000 inch.)

### THE CHOKE SECTION

### THE PERCENTAGES OF CHOKE
| | |
|---|---|
| Cylinder | 45% |
| Improved Cylinder | 50% |
| 1/4 Choke | 55% |
| 1/2 Choke | 60% |
| 3/4 or Modified Choke | 65% |
| Choke | 70% |
| Full Choke | 75% |
| Skeet (2) | 45% |
| Skeet (1) | 40% |

### 12 Bore 2.75" 1.25 oz No.6
| | |
|---|---|
| FULL CHOKE | .038 - .040 |
| CHOKE | .035 |
| .75 (MOD) | .022 |
| .5 CHOKE | .016-.017 |
| .25 CHOKE | .010-.01 |
| IMP CYL | 7-8 |
| CYL | 3 |
| SKEET | Open Bore |

### 12 Bore 2.5" 1 oz. No. 6
| | |
|---|---|
| FULL CHOKE | .038 - .040 |
| CHOKE | .030 |
| .75 (MOD) | .018-.019 |
| .5 CHOKE | .012-.013 |
| .25 CHOKE | 6-7 |
| IMP CYL | 3 |
| CYL | 2 |

### 20 Bore 2.75"
| | |
|---|---|
| FULL CHOKE | .038 - .040 |
| CHOKE | .030 |
| .75 (MOD) | .018-.019 |
| .5 CHOKE | .012-.013 |
| .25 CHOKE | 7-8 |
| IMP CYL | 6 |
| CYL | 3 |
| SKEET | Open Bore |

### 28 Bore 2.75"
| | |
|---|---|
| FULL CHOKE | .026 |
| CHOKE | .020 |
| .75 (MOD) | .018 |
| .5 CHOKE | .015 |
| .25 CHOKE | .011 |
| IMP CYL | 7 |
| CYL | 3 |
| SKEET | Open |

SHOTGUNS

# Remington Shotguns

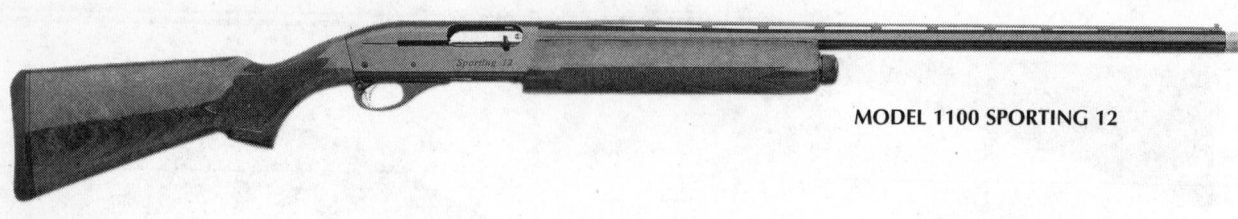

MODEL 1100 SPORTING 12

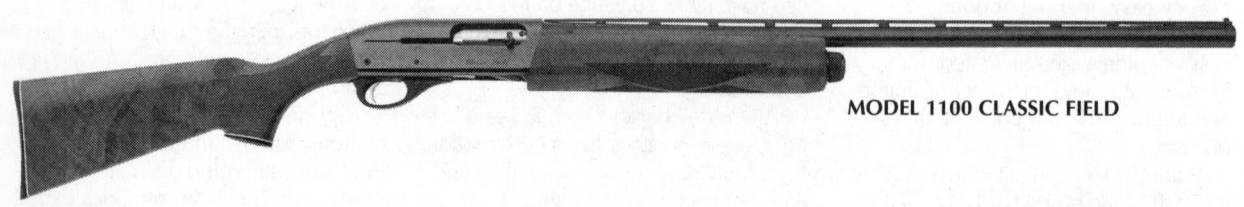

MODEL 1100 CLASSIC FIELD

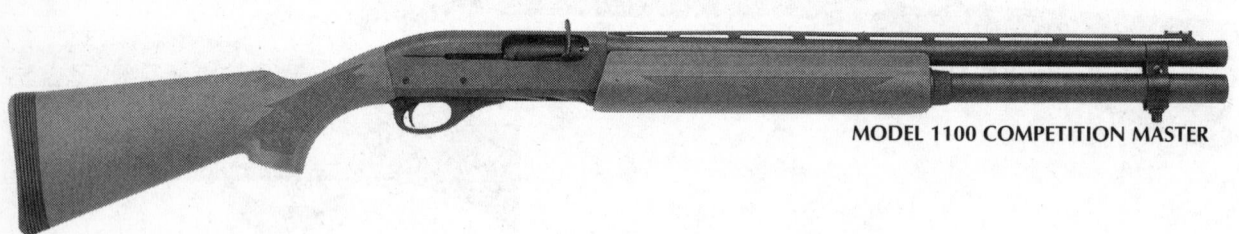

MODEL 1100 COMPETITION MASTER

### MODEL 1100 SYNTHETIC

*Action:* autoloader
*Stock:* synthetic or walnut Classic Field
*Barrel:* 21, 26 or 28 in.
*Chokes:* screw-in tubes
*Weight:* 7.0lbs.
*Bore/Gauge:* 12, 16, 20
*Magazine:* 4
*Features:* chambered for 2 $^3/_4$-inch shells; available in Deer, Youth and Youth Turkey variations with 21-inch barrels.

1100 Synthetic. . . . . . . . . . . . $549
Cantilever Deer Synthetic. . . . . $629
Youth Turkey, 20 ga. . . . . . . . . $612
Model 1100 Target Sporting. . $868-901
Model 1100 Tournament Skeet . $868
Model 1100 Classic Trap. . . . . . $901

### MODEL 1100 CLASSIC FIELD

*Action:* autoloader
*Stock:* walnut
*Barrel:* 26 or 28 in.
*Chokes:* screw-in tubes
*Weight:* 7.1lbs.
*Bore/Gauge:* 16 and 20 (26 in. only)
*Magazine:* 4
*Features:* gas-operated autoloading, vent rib
Classic Field. . . . . . . . . . . . . . $765

### MODEL 1100 COMPETITION MASTER

*Action:* autoloader
*Stock:* synthetic matte gray
*Barrel:* 22 in.
*Chokes:* screw-in tubes
*Weight:* 8.25 lbs.
*Bore/Gauge* 12 (2 3/4 in. only)
*Magazine*: 8 + 1
*Features:* vent rib, fiber optic sight; receiver mounted ammo carrier and release, designed for speed loading.
Model 1100
Competition Master . . . . . . . . $932

SHOTGUNS

# Remington Shotguns

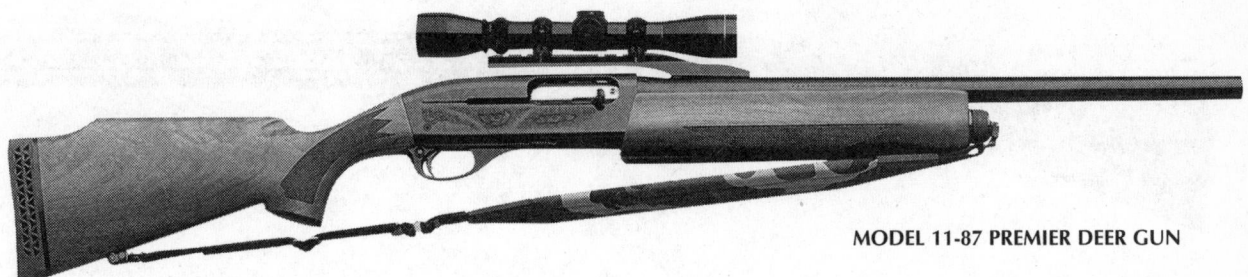

**MODEL 11-87 PREMIER DEER GUN**

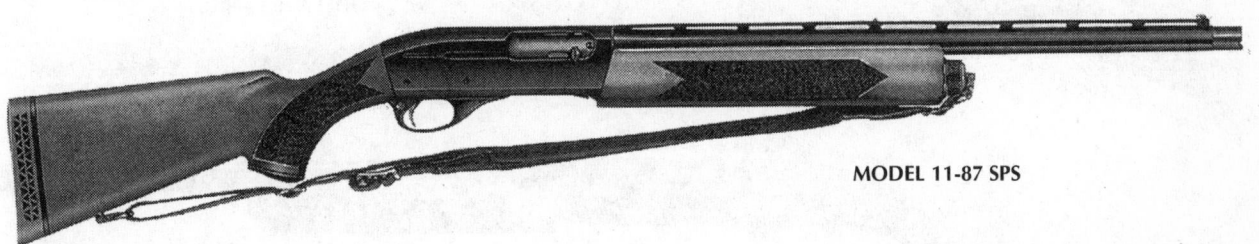

**MODEL 11-87 SPS**

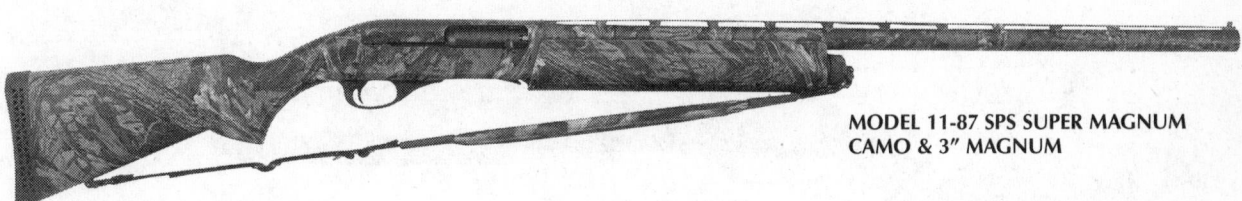

**MODEL 11-87 SPS SUPER MAGNUM
CAMO & 3" MAGNUM**

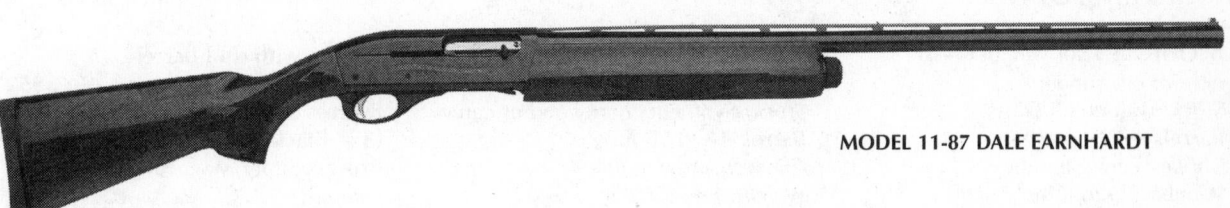

**MODEL 11-87 DALE EARNHARDT**

## MODEL 11-87 PREMIER
**Action:** autoloader
**Stock:** walnut
**Barrel:** 21, 23, 26, 28 or 30 in.
**Chokes:** screw-in tubes
**Weight:** 7.5lbs.
**Bore/Gauge:** 12 & 20

**Magazine:** 5
**Features:** gas-operated, handles 2 ³/₄ and 3-inch shells interchangeably; deer gun has cantilever scope mount, rifled bore; Upland Special has straight grip; SPS Super Magnum chambers 3.5-inch shells

| | |
|---|---|
| 11-87 Premier | $793 |
| Deer Gun. | $875 |
| Upland Special. | $793 |
| Premier Super Mag. | $865 |
| Left-Hand. | $860 |
| Model 11-87 SPS (Dale EarnhardtTribute) | $972 |

# Remington Shotguns

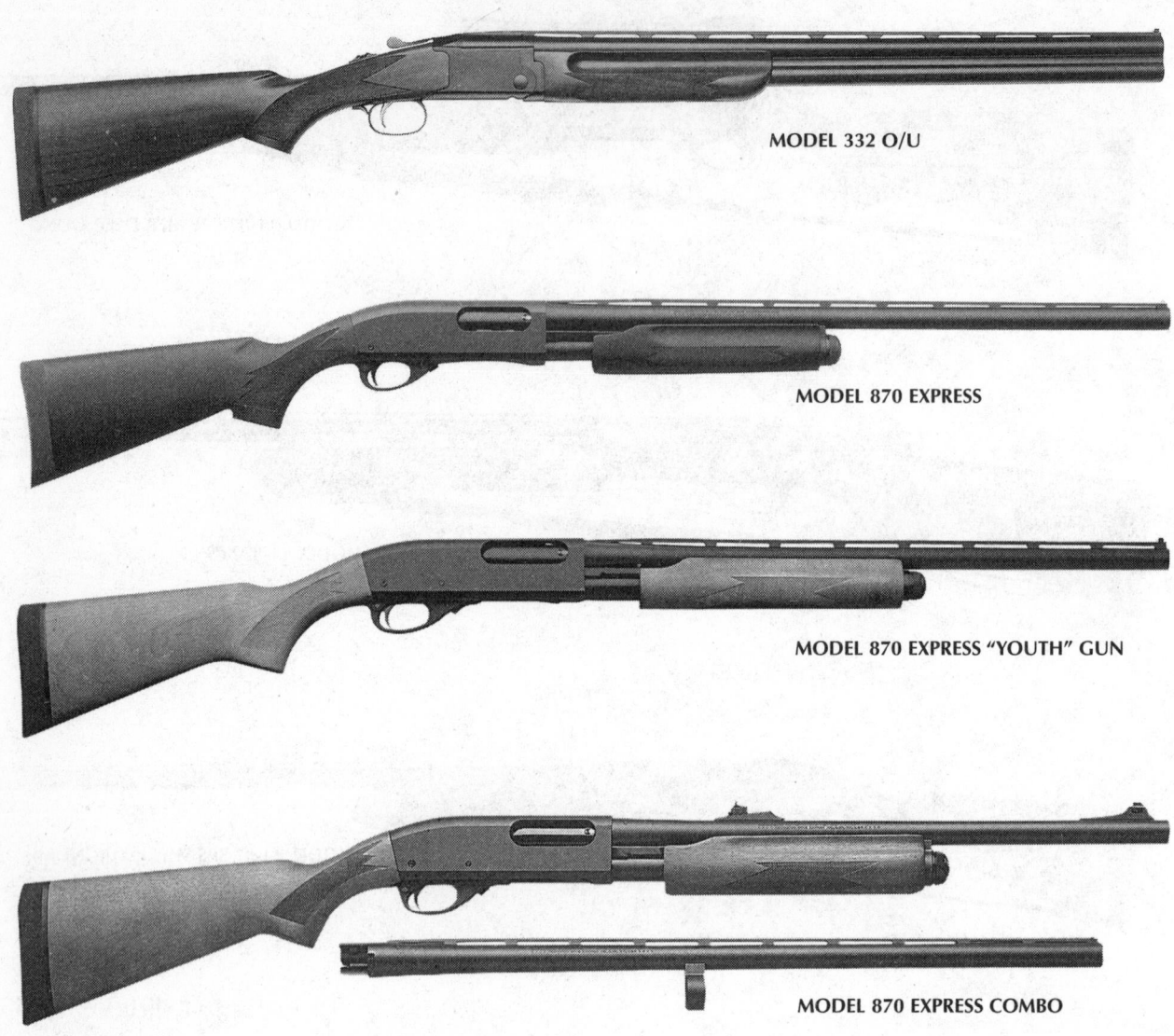

MODEL 332 O/U

MODEL 870 EXPRESS

MODEL 870 EXPRESS "YOUTH" GUN

MODEL 870 EXPRESS COMBO

## MODEL 332

*Action:* over/under
*Stock:* walnut, Hi-Gloss
*Barrel:* 26, 28 or 30 in.
*Chokes:* screw-in tubes
*Weight:* 7.5 to 8 lbs.
*Bore/Gauge:* 12
*Magazine:* none
*Features:* boxlock; ventilated rib;
Model 332 patterned after
classic Model 32
**Model 332** . . . . . . . . . . . . . . . **$1624**

## MODEL 870 EXPRESS

*Action:* pump
*Stock:* Synthetic, hardwood or camo
*Barrel:* 18 to 30 in.
*Chokes:* screw-in tubes
*Weight:* 6 to 7.5 lbs.
*Bore/Gauge:* 12, 16, 20, 28, .410
*Magazine:* 5
*Features:* Super Magnum chambered
for 3.5-inch shells; deer gun has rifled
barrel, open sights
**Express** . . . . . . . . . . . . . . . . . **$332**
**Express (28 ga. or .410)** . . . . . . **$359**
**Express Super Magnum** . . . . . . . **$376**
**Express Lightweight**
**Youth 20 ga.** . . . . . . . . . . . . . . . **$332**

Combo with shot barrel
and slug barrel . . . . . . . . . . . . . **$523**
**Express Super Mag. Turkey**
**(3½" Black synthetic )** . . . . . . . . **$389**
**Express Super Mag. Turkey,**
**camo** . . . . . . . . . . . . . . . . . . . . **$500**
**Express Super Mag. Combo**
**with deer barrel** . . . . . . . . . . . **$523**

SHOTGUNS

# Remington Shotguns

MODEL 870 MARINE MAGNUM

MODEL 870 SPS

SP-10 MAGNUM SHOTGUN

### MODEL 870 MARINE MAGNUM

*Action:* pump
*Stock:* synthetic
*Barrel:* 18 in.
*Chokes:* none, cylinder bore
*Weight:* 7.5lbs.
*Bore/Gauge:* 12
*Magazine:* 7
*Features:* nickel-plated exterior metal; R3 recoil pad

**Marine Magnum. . . . . . . . . . . $573**

### MODEL 870 SPS

*Action:* pump
*Stock:* camo or black synthetic
*Barrel:* 18 to 28 in..
*Chokes:* screw-in tubes
*Weight:* 6.25 to 8 lbs.
*Bore/Gauge:* 12
*Magazine:* 4 (3: 3.5-inch)
*Features:* slug, turkey and Marine Mag. models available; also 20 gauge rifled slug; R3 recoil pad

**Turkey. . . . . . . . . . . . . . . $591 - 595**
**Cantilever slug . . . . . . . . . . . . . $580**
**Super Magnum. . . . . . . . . . . . $591**

### MODEL SP-10

*Action:* autoloader
*Stock:* walnut or synthetic
*Barrel:* 26 or 30 in.
*Chokes:* screw-in tubes
*Weight:* 10.75 - 11.0lbs.
*Bore/Gauge:* 10
*Magazine:* 2
*Features:* the only gas-operated 10 gauge made; stainless piston and sleeve; R3 recoil pad.

**SP-10. . . . . . . . . . . . . . . . . . $1331**
**camo . . . . . . . . . . . . . . . . . . $1468**

SHOTGUNS

# Renato Gamba Shotguns

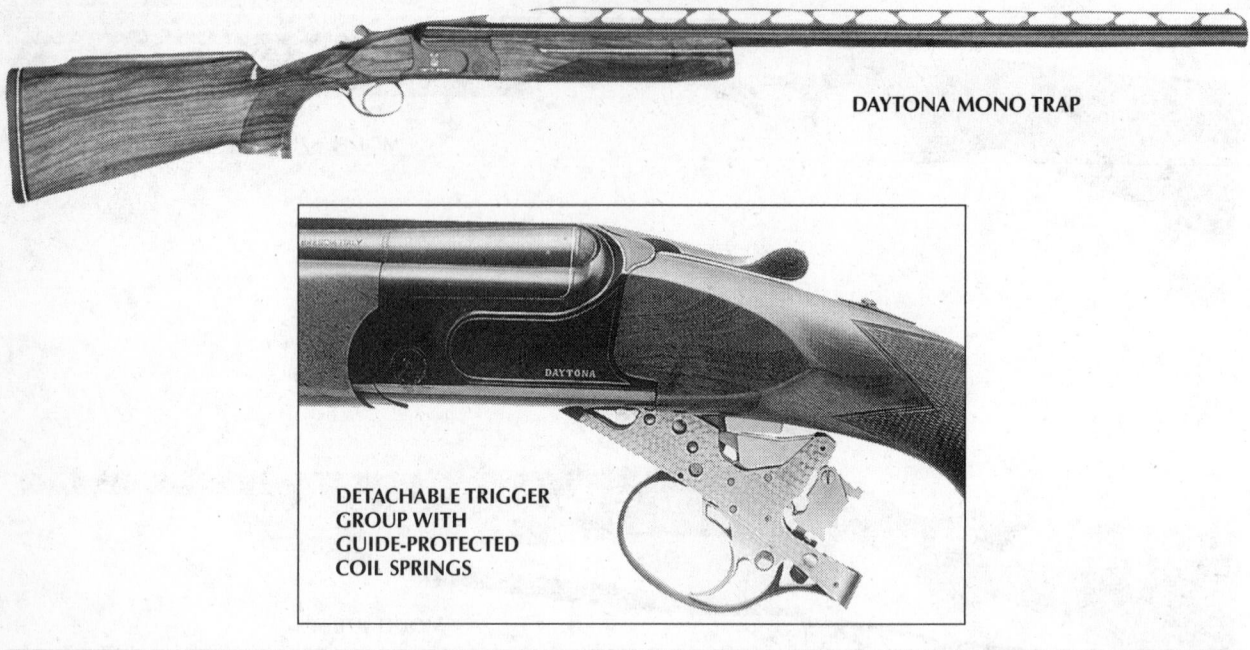

**DAYTONA MONO TRAP**

**DETACHABLE TRIGGER GROUP WITH GUIDE-PROTECTED COIL SPRINGS**

|  | TRAP | DOUBLE TRAP | SKEET | SPORTING CLAYS | HUNTING | MONO TRAP |
|---|---|---|---|---|---|---|
| **GAUGE** | 12 - 20 | | | | | |
| **BARRELS** | heat treated special chrome-nickel-molybdenum steel | | | | | |
| **CHANBER** | mm 70 (2"3/4) • mm 79 (3") on request | | | | | |
| **BARRELS LENGTH** | cm. 76 - cm.81 30" - 32" | cm. 76 30" | cm. 68-71 26"3/4 - 28" | cm. 71-74cm 76 - cm.81 28"- 29"- 30"- 32" | cm. 68- cm. 71 26"3/4 - 28" | cm. 81- cm. 86 32" - 34" |
| **CHOKES** | imp. mod/ full-mac/full | imp. cil./full | SK/SK | mod./full | imp. cit./imp.mod. mod./full | full |
| **INTERCH. CHOKES** | 5 screw-in choke tubes set available on request | | | | | |

## THE DAYTONA SHOTGUN

The Daytona shotgun is available in several styles oriented specifically to American Trap, International Trap, American Skeet, International Skeet, and Sporting Clays. The Daytona SL, (the side plate model), and the Daytona SLHH, (the side lock model), are the top of the Daytona line. All employ the Boss locking system in a breech milled from one massive block of steel.

**The trigger group:** The trigger group is detachable and is removable without the use of tools. The frame that contains the hammers, sears and springs is milled from a single block of special steel and jeweled for oil retention. On special order, an adjustable trigger may be produced with one inch of movement that can accomodate shooters with exceptionally large or small hands. Internally, the hammer springs are constructed from coils that are

contained in steel sleeves placed directly behind the hammers. With the fail safe capsule surrounding the springs, the shotgun will fire even if breakage occurs.

**Hunter o/u** . . . . . . . . . . . **from $1390**
**Le Maus o/u** . . . . . . . . . . . **from 1580**
**Concorde o/u** . . . . . . . . . . **from 6100**
**Daytona 2K o/u** . . . . . . . . **from 7600**

*Back-bored barrels are simply those with oversize dimensions forward of the chamber. The advantage: less friction as the shot charge leaves, less pellet deformation. Also, lower pressures.*

**SHOTGUNS**

# Rossi Shotguns

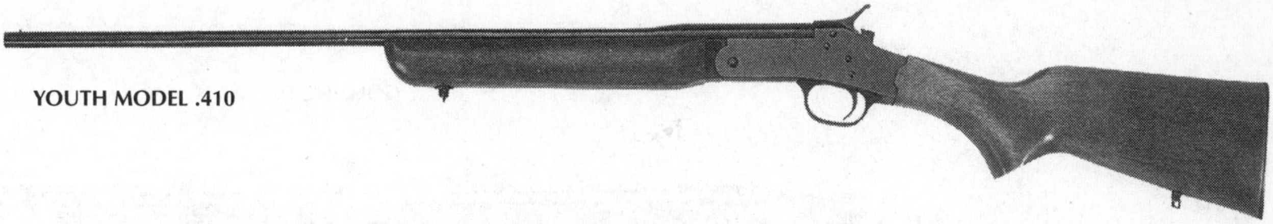

**YOUTH MODEL .410**

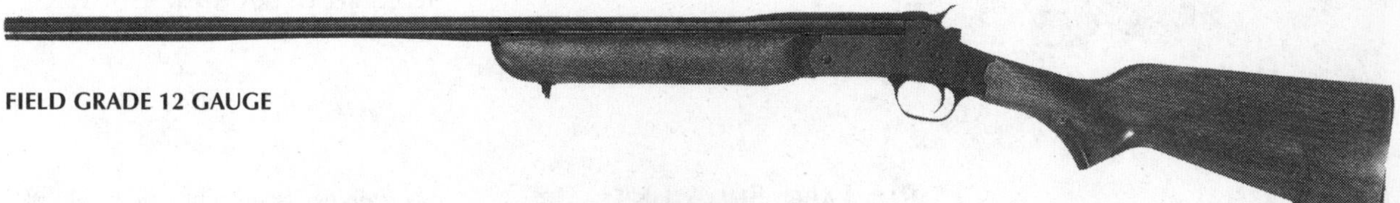

**FIELD GRADE 12 GAUGE**

**MATCHED PAIR**

## SINGLE BARREL SHOTGUNS
**Action:** hinged single-shot
**Stock:** hardwood
**Barrel:** 28 in.
**Chokes:** modified, full
**Weight:** 5.3lbs.
**Bore/Gauge:** 12, 20, .410
**Magazine:** none

**Features:** exposed-hammer, transfer-bar action; Youth model available; rifle barrels have open sights

| | |
|---|---:|
| Single-Shot | $106 |
| Youth, 22" barrel | $106 |
| two-barrel sets with 12 ga/.22 WMR, 12/.22 LR, 20/.22LR | $144 |
| two-barrel sets with .410/.22 | $152 |
| two-barrel sets with .410/.17 | $180 |
| two barrel set with stainless bbl .410/.22LR | $195 |
| .410/.17HMR | $224 |
| 12 ga/.17 HMR | $180 |
| 12 or 20 ga./.223, .243 or .308 | $231 |

*Some shooters prefer mechanical single triggers on double guns because they work even if you have a misfire in the first barrel. A recoil-operated trigger won't switch unless the round fires.*

# Ruger Shotguns

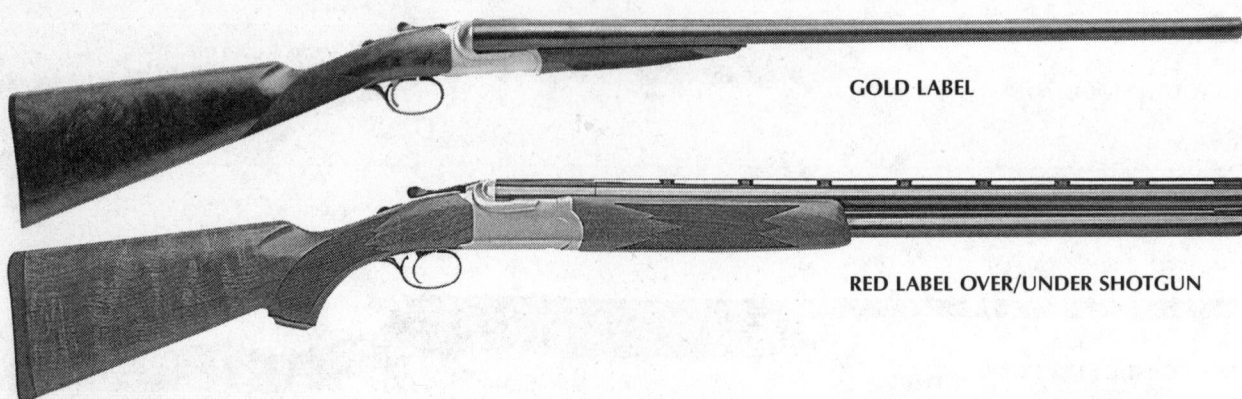

GOLD LABEL

RED LABEL OVER/UNDER SHOTGUN

## GOLD LABEL
*Action:* over/under
*Stock:* walnut, straight or pistol grip
*Barrel:* 28 in.
*Chokes:* screw-in tubes
*Weight:* 6.5lbs.
*Bore/Gauge:* 12
*Magazine:* none
*Features:* boxlock; round stainless frame
**Gold Label** . . . . . . . . . . . . . . . **$1950**

## RED LABEL SHOTGUNS
*Action:* over/under
*Stock:* walnut or synthetic, straight or pistol grip
*Barrel:* 26, 28, 30 in.
*Chokes:* screw-in tubes
*Weight:* 7.4lbs.
*Bore/Gauge:* 12, 20, 28
*Magazine:* none
*Features:* boxlock; All-Weather version

has stainless steel, synthetic stock; 28 ga. only available in 26" or 28" barrel
**standard or All-Weather** . . . . . **$1545**
**engraved** . . . . . . . . . . . . . . . . **$1725**

# Savage Shotguns

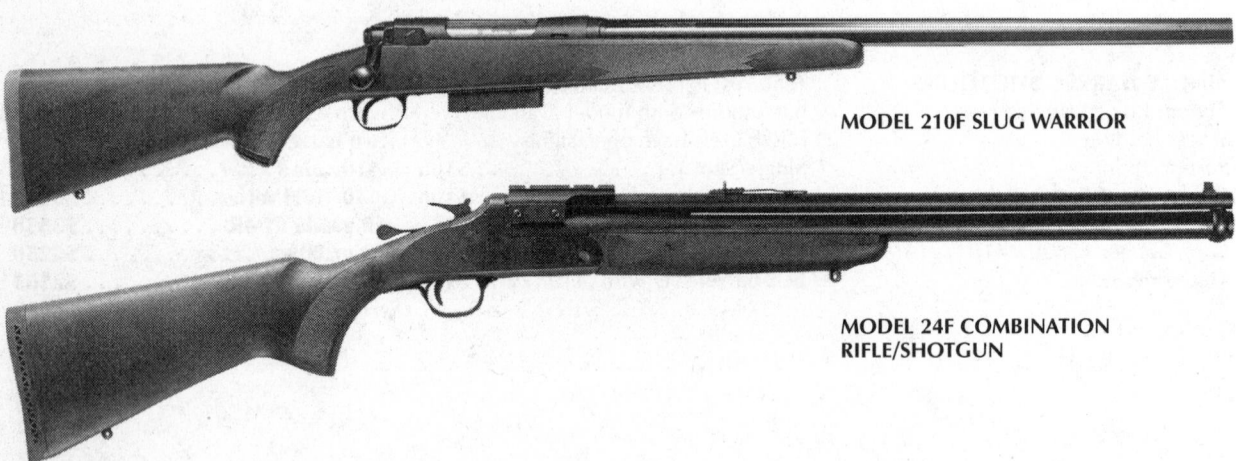

MODEL 210F SLUG WARRIOR

MODEL 24F COMBINATION RIFLE/SHOTGUN

## MODEL 210F SLUG WARRIOR
*Action:* bolt
*Stock:* synthetic
*Barrel:* rifled, 24 in.
*Chokes:* none
*Weight:* 7.5lbs.
*Bore/Gauge:* 12
*Magazine:* 2
*Features:* top tang safety, no sights,

new camo version available
**210F** . . . . . . . . . . . . . . . . . . . . **$458**
**Camo** . . . . . . . . . . . . . . . . . . . . **$495**

## MODEL 24F
*Action:* hinged single-shot
*Stock:* synthetic
*Barrel:* rifle over shotgun, 24 in.
*Chokes:* none

*Weight:* 8.0lbs.
*Bore/Gauge:* 12, 20
*Magazine:* none
*Features:* open sights, hammer-mounted barrel selector; available in 20 ga./.22LR, 20/.22 Hornet, 20/.223, 12 ga./.22 Hornet, 12/.223, 12/.30-30
**20 gauge** . . . . . . . . . . . . . . . . **$598**
**12 gauge** . . . . . . . . . . . . . . . . **$629**

SHOTGUNS

# SIG Arms Shotguns

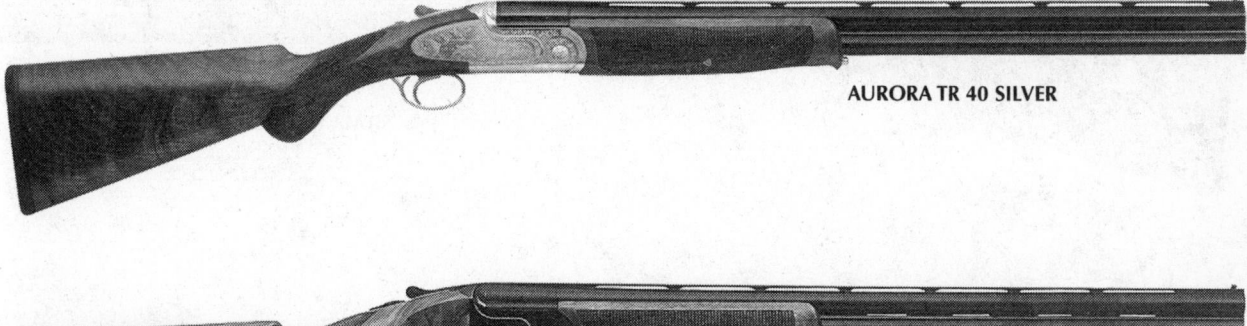

AURORA TR 40 SILVER

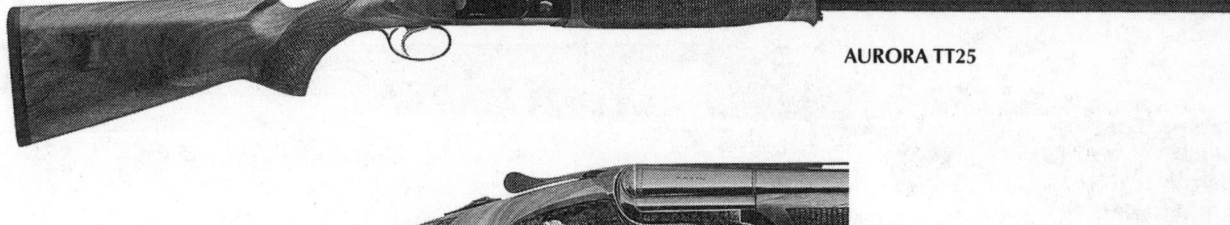

AURORA TT25

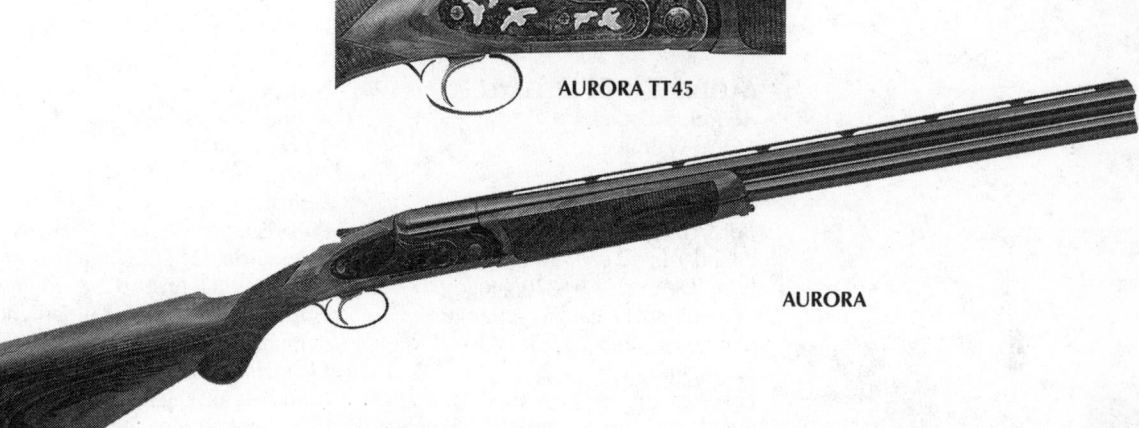

AURORA TT45

AURORA

## AURORA

*Action:* over/under
*Stock:* walnut
*Barrel:* 26 or 28 in.
*Chokes:* screw-in tubes
*Weight:* 7.3lbs.
*Bore/Gauge:* 12, 20, 28, 410
*Magazine:* none
*Features:* boxlock, single selective trigger, automatic ejectors, replaceable hingepin; 20 gauge weighs 6.3 lbs., 28 ga. and .410 6.0 lbs.

| | |
|---|---|
| 12, 20, 28, .410 . . . . . . . . . . | $2250 |
| high-grade TT 25: . . . . . . . . . . | $2950 |
| TR 40 Gold series . . . . . . . . . . | $3050 |
| best-grade TT 45: . . . . . . . . . . | $3350 |
| series 20 . . . . . . . . . . . . . . . | $2250 |
| New Englander . . . . . . . . . . . . | $2161 |
| Series 30 . . . . . . . . . . . . . . . | $2650 |
| Compeition . . . . . . . . | $2950 to 3350 |

*Repeating shotguns give you more shots, but doubles are shorter overall for their barrel length, and, say many connoisseurs, much better balanced.*

# Silma Shotguns

**SILMA DELUXE 20 GAUGE**

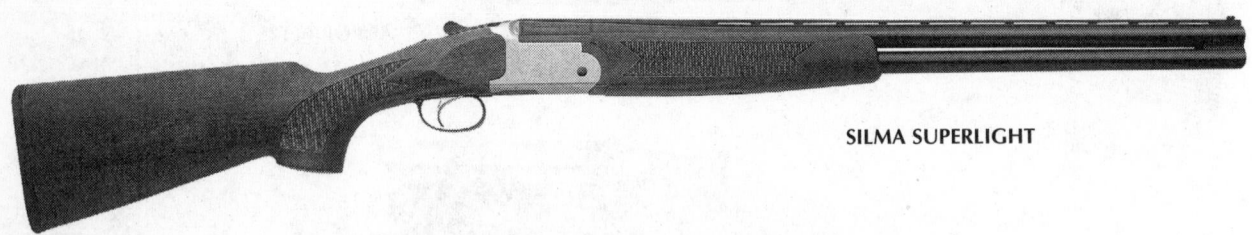

**SILMA SUPERLIGHT**

## MODEL 70 EJ DELUXE

*Action:* box lock
*Stock:* walnut
*Barrel:* 28 in.
*Sights:*
*Bore/Gauge:* 12 and 20 gauges (Standard); 12, 20, 28 gauges and .410 bore (Deluxe); 12 & 20 gauge (Superlight);12 gauge (Superlight deluxe); 12 and 20 (Clays)
*Magazine:* none
*Features:* all 12 gauge models, except Superlight, come with 3.5 inch chambers, high grade steel barrels and are proofed for steel shot. All models come with single selective trigger, automatic safety, automatic ejectors, ventilated rib, and recoil pad, gold plated.

| | |
|---|---|
| **Standard, 12 ga** | **$940** |
| **Standard, 20 ga** | **$865** |
| **Deluxe, 12 ga.** | **$1020** |
| **Deluxe, 20 ga.** | **$945** |
| **28 gauge & .410:** | **$1060** |
| **Superlight:** | **$1105** |
| **Clays:** | **$1305** |

## SILMA

*Action:* box lock
*Stock:* walnut
*Barrel:* 28 in.
*Sights:*
*Bore/Gauge:* 12 and 20 gauges (Standard); 12, 20, 28 gauges and .410 bore (Deluxe); 12 & 20 gauge (Superlight);12 gauge (Superlight deluxe); 12 and 20 (Clays)
*Magazine:* none
*Features:* all 12 gauge models, except Superlight, come with 3.5 inch chambers, high grade steel barrels and are proofed for steel shot. All models come with mechanical single trigger, automatic safety, automatic ejectors, ventilated rib, and recoil pad.

| | |
|---|---|
| **Standard:** | **$765** |
| **Deluxe** | |
| **12 & 20gauge:** | **$823** |
| **28 gauge & .410:** | **$961** |
| **Superlight:** | **$1004** |
| **Superlight Deluxe:** | **$1004** |
| **Clays:** | **$1237** |

*Recoil – or anticipation of it – can cause flinching and missing. A soft, thick recoil pad can pay big dividends, especially if you insist on shooting very lightweight guns with heavy loads.*

SHOTGUNS

# SKB Shotguns

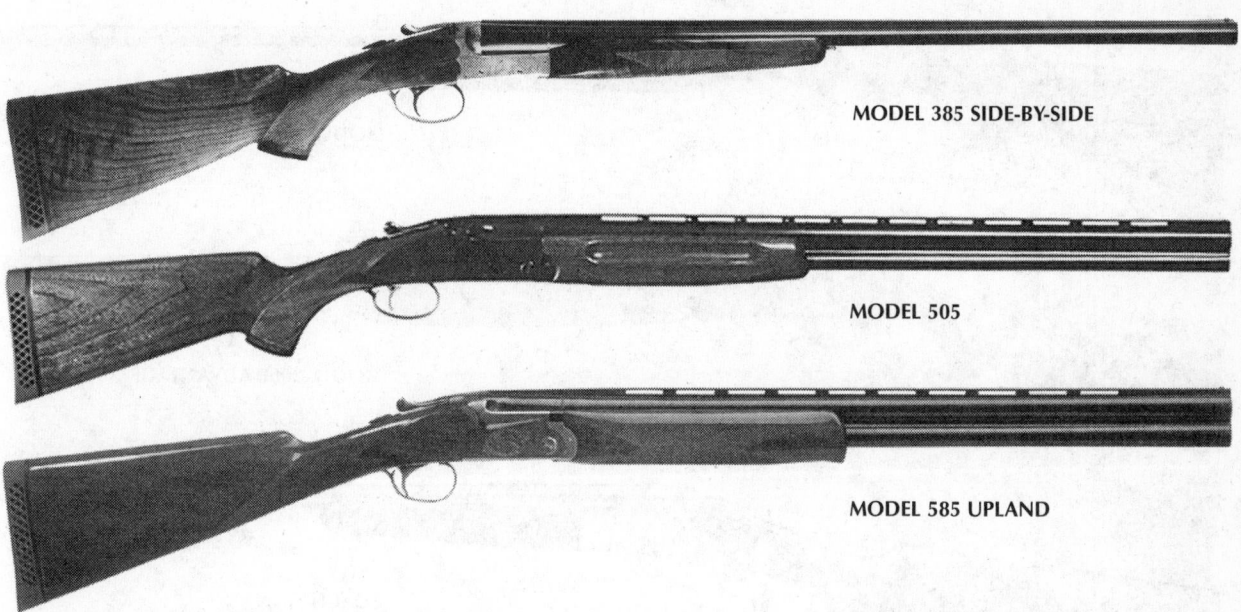

MODEL 385 SIDE-BY-SIDE

MODEL 505

MODEL 585 UPLAND

## MODEL 385 AND 485
*Action:* side-by-side
*Stock:* walnut, straight or pistol grip
*Barrel:* 26 or 28 in.
*Chokes:* screw-in tubes
*Weight:* 7.2lbs.
*Bore/Gauge:* 12, 20, 28
*Magazine:* none
*Features:* boxlock; single selective trigger, automatic ejectors; two-barrel sets also available
**standard. . . . . . . . . . . . . . . $2049**
**Model 485 deluxe. . . . . . . . . $2769**
**Model 485 two-barrel set . . . . $3949**

## MODEL 505
*Action:* over/under
*Stock:* walnut
*Barrel:* 26 or 28 in.
*Chokes:* screw-in tubes
*Weight:* 8.4lbs.
*Bore/Gauge:* 12, 20
*Magazine:* none
*Features:* boxlock; ventilated rib, automatic ejectors
**Model 505 Field . . . . . . . . . . $1229**

## MODEL 585 FIELD
*Action:* over/under
*Stock:* walnut, straight or pistol grip
*Barrel:* 26 or 28 in.
*Chokes:* screw-in tubes
*Weight:* 9.0lbs.
*Bore/Gauge:* 12, 20, 28, .410
*Magazine:* none
*Features:* boxlock; Field, Upland and Youth.
**Field, Upland, Youth**
**(12 and 20 ga.) . . . . . . . . . . . $1499**
**28 ga. or .410 . . . . . . . . . . . . $1569**
**Field Set (12 and 20) . . . . . . . $2399**
**Field Set (20 and 28) . . . . . . . $2469**
**Field Set (28 and .410) . . . . . . $2469**

# Stevens Shotguns

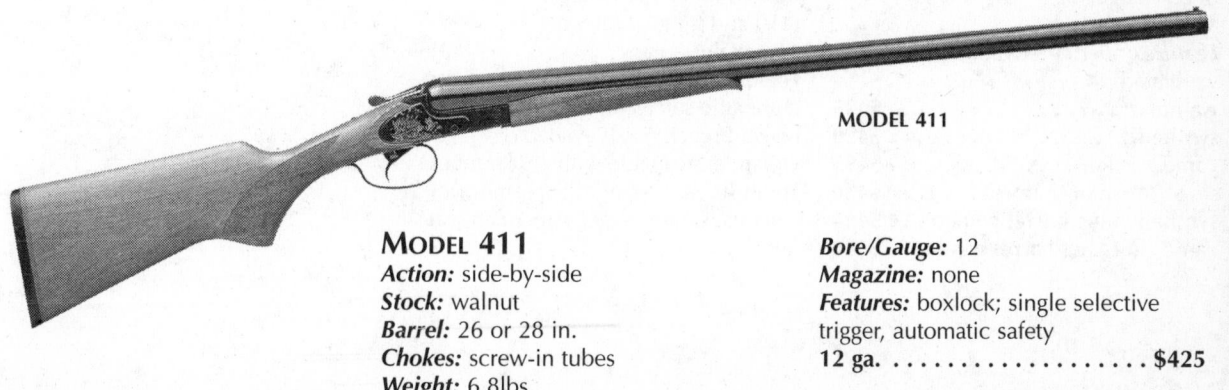

MODEL 411

## MODEL 411
*Action:* side-by-side
*Stock:* walnut
*Barrel:* 26 or 28 in.
*Chokes:* screw-in tubes
*Weight:* 6.8lbs.
*Bore/Gauge:* 12
*Magazine:* none
*Features:* boxlock; single selective trigger, automatic safety
**12 ga. . . . . . . . . . . . . . . . . . $425**

# Stoeger Shotguns

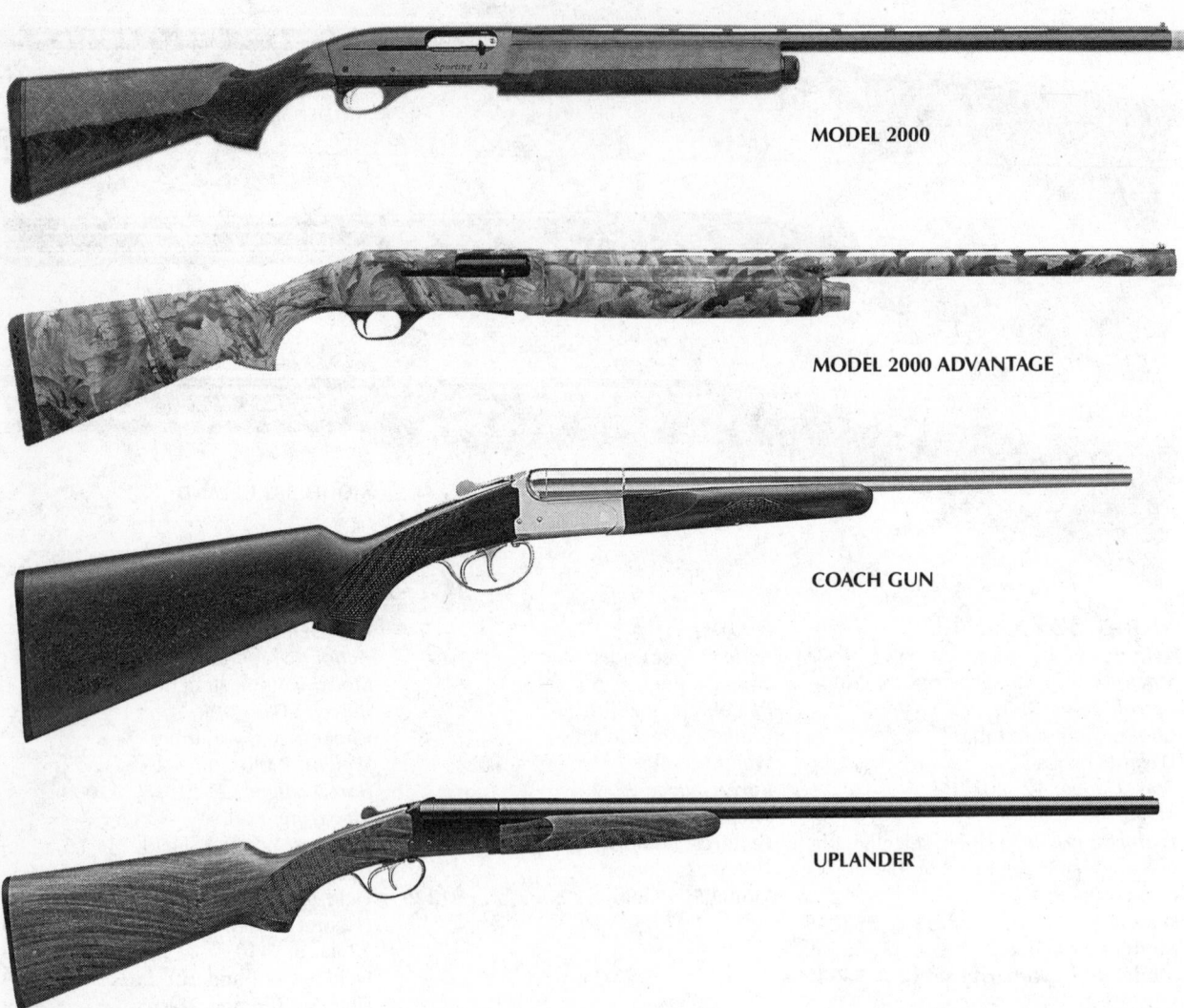

MODEL 2000

MODEL 2000 ADVANTAGE

COACH GUN

UPLANDER

## MODEL 2000
*Action:* autoloader
*Stock:* walnut or synthetic
*Barrel:* 24, 26, 28 or 30 in.
*Chokes:* screw-in tubes
*Weight:* 7.0lbs.
*Bore/Gauge:* 12
*Magazine:* 4
*Features:* inertia-recoil system, ventilated rib.
walnut . . . . . . . . . . . . . . . . . . $435
synthetic . . . . . . . . . . . . . . . . $420
camo . . . . . . . . . . . . . . . . . . . . $495
slug (24" smooth bore) . . . . . . . $430
synthetic/slug barrel combo . . . $495
camo shot/slug barrel combo . . $580

## COACH GUN AND UPLANDER
*Action:* side-by-side
*Stock:* Brazilian hardwood
*Barrel:* 20 in. (Uplander 26 or 28 in.)
*Chokes:* improved cylinder, modified
*Weight:* 6.4lbs.
*Bore/Gauge:* 12, 16, 20, .410 and 28 ga. Uplander
*Magazine:* none
*Features:* boxlock; double triggers, automatic safety, nickel and matte nickel breech finish available; Uplander available with choke tubes, Youth stock; Uplander Supreme with ejectors, single trigger, American walnut stock

Coach Gun. . . . . . . . . . . . . . . $320
nickel finish . . . . . . . . . . . . . . $375
Uplander . . . . . . . . . . . . . . . . $335
Uplander Youth . . . . . . . . . . . $335
Uplander with choke tubes. . . . $350
Uplander Supreme . . . . . . . . . $445

SHOTGUNS

# Stoeger Shotguns

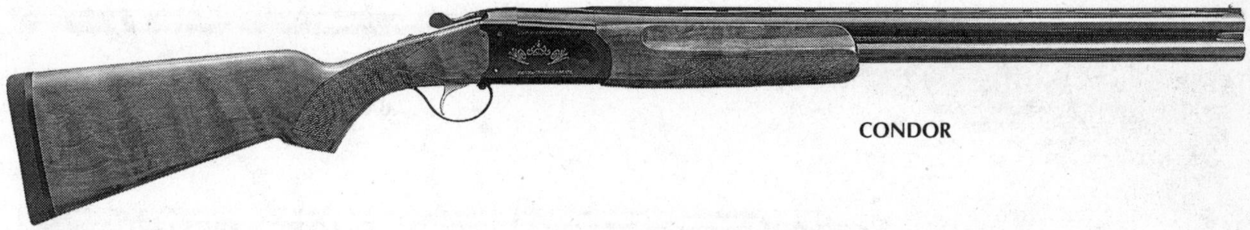

**CONDOR**

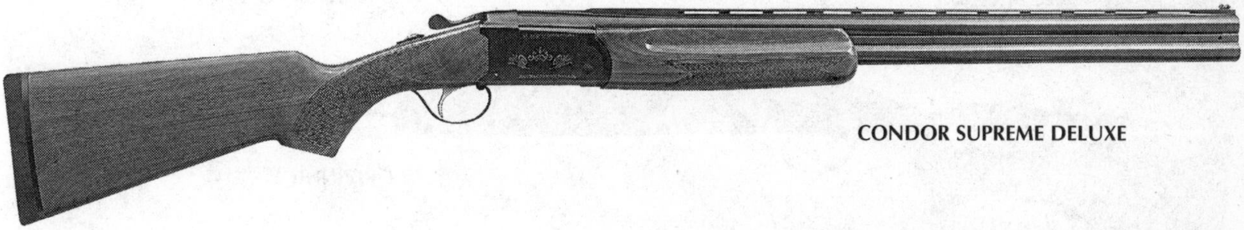

**CONDOR SUPREME DELUXE**

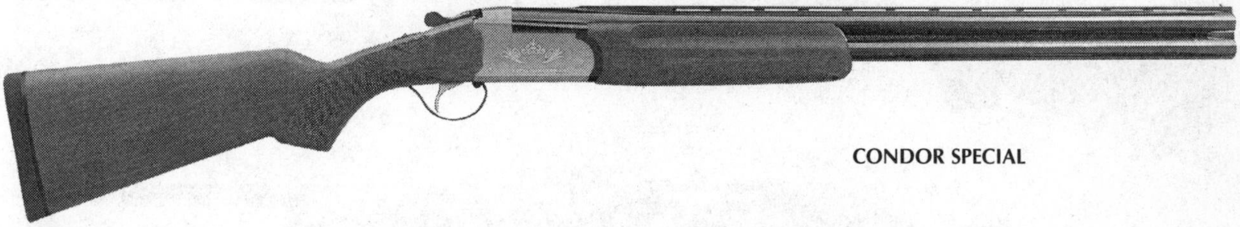

**CONDOR SPECIAL**

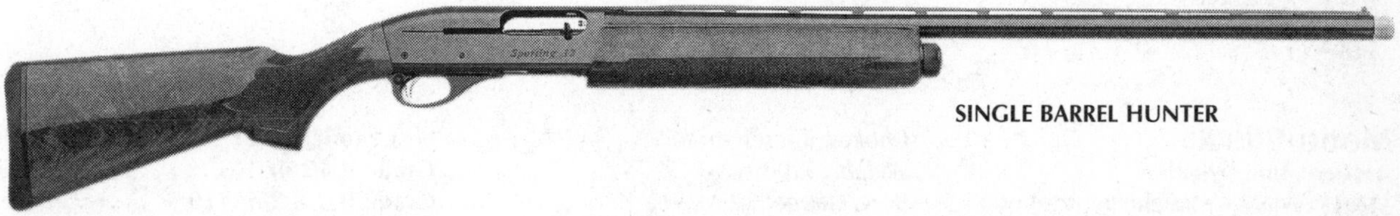

**SINGLE BARREL HUNTER**

## CONDOR
*Action:* over/under
*Stock:* Brazilian hardwood
*Barrel:* 26 or 28 in.
*Chokes:* improved cylinder, modified
*Weight:* 7.7lbs.
*Bore/Gauge:* 12, 20
*Magazine:* none
*Features:* boxlock; single trigger
**Condor** . . . . . . . . . . . . . . . . . **$390**

**Special with stainless receiver. . $440**
**Supreme with American walnut**
**stock,automatic ejectors** . . . . . . **$500**

## SINGLE-BARREL SHOTGUN
*Action*: hinged single-shot
*Stock*: hardwood
*Barrel*: 22, 24, 26 or 28 in.
*Chokes*: screw-in tubes
*Weight*: 5.4lbs.

*Bore/Gauge*: 12, 20, .410
*Magazine*: none
*Features*: vent rib, crossbolt and transfer bar safety; .410 has fixed choke.
**standard or Youth** . . . . . . . . . . **$119**

*Some crack shotgun competitors lay their left center
finger under the forend, pointing it at the target
instead of wrapping it around the gun. The pointing
and loose grip both help your accuracy.*

SHOTGUNS

# Tristar Sporting Arms Shotguns

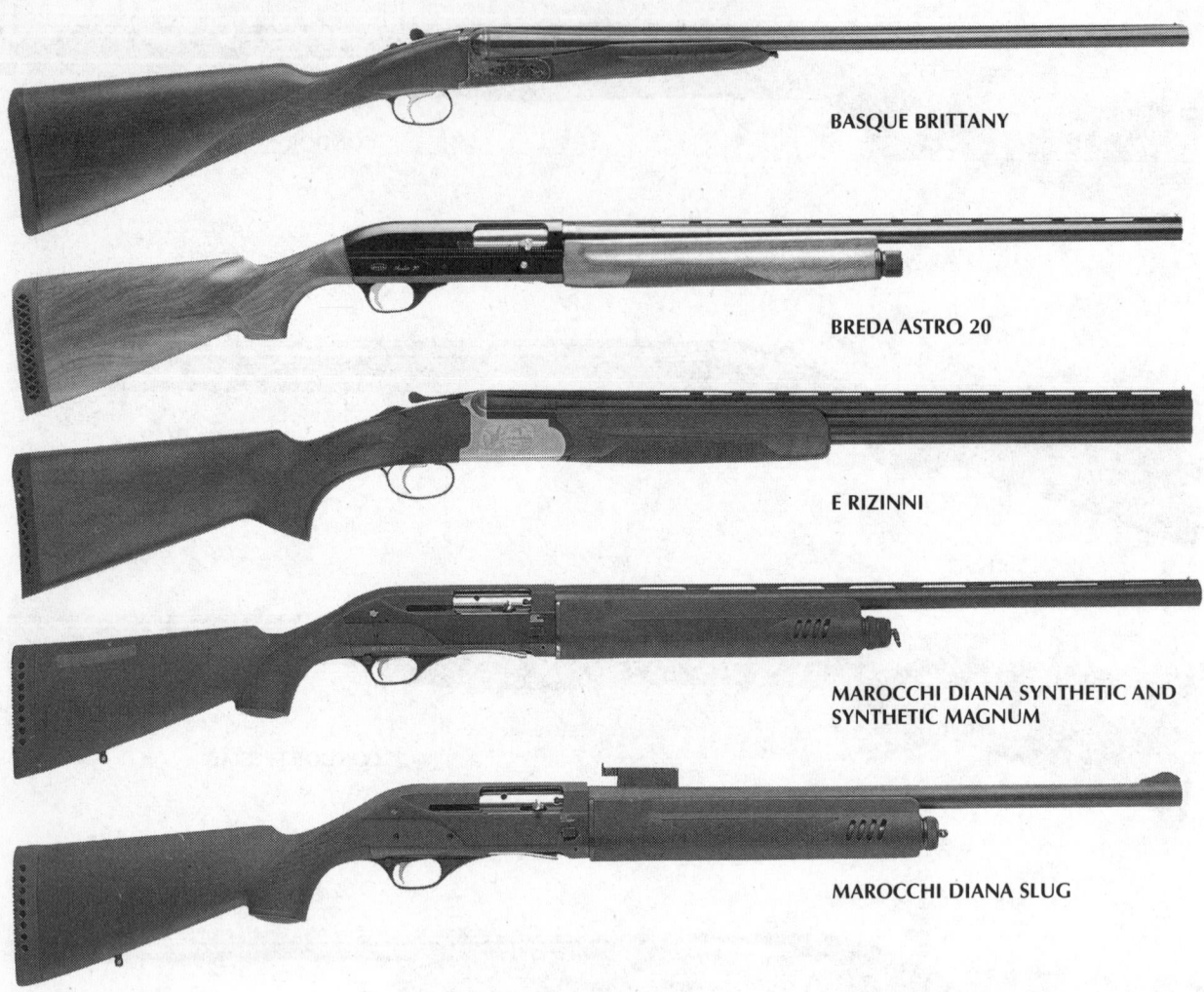

**BASQUE BRITTANY**

**BREDA ASTRO 20**

**E RIZINNI**

**MAROCCHI DIANA SYNTHETIC AND SYNTHETIC MAGNUM**

**MAROCCHI DIANA SLUG**

## BASQUE SERIES
*Action:* side-by-side
*Stock:* walnut, straight or pistol grip
*Barrel:* 26 or 28 in.
*Chokes:* screw-in tubes
*Weight:* 6.8lbs.
*Bore/Gauge:* 12, 16, 20, 28, 410
*Magazine:* none
*Features:* boxlock, single selective trigger, automatic ejectors, chromed bores, also: 20-inch Coach gun; chokes in 16 gauge: M/F and IC/M in 28 gauge and .410.
Gentry . . . . . . . . . . . . . . . . . . **$679**
Brittany . . . . . . . . . . . . . . . . . **$749**
Brittany Sporting . . . . . . . . . . **$866**

## BREDA
*Action:* autoloader
*Stock:* walnut or camo
*Barrel:* 28 or 30 in.
*Chokes:* screw-in tubes
*Weight:* 7.0lbs.
*Bore/Gauge:* 12
*Magazine:* 4
*Features:* gas-operated, rotary bolt, stock shims, hard case. Also 6 pound inertia-operated 20 gauge, 26 in. barrel
camo . . . . . . . . . . . . . . . . . . . . **$879**
20-gauge . . . . . . . . . . . . . . . **$1142**
12-gauge black and walnut . . . **$1259**

## E. RIZINNI
*Action:* over/under
*Stock:* walnut
*Barrel:* 24, 26 or 28 in.
*Chokes:* screw-in tubes
*Weight:* 7.3lbs.
*Bore/Gauge:* 12, 16, 20, 28, 410
*Magazine:* none
*Features:* boxlock, camo and magnum and Sporting Clays models available

base model 12 or 20 . . . . . . . . **$779**
Grade II 12 or 16 . . . . . . . . . . **$919**
Grade II 20, 20, .410 . . . . . . . . **$969**

## MAROCCHI DIANA
*Action:* autoloader
*Stock:* walnut, synthetic or camo
*Barrel:* 24, 26, 28 or 30 in.
*Chokes:* screw-in tubes
*Weight:* 7.0lbs.
*Bore/Gauge:* 12, 20, 28
*Magazine:* 4
*Features:* gas-operated, stock shims, slug model has sights, scope mount on rifled barrel
synthetic . . . . . . . . . . . . . . . . . **$399**
walnut . . . . . . . . . . . . . . . . . . . **$425**
synthetic magnum . . . . . . . . . . **$487**
camo magnum . . . . . . . . . . . . . **$576**
slug . . . . . . . . . . . . . . . . . . . . . **$425**

# Verona Shotguns

**LX 1001-308/20 EXPRESS**

**LX 1001-20 GA OVER/UNDER BARREL SET**

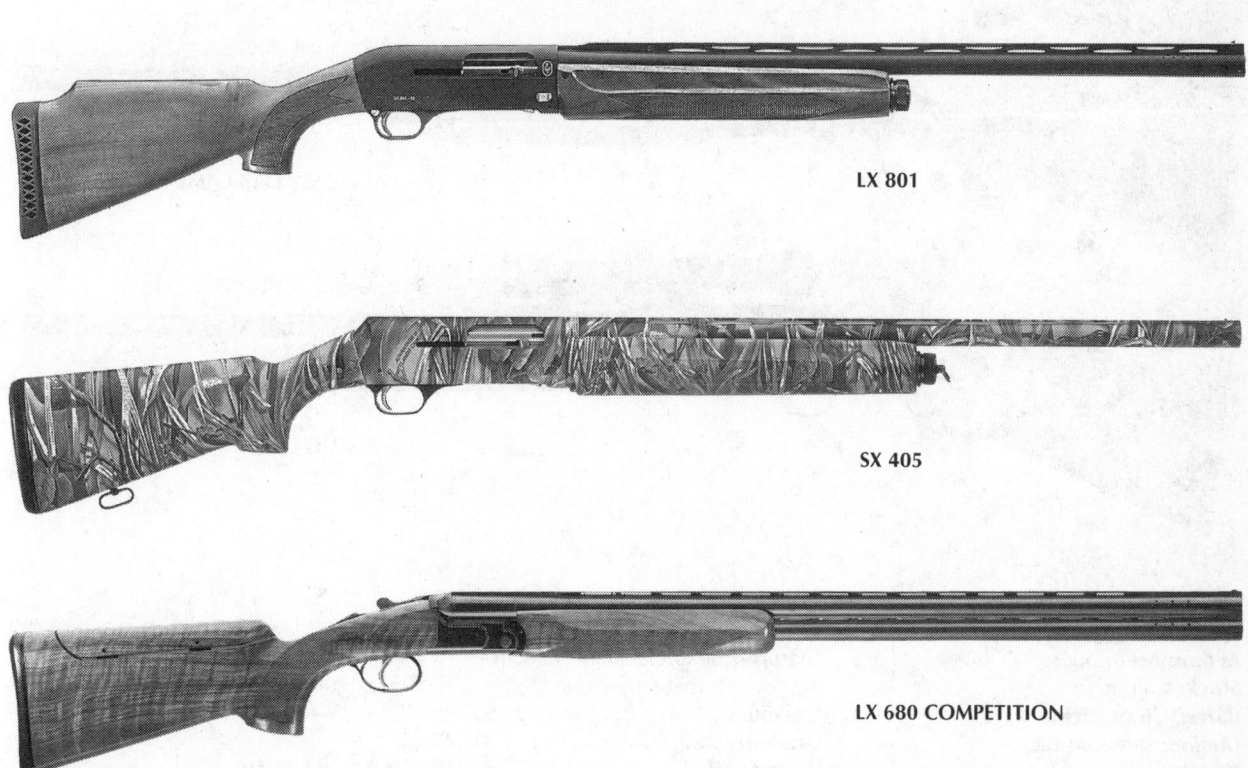

LX 801

SX 405

LX 680 COMPETITION

## MODEL LX EXPRESS
**Action:** over/under
**Stock:** Turkish walnut
**Barrel:** 28 in.
**Chokes:** screw-in tubes
**Weight:** 8.0lbs.
**Bore/Gauge:** .223, .243, .270, .308 or .30-06 over 20 gauge
**Magazine:** none
**Features:** single selective tirgger, automatic ejectors
**Express Combo with Express and 20 . gauge over/under set:** . . . . . . P.O.R.

## MODEL LX 801
**Action:** autoloader
**Stock:** walnut
**Barrel:** 28 or 30 in.
**Chokes:** screw-in tubes
**Weight:** 6.8lbs.
**Bore/Gauge** 12
**Magazine:** 3
**Features:** gas-operated, alloy receiver, sporting and competition models available; also model SX405: synthetic or camo, 22 in. slug or 26 in. field
**Verona LX 801 . . . . . price on request**
**Verona SX 405 . . . . . . . . . . . . . $353**

## MODEL LX 680 COMPETITION SERIES
**Action:** over/under
**Stock:** Turkish walnut
**Barrel:** 30 in. 932 on Trap Model)
**Chokes:** screw-in tubes
**Weight:** 7.5lbs.
**Bore/Gauge:** 12
**Magazine:** none
**Features:** boxlock; removable competition trigger, ported barrels, deluxe case; also multiple-barrel sets
**Verona LX 680 . . . . . . . . . . . . $1737**

SHOTGUNS

# Weatherby Shotguns

**ATHENA GRADE III CLASSIC FIELD**

**SAS FIELD**

**SAS MOSSY OAK CAMO**

**SAS SLUG GUN**

**ATHENA**
*Action:* over/under
*Stock:* walnut
*Barrel:* 26 or 28 in.
*Chokes:* screw-in tubes
*Weight:* 8.0lbs.
*Bore/Gauge:* 12, 20, 28
*Magazine:* none
*Features:* boxlock; single selective
mechanical trigger, automatic ejectors
Grade III . . . . . . . . . . . . . . . $2173
Grade V . . . . . . . . . . . . . . . . $3037

**ORION**
*Action:* over/under
*Stock:* walnut, straight or pistol grip
*Barrel:* 26, 28, 30 or 32 in.
*Chokes:* screw-in tubes
*Weight:* 8.0lbs.
*Bore/Gauge:* 12, 20 or 28

*Magazine:* none
*Features:* boxlock; single selective
trigger, automatic ejectors
Upland. . . . . . . . . . . . . . . . . $1299
Grade II . . . . . . . . . . . . . . . . $1622
Sporting Clays . . . . . . . . . . . $2059
Grade III . . . . . . . . . . . . . . . $1955

**SAS**
*Action:* autoloader
*Stock:* walnut, synthetic or camo
*Barrel:* 24, 26, 28 or 30 in., vent rib
*Chokes:* screw-in tubes
*Weight:* 7.8lbs.
*Bore/Gauge:* 12
*Magazine:* 4
*Features:* gas-operated, 3-inch cham-
ber, magazine cutoff
walnut . . . . . . . . . . . . . . . . . $749
synthetic . . . . . . . . . . . . . . . $699

camo . . . . . . . . . . . . . . . . . . $799
Sporting Clays . . . . . . . . . . . . $849
Slug gun (22" rifled bbl.). . . . . $799

**SAS SLUG GUN**
*Action:* autoloader
*Stock:* walnut
*Barrel:* 22 in. rifled
*Chokes:* none
*Weight:* 7.3lbs.
*Bore/Gauge:* 12
*Magazine:* 4
*Features:* self-compensating gas sys-
tem; cantilever scope base included;
"smart" follower, magazine cutoff,
stock has shims to alter drop, pitch,
cast-off
SAS Slug Gun. . . . . . . . . . . . . $799

**SHOTGUNS**

# Winchester Shotguns

MODEL 1300 UNIVERSAL HUNTER

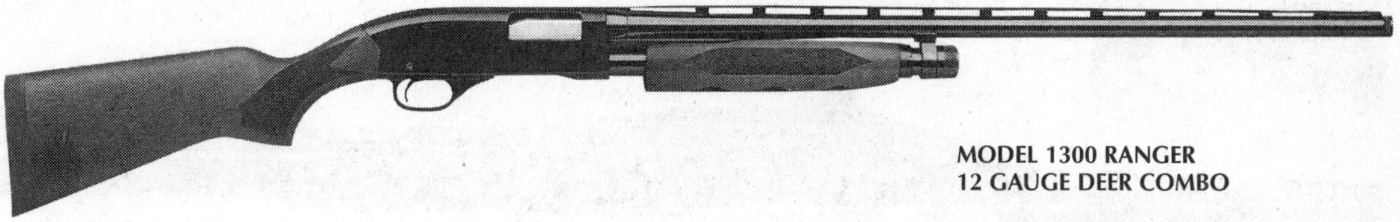

MODEL 1300 RANGER
12 GAUGE DEER COMBO

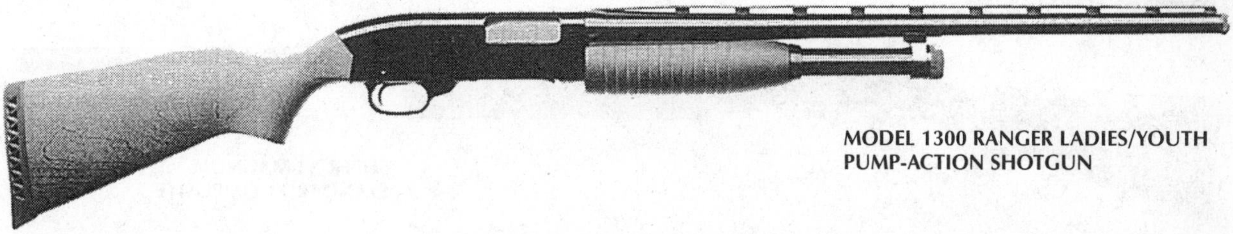

MODEL 1300 RANGER LADIES/YOUTH
PUMP-ACTION SHOTGUN

MODEL 9410 PACKER SHOTGUN

## MODEL 1300
*Action:* pump
*Stock:* walnut or synthetic
*Barrel:* 18, 22, 24, 26 or 28 in.
*Chokes:* screw-in tubes
*Weight:* 7.5lbs.
*Bore/Gauge:* 12, 20
*Magazine:* 4
*Features:* Deer versions feature either smooth or rifled 22-inch barrels, rifle sights

synthetic . . . . . . . . . . . . . . . . . $353
walnut . . . . . . . . . . . . . . . . . . . $439
Ranger, hardwood . . . . . . . . . . $367
Turkey, camo . . . . . . . . . . . . . . $554
Deer, synthetic . . . . . . . . . . . . . $392
Deer, synthetic
with cantilever mount . . . . . . . $422
Deer, combo . . . . . . . . . . . . . . $455
Universal Hunter . . . . . . . . . . . $472

## MODEL 9410
*Action:* lever
*Stock:* walnut
*Barrel:* 20 or 24 in.
*Chokes:* full
*Weight:* 7.0lbs.
*Bore/Gauge:* 410
*Magazine:* 9
*Features:* 2.5-inch chamber; Truglo front sight, shallow V rear
9410 . . . . . . . . . . . . . . . . . . . $645
**Packer with 20-inch barrel** . . . . $667

*Pull the shotgun firmly into your shoulder with your right hand; let the left gently and smoothly guide the muzzle.*

# Winchester Shotguns

**NEW SUPER X2 UNIVERSAL HUNTER**

**SUPER X2 SPORTING CLAYS 3"**

**SUPER X2 PRACTICAL MK II**

**SUPER X2 MAGNUM STANDARD COMPOSITE**

**SUPER X2 MAGNUM UNIVERSAL HUNTER**

**SUPER X2 SIGNATURE RED**

## SUPER X2

*Action:* autoloader
*Stock:* walnut or synthetic
*Barrel:* 22, 24, 26, 28 or 30 in.
*Chokes:* screw-in tubes
*Weight:* 8.0lbs.
*Bore/Gauge:* 12
*Magazine:* 4
*Features:* gas-operated mechanism, back-bored barrels; Universal Hunter, Greenhead, Turkey and other versions available, all with "Dura-Touch" finish, some with Tru-Glo sights

Super X2 Field . . . . . . . . . . . . . $874
Sporting Clays . . . . . . . . . . . . . $959
Deer, rifled barrel with sights . . $920
Practical MK II,
extended magazine. . . . . . . . . $1237
3.5-inch synthetic. . . . . . . . . . $988
3.5-inch camo . . . . . . . . . . . . $1139
Greenhead. . . . . . . . . . . . . . . $996
Turkey . . . . . . . . . . . . . . . . . $1165
Universal Hunter Turkey . . . . . $1179

## SUPER X2 SIGNATURE RED

*Action:* autoloader
*Stock:* hardwood, "Dura-Touch" finish
*Barrel:* 28 or 30 in.
*Chokes:* screw-in tubes
*Weight:* 8.0lbs.
*Bore/Gauge:* 12
*Magazine:* 4
Features: shims adjust buttstock; back-bored barrel; "Dura-Touch" armor coating now available on many other Winchesters
Signature Red. . . . . . . . . . . . . $976

SHOTGUNS

# American Derringer Handguns

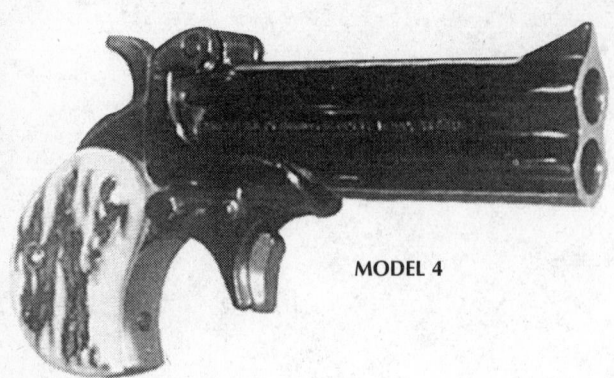

MODEL 4

## MODEL 4
*Action:* hinged breech
*Grips:* stag
*Barrel:* 4 in.
*Sights:* fixed open
*Weight:* 16.5oz.

*Caliber:* .32 H&R, .357 Mag., .357
Max., .44 Mag., .45 Colt/.410, .45-70
*Capacity:* 2
*Features:* over/under Derringer also
available with .45-70 over .45
Colt/.410

| | |
|---|---|
| .357 Mag. | $435 |
| .357 Max. | $440 |
| .44 Mag. | $540 |
| .45 Colt/.410 | $460 |

# Auto Ordnance Handguns

MODEL 1911A1                          1911WGS

## MODEL 1911A1
*Action:* autoloader
*Grips:* plastic
*Barrel:* 5 in.
*Sights:* fixed open

*Weight:* 39.0oz.
*Caliber:* .45 ACP.
*Capacity:* 7 + 1
*Features:* single-action 1911 Colt
design; Deluxe version has rubber

wrap-around grips, 3-dot sights
| | |
|---|---|
| **standard.** | $581 |
| **WWII Parkerized** | $581 |
| **Deluxe.** | $597 |
| **Thompson 1911C 45 cal.** | $701 |

MODEL 21 BOBCAT

MODEL 8000 SERIES COUGAR

MODEL 3032 TOMCAT

MODEL U22 NEOS

## MODEL 21 BOBCAT

**Action:** autoloader
**Grips:** plastic or walnut
**Barrel:** 2.4 in.
**Sights:** fixed open
**Weight:** 11.5oz.
**Caliber:** .22 LR, .25 Auto
**Capacity:** 7 (.22) or 8 (.25)
**Features:** double action, tip-up barrel, alloy frame, walnut grips extra

matte . . . . . . . . . . . . . . . . . . . . $265
blued . . . . . . . . . . . . . . . . . . . . $300
stainless . . . . . . . . . . . . . . . . . $329

## MODEL 8000 SERIES COUGAR

**Action:** autoloader
**Grips:** composite
**Barrel:** 3.6 in.
**Sights:** fixed open
**Weight:** 32.6oz.
**Caliber:** 9mm, .357 Sig, .40 S&W,

.45 ACP
**Capacity:** 10 + 1 and 8 + 1 (.45 ACP)
**Features:** locked-breech, rotating barrel mechanism, double action, chrome-lined bore; also mini-Cougar (27.5 oz.) with 8-shot magazine in 9mm, .40 S&W

Cougar . . . . . . . . . . . . . . . . . . $729
.45 ACP . . . . . . . . . . . . . . . . . . $779
Cougar Inox . . . . . . . . . . . . . . $794

## MODEL 3032 TOMCAT

**Action:** autoloader
**Grips:** plastic
**Barrel:** 2.5 in.
**Sights:** fixed open
**Weight:** 14.5oz.
**Caliber:** .32 Auto
**Capacity:** 7 + 1
**Features:** double action; tip-up barrel

matte . . . . . . . . . . . . . . . . . . . . $358

blue . . . . . . . . . . . . . . . . . . . . . $393
stainless . . . . . . . . . . . . . . . . . $443
Titanium . . . . . . . . . . . . . . . . . $436

## MODEL U22 NEOS

**Action:** autoloader
**Grips:** plastic
**Barrel:** 4.5 or 6 in.
**Sights:** target
**Weight:** 31.7oz.
**Caliber:** .22 LR
**Capacity:** 10 + 1
**Features:** single action; removable colored grip inserts; model with 6 in. barrel weighs 36.2 oz.; Deluxe model features adjustable trigger, replaceable sights; optional 7.5-inch barrel

U22 Neos . . . . . . . . . . . . . . . . $279
Inox . . . . . . . . . . . . . . . . . . . . . $329
DLX . . . . . . . . . . . . . . . . . . . . . $350
Inox DLX . . . . . . . . . . . . . . . . . $400

HANDGUNS

# Beretta Handguns

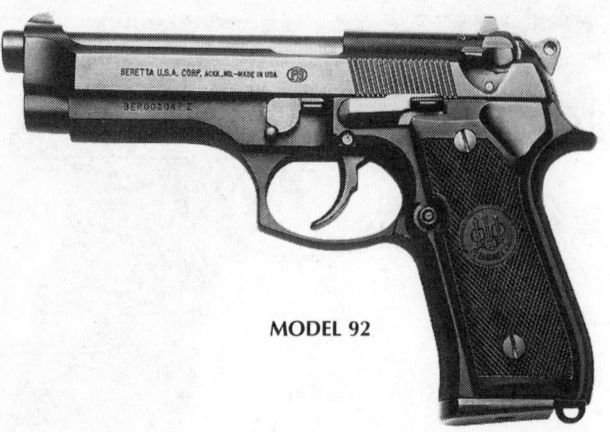

MODEL 92

MODEL 92/96 VERTEC

MODEL 96

MODEL 84 CHEETAH

## MODEL 92

*Action:* autoloader
*Grips:* wood or plastic
*Barrel:* 4.3
*Sights:* 3-dot
*Weight:* 34.4oz.
*Caliber:* 9mm and .40 S&W
*Capacity:* 10 + 1 (8 + 1 compact)
*Features:* chrome-lined bore; double action tritium sights available; reversible magazine catch

Model 92 . . . . . . . . . . . . . . . . $712
stainless . . . . . . . . . . . . . . . . . $772
compact stainless . . . . . . . . . . $748
Brigadier . . . . . . . . . . . . . . . $748
Brigadier stainless . . . . . . . . . $798

## MODEL 92/96 VERTEC

*Action:* autoloader
*Grips:* thin, vertical, dual-textured panels

*Barrel:* 4.7
*Sights:* fixed open
*Weight:* 32.2oz.
*Caliber:* 9mm and .40 S&W
*Capacity:* 10 + 1
*Features:* double action, accessory rail for laser sight, flashlight
Vertec . . . . . . . . . . . . . . . . . $751
Inox . . . . . . . . . . . . . . . . . . . $801

## MODEL 96

*Action:* autoloader
*Grips:* composite
*Barrel:* 5.9 in.
*Sights:* target
*Weight:* 40.0oz.
*Caliber:* .40 S&W
*Capacity:* 10 + 1 (8 + 1 compact)
*Features:* double action, rubber magazine bumpers, competition-tuned trigger; tool set and ABS case

Model 96 . . . . . . . . . . . . . . . . $712
stainless . . . . . . . . . . . . . . . . . $772

## MODEL 84 CHEETAH

*Action:* autoloader
*Grips:* plastic or wood
*Barrel:* 3.8 or 4.4 in. (M86)
*Sights:* fixed open
*Weight:* 23.3oz.
*Caliber:* .380 Auto
*Capacity:* 10 + 1
*Features:* double action, ambidextrous safety

Cheetah 84 . . . . . . . . . . . . . . $615
M84 nickel . . . . . . . . . . . . . . . $694
M85 nickel . . . . . . . . . . . . . . . $658
M85 with 8-round
single-stack magazine . . . . . . . $579

# Beretta Handguns

MODEL 87 TARGET

MODEL 9000 S

## MODEL 87 TARGET
*Action:* autoloader
*Grips:* plastic or wood
*Barrel:* 3.8 or 5.9 in. (Target)
*Sights:* fixed open
*Weight:* 20.1oz.
*Caliber:* .22 LR
*Capacity:* 10 + 1

*Features:* blowback design; Target weighs 40.9 oz. with target sights
Model 87 . . . . . . . . . . . . . . . . . $615
Target . . . . . . . . . . . . . . . . . . $708

## MODEL 9000 S
*Action:* autoloader
*Grips:* soft polymer

*Barrel:* 3.5 in.
*Sights:* fixed open
*Weight:* 27.0oz.
*Caliber:* 9mm and .40 S&W
*Capacity:* 10 + 1
*Features:* double action, polymer frame, firing pin block
9000 S . . . . . . . . . . . . . . . . . . $472

# Bersa Handguns

## MODEL 380 THUNDER
*Action:* autoloader
*Grips:* composite
*Barrel:* 3.5 in.
*Sights:* fixed open
*Weight:* 23.0oz.
*Caliber:* .380 ACP
*Capacity:* 7 + 1
*Features:* double action;
also Thunder .45
.380 . . . . . . . . . . . . . . . . . . . . $275
.380 nickel . . . . . . . . . . . . . . . $300
.380, 9-shot . . . . . . . . . . . . . . $309
9mm, 10-shot matte . . . . . . . . $425
9mm, 10-shot stainless . . . . . . . $465
.45 . . . . . . . . . . . . . . . . . . . . . $425
.45 nickel . . . . . . . . . . . . . . . . $450
.45 stainless . . . . . . . . . . . . . . $465

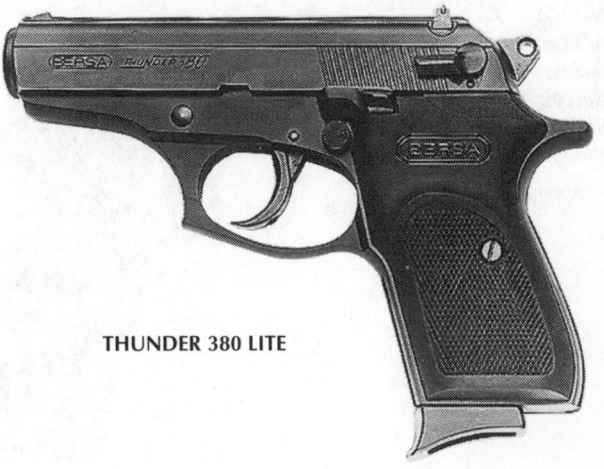

THUNDER 380 LITE

# Bond Arms Handguns

**TEXAS DEFENDER**

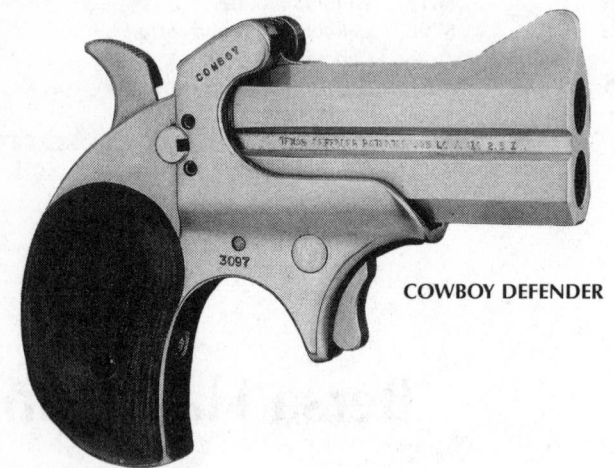

**COWBOY DEFENDER**

**CENTURY 2000 DEFENDER**

## TEXAS DEFENDER
*Action:* hinged breech
*Grips:* composite
*Barrel:* 3 in.
*Sights:* fixed open
*Weight:* 20.0oz.
*Caliber:* .450 Autobond, .45
*Capacity:* 2
*Features:* double barrel, stainless steel; also available: Cowboy Defender at 19 oz., with no trigger guard
**Texas Defender** . . . . . . . . . . . . **$379**
**Cowboy Defender** . . . . . . . . . . **$379**

## CENTURY 2000 DEFENDER
*Action:* hinged breech
*Grips:* Rosewood
*Barrel:* 3.5 in.
*Sights:* fixed open
*Weight:* 21 oz.
*Caliber:* .45 Colt or .410 Shot Shell
*Capacity:* 2
*Features:* 16 interchangeable barrels, stainless steel
**Century 2000 Defender** . . . . . . **$394**

*The .357 Magnum and .38 Special use the same-diameter bullets (.357); the .38 Special cartridge can be fired safely in the longer chambers of 357 Magnum revolvers.*

# Browning Handguns

**BUCK MARK STANDARD
(5.5" BARREL)**

**BUCK MARK CLASSIC**

**BUCK MARK 5.5 TARGET**

**BUCK MARK BULLSEYE**

**HI-POWER**

**PRO-9**

## BUCK MARK

*Action:* autoloader
*Grips:* composite, laminated or wood
*Barrel:* 5.5 in.
*Sights:* target
*Weight:* 32.0oz.
*Caliber:* .22 LR
*Capacity:* 10 + 1
*Features:* standard, camper, target, bullseye models available with various grips, barrel contours
**Buck Mark . . . . . . . . . . . . . . . $310**

Nickel . . . . . . . . . . . . . . . . . . $366
Camper . . . . . . . . . . . . . . . . . $279
Camper nickel . . . . . . . . . . . . $311
Bullseye . . . . . . . . . . . . . . . . . $454
Target . . . . . . . . . . . . . . . . . . $496
Micro (4 in. bbl.) . . . . . . . . . . $310
Micro nicket . . . . . . . . . . . . . $366

## PRO-9 AND HI-POWER

*Action:* autoloader
*Grips:* walnut, rubber or composite
*Barrel:* 4.75 in.

*Sights:* fixed
*Weight:* 30-35 oz.
*Caliber:* 9mm, .40 S& W
*Features:* Pro-9 (9mm only) has stainless steel slide and replaceable backstrap inserts. Hi-Power has optional adjustable sights.
**Pro-9 . . . . . . . . . . . . . . . . . . . $628**
**Hi-Power . . . . . . . . . . . $730 – 791**
**Hi-Power, adjustable sights . . . . $805**

# Charles Daly Handguns

MODEL 1911

MODEL 1911
TARGET STAINLESS

## MODEL 1911
*Action:* autoloader
*Grips:* walnut
*Barrel:* 3.5, 4.0 or 5.0 in.
*Sights:* target
*Weight:* 33.0oz.
*Caliber:* .45 ACP
*Capacity:* 7 + 1
Features: stainless and target models
available (weights vary to 39 oz.)
Model 1911 . . . . . . . . . . . . . . . $529
**Target** . . . . . . . . . . . . . . . . . . $619
**Target stainless** . . . . . . . . . . . . $699

# Cimarron Handguns

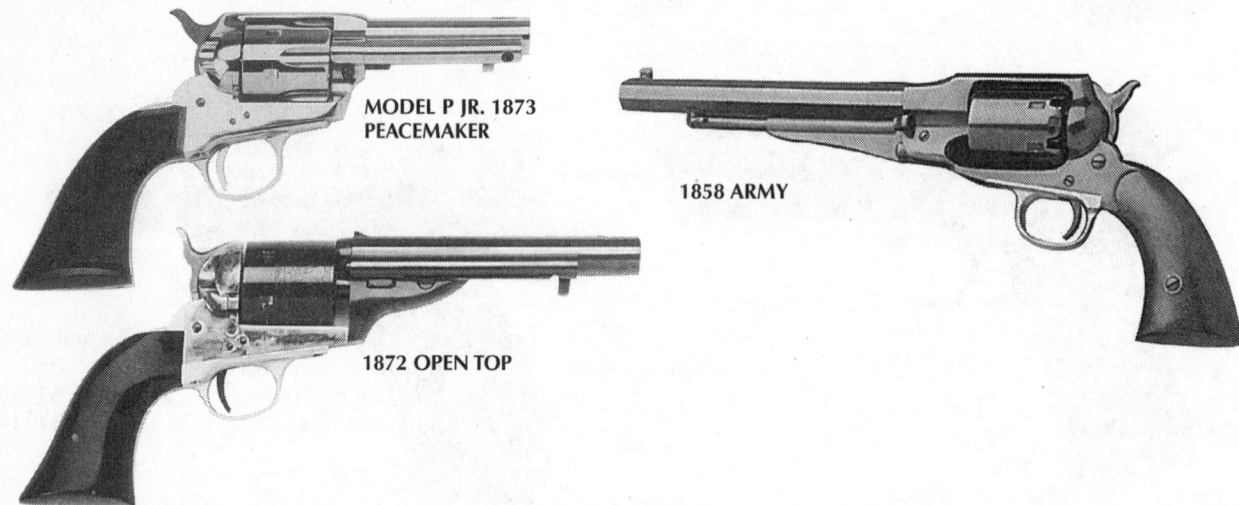

MODEL P JR. 1873
PEACEMAKER

1858 ARMY

1872 OPEN TOP

## MODEL 1858 ARMY
*Action:* single-action revolver
*Grips:* walnut
*Barrel:* 7.5 in.
*Sights:* fixed open
*Weight:* 50.0oz.
*Caliber:* .44
*Capacity:* 6
Features: black powder single action
revolver also available in .36 Paterson
**1858 Army** . . . . . . . . . . . . . . . $329

## MODEL 1872 OPEN TOP
*Action:* single-action revolver
*Grips:* walnut
*Barrel:* 5.5 and 7.5 in.
*Sights:* fixed open
*Weight:* 40.0oz.
*Caliber:* .38 Colt and S&W, .44 Colt
and Russian, .45 Schofield
*Capacity:* 6
*Features:* modern steel, traditional
design; weight varies up to 46 oz.
**1872** . . . . . . . . . . . . . . . . . . . $529

## MODEL P JR. 1873 PEACEMAKER
*Action:* single-action revolver
*Grips:* composite
*Barrel:* 4.8, 5.5 and 7.5 in.
*Sights:* none
*Weight:* 44.0oz.
*Caliber:* .32 WCP, .38 WCF, .357, .44
WCF, .45 LC
*Capacity:* 6
*Features:* fashioned after the 1873 Colt
SAA but 20 percent smaller
**Peacemaker** . . . . . . . . . . . . . . $499

**GOVERNMENT 1991 MATTE**

**XSE COMMANDER**

**GOLD CUP**

**DEFENDER**

## SERIES 70
Action: autoloader
Grips: walnut
Barrel: 5 in.
Sights: fixed open
Weight: 39.0oz.
Caliber: .45 ACP
Capacity: 7 + 1
Features: single-action M1911 design
**Model 70** . . . . . . . . . . . . . . . . **$599**

## .38 SUPER
Action: autoloader
Grips: rosewood or composite
Barrel: 5 in.
Sights: fixed open
Weight: 39.0oz.
Caliber: .38 Super
Capacity: 9 + 1
Features: M1911 stainless models
available, aluminum trigger
**blue** . . . . . . . . . . . . . . . . . . . . . **$864**
**stainless** . . . . . . . . . . . . . . . . . . **$943**
**bright stainless** . . . . . . . . . . . . **$1152**

## 1991 SERIES
Action: autoloader
Grips: rosewood or composite
*Barrel:* 5 in.
*Sights:* fixed open
*Weight:* 39.0oz.
*Caliber:* .45 ACP
*Capacity:* 7 + 1
*Features:* M1911 Commander with
4.3 in. barrel available; both versions
in stainless or chrome moly
**1991** . . . . . . . . . . . . . . . . . . . **$699**
**stainless** . . . . . . . . . . . . . . . . . **$800**

## MODEL XSE
*Action:* autoloader
*Grips:* rosewood
*Barrel:* 5 in.
*Sights:* 3-dot
*Weight:* 39.0oz.
*Caliber:* .45 ACP
*Capacity:* 8 + 1
*Features:* stainless, M1911 with
extended ambidextrous safety,
upswept beavertail, slotted hammer
and trigger; also available as 4.3-in.
barreled Commander
**XSE** . . . . . . . . . . . . . . . . . . . . . **$950**

## GOLD CUP
*Action:* autoloader
*Grips:* black composite
*Barrel:* 5 in.
*Sights:* target
*Weight:* 39.0oz.
*Caliber:* .45 ACP
*Capacity:* 8 + 1
*Features:* stainless or chome-moly; Bo-
Mar or Eliason sights
**Gold Cup, blue.** . . . . . . . . . . . **$1050**
**stainless** . . . . . . . . . . . . . . . . . **$1116**

## DEFENDER
*Action:* autoloader
*Grips:* rubber finger-grooved
*Barrel:* 3 in.
*Sights:* 3-dot
*Weight:* 30.0oz.
*Caliber:* .45 ACP
*Capacity:* 7 + 1
*Features:* stainless M1911, extended
safety, upswept beavertail, beveled
magazine well
**Defender** . . . . . . . . . . . . . . . . **$842**

# Colt Handguns

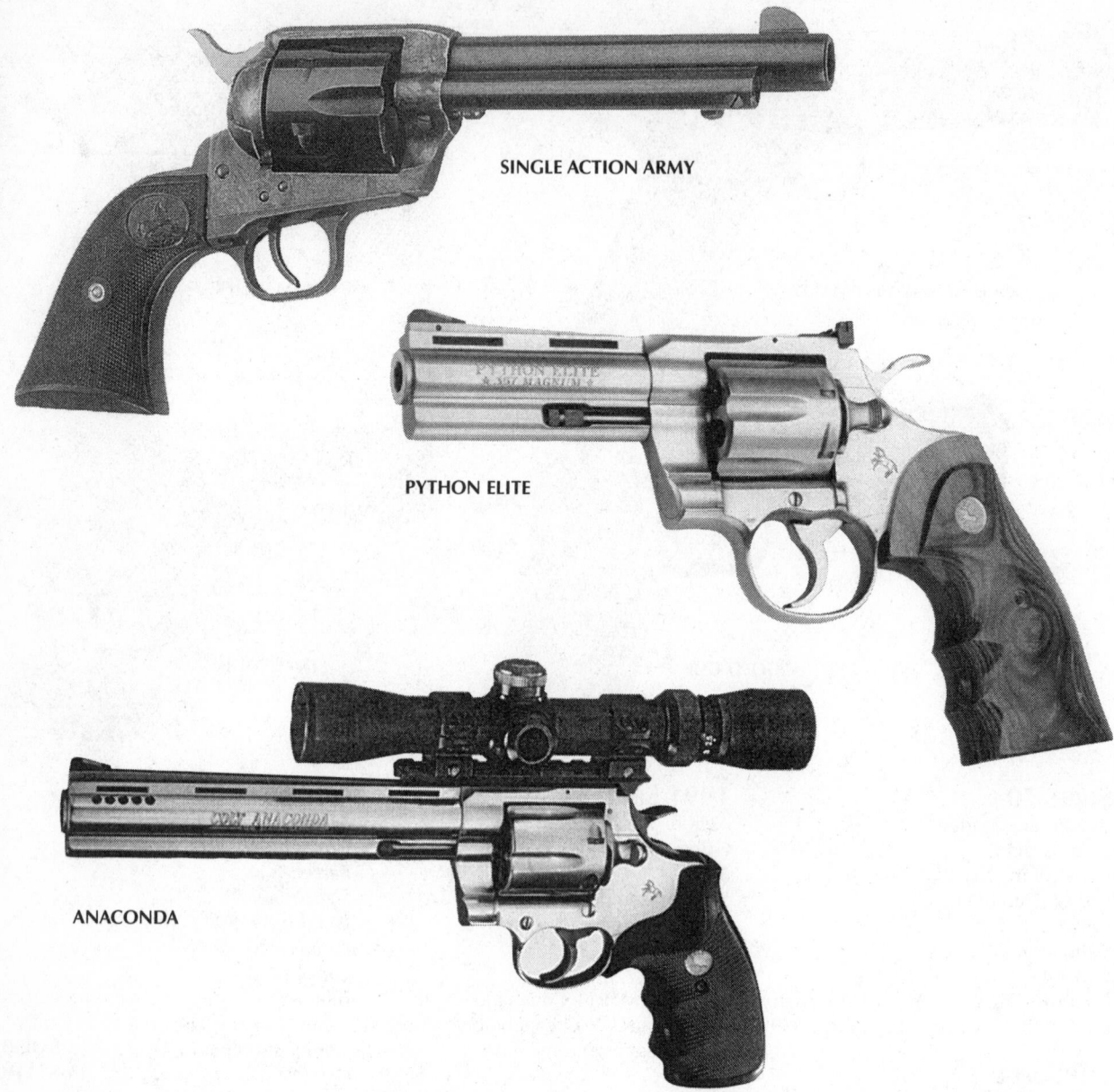

SINGLE ACTION ARMY

PYTHON ELITE

ANACONDA

### SINGLE ACTION ARMY
*Action:* single-action revolver
*Grips:* composite
*Barrel:* 4.3, 5.5 or 7.5 in.
*Sights:* fixed open
*Weight:* 46.0oz.
*Caliber:* .357 Mag., .44-40, .45 Colt
*Capacity:* 6
*Features:* case-colored frame, transfer bar, weight for .44-40, 48 oz. and 50 oz. for .45 Colt
**Single Action Army. . . . . . . . $1380**

### PYTHON ELITE
*Action:* double-action revolver
*Grips:* wood
*Barrel:* 4 or 6 in. (47 oz.)
*Sights:* target
*Weight:* 44.0oz.
*Caliber:* .357 Mag.
*Capacity:* 6
*Features:* stainless or chrome-moly;
**Python Elite . . . . . . . . . . . . . $1150**

### ANACONDA
*Action:* double-action revolver
*Grips:* rubber combat-style
*Barrel:* 4, 6 or 8 in. (ported)
*Sights:* target
*Weight:* 47.0oz.
*Caliber:* .44 Mag.
*Capacity:* 6
*Features:* ventilated rib, target trigger and hammer (weight depends on barrel length)
**4 or 6 in. . . . . . . . . . . . . . . . $1000**
**8 in. ported . . . . . . . . . . . . . $1050**

# Comanche Handguns

## MODEL II

*Action:* double-action revolver
*Grips:* rubber
*Barrel:* 3 or 6 in.
*Sights:* target
*Weight:* 22.0oz.
*Caliber:* .38 Spl.
(also in .22, .357, and .44)
*Capacity:* 6
*Features:* stainless or blue

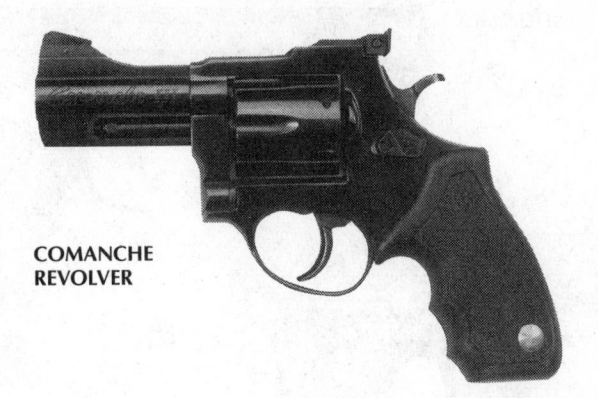

**COMANCHE REVOLVER**

| | |
|---|---|
| **Blue, 3 or 4 in.** | **$225** |
| **Stainless, 3 or 4 in.** | **$242** |
| **.22 blue, 6 in.** | **$242** |
| **.22 stainless, 6 in.** | **$267** |
| **.357 blue, 3, 4 or 6 in.** | **$259** |
| **.357 stainless, 3, 4 or 6 in.** | **$284** |
| **.44 Mag, 6 in. blue** | **$309** |
| **.44 Mag, 6 in. stainless** | **$334** |

## SUPER SINGLE SHOT

*Action:* hinged breech
*Grips:* composite
*Barrel:* 10 in.
*Sights:* target
*Weight:* 48.0oz.
*Caliber:* .45 LC/.410
*Capacity:* 1
*Features:* satin nickel finish (also in blue)

| | |
|---|---|
| **nickel.** | **$192** |
| **blue.** | **$175** |

**SUPER COMANCHE SINGLE SHOT**

 *Don't store handguns in leather; chemicals in leather can damage the steel.*

# CZ Handguns

MODEL 75B

MODEL 100B

MODEL 75 CHAMPION

MODEL 75 IPSC

MODEL 83

## MODEL 100

*Action:* autoloader
*Grips:* composite
*Barrel:* 3.9 in.
*Sights:* target
*Weight:* 24.0oz.
*Caliber:* 9mm, .40 S&W
*Capacity:* 10 + 1
*Features:* single or double action, decocking lever
Model 100 . . . . . . . . . . . . . . . $436

## MODEL 75

*Action:* autoloader
*Grips:* composite
*Barrel:* 4.7 in.
*Sights:* 3-dot
*Weight:* 35.0oz.
*Caliber:* 9mm or .40 S&W
*Capacity:* 10 + 1
*Features:* single or double action
9mm . . . . . . . . . . . . . . . . . . . $494
.40 S&W . . . . . . . . . . . . . . . . $510

## MODEL 75 CHAMPION

*Action:* autoloader
*Grips:* composite
*Barrel:* 4.5 in.
*Sights:* target
*Weight:* 35.0oz.
*Caliber:* 9 mm or .40 S&W
*Capacity:* 10 + 1
*Features:* also available: IPSC version with 5.4-in. barrel
Champion . . . . . . . . . . . . . . . $1598
IPSC. . . . . . . . . . . . . . . . . . . . $1118

## MODEL 83

*Action:* autoloader
*Grips:* composite
*Barrel:* 3.8 in.
*Sights:* fixed open
*Weight:* 26.0oz.
*Caliber:* 9mm
*Capacity:* 10 + 1
*Features:* single or double action
Model 83 . . . . . . . . . . . . . . . $408

## MODEL 85 COMBAT

*Action:* autoloader
*Grips:* composite
*Barrel:* 4.7 in.
*Sights:* target
*Weight:* 35.0oz.
*Caliber:* 9 mm
*Capacity:* 10 + 1
*Features:* single or double action
Combat . . . . . . . . . . . . . . . . . $582

## MODEL 97

*Action:* autoloader
*Grips:* composite
*Barrel:* 4.8 in.
*Sights:* fixed open
*Weight:* 41.0oz.
*Caliber:* .45 ACP
*Capacity:* 10 + 1
*Features:* single or double action
Model 97 . . . . . . . . . . . . . . . . $644

## COMPACT MODEL 75

*Action:* autoloader
*Grips:* composite
*Barrel:* 3.9 in.
*Sights:* fixed open
*Weight:* 32.0oz.
*Caliber:* 9 mm
*Capacity:* 10 + 1
*Features:* single or double action
Compact . . . . . . . . . . . . . . . . $523

## KADET MODEL 75

*Action:* autoloader
*Grips:* composite
*Barrel:* 4.9 in.
*Sights:* target
*Weight:* 38.0oz.
*Caliber:* .22 LR
*Capacity:* 10 + 1
*Features:* single or double action
Kadet. . . . . . . . . . . . . . . . . . . $495
.22 conversion kit
for CZ 75/85 . . . . . . . . . . . . . $291

MODEL 85 COMBAT

MODEL 97

MODEL 75
COMPACT

KADET MODEL 75

THE KADET
ADAPTER IN
ITS REAR
(COCKED)
POSITION

# Downsizer Handguns

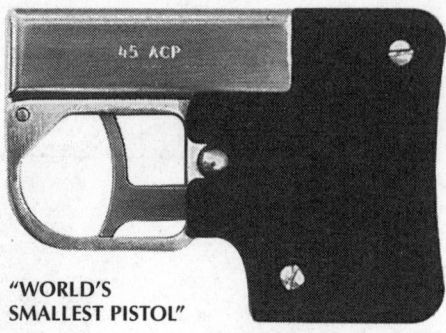

"WORLD'S SMALLEST PISTOL"

**WSP**
*Action:* hinged breech
*Grips:* composite
*Barrel:* 2.1 in.
*Sights:* none
*Weight:* 11.0oz.
*Caliber:* .357 Mag., .45 ACP
*Capacity:* 1
*Features:* double action only, stainless steel
**WSP** . . . . . . . . . . . . . . . . . . . **$499**

# Ed Brown Handguns

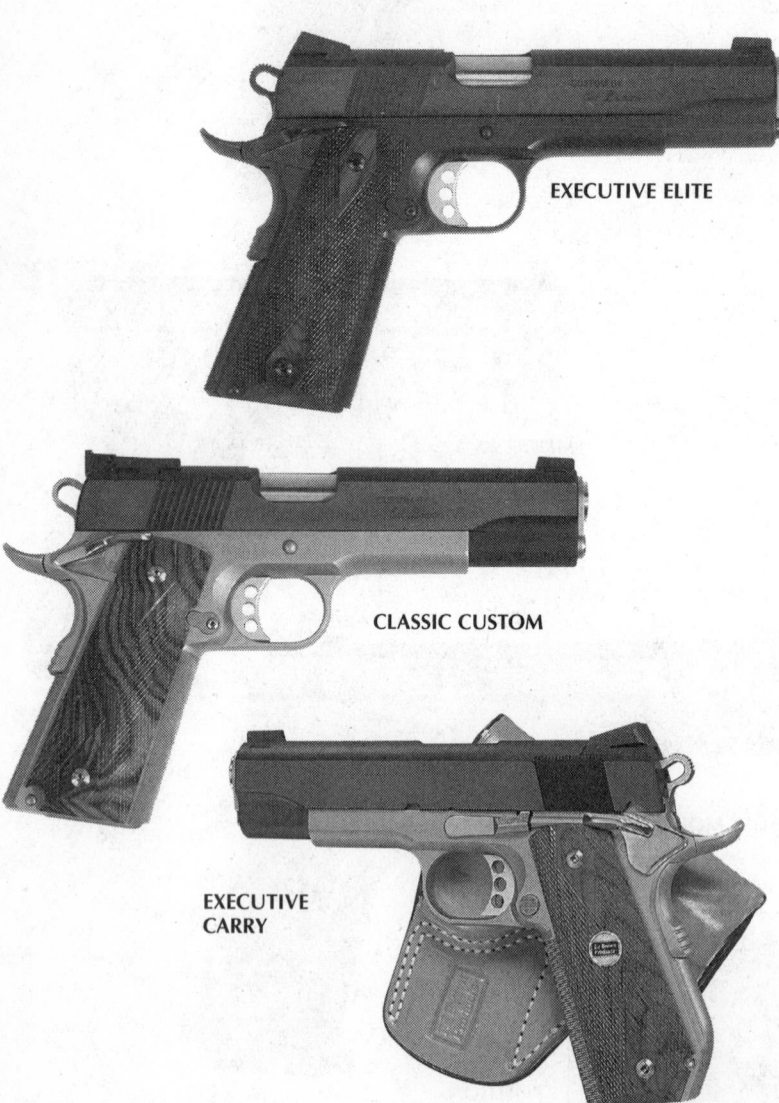

EXECUTIVE ELITE

CLASSIC CUSTOM

EXECUTIVE CARRY

### EXECUTIVE ELITE
*Action:* autoloader
*Grips:* Hogue wood
*Barrel:* 5 in.
*Sights:* to order
*Weight:* 34.0oz.
*Caliber:* .45 ACP
*Capacity:* 7 + 1 or more
*Features:* custom-grade M1911 Colt with many options to order
**base model.** . . . . . . . . . . . . . . **$2195**

### CLASSIC CUSTOM
*Action:* autoloader
*Grips:* Hogue wood
*Barrel:* 5 in.
*Sights:* target
*Weight:* 39.0oz.
*Caliber:* .45 ACP
*Capacity:* 7 + 1
*Features:* single action, M1911 Colt design, Bo-Mar sights; checkered forestrap, ambidextrous safety
**Classic Custom.** . . . . . . . . . . . **$2895**

### EXECUTIVE CARRY
*Action:* autoloader
*Grips:* Hogue exotic wood
*Barrel:* 4.3 in.
*Sights:* low-profile combat
*Weight:* 34.0oz.
*Caliber:* .45 ACP
*Capacity:* 7 + 1
*Features:* Bob-tail butt, checkered forestrap, stainless optional
**Commander Bobtail** . . . . . . . . **$2295**

# Ed Brown Handguns

## KOBRA

*Action:* autoloader
*Grips:* Hogue wood
*Barrel:* 5 in.
*Sights:* low-profile combat
*Weight:* 39.0oz.
*Caliber:* .45 ACP
*Capacity:* 7 + 1
*Features:* single-action M1911 Colt design, stainless models available

Kobra. . . . . . . . . . . . . . . . . . $1895

Kobra Carry
with 4.3-in. barrel . . . . . . . . $1995

KOBRA

KOBRA CARRY

# EMF Handguns

## MODEL 1873 DAKOTA

*Action:* single-action revolver
*Grips:* walnut
*Barrel:* 4.8, 5.5 and 7.5 in.
*Sights:* fixed open
*Weight:* 46.0oz.
*Caliber:* .357 Mag., .44-40, .45 Colt
*Capacity:* 6
*Features:* case-colored frame; barrel length determines weight

1873 Dakota . . . . . . . . . . . . . . $375

Buntline with
12 in. barrel, 55 oz. . . . . . . . . . $430

1873 DAKOTA SINGLE ACTION
WITH 5.5" BARREL

1873 HARTFORD "BUNTLINE"

# EMF Handguns

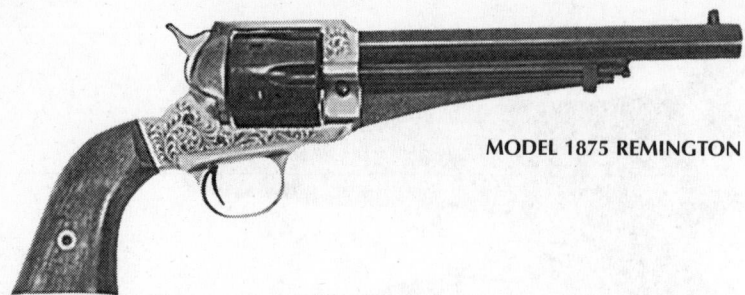

MODEL 1875 REMINGTON

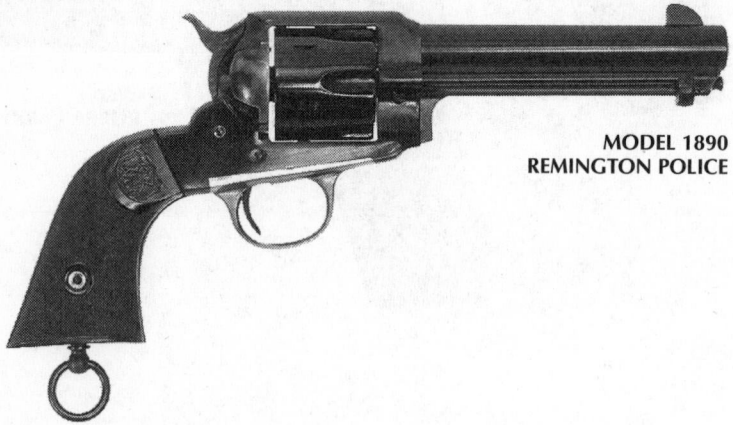

MODEL 1890
REMINGTON POLICE

HARTFORD
PINKERTON

### MODEL 1875 REMINGTON
*Action:* single-action revolver
*Grips:* walnut
*Barrel:* 5.5 or 7.5 in.
*Sights:* fixed open
*Weight:* 48.0oz.
*Caliber:* .357 Mag., .44, .45 Colt
*Capacity:* 6
*Features:* case-colored frame
Model 1875 . . . . . . . . . . . . . . $435
engraved . . . . . . . . . . . . . . . . $750

### MODEL 1890 REMINGTON POLICE
*Action:* single-action revolver
*Grips:* walnut
*Barrel:* 5.8 in.
*Sights:* fixed open
*Weight:* 48.0oz.
*Caliber:* .357 Mag., .44-40, .45 Colt
*Capacity:* 6
*Features:* lanyard loop,
case-colored frame
Model 1890 . . . . . . . . . . . . . . $450
engraved . . . . . . . . . . . . . . . . $750

### HARTFORD PINKERTON
*Action:* single-action revolver
*Grips:* walnut, birds-head
*Barrel:* 4 in.
*Sights:* fixed open
*Weight:* 44.0oz.
*Caliber:* .357, .45 Colt
*Capacity:* 6
*Features:* case-colored frame
Hartford Pinkerton . . . . . . . . $410

*Revolvers naturally point high when you jam the web of your hand firmly into the top of the grip. Locking the wrist brings them on target. Hold the grip low and you'll lose control.*

**BOXER P500**

**TACTICAL P325 PLUS**

## MODEL 500 BOXER

Action: autoloader
Grips: composite
Barrel: 5 in.
Sights: target
Weight: 44.0oz.
Caliber: .40 S&W, .45 ACP
Capacity: 10 + 1
Features: match-grade components
and fitting, stainless one-piece guide
*rod, lapped slide, flared ejection port*
*.45 ACP* . . . . . . . . . . . . . . . . . *$1399*
*.40 S&W*. . . . . . . . . . . . . . . . . *$1499*

## MEDALIST

*Action:* autoloader
*Grips:* composite
*Barrel:* 5 in.
*Sights:* target
*Weight:* 44.0oz.
*Caliber:* .40 S&W, .45 ACP

*Capacity:* 10 + 1
*Features:* up-turned beavertail, stainless hammer and sear, flared ejection
port, match trigger, lapped slide
**.45**. . . . . . . . . . . . . . . . . . . . . **$979**
**.40 S&W** . . . . . . . . . . . . . . . **$1099**

## TACTICAL P325 PLUS

*Action: autoloader*
*Grips:* composite
*Barrel:* 3.3 in.
*Sights:* low-profile combat
*Weight:* 37.0oz.
*Caliber:* .45 ACP
*Capacity:* 10 + 1
*Features:* extended ambidextrous safety,
lapped slide, up-turned beavertail,
skeleton trigger and hammer; Tactical
Ghost Ring or Novak sights; (also avail-
able with 4.3 and 5.0-inch barrels)
**Tactical** . . . . . . . . . . . . . . . . . **$979**

## TOURNAMENT

*Action:* autoloader
*Grips:* composite
*Barrel:* 5 in.
*Sights:* target
*Weight:* 44.0oz.
*Caliber:* .38 Super, .40 S&W, .45 ACP
*Capacity:* 10 + 1
*Features:* up-turned beavertail, extend-
ed thumb safety, front cocking
grooves, checkered front strap, all
match components; 2-lb. trigger
**TI with stainless bull barrel**. . . **$2300**
**TII with long slide** . . . . . . . . . **$2000**
**TIII ported, hard chromed,**
**fashioned for scope use** . . . . . **$2700**

# European American Armory Handguns

**WITNESS**

**BIG BORE BOUNTY HUNTER SINGLE ACTION**

**SMALL BORE BOUNTY HUNTER**

**WITNESS P COMPACT**

**WINDICATOR REVOLVER**

## BIG BORE BOUNTY HUNTER
*Action:* single-action revolver
*Grips:* walnut
*Barrel:* 4.5 or 7.5 in.
*Sights:* fixed open
*Weight:* 39 to 41 oz.
*Caliber:* .357 Mag., .44 Mag., .45 Colt
*Capacity:* 6
*Features:* case-colored or blued or nickel frame; version with 7.5 in. barrel weighs 42 oz.
Bounty Hunter . . . . . . . . . . . . $379
nickel. . . . . . . . . . . . . . . . . . . $399
Also available:
Small Bore Bounty Hunter
(.22 LR or .22 WMR) . . . . . . . $269
nickel. . . . . . . . . . . . . . . . . . . $299

## WINDICATOR
*Action:* double-action revolver
*Grips:* rubber
*Barrel:* 2 or 4 in.
*Sights:* fixed open
*Weight:* 36.0oz.
*Caliber:* .357 Mag., .38 Special
*Capacity:* 6
*Features:* transfer bar
.38, 2-inch . . . . . . . . . . . . . . . $249
.38, 4-inch; .357, 2-inch . . . . . $259
.357, 4-inch . . . . . . . . . . . . . . $279

## WITNESS
*Action:* autoloader
*Grips:* rubber
*Barrel:* 4.5 in.
*Sights:* 3-dot
*Weight:* 33.0oz.
*Caliber:* 9mm, .38 Super, .40 S&W, 10 mm, .45 ACP
*Capacity:* 10 + 1
*Features:* double action, polymer frame available

steel. . . . . . . . . . . . . . . . . . . . $449
polymer . . . . . . . . . . . . . . . . . $429
"Wonder" finish . . . . . . . . . . . $459

## WITNESS COMPACT
*Action:* autoloader
*Grips:* rubber
*Barrel:* 3.6 in.
*Sights:* 3-dot
*Weight:* 29.0oz.
*Caliber:* 9mm, .38 Super, .40 S&W, 10 mm, .45 ACP
*Capacity:* 10 + 1
*Features:* double action, polymer frame and ported barrels available
steel. . . . . . . . . . . . . . . . . . . . $449
polymer . . . . . . . . . . . . . . . . . $429
"Wonder" finish or
polymer ported . . . . . . . . . . . $459
"Wonder" finish, ported . . . . . $479

# Firestorm Handguns

## MODEL 380

*Action:* autoloader
*Grips:* rubber
*Barrel:* 3.5 in.
*Sights:* 3-dot
*Weight:* 23.0oz.
*Caliber:* .380
*Capacity:* 7 + 1
*Features:* double action, also available in .22 LR, 10-shot magazine
Model 380 . . . . . . . . . . . . . . . $265
Duotone . . . . . . . . . . . . . . . . $275

## MODEL 45

*Action:* autoloader
*Grips:* rubber
*Barrel:* 4.3 or 5.2 in.
*Sights:* 3-dot
*Weight:* 34.0oz.
*Caliber:* .45 ACP
*Capacity:* 7 + 1
*Features:* single action, 1911 Colt design, from cocking grooves
Model 45 . . . . . . . . . . . . . . . . $325
Duotone . . . . . . . . . . . . . . . . $334

## MINI

*Action:* autoloader
*Grips:* polymer
*Barrel:* 3.5 in.
*Sights:* target
*Weight:* 24.5oz.
*Caliber:* 9mm, .40 S&W, .45 ACP
*Capacity:* 10 + 1 (7 + 1 in .45)
*Features:* double action
Mini . . . . . . . . . . . . . . . . . . . . $384
Duotone . . . . . . . . . . . . . . . . $392
Duotone .45 . . . . . . . . . . . . . . $400
nickel . . . . . . . . . . . . . . . . . . $409
.45 nickel . . . . . . . . . . . . . . . $417

**MODEL 380**

**MODEL 45**

**MINI**

# Freedom Arms Handguns

HANDGUNS

**MODEL 83
454 CASULL FIELD GRADE**

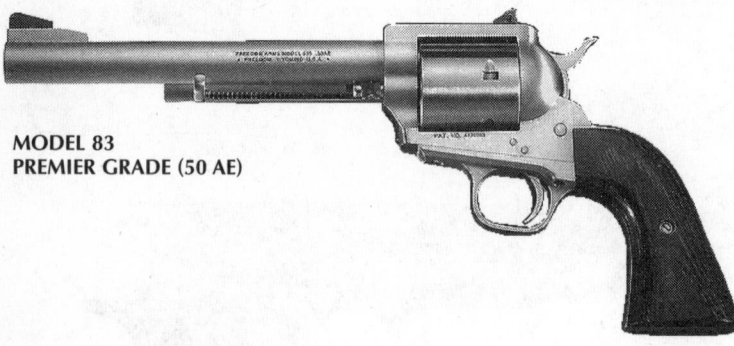

**MODEL 83
PREMIER GRADE (50 AE)**

**MODEL 83 RIMFIRE
SILHOUETTE CLASS 10" BARREL**

**MODEL 97
PREMIER GRADE**

## MODEL 83

*Action:* single-action revolver
*Grips:* Pachmayr rubber or hardwood
*Barrel:* 4.8, 6.0, 7.5 or 10 in.
*Sights:* target
*Weight:* 50.0oz.
*Caliber:* .357 Mag., .41 Mag., .44
Mag., .454 Casull, .475 Linebaugh, .50
AE
*Capacity:* 5
*Features:* sights and scope mounts and
extra cylinders optional
field grade . . . . . . . . . . . . . . $1527
field grade, adjustable sights . . $1591
premier grade. . . . . . . . . . . . $1976
premier grade,
adjustable sights . . . . . . . . . . $2058

## MODEL 83 RIMFIRE

*Action:* single-action revolver
*Grips:* Micarta or laminated
*Barrel:* heavy 5.1, 7.5 or 10 in.
*Sights:* target
*Weight:* 50.0oz.
*Caliber:* .22 LR
*Capacity:* 6
*Features:* dual firing pin, version with
7.5 in. barrel weighs 58 oz., 10-inch
barrel, 63 oz.; magnum cylinder avail-
able
Model 83 . . . . . . . . . . . . . . . $1828
with 10-inch barrel. . . . . . . . . $1902

## MODEL 97 PREMIER

*Action:* single-action revolver
*Grips:* Micarta or laminated
*Barrel:* 4.5, 5.5, 7.5 or 10 in.
*Sights:* target
*Weight:* 36.0oz.
*Caliber:* .17 HMR, .32 H&R, .357
Mag., .41 Mag., .44 Mag., .45 Colt
*Capacity:* 5
*Features:* weight varies to 42 oz.
depending on barrel length; .22 rimfire
version available
Premier . . . . . . . . . . . . . . . . $1668
.22 . . . . . . . . . . . . . . . . . . . $1732

# Glock Handguns

**MODEL G19**

**MODEL G17**

**9X19**

**MODEL G27**

**MODEL G23**

**PORTED BARREL**

**MODEL G22**

**.40**

**MODEL G33**

**MODEL G26**

**MODEL G31**

**.357**

**MODEL G29**

**MODEL G20**

**10MM**

**9X19**

**MODEL G34**

**MODEL G30**

**MODEL G17**

**9X19**

**.40**

**MODEL G35**

## COMPACT PISTOLS
*Action:* autoloader
*Grips:* composite
*Barrel:* 3.8 in.
*Sights:* fixed open
*Weight:* 21.2oz.
*Caliber:* 9mm, .40 S&W, .357 Mag., 10 mm, .45 ACP
*Capacity:* 9, 10, 13, 15 depending on cartridge, magazine
*Features:* trigger safety, double action, 10 mm and .45 ACP weigh 24.0 oz.
*Compact Pistols . . . . price on request*

## FULL-SIZE PISTOLS
*Action:* autoloader
*Grips:* composite
*Barrel:* 4.5 in.
*Sights:* fixed open
*Weight:* 22.3oz.
*Caliber:* 9 mm, .40 S&W, .357 Mag., 10 mm, .45 ACP
*Capacity:* 10, 13, 15, 17 depending on cartridge
*Features:* trigger safety, double action, 10 mm and .45 ACP weigh 26.3 oz.
*Full-Size . . . . . . . . . price on request*

## SUBCOMPACT PISTOLS
*Action:* autoloader
*Grips:* composite
*Barrel:* 3.5 in.
*Sights:* fixed open
*Weight:* 19.8oz.
*Caliber:* 9mm, .40 S&W, .357, .45
*Capacity:* 9, 10, 6, depending on cartridge, magazine
*Features:* trigger safety, double action
*Subcompact . . . . . . price on request*

# Glock Handguns

**G36 SLIMLINE**

### G-36 SLIMLINE
*Action:* autoloader
*Grips:* synthetic
*Barrel:* 3.8 in.
*Sights:* fixed open
*Weight:* 21.0oz.
*Caliber:* .45 ACP
*Capacity:* 6 + 1
*Features:* single-stack magazine for thinner grip
G36 . . . . . . . . . . . **price on request**

### G-37 SLIMLINE
*Action*: autoloader
*Grips*: synthetic
*Barrel*: 24-30 in.
*Sights:fixed* open
*Weight*:
*Caliber*:  .45 Glock
*Capacity*:  10 + 1
*Features*:  chambered for .45 Glock shortened 45 ACP cartridge
G-37: . . . . . . . . . . . **price on request**

**G37 SLIMLINE**

*The new .45 GAP – Glock Automatic Pistol – delivers the punch of a .45 ACP in a slightly shorter case, which fits more compact pistols designed around the 9mm Parabellum.*

# Hammerli Handguns

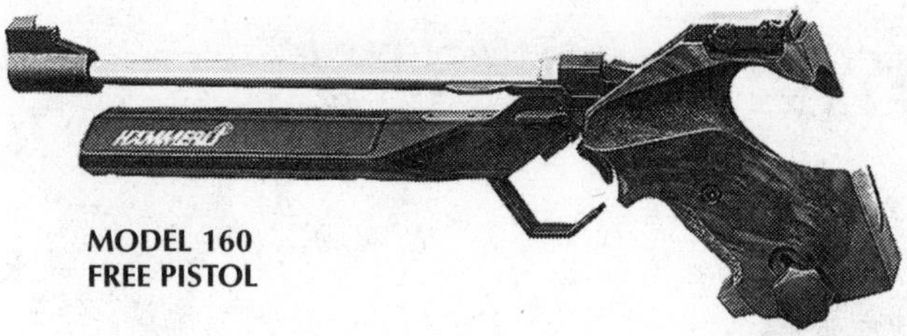

MODEL 160
FREE PISTOL

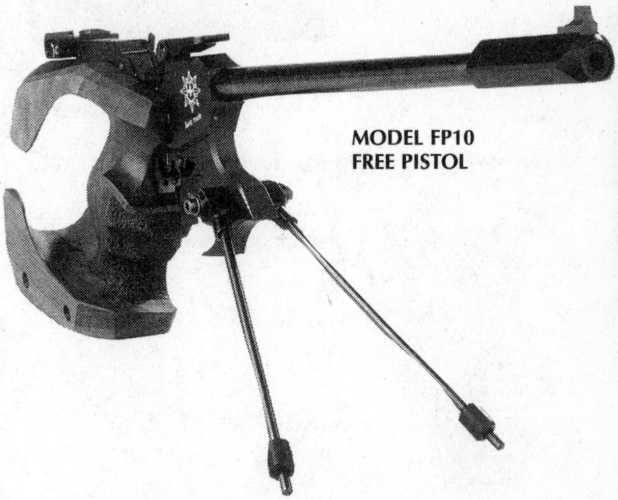

MODEL FP10
FREE PISTOL

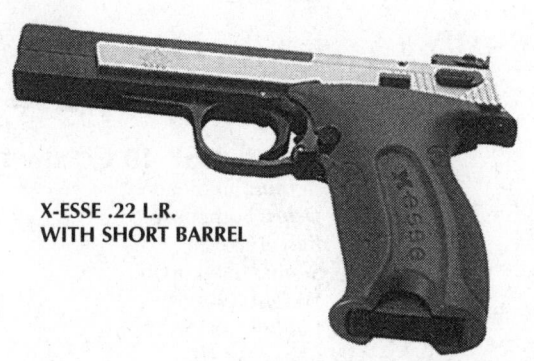

HAMMERLI SP 20

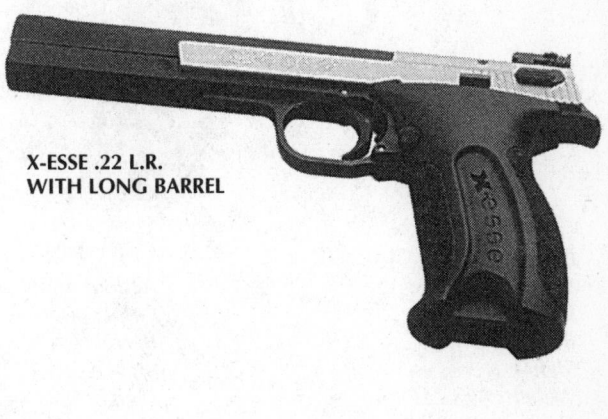

X-ESSE .22 L.R.
WITH LONG BARREL

X-ESSE .22 L.R.
WITH SHORT BARREL

## MODEL FP10 FREE PISTOL
*Action:* Martini
*Grips:* walnut target
*Barrel:* 11.3 in.
*Sights:* target
*Weight:* 45.0oz.
*Caliber:* .22 LR
*Capacity:* 1
*Features:* side-mounted locking lever, fully adjustable trigger
**Model FP10 with integral compensator** . . . . . . . . . . . . . . . . . . . $2041

## MODEL SP20
### ACTION: AUTOLOADER
*Grips:* synthetic
*Barrel:* 4.6 in.
*Sights:* target
*Weight:* 40.0oz.
*Caliber:* .22 LR, .32 S&W
*Capacity:* 5
*Features:* front-end magazine
**.22** . . . . . . . . . . . . . . . . . . . . . $1668
**.32** . . . . . . . . . . . . . . . . . . . . . $1743

## MODEL X-ESSE SPORT
### ACTION: AUTOLOADER
*Grips:* composite
*Barrel:* 4.5 or 5.5 in.
*Sights:* target
*Weight:* 36.0oz.
*Caliber:* .22 LR
*Capacity:* 10
*Features:* single action
**X-ESSE** . . . . . . . . . . . . . . . . . $710

# Heckler & Koch Handguns

MARK 23
SPECIAL OP

USP 45 TACTICAL
PISTOL

MODEL P7M8

COMPACT LEM

USP 45
UNIVERSAL
SELF-LOADING PISTOL

USP EXPERT

## Mark 23 Special OP

*Action:* autoloader
*Grips:* polymer
*Barrel:* 5.9 in.
*Sights:* 3-dot
*Weight:* 42.0oz.
*Caliber:* .45 ACP
*Capacity:* 10 + 1
*Features:* military version of USP
Mark 23 Special OP . . . . . . . . $2212

## Model P7M8

*Action:* autoloader
*Grips:* polymer
*Barrel:* 4.1 in.
*Sights:* target
*Weight:* 28.0oz.
*Caliber:* 9mm
*Capacity:* 8 + 1
*Features:* blue or nickel finish
Model P7M8 . . . . . . . . . . . . . $1515

## USP 45

*Action:* autoloader
*Grips:* polymer
*Barrel:* 4.4 in.
*Sights:* 3-dot
*Weight:* 30.0oz.
*Caliber:* .45 ACP
*Capacity:* 10 + 1
*Features:* short-recoil action
USP 45 . . . . . . . . . . . . . . . . . $839

## USP 9 & 40

*Action:* autoloader
*Grips:* polymer
*Barrel:* 4.25 in.
*Sights:* 3-dot
*Weight:* 27.0oz.
*Caliber:* 9mm, .40 S&W
*Capacity:* 10 + 1
*Features:* short-recoil action,
also in kit form
USP . . . . . . . . . . . . . . . . . . . . $769

## Model USP 40 Compact LEM

*Action:* autoloader
*Grips:* composite
*Barrel:* 3.6 in.
*Sights:* fixed open
*Weight:* 24.0oz.
*Caliber:* .40 S&W
*Capacity:* 10
*Features:* double-action only with
improved trigger pull; also in 9mm
USP40 . . . . . . . . . . . . . . . . . $821

## Model USP Elite

*Action:* autoloader
*Grips:* composite
*Barrel:* 6.2 in.
*Sights:* target
*Weight:* 36.0oz.
*Caliber:* 9mm, .45 ACP
*Capacity:* 10
*Features:* short recoil action, fiber-
reinforced polymer frame; universal
scope mounting groves, ambidextrous
magazine release
USP Elite . . . . . . . . . . . . . . . $1533

# Heckler & Koch Handguns

## USP 40 COMPACT LEM

*Action:* autoloader
*Grips:* composite
*Barrel:* 3.6 in.
*Sights:* fixed open
*Weight:* 24.0oz.
*Caliber:* .40 S&W
*Capacity:* 10
*Features:* double-action only with improved trigger pull; also in 9mm
**USP40** . . . . . . . . . . . . . . . . . . . **$821**

## USP ELITE

*Action:* autoloader
*Grips:* composite
*Barrel:* 6.2 in.
*Sights:* target
*Weight:* 36.0oz.
*Caliber:* 9mm, .45 ACP
*Capacity:* 10
*Features:* short recoil action, fiber-reinforced polymer frame; universal scope mounting groves, ambidextrous magazine release
**USP Elite** . . . . . . . . . . . . . . . **$1533**

USP 40 COMPACT LEM

USP ELITE

# Heritage Handguns

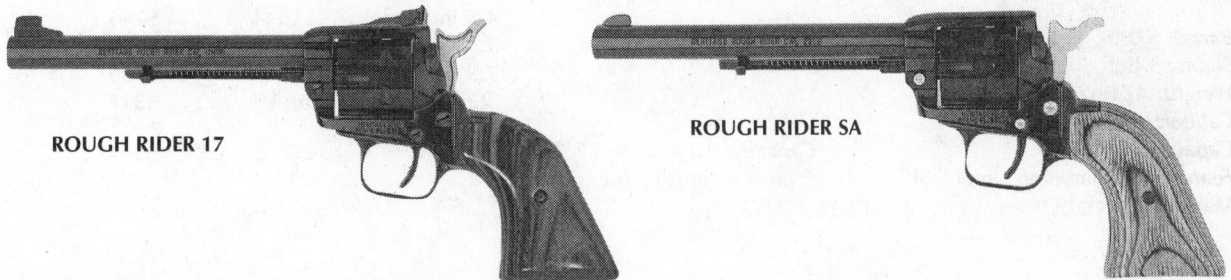

ROUGH RIDER 17

ROUGH RIDER SA

## ROUGH RIDER

*Action:* single-action revolver
*Grips:* hardwood, regular or birdshead
*Barrel:* 3.5, 4.75, 6.5, 9 in.
*Sights:* fixed open
*Weight:* 31.0oz.
*Caliber:* .22, .22 LR (.22 WMR cylinder available)
*Capacity:* 6
*Features:* action on Colt 1873 pattern, transfer bar, satin or blued finish,

weight to 38 oz. dependent on barrel length
**Rough Rider** . . . . . . . . . . . . . . **$145**
**with WMR cylinder** . . . . . . . . . **$160**
**satin, with WMR cylinder** . . . . . **$200**
**satin, adjustable sights,**
**WMR cylinder** . . . . . . . . . . . . . **$240**

## ROUGH RIDER IN .17 HMR

*Action:* single-action revolver
*Grips:* laminated camo
*Barrel:* 6.5 or 9 in.
*Sights:* adjustable
*Weight:* 38.0oz.
*Caliber:* .17 HMR
*Capacity:* 6
*Features:* Williams Fire Red ramp front sight and Millet rear
**Rough Rider** . . . . . . . . . . . . . . **$240**

# High Standard Handguns

**SUPERMATIC CITATION MS**

**SUPERMATIC TROPHY**

**VICTOR**

### SUPERMATIC CITATION
*Action:* autoloader
*Grips:* walnut
*Barrel:* 10 in.
*Sights:* target
*Weight:* 54.0oz.
*Caliber:* .22 LR
*Capacity:* 10 + 1
*Features:* optional scope mount, slide conversion kit for .22 short
**Citation . . . . . . . . . . . . . . . . . $775**
**slide conversion kit . . . . . . . . . $317**

### SUPERMATIC TROPHY
*Action:* autoloader
*Grips:* walnut
*Barrel:* 5.5 (bull) or 7.3 (fluted) in.
*Sights:* target
*Weight:* 44.0oz.
*Caliber:* .22 LR
*Capacity:* 10 + 1
*Features:* left-hand grip optional
**5.5 in. barrel . . . . . . . . . . . . . . $795**
**7.3 in barrel (46 oz.) . . . . . . . . $845**

### VICTOR
*Action:* autoloader
*Grips:* walnut
*Barrel:* 4.5 or 5.5 in.
*Sights:* target
*Weight:* 45.0oz.
*Caliber:* .22 LR
*Capacity:* 10 + 1
*Features:* optional slide conversion kit for .22 Short
**4.5 in. barrel . . . . . . . . . . . . . . $745**
**5.5 in. barrel (46 oz.) . . . . . . . . $745**
**7.5 in. barrel . . . . . . . . . . . . . . $755**
**.22 Short conversion kit . . . . . . $317**

*Pistoleers concentrate on three things: sight alignment, sight alignment and sight alignment. A bit of wobble, slight movement of the sight off target matter little. Poor sight alignment is fatal.*

# High Standard Handguns

### OLYMPIC MILITARY
*Action:* autoloader
*Grips:* walnut
*Barrel:* 5.5 in.
*Sights:* target
*Weight:* 44.0oz.
*Caliber:* .22 LR
*Capacity:* 10 + 1
*Features:* single action, blowback mechanism
**Olympic Military** . . . . . . . . . . **$795**

OLYMPIC

### OLYMPIC RAPID-FIRE
*Action:* autoloader
*Grips:* walnut
*Barrel:* 4 in.
*Sights:* target
*Weight:* 46.0oz.
*Caliber:* .22 short
*Capacity:* 5
*Features:* push-button take-down, adjustable match trigger
**Rapid-Fire** . . . . . . . . . . . . . . **$1027**

OLYMPIC RAPID FIRE

# Hi-Point Handguns

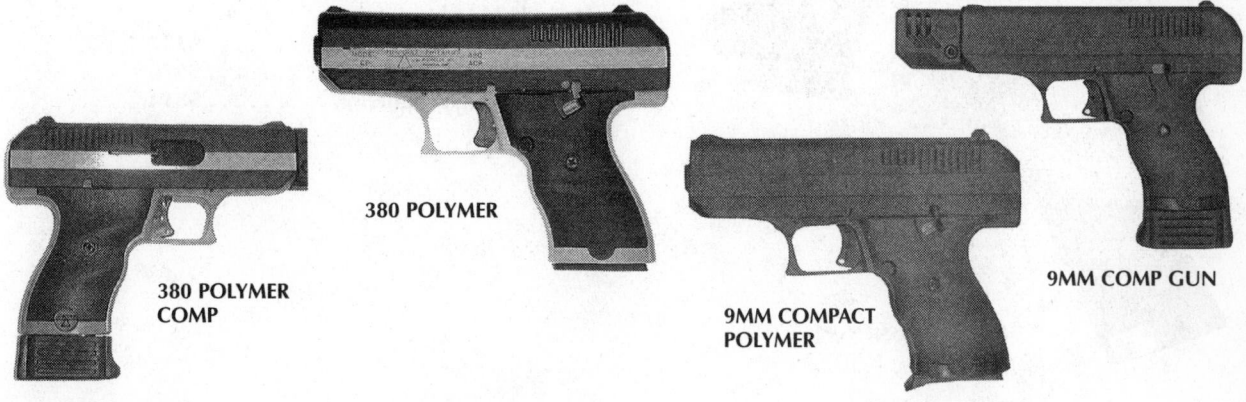

380 POLYMER

380 POLYMER COMP

9MM COMPACT POLYMER

9MM COMP GUN

### 380 POLYMER
*Action:* autoloader
*Grips:* polymer
*Barrel:* 3.5 in.
*Sights:* 3-dot
*Weight:* 30.0oz.
*Caliber:* .380
*Capacity:* 8 + 1 (10-shot magazine available)
*Features:* last-round lock-open; comp model has 4 in. barrel
**380 Polymer**. . . . . . . . . . . . . . **$100**
**comp**. . . . . . . . . . . . . . . . . . . . **$125**
**with laser sight**. . . . . . . . . . . . **$190**

### 9MM POLYMER
*Action:* autoloader
*Grips:* polymer
*Barrel:* 3.5 in.
*Sights:* 3-dot
*Weight:* 30.0oz.
*Caliber:* 9mm
*Capacity:* 8 + 1 (10-shot magazine available)
*Features:* last-round lock-open, comp model has 4 in. barrel
**9mm Polymer**. . . . . . . . . . . . . **$137**
**comp**. . . . . . . . . . . . . . . . . . . . **$159**
**with laser sight**. . . . . . . . . . . . **$219**

### BIG BORE PISTOL
*Action:* autoloader
*Grips:* polymer
*Barrel:* 4.5 in.
*Sights:* 3-dot
*Weight:* 32.0oz.
*Caliber:* .45 ACP, .40 S&W
*Capacity:* 9 + 1, 10 + 1
*Features:* last-round lock-open
**Big Bore**. . . . . . . . . . . . . . . . . **$169**
**.45 ACP with laser** . . . . . . . . . . **$239**
**.40 S&W with laser** . . . . . . . . . **$239**

# Kahr Handguns

MODEL P40

MODEL P9

## MODEL P40

*Action:* autoloader
*Grips:* polymer
*Barrel:* 3.5 in.
*Sights:* fixed open
*Weight:* 18.7oz.
*Caliber:* .40 S&W
*Capacity:* 6 + 1
*Features:* hammerless double action

| | |
|---|---|
| P40 | $676 |
| stainless | $719 |
| Elite stainless | $783 |
| P40 with 3 in. bbl. | $707 |
| Stainless. | $719 |
| Elite stainless | $783 |

## MODEL P9

*Action:* autoloader
*Grips:* polymer
*Barrel:* 3.5 in.
*Sights:* fixed open
*Weight:* 17.7oz.
*Caliber:* 9mm
*Capacity:* 7 + 1
*Features:* hammerless double action

| | |
|---|---|
| P9 | $676 |
| stainless | $719 |
| Elite stainless | $783 |
| PM9 (3″ bbl., black frame, stainless slide) | $737 |
| 4 in. target bbl. | $676 |
| with night sights | $814 |

*Before transporting handguns across state lines, be aware of laws that may require you to case or otherwise secure the gun in your car. Concealed-carry rules differ too.*

# Kel-Tec Handguns

**P-11 CALIBER**

**P-32 CALIBER .32 AUTO**

**SUB RIFLE 2000 (READY TO FIRE)**

**SUB RIFLE 2000
CALIBERS 9MM
& 40 S&W**

## MODEL P-11
*Action:* autoloader
*Grips:* polymer
*Barrel:* 3.1 in.
*Sights:* fixed open
*Weight:* 14.4oz.
*Caliber:* 9mm
Capacity: 10 + 1
*Features:* locked-breech mechanism
**P-11** . . . . . . . . . . . . . . . . . . . **$314**
**parkerized** . . . . . . . . . . . . . . . **$355**
**chrome** . . . . . . . . . . . . . . . . . . **$368**

## MODEL P-32
*Action:* autoloader
*Grips:* polymer
*Barrel:* 2.7 in.
*Sights:* fixed open
*Weight:* 6.6oz.
*Caliber:* .32 Auto
*Capacity:* 7 + 1
*Features:* locked-breech mechanism
**P-3AT** . . . . . . . . . . . . . . . . . . . **$300**
**parkerized** . . . . . . . . . . . . . . . **$340**
**chrome** . . . . . . . . . . . . . . . . . . **$355**

## MODEL P-3AT
*Action:* autoloader
*Grips:* polymer
*Barrel:* 2.8 in.
*Sights:* fixed open
*Weight:* 7.3oz.
*Caliber:* .380
*Capacity:* 6 + 1

*Features:* locked-breech mechanism
**P-3AT** . . . . . . . . . . . . . . . . . . . **$305**
**parkerized** . . . . . . . . . . . . . . . **$345**
**chrome** . . . . . . . . . . . . . . . . . . **$355**

## SUB RIFLE 2000
*Action:* autoloader
*Grips:* polymer
*Barrel:* 16 in.
*Sights:* target
*Weight:* 64.0oz.
*Caliber:* 9mm and .40 S&W
*Capacity:* 10 + 1
*Features:* take-down,
uses pistol magazines
**Sub Rifle** . . . . . . . . . . . . . . . . . **$383**
**SU-16 in .223** . . . . . . . . . . . . . **$640**

# Kimber Handguns

**CUSTOM CDP II**

**COMPACT II & PRO CARRY II**

**CUSTOM II & CUSTOM TARGET II**

**ECLIPSE TARGET II**

In 1995, following bankruptcy proceedings at Kimber of Oregon, handgun sports were becoming more popular, and many people were concerned with the effect of stricter regulations on the availability of handguns. New Kimber owner, Les Edelman thought there'd be a market for high-quality pistols based on the 1911 Colt. He enlisted the reputation and expertise of ace pistol shooter Chip McCormick, bought a factory in Yonkers and began turning out pistols, projecting a run of 5000. His projection proved conservative; in 2002 the Kimber plant sold more than 44,000 Model 1911-style pistols, eclipsing its closest seven competitors combined. Since then the Kimber line has grown to include target and tactical pistols, as well as those for sporting use, home defense and concealed carry.

## CDP 11 SERIES
**Action:** autoloader
**Grips:** rosewood
**Barrel:** 3, 4, or 5 in.
**Sights:** low-profile night
**Weight:** 25 – 31 oz.
**Caliber:** .45 ACP

**Capacity:** 7 + 1
**Features:** alloy frame, stainless slide; also in 4 in. (Pro Carry and Compact) and 3 in. (Ultra) configurations
CDP . . . . . . . . . . . . . . . . . . . . . **$1141**

## COMPACT STAINLESS II
**Action:** autoloader
**Grips:** synthetic
**Barrel:** 4 in.
**Sights:** low-profile combat
**Weight:** 34.0oz.
**Caliber:** .45 ACP
**Capacity:** 7 + 1
**Features:** shortened single action 1911 Colt design; also Pro Carry with alloy frame at 28 oz.; match-grade bushingless bull barrel
Compact II . . . . . . . . . . . . . . . . **$889**
Pro Carry II . . . . . . . . . . . . . . . **$789**
Pro Carry II stainless . . . . . . . . **$862**
Pro Carry HD II . . . . . . . . . . . . **$897**

## CUSTOM II
**Action:** autoloader
**Grips:** synthetic or rosewood
**Barrel:** 5 in.
**Sights:** target
**Weight:** 38.0oz.
**Caliber:** .38 Super, .40 S&W, .45 ACP
**Capacity:** 7 + 1

**Features:** single action, 1911 Colt design, front cocking serrations, skeleton trigger and hammer
Custom II . . . . . . . . . . . . . . . . . **$745**
Stainless II . . . . . . . . . . . . . . . . **$848**
Target II . . . . . . . . . . . . . . . . . . **$854**
Target II stainless . . . . . . . . . . . **$964**

## ECLIPSE II
**Action:** autoloader
**Grips:** laminated
**Barrel:** 5 in.
**Sights:** 3-dot night
**Weight:** 38.0oz.
**Caliber:** .45 ACP
**Capacity:** 7 + 1
**Features:** matte-black oxide finish polished bright on flats; also 3-inch Ultra and 4-inch Pro Carry versions; sights also available in low profile combat or target
Eclipse II . . . . . . . . . . . . . . . . . **$1074**
Target II . . . . . . . . . . . . . . . . . . **$1177**
Ultra II . . . . . . . . . . . . . . . . . . . **$1074**
Pro II . . . . . . . . . . . . . . . . . . . . **$1074**
Pro Target II . . . . . . . . . . . . . . . **$1177**

GOLD COMBAT II

STAINLESS GOLD
MATCH II

STAINLESS
ULTRA CARRY II

## GOLD COMBAT II

*Action:* autoloader
*Grips:* rosewood
*Barrel:* 5 in.
*Sights:* low-profile night
*Weight:* 38.0oz.
*Caliber:* .45 ACP
*Capacity:* 7 + 1
*Features:* M1911 Colt design with many refinements: checkered front strap, match bushing, ambidextrous safety, stainless match barrel
Gold Combat II . . . . . . . . . . . $1716
Gold Combat Stainless II . . . . $1657

## GOLD MATCH II

*Action:* autoloader
*Grips:* rosewood
*Barrel:* 5 in.
*Sights:* adjustable target

*Weight:* 38.0oz.
*Caliber:* .45 ACP
*Capacity:* 7 + 1
*Features:* single action 1911 Colt design; match components, ambidextrous safety
Gold Match II . . . . . . . . . . . . $1192
Stainless. . . . . . . . . . . . . . . . $1342
Stainless in .40 S&W. . . . . . . $1373
Team Match II . . . . . . . . . . . . . . . . $1310

## TEN II HIGH CAPACITY

*Action:* autoloader
*Grips:* polymer
*Barrel:* 5 in.
*Sights:* low-profile combat
*Weight:* 34.0oz.
*Caliber:* .45 ACP
*Capacity:* 10 + 1

*Features:* double-stack magazine, polymer frame; also in 4 in. (Pro Carry) configuration, from 32 oz.
Stainless Ten II . . . . . . . . . . . . $771
Pro Carry Ten II . . . . . . . . . . . . $786
Gold Match Ten II . . . . . . . . . $1061

## ULTRA CARRY II

*Action:* autoloader
*Grips:* synthetic
*Barrel:* 3 in.
*Sights:* low-profile combat
*Weight:* 25.0oz.
*Caliber:* .40 S&W, .45 ACP
*Capacity:* 7 + 1
*Features:* smallest commercial 1911-style pistol
Ultra Carry II. . . . . . . . . . . . . $783
Stainless II . . . . . . . . . . . . . . . $858
Stainless II in .40 S&W . . . . . . . $903

# Llama Handguns

**MAX-I 45
GOVERNMENT
DUOTONE FINISH**

**MICROMAX .380
MATTE FINISH**

**MINIMAX .45 SATIN
CHROME FINISH**

## MAX-I GOVERNMENT
*Action:* autoloader
*Grips:* rubber
*Barrel:* 5 in.
*Sights:* 3-dot
*Weight:* 38.0oz.
*Caliber:* .45 ACP
*Capacity:* 7 + 1
*Features:* single action M1911 Colt design; extended safety, beavertail, Duotone finish
**Max-I. . . . . . . . . . . . . . . . . . . $389**

## MICROMAX .380
*Action:* autoloader
*Grips:* polymer
*Barrel:* 4 in.
*Sights:* 3-dot
*Weight:* 29.0oz.
*Caliber:* .380, .32 ACP
*Capacity:* 7 + 1, 8 + 1
*Features:* extended safety
**matte. . . . . . . . . . . . . . . . . . . $292**
**satin chrome . . . . . . . . . . . . . $309**

## MINIMAX .45
*Action:* autoloader
*Grips:* rubber
*Barrel:* 3 in.
*Sights:* 3-dot
*Weight:* 28.0oz.
*Caliber:* .40 S&W, .45 ACP
*Capacity:* 7 + 1 (.40), 6 + 1 (.45)
*Features:* single-action M1911 Colt design; extended beavertail grip
**matte. . . . . . . . . . . . . . . . . . . $342**
**Duo-Tone. . . . . . . . . . . . . . . . $350**
**satin chrome . . . . . . . . . . . . . $359**

*Autoloaders with a de-cocking device can be carried safely with a round in the chamber.*

# Magnum Research Handguns

## BABY EAGLE

*Action:* autoloader
*Grips:* plastic composite
*Barrel:* 3.5, 4, 4.5 in.
*Sights:* 3-dot combat
*Weight:* 26.8 – 39.8 oz.
*Caliber:* 9mm, .40 S&W, .45 ACP
*Capacity:* 10
*Features:* squared,
serrated trigger guard
**Baby Eagle** . . . . . . . . . . . . . . . . **$499**

## MARK XIX DESERT EAGLE

*Action:* autoloader
*Grips:* plastic composite
*Barrel:* 6 or 10 in.
*Sights:* fixed combat
*Weight:* 70.2 oz.
*Caliber:* .357 Mag., .44 Mag., .50 AE
*Capacity:* 9 + 1, 8 + 1, 7 + 1
*Features:* gas operated; all with polyg-
onal rifling, integral scope bases
**Desert Eagle, 6 in. barrel** . . . . **$1249**
**10 in. barrel (79 oz.)** . . . . . . . **$1349**
**6 in. chrome or nickel** . . . . . . **$1489**
**6 in. Titaniums/gold** . . . . . . . . **$1749**

## BFR (BIGGEST FINEST REVOLVER)

*Action:* single-action revolver
*Grips:* rubber
*Barrel:* 6.5, 7.5 or 10 in.
*Sights:* open adjustable
*Weight:* 50 – 67.3 oz.
*Caliber:* .45/70, .444, .450, .500 S&W,
.30-30 Win. (long cylinder), .480
Ruger, .475 Linbaugh, .22 Hornet,
.45 Colt/.410, .50 AE  (short cylinder)
*Capacity:* 5
*Features:* both short and long-cylinder
models entirely of stainless steel
**BRF** . . . . . . . . . . . . . . . . . . . . . **$999**

BABY EAGLE

DESERT EAGLE PISTOL
MARK XIX .50 MAGNUM
TITANIUM FINISH

MARK XIX
COMPONENT SYSTEM

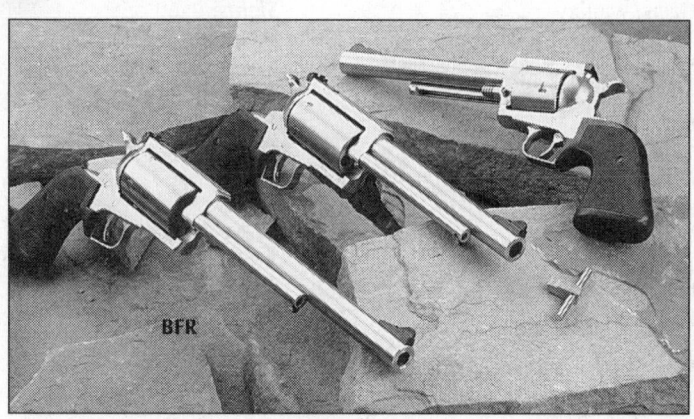

BFR

# MOA Handguns

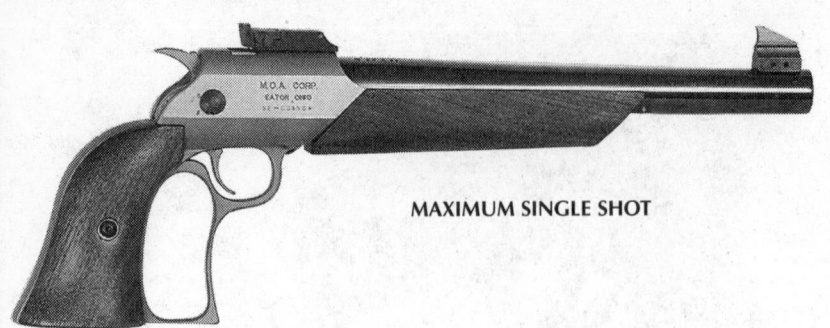

**MAXIMUM SINGLE SHOT**

**MAXIMUM**
*Action:* hinged breech
*Grips:* walnut
*Barrel:* 8.5, 10.5 or 14 in.
*Sights:* target
*Weight:* 56.0oz.
*Caliber:* most rifle chamberings from .22 Hornet to .375 H&H
*Capacity:* 1
*Features:* stainless breech, Douglas barrel; extra barrels, muzzle brake available
**Maximum. . . . . . . . . . . . . . . . . $823**
**with stainless barrel . . . . . . . . . $919**
**extra barrels. . . . . . . . . . . . . . . $269**

# Navy Arms Handguns

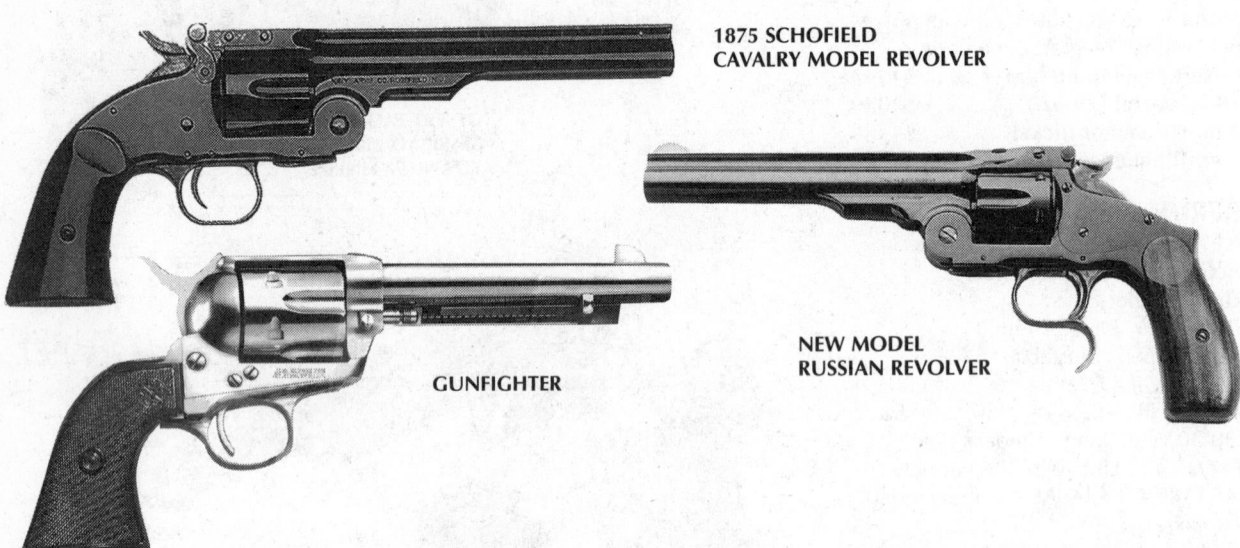

**1875 SCHOFIELD CAVALRY MODEL REVOLVER**

**GUNFIGHTER**

**NEW MODEL RUSSIAN REVOLVER**

## MODEL 1875 SCHOFIELD
*Action:* double-action revolver
*Grips:* walnut
*Barrel:* 3.5, 5.0 or 7.0 in.
*Sights:* fixed open
*Weight:* 35.0oz.
*Caliber:* .44-40, .45 Colt
*Capacity:* 6
*Features:* top-break action, automatic ejectors; 5 in barrel (37 oz.) and 7 in. barrel (39 oz.)
**1875 Schofield . . . . . . . . . . . . $810**
**U.S. Cavalry Model (7.5 in.) . . . $550**
**Flat Top target (7.5 in.) . . . . . . . $514**

## BISLEY
*Action:* single-action revolver
*Grips:* walnut
*Barrel:* 4.8, 5.5 or 7.5 in.
*Sights:* fixed open
*Weight:* 45.0oz.
*Caliber:* .44-40, .45 Colt
*Capacity:* 6
*Features:* Bisley grip case-colored frame; weight to 48 oz.
**Bisley. . . . . . . . . . . . . . . . . . . $501**

## NEW MODEL RUSSIAN
*Action:* double-action revolver
*Grips:* walnut
*Barrel:* 6.5 in.
*Sights:* fixed open
*Weight:* 40.0oz.
*Caliber:* .44 Russian

*Capacity:* 6
*Features:* top-break action
**New Model Russian . . . . . . . . . $893**

## GUNFIGHTER SERIES
*Action:* single-action revolver
*Grips:* walnut
*Barrel:* 4.8, 5.5, 7.5 in.
*Sights:* fixed open
*Weight:* 47.0oz.
*Caliber:* .357, .44-40, .45 Colt
*Capacity:* 6
*Features:* case-colored frames, after 1873 Colt design
**Gunfighter . . . . . . . . . . . . . . . $478**
**stainless . . . . . . . . . . . . . . . . . $566**

# North American Arms Handguns

## GUARDIAN .32
*Action:* autoloader
*Grips:* polymer
*Barrel:* 2.5 in.
*Sights:* fixed open
*Weight:* 12.0oz.
*Caliber:* .32 Auto, .32 NAA
*Capacity:* 6 + 1
*Features:* stainless, double action
Guardian . . . . . . . . . . . . . . . $402
.32 NAA. . . . . . . . . . . . . . . . $449

## MINI REVOLVER
*Action:* single-action revolver
*Grips:* laminated rosewood
*Barrel:* 1.2 in.
*Sights:* fixed open
*Weight:* 5.0oz.
*Caliber:* .22 Short, .22 LR, .22 WMR
*Capacity:* 5
*Features:* holster grip
.22 Short or .22 LR. . . . . . . . . $193
   with holster grip . . . . . . . . . $215
.22 Magnum. . . . . . . . . . . . . . $208
.22 Magnum
   with holster grip . . . . . . . . . $229

## MINI MASTER SERIES REVOLVER
*Action:* single-action revolver
*Grips:* rubber
*Barrel:* 2 or 4 in.
*Sights:* fixed or adjustable
*Weight:* 8.8 oz (2 in.) or 10.7 oz (4 in.)
*Caliber:* .22LR or .22 Mag.
*Capacity:* 5
*Features:* conversion cylinder or
adjustable sights available
.22 Mag or .22 LR (2 in.) . . . . . . . $258
.22 Mag w/conversion
.22 LR (2 in.) . . . . . . . . . . . . . $287
.22 Mag or LR
(4 in.) . . . . . . . . . . . . . . . . $272
.22 Mag w/conversion
.22 LR (4 in.) . . . . . . . . . . . . . $301

## GUARDIAN .380
*Action:* autoloader
*Grips:* composite
*Barrel:* 2.5 in.
*Sights:* fixed open
*Weight:* 18.8oz.
*Caliber:* .380
*Capacity:* 6
*Features:* manufactured with Kahr
Arms
Guardian . . . . . . . . . . . . . . . $449

GUARDIAN 32

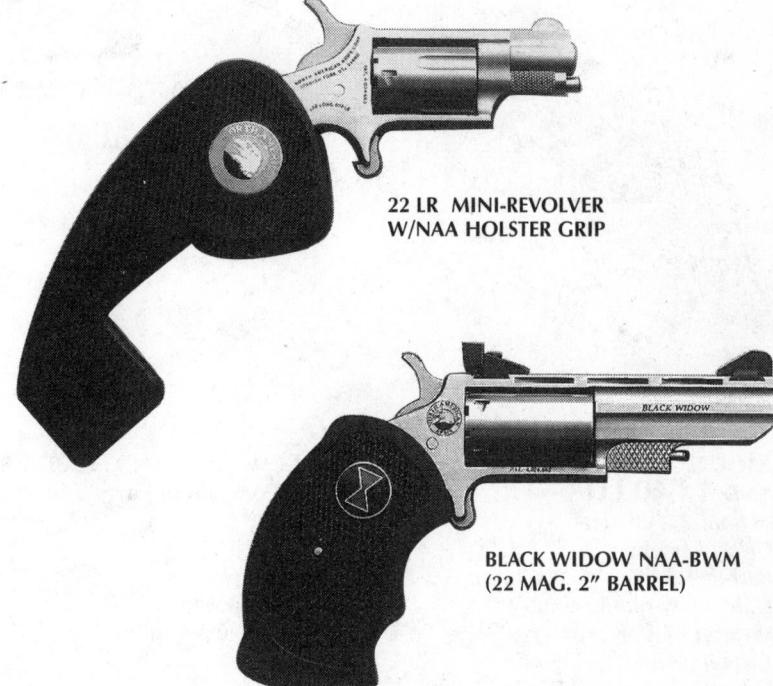

22 LR  MINI-REVOLVER
W/NAA HOLSTER GRIP

BLACK WIDOW NAA-BWM
(22 MAG. 2″ BARREL)

GUARDIAN.380

# Para Ordnance Handguns

MODEL P12•45 ACP
(3.5" BARREL, STAINLESS)

PARA CARRY C6.45 LDA

TAC-FOUR

LDA

## MODEL 12.45 LDA AND 14.40 LDA

*Action:* autoloader
*Grips:* Cocobolo
*Barrel:* 3.5 in.
*Sights:* low-profile combat
*Weight:* 34.0oz.
*Caliber:* .40 S&W, .45 ACP
*Capacity:* 14 + 1 (.40), 12 + 1 (.45)
*Features:* double action, stainless, flush hammer, bobbed beavertail
**LDA**. . . . . . . . . . . . . . . . . . . . **$1095**

## CCW AND COMPANION CARRY

*Action:* autoloader
*Grips:* rosewood
*Barrel:* 3.5 or 4.3 in.
*Sights:* low-profile combat
*Weight:* 32.0oz.
*Caliber:* .45 ACP
*Capacity:* 7 + 1
*Features:* double action, stainless; Tritium night sights available

4 in. CCW . . . . . . . . . . . . . . . $953
3.5 in. Companion Carry . . . . $1009

## LDA SERIES

*Action:* autoloader
*Grips:* composite
*Barrel:* 3.5 or 5.0 in.
*Sights:* target
*Weight:* 34.0oz.
*Caliber:* 9mm, .40 S&W or .45 ACP
*Capacity:* 12 + 1, 14 + 1, 16 + 1, 18 + 1
*Features:* double action, double-stack magazine; 40 oz. with 5 in. barrel
**LDA**. . . . . . . . . . . . . . . . . . . . . **$878**

## P-SERIES

*Action:* autoloader
*Grips:* composite
*Barrel:* 3.0, 3.5, 4.3, or 5.0 in.
*Sights:* fixed open
*Weight:* 24.0oz.
*Caliber:* 9mm, .40 S&W, .45 ACP
*Capacity:* 10 + 1

*Features:* customized 1911 Colt design, beveled magazine well, polymer magazine; also available with 3-dot or low-profile combat sights; weight to 40 oz. depending on barrel length
**.45 ACP** . . . . . . . . . . . . . . . . . **$840**
    **stainless .45** . . . . . . . . . . . . **$915**
**"Limited" .40 or .45**
**with adj. sights** . . . . . . . . . . . **$1020**
    **stainless "Limited"** . . . . . . . **$1095**

## TAC-FOUR

*Action:* autoloader
*Grips:* Cocobolo
*Barrel:* 4.3 in.
*Sights:* low-profile combat
*Weight:* 36.0oz.
*Caliber:* .45 ACP
*Capacity:* 13 + 1
*Features:* double action, stainless; flush hammer, bobbed beavertail
**Tac-Four**. . . . . . . . . . . . . . . . . **$968**

# Rossi Handguns

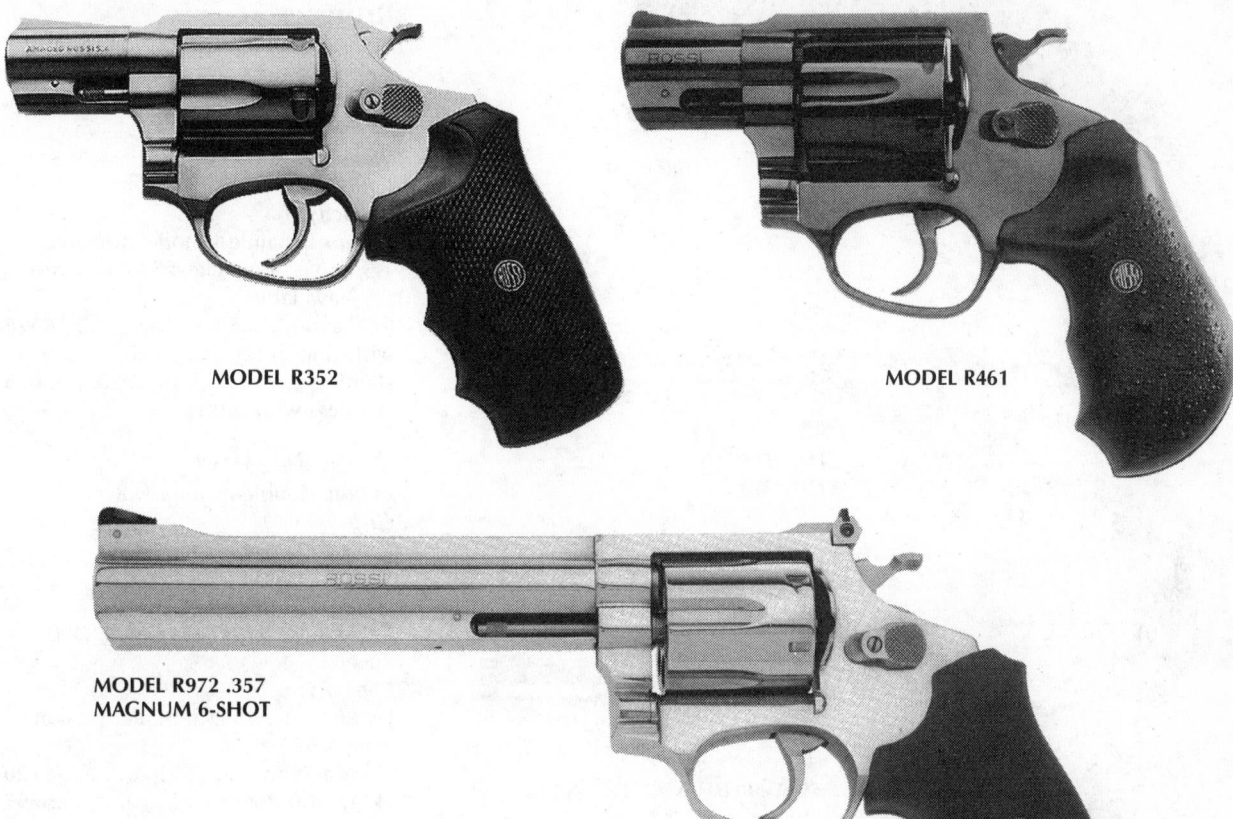

MODEL R352

MODEL R461

MODEL R972 .357
MAGNUM 6-SHOT

## MODEL R352

**Action:** double-action revolver
**Grips:** rubber
**Barrel:** 2 in.
**Sights:** fixed open
**Weight:** 24.0oz.
**Caliber:** .38 Spl.
**Capacity:** 6
**Features:** stainless; R351 chrome-moly
also available
R352 . . . . . . . . . . . . . . . . . . . . $345
R351 . . . . . . . . . . . . . . . . . . . . $298
R851, 4 in. barrel . . . . . . . . . . $298

## MODEL R462

**Action:** double-action revolver
**Grips:** rubber
**Barrel:** 2 in.
**Sights:** fixed open
**Weight:** 26.0oz.
**Caliber:** .357 Mag.
**Capacity:** 6
Features: stainless; R461 chrome-moly
also available
R462 . . . . . . . . . . . . . . . . . . . . $298
R461 . . . . . . . . . . . . . . . . . . . . $298

## MODEL R972

**Action:** double-action revolver
**Grips:** rubber
**Barrel:** 6
**Sights:** target
**Weight:** 34.0oz.
**Caliber:** .357 Mag.
**Capacity:** 6
**Features:** stainless after S&W M19 pattern; also R971 chrome-moly with 4
in. barrel
R972 . . . . . . . . . . . . . . . . . . . . $391
R971 . . . . . . . . . . . . . . . . . . . . $345

*Wadcutter pistol bullets are so named because they
make neat, clean-edged holes in paper. They are typically accurate at target distances but decelerate quickly
and aren't made to upset in game.*

# Ruger Handguns

**REDHAWK REVOLVER**

**STAINLESS REDHAWK**

**SUPER REDHAWK**

**SUPER REDHAWK GREY STAINLESS**

**VAQUERO SINGLE ACTION**

## REDHAWK

*Action:* double-action revolver
*Grips:* walnut
*Barrel:* 5.5 or 7.5 in.
*Sights:* target
*Weight:* 49.0oz.
*Caliber:* .44 Mag., .45 Colt
*Capacity:* 6
*Features:* stainless model available;
7.5 in. version weighs 54 oz.; scope
rings available
Redhawk . . . . . . . . . . . . . . . . $615
with rings. . . . . . . . . . . . . . . $655
stainless . . . . . . . . . . . . . . . . $675
stainless with rings . . . . . . . . . $720

## SUPER REDHAWK

*Action:* double-action revolver
*Grips:* walnut
*Barrel:* 7.5 or 8.5 in.
*Sights:* target
*Weight:* 53.0oz.
*Caliber:* .44 Mag., .454 Casull, .480
Ruger
*Capacity:* 6
*Features:* gray finish; 9.5 in. version
weighs 58 oz.
.44 Magnum. . . . . . . . . . . . . . $720
.454, .480 Ruger . . . . . . . . . . . $795

## VAQUERO

*Action:* single-action revolver
*Grips:* Micarta or rosewood
*Barrel:* 4.6 or 7.5 in.
*Sights:* fixed open
*Weight:* 40.0oz.
*Caliber:* .357, .44-40, .44 Mag., .45 Colt
*Capacity:* 6
Features: Bisley, birds-head grips also
available
Vaquero . . . . . . . . . . . . . . . . . $555
Bisley, blue. . . . . . . . . . . . . . . $555
Bisley, stainless. . . . . . . . . . . . $575
birds-head grips . . . . . . . . . . . $595

# Ruger Handguns

## NEW MODEL SUPER BLACKHAWK

*Action:* single-action revolver
*Grips:* walnut
*Barrel:* 4.6, 5.5, 7.5 or 10.5 in.
*Sights:* target
*Weight:* 45.0oz.
*Caliber:* .44 Mag.
*Capacity:* 6
*Features:* weight to 51 oz. depending on barrel length; also available: Super Blackhawk Hunter, stainless with 7.5 in. barrel, black laminated grips, rib, scope rings
**blue . . . . . . . . . . . . . . . . . . . . $540**
**stainless . . . . . . . . . . . . . . . . . $555**
**Super Blackhawk Hunter . . . . . $650**

## NEW MODEL SINGLE SIX

*Action:* single-action revolver
*Grips:* rosewood or Micarta
*Barrel:* 4.6, 5.5, 6.5 or 9.5 in.
*Sights:* fixed open
*Weight:* 33.0oz.
*Caliber:* .22 LR, .22 WMR, .17 HMR, .32 H&R
*Capacity:* 6
*Features:* adjustable sights available; weight to 38 oz. depending on barrel length
**Single Six . . . . . . . . . . . . . . . . $399**
**stainless . . . . . . . . . . . . . . . . . $599**
**.32 H&R . . . . . . . . . . . . . . . . . $576**

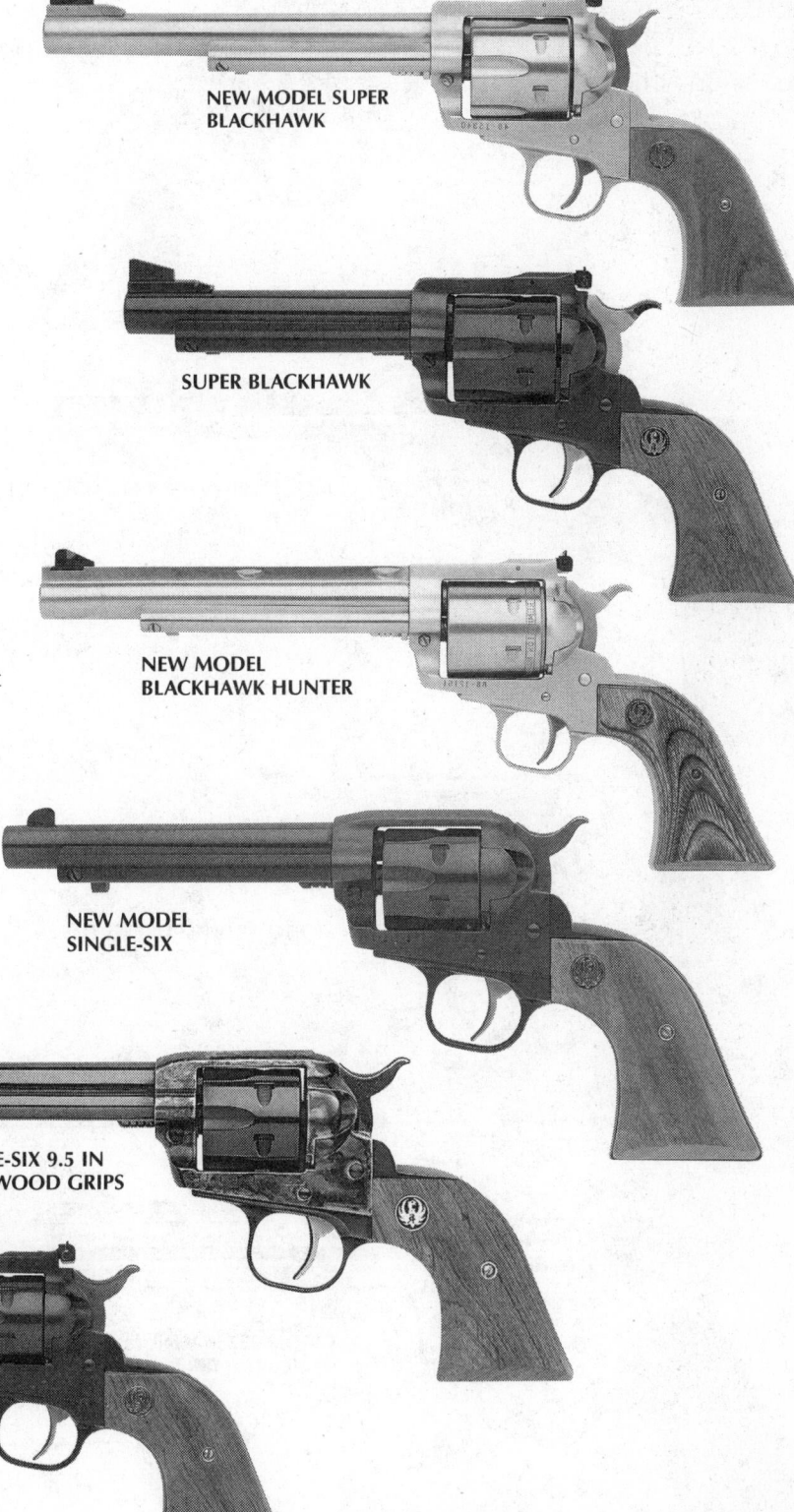

NEW MODEL SUPER BLACKHAWK

SUPER BLACKHAWK

NEW MODEL BLACKHAWK HUNTER

NEW MODEL SINGLE-SIX

NEW MODEL SINGLE-SIX 9.5 IN BARREL WITH ROSEWOOD GRIPS

NEW MODEL SUPER SINGLE-SIX

# Ruger Handguns

BISLEY SINGLE-ACTION
TARGET

## BISLEY
*Action:* single-action revolver
*Grips:* walnut
*Barrel:* 6.5 or 7.5 in.
*Sights:* target
*Weight:* 41.0oz.
*Caliber:* .22 LR, .357 Mag.,
.44 Mag., .45 Colt
*Capacity:* 6
*Features:* rimfire and centerfire (48
oz.); low-profile hammer
**.22 . . . . . . . . . . . . . . . . . . . . . . $445**
**.357, .44, .45 . . . . . . . . . . . . . . $560**

MODEL SBC-4 NEW BEARCAT

## MODEL SBC-4 NEW BEARCAT
*Action:* single-action revolver
*Grips:* rosewood
*Barrel:* 4 in.
*Sights:* fixed open
*Weight:* 24.0oz.
*Caliber:* .22 LR
*Capacity:* 6
*Features:* transfer bar
**New Bearcat . . . . . . . . . . . . . . $379**
**stainless . . . . . . . . . . . . . . . . . . $429**

MODEL SP101 SPURLESS DA

## MODEL SP101 AND GP100
*Action:* single-action revolver
*Grips:* composite and walnut
*Barrel:* 2.3, 3.0, 4.0 or 6.0 in.
*Sights:* fixed open
*Weight:* 25.0oz.
*Caliber:* .22 LR, .32 H&R,
.38 Spl., .357
*Capacity:* 6 (5 in some SP101s)
*Features:* SP101 stainless, GP100
chrome-moly or stainless; weight to 46
oz. depending on barrel length; target
sights on GP100
**SP101 . . . . . . . . . . . . . . . . . . . $505**
**GP100 . . . . . . . . . . . . . . . . . . . $520**
**GP100, stainless . . . . . . . . . . . $580**

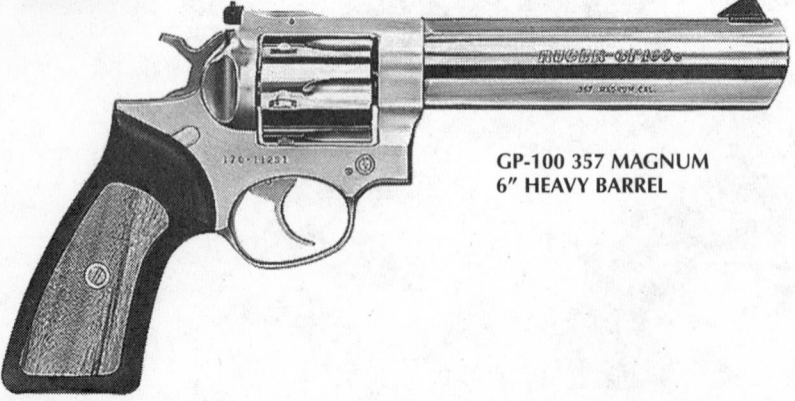

GP-100 357 MAGNUM
6" HEAVY BARREL

# Ruger Handguns

MARK II

MARK II 22/45
W/ZYTEL FRAME

MARK II 22/45 TARGET
MODEL P-512

MODEL P95D

MODEL P94

MODEL P89D

## MARK II

**Action:** autoloader
**Grips:** polymer
**Barrel:** 4 to 10 in.
**Sights:** target
**Weight:** 28.0oz.
**Caliber:** .22 LR
**Capacity:** 10 + 1
**Features:** blowback, Mark I and
.22/.45 designs, many barrel options;
bull barrels extra

| | |
|---|---|
| Mark II | $299 |
| stainless | $390 |
| Target stainless | $460 |

## P-SERIES

**Action:** autoloader
**Grips:** polymer
**Barrel:** 3 in.
**Sights:** fixed open
**Weight:** 30.0oz.
**Caliber:** 9mm, .40 S&W, .45 ACP
**Capacity:** 10 + 1 (8 + 1 in .45)
**Features:** double action, ambidextrous
grip, safety; decocker on some models,
manual safety on others.

| | |
|---|---|
| blued | $425 - 525 |
| stainless | $525 - 575 |
| blued .45 | $525 |
| stainless .45 | $565 |

# Safari Arms Handguns

COHORT

ENFORCER

MATCHMASTER

## COHORT
*Action:* autoloader
*Grips:* walnut
*Barrel:* 4 in.
*Sights:* target
*Weight:* 38.0oz.
*Caliber:* .45 ACP
*Capacity:* 7 + 1
*Features:* single action on 1911 Colt design, extended beavertail, stainless or parkerized
**Cohort** . . . . . . . . . . . . . . . . . **$649**

## ENFORCER
*Action:* autoloader
*Grips:* walnut
*Barrel:* 4.8 in.
*Sights:* low-profile combat
*Weight:* 36.0oz.
*Caliber:* .45 ACP
*Capacity:* 6 + 1
*Features:* single action on 1911 Colt design; extended beavertail, stainless or parkerized
**Enforcer** . . . . . . . . . . . . . . . . **$625**

## MATCHMASTER
*Action:* autoloader
*Grips:* walnut
*Barrel:* 5 or 6 in.
*Sights:* target
*Weight:* 40.0oz.
*Caliber:* .45 ACP
*Capacity:* 7 + 1
*Features:* single action on 1911 Colt design; extended beavertail, stainless or parkerized
**Matchmaster** . . . . . . . . . . . . . **$595**
**Two-tone** . . . . . . . . . . . . . . . . **$645**
**6 in. barrel (44 oz.)** . . . . . . . . . **$645**
**Big Deuce** . . . . . . . . . . . . . . . **$695**

# Savage Handguns

## STRIKER 501, 502, 503

**Action:** bolt
**Grips:** synthetic
**Barrel:** 10 in.
**Sights:** none
**Weight:** 64.0oz.
**Caliber:** .22 LR, .22 WMR, .17 HMR
**Capacity:** 5 + 1
**Features:** left-hand bolt, right-hand ejection

.22 LR . . . . . . . . . . . . . . . . . . $236
.22 WMR . . . . . . . . . . . . . . . $260
.17 HMR . . . . . . . . . . . . . . . . $285
.17 HMR stainless . . . . . . . . . . $335

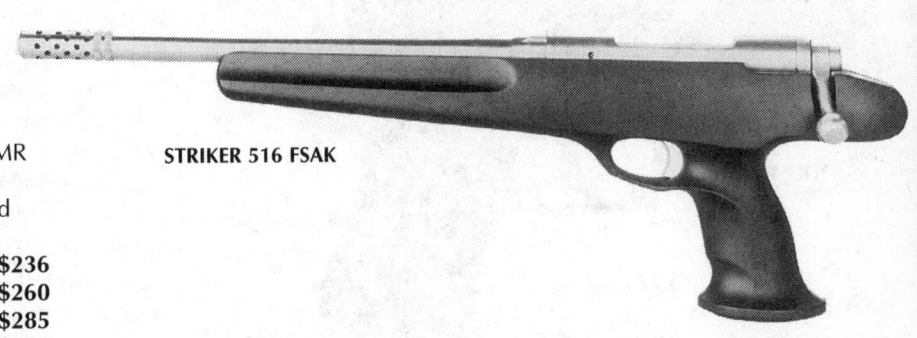

STRIKER 516 FSAK

## STRIKER 516 FSAK

**Action:** bolt
**Grips:** synthetic
**Barrel:** 14 in.
**Sights:** none
**Weight:** 78.0oz.
**Caliber:** .243, 7mm-08, .308, .270 WSM, 7mm WSM, .300 WSM
**Capacity:** 2 + 1
**Features:** stainless, with muzzle brake
FSAK . . . . . . . . . . . . . . . . . . . $598

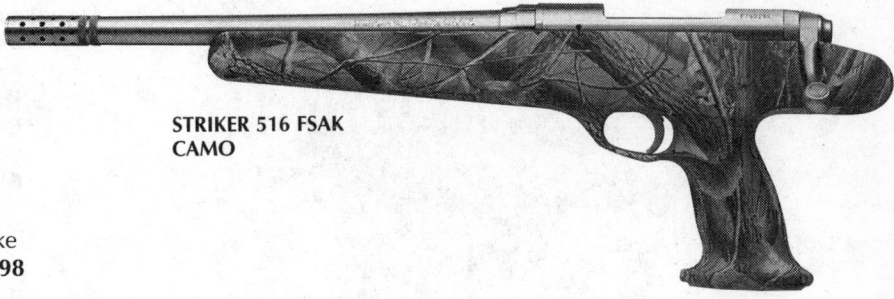

STRIKER 516 FSAK
CAMO

*Back-up for bear country? Few handgun rounds will stop a grizzly, and you'll need a very heavy pistol to shoot them. Besides, hitting a charging bear is very difficult. Better to tote pepper spray.*

# Sig Handguns

MODEL P226

MODEL P229

MODEL P232

## MODEL P229

*Action:* autoloader
*Grips:* polymer
*Barrel:* 3.9 in.
*Sights:* fixed open
*Weight:* 24.5oz.
*Caliber:* 9mm, .357 Sig, .40 S&W
*Capacity:* 10 + 1
*Features:* "Nitron" stainless finish; tac rail,Siglite night sights available for about $100 extra; also P226 with 4.4 in. barrel

P229 . . . . . . . . . . . . . . . . . . . . $840
two-Tone . . . . . . . . . . . . . . . . $896

## MODEL P232

*Action:* autoloader
*Grips:* polymer
*Barrel:* 3.6 in.
*Sights:* fixed open
*Weight:* 16.2oz.
*Caliber:* .380
*Capacity:* 7 + 1
*Features:* double action, available with Siglite night sights

P232 . . . . . . . . . . . . . . . . . . . . $516
two-tone . . . . . . . . . . . . . . . . $535
stainless . . . . . . . . . . . . . . . . . $559

*When using a two-handed grip, push with your right arm and pull with your left. The tension helps "lock" the pistol on target.*

# Sig Handguns

### MODEL P239
Action: autoloader
Grips: polymer
Barrel: 3.6 in.
Sights: target
Weight: 27.0oz.
Caliber: 9mm, .357 Sig, .40 S&W
Capacity: 7 + 1
Features: stainless, double action
**P239 . . . . . . . . . . . . . . . . . . . . . $642**
**with Siglite night sights . . . . . . $745**
**two-tone . . . . . . . . . . . . . . . . . $696**
**with night sights . . . . . . . . . . . $800**

### MODEL PL22 TRAILSIDE
*Action:* autoloader
*Grips:* rubber or walnut
*Barrel:* 4.5 or 6.0 in.
*Sights:* target
*Weight:* 26.0oz.
*Caliber:* .22 LR
*Capacity:* 10 + 1
*Features:* all versions have a top rail for scope mounts
**4.5 in. standard . . . . . . . . . . . $455**
**4.5 in. target . . . . . . . . . . . . . . $534**
**6 in. standard . . . . . . . . . . . . . $540**
**6 in. target . . . . . . . . . . . . . . . $559**
**6 in. competition . . . . . . . . . . $710**

### PRO
*Action:* autoloader
*Grips:* polymer
*Barrel:* 3.9 in.
*Sights:* fixed open
*Weight:* 29.0oz.
*Caliber:* .357 Sig, .40 S&W, 9mm
*Capacity:* 10 + 1
*Features:* polymer frame, stainless slide, double action; Siglite night sights available
**Pro . . . . . . . . . . . . . . . . . . . . . $640**
**Two-Tone . . . . . . . . . . . . . . . . . $671**
**Pro with night sights . . . . . . . . $700**
**Two-Tone with night sights . . . . $717**

MODEL P239

MODEL PL 22
TRAILSIDE
COMPETITION

PRO PISTOL
TWO TONE

# Smith & Wesson Handguns

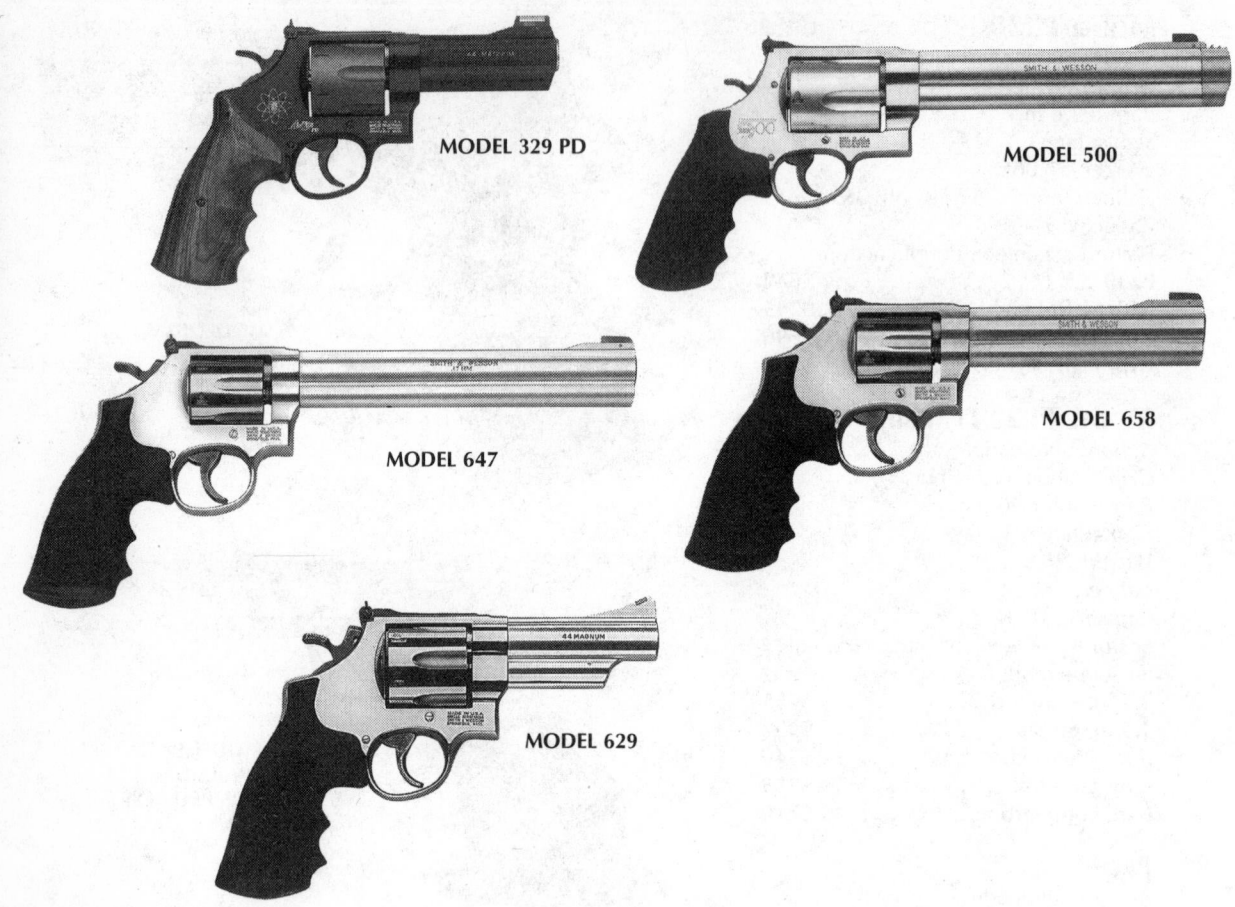

MODEL 329 PD

MODEL 500

MODEL 647

MODEL 658

MODEL 629

## MODEL 329 PD

**Action:** double-action revolver
**Grips:** wood
**Barrel:** 4 in.
**Sights:** adjustable fiber optic
**Weight:** 27.0oz.
**Caliber:** .44 Mag.
**Capacity:** 6
**Features:** scandium frame, titanium cylinder
**329 PD** . . . . . . . . . . . . . . . . . $927

## MODEL 500

**Action:** double-action revolver
**Grips:** Hogue Sorbathane
**Barrel:** ported 8.4 in.
**Sights:** target
**Weight:** 72.5oz.
**Caliber:** .500 S&W
**Capacity:** 5
**Features:** X-Frame, double-action stainless revolver
**Model 500** . . . . . . . . . . . . . $1150

## MODEL 647

**Action:** double-action revolver
**Grips:** rubber
**Barrel:** 8.4 in.
**Sights:** target
**Weight:** 52.5oz.
**Caliber:** .17 HMR
**Capacity:** 6
**Features:** stainless, full-lug, K-frame
**Model 647** . . . . . . . . . . . . . . . $697

## MODEL 658

**Action:** double-action revolver
**Grips:** rubber
**Barrel:** 6 in.
**Sights:** target
**Weight:** 45.0oz.
**Caliber:** .22 WMR
**Capacity:** 6
**Features:** stainless, full-lug, K-frame
**Model 648** . . . . . . . . . . . . . . . $659

## MODEL 625

**Action:** double-action revolver
**Grips:** Hogue rubber, round butt
**Barrel:** 4 or 5 in.
**Sights:** target
**Weight:** 49.0oz.
**Caliber:** .45 ACP
**Capacity:** 6
**Features:** N-frame, stainless; also in Model 610 10mm with 4 in. barrel; 5 in. barrel: 51 oz.
**Model 625** . . . . . . . . . . . . . . . $790
**10 mm** . . . . . . . . . . . . . . . . . $833

## MODEL 629

**Action:** double-action revolver
**Grips:** Hogue rubber
**Barrel:** 4 or 6 in.
**Sights:** target
**Weight:** 44.0oz.
**Caliber:** .44 Mag.
**Capacity:** 6
**Features:** N-frame, stainless; 6 in. weighs 47 oz.
**4 in.** . . . . . . . . . . . . . . . . . . . $760

# Smith & Wesson Handguns

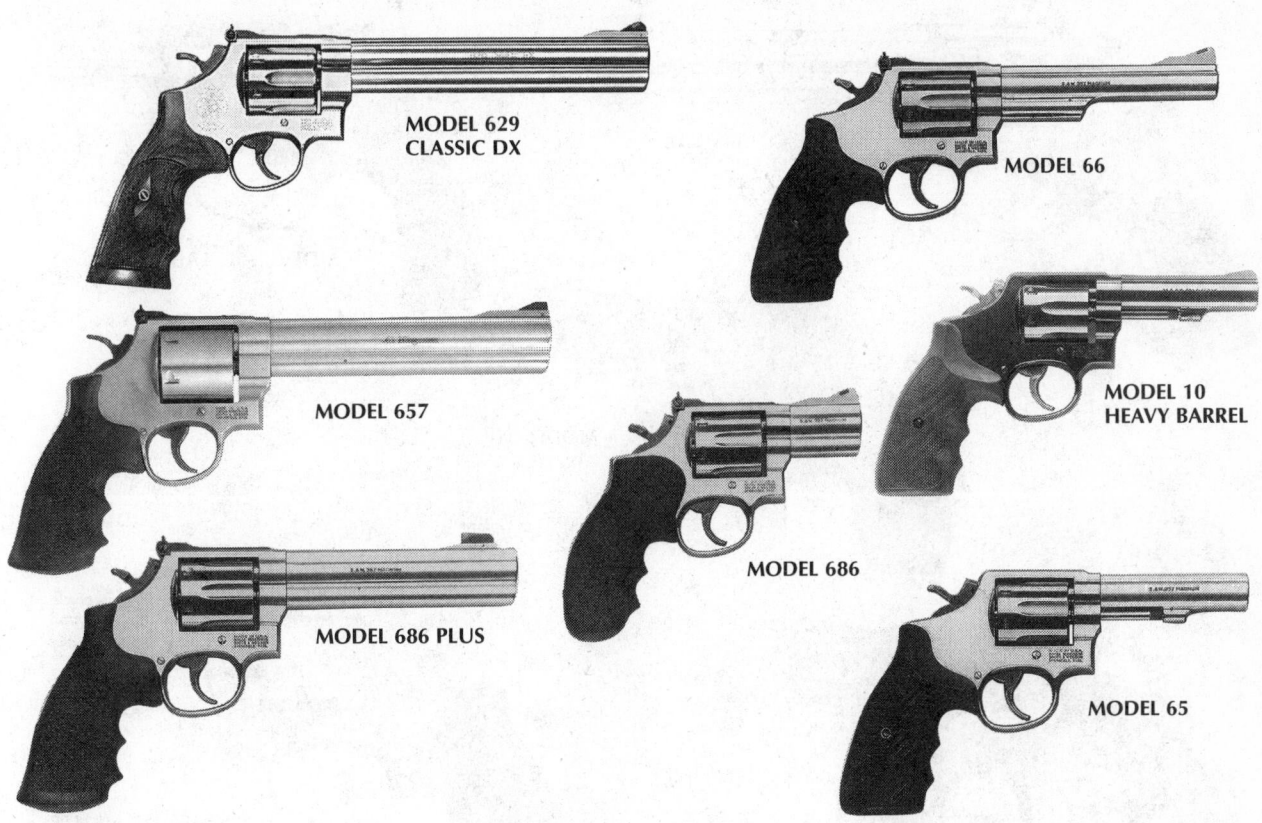

MODEL 629
CLASSIC DX

MODEL 66

MODEL 657

MODEL 10
HEAVY BARREL

MODEL 686

MODEL 686 PLUS

MODEL 65

## MODEL 629 CLASSIC

*Action:* double-action revolver
*Grips:* Hogue rubber
*Barrel:* 5.0, 6.5 or 8.4 in.
*Sights:* target
*Weight:* 51.0oz.
*Caliber:* .44 Mag.
*Capacity:* 6
*Features:* N-frame, stainless, full lug;
weight to 54 oz. depending on
barrel length
**5.0 or 6.5 in.** . . . . . . . . . . **$815 - 839**
**8.4 in.** . . . . . . . . . . . . . . . . . **$841**

## MODEL 66

*Action:* double-action revolver
*Grips:* Uncle Mike's Combat
*Barrel:* 2.5 or 4 in.
*Sights:* target
*Weight:* 30.5oz.
*Caliber:* .357 Mag.
*Capacity:* 6
*Features:* stainless K-frame; 4 in.
barrel: 36 oz.
**4 in.** . . . . . . . . . . . . . . . . . . . **$614**
**2.5 in.** . . . . . . . . . . . . . . . . . . **$625**

## MODEL 657

*Action:* double-action revolver
*Grips:* Hogue rubber
*Barrel:* 7.5 in.
*Sights:* target
*Weight:* 52.0oz.
*Caliber:* .41 Mag.
*Capacity:* 6
*Features:* N-frame stainless
**Model 657** . . . . . . . . . . . . . . . **$748**

## MODEL 686

*Action:* single-action revolver
*Grips:* combat or target
*Barrel:* 2.5, 4, 6, 8.4 in.
*Sights:* target
*Weight:* 34.5oz.
*Caliber:* .357 mag.
*Capacity:* 6
*Features:* stainless, K-frame 686 Plus
holds 7 rounds; to 48 oz. depending
on barrel length
**2.5 in.** . . . . . . . . . . . . . . . . . . **$644**
**4 in.** . . . . . . . . . . . . . . . . . . . . **$670**
**6 in.** . . . . . . . . . . . . . . . . . . . . **$676**
**6 in. ported** . . . . . . . . . . . . . . **$722**
**2.5 in. Plus** . . . . . . . . . . . . . . **$669**
**4 in. Plus** . . . . . . . . . . . . . . . . **$692**
**6 in. Plus** . . . . . . . . . . . . . . . . **$703**

## MODEL 65

*Action:* double-action revolver
*Grips:* Uncle Mike's Combat
*Barrel:* 4 in.
*Sights:* fixed open
*Weight:* 34.0oz.
*Caliber:* .357 Mag.
*Capacity:* 6
*Features:* K-frame; also as LadySmith
with 3 in. barrel, rosewood grips
**Model 65** . . . . . . . . . . . . . . . . **$563**

## MODEL 10

*Action:* double-action revolve
*Grips:* Uncle Mike's Combat
*Barrel:* 4.0 in. heavy
*Sights:* fixed open
*Weight:* 33.5oz.
*Caliber:* .38 Spl.
*Capacity:* 6
*Features:* "military and police" model;
also in stainless, K-frame
**Model 10** . . . . . . . . . . . . . . . . **$526**
**stainless Model 64** . . . . . . . . . . **$563**
**stainless with 2 in. barrel,**
**round butt** . . . . . . . . . . . . . . . **$553**

# Smith & Wesson Handguns

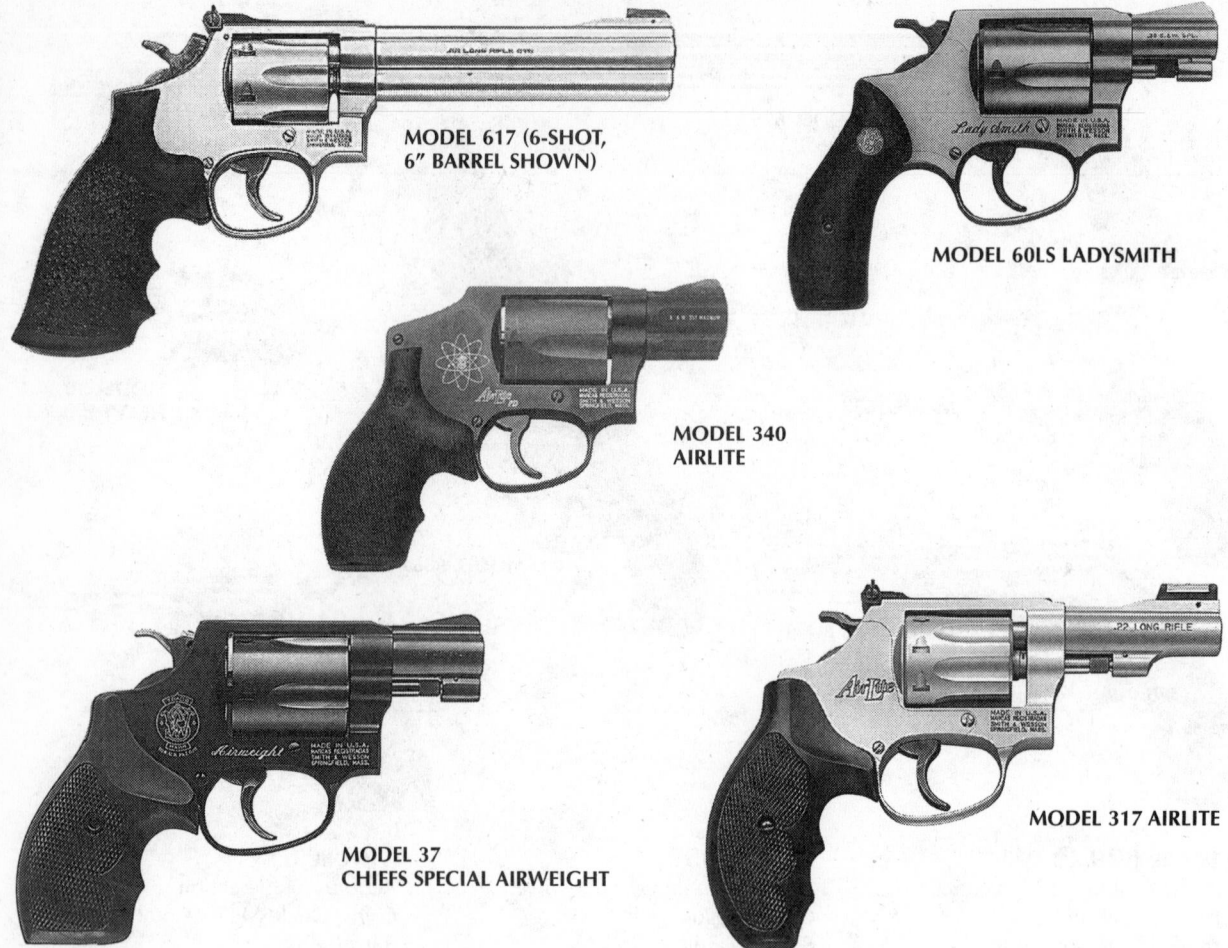

MODEL 617 (6-SHOT,
6" BARREL SHOWN)

MODEL 60LS LADYSMITH

MODEL 340
AIRLITE

MODEL 317 AIRLITE

MODEL 37
CHIEFS SPECIAL AIRWEIGHT

## MODEL 617

**Action:** double-action revolver
**Grips:** Hogue rubber
**Barrel:** 4.0, 6.0, 8.4 in.
**Sights:** target
**Weight:** 42.0oz.
**Caliber:** .22 LR
**Capacity:** 6
**Features:** stainless, target hammer and trigger, K-frame; weight to 54 oz. depending on barrel length
**4 in.** . . . . . . . . . . . . . . . . . . . . **$683**
**6 in.** . . . . . . . . . . . . . . . . . . . . **$663**
**6 in., 10-shot** . . . . . . . . . . . . . **$709**

## MODEL 36-LS

**Action:** double-action revolver
**Grips:** laminated rosewood, round butt
**Barrel:** 1.8, 2.2, 3 in.
**Sights:** fixed open
**Weight:** 20.0oz.
**Caliber:** .38 Spl.
**Capacity:** 5
**Features:** weight to 24 oz. depending on barrel length; stainless version in .357 Mag. available (60 LS)
**Model 36 LS** . . . . . . . . . . . . . . **$549**
**60 LS** . . . . . . . . . . . . . . . . . . **$609**

## MODEL 37 CHIEF'S

Special Airweight
**Action:** double-action revolver
**Grips:** uncle Mike's boot
**Barrel:** 1.8
**Sights:** fixed open
**Weight:** 11.9oz.
**Caliber:** .38 Spl.
**Capacity:** 5
**Features:** alloy frame (also M37 in blue finish)
**Model 637** . . . . . . . . . . . . . . . **$450**
**Model 37** . . . . . . . . . . . . . . . . **$554**

## MODEL 317

**Action:** double-action revolver
**Grips:** rubber
**Barrel:** 1.8 or 3 in.
**Sights:** fixed open
**Weight:** 10.5oz.
**Caliber:** .22 LR
**Capacity:** 8
**Features:** alloy frame
**1.8 in.** . . . . . . . . . . . . . . . . . **$582**
**3 in.** . . . . . . . . . . . . . . . . . . . **$636**

## MODEL 340 AIRLITE

**Action:** double-action revolver
**Grips:** rubber
**Barrel:** 1.8 in.
**Sights:** fixed open
**Weight:** 12.0oz.
**Caliber:** .357 Mag.
**Capacity:** 5
**Features:** Scandium alloy frame, titanium cylinder
**Model 340** . . . . . . . . . . . . . . . **$809**
**with Hi-Viz sight** . . . . . . . . . . **$847**

# Smith & Wesson Handguns

## MODEL 442 AIRWEIGHT
*Action:* double-action revolver
*Grips:* rubber
*Barrel:* 1.8 in.
*Sights:* fixed open
*Weight:* 15.0oz.
*Caliber:* .38 Spl.
*Capacity:* 5
*Features:* stainless Model 642 and 442 are concealed-hammer, double-action only
**Model 442** . . . . . . . . . . . . . . . **$580**

## MODEL 640 CENTENNIAL
*Action:* double-action revolver
*Grips:* rubber
*Barrel:* 2.2
*Sights:* fixed open
*Weight:* 23.0oz.
*Caliber:* .357
*Capacity:* 5
*Features:* stainless, concealed-hammer, double-action-only; also M649 Bodyguard single or double-action
**M640.** . . . . . . . . . . . . . . . . . . **$635**
**M649.** . . . . . . . . . . . . . . . . . . **$629**

## MODEL 386
*Action:* double-action revolver
*Grips:* rubber
*Barrel:* 3.2 in.
*Sights:* low-profile combat
*Weight:* 18.5oz.
*Caliber:* .357 Mag.
*Capacity:* 7
*Features:* Scandium alloy frame, titanium cylinder
**Model 386** . . . . . . . . . . . . . . . **$847**

## MODEL 360 AIRLITE
*Action:* double-action revolver
*Grips:* rubber
*Barrel:* 1.8 in.
*Sights:* fixed open
*Weight:* 12.0oz.
*Caliber:* .357 Mag.
*Capacity:* 5
*Features:* Scandium alloy frame, titanium cylinder
**Model 360** . . . . . . . . . . . . . . . **$790**
**with Hi-Viz sight** . . . . . . . . . . . **$829**
**3.2 in. Kit Gun**
**with Hi-Viz sight** . . . . . . . . . . . **$836**

MODEL 442

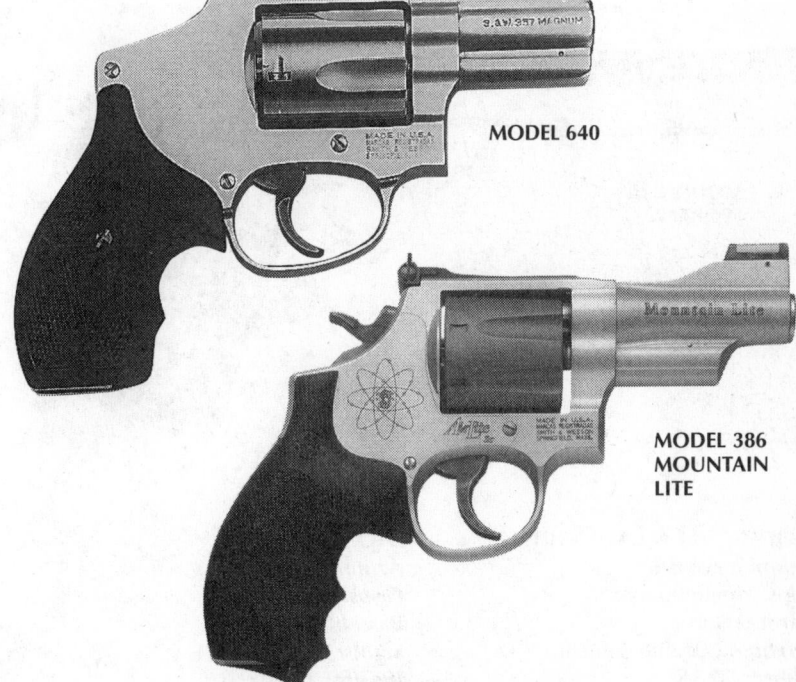

MODEL 640

MODEL 386
MOUNTAIN
LITE

MODEL 360 PD
AIRLITE

# Smith & Wesson Handguns

MODEL 41

MODEL 3913
LADYSMITH

MODEL 22A
SPORT

SW9VE

## Model 3913 LadySmith
*Action:* autoloader
*Grips:* Hogue rubber
*Barrel:* 3.5 in.
*Sights:* low-profile combat
*Weight:* 24.8oz.
*Caliber:* 9mm
*Capacity:* 8 + 1
*Features:* double action, stainless
Model 3913 . . . . . . . . . . . . . . $829

## Model SW40G, P and VE
*Action:* autoloader
*Grips:* polymer
*Barrel:* 4 in.
*Sights:* 3-dot
*Weight:* 24.4oz.
*Caliber:* .40 S&W
*Capacity:* 10 + 1
*Features:* double action stainless slide,
polymer frame, finish options
standard. . . . . . . . . . . . . . . . $379
with night sights. . . . . . . . . . . $524

## Model SW VE
*Action:* autoloader
*Grips:* polymer
*Barrel:* 4 in.
*Sights:* 3-dot
*Weight:* 24.7oz.
*Caliber:* 9mm
*Capacity:* 10 + 1
*Features:* double action, stainless
slide, polymer frame, finish options
SW9 VE . . . . . . . . . . . . . . . . . $379

## Model 41
*Action:* autoloader
*Grips:* walnut
*Barrel:* 5.5 or 7 in.
*Sights:* target
*Weight:* 41.0oz.
*Caliber:* .22 LR
*Capacity:* 12 + 1
*Features:* adjustable trigger;
7 in. barrel: 44 oz.
Model 41 . . . . . . . . . . . . . . . $1026

## Model 22A Sport
*Action:* autoloader
*Grips:* polymer
*Barrel:* 4, 5.5 or 7 in.
*Sights:* target
*Weight:* 28.0oz.
*Caliber:* .22 LR
*Capacity:* 10 + 1
*Features:* scope mounting rib;
5.5 in. bull barrel available
4 in.. . . . . . . . . . . . . . . . . . . . $283
5.5 in. (31 oz.) . . . . . . . . . . . . $313
5.5 in. bull. . . . . . . . . . . . . . . $393
5.5 in. bull, Hi-Viz sights . . . . $465
7 in. (33 oz.) . . . . . . . . . . . . . $355
7 in. stainless . . . . . . . . . . . . . $423

**MODEL 3913TSW**

**MODEL 4013TSW**

**MODEL 4513TSW**

**MODEL 5906 DA STAINLESS**

## MODEL 3913 TSW

*Action*: autoloader
*Grips*: rubber
*Barrel*: 3.5 in.
*Sights*: 3-dot
*Weight*: 24.8oz.
*Caliber*: 9mm
*Capacity*: 8 + 1
*Features*: alloy frame, stainless slide;
also: 3953TSW double-action-only
**Model 3913TSW** . . . . . . . . . . **$806**

## MODEL 4013TSW

*Action*: autoloader
*Grips*: rubber
*Barrel*: 3.5 in.
*Sights*: 3-dot
*Weight*: 26.8oz.
*Caliber*: .40 S&W
*Capacity*: 9 + 1
*Features*: alloy frame, stainless slide,
ambidextrous safety; also: 4053TSW

double-action-only
**Model 4013TSW** . . . . . . . . . . **$940**

## MODEL 4513TSW

*Action*: autoloader
*Grips*: rubber
*Barrel*: 3.5 in.
*Sights*: 3-dot
*Weight*: 28.6oz.
*Caliber*: .45 ACP
*Capacity*: 7 + 1
*Features*: alloy frame, stainless slide,
ambidextrous safety
**Model 4513TSW** . . . . . . . . . . **$980**

## MODEL 5903TSW

*Action*: autoloader
*Grips*: rubber
*Barrel*: 4 in.
*Sights*: 3-dot
*Weight*: 29.0oz.
*Caliber*: 9mm

*Capacity*: 10 + 1
*Features*: alloy frame, stainless slide;
also 5906 with stainless frame, 38.3 oz.
**Model 5903** . . . . . . . . . . . . . . **$892**
**Model 5906** . . . . . . . . . . . . . . **$959**

## MODEL 4003TSW

*Action*: autoloader
*Grips*: rubber
*Barrel*: 4 in.
*Sights*: 3-dot
*Weight*: 28.5oz.
*Caliber*: .40 S&W
*Capacity*: 10 + 1
*Features*: alloy frame, stainless slide;
also 4006 with stainless frame, 37.8 oz.
**Model 4003** . . . . . . . . . . . . . . **$940**
**Model 4006** . . . . . . . . . . . . . . **$1001**

# Smith & Wesson Handguns

MODEL 4563T

MODEL 410

## MODEL 4563

**Action:** autoloader
**Grips:** rubber
**Barrel:** 4 in.
**Sights:** 3-dot
**Weight:** 30.6oz.
**Caliber:** .45 ACP
**Capacity:** 8 + 1
**Features:** alloy frame, stainless slide; also 4566 with stainless frame, 39.1 oz.
Model 4563 . . . . . . . . . . . . . . . $977
Model 4566 . . . . . . . . . . . . . $1000

## MODEL 4040 PD

**Action:** double-action revolver
**Grips:** Hogue rubber
**Barrel:** 3.5 in.
**Sights:** 3-dot
**Weight:** 25.6oz.
**Caliber:** .40 S&W
**Capacity:** 7 + 1
**Features:** first scandium-frame pistol
4040 PD . . . . . . . . . . . . . . . . . $812

## MODEL SW1911

**Action:** autoloader
**Grips:** rubber
**Barrel:** 5 in.
**Sights:** low-profile combat
**Weight:** 39.0oz.
**Caliber:** .45 ACP
**Capacity:** 8 + 1
**Features:** stainless, extended beaver-tail, match trigger; single action
SW 1911 . . . . . . . . . . . . . . . $1049

## MODEL SW99

**Action:** autoloader
**Grips:** polymer
**Barrel:** 4.3 in.
**Sights:** low-profile combat
**Weight:** 25.6oz.
**Caliber:** .45 ACP
**Capacity:** 9 + 1
**Features:** double action pistol made in collaboration with Walther; also new: 23-ounce compact version in 9mm and .40 S&W, 3.5 in. barrel
Model 99 . . . . . . . . . . . . . . . . . $708

## MODEL 910, 410

**Action:** autoloader
**Grips:** rubber
**Barrel:** 4 in.
**Sights:** 3-dot
**Weight:** 28.5oz.
**Caliber:** 9mm, .40 S&W
**Capacity:** 10 + 1
**Features:** alloy frame, chrome-moly slide, decocking lever; also M457 in .45 ACP, 7 + 1 capacity; Hi-Viz sights extra
Model 910 . . . . . . . . . . . . . . . $567
Model 410 . . . . . . . . . . . . . . . $627
Model 457 . . . . . . . . . . . . . . . $627

# Springfield Handguns

MODEL 1911-A1
TROPHY MATCH

MODEL XD 9801

MODEL 1911-A1
CHAMPION
4-INCH

MICRO
COMPACT
1911-A1

MODEL 1911-A1
STANDARD &
LIGHTWEIGHT

1911-A1
ULTRA COMPACT
BI-TONE V-10

X-TREME DUTY (XD)

## MODEL XD 9801

*Action:* autoloader
*Grips:* composite
*Barrel:* 3 in.
*Sights:* fixed open
*Weight:* 20.5oz.
*Caliber:* 9mm
*Capacity:* 10
*Features:* lightweight polymer frame, stainless magazines
XD 9801 . . . . . . . . . . . . . . . . $489
with Tritium sights . . . . . . . . . $569

## MODEL 1911 CHAMPION

*Action:* autoloader
*Grips:* walnut
*Barrel:* 4 in.
*Sights:* fixed open
*Weight:* 34.0oz.
*Caliber:* .45 ACP
*Capacity:* 7 + 1
*Features:* Ultra Compact with 3.5 in. barrel, Novak sights, Bi-Tone finish option

Champion . . . . . . . . . . . . . . . $906
Ultra Compact . . . . . . . . . . . . $923

## MODEL 1911 TROPHY MATCH

*Action:* autoloader
*Grips:* Cocobolo
*Barrel:* match-grade, 5 in.
*Sights:* target
*Weight:* 40.0oz.
*Caliber:* .45 ACP
*Capacity:* 7 + 1
*Features:* Videcki speed trigger, serrated front strap, stainless
Trophy Match. . . . . . . . . . . . . $1393

## MODEL 1911-A1

*Action:* autoloader
*Grips:* Cocobolo
*Barrel:* 5 in.
*Sights:* fixed open
*Weight:* 38.5oz.
*Caliber:* .45 ACP, 9mm
*Capacity:* 7 + 1
*Features:* also Lightweight (31.5 oz.)

and 3 in. Micro Compact (24 oz.) with alloy frames, stainless
M1911-A1 . . . . . . . . . . . . . . . $875
Adjustable sights . . . . . . . . . . $923
Lightweight . . . . . . . . . . . . . . $892
Micro Compact . . . . . . . . . . . $1058

## X-TREME DUTY

*Action:* autoloader
*Grips:* walnut
*Barrel:* 4 in.
*Sights:* fixed open
*Weight:* 22.8oz.
*Caliber:* 9mm, .357 Sig, .40 S&W
*Capacity:* 10 + 1
*Features:* short recoil, single action, black or OD green
X-Treme Duty. . . . . . . . . . . . . $498
Bi-tone. . . . . . . . . . . . . . . . . $525

# Swiss Arms Handguns

P210-8-9

## MODEL P210 SPORT

*Action:* autoloader
*Grips:* wood
*Barrel:* 4.8 in.
*Sights:* target
*Weight:* 24.0oz.
*Caliber:* 9mm
*Capacity:* 8 + 1
*Features:* chrome-moly, single action
**Swiss Army Service Model . . . $3031**
**Target grade. . . . . . . . . . . . . $2695**

# Taurus Handguns

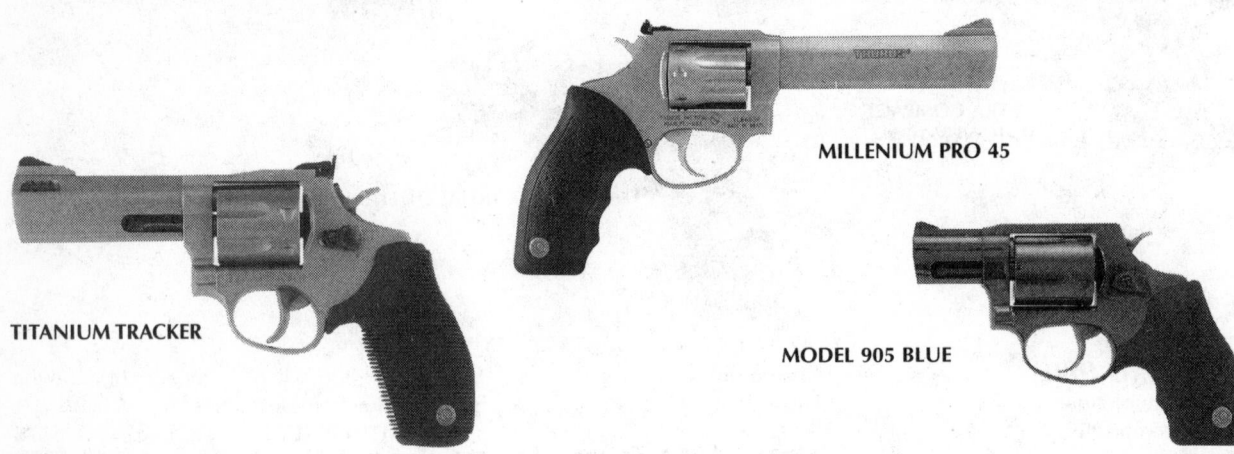

MILLENIUM PRO 45

TITANIUM TRACKER

MODEL 905 BLUE

## TITANIUM TRACKER

*Action*: double-action revolver
*Grips*: rubber
*Barrel*: 4 or 6 in.
*Sights*: target
*Weight*: 21.0oz.
*Caliber*: .357 Mag or .41 Mag. (4 in. only)
*Capacity*: 7 (.357) or 5 9.41)
*Features*: Titanium frame; 23 oz. with 6 in. barrel
**Tracker . . . . . . . . . . . . . . . . $688**

## MODEL 905 AND 455

*Action:* double-action revolver
*Grips:* rubber
*Barrel:* 2 in.
*Sights:* fixed open
*Weight:* 21.0oz.
*Caliber:* 9mm, .40 S&W, .45 ACP
9with 2, 4 or 6.5 inch barrel)

*Capacity:* 5
*Features:* stellar clips furnished; UltraLite weighs 17 oz.
**blue. . . . . . . . . . . . . . . . . . . $383**
**stainless. . . . . . . . . . . . . . . . $430**
**UltraLite, blue . . . . . . . . . . . . $414**
**UltraLite, stainless . . . . . . . . . $461**
**.45 ACP . . . . . . . . . . . . . . . . . $523**

## MODEL PT911 COMPACT

*Action*: autoloader
*Grips*: polymer
*Barrel*: 4 in.
*Sights*: 3-dot
*Weight*: 28.2oz.
*Caliber*: 9mm
*Capacity*: 10 + 1
*Features*: double action only; ambidextrous decocker
**blue. . . . . . . . . . . . . . . . . . . $523**

**stainless. . . . . . . . . . . . . . . . $539**
**PT III blue . . . . . . . . . . . . . . . $422**
**PT III stainless . . . . . . . . . . . . $438**

## MODEL MILLENIUM PRO

*Action:* autoloader
*Grips:* composite, wood, mother of pearl
*Barrel:* 3.5 in.
*Sights:* low-profile combat
*Weight:* 18.7oz.
*Caliber:* .40 S&W, .45 ACP
*Capacity:* 10 + 1
*Features:* double action, polymer frame; also comes with night sights (add $78); .45 ACP weighs 23 oz.
**.40 blue/composite. . . . . . . . . $461**
**.40 stainless/composite. . . . . . $477**
**.45 blue/composite. . . . . . . . . $484**
**.45 stainless/compo site . . . . . . $500**

# Taurus Handguns

MODEL PT-92

MODEL PT 22

PT-145

MODEL PT-945

MODEL M17CSS

## MODEL PT22

**Action:** autoloader
**Grips:** rosewood
**Barrel:** 2.8 in.
**Sights:** fixed open
**Weight:** 12.3oz.
**Caliber:** .22 LR
**Capacity:** 8 + 1
**Features:** double action only, blue, nickel or DuoTone finish; also in .25 ACP (PT25)
PT22 . . . . . . . . . . . . . . . . . . . $219
with gold trim . . . . . . . . . . . . . $234
with Mother of Pearl grips . . . . $250

## MODEL PT145

**Action:** autoloader
**Grips:** polymer
**Barrel:** 1.8 in.
**Sights:** fixed open
**Weight:** 22.0oz.
**Caliber:** .45 ACP
**Capacity:** 10 + 1
**Features:** double action, double-stack magazine
blue . . . . . . . . . . . . . . . . . . . . . $484

stainless . . . . . . . . . . . . . . . . . . $500
blue with night sights . . . . . . . . $563
stainless with night sights . . . . . $578

## MODEL PT945

**Action:** autoloader
**Grips:** rubber or rosewood
**Barrel:** 4.3 in.
**Sights:** 3-dot
**Weight:** 29.5oz.
**Caliber:** .45 ACP
**Capacity:** 8 + 1
**Features:** double action; also PT940 in .40 S&W (28.2 oz., 10 + 1 capacity)
blue . . . . . . . . . . . . . . . . . . . . . $563
stainless . . . . . . . . . . . . . . . . . . $578
blue with night sights . . . . . . . . $641
stainless with night sights . . . . . $656
Model 940 blue . . . . . . . . . . . . $523
Model 940 stainless . . . . . . . . . $539

## MODEL PT92

**Action:** autoloader
**Grips:** walnut
**Barrel:** 5 in.
**Sights:** fixed open

**Weight:** 34.0oz.
**Caliber:** 9mm
**Capacity:** 15 + 1
**Features:** double action; also PT99 with adjustable sights
blue . . . . . . . . . . . . . . . . . . . . . $578
stainless . . . . . . . . . . . . . . . . . . $594
blue with night sights . . . . . . . . $656
stainless with night sights . . . . . $672

## MODEL M17C

**Action:** double-action revolver
**Grips:** composite
**Barrel:** 2, 4, 5, 6.5 or 12 in.
**Sights:** target
**Weight:** 18.5oz.
**Caliber:** .17 HMR
**Capacity:** 7 or 8
**Features:** 10 models available in blued and stainless steel; weight varies with barrel length to 49.8 oz.
blue, 2, 4 or 5 in. barrel . . . . . . $359
most stainless models . . . . . . . . $406
12 in. barrel . . . . . . . . . . . . . . . $430

# Taurus Handguns

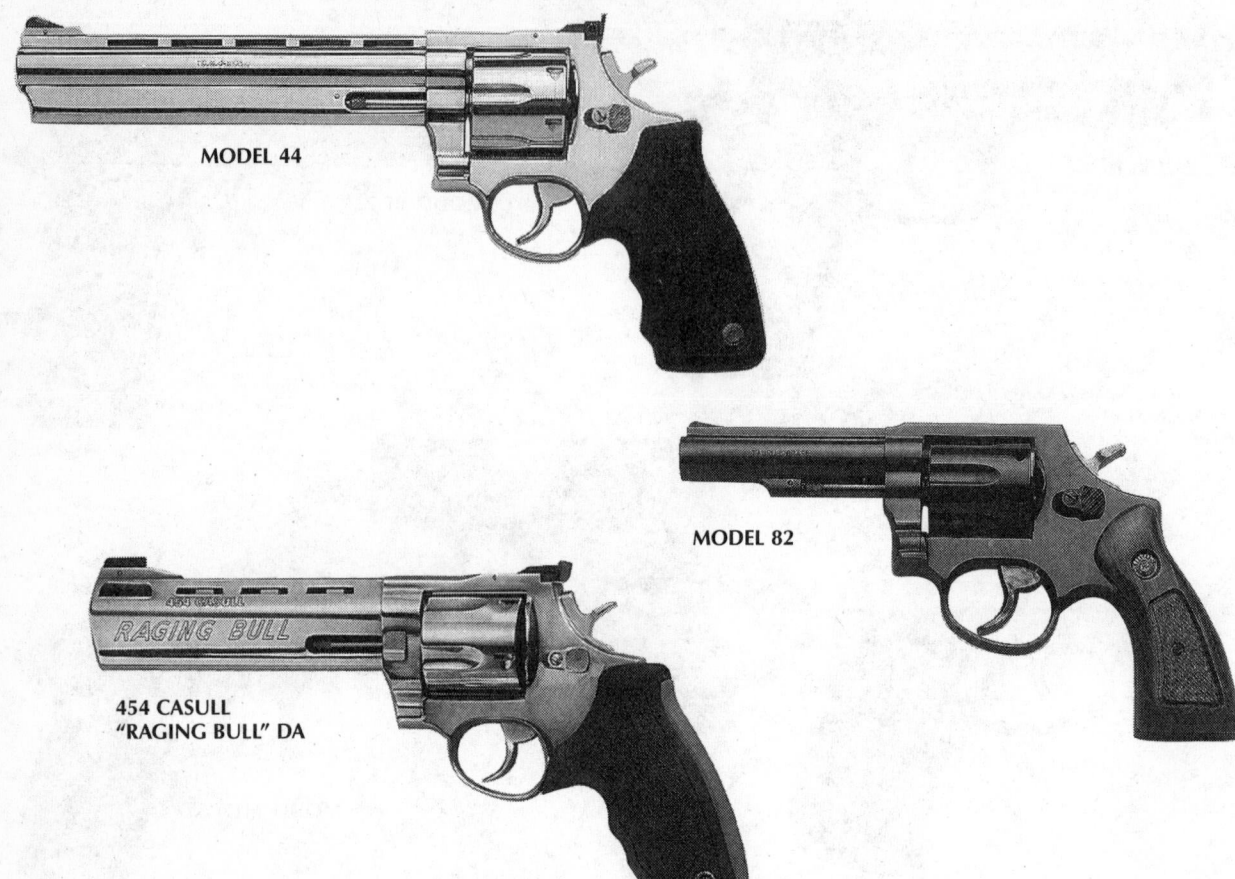

MODEL 44

MODEL 82

454 CASULL
"RAGING BULL" DA

## MODEL PT938 COMPACT

*Action:* autoloader
*Grips:* rubber
*Barrel:* 3 in.
*Sights:* fixed open
*Weight:* 27.0oz.
*Caliber:* .380
*Capacity:* 10 + 1
*Features:* double action only
blue . . . . . . . . . . . . . . . . . . . . . $516
stainless . . . . . . . . . . . . . . . . . . $531

## MODEL 44

Action: double-action revolver
*Grips:* rubber
*Barrel:* 4, 6 or 8.4 in.
*Sights:* target
*Weight:* 44.0oz.
*Caliber:* .44 Mag.
*Capacity:* 6
*Features:* vent rib, porting; weight to
57 oz. depending on barrel length
blue, **4 in.** . . . . . . . . . . . . . . . . $500
**stainless, 4 in.** . . . . . . . . . . . . . $563

blue, 6 or 8.4 in. . . . . . . . . . . . $523
stainless, 6 or 8.4 in. . . . . . . . . $578

## MODEL 454 RAGING BULL

*Action:* double-action revolver
*Grips:* rubber
*Barrel:* 6.5 or 8.4 in.
*Sights:* target
*Weight:* 53.0oz.
*Caliber:* .454 Casull
*Capacity:* 5
*Features:* stainless or chrome-moly,
vent rib, ported; 8.4 in. weighs 63 oz.
blue . . . . . . . . . . . . . . . . . . . . . $797
stainless . . . . . . . . . . . . . . . . . . $859

## MODEL 82

*Action:* double-action revolver
*Grips:* rubber
*Barrel:* 4 in.
*Sights:* fixed open
*Weight:* 34.0oz.
*Caliber:* .38 Spl.
*Capacity:* 6

*Features:* also, 21-ounce model 85 in
.38 Spl and .32 H&R, with 2 or 3 in.
barrel, grip options
Model 82, blue . . . . . . . . . . . . . $352
Model 82, stainless . . . . . . . . . . $398
Model 85, blue . . . . . . . . . . . . . $375
Model 85, stainless . . . . . . . . . . $422

## PROTECTOR

*Action:* double-action revolver
*Grips:* rubber
*Barrel:* 2 in.
*Sights:* fixed open
*Weight:* 24.5oz.
*Caliber:* .357 Mag.
*Capacity:* 5
*Features:* shrouded but accessible
hammer; also Titanium and UltraLight
versions to 17 oz.
blue . . . . . . . . . . . . . . . . . . . . . $383
stainless . . . . . . . . . . . . . . . . . . $430
**Shadow Gray Titanium** . . . . . . . $547

## MODEL 416 RAGING BULL

*Action:* double-action revolver
*Grips:* rubber
*Barrel:* 6.5 in.
*Sights:* target
*Weight:* 62.0oz.
*Caliber:* .41 Mag.
*Capacity*: 6
*Features:* stainless vent rib, ported; also 72-ounce 8-shot Raging Bee (.218) and Thirty (.30 Carbine) with 10 in. barrel

| | |
|---|---|
| .41 | $641 |
| .218 Raging Bee | $898 |
| .30 | $898 |
| .22 Hornet | $898 |

MODEL 416
RAGING BULL

## MODEL 455 STELLAR TRACKER

*Action:* double-action revolver
*Grips:* rubber
*Barrel:* 2, 4 or 6 in.
*Sights:* target
*Weight:* 28.0oz.
*Caliber:* .45 ACP
*Capacity:* 5 (full-moon clips)
*Features:* ported barrel, to 38 ounces depending on barrel length; also M460 Tracker in .45 Colt with 4 or 6 in. barrel

| | |
|---|---|
| Model 455 | $523 |
| Model 460 | $516 |

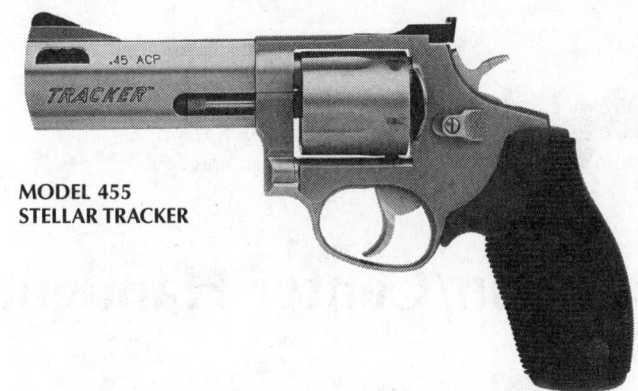

MODEL 455
STELLAR TRACKER

## 218 TARGET SILHOUETTE

*Action:* double-action revolver
*Grips:* rubber
*Barrel:* 12 in.
*Sights:* target
*Weight:* 52.3oz.
*Caliber:* .218 Bee
*Capacity:* 7
*Features:* vent rib, stainless

| | |
|---|---|
| Model 218 | $461 |

## MODEL 94/941

*Action:* double-action revolver
*Grips:* hardwood
*Barrel:* 2, 4 or 5 in.
*Sights:* target
*Weight:* 25.0oz.
*Caliber:* .22 LR
*Capacity:* 9
*Features:* solid rib; also .22 WMR with 8-shot cylinder

| | |
|---|---|
| blue | $328 |
| stainless | $375 |
| Magnum, blue | $344 |
| Magnum, stainless | $391 |

MODEL 941

# Taurus Handguns

**MODEL 605**

**MODEL 608 DOUBLE ACTION**

## MODEL 605
**Action:** double-action revolver
**Grips:** rubber
**Barrel:** 2.3 in.
**Sights:** fixed open
**Weight:** 24.5oz.
**Caliber:** .357 Mag.
**Capacity:** 5
**Features:** transfer bar; porting optional;

also 605CH with concealed hammer
Model 605 . . . . . . . . . . . . . . . . $375
stainless . . . . . . . . . . . . . . . . . $422

## MODEL 608
**Action:** double-action revolver
**Grips:** rubber
**Barrel:** 4, 6.5 or 8.4 in.
**Sights:** target

**Weight:** 49.0oz.
**Caliber:** .357 Mag.
**Capacity:** 8
**Features:** transfer bar, weight to 53 oz. depending on barrel length
blue, 4 in. . . . . . . . . . . . . . . $469
stainless, 4 in. . . . . . . . . . . . $523
blue, 6.5 or 8.4 in. . . . . . . . . . $484
stainless, 6.5 or 8.4 in. . . . . . . $547

# Thompson/Center Handguns

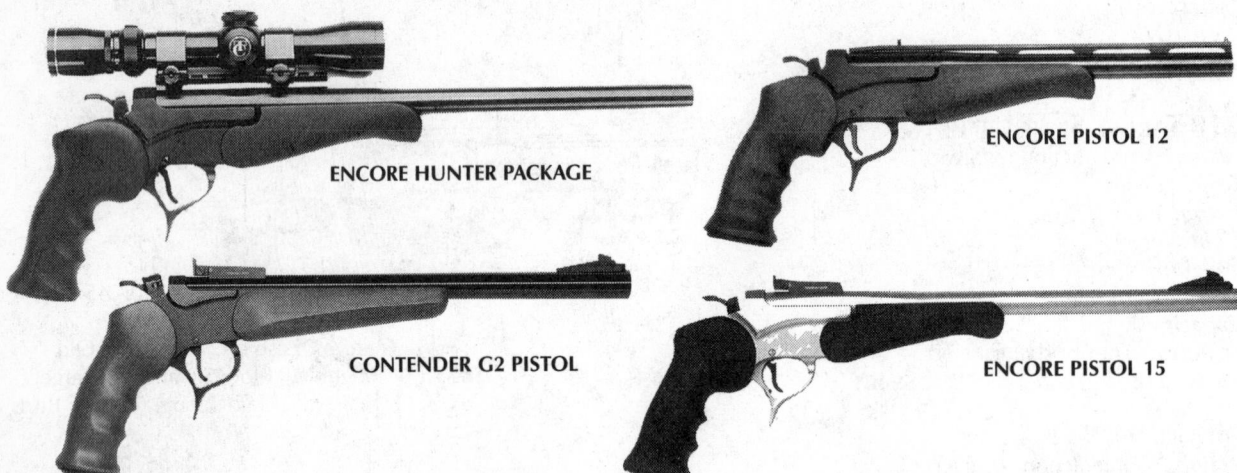

**ENCORE HUNTER PACKAGE**

**ENCORE PISTOL 12**

**CONTENDER G2 PISTOL**

**ENCORE PISTOL 15**

## CONTENDER G2
**Action:** hinged breech
**Grips:** walnut
**Barrel:** 12 or 14 in.
**Sights:** target
**Weight:** 60.0oz.
**Caliber:** .22 LR, .22 Hornet, .357 Mag., .44 Mag., .45/.410 (12 in.), .17 HMR, .22 LR, .22 Hornet, .223, 7-30, .30-30, .44 Mag., .45/.410, .45-70 (15 in.), .204 Ruger, .375 JDJ

**Capacity:** 1
**Features:** improved, stronger version of Contender
12 in. . . . . . . . . . . . . . . $555 – 585
14 in. (64 oz.) . . . . . . . . $563 – 600

## ENCORE
**Action:** hinged breech
**Grips:** walnut or rubber
**Barrel:** 12 or 15 in.
**Sights:** target
**Weight:** 68.0oz.

**Caliber:** many popular rifle and big-bore pistol rounds, from the .22 Hornet to the .30-06 and .45-70, the .454 Casull and .480 Ruger
**Capacity:** 1
**Features:** also in package with 2-7x scope, carry case; prices vary with caliber, options
12 in. . . . . . . . . . . . . . . . . . $583
15 in. (72 oz.) . . . . . . . . . . . . $588
.45/.410 with rib . . . . . . . . . . $615
stainless with rubber grips . . . . $641

# Uberti Handguns

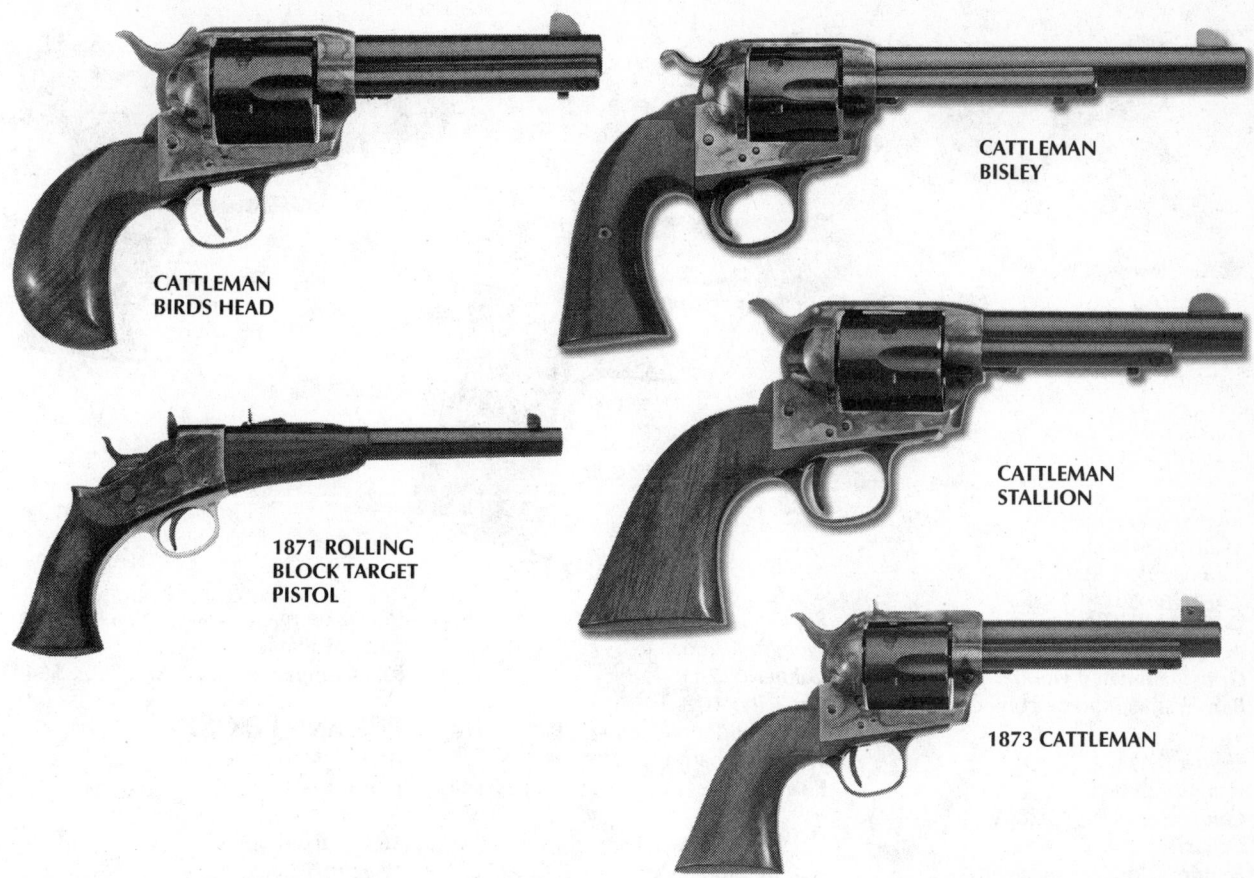

CATTLEMAN BIRDS HEAD

CATTLEMAN BISLEY

1871 ROLLING BLOCK TARGET PISTOL

CATTLEMAN STALLION

1873 CATTLEMAN

## 1873 CATTLEMAN BIRD'S HEAD

*Action*: single-action revolver
*Grips*: walnut
*Barrel*: 3½, 4, 4½ or 5½ in.
*Sights*: fixed open
*Weight*: 2.31 lbs.
*Caliber*: .357 Mag., .44/40, .45 LC
*Capacity*: 6
*Features*: fluted cylinder, round tapered barrel, forged steel, color case-hardened frame, curved grip frame and grip, Flattop available with adjustable sights.
1873 Bird's Head . . . . . . . . . . .$430

## BISLEY

*Action*: single-action revolver
*Grips*: walnut
*Barrel*: 4³/₄, 5½", 7½ in.
*Sights*: adjustable
*Weight*: 2.51 lbs.
*Caliber*: .357 Mag., .44/40, .45 LC
*Capacity*: 6
*Features*: Bisley style grip, color case hardened frame, fluted cylinder.
Bisley . . . . . . . . . . . . . . . . .$430
Bisley Flattop . . . . . . . . . . . . .$435

## 1873 STALLION

*Action*: single-action revolver
*Grips*: walnut
*Barrel*: 5½ in.
*Sights*: open fixed
*Weight*: 1.98 lbs.
*Caliber*: .22 LR, .38 SP
*Capacity*: 6
*Features*: color case-hardened steel frame, fluted cylender
1873 Stallion . . . . . . . . . . . . .$375

## MODEL 1871 ROLLING BLOCK PISTOL

*Action:* rolling block
*Grips:* walnut
*Barrel:* 9.5 in.
*Sights:* target
*Weight:* 45.0oz.
*Caliber:* .22 LR, .22 Mag.
*Capacity:* 1
*Features:* case-colored breech, brass guard
1871 Rolling Block . . . . . . . . . $410

## MODEL 1873 SINGLE ACTION REVOLVER

*Action:* single-action revolver
*Grips:* walnut
*Barrel:* 4.8, 5.5, 7.5 or 18 in.
*Sights:* fixed open
*Weight:* 37.0oz. (5.5 in.)
*Caliber:* .357 Mag., .44-40, .45 Colt
*Capacity:* 6
*Features:* case colored frame, Old Model/New Model available. Target sights available on some models; Birds Head or Bisley grips available
1873 . . . . . . . . . . . . . . . . . . . . . $395
nickel finish . . . . . . . . . . . . . . $470
brass backstrap and guard. . . . . $340
Old West antique finish . . . . . . $470
Matte black millennium . . . . . . $260
stainless steel . . . . . . . . . . . . . . $475
charcoal blue . . . . . . . . . . . . . . $440

# Walther Handguns

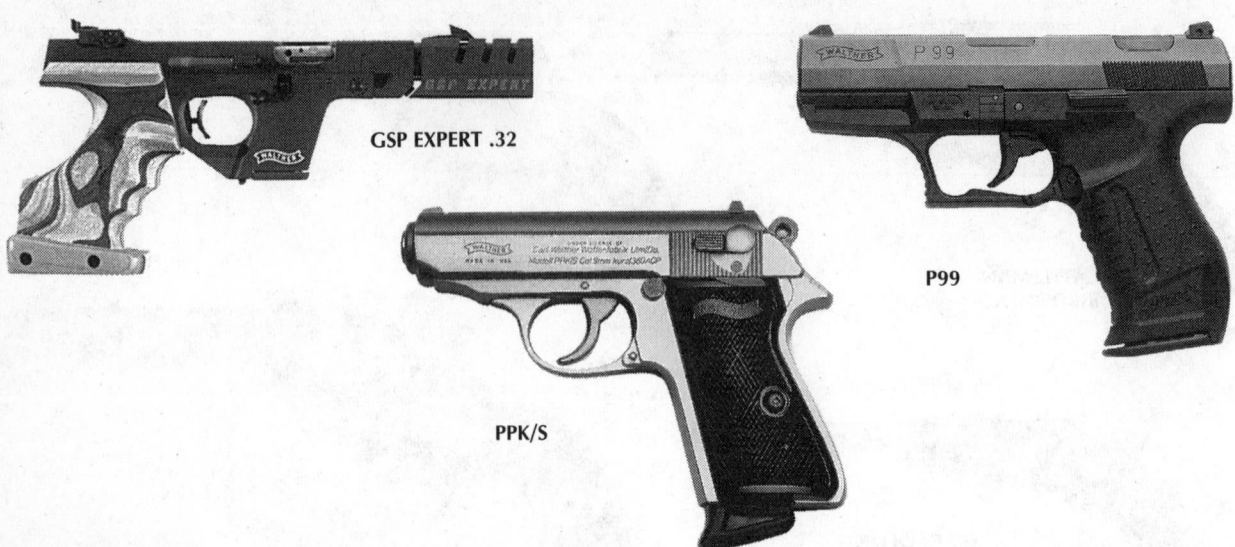

GSP EXPERT .32

PPK/S

P99

## GSP EXPERT

*Action:* autoloader
*Grips:* laminated wood
*Barrel:* match-grade compensated 4.2 in.
*Sights:* target
*Weight:* 29.0oz.
*Caliber:* .22 LR, .32 S&W
*Capacity:* 5
*Features:* forward magazine
.22.....................$1240
.32.....................$1420

## P22

*Action:* autoloader
*Grips:* polymer
*Barrel:* 3.4 or 5 in.

*Sights:* 3-dot
*Weight:* 19.6oz.
*Caliber:* .22 LR
*Capacity:* 10 + 1
*Features:* double action; 20.3 ounces with 5 in. barrel
P22.....................$249

## P99 COMPACT

*Action:* autoloader
*Grips:* polymer
*Barrel:* 4 in.
*Sights:* low-profile combat
*Weight:* 25.0oz.
*Caliber:* 9mm, .40 S&W
*Capacity:* 10 + 1
*Features:* double action, ambidextrous

magazine release, high-capacity magazines available
P99 Compact.............$644

## PPK AND PPK/S

*Action:* autoloader
*Grips:* polymer
*Barrel:* 3.4 in.
*Sights:* fixed open
*Weight:* 22.0oz.
*Caliber:* .380 and .32 ACP
*Capacity:* 7 + 1
*Features:* double action, blue or stainless, decocker
PPK.....................$543

# Wildey Handguns

## WILDEY AUTOMATIC PISTOL

*Action:* autoloader
*Grips:* composite
*Barrel:* 5, 6, 7, 8, 10, 12 or 14 in.
*Sights:* target
*Weight:* 64.0oz.
*Caliber:* .45 Win. Mag., .44 Auto Mag, .45 and .475 Wildey
*Capacity:* 7 + 1
*Features:* gas operated, ribbed barrel
starting at ...............$1385

# Austin & Halleck Black Powder

MODEL 320 REALTREE-HARDWOODS CAMO

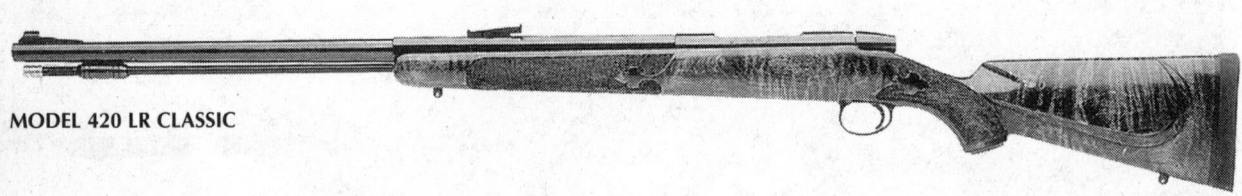

MODEL 420 LR CLASSIC

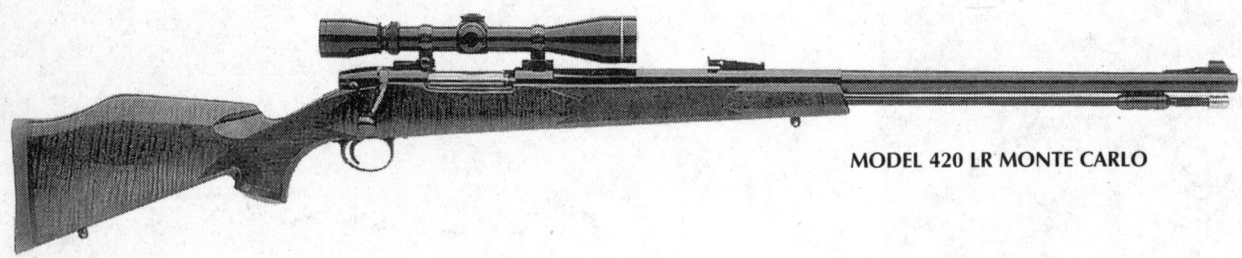

MODEL 420 LR MONTE CARLO

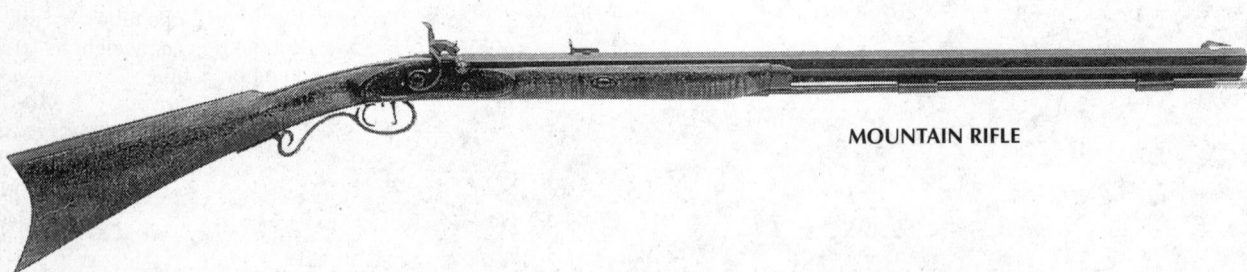

MOUNTAIN RIFLE

## BOLT ACTION M320, 420
**Lock**: in-line
**Stock**: curly maple, synthetic, camo
**Barrel**: 26 in., 1:28 twist
**Sights**: adjustable open
**Weight**: 7.8lbs.
**Bore/Caliber**: .50
**Features**: match trigger
synthetic . . . . . . . . . . . . . . . . . . $419
stainless synthetic . . . . . . . . . . $449

camo . . . . . . . . . . . . . . . . . . . . $459
stainless camo . . . . . . . . . . . . . $489
maple . . . . . . . . . . . . . . . . . . . $549
stainless maple . . . . . . . . . . . . $579

## MOUNTAIN RIFLE
**Lock:** traditional cap or flint
**Stock:** curly maple
**Barrel:** 32 in., 1:66 or 1:28 twist
**Sights:** fixed
**Weight:** 7.5lbs.

**Bore/Caliber:** .50
**Features:** double set triggers
percussion . . . . . . . . . . . . . . . . $539
select percussion . . . . . . . . . . . $719
flint . . . . . . . . . . . . . . . . . . . . . $589
select flint . . . . . . . . . . . . . . . . $769

# Cabela's Black Powder

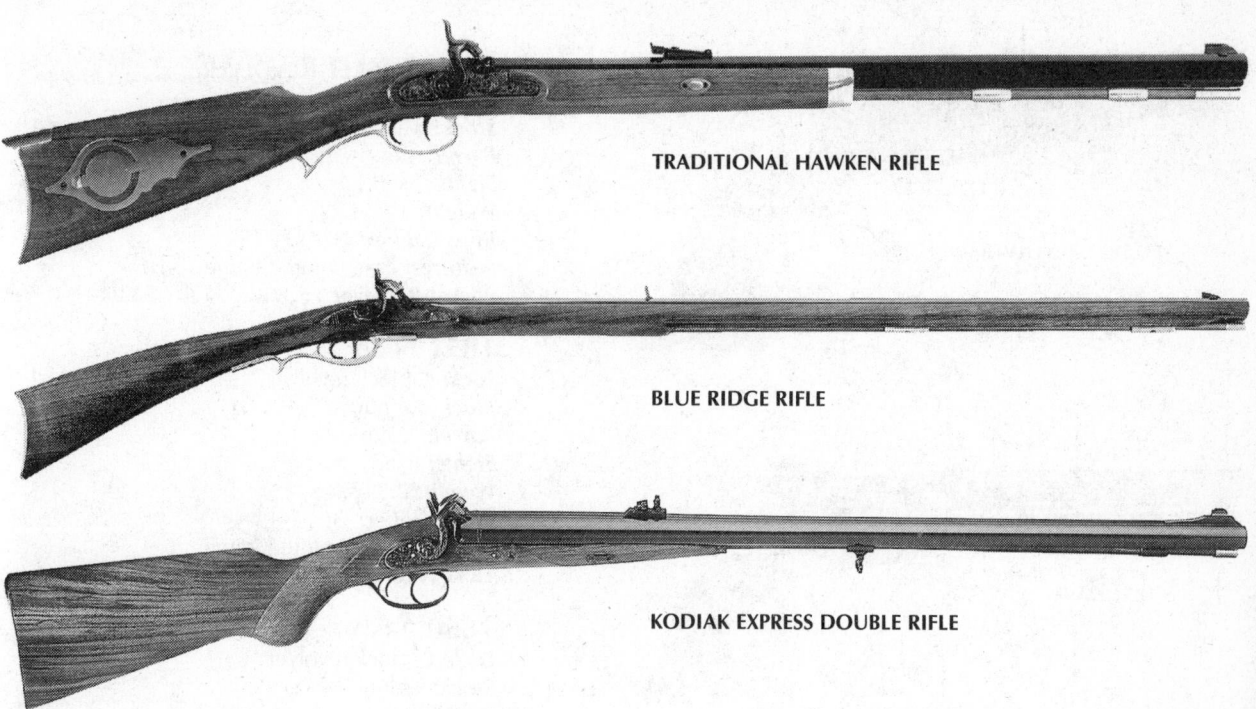

TRADITIONAL HAWKEN RIFLE

BLUE RIDGE RIFLE

KODIAK EXPRESS DOUBLE RIFLE

## HAWKEN
*Lock:* traditional cap or flint
*Stock:* walnut
*Barrel:* 24 in., 1:28 twist
*Sights:* adjustable open
*Weight:* 9.0lbs.
*Bore/Caliber:* .50 or .54
*Features:* brass furniture,
double-set trigger
**percussion (right or left-hand). . $270**
**flint** . . . . . . . . . . . . . . . . . . . **$300**

## BLUE RIDGE
*Lock:* side-hammer caplock
*Stock:* walnut

*Barrel:* 39 in., 1:48 twist
*Sights:* none
*Weight:* 7.8lbs.
*Bore/Caliber:* .32, .36, .45 and .50
*Features:* double set triggers,
case-colored locks
**caplock** . . . . . . . . . . . . . . . . . **$479**
**flint** . . . . . . . . . . . . . . . . . . . **$499**

## KODIAK EXPRESS DOUBLE RIFLE
*Lock:* traditional caplock
*Stock:* walnut, pistol grip
*Barrel:* 28 in., 1:48 twist
*Sights:* folding leaf
*Weight:* 9.3lbs.

*Bore/Caliber:* .50, .54, .58 and .72
*Features:* double triggers
**from** . . . . . . . . . . . . . . . . . . **$900**

## DOUBLE SHOTGUN
*Lock:* traditional caplock
*Stock:* walnut
*Barrel:* 27, 28 or 30 in.
*Sights:* none
*Weight:* 7.0lbs.
*Bore/Caliber:* 20, 12 or 10 ga.
*Features:* screw-in choke tubes: X-Full,
Mod, IC, double triggers; weight to 10
lbs. depending on gauge
**from** . . . . . . . . . . . . . . . . . . **$660**

*Pyrodex pellets make loading faster and easier
than measuring black powder or granular Pyrodex
(a black powder substitute).*

# Colt Black Powder

**1849
POCKET REVOLVER**

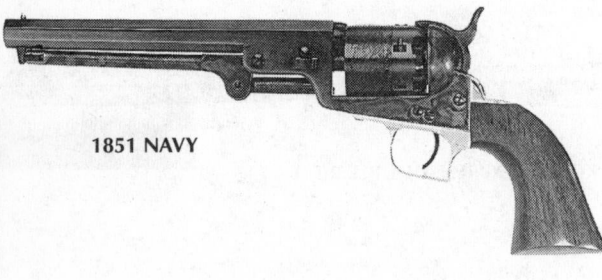

**1851 NAVY**

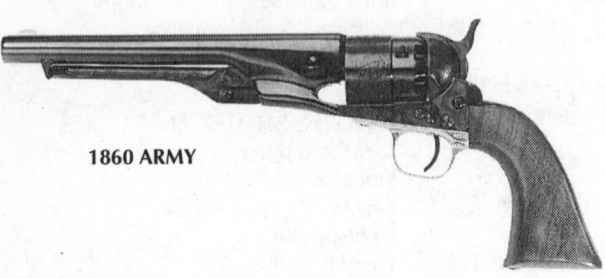

**1860 ARMY**

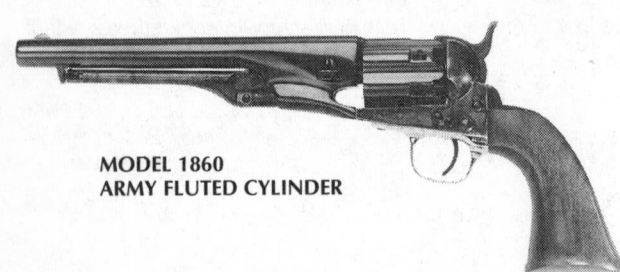

**MODEL 1860
ARMY FLUTED CYLINDER**

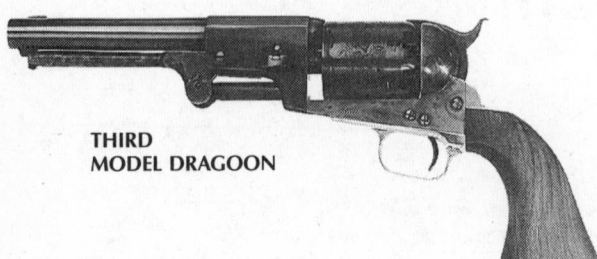

**THIRD
MODEL DRAGOON**

### 1849 POCKET REVOLVER
*Lock:* caplock revolver
*Stock:* walnut
*Barrel:* 4 in.
*Sights:* fixed
*Weight:* 1.5lbs.
*Bore/Caliber:* .31
*Features:* case-colored frame
**Pocket Revolver . . . . . . . . . . . . $430**

### 1851 NAVY
*Lock:* caplock revolver
*Stock:* walnut
*Barrel:* 7.5 in.
*Sights:* fixed
*Weight:* 2.5lbs.
*Bore/Caliber:* .36
*Features:* case-colored frame
**1851 Navy . . . . . . . . . . . . . . . $450**

### 1860 ARMY
*Lock:* caplock revolver
*Stock:* walnut
*Barrel:* 8 in.
*Sights:* fixed
*Weight:* 2.6lbs.
*Bore/Caliber:* ..44
*Features:* case-colored frame, hammer,
plunger; also with fluted cylinder and
adapted for shoulder stock
**1860 Army . . . . . . . . . . . . . . . $450**

### THIRD MODEL DRAGOON
*Lock:* caplock revolver
*Stock:* walnut
*Barrel:* 7.5 in.
*Sights:* fixed
*Weight:* 4.1lbs.
*Bore/Caliber:* .44
*Features:* case-colored frame, hammer,
lever, plunger
**Dragoon . . . . . . . . . . . . . . . $500**

# Colt Black Powder

## WALKER
*Lock:* caplock revolver
*Stock:* walnut
*Barrel:* 9 in.
*Sights:* fixed
*Weight:* 4.6lbs.
*Bore/Caliber:* .44
*Features:* case-colored frame, authentic remake of 1847 Walker
**Walker. . . . . . . . . . . . . . . . . . $500**

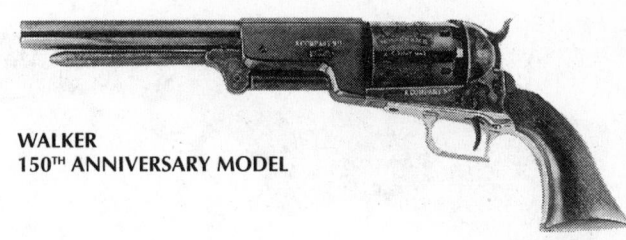

WALKER
150TH ANNIVERSARY MODEL

## 1861 NAVY
*Lock:* caplock revolver
*Stock:* walnut
*Barrel:* 7.5 in.
*Sights:* fixed
*Weight:* 2.6lbs.
*Bore/Caliber:* .36
*Features:* revolver with case-colored frame, hammer, lever, plunger
**1861 Navy . . . . . . . . . . . . . . . . $450**

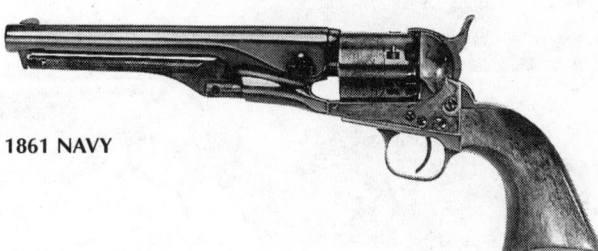

1861 NAVY

## TRAPPER 1862 POCKET POLICE
*Lock:* caplock revolver
*Stock:* walnut
*Barrel:* 3.5 in.
*Sights:* fixed
*Weight:* 1.25lbs.
*Bore/Caliber:* .36
*Features:* revolver with case-colored frame, separate brass ramrod
**Pocket Police . . . . . . . . . . . . . $430**

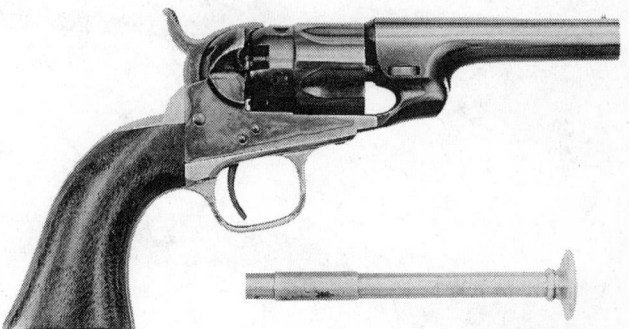

TRAPPER
1862 POCKET POLICE

## COLT 1861 RIFLE
*Lock:* traditional caplock
*Stock:* walnut
*Barrel:* 40 in.
*Sights:* folding leaf
*Weight:* 9.2lbs.
*Bore/Caliber:* .58
*Features:* authentic reproduction of 1861 Springfield
**1861 Musket. . . . . . . . . . . . . . $800**

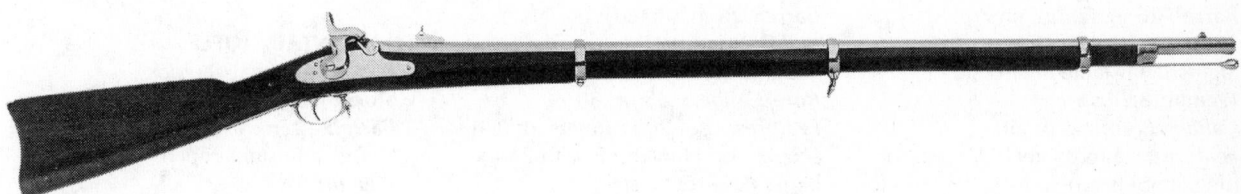

COLT 1861 RIFLE

BLACK POWDER

# CVA Black Powder

**OPTIMA 209 SYNTHETIC/BLUE**

**OPTIMA 209 CAMO/BLUE**

**OPTIMA 209 CAMO/NICKEL**

**FIREBOLT ULTRAMAG**

**MOUNTAIN RIFLE**

### OPTIMA AND OPTIMA PRO
*Lock:* traditional caplock
*Stock:* synthetic or camo
*Barrel:* 26 in. (29 in. on Pro), 1:28 twist
*Sights:* adjustable fiber optic
*Weight:* 8.2lbs.
*Caliber/Bore:* .45 or .50
*Features:* stainless steel 209 breech plug, ambidextrous stock; add $65 for Pro (8.8 lbs.)

Optima, synthetic/blue . . . . . . . $225
synthetic/nickel . . . . . . . . . . . . $255
camo/blue . . . . . . . . . . . . . . . . $280
camo/nickel . . . . . . . . . . . . . . . $300

### FIREBOLT ULTRAMAG RIFLE
*Lock:* inline
*Stock:* synthetic or camo
*Barrel:* 26 in., fluted
*Sights:* none
*Weight:* 7.0lbs.
*Bore/Caliber:* .45 or .50
*Features:* uses 209 primers, drilled for scope; also Hunterbolt with 24-inch barrel, fiber optic sights

Firebolt, synthetic blue . . . . . . . $200
synthetic nickel . . . . . . . . . . . . $250
camo blue . . . . . . . . . . . . . . . . $240
camo nickel . . . . . . . . . . . . . . . $260
Hunterbolt, synthetic blue . . . . $140

synthetic nickel . . . . . . . . . . . . $195
camo blue . . . . . . . . . . . . . . . . $220
camo nickel . . . . . . . . . . . . . . . $235

### MOUNTAIN RIFLE
*Lock:* traditional caplock
*Stock:* maple
*Barrel:* 32 in., 1:48 twist
*Sights:* adjustable open
*Weight:* 9.0lbs.
*Bore/Caliber:* .50
*Features:* blued steel hardware, limited production
**Mountain Rifle** . . . . . . . . . . . $260

# CVA Black Powder

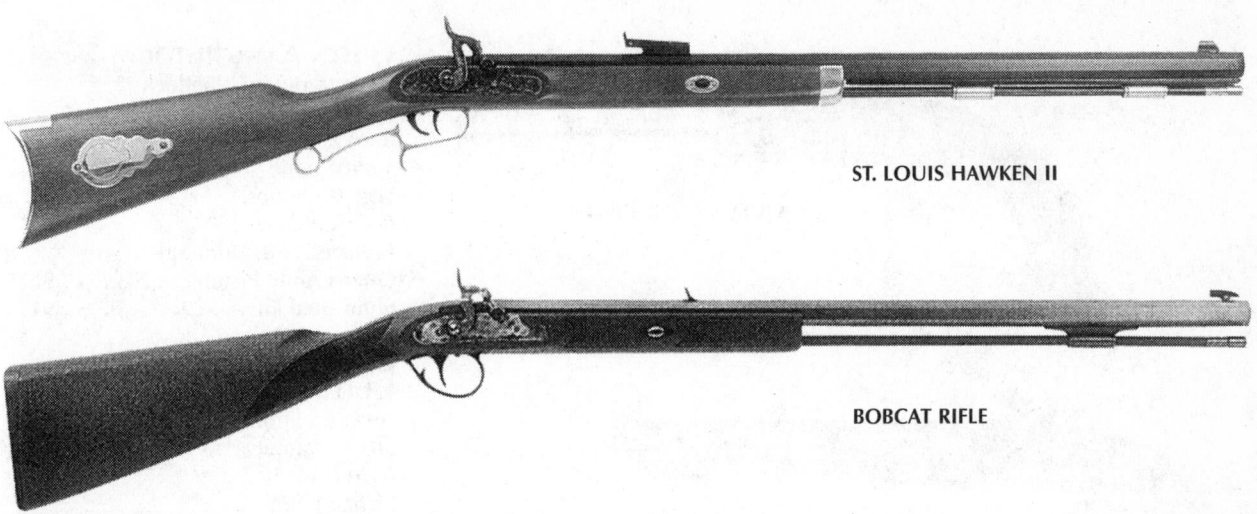

**ST. LOUIS HAWKEN II**

**BOBCAT RIFLE**

### St. Louis Hawken II
*Lock:* traditional caplock
*Stock:* hardwood
*Barrel:* 28 in.; 1:48 twist
*Sights:* adjustable open
*Weight:* 8.0lbs.
*Bore/Caliber:* .40 or .54
*Features:* brass furniture,
double set trigger
**St. Louis Hawken II . . . . . . . . . $230**

### Bobcat
*Lock:* traditional caplock
*Stock:* hardwood or synthetic
*Barrel:* 26 in., 1:48 twist
*Sights:* fixed
*Weight:* 6.0lbs.
*Bore/Caliber:* .50

*Features:* basic muzzleloader with versatile deep-groove rifling; also,
Plainsman flintlock with wood stock
**synthetic . . . . . . . . . . . . . . . . . . . $70**
**hardwood . . . . . . . . . . . . . . . . $100**

**Warning: Continuation of 1997 Recall**
**Do not use CVA In-Line rifles with 1995 or 1996 serial numbers**
**Serious injury may result**

In 1997, Connecticut Valley Arms, Inc., voluntarily implemented a recall of in-line muzzleloading rifles manufactured in 1995 and 1996. If you currently own or possess a CVA in-line rifle with a 95 or 96 serial number, or you purchased one or gave it or sold it to another person, and the barrel has not been replaced, you should contact a Company Representative immediately by calling the customer service number below:
**1-770-449-4687 (8:30 a.m. to 4:00 p.m. EST)**
sample serial # 61-13-xxxxxx-95
sample serial # 61-13-xxxxxx-96

To identify the rifle, read the serial number on the barrel opposite the firing bolt. The only CVA rilfes subject to the voluntary recall are in-line models with serial numbers ending with the last two digits of 95 or 96. No other firearm models within the CVA product line are affected by the voluntary recall.

Blackpowder Products, Inc. purchased the assets of Connecticut Valley Arms, Inc. in May, 1999. Blackpowder products, Inc. assumed no liability for any product manufactured or sold prior to January 1, 1998. Blackpowder Products, Inc. is continuing the Connecticut Valley Arms, Inc. recall, and will cover all reasonable related shipping charges. Please do not return your in-line rifle before contacting a Company Representative at the above customer service number.

*Before loading a caplock rifle, hold the muzzle close to a patch of grass and fire a primer only. If the grass shudders, the nipple is clear and the gun ready for loading.*

# Dixie Black Powder

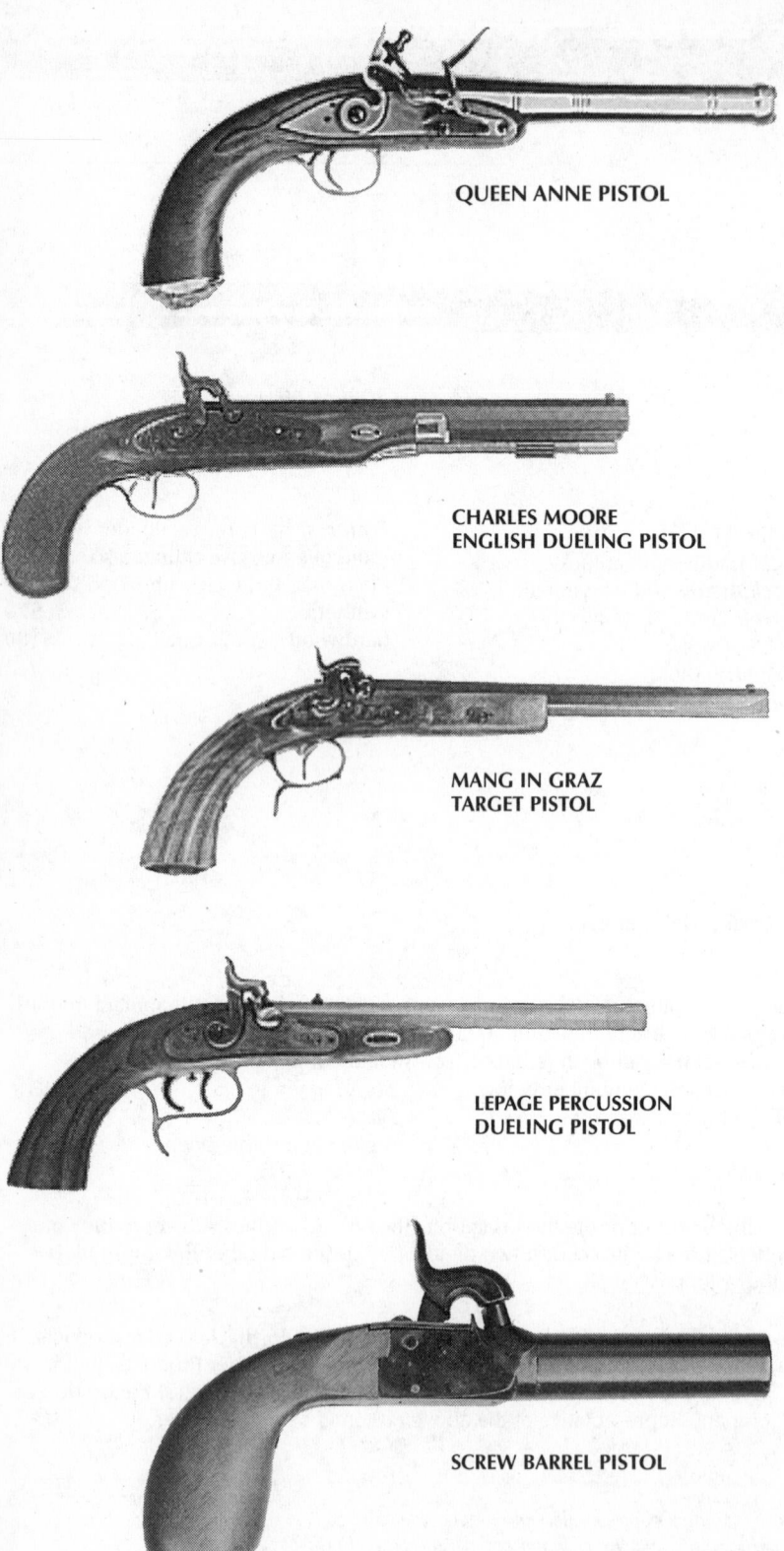

QUEEN ANNE PISTOL

CHARLES MOORE
ENGLISH DUELING PISTOL

MANG IN GRAZ
TARGET PISTOL

LEPAGE PERCUSSION
DUELING PISTOL

SCREW BARREL PISTOL

## QUEEN ANNE PISTOL
*Lock:* traditional flintlock
*Stock:* walnut
*Barrel:* 7.5 in.
*Sights:* none
*Weight:* 2.2lbs.
*Bore/Caliber:* .45
*Features:* brass furniture
**Queen Anne Pistol** . . . . . . . . . . **$275**
**unfinished kit** . . . . . . . . . . . . . **$195**

## CHARLES MOORE
## DUELING PISTOL
*Lock:* traditional cap or flint
*Stock:* walnut
*Barrel:* 11 in.
*Sights:* fixed
*Weight:* 2.8lbs.
*Bore/Caliber:* .45
*Features:* silver-plated furniture,
case-colored
**cap** . . . . . . . . . . . . . . . . . . . . . **$375**
**flint** . . . . . . . . . . . . . . . . . . . . **$425**

## MANG TARGET PISTOL
*Lock:* traditional caplock
*Stock:* hardwood
*Barrel:* 10.4 in., 1:15 twist
*Sights:* fixed
*Weight:* 2.5lbs.
*Bore/Caliber:* .38
*Features:* half-stock, finger rest on
guard
**Mang Target Pistol** . . . . . . . . . . **$925**

## LEPAGE DUELING PISTOL
*Lock:* traditional caplock
*Stock:* hardwood
*Barrel:* 9 in.
*Sights:* fixed
*Weight:* 2.5lbs.
*Bore/Caliber:* .45
*Features:* double set trigger
**LePage Dueling Pistol** . . . . . . . . **$545**

## SCREW BARREL PISTOL
*Lock:* traditional caplock
*Stock:* hardwood
*Barrel:* 3 in.
*Sights:* none
*Weight:* 0.75lbs.
*Bore/Caliber:* .445
*Features:* barrel detaches for loading;
folding trigger
**Screw Barrel Pistol** . . . . . . . . . . **$115**
**unfinished kit** . . . . . . . . . . . . . **$95**

# Dixie Black Powder

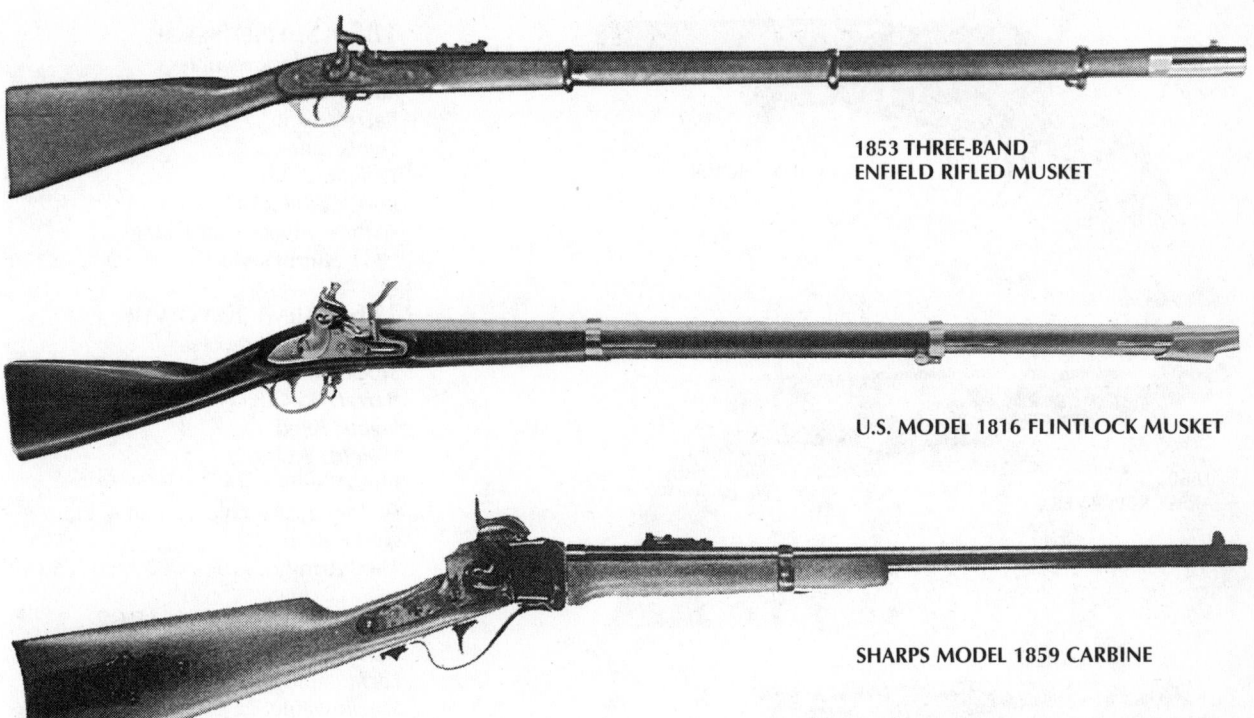

**1853 THREE-BAND
ENFIELD RIFLED MUSKET**

**U.S. MODEL 1816 FLINTLOCK MUSKET**

**SHARPS MODEL 1859 CARBINE**

## PENNSYLVANIA RIFLE

*Lock:* traditional cap or flint
*Stock:* walnut
*Barrel:* 41 in.
*Sights:* fixed
*Weight:* 8.0lbs.
*Bore/Caliber:* .45
*Features:* brass furniture
**Pennsylvania Rifle . . . . . . . . . . . $575**
**unfinished kit . . . . . . . . . . . . . . $465**

## WAADTLANDER RIFLE

*Lock:* traditional caplock
*Stock:* walnut
*Barrel:* 31 in., 1;48 twist
*Sights:* aperture
*Weight:* 10.5lbs.
*Bore/Caliber:* .45
*Features:* recreation of Swiss Target
rifle, circa 1839 - 1860, case-colored
hardware, double set trigger
**Waadtlander . . . . . . . . . . . . . $1600**

## 1853
### THREE-BAND ENFIELD

*Lock:* traditional caplock
*Stock:* walnut
*Barrel:* 39 in.
*Sights:* fixed
*Weight:* 10.5lbs.
*Bore/Caliber:* .58
*Features:* case-colored lock, brass fur-
niture; also 1858 two-band Enfield
with 33 in. barrel
**three-band . . . . . . . . . . . . . . . . $575**
**unfinished kit . . . . . . . . . . . . . . $525**
**two-band . . . . . . . . . . . . . . . . . $580**

## MODEL U.S. 1816
### FLINTLOCK MUSKET

*Lock:* traditional flintlock
*Stock:* walnut
*Barrel:* 42 in. smoothbore
*Sights:* fixed
*Weight:* 9.8lbs.

*Bore/Caliber:* .69
*Features:* most common military flintlock from U.S. armories, complete
with bayonet lug and swivels
**Musket . . . . . . . . . . . . . . . . . . $875**

## MODEL 1859
### SHARPS CARBINE

*Lock:* dropping block
*Stock:* walnut
*Barrel:* 22 in.
*Sights:* adjustable open
*Weight:* 7.8lbs.
*Bore/Caliber:* .54
*Features:* case-colored furniture,
including saddle ring; also 1859 mili-
tary rifle with 30-inch barrel (9 lbs.);
both by Pedersoli
**Sharps Carbine . . . . . . . . . . . . . $850**
**with 30 in. barrel . . . . . . . . . . . $995**

# EMF Hartford Black Powder

BLACK POWDER

**1851 SHERIFF'S**

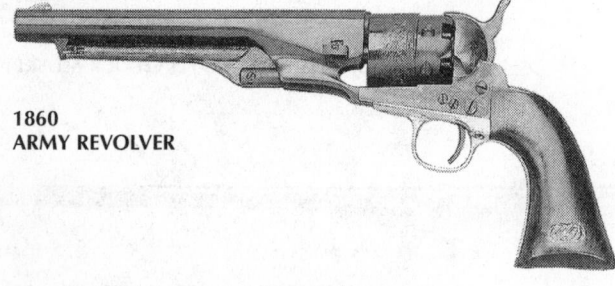

**1860 ARMY REVOLVER**

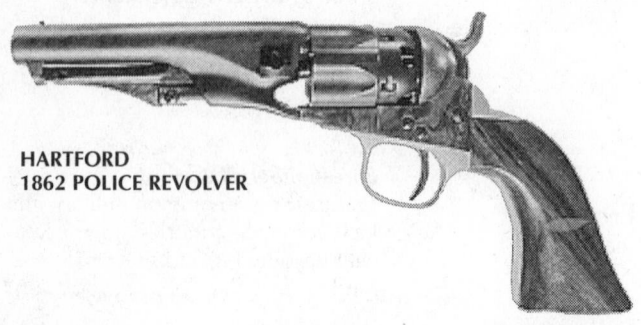

**HARTFORD 1862 POLICE REVOLVER**

**1851 BUNTLINE SPECIAL**

## 1851 SHERIFF'S
*Lock:* caplock revolver
*Stock:* walnut
*Barrel:* 5 in.
*Sights:* none
*Weight:* 2.4lbs.
*Bore/Caliber:* .44
*Features:* brass guard, strap
**1851 Sheriff's Model** . . . . . . . . $130

## 1860 ARMY REVOLVER
*Lock:* caplock revolver
*Stock:* walnut
*Barrel:* 8 in.
*Sights:* fixed
*Weight:* 2.6lbs.
*Bore/Caliber:* .44
*Features:* case-colored frame, brass guard, strap
**1860 Army** . . . . . . . . . . . . . . $160

## HARTFORD MODEL 1862 POLICE REVOLVER
*Lock:* caplock revolver
*Stock:* walnut
*Barrel:* 5.5 in.
*Sights:* fixed
*Weight:* 2.1lbs.
*Bore/Caliber:* .36
*Features:* 5-shot cylinder
**1862 Police Revolver.** . . . . . . . . $210

## 1851 BUNTLINE SPECIAL
*Lock:* caplock revolver
*Stock:* walnut
*Barrel:* 12 in.
*Sights:* fixed
*Weight:* 3.4lbs.
*Bore/Caliber:* .44
*Features:* brass frame
**1851 Buntline Special** . . . . . . . . $130

*Conical lead bullets need fast-twist barrels: 1 turn in 28 inches. Patched balls typically shoot best with slow twist: 1 in 66. The popular compromise in many muzzleloaders: 1-in-48 twist.*

# EMF Hartford Black Powder

## 1858 REMINGTON
*Lock:* caplock revolver
*Stock:* walnut
*Barrel:* 8 in.
*Sights:* fixed
*Weight:* 2.5lbs.
*Bore/Caliber:* .44
*Features:* brass or stainless steel frame
**brass** . . . . . . . . . . . . . . . . . . . **$160**
**stainless steel** . . . . . . . . . . . . . **$230**

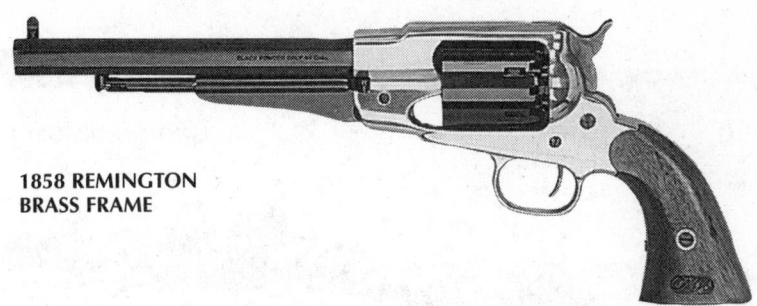

1858 REMINGTON
BRASS FRAME

## 1851 NAVY
*Lock:* caplock revolver
*Stock:* walnut
*Barrel:* 7.5 in.
*Sights:* fixed
*Weight:* 2.5lbs.
*Bore/Caliber:* .36 or .44
*Features:* brass frame
**1851 Navy** . . . . . . . . . . . . . . . **$130**

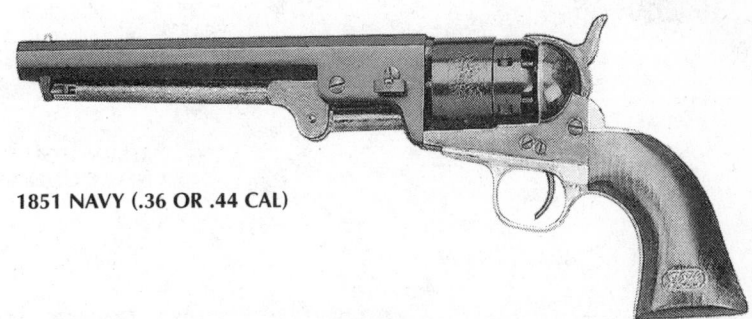

1851 NAVY (.36 OR .44 CAL)

## 1847 WALKER
*Lock:* caplock revolver
*Stock:* walnut
*Barrel:* 9 in.
*Sights:* fixed
*Weight:* 4.6lbs.
*Bore/Caliber:* .44
*Features:* largest commercial Colt single-action, named after Texas Ranger
**1847 Walker** . . . . . . . . . . . . . . **$270**

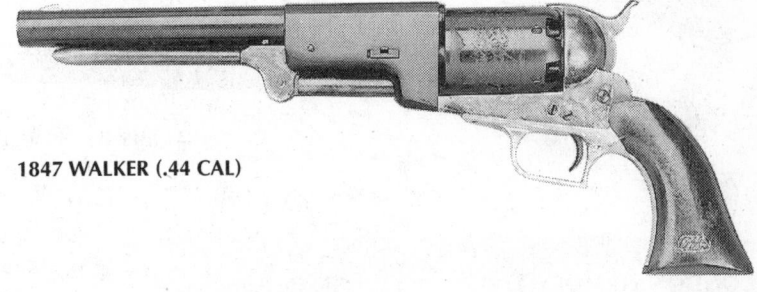

1847 WALKER (.44 CAL)

## 1848 DRAGOON
*Lock:* caplock revolver
*Stock:* walnut
*Barrel:* 7.5 in.
*Sights:* fixed
*Weight:* 2.9lbs.
*Bore/Caliber:* .44
*Features:* case-colored frame
**1848 Dragoon** . . . . . . . . . . . . . **$270**

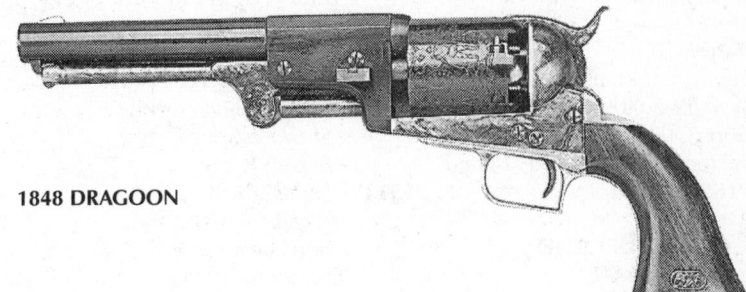

1848 DRAGOON

BLACK POWDER

*Be sure you check state game regulations before buying an in-line muzzleloader or scoping your smokepole. Some states insist that "primitive weapons" be primitive!*

# Euroarms of America Black Powder

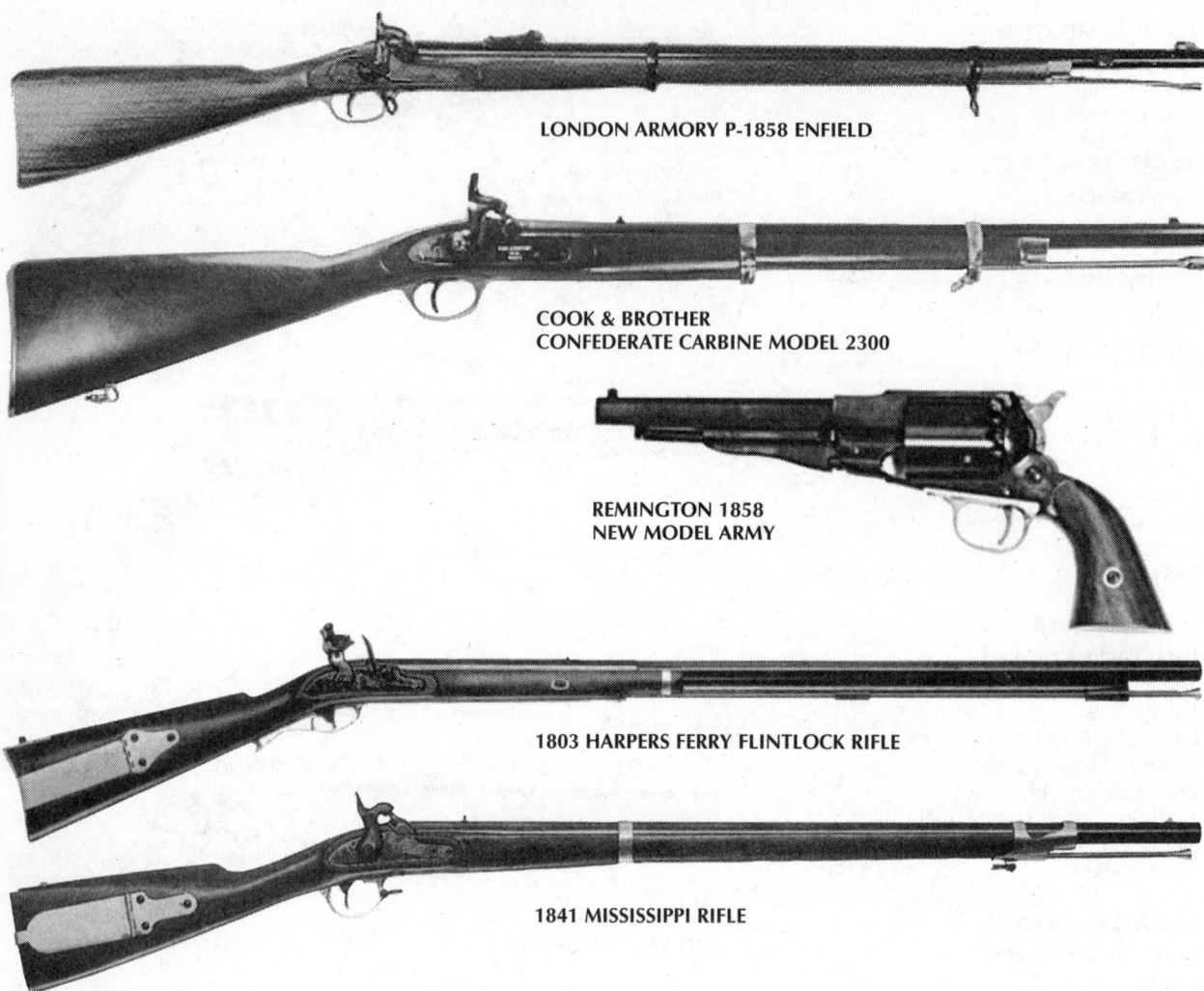

LONDON ARMORY P-1858 ENFIELD

COOK & BROTHER
CONFEDERATE CARBINE MODEL 2300

REMINGTON 1858
NEW MODEL ARMY

1803 HARPERS FERRY FLINTLOCK RIFLE

1841 MISSISSIPPI RIFLE

BLACK POWDER

### LONDON ARMORY P1858 ENFIELD
*Lock:* traditional caplock
*Stock:* walnut
*Barrel:* 33 in.
*Sights:* adjustable open
*Weight:* 8.8lbs.
*Bore/Caliber:* .58
*Features:* steel ramrod, 2-band
P1858 Enfield . . . . . . . . . . . . . $513

### COOK & BROTHER CONFEDERATE
*Lock:* traditional caplock
*Stock:* walnut
*Barrel:* 24 in.
*Sights:* fixed
*Weight:* 7.9lbs.
*Bore/Caliber:* .577
*Features*: carbine; also rifle with

33 in. barrel
carbine . . . . . . . . . . . . . . . . . $513
rifle . . . . . . . . . . . . . . . . . . . . $552

### REMINGTON 1858 NEW MODEL ARMY
*Lock:* caplock revolver
*Stock:* walnut
*Barrel:* 8 in.
*Sights:* fixed
*Weight:* 2.5lbs.
*Bore/Caliber:* .44
*Features:* brass guard; also engraved version
New Model Army . . . . . . . . . . . $220
engraved . . . . . . . . . . . . . . . . . $302

### 1803 HARPER'S FERRY FLINTLOCK
*Lock:* traditional flintlock
*Stock:* walnut
*Barrel:* 35 in.
*Sights:* fixed
*Weight:* 10.0lbs.
*Bore/Caliber:* .54
*Features:* half-stock, browned steel
1803 Harper's Ferry . . . . . . . . . $735

### 1841 MISSISSIPPI RIFLE
*Lock:* traditional caplock
*Stock:* walnut
*Barrel:* 33 in.
*Sights:* fixed
*Weight:* 9.5lbs.
*Bore/Caliber:* .54 or .58
*Features:* brass furniture
1841 Mississippi . . . . . . . . . . . $575

# Euroarms of America Black Powder

J.P. MURRAY CARBINE

C.S. RICHMOND MUSKET

ROGERS AND SPENCER

ROGERS AND SPENCER TARGET

U.S. 1863 REMINGTON ZOUAVE RIFLE

U.S. 1861 SPRINGFIELD RIFLE

## J.P. MURRAY CARBINE
**Lock:** traditional caplock
**Stock:** walnut
**Barrel:** 23 in.
**Sights:** fixed
**Weight:** 7.5lbs.
**Bore/Caliber:** .58
**Features:** brass furniture, replica of rare Confederate Cavalry Carbine
**J.P. Murray Carbine** . . . . . . . . . . **$521**

## C.S. RICHMOND MUSKET
**Lock:** traditional caplock
**Stock:** walnut
**Barrel:** 40 in.
**Sights:** fixed
**Weight:** 9.0lbs.
**Bore/Caliber:** .58
**Features:** 3-band furniture, swivels
**C.S. Richmond Musket** . . . . . . . **$579**

## ROGERS AND SPENCER
**Lock:** caplock revolver
**Stock:** walnut
**Barrel:** 7.5 in.
**Sights:** fixed
**Weight:** 2.9lbs.
**Bore/Caliber:** .44
**Features:** recommended ball diameter .451; also target model with adjustable sight
**Rogers and Spencer** . . . . . . . . . **$260**
**with London gray finish** . . . . . . **$283**
**Target** . . . . . . . . . . . . . . . . . . . **$275**

## U.S. 1841 MISSISSIPPI RIFLE
**Lock:** traditional caplock
**Stock:** walnut
**Barrel:** 33 in.
**Sights:** fixed
**Weight:** 9.5lbs.
**Bore/Caliber:** .54 or .58
**Features:** brass furniture; also 1863 Remington Zouave rifle
**Mississippi** . . . . . . . . . . . . . . . **$575**
**Zouave** . . . . . . . . . . . . . . . . . . **$469**

## U.S. 1861 SPRINGFIELD
**Lock:** traditional caplock
**Stock:** walnut
**Barrel:** 40 in.
**Sights:** fixed
**Weight:** 10.0lbs.
**Bore/Caliber:** .58
**Features:** sling swivels; also London P-1852 rifled musket, London Enfield P-1861 (7.5 lbs.)
**Springfield** . . . . . . . . . . . . . . . **$579**
**1852 rifled musket** . . . . . . . . . . **$528**
**1861 London Enfield** . . . . . . . . **$475**

# Gonic Black Powder

MODEL 93 MAG

STANDARD

THUMBHOLE

TK 2000 SHOTGUN

WOLVERINE 209

## MODEL 93
*Lock:* in-line
*Stock:* laminated or synthetic, pillar bedded
*Barrel:* 26 in. stainless, 1:24 twist
*Sights:* adjustable open
*Weight:* 7.0lbs.
*Bore/Caliber:* .50
*Features:* various stock configurations, including thumbhole; scope mounting provisions
**Model 93** . . . . . . . . . . . . . . . . **$999**

## MODEL TK 2000 SHOTGUN
*Lock:* in-line
*Stock:* synthetic or camo
*Barrel:* 26 in.
*Sights:* fiber optic
*Weight:* 7.6lbs.
*Bore/Caliber:* 12 ga.
*Features:* adjustable trigger, screw-in choke tubes; uses 209 primers
**synthetic** . . . . . . . . . . . . . . . . . **$350**
**camo** . . . . . . . . . . . . . . . . . . . . **$400**

## WOLVERINE 209
*Lock:* in-line
*Stock:* synthetic or camo
*Barrel:* 22 in., 1:28 twist
*Sights:* fiber optic
*Weight:* 7.0lbs.
*Bore/Caliber:* .50
*Features:* Full Plastic Jacket ignition
**Wolverine** . . . . . . . . . . . . . . . . **$290**
**Camo** . . . . . . . . . . . . . . . . . . . . **$354**

# Knight Black Powder

**AMERICAN KNIGHT**

**DISC EXTREME**

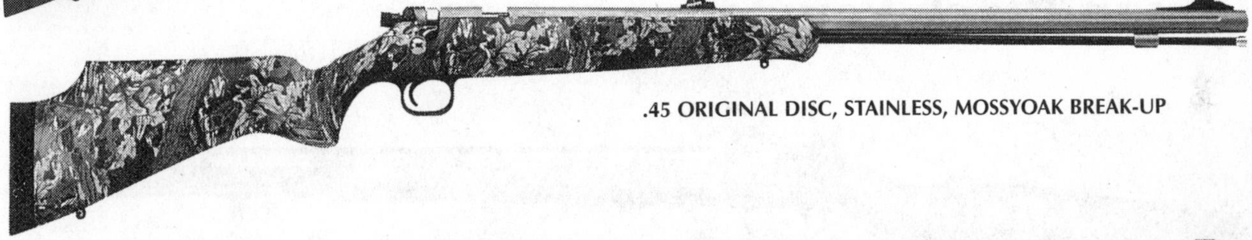

**.45 ORIGINAL DISC, STAINLESS, MOSSYOAK BREAK-UP**

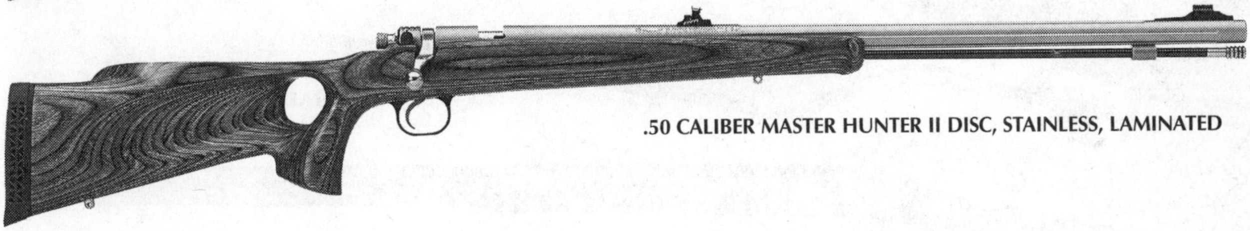

**.50 CALIBER MASTER HUNTER II DISC, STAINLESS, LAMINATED**

BLACK POWDER

## AMERICAN KNIGHT

*Lock:* in-line
*Stock:* synthetic
*Barrel:* 22 in., 1:28 twist
*Sights:* fiber optic
*Weight:* 6.2lbs.
*Bore/Caliber:* .50
*Features:* basic Knight hunting rifle
**American Knight** . . . . . . . . . . **$210**

## DISC EXTREME

*Lock:* in-line
*Stock:* walnut or synthetic thumbhole
*Barrel:* 26 in., 1:28 twist air-gauged
Green Mtn.
*Sights:* fiber optic
*Weight:* 7.3lbs.
*Bore/Caliber:* .45 or .50
*Features:* Full Plastic Jacket ignition, blue
or stainless, adjustable trigger; also origi-
nal DISC rifle with 1:20 twist (8.2 lbs.)
**Extreme, walnut** . . . . . . . . . . . **$610**
**blue/synthetic** . . . . . . . . . . . . . **$537**
**blue/camo** . . . . . . . . . . . . . . . **$537**
**stainless/synthetic** . . . . . . . . . **$610**
**stainless/camo** . . . . . . . . . . . . **$652**

## MASTER HUNTER II DISC

*Lock:* in-line
*Stock:* laminated thumbhole or synthetic
*Barrel:* 26 in., 1:28 twist
*Sights:* fiber optic
*Weight:* 7.5lbs.
*Bore/Caliber:* .45 or .50
*Features:* adjustable trigger, top of
Knight line
**Master Hunter II** . . . . . . . . . . **$1053**

*Traditional #11 percussion caps are being replaced with
musket caps and #209 shotshell primers because these
options are "hotter" and provide surer ignition in guns
that accept them.*

# Lenartz Black Powder

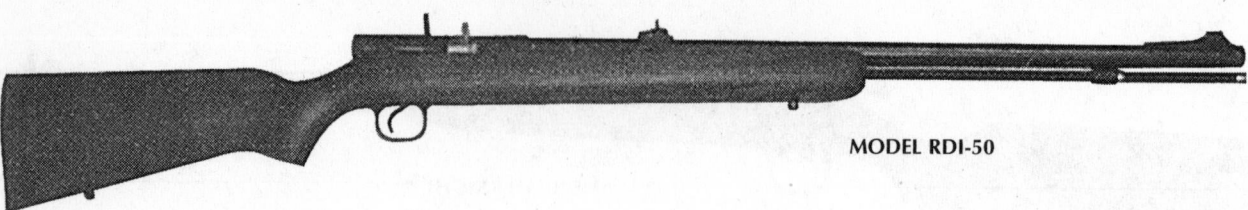

MODEL RDI-50

## MODEL RDI-50
**Lock:** in-line
**Stock:** walnut
**Barrel:** 26 in., 1:28 twist
**Sights:** adjustable open

**Weight:** 7.5lbs.
**Bore/Caliber:** .50
**Features:** adjustable trigger; uses 209 primers, converts to #11
**RDI-5** . . . . . . . . . . **price on request**

# Lyman Black Powder

DEERSTALKER RIFLE

GREAT PLAINS RIFLE

GREAT PLAINS HUNTER
WITH TANG SIGHT

## DEERSTALKER
**Lock:** traditional cap or flint
**Stock:** walnut
**Barrel:** 24 in.
**Sights:** aperture
**Weight:** 7.5lbs.
**Bore/Caliber:** .50 or .54
**Features:** left-hand models available
**caplock** . . . . . . . . . . . . . . . . . . **$305**
**left-hand** . . . . . . . . . . . . . . . . . **$330**

stainless caplock . . . . . . . . . . . **$395**
flintlock . . . . . . . . . . . . . . . . . **$350**
left-hand . . . . . . . . . . . . . . . . **$360**

## GREAT PLAINS RIFLE
**Lock:** traditional cap or flint
**Stock:** walnut
**Barrel:** 32 in., 1:66 twist
**Sights:** adjustable open
**Weight:** 8.0lbs.

**Bore/Caliber:** .50 or .54
**Features:** double set triggers, left-hand models available; also Great Plains Hunter with 1:32 twist
**caplock** . . . . . . . . . . . . . . . . . . **$475**
**unfinished kit** . . . . . . . . . . . . . . **$365**
**flintlock** . . . . . . . . . . . . . . . . . **$500**
**unfinished kit** . . . . . . . . . . . . . . **$390**

BLACK POWDER

# Lyman Black Powder

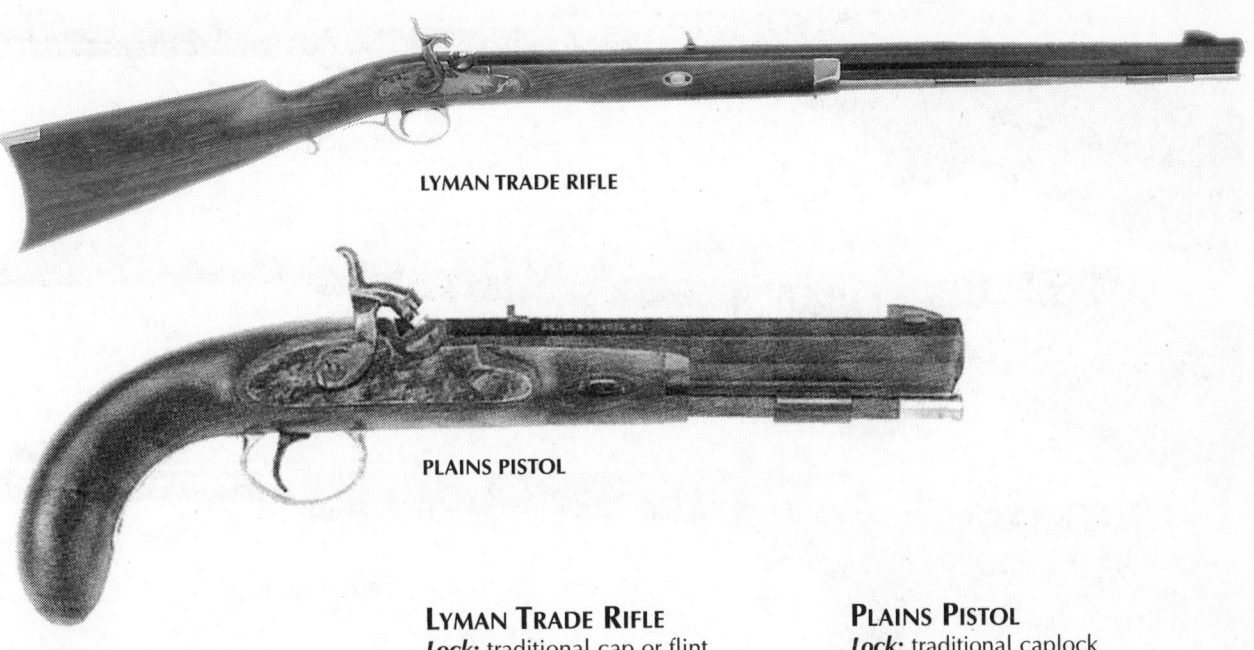

**LYMAN TRADE RIFLE**

**PLAINS PISTOL**

### LYMAN TRADE RIFLE
*Lock:* traditional cap or flint
*Stock:* walnut
*Barrel:* 28 in., 1:48 twist
*Sights:* adjustable open
*Weight:* 8.0lbs.
*Bore/Caliber:* .50 or .54
*Features:* brass furniture
**Lyman** . . . . . . . . . . . . . . . . . . . . $315
**flint** . . . . . . . . . . . . . . . . . . . . . $340

### PLAINS PISTOL
*Lock:* traditional caplock
*Stock:* walnut
*Barrel:* 6 in.
*Sights:* fixed
*Weight:* 2.2lbs.
*Bore/Caliber:* .50 or .54
*Features:* iron furniture
**Plains Pistol** . . . . . . . . . . . . . . $245
**unfinished kit** . . . . . . . . . . . . . $195

*When you seat a ball or bullet, make sure it's in contact with the powder. Let the ramrod drop a few inches onto the charge. If it bounces, the ball or bullet is probably seated properly.*

# Marksbery Black Powder

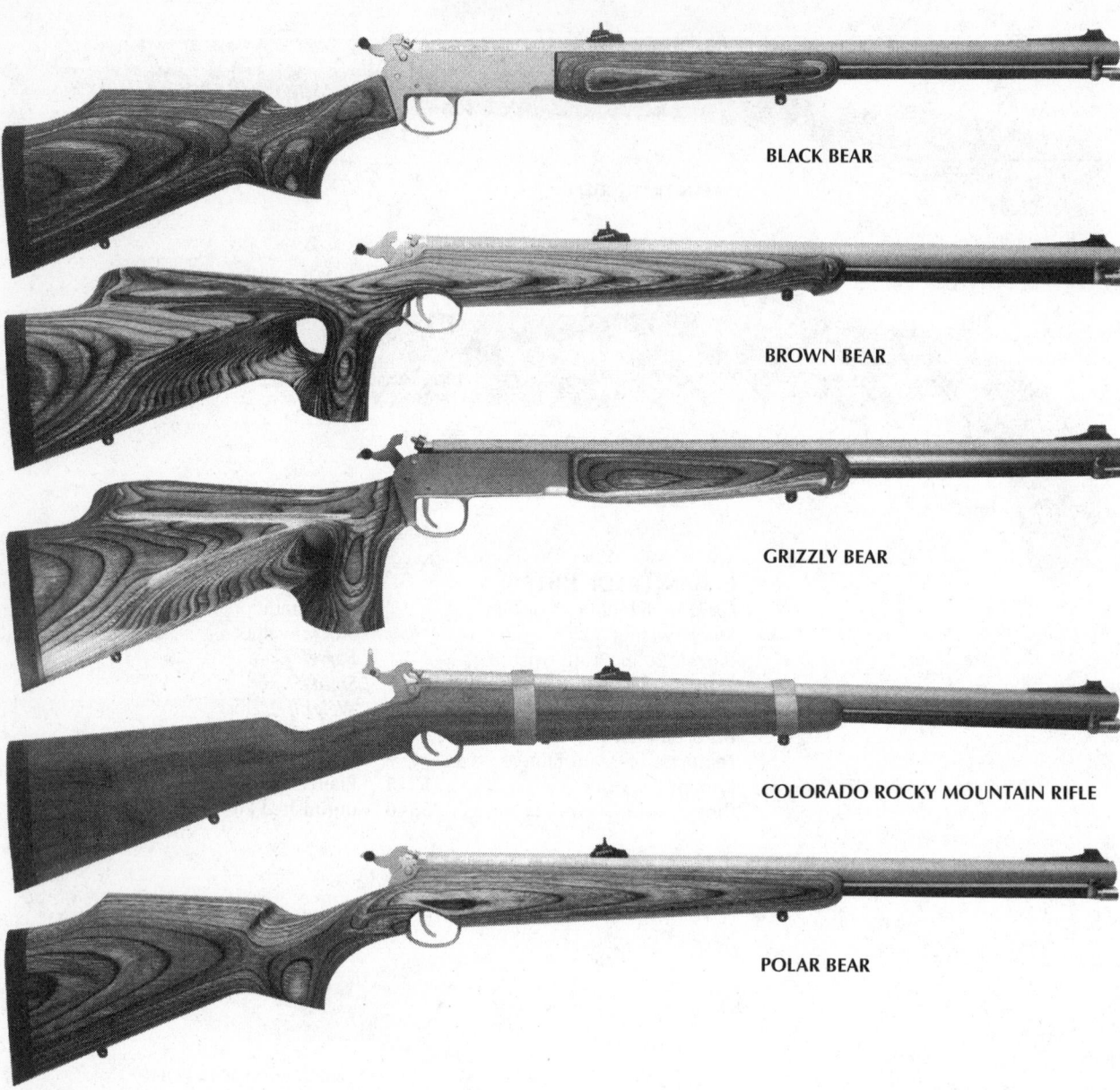

BLACK BEAR

BROWN BEAR

GRIZZLY BEAR

COLORADO ROCKY MOUNTAIN RIFLE

POLAR BEAR

## BLACK BEAR
*Lock:* in-line
*Stock:* two-piece laminated
*Barrel:* 24 in., 1:26 twist
*Sights:* adjustable open
*Weight:* 6.5lbs.
*Bore/Caliber:* .36, .45, .50, .54
*Features:* also Grizzly Bear with thumbhole stock, Brown Bear with one-piece thumbhole stock, both checkered, aluminum ramrod

| | |
|---|---|
| Black Bear, blue | $537 |
| stainless | $553 |
| camo | $557 |
| camo stainless | $574 |

| | |
|---|---|
| Brown Bear | $659 |
| stainless | $676 |
| camo stainless | $698 |
| Grizzly Bear | $643 |
| stainless | $665 |
| camo stainless | $684 |

## COLORADO ROCKY MOUNTAIN RIFLE
*Lock:* in-line
*Stock:* walnut, laminated
*Barrel:* 24 in., 1:26 twist
*Sights:* adjustable open
*Weight:* 7.0lbs.
*Bore/Caliber:* .36, .45, .50, .54
*Features:* #11 or magnum ignition

| | |
|---|---|
| Rocky Mountain Rifle | $549 |
| stainless | $567 |

## POLAR BEAR
*Lock:* in-line
*Stock:* laminated
*Barrel:* 24 in., 1:26 twist
*Sights:* adjustable open
*Weight:* 7.8lbs.
*Bore/Caliber:* .36, .45, .50, .54
*Features:* one-piece stock

| | |
|---|---|
| Polar Bear | $540 |
| stainless | $556 |
| camo stainless | $574 |

# Navy Arms Black Powder Handguns

## 1847 Colt Walker
**Lock:** caplock revolver
**Stock:** walnut
**Barrel:** 9 in.
**Sights:** fixed
**Weight:** 4.5lbs.
**Bore/Caliber:** .44
**Features:** case-colored frame, brass guard
**1847 Colt Walker** . . . . . . . . . **$347**

## Le Mat Calvary Model
**Lock:** caplock revolver
**Stock:** walnut
**Barrel:** 7.6 in.
**Sights:** fixed
**Weight:** 3.4lbs.
**Bore/Caliber:** .44
**Features:** 9-shot cylinder; Navy, Cavalry, Army models available
**Le Mat** . . . . . . . . . . . . . . . . . **$748**

## Colt 1862
## New Model Police
**Lock:** caplock revolver
**Stock:** walnut
**Barrel:** 5.5 in.
**Sights:** fixed
**Weight:** 2.7lbs.
**Bore/Caliber:** .36
**Features:** last of the percussion Colts, has brass guard, case-colored frame
**New Model Police** . . . . . . . . . **$266**

## Rogers and Spencer
**Lock:** caplock revolver
**Stock:** walnut
**Barrel:** 7.5 in.
**Sights:** fixed
**Weight:** 3.0lbs.
**Bore/Caliber:** .44
**Features:** octagonal barrel, 6-shot cylinder
**Rogers and Spencer** . . . . . . . . **$363**

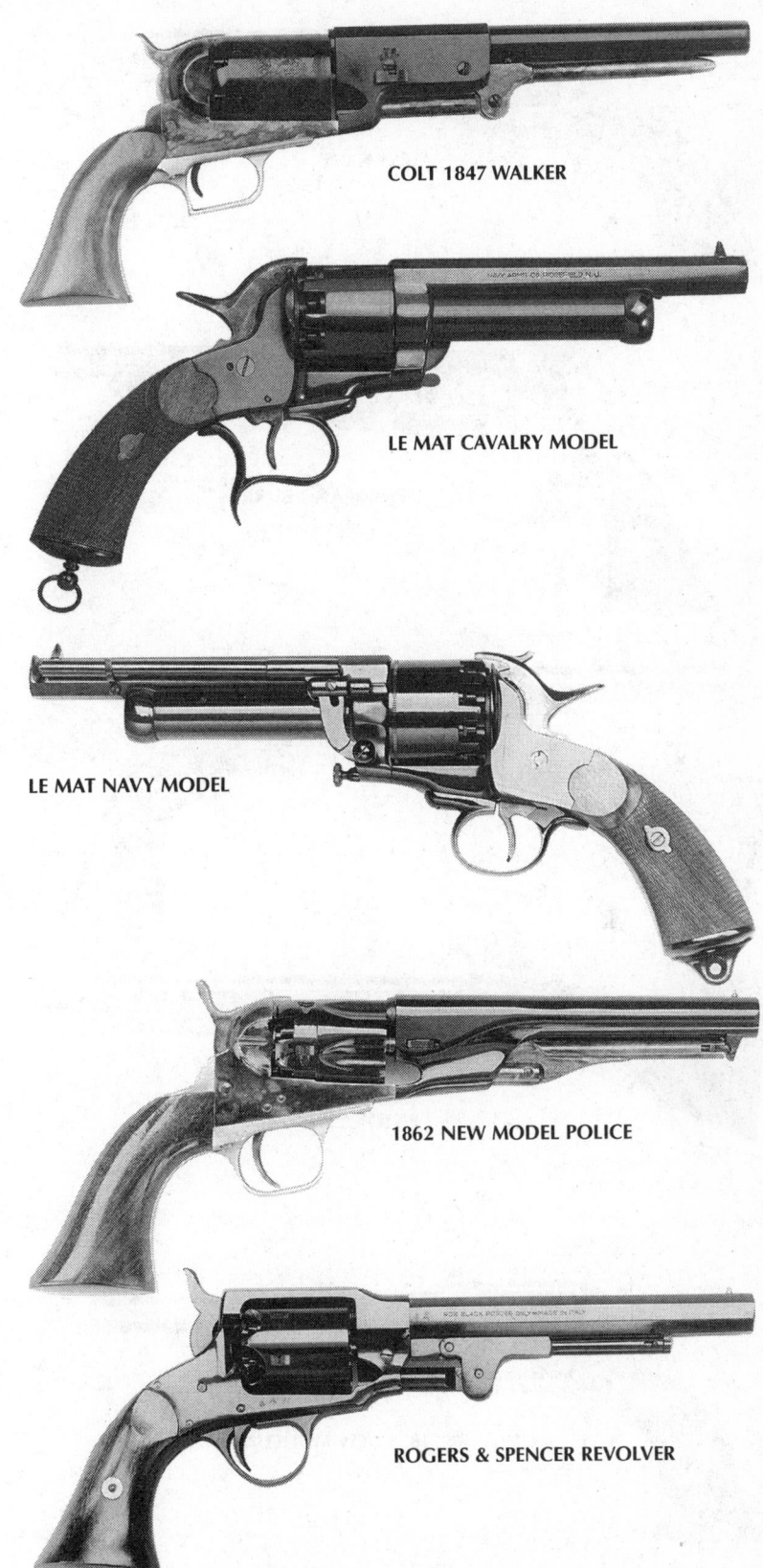

COLT 1847 WALKER

LE MAT CAVALRY MODEL

LE MAT NAVY MODEL

1862 NEW MODEL POLICE

ROGERS & SPENCER REVOLVER

# Navy Arms Black Powder Handguns

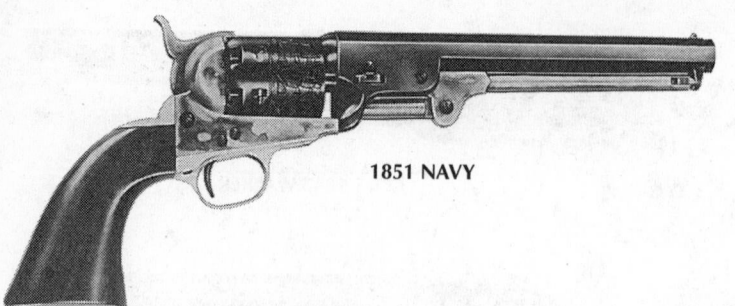

**1851 NAVY**

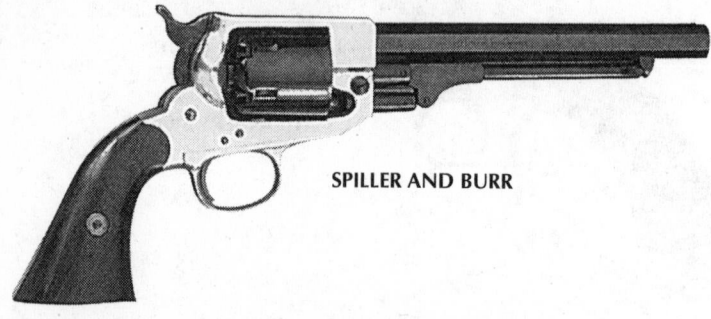

**SPILLER AND BURR**

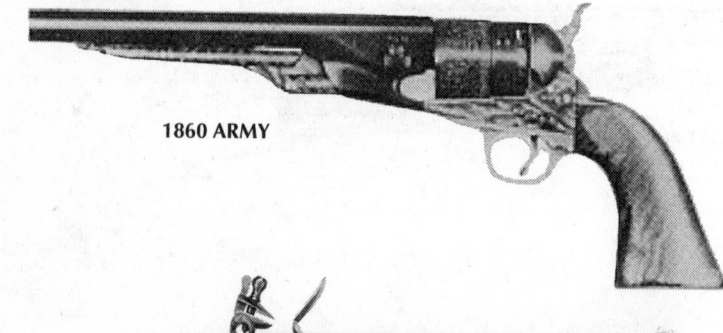

**1860 ARMY**

**1805 HARPER'S FERRY FLINTLOCK PISTOL**

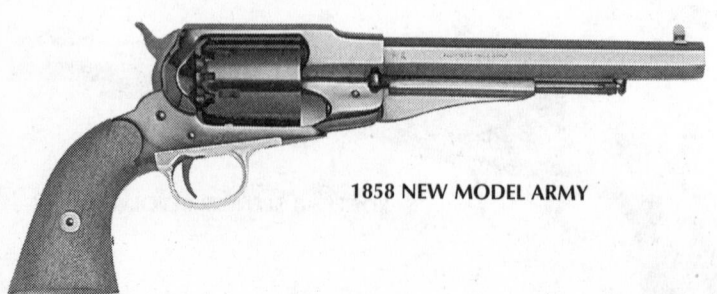

**1858 NEW MODEL ARMY**

## 1851 NAVY
*Lock:* caplock revolver
*Stock:* walnut
*Barrel:* 7.5 in.
*Sights:* fixed
*Weight:* 2.7lbs.
*Bore/Caliber:* .36 and .44
*Features:* brass guard and strap
**1851 Navy . . . . . . . . . . . . . . . $242**

## SPILLER AND BURR
*Lock:* caplock revolver
*Stock:* walnut
*Barrel:* 7 in.
*Sights:* fixed
*Weight:* 2.6lbs.
*Bore/Caliber:* .36
*Features:* brass frame
**Spiller and Burr . . . . . . . . . . . $196**

## 1860 ARMY
*Lock:* caplock revolver
*Stock:* walnut
*Barrel:* 8 in.
*Sights:* fixed
*Weight:* 2.6lbs.
*Bore/Caliber:* .44
*Features:* brass guard, steel backstrap
**1860 Army . . . . . . . . . . . . . . . $220**

## HARPER'S FERRY FLINTLOCK PISTOL
*Lock:* traditional flintlock
*Stock:* walnut
*Barrel:* 10 in.
*Sights:* fixed
*Weight:* 2.6lbs.
*Bore/Caliber:* .58
*Features:* case-colored lock, brass furniture, browned barrel
**Harper's Ferry . . . . . . . . . . . . $411**

## 1858 NEW MODEL ARMY REMINGTON
*Lock:* caplock revolver
*Stock:* walnut
*Barrel:* 8 in.
*Sights:* fixed
*Weight:* 2.5lbs.
*Bore/Caliber:* .44
*Features:* brass guard, steel frame with top strap
**1858 New Model Army Rem. . . $269**
**with brass frame . . . . . . . . . . $183**
**stainless . . . . . . . . . . . . . . . $358**
**color, case-hardened . . . . . . . $320**

# Navy Arms Black Powder Handguns

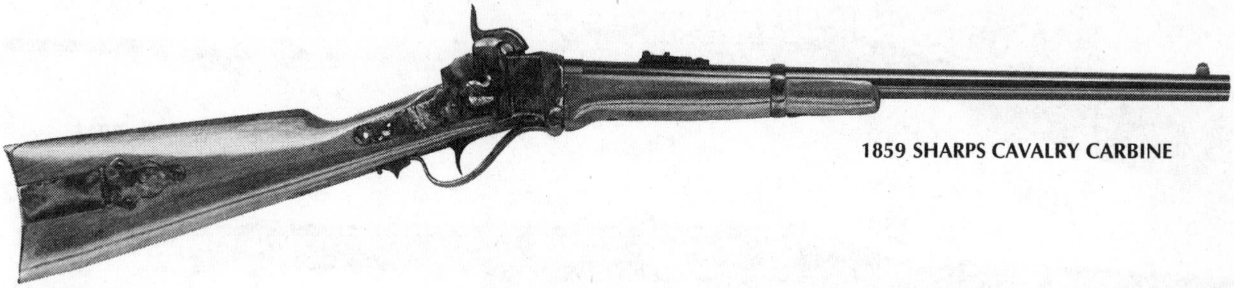

**1859 SHARPS CAVALRY CARBINE**

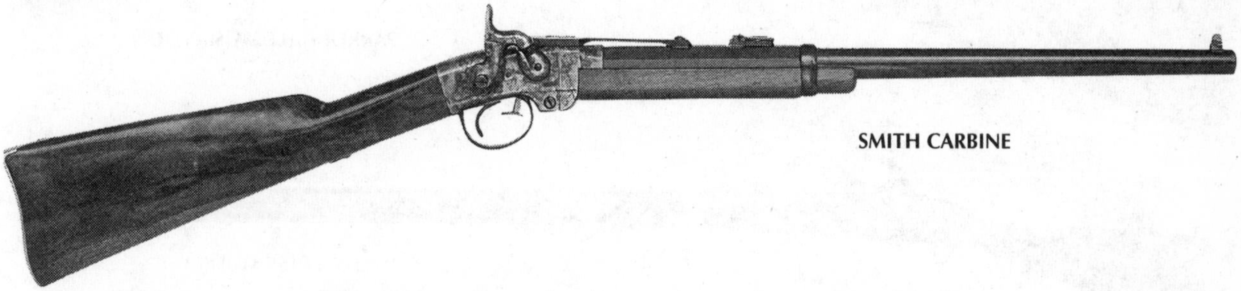

**SMITH CARBINE**

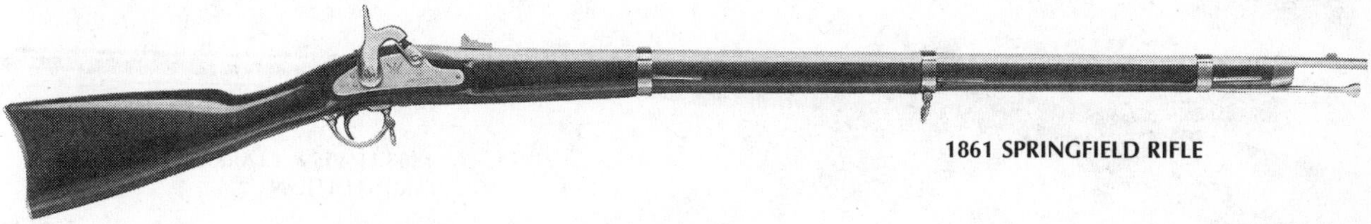

**1861 SPRINGFIELD RIFLE**

**C.S. RICHMOND RIFLE**

## 1859
### SHARPS CAVALRY CARBINE
*Lock:* traditional caplock
*Stock:* walnut
*Barrel:* 22 in.
*Sights:* adjustable open
*Weight:* 7.8lbs.
*Bore/Caliber:* .54
*Features:* infantry rifle also available
carbine . . . . . . . . . . . . . . . . $1187
rifle . . . . . . . . . . . . . . . . . . . $1386

### SMITH CARBINE
*Lock:* traditional caplock
*Stock:* walnut
*Barrel:* 22 in.
*Sights:* adjustable open

*Weight:* 7.8lbs.
*Bore/Caliber:* .50
*Features:* cavalry and artillery models available
Smith Carbine . . . . . . . . . . . . . $790

### 1861 SPRINGFIELD
*Lock:* traditional caplock
*Stock:* walnut
*Barrel:* 40 in.
*Sights:* fixed
*Weight:* 10.0lbs.
*Bore/Caliber:* .58
*Features:* three-band furniture polished bright
1861 Springfield . . . . . . . . . . . $926

### C.S. RICHMOND RIFLE
*Lock:* traditional caplock
*Stock:* walnut
*Barrel:* 40 in.
*Sights:* fixed
*Weight:* 10.0lbs.
*Bore/Caliber:* .58
*Features:* polished furniture
C.S. Richmond . . . . . . . . . . . . $862

# Navy Arms Black Powder Rifles

PARKER-HALE 1858 ENFIELD RIFLE

PARKER-HALE MUSKETOON

BROWN BESS MUSKET

1803 LEWIS & CLARK HARPERS
FERRY EDITION

BERDAN 1859 SHARPS RIFLE

## PARKER-HALE 1858 ENFIELD RIFLE
*Lock:* traditional caplock
*Stock:* walnut
*Barrel:* 33 in.
*Sights:* adjustable open
*Weight:* 9.6lbs.
*Bore/Caliber:* .58
*Features:* brass furniture
**Parker-Hale Enfield . . . . . . . . . $762**

## PARKER-HALE MUSKETOON
*Lock:* traditional caplock
*Stock:* walnut
*Barrel:* 24 in.
*Sights:* adjustable open
*Weight:* 7.5lbs.
*Bore/Caliber:* .58

*Features:* brass furniture
**Parker-Hale Musketoon . . . . . . $684**

## BROWN BESS MUSKET
*Lock:* traditional flintlock
*Stock:* walnut
*Barrel:* 42 in.
*Sights:* fixed
*Weight:* 9.5lbs.
*Bore/Caliber:* .75
*Features:* full stock without bands
**Brown Bess Musket . . . . . . . . $1061**

## 1803 LEWIS & CLARK HARPER'S FERRY EDITION
*Lock:* traditional flintlock
*Stock:* walnut
*Barrel:* 35 in.
*Sights:* fixed

*Weight:* 8.5lbs.
*Bore/Caliber:* .54
*Features:* case-colored lock, brass patch box
**1803 Harper's Ferry . . . . . . . . $882**

## BERDAN 1859 SHARPS RIFLE
*Lock:* traditional caplock
*Stock:* walnut
*Barrel:* 30 in.
*Sights:* adjustable open
*Weight:* 8.5lbs.
*Bore/Caliber:* .54
*Features:* case-colored receiver, double set trigger
**Berdan 1859 Sharps . . . . . . . $1386**

# Pedersoli Black Powder

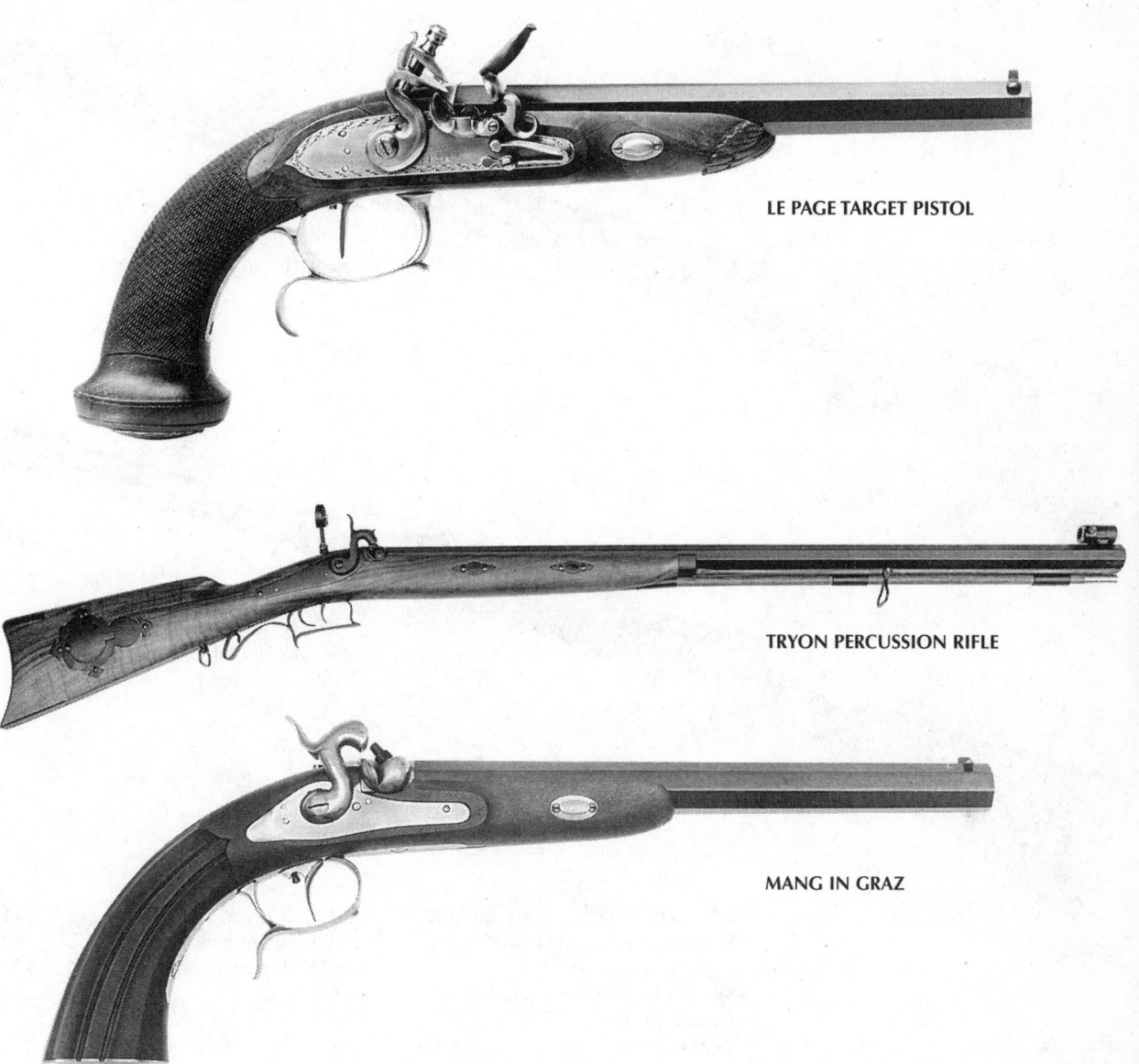

LE PAGE TARGET PISTOL

TRYON PERCUSSION RIFLE

MANG IN GRAZ

## LePage Target Pistol
**Lock:** traditional flintlock
**Stock:** walnut
**Barrel:** 10.5 in., 1:18 twist
**Sights:** fixed
**Weight:** 2.5lbs.
**Bore/Caliber:** .44 or .45
**Features:** smoothbore .45 available
**LePage** . . . . . . . . . . . . . . . . . . $780
**caplock in .36, .38, .44** . . . . . . . $675

## "Mang in Graz"
**Lock:** traditional caplock
**Stock:** walnut
**Barrel:** 11 in., 1:15 or 1:18 (.44) twist
**Sights:** fixed
**Weight:** 2.5lbs.
**Bore/Caliber:** .38 or .44
**Features:** grooved butt
**Price:** . . . . . . . . . . . . . . . . . $1195

## Mortimer Target Rifle
**Lock:** flintlock
**Stock:** English-style European walnut
**Barrel:** octagon to round 36 in.
**Sights:** target
**Weight:** 8.8lbs.
**Bore/Caliber:** .54
**Features:** case-colored lock; stock has cheekpiece and hand checkering; 7-groove barrel
**Mortimer Target** . . . . . . . . . . $1150

## Tryon-Percussion Rifle
**Lock:** traditional caplock
**Stock:** walnut
**Barrel:** 32 in., 1:48 or 1:66 (.54) twist
**Sights:** adjustable open
**Weight:** 9.5lbs.
**Bore/Caliber:** .45, .50, .54
**Features:** Creedmoor version with aperture sight available
**Tryon-Percussion** . . . . . . . . . . . $650
**Creedmoor** . . . . . . . . . . . . . . . $960

# Remington Arms Black Powder

**MODEL 700 BLACKPOWDER**

**MODEL 700 MLS STAINLESS**

### MODEL 700 IN-LINE BLACK POWDER MUZZLELOADER

**Lock:** in-line
**Stock:** black or camo synthetic
**Barrel:** 24 in.
**Sights:** open
**Weight:** 7.75 lbs.
**Bore/Caliber:** .45, .50
**Features:** 1:28 twist, full set of nipples for percussion caps, musket caps or 209 primers included; also magnum version with stainless 26 in. barrel

ML .50 . . . . . . . . . . . . . . . . . . $415
MLS Magnum .45 or .50 . . . . . . $533
MLS Magnum camo .50 . . . . . . $569

*When hunting with a traditional caplock blackpowder rifle in cold or wet weather, you can decrease the chance of a misfire by seating the percussion cap carefully and sealing it around the flange with a light coating of beeswax or bowstring wax.*

**MODEL 77/50 BLACK POWDER RIFLE**

**MODEL 77/50 RS**

**OLD ARMY CAP AND BALL**

## MODEL 77/50 BLACK POWDER RIFLE
*Lock:* in-line
*Stock:* synthetic or laminated
*Barrel:* 22 in., 1:28 twist
*Sights:* folding leaf
*Weight:* 6.5lbs.
*Bore/Caliber:* .50
*Features:* comes with 1-inch scope rings
synthetic blue . . . . . . . . . . . . $562
hardwood blue . . . . . . . . . . . . $616
walnut blue . . . . . . . . . . . . . $662
stainless synthetic. . . . . . . . . . $604
stainless laminated . . . . . . . . . $674

## OLD ARMY CAP AND BALL
*Lock:* caplock revolver
*Stock:* walnut
*Barrel:* 5.5 or 7.5 in.
*Sights:* fixed
*Weight:* 2.9lbs.
*Bore/Caliber:* .45
*Features:* Civil War-era reproduction in modern steel, music wire springs
blue . . . . . . . . . . . . . . . . . . . . $525
stainless . . . . . . . . . . . . . . . . $560
gloss stainless with ivory grips . . $605

*Whether you hunt with a traditional flintlock or caplock rifle, always remember to carry some kind of vent pick. A fouled touchhole or percussion cone can block a successful shot.*

# Savage Black Powder

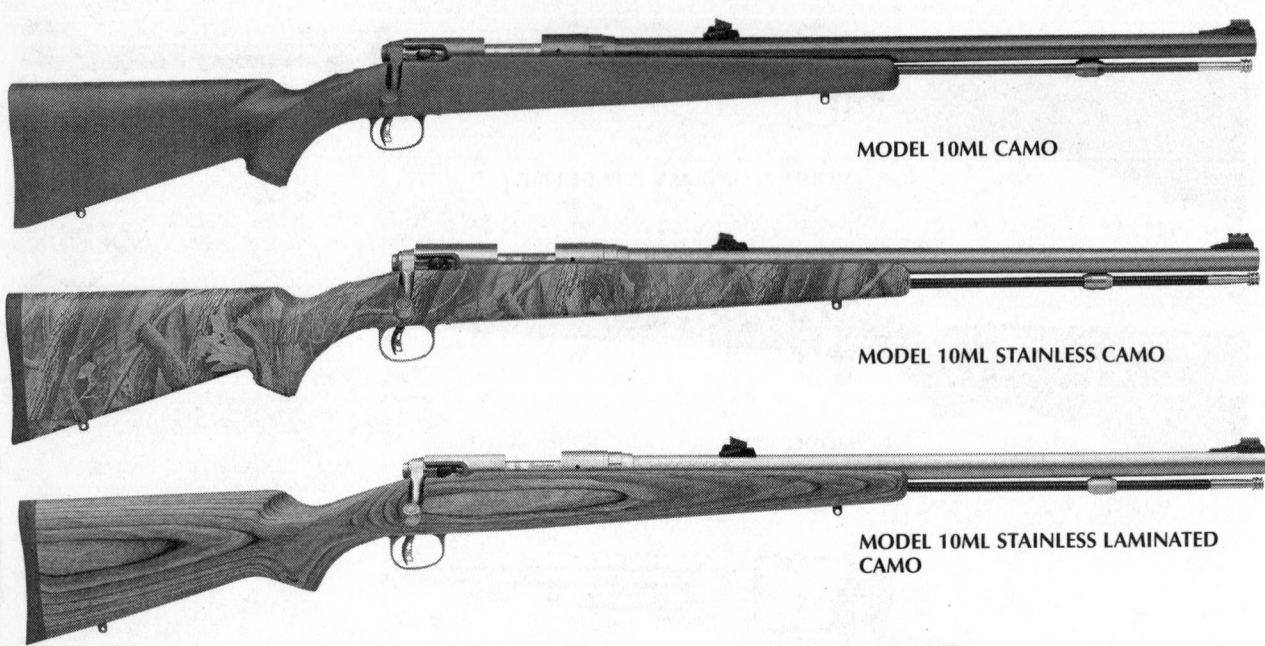

**MODEL 10ML CAMO**

**MODEL 10ML STAINLESS CAMO**

**MODEL 10ML STAINLESS LAMINATED CAMO**

### MODEL M10ML MUZZLELOADER
*Lock:* in-line
*Stock:* synthetic, camo or laminated
*Barrel:* 24 in.

*Sights:* adjustable fiber optic
*Weight:* 8.0lbs.
*Bore/Caliber:* .50
*Features:* bolt action mechanism, 209 priming

blue synthetic . . . . . . . . . . . . $512
stainless . . . . . . . . . . . . . . . . $571
blue camo . . . . . . . . . . . . . . $549
stainless camo . . . . . . . . . . . . $607
stainless laminated . . . . . . . . . $645

# Shiloh Black Powder

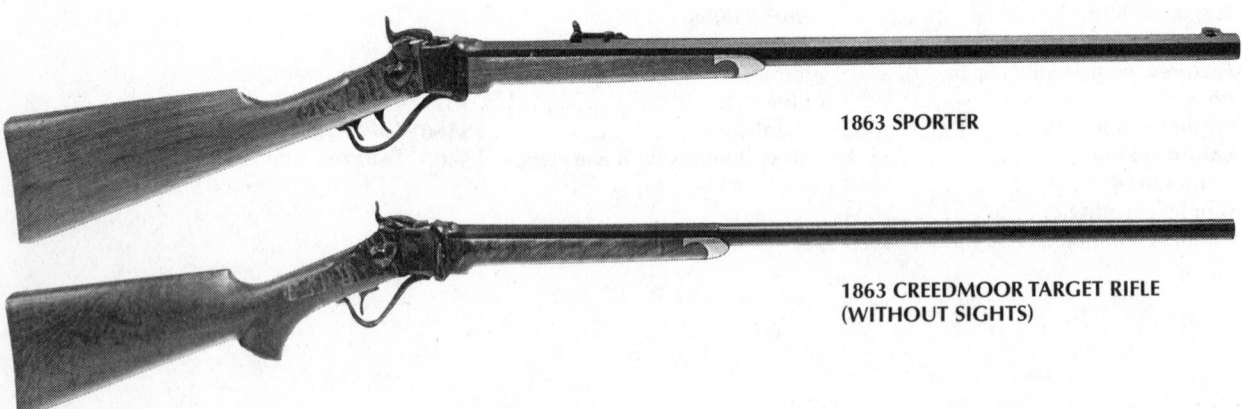

**1863 SPORTER**

**1863 CREEDMOOR TARGET RIFLE (WITHOUT SIGHTS)**

### MODEL 1863 SHARPS
*Lock:* traditional caplock
*Stock:* walnut
*Barrel:* 30 in.
*Sights:* adjustable open

*Weight:* 9.5lbs.
*Bore/Caliber:* .50 or .54
*Features:* sporting model with half-stock, double set trigger military model with 3-band full stock; also car-

bine with 22 in. barrel (7.5 lbs.)
**sporting rifle and carbine** . . . . $1504
**military rifle** . . . . . . . . . . . . . $1750

# Thompson/Center Black Powder

**NEW BLACK DIAMOND XR**

**BLACK DIAMOND MUZZLE-LOADING RIFLE**

**ENCORE 209 X 50 MAGNUM MUZZLELOADING RIFLE**

**EVOLUTION SYNTHETIC**

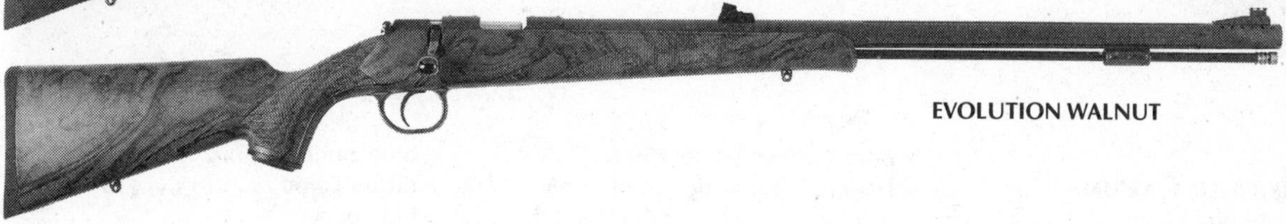

**EVOLUTION WALNUT**

## BLACK DIAMOND RIFLE
*Lock:* in-line
*Stock:* walnut or synthetic
*Barrel:* 26 in., 1:28 twist
*Sights:* adjustable fiber optic
*Weight:* 6.6lbs.
*Bore/Caliber:* .50
*Features:* musket, cap or no. 11 nipple
blue synthetic . . . . . . . . . . . . . . $337
blue walnut. . . . . . . . . . . . . . . $413
stainless camo. . . . . . . . . . . . . $440

## ENCORE 209x50 RIFLE
*Lock:* in-line
*Stock:* walnut or synthetic
*Barrel:* 26 in., 1:28 twist
*Sights:* adjustable fiber optic
*Weight:* 7.0lbs.

*Bore/Caliber:* .50
*Features:* automatic safety, interchange-able barrel with Encore centerfire barrels; also available 209x45 9.45)
blue synthetic . . . . . . . . . . . . . $635
stainless synthetic. . . . . . . . . . $706
blue walnut . . . . . . . . . . . . . . . $665
blue camo . . . . . . . . . . . . . . . $694
stainless camo . . . . . . . . . . . . $765
blue walnut .45 . . . . . . . . . . . $680
stainless synthetic .45 . . . . . . . $721

## MODEL EVOLUTION PREMIER SERIES
*Lock:* in-line
*Stock:* hardwood, synthetic, camo or laminated

*Barrel:* 26 in., 1:28 twist, internally ported
*Sights:* fiber optic
*Weight:* 7.0lbs.
*Caliber/Bore:* .50
*Features:* stainless steel 209 priming; "LD" Long Distance Models have Tru-Glo instead of Williams sights, cost less; standard models have 24 in. bar-rels, laminated version weighs 7.8 lbs.
synthetic . . . . . . . . . . . . . . . . $279
hardwood . . . . . . . . . . . . . . . $349
camo . . . . . . . . . . . . . . . . . . . $369
laminated. . . . . . . . . . . . . . . . $469

*Keep both eyes open when shooting any firearm, squinting slightly or using a patch or tape only if you must to avoid "doubling" the sight picture. A severe squint impairs vision in the open eye.*

# Thompson/Center Black Powder

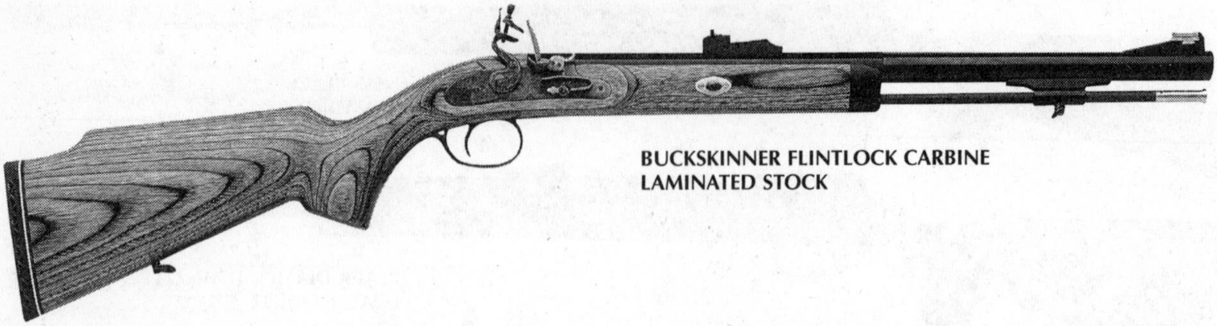

**BUCKSKINNER FLINTLOCK CARBINE LAMINATED STOCK**

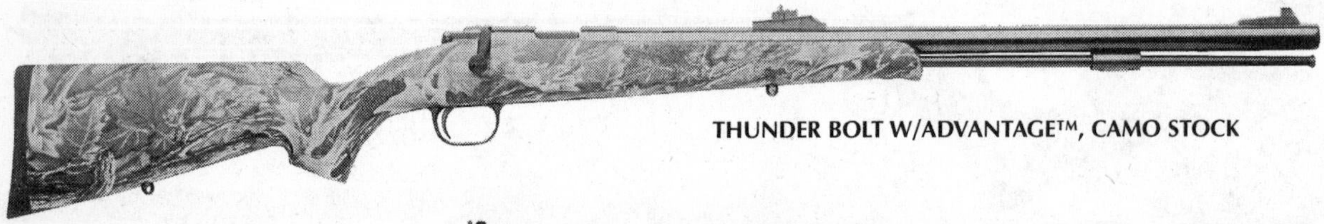

**THUNDER BOLT W/ADVANTAGE™, CAMO STOCK**

**FIRE STORM**

## BUCKSKINNER CARBINE

*Lock:* traditional flintlock
*Stock:* hardwood or laminated
*Barrel:* 21 in., 1:48 twist
*Sights:* fiber optic
*Weight:* 6.0lbs.
*Bore/Caliber:* .50
*Features:* German silver hardware
hardwood . . . . . . . . . . . . . . . $249
laminated. . . . . . . . . . . . . . . $339
laminated nickel. . . . . . . . . . . $349

## THUNDER BOLT

*Lock:* in-line
*Stock:* synthetic or camo
*Barrel:* 24 in., 1:28 twist
*Sights:* fiber optic
*Weight:* 6.8lbs.

*Bore/Caliber:* .45 or .50
*Features:* bolt action, 209 primer
ignition; also 21 in. Youth Model
**blue synthetic and Youth** . . . . . . $179
nickel synthetic. . . . . . . . . . . $189
blue camo. . . . . . . . . . . . . . $199
nickel camo . . . . . . . . . . . . . $219

## EVOLUTION

*Lock:* in-line
*Stock:* beech, walnut, synthetic or camo
*Barrel:* 24 in., 1:28 twist (1:48 .54)
*Sights:* fiber optic
*Weight:* 7.0lbs.
*Bore/Caliber:* .50 or .54 (with brake)
*Features:* 209 primer ignition, drilled
for scope
blue synthetic . . . . . . . . . . . $239
nickel synthetic . . . . . . . . . . . $249

blue camo . . . . . . . . . . . . . . $259
nickel camo . . . . . . . . . . . . . $289
blue beech. . . . . . . . . . . . . . $289
blue walnut . . . . . . . . . . . . . $309
fluted stainless synthetic .54 . . . $309
fluted stainless camo .54 . . . . . $349

## FIRE STORM

*Lock:* traditional cap or flint
*Stock:* synthetic
*Barrel:* 26 in., 1:48 twist
*Sights:* adjustable fiber optic
*Weight:* 7.0lbs.
*Bore/Caliber:* .50
*Features:* aluminum ramrod
blue. . . . . . . . . . . . . . . . . . $337
stainless . . . . . . . . . . . . . . . $474

*Traditional blackpowder open choked shotguns perform
best when loaded with a combination of wads rather
than a modern one-piece plastic wad. One effective
combination consists of a heavy over-powder card wad,
a fiber cushion wad and a thin card over shot wad.*

# Traditions Black Powder

NEW OMEGA 50

DEERHUNTER

PANTHER RIFLE ALL-WEATHER

TRACKER 209 IN-LINE RIFLE

### NEW OMEGA 50
**Lock:** in-line
**Stock:** synthetic or laminated
**Barrel:** 28 in., fast twist
**Sights:** adjustable fiber optic
**Weight:** 7.0lbs.
**Bore/Caliber:** .50
**Features:** swinging breech block mechanism
blue synthetic . . . . . . . . . . . . . $418
stainless synthetic . . . . . . . . . . $468
stainless laminated . . . . . . . . . $504
stainless camo. . . . . . . . . . . . . $527
also available:
Omega 45 synthetic blue, . . . . . . . .
  .45 cal. . . . . . . . . . . . . . . $433
SST synthetic, . . . . . . . . . . . . . . .
  .45 cal. . . . . . . . . . . . . . . $482

### DEERHUNTER RIFLE
**Lock:** traditional cap or flint
**Stock:** hardwood, synthetic or camo
**Barrel:** 24 in., 1:48 twist
**Sights:** fixed
**Weight:** 6.0lbs.
**Bore/Caliber:** .32, .50, .54
**Features:** blackened furniture; also economy-model Panther, 24 in .50 or .54
caplock blue, . . . . . . . . . . . . . . . .
  flint nickel synthetic. . . . . . . $199
flintlock blue hardwood . . . . . . $209
flintlock blue camo . . . . . . . . . . $239

### PANTHER RIFLE
**Action:** traditional cap lock
**Stock:** synthetic
**Barrel:** 24 in., 1:48 twist
**Sights:** fixed

**Weight:** 6.0 lbs.
**Bore/Caliber:** 50, .54
**Features:** #11 Percussion ignition; sling swivels; synthetic ramrod.
50cal Percussion Rifle: . . . . . . . $129
54cal Percussion Rifle: . . . . . . . $129

### TRACKER 209
**Lock:** in-line
**Stock:** synthetic or camo
**Barrel:** 22 in., 1:28 twist (1:24 .45)
**Sights:** fiber optic
**Weight:** 6.5lbs.
**Bore/Caliber:** .45 or .50
**Features:** 209 primer ignition
blue synthetic . . . . . . . . . . . . . $129
nickel synthetic. . . . . . . . . . . . . $139
nickel camo . . . . . . . . . . . . . . . $189

# Traditions Black Powder

**HAWKEN BEECH**

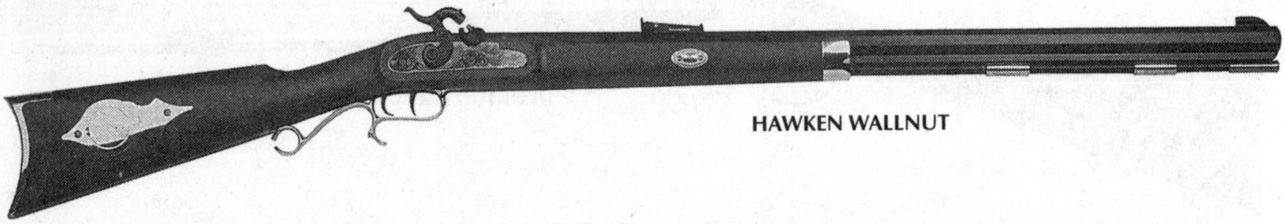

**HAWKEN WALLNUT**

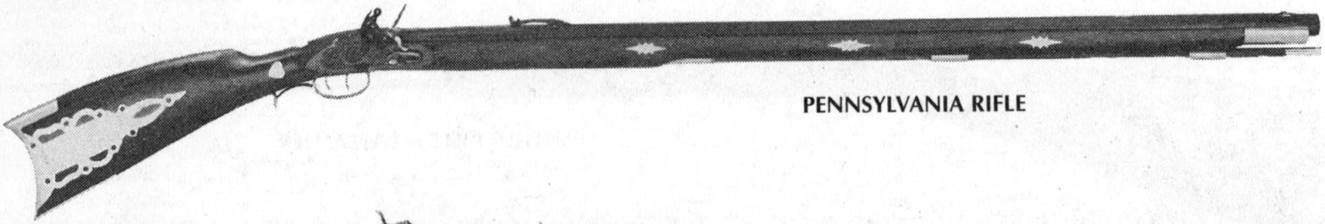

**PENNSYLVANIA RIFLE**

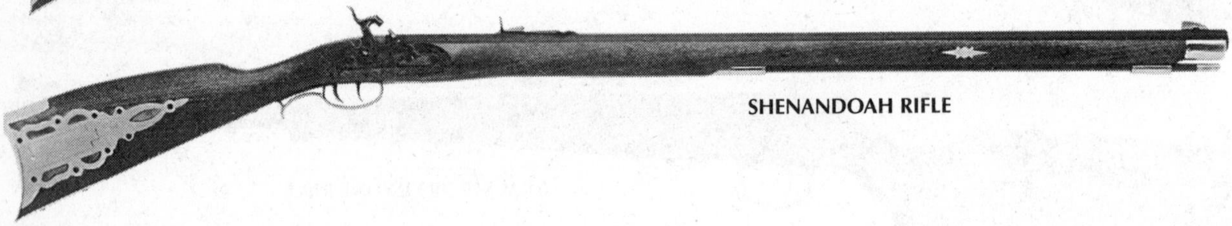

**SHENANDOAH RIFLE**

### HAWKEN
*Lock:* traditional cap or flint
*Stock:* beech
*Barrel:* 28 in., 1:48 twist
*Sights:* adjustable open
*Weight:* 7.7lbs.
*Bore/Caliber:* .50 or .54
*Features:* brass furniture
caplock. . . . . . . . . . . . . . . . . . $259
lefthand caplock. . . . . . . . . . . $279
flintlock . . . . . . . . . . . . . . . . . $299

### HAWKEN RIFLE
*Lock:* traditional cap or flint
*Stock:* walnut
*Barrel:* 26 in., 1:28 twist
*Sights:* adjustable open

*Weight:* 8.5lbs.
*Bore/Caliber:* .45, .50, .54
*Features:* brass furniture
caplock. . . . . . . . . . . . . . . . . . $562
flintlock . . . . . . . . . . . . . . . . . $586

### PENNSYLVANIA RIFLE
*Lock:* traditional cap or flint
*Stock:* walnut
*Barrel:* 20 in., 1:66 twist
*Sights:* adjustable open
*Weight:* 8.5lbs.
*Bore/Caliber:* .50
*Features:* brass furniture
caplock . . . . . . . . . . . . . . . . . $519
flintlock. . . . . . . . . . . . . . . . . $529

### SHENANDOAH RIFLE
*Lock:* traditional cap or flint
*Stock:* beech
*Barrel:* 33 in., 1:66 twist
*Sights:* fixed
*Weight:* 7.2lbs.
*Bore/Caliber:* .50
*Features:* brass furniture; squirrel rifle in .36
caplock . . . . . . . . . . . . . . . . . $399
flintlock. . . . . . . . . . . . . . . . . $429
caplock .36 . . . . . . . . . . . . . . $419
flintlock .36 . . . . . . . . . . . . . . $449

*Pistoleers concentrate on three things: sight alignment, sight alignment and sight alignment. A bit of wobble, slight movement of the sight off target matter little. Poor sight alignment is fatal.*

## KENTUCKY PISTOL

*Lock:* traditional caplock
*Stock:* beech
*Barrel:* 10 in.
*Sights:* fixed
*Weight:* 2.5lbs.
*Bore/Caliber:* .50
*Features:* brass furniture
**Kentucky Pistol. . . . . . . . . . . . $159**
**unfinished kit . . . . . . . . . . . . . $119**

## IN-LINE PISTOLS (BUCKHUNTER)

*Lock:* in-line
*Stock:* walnut or synthetic
*Barrel:* 9.5 or 12.5 in.
*Sights:* adjustable open
*Weight:* 2.1lbs.
*Bore/Caliber:* .50
*Features:* blue or nickel furniture; also
with extra-long barrel and brake
**9.5 in. . . . . . . . . . . . . . . . . $259**
**12.5 in. . . . . . . . . . . . . . . . $279**
**14.8 in. with brake (also in .45) $309**

## PIONEER PISTOL

*Lock:* traditional caplock
*Stock:* walnut
*Barrel:* 9.6 in.
*Sights:* fixed
*Weight:* 1.9lbs.
*Bore/Caliber:* .45
*Features:* German silver furniture
**Pioneer . . . . . . . . . . . . . . . . . $159**
**unfinished kit . . . . . . . . . . . . . $129**

## WILLIAM PARKER PISTOL

*Lock:* traditional caplock
*Stock:* walnut
*Barrel:* 10.4 in.
*Sights:* fixed
*Weight:* 2.3lbs.
*Bore/Caliber:* .50
*Features:* checkered with brass furniture
**William Parker . . . . . . . . . . . . . $279**

## TRAPPER PISTOL

*Lock:* traditional cap or flint
*Stock:* beech
*Barrel:* 9.8 in.
*Sights:* adjustable open
*Weight:* 2.9lbs.
*Bore/Caliber:* .50
*Features:* brass furniture
**Trapper . . . . . . . . . . . . . . . . . $209**
**flintlock . . . . . . . . . . . . . . . . $219**
**caplock unfinished kit. . . . . . . $159**

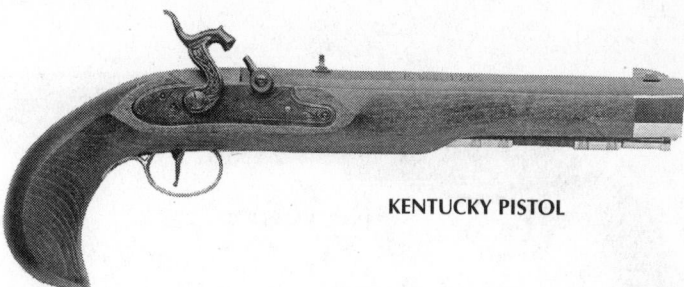

KENTUCKY PISTOL

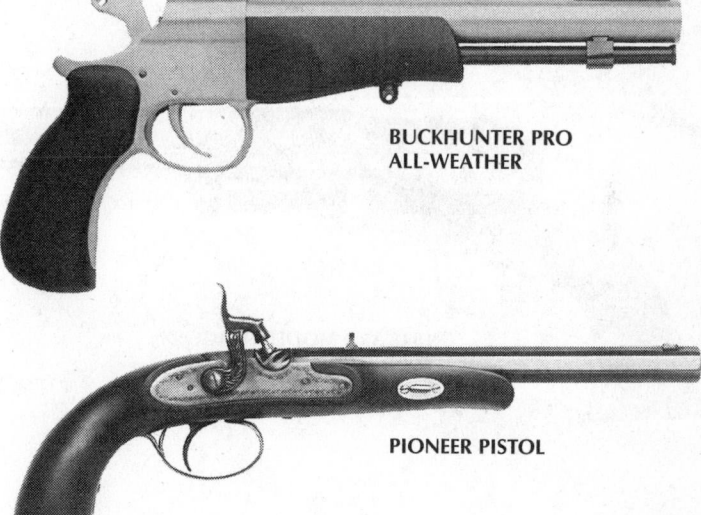

BUCKHUNTER PRO
ALL-WEATHER

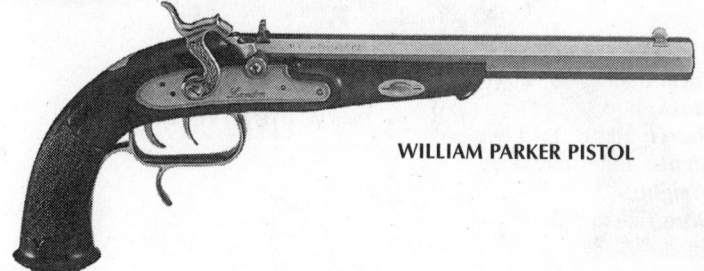

PIONEER PISTOL

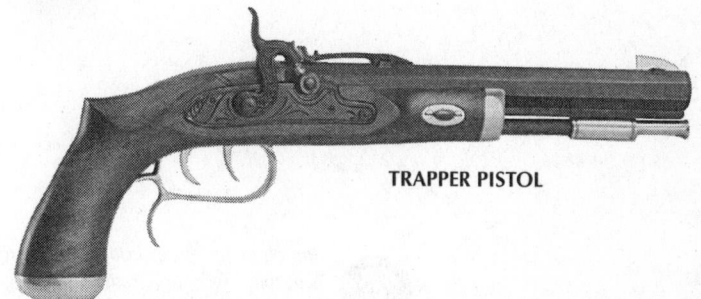

WILLIAM PARKER PISTOL

TRAPPER PISTOL

BLACK POWDER

# Uberti Black Powder

1847 WALKER 9

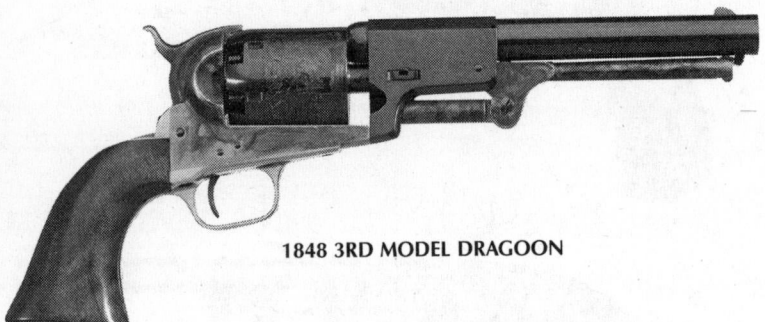

1848 3RD MODEL DRAGOON

1848 WHITENEYVILLE DRAGOON

### 1847 WALKER
*Lock*: caplock revolver
*Grips*: walnut grips
*Barrel*: 9 in.
*Sights*: fixed
*Weight*: 4.45 lbs.
*Caliber*: .44
*Features*: color, case-hardened frame, brass trigger guard
**1847 Walker** . . . . . . . . . . . . . . **$305**

### 1848 DRAGOON
*Lock*: caplock revolver
*Grips*: walnut
*Barrel*: 7.5 in.
*Sights*: fixed
*Weight*: 4.06 lbs.
*Caliber*: .44
*Features*: comes in 1st, 2nd and 3rd models, color, case-hardened frame, brass trigger guard
**1848 Dragoon** . . . . . . . . . . . . . **$285**
**1848 Whiteneyville Dragoon**. . . **$340**

*Bench technique is critical to accurate shooting. Sandbags won't guarantee a tight group if your body position and pressure on the rifle is not identical with each shot.*

# Uberti Black Powder

**1858 REMINGTON NEW ARMY**

**1860 ARMY REVOLVER**

## 1858 REMINGTON NEW ARMY
*Lock*: caplock revolver
*Grips*: walnut
*Barrel:* 8 in.
*Sights*: fixed
*Weight*: 2.8lbs.
*Bore/Caliber*: .44
*Features*: octagonal barrel, brass guard
**New Army** . . . . . . . . . . . . . . . $260
**stainless** . . . . . . . . . . . . . . . . $310
**with 18 in. barrel, carbine** . . . . $395

## 1860 ARMY REVOLVER
*Lock*: caplock revolver
*Grips*: walnut
*Barrel:* 8 in.
*Sights*: fixed
*Weight*: 2.6lbs.
*Bore/Caliber*: .44
*Features*: case-colored frame
**1860 Army** . . . . . . . . . . . . . . . $260
**with fluted cylinder** . . . . . . . . $260

*A CO2 bullet discharger will remove an unfired load
safely by blowing it out of the bore with a blast of
compressed gas. The device, which contains a CO2
cartridge, screws into the percussion bolster.*

# Uberti Black Powder

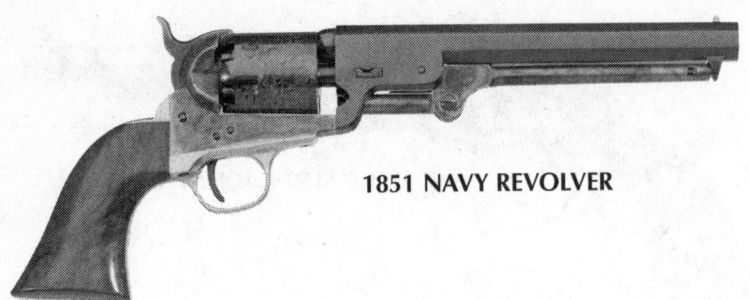

**1851 NAVY REVOLVER**

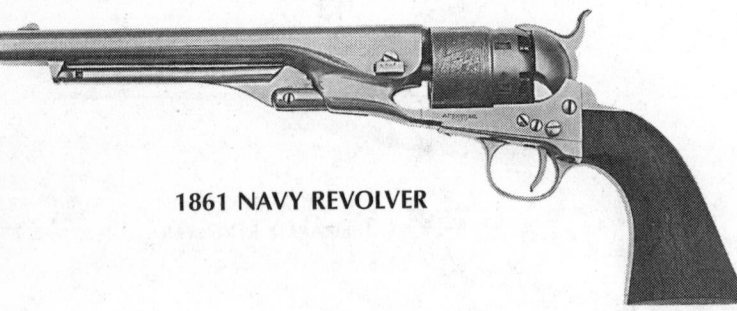

**1861 NAVY REVOLVER**

**1862 POCKET NAVY 5.5**

**1862 POLICE 5.5**

### 1851 NAVY REVOLVER
*Lock*: caplock revolver
*Grips*: walnut
*Barrel*: 7.5 in.
*Sights*: fixed
*Weight*: 2.8lbs.
*Bore/Caliber*: .36
*Features*: case-colored frame; brass round or square trigger-guard
**1851 Navy** . . . . . . . . . . . . . . . . **$240**

### 1861 NAVY REVOLVER
*Lock*: caplock revolver
*Grips*: walnut
*Barrel*: 7.5 in.
*Sights*: fixed
*Weight*: 2.8lbs.
*Bore/Caliber*: .36
*Features*: case-colored frame; brass or steel trigger-guard
**1861 Navy** . . . . . . . . . . . . . . . . **$260**

### 1862 POCKET NAVY
*Lock*: caplock revolver
*Grips*: walnut
*Barrel*: 5.5,.
*Sights*: fixed
*Weight*: 1.68 lbs.
*Bore/Caliber*: .36
*Features*: color case-colored frame, 6-shot cylinder, forged steel barrel,
**Pocket Navy** . . . . . . . . . . . . . . **$260**

### 1862 POLICE
*Lock*: caplock revolver
*Grips*: walnut
*Barrel*: 6.5 in
*Sights*: fixed
*Weight*: 1.59 lbs.
*Bore/Caliber*: .36
*Features*: color case-colored frame, 6-shot cylinder, forged steel barel,
**1862 Pocket Police** . . . . . . . . . **$260**

BLACK POWDER

# Uberti Black Powder

## PATERSON REVOLVER

*Lock*: caplock revolver
*Grips*: walnut
*Barrel*: 7.5 in.
*Sights*: none
*Weight*: 2.6lbs.
*Bore/Caliber*: .36
*Features*: 5-shot cylinder

**Paterson** . . . . . . . . . . . . . . . . . **$360**
**with load lever** . . . . . . . . . . . . **$390**

## POCKET REVOLVERS

*Lock*: caplock revolver
*Grips*: walnut
*Barrel*: 4 in.
*Sights*: fixed
*Weight*: 1.46 to 1.56 lbs.
*Bore/Caliber*: .31
*Features*: color case-colored frame,
5-shot cylinders, forged steel barrel

**1848 Baby Dragoon** . . . . . . . . **$260**
**1849 Wells Fargo 4"** . . . . . . . . **$260**
**1849 Pocket 4"** . . . . . . . . . . . . **$260**

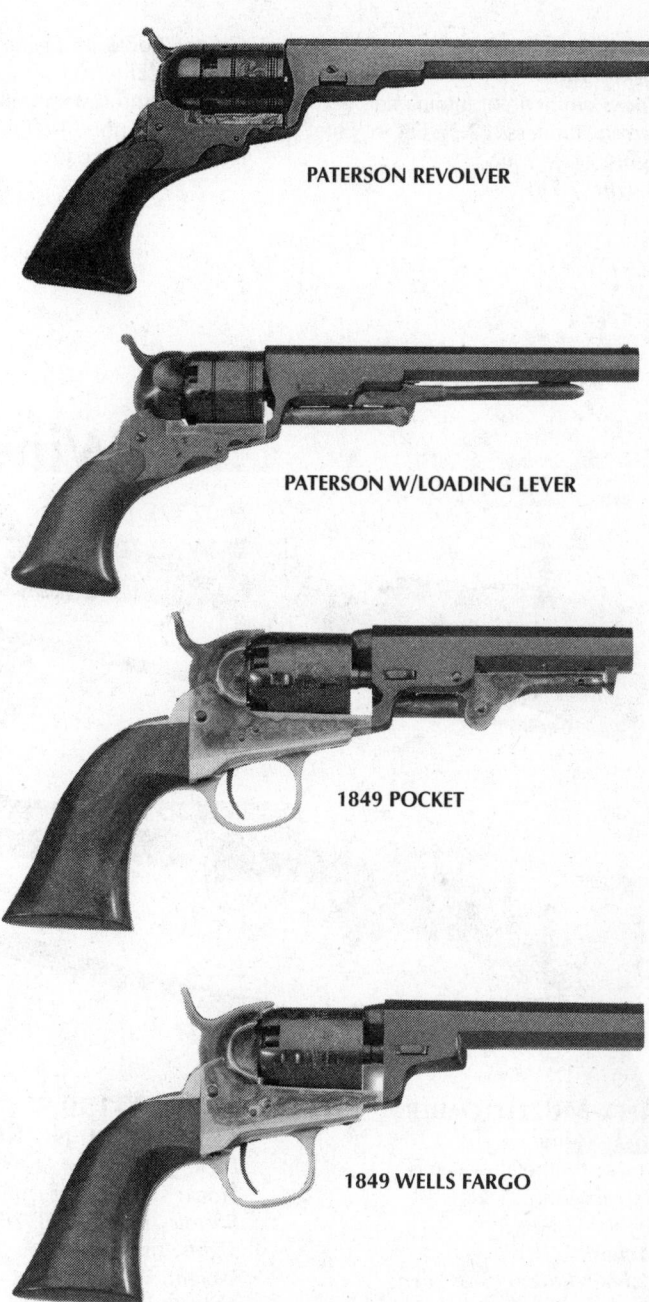

PATERSON REVOLVER

PATERSON W/LOADING LEVER

1849 POCKET

1849 WELLS FARGO

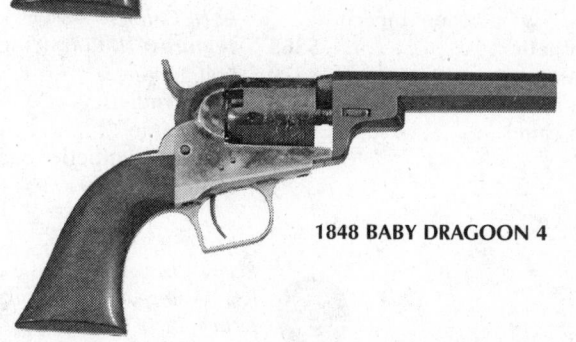

1848 BABY DRAGOON 4

# White Rifles Black Powder

## HUNTER SERIES

**Lock:** in-line
**Stock:** synthetic or laminated
**Barrel:** stainless, 22 in. (24 in. Elite)
**Sights:** fiber-optic
**Weight:** 7.7lbs.

**Caliber/Bore:** .45 or .50
**Features:** Elite weighs 8.6 lbs., aluminum ramrod with bullet extractor, also: Thunderbolt bolt action with 209 ignition, 26 in. barrel

Whitetail . . . . . . . . . . . . . . . . $430
Blacktail and Elite. . . . . . . . . . $500
Thunderbolt . . . . . . . . . . . . . . $600

# Winchester Black Powder

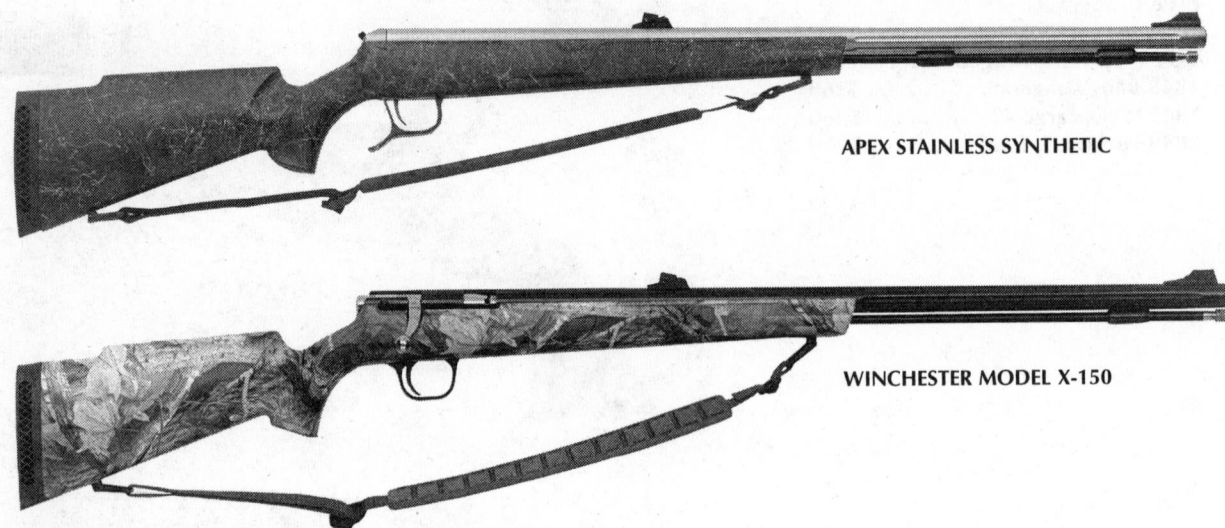

**APEX STAINLESS SYNTHETIC**

**WINCHESTER MODEL X-150**

## APEX MUZZLELOADER

**Lock:** in-line
**Stock:** synthetic or camo
**Barrel:** 28 in., 1:28 twist
**Sights:** fiber optic
**Weight:** 7.2 lbs.
**Caliber/Bore:** .45 or .50
**Features:** "swing-action" breech

blue synthetic . . . . . . . . . . . . . $365
blue camo . . . . . . . . . . . . . . . . $470
stainless synthetic. . . . . . . . . . $450
stainless camo . . . . . . . . . . . . . $490

## MODEL X-150
## MUZZLELOADING RIFLE

**Lock:** in-line
**Stock:** synthetic or camo
**Barrel:** 26 in. fluted, 1:28 twist
**Sights:** fiber optic
**Weight:** 7.9lbs.
**Bore/Caliber:** .45 or .50
**Features:** 209 primer ignition, stainless bolt action

blue synthetic . . . . . . . . . . . . . $230
blue camo . . . . . . . . . . . . . . . . $280
stainless synthetic. . . . . . . . . . $300
stainless camo . . . . . . . . . . . . . $350

*Before taking a shot, inhale deeply, then let your lungs relax. A surge of oxygen improves your vision and sight picture; but if you hold your breath, you tense up and pulse becomes a problem.*

# SIGHTS & SCOPES

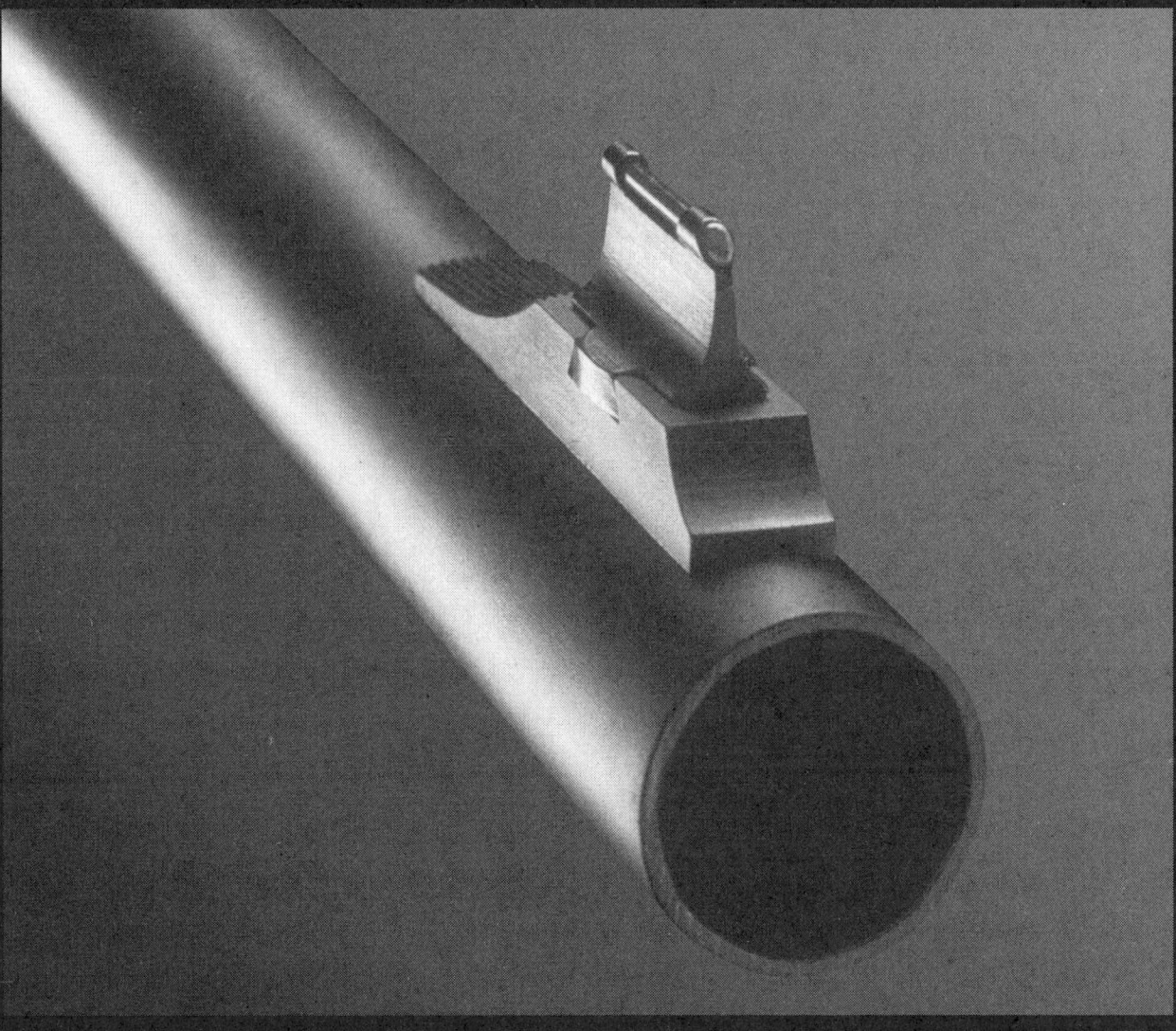

# Aimpoint Sights

**7000S SIGHT**

**COMP M2 AND COMP ML2**

**SERIES 3000 UNIVERSAL**

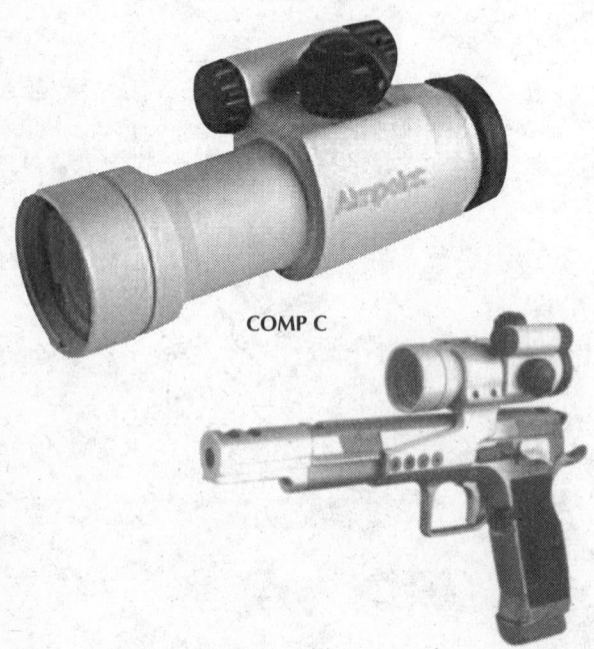

**COMP C**

## 7000S SIGHT

### SPECIFICATIONS
*System:* Parallax free
*Optical:* Anti-reflex coated lenses
*Adjustment:* 1 click = 1/2 inch at 100 yards
*Length:* 6.3"  Weight: 7.4 oz.  Objective diameter: 36mm
*Mounting system:* 30mm rings  Magnification: 1X
*Material:* Anodized aluminum; black finish
*Diameter of dot:* Red dot, 4 MOA
Price:. . . . . . . . . . . . . . . . . . . . . . . . . . . . . . . . .$298
Also Available:
7000L (length: 7.9") . . . . . . . . . . . . . . . . . . . . . . . . 298
7000S 2X (fixed 2X) . . . . . . . . . . . . . . . . . . . . . . . . 378
7000L 2X (fixed2X) . . . . . . . . . . . . . . . . . . . . . . . . 378

## COMP C2X

### SPECIFICATIONS
*System:* Parallax free  Optical: Anti-reflex coated lens
*Adjustment:* 1 click = 1/2" at 100 yards  Length: 4.7"
*Weight:* 6.5 oz.
*Objective diameter:* 36 mm
*Diameter of dot:* 2 MOA
*Mounting system:* 30mm ring
*Magnification:* 2X fixed
*Material:* Anodized aluminum; black finish
Price:
   Comp ML2 . . . . . . . . . . . . . . . . . . . . . . . . . . . . .$368
   Comp M2 . . . . . . . . . . . . . . . . . . . . . . . . . . . . . . 410
   Comp M2 2X . . . . . . . . . . . . . . . . . . . . . . . . . . . . 521
   Comp ML2 2X . . . . . . . . . . . . . . . . . . . . . . . . . . . 467

## SERIES 3000 UNIVERSAL

### SPECIFICATIONS
*System:* 100% parallax free
*Weight:* 6 oz.
*Length:* 6.25"
*Magnification:* 1X
*Scope attachment:* 3X
*Eye relief:* Unlimited
*Battery choices:* 2X Mercury SP 675 1X Lithium or DL 1/3N
*Material:* Anodized aluminum, black finish
*Mounting:* 1" Rings (Medium or High)
Price: Black . . . . . . . . . . . . . . . . . . . . . . . . . . . . .$232

## COMP C

### SPECIFICATIONS
*System:* 100% Parallax free
*Optics:* Anti-reflex coated lenses
*Eye relief:* Unlimited  Batteries: 3V Lithium
*Adjustment:* 1 click = 1/2-inch at 100 yards
*Length:* 43/4"  Weight: 6.5 oz.
*Objective diameter:* 36mm
*Dot diameter:* 4 MOA
*Mounting system:* 30mm ring Magnification: 1X
*Material:* Black or stainless finish
Price:. . . . . . . . . . . . . . . . . . . . . . . . . . . . . . . . .$324
Also Available: heavy-duty, hard anodized, graphite
   gray, submersible to 80' . . . . . . . . . . . . . . . . . . . . 411

SIGHTS & SCOPES

**HUNTSMAN 3-9X40**

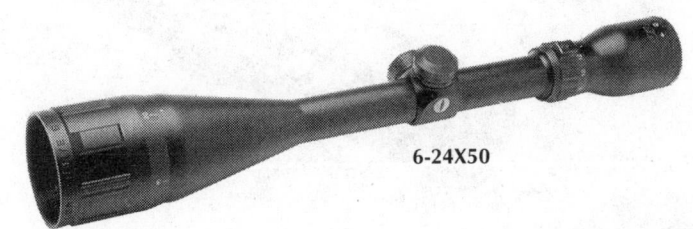

**6-24X50**

## BSA SCOPES

The BSA name once reserved for superior rifles and motor-cycles is now appearing on rifle scopes. The Catseye line, with multi-coated objective and ocular lenses and a European-style reticle for shooting in dim light, includes two new looks for 2001. The PowerBright has the features of a BSA Catseye plus a PowerBright reticle that lights up bright red against dark backgrounds. The Big Cat has all the features wanted in a hunting scope: long eye relief, fully multicoated, very bright three piece objective lens.

**Prices: Catseye**
| | |
|---|---|
| 1.5-4x32 | $92 |
| 3-10x44 | 152 |
| 3.5-10x50 | 172 |
| 4-16x50 AO | 192 |
| 6-24x50 AO | 223 |

## BSA CATSEYE CE 6-24x50
### SPECIFICATIONS
Magnification: 6x-24x  Objective Lens Diameter: 50mm
Exit Pupil Range: 8.3-2.0  Field of View at 100 yd: 16-3'
Optimum Eye Relief: 4.5"  Length/Weight: 16"/23 oz.
**Price:** . . . . . . . . . . . . . . . . . . . . . . . . . . . . . . . **$223**

## HUNTSMAN SERIES

The Huntsman series includes three 3-9x and a 6-18x AO, plus fixed-power and low-power variable models.  A 3-12x and 4-16x have 50mm objectives.  All tubes are 1-inch alloy, of one-piece construction.  They feature finger-adjustable windage and elevation dials and generous eye relief.  Multi-coated lenses are standard.  Huntsman scopes are warranted waterproof, fog proof and shock-proof.

**Price:** . . . . . . . . . . . . . . . . . . . . . . . . . . . . . **$90 to 172**

## BSA PLATINUM TARGET SCOPES

BSA Platinum target scopes are fitted with finger-adjustable windage and elevation dials that move point of impact in 1/8-minute clicks. BSA's Big Wheel is for long distance shooting when parallax adjustments are extremely critical. It has a convenient sidewheel for extra-sensitive focusing. Actually the side wheel is two wheels in one. The larger outer wheel is best for off-hand or prone shooting, and the smaller wheel for benchrest. You just snap off the outer wheel to use the smaller focusing wheel. These new scopes are more compact than older models and have three-piece objective lens systems for sharper resolution, better color and less distortion.

**Prices: PT 6-24x44 AO** . . . . . . . . . . . . . . . . . . . . . . **$222**
**PT 8-32x44 AO** . . . . . . . . . . . . . . . . . . . . . . . . . . . 242
**PT 6-24x44 AO Mildot reticle** . . . . . . . . . . . . . . . . . . 200
**PT 8-32x44 AO Mildot reticle** . . . . . . . . . . . . . . . . . . 23

# BSA Scopes

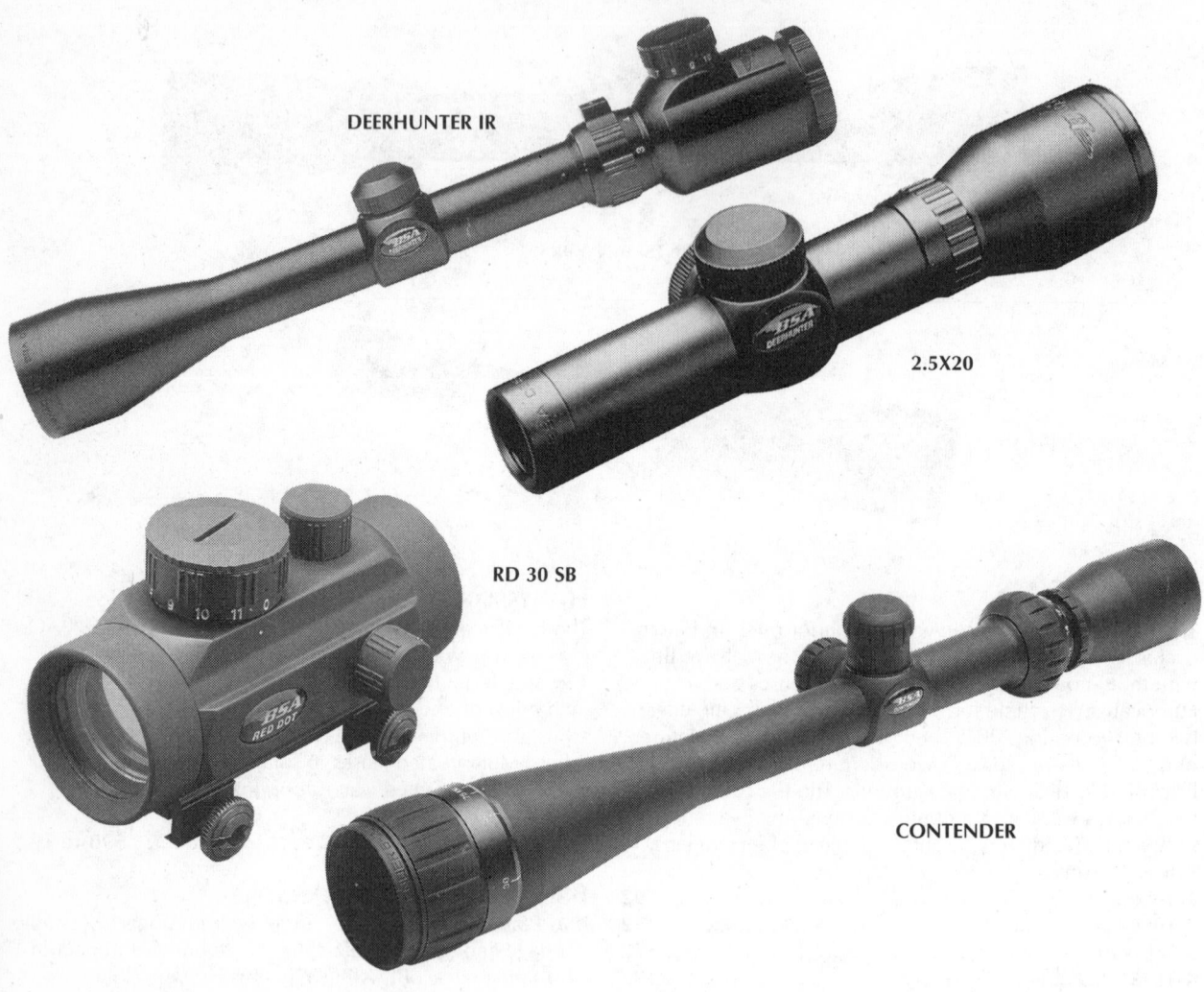

DEERHUNTER IR

2.5X20

RD 30 SB

CONTENDER

## DEERHUNTER 3-9x40 ILLUMINATED RETICLE
### SPECIFICATIONS
*Magnification:* 3x-9x  *Objective Lens Diameter:* 40mm
*Exit Pupil Range:* 13.3-4.4  *Field of View at 100 yd:* 26'
*Eye Relief:* 4.5"  *Weight:* 13 oz.
Price:.................................$130

BSA Deer Hunter scopes, from a 2.5x20 (shown) to a
3-9x50 offer value for the big game hunter on a budget.
Prices: from.........................$60 to 130

## RED DOT SCOPE
Prices: RD30 (30mm black matte or silver) .......$60
RD30SB (30mm shadow black)..................70
RD42 (42mm black matte) .....................80
RD42SB (42mm shadow black)..................90
RD50SB (50mm shadow black)................110

## DEERHUNTER DH 2.5x20
### SPECIFICATIONS
*Magnification:* 2.5x  *Objective Lens Diameter:* 20mm
*Exit Pupil Range:* 8  *Field of View at 100 yd:* 72'
*Optimum Eye Relief:* 6"  *Length/Weight:* 7.5"/7.5 oz.
Price:.................................$60

## CONTENDER CT 6-24x40 TS
### SPECIFICATIONS
*Magnification:* 6x-24x  *Objective Lens Diameter:* 40mm
*Exit Pupil Range:* 6.7-1.7  *Field of View at 100 yd:* 16'-4'
*Optimum Eye Relief:* 3"  *Length/Weight:* 15.5"/20 oz.
Price:.................................$150
Also Available: 3-12x40 .....................130
4-16x40.................................132
8-32x40.................................172
3-12x50.................................132
4-16x50.................................152
6-24x50.................................172
8-32x50.................................192

# Burris Scopes
## Black Diamond Riflescopes

**BLACK DIAMOND T-PLATE**

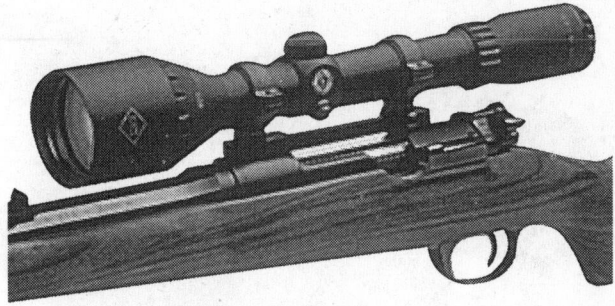

**MODEL 3X-12X-50MM**

## BLACK DIAMOND™ T-PLATE SCOPES

The popularity of Black Diamond scopes and T-Plate lens coating technology on Mr. T riflescopes created a significant number of requests to apply T-Plate to Black Diamond riflescopes. Available in 2.5x-10x and 4x-16x, these scopes are essentially the same as the Mr. T offering, except Black Diamonds are built on a foundation of 6061-T6 Aluminum instead of Titanium.

## 4X-16X BLACK DIAMOND

The Burris Black Diamond is designed for long-range big game rifles and dual-purpose big game/varmint rifles, it has a 50mm objective and Burris' best optics. It is available with the trajectory-compensating Ballistic Mil-Dot reticle. The heavy 30mm tube is notable for its ruggedness.

Burris's Black Diamond line includes three models of a 30mm main tube 3-12X50mm with various finishes, reticles, and adjustment knobs. These riflescopes have easy-to-grip rubber-armored parallax-adjust rings, an adjustable and resettable adjustment dial, and an internal focusing eyepiece.

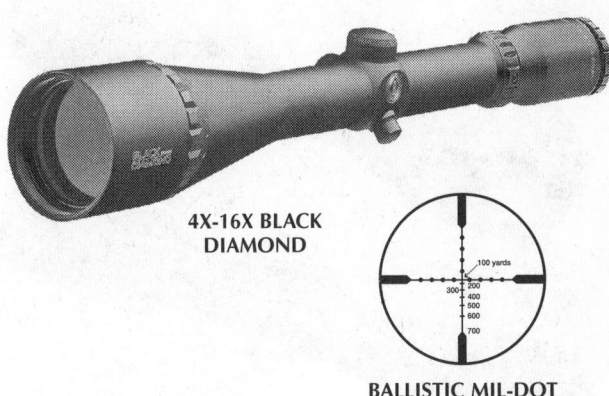

**4X-16X BLACK DIAMOND**

**BALLISTIC MIL-DOT**

### SPECIFICATIONS

**Models:** 3-12X50mm/4-16x50/6-24x50/8-32x50
**Field of View (feet @ 100yds.):** 34'-12'/18-6
**Optimum eye relief:** 3.5"-4.0"/3.5-4
**Exit Pupil:** 13.7mm-4.2mm/7.6-2.1
**Click adjust value (@ 100 yds.):** .25"/.125
**Max. internal adj. (@ 100 yds.):** 100"/52
**Clear objective diameter:** 50mm/50mm
**Ocular end diameter:** 42mm/42mm
**Weight:** 25 oz./25 oz.
**Length:** 13.8"/16.2"
**Reticles available:** Plex, Mil-Dot, Ballistic MDot, and Fine Plex

## SCOUT SCOPES

For hunters who need a 7- to 14-inch eye relief for mounting in front of the ejection port; allows you to shoot with both eyes open. The 15-foot field of view and 2.75X magnification are ideal for brush guns and shotgunners. Rugged, reliable and fog proof.

## SPEEDDOT 135

1x35mm pistol and shotgun sight. Electronic red dot reticle, 3 moa or 11 moa

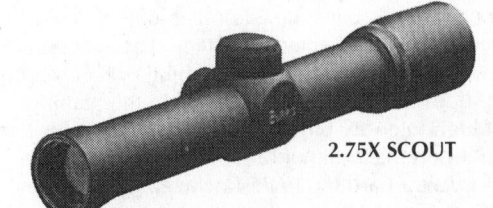

**2.75X SCOUT**

**SPEEDDOT 135**

# Burris Riflescopes

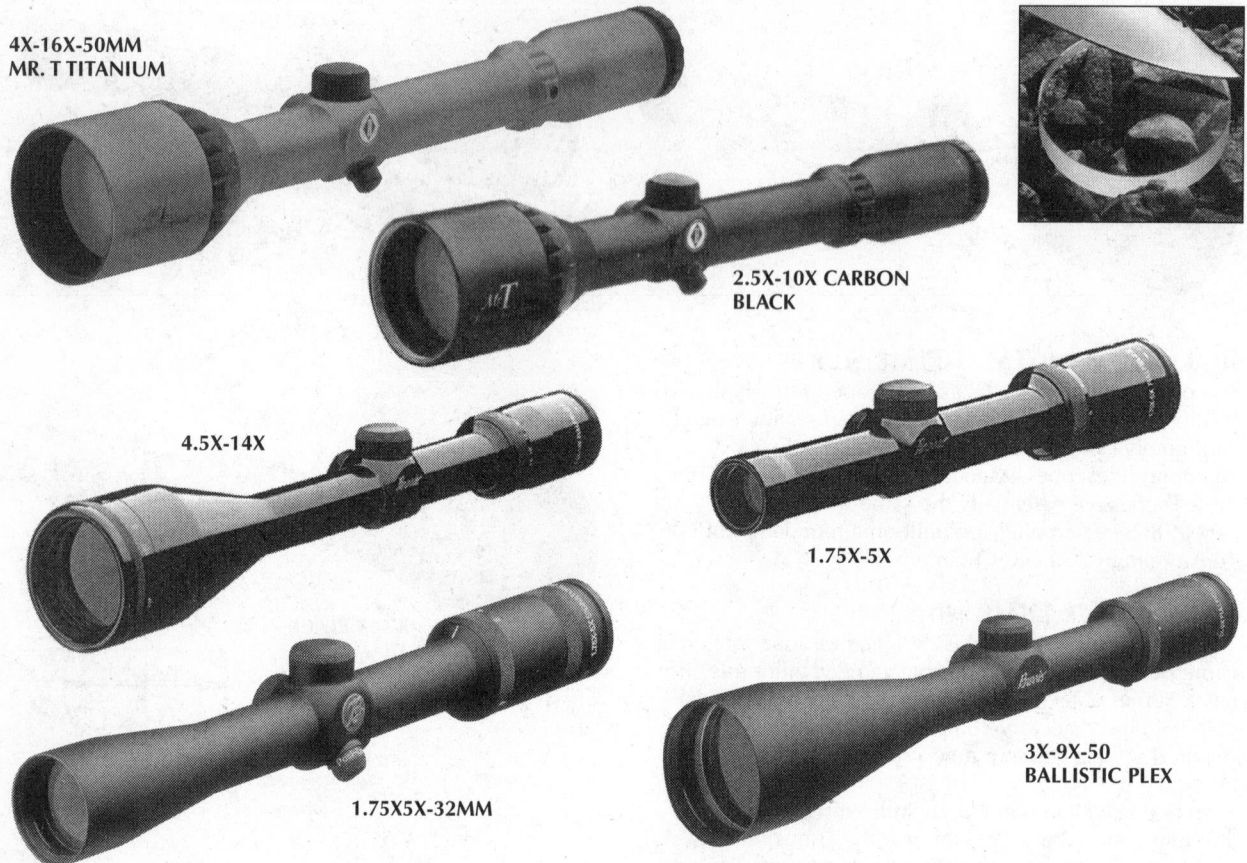

**4X-16X-50MM
MR. T TITANIUM**

**2.5X-10X CARBON
BLACK**

**4.5X-14X**

**1.75X-5X**

**1.75X5X-32MM**

**3X-9X-50
BALLISTIC PLEX**

## BURRIS "MR T"
### TITANIUM BLACK • DIAMOND SCOPES

This scope's tube is constructed of titanium, stronger than aluminum and much lighter than steel. Each scope is coated with a nitride harder than carbide or hard chrome. These nitrides are molecularly bonded to the titanium through high intensity physical vapor deposition for maximum adhesion that will not blister, flake, or chip. The result is an ultra-hard (up to 85 Rockwell C), abrasion resistant surface.

The lenses in this scope are as tough as the tube. A scratch-proof T-Plate coating applied to the objective and eyepiece lenses is remarkable. These lenses do not come with the warning of other "scratch-resistant" coatings about removing all dust before cleaning. T-plated lenses do not require a "soft clean lens cloth". Just knock the mud off the lens and wipe it clean with a dirty shirt tail. Ordinary dirt, dust, and grit won't touch it. This coating technology is prohibitively expensive for ordinary scopes. Mr. T is a premium - quality sight for discriminating hunters.

## 1.75X-5X-32MM
### SIGNATURETM SAFARI

A new optic system was designed to integrate a host of features into the ultimate riflescope for hunting in heavy brush, for heavy recoiling dangerous game rifles, and for magnum slug shotguns. The 1.75X-5X Signature SafariTM provides 3/4" additional eye relief to save your brow while shooting from awkward positions. The 32mm objective allows for ultra-flexibility in eye position. The eyepiece and power ring are combined into a single sturdy unit that makes changing magnifications faster. The Post and Crosshair reticle is the fastest and most instinctive reticle pattern available. Because of its size, shape, ruggedness, and lighter weight, the 1.75X-5X also makes a great scope for all the new short magnum rifles.

## BURRIS FULLFIELD II VARIABLE SCOPES

Now one of the most popular big game scopes around, the Fullfield II is more forgiving for eye positioning both fore and aft, and left and right, than its predecessor. Burris has shaved 4 ounces of weight off each model without affecting durability or optical performance. Overall, the Fullfield is about one inch shorter too -- for a more compact look and feel. Like the Fullfield, and unlike other scopes, Fullfield II eyepieces are sealed with special quad seals rather than old-tech O-rings. And the eyepiece is now part of the power ring. To change magnification, simply turn the entire eyepiece. A European-style adjustable eyepiece is easy to use and requires no locking mechanism.

# Burris Scopes
## Signature Series

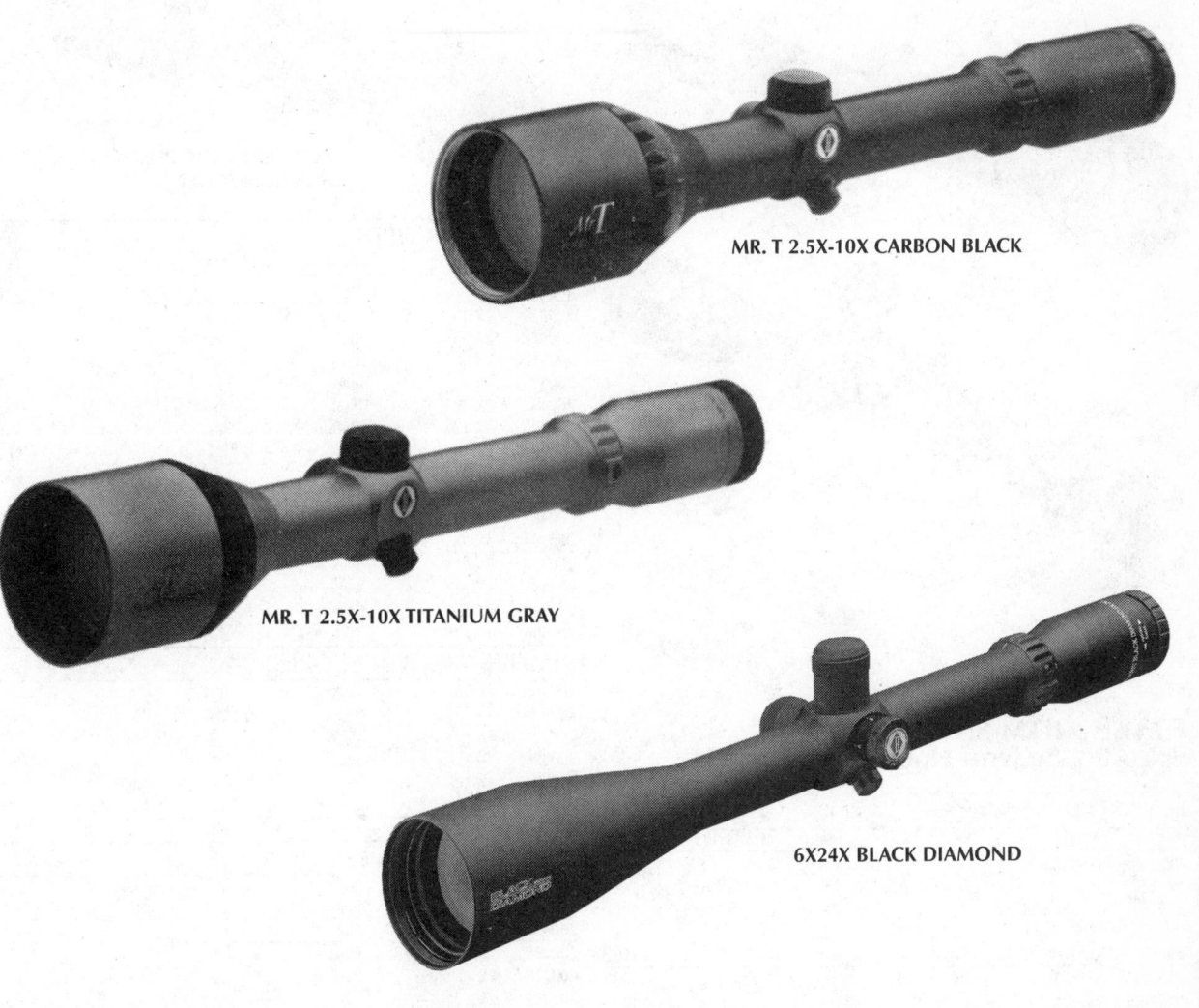

MR. T 2.5X-10X CARBON BLACK

MR. T 2.5X-10X TITANIUM GRAY

6X24X BLACK DIAMOND

## SIGNATURE SERIES SCOPES

| Item | Model | Reticle | Finish | Features | List |
|---|---|---|---|---|---|
| 200707 | 1.75X-5X-Safari | Taper Plex | mat | - | $601 |
| 200708 | 1.75X-5X-Safari | Taper Plex | mat | Posi-Lock | 649 |
| 200709 | 1.75X-5X-Safari | Post Crosshair | mat | Posi-Lock | 667 |

### MR. T BLACK DIAMOND TITANIUM SCOPES (30MM)

| | | | | | |
|---|---|---|---|---|---|
| 200920 | 2.5X-10X-50mm | Plex | titanium gray | | $1,518 |
| 200928 | 4X-16X-50mm | Plex | titanium gray | PA | 1,594 |
| 200956 | 4X-16X-50mm | Ballistic MDot | titanium gray | PA | 1,670 |

### BLACK DIAMOND T-PLATES SCOPES (30MM)

| | | | | | |
|---|---|---|---|---|---|
| 200912 | 2.5X-10X-55mm | Plex | mat | PA | $1,165 |
| 200929 | 4X-16X-50mm | Ballistic MDot | mat | PA | 1,351 |

### BLACK DIAMOND SCOPES (30MM)

| | | | | | |
|---|---|---|---|---|---|
| 200906 | 6X-50mm | Plex | mat | | $756 |
| 200900 | 3X-12X-50mm | Plex | mat | | $974 |
| 200901 | 3X-12X-50mm | Plex | mat | Posi-Lock /PA | 1,046 |
| 200954 | 4X-16X-50mm | Plex | mat | Side PA | 888 |
| 200955 | 4X-16X-50mm | Ballistic MDot | mat | Side PA | 1,119 |
| 200957 | 4X-16X-50mm | German 3P#4 | mat | Side PA | 1,024 |
| 200958 | 4X-16X-50mm | Ballistic MDot | mat | PLOCK/Side P | 1,190 |

| | | | | | |
|---|---|---|---|---|---|
| 200933 | 6X-24X-50mm | Fine Plex | mat | Tar-Side /PA | 1,098 |
| 200934 | 6X-24X-50mm | Ballistic MDot | mat | Tar-Side /PA | 1,237 |
| 200942 | 8X-32X-50mm | Fine Plex | mat | Tar-Side /PA | 1,149 |
| 200943 | 8X-32X-50mm | Ballistic MDot | mat | Tar-Side /PA | 1,308 |

### LRS LIGHTED RETICLE SCOPES

| | | | | | |
|---|---|---|---|---|---|
| 200167 | 3X-9X Fullfield II | Electro-Dot | mat | | $520 |
| 200168 | 3X-9X FFII LRS | LRS Ball Plex | mat | | 558 |
| 200173 | 3.5X-10X-50 FFII LRS | LRS Ball Plex | mat | | 672 |
| 200710 | 1.75X-5X Sig LRS | LRS Fast Plex | mat | | $769 |
| 200711 | 1.5X-6X Signature | Electro-Dot | mat | | 667 |
| 200712 | 1.5X-6X Signature | Electro-Dot | mat | Posi-Lock | 719 |
| 200581 | 3X-9X Signature | Electro-Dot | mat | | $763 |
| 200590 | 3X-9X Signature | Electro-Dot | blk | Posi-Lock | 794 |
| 200591 | 3X-9X Signature | Electro-Dot | mat | Posi-Lock | 815 |
| 200765 | 4X-16X Signature | Electro-Dot | mat | PA | $887 |
| 200766 | 4X-16X Signature | Electro-Dot | mat | Posi-Lock/PA | 942 |
| 200580 | 3X-9X-40 Signature | Electro-Dot | blk | | 763 |
| 200179 | 3X-9X-40 Fullfield II | Plex | mat | | 558 |
| 200175 | 3X-10X-50 FFII | Plex | mat | | 672 |
| 200185 | 4.5X-14X-42 FFII | Ballistic Plex | mat | | 767 |
| 200186 | 4.5X-14X-42 FFII | Plex | mat | | 767 |

SIGHTS & SCOPES

Sights & Scopes • 391

# Burris Scopes

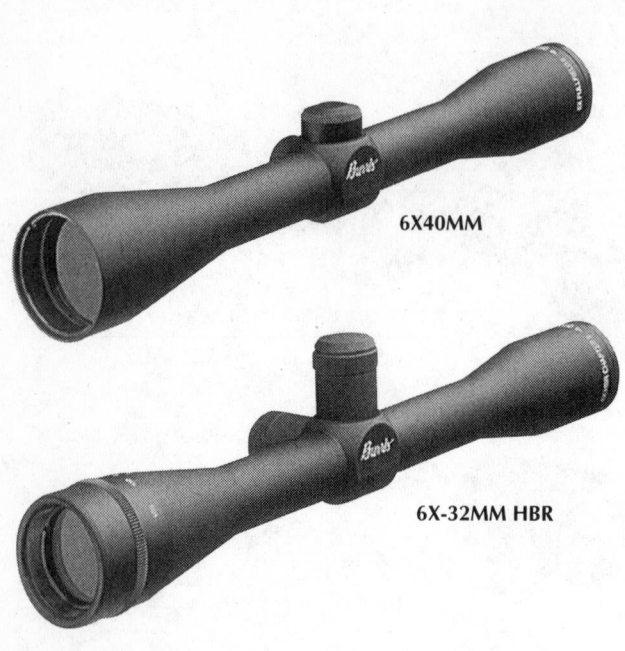

6X40MM

6X-32MM HBR

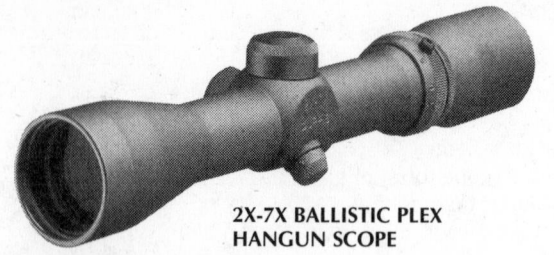

2X-7X BALLISTIC PLEX
HANGUN SCOPE

## FULLFIELD IITM SCOPES
## FIXED POWER WITH HI-LUME LENSES

### FULLFIELD II SCOPES

| ITEM | MODEL | RETICLE | FINISH | FEATURES | LIST |
|---|---|---|---|---|---|
| 200052 | 6X-40mm | Plex | mat | - | $386 |
| 200057 | 6X-32mm HBRII | Superfine XHr | mat | Target /PA | 515 |
| 200056 | 6X-32mm HBRII | .375 Dot | mat | Target /PA | 538 |
| 200153 | 3X-9X-50mm | Plex | mat | - | 481 |
| 200154 | 3X-9X-50mm | Ballistic Plex | mat | - | 490 |
| 200086 | 1.75-5X | Plex | blk | | $400 |
| 200087 | 1.75-5X | Plex | mat | | 420 |
| 200160 | 3X-9X-40mm | Plex | blk | | $336 |
| 200161 | 3X-9X-40mm | Plex | mat | | 336 |
| 200162 | 3X-9X-40mm | Ballistic Plex | mat | | $354 |
| 200163 | 3X-9X-40mm | Plex | nic | | 372 |
| 200164 | 3X-9X-40mm | German 3P#4 | mat | | 372 |
| 200166 | 3X-9X-40mm | Ballistic Plex | blk | | 354 |
| 200169 | 3X-9X-40mm | Ballistic Plex | nic | | 390 |
| 200170 | 3.5X-10X-50mm | Plex | blk | | $542 |
| 200171 | 3.5X-10X-50mm | Plex | mat | | 561 |
| 200172 | 3.5X-10X-50mm | Ballistic Plex | mat | | $570 |
| 200180 | 4.5X-14X | Plex | blk | PA | $585 |
| 200181 | 4.5X-14X | Plex | mat | PA | 585 |
| 200182 | 4.5X-14X | Fine Plex | mat | PA | $602 |
| 200183 | 4.5X-14X-42mm | Ballistic Plex | mat | PA | 602 |
| 200184 | 4.5X-14X-42 | German 3P#4 | mat | PA | 620 |
| 200190 | 6.5X-20X-50mm | Fine Plex | blk | PA | 656 |
| 200191 | 6.5X-20X-50mm | Fine Plex | mat | PA | 674 |
| 200192 | 6.5X-20X-50mm | Fine Plex | mat | Target /PA | 715 |
| 200193 | 6.5X-20X-50mm | Ballistic MDot | mat | PA | 808 |

### FULLFIELD SCOPES

| ITEM | MODEL | RETICLE | FINISH | FEATURES | LIST |
|---|---|---|---|---|---|
| 200413 | 2.5X shotgun | Plex | mat | | $307 |
| 200103 | 6X-18X | Fine Plex | blk | PA | $543 |
| 200109 | 6X-18X | Fine Plex | mat | PA | 561 |
| 200104 | 6X-18X | Fine Plex | blk | Target /PA | 581 |

### COMPACT SCOPES

| ITEM | MODEL | RETICLE | FINISH | FEATURES | LIST |
|---|---|---|---|---|---|
| 1X XER | Plex | mat | | $320 | |
| 200379 | 2X-7X | Ballistic Plex | mat | | 456 |
| 200382 | 2X-9X | Ballistic Plex | mat | | 467 |
| 200310 | 4X | Plex | blk | | $307 |
| 200311 | 4X | Plex | mat | | 329 |
| 200432 | 1X-4X | XER | mat | | 397 |
| 200396 | 4X-12X | Ballistic Plex | mat | PA | 561 |
| 200375 | 2X-7X | Plex | blk | | 415 |
| 200376 | 2X-7X | Plex | mat | | 438 |
| 200387 | 3X-9X | Plex | mat | | 449 |
| 200388 | 3X-9X | Plex | nic | | 458 |
| 200384 | 3X-9X | Plex | mat | PA | 456 |
| 200390 | 4X-12X | Plex | blk | PA | $534 |
| 200395 | 4X-12X | Plex | mat | PA | 542 |
| 200393 | 4X-12X | Fine Plex | blk | Target /PA | 576 |
| 200394 | 4X-12X | Fine Plex | mat | Target /PA | 595 |

### RIMFIRE/AIRGUN SCOPES

| ITEM | MODEL | RETICLE | FINISH | FEATURES | LIST |
|---|---|---|---|---|---|
| 200384 | 3X-9X | Plex | mat | PA | $456 |
| 200390 | 4X-12X | Plex | blk | PA | 534 |
| 200395 | 4X-12X | Plex | mat | PA | 542 |
| 200396 | 4X-12X | Ballistic Plex | mat | PA | 561 |
| 200393 | 4X-12X | Fine Plex | blk | Target /PA | 576 |
| 200394 | 4X-12X | Fine Plex | mat | Target /PA | 595 |
| 200858 | 8X-32X | Plex | blk | Target /PA | $835 |

### HANDGUN SCOPES

| ITEM | MODEL | RETICLE | FINISH | FEATURES | LIST |
|---|---|---|---|---|---|
| 200299 | 2X-7X | Ballistic Plex | mat | Posi-Lock | $527 |
| 200309 | 3X-12X | Ballistic Plex | mat | PA | 586 |
| 200424 | 1X XER | Plex | mat | | $320 |
| 200220 | 2X | Plex | blk | | $286 |
| 200218 | 2X | Plex | mat | | 279 |
| 200229 | 2X | Plex | nic | | 306 |
| 200228 | 2X | Plex | mat | Posi-Lock | 334 |
| 200235 | 4X | Plex | blk | | $338 |
| 200263 | 10X Target /PA | Plex | blk | Target | $515 |
| 200214 | 1.5X-4X | Plex | nic | | $411 |
| 200207 | 1.5X-4X | Plex | mat | Posi-Lock | 449 |
| 200213 | 1.5X-4X | Plex | nic | Posi-Lock | 450 |
| 200290 | 2X-7X | Plex | blk | | $458 |
| 200291 | 2X-7X | Plex | mat | | 468 |
| 200293 | 2X-7X | Plex | blk | PA | 506 |
| 200298 | 2X-7X | Plex | nic | | 479 |
| 200294 | 2X-7X | Plex | blk | Posi-Lock | 501 |
| 200297 | 2X-7X | Plex | nic | Posi-Lock | 520 |
| 200306 | 3X-12X | Plex | blk | PA | $558 |
| 200307 | 3X-12X | Plex | mat | PA | 568 |
| 200308 | 3X-12X | Plex | blk | PA | 577 |
| 200305 | 3X-12X | Fine Plex | blk | Target /PA | 570 |
| 200303 | 3X-12X | Plex | mat | Posi-Lock | 608 |

### SPEEDDOT 135 SIGHTS

| | | | | | |
|---|---|---|---|---|---|
| 300200 | 1X-35mm | 3 MOA Dot | mat | | $291 |
| 300201 | 1X-35mm | 11 MOA Dot | mat | | 291 |

### SCOUT SCOPES

| | | | | | |
|---|---|---|---|---|---|
| 200424 | 1X XER | Plex | mat | | $320 |
| 200269 | 2.75X | Heavy Plex | mat | | 356 |

# Bushnell Riflescopes

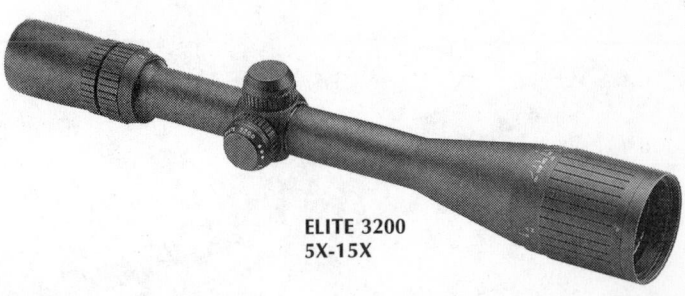

**ELITE 3200
5X-15X**

## FIREFLY RETICLE

The Firefly reticle is available in Elite 3200 scopes, from 1.5-4x32 to 3-9x50. Firefly requires no batteries. You "energize" it by shining a flashlight beam into the scope for a minute. The reticle glows green for a short time, then fades to black. As shooting light diminishes, even hours later, the green glow returns, enabling you to see the reticle more clearly.

### ELITE 3200

| Model | Finish | Power / Obj. Lens (MM) | Reticle | Field-of-view (FT@100YDS) | Weight (OZ) | Length (IN) | Eye Relief (IN) | Exit Pupil (MM) | Click Value (IN@100YDS) | Adj. Range (IN@100YDS) | Suggested Retail |
|---|---|---|---|---|---|---|---|---|---|---|---|
| 32-1040M | Matte | 10 x 40 | Mil Dot | 11 | 15.5 | 11.7 | 3.5 | 4.0 | .25 | 100 | $279.95 |
| 32-1546M | Matte | 1.5–4.5 x 32 | FireFly™ | 63/21@1.5x | 13 | 12.5 | 3.6 | 21–7.6 | .25 | 100 | 307.95 |
| 32-2632M | Matte | 2–6 x 32 | Multi-X® | 10/3@2x | 10 | 9 | 20 | 16–5.3 | .25 | 50 | 389.95 |
| 32-2632S | Silver | 2–6 x 32 | Multi-X® | 10/3@2x | 10 | 9 | 20 | 16–5.3 | .25 | 50 | 389.95 |
| *32-2636M | Matte | 2–6 x 32 | FireFly™ | 10/3@2x | 10 | 9 | 20 | 16–5.3 | .25 | 50 | 431.95 |
| 32-2732M | Matte | 2–7 x 32 | Multi-X® | 44.6/15@2x | 12 | 11.6 | 3.0 | 12.2–4.6 | .25 | 50 | 265.95 |
| 32-3940G | Gloss | 3–9 x 40 | Multi-X® | 33.8/11@3x | 13 | 12.6 | 3.3 | 13.3–4.4 | .25 | 50 | 279.95 |
| 32-3940S | Silver | 3–9 x 40 | Multi-X® | 33.8/11@3x | 13 | 12.6 | 3.3 | 13.3–4.4 | .25 | 50 | 279.95 |
| 32-3944M | Matte | 3–9 x 40 | Multi-X® | 33.8/11@3x | 13 | 12.6 | 3.3 | 13.3–4.4 | .25 | 50 | 279.95 |
| 32-3946M | Matte | 3–9 x 40 | FireFly™ | 33.8/11@3x | 13 | 12.6 | 3.3 | 13.3–4.4 | .25 | 50 | 321.95 |
| 32-3954M | Matte | 3–9 x 50 | Multi-X® | 31.5/10@3x | 19 | 15.7 | 3.3 | 16–5.6 | .25 | 50 | 335.95 |
| 32-3955E | Matte | 3–9 x 50 | European | 31.5/10@3x | 22 | 15.6 | 3.3 | 16–5.6 | .36 | 70 | 561.95 |
| 32-3956M | Matte | 3–9 x 50 | FireFly™ | 31.5/1.50@3x | 19 | 15.7 | 3.3 | 16.7–5.6 | .25 | 50 | 377.95 |
| 32-3957M | Matte | 3–9 x 50 | FireFly™ | 31.5/10.5@3x | 22 | 15.6 | 3.3 | 16.7–5.6 | .25 | 70 | 603.95 |
| 32-4124A | Matte | 4–12 x 40 | Multi-X® | 26.9/9@4x | 15 | 13.2 | 3.3 | 10–3.33 | .25 | 50 | 411.95 |
| 32-5154M | Matte | 5–15 x 40 | Multi-X® | 21/7@5x | 19 | 14.5 | 4.3 | 9–2.7 | .25 | 50 | 439.95 |
| 32-5155M | Matte | 5–15 x 50 | Multi-X® | 21/7@5x | 24 | 15.9 | 3.4 | 10–3.3 | .25 | 40 | 463.95 |
| *32-5156M | Matte | 5–15 x 40 | FireFly™ | 21/7@5x | 19 | 14.5 | 4.3 | 9–2.7 | .25 | 50 | 481.95 |

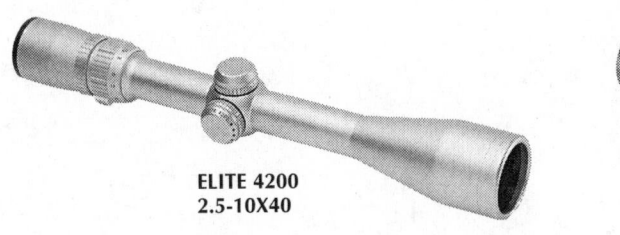

**ELITE 4200
2.5-10X40**

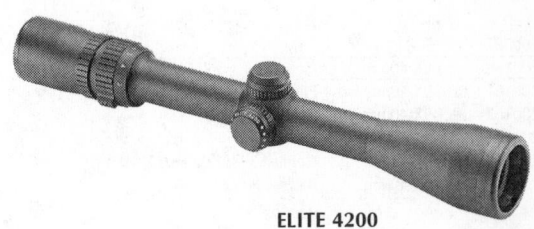

**ELITE 4200**

### ELITE 4200

| Model | Finish | Power / Obj. Lens (MM) | Reticle | Field-of-view (FT@100YDS) | Weight (OZ) | Length (IN) | Eye Relief (IN) | Exit Pupil (MM) | Click Value (IN@100YDS) | Adj. Range (IN@100YDS) | Suggested Retail |
|---|---|---|---|---|---|---|---|---|---|---|---|
| 42-1636M | Matte | 1.5–6 x 36 | Multi-X® | 61.8/20.6@1.5x | 15.4 | 12.8 | 3.3 | 14.6–6 | .25 | 60 | $533.95 |
| 42-2104M | Matte | 2.5–10 x 40 | Multi-X® | 41.5/13.8@2.5x | 16 | 13.5 | 3.3 | 15.6–4 | .25 | 50 | 563.95 |
| 42-2104G | Gloss | 2.5–10 x 40 | Multi-X® | 41.5/13.8@2.5x | 16 | 13.5 | 3.3 | 15.6–4 | .25 | 50 | 563.95 |
| 42-2104S | Silver | 2.5–10 x 40 | Multi-X® | 41.5/13.8@2.5x | 16 | 13.5 | 3.3 | 15.6–4 | .25 | 50 | 563.95 |
| 42-2105M | Matte | 2.5–10 x 50 | Multi-X® | 40.3/13.4@2.5x | 18 | 14.3 | 3.3 | 15–5 | .25 | 50 | 669.95 |
| 42-2146M | Matte | 2.5–10 x 40 | FireFly™ | 41.5/13.8@2.5x | 16 | 13.5 | 3.3 | 15.6–4 | .25 | 50 | 605.95 |
| 42-2151M | Matte | 2.5–10 x 50 | 4A w/1 M.O.A Dot | 40/13.3@2.5x | 22 | 14.5 | 3.3 | 5–15 | .25 | 60 | 699.95 |
| 42-4164M | Matte | 4–16 x 40 | Multi-X® | 26/8.7@4x | 18.6 | 14.4 | 3.3 | 10–25 | .125 | 40 | 565.95 |
| 42-4165M | Matte | 4–16 x 50 | Multi-X® | 26/9@4x | 22 | 15.6 | 3.3 | 12.5–3.1 | .125 | 50 | 731.95 |
| 42-6242M | Matte | 6–24 x 40 | Mil Dot | 18/6@6x | 20.2 | 16.9 | 3.3 | 6.7–1.7 | .125 | 26 | 659.95 |
| 42-6243A | Matte | 6–24 x 40 | 1/4 M.O.A. Dot | 18/6@6x | 20.2 | 16.9 | 3.3 | 6.7–1.7 | .125 | 26 | 639.95 |
| 42-6244M | Matte | 6–24 x 40 | Multi-X® | 18/4.5@6x | 20.2 | 16.9 | 3.3 | 6.7–1.7 | .125 | 26 | 639.95 |
| 42-8324M | Matte | 8–32 x 40 | Multi-X® | 14/4.7@8x | 22 | 18 | 3.3 | 5–1.25 | .125 | 20 | 703.95 |

# Bushnell Riflescopes

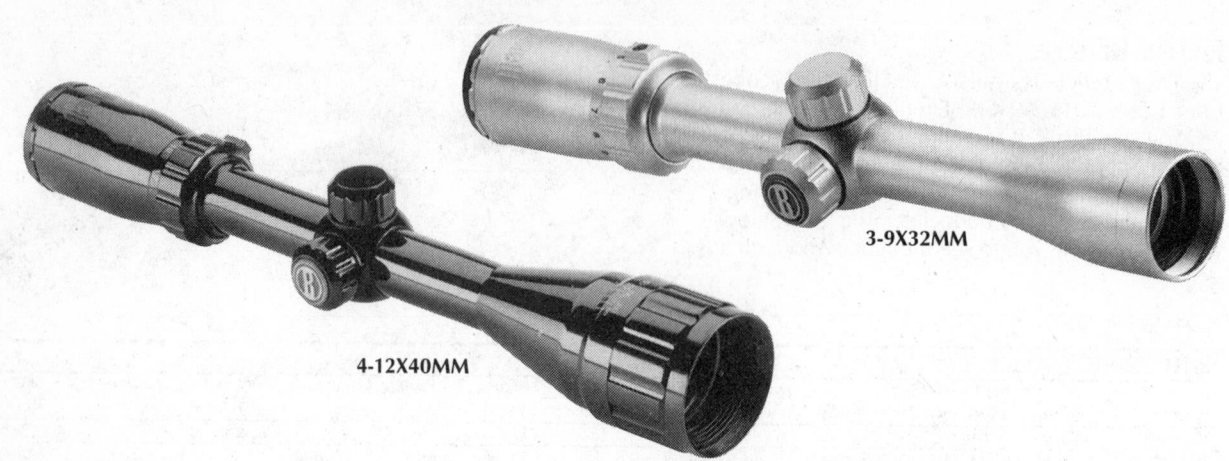

3-9X32MM

4-12X40MM

## SPORTSMAN RIFLESCOPES

Sportsman Riflescopes have multi-coated optics, plus a long list of standard features, including a fast-focus eyepiece and 1/4 M.O.A. fingertip windage and elevation adjustments. The easy-grip power change ring makes changing magnifications fast and easy. The rigid one-piece 1" tube is waterproof, fogproof and shockproof.
3-9x32mm: Gloss, 72-1393; Silver, 72-1393S; Matte, 72-13984-12x40mm: Gloss, 72-0412

## BUSHNELL SPORTSMAN® RIFLESCOPES

| MODEL | FINISH | POWER / OBJ. LENS (MM) | RETICLE | FIELD-OF-VIEW (FT@100YDS) | WEIGHT (OZ) | LENGTH (IN) | EYE RELIEF (IN) | EXIT PUPIL (MM) | CLICK VALUE (IN@100YDS) | ADJ. RANGE (IN@100YDS) | SUGGESTED RETAIL |
|---|---|---|---|---|---|---|---|---|---|---|---|
| 72-0038 | Matte | 3–9 x 32 | Multi-X® | 37–14 | 13.5 | 12 | 3.5 | 10.6–3.6 | .25 | 100 | $69.96 |
| 72-0039 | Gloss | 3–9 x 32 | Multi-X® | 40 13.1 | 163 | 12.2 | 430 | 3.6–11 | .25 | 100 | 101.95 |
| 72-0130 | Matte | 1 x 23 | 6 M.O.A. Red Dot | 60 | 4.9 | 5.5 | Unlimited | 2.3 | .5 | 50 | 73.95 |
| 72-1393 | Gloss | 3–9 x 32 | Multi-X® | 37–14 | 13.5 | 12 | 3.5 | 10–3.6 | .25 | 100 | 59.95 |
| 72-1393S | Silver | 3–9 x 32 | Multi-X® | 37–14 | 13.5 | 12 | 3.5 | 10–3.6 | .25 | 100 | 59.95 |
| 72-1398 | Matte | 3–9 x 32 | Multi-X® | 37–14 | 13.5 | 12 | 3.5 | 10–3.6 | .25 | 100 | 59.95 |
| 72-1403 | Matte | 4 x 32 | Multi-X® | 29 | 11 | 11.7 | 3.4 | 8 | .25 | 110 | 49.95 |
| 72-1545 | Matte | 1.5–4.5 x 21 | Multi-X® | 24–69 | 11.7 | 10.1 | 3.3 | 10–3.6 | .25 | 210 | 75.95 |
| 72-1548R | Camo | 1.5–4.5 x 32 | Circle-X® | 46.2–19.3 | 13.5 | 11.7 | 4.3 | 21–7.1 | .25 | 100 | 95.95 |
| 72-3940M | Matte | 3–9 x 40 | Multi-X® | 37–12 | 15 | 13 | 3.5 | 13–4.4 | .25 | 100 | 83.95 |

# Bushnell Riflescopes

**3X-9X (40MM) TROPHY®
WIDE ANGLE RIFLESCOPE**

## BUSHNELL TROPHY® RIFLESCOPES

| MODEL | FINISH | POWER / OBJ. LENS (MM) | RETICLE | FIELD-OF-VIEW (FT@100YDS) | WEIGHT (OZ) | LENGTH (IN) | EYE RELIEF (IN) | EXIT PUPIL (MM) | CLICK VALUE (IN@100YDS) | ADJ. RANGE (IN@100YDS) | SUGGESTED RETAIL |
|---|---|---|---|---|---|---|---|---|---|---|---|
| 73-0131 | Matte | 1 x 28 | 6 M.O.A. Red Dot | 68–22.6 | 6 | 5.5 | Unlimited | 28 | .5 | 50 | $89.95 |
| 73-0134 | Matte | 1 x 28 | 4 Dial-In Electronic | 68–22.6 | 6 | 5.5 | Unlimited | 28 | .5 | 50 | 119.95 |
| 73-0232S | Silver | 2 x 32 | Multi-X® | 20–7 | 7.7 | 8.7 | 18 | 16 | .25 | 90 | 191.95 |
| 73-1421 | Matte | 1.75–4 x 32 | Circle-X® | 73–30 | 10.9 | 10.8 | 4.1 | 18@1.75x / 8@4x | .25 | 120 | 149.95 |
| 73-1422MO | Camo | 1.75–4 x 32 | Circle-X® | 73–30 | 10.9 | 10.8 | 4.1 | 18@1.75x / 8@4x | .25 | 120 | 163.95 |
| 73-1500 | Gloss | 1.75–5 x 32 | Multi-X® | 68–23 | 12.3 | 10.8 | 4.1 | 18.3@1.75x / 6.4@5x | .25 | 120 | 155.95 |
| 73-2632 | Matte | 2–6 x 32 | Multi-X® | 11–4 | 10.9 | 9.1 | 9–26 | 16@2x / 5.3@6x | .25 | 50 | 251.95 |
| 73-2632S | Silver | 2–6 x 32 | Multi-X® | 11–4 | 10.9 | 9.1 | 9–26 | 16@2x / 5.3@6x | .25 | 50 | 251.95 |
| 73-3940 | Gloss | 3–9 x 40 | Multi-X® | 42–14 | 13.2 | 11.7 | 3.4 | 13.3@3x / 4.4@9x | .25 | 60 | 139.95 |
| 73-3940S | Silver | 3–9 x 40 | Multi-X® | 42–14 | 13.2 | 11.7 | 3.4 | 13.3@3x / 4.4@9x | .25 | 60 | 139.95 |
| 73-3946 | Matte | 3–9 x 40 | Mil Dot | 42–14 | 13.2 | 11.7 | 3.4 | 13.3@3x / 4.4@9x | .25 | 60 | 149.95 |
| 73-3948 | Matte | 3–9 x 40 | Multi-X® | 42–14 | 13.2 | 11.7 | 3.4 | 13.3@3x / 4.4@9x | .25 | 60 | 139.95 |
| 73-3949 | Matte | 3–9 x 40 | Circle-X® | 42–14 | 13.2 | 11.7 | 3.4 | 13.3@3x / 4.4@9x | .25 | 60 | 149.95 |
| 73-4124 | Gloss | 4–12 x 40 | Multi-X® | 32–11 | 16.1 | 12.6 | 3.4 | 10@4x / 3.3@12x | .25 | 60 | 263.95 |
| 73-4124M | Matte | 4–12 x 40 | Multi-X® | 32–11 | 16.1 | 12.6 | 3.4 | 10@4x / 3.3@12x | .25 | 60 | 263.95 |
| 73-6184 | Matte | 6–18 x 40 | Multi-X® | 17.3–6 | 17.9 | 14.8 | 3.0 | 6.6@6x / 2.2@18x | .125 | 40 | 331.95 |

*An adjustable objective (AO) enables you to eliminate parallax (image shift relative to the reticle) at a given range. It also allows you to bring the target sharply into focus*

**SIGHTS & SCOPES**

# Bushnell Riflescopes

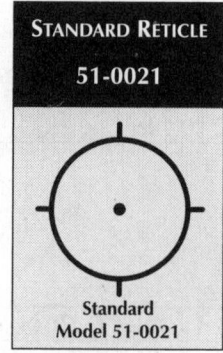

**STANDARD RETICLE**

**51-0021**

Standard
Model 51-0021

**HOLOSIGHT**

## HOLOsight

Unlike conventional sights, HOLOsight projects the appearance of an illuminated crosshair 50 yards in front of your gun, yet no forward light is projected. Sight from any distance behind the gun – with both eyes on the target. This fastest of all optical sights offers unlimited field of view and eye relief. Shockproof, waterproof and fogproof. Half the length and weight of conventional scopes. Fits easily on handguns, shotguns and rifles with a standard Weaver style mount. Available in two battery styles – N cell or AA.

### HOLOsight

| Model | Finish | Power / Obj. Lens (mm) | Reticle | Field-of-View (ft@100yds) | Weight (oz) | Length (in) | Eye Relief (in) | Exit Pupil (mm) | Click Value (in@100yds) | Adj. Range (in@100yds) | Suggested Retail |
|---|---|---|---|---|---|---|---|---|---|---|---|
| *75-2732M | Matte | 2–7 x 32 | Multi-X® | 56–16 | 11.6 | 11.6 | 3.5 | 14.4–4.6 | .25 | 60 | $187.95 |
| 75-3940M | Matte | 3–9 x 40 | Multi-X® | 36–13 | 14.6 | 13.1 | 3.5 | 13.3–4.4 | .25 | 80 | 207.95 |
| 75-3950M | Matte | 3–9 x 50 | Multi-X® | 36–13 | 16 | 13.1 | 3.5 | 16.7–5.6 | .25 | 80 | 227.95 |
| 75-5154M | Matte | 5–15 x 40 | Mil Dot | 23–8 | 17.7 | 14.6 | 3.5 | 8–2.7 | .25 | 50 | 277.95 |

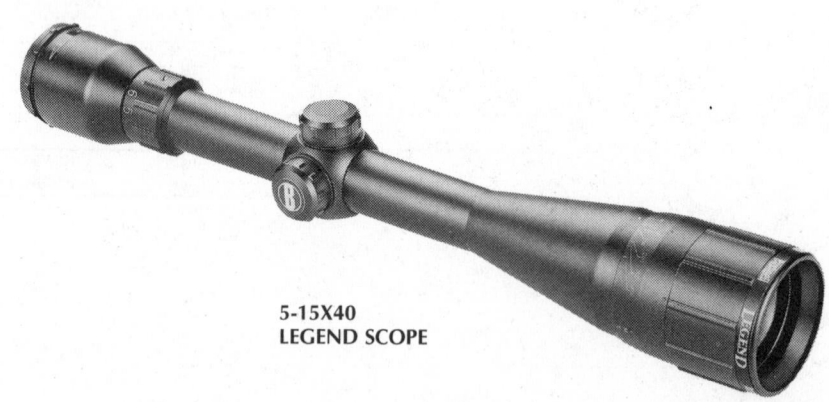

**5-15X40**
**LEGEND SCOPE**

### Legend

| Model | Finish | Power / Obj. Lens (mm) | Reticle | Field-of-View (ft@100yds) | Weight (oz / g) | Length (in) | Eye Relief (in) | Exit Pupil (mm) | Click Value (in@100yds) | Adj. Range (in@100yds) | Suggested Retail |
|---|---|---|---|---|---|---|---|---|---|---|---|
| *75-2732M | Matte | 2–7 x 32 | Multi-X® | 56–16 | 11.6 | 11.6 | 3.5 | 14.4–4.6 | .25 | 60 | $187.95 |
| 75-3940M | Matte | 3–9 x 40 | Multi-X® | 36–13 | 14.6 | 13.1 | 3.5 | 13.3–4.4 | .25 | 80 | 207.95 |
| 75-3950M | Matte | 3–9 x 50 | Multi-X® | 36–13 | 16 | 13.1 | 3.5 | 16.7–5.6 | .25 | 80 | 227.95 |
| 75-5154M | Matte | 5–15 x 40 | Mil Dot | 23–8 | 17.7 | 14.6 | 3.5 | 8–2.7 | .25 | 50 | 277.95 |

SIGHTS & SCOPES

# Bushnell Riflescopes

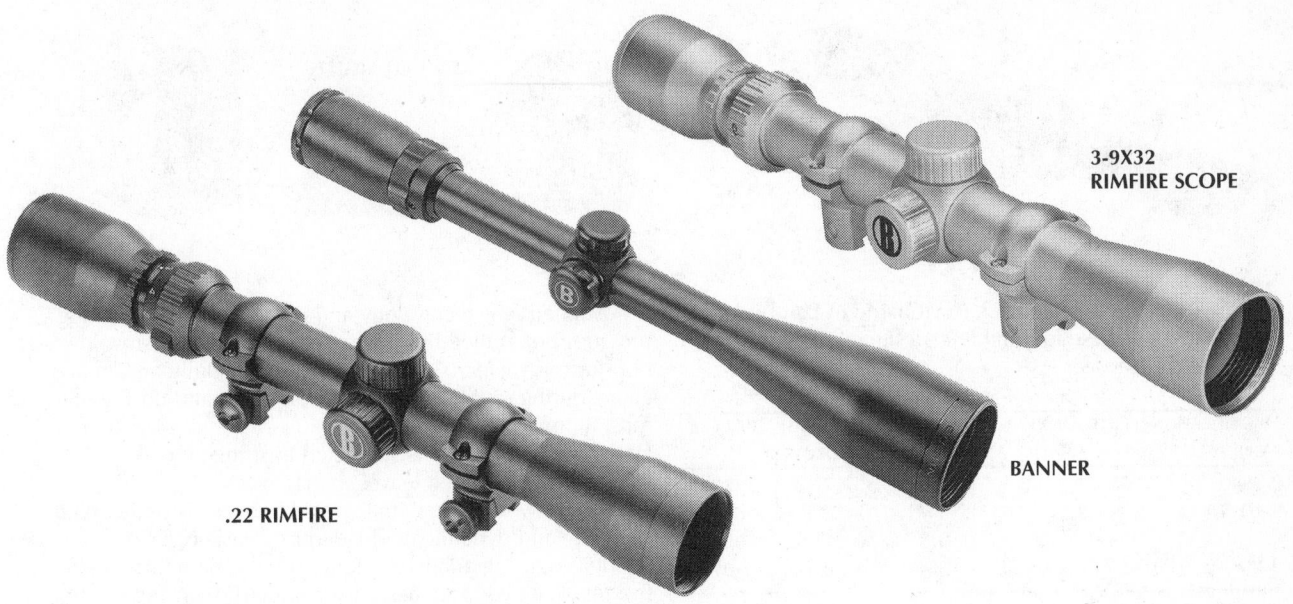

**3-9X32 RIMFIRE SCOPE**

**BANNER**

**.22 RIMFIRE**

## .22 RIMFIRE

Bushnell .22 Rimfire scopes are designed with a 50-yard parallax setting and fully coated optics for low-light shooting The one-piece 1″ tube is waterproof and fogproof; 1/4 M.O.A. windage and elevation adjustments are fingertip-easy to turn. These scopes come with rings for grooved receivers.

## BANNER

Bushnell's Banner Dusk & Dawn riflescopes feature DDB multi-coated lenses to maximize dusk and dawn brightness for clarity in low and full light. A fast-focus eyepiece and wide-angle field of view complement a one-piece tube and 1/4″ M.O.A. resettable windage and elevation adjustments. An easy-trip power change ring allows fast power changes. This scope is waterproof, fogproof and shockproof.

### .22 RIMFIRE

| Model | Finish | Power / Obj. Lens (mm) | Reticle | Field-of-View (ft@100yds) | Weight (oz) | Length (in) | Eye Relief (in) | Exit Pupil (mm) | Click Value (in@100yds) | Adj. Range (in@100yds) | Suggested Retail |
|---|---|---|---|---|---|---|---|---|---|---|---|
| 76-2239 | Matte | 3–9 x 32 | Multi-X® | 40–13 | 11.2 | 11.75 | 3.0 | 10.6–3.6 | .25 | 40 | $53.95 |
| 76-2239S | Silver | 3–9 x 32 | Multi-X® | 40–13 | 11.2 | 11.75 | 3.0 | 10.6–3.6 | .25 | 40 | 53.95 |
| 76-2243 | Matte | 4 x 32 | Multi-X® | 30 / 10@4x | 10 | 11.5 | 3.0 | 8 | .25 | 40 | 45.95 |
| 76-2243S | Silver | 4 x 32 | Multi-X® | 30 / 10@4x | 10 | 11.5 | 3.0 | 8 | .25 | 40 | 45.95 |

### BANNER DUSK & DAWN

| Model | Finish | Power / Obj. Lens (mm) | Reticle | Field-of-View (ft@100yds) | Weight (oz) | Length (in) | Eye Relief (in) | Exit Pupil (mm) | Click Value (in@100yds) | Adj. Range (in@100yds) | Suggested Retail |
|---|---|---|---|---|---|---|---|---|---|---|---|
| 71-0432 | Matte | 4 x 32 | Circle-X® | 31.5–10.5@4x | 11.1 | 11.3 | 3.3 | 8@4x | .25 | 50 | $89.95 |
| 71-1432 | Matte | 1–4 x 32 | Circle-X® | 78.5–24.9 | 12.2 | 10.5 | 4.3 | 16.9@1x / 8@4x | .25 | 50 | 107.95 |
| 71-1436 | Matte | 1.75–4 x 32 | Circle-X® | 35–16 | 12.1 | 10.8 | 6 | 18.3@1.75x –6.4@4x | .25 | 100 | 101.95 |
| 71-1545 | Matte | 1.5–4.5 x 32 | Multi-X® | 67v23 | 10.5 | 10.5 | 4.0 | 17@1.5x / 7@4.5x | .25 | 60 | 101.95 |
| 71-3944 | Matte | 3–9 x 40 | Circle-X® | 36–13 | 12.5 | 11.5 | 4.0 | 13@3x / 4.4@9x | .25 | 60 | 109.95 |
| 71-3946 | Matte | 3–9 x 40 | Multi-X® | 40–14 | 13 | 12 | 4.0 | 13@3x / 4.4@9x | .25 | 60 | 101.95 |
| *71-3947 | Matte | 3–9 x 40 | Multi-X® | 40–13.6 | 13 | 12 | 3.3 | 13@3x / 4.4@9x | .25 | 60 | 111.95 |
| 71-3948 | Matte | 3–9 x 40 | Multi-X® | 40–14 | 13 | 12 | 3.3 | 13.3@3x / 4.4@9x | .25 | 60 | 105.95 |
| 71-3950 | Matte | 3–9 x 50 | Multi-X® | 26–12 | 19 | 16 | 3.8 | 16@3x / 5.6@9x | .25 | 50 | 163.95 |
| 71-3951 | Matte | 3–9 x 50 | 3-2-1 Low Light™ | 26–12 | 19 | 16 | 3.8 | 16@3x / 5.6@9x | .25 | 50 | 163.95 |
| 71-4124 | Matte | 4–12 x 40 | Multi-X® | 29–11 | 15 | 12 | 3.3 | 10@4x / 3.3@12x | .25 | 60 | 138.95 |
| 71-6185 | Matte | 6–18 x 50 | Multi-X® | 17–6 | 18 | 16 | 3.5 | 8.3@6x / 2.8@18x | .25 | 40 | 183.95 |
| *71-6244 | Matte | 6–24 x 40 | Mil Dot | 17–5 | 19.6 | 16.1 | 3.4 | 6.7@6x / 1.7@24x | .25 | 36 | 189.95 |

# Docter Sports Optics

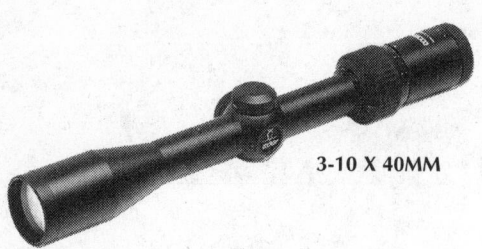

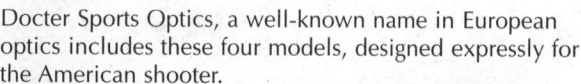

**3-10 X 40MM**

**RED DOT SIGHT**

Docter Sports Optics, a well-known name in European optics includes these four models, designed expressly for the American shooter.

| MAGNIFICATION X OBJ. DIA. | FIELD OF VIEW (FT., 100 YDS) | DIA./LENGTH (IN.) | WEIGHT (OZ.) | PRICE |
|---|---|---|---|---|
| 3-9x40 | 31-13 | 1/12.5 | 17 | $378.00 |
| 3-10x40 | 34-12 | 1/13 | 18.5 | 626.00 |
| 4.5-14x40 | 23-8 | 1/13.5 | 21.5 | 652.00 |
| 8-25x50 | 13-4 | 1/16 | 26.5 | 901.00 |

Some of Docter Optic 30mm scopes feature aspherical lenses, as do the company's binoculars. All Docter scopes offer these advantages:

## RIFLE SCOPE SPECIFICATIONS

• High strength, one-piece tube construction of aircraft-grade aluminum eliminates weak screw-together joints that can leak or break, won't rust or corrode in adverse weather.
• Precise click-stop adjustments of 1/4" at 100 yards for windage and elevation. Wide range of adjustment (50") makes it easier to compensate for mounting errors.

• Advanced lens technology and high grade multi-coating provides unparalled light transmission and image resolution for crisp, clear sighting picture - especially advantageous during low light conditions at dawn and dusk when most animal movement occurs.

Every DOCTER scope is subjected to stringent leak and shock testing before it leaves the factory.

Every joint where a leak may possibly occur is sealed with statically and dynamically loaded ring gaskets.

Diopter focusing adapts the focus to your particular needs. Eye relief of over 3 inches, plus a wide rubber ring on the eye-piece protects the shooter from half-moon cuts, even with heavy calibers.

## DOCTER RED DOT SIGHT

A red dot sight is now available from Docter Sports Optics. Weighing just one ounce, it is not much bulkier than a standard rear aperture. A red dot appears to project itself on the target—there's nothing to line up. You can shoot more quickly than with any other type of sight. Coated, high-quality lenses ensure a clear sight picture. There is no battery switch; batteries last up to five years without rest. Available in 3.5 or 7 M.D.A.

## ONE-INCH TUBE SCOPES

| DESCRIPTION | MAGNI-FICATION | OBJECTIVE LENS DIA. | COLOR | RETICLE |
|---|---|---|---|---|
| 3-9 x 40 Variable | 3x to 9x | 40 mm | Matte Black | Plex |
| 3-9 x 40 Variable | 3x to 9x | 40 mm | Matte Black | German #4 |
| 3-10 x 40 Variable | 3x to 10x | 40 mm | Matte Black | Plex |
| 3-10 x 40 Variable | 3x to 10x | 40 mm | Matte Black | German #4 |
| 4.5-14 x 40 Variable | 4.5x to 14x | 40 mm | Matte Black | Plex |
| 4.5-14 x 40 Variable | 4.5x to 14x | 40 mm | Matte Black | Dot |
| 8-25 x 50 Variable | 8x to 25x | 50 mm | Matte Black | Dot |
| 8-25 x 50 Variable | 8x to 25x | 50 mm | Matte Black | Plex |
| **30 mm TUBE SCOPES** | | | | |
| 1.5-6 x 42 Variable | 1.5x to 6x | 42 mm | Matte Black | Plex |
| 1.5-6 x 42 Variable | 1.5x to 6x | 42 mm | Matte Black | German #4 |
| 1.5-6 x 42 Var., Aspherical Lens | 1.5x to 6x | 42 mm | Matte Black | Plex |
| 1.5-6 x 42 Var., Aspherical Lens | 1.5x to 6x | 42 mm | Matte Black | German #4 |
| 2.5-10 x 48 Variable | 2.5x to 10x | 48 mm | Matte Black | Plex |
| 2.5-10 x 48 Variable | 2.5x to 10x | 48 mm | Matte Black | German #4 |
| 2.5-10 x 48 Var., Aspherical Lens | 2.5x to 10x | 48 mm | Matte Black | Plex |
| 2.5-10 x 48 Var., Aspherical Lens | 2.5x to 10x | 48 mm | Matte Black | German #4 |
| 3-12 x 56 Variable | 3x to 12x | 56 mm | Matte Black | Plex |
| 3-12 x 56 Variable | 3x to 12x | 56 mm | Matte Black | German #4 |
| 3-12 x 56 Var., Aspherical Lens | 3x to 12x | 56 mm | Matte Black | Plex |
| 3-12 x 56 Var., Aspherical Lens | 3x to 12x | 56 mm | Matte Black | German #4 |

# Kahles Riflescopes

2-7X36MM AMERICAN HUNTER

HELIA COMPACT C 4X36

HELIA COMPACT C 1,1-4X24

## AMERICAN HUNTER

Kahles rifle scopes, manufactured in Austria, are compact and lightweight with excellent optical performance. The 1-inch tubes are of one piece construction, with hard anodized, scratch resistant finish. Shockproof and fogproof these scopes offer generous eye relief. The AH's reticle is mounted in the second image focal plane, so the reticle appears the same size at every power setting.

| | |
|---|---|
| Prices: AH 2-7x36 (4A) | $554 |
| AH 2-7x36 (Plex) | 554 |
| AH 2-7x36 (Circle Plex) | 566 |
| AH 2-7x36 (TDS) | 610 |
| AH 2-7x36RF (Rimfire) 4A | 554 |
| AH 2-7x36RF (Rimfire) Plex | 554 |
| AH 3-9x42 (4A) | 654 |
| AH 3-9x42 (Plex) | 654 |
| AH 3-9x42 (TDS) | 721 |
| AH 3.5-10x50 (4A) | 766 |
| AH 3.5-10x50 (Plex) | 766 |
| AH 3.5-10x50 (TDS) | 843 |

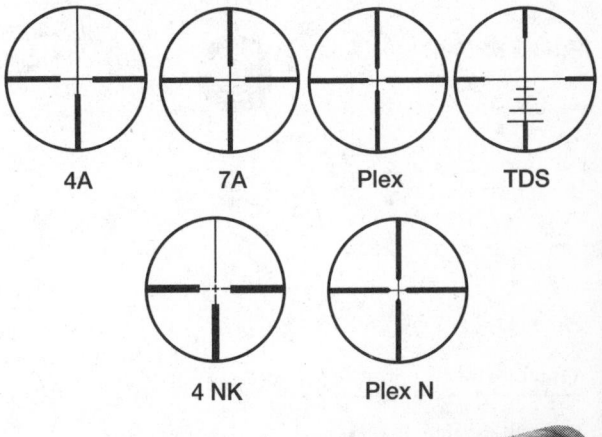

4A    7A    Plex    TDS

4 NK    Plex N

## HELIA COMPACT

Kahles AMV-multi-coatings transmit up to 99.5% per air-to-glass surface. This ensures optimum use of incident light, especially in low light level conditions or at twilight. These 30mm Kahles rifle scopes are shockproof, waterproof and fogproof, nitrogen purged several times to assure the elimination of any moisture.

| | |
|---|---|
| Prices:C 1.1-4x24 (4A or 7A) | $877 |
| CSX 1.1-4x24 (circle, Post or D-Dot) | 1478 |
| C 1.5-6x42 (4A or 7A) | 966 |
| CSX 1.5-42 (circle, Post or D-Dot) | 1667 |
| C 2.5-10x50 (7A or Plex) | 1110 |
| C 3-12x56 (7A, Plex or 4A) | 1254 |
| C 4x36 (1" tube, 4A or 7A) | 632 |
| C 6x42 (1" tube, 4A or 7A) | 810 |

HELIA CB ILLUMINATED CB 3-12X56

## HELIA CB ILLUMINATED

When you don't have the light to see a standard reticle, the illuminated crosswire of the Helia comes through. It's adjustable for illumination, and minimizes stray light. Battery life: 110 hours.

| | |
|---|---|
| Prices: CB 1.5-6x42 (4NK or PlexN) | $1388 |
| CB 2.5-10x50 (4NK or PlexN) | 1499 |
| CB 3-12x56 (PlexN or 4NK) | 1632 |

# Kaps Optics

**KAPS SCOPES**

A 50-year-old German company headquartered in Asslar/Wetzlar, Kap has manufactured optics for military and police units, and for hunters. It now brings its riflescope line Stateside, with 4x36, 6x42 and 8x56 fixed-power models and five variables: 1-4x22, 1.5-6x42, 1-8x42, 2.5-10x50, 2.5-10x56. Pick illuminated reticles in 8x56, 2.5-10x50 and 2.5-10x56. The 30mm alloy tubes wear a satin finish. High-quality glass and state-of-the-art coatings complement reticles in the first focal plane – traditional in European scopes.

*A big objective (front) lens will help you aim only if the scope is set at high magnification and the light is dim. Otherwise, it's a liability because it adds weight and bulk and raises line of sight.*

SIGHTS & SCOPES

# Laseraim Technologies Inc. Sights

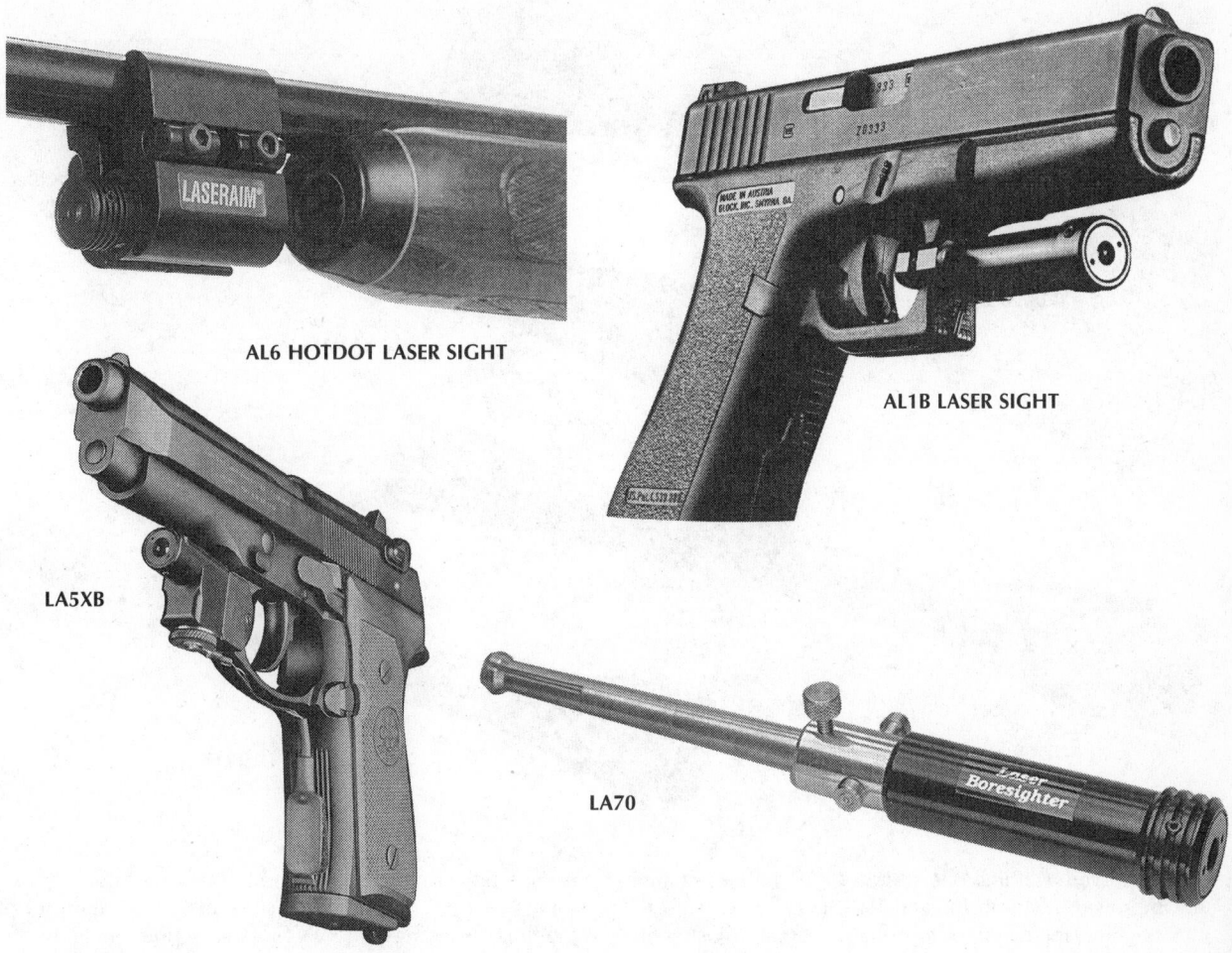

AL6 HOTDOT LASER SIGHT

AL1B LASER SIGHT

LA5XB

LA70

## AL1B LASER SIGHT
The AL1B sight mounts quickly and easily to most pistols and revolvers and produces a 2" dot at 100 yds. Four button cell batteries power the water- and shock-resistant sight up to one hour's continuous use. Windage and elevation range is 9 feet at 25 yards. Adaptable to rifles, shotguns, muzzleloaders, and bows. Available in black. Universal mount included. *Length*: 2.75" *Diameter*: ⅝" *Weight* (approx.): 2 oz.
Price:...................................... $99

## LA70 SHOTLESS LASER BORE SIGHTER™
The LA70 Shotless Laser Bore SighterTM makes sighting in easier and quicker. To check the center of the bore, simply rotate the laser on axis of the gun bore. The LA70 is equipped with a rotational Laseraim™ with constant ON switch and six arbors fitting calibers 22 thru 45, 12-gauge shotguns and muzzleloaders (50 and 54 cal.). *Length:* 8" (w/laser and arbor).
Price:...................................... 169

## AR15 CUSTOM LASER SIGHT
The AR15 laser sight is custom designed to fit all AR15/M16 rifles equipped with triangular front sight post. Laser provides three hours of continuous battery life with convenient replaceable battery. Machined from aircraft grade alminum.

*Weight:* 3 oz. *Length:* 2"
Price:...................................... $199

## AL6 HOTDOT LASER SIGHT
Ten times brighter than many other laser sights, this laser produces a 2-inch dot at 100 yards. The remote pressure switch provides operation for up to 2 hours of continuous power. The laser features Laseraim's unique 3-way micro-lock windage and elevation adjustment. Fits Laseraim mounts with no gunsmithing required and is suitable for handguns, rifles, shotguns, muzzle loaders, and bows. Uses convenient replaceable watch batteries.
Price: AL6 Hotdot laser sight .................... 99

## LA5XB
### HOTDOT MIGHTY SIGHT
Up to 10 times brighter than other laser sights, Laseraim's Hotdot Lasersights include a rechargeable NICad battery and in-field charger. Produce a 2" dot at 100 yards with a 500-yard range. *Length:* 2". *Diameter:* .75". Can be used with handguns, rifles, shotguns and bows. Fit all Laseraim mounts. Available in black or satin.
Price:...................................... 139

# Leupold Scopes
## VXII Line

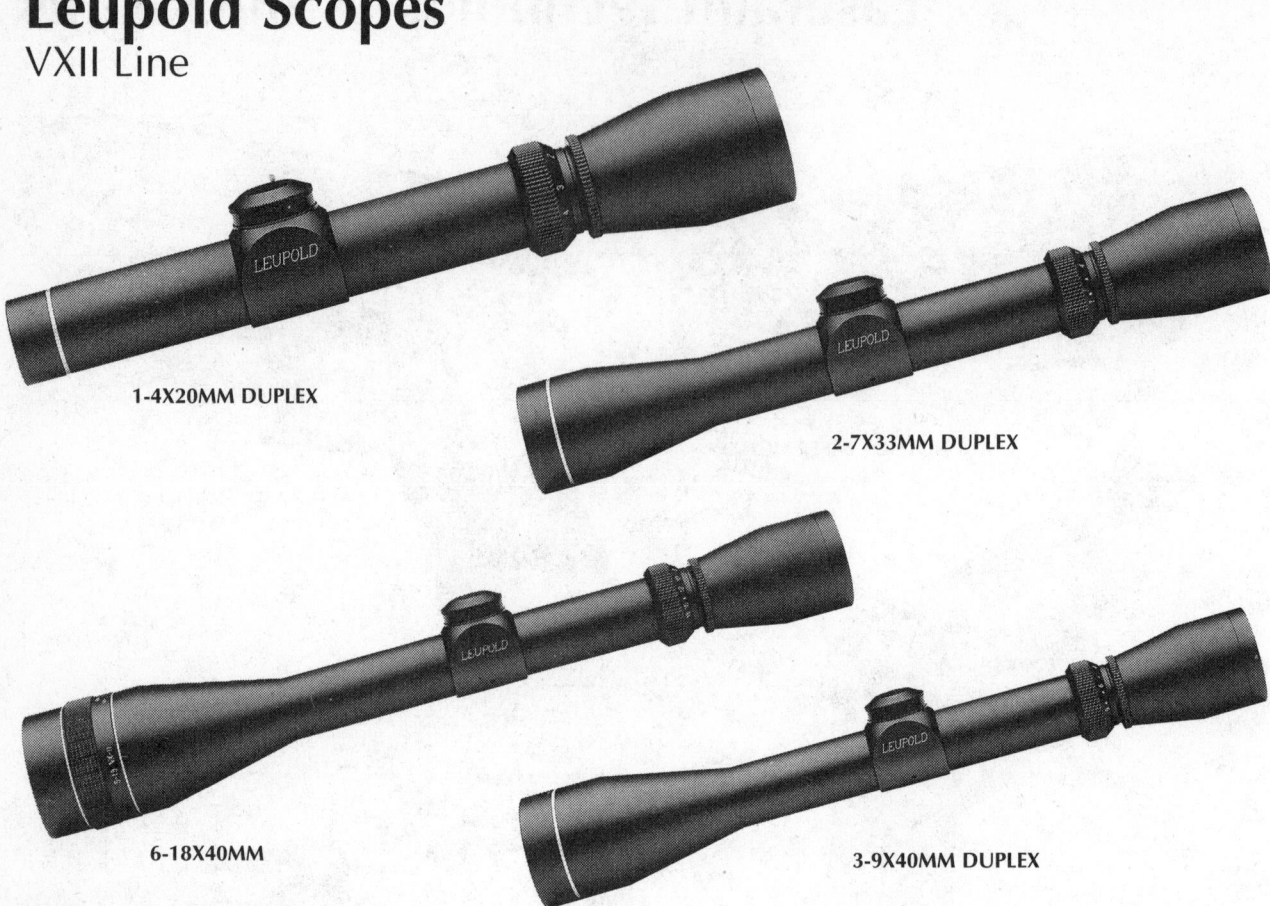

**1-4X20MM DUPLEX**

**2-7X33MM DUPLEX**

**6-18X40MM**

**3-9X40MM DUPLEX**

The improved VXII line offers Multi-Coated 4 lens coatings for improved light transmission, 1/4 M.O.A. click adjustments, a locking eyepiece for reliable ocular adjustment, and a sealed, nitrogen-filled interior for fog-free sighting.

### VX-II 1-4X20MM
This scope, the smallest of Leupold's VARI-X II line, is noted for its large field of view: 70 feet at 100 yards.

Matte finish only(Duplex) . . . . . . . . . . . . . . . . . . . $325
CPC . . . . . . . . . . . . . . . . . . . . . . . . . . . . . . . . . . . 375

### VX-II 2-7X33MM
A compact scope, no larger than the Leupold M8-4X, the 2-7x33 is arguably the most useful big game scope.

VX II 2-7x 33 Shotgun (Duplex) matte . . . . . . . . . $350
Leupold Dot. . . . . . . . . . . . . . . . . . . . . . . . . . . . . 400

### VX-II 3-9X50MM
This LOV scope delivers a 5.5mm exit pupil for low-light visibility:

Gloss (Duplex) . . . . . . . . . . . . . . . . . . . . . . . . . . . $415
Matte finish (Duplex) . . . . . . . . . . . . . . . . . . . . . . 440
German reticles or Leupold dot (Matte) . . . . . . . . . 490

### VX-II 3-9X40MM

A wide power range makes the 3-9 the most popular of hunting scopes. Many hunters use the 3X setting most of the time, cranking up to 9X for positive identification of game or for extremely long shots. The adjustable objective eliminates parallax and permits precise focusing on any object from less than 50 yards to infinity.

Gloss finish . . . . . . . . . . . . . . . . . . . . . . . . . . . . . $350
In matte, silver (Duplex). . . . . . . . . . . . . . . . . . . . . 375
Matte (CPC, Leupold Dot, German, Post & Duplex). . 425

### VX-II 4-12X40MM
(Adj. Objective)
The ideal answer for big game and varmint hunters alike. At 12.25 inches, the 4X12 is virtually the same length as Vari-X II 3X9. New fixed objective has same long eye relief and is factory-set to be free of parallax at 150 yds.

Matte or silver finish (Duplex) . . . . . . . . . . . . . . . $500
Leupold Dot or German 4 . . . . . . . . . . . . . . . . . . . 550

### VX-II 6-18X40MM ADJ. OBJ. TARGET
Features target-style click adjustments, fully coated lenses, adjustable objective for parallax-free shooting from 50 yards to infinity.

In matte, Fine or wide Duplex . . . . . . . . . . . . . . . . $540
Target Dot . . . . . . . . . . . . . . . . . . . . . . . . . . . . . . 590
Dot w/Target knobs . . . . . . . . . . . . . . . . . . . . . . . 615
Duplex w/Target knobs. . . . . . . . . . . . . . . . . . . . . 565

# Leupold Scopes
## VXI Line

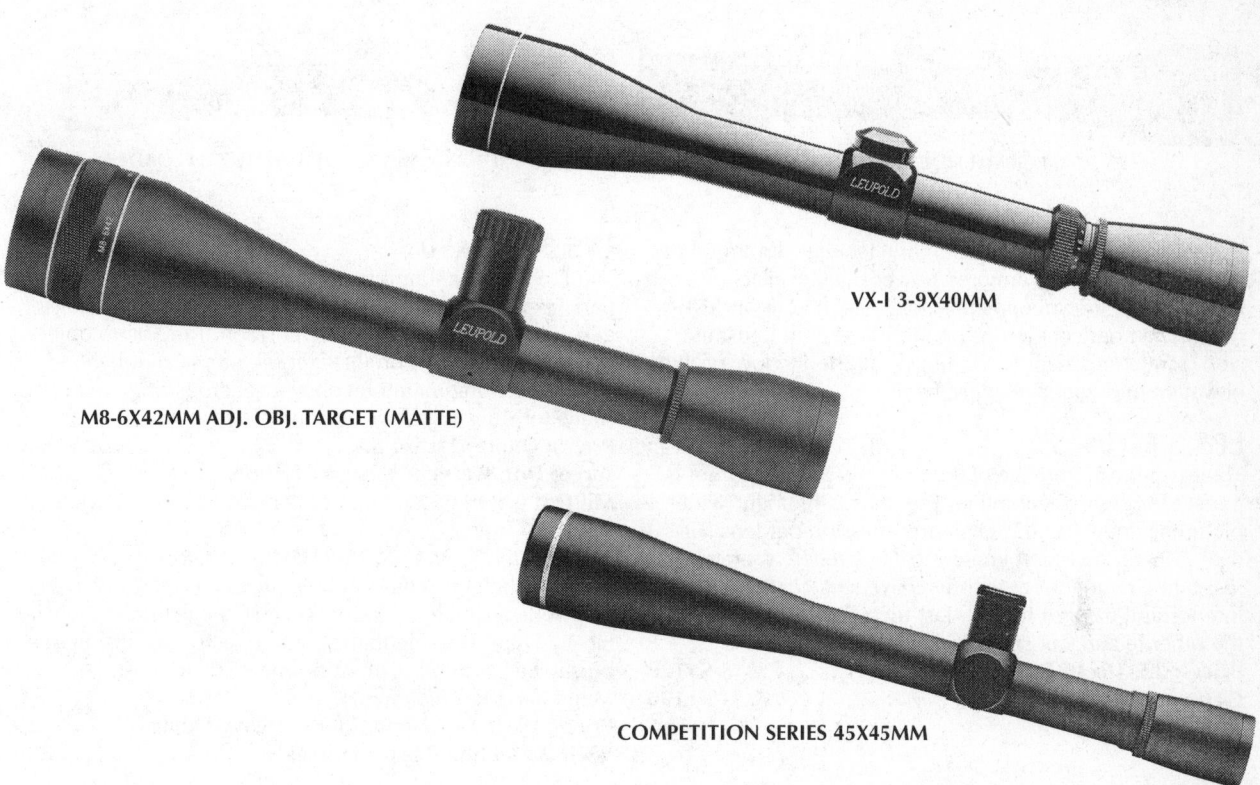

VX-I 3-9X40MM

M8-6X42MM ADJ. OBJ. TARGET (MATTE)

COMPETITION SERIES 45X45MM

## VX-I SERIES

A tough, gloss black finish and Duplex reticle. Leupold's high quality at an affordable price. Available in 2-7x33, 3-9x40 and 4-12x40mm

Gloss . . . . . . . . . . . . . . . . . . . . . . . . . . . . . . $225-310
Matte . . . . . . . . . . . . . . . . . . . . . . . . . . . . . . 250-340

## LEUPOLD 6 X 42 AO TARGET SCOPE

The Leupold M8 6x42mm Adjustable Objective Target Scope offers all the features needed by hunters and benchrest shooters. Both the elevation and windage dials of this scope feature 1/4-minute, target-style click adjustments. An adjustable objective dial offers parallax correction from a distance of 50 yards to infinity.

Price: Matte w/Duplex . . . . . . . . . . . . . . . . . . . . . . $500

## COMPETITION SERIES SCOPES

Leupold's new Competition series includes the 35x45mm, 40x45mm and 45x45mm. Shooters get a bright, crisp sight picture with outstanding contrast, at extremely high magnification. The side-focus parallax adjustment knob allows you to adjust your scope to be parallax-free at distances from 40 yards to infinity. Available in matte finish with target dot or target crosshair reticle.

Price . . . . . . . . . . . . . . . . . . . . . . . . . . . . . . . . . . $1190

**SIGHTS & SCOPES**

# Leupold Scopes
## Leupold Premier Scopes (LPS)

**LPS 3.5-14X50MM SIDE FOCUS (SATIN FINISH)**

**VX-II 1-4X20MM SHOTGUN/MUZZLELOADER**

Leupold's Premiere Scope (LPS) line features 30mm tubes, fast-focus eyepieces, armored power selector dials that can be read from the shooting position, 4-inch constant eye relief, Diamondcoat lenses for increased light transmission, scratch resistance, and finger adjustable, low-profile elevation and windage adjustments.

### LPS 2.5-10x45
The magnification range of the new LPS 2.5-10x45mm is perfect for big game hunting. The unusually bright sight picture is due to 99.65% light transmission per lens surface. You get constant, non-critical eye relief, a scratch-resistant DiamondCoat anti-reflective lens coating on all interior and exterior lenses; fast-focus eyepiece; and all the other features of Leupold Premier Scopes.
**Prices: 2.5-10x45 Duplex (satin)** . . . . . . . . . . . . . **$1120**
**German #1 or #4 (satin)** . . . . . . . . . . . . . . . . . . . . **1120**

### LPS 3.5-14x50
The LPS 3.5-14x50mm has a turret-mounted side-focus parallax adjustment so you can change parallax settings easily, even from the shooting position. The 50mm objective lens produces a bright sight picture, in dim light. Finally, the long maintube allows generous ring mount space for rifles with long actions.
**Prices: Duplex (satin)** . . . . . . . . . . . . . . . . . . . . . **$1250**
**Target Dot, German #1 or #4 (satin)** . . . . . . . . . . . . **1250**
**Mil Dot (satin)** . . . . . . . . . . . . . . . . . . . . . . . . . . . **1250**

### SHOTGUN & MUZZLELOADERS SCOPES
Leupold shotgun scopes are parallax-adjusted to deliver precise focusing at 75 yards. Each scope features a special Heavy Duplex reticle that is more effective against heavy, brushy backgrounds. All scopes have matte finish and Multicoat 4 lens coating.
**Prices: VX II 1-4X20mm Model Heavy Duplex** . . . . . **$325**
**VX II 2-7X33mm Heavy Duplex** . . . . . . . . . . . . . . . . **350**

## Compact Scopes

**M8 - 2.5X20MM COMPACT**

**M8 4X28 COMPACT RF SPECIAL**

**VARI-X 2-7X28 & RF SPECIAL**

**VARI-X 3-9X33 COMPACT**

### M8 2.5-20MM COMPACT
This small scope presents the shooter with an enormous field of view for fast target acquisition. It also features generous elevation and windage adjustment. Standard models are parallax adjusted to 100 yards. The Turkey Ranger model, with a special Post & Duplex reticle designed to subtend 9 inches from the post to crosswire at 40 yards, is parallax adjusted to 40 yards. Offered in a matte finish.
**Duplex or Heavy Duplex (matte)** . . . . . . . . . . . . . . **$250**
**M8 4x28mm Compact Rimfire Special**
   **Fine Duplex (gloss)** . . . . . . . . . . . . . . . . . . . . . . **290**
**Vari-X 2-7x28mm Compact**
   **Duplex (gloss)** . . . . . . . . . . . . . . . . . . . . . . . . . . **$300**
**Vari-X 2-7x28mm Compact Rimfire Special**

   **Fine Duplex (gloss)** . . . . . . . . . . . . . . . . . . . . . . . **300**
**Vari-X 3-9x33mm Compact Duplex**
   **(matte, silver)** . . . . . . . . . . . . . . . . . . . . . . . . . . . **315**

### VARI-X 3-9x33MM COMPACT E.F.R.
With an adjustable objective capable of correcting parallax as close as 10 meters, this scope is perfectly suited to .22 rimfire silhouette and air rifle shooting.
**Duplex (gloss)** . . . . . . . . . . . . . . . . . . . . . . . . . . . **$455**
Also available:
**VX-III 6.5-20x40mm E.F.R. Target**
   **matte, fine duplex** . . . . . . . . . . . . . . . . . . . . . . . **$750**
   **matte, target dot** . . . . . . . . . . . . . . . . . . . . . . . . . **800**

SIGHTS & SCOPES

# Leupold Scopes

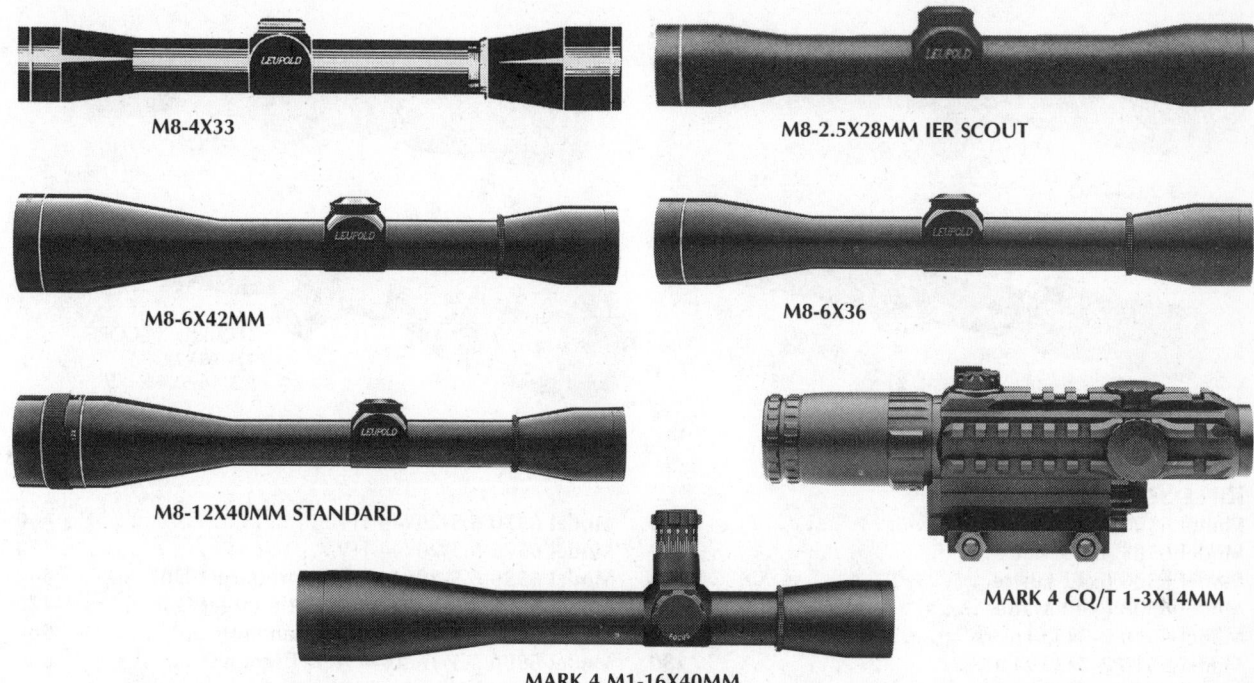

M8-4X33

M8-2.5X28MM IER SCOUT

M8-6X42MM

M8-6X36

M8-12X40MM STANDARD

MARK 4 CQ/T 1-3X14MM

MARK 4 M1-16X40MM

## LEUPOLD TACTICAL SCOPES
### FIXED AND VARIABLE POWER
Repeatable accuracy on all powers. 1/4 MOA audible click windage and elevation adjustments (Except M-3s). Superior image quality and excellent light transmission. Duplex or Mil Dot reticle. Waterproof.

## M8-2.5x28MM
Shooters worldwide are rediscovering the classic lever-action rifle, and for that, the M8-2.5x28mm IER Scout is the ideal sight. Designed specifically for lever- and scout-style rifles, it offers 9 to 17 inches of eye relief (IER stands for "Intermediate Eye Relief"). The Scout is mounted on the barrel, in front of the receiver.
**Matte finish (Duplex)** . . . . . . . . . . . . . . . . . . . . . . . . $275
**Matte or silver (Duplex)** . . . . . . . . . . . . . . . . . . . . . . . 275

## M8-4X
The 4X delivers a widely used magnification and a generous field of view.
**(Gloss)** . . . . . . . . . . . . . . . . . . . . . . . . . . . . . . . $250-300
**In black matte finish (Duplex).** . . . . . . . . . . . . . . . . . 275

## M8-6X 36MM
The 6X extends the range for big-game hunting and doubles in some cases as a varmint scope.
**gloss, duplex** . . . . . . . . . . . . . . . . . . . . . . . . . . . . . $315
**gloss, Post & Duplex or Leupold Dot.** . . . . . . . . . . . . 365

## M8-6X42MM
Large 42mm objective lens features a 7mm exit pupil for increased light-gathering capability. Recommended for varmint shooting at night.
**Duplex or Heavy Duplex** . . . . . . . . . . . . . . . . . . . . . $425
**matte, Post & Duplex or German** . . . . . . . . . . . 450-490

## M8-12X40MM STANDARD (ADJ. OBJ.)
Outstanding optical qualities, resolution and magnification make the 12X a natural for the varmint shooter. Adjustable objective is standard for parallax-free focusing.
**Fine Duplex** . . . . . . . . . . . . . . . . . . . . . . . . . . . . . . $475
**Leupold Dot.** . . . . . . . . . . . . . . . . . . . . . . . . . . . . . . 500

## MARK 4 LR/T (LONG RANGE/TACTICAL)

Mark 4 M1 10X40 (Matte)/Mark 4 M1 16X40 (Matte)
**Duplex.** . . . . . . . . . . . . . . . . . . . . . . . . . . . . . . . . . $1510
**Mil Dot** . . . . . . . . . . . . . . . . . . . . . . . . . . . . . . . . . 1610
Mark 4 8.5-25x50, mil Dot. . . . . . . . . . . . . . . . . . . . . 1250
Mark 4 6.5-20x50, mil Dot. . . . . . . . . . . . . . . . . . . . . 1199
Mark 4 4.5-14x50, Duplex or mil Dot . . . . . . 1000-1115
Mark 4 3.5-10x40, Duplex or mil Dot . . . . . . . 940-1050
    with illuminated reticle . . . . . . . . . . . . . . . . . . . . 1125

## MARK 4 CQ/T
The Leupold Mark 4 CQ/T 1-3x14mm is a revolutionary optical sight for tactical firearms. It combines the strengths of a red dot sight and variable-power riflescopes. Ten illumination settings match any light conditions; two low-intensity settings work with night-vision devices.
**Price** . . . . . . . . . . . . . . . . . . . . . . . . . . . . . . . . . . . $875

# Nikon Monarch Scopes

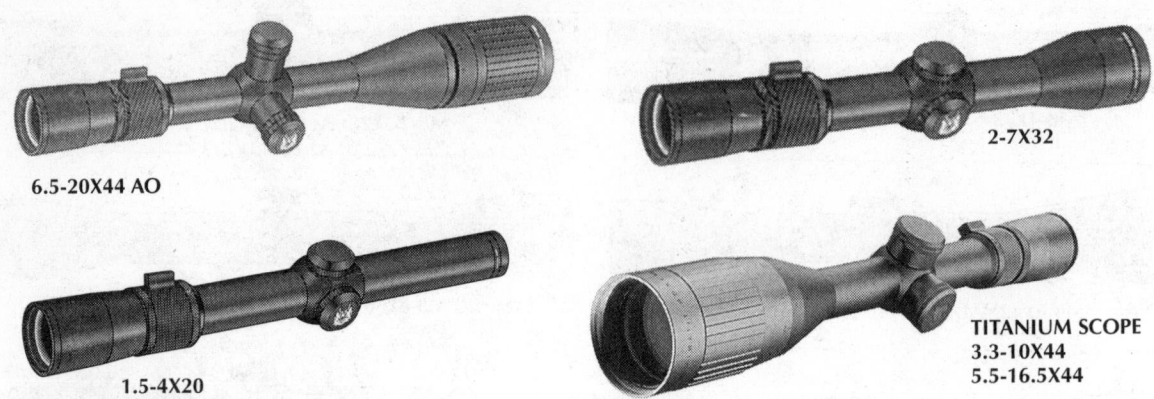

**6.5-20X44 AO**

**2-7X32**

**1.5-4X20**

**TITANIUM SCOPE
3.3-10X44
5.5-16.5X44**

## RIFLE SCOPES

Model 6500 4x40 Lustre . . . . . . . . . . . . . . . . . . . $230
Model 6505 4x40 Matte . . . . . . . . . . . . . . . . . . . 240
Model 6506 6x42 Lustre . . . . . . . . . . . . . . . . . . . 240
Model 6508 6x42 Matte . . . . . . . . . . . . . . . . . . . 250
Model 6510 2-7x32 Lustre . . . . . . . . . . . . . . . . . 270
Model 6515 2-7x32 Matte . . . . . . . . . . . . . . . . . 280
Model 6520 3-9x40 Lustre . . . . . . . . . . . . . . . . . 290
Model 6525 3-9x40 Matte . . . . . . . . . . . . . . . . . 300
Model 6528 3-9x40 Silver Matte . . . . . . . . . . . . . 310
Model 6530 3.5-10x50 Lustre . . . . . . . . . . . . . . . 430
Model 6535 3.5-10x50 Matte . . . . . . . . . . . . . . . 440
Model 6537 3.3-10x44AO Lustre . . . . . . . . . . . . . 380
Model 6538 3.3-10X44AO Matte (Mildot) . . . . . . . 390
Model 6539 3.3-10x44AO Matte . . . . . . . . . . . . . 390
Model 6540 4-12x40 AO Lustre . . . . . . . . . . . . . . 370
Model 6545 4-12x40 AO Matte . . . . . . . . . . . . . . 380
Model 6580 5.5-16.5x44 AO Black Lustre . . . . . . . . 390
Model 6585 5.5-16.5x44 AO Black Matte . . . . . . . . 400
Model 6550 6.5-20x44 AO Lustre . . . . . . . . . . . . . 460
Model 6555 6.5-20x44 AO Matte . . . . . . . . . . . . . 470

Model 6570 6.5-20x44 HV . . . . . . . . . . . . . . . . . . 460
Model 6575 6.5-20x44 HV . . . . . . . . . . . . . . . . . . 470
Model 6556 6.5-20x44 AO Lustre target Dot . . . . . . 460
Model 6558 6.5-20x44 AO Matte target Dot . . . . . . 470
Model 6630 3.3-10x44 AO (Titanium) . . . . . . . . . . 580
Model 6680 5.5-16.5x44 AO (Titanium) . . . . . . . . . 600

### Handgun and Shotgun Scopes

Model 6560 2x20 EER Black Lustre . . . . . . . . . . . . 170
Model 6562 2x20 EER Matte . . . . . . . . . . . . . . . . 180
Model 6565 2x20 EER Silver . . . . . . . . . . . . . . . . 180
Model 6590 1.5-4.5x20 Shotgun Black Matte . . . . . . 240
Model 6595 1.5-4.5x20 Sabot/Slug Black Matte . . . . 240

### Also Available:

### Illuminated Scopes

3.5-10x50 (Nikoplex or Mildot) . . . . . . . . . . . . . 600
6.5-20x44 (Nikoplex or Mildot) . . . . . . . . . . . . . 680

### Monarch Gold

1.5-6x42 . . . . . . . . . . . . . . . . . . . . . . . . . . . . . 500
2.5-10x50 . . . . . . . . . . . . . . . . . . . . . . . . . . . . . 600
2.5-10x56 . . . . . . . . . . . . . . . . . . . . . . . . . . . . . 700

## MONARCH™ UCC RIFLESCOPE SPECIFICATIONS

| MODEL | 4x40 | 1.5-4.5x20 | 2-7x32 | 3-9x40 | 3.5-10x50 | 4-12x40AO | 5.5-16.5x44AO | 6.5-20x44AO | 2x20EER |
|---|---|---|---|---|---|---|---|---|---|
| Lustre | 6500 | N/A | 6510 | 6520 | 6530 | 6540 | 6580 | 6550/6556 | 6560 |
| Matte | 6505 | 6595 | 6515 | 6525 | 6535 | 6545 | 6585 | 6555/6558 | 6562 |
| Silver | N/A | N/A | N/A | 6528 | N/A | N/A | N/A | N/A | 6565 |
| Actual Magnification | 4x | 1.5-4.5x | 2x-7x | 3x-9x | 3.5x-10x | 4x-12x | 5.5x-16.5x | 6.5x-19.46x | 1.75x |
| Objective Diameter | 40mm | 20mm | 32mm | 40mm | 50mm | 40mm | 44mm | 44mm | 20mm |
| Exit Pupil (mm) | 10 | 13.3-4.4 | 16-4.6 | 13.3-4.4 | 14.3-5 | 10-3.3 | 8-2.7 | 6.7-2.2 | 11.4 |
| Eye Relief (in) | 3.5 | 3.7-3.5 | 3.9-3.6 | 3.6-3.5 | 3.9-3.8 | 3.6-3.4 | 3.2-3.0 | 3.5-3.1 | 26.4-10.5 |
| FOV @ 100 yds (ft) | 26.9 | 50.3-16.7* | 44.5-12.7 | 33.8-11.3 | 25.5-8.9 | 25.6-8.5 | 19.1-6.4 | 16.1-5.4 | 22 |
| Tube Diameter | 1 in. | 1 in. | 1 in. | 1 in. | 1 in. | 1 in. | 1 in. | 1 in. | 1 in. |
| Objective Tube(mm/in) | 47.3-1.86 | 25.4/1 | 39.3-1.5 | 47.3-1.86 | 57.3-2.2 | 53.1-2.09 | 54-2.13 | 54-2.13 | 25, 4/1 |
| Eyepiece O.D. (mm) | 38 | 38 | 38 | 38 | 38 | 38 | 38 | 38 | 38 |
| Length (in) | 11.7 | 10 | 11.1 | 12.3 | 13.7 | 13.7 | 13.4 | 14.6 | 8.1 |
| Weight (oz) | 11.2 | 9.3 | 11.2 | 12.6 | 15.5 | 16.9 | 18.4 | 20.1 | 6.6 |
| Adjustment Gradation | 1/4 MOA | 1/4 MOA | 1/4 MOA | 1/4 MOA | 1/4 MOA | 1/4 MOA | 1/4 MOA | 1/8 MOA | 1/4 MOA |
| Max Internal Adjustment | 120 MOA | 120 MOA | 70 MOA | 55 MOA | 45 MOA | 45 MOA | 40 MOA | 38 MOA | 120 MOA |
| Parallax Setting (yds) | 100 | 75 | 100 | 100 | 100 | 50 to ∞ | 50 to ∞ | 50 to ∞ | 100 |

*FOV @ 75 yds (ft)     *FOV @ 50 yds (ft)

# Nikon Buckmasters® Scopes

**SPECIAL LIMITED EDITION 3-9X40**

4.5-14

Built to withstand the toughest hunting conditions, Nikon buckmaster scopes integrate shockproof, fogproof and waterproof construction, plus other features seldom found on riflescopes in this price range. Nikon's Brightvue™ anti-reflective system of high-quality, multicoated lenses provides over 93% anti-reflection capability for high levels of light transmission and dawn-to-dusk big game hunting. These riflescopes are parallax-adjusted at 100 yards and have durable matte finishes that reduce glare while afield. They also feature positive steel-to-brass, quarter-minute-click windage and elevation adjustments for instant, repeatable accuracy and a Nikoplex® reticle for quick target acquisition.

**Prices:**

Model 6465 1x20 . . . . . . . . . . . . . . . . . . . . . . . . . . $160
Model 6405 4x40 . . . . . . . . . . . . . . . . . . . . . . . . . . 160
Model 6425 3-9x40 Black Matte . . . . . . . . . . . . . . 200
Model 6415 3-9x40 Silver . . . . . . . . . . . . . . . . . . . 210
Model 6435 3-9x50 . . . . . . . . . . . . . . . . . . . . . . . . 300
Model 6450 4.5-14x40 AO Blck Matte . . . . . . . . . . 280
Model 6455 4.5-14x40 AO Silver . . . . . . . . . . . . . . 290
Model 6466 4.5-14X40AO Matte Adj. Mildot . . . . . . 280
Model 6440 4-12x50 AO Matte . . . . . . . . . . . . . . . . 330
Model 6470 6-18x40 AO Matte . . . . . . . . . . . . . . . . 330
Model 6475 6-18x40 AO Matte . . . . . . . . . . . . . . . . 330

## BUCKMASTERS SCOPES

| Model | 1x20 | 4x40 | 3-9x40 | 3-9x50 | 4.5-14x40AO |
|---|---|---|---|---|---|
| Matte | 6465 | 6405 | 6425 | 6435 | 6450 |
| Silver | N/A | N/A | 6415 | N/A | 6455 |
| Actual Magnification | 1x | 4x | 3.3-8.5x | 3.3-8.5x | 4.5-13.5x |
| Objective Diameter | 20mm | 40mm | 40mm | 50mm | 40mm |
| Exit Pupil (mm) | 20 | 10 | 12.1-4.7 | 15.1-5.9 | 8.9-2.9 |
| Eye Relief (in) | 4.3-13.0 | 3.5 | 3.5-3.4 | 3.5-3.4 | 3.6-3.4 |
| FOV @ 100 yds (ft) | 52.5 | 30.6 | 33.9-12.9 | 33.9-12.9 | 22.5-7.5 |
| Tube Diameter | 1 in. | 1 in. | 1 in. | 1 in. | 1 in. |
| Objective Tube (mm/in) | 27/1.06 | 47.3/1.86 | 47.3/1.86 | 58.7/2.3 | 53/2.1 |
| Eyepiece O.D. (mm) | 37 | 42.5 | 42.5 | 42.5 | 38 |
| Length (in) | 8.8 | 12.7 | 12.7 | 12.9 | 14.8 |
| Weight (oz) | 9.2 | 11.8 | 13.4 | 18.2 | 18.7 |
| Adjustment Gradation | 1/4: 1 click | 1/4: 1 click | 1/4: 1 click | 1/4: 1 click | |
| Max Internal Adjustment | 50 | 80 | 80 | 70 | 40 |
| Parallax Setting (yds) | 75 | 100 | 100 | 100 | 50 to ∞ |

# Nikon Scopes

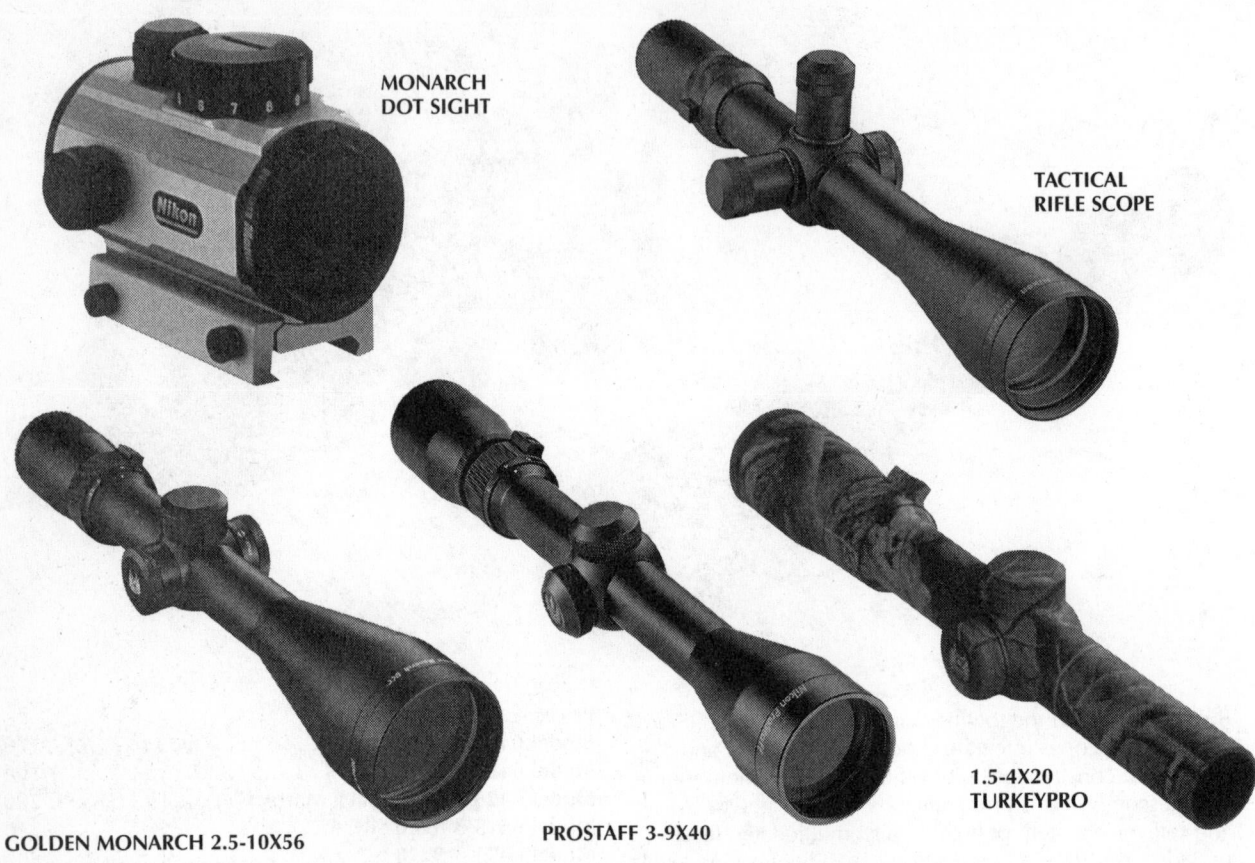

MONARCH DOT SIGHT

TACTICAL RIFLE SCOPE

1.5-4X20 TURKEYPRO

GOLDEN MONARCH 2.5-10X56

PROSTAFF 3-9X40

### TACTICAL RIFLESCOPE

Nikon's Tactical Riflescopes are available in 2.5-10x44 and 4-16x50. The 2.5-10x44 features a choice of reticles: Nikoplex, Mildot, and Dual Illuminated Mildot. The 4-16 is offered with Nikoplex or Mildot. Both are equipped with turret mounted parallax adjustment knobs, have a tough, black-anodized matte finish and have easy-to-grip windage and elevation knobs for accurate field adjustments.
Prices:

| | |
|---|---|
| Tactical 2.5-10x44 (Nikoplex or Mildot) | $900 |
| With Illuminated Mildot | 1050 |
| Tactical 4-16x50 (Mildot or Nikoplex) | 1000 |

### PROSTAFF

Nikon's Prostaff line inclues the 4x32, 2-7x32 and 3-9x40 scopes. The 4x is parallax-corrected at 50 yards. It measures 11.2 inches long and weighs just 11.6 ounces, in silver, matte black or Realtree camo finish. The 2-7x, parallax-free at 75 yards, is a 12-ounce scope available in matte black or camo. You can get the 13-ounce 3-9x in all three finishes. The Prostaff scopes have multicoated lenses and quarter-minute adjustments. They're waterproof, fog proof and carry Nikon's Full Lifetime Warranty.

| | |
|---|---|
| Prostaff 4x32 | $100 |
| 2-7x32 | 130 |
| 309x40 | 150 |

### MONARCH DOT SIGHT

As fast a sight as you'll ever find, the Monarch Dot is fully waterproof, fogproof and shockproof. Objective and ocular lenses are 30mm diameter and are fully multicoated. Nikon Dot sights have zero magnification, providing unlimited eye relief and a 47.2' field of view at 100 yards, perfect for close up, fast shots. Brightness is controlled by a lithium battery. The standard Monarch Dot Sight is available in silver and black and has a 6 MOA dot. It is also available in Realtree camouflage.

| | |
|---|---|
| Price: Standard | $250 |
| VSD | 280 |
| VSD in camo | 290 |

### 1.5-4.5x20 TURKEYPRO

Now available in Realtree Hardwoods camo, the 1.5-4x20 Monarch TurkeyPro is parallax-free at 50 yards. Kill more toms with precise pattern placement!

| | |
|---|---|
| Price: | $270 |

### 2.5-8x28 EER HANDGUN SCOPE

Nikon's 2.5-8x28 EER (Extended Eye Relief) should find favor with hunters, varminters and competitors. It has a wide field of view at low power, but a twist of the power ring instantly supplies 8x magnification for long shots.

| | |
|---|---|
| Price: Matte | $280 |
| Silver | 290 |

# Pentax Scopes

**4X-16XAO LIGHTSEEKER 30**

**8.5X-32XAO LIGHTSEEKER 30**

**6X-24XAO LIGHTSEEKER 30**

**WHITETAILS UNLIMITED**

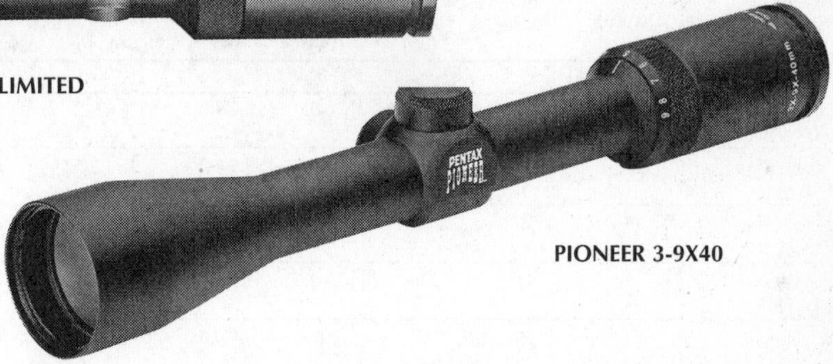

**PIONEER 3-9X40**

## PIONEER
The 3-9x40 Pioneer offers fully coated optics in a one-piece, 1-inch alloy tube. It comes in matte black finish with a Penta-:lex reticle. Weighing just 13 ounces, the scope offers 50 inches of elevation adjustment in quarter-minute graduations.

**Pioneer . . . . . . . . . . . . . . . . . . . . . . . . . . . . . $310-320**

Among the brightest scopes available, Pentax sights are durable as well. The Lghtseeker features:
- Scratch-resistant outer tube. Under ordinary wear and tear, the outer tube is almost impossible to scratch.
- High Quality cam zoom tube. No plastics are used. The tube is made of a bearing-type brass with precision machined cam slots. The zoom control screws are precision-ground to 1/2 of one thousandth tolerance.
- Leak Prevention. Power rings are sealed on a separate precision-machined seal tube. The scopes are then filled with nitrogen and double-sealed with heavy-duty "O" rings, making them leak-proof and fog-proof.
- Optics. Fully multi-coated, Lightseekers' optics are

among the best in the industry, giving you a bright, sharp picture even in poor light.

The Lightseeker-30 has the same features as the Light-seeker II, but with a 30mm tube.
The purchase of every Pentax Whitetails Unlimited rifle or shotgun scope includes a free one-year membership in Whitetails Unlimited, and a portion of the purchase price goes to the organization to support its conservation efforts. Ballistic Plex reticles are available on the 3X-9X and 6.5X-20X Whitetails Unlimited Scopes.

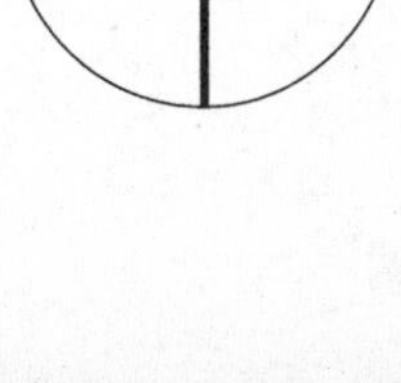

The Ballistic Plex Reticle is a copyrighted design on the lower vertical crosshair that compensates for bullet drop. The Ballistic Plex reticle is set to provide dead-on aiming from 100 yards to 500 yards for many of the most common hunting cartridges.

# Pentax Rifle Scopes

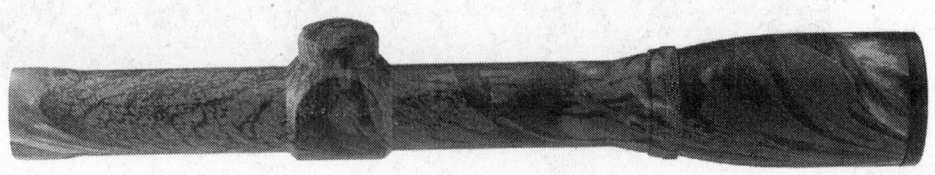

**LIGHTSEEKER 2.5xSG PLUS
MOSSY OAK® BREAK-UP SCOPE**

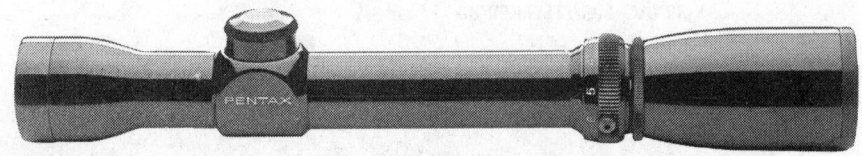

**LIGHTSEEKER 1.75X-6X**

## LIGHTSEEKER RIFLESCOPE AND WHITETAILS UNLIMITED

| | TUBE DIAMETER (IN) | OBJECTIVE DIAMETER (MM) | EYEPIECE DIAMETER (MM) | EXIT PUPIL (MM) | EYE RELIEF (IN) | FIELD OF VIEW (FT@100 YD) | ADJUSTMENT GRADUATION (IN@100 YD) | MAXIMUM ADJUSTMENT (IN@100 YD) | LENGTH (IN) | WEIGHT (OZ) | RETICLE | PRICE |
|---|---|---|---|---|---|---|---|---|---|---|---|---|
| **RIFLE SCOPES** | | | | | | | | | | | | |
| Lightseeker 3X - 9X | 1 | 43 | 39 | 12.0-5.0 | 3.5-4.0 | 36-14 | 1/4 | 50 | 12.7 | 15 | P, MD | 495-523 |
| Lightseeker 3X - 9X | 1 | 50 | 39 | 16.1-5.6 | 3.5-4.0 | 35-12 | 1/4 | 50 | 13.0 | 19 | TW, BP | 582 |
| Lightseeker 2.5X - 10X | 1 | 50 | 39 | 16.3-4.6 | 4.2-4.7 | 35-10 | 1/4 | 100 | 14.1 | 23 | TW | 665 |
| Lightseeker 4X - 16X | 1 | 44 | 36 | 10.4-2.8 | 3.5-4.0 | 33-9 | 1/4 | 35 | 15.4 | 23.7 | BP | 682 |
| Lightseeker 2.5X SG Plus | 1 | 25 | 39 | 7.0 | 3.5-4.0 | 55 | 1/2 | 60 | 10.0 | 9 | DW | 292-303 |
| **LIGHTSEEKER-30** | | | | | | | | | | | | |
| 3X-10X AO | 30MM | 40 | 35 | 13.3-4.4 | 3.5-4.0 | 34-14 | 1/4 | 90 | 13.1 | 20.0 | BP | $599 |
| 4X-16X AO | 30mm | 50 | 42 | 12-3.1 | 3.3-3.8 | 27-7.5 | 1/4 | 74 | 15.2 | 23 | TW, MD | 715-798 |
| 6X-24X AO | 30mm | 50 | 42 | 7.6-2.1 | 3.2-3.7 | 18-5 | 1/8 | 52 | 16.9 | 27 | MD, FP | 746-832 |
| 8.5X-32X AO | 30mm | 50 | 42 | 6.2-1.7 | 3.0-3.5 | 14-4 | 1/8 | 39 | 18.0 | 27 | MD, FP | 782-865 |
| **WHITETAILS UNLIMITED** | | | | | | | | | | | | |
| 2X-5X WTU | 1 | 20 | 39 | 11.1-4.2 | 3.1-3.8 | 65-23 | 1/2 | 70 | 10.7 | 10 | TW | 332-348 |
| 3X-9X WTU | 1 | 40 | 39 | 12.9-4.7 | 3.1-3.8 | 31-13 | 1/4 | 50 | 12.4 | 13 | TW | 348 |
| 3.5X-10X WTU | 1 | 50 | 39 | 13-5.1 | 3.1-3.8 | 28-11 | 1/4 | 50 | 13.1 | 15 | LBP | 582 |
| 3.7X-11X WTU | 1 | 42 | 39 | 13-5.1 | 3.1-3.8 | 28-11 | 1/4 | 50 | 13.1 | 15 | TW | 465 |
| 4.5X-14X WTU | 1 | 42 | 39 | 9.3-3.0 | 3.7-4.2 | 23-8 | 1/4 | 52 | 12.9 | 17 | BP | 497 |
| 6.5X-20X WTU | 1 | 50 | 39 | 7.6-2.6 | 3.1-3.6 | 17-6 | 1/4 | 30 | 14.6 | 19 | BP | 598 |
| 3X-9X WTU | 1 | 50 | 39 | 16.0-5.3 | 3.1-3.8 | 32-13 | 1/4 | 50 | 13.2 | 17 | BP | 398 |

*Scopes are available in high gloss black, matte black, or camouflage, depending on model.*
*P=Penta-Plex, FP=Fine-Plex, DW=Deepwoods Plex, MD=Mil-Dot, CP=Comp-Plex, TW=Twilight Plex, BP=Ballistic Plex, LBP=Laser Ballistic Plex*

**SIGHTS & SCOPES**

# Redfield Scopes

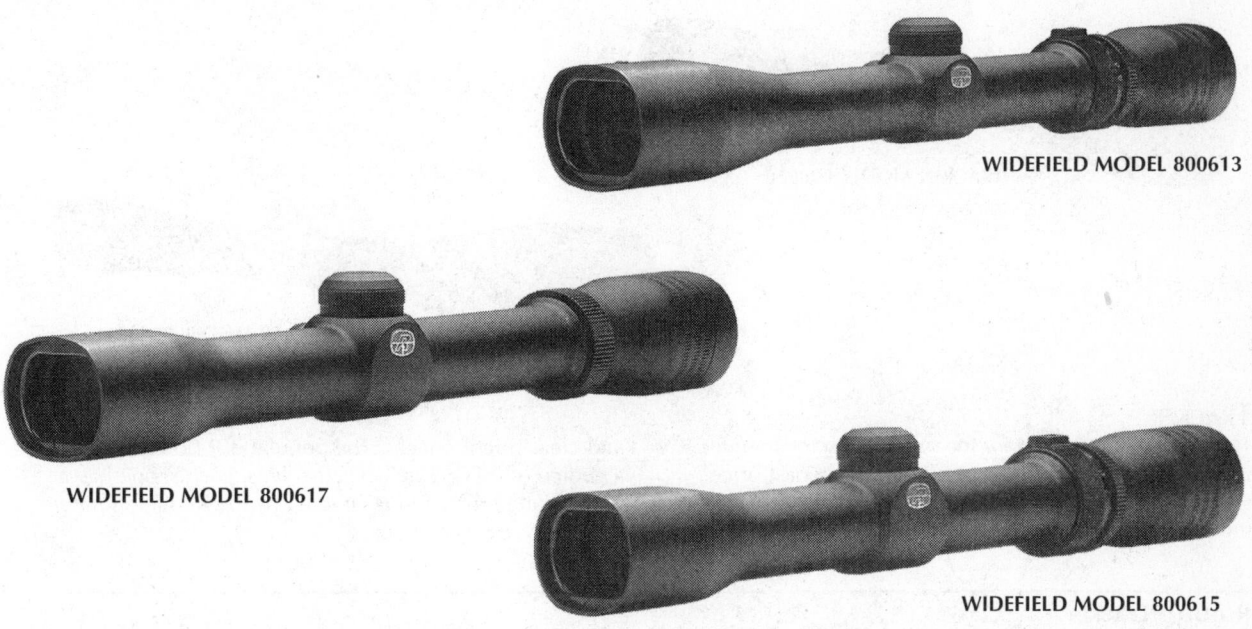

WIDEFIELD MODEL 800613

WIDEFIELD MODEL 800617

WIDEFIELD MODEL 800615

## WIDEFIELD

Widefield's field of view is 30% wider than that of conventional scopes - over 40 feet at 100 yards on two models. It helps scan more area to detect the flick of an ear, or to pick the best shooting lane on running game. It's also designed to mount low on the receiver, a quicker sight picture when mounting the rifle. Choose a 2-7 power, 3-9 power or a fixed 4 power, in gloss or matte finish.

### REDFIELD WIDEFIELD

| Model | Magnification Object Lens Dia-mm | Finish | Exit Pupil Range In Variable MM | Field of View in Feet @ 100 yds | Optimum Eye Relief Inches | Overall Length Inches | Weight Ounces | Reticle | Price |
|---|---|---|---|---|---|---|---|---|---|
| 800612 | 3-9x27x36 | Black gloss | 12x10-4x3 | 42.5x33-14.3x10.9 | 3.25-3 | 12.38 | 15 | Truplex TV Oval | $443 |
| 800613 | 3-9x27x36 | Black matte | 12x10-4x3 | 42.5x33-14.3x10.9 | 3.25-3 | 12.38 | 15 | Truplex TV Oval | 443 |
| 800614 | 2-7x22x30 | Black gloss | 9x75x11.75-3.1x4 | 43.27x57.78-13.53x18.34 | 3.75-2.88 | 11.5 | 13.7 | Truplex TV Oval | 412 |
| 800615 | 2-7x22x30 | Black matte | 9x75x11.75-3.1x4 | 43.27x57.78-13.53x18.34 | 3.75-2.88 | 11.5 | 13.7 | Truplex TV Oval | 412 |
| 800616 | 4x22x30 | Black gloss | 5.3x7.4 | 29.75x35.95 | 2.88 | 11.38 | 12.4 | Truplex TV Oval | 360 |
| 800617 | 4x22x30 | Black matte | 5.3x7.4 | 29.75x35.95 | 2.88 | 11.38 | 12.4 | Truplex TV Oval | 360 |

# Redfield Scopes

**TRACKER MODEL 800618**

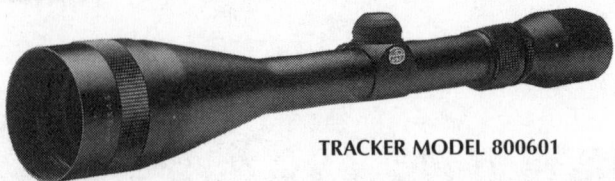

**TRACKER MODEL 800601**

## TRACKER

The Tracker is designed for the value-conscious hunter who wants a rugged Redfield scope at a modest price. Each Tracker is built from strong, lightweight aircraft aluminum and fine optical glass for maximum performance and clear bright images. The popular 3-9 power gives you a choice of 40 or 50m objective lens. Each scope has a black matte finish and is covered by the Redfield limited lifetime warranty.

## REDFIELD TRACKER

| MODEL | MAGNIFICATION OBJECT LENS DIA-MM | FINISH | EXIT PUPIL RANGE IN VARIABLE MM | FIELD OF VIEW IN FEET @ 100 YDS | OPTIMUM EYE RELIEF INCHES | OVERALL LENGTH INCHES | WEIGHT OUNCES | RETICLE | PRICE |
|---|---|---|---|---|---|---|---|---|---|
| 800631 | 3-9x40 | Black matte | 13.3-4.5 | 35-11.3 | 3.25-3.13 | 12.75 | 13.5 | Truplex | $216 |
| 800632 | 3-9x40 | Black matte | 15.8-6.3 | 35-11.75 | 3.25-3 | 13 | 1 lb. 2.5 oz. | Truplex | 237 |
| 800618 | 3-12x44 | Black matte | 5.5-3.0 | 33-8.7 | 3-2.75 | 12.38 | 13.5 | Truplex | 268 |
| 800601 | 3-12x44 | Black matte | 5.5-2.7 | 26.2-7.42 | 3-2.625 | 14.375 | 16 | Truplex | 299 |

*Eye relief is the distance from your eye to the scope's rear or ocular lens. Mount the scope well forward, to protect your brow and speed your aim as you shove your face forward on the comb.*

SIGHTS & SCOPES

# Schmidt & Bender Rifle Scopes

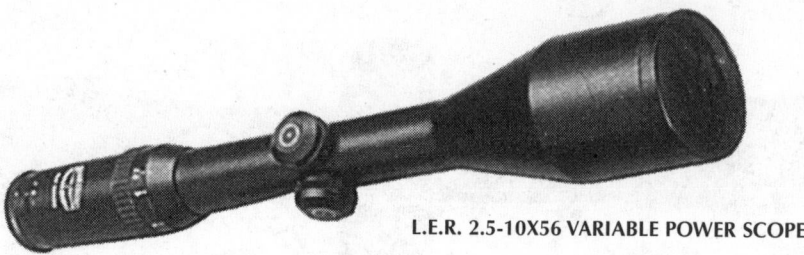

**L.E.R. 2.5-10X56 VARIABLE POWER SCOPE**

This German firm manufactures carriage-class optics for discriminating sportsmen and tactical shooters. Variable scopes have 30mm and 34mm tubes.

## L.E.R. 2.5-10X56 VARIABLE POWER SCOPE
Price:. . . . . . . . . . . . . . . . . . . . . . . . . . . . . .$1499
Also available:
1.25-4X20 Variable Power Scope . . . . . . . . . . . . . 1199
1.5-6X42 Variable Power Scope. . . . . . . . . . . . . . . 1299
3-12X42 Variable Power Scope . . . . . . . . . . . . . . . 1479
3-12X50 Variable Power Scope . . . . . . . . . . . . . . . 1479
4-16X50 Variable Power Scope . . . . . . . . . . . . . . . 1799

Note: All variable power scopes have glass reticles and aluminum tubes.
Also available:
**4X36 Fixed Power Scope**
1" Steel Tube w/o Mounting Rail . . . . . . . . . . . . . . $859
6X42 Fixed Power . . . . . . . . . . . . . . . . . . . . . . . 959
8X56 Fixed Power. . . . . . . . . . . . . . . . . . . . . . . 1099
10X42 Fixed Power. . . . . . . . . . . . . . . . . . . . . . . 999

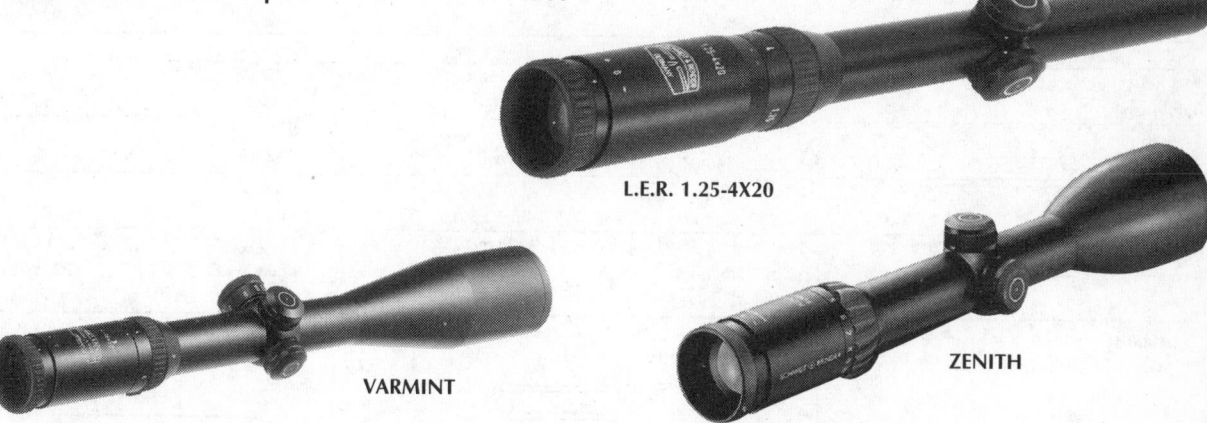

**L.E.R. 1.25-4X20**

**VARMINT**

**ZENITH**

## ILLUMINATED SCOPES
This 1.25-4x is designed for use on magnum rifles and for quick shots at dangerous game. Long eye relief, and a wide field of view (31.5 yards at 200 yards) speed your aim. The Flash Dot reticle shows up bright against the target at the center of the crosswire.
*Magnification:* 1.25-4X
*Objective lens diameter:* 12.7-20mm
*Field of view at 100m:* 32m-10m; *at 100 yards:* 96'-16'
*Objective housing diameter:* 30mm
*Scope tube diameter:* 30mm
*Twilight factor:* 3,7-8,9 **Lenses:** hard multi-coating
*Click value 1 click @100 meters:* 15mm; @100 yards: .540"
Price:. . . . . . . . . . . . . . . . . . . . . . . . . . . . . .$1649
Also available:
**Illuminated reticles**
1.5-6x42 . . . . . . . . . . . . . . . . . . . . . . . . . . . . 1699
3-12x50 or 3-12X42. . . . . . . . . . . . . . . . . . . . . 1879
2.5-10x56 . . . . . . . . . . . . . . . . . . . . . . . . . . . 1899

## ZENITH SERIES
3.5-12x50 or 2.5-10X56 . . . . . . . . . . . . . . . . . . . $1599
2.5-10x56 Illuminated or 3-12X50 Ill. . . . . . . . . . . . 1999

Designed for long-range target shooters and varmint hunters, Schmidt & Bender 4-16X50 "Varmint" riflescope features a precise parallax adjustment located in a third turret on the left side of the scope, making setting adjustments quick and convenient. The fine crosshairs of Reticle No. 6 and 8 cover only 1.5mm at 100 meters (.053" at 100 yards) throughout the entire magnification range.
*Magnification:* 4-16X
*Objective lens diameter:* 50mm
*Field of view at 100m:* 7.5-2.5m; *at 100 yards:* 22.5'-7.5'
*Objective housing diameter:* 57mm
*Scope tube diameter:* 30mm
*Twilight factor:* 14-28
*Lenses:* Hard multi-coating
*Click value 1 click @100 meters:* 10mm; *@100 yards:* .360"
Price:. . . . . . . . . . . . . . . . . . . . . . . . . . . . . .$1799

# Schmidt & Bender Scopes
## Police/Marksman II

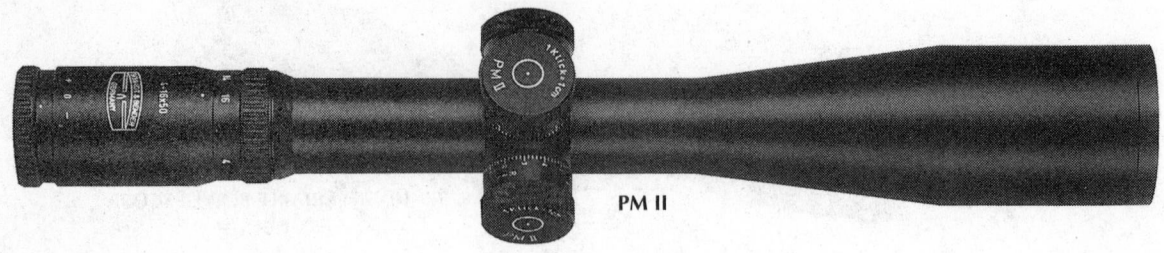

PM II

## SPECIFICATIONS

| | 10 x 42 | 3-12 x 50/50 CAL | 3-12 x 50 W/PARALLAX ADJ. | 3-12 x 50 LP ILLUMINATED W/PARALLAX ADJ. | 4-16 x 50 W/PARALLAX ADJ. |
|---|---|---|---|---|---|
| Price | $1699 | 2799 | 2299 | 2699 | 2399 |
| Magnification | 10x | 3-12x | 3-12x | 3-12x | 4-16x |
| Field of View | 4m | 11.1-4.2m | 11.1-4.2m | 11.1-4.2m | 7.5-2.5m |
| (100m/100yd) | 12' | 33.3-12.6' | 33.3-12.6' | 33.3-12.6' | 22.5-7.5' |
| Objective Diameter | 42mm | 50mm | 50mm | 50mm | 5mm |
| Exit Pupil | 4.2mm | 14.3-4.3mm | 14.3-4.3mm | 14.3-4.3mm | 12.5-3.1mm |
| (mm/inches) | .165" | .563-.169" | .563-.169" | .563-.169" | .492"-.122" |
| Twilight Factor | 20.5 | 11.4-24.5 | 11.4-24.5 | 11.4-24.5 | 14-28 |
| Eye Relief | 95mm | 995mm | 95mm | 95mm | 95mm |
| (mm/inches) | 3.74" | 3.74" | 3.74" | 3.74" | 3.74" |
| Middle Tube Diameter | 30mm | 34mm | 34mm | 34mm | 34mm |
| Weight | 520g | 820g | 810g | 780g | 880g |
| (gram/lb., oz.) | 1 lb. 2 oz. | 1 lb. 13 oz. | 1 lb. 12.5 oz. | 1 lb. 11.5 oz. | 1 lb. 15 oz. |
| Adj. Range @ | *270 cm/97" | adjustment for 1500 meters | 200 cm/72" | 200 cm/72" | 185 cm/67" |
| (100m/100 yd) | **250 cm/990" | of reach (22miliradians of adj.) | 180 cm/64.8" | 180 cm/64.8" | 170 cm/61.2" |
| | ***130 cm/46.8" | 130 cm/46.8" | 130 cm/46.8" | 130 cm/46.8" | 130 cm/46.8" |

*Using the very ends of the elevation adjustment will reduce the windage adjustment range   **Sighting-in adjustment range without restriction of windage
***With adjustment knob locked in place

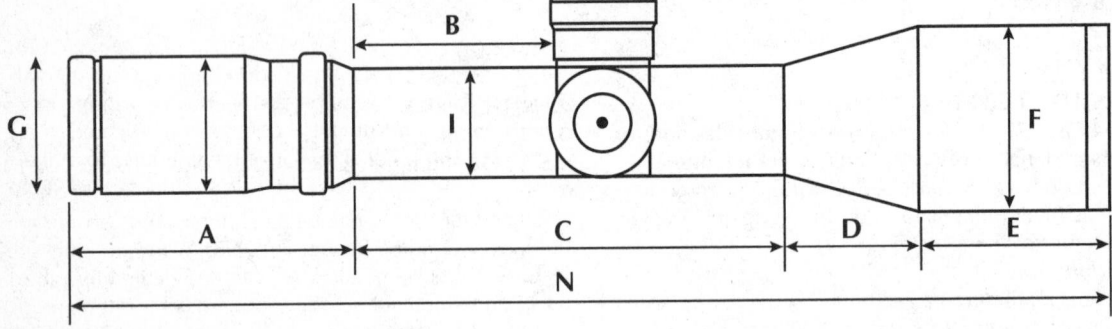

## DIMENSIONS

| MODEL | A | B | C | D | E | F | G | I | N |
|---|---|---|---|---|---|---|---|---|---|
| 10x42 | 98mm | 56mm | 139mm | 55mm | 54mm | 50mm | 43mm | 30mm | 346mm |
| | 3.858" | 2,204" | 5.472" | 2.165" | 2.126" | 1.969" | 1.693" | | 13.622" |
| 3-12x50 | 101.3mm | 68.3mm | 145.4mm | 43.5mm | 64.8mm | 57mm | 43mm | 34mm | 355mm |
| | 3.988" | 2.689" | 6.076" | 1.713" | 3.354" | 2.244" | 1.693" | | 13.976" |
| 4-16x50 | 101.3mm | 68.3mm | 145.4mm | 85.2mm | 75.5mm | 57mm | 43mm | 34mm | 405.7mm |
| | 3.988" | 2.689" | 6.076" | 1.713" | 3.354" | 2.244" | 1.693" | | 15.972" |

SIGHTS & SCOPES

# Schmidt & Bender Scopes
## Scopes For Long Range Shooting

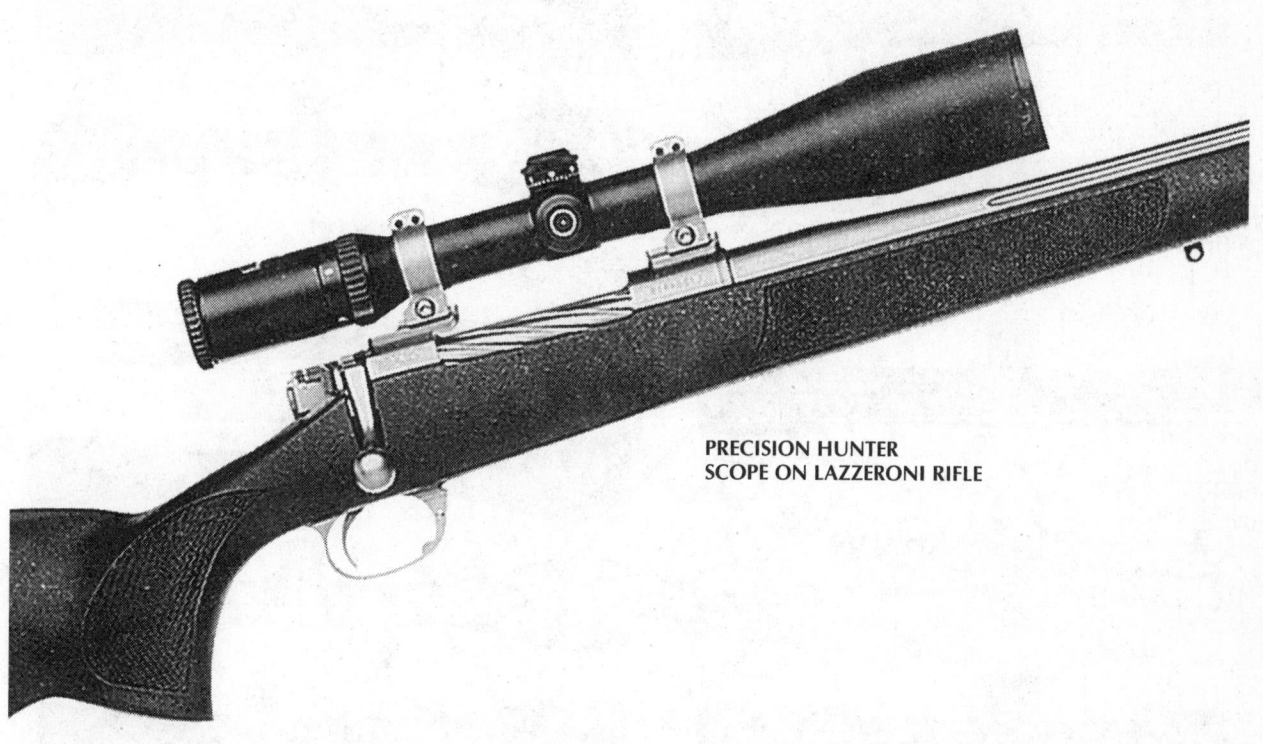

**PRECISION HUNTER
SCOPE ON LAZZERONI RIFLE**

## PRECISION HUNTER

Accurate rifles, high-speed cartridges and modern bullets make long-range hits possible. But the scope matters too. It must deliver a clear image but also help with range estimation and holdover.

Precision Hunter scopes combine the optical quality of S&B hunting scopes, with a sophisticated mil-dot reticle (developed by the U.S. Marine Corps) with a bullet drop compensator to give shooters the ability and confidence to place an accurate shot at up to 500 yards. Three models are available:

## 4-16 x 50 PRECISION HUNTER SCOPE
### WITH PARALLAX ADJUSTMENT

At 4 power, the mil-dot reticle with fine crosshairs and four posts allows quick target acquisition. This scope can be used in thickets or on the prairie. Turned up to 16 power, the mil-dots become visible and can be used for range, trajectory and windage calculations. The top-mounted bullet drop compensator has 5mm (1/5") clicks, permitting quick adjustments up to 500 yards. The windage adjustment also has 5mm (1/5") clicks, allowing for precise sighting in.

The standard elevation adjustment knob has graduations and numbers for creating a meaningful distance chart for preferred caliber. A blank elevation knob can be special-ordered with markings to be specified after sighting in rifle. A parallax adjustment is conveniently located in a third turret on the left side. This allows shooter to make necessary adjustments with the rifle shouldered, ready to shoot.
**Price:**. . . . . . . . . . . . . . . . . . . . . . . . . . . . . . . . . . **$1999**

## 3-12 x 50 PRECISION HUNTER & 3-12x42

Identical to the 4-16 x 50 with mil-dot reticle but 1cm (2/5") clicks and no parallax adjustment. It is factory-adjusted to be parallax free at 200 meters.
**Price:**. . . . . . . . . . . . . . . . . . . . . . . . . . . . . . . . . . **$1679**

## 2.5-10 x 56 PRECISION HUNTER

Identical to the 3-12 x 50, but with 1 cm (2/5") clicks for windage and elevation adjustment and with our Reticle No. 9, which makes it suitable for dangerous game.
**Price:**. . . . . . . . . . . . . . . . . . . . . . . . . . . . . . . . . . **$1699**

# Sightron Scopes

**SIGHTRON SHOTGUN SCOPES**

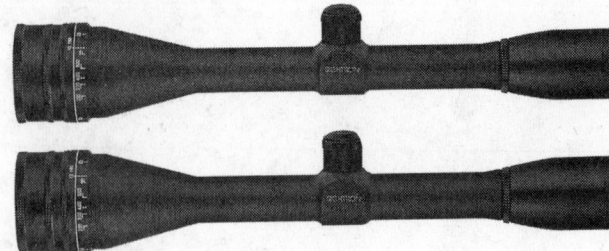

**SIGHTRON BENCHREST SCOPES**

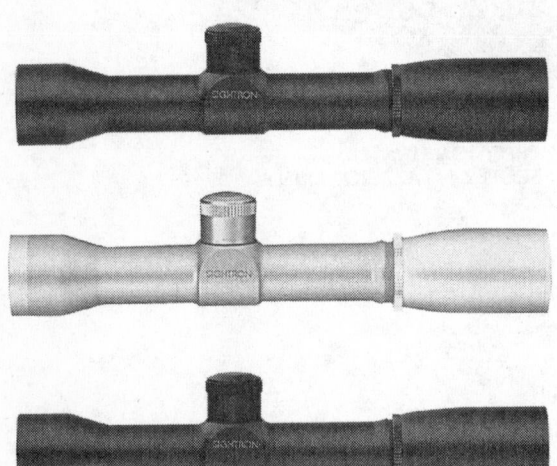

**SIGHTRON PISTOL SCOPES**

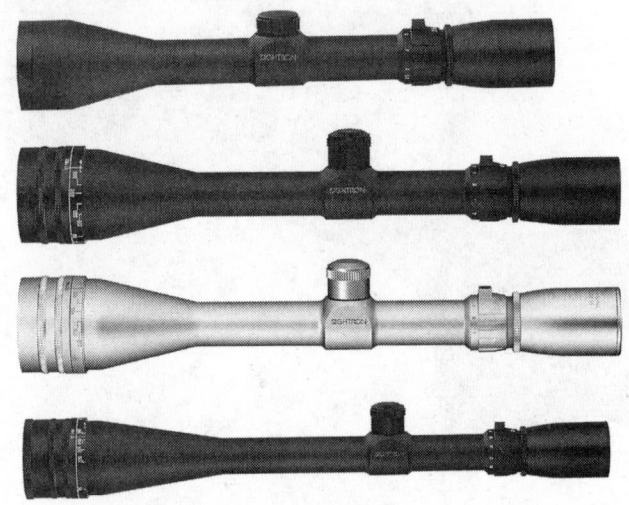

**SIGHTRON HUNTING SCOPES**

## SIGHTRON SERIES III
### WITH SIDE-MOUNTED ("SADDLE") PARALLAX ADJUSTMENT

Sightron's expanded scope line offers nearly 40 models in fixed and variable power at modest prices. The SII series features 1-inch alloy tubes; the SIII series has 30 mm aluminum tubes, multicoated lenses, and "saddle" mounted parallax adjustments. Most target and competition scopes feature 1/8-minute clicks. Sightron offers stainless finish and a broad choice of reticles including the mil dot.

**Prices:**

| | |
|---|---|
| SIII 3.5-10x44 mil dot | $757 |
| SIII 1.5-6x50 plex | 902 |
| SII shotgun 2.5-7x32 | 315 |

**SII hunting scopes:**

| | |
|---|---|
| 3-9x42 | 356 |
| 3-9x42 dot | 419 |
| 3-9x50 | 440 |
| 1.5-6x42 | 372 |
| 3-12x42 | 422 |
| 3-12x50 | 443 |
| 3.5-10x42 | 421 |
| 3.5-10x50 | 446 |
| 4.5-14x42 | 481 |
| 4.5-14x50 | 474 |

**SII target scopes:**

| | |
|---|---|
| 4-16x42 | 481 |
| 4-16x42 dot | 534 |
| 6-24x42 | 510 |
| 6-24x42 dot | 563 |

**SII competition scopes:**

| | |
|---|---|
| 3-12x42 mil dot | 428 |
| 4-16x42 mil dot | 568 |
| 4.5-14x42 mil dot | 730 |
| 6-24x42 mil dot | 599 |
| 24x44 Dot | 442 |
| 6x42 AO HBRD | 442 |
| 6-24x42 | 510 |
| 36x42 | 534 |

**SII compact scopes:**

| | |
|---|---|
| 4x32 | 267 |
| 2.5-10x32 | 338 |
| 2.5-7x32 | 315 |
| 6x42 | 291 |
| 12x42 Dot | 474 |

SIGHTS & SCOPES

# Sightron Scopes

**SI 3.510X50**

## SERIES 1

S1 scopes in the Sightron line include: 3-9x40, 3-9x50 and 3.5-10x50. The 3-9x40 MD features a mil dot range-finding reticle. All have multi-coated optics and come with Sightron's Lifetime Replacement Warranty. The 4.5-14x42 IRMD has a three-position brightness switch. Battery life ranges from 100 to 400 hours, depending on intensity. The 3-9x features a plex reticle with a lighted center.

Series 1 1x20 . . . . . . . . . . . . . . . . . . . . . . . . . . . . . . . $162
2.5-10x44 . . . . . . . . . . . . . . . . . . . . . . . . . . . . . . . . . 249
3-9x32RF . . . . . . . . . . . . . . . . . . . . . . . . . . . . . . . . . . 156
3-9x40 . . . . . . . . . . . . . . . . . . . . . . . . . . . . . . . . . . . . 205
3-9x40GL . . . . . . . . . . . . . . . . . . . . . . . . . . . . . . . . . . 205
3-9x40MD . . . . . . . . . . . . . . . . . . . . . . . . . . . . . . . . . . 248
3.5-10x50 . . . . . . . . . . . . . . . . . . . . . . . . . . . . . . . . . . 276

*To perfectly align scope rings use a ring alignment tool. Just mount each half as you would a scope and line them up. For gunsmithing tips like this, check out the latest edition of Shooter's Bible, by Stoeger Publishing.*

**SIGHTS & SCOPES**

# Sightron Scopes

In conventional scopes a curved erector tube surface contacts the flat surface of the adjustment peg. This contact is only complete at zero adjustment. As the adjustments press the erector tube in any direction, the contact becomes imperfect, causing the reticle to drift from the optical center. In many cases, since the point of contact is less than what is required to hold the erector tube in position, point of impact can shift. Sightron has developed a new erector tube with an integral ring. ExacTrack will keep constant and perfect point-of-impact, at or off zero. This constant pressure point will ensure the accuracy of all Sightron scopes under heavy recoil and severe use afield.

## SIGHTRON COMPACT SCOPES

**RETICLE DIMENSION REFERENCES**

 Plex Reticle
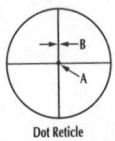 Dot Reticle
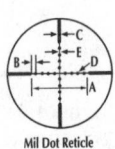 Mil Dot Reticle
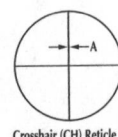 Crosshair (CH) Reticle
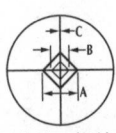 Double Diamond Reticle
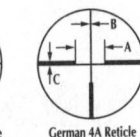 German 4A Reticle

| Item Number | Magnification | Objective Dia. (mm) | Field of View (ft @ 100 yds) | Eye Relief (in.) | Reticle Type | Reticle Subtensions (in. @ 100 yds) Min. Power A/B/C/D/E | Max. Power A/B/C/D/E | Click Value | Windage/ Elevation Travel (in.) | Tube (Dia.) | Weight (oz.) | Finish |
|---|---|---|---|---|---|---|---|---|---|---|---|---|
| **SIII SERIES RIFLE SCOPES** | | | | | | | | | | | | |
| *30mm Side Saddle Rifle Scopes* | | | | | | | | | | | | |
| SIII3.510X44MD | 3.5-10X | 44 | 28-9.2 | 3.5 | Mil-Dot | 102.6/10.26/3.25/2.2/.69 | 36/3.6/1.15/.8/.23 | 1/4 MOA | 80 | 30mm | 24.60 | Satin Black |
| SIII1.56X50 | 1.5-6X | 50 | 64-17 | 4.3-3.7 | Plex | 79.0/1.33/5.32 | 19.8/.33/1.32 | 1/4 MOA | 70 | 30mm | 21.00 | Satin Black |
| **SII SERIES RIFLE SCOPES** | | | | | | | | | | | | |
| *Variable Power Rifle Scopes* | | | | | | | | | | | | |
| SII1.56X42 | 1.5-6X | 42 | 50-15 | 4.0-3.8 | Plex | 79.0/1.33/5.32 | 19.8/.33/1.32 | 1/4 MOA | 70 | 1.0 in. | 14.00 | Satin Black |
| SII2.58X42 | 2.5-8X | 42 | 36-12 | 3.6-4.2 | Plex | 48.0/.80/3.20 | 15.0/.25/1.0 | 1/4 MOA | 90 | 1.0 in. | 12.82 | Satin Black |
| SII39X42 | 3-9X | 42 | 34-12 | 3.6-4.2 | Plex | 39.9/.66/2.66 | 13.2/.22/.88 | 1/4 MOA | 95 | 1.0 in. | 13.22 | Satin Black |
| SII39X42ST | 3-9X | 42 | 34-12 | 3.6-4.2 | Plex | 39.9/.66/2.66 | 13.2/.22/.88 | 1/4 MOA | 95 | 1.0 in. | 13.22 | Stainless |
| SII39X42D | 3-9X | 42 | 34-12 | 3.6-4.2 | Dot | 4/.66 | 1.3/.22 | 1/4 MOA | 95 | 1.0 in. | 13.22 | Satin Black |
| SII312X42 | 3-12X | 42 | 32-9 | 3.6-4.2 | Plex | 39.9/.66/2.66 | 9.9/.16/.66 | 1/4 MOA | 80 | 1.0 in. | 12.99 | Satin Black |
| SII3.510X42 | 3.5-10X | 42 | 32-11 | 3.6 | Plex | 34.2/.57/2.28 | 12.0/.20/.80 | 1/4 MOA | 60 | 1.0 in. | 13.80 | Satin Black |
| SII4.514X42 | 4.5-14X | 42 | 22-7.9 | 3.6 | Plex | 26.4/.44/1.76 | 8.5/.14/.56 | 1/4 MOA | 50 | 1.0 in. | 16.07 | Satin Black |
| SII39X50 | 3-9X | 50 | 34-12 | 4.2-3.6 | Plex | 39.9/.66/2.66 | 13.2/.22/.88 | 1/4 MOA | * | 1.0 in. | 15.40 | Satin Black |
| SII312X50 | 3-12X | 50 | 34-8.5 | 4.5-3.7 | Plex | 39.9/.66/2.66 | 9.9/.16/.66 | 1/4 MOA | * | 1.0 in. | 16.30 | Satin Black |
| SII3.510X50 | 3.5-10X | 50 | 30-10 | 4.0-3.4 | Plex | 34.2/.57/2.28 | 12.0/.20/.80 | 1/4 MOA | 50 | 1.0 in. | 15.10 | Satin Black |
| SII4.514X50 | 4.5-14X | 50 | 23-8 | 3.9-3.25 | Plex | 26.4/.44/1.76 | 8.4/.14/.56 | 1/4 MOA | 60 | 1.0 in. | 15.20 | Satin Black |
| **VARIABLE POWER TARGET SCOPES** | | | | | | | | | | | | |
| SII416X42 | 4-16X | 42 | 26-7 | 3.6 | Plex | 30/.50/2.0 | 7.5/.125/.50 | 1/8 MOA | 56 | 1.0 in. | 16.00 | Satin Black |
| SII416X42ST | 4-16X | 42 | 26-7 | 3.6 | Plex | 30/.50/2.0 | 7.5/.125/.50 | 1/8 MOA | 56 | 1.0 in. | 16.00 | Stainless |
| SII416X42D | 4-16X | 42 | 26-7 | 3.6 | Dot | 1.7/.10 | .425/.025 | 1/8 MOA | 56 | 1.0 in. | 16.00 | Satin Black |
| SII416X42DST | 4-16X | 42 | 26-7 | 3.6 | Dot | 1.7/.10 | .425/.025 | 1/8 MOA | 56 | 1.0 in. | 16.00 | Stainless |
| SII624X42 | 6-24X | 42 | 15.7-4.4 | 3.6 | Plex | 19.8/.33/1.32 | 4.8/.08/.32 | 1/8 MOA | 40 | 1.0 in. | 18.70 | Satin Black |
| SII624X42ST | 6-24X | 42 | 15.7-4.4 | 3.6 | Plex | 19.8/.33/1.32 | 4.8/.08/.32 | 1/8 MOA | 40 | 1.0 in. | 18.70 | Stainless |
| SII624X42D | 6-24X | 42 | 15.7-4.4 | 3.6 | Dot | 1.12/.066 | .27/.016 | 1/8 MOA | 40 | 1.0 in. | 18.70 | Satin Black |
| SII624X42DST | 6-24X | 42 | 15.7-4.4 | 3.6 | Dot | 1.12/.066 | .27/.016 | 1/8 MOA | 40 | 1.0 in. | 18.70 | Stainless |
| **COMPETITION/TACTICAL SCOPES** | | | | | | | | | | | | |
| SII312X42MD | 3-12X | 42 | 32-9 | 3.6-4.2 | Mil-Dot | 144/14/4.7/3.1/.7 | 36/3.6/1.2/.79/.1 | 1/4 MOA | 80 | 1.0 in. | 12.99 | Satin Black |
| SII416X42MD | 4-16X | 42 | 26-7 | 3.6 | Mil-Dot | 144/14/4.7/3.1/.6 | 36/3.6/1.2/.79/.1 | 1/8 MOA | 56 | 1.0 in. | 16.00 | Satin Black |
| SII416X42MDST | 4-16X | 42 | 26-7 | 3.6 | Mil-Dot | 144/14/4.7/3.1/.6 | 36/3.6/1.2/.79/.1 | 1/8 MOA | 56 | 1.0 in. | 16.00 | Stainless |
| SII624X42MD | 6-24X | 42 | 15.7-4.4 | 3.6 | Mil-Dot | 144/14/4.7/3.1/.4 | 36/3.6/1.2/.79/.1 | 1/8 MOA | 40 | 1.0 in. | 18.70 | Satin Black |
| SII624X42MDST | 6-24X | 42 | 15.7-4.4 | 3.6 | Mil-Dot | 144/14/4.7/3.1/.4 | 36/3.6/1.2/.79/.1 | 1/8 MOA | 40 | 1.0 in. | 18.70 | Stainless |
| SII24X44D | 24X | 44 | 4.4 | 4.33 | Dot | | .27/.016 | 1/8 MOA | 60 | 1.0 in. | 15.87 | Satin Black |
| SII6X42HBRD | 6X | 42 | 20 | 4.00 | Dot | | .375/.070 | 1/8 MOA | 100 | 1.0 in. | 16.00 | Satin Black |
| **COMPACT RIFLE SCOPES** | | | | | | | | | | | | |
| SII4X32 | 4X | 32 | 25 | 4.52 | Plex | | 30/.50/2.0 | 1/4 MOA | 120 | 1.0 in. | 9.80 | Satin Black |
| SII2.57X32 | 2.5-7X | 32 | 41-11.8 | 3.8-3.2 | Plex | 48/.80/3.20 | 17.2/.29/1.2 | 1/4 MOA | 120 | 1.0 in. | 11.60 | Satin Black |
| SII2.510X32 | 2.5-10X | 32 | 41-10.5 | 3.8-3.5 | Plex | 48/.80/3.20 | 12/.20/.80 | 1/4 MOA | 120 | 1.0 in. | 10.93 | Satin Black |
| SII6X42 | 6X | 42 | 20 | 3.60 | Plex | | 19.8/.33/1.32 | 1/4 MOA | 100 | 1.0 in. | 12.69 | Satin Black |
| *Shotgun Scopes* | | | | | | | | | | | | |
| SII2.5X20SG | 2.5X | 20 | 41 | 4.33 | Plex | | 48.0/.80/3.20 | 1/4 MOA | 160 | 1.0 in. | 9.00 | Satin Black |
| SII2.57X32SG | 2.5-7X | 32 | 41-11.8 | 3.8-3.2 | DD | 48/24/.60 | 17/8.5/.26 | 1/4 MOA | 120 | 1.0 in. | 11.60 | Satin Black |

*Specifications not available at press time

SIGHTS & SCOPES

AETEC MODEL 800865

# Simmons Scopes
## Aetec

Sleek and durable, with bright, coated lenses, Simmons scopes offers great value for the dollar.

## MODEL 2100/2101/2102
2.8-10X44 WA Length: 11.9" Weight: 15.5 oz. Reticle: Truplex
Price: . . . . . . . . . . . . . . . . . . . . . . . . . . . . . . . . . . . . $190
   Model 2104 3.8-12x44mm AO . . . . . . . . . . . . . . 200

## MODEL 800865/800866
Illuminated Reticle, black matte
Prices: Model 800865 (2.8-10x44) . . . . . . . . . . . . $230

## 44 Mag Riflescopes

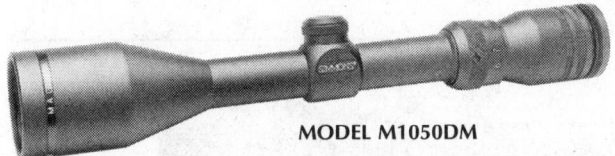

MODEL M1050DM

## MODEL M1044 (BLACK MATTE)
3-10X44mm  Length: 12.75"  Weight: 15.5 oz.
Price: . . . . . . . . . . . . . . . . . . . . . . . . . . . . . . . . . $150

## MODEL M1050DM
## 44 DIAMOND MG (BLACK MATTE)
## RANGE-CALCULATING SMART RETICLE
## (BLACK MATTE)
3.8-12X44mm  Length: 13.08"  Weight: 16.75 oz.
Price: . . . . . . . . . . . . . . . . . . . . . . . . . . . . . . . . . $190

Model M1045 (black MATTE)
4-12X44mm  Length: 13.2"  Weight: 18.25 oz.
Price: . . . . . . . . . . . . . . . . . . . . . . . . . . . . . . . . . $170

## MODEL M1047 (BLACK MATTE)
6.5-20X44mm  Length: 12.8" Weight: 19.5 oz.
Price: . . . . . . . . . . . . . . . . . . . . . . . . . . . . . . . . . $200
*Also available:*

## MODEL M1048
6.5-20X44 Target Turrets
   Black Matte (1/8" MOA) . . . . . . . . . . . . . . . . . . $220

## MODEL M1055
3-10X44 Mildot . . . . . . . . . . . . . . . . . . . . . . . . . $170

## MODEL M1056
6.5-20X44 Mildot . . . . . . . . . . . . . . . . . . . . . . . . $240

## MODEL M1057
6.5-20x44 Mildot, illum . . . . . . . . . . . . . . . . . . . . $250

## ProHunter Riflescopes

PRO 50 MODEL 8800

PROHUNTER SE MODEL 807729

## MODEL 7710
*3-9X40mm Wide Angle Riflescope*
**Length:** 12.6"
**Weight:** 13.5 oz.
**Features:** Truplex reticle; silver matte finish
Price: . . . . . . . . . . . . . . . . . . . . . . . . . . . . . . . . . $110
(Same in black matte or black polish, Models 7711 and 7712) *Also available:*
Model 7700 2-7X32 Black Matte . . . . . . . . . . . . . . 100
Model 7716 4-12X40 Black Matte AO . . . . . . . . . . . 130
Model 7721 6-18X40 AO Black Matte . . . . . . . . . . . 140
Model 7722 6-18X40 AO Target Gray . . . . . . . . . . . 140

Model 7740 6X40 Black Matte . . . . . . . . . . . . . . . . . 90
Model 7711 3-9X40 WA Matte . . . . . . . . . . . . . . . 110
Model 7702 3-9X40 Illum. . . . . . . . . . . . . . . . . . . 140
Model 7712 3-9X40 Gloss . . . . . . . . . . . . . . . . . . 110
Model 7703 6-24X42 Mildot. . . . . . . . . . . . . . . . . 160

## PRO50
Pro 50's have all the features of the Prohunter models, only with a 50mm lens.
Prices:
Model 8800 4-12x50mm, AO Black Matte . . . . . . . $180
Model 8810 6-18x50mm, AO Black Matte . . . . . . . 175

# Simmons Scopes

### 1022T RIMFIRE TARGET SCOPE
*Magnification:* 3-9X32mm WA/AO *Finish:* Black matte or silver *Features:* Adjustable for windage and elevation; adjustable objective lens, target knobs

Price:............................................$170
*Also available:*
1022 4X32 black matte w/22 rings.................50
1031 4X28 22 Mag Mini black matte w/22 rings.....50
1032 4X28 22 Mag Mini silver matte w/22 rings....50
1033 4X32 silver matte w/22 rings...............50
1037 3-9X32 silver matte w/22 rings ............60
1039 3-9X32 black matte w/22 rings .............60

**1022T RIMFIRE TARGET SCOPE**

## Black Powder Scopes

**MODEL BP2732M**

### MODEL BP2732M
*Magnification:* 2-7X32  *Finish:* Black matte
*Field of view:* 57.7'-16.6' 100 yards  *Eye relief:* 3"
*Reticle:* Truplex  *Length:* 11.6"  *Weight:* 12.4 oz.
Price:.......................................$130

*Also available: Models BP400M/400S*
4X20 Black Matte or Silver Matte, Long Body
*Field of view:* 28'  *Eye relief:* 5.0"  *Length:* 10.25"
*Weight:* 8.7 oz.  *Reticle:* Truplex
Price:........................................$60

## ProDiamond Shotgun Scopes

**MODEL 7790D**

### MODELS 7790D
Magnification: 4X32  Finish: Black matte
Field of view: 17' Eye relief: 5.5" Reticle: ProDiamond
Length: 8.5" Weight: 9.1 oz.
Prices:
Model 7790D............................$110

*Also available:*
Model 7789D 2X32 Black matte
  (ProDiamond reticle) ......................100
Model 7791D 1.5-5X20 WA Black matte
  (ProDiamond reticle) ......................130
Model 7792D 1.5-5X32 Camo Pro Diamond ......130
Model 807787 1.5-5x32 illum. Pro Diamond.......170
Model 7788 1x32 Truplex......................113
Model 899738 3-9x40 ........................130

**SIMMONS 8 POINT
4X32 BLACK**

The Simmons 8-Point series is aimed at the entry level or budget-minded shooter who needs a reliable scope at an affordable price. The 8-Point family includes seven scopes in popular configurations: 3-9x32mm, 3-9x40mm, 3-9x50mm, 4x32mm, 4-12x40mm AO, and 4x32 mm shotgun. All versions are offered in black matte finish, and the 3-9x40mm is also available in silver. Fully coated lenses enhance light transmission for low-light viewing and reduce reflections. Simmons' popular Truplex reticle is standard. Windage and elevation are adjusted in 1/4-MOA increments. The new 8-Point scopes are shockproof, waterproof, and fogproof.

## 8-POINT SCOPE 4-12X40MM AO

*Magnification:* 4-12X
*Field of View:* 29 - 10 ft. at 100 yards
*Eye Relief:* 3 inches at 4X and 27/8 inches at 12X
*Length:* 13.5 inches
*Weight:* 15.75 oz.
*Reticle:* Duplex
*Finish:* Black Matte
*Price:*. . . . . . . . . . . . . . . . . . . . . . . . . . . . . . . .$100

## 8-POINT SCOPE 4X32MM

*Magnification:* 4X
*Field of View:* 28.75 ft. at 100 yards
*Eye Relief:* 3 inches
*Length:* 11.625 inches
*Weight:* 14.25 oz.
*Reticle:* Duplex
*Finish:* Black Matte
*Price:*. . . . . . . . . . . . . . . . . . . . . . . . . . . . . . . .$35

## 8-POINT SCOPE 3-9X32 MM

*Magnification:* 3-9X
*Field of View:* 37.5 - 13 ft. at 100 yards
*Eye Relief:* 3 inches at 3X and 27/8 inches at 9X
*Length:* 11.875 inches
*Weight:* 11.5 oz.
*Reticle:* Duplex
*Finish:* Black Matte
*Price:*. . . . . . . . . . . . . . . . . . . . . . . . . . . . . . . .$45

## 8-POINT SCOPE 3-9X40MM

*Magnification:* 3-9X
*Field of View:* 37 - 13 ft. at 100 yards
*Eye Relief:* 3 inches at 3X and 27/8 inches at 9X
*Length:* 12.25 inches
*Weight:* 12.25 oz.
*Reticle:* Duplex
*Finish:* Black Matte or Silver
*Price: Black Matte or Silver* . . . . . . . . . . . . . . . . . .$50
Camo . . . . . . . . . . . . . . . . . . . . . . . . . . . . . . . . 80

## 8-POINT SCOPE 3-9X50MM

*Magnification:* 3-9X
*Field of View:* 32 - 11.75 ft. at 100 yards
*Eye Relief:* 3 inches at 3X and 27/8 inches at 9X
*Length:* 13 inches
*Weight:* 15.25 oz.
*Reticle:* Duplex
*Finish:* Black Matte
*Price:*. . . . . . . . . . . . . . . . . . . . . . . . . . . . . . . .$80

*Also available: 8-Point Shotgun Scopes*
2.5x20, matte . . . . . . . . . . . . . . . . . . . . . . . . . . . .$50
4x32, matte . . . . . . . . . . . . . . . . . . . . . . . . . . . . . 60
1.5-5x32, matte . . . . . . . . . . . . . . . . . . . . . . . . . . 80
1.5-5x32, camo . . . . . . . . . . . . . . . . . . . . . . . . . 110

SIGHTS & SCOPES

# Simmons Scopes
## Prohunter Handgun Scopes

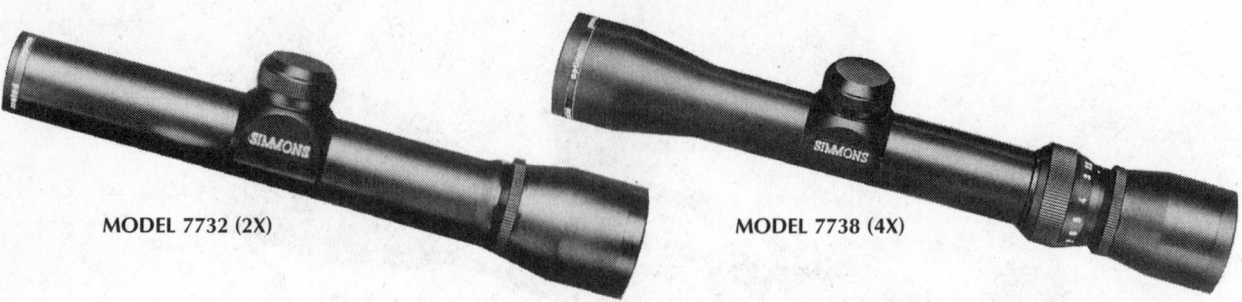

**MODEL 7732 (2X)**

**MODEL 7738 (4X)**

### MODEL #7732/7733 (SILVER MATTE)
**SPECIFICATIONS**
*Magnification:* 2X  *Field Of View:* 22'  *Eye Relief:* 9-17"
*Length:* 8.75"  *Weight:* 7 oz.  *Reticle:* Truplex *Finish:* Black matte
**Price:**...................................$110

### MODEL #7738/7739 (SILVER MATTE)
**SPECIFICATIONS**
*Magnification:* 4X  *Field Of View:* 15'  *Eye Relief:* 11.8-17.6"  *Length:* 9"  *Weight:* 8 oz.  *Reticle:* Truplex
*Finish:* Black matte
**Price:**...................................$130
**Also:** Prohunter 2-6X32, Matte or Silver ..........160

*A smooth, perfectly aligned bearing surface is critical to holding power in scope rings. Accomplish this by using a lapping tool and rubbing compound. This removes high spots and produces a vice-like grip. Check out Gunsmithing at Home, by Stoeger Publishing.*

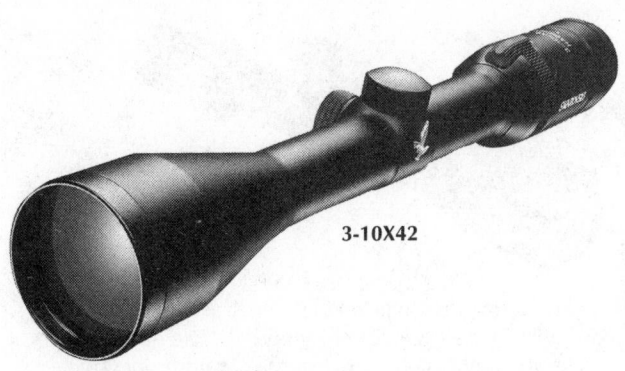

3-10X42

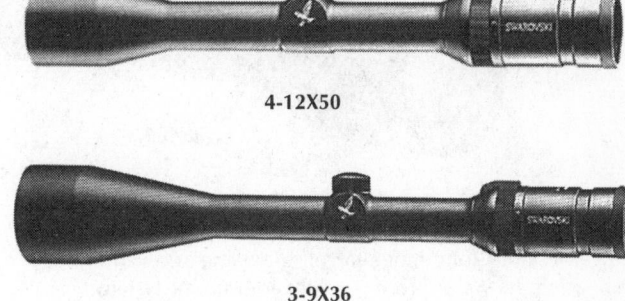

4-12X50

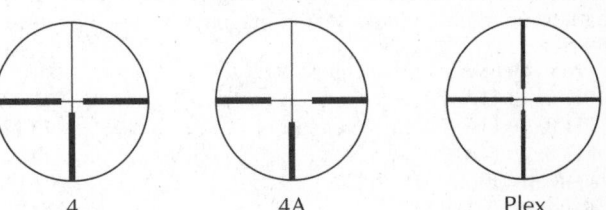

3-9X36

Top-grade optics and attention to the needs of American hunters have made Swarovski scopes a best-selling brand. When performance matters more than price, sportsmen are turning to Swarovski.

### SWAROVSKI A-LINE SERIES LIGHTWEIGHT 1-INCH SCOPES

Developed for American hunters, the A-Line scopes feature constant-size reticles, lightweight alloy tubes and satin finish. Totally waterproof even with caps removed, these scopes have fully multi-coated lenses and the quality that has made Swarovski famous.

***Prices:***

```
3-10x42 (TDS) . . . . . . . . . . . . . . . . . . . . . . . . . . . . $943
3-10 x 42 (4A, Plex) . . . . . . . . . . . . . . . . . . . . . . . . . 877
4-12 x 50 (4A, Plex) . . . . . . . . . . . . . . . . . . . . . . . . . 921
3-9 x 36 (4A, Plex) . . . . . . . . . . . . . . . . . . . . . . . . . . 799
6-18x50 (4A, Plex) . . . . . . . . . . . . . . . . . . . . . . . . . . 977
6-18x50 (TDS)1032
4-12X50 (TDS) . . . . . . . . . . . . . . . . . . . . . . . . . . . . . 988
```

### 6-18x50

Swarovski's 6-18x50 incorporates a parallex adjustment ring that insures parallex free accuracy from 50 yds to beyond 500. The objective bell, 1" tube, turret housing and ocular bell are machined out of one solid piece of alloy bar stock for strength, weight and waterproof integrity.

**Price:** . . . . . . . . . . . . . . . . . . . . . . . . . . . . . . . . $977

**A-LINE RETICLES AVAILABLE:**

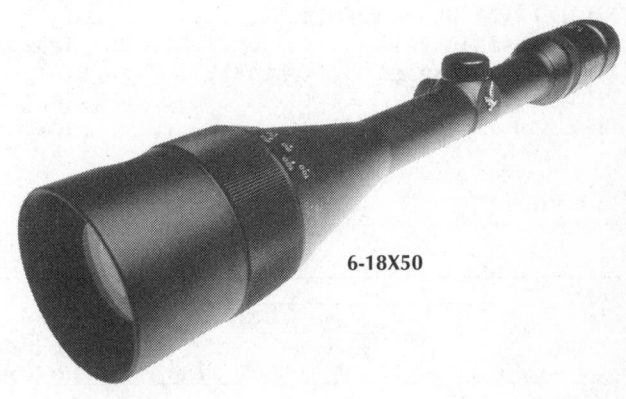

| 4 | 4A | Plex |

6-18X50

|  | 3-9x36 | 3-10x42 | 4-12x50 | 6-18x50 |
|---|---|---|---|---|
| Magnification | 3-9x | 3.3-10x | 4-12x | 6-18x |
| Objective lens diameter: mm | 36 | 42 | 50 | 50 |
| in | 1.42 | 1.55 | 1.97 | 1.97 |
| Exit pupil, diameter: mm | 12-4 | 12.6-4.2 | 12.5-4.2 | 8.3-2.8 |
| Eye relief: in | 3.5 | 3.5 | 3.5 | 3.5 |
| Field of view, real: m/100m | 13-4.5 | 11-3.9 | 9.7-3.3 | 17.4-6.5 |
| ft/100yds | 39-13.5 | 33-11.7 | 29.1-9.9 | 17.4-6.5 |
| Diopter compensation (dpt) | ± 2.6 | ± 2.5 | ± 2.5 | ± 2.5 |
| Transission (%) | 94 | 94 | 94 | 92 |
| Twilight factor (DIN 58388) | 9-18 | 9-21 | 11-25 | 17-30 |
| Impact Point correction per click: in/100yds | 0.25 | 0.25 | 0.25 | 0.25 |
| Max. elevation/windage adjustment range: ft/100yds | 4.8 | 4.2 | 3.6 | 3.9 |
| Length, approx: in | 11.8 | 12.44 | 13.5 | 14.85 |
| Weight, approx (oz.): L | 11.6 | 12.7 | 13.9 | 20.3 |
| LS | – | 13.6 | 15.2 | – |

L=light alloy • LS=light alloy with rail

SIGHTS & SCOPES

# Swarovski Scopes

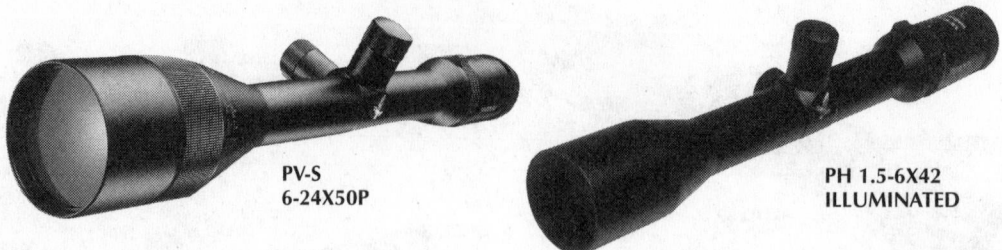

**PV-S**
**6-24X50P**

**PH 1.5-6X42**
**ILLUMINATED**

The 6-24X50mm "PH" riflescope was developed by Swarovski for long-range target, big-game and varmint shooting. Its water-proof parallax adjustment system should be popular with whitetail "Bean Field Shooters" and long-range varmint hunters looking for a choice of higher powers in a premium rifle scope and still deliver accuracy. The scope will also appeal to many bench rest shooters who compete in certain classes where power and adjustment are limited. A non-magnifying, fine plex reti-cle and a fine crosshair reticle with 1/ 8" MOA dot are available in the 6-24x50mm scope. Reticle adjustment clicks are 1/ 6" (minute) by external, waterproof target knobs. The internal optical system features a patented coil spring suspension system for dependable accuracy and positive reticle adjustment. The objective bell, 30mm middle tube, turret housing and ocular bell are machined from one solid bar of aluminum.

### Prices PH Series Riflescopes

| | |
|---|---:|
| PH 6x42 (4A, 7A) | $1088 |
| PH 8x50 (4A, 7A) | 1132 |
| PH 8x56 (4A) | 1188 |
| PH8x56 (Illum. ret. PLEXN) | 1610 |
| PH 1.25-4x24 (4A) | 1199 |
| PH 1.25-4x24 (#24) | 1221 |
| PH 1.25-4x24 (Ill. ret. #24N) | 1521 |
| PH 1.5-6x42 (4A, 7A) | 1332 |
| PH 1.5-6x42 (Illum. ret. #24N, 4A-1K) | 1643 |
| PH 1.5-6x42 (#24) | 1377 |
| PH 2.5-10x42 (4A, 7A, PLEX) | 1488 |
| illum reticle (4NK) | 1854 |
| PH 2.5-10x56 (4A, 7A PLEX) | 1543 |
| w/illum reticle (4NK, PLEXN) | 1999 |
| PH 3-12x50 (4A, 7A, PLEX) | 1577 |
| TDS reticle | 1643 |
| w/illum reticle (4NK, PLEXN) | 1999 |
| PH 6-24x50 (4A, PLEX) with low turret | 1743 |
| PH 6-24x50 (low turrets, TDS) | 1866 |
| PH 4-16x50 (4A, PLEX) | 1643 |
| PH 4-16x50 (TDS) | 1721 |

### PF& PV

| | PF 6x42 | PF/PF-N 8x50 | PF/PF-N 8x56 | PV/PV-1 1.25-4x24 | PV 1.5-6x42 | PV/PV-N 2.5-10x42 | PV/PV-N 2.5-10x56 | PV/PV-N 3-12x50 | PV 4-16x50P | PV 6-24x50P | PV-S 6-24x50P |
|---|---|---|---|---|---|---|---|---|---|---|---|
| Magnification | 6x | 8x | 8x | 1.25-4x | 1.5-6x | 2.5-10x | 2.5-10x | 3-12x | 4-16x | 6-24x | 6-24x |
| **Objective lens diameter: mm** | 42 | 50 | 56 | 17-24 | 20-42 | 33-42 | 33-56 | 39-50 | 50 | 50 | 50 |
| in | 1.65 | 1.97 | 2.20 | 0.67-0.94 | 0.79-1.65 | 1.3-1.65 | 1.3-2.20 | 1.54-1.97 | 1.97 | 1.97 | 1.97 |
| **Exit pupil, diameter: mm** | 7 | 6.25 | 7 | 12.5-6 | 13.1-7 | 13.1-4.2 | 13.1-5.6 | 13.1-4.2 | 12.5-3.1 | 8.3-2.1 | 8.3-2.1 |
| Eye relief: in | 3.15 | 3.15 | 3.15 | 3.15 | 3.15 | 3.15 | 3.15 | 3.15 | 3.15 | 3.15 | 3.15 |
| **Field of view, real: m/100m** | 7 | 5.2 | 5 | 32.8-10.4 | 21.8-7 | 13.2-4.2 | 13.2-4.1 | 11-3.5 | 9.1-2.6 | 6.2-1.8 | 6.2-1.8 |
| ft/100yds | 21 | 15.6 | 15.6 | 98.4-31.2 | 65.4-21 | 39.6-12.6 | 39.6-12.3 | 33-10.5 | 27.3-7.8 | 18.6-5.4 | 18.6-5.4 |
| **Diopter compensation (dpt)** | +2. -3 | +2. -3 | +2. -3 | +2. -3 | +2. -3 | +2. -3 | +2. -3 | +2. -3 | +2. -3 | +2. -3 | +2. -3 |
| Transission (%) | 94 | 94/92 | 93/91 | 93/91 | 93 | 94/92 | 93/91 | 94/92 | 90 | 90 | 90 |
| **Twilight factor (DIN 58388)** | 16 | 20 | 21 | 4-10 | 4-16 | 7-21 | 7-24 | 9-25 | 11-28 | 17-35 | 17-35 |
| **Impact Point correction per click: in/100yds** | 0.36 | 0.36 | 0.36 | 0.54 | 0.36 | 0.36 | 0.36 | 0.36 | 0.18 | 0.18 | 0.17 |
| **Max. elevation/windage adjustment range: ft/100yds** | 3.9 | 3.3 | 3.9 | 9.9 | 6.6 | 3.9 | 3.9 | 3.3 | E:5.4/W:3 | E:3.6/W:2.1 | E:3.6/W:2.1 |
| Length, approx: in | 12.83 | 13.94 | 13.27 | 10.63 | 12.99 | 13.23 | 13.62 | 14.33 | 14.21 | 15.43 | 15.43 |
| Weight, approx (oz.): L | 12.0 | 14.8 | 15.9 | 12.7 | 16.2 | 15.2 | 18.0 | 16.9 | 22.2 | 23.6 | 24.5 |
| LS | 13.4 | 15.9 | 16.9 | 13.8 | 17.5 | 16.4 | 19.0 | 18.3 | — | — | — |

L=light alloy • LS=light alloy with rail

SIGHTS & SCOPES

686M 6.5-20X44

687M 4.5-14X44

688M 6-18X44

685M 3-9X40

Swift Model's 685M and 686M were both designed for the rigors of airgun use. Strength and durability are the best terms used to describe these two scopes as they are constructed to withstand the severe reverse recoil of spring-loaded airguns. These versatile scopes have the Swift Quadraplex reticle, have been shock tested and are airgun rated.

## MODEL 685M: SWIFT PREMIER
3-9x,40mm Air Gun Rated Riflescope
Waterproof – Fully Multi-Coated – Speed Focus
Adjustable Objective
Comes Complete with Sunshade
Price:. . . . . . . . . . . . . . . . . . . . . . . . . . . . . . . . . $190

## MODEL 686M: SWIFT PREMIER
6.5-20x,44mm Air Gun Rated Riflescope
Waterproof – Fully Multi-Coated – Speed Focus
Adjustable Objective
Comes Complete with Sunshade
Price:. . . . . . . . . . . . . . . . . . . . . . . . . . . . . . . . . $250

Swift Model's 687M and 688M both feature a mil-dot reticle for pinpoint accuracy in long-range varmint or target shooting. The 44mm objective lens on these scopes allows for an exceptional light gathering capability.

## MODEL 687M: SWIFT PREMIER
4.5-14x,44mm Mil-Dot Riflescope
Waterproof – Fully Multi-Coated – Speed Focus
Comes Complete with Sunshade
Price:. . . . . . . . . . . . . . . . . . . . . . . . . . . . . . . . . $220

## MODEL 688M: SWIFT PREMIER
6-18x,44mm Mil-Dot Riflescope
Waterproof – Fully Multi-Coated – Speed Focus
Comes Complete with Sunshade
Price: . . . . . . . . . . . . . . . . . . . . . . . . . . . . . . . . . $240

Produced for the youth market, Swift's new Model 587 is a 4x, 32mm with a quadraplex reticle, this lightweight scope is designed for smaller caliber rimfires rifles.

## MODEL 587: SWIFT
4x,32mm Rimfire Riflescope
Waterproof – Fully Coated
**Comes Complete with Rings**
Price:. . . . . . . . . . . . . . . . . . . . . . . . . . . . . . . . . $50

The Swift Model 660M with a 2 - 6X zoom is a very versatile pistol scope that features full saddle construction and the Swift Speed Focus feature for optimum focusing ability at any power setting. Quadraplex reticle.

## MODEL 660M: SWIFT PREMIER
2-6x,32mm Pistol Scope
Waterproof – Fully Multi-Coated – Speed Focus
Price:. . . . . . . . . . . . . . . . . . . . . . . . . . . . . . . . . $250

SIGHTS & SCOPES

# Swift Scopes

658M 2-7X40

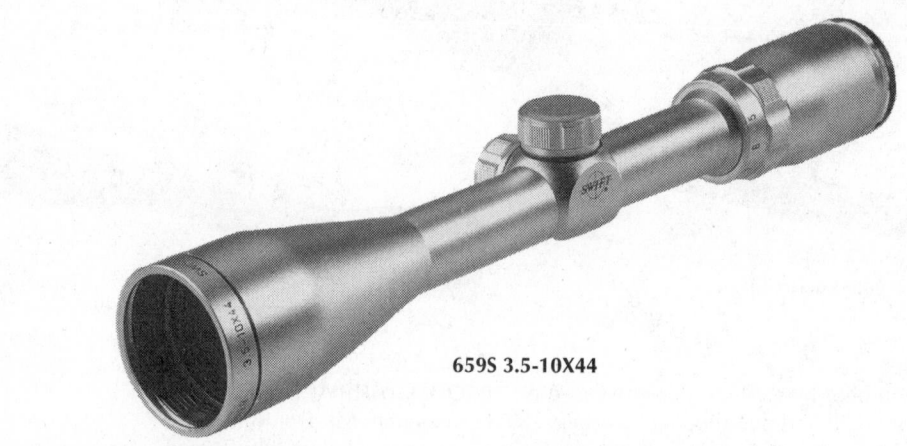

659S 3.5-10X44

669MA 6-18X44

Three of Swifts best selling standard line of riflescopes, models 658M, 659M, and 669MA will be upgraded to become part of the Swift Premier line. The upgrades to these scopes will include; full saddle construction, for added strength; 'Speed Focus', for a quick focus at any power setting; fully multi-coated optics for a brighter, glare free view at dawn and dusk, and; clear dust caps that will allow hunters to get off a quick shot if the need arises, without losing the time it takes to remove their dust caps.

## MODEL 658M: SWIFT PREMIER 2-7x,40MM RIFLESCOPE
Waterproof – Fully Multi-Coated – Speed Focus
Finger Tip Adjustment System
**Price:**. . . . . . . . . . . . . . . . . . . . . . . . . . . . . . . $175

## MODEL 659M: SWIFT PREMIER 3.5-10x,44MM RIFLESCOPE
Waterproof – Fully Multi-Coated – Speed Focus
*Also available in "blue" and "silver" finishes*
**Price:**. . . . . . . . . . . . . . . . . . . . . . . . . . . . . . . $210

## MODEL 669MA: SWIFT PREMIER 6-18x,44MM RIFLESCOPE
Waterproof – Fully Multi-Coated – Speed Focus w/target turrets
**Price:**. . . . . . . . . . . . . . . . . . . . . . . . . . . . . . . $250

# Tasco Scopes

**PROPOINT 1X25**

This past year, the Tasco name and inventory was purchased by Bushnell. Tasco's line has since been winnowed, only the top-performing scopes and best bargains retained. Bushnell will not integrate the Tasco fleet but keep it as a separate name. Plans are to boost Tasco's image while maintaining quality and increasing the number of scopes designed to deliver great value, especially to hunters on a budget.

## PROPOINT RED DOT SIGHTING DEVICE

Propoint Red Dot Sights have been the choice for competitive shooters, turkey hunters and slug gun enthusiasts for years. Built to last, the Propoint features solid construction, flawless tracking and a rheostat-controlled illuminated red dot. Included accessories: rings to fit standard 5/8" bases, extension tubes, polarizing filter and one lithium battery.

## PROPOINT SCOPES

| Model | Power | Objective Diameter | Finish | Reticle | Field of View @ 100 Yds. | Eye Relief | Tube Diam. | Scope Length | Scope Weight | Prices |
|-------|-------|--------------------|--------|---------|--------------------------|------------|------------|--------------|--------------|--------|
| PDP2 | 1X | 25mm | Black Matte | 5 M.O.A. Dot | 40' | Unlimited | 30mm | 5" | 5.5 oz. | $118 |
| PDP3 | 1X | 25mm | Black Matte | 5 M.O.A. Dot | 52' | Unlimited | 30mm | 5" | 5.5 oz. | 138 |
| PDP3ST | 1X | 25mm | Stainless | 10 M.O.A. Dot | 52' | Unlimited | 30mm | 5" | 5.5 oz. | 144 |
| PDP3CMP | 1X | 30mm | Black Matte | 10 M.O.A. Dot | 68' | Unlimited | 33mm | 4.75" | 5.4 oz. | 156 |
| PDPRG | 1X | 26mm | Black Matte | 5 M.O.A. Dot | 60' | Unlimited | 38mm | 5.4" | 5.7 oz. | 92 |
| **RED DOT SIGHTS** | | | | | | | | | | |
| BKRD30 | 1X | 30mm | Black Matte AWF | Illum. Red Dot | 57" | Unlimited | 38mm | 3.75" | 6 oz. | $46 |
| BKRD30/22 | 1X | 30mm | Black Matte AWF | Illum. Red Dot | 57" | Unlimited | 38mm | 3.75" | 6 oz. | 46 |
| BKRD42 | 1X | 42mm | Black Matte AWF | Illum. Red Dot | 62" | Unlimited | 47mm | 3.75" | 6.7 oz. | 58 |

*Sharp recoil can put a divot in your eyebrow if you're too close to the scope. Look for scope care and mounting tips in Stoeger Publishing's Home Gunsmithing video on Sight Systems.*

# Tasco Scopes

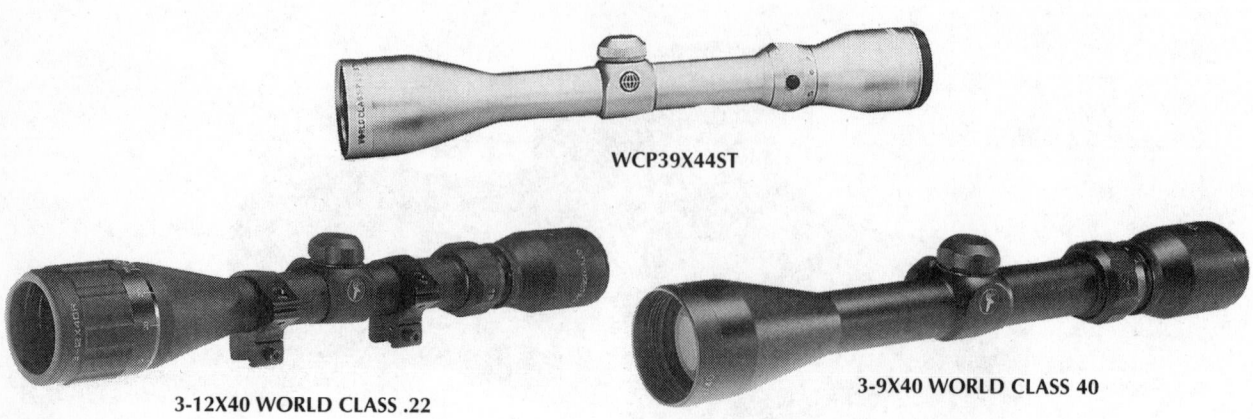

**WCP39X44ST**

**3-12X40 WORLD CLASS .22**

**3-9X40 WORLD CLASS 40**

## WORLD CLASS RIFLESCOPES

Wide-angle World Class Riflescopes have 1" Advanced Monotube Construction to make them strong and shock resistant. SuperCon multi-layered coating on the objective and ocular lenses and fully-coated optics throughout increase light transmission. World Class Riflescopes are waterproof, fogproof and shock proof.

## TITAN RIFLESCOPES

Titan 30mm riflescopes feature multi-coated lenses, finger adjustable windage and elevation controls and a fast-focus eyepiece. Available with a 30/30 or German-style 4A reticle, the Titan is waterproof, fogproof and shockproof.

## TASCO RIFLESCOPES

| Model | Power | Objective Diameter | F.O.V. @ 100 Yd.s | Eye Relief (Inches) | Length | Weight | Prices |
|---|---|---|---|---|---|---|---|
| **TITAN** | | | | | | | |
| DWCP351050 | 3.5-10 | 50 | 30-10.5 | 3.75 | 13 | 17.1 | $191.95 |
| DWCP39X44 | 3-9 | 44 | 39-14 | 3.5 | 12.75 | 16.5 | 173.95 |
| T156X42N | 1.5-6 | 42 | 59-20 | 3.5 | 12 | 16.4 | 293.95 |
| T14526N4A | 1.5-6 | 42 | 59-20 | 3.5 | 12 | 16.4 | 293.95 |
| T14526N4A | 1.25-4.5 | 26 | 77.5-22 | 3.25 | 10.5 | 15.2 | 273.95 |
| T312X52N | 3-12 | 52 | 27-10 | 4.5 | 14 | 20.7 | 335.95 |
| T312X52N4A | 3-12 | 52 | 27—10 | 4.5 | 14 | 20.7 | 335.95 |
| T39X42N | 3-9 | 42 | 37-13 | 3.5 | 12.5 | 16 | 281.95 |
| T39X42N4A | 3-9 | 42 | 37-13 | 3.5 | 12.5 | 16 | 281.95 |
| **TARGET & VARMINT** | | | | | | | |
| VAR251042M | 2.5-10 | 42 | 35-9 | 3 | 14 | 19.1 | $ 89.95 |
| MAG624x40 | 6-24 | 40 | 17-4 | 3 | 16 | 19.1 | 113.95 |
| VAR624X42M | 6-24 | 42 | 13-3.7 | 7 | 16 | 19.6 | 113.95 |
| TG624X44DS | 6-24 | 44 | 15-4.5 | 3 | 16.5 | 19.6 | 199.95 |
| TG104050DS | 10-40 | 50 | 11-2.5 | 3.25 | 15.5 | 25.5 | 211.95 |
| TG832X44DS | 8-32 | 44 | 11-3.5 | 3.25 | 17 | 20 | 219.95 |
| **WORLD CLASS** | | | | | | | |
| BA1545X32 | 1.5-4.5 | 32 | 77-23 | 4 | 11.25 | 12 | $59.95 |
| DWC28X32 | 2-8 | 32 | 50-17 | 4 | 10.5 | 12.5 | 69.96 |
| DWC39X40N | 3-9 | 40 | 41-15 | 3.5 | 12.75 | 13 | 73.95 |
| WA39X40N | 3-9 | 40 | 41-15 | 3.5 | 12.75 | 13 | 73.95 |
| WA39X40STN | 3-9 | 40 | 41-15 | 3.5 | 12.75 | 13 | 73.95 |
| DWC39X50N | 3-9 | 40 | 41-13 | 3 | 12.5 | 15.8 | 87.95 |
| DWC39X40M | 3-9 | 40 | 41-15 | 3.5 | 12.75 | 13 | 73.95 |
| MAG312X40 | 2-12 | 40 | 26.5-7.3 | 3 | 14 | 18 | 95.95 |
| DWC416X40 | 4-16 | 40 | 22.5-5.9 | 3.7 | 14 | 16 | 103.95 |
| DWC416X50 | 4-16 | 50 | 28-7 | 3 | 16 | 20.5 | 123.95 |
| **PRONGHORN** | | | | | | | |
| PH39X40D | 3-9 | 40 | 39-13 | 3 | 13 | 12.1 | $47.95 |
| PH39X32D | 3-9 | 32 | 39-13 | 3 | 12 | 11 | 41.95 |
| PH4x32D | 4 | 32 | 32 | 3 | 12 | 11 | 32.95 |
| PH2533D | 2.5 | 32 | 43 | 3.2 | 11.4 | 10.1 | 31.95 |
| PH3950D | 3-9 | 50 | 33 | 3.3 | 13 | 14.8 | 57.95 |

# Tasco Riflescopes

### VARMINT/TACTICAL SCOPES

Long range shooting is easier with Tasco's True Mil-Dot system. SuperCon multi-layered lens coatings and fully coated optics throughout provide clear resolution. With extra large 42mm objectives, this line of Varmint riflescopes transmit more light than standard 40mm scopes.

### LER

Tasco's new LER (Long Eye Relief) combines a lightweight, compact scope with illuminated technology (IT) to make these riflescopes perfect for rifles, shotgun, black powder, slug and brush. Available in fixed 4 power and variable 1.5 to 6 power.

### MAG IV RIFLESCOPES

The large 40mm objective of MAG IV riflescopes delivers a full four times magnification with more zooming range than most variable scopes. In addition, a focusing objective provides valuable parallax correction. MAG IV scopes feature 1/4-minute windage/elevation click stops and black matte finish. The result is a line of scopes that provide superior light transmission and clarity even at high magnifications. Waterproof, fogproof and shockproof.

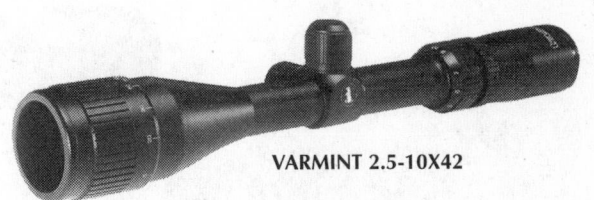

VARMINT 2.5-10X42

LER4X32

3-12X40

## TASCO RIFLESCOPES

| MODEL | POWER | OBJECTIVE DIAMETER | F.O.V. @ 100 YD.S | EYE RELIEF (INCHES) | LENGTH | WEIGHT | PRICES |
|---|---|---|---|---|---|---|---|
| **.22 RIFLESCOPES** | | | | | | | |
| MAG39X32D | 3-9 | 32 | 17.75-6 | 3 | 12.75 | 11.3 | 55.95 |
| MAG38X32SD | 3-9 | 32 | 17.75-6 | 3 | 12.75 | 11.3 | 55.95 |
| MAG4X32SD | 4 | 32 | 13.5 | 3 | 12.25 | 12.1 | 43.95 |
| MAG4X32STD | 4 | 32 | 13.5 | 3 | 12.25 | 12.1 | 43.95 |
| **RIMFIRE** | | | | | | | |
| EZ01D | 1 | 20 | 35 | Unltd. | 4.75 | 2.5 | 17.95 |
| RF37X20D | 3-7 | 20 | 24 | 2.5 | 11.5 | 5.7 | 23.95 |
| RF4X15D | 4 | 15 | 20.5 | 2.5 | 11 | 4 | 7.95 |
| RF4X20WAD | 4 | 20 | 23 | 2.5 | 10.5 | 3.8 | 9.95 |
| **GOLDEN ANTLER** | | | | | | | |
| DMGA39X32T | 3-9 | 32 | 39-13 | 3 | 13.25 | 12.2 | 49.95 |
| DMGA4X32T | 4 | 32 | 32 | 3 | 12.75 | 11. | 37.95 |
| GA3940 | 3-9 | 40 | 41-15 | 3 | 12.75 | 13 | 57.95 |
| GA2532 | 2.5 | 32 | 43 | 3.2 | 11.4 | 10.1 | 43.95 |
| GA3932AGD | 3-9 | 32 | 39 | 3 | 13.25 | 12 | 43.95 |

# Trijicon Sights & Scopes
## Fiber-Optic

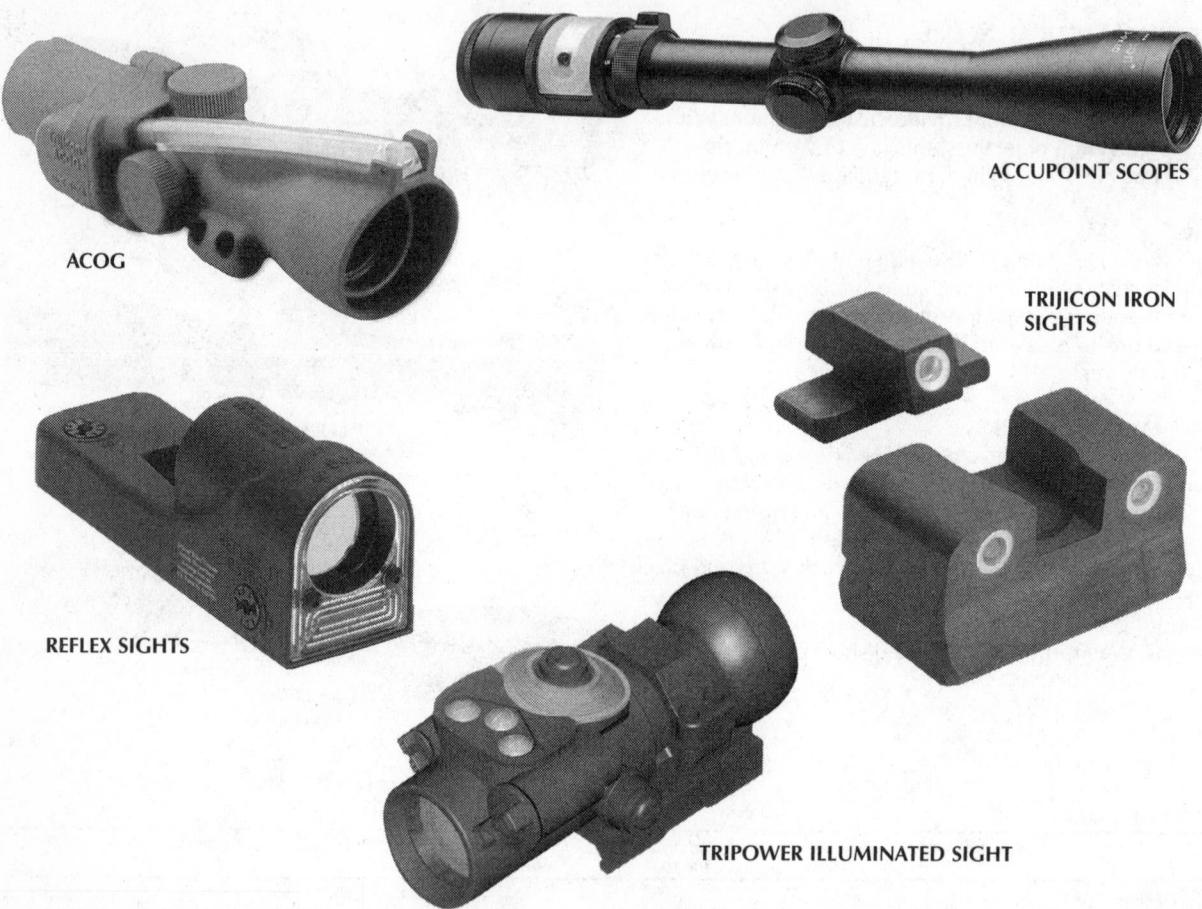

ACOG

ACCUPOINT SCOPES

TRIJICON IRON SIGHTS

REFLEX SIGHTS

TRIPOWER ILLUMINATED SIGHT

## ACOG

The ACOGs are internally-adjustable, compact telescopic sights with tritium illuminated reticle patterns for use in low light or at night. Many models are dual-illuminated, featureing fiber optics which collect ambient light for maximum brightness in day-time shooting. The ACOGs combine traditional, precise distance marksmanship with close-in aiming speed.

Prices:...........................$950 to 1672
Compact ACOG............................950

### Accupoint Scopes

AccuPoint's dual-illuminated aiming point offers a major advancement over crosshairs that can disappear due to lack of contrast when aiming at a dark animal, or in low-light conditions. Reticle illumination is supplied by advanced fiber optics or, in low-light conditions, by a self-contained tritium lamp.

Prices: 3-9x40, red or amber triangle ...........$720
    1.2-4x24, red or amber triangle...............700

## REFLEX SIGHTS

The dual-illuminated, Trijicon Reflex sight gives shooters next-generation technology for super-fast, any-light aiming-without batteries.

Developed for the military for use in both-eyes-open Close Quarters Battle (CQB) situations, the Reflex sight features an amber aiming dot or triangle that is illuminated both by light from the target area and from a tritium lamp.

Price: ..............................$350 to 599

## TRIJICON IRON SIGHTS

Trijicon self-luminous iron sights give shooters greater night fire accuracy-with the same speed as instinctive shooting. Trijicon Bright & Tough night sights are the first choice of major handgun manufacturers and standard issue with hundreds of municipal and county departments, numerous state and police departments and several Federal agencies.

Price: ..............................$99 to 119

## TRIPOWER ILLUMINATED SIGHT

The new TriPower features a red chevron-shaped reticle illuminated by three lighting sources: an integrated fiber optic system, a Tritium-Illuminated reticle and on-call battery backup. The TriPower has a 30mm tube, coated lenses, and is sealed for underwater use up to 100 feet. The TriPower is 5 inches long and weighs 6 oz.

Price:...................................550

# Weaver Scopes
## T-Series

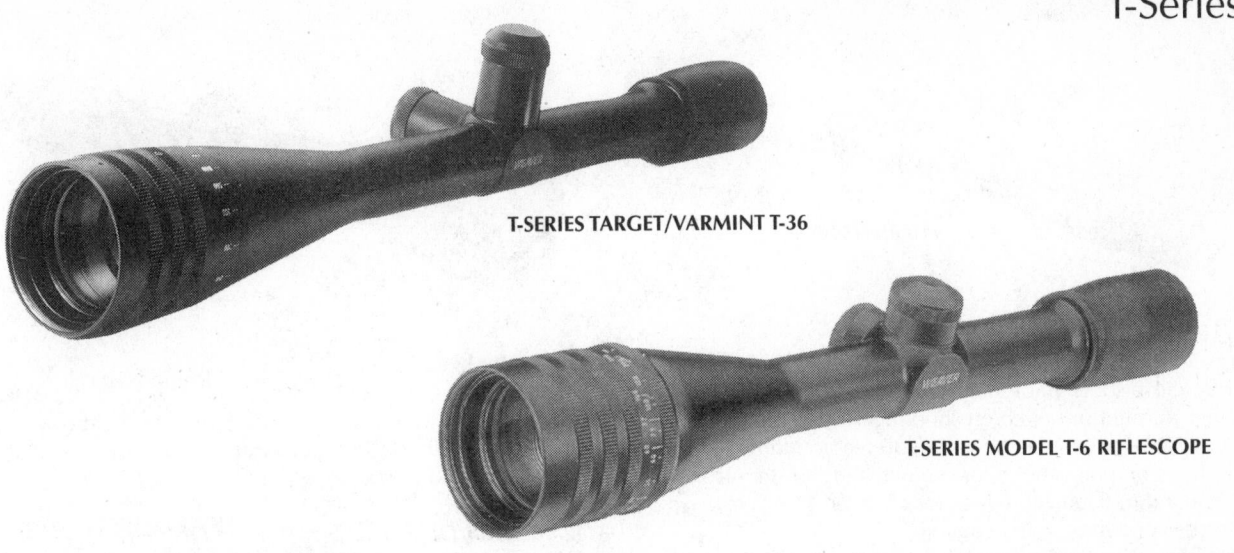

**T-SERIES TARGET/VARMINT T-36**

**T-SERIES MODEL T-6 RIFLESCOPE**

## T-SERIES TARGET/VARMINT T-36

You need high magnification for the greatest possible precision. Weaver's 36x gives it to you with patented Micro-Trac adjustments in a dual-spring, four-bearing housing that allows independent movement of windage and elevation. Optics are fully multi-coated, delivering premium image clarity in virtually all light conditions. An adjustable objective allows for parallax zero from 50' to infinity. Choice of fine crosshair or dot reticles. Scopes come with sunshade, an extra pair of oversize benchrest adjustment knobs, and screw-in metal lens caps.

*Model:* T-36 *Magnification/Objective:* 36X40mm *Field Of View:* 3.0' *Eye Relief:* 3.0" *Length:* 15.1" *Weight:* 16.7 oz. *Reticle:* 1/8 MOA Dot, Fine Crosshair *Finish:* Matte black or silver

Price: Matte . . . . . . . . . . . . . . . . . . . . . . . . . . . . . . $480
Silver or Matte Dot . . . . . . . . . . . . . . . . . . . . . . . . . 490
Silver Dot . . . . . . . . . . . . . . . . . . . . . . . . . . . . . . . . 500

## T-SERIES MODEL T-6 RIFLESCOPE

Weaver's T-6 competition 6x scope is only 12.7 inches long and weighs less than 15 ounces. All optical surfaces are fully multi-coated for maximum clarity and light transmission. The T-6 features Weaver's Micro-Trac precision adjustments in 1/8-minute clicks to ensure parallel tracking. The protected target-style turrets are a low-profile configuration combining ease of adjustment with weight reduction. A 40mm adjustable objective permits parallax correction from 50 feet to infinity without shifting the

point of impact. A special AO lock ring eliminates bell vibration or shift. The T-6 comes with screw-in metal lens caps and features a competition matte black finish.
Reticles: dot, Fine Crosshair
**Price: 6x40 Satin Black** . . . . . . . . . . . . . . . . . . . . . **$340**

## WEAVER TACTICAL SCOPES (NOT SHOWN)

These tactical scopes have a first-plane reticle, meaning the crosshair measurement maintains the same size relative to the size of the target at any power. The range-finding reticle of the Tactical scope is etched into the glass in front of the adjustment housing. At the center of the reticle is a small diamond that covers one inch outside. Marks beyond the diamond on the crosspieces can be used to bracket a target and determine range.

Tactical scopes have 1/8-minute-of-angle windage and elevation adjustments with target-style knobs. The knobs also offer a "guaranteed zero" feature that allows the shooter to move the reticle for a specific shooting need, then return the scope to zero without sighting in again. An adjustable objective lens is also included on the 4.5-14x44mm scope for precise parallax-free adjustments. All air-to-glass lens surfaces are fully multi-coated, and the scopes are waterproof to 10,000 feet and to 120 degrees with 100% humidity. Weaver's Tactical scopes are offered in black matte finish.
**Price: 4.5-14x44** . . . . . . . . . . . . . . . . . . . . . . . . . . . **540**
**Also: 3-9x40** . . . . . . . . . . . . . . . . . . . . . . . . . . . . . **480**

## SPECIFICATIONS

| MAGNIFICATION X OBJ. DIAM. (MM) | EXIT PUPIL (MM) | FOV (FT. @ 100 YDS.) | EYE RELIEF (IN.) | OVERALL LENGTH (IN.) | WEIGHT (OZ.) | RETICLE |
|---|---|---|---|---|---|---|
| 3-9x40 | 13.3-4.4 | 33-14.5 | 4.17-3.02 | 12.5 | 17.0 | Diamond |
| 4.5-14x44 | 10-3 | 22-9.4 | 4.1-2.8 | 15.2 | 20.6 | Diamond |

# Weaver Scopes

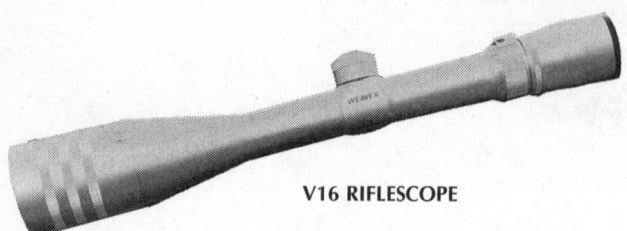

**V16 RIFLESCOPE**

**CLASSIC V9**

V16 Riflescopes

The V16 is popular for a variety of shooting applications, from close shots that require a wide field of view to long-range varmint or benchrest shooting. Adjustable objective allows a parallax-free view from 30 feet to infinity. Features one-piece tube for strength and moisture resistance and multicoated lenses for clear, crisp images. Two finishes and three reticle options.

*Magnification/Objective:* 4-16X42mm *Field Of View:* 26.8'-6.8' *Eye Relief:* 3.1" *Length:* 13.9" *Weight:* 16.5 oz. *Reticle:* Choice of Dual-X, 1/4 MOA Dot, or Fine Crosshair *Finish:* Matte black

| | |
|---|---|
| **Price:** | **$330** |
| **V24 6-24x42 (not shown) black matte** | **380** |
| **V24 6-24x42 with mil dot** | **400** |

## V10 (NOT SHOWN)

*Magnification/Objective:* 2-10X38mm *Field Of View:* 38.5-9.5 *Eye Relief:* 3.5" *Length:* 12.2" *Weight:* 11.2 oz. *Reticle:* Dual-X *Finish:* Matte black, silver

| | |
|---|---|
| **Price: Matte black** | **$210** |
| **Silver** | **210** |
| **In gloss black** | **210** |
| **V10x50 (2-10x50) Matte** | **280** |

## V9

*Magnification/Objective:* 3-9x38 *Field Of View:* 34-11' *Eye Relief:* 3.5" *Length:* 12" *Weight:* 11 oz. *Finish:* Matte black, gloss

| | |
|---|---|
| **Price: Matte black** | **$190** |
| **Gloss** | **190** |
| **V9XX50 (3-9x50) Matte** | **240** |

## V3 (NOT SHOWN)

*Magnification/Objective:* 1-3x20 *Field Of View:* 100x34 *Eye Relief:* 3.5" *Length:* 9" *Weight:* 9 oz. *Finish:* Matte black

| | |
|---|---|
| **Price: Matte black** | **$190** |

**CLASSIC HANDGUN 1.5-4X20**

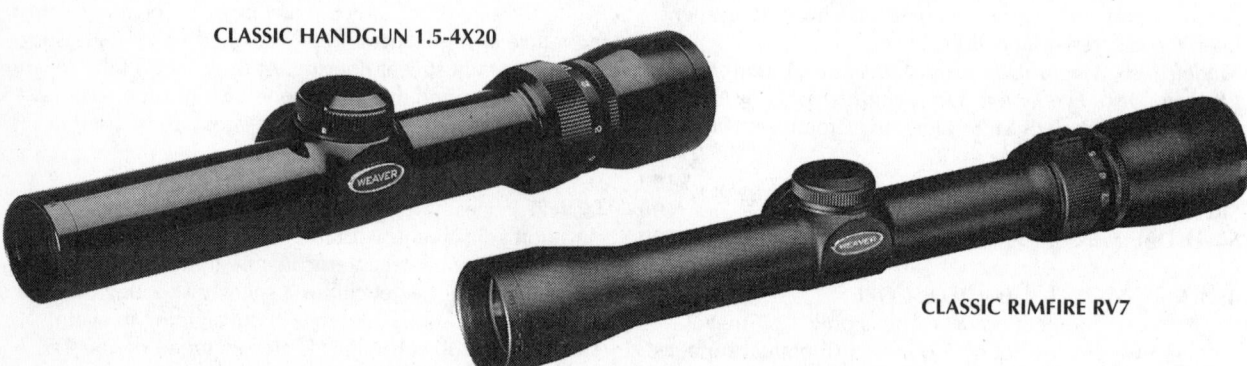

**CLASSIC RIMFIRE RV7**

## WEAVER CLASSIC HANDGUN SCOPES

Fixed-power scopes include 2x28 and 4x28 scopes in gloss black or silver. Variables in 1.5-4x20 and 2.5-8x28 come with a gloss black finish. The 2.5-8x28 is also available in black matte. One-piece tubes, fully multi-coated lenses and generous eye relief (4-29") make these scopes top performers on hunting handguns.

| | |
|---|---|
| **Prices: 2x28** | **$190** |
| **4x28** | **200** |
| **1.5-4x20** | **250** |
| **2.5-8x28** | **260** |
| **2.5-8x28 matte** | **260** |

## CLASSIC RIMFIRE RV7

Lenses are multi-coated for bright, clear low-light performance and the one-piece tube design is shockproof and waterproof.

| | |
|---|---|
| **Prices:** | |
| **2.5-7x28 Rimfire Matte** | **$160** |
| **2.5-7x28 Rimfire Silver** | **160** |

## RIMFIRE SCOPE RV4 (NOT SHOWN)

This fixed 4x scope is ideal for a variety of shooting applications. It's durable, light-weight and waterproof.

| | |
|---|---|
| **Prices:** | |
| **Rimfire Matte Black 4x28** | **150** |

**GRAND SLAM SCOPE
6-20X40**

**SILVER GRAND SLAM**

## WEAVER GRAND SLAM SCOPES

The Grand Slam series features Weaver's best optics, with an advanced one-piece tube design. A "sure-grip" power ring and AO adjustment let you easily adjust the variable scopes, even while wearing heavy gloves. An offset parallax indicator lets you remain in shooting position while adjusting the scope. The eyepiece has a fast-focus adjustment ring. Simply rotate the ring until the reticle becomes sharp.

Grand Slam configurations include: 4.75x40mm, a fixed-power scope with sufficient magnification for longer shots, yet a wide field of view for finding running game close in; 1.5-5x32mm, the ideal scope for short-range rifles and fast target acquisition in brushy country; 3.5-10x40mm, the traditional choice of big-game hunters for short- or long-range shooting; 3.5-10x50mm, which provides the brightest view in low-light situations; 4.5-14x40mm AO, possibly the most versatile Grand Slam scope, with a low range suitable for stand hunting and high enough magnification for target shooting or varmint hunting; and 6-20x40mm AO, two target/varminter models.

Windage and elevation knobs have target-type finger adjustments so 1/4-MOA adjustments can be made by gripping the rim of the knob between the thumb and index finger. The Grand Slam scopes are also equipped with Micro-Trac, Weaver's patented four-point adjustment system.

All Grand Slam scopes are offered with a plex reticle (except the 6-20x model, which is offered with a choice of Weaver's Varminter reticle or fine crosshairs with a dot). The scopes have a non-glare black matte or silver and black finish, featuring the new green and gold oval Weaver logo medallion on the scope saddle and green ring inside the objective lens hood.

**Price: 6-20x40 AO** . . . . . . . . . . . . . . . . . . . . . . . . . . . **$420**
**4.5-14x40 AO** . . . . . . . . . . . . . . . . . . . . . . . . . . . . . . . 400
**3.5-10x50** . . . . . . . . . . . . . . . . . . . . . . . . . . . . . . . . . . 390
**3-10x40** . . . . . . . . . . . . . . . . . . . . . . . . . . . . . . . . . . . . 330
**1.5-5x32** . . . . . . . . . . . . . . . . . . . . . . . . . . . . . . . . . . . 350
**4.75x40** . . . . . . . . . . . . . . . . . . . . . . . . . . . . . . . . . . . . 300

**CLASSIC 2.5 2.5X20MM**

## WEAVER CLASSIC K SERIES

Classic American scopes, the K2.5, K4 and K6 now have a sleeker look. They weigh less but deliver brighter images than ever before. New logos distinguish these versatile hunting scopes at a glance. Reasonably priced and great values, K scopes–including the target model, KT-15–have one-piece tubes.

**Prices: KT-15 (15x40 gloss)** . . . . . . . . . . . . . . . . . . . . **$330**
**K6 (gloss)** . . . . . . . . . . . . . . . . . . . . . . . . . . . . . . . . . . 160
**K6 (matte)** . . . . . . . . . . . . . . . . . . . . . . . . . . . . . . . . . . 160
**K4 (gloss)** . . . . . . . . . . . . . . . . . . . . . . . . . . . . . . . . . . 150
**K4 (matte)** . . . . . . . . . . . . . . . . . . . . . . . . . . . . . . . . . . 150
**K2.5 (2.5x20 gloss)** . . . . . . . . . . . . . . . . . . . . . . . . . . . 150

**SIGHTS & SCOPES**

# Williams Sights
## FP Series

The "Foolproof" series of aperture sights have internal micrometer adjustments with positive internal locks. The alloy used to manufacture this sight has a tensile strength of 85,000 pounds. Yet, the FP is light and compact, weighing only 1½ ounces. Target knobs are available on all models.

Prices:

For most models. . . . . . . . . . . . . . . . . . . . . . . . . . . . $70

With target knobs . . . . . . . . . . . . . . . . . . . . . . . . . 82

**FP-GR-TK
ON REMINGTO 581**

**FP-KNIGHT-TK
SILVER ON MK-85**

**FP-AG-TK
ON BEEMAN
AIR RIFLE**

**FP-94 SE SHOWN ON
WINCHESTER
94 SIDE EJECT**

**FP MINI-14-TK
WITH SUB-BASE**

## FP RECEIVER SIGHT OPTIONS

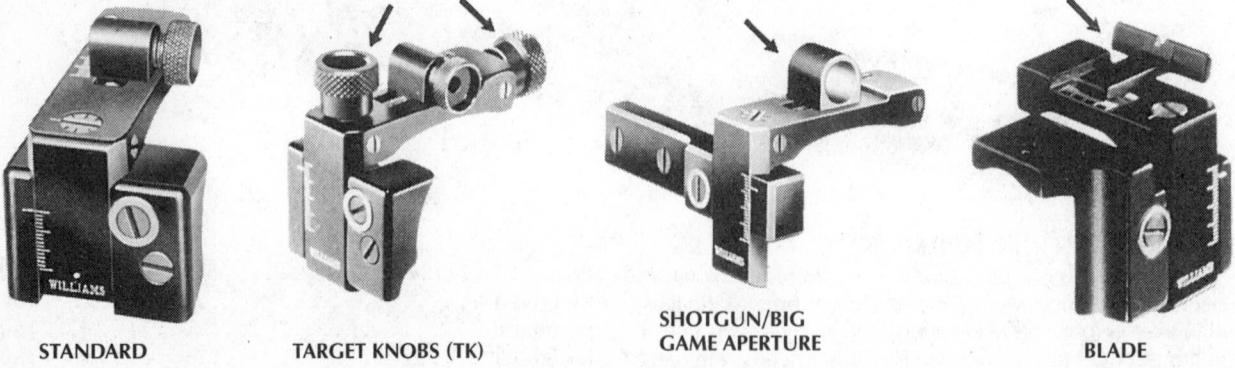

**STANDARD**

**TARGET KNOBS (TK)**

**SHOTGUN/BIG
GAME APERTURE**

**BLADE**

# Williams Sights
## Open Sights

### WGOS Series
• Made from high tensile strength aluminum. Will not rust.
• All parts milled - no stampings.
• Streamlined and lightweight with tough anodized finish.
• Dovetailed windage and elevation - Easy to adjust, positive locks.
• Interchangeable blades available in four heights and four styles.
**Price:** .................................$20-27

Blades are sold separately, except "U" blades are available installed on WGOS octagon T/C and CVA.
**Price:**.....................................$7

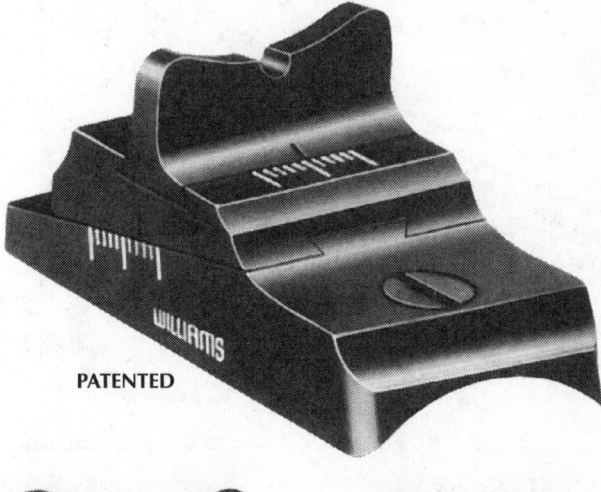

PATENTED

"SQ"

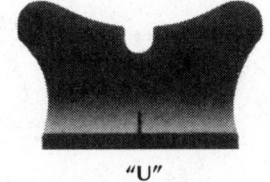

"U"

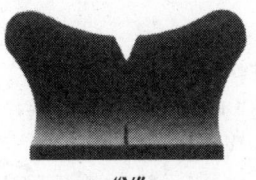

"V"

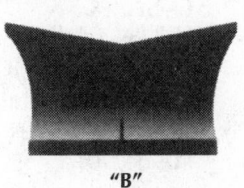

"B"

## Receiver Sights

### Military Sights
Open and aperture for:
• SKS (no drilling required)
• AK47 (no drilling required)
• **Mauser 96** ...........................$20-26

### WGRS Series
• Compact Low Profile
• Lightweight, Strong, Rustproof
• Positive Windage and Elevation Locks
In most cases these sights utilize dovetail or existing screws on top of the receiver for installation. They are made from an aluminum alloy that is stronger than many steels. Light. Rustproof. Williams quality throughout.
**Price: most models**.....................$35

### Fire Sights
Williams has introduced new "Fire Sights". These sights are machined from aircraft-strength aluminum and steel. This sight is lightweight, durable and brightens in low-light situations.
**Prices:**
**Pistol Fire Sight Sets**.......................$45
**Shotgun Fire Sight Sets** ............29 to 38
**Muzzleloader Fire Sight Sets** ........29 to 50
**Rifle Fire Sight Sets** ...............29 to 39
**Peep Sets** ........................40 to 81
**Rifle Beads**..............................18

WGRS-CVA ON CVA APOLLLO

"GHOST RING" SHOTGUN APERTURE AVAILABLE FOR WGRS RECEIVER SIGHTS. SOLD SEPARATELY.

FIRE SIGHTS

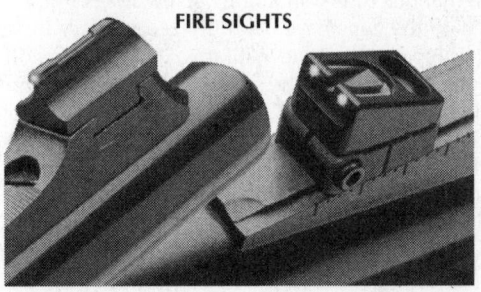

SIGHTS & SCOPES

# Williams Sights
## 5D Series

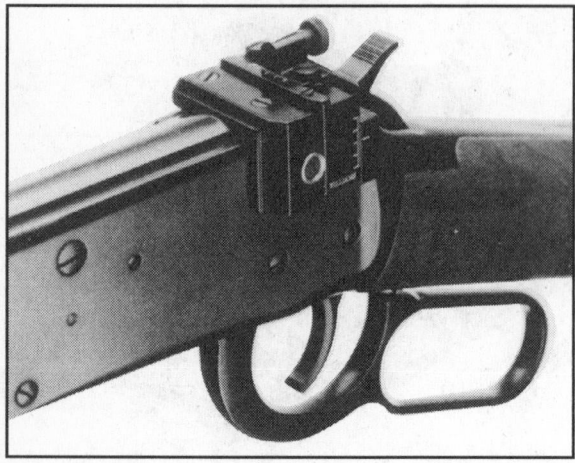

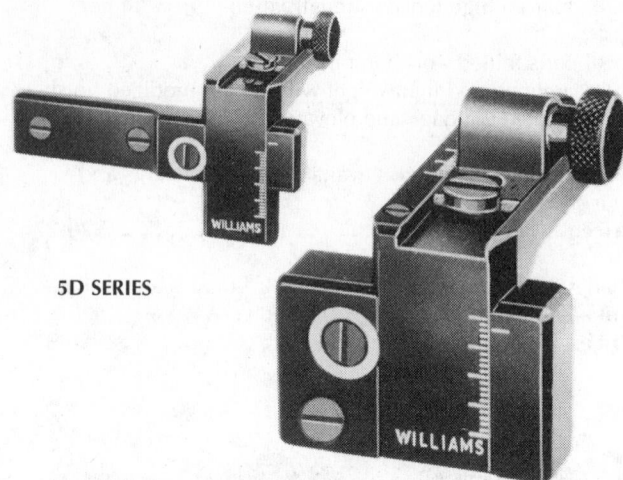

**5D SERIES**

### 5D SERIES
- FOR BIG GAME RIFLES, 22'S, SHOTGUNS
- POSITIVE WINDAGE AND ELEVATION LOCKS
- LIGHTWEIGHT, STRONG, ACCURATE
- WILLIAMS QUALITY THROUGHOUT - RUSTPROOF

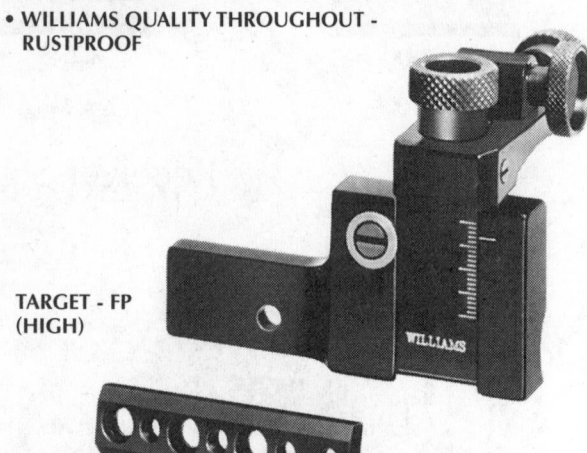

**TARGET - FP (HIGH)**

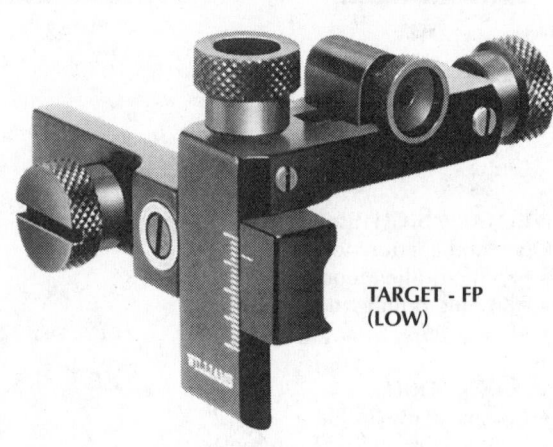

**TARGET - FP (LOW)**

Williams has offered the inexpensive, high-quality 5D sight for decades. Models are available for most popular rifles and shotguns. These sights have the strength, light weight, and neat appearance of the FP, without the micrometer adjustments. Designed for rugged hunting use, 5D sights offer unobstructed vision. No knobs or side plates to blot out shooter's field of vision. Wherever possible, the manufacturers' mounting screw holes in the receivers of the guns have been utilized for easy installation. The upper staff of the Williams 5D sight is readily detachable. Just loosen one screw. The angular bushing locks this upper staff. A set screw is provided as a stop screw so that the sight will return to absolute zero after reattaching. The Williams 5D sight is made of one of the highest grade alloys obtainable. Laboratory tests show that the material used has a tensile strength approximately 25% greater than mild steels.
**Price: Most 5D models. . . . . . . . . . . . . . . . . . . . . . $37**

### TARGET - FP (HIGH)
Adjustable From 1.250" to 1.750"
Above Centerline of Bore.
**Price:. . . . . . . . . . . . . . . . . . . . . . . . . . . . . . . . . $78**

### TARGET FP-ANSCHUTZ
Designed to fit many of the Anschutz Lightweight .22 Cal. Target and Sporter Models. No Drilling and Tapping required.
**Price:. . . . . . . . . . . . . . . . . . . . . . . . . . . . . . . . . $82**

### TARGET - FP (LOW)
Adjustable From .750" to 1.250"
Above Centerline of Bore.
**Price:. . . . . . . . . . . . . . . . . . . . . . . . . . . . . . . . . $78**

# XS Sight Systems

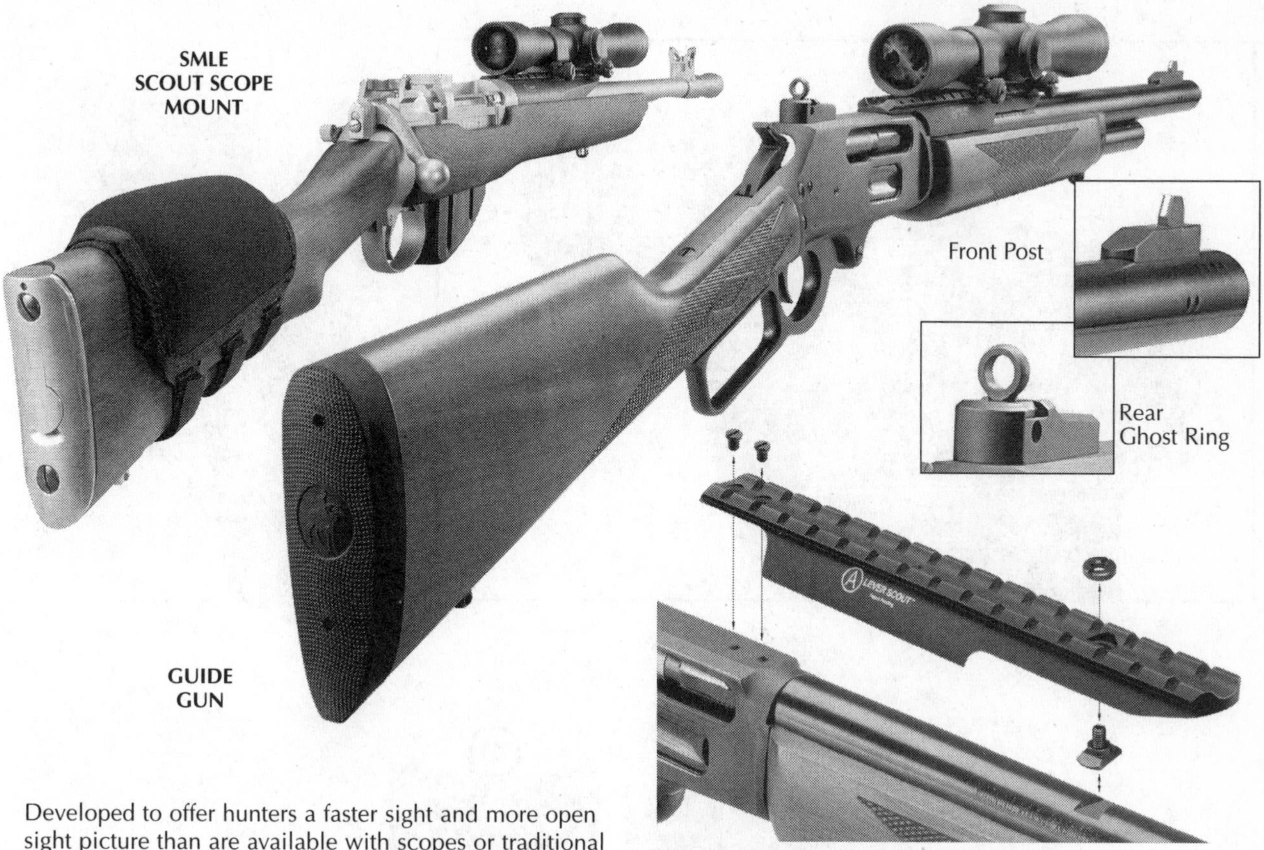

**SMLE SCOUT SCOPE MOUNT**

**GUIDE GUN**

Front Post

Rear Ghost Ring

**MOUNT INSTALLATION**

Developed to offer hunters a faster sight and more open sight picture than are available with scopes or traditional iron sights, XS models fit most popular hunting rifles and shotguns.

## XS SIGHT SYSTEMS GHOST-RING SIGHTS & LEVER SCOUT MOUNTS

• Scout Scope Mount with 8" long Weaver-style rail and cross slots on 1/2" Centers • Scope mounts 1/8" lower than previously possible on Marlin Lever Guns • Drop-in installation, no gunsmithing required • Installs using existing rear dovetail & front two screw holes on receiver • Allows fast target acquisition with both eyes open—better peripheral vision • Affords use of Ghost-Ring Sights with Scope dismounted • Recoil tested for even the stout 45/70 and .450 Loads • Available for Marlin Lever Models: 1895 Guide Series, new .450, .444P, the 336, and 1894.

**Price:. . . . . . . . . . . . . . . . . . . . . . . . . . . . . . . $50**
**XS Lever Scout Mount for**
**Win 94. . . . . . . . . . . . . . . . . . . . . . . . . . . . . . 55**

## XS GHOST-RING HUNTING SIGHTS

• Fully adjustable for windage & elevation • Available for most rifles, including blackpowder • Minimum gunsmithing for most installations; matches most existing mounting holes • Compact design, CNC machined from steel and heat treated • Perfect for low light hunting conditions and brush/timer hunting, offers minimal target obstruction.

**Price: AO Ghost-Ring Hunting Sight Set . . . . . . . . . $90**

## SMLE SCOUT SCOPE MOUNTS

• Offers Scout Scope Mount with 7" long Weaver style rail
• Requires no machining of barrel to fit—no drilling or tapping
• Tapered counter bore for snug fit of SMLE Barrels
• Circular Mount is final filled with Brownells Acraglass
**Price:**
**SMLE Scout Mount. . . . . . . . . . . . . . . . . . . . . . . . . $60**

.191    .230    .150    .218

## XS GHOST-RING HUNTING SIGHTS

• Fully adjustable for windage & elevation • Available for most rifles, including blackpowder • Minimum gunsmithing for most installations; matches most existing mounting holes • Compact design, CNC machined from steel and heat treated • Perfect for low light hunting conditions and brush/timer hunting, offers minimal target obstruction.

**Price: AO Ghost-Ring Hunting Sight Set . . . . . . . . . $90**

# XS Sight Systems

GLOCK 36
W/BIG DOT
TRITIUM

BIG DOT TRITIUM W/TRITIUM REAR

### SMLE SCOUT SCOPE MOUNTS
• Offers Scout Scope Mount with 7" long Weaver style rail
• Requires no machining of barrel to fit—no drilling or tapping
• Tapered counter bore for snug fit of SMLE Barrels
• Circular Mount is final filled with Brownells Acraglass
**Price:**
**SMLE Scout Mount**. . . . . . . . . . . . . . . . . . . . . . . . **$60**

### XS EXPRESS SIGHTS
Extremely Fast Front Sight using proven Express Sight Principles. Low profile Shallow V Express rear with white vertical line, front white dot available with or without Tritium. Machined steel sights in matte black finish. Rear sight available in different heights. Made for most pistols, and limited styles of revolvers. Rear available in double set-screw for most installations.
**Prices:**
**Big Dot Tritium Set**. . . . . . . . . . . . . . . . . . . . . . . . **$90**
**Standard Dot Tritium Set** . . . . . . . . . . . . . . . . . . . . . 90

### XS 24/7 EXPRESS SIGHTS
The original fast aacquisition sight. Now enhanced with new 24/7 tritium sight.

24/7 Express sights are the finest sights made for fast sight acquisition under any light conditions. Light or dark just "dot the i" and put the dot on the target.
• Enhances low light sight acquisition
• Improves Low Light accuracy
• Low profile, snag free design
• Available for most pistols
**Prices: XS 24/7 Big Dot Express Sets** . . . . . . . . . . . **$120**
**XS 24/7 Standard Dot Express Sets** . . . . . . . . . . . . . 120

### XS ADJUSTABLE EXPRESS SIGHT SETS
Incorporates Adjustable Rear Express Sight with a white stripe rear, or Pro Express Rear with a Vertical Tritium Bar, fits Bomar style cut, LPA style cut, or a Kimber Target cut rear sight. Affords same Express Sight principles as fixed sight models.
**Prices:**
**Adjustable Express w/White Stripe Rear and**
    **Big Dot Front or Standard Dot Front** . . . . . . . . . **$120**
**Adjustable Express w/White Stripe Rear and**
    **Big Dot Tritium or Standard Dot Tritium Front** . . . . 150
**Adjustable Pro Express w/Tritium Rear and Big**
    **Dot Tritium or Standard Dot Tritium Front** . . . . . . 150

# Zeiss Scopes

**CONQUEST 3.5-10X44 STAINLESS STEEL FINISH**

**CONQUEST 3-9X40**

## ZEISS CONQUEST SERIES RIFLESCOPES

The Conquest series has Zeiss' proprietary MC anti-reflective coating and is backed by a Lifetime Transferable Warranty. Couple this with Zeiss' world renowned low-light performance, new arsenic/lead-free glass technology, precision engineering, quick focus and constant eye relief design and you have one of the world's highest performance riflescope series.

## CONQUEST 3-9x40

The 3-9x40 Conquest is the most versatile scope in the series, featuring a 4-inch eye-relief with unique European quick focus and advanced internal design, enabling the widest windage/elevation adjustment to 64 inches. All this combined with a solid one-piece alloy body manufactured to German standards makes the 3-9x40 Conquest a practical hunting sight.

**Price: 3-9x40 MC** . . . . . . . . . . . . . . . . . . . . . . . **$500**
**Stainless** . . . . . . . . . . . . . . . . . . . . . . . . . . . . . . 530

## CONQUEST 3-9x40S (NOT SHOWN)

The 3-9x40S Conquest is designed to support sportsmen who demand a shotgun, airgun, or muzzleloader scope with heavy reticle. The 3-9x40S has the same glass and coating as the 3-9, with a safe 4-inch eye relief, etched glass reticle and one-piece alloy tube.

**Price: 3-9x40S** . . . . . . . . . . . . . . . . . . . . . . . . . . **$500**
**w/turkey reticle** . . . . . . . . . . . . . . . . . . . . . . . . . . 500

## CONQUEST 3.5-10x44

The 3.5-10x44 Conquest, designed to replace Zeiss' Diavari C 3-9x36, is superior in design and has all the standard Conquest features. Additionally, the 3.5-10x44 Conquest offers a 22-percent larger objective and a 66-inch windage/ elevation adjustment. Combine these features with a weight of just 14 oz., the 3.5-10x44 Conquest makes it suitable for general big game hunting.

**Price: 3.5-10x44 MC** . . . . . . . . . . . . . . . . . . . . . . **$650**
**Stainless** . . . . . . . . . . . . . . . . . . . . . . . . . . . . . . 680
**Target** . . . . . . . . . . . . . . . . . . . . . . . . . . . . . . . . 750

## CONQUEST 4.5-14x44 (NOT SHOWN)

The 4.5-14x44 Conquest offers the first turret-mounted parallax adjustment from Zeiss. The 64-inch windage/elevation adjustment coupled with the 25-foot to 8.3-foot field of view made the 4.5-14x44 Conquest the selection of choice. The objective clarity and light transmission exceeds most models that have larger objectives and provides for perfect balance without adding weight or requiring raised mounts. Conquest riflescopes are water- and fog-proof, are free of lead and arsenic, and are backed by Zeiss' lifetime transferable warranty.

**Price: 4.5-14x44 AO** . . . . . . . . . . . . . . . . . . . . . . **$750**
**w/crosshair reticle** . . . . . . . . . . . . . . . . . . . . . . . 750
**Stainless** . . . . . . . . . . . . . . . . . . . . . . . . . . . . . . 780
**Target** . . . . . . . . . . . . . . . . . . . . . . . . . . . . . . . . 850

## CONQUEST 6.5-20X50 MC (NOT SHOWN)

The latest addition to the Conquest line of riflescopes is the 6.5-20X50. Developed for the American long-range shooter, this riflescope is ideal for big game hunting, varmint shooting or competition at great distances. Equipped with a turret-mounted parallax adjustment, the new 6.5-20X50 eliminates the need for the shooter to take his eye off the target. The external target turret knobs have no caps to lose and make it easier to view the windage and elevation. The riflescope does not require high mounts, allowing for a compact rifle profile and low line of sight.

**Reticle:** Z Plex or Fine Crosshair **Eye Relief:** 3.5"
**F.O.V.:** 17.6'-5.8' at 100 yds. **Weight:** 21.5 oz.
**Price: Matte Black** . . . . . . . . . . . . . . . . . . . . . . . **$950**
**Stainless** . . . . . . . . . . . . . . . . . . . . . . . . . . . . . . 970

| SPECIFICATIONS | ZEISS CONQUEST 3-9x40 | ZEISS CONQUEST 3-9x40S | ZEISS CONQUEST 3.5-10x44 | ZEISS CONQUEST 4.5-14x44 | ZEISS CONQUEST 6.5-20x50AO |
|---|---|---|---|---|---|
| Magnification | 3-9x | 3-9x | 3.5-10x | 4.5-14X | 6.5-20X |
| Objective | 40 | 40 | 44 | 44 | 50 |
| Tube diameter | 1" | 1" | 1" | 1" | 1" |
| Field of View(ft.@100yards) | 11.01'-34' | 11.01'-34' | 11.61'-35.1' | 8.31'-24.99' | 17.6'-5.8' |
| Parallax (yards) | 100 | 50 | 100 | 30-Infinity | 50-Infinity |
| Exit Pupil (mm) | 13.3-4.4 | 13.3-4.4 | 12.57-4.4 | 9.7-3.14 | 7.7-2.5 |
| Eye Relief | 4" | 4" | 3.5" | 3.5" | 3.5" |
| Length | 13.15" | 13.15" | 12.7" | 13.86" | 15.6" |
| Weight | 15 oz. | 15 oz. | 15.8 oz. | 17.5 oz. | 21.5 oz. |
| MOA | 1/4 | 1/4 | 1/4 | 1/4 | 1/4 |

# Zeiss Scopes
## Zeiss Premuim Sports Optics

**1.1-4 X 24 T***

### DIAVARI 1.1-4 X 24 T* VM/V
- Compact riflescope with 108 ft. field of view at 1.1 power
- Extremely lightweight - ideal for safari rifles
- With illuminated varipoint reticle for fast target acquisition clearly visible also in critical lighting conditions
- Especially designed for running shots and hunting in heavy brush
- Available with bullet drop compensator
- Eye relief: 3.74 in.

**Price:** . . . . . . . . . . . . . . . . . . . . . . . . . . . . . . . . . **$1800**

**1.5-6 X 42 T***

### DIAVARI 1.5-6 X 42 T* VM/V
- Excellent choice for white-tail or moose hunter
- Compact and easy to handle
- Lightest scope of its class
- 72 ft. field of view - largest field of view in premium class
- Easy-grip adjustment knob
- Available with bullet drop compensator
- Eye relief: 3.54 in.

**Price:** . . . . . . . . . . . . . . . . . . . . . . . . . . . . . . . . . **$1350**
    **w/Varipoint, reticle** . . . . . . . . . . . . . . . . . . . . . . . . 1850
    **w/Varipoint 54 reticle** . . . . . . . . . . . . . . . . . . . . . 1900

### DIAVARI VM/V 3-9x42 T*

Over the years, the 3-9x power range has proven its staying power. It is still the favorite power range of North American hunters. The 42 mm objective, coupled with the Zeiss T* coat-ing, extends the hunting day. Whether the quarry is elk, Dall sheep or Boone and Crockett white-tail, the VM/V Diavari 3-9 x 42T* offers top quality and the right magnification.

| | |
|---|---|
| Power | 3-9x |
| Effective Objective Diameter (mm) | 30-42 |
| Exit Pupil Diameter (mm) | 10-4.7 |
| Twilight Factor | 8.5-18.4 |
| Field Of View At 100 Yards (feet) | 36-12.9 |
| Minimum Square Adjustment Range | |
| At 100 Yards (inch) | 49.7 |
| Eye Relief (inch) | 3.74 |
| Center Tube Diameter (inch) | 1 |
| Objective Bell Diameter (inch) | 1.89 |
| Length (inch) | 13.3 |
| Weight (ounces) | 15.2 |
| Parallax Free (yards) | 109.4 |
| Price: | $1200 |

**2.5-10 X 50 T***

### DIAVARI 2.5-10 X 50 T* VM/V

- High powered riflescope with superior twilight performance
- Light, compact with a wide field of view
- Available with an illuminated reticle
- Easy-grip adjustment knob
- Excellent choice for world-wide all-round hunting
- Available with bullet drop compensator
- Eye relief: 3.54 in.

| | |
|---|---|
| Price: | $1550 |
| w/illuminated reticle | 2000 |

**SIGHTS & SCOPES**

# Zeiss Scopes
## Zeiss Premuim Sports Optics

### DIAVARI VM/V 5-15x42 T*

Precise windage and elevation adjustments make the Diavari VM/V 5 - 15 x 42 T* the perfect companion for a target or varmint rifle. The rugged adjustment system pro- vides fast, accurate and repeatable adjustments. By align- ing the optical and mechanical axes, Zeiss ensures full range of adjustment.

Power . . . . . . . . . . . . . . . . . . . . . . . . . . . . . . . . . . 5-15x
Effective Objective Diameter (mm) . . . . . . . . . . . 42-42
Exit Pupil Diameter (mm) . . . . . . . . . . . . . . . . . 8.4-2.8
Twilight Factor . . . . . . . . . . . . . . . . . . 14.1-25.1
Field Of View At 100 Yards (feet) . . . . . . . . . . 23.7-7.8
Minimum Square Adjustment Range . . . . . . . . . . . . . . .
At 100 Yards (inch). . . . . . . . . . . . . . . . . . . . . . . . . 30

Eye Relief (inch). . . . . . . . . . . . . . . . . . . . . . . . . . 3.74
Center Tube Diameter (inch) . . . . . . . . . . . . . . . . . . . 1
Objective Bell Diameter (inch) . . . . . . . . . . . . . . . 1.89
Length (inch) . . . . . . . . . . . . . . . . . . . . . . . . . . . 13.3
Weight (ounces) . . . . . . . . . . . . . . . . . . . . . . . . . . 14
Parallax Free (yards) . . . . . . . . . . . . . . . . . . . . . 109.4
Price: . . . . . . . . . . . . . . . . . . . . . . . . . . . . . . . . $1500

### DIAVARI VM/V 3-12x56 T*

In the quiet haze of dawn or the fleeting light of sunset, a riflesope is put to the ultimate test. Under these conditions, the Diavari VM/V 3-12x56 T* excels. The patented Zeiss T* anti-reflection coating is designed to transmit the optimum percentage of light throughout the spectral range to take full advantage of your eye's sensitivity. Weighing in at 13.5 ounces, the VM/V 3-12x56 T* won't slow you down.

Power . . . . . . . . . . . . . . . . . . . . . . . . . . . . . . . . . 3-12x
Effective Objective Diameter (mm) . . . . . . . . . . 44.0-56
Exit Pupil Diameter (mm) . . . . . . . . . . . . . . . 14.7-4.7
Twilight Factor . . . . . . . . . . . . . . . . . . . . 8.5-25.9
Field Of View At 100 Yards (feet) . . . . . . . . . 37.5-10.4
Minimum Square . . . . . . . . . . . . . . . . . . . . . . . . . . . .
Adjustment Range . . . . . . . . . . . . . . . . . . . . . . . . . . .
At 100 Yards (inch) . . . . . . . . . . . . . . . . . . . . . . 36.7

Eye Relief (inch) . . . . . . . . . . . . . . . . . . . . . . . . . 3.54
Center Tube Diameter (inch) . . . . . . . . . . . . . . . . 1.18
Objective Bell Diameter (inch) . . . . . . . . . . . . . . 2.44
Length (inch). . . . . . . . . . . . . . . . . . . . . . . . . . 13.54
Weight (ounces) . . . . . . . . . . . . . . . . . . . . 17.8/16.8
Parallax Free (yards) . . . . . . . . . . . . . . . . . . . . 109.4
Price: . . . . . . . . . . . . . . . . . . . . . . . . . . . . . . . . $1500
  w/illuminated reticle . . . . . . . . . . . . . . . . . . . $1900

**SIGHTS & SCOPES**

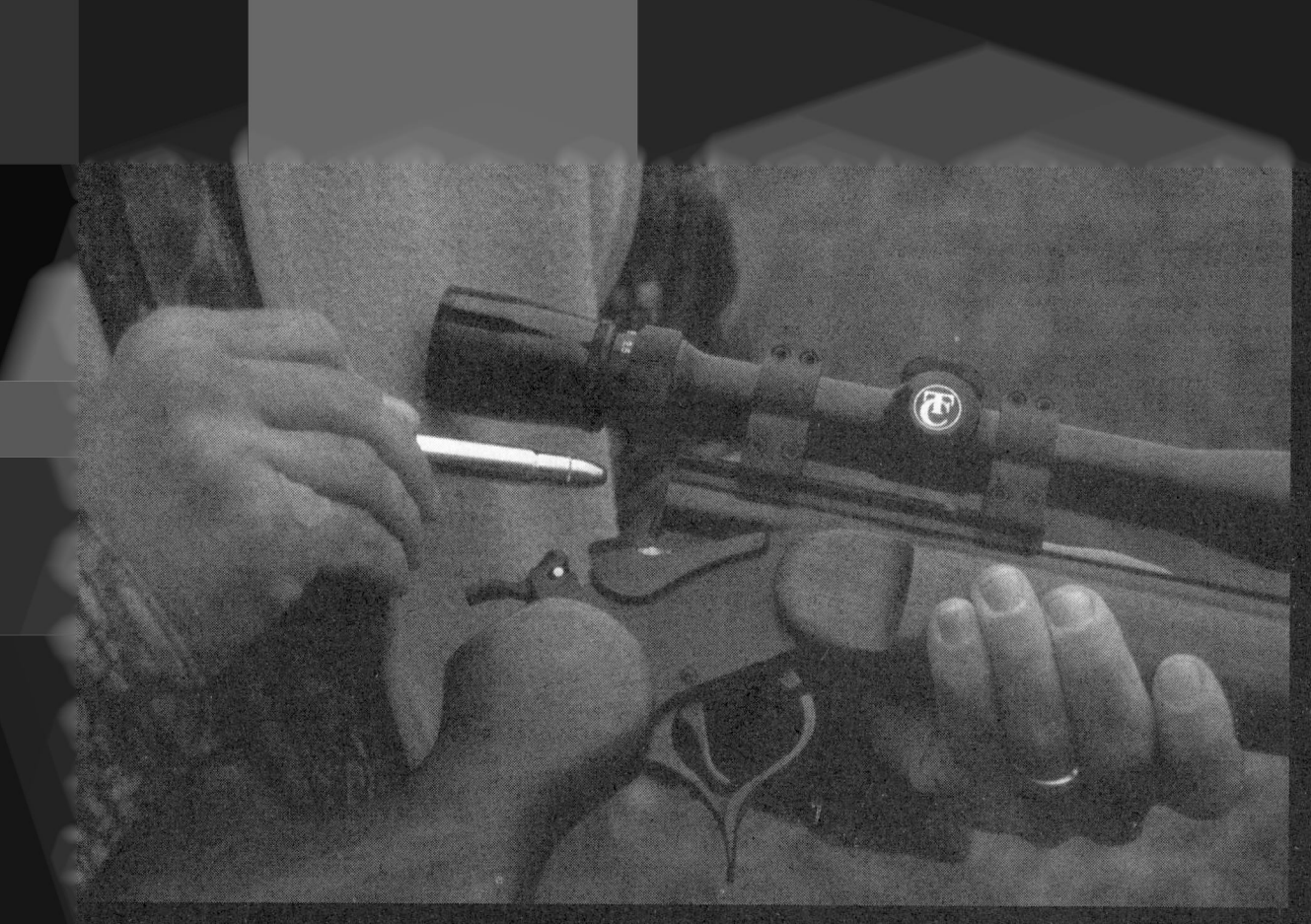

AMMUNITION

# Black Hills Ammunition

Noted for varmint and tactical ammo, Black Hills has expanded its big game hunting line to include softpoint offerings beginning with the .223 loaded with 60-grain Nosler Partition bullets. Velocity is 3150 fps from a 24-inch barrel. You'll also find a broad selection in the Black Hills Gold big game series. The .25-06 comes with 100-grain Nosler Ballistic Tips and 115-grain Barnes X-Bullets. Get 140-grain Ballistic Tips and X-Bullets in 7mm Remington Magnum cartridges. Another offering at Black Hills augments the Cowboy line, which includes modern and traditional rounds from the .32 H&R to the .45-70. The latest entry is a .38-55 with 255-grain lead bullets at 1250 fps.

Black Hills, offers an expanding line of factory-new and remanufactured ammunition for handguns and rifles. The Cowboy Action Line includes loads for the .32 H+R, .357 Magnum, .38-40, .44-40, .45 Colt, .32-20, .44 Colt, .44 Spl., .45 Schofield, .38 Spl, .38 Long Colt, .44 Russian, .45-70. Modern handgun ammunition, from .40 S+W to .44 Magnum, features a variety of bullet types. Black Hills rifle cartridges include the popular .223, .308, 6.5-284, .300 Win. Mag, and the potent long-range tactical round, the .338 Lapua. There's also specialty ammo, with frangible or moly-coated bullets. Black Hills Gold hunting rounds are available in 243 Win, 270 Win, 308 Win, 30-06, and 300 Win Mag.

# Brenneke USA Cartridges

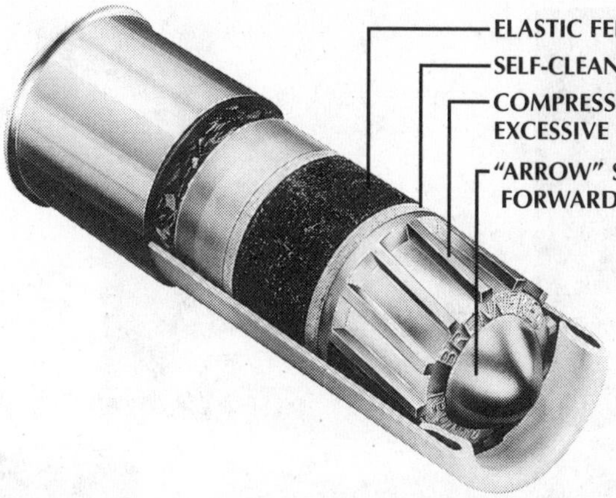
ELASTIC FELT WAD FOR OPTIMUM GAS PRESSURE RISE
SELF-CLEANING WAD PREVENTS LEAD BUILD-UP IN BORE
COMPRESSIBLE GUIDING RIBS PREVENT EXCESSIVE PRESSURE ON THE MUZZLE
"ARROW" STABILIZATION PROVIDED BY FORWARD CENTER OF GRAVITY

**The Original Brenneke has been the standard against which other slugs have been measured for 100 years.**

## Specifications

| Brenneke USA Load | Barrel | Distance (yds) | Velocity (ft./sec.) | Energy (ft./lbs.) | Trajectory (in) |
|---|---|---|---|---|---|
| SuperSabot 12 GA | Rifled only | Muzzle | 1407 | 2157 | -2.0 |
| 2¾" | | 25 | 1274 | 1770 | +0.4 |
| 1⅛oz | | 50 | 1165 | 1478 | +1.6 |
| | | 75 | 1080 | 1272 | +1.1 |
| | | 100 | 1017 | 1127 | -1.3 |
| SuperSabot 12 GA | Rifled only | Muzzle | 1526 | 2536 | -2.0 |
| 3" | | 25 | 1376 | 2064 | +0.2 |
| 1⅛ oz | | 50 | 1248 | 1697 | +1.2 |
| | | 75 | 1144 | 1426 | +0.9 |
| | | 100 | 1065 | 1236 | -1.1 |
| K.O. Sabot 12 GA | Smooth or rifled | Muzzle | 1509 | 2184 | -2.0 |
| 2¾" | | 25 | 1344 | 1733 | +0.3 |
| 1 oz | | 50 | 1206 | 1395 | +1.3 |
| | | 75 | 1101 | 1162 | +0.9 |
| | | 100 | 1024 | 1007 | -1.3 |
| K.O. Sabot 12 GA | Smooth or rifled | Muzzle | 1673 | 2686 | -2.0 |
| 3" | | 25 | 1487 | 2122 | +0.0 |
| 1 oz | | 50 | 1325 | 1685 | +1.0 |
| | | 75 | 1191 | 1361 | +0.7 |
| | | 100 | 1090 | 1139 | -1.1 |
| Super Magnum 12 GA | Rifled only | Muzzle | 1502 | 3014 | -2.0 |
| 3" | | 25 | 1295 | 2241 | +0.4 |
| 1⅜ oz | | 50 | 1136 | 1724 | +1.6 |
| | | 75 | 1030 | 1418 | +1.0 |
| | | 100 | 955 | 1219 | -1.5 |
| Black Magic | Smooth or rifled | Muzzle | 1502 | 3014 | -2.0 |
| Magnum 12 GA | | 25 | 1295 | 2241 | +0.4 |
| 3" | | 50 | 1136 | 1724 | +1.6 |
| 1⅜ oz | | 75 | 1030 | 1418 | +1.0 |
| | | 100 | 955 | 1219 | -1.5 |
| Magnum 20 GA | Smooth or rifled | Muzzle | 1476 | 2120 | -2.0 |
| 3" | | 25 | 1322 | 1701 | +0.4 |
| 1 oz | | 50 | 1193 | 1385 | +1.5 |
| | | 75 | 1094 | 1165 | +1.2 |
| | | 100 | 1022 | 1016 | -1.0 |
| K.O. 12 GA | Smooth or rifled | Muzzle | 1600 | 2491 | -2.0 |
| 2¾" | | 25 | 1377 | 1845 | +0.3 |
| 1 oz | | 50 | 1199 | 1399 | +1.5 |
| | | 75 | 1072 | 1118 | +1.2 |
| | | 100 | 987 | 948 | -1.0 |
| Heavy Field Short | Smooth or rifled | Muzzle | 1476 | 2538 | -2.0 |
| Magnum 12 GA | | 25 | 1310 | 2000 | +0.4 |
| 2¾" | | 50 | 1174 | 1606 | +1.5 |
| 1¼oz | | 75 | 1075 | 1346 | +1.0 |
| | | 100 | 1002 | 1170 | -1.4 |
| Low Recoil | Smooth or rifled | Muzzle | 1246 | 1511 | -2.0 |
| 12 GA | | 25 | 1104 | 1186 | +0.7 |
| 2¾" | | 50 | 1009 | 991 | +1.6 |
| 1 oz | | 75 | 941 | 862 | +0.4 |
| | | 100 | 886 | 764 | -3.2 |
| Magnum .410 | Smooth or rifled | Muzzle | 1755 | 781 | -2.0 |
| 3" | | 25 | 1427 | 517 | +0.2 |
| ¼oz | | 50 | 1179 | 352 | +1.4 |
| | | 75 | 1025 | 266 | +1.0 |
| | | 100 | 930 | 219 | -1.4 |
| Buckshot | Smooth only | Muzzle | N.A. | | |
| 2¾" | | | | | |
| 1⅛ oz (9 pellets) | | | | | |

# Federal Ammunition

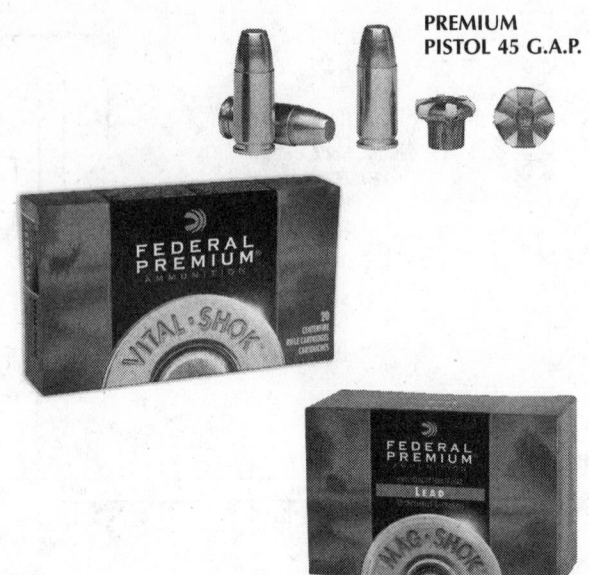

**PREMIUM PISTOL 45 G.A.P.**

Last year Federal overhauled its ammunition line and packaging. Shotgunners found Speed•Shok steel ammo in 12 and 20 gauge, with shot sizes from #7 to BB and Ultra•Shok shells with zinc-plated pellets, in 10, 12, 16 and 20 gauges, shot sizes #6 to T. Riflemen were introduced to Power•Shok cartridges from .243 to .300 Winchester Magnum, feature Speer Grand Slam bullets.

## PREMIUM MAG•SHOK TURKEY LOAD
### Features & Benefits
- High velocity provides increased downrange pellet energy and deep penetration
- Copper-plated extra hard shot for tight patterns
- Granulated plastic shot buffer cushions the shot for dense, uniform patterns
- Triple-Plus wad column provides positive gas sealing for uniform ballistics
- High base hull with high output 209A primer for consistant reliable ignition
- Portion of the proceeds from the sales go to the National Wild Turkey Federation

## ULTRA•SHOK - HEAVY HIGH VELOCITY
### Features & Benefits
- Increased shot payload with more downrange energy
- High velocity so it is quicker to target
- Three watertight seals at crimp, wad and primer
- High density shot cup prevents pellets from contacting bore surface
- High output 209A Primer provides consistent ballistic performance at all temperatures
- New box design
- Water resistant packaging

## PREMIUM PISTOL 45 G.A.P.
### Features & Benefits

- No hollowpoint to fill and block expansion, insuring consistent expansion through barriers
- Internally skived jacket gives consistent, symmetrical expansion with a large diameter
- Rubber front core performs well under a wide range of operating velocities and temperatures
- Works well in short barreled and standard barrel length handguns
- Low flash propellant for low light tactical use
- Reliable feed and function in semi-auto and automatic firearms

## PREMIUM RIFLE 300 WIN. SHORT MAGNUM
### Features & Benefits
- Designed for short action rifles
- Beltless high capacity case provides ballistics equal to the longer 300 Win Magnum
- Available with Trophy Bonded Bear Claw or Speer Grand Slam bullets

**Trophy Bonded Bear Claw:**
- 100% fusion bonded jacket and core
- 95% weight return
- Reliable expansion from 25 yards to extreme ranges
- Better penetration through bone and muscle with no fragmentation

**Speer Grand Slam:**
- Exclusive hot core process insures reliable expansion and penetration
- Excellent retained weight and flat trajectory

## AMERICAN EAGLE PISTOL
### Features & Benefits
- Gives price conscious customers top value for their money
- Federal brass for easy reloading
- Made in USA
- Quality components with reliable performance

AMMUNITION

# Federal Ammunition

## TROPHY BONDED BEAR CLAW®

This legendary Jack Carter design is ideal for medium to large dangerous game and is loaded exclusivly by Federal. The jacket and core are 100% fusion-bonded for reliable bullet expansion from 25 yards to extreme ranges. The bullet retains 95% of its weight, assuring deep penetration. The bullet jacket features a hard solid copper base tapering to a soft, copper nose section for controlled expansion.

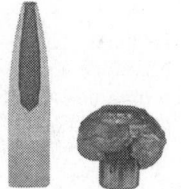

## TROPHY BONDED SLEDGEHAMMER®

Use it on the largest, most dangerous game in the world. This Jack Carter design maximizes stopping power and your confidence. It's a bonded bronze solid with a flat nose that minimizes deflection off bone and muscle for a deep, straight wound channel.

## SIERRA® GAMEKING® BOAT-TAIL

Long ranges are its specialty. With varying calibers, it's an excellent choice for everything from varmints to big game animals. The GameKings's tapered, boat-tail design provides extremely flat trajectories. The design also gives it a higher downrange velocity, so there's more energy at the point of impact. Reduced wind drift makes it a good choice for long-range shots.

## WOODLEIGH® WELDCORE

Safari hunters have long respected this bonded Australian bullet for its superb accuracy and excellent stopping power. Its special heavy jacket provides 80-85% weight retention. These bullets are favored for large or dangerous game.

## NOSLER® PARTITION®

This Nosler design is a proven choice for medium to large game animals. A partioned copper jacket allows the front half of the bullet to mushroom, while the rear core remains intact, driving forward for deep penetration and stopping power.

## NOSLER® BALLISTIC TIP®

With proven fast, flat-shooting wind-defying performance, it's specially designed for long-range shots at varmints, predators and small to medium game. A color-coded polycarbonate tip provides easy identification, prevents deformation in the magazine and drives back on impact for expansion and immediate energy transfer.

## SPEER® AFRICAN GRAND SLAM®

For big, dangerous game, you need a bullet that penetrates deep without excessive expansion. That's precisely the nature of our African Grand Slam bullet. A massive solid gilding metal jacket helps the bullet maintain its length and weight, while a "stop shoulder" prevents tip rollback. The Hot-Cor is firmly held by multi-lock serrations which help lock the core to the jacket.

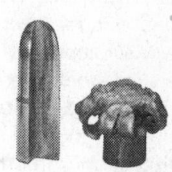

## SPEER® AFRICAN GRAND SLAM® SOLID

The African Grand Slam features a Tungsten-Carbide core to keep the weight up without making the bullet too long. A flat tip ensures stability and straight line penetration.

## SPEER® TNT®

Varmint hunters require two things from a bullet: tight groups and quick expansion. The Speer TNT gives you both. For rapid expansion, TNT jackets are fluted more than 90% of their length and have a dead-soft lead core.

# Federal Ammunition

## POWER•SHOK CENTERFIRE RIFLE
### SOFT POINT

It's a proven performer on small game and thin-skinned medium game. It has an aerodynamic tip for a flat trajectory. The exposed soft point expands rapidly for hard hits, even as velocity slows at longer ranges.

### SOFT POINT ROUND NOSE

For generations, hunters have made this bullet the choice for deer and bear in heavy cover. Its large exposed tip, good weight retention and specially tapered jacket provide controlled expansion for deep penetration.

### SOFT POINT FLAT NOSE

This is the bullet hunters traditionally choose when headed into thick cover. It expands reliably and penetrates deep on light to medium game. The flat nose prevents accidental discharge in tubular magazines.

### SPEER® GRAND SLAM®

An excellent all-around choice for medium to large game. When hunting both woods and clearings, you need a bullet that handles any situation. The Speer Grand Slam features a slim profile, yet thicker metal on the jacket's shank and internal flutes at the bullet's tip. This gives you flat shooting capability, a tip that mushrooms perfectly on impact and a bullet that stays in one piece.

### FULL METAL JACKET BOAT-TAIL

These accurate, non-expanding bullets give you a flat shooting trajectory, leave a small exit hole in game, and puts clean holes in paper - great for sharpening your shooting eye. And they're famous for smooth, reliable feeding into semi-automatics too.

## HANDGUN BULLET STYLES
### LEAD ROUND NOSE

A great economical training round for practicing at the range. It dates back to the early part of this century. This bullet is 100% lead with no jacket. It provides excellent accuracy and is very economical.

### FULL METAL JACKET

A good choice for range practice and reducing lead fouling in the barrel. The jacket extends from the nose to the base, preventing bullet expansion and barrel leading. It is used primarily as military ammunition and for recreational shooting.

### HI-SHOK® JACKETED SOFT POINT

It's a proven performer on small to medium-sized game.

### LEAD SEMI-WADCUTTER

The most popular all-around choice for target and personal defense. a versatile design which cuts clean holes in targets and efficiently transfers energy.

### JACKETED HOLLOW POINT

It's an ideal personal defense round in revolvers and semi-autos. Creates quick, positive expansion with proven accuracy. Specially designed jacket ensures smooth feeding into autoloading firearms.

### SEMI-WADCUTTER HOLLOW POINT

A good combination for both small game and personal defense. Hollow point design promotes uniform expansion.

## PREMIUM® HANDGUN BULLET STYLES
### HYDRA-SHOK®

The choice of law enforcement agencies nationwide. Federal's unique center-post design delivers controlled expansion, and the notched jacket provides efficient energy transfer to penetrate barriers while retaining stopping power. The deep penetration of this jacketed bullet satisfies even the FBI's stringent testing requirements.

### PREMIUM® PERSONAL DEFENSE®

We hope you never have to use our Premium Personal Defense ammunition in a critical situation. But, if you do, you'll appreciate the increased muzzle velocity and energy compared to standard loads, and the rapid bullet expansion that delivers instant stopping power. You'll also appreciate that recoil is significantly reduced. In addition, our unique clear packaging lets you see the ammo before you open the box.

### PREMIUM EXPANDING FULL METAL JACKET

An ideal choice for agencies that don't permit hollow point ammunition, this revolutionary barrier-penetrating design combines a scored metal nose over an internal rubber tip that collapses on impact. It never fills with barrier material and assures expansion on every shot. A lead core at the base maintains weight retension.

### CASTCORE

Premium CastCore gives you a heavyweight, flat nosed, hard cast-lead bullet that smashes through bone, without breaking apart.

### TROPHY BONDED BEAR CLAW

The Trophy Bonded Bear Claw handgun bullet has a fusion-bonded jacket and core for up to 95% weight retention, better penetration and more knockdown power.

AMMUNITION

# Fiocchi Ammunition

Known for its shotshells and .22 rimfire ammunition, Fiocchi also markets centerfire pistol and rifle cartridges. This Italian firm has been in business since 1876.

Fiocchi Target Loads offer you many choices to suit the shell to your game: Standard 1⅛-ounce loads for everything from registered trap and skeet to sporting clays. One-ounce loads that deliver superior performance with less recoil than a comparable 1⅛-ounce load. Also, a ⅞-ounce training load for new or recoil sensitive shooters. Fiocchi lilac-colored hulls are fully reloadable.

| STOCK # | | GAUGE | SHELL LENGTH | DRAM. EQUIV. | MUZZLE VELOCITY | SHOT OZ. | SHOT SIZES | RDS./BOX | SHOT TYPE |
|---|---|---|---|---|---|---|---|---|---|
| **STEEL (WATERFOWL LOADS)** | | | | | | | | | |
| 1235ST | Speed Steel | 12 | 3 1/2" | Max. | 1520 | 1 3/8 | T BBB BB 1 2 | 25 | Treated Steel |
| 1235SH | Heavy Steel | 12 | 3 1/2" | Max. | 1470 | 1 9/16 | T BBB BB 1 | 25 | Treated Steel |
| 123ST | Speed Steel | 12 | 3" | Max. | 1475 | 1 1/8 | BBB BB 1 2 3 4 | 25 | Treated Steel |
| 123S | Steel | 12 | 3" | Max. | 1320 | 1 1/4 | T BBB BB 1 2 3 4 | 25 | Treated Steel |
| 123SH | Heavy Steel | 12 | 3" | Max. | 1300 | 1 3/8 | 2 3 4 | 25 | Treated Steel |
| 12S78 | Training Load | 12 | 2 3/4" | Max. | 1440 | 7/8 | 7 | 25 | Treated Steel |
| 12S1OZ | Upland Steel | 12 | 2 3/4" | Max. | 1400 | 1 | 4 6 7 | 25 | Treated Steel |
| 12S118 | Steel | 12 | 2 3/4" | Max. | 1375 | 1 1/8 | BB 1 2 3 4 6 | 25 | Treated Steel |
| 12S114 | Heavy Steel | 12 | 2 3/4" | Max. | 1275 | 1 1/4 | 2 3 4 | 25 | Treated Steel |
| 20S | Upland Steel | 20 | 2 3/4" | Max. | 1470 | 3/4 | 3 4 6 7 | 25 | Treated Steel |
| 203ST | Speed Steel | 20 | 3" | Max. | 1500 | 7/8 | 2 3 4 | 25 | Treated Steel |
| **FIELD LOADS (UPLAND GAME LOADS)** | | | | | | | | | |
| 12HF | Heavy Field | 12 | 2 3/4" | 3 1/4 | 1225 | 1 1/4 | 6 7-1/2/ 8 9 | 25 | Lead |
| 12FLD | Field Load | 12 | 2 3/4" | 3 1/4 | 1255 | 1 1/8 | 6 7-1/2 8 9 | 25 | Lead |
| 16FLD | Field Load | 16 | 2 3/4" | 2 3/4 | 1185 | 1 1/8 | 6 7-12 8 | 25 | Lead |
| 20FLD | Field Load | 20 | 2 3/4" | 2 1/2 | 1165 | 1 | 6 7-1/2 8 9 | 25 | Lead |
| **DOVE LOADS** | | | | | | | | | |
| 12MS3 | Multi-Sport | 12 | 2 3/4" | 3 | 1250 | 1 | 7-1/2 8 9 | 25 | Lead |
| 12GT1 | Game & Target | 12 | 2 3/4" | 3 1/4 | 1290 | 1 | 6 7-1/2 8 9 | 25 | Lead |
| 12GT118 | Game & Target | 12 | 2 3/4" | 3 | 1200 | 1 1/8 | 7-1/2 8 | 25 | Lead |
| 16GT | Game & Target | 16 | 2 3/4" | 2 1/2 | 1165 | 1 | 7-1/2 8 9 | 25 | Lead |
| 20GT | Game & Target | 20 | 2 3/4" | 2 1/2 | 1210 | 7/8 | 7-1/2 8 9 | 25 | Lead |
| 28GT | Game & Target | 28 | 2 3/4" | 2 | 1200 | 3/4 | 8 9 | 25 | Lead |
| 410GT | Game & Target | 410 | 2 1/2" | Max | 1200 | 1/2 | 8 9 | 25 | Lead |
| **TARGET LOADS** | | | | | | | | | |
| 12TL | Target Light | 12 | 2 3/4" | 2 3/4 | 1150 | 1 | 7-1/2 8 8-1/2 9 | 25 | Hi-Antimony Lead |
| 12TH | Target Heavy | 12 | 2 3/4" | 3 | 1200 | 1 | 7-1/2 8 8-1/2 | 25 | Hi-Antimony Lead |
| 12TX | Little Rhino | 12 | 2 3/4" | HDCP | 1250 | 1 | 7-1/2 8 8-1/2 | 25 | Hi-Antimony Lead |
| 12CRSR | Crusher | 12 | 2 3/4" | Max | 1300 | 1 | 7-1/2 8 8-1/2 9 | 25 | Hi-Antimony Lead |
| 12LITE | Lite | 12 | 2 3/4" | 2 7/8 | 1165 | 1 1/8 | 7-1/2 8 9 | 25 | Hi-Antimony Lead |
| 12VIPL | VIP Light | 12 | 2 3/4" | 2 3/4 | 1150 | 1 1/8 | 7-1/2 8 9 | 25 | Hi-Antimony Lead |
| 12VIPH | VIP Heavy | 12 | 2 3/4" | 3 | 1200 | 1 1/8 | 7-1/2 8 9 | 25 | Hi-Antimony Lead |
| 12WRNO | White Rhino | 12 | 2 3/4" | HDCP | 1250 | 1 1/8 | 7-1/2 8 8-1/2 9 | 25 | Hi-Antimony Lead |
| 1278OZ | Training Load | 12 | 2 3/4" | 3 | 1200 | 7/8 | 7-1/2 8 | 25 | Hi-Antimony Lead |
| 12IN24 | International | 12 | 2 3/4" | Max | 1350 | 24 grams | 7-1/2 8 9 | 25 | Hi-Antimony Lead |
| **SUB-GAUGE** | | | | | | | | | |
| 20VIP | VIP | 20 | 2 3/4" | 2 1/2 | 1200 | 7/8 | 7-1/2 8 9 | 25 | Hi-Antimony Lead |
| 28GT | Game & Target | 28 | 2 3/4" | 2 | 1200 | 3/4 | 8 9 | 25 | Lead |
| 28HV | High Velocity | 28 | 2 3/4" | 2 1/4 | 1300 | 3/4 | 6 7-1/2 8 9 | 25 | Lead |
| 410GT | Game & Target | 410 | 2 1/2" | Max | 1200 | 1/2 | 8 9 | 25 | Lead |
| **HIGH VELOCITY** | | | | | | | | | |
| 12HV | High Velocity | 12 | 2 3/4" | 3 3/4 | 1330 | 1 1/4 | 4 5 6 7-1/2 8 9 | 25 | Lead |
| 16HV | High Velocity | 16 | 2 3/4" | 3 1/8 | 1300 | 1 1/8 | 4 6 7-1/2 8 | 25 | Lead |
| 20HV | High Velocity | 20 | 2 3/4" | 2 3/4 | 1220 | 1 | 4 5 6 7-1/2 8 9 | 25 | Lead |
| 28HV | High Velocity | 28 | 2 3/4" | 2 1/4 | 1300 | 3/4 | 6 7-1/2 8 9 | 25 | Lead |
| 410HV | High Velocity | 410 | 3" | Max | 1140 | 11/16 | 6 7-1/2 8 9 | 25 | Lead |

# Fiocchi Ammunition

## SHOTSHELL APPLICATION GUIDE

| GAME | LEAD SHOT SIZE | STEEL SHOT SIZE | RECOMMENDED LOADS |
|---|---|---|---|
| Geese | NA | T-BBB-BB-1 | Heavy Steel, Speed Steel |
| Ducks | NA | BB-1-2-3-4-6 | Heavy Steel, Speed Steel, Upland Steel |
| Pheasant | 4-5-6 | 3-4-5-6 | Golden Pheasant, HV, Speed Steel, Upland Steel, HVN |
| Turkey | 4-5-6 | 4-5 | Turkey Tunder, HV, HVN |
| Grouse/Partridge | 5-6-7 1/2-8 | 4-6-7 | Field Loads, Upland Steel, HV, HVN, HFN |
| Quail | 7 1/2-8-9 | 7 | Field Loads, HV, Upland Steel, HVN, HFN |
| Dove/Pigeon | 6-7 1/2-8-9 | 6-7 | Field Loads, GT, Dove, HV, HFN, HVN |
| Rabbit/Squirrel | 4-5-6-7 1/2 | 6-7 | Field Loads, HV, GT, Upland Steel, HFN, HVN |
| Deer/Boar | 00-Slug | NA | 12HV00BK, 12 Gauge Slug, 20 Gauge Slug |
| Trap | 7 1/2-8-8 1/2 | 6-7 | TL, TH, TX, VIP, LITE, WRNO, MS, TRAPH, TRAPL |
| Skeet | 8-8 1/2-9 | 7 | TL, TH, TX, VIP, LITE, WRNO, MS |
| Sporting Clays | 7 1/2-8-8 1/2-9 | 7 | TL, TH, TX, TIP, LITE, WRNO, MS |
| Steel Target | | | Upland Steel, Training Load |

## SHOT PELLET SIZES

| Size # | 9 | 8-1/2 | 8 | 7-1/2 | 6 | 5 | 4 | 3 | 2 | 1 | BB | BBB | T | #4 | 00 |
|---|---|---|---|---|---|---|---|---|---|---|---|---|---|---|---|
| DIA.IN. | .08 | .085 | .09 | .095 | .11 | .12 | .13 | .14 | .15 | .16 | .18 | .19 | .20 | .24 | .33 |
| DIA.MM | 2.03 | 2.16 | 2.29 | 2.41 | 2.79 | 3.05 | 3.30 | 3.56 | 3.81 | 4.06 | 4.57 | 4.83 | 5.08 | 6.10 | 8.38 |

## LEAD SHOT

| SHOT SIZE | 1/2 | 1/16 | 3/4 | 7/8 | 1 | 1 1/8 | 1 1/4 | 1 3/8 | 1 3/4 | 2 |
|---|---|---|---|---|---|---|---|---|---|---|
| 9 | | 290 | 398 | 434 | 507 | 579 | 685 | 724 | | |
| 8 1/2 | | | | | 423 | 483 | | | | |
| 8 | | 204 | 280 | 305 | 356 | 407 | 458 | 509 | | |
| 7 1/2 | | | 238 | 260 | 303 | 346 | 389 | 433 | | |
| 6 | | | 153 | 167 | 194 | 222 | 250 | 278 | 305 | 389 | 444 |
| 5 | | | 118 | | | 171 | 192 | 214 | 235 | 299 | 342 |
| 4 | | | | | | 135 | 152 | 169 | 186 | 236 | 270 |

## STEEL SHOT

| SHOT SIZE | 3/4 | 7/8 | 1 | 1 1/8 | 1 1/4 | 1 3/8 | 1 9/16 |
|---|---|---|---|---|---|---|---|
| 7 | 315 | 368 | 420 | | | | |
| 6 | 237 | | 316 | 356 | | | |
| 4 | 143 | 167 | 191 | 215 | 239 | 263 | |
| 3 | 115 | 134 | | 172 | 191 | 210 | |
| 2 | | 109 | | 141 | 156 | 172 | |
| 1 | | | | 116 | 129 | 142 | 161 |
| BB | | | | 81 | 90 | 99 | 113 |
| BBB | | | | 69 | 76 | 84 | 95 |
| T | | | | | 66 | 73 | 83 |

**Note:** When comparing steel shot to lead shot, increase shot size by two to get similar downrange results (i.e. Lead #4 to Steel #2). Check your shotgun and choke manufacturer for steel shot compatibility.

# Fiocchi Ammunition

The three-shot group here measures .450 inches; it was fired at 50 yds. from a bench rest with a Mossberg 500 Crown Grade 24″ fully rifled barrel and 4 power scope.

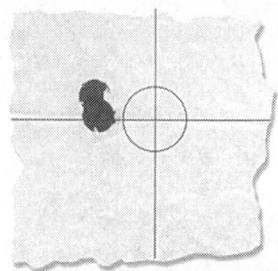

| STOCK # | | GAUGE | SHELL LENGTH | DRAM. EQUIV. | MUZZLE VELOCITY | PELLET CT. | SHOT SIZES | RDS. BOX | SHOT TYPE |
|---|---|---|---|---|---|---|---|---|---|
| **BUCKSHOT** | | | | | | | | | |
| 12HV4BK Buckshot | | 12 | 2 3/4″ | Max | 1325 | 27 pell. | 4 Buck | 10 | Hi-Antimony Nicke-Plated |
| 12HV00BK Buckshot | | 12 | 2 3/4″ | Max | 1325 | 9 pell. | 00 Buck | 10 | Hi-Antimony Nickel-Plated |
| 12LE00BK Reduced Recoil* | | 12 | 2 3/4″ | Lite | 1150 | 9 pell. | 00 Buck | 10 | Hi-Antimony Nickel-Plated |

| STOCK # | | GAUGE | SHELL LENGTH | MM | DRAM. EQUIV. | MUZZLE VELOCITY | SHOT OZ. | SHOT SIZES | RDS. BOX | SHOT TYPE |
|---|---|---|---|---|---|---|---|---|---|---|
| **SLUGS** | | | | | | | | | | |
| 12TS1 | Trophy Slug | 12 | 2 3/4″ | 70 | Max | 1560 | 1 | Rifled Slug | 5 | Lead w/attached Wad |
| 20TS78 | Trophy Slug | 20 | 2 3/4″ | 70 | Max | 1650 | 7/8 | Rifled Slug | 5 | Lead w/attached Wad |

| STOCK # | | GAUGE | SHELL LENGTH | DRAM. EQUIV. | MUZZLE VELOCITY | SHOT OZ. | SHOT SIZES | RDS. BOX | SHOT TYPE |
|---|---|---|---|---|---|---|---|---|---|
| **NICKEL PLATED HUNTING LOADS** | | | | | | | | | |
| 12HFN Heavy Field Nickel | | 12 | 2 3/4″ | 3 1/4 | 1225 | 1 1/4 | 7-1/2 8 | 25 | Nickel-Plated Lead |
| 12HVN High Velocity Nickel | | 12 | 2 3/4″ | 3 3/4 | 1330 | 1 1/4 | 4 5 6 7-1/2 8 | 25 | Nickel-Plated Lead |
| 12GP Golden Pheasant | | 12 | 2 3/4″ | Max | 1250 | 1 3/8 | 4 5 6 | 25 | Nickel-Plated Lead |
| 203GP Golden Pheasant 20 | | 20 | 3″ | Max | 1200 | 1 1/4 | 4 5 6 | 25 | Nickel-Plated Lead |
| **FITASC** | | | | | | | | | |
| 12HFN | | 12 | 2 3/4″ | 3 1/4 | 1225 | 1 1/4 | 7-1/2 8 | 25 | Nickel-Plated Lead |
| 12HFN Heavy Field | | 12 | 2 3/4″ | 3 1/4 | 1225 | 1 1/4 | 7-1/2 8 | 25 | Lead |
| **INTERCEPTOR SPREADER** | | | | | | | | | |
| 12CPTR Interceptor | | 12 | 2 3/4″ | Max | 1300 | 1 | 7-1/2 8 8-1/2 9 | 25 | Lead |
| **SPORTING CLAYS POWER SPREADERS** | | | | | | | | | |
| 12SSCH Power Spreader | | 12 | 2 3/4″ | 3 | 1200 | 1 1/8 | 8 8-1/2 | 25 | Lead |
| 12SSCX Power Spreader | | 12 | 2 3/4″ | Max | 1250 | 1 1/8 | 8 8-1/2 9 | 25 | Lead |
| **SPORTING TARGET LOAD** | | | | | | | | | |
| 12S78 Steel Target Load | | 12 | 2 3/4″ | Max | 1440 | 7/8 | 7 | 25 | Steel |
| 12S1OZ Steel Target Load | | 12 | 2 3/4″ | Max | 1400 | 1 | 4 6 7 | 25 | Steel |
| 20S Steel Target Load | | 20 | 2 3/4″ | Max | 1470 | 3/4 | 3 4 6 7 | 25 | Steel |
| **ULTRA LOW RECOIL LOADS** | | | | | | | | | |
| 1278OZ Trainer | | 12 | 2 3/4″ | Lite | 1200 | 7/8 | 7-1/2 8 | 25 | Hi-Antimony Lead |
| **MULTI-SPORT LOADS-GAME & TARGET** | | | | | | | | | |
| 12MS3 Multi-Sport | | 12 | 2 3/4″ | 3 | 1250 | 1 | 7-1/2 8 9 | 25 | Lead |
| 12GT Game & Target | | 12 | 2 3/4″ | 3 1/4 | 1290 | 1 | 6 7-1/2 8 9 | 25 | Lead |
| 12GT118 Game & Target | | 12 | 2 3/4″ | 3 | 1200 | 1 1/8 | 7-1/2 8 | 25 | Lead |
| **LOW RECOIL TRAP LOADS** | | | | | | | | | |
| 12TRAPL Low-Recoil Trap Light | | 12 | 2 3/4″ | 2 3/4 | 1140 | 1 1/8 | 7-1/2 8 | 25 | Hi-Antimony Lead |
| 12TRAPH Low-Recoil Trap Heavy | | 12 | 2 3/4″ | 3 | 1185 | 1 1/8 | 7-1/2 8 | 25 | Hi-Antimony Lead |

# Hornady

Hornady is becoming known for high-performance loaded ammo, like a 265-grain .444 Marlin that clocks 2335 fps at the muzzle. It has also produced the first .450 Marlin rounds and recently reintroduced the .405 Winchester.

Hornady loads the .458 Lott too. Those 500-grain softpoints leave at 2300 fps and generate nearly 5900 footpounds of energy at the muzzle. Hornady offers a 500-grain solid bullet with the same punch.

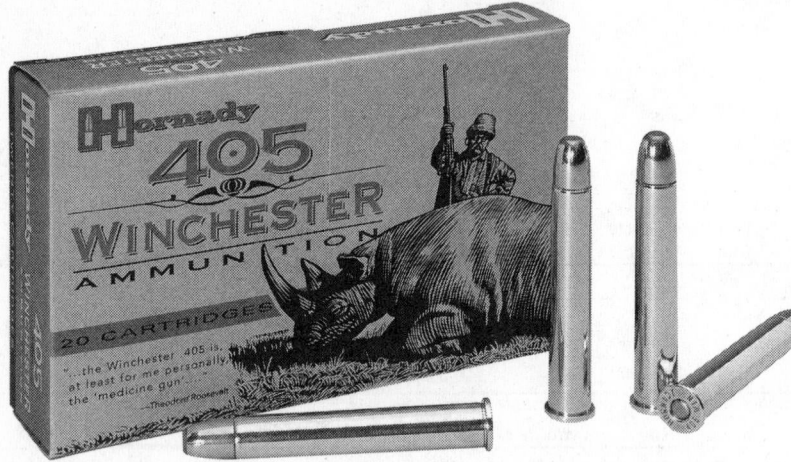

### HORNADY .405 WINCHESTER
Hornady has brought the old warhorse favored by Teddy Roosevelt into the 21st century by designing a high-performance cartridge that delivers amazing power and accuracy from the .405 Winchester. The .405 Winchester cartridge is loaded with a 300-grain FP bullet from Hornady.

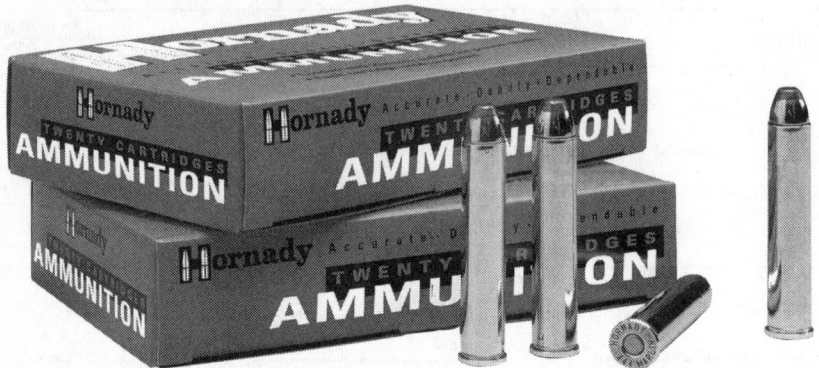

### .444 MARLIN LIGHT MAG
When the .444 Marlin was born as a joint project between Marlin and Remington, shooters quickly fell in love with the combination of a high-performance cartridge in a lever-action rifle. Now, Hornady has gone the original one better by loading the .444 Marlin with the high-performance 265-grain bullet that has been a staple of the line since 1964.

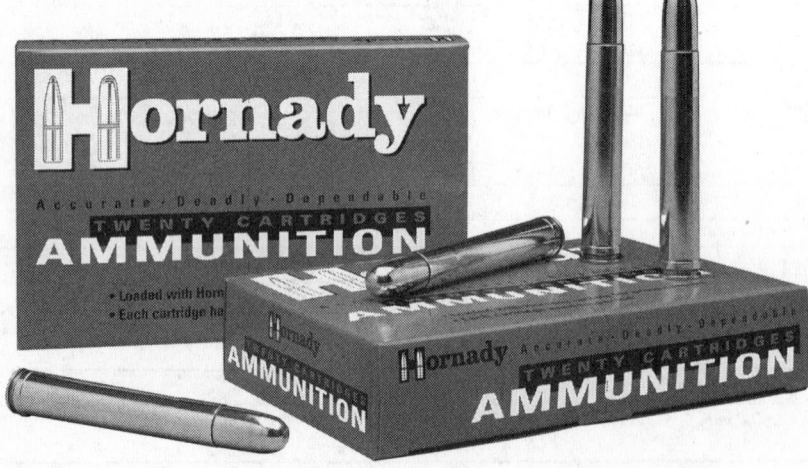

### .458 LOTT
Developed by Jack Lott and a favorite of custom rifle builders and African hunters.

## NITRO-EXPRESS-SPORTING AMMUNITION

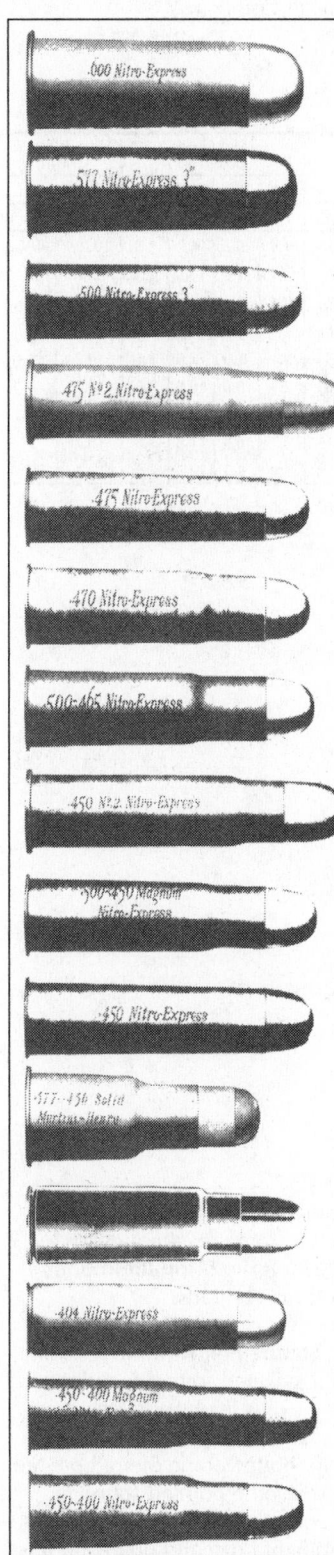

**.600 NE**
900 gr Solid or SN

**.577 NE 3"**
750 gr Solid or SN

**.500 NE 3"**
570 gr Solid or SN

**.475 No. 2 NE**
480 gr Solid or SN for
Jeffery Rifles: 500 gr
Solid or SN

**.475 NE**
480 gr Solid or SN

**.470 NE**
500 gr Solid or SN

**.500/.465 NE**
480 gr Solid or SN

**.450 No. 2 NE**
480 gr Solid or SN

**.500/.450**
Magnum NE
480 gr Solid or SN

**.450 NE**
480 gr Solid or SN

**.577/.450 MH**
480 gr Solid Lead

**.416 Rigby**
410 gr Solid or SN

**.404 Rimless NE**
400 gr Solid or SN

**.450/.400**
Magnum NE
400 gr Solid or SN

**.450/.440 NE**
400 gr Solid or SN

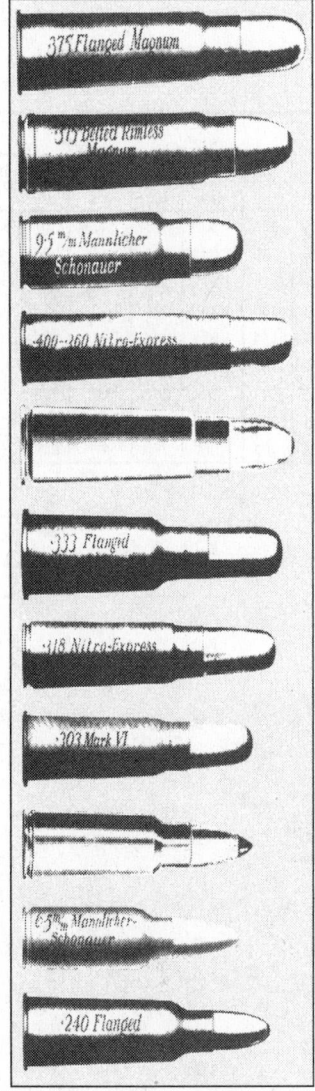

**.375 Flanged Magnum**
300, 270 or 235 gr
Solid or SN

**.375 Belted Magnum**
300, 270 or 235 gr
Solid or SN

**9.5 mm Mannlicher**
Schonauer 270 gr Solid or SN

**.400/.360 NE for Purdey
Rifles:** 300 gr for Westley
Richards: 314 gr. Solid or SN

**.350 Rigby Magnum**
225 gr or 250 gr, Solid or SN

**.333 Jeffrey Flanged NE**
300 gr Solid or SN

**.318 Rimless NE**
250 gr Solid or SN
180 gr SN

**.303 British**
215 gr Solid or SN

**.275 Rigby Rimless**
140 gr SN

**6.5 m/m Mannlicher**
Schonauer 160 gr SN

**.240 H&H Flanged**
100 gr SN

## ADDITIONAL PROPRIETARY CALIBERS AVAILABLE:

**.700 NE**
1000 gr Solid

**.500 Jeffery**
535 gr Solid or SN

**.450 Rigby Rimless Magnum**
480 gr Solid or SN

**.400 - 3" Purdey**
230 gr SN

**.505 Gibbs Magnum**
525 gr Solid or SN

**.425 Westley Richards
Magnum**
410 gr Solid or SN

**.300 H&H Flanged Magnum**
220 gr Solid or SN

# Magtech Ammunition

Magtech Ammunition Co. imports and distributes high-quality rifle and pistol cartridges manufactured by Companhia Brasileira de Cartuchos (CBC). in Sao Paulo, Brazil. Before 1976, it was owned and managed by Remington Arms and ICI - the UK's Imperial Chemical Company.

| Symbol | Caliber | Bullet | | | Velocity | | | | | | Energy | | | | | | Mid-Range Trajectory | | | | Test Barrel Length | |
|---|---|---|---|---|---|---|---|---|---|---|---|---|---|---|---|---|---|---|---|---|---|---|
| | | Style | Weight | | Muzzle | | 50M | 50YD | 100M | 100YD | Muzzle | | 50M | 50YD | 100M | 100YD | 50M | 50YD | 100M | 100YD | | |
| | | | G | GR | M/S | FPS | M/S | FPS | M/S | FPS | J | FT/LBS | J | FT/LBS | J | FT/LBS | CM | INCH | CM | INCH | CM | INCH |
| GG357A | .357 Mag | JHP | 8.10 | 125 | 420 | 1,378 | 353 | 1,170 | 307 | 1,020 | 714 | 527 | 505 | 381 | 382 | 289 | 1.5 | 0.5 | 7.5 | 2.5 | 10.2V | 4-V |
| GG380A | .380 Auto+P | JHP | 5.5 | 85 | 330 | 1,082 | 303 | 999 | 282 | 936 | 300 | 221 | 252 | 188 | 219 | 166 | 3.1 | 1.0 | 13.3 | 4.3 | 9.5 | 3¾ |
| GG38A | .38 SPL+P | JHP | 8.10 | 125 | 310 | 1,017 | 295 | 971 | 282 | 931 | 389 | 287 | 352 | 262 | 322 | 241 | 3.4 | 1.1 | 14.3 | 4.6 | 10.2 | 4 |
| GG9A | 9mm Luger+P | JHP | 7.45 | 115 | 380 | 1,246 | 344 | 1,137 | 318 | 1,056 | 538 | 397 | 441 | 330 | 377 | 285 | 2.4 | 0.8 | 10.5 | 3.4 | 10.2 | 4 |
| GG9B | 9mm Luger | JHP | 8.03 | 124 | 334 | 1,096 | 304 | 1,017 | 286 | 958 | 448 | 331 | 371 | 285 | 328 | 253 | 3.1 | 1.0 | 12.5 | 4.1 | 10.2 | 4 |
| GG40A | .40 S&W | JHP | 10.0 | 155 | 367 | 1,205 | 338 | 1,118 | 317 | 1,052 | 677 | 500 | 571 | 430 | 523 | 381 | 2.5 | 0.8 | 10.9 | 3.5 | 10.2 | 4 |
| GG40B | .40 S&W | JHP | 11.66 | 180 | 302 | 990 | 282 | 938 | 268 | 891 | 532 | 392 | 463 | 352 | 419 | 318 | 3.7 | 1.2 | 13.4 | 4.5 | 10.2 | 4 |
| GG45A | .45 Auto+P | JHP | 12.0 | 185 | 350 | 1,148 | 323 | 1,066 | 303 | 1,005 | 735 | 540 | 626 | 467 | 551 | 415 | 2.7 | 0.9 | 11.8 | 3.8 | 12.7 | 5 |
| GG45B | .45 Auto+P | JHP | 14.90 | 230 | 307 | 1,007 | 290 | 965 | 279 | 927 | 702 | 518 | 626 | 467 | 580 | 440 | 4.0 | 1.3 | 12.5 | 4.0 | 12.7 | 5 |

# PMC

**PMC RIFLE CARTRIDGES**

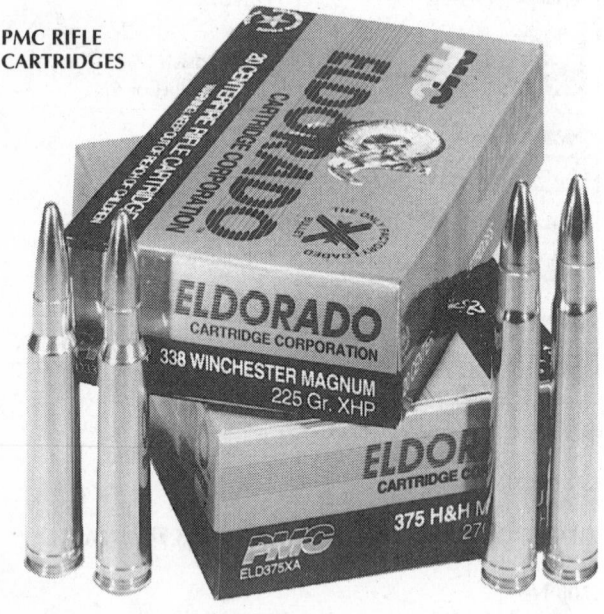

## PRECISION MADE CARTRIDGES

PMC (Precision Made Cartridges) is the same firm as Eldorado Cartridge Company. It is a growing enterprise whose product line has expanded substantially this year, offering new sporting and tactical centerfire rounds from its rural Nevada digs. Handgun ammo, from .25 Auto to .44 Magnum, includes loads specifically for Cowboy Action shooting. The centerfire rifle stable has cowboy action loads in .30-30 and .45-70, plus a wide variety of hunting and match ammunition from .222 Remington to .375 H&H Magnum. The selection of .22 rimfire rounds features hunting, plinking and match loads.

A broad choice of pistol bullets is available from PMC. There's the quick-opening Starfire hollowpoint, a traditional jacketed hollowpoint, a jacketed softpoint and a full-metal-jacket (hardball) bullet — plus lead wadcutter, semi-wadcutter and round-nose options. Rifle bullets include the Barnes X-Bullet, .30-30 Starfire hollowpoint, Sierra boat-tail hollowpoint, Sierra boat-tail softpoint, pointed softpoint, softpoint, flat-nose softpoint and full metal jacket. PMC also manufactures shotshells, from light dove and quail and target loads to heavy steel-shot loads for geese

**CENTERFIRE RIFLE AMMUNITION**

**FIELD AND TARGET**

**LESS LETHAL RUBBER FIN BATON**

**LESS LETHAL RUBBER BUCK SHOT**

## PMC GOLD LINE NOW FEATURES THE BARNES XLC COATED X-BULLET

Premier-performance PMC Gold Line rifle cartridges feature the Barnes SLC Coated X-Bullet. The solid-copper X-Bullet has a reputation for deep penetration and reliable expansion. The exclusive blue XLC coating is a high-tech, dry-film lubricant that will decrease the friction within the rifle bore. The barrel stays cooler and copper fouling is reduced.

## PMC FIELD & TARGET SHOTSHELLS

The PMC Field & Target shell combines the dense patterning and target-smashing performance of a PMC Clay Target shell with the solid penetration necessary for taking lighter upland birds and small game. It's the perfect all-purpose load for shooters who wish to use the same load for clay targets and wing shooting. Features include clean-burning powder to keep your shotgun functioning smoothly, high antimony, chilled lead shot to give good penetration, reliable ignition primers and a tough, reloadable ribbed plastic hull.

## PMC LESS-LETHAL SHOTSHELLS

PMC has a shotshell line for law enforcement and home defense. The rubber projectiles discourage home intruders when lethal force may not be desirable.

## FIN-STABILIZED RUBBER BATON

The rubber projectile in this shell utilizes canted fins and a bore-riding band, both of which contribute to stable flight and enhanced accuracy. It will produce groups of 2-4 inches at 20 yards. Available in 12 gauge only.

## 000 RUBBER BUCKSHOT

Low-energy shell loaded with twelve 3/8th-inch rubber balls. Available in 12 gauge only.

# Remington Ammunition

## PREMIER® HEVI-SHOT MAGNUM TURKEY LOADS

If you're passionate about turkey hunting, new Premier Hevi-Shot is the load for you. This load won all event classes at the 2001 National Wild Turkey Federation Annual Turkey Shoot. It routinely achieves patterns in excess of 90%. Shot material alloy of tungsten, nickel and iron fea- tures a 10% higher density than lead, which yields denser patterns and higher energy - a lead improve- ment. A superior product for serious turkey hunters.

### PREMIER® HEVI-SHOT® HIGH VELOCITY MAGNUM TURKEY BUFFERED LOADS

| INDEX/ EDI No. | GAUGE | SHELL LENGTH | POWDER DR. EQ. | VELOCITY (FT./SEC.@3 FT.) | OUNCES OF SHOT | SHOT SIZES |
|---|---|---|---|---|---|---|
| PRHSHV12M | 12 | 3" | Max | 1300 | 1 1/2 | 4, 5, 6 |
| PRHSHV1235M | 12 | 3 1/2" | Max | 1300 | 1 3/4 | 4, 5, 6 |

### PREMIER® HEVI-SHOT® MAGNUM TURKEY BUFFERED LOADS

| INDEX/ EDI No. | GAUGE | SHELL LENGTH | POWDER DR. EQ. | VELOCITY (FT./SEC.@3 FT.) | OUNCES OF SHOT | SHOT SIZES |
|---|---|---|---|---|---|---|
| PRHS12SM | 12 | 2 3/4" | Max | 1250 | 1 3/8 | 4, 5, 6 |
| PRHS12HM | 12 | 3" | Max | 1225 | 1 5/8 | 4, 5, 6 |
| PRHS1235M | 12 | 3 1/2" | Max | 1225 | 1 7/8 | 4, 5, 6 |

## PREMIER® HEVI-SHOT NITRO MAGNUM WATERFOWL LOADS

Premier Hevi-Shot Nitro Magnums are manufactured of a non-toxic tungsten-nickel-iron alloy, Hevi-Shot is 10% denser than lead and an amazing 54% denser than steel. Shooting an equal payload and shot size, Hevi-Shot pel- lets have 25% more energy at 50 yards than steel pellets have at 30 yards. This allows you to drop down three shot sizes to maintain pattern energy and dramatically increase on-game pellet count. The resulting Hevi-Shot patterning, with full chokes, yields an average of 88% efficiency.

### DENSITY COMPARISON

| Density Of Steel | 7.8 |
|---|---|
| Density Of Lead | 10.9 |
| Density Of Hevi-Shot | 12.0 |

### PREMIER® HEVI-SHOT® NITRO MAGNUM WATERFOWL LOADS

| INDEX/ EDI No. | GAUGE | SHELL LENGTH | POWDER DR. EQ. | VELOCITY (FT./SEC.@3 FT.) | OUNCES OF SHOT | SHOT SIZES |
|---|---|---|---|---|---|---|
| PRHSN10M | 10 | 3 1/2" | Magnum | 1300 | 1 3/4 | 2,4 |
| PRHSN12SM | 12 | 2 3/4" | Magnum | 1325 | 1 1/4 | 4, 6, 7 1/2 |
| PRHSN12HM | 12 | 3" | Magnum | 1300 | 1 1/2 | 2, 4, 6 |
| PRHSN1235 | 12 | 3 1/2" | Magnum | 1300 | 1 3/4 | 2, 4, 6 |
| PRHSN20M | 20 | 3" | Magnum | 1300 | 1 1/8 | 4, 6 |

AMMUNITION

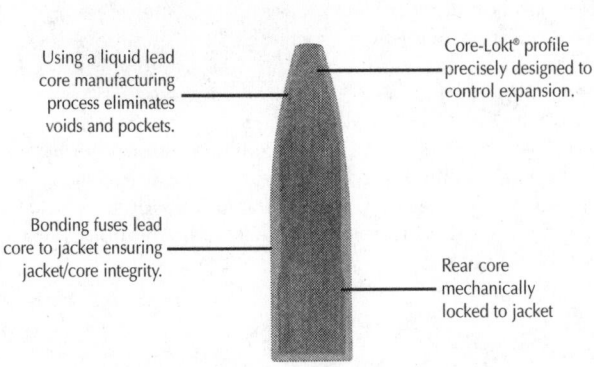

Using a liquid lead core manufacturing process eliminates voids and pockets.

Core-Lokt® profile precisely designed to control expansion.

Bonding fuses lead core to jacket ensuring jacket/core integrity.

Rear core mechanically locked to jacket

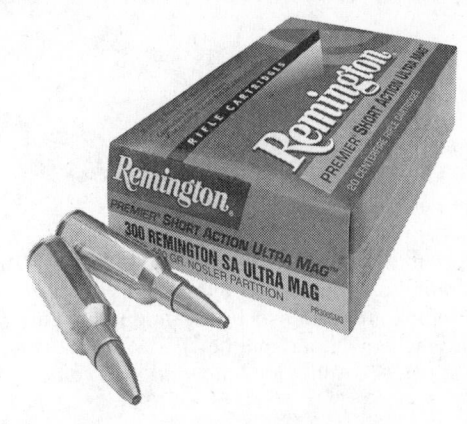

### PREMIER SHORT-ACTION ULTRA MAG

Designed to offer belted magnum performance in a .308-length action, SA Ultra Mag cartridges headspace off the shoulder, rather than a belt, promoting more precise bore alignment and improved accuracy. Furthermore, the highly efficient case design duplicates or exceeds belted magnum ballistics with less powder, which in turn means less felt recoil. Finally, the entire package achieves greater down-range velocity and energy than traditional 300 Win Mag and 7mm Remington Mag calibers. SA Ultra Mag ammo will be available to match Remington's Model Seven Magnum rifles in two popular calibers: 300 Remington SA Ultra Mag and 7mm Remington SA Ultra Mag.

### PREMIER® SHORT ACTION ULTRA MAG™

| CALIBER | INDEX/EDI NO. | BULLET WEIGHT | BULLET TYPE |
|---|---|---|---|
| 7mm Rem. SA UM | PR7SM1 | 140 | PSP Core-Lokt® Ultra |
| 7mm Rem. SA UM | PR7SM2 | 150 | PSP Core-Lokt® |
| 7mm Rem. SA UM | PR7SM3 | 160 | Nosler® Partition® |
| 300 Rem. SA UM | PR300SM1 | 150 | PSP Core-Lokt® Ultra |
| 300 Rem. SA UM | PR300SM2 | 165 | PSP Core-Lokt® |
| 300 Rem. SA UM | PR300SM3 | 180 | Nosler® Partition® |

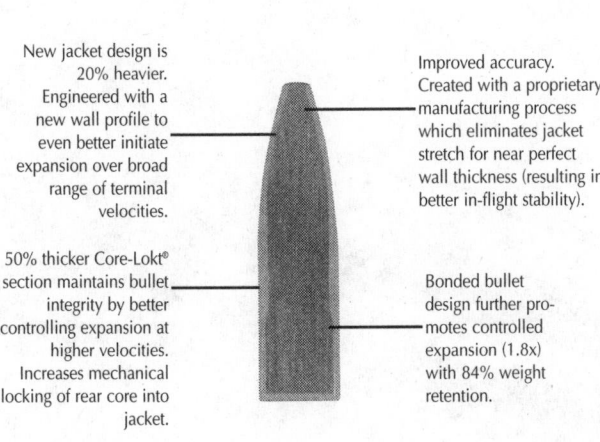

New jacket design is 20% heavier. Engineered with a new wall profile to even better initiate expansion over broad range of terminal velocities.

50% thicker Core-Lokt® section maintains bullet integrity by better controlling expansion at higher velocities. Increases mechanical locking of rear core into jacket.

Improved accuracy. Created with a proprietary manufacturing process which eliminates jacket stretch for near perfect wall thickness (resulting in better in-flight stability).

Bonded bullet design further promotes controlled expansion (1.8x) with 84% weight retention.

### PREMIER CORE-LOKT ULTRA

Introduced in 2003, Core-Lokt Ultra bonded bullets retain up to 90% of their original weight for maximum penetration and energy transfer. Featuring a progressively-tapered jacket, the Core-Lokt Ultra bullet initiates and controls expansion up to 1.8X. The unique design of the bullet, combined with the bonded lead core, provides the hunter with a Premier bullet that yields unmatched performance from 50 yards to 500 yards and all yardages in between.

### PREMIER® CORE-LOKT® ULTRA

| CALIBER | INDEX/EDI NO. | BULLET WEIGHT | BULLET TYPE |
|---|---|---|---|
| 270 Win | PRC270WB | 140 | Core-Lokt® Ultra PSP |
| 7mm Remington Mag | PRC7MMRA | 140 | Core-Lokt® Ultra PSP |
| 30-06 Springfield | PRC3006C | 180 | Core-Lokt® Ultra PSP |
| 300 Win Mag | PRC300WC | 180 | Core-Lokt® Ultra PSP |
| 308 Winchester | PRC308WC | 180 | Core-Lokt® Ultra PSP |

AMMUNITION

# RWS Centerfire Cartridges
## Bullets and Ballistics for Norma

### VULKAN

Vulkan big game bullets are strengthened by the folded jacket at the front. The folds protect the tip from deforma-

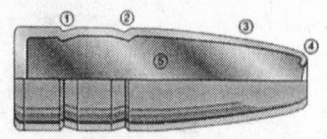

tion. The bullet penetrates before expansion starts. Subsequently, mushrooming to double the original diameter follows rapidly. 1. Reinforced rear jacket with lead core lock. 2. Crimping groove for secure seating in the case. 3. Thin forward jacket with internal notches. 4. Jacket folded into the lead core. 5. Antimony hardened lead core.

### SOFT POINT

Norma's Soft Point bullets have optimum ballistic shape. They offer good penetration and mush-room well, even on small-

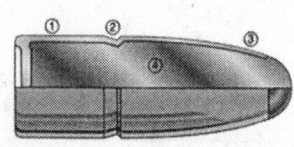

er game. The Soft Point is an excellent all-around bullet particularly suitable for small and medium game. 1. Reinforced rear jacket. 2. Crimping groove for secure seating in the case. 3. Thin forward jacket. 4. Antimony hard-ened lead core.

### DK

Manufactured at considerable expense, DK bullets barely splinter, mushroom in a controlled manner, have a residue body of over 50 percent, and usually produce an exit hole. A true twin core that separates to perform two separate functions upon impact, penetration and a high degree of impact force, combine to give the DK a clear advantage over traditional bullets, especially for large game with heavy bones and muscles.

### RWS

The RWS cone point bullet was designed and developed after exhaustive studies in the laboratory as well as in the field. A carefully engineered matching of casing and core material and an aerodynamically favorable bullet shape have been paired to produce a controlled mushrooming to almost twice caliber size. The rear groove, which joins the lead core and casing, controls mushrooming and preserves effective residual body to give it killing power.

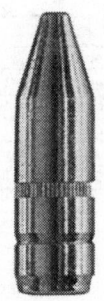

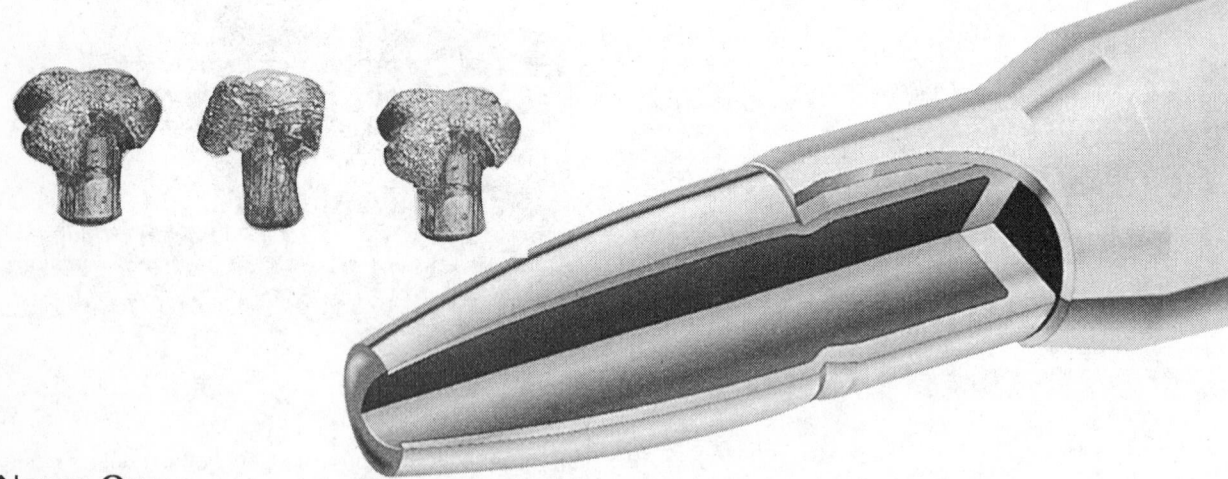

### NORMA ORYX

Relatively recent but already well-proven, the Oryx bullet is designed to penetrate deep. Jacket and core are bonded together through a chemical process to ensure a very high residual weight, even in tough targets. Despite the solid construction, mushrooming starts early. The Oryx bullet delivers excellent deep energy transfer and is suitable for big and medium sized game.
**Price: box of 20 cartridges. . . . . . . . . . . . . . . . . $42-66**

AMMUNITION

# RWS Rimfire Cartridges

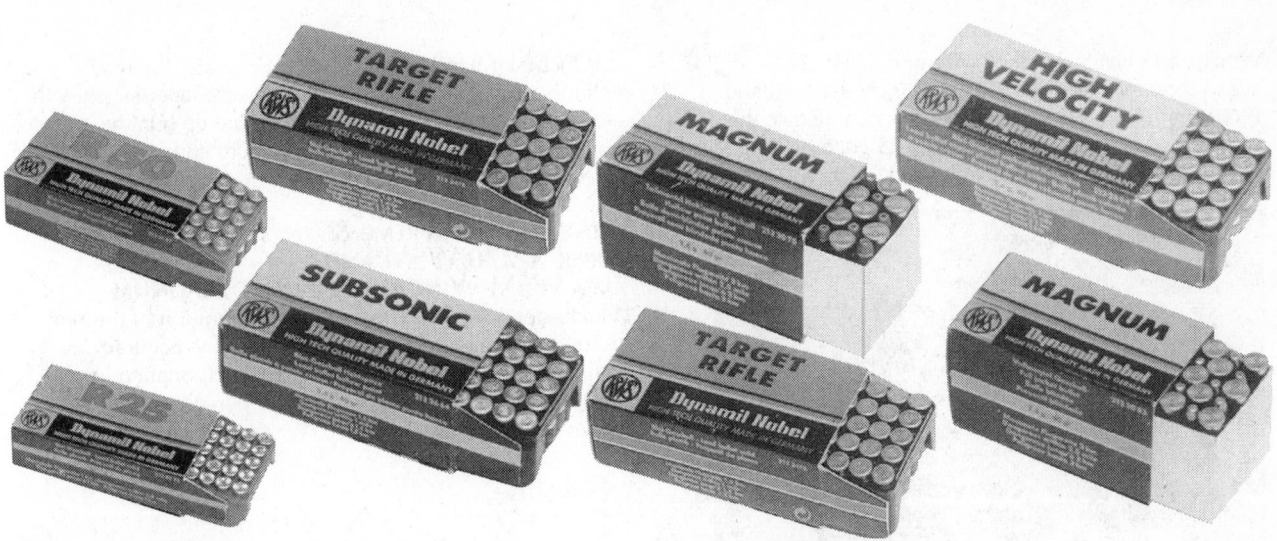

## RWS .22 R50

For competitive shooters demanding the ultimate in precision. This cartridge has been used to establish several world records and is used by Olympic Gold Medalists. No finer cartridge can be bought at any price.

Price:................................ $13/box

## RWS .22 L.R. RIFLE MATCH

Perfect for the club level target competitor. Accurate and affordable.

Price:................................ $8/box

## RWS .22 L.R. SUBSONIC HOLLOW POINT

Subsonic ammunition is a favorite ammunition of shooters whose shooting range is limited to where the noise of a conventional cartridge would be a problem.

Price:................................ $5/box

## RWS .22 MAGNUM HOLLOW POINT

The soft point allows good expansion on impact, while preserving the penetration characteristics necessary for larger vermin and game.

Price:................................ $24/box

## RWS .22 SHORT R25

Designed for world class Rapid Fire Pistol events, this cartridge provides the shooter with outstanding accuracy and minimal recoil. Manufactured to exacting standards, the shooter can be assured of consistent performance.

Price:................................ $9/box

## RWS .22 L.R. TARGET RIFLE

An ideal training and field cartridge, the .22 Long Rifle Target also excels in informal competitions. The target .22 provides the casual shooter with accuracy at an economical price.

Price:................................ $4/box

## RWS .22 L.R. HV HOLLOW POINT

A higher velocity hollow point offers the shooter greater shocking power in game, suitable for both small game and vermin.

Price:................................ $6/box

## RWS .22 MAGNUM FULL JACKET

Outstanding penetration characteristics of this cartridge allow the shooter to easily tackle game where penetration is necessary.

Price:................................ $24/box

## TECHNICAL DATA

| Cartridges | Bullet Style | Bullet Weight (Grains) | Max. Chamber Pressure (psi) | Velocity (ft./sec.) Muzzle | 50y | 100y | Energy (ft./lbs.) Muzzle | 50y | 100y | Open Sight At | 25 yds | 50 yds | 75 yds | 100yds | Scope Sighted In At | 25 yds | 50 yds | 75 yds | 100 yds |
|---|---|---|---|---|---|---|---|---|---|---|---|---|---|---|---|---|---|---|---|
| .22 L.R. R 50 | Lead | 40 | 25.600 | 1.070 | 970 | 890 | 100 | 80 | 70 | -- | -- | -- | -- | -- | -- | -- | -- | -- | -- |
| .22 Short R 25 | Lead | 28 | 18.500 | 560 | 490 | --- | 20 | 15 | -- | -- | -- | -- | -- | -- | -- | -- | -- | -- | -- |
| .22 L.R. Rifle Match | Lead | 40 | 25.600 | 1.035 | 945 | 860 | 95 | 80 | 65 | 50 yds. | +0.7 | | -3.2 | -9.0 | 50 yds | +0.1 | | -2.6 | -7.8 |
| .22 L.R. Target Rifle | Lead | 40 | 25.600 | 1.080 | 990 | 900 | 100 | 85 | 70 | 50 yds. | +0.6 | | -3.1 | -8.7 | 50 yds | +0.1 | | -2.5 | -7.5 |
| .22 L.R. Subsonic | Hollow Point | 40 | 25.600 | 1.000 | 915 | 835 | 90 | 75 | 60 | 50 yds. | +0.8 | | -3.4 | -4.7 | 50 yds | +0.2 | | +2.8 | -8.5 |
| .22 L.R. HV | Lead | 40 | 25.600 | 1.310 | 1.120 | 990 | 150 | 110 | 85 | | -- | -- | -- | -- | -- | -- | -- | -- | -- |
| Hollow point | coppered | | | | | | | | | | | | | | | | | | |
| .22 Magnum | Soft Point | 40 | 25.600 | 2.020 | 1.710 | 1.430 | 360 | 260 | 180 | 100 yds. | +0.6 | +1.3 | +1.1 | 0 | 100 yds | -0.3 | +0.7 | +0.8 | 0 |
| .22 Magnum | Full Jacket | 40 | 25.600 | 2.020 | 1.710 | 1.430 | 360 | 260 | 180 | 100 yds. | +0.6 | +1.3 | +1.1 | 0 | 100 yds | -0.3 | +0.7 | +0.8 | 0 |
| .22 LR R100 | Lead | 40 | 25.600 | 1.175 | 1.065 | 970 | 100 | 80 | 70 | 100 yds. | +0.6 | +13 | +1.1 | 0 | 100 yds | -0.3 | +0.7 | +0.8 | 0 |

# Winchester Ammunition

Winchester's first Super Short Magnums – the .223 and .243 – are so short that new rifle actions (Winchester M70 and Browning A-Bolt) were developed to accommodate them. The .223 is loaded with three bullets: the 55-grain Ballistic Silvertip, the 55-grain Pointed Soft Point and 64-grain Power Point.

**Z-HAT MIS DIES**

Winchester handgun ammunition includes the new Platinum tip bullet with a notched, reverse-taper jacket with a two-step nose cavity. Supreme Platinum tip hunting ammo is available in .41 Magnum, .44 Magnum and .454 Casull.

### WINCHESTER SUPREME & SUPER-X 270 WSM AND 7MM WSM WINCHESTER SHORT MAGNUM

Winchester's 300 WSM won the "Ammunition of the Year" in 2002. These cartridges deliver incredible accuracy as well as magnum energy and velocity performance in a short-action cartridge, all with lower perceived recoil in lighter-weight rifles.

### WINCHESTER SUPREME PLATINUM TIP HUNTING AMMUNITION

Winchester's Platinum Tip Hollow Point Hunting Ammunition is ideal for deer hunting. Available in 12 gauge sabot slug shotshell and as a 50-caliber Muzzleloading sabot bullet, the Platinum Tip Hollow Point bullet has a reverse taper jacket that delivers superior accuracy, uniform expansion and on-target energy delivery.

### WINCHESTER SUPER-X DRYLOK HI-VELOCITY STEEL WATERFOWL LOADS

Available in 12 gauge 3" and 3 ½", these steel shotshells give a performance boost, with 1550 feet-per-second muzzle velocity. Add the exclusive water-resistant Super-X Drylok wad system, and you have a traditional steel load delivering greater per-pellet energy on target for superior bird hunting in harsh conditions.

### HAWK CARTRIDGES:

**240 Hawk • 257 Hawk • 264 Hawk • 270 Hawk • 284 Hawk • 300 Hawk • 8mm Hawk • 338 Hawk • 358 Hawk • 9.3 Hawk • 375 Hawk • 411 Hawk**

Fred Zeglin offers Hawk cartridges based on the .30-06 case, plus offers formed brass for all 12 Hawk cartridges, at $31.97 per 20. Loaded rounds are available at $69.95 per box, in .338, .358 and .375 Hawk. Custom loads for your rifle can be developed at Z-Hat (www.Z-Hat.com, or phone 307-577-7443).

Fred also sells custom sizing dies with Z-Hat custom rifles.

**Prices:**
**In-Line Seater set up for one cartridge** . . . . . . . . . . $99
**Caliber inserts** . . . . . . . . . . . . . . . . . . . . . . . . . . 17

# BALLISTICS

# Centerfire Rifle Ballistics

## Comprehensive Ballistics Tables for Currently Manufactured Sporting Rifle Cartridges

No need to assemble catalogs and squint at tiny print to find a factory load you want to try, or see how it compares with other loads! Shooter's Bible has all the data right here and it's updated every year.

Data is taken from manufacturers' charts; your chronograph readings may vary. Listings are current as of February the year *Shooter's Bible* appears (not the cover year). Listings are not intended as recommendations. For example, the data for the .44 Magnum at 400 yards shows its effective range is much shorter. The lack of data for a 285-grain .375 H&H bullet beyond 300 yards does not mean the bullet has no authority farther out. Besides ammunition, the rifle, sights, conditions and shooter ability all must be considered when contemplating a long shot. Accuracy and bullet energy both matter when big game is in the offing.

Barrel length affects velocity, and at various rates depending on the load. As a rule, figure 50 fps per inch of barrel, plus or minus, if your barrel is longer or shorter than 22 inches.

Bullets are given by make, weight (in grains) and type. Most type abbreviations are self-explanatory: BT=Boat-Tail, FMJ=Full Metal Jacket, HP=Hollow Point, SP=Soft Point – except in Hornady listings, where SP is the firm's Spire Point. TNT and TXP are trademarked designations of Speer and Norma. XLC identifies a coated Barnes X bullet. HE indicates a Federal High Energy load, similar to the Hornady LM (Light Magnum) and HM (Heavy Magnum) cartridges.

Arc (trajectory) is based on a zero range published by the manufacturer, from 100 to 300 yards. If a zero does not fall in a yardage column, it lies halfway between – at 150 yards, for example, if the bullet's strike is "+" at 100 yards and "-" at 200.

## .17 REMINGTON TO .222 REMINGTON

| CARTRIDGE BULLET | RANGE, YARDS: | 0 | 100 | 200 | 300 | 400 |
|---|---|---|---|---|---|---|
| **.17 REMINGTON** | | | | | | |
| Rem. 20 AccuTip BT | velocity, fps: | 4250 | 3594 | 3028 | 2529 | 2081 |
| | Energy, ft-lb: | 802 | 574 | 407 | 284 | 192 |
| | Arc, inches: | | +1.3 | +1.3 | -2.5 | -11.8 |
| Rem. 25 HP Power-Lokt | velocity, fps: | 4040 | 3284 | 2644 | 2086 | 1606 |
| | energy, ft-lb: | 906 | 599 | 388 | 242 | 143 |
| | arc, inches: | | +1.8 | 0 | -3.3 | -16.6 |
| **.204 RUGER** | | | | | | |
| Hornady 32 V-Max | velocity, fps: | 4225 | 3632 | 3114 | 2652 | 2234 |
| | energy, ft-lb: | 1268 | 937 | 689 | 500 | 355 |
| | arc, inches: | | +0.6 | 0 | -4.2 | -13.4 |
| Hornady 40 V-Max | velocity, fps: | 3900 | 3451 | 3046 | 2677 | 2335 |
| | energy, ft-lb: | 1351 | 1058 | 824 | 636 | 485 |
| | arc, inches: | | +0.7 | 0 | -4.5 | -13.9 |
| **.218 BEE** | | | | | | |
| Win. 46 Hollow Point | velocity, fps: | 2760 | 2102 | 1550 | 1155 | 961 |
| | energy, ft-lb: | 778 | 451 | 245 | 136 | 94 |
| | arc, inches: | | 0 | -7.2 | -29.4 | |
| **.22 HORNET** | | | | | | |
| Hornady 35 V-Max | velocity, fps: | 3100 | 2278 | 1601 | 1135 | 929 |
| | energy, ft-lb: | 747 | 403 | 199 | 100 | 67 |
| | arc, inches: | | +2.8 | 0 | -16.9 | -60.4 |
| Rem. 45 Pointed Soft Point | velocity, fps: | 2690 | 2042 | 1502 | 1128 | 948 |
| | energy, ft-lb: | 723 | 417 | 225 | 127 | 90 |
| | arc, inches: | | 0 | -7.1 | -30.0 | |
| Rem. 45 Hollow Point | velocity, fps: | 2690 | 2042 | 1502 | 1128 | 948 |
| | energy, ft-lb: | 723 | 417 | 225 | 127 | 90 |
| | arc, inches: | | 0 | -7.1 | -30.0 | |
| Win. 34 Jacketed HP | velocity, fps: | 3050 | 2132 | 1415 | 1017 | 852 |
| | energy, ft-lb: | 700 | 343 | 151 | 78 | 55 |
| | arc, inches: | | 0 | -6.6 | -29.9 | |
| Win. 45 Soft Point | velocity, fps: | 2690 | 2042 | 1502 | 1128 | 948 |
| | energy, ft-lb: | 723 | 417 | 225 | 127 | 90 |
| | arc, inches: | | 0 | -7.7 | -31.3 | |
| Win. 46 Hollow Point | velocity, fps: | 2690 | 2042 | 1502 | 1128 | 948 |
| | energy, ft-lb: | 739 | 426 | 230 | 130 | 92 |
| | arc, inches: | | 0 | -7.7 | -31.3 | |
| **.221 REMINGTON FIREBALL** | | | | | | |
| Rem. 50 AccuTip BT | velocity, fps: | 2995 | 2605 | 2247 | 1918 | 1622 |
| | energy, ft-lb: | 996 | 753 | 560 | 408 | 292 |
| | arc, inches: | | +1.8 | 0 | -8.8 | -27.1 |
| **.222 REMINGTON** | | | | | | |
| Federal 50 Hi-Shok | velocity, fps: | 3140 | 2600 | 2120 | 1700 | 1350 |
| | energy, ft-lb: | 1095 | 750 | 500 | 320 | 200 |
| | arc, inches: | | +1.9 | 0 | -9.7 | -31.6 |
| Federal 55 FMJ boat-tail | velocity, fps: | 3020 | 2740 | 2480 | 2230 | 1990 |
| | energy, ft-lb: | 1115 | 915 | 750 | 610 | 484 |
| | arc, inches: | | +1.6 | 0 | -7.3 | -21.5 |
| Hornady 40 V-Max | velocity, fps: | 3600 | 3117 | 2673 | 2269 | 1911 |
| | energy, ft-lb: | 1151 | 863 | 634 | 457 | 324 |
| | arc, inches: | | +1.1 | 0 | -6.1 | -18.9 |
| Hornady 50 V-Max | velocity, fps: | 3140 | 2729 | 2352 | 2008 | 1710 |
| | energy, ft-lb: | 1094 | 827 | 614 | 448 | 325 |
| | arc, inches: | | +1.7 | 0 | -7.9 | -24.4 |
| Norma 50 Soft Point | velocity, fps: | 3199 | 2667 | 2193 | 1771 | |
| | energy, ft-lb: | 1136 | 790 | 534 | 348 | |
| | arc, inches: | | +1.7 | 0 | -9.1 | |

BALLISTICS

| CARTRIDGE BULLET | RANGE, YARDS: | 0 | 100 | 200 | 300 | 400 |
|---|---|---|---|---|---|---|
| Norma 50 FMJ | velocity, fps: | 2789 | 2326 | 1910 | 1547 | |
| | energy, ft-lb: | 864 | 601 | 405 | 266 | |
| | arc, inches: | | +2.5 | 0 | -12.2 | |
| Norma 62 Soft Point | velocity, fps: | 2887 | 2457 | 2067 | 1716 | |
| | energy, ft-lb: | 1148 | 831 | 588 | 405 | |
| | arc, inches: | | +2.1 | 0 | -10.4 | |
| PMC 50 Pointed Soft Point | velocity, fps: | 3044 | 2727 | 2354 | 2012 | 1651 |
| | energy, ft-lb: | 1131 | 908 | 677 | 494 | 333 |
| | arc, inches: | | +1.6 | 0 | -7.9 | -24.5 |
| PMC 55 Pointed Soft Point | velocity, fps: | 2950 | 2594 | 2266 | 1966 | 1693 |
| | Energy, ft-lb: | 1063 | 822 | 627 | 472 | 350 |
| | Arc, inches: | | +1.9 | 0 | -8.7 | -26.3 |
| Rem. 50 Pointed Soft Point | velocity, fps: | 3140 | 2602 | 2123 | 1700 | 1350 |
| | energy, ft-lb: | 1094 | 752 | 500 | 321 | 202 |
| | arc, inches: | | +1.9 | 0 | -9.7 | -31.7 |
| Rem. 50 HP Power-Lokt | velocity, fps: | 3140 | 2635 | 2182 | 1777 | 1432 |
| | energy, ft-lb: | 1094 | 771 | 529 | 351 | 228 |
| | arc, inches: | | +1.8 | 0 | -9.2 | -29.6 |
| Rem. 50 AccuTip BT | velocity, fps: | 3140 | 2744 | 2380 | 2045 | 1740 |
| | energy, ft-lb: | 1094 | 836 | 629 | 464 | 336 |
| | arc, inches: | | +1.6 | 0 | -7.8 | -23.9 |
| Win. 40 Ballistic Silvertip | velocity, fps: | 3370 | 2915 | 2503 | 2127 | 1786 |
| | energy, ft-lb: | 1009 | 755 | 556 | 402 | 283 |
| | arc, inches: | | +1.3 | 0 | -6.9 | -21.5 |
| Win. 50 Pointed Soft Point | velocity, fps: | 3140 | 2602 | 2123 | 1700 | 1350 |
| | energy, ft-lb: | 1094 | 752 | 500 | 321 | 202 |
| | arc, inches: | | +2.2 | 0 | -10.0 | -32.3 |

## .223 REMINGTON

| CARTRIDGE BULLET | RANGE, YARDS: | 0 | 100 | 200 | 300 | 400 |
|---|---|---|---|---|---|---|
| Black Hills 40 Nosler B. Tip | velocity, fps: | 3600 | | | | |
| | energy, ft-lb: | 1150 | | | | |
| | arc, inches: | | | | | |
| Black Hills 50 V-Max | velocity, fps: | 3300 | | | | |
| | energy, ft-lb: | 1209 | | | | |
| | arc, inches: | | | | | |
| Black Hills 52 Match HP | velocity, fps: | 3300 | | | | |
| | energy, ft-lb: | 1237 | | | | |
| | arc, inches: | | | | | |
| Black Hills 55 Softpoint | velocity, fps: | 3250 | | | | |
| | energy, ft-lb: | 1270 | | | | |
| | arc, inches: | | | | | |
| Black Hills 60 SP or V-Max | velocity, fps: | 3150 | | | | |
| | energy, ft-lb: | 1322 | | | | |
| | arc, inches: | | | | | |
| Black Hills 60 Partition | velocity, fps: | 3150 | | | | |
| | energy, ft-lb: | 1322 | | | | |
| | arc, inches: | | | | | |
| Black Hills 68 Heavy Match | velocity, fps: | 2850 | | | | |
| | energy, ft-lb: | 1227 | | | | |
| | arc, inches: | | | | | |
| Black Hills 69 Sierra MK | velocity, fps: | 2850 | | | | |
| | energy, ft-lb: | 1245 | | | | |
| | arc, inches: | | | | | |
| Black Hills 73 Berger BTHP | velocity, fps: | 2750 | | | | |
| | energy, ft-lb: | 1226 | | | | |
| | arc, inches: | | | | | |
| Black Hills 75 Heavy Match | velocity, fps: | 2750 | | | | |
| | energy, ft-lb: | 1259 | | | | |
| | arc, inches: | | | | | |

| CARTRIDGE BULLET | RANGE, YARDS: | 0 | 100 | 200 | 300 | 400 |
|---|---|---|---|---|---|---|
| Black Hills 77 Sierra MKing | velocity, fps: | 2750 | | | | |
| | energy, ft-lb: | 1293 | | | | |
| | arc, inches: | | | | | |
| Federal 50 Jacketed HP | velocity, fps: | 3400 | 2910 | 2460 | 2060 | 1700 |
| | energy, ft-lb: | 1285 | 940 | 675 | 470 | 320 |
| | arc, inches: | | +1.3 | 0 | -7.1 | -22.7 |
| Federal 50 Speer TNT HP | velocity, fps: | 3300 | 2860 | 2450 | 2080 | 1750 |
| | energy, ft-lb: | 1210 | 905 | 670 | 480 | 340 |
| | arc, inches: | | +1.4 | 0 | -7.3 | -22.6 |
| Federal 52 Sierra MatchKing BTHP | velocity, fps: | 3300 | 2860 | 2460 | 2090 | 1760 |
| | energy, ft-lb: | 1255 | 945 | 700 | 505 | 360 |
| | arc, inches: | | +1.4 | 0 | -7.2 | -22.4 |
| Federal 55 Hi-Shok | velocity, fps: | 3240 | 2750 | 2300 | 1910 | 1550 |
| | energy, ft-lb: | 1280 | 920 | 650 | 445 | 295 |
| | arc, inches: | | +1.6 | 0 | -8.2 | -26.1 |
| Federal 55 FMJ boat-tail | velocity, fps: | 3240 | 2950 | 2670 | 2410 | 2170 |
| | energy, ft-lb: | 1280 | 1060 | 875 | 710 | 575 |
| | arc, inches: | | +1.3 | 0 | -6.1 | -18.3 |
| Federal 55 Sierra GameKing BTHP | velocity, fps: | 3240 | 2770 | 2340 | 1950 | 1610 |
| | energy, ft-lb: | 1280 | 935 | 670 | 465 | 315 |
| | arc, inches: | | +1.5 | 0 | -8.0 | -25.3 |
| Federal 55 Trophy Bonded | velocity, fps: | 3100 | 2630 | 2210 | 1830 | 1500 |
| | energy, ft-lb: | 1175 | 845 | 595 | 410 | 275 |
| | arc, inches: | | +1.8 | 0 | -8.9 | -28.7 |
| Federal 55 Nosler Bal. Tip | velocity, fps: | 3240 | 2870 | 2530 | 2220 | 1920 |
| | energy, ft-lb: | 1280 | 1005 | 780 | 600 | 450 |
| | arc, inches: | | +1.4 | 0 | -6.8 | -20.8 |
| Federal 55 Sierra BlitzKing | velocity, fps: | 3240 | 2870 | 2520 | 2200 | 1910 |
| | energy, ft-lb: | 1280 | 1005 | 775 | 590 | 445 |
| | arc, inches: | | +-1.4 | 0 | -6.9 | -20.9 |
| Federal 62 FMJ | velocity, fps: | 3020 | 2650 | 2310 | 2000 | 1710 |
| | energy, ft-lb: | 1225 | 970 | 735 | 550 | 405 |
| | arc, inches: | | +1.7 | 0 | -8.4 | -25.5 |
| Federal 64 Hi-Shok SP | velocity, fps: | 3090 | 2690 | 2325 | 1990 | 1680 |
| | energy, ft-lb: | 1360 | 1030 | 770 | 560 | 400 |
| | arc, inches: | | +1.7 | 0 | -8.2 | -25.2 |
| Federal 69 Sierra MatchKing BTHP | velocity, fps: | 3000 | 2720 | 2460 | 2210 | 1980 |
| | energy, ft-lb: | 1380 | 1135 | 925 | 750 | 600 |
| | arc, inches: | | +1.6 | 0 | -7.4 | -21.9 |
| Hornady 40 V-Max | velocity, fps: | 3800 | 3305 | 2845 | 2424 | 2044 |
| | energy, ft-lb: | 1282 | 970 | 719 | 522 | 371 |
| | arc, inches: | | +0.8 | 0 | -5.3 | -16.6 |
| Hornady 53 Hollow Point | velocity, fps: | 3330 | 2882 | 2477 | 2106 | 1710 |
| | energy, ft-lb: | 1305 | 978 | 722 | 522 | 369 |
| | arc, inches: | | +1.7 | 0 | -7.4 | -22.7 |
| Hornady 55 V-Max | velocity, fps: | 3240 | 2859 | 2507 | 2181 | 1891 |
| | energy, ft-lb: | 1282 | 998 | 767 | 581 | 437 |
| | arc, inches: | | +1.4 | 0 | -7.1 | -21.4 |
| Hornady 55 Urban Tactical | velocity, fps: | 2970 | 2626 | 2307 | 2011 | 1739 |
| | energy, ft-lb: | 1077 | 842 | 650 | 494 | 369 |
| | arc, inches: | | +1.5 | 0 | -8.1 | -24.9 |
| Hornady 60 Soft Point | velocity, fps: | 3150 | 2782 | 2442 | 2127 | 1837 |
| | energy, ft-lb: | 1322 | 1031 | 795 | 603 | 450 |
| | arc, inches: | | +1.6 | 0 | -7.5 | -22.5 |
| Hornady 60 Urban Tactical | velocity, fps: | 2950 | 2619 | 2312 | 2025 | 1762 |
| | energy, ft-lb: | 1160 | 914 | 712 | 546 | 413 |
| | arc, inches: | | +1.6 | 0 | -8.1 | -24.7 |
| Hornady 75 BTHP Match | velocity, fps: | 2790 | 2554 | 2330 | 2119 | 1926 |
| | energy, ft-lb: | 1296 | 1086 | 904 | 747 | 617 |
| | arc, inches: | | +2.4 | 0 | --8.8 | -25.1 |

# Centerfire Rifle Ballistics

## .223 REMINGTON TO .22-250 REMINGTON

| CARTRIDGE BULLET | RANGE, YARDS: | 0 | 100 | 200 | 300 | 400 |
|---|---|---|---|---|---|---|
| Hornady 75 BTHP Tactical | velocity, fps: | 2630 | 2409 | 2199 | 2000 | 1814 |
|  | energy, ft-lb: | 1152 | 966 | 805 | 666 | 548 |
|  | arc, inches: |  | -2.0 | 0 | -9.2 | -25.9 |
| PMC 40 non-toxic | velocity, fps: | 3500 | 2606 | 1871 | 1315 |  |
|  | energy, ft-lb: | 1088 | 603 | 311 | 154 |  |
|  | arc, inches: |  | +2.6 | 0 | -12.8 |  |
| PMC 50 Sierra BlitzKing | velocity, fps: | 3300 | 2874 | 2484 | 2130 | 1809 |
|  | energy, ft-lb: | 1209 | 917 | 685 | 504 | 363 |
|  | arc, inches: |  | +1.4 | 0 | -7.1 | -21.8 |
| PMC 52 Sierra HPBT Match | velocity, fps: | 3200 | 2808 | 2447 | 2117 | 1817 |
|  | energy, ft-lb: | 1182 | 910 | 691 | 517 | 381 |
|  | arc, inches: |  | +1.5 | 0 | -7.3 | -22.5 |
| PMC 53 Barnes XLC | velocity, fps: | 3200 | 2815 | 2461 | 2136 | 1840 |
|  | energy, ft-lb: | 1205 | 933 | 713 | 537 | 398 |
|  | arc, inches: |  | +1.5 | 0 | -7.2 | -22.2 |
| PMC 55 HP boat-tail | velocity, fps: | 3240 | 2717 | 2250 | 1832 | 1473 |
|  | energy, ft-lb: | 1282 | 901 | 618 | 410 | 265 |
|  | arc, inches: |  | +1.6 | 0 | -8.6 | -27.7 |
| PMC 55 FMJ boat-tail | velocity, fps: | 3195 | 2882 | 2525 | 2169 | 1843 |
|  | energy, ft-lb: | 1246 | 1014 | 779 | 574 | 415 |
|  | arc, inches: |  | +1.4 | 0 | -6.8 | -21.1 |
| PMC 55 Pointed Soft Point | velocity, fps: | 3112 | 2767 | 2421 | 2100 | 1806 |
|  | energy, ft-lb: | 1182 | 935 | 715 | 539 | 398 |
|  | arc, inches: |  | +1.5 | 0 | -7.5 | -22.9 |
| PMC 64 Pointed Soft Point | velocity, fps: | 2775 | 2511 | 2261 | 2026 | 1806 |
|  | energy, ft-lb: | 1094 | 896 | 726 | 583 | 464 |
|  | arc, inches: |  | +2.0 | 0 | -8.8 | -26.1 |
| PMC 69 Sierra BTHP Match | velocity, fps: | 2900 | 2591 | 2304 | 2038 | 1791 |
|  | energy, ft-lb: | 1288 | 1029 | 813 | 636 | 492 |
|  | arc, inches: |  | +1.9 | 0 | -8.4 | -25.3 |
| Rem. 50 AccuTip BT | velocity, fps: | 3300 | 2889 | 2514 | 2168 | 1851 |
|  | energy, ft-lb: | 1209 | 927 | 701 | 522 | 380 |
|  | arc, inches: |  | +1.4 | 0 | -6.9 | -21.2 |
| Rem. 55 Pointed Soft Point | velocity, fps: | 3240 | 2747 | 2304 | 1905 | 1554 |
|  | energy, ft-lb: | 1282 | 921 | 648 | 443 | 295 |
|  | arc, inches: |  | +1.6 | 0 | -8.2 | -26.2 |
| Rem. 55 HP Power-Lokt | velocity, fps: | 3240 | 2773 | 2352 | 1969 | 1627 |
|  | energy, ft-lb: | 1282 | 939 | 675 | 473 | 323 |
|  | arc, inches: |  | +1.5 | 0 | -7.9 | -24.8 |
| Rem. 55 AccuTip BT | velocity, fps: | 3240 | 2854 | 2500 | 2172 | 1871 |
|  | energy, ft-lb: | 1282 | 995 | 763 | 576 | 427 |
|  | arc, inches: |  | +1.5 | 0 | -7.1 | -21.7 |
| Rem. 55 Metal Case | velocity, fps: | 3240 | 2759 | 2326 | 1933 | 1587 |
|  | energy, ft-lb: | 1282 | 929 | 660 | 456 | 307 |
|  | arc, inches: |  | +1.6 | 0 | -8.1 | -25.5 |
| Rem. 62 HP Match | velocity, fps: | 3025 | 2572 | 2162 | 1792 | 1471 |
|  | energy, ft-lb: | 1260 | 911 | 643 | 442 | 298 |
|  | arc, inches: |  | +1.9 | 0 | -9.4 | -29.9 |
| Win. 40 Ballistic Silvertip | velocity, fps: | 3700 | 3166 | 2693 | 2265 | 1879 |
|  | energy, ft-lb: | 1216 | 891 | 644 | 456 | 314 |
|  | arc, inches: |  | +1.0 | 0 | -5.8 | -18.4 |
| Win. 45 JHP | velocity, fps: | 3600 |  |  |  |  |
|  | energy, ft-lb: | 1295 |  |  |  |  |
|  | arc, inches: |  |  |  |  |  |
| Win. 50 Ballistic Silvertip | velocity, fps: | 3410 | 2982 | 2593 | 2235 | 1907 |
|  | energy, ft-lb: | 1291 | 987 | 746 | 555 | 404 |
|  | arc, inches: |  | +1.2 | 0 | -6.4 | -19.8 |
| Win. 53 Hollow Point | velocity, fps: | 3330 | 2882 | 2477 | 2106 | 1770 |
|  | energy, ft-lb: | 1305 | 978 | 722 | 522 | 369 |
|  | arc, inches: |  | +1.7 | 0 | -7.4 | -22.7 |
| Win. 55 Pointed Soft Point | velocity, fps: | 3240 | 2747 | 2304 | 1905 | 1554 |
|  | energy, ft-lb: | 1282 | 921 | 648 | 443 | 295 |
|  | arc, inches: |  | +1.9 | 0 | -8.5 | -26.7 |
| Win. 55 Super Clean NT | velocity, fps: | 3150 | 2520 | 1970 | 1505 | 1165 |
|  | energy, ft-lb: | 1212 | 776 | 474 | 277 | 166 |
|  | arc, inches: |  | +2.8 | 0 | -11.9 | -38.9 |
| Win. 55 FMJ | velocity, fps: | 3240 | 2854 |  |  |  |
|  | energy, ft-lb: | 1282 | 995 |  |  |  |
|  | arc, inches: |  |  |  |  |  |
| Win. 55 Ballistic Silvertip | velocity, fps: | 3240 | 2871 | 2531 | 2215 | 1923 |
|  | energy, ft-lb: | 1282 | 1006 | 782 | 599 | 451 |
|  | arc, inches: |  | +1.4 | 0 | -6.8 | -20.8 |
| Win. 64 Power-Point | velocity, fps: | 3020 | 2656 | 2320 | 2009 | 1724 |
|  | energy, ft-lb: | 1296 | 1003 | 765 | 574 | 423 |
|  | arc, inches: |  | +1.7 | 0 | -8.2 | -25.1 |
| Win. 64 Power-Point Plus | velocity, fps: | 3090 | 2684 | 2312 | 1971 | 1664 |
|  | energy, ft-lb: | 1357 | 1024 | 760 | 552 | 393 |
|  | arc, inches: |  | +1.7 | 0 | -8.2 | -25.4 |

## .5.6 x 52 R

| CARTRIDGE BULLET | RANGE, YARDS: | 0 | 100 | 200 | 300 | 400 |
|---|---|---|---|---|---|---|
| Norma 71 Soft Point | velocity, fps: | 2789 | 2446 | 2128 | 1835 |  |
|  | energy, ft-lb: | 1227 | 944 | 714 | 531 |  |
|  | arc, inches: |  | +2.1 | 0 | -9.9 |  |

## .22 PPC

| CARTRIDGE BULLET | RANGE, YARDS: | 0 | 100 | 200 | 300 | 400 |
|---|---|---|---|---|---|---|
| A-Square 52 Berger | velocity, fps: | 3300 | 2952 | 2629 | 2329 | 2049 |
|  | energy, ft-lb: | 1257 | 1006 | 798 | 626 | 485 |
|  | arc, inches: |  | +1.3 | 0 | -6.3 | -19.1 |

## .225 WINCHESTER

| CARTRIDGE BULLET | RANGE, YARDS: | 0 | 100 | 200 | 300 | 400 |
|---|---|---|---|---|---|---|
| Win. 55 Pointed Soft Point | velocity, fps: | 3570 | 3066 | 2616 | 2208 | 1838 |
|  | energy, ft-lb: | 1556 | 1148 | 836 | 595 | 412 |
|  | arc, inches: |  | +2.4 | +2.0 | -3.5 | -16.3 |

## .224 WEATHERBY MAGNUM

| CARTRIDGE BULLET | RANGE, YARDS: | 0 | 100 | 200 | 300 | 400 |
|---|---|---|---|---|---|---|
| Wby. 55 Pointed Expanding | velocity, fps: | 3650 | 3192 | 2780 | 2403 | 2056 |
|  | energy, ft-lb: | 1627 | 1244 | 944 | 705 | 516 |
|  | arc, inches: |  | +2.8 | +3.7 | 0 | -9.8 |

## .22-250 REMINGTON

| CARTRIDGE BULLET | RANGE, YARDS: | 0 | 100 | 200 | 300 | 400 |
|---|---|---|---|---|---|---|
| Federal 40 Sierra Varminter | velocity, fps: | 4000 | 3320 | 2720 | 2200 | 1740 |
|  | energy, ft-lb: | 1420 | 980 | 660 | 430 | 265 |
|  | arc, inches: |  | +0.8 | 0 | -5.6 | -18.4 |
| Federal 55 Hi-Shok | velocity, fps: | 3680 | 3140 | 2660 | 2220 | 1830 |
|  | energy, ft-lb: | 1655 | 1200 | 860 | 605 | 410 |
|  | arc, inches: |  | +1.0 | 0 | -6.0 | -19.1 |
| Federal 55 Sierra BlitzKing | velocity, fps: | 3680 | 3270 | 2890 | 2540 | 2220 |
|  | energy, ft-lb: | 1655 | 1300 | 1020 | 790 | 605 |
|  | arc, inches: |  | +0.9 | 0 | -5.1 | -15.6 |
| Federal 55 Sierra GameKing BTHP | velocity, fps: | 3680 | 3280 | 2920 | 2590 | 2280 |
|  | energy, ft-lb: | 1655 | 1315 | 1040 | 815 | 630 |
|  | arc, inches: |  | +0.9 | 0 | -5.0 | -15.1 |
| Federal 55 Trophy Bonded | velocity, fps: | 3600 | 3080 | 2610 | 2190 | 1810 |
|  | energy, ft-lb: | 1585 | 1155 | 835 | 590 | 400 |
|  | arc, inches: |  | +1.1 | 0 | -6.2 | -19.8 |
| Hornady 40 V-Max | velocity, fps: | 4150 | 3631 | 3147 | 2699 | 2293 |
|  | energy, ft-lb: | 1529 | 1171 | 879 | 647 | 467 |
|  | arc, inches: |  | +0.5 | 0 | -4.2 | -13.3 |
| Hornady 50 V-Max | velocity, fps: | 3800 | 3349 | 2925 | 2535 | 2178 |
|  | energy, ft-lb: | 1603 | 1245 | 950 | 713 | 527 |
|  | arc, inches: |  | +0.8 | 0 | -5.0 | -15.6 |

**BALLISTICS**

| CARTRIDGE BULLET | RANGE, YARDS: | 0 | 100 | 200 | 300 | 400 |
|---|---|---|---|---|---|---|
| Hornady 53 Hollow Point | velocity, fps: | 3680 | 3185 | 2743 | 2341 | 1974 |
| | energy, ft-lb: | 1594 | 1194 | 886 | 645 | 459 |
| | arc, inches: | | +1.0 | 0 | -5.7 | -17.8 |
| Hornady 55 V-Max | velocity, fps: | 3680 | 3265 | 2876 | 2517 | 2183 |
| | energy, ft-lb: | 1654 | 1302 | 1010 | 772 | 582 |
| | arc, inches: | | +0.9 | 0 | -5.3 | -16.1 |
| Hornady 60 Soft Point | velocity, fps: | 3600 | 3195 | 2826 | 2485 | 2169 |
| | energy, ft-lb: | 1727 | 1360 | 1064 | 823 | 627 |
| | arc, inches: | | +1.0 | 0 | -5.4 | -16.3 |
| Norma 53 Soft Point | velocity, fps: | 3707 | 3234 | 2809 | 1716 | |
| | energy, ft-lb: | 1618 | 1231 | 928 | 690 | |
| | arc, inches: | | +0.9 | 0 | -5.3 | |
| PMC 50 Sierra BlitzKing | velocity, fps: | 3725 | 3264 | 2641 | 2455 | 2103 |
| | energy, ft-lb: | 1540 | 1183 | 896 | 669 | 491 |
| | arc, inches: | | +0.9 | 0 | -5.2 | -16.2 |
| PMC 50 Barnes XLC | velocity, fps: | 3725 | 3280 | 2871 | 2495 | 2152 |
| | energy, ft-lb: | 1540 | 1195 | 915 | 691 | 514 |
| | arc, inches: | | +0.9 | 0 | -5.1 | -15.9 |
| PMC 55 HP boat-tail | velocity, fps: | 3680 | 3104 | 2596 | 2141 | 1737 |
| | energy, ft-lb: | 1654 | 1176 | 823 | 560 | 368 |
| | arc, inches: | | +1.1 | 0 | -6.3 | -20.2 |
| PMC 55 Pointed Soft Point | velocity, fps: | 3586 | 3203 | 2852 | 2505 | 2178 |
| | energy, ft-lb: | 1570 | 1253 | 993 | 766 | 579 |
| | arc, inches: | | +1.0 | 0 | -5.2 | -16.0 |
| Rem. 50 AccuTip BT (also in EtronX) | velocity, fps: | 3725 | 3272 | 2864 | 2491 | 2147 |
| | energy, ft-lb: | 1540 | 1188 | 910 | 689 | 512 |
| | arc, inches: | | +1.7 | +1.6 | -2.8 | -12.8 |
| Rem. 55 Pointed Soft Point | velocity, fps: | 3680 | 3137 | 2656 | 2222 | 1832 |
| | energy, ft-lb: | 1654 | 1201 | 861 | 603 | 410 |
| | arc, inches: | | +1.9 | +1.8 | -3.3 | -15.5 |
| Rem. 55 HP Power-Lokt | velocity, fps: | 3680 | 3209 | 2785 | 2400 | 2046 |
| | energy, ft-lb: | 1654 | 1257 | 947 | 703 | 511 |
| | arc, inches: | | +1.8 | +1.7 | -3.0 | -13.7 |
| Rem. 60 Nosler Partition (also in EtronX) | velocity, fps: | 3500 | 3045 | 2634 | 2258 | 1914 |
| | energy, ft-lb: | 1632 | 1235 | 924 | 679 | 488 |
| | arc, inches: | | +2.1 | +1.9 | -3.4 | -15.5 |
| Win. 40 Ballistic Silvertip | velocity, fps: | 4150 | 3591 | 3099 | 2658 | 2257 |
| | energy, ft-lb: | 1530 | 1146 | 853 | 628 | 453 |
| | arc, inches: | | +0.6 | 0 | -4.2 | -13.4 |
| Win. 50 Ballistic Silvertip | velocity, fps: | 3810 | 3341 | 2919 | 2536 | 2182 |
| | energy, ft-lb: | 1611 | 1239 | 946 | 714 | 529 |
| | arc, inches: | | +0.8 | 0 | -4.9 | -15.2 |
| Win. 55 Pointed Soft Point | velocity, fps: | 3680 | 3137 | 2656 | 2222 | 1832 |
| | energy, ft-lb: | 1654 | 1201 | 861 | 603 | 410 |
| | arc, inches: | | +2.3 | +1.9 | -3.4 | -15.9 |
| Win. 55 Ballistic Silvertip | velocity, fps: | 3680 | 3272 | 2900 | 2558 | 2240 |
| | energy, ft-lb: | 1654 | 1307 | 1027 | 799 | 613 |
| | arc, inches: | | +0.9 | 0 | -5.0 | -15.4 |

## .220 SWIFT

| CARTRIDGE BULLET | RANGE, YARDS: | 0 | 100 | 200 | 300 | 400 |
|---|---|---|---|---|---|---|
| Federal 52 Sierra MatchKing BTHP | velocity, fps: | 3830 | 3370 | 2960 | 2600 | 2230 |
| | energy, ft-lb: | 1690 | 1310 | 1010 | 770 | 575 |
| | arc, inches: | | +0.8 | 0 | -4.8 | -14.9 |
| Federal 55 Sierra BlitzKing | velocity, fps: | 3800 | 3370 | 2990 | 2630 | 2310 |
| | energy, ft-lb: | 1765 | 1390 | 1090 | 850 | 650 |
| | arc, inches: | | +0.8 | 0 | -4.7 | -14.4 |
| Federal 55 Trophy Bonded | velocity, fps: | 3700 | 3170 | 2690 | 2270 | 1880 |
| | energy, ft-lb: | 1670 | 1225 | 885 | 625 | 430 |
| | arc, inches: | | +1.0 | 0 | -5.8 | -18.5 |

| CARTRIDGE BULLET | RANGE, YARDS: | 0 | 100 | 200 | 300 | 400 |
|---|---|---|---|---|---|---|
| Hornady 40 V-Max | velocity, fps: | 4200 | 3678 | 3190 | 2739 | 2329 |
| | energy, ft-lb: | 1566 | 1201 | 904 | 666 | 482 |
| | arc, inches: | | +0.5 | 0 | -4.0 | -12.9 |
| Hornady 50 V-Max | velocity, fps: | 3850 | 3396 | 2970 | 2576 | 2215 |
| | energy, ft-lb: | 1645 | 1280 | 979 | 736 | 545 |
| | arc, inches: | | +0.7 | 0 | -4.8 | -15.1 |
| Hornady 50 SP | velocity, fps: | 3850 | 3327 | 2862 | 2442 | 2060 |
| | energy, ft-lb: | 1645 | 1228 | 909 | 662 | 471 |
| | arc, inches: | | +0.8 | 0 | -5.1 | -16.1 |
| Hornady 55 V-Max | velocity, fps: | 3680 | 3265 | 2876 | 2517 | 2183 |
| | energy, ft-lb: | 1654 | 1302 | 1010 | 772 | 582 |
| | arc, inches: | | +0.9 | 0 | -5.3 | -16.1 |
| Hornady 60 Hollow Point | velocity, fps: | 3600 | 3199 | 2824 | 2475 | 2156 |
| | energy, ft-lb: | 1727 | 1364 | 1063 | 816 | 619 |
| | arc, inches: | | +1.0 | 0 | -5.4 | -16.3 |
| Norma 50 Soft Point | velocity, fps: | 4019 | 3380 | 2826 | 2335 | |
| | energy, ft-lb: | 1794 | 1268 | 887 | 605 | |
| | arc, inches: | | +0.7 | 0 | -5.1 | |
| Rem. 50 Pointed Soft Point | velocity, fps: | 3780 | 3158 | 2617 | 2135 | 1710 |
| | energy, ft-lb: | 1586 | 1107 | 760 | 506 | 325 |
| | arc, inches: | | +0.3 | -1.4 | -8.2 | |
| Rem. 50 V-Max boat-tail (also in EtronX) | velocity, fps: | 3780 | 3321 | 2908 | 2532 | 2185 |
| | energy, ft-lb: | 1586 | 1224 | 939 | 711 | 530 |
| | arc, inches: | | +0.8 | 0 | -5.0 | -15.4 |
| Win. 40 Ballistic Silvertip | velocity, fps: | 4050 | 3518 | 3048 | 2624 | 2238 |
| | energy, ft-lb: | 1457 | 1099 | 825 | 611 | 445 |
| | arc, inches: | | +0.7 | 0 | -4.4 | -13.9 |
| Win. 50 Pointed Soft Point | velocity, fps: | 3870 | 3310 | 2816 | 2373 | 1972 |
| | energy, ft-lb: | 1663 | 1226 | 881 | 625 | 432 |
| | arc, inches: | | +0.8 | 0 | -5.2 | -16.7 |

## .223 WSSM

| CARTRIDGE BULLET | RANGE, YARDS: | 0 | 100 | 200 | 300 | 400 |
|---|---|---|---|---|---|---|
| Win. 55 Ballistic Silvertip | velocity, fps: | 3850 | 3438 | 3064 | 2721 | 2402 |
| | energy, ft-lb: | 1810 | 1444 | 1147 | 904 | 704 |
| | arc, inches: | | +0.7 | 0 | -4.4 | -13.6 |
| Win. 55 Pointed Softpoint | velocity, fps: | 3850 | 3367 | 2934 | 2541 | 2181 |
| | energy, ft-lb: | 1810 | 1384 | 1051 | 789 | 581 |
| | arc, inches: | | +0.8 | 0 | -4.9 | -15.1 |
| Win. 64 Power-Point | velocity, fps: | 3600 | 3144 | 2732 | 2356 | 2011 |
| | energy, ft-lb: | 1841 | 1404 | 1061 | 789 | 574 |
| | arc, inches: | | +1.0 | 0 | -5.7 | -17.7 |

## 6MM PPC

| CARTRIDGE BULLET | RANGE, YARDS: | 0 | 100 | 200 | 300 | 400 |
|---|---|---|---|---|---|---|
| A-Square 68 Berger | velocity, fps: | 3100 | 2751 | 2428 | 2128 | 1850 |
| | energy, ft-lb: | 1451 | 1143 | 890 | 684 | 516 |
| | arc, inches: | | +1.5 | 0 | -7.5 | -22.6 |

## 6x70 R

| CARTRIDGE BULLET | RANGE, YARDS: | 0 | 100 | 200 | 300 | 400 |
|---|---|---|---|---|---|---|
| Norma 90 Nosler Bal. Tip | velocity, fps: | 2461 | 2231 | 2013 | 1809 | |
| | energy, ft-lb: | 1211 | 995 | 810 | 654 | |
| | arc, inches: | | +2.7 | 0 | -11.3 | |

## .243 WINCHESTER

| CARTRIDGE BULLET | RANGE, YARDS: | 0 | 100 | 200 | 300 | 400 |
|---|---|---|---|---|---|---|
| Black Hills 55 Nosler B. Tip | velocity, fps: | 3800 | | | | |
| | energy, ft-lb: | 1763 | | | | |
| | arc, inches: | | | | | |
| Black Hills 90 Nosler B. Tip | velocity, fps: | 2950 | | | | |
| | energy, ft-lb: | 1836 | | | | |
| | arc, inches: | | | | | |
| Federal 70 Nosler Bal. Tip | velocity, fps: | 3400 | 3070 | 2760 | 2470 | 2200 |
| | energy, ft-lb: | 1795 | 1465 | 1185 | 950 | 755 |
| | arc, inches: | | +1.1 | 0 | -5.7 | -17.1 |

# Centerfire Rifle Ballistics

## .243 WINCHESTER TO 6MM REMINGTON

| CARTRIDGE BULLET | RANGE, YARDS: | 0 | 100 | 200 | 300 | 400 |
|---|---|---|---|---|---|---|
| Federal 70 Speer TNT HP | velocity, fps: | 3400 | 3040 | 2700 | 2390 | 2100 |
| | energy, ft-lb: | 1795 | 1435 | 1135 | 890 | 685 |
| | arc, inches: | | +1.1 | 0 | -5.9 | -18.0 |
| Federal 80 Sierra Pro-Hunter | velocity, fps: | 3350 | 2960 | 2590 | 2260 | 1950 |
| | energy, ft-lb: | 1995 | 1550 | 1195 | 905 | 675 |
| | arc, inches: | | +1.3 | 0 | -6.4 | -19.7 |
| Federal 85 Sierra GameKing BTHP | velocity, fps: | 3320 | 3070 | 2830 | 2600 | 2380 |
| | energy, ft-lb: | 2080 | 1770 | 1510 | 1280 | 1070 |
| | arc, inches: | | +1.1 | 0 | -5.5 | -16.1 |
| Federal 90 Trophy Bonded | velocity, fps: | 3100 | 2850 | 2610 | 2380 | 2160 |
| | energy, ft-lb: | 1920 | 1620 | 1360 | 1130 | 935 |
| | arc, inches: | | +1.4 | 0 | -6.1 | -19.2 |
| Federal 100 Hi-Shok | velocity, fps: | 2960 | 2700 | 2450 | 2220 | 1990 |
| | energy, ft-lb: | 1945 | 1615 | 1330 | 1090 | 880 |
| | arc, inches: | | +1.6 | 0 | -7.5 | -22.0 |
| Federal 100 Sierra GameKing BTSP | velocity, fps: | 2960 | 2760 | 2570 | 2380 | 2210 |
| | energy, ft-lb: | 1950 | 1690 | 1460 | 1260 | 1080 |
| | arc, inches: | | +1.5 | 0 | -6.8 | -19.8 |
| Federal 100 Nosler Partition | velocity, fps: | 2960 | 2730 | 2510 | 2300 | 2100 |
| | energy, ft-lb: | 1945 | 1650 | 1395 | 1170 | 975 |
| | arc, inches: | | +1.6 | 0 | -7.1 | -20.9 |
| Hornady 58 V-Max | velocity, fps: | 3750 | 3319 | 2913 | 2539 | 2195 |
| | energy, ft-lb: | 1811 | 1418 | 1093 | 830 | 620 |
| | arc, inches: | | +1.2 | 0 | -5.5 | -16.4 |
| Hornady 75 Hollow Point | velocity, fps: | 3400 | 2970 | 2578 | 2219 | 1890 |
| | energy, ft-lb: | 1926 | 1469 | 1107 | 820 | 595 |
| | arc, inches: | | +1.2 | 0 | -6.5 | -20.3 |
| Hornady 100 BTSP | velocity, fps: | 2960 | 2728 | 2508 | 2299 | 2099 |
| | energy, ft-lb: | 1945 | 1653 | 1397 | 1174 | 979 |
| | arc, inches: | | +1.6 | 0 | -7.2 | -21.0 |
| Hornady 100 BTSP LM | velocity, fps: | 3100 | 2839 | 2592 | 2358 | 2138 |
| | energy, ft-lb: | 2133 | 1790 | 1491 | 1235 | 1014 |
| | arc, inches: | | +1.5 | 0 | -6.8 | -19.8 |
| Norma 80 FMJ | velocity, fps: | 3117 | 2750 | 2412 | 2098 | |
| | energy, ft-lb: | 1726 | 1344 | 1034 | 782 | |
| | arc, inches: | | +1.5 | 0 | -7.5 | |
| Norma 100 FMJ | velocity, fps: | 3018 | 2747 | 2493 | 2252 | |
| | energy, ft-lb: | 2023 | 1677 | 1380 | 1126 | |
| | arc, inches: | | +1.5 | 0 | -7.1 | |
| Norma 100 Soft Point | velocity, fps: | 3018 | 2748 | 2493 | 2252 | |
| | energy, ft-lb: | 2023 | 1677 | 1380 | 1126 | |
| | arc, inches: | | +1.5 | 0 | -7.1 | |
| PMC 80 Pointed Soft Point | velocity, fps: | 2940 | 2684 | 2444 | 2215 | 1999 |
| | energy, ft-lb: | 1535 | 1280 | 1060 | 871 | 709 |
| | arc, inches: | | +1.7 | 0 | -7.5 | -22.1 |
| PMC 85 Barnes XLC | velocity, fps: | 3250 | 3022 | 2805 | 2598 | 2401 |
| | energy, ft-lb: | 1993 | 1724 | 1485 | 1274 | 1088 |
| | arc, inches: | | +1.6 | 0 | -5.6 | 16.3 |
| PMC 85 HP boat-tail | velocity, fps: | 3275 | 2922 | 2596 | 2292 | 2009 |
| | energy, ft-lb: | 2024 | 1611 | 1272 | 991 | 761 |
| | arc, inches: | | +1.3 | 0 | -6.5 | -19.7 |
| PMC 100 Pointed Soft Point | velocity, fps: | 2743 | 2507 | 2283 | 2070 | 1869 |
| | energy, ft-lb: | 1670 | 1395 | 1157 | 951 | 776 |
| | arc, inches: | | +2.0 | 0 | -8.7 | -25.5 |
| PMC 100 SP boat-tail | velocity, fps: | 2960 | 2742 | 2534 | 2335 | 2144 |
| | energy, ft-lb: | 1945 | 1669 | 1425 | 1210 | 1021 |
| | arc, inches: | | +1.6 | 0 | -7.0 | -20.5 |
| Rem. 75 AccuTip BT | velocity, fps: | 3375 | 3065 | 2775 | 2504 | 2248 |
| | energy, ft-lb: | 1897 | 1564 | 1282 | 1044 | 842 |
| | arc, inches: | | +2.0 | +1.8 | -3.0 | -13.3 |
| Rem. 80 Pointed Soft Point | velocity, fps: | 3350 | 2955 | 2593 | 2259 | 1951 |
| | energy, ft-lb: | 1993 | 1551 | 1194 | 906 | 676 |
| | arc, inches: | | +2.2 | +2.0 | -3.5 | -15.8 |
| Rem. 80 HP Power-Lokt | velocity, fps: | 3350 | 2955 | 2593 | 2259 | 1951 |
| | energy, ft-lb: | 1993 | 1551 | 1194 | 906 | 676 |
| | arc, inches: | | +2.2 | +2.0 | -3.5 | -15.8 |
| Rem. 90 Nosler Bal. Tip (also in EtronX) or Scirocco | velocity, fps: | 3120 | 2871 | 2635 | 2411 | 2199 |
| | energy, ft-lb: | 1946 | 1647 | 1388 | 1162 | 966 |
| | arc, inches: | | +1.4 | 0 | -6.4 | -18.8 |
| Rem. 95 AccuTip | velocity, fps: | 3120 | 2847 | 2590 | 2347 | 2118 |
| | energy, ft-lb: | 2053 | 1710 | 1415 | 1162 | 946 |
| | arc, inches: | | +1.5 | 0 | -6.6 | -19.5 |
| Rem. 100 PSP Core-Lokt (also in EtronX) | velocity, fps: | 2960 | 2697 | 2449 | 2215 | 1993 |
| | energy, ft-lb: | 1945 | 1615 | 1332 | 1089 | 882 |
| | arc, inches: | | +1.6 | 0 | -7.5 | -22.1 |
| Rem. 100 PSP boat-tail | velocity, fps: | 2960 | 2720 | 2492 | 2275 | 2069 |
| | energy, ft-lb: | 1945 | 1642 | 1378 | 1149 | 950 |
| | arc, inches: | | +2.8 | +2.3 | -3.8 | -16.6 |
| Speer 100 Grand Slam | velocity, fps: | 2950 | 2684 | 2434 | 2197 | |
| | energy, ft-lb: | 1932 | 1600 | 1315 | 1072 | |
| | arc, inches: | | +1.7 | 0 | -7.6 | -22.4 |
| Win. 55 Ballistic Silvertip | velocity, fps: | 4025 | 3597 | 3209 | 2853 | 2525 |
| | energy, ft-lb: | 1978 | 1579 | 1257 | 994 | 779 |
| | arc, inches: | | +0.6 | 0 | -4.0 | -12.2 |
| Win. 80 Pointed Soft Point | velocity, fps: | 3350 | 2955 | 2593 | 2259 | 1951 |
| | energy, ft-lb: | 1993 | 1551 | 1194 | 906 | 676 |
| | arc, inches: | | +2.6 | +2.1 | -3.6 | -16.2 |
| Win. 95 Ballistic Silvertip | velocity, fps: | 3100 | 2854 | 2626 | 2410 | 2203 |
| | energy, ft-lb: | 2021 | 1719 | 1455 | 1225 | 1024 |
| | arc, inches: | | +1.4 | 0 | -6.4 | -18.9 |
| Win. 100 Power-Point | velocity, fps: | 2960 | 2697 | 2449 | 2215 | 1993 |
| | energy, ft-lb: | 1945 | 1615 | 1332 | 1089 | 882 |
| | arc, inches: | | +1.9 | 0 | -7.8 | -22.6 |
| Win. 100 Power-Point Plus | velocity, fps: | 3090 | 2818 | 2562 | 2321 | 2092 |
| | energy, ft-lb: | 2121 | 1764 | 1458 | 1196 | 972 |
| | arc, inches: | | +1.4 | 0 | -6.7 | -20.0 |

## 6MM REMINGTON

| CARTRIDGE BULLET | RANGE, YARDS: | 0 | 100 | 200 | 300 | 400 |
|---|---|---|---|---|---|---|
| Federal 80 Sierra Pro-Hunter | velocity, fps: | 3470 | 3060 | 2690 | 2350 | 2040 |
| | energy, ft-lb: | 2140 | 1665 | 1290 | 980 | 735 |
| | arc, inches: | | +1.1 | 0 | -5.9 | -18.2 |
| Federal 100 Hi-Shok | velocity, fps: | 3100 | 2830 | 2570 | 2330 | 2100 |
| | energy, ft-lb: | 2135 | 1775 | 1470 | 1205 | 985 |
| | arc, inches: | | +1.4 | 0 | -6.7 | -19.8 |
| Federal 100 Nosler Partition | velocity, fps: | 3100 | 2860 | 2640 | 2420 | 2220 |
| | energy, ft-lb: | 2135 | 1820 | 1545 | 1300 | 1090 |
| | arc, inches: | | +1.4 | 0 | -6.3 | -18.7 |
| Hornady 100 SP boat-tail | velocity, fps: | 3100 | 2861 | 2634 | 2419 | 2231 |
| | energy, ft-lb: | 2134 | 1818 | 1541 | 1300 | 1088 |
| | arc, inches: | | +1.3 | 0 | -6.5 | -18.9 |
| Hornady 100 SPBT LM | velocity, fps: | 3250 | 2997 | 2756 | 2528 | 2311 |
| | energy, ft-lb: | 2345 | 1995 | 1687 | 1418 | 1186 |
| | arc, inches: | | +1.6 | 0 | -6.3 | -18.2 |
| Rem. 75 V-Max boat-tail | velocity, fps: | 3400 | 3088 | 2797 | 2524 | 2267 |
| | energy, ft-lb: | 1925 | 1587 | 1303 | 1061 | 856 |
| | arc, inches: | | +1.9 | +1.7 | -3.0 | -13.1 |
| Rem. 100 PSP Core-Lokt | velocity, fps: | 3100 | 2829 | 2573 | 2332 | 2104 |
| | energy, ft-lb: | 2133 | 1777 | 1470 | 1207 | 983 |
| | arc, inches: | | +1.4 | 0 | -6.7 | -19.8 |

BALLISTICS

# Centerfire Rifle Ballistics

## 6MM REMINGTON TO .25-06 REMINGTON

| CARTRIDGE BULLET | RANGE, YARDS: | 0 | 100 | 200 | 300 | 400 |
|---|---|---|---|---|---|---|
| Rem. 100 PSP boat-tail | velocity, fps: | 3100 | 2852 | 2617 | 2394 | 2183 |
| | energy, ft-lb: | 2134 | 1806 | 1521 | 1273 | 1058 |
| | arc, inches: | | +1.4 | 0 | -6.5 | -19.1 |
| Win. 100 Power-Point | velocity, fps: | 3100 | 2829 | 2573 | 2332 | 2104 |
| | energy, ft-lb: | 2133 | 1777 | 1470 | 1207 | 983 |
| | arc, inches: | | +1.7 | 0 | -7.0 | -20.4 |

### .243 WSSM

| | | | | | | |
|---|---|---|---|---|---|---|
| Win. 55 Ballistic Silvertip | velocity, fps: | 4060 | 3628 | 3237 | 2880 | 2550 |
| | energy, ft-lb: | 2013 | 1607 | 1280 | 1013 | 794 |
| | arc, inches: | | +0.6 | 0 | -3.9 | -12.0 |
| Win. 95 Ballistic Silvertip | velocity, fps: | 3250 | 3000 | 2763 | 2538 | 2325 |
| | energy, ft-lb: | 2258 | 1898 | 1610 | 1359 | 1140 |
| | arc, inches: | | +1.2 | 0 | 5.7 | 16.9 |
| Win. 100 Power Point | velocity, fps: | 3110 | 2838 | 2583 | 2341 | 2112 |
| | energy, ft-lb: | 2147 | 1789 | 1481 | 1217 | 991 |
| | arc, inches: | | +1.4 | 0 | -6.6 | -19.7 |

### .240 WEATHERBY MAGNUM

| | | | | | | |
|---|---|---|---|---|---|---|
| Wby. 87 Pointed Expanding | velocity, fps: | 3523 | 3199 | 2898 | 2617 | 2352 |
| | energy, ft-lb: | 2397 | 1977 | 1622 | 1323 | 1069 |
| | arc, inches: | | +2.7 | +3.4 | 0 | -8.4 |
| Wby. 90 Barnes-X | velocity, fps: | 3500 | 3222 | 2962 | 2717 | 2484 |
| | energy, ft-lb: | 2448 | 2075 | 1753 | 1475 | 1233 |
| | arc, inches: | | +2.6 | +3.3 | 0 | -8.0 |
| Wby. 95 Nosler Bal. Tip | velocity, fps: | 3420 | 3146 | 2888 | 2645 | 2414 |
| | energy, ft-lb: | 2467 | 2087 | 1759 | 1475 | 1229 |
| | arc, inches: | | +2.7 | +3.5 | 0 | -8.4 |
| Wby. 100 Pointed Expanding | velocity, fps: | 3406 | 3134 | 2878 | 2637 | 2408 |
| | energy, ft-lb: | 2576 | 2180 | 1839 | 1544 | 1287 |
| | arc, inches: | | +2.8 | +3.5 | 0 | -8.4 |
| Wby. 100 Partition | velocity, fps: | 3406 | 3136 | 2882 | 2642 | 2415 |
| | energy, ft-lb: | 2576 | 2183 | 1844 | 1550 | 1294 |
| | arc, inches: | | +2.8 | +3.5 | 0 | -8.4 |

### .25-20 WINCHESTER

| | | | | | | |
|---|---|---|---|---|---|---|
| Rem. 86 Soft Point | velocity, fps: | 1460 | 1194 | 1030 | 931 | 858 |
| | energy, ft-lb: | 407 | 272 | 203 | 165 | 141 |
| | arc, inches: | | 0 | -22.9 | -78.9 | -173.0 |
| Win. 86 Soft Point | velocity, fps: | 1460 | 1194 | 1030 | 931 | 858 |
| | energy, ft-lb: | 407 | 272 | 203 | 165 | 141 |
| | arc, inches: | | 0 | -23.5 | -79.6 | -175.9 |

### .25-35 WINCHESTER

| | | | | | | |
|---|---|---|---|---|---|---|
| Win. 117 Soft Point | velocity, fps: | 2230 | 1866 | 1545 | 1282 | 1097 |
| | energy, ft-lb: | 1292 | 904 | 620 | 427 | 313 |
| | arc, inches: | | +2.1 | -5.1 | -27.0 | -70.1 |

### .250 SAVAGE

| | | | | | | |
|---|---|---|---|---|---|---|
| Rem. 100 Pointed SP | velocity, fps: | 2820 | 2504 | 2210 | 1936 | 1684 |
| | energy, ft-lb: | 1765 | 1392 | 1084 | 832 | 630 |
| | arc, inches: | | +2.0 | 0 | -9.2 | -27.7 |
| Win. 100 Silvertip | velocity, fps: | 2820 | 2467 | 2140 | 1839 | 1569 |
| | energy, ft-lb: | 1765 | 1351 | 1017 | 751 | 547 |
| | arc, inches: | | +2.4 | 0 | -10.1 | -30.5 |

### .257 ROBERTS

| | | | | | | |
|---|---|---|---|---|---|---|
| Federal 120 Nosler Partition | velocity, fps: | 2780 | 2560 | 2360 | 2160 | 1970 |
| | energy, ft-lb: | 2060 | 1750 | 1480 | 1240 | 1030 |
| | arc, inches: | | +1.9 | 0 | -8.2 | -24.0 |

| Hornady 117 SP boat-tail | velocity, fps: | 2780 | 2550 | 2331 | 2122 | 1925 |
|---|---|---|---|---|---|---|
| | energy, ft-lb: | 2007 | 1689 | 1411 | 1170 | 963 |
| | arc, inches: | | +1.9 | 0 | -8.3 | -24.4 |
| Hornady 117 SP boat-tail LM | velocity, fps: | 2940 | 2694 | 2460 | 2240 | 2031 |
| | energy, ft-lb: | 2245 | 1885 | 1572 | 1303 | 1071 |
| | arc, inches: | | +1.7 | 0 | -7.6 | -21.8 |
| Rem. 117 SP Core-Lokt | velocity, fps: | 2650 | 2291 | 1961 | 1663 | 1404 |
| | energy, ft-lb: | 1824 | 1363 | 999 | 718 | 512 |
| | arc, inches: | | +2.6 | 0 | -11.7 | -36.1 |
| Win. 117 Power-Point | velocity, fps: | 2780 | 2411 | 2071 | 1761 | 1488 |
| | energy, ft-lb: | 2009 | 1511 | 1115 | 806 | 576 |
| | arc, inches: | | +2.6 | 0 | -10.8 | -33.0 |

### .25-06 REMINGTON

| | | | | | | |
|---|---|---|---|---|---|---|
| Black Hills 100 Nosler B. Tip | velocity, fps: | 3200 | | | | |
| | energy, ft-lb: | 2259 | | | | |
| | arc, inches: | | | | | |
| Black Hills 115 Barnes X | velocity, fps: | 2975 | | | | |
| | energy, ft-lb: | 2259 | | | | |
| | arc, inches: | | | | | |
| Federal 90 Sierra Varminter | velocity, fps: | 3440 | 3040 | 2680 | 2340 | 2030 |
| | energy, ft-lb: | 2365 | 1850 | 1435 | 1100 | 825 |
| | arc, inches: | | +1.1 | 0 | -6.0 | -18.3 |
| Federal 100 Barnes XLC | velocity, fps: | 3210 | 2970 | 2750 | 2540 | 2330 |
| | energy, ft-lb: | 2290 | 1965 | 1680 | 1430 | 1205 |
| | arc, inches: | | +1.2 | 0 | -5.8 | -17.0 |
| Federal 100 Nosler Bal. Tip | velocity, fps: | 3210 | 2960 | 2720 | 2490 | 2280 |
| | energy, ft-lb: | 2290 | 1940 | 1640 | 1380 | 1150 |
| | arc, inches: | | +1.2 | 0 | -6.0 | -17.5 |
| Federal 115 Nosler Partition | velocity, fps: | 2990 | 2750 | 2520 | 2300 | 2100 |
| | energy, ft-lb: | 2285 | 1930 | 1620 | 1350 | 1120 |
| | arc, inches: | | +1.6 | 0 | -7.0 | -20.8 |
| Federal 115 Trophy Bonded | velocity, fps: | 2990 | 2740 | 2500 | 2270 | 2050 |
| | energy, ft-lb: | 2285 | 1910 | 1590 | 1310 | 1075 |
| | arc, inches: | | +1.6 | 0 | -7.2 | -21.1 |
| Federal 117 Sierra Pro Hunt. | velocity, fps: | 2990 | 2730 | 2480 | 2250 | 2030 |
| | energy, ft-lb: | 2320 | 1985 | 1645 | 1350 | 1100 |
| | arc, inches: | | +1.6 | 0 | -7.2 | -21.4 |
| Federal 117 Sierra GameKing BTSP | velocity, fps: | 2990 | 2770 | 2570 | 2370 | 2190 |
| | energy, ft-lb: | 2320 | 2000 | 1715 | 1465 | 1240 |
| | arc, inches: | | +1.5 | 0 | -6.8 | -19.9 |
| Hornady 117 SP boat-tail | velocity, fps: | 2990 | 2749 | 2520 | 2302 | 2096 |
| | energy, ft-lb: | 2322 | 1962 | 1649 | 1377 | 1141 |
| | arc, inches: | | +1.6 | 0 | -7.0 | -20.7 |
| Hornady 117 SP boat-tail LM | velocity, fps: | 3110 | 2855 | 2613 | 2384 | 2168 |
| | energy, ft-lb: | 2512 | 2117 | 1774 | 1476 | 1220 |
| | arc, inches: | | +1.8 | 0 | -7.1 | -20.3 |
| PMC 100 Barnes XLC | velocity, fps: | 3150 | 2978 | 2811 | 2651 | 2497 |
| | energy, ft-lb: | | 2203 | 1969 | 1755 | 1561 |
| | arc, inches: | | +1.2 | 0 | -5.6 | -16.2 |
| PMC 117 PSP | velocity, fps: | | | | | |
| | energy, ft-lb: | | | | | |
| | arc, inches: | | | | | |
| Rem. 100 PSP Core-Lokt | velocity, fps: | 3230 | 2893 | 2580 | 2287 | 2014 |
| | energy, ft-lb: | 2316 | 1858 | 1478 | 1161 | 901 |
| | arc, inches: | | +1.3 | 0 | -6.6 | -19.8 |
| Rem. 115 Core-Lokt Ultra | velocity, fps: | 3000 | 2751 | 2516 | 2293 | 2081 |
| | energy, ft-lb: | 2298 | 1933 | 1616 | 1342 | 1106 |
| | arc, inches: | | +1.6 | 0 | -7.1 | -20. |

# Centerfire Rifle Ballistics

## .25-06 Remington to 6.5x55 Swedish

| CARTRIDGE BULLET | RANGE, YARDS: | 0 | 100 | 200 | 300 | 400 |
|---|---|---|---|---|---|---|
| Rem. 120 PSP Core-Lokt | velocity, fps: | 2990 | 2730 | 2484 | 2252 | 2032 |
| | energy, ft-lb: | 2382 | 1985 | 1644 | 1351 | 1100 |
| | arc, inches: | | +1.6 | 0 | -7.2 | -21.4 |
| Speer 120 Grand Slam | velocity, fps: | 3130 | 2835 | 2558 | 2298 | |
| | energy, ft-lb: | 2610 | 2141 | 1743 | 1407 | |
| | arc, inches: | | +1.4 | 0 | -6.8 | -20.1 |
| Win. 90 Pos. Exp. Point | velocity, fps: | 3440 | 3043 | 2680 | 2344 | 2034 |
| | energy, ft-lb: | 2364 | 1850 | 1435 | 1098 | 827 |
| | arc, inches: | | +2.4 | +2.0 | -3.4 | -15.0 |
| Win. 115 Ballistic Silvertip | velocity, fps: | 3060 | 2825 | 2603 | 2390 | 2188 |
| | energy, ft-lb: | 2391 | 2038 | 1729 | 1459 | 1223 |
| | arc, inches: | | +1.4 | 0 | -6.6 | -19.2 |

## .25 Winchester Super Short Mag.

| CARTRIDGE BULLET | | 0 | 100 | 200 | 300 | 400 |
|---|---|---|---|---|---|---|
| Win. 85 Ballistic Silvertip | velocity, fps: | 3470 | 3156 | 2863 | 2589 | 2331 |
| | energy, ft-lb: | 2273 | 1880 | 1548 | 1266 | 1026 |
| | arc, inches: | | +1.0 | 0 | -5.2 | -15.7 |
| Win. 115 Ballistic Silvertip | velocity, fps: | 3060 | 2844 | 2639 | 2442 | 2254 |
| | energy, ft-lb: | 2392 | 2066 | 1778 | 1523 | 1298 |
| | arc, inches: | | +1.4 | 0 | -6.4 | -18.6 |
| Win. 120 Pos. Pt. Exp. | velocity, fps: | 2990 | 2717 | 2459 | 2216 | 1987 |
| | energy, ft-lb: | 2383 | 1967 | 1612 | 1309 | 1053 |
| | arc, inches: | | +1.6 | 0 | -7.4 | -21.8 |

## .257 Weatherby Magnum

| CARTRIDGE BULLET | | 0 | 100 | 200 | 300 | 400 |
|---|---|---|---|---|---|---|
| Federal 115 Nosler Partition | velocity, fps: | 3150 | 2900 | 2660 | 2440 | 2220 |
| | energy, ft-lb: | 2535 | 2145 | 1810 | 1515 | 1260 |
| | arc, inches: | | +1.3 | 0 | -6.2 | -18.4 |
| Federal 115 Trophy Bonded | velocity, fps: | 3150 | 2890 | 2640 | 2400 | 2180 |
| | energy, ft-lb: | 2535 | 2125 | 1775 | 1470 | 1210 |
| | arc, inches: | | +1.4 | 0 | -6.3 | -18.8 |
| Wby. 87 Pointed Expanding | velocity, fps: | 3825 | 3472 | 3147 | 2845 | 2563 |
| | energy, ft-lb: | 2826 | 2328 | 1913 | 1563 | 1269 |
| | arc, inches: | | +2.1 | +2.8 | 0 | -7.1 |
| Wby. 100 Pointed Expanding | velocity, fps: | 3602 | 3298 | 3016 | 2750 | 2500 |
| | energy, ft-lb: | 2881 | 2416 | 2019 | 1680 | 1388 |
| | arc, inches: | | +2.4 | +3.1 | 0 | -7.7 |
| Wby. 115 Nosler Bal. Tip | velocity, fps: | 3400 | 3170 | 2952 | 2745 | 2547 |
| | energy, ft-lb: | 2952 | 2566 | 2226 | 1924 | 1656 |
| | arc, inches: | | +3.0 | +3.5 | 0 | -7.9 |
| Wby. 115 Barnes X | velocity, fps: | 3400 | 3158 | 2929 | 2711 | 2504 |
| | energy, ft-lb: | 2952 | 2546 | 2190 | 1877 | 1601 |
| | arc, inches: | | +2.7 | +3.4 | 0 | -8.1 |
| Wby. 117 RN Expanding | velocity, fps: | 3402 | 2984 | 2595 | 2240 | 1921 |
| | energy, ft-lb: | 3007 | 2320 | 1742 | 1302 | 956 |
| | arc, inches: | | +3.4 | +4.31 | 0 | -11.1 |
| Wby. 120 Nosler Partition | velocity, fps: | 3305 | 3046 | 2801 | 2570 | 2350 |
| | energy, ft-lb: | 2910 | 2472 | 2091 | 1760 | 1471 |
| | arc, inches: | | +3.0 | +3.7 | 0 | -8.9 |

## 6.53 (.257) Scramjet

| CARTRIDGE BULLET | | 0 | 100 | 200 | 300 | 400 |
|---|---|---|---|---|---|---|
| Lazzeroni 85 Nosler Bal. Tip | velocity, fps: | 3960 | 3652 | 3365 | 3096 | 2844 |
| | energy, ft-lb: | 2961 | 2517 | 2137 | 1810 | 1526 |
| | arc, inches: | | +1.7 | +2.4 | 0 | -6.0 |
| Lazzeroni 100 Nosler Part. | velocity, fps: | 3740 | 3465 | 3208 | 2965 | 2735 |
| | energy, ft-lb: | 3106 | 2667 | 2285 | 1953 | 1661 |
| | arc, inches: | | +2.1 | +2.7 | 0 | -6.7 |

## 6.5x50 Japanese

| CARTRIDGE BULLET | | 0 | 100 | 200 | 300 | 400 |
|---|---|---|---|---|---|---|
| Norma 156 Alaska | velocity, fps: | 2067 | 1832 | 1615 | 1423 | |
| | energy, ft-lb: | 1480 | 1162 | 904 | 701 | |
| | arc, inches: | | +4.4 | 0 | -17.8 | |

## 6.5x52 Carcano

| CARTRIDGE BULLET | | 0 | 100 | 200 | 300 | 400 |
|---|---|---|---|---|---|---|
| Norma 156 Alaska | velocity, fps: | 2428 | 2169 | 1926 | 1702 | |
| | energy, ft-lb: | 2043 | 1630 | 1286 | 1004 | |
| | arc, inches: | | +2.9 | 0 | -12.3 | |

## 6.5x55 Swedish

| CARTRIDGE BULLET | | 0 | 100 | 200 | 300 | 400 |
|---|---|---|---|---|---|---|
| Federal 140 Hi-Shok | velocity, fps: | 2600 | 2400 | 2220 | 2040 | 1860 |
| | energy, ft-lb: | 2100 | 1795 | 1525 | 1285 | 1080 |
| | arc, inches: | | +2.3 | 0 | -9.4 | -27.2 |
| Federal 140 Trophy Bonded | velocity, fps: | 2550 | 2350 | 2160 | 1980 | 1810 |
| | energy, ft-lb: | 2020 | 1720 | 1450 | 1220 | 1015 |
| | arc, inches: | | +2.4 | 0 | -9.8 | -28.4 |
| Federal 140 Sierra MatchKg. BTHP | velocity, fps: | 2630 | 2460 | 2300 | 2140 | 2000 |
| | energy, ft-lb: | 2140 | 1880 | 1640 | 1430 | 1235 |
| | arc, inches: | | +16.4 | +28.8 | +33.9 | +31.8 |
| Hornady 129 SP LM | velocity, fps: | 2770 | 2561 | 2361 | 2171 | 1994 |
| | energy, ft-lb: | 2197 | 1878 | 1597 | 1350 | 1138 |
| | arc, inches: | | +2.0 | 0 | -8.2 | -23.2 |
| Hornady 140 SP Interlock | velocity, fps | 2525 | 2341 | 2165 | 1996 | 1836 |
| | energy, ft-lb: | 1982 | 1704 | 1457 | 1239 | 1048 |
| | arc, inches: | | +2.4 | 0 | -9.9 | -28.5 |
| Hornady140 SP LM | velocity, fps: | 2740 | 2541 | 2351 | 2169 | 1999 |
| | energy, ft-lb: | 2333 | 2006 | 1717 | 1463 | 1242 |
| | arc, inches: | | +2.4 | 0 | -8.7 | -24.0 |
| Norma 120 Nosler Bal. Tip | velocity, fps: | 2822 | 2609 | 2407 | 2213 | |
| | energy, ft-lb: | 2123 | 1815 | 1544 | 1305 | |
| | arc, inches: | | +1.8 | 0 | -7.8 | |
| Norma 139 Vulkan | velocity, fps: | 2854 | 2569 | 2302 | 2051 | |
| | energy, ft-lb: | 2515 | 2038 | 1636 | 1298 | |
| | arc, inches: | | +1.8 | 0 | -8.4 | |
| Norma 140 Nosler Partition | velocity, fps: | 2789 | 2592 | 2403 | 2223 | |
| | energy, ft-lb: | 2419 | 2089 | 1796 | 1536 | |
| | arc, inches: | | +1.8 | 0 | -7.8 | |
| Norma 156 TXP Swift A-Fr. | velocity, fps: | 2526 | 2276 | 2040 | 1818 | |
| | energy, ft-lb: | 2196 | 1782 | 1432 | 1138 | |
| | arc, inches: | | +2.6 | 0 | -10.9 | |
| Norma 156 Alaska | velocity, fps: | 2559 | 2245 | 1953 | 1687 | |
| | energy, ft-lb: | 2269 | 1746 | 1322 | 986 | |
| | arc, inches: | | +2.7 | 0 | -11.9 | |
| Norma 156 Vulkan | velocity, fps: | 2644 | 2395 | 2159 | 1937 | |
| | energy, ft-lb: | 2422 | 1987 | 1616 | 1301 | |
| | arc, inches: | | +2.2 | 0 | -9.7 | |
| Norma 156 Oryx | velocity, fps: | 2559 | 2308 | 2070 | 1848 | |
| | energy, ft-lb: | 2269 | 1845 | 1485 | 1183 | |
| | arc, inches: | | +2.5 | 0 | -10.6 | |
| PMC 139 Pointed Soft Point | velocity, fps: | 2850 | 2560 | 2290 | 2030 | 1790 |
| | energy, ft-lb: | 2515 | 2025 | 1615 | 1270 | 985 |
| | arc, inches: | | +2.2 | 0 | -8.9 | -26.3 |
| PMC 140 HP boat-tail | velocity, fps: | 2560 | 2398 | 2243 | 2093 | 1949 |
| | energy, ft-lb: | 2037 | 1788 | 1563 | 1361 | 1181 |
| | arc, inches: | | +2.3 | 0 | -9.2 | -26.4 |
| PMC 140 SP boat-tail | velocity, fps: | 2560 | 2386 | 2218 | 2057 | 1903 |
| | energy, ft-lb: | 2037 | 1769 | 1529 | 1315 | 1126 |
| | arc, inches: | | +2.3 | 0 | -9.4 | -27.1 |
| PMC 144 FMJ | velocity, fps: | 2650 | 2370 | 2110 | 1870 | 1650 |
| | energy, ft-lb: | 2425 | 1950 | 1550 | 1215 | 945 |
| | arc, inches: | | +2.7 | 0 | -10.5 | -30.9 |
| Rem. 140 PSP Core-Lokt | velocity, fps: | 2550 | 2353 | 2164 | 1984 | 1814 |
| | energy, ft-lb: | 2021 | 1720 | 1456 | 1224 | 1023 |
| | arc, inches: | | +2.4 | 0 | -9.8 | -27.0 |

| CARTRIDGE BULLET | RANGE, YARDS: | 0 | 100 | 200 | 300 | 400 |
|---|---|---|---|---|---|---|
| Speer 140 Grand Slam | velocity, fps: | 2550 | 2318 | 2099 | 1892 | |
| | energy, ft-lb: | 2021 | 1670 | 1369 | 1112 | |
| | arc, inches: | | +2.5 | 0 | -10.4 | -30.6 |
| Win. 140 Soft Point | velocity, fps: | 2550 | 2359 | 2176 | 2002 | 1836 |
| | energy, ft-lb: | 2022 | 1731 | 1473 | 1246 | 1048 |
| | arc, inches: | | +2.4 | 0 | -9.7 | -28.1 |

## .260 REMINGTON

| CARTRIDGE BULLET | RANGE, YARDS: | 0 | 100 | 200 | 300 | 400 |
|---|---|---|---|---|---|---|
| Federal 140 Sierra GameKing BTSP | velocity, fps: | 2750 | 2570 | 2390 | 2220 | 2060 |
| | energy, ft-lb: | 2350 | 2045 | 1775 | 1535 | 1315 |
| | arc, inches: | | +1.9 | 0 | -8.0 | -23.1 |
| Federal 140 Trophy Bonded | velocity, fps: | 2750 | 2540 | 2340 | 2150 | 1970 |
| | energy, ft-lb: | 2350 | 2010 | 1705 | 1440 | 1210 |
| | arc, inches: | | +1.9 | 0 | -8.4 | -24.1 |
| Rem. 120 Nosler Bal. Tip | velocity, fps: | 2890 | 2688 | 2494 | 2309 | 2131 |
| | energy, ft-lb: | 2226 | 1924 | 1657 | 1420 | 1210 |
| | arc, inches: | | +1.7 | 0 | -7.3 | -21.1 |
| Rem. 120 AccuTip | velocity, fps: | 2890 | 2697 | 2512 | 2334 | 2163 |
| | energy, ft-lb: | 2392 | 2083 | 1807 | 1560 | 1340 |
| | arc, inches: | | +1.6 | 0 | -7.2 | -20.7 |
| Rem. 125 Nosler Partition | velocity, fps: | 2875 | 2669 | 2473 | 2285 | 2105 |
| | energy, ft-lb: | 2294 | 1977 | 1697 | 1449 | 1230 |
| | arc, inches: | | +1.71 | 0 | -7.4 | -21.4 |
| Rem. 140 PSP Core-Lokt (and C-L Ultra) | velocity, fps: | 2750 | 2544 | 2347 | 2158 | 1979 |
| | energy, ft-lb: | 2351 | 2011 | 1712 | 1448 | 1217 |
| | arc, inches: | | +1.9 | 0 | -8.3 | -24.0 |
| Speer 140 Grand Slam | velocity, fps: | 2750 | 2518 | 2297 | 2087 | |
| | energy, ft-lb: | 2351 | 1970 | 1640 | 1354 | |
| | arc, inches: | | +2.3 | 0 | -8.9 | -25.8 |

## 6.5/284

| CARTRIDGE BULLET | RANGE, YARDS: | 0 | 100 | 200 | 300 | 400 |
|---|---|---|---|---|---|---|
| Norma 120 Nosler Bal. Tip | velocity, fps: | 3117 | 2890 | 2674 | 2469 | |
| | energy, ft-lb: | 2589 | 2226 | 1906 | 1624 | |
| | arc, inches: | | +1.3 | 0 | -6.2 | |
| Norma 140 Nosler Part. | velocity, fps: | 2953 | 2750 | 2557 | 2371 | |
| | energy, ft-lb: | 2712 | 2352 | 2032 | 1748 | |
| | arc, inches: | | +1.5 | 0 | -6.8 | |

## 6.5 REMINGTON MAGNUM

| CARTRIDGE BULLET | RANGE, YARDS: | 0 | 100 | 200 | 300 | 400 |
|---|---|---|---|---|---|---|
| Rem. 120 Core-Lokt PSP | velocity, fps: | 3210 | 2905 | 2621 | 2353 | 2102 |
| | energy, ft-lb: | 2745 | 2248 | 1830 | 1475 | 1177 |
| | arc, inches: | | +2.7 | +2.1 | -3.5 | -15.5 |

## .264 WINCHESTER MAGNUM

| CARTRIDGE BULLET | RANGE, YARDS: | 0 | 100 | 200 | 300 | 400 |
|---|---|---|---|---|---|---|
| Rem. 140 PSP Core-Lokt | velocity, fps: | 3030 | 2782 | 2548 | 2326 | 2114 |
| | energy, ft-lb: | 2854 | 2406 | 2018 | 1682 | 1389 |
| | arc, inches: | | +1.5 | 0 | -6.9 | -20.2 |
| Win. 140 Power-Point | velocity, fps: | 3030 | 2782 | 2548 | 2326 | 2114 |
| | energy, ft-lb: | 2854 | 2406 | 2018 | 1682 | 1389 |
| | arc, inches: | | +1.8 | 0 | -7.2 | -20.8 |

## 6.8MM REMINGTON SPC

| CARTRIDGE BULLET | RANGE, YARDS: | 0 | 100 | 200 | 300 | 400 |
|---|---|---|---|---|---|---|
| Rem. 115 Open Tip Match (and HPBT Match) | velocity, fps: | 2800 | 2535 | 2285 | 2049 | 1828 |
| | energy, ft-lb: | 2002 | 1641 | 1333 | 1072 | 853 |
| | arc, inches: | | +2.0 | 0 | -8.7 | -25.6 |
| Rem. 115 Metal Case | velocity, fps: | 2800 | 2523 | 2262 | 2017 | 1789 |
| | energy, ft-lb: | 2002 | 1625 | 1307 | 1039 | 817 |
| | arc, inches: | | +2.0 | 0 | -8.8 | -26.2 |

## .270 WINCHESTER

| CARTRIDGE BULLET | RANGE, YARDS: | 0 | 100 | 200 | 300 | 400 |
|---|---|---|---|---|---|---|
| Black Hills 130 Barnes X | velocity, fps: | 2950 | | | | |
| | energy, ft-lb: | 2184 | | | | |
| | arc, inches: | | | | | |
| Black Hills 130 Nosler B. Tip | velocity, fps: | 2950 | | | | |
| | energy, ft-lb: | 2184 | | | | |
| | arc, inches: | | | | | |
| Federal 130 Hi-Shok | velocity, fps: | 3060 | 2800 | 2560 | 2330 | 2110 |
| | energy, ft-lb: | 2700 | 2265 | 1890 | 1565 | 1285 |
| | arc, inches: | | +1.5 | 0 | -6.8 | -20.0 |
| Federal 130 Sierra Pro-Hunt. | velocity, fps: | 3060 | 2830 | 2600 | 2390 | 2190 |
| | energy, ft-lb: | 2705 | 2305 | 1960 | 1655 | 1390 |
| | arc, inches: | | +1.4 | 0 | -6.4 | -19.0 |
| Federal 130 Sierra GameKing | velocity, fps: | 3060 | 2830 | 2620 | 2410 | 2220 |
| | energy, ft-lb: | 2700 | 2320 | 1980 | 1680 | 1420 |
| | arc, inches: | | +1.4 | 0 | -6.5 | -19.0 |
| Federal 130 Nosler Bal. Tip | velocity, fps: | 3060 | 2840 | 2630 | 2430 | 2230 |
| | energy, ft-lb: | 2700 | 2325 | 1990 | 1700 | 1440 |
| | arc, inches: | | +1.4 | 0 | -6.5 | -18.8 |
| Federal 130 Barnes XLC | velocity, fps: | 3060 | 2840 | 2620 | 2420 | 2220 |
| | energy, ft-lb: | 2705 | 2320 | 1985 | 1690 | 1425 |
| | arc, inches: | | +1.4 | 0 | -6.4 | -18.9 |
| Federal 130 Trophy Bonded | velocity, fps: | 3060 | 2810 | 2570 | 2340 | 2130 |
| | energy, ft-lb: | 2705 | 2275 | 1905 | 1585 | 1310 |
| | arc, inches: | | +1.5 | 0 | -6.7 | -19.8 |
| Federal 140 Trophy Bonded | velocity, fps: | 2940 | 2700 | 2480 | 2260 | 2060 |
| | energy, ft-lb: | 2685 | 2270 | 1905 | 1590 | 1315 |
| | arc, inches: | | +1.6 | 0 | -7.3 | -21.5 |
| Federal 140 Tr. Bonded HE | velocity, fps: | 3100 | 2860 | 2620 | 2400 | 2200 |
| | energy, ft-lb: | 2990 | 2535 | 2140 | 1795 | 1500 |
| | arc, inches: | | +1.4 | 0 | -6.4 | -18.9 |
| Federal 150 Hi-Shok RN | velocity, fps: | 2850 | 2500 | 2180 | 1890 | 1620 |
| | energy, ft-lb: | 2705 | 2085 | 1585 | 1185 | 870 |
| | arc, inches: | | +2.0 | 0 | -9.4 | -28.6 |
| Federal 150 Sierra GameKing | velocity, fps: | 2850 | 2660 | 2480 | 2300 | 2130 |
| | energy, ft-lb: | 2705 | 2355 | 2040 | 1760 | 1510 |
| | arc, inches: | | +1.7 | 0 | -7.4 | -21.4 |
| Federal 150 Sierra GameKing HE | velocity, fps: | 3000 | 2800 | 2620 | 2430 | 2260 |
| | energy, ft-lb: | 2995 | 2615 | 2275 | 1975 | 1700 |
| | arc, inches: | | +1.5 | 0 | -6.5 | -18.9 |
| Federal 150 Nosler Partition | velocity, fps: | 2850 | 2590 | 2340 | 2100 | 1880 |
| | energy, ft-lb: | 2705 | 2225 | 1815 | 1470 | 1175 |
| | arc, inches: | | +1.9 | 0 | -8.3 | -24.4 |
| Hornady 130 SST (or Interbond) | velocity, fps: | 3060 | 2845 | 2639 | 2442 | 2254 |
| | energy, ft-lb: | 2700 | 2335 | 2009 | 1721 | 1467 |
| | arc, inches: | | +1.4 | 0 | -6.6 | -19.1 |
| Hornady 130 SST LM (or Interbond) | velocity, fps: | 3215 | 2998 | 2790 | 2590 | 2400 |
| | energy, ft-lb: | 2983 | 2594 | 2246 | 1936 | 1662 |
| | arc, inches: | | +1.2 | 0 | -5.8 | -17.0 |
| Hornady 140 SP boat-tail | velocity, fps: | 2940 | 2747 | 2562 | 2385 | 2214 |
| | energy, ft-lb: | 2688 | 2346 | 2041 | 1769 | 1524 |
| | arc, inches: | | +1.6 | 0 | -7.0 | -20.2 |
| Hornady 140 SP boat-tail LM | velocity, fps: | 3100 | 2894 | 2697 | 2508 | 2327 |
| | energy, ft-lb: | 2987 | 2604 | 2261 | 1955 | 1684 |
| | arc, inches: | | +1.4 | 0 | 6.3 | -18.3 |
| Hornady 150 SP | velocity, fps: | 2800 | 2684 | 2478 | 2284 | 2100 |
| | energy, ft-lb: | 2802 | 2400 | 2046 | 1737 | 1469 |
| | arc, inches: | | +1.7 | 0 | -7.4 | -21.6 |
| Norma 130 SP | velocity, fps: | 3140 | 2862 | 2601 | 2354 | |
| | energy, ft-lb: | 2847 | 2365 | 1953 | 1600 | |
| | arc, inches: | 0 | +1.3 | 0 | -6.5 | |
| Norma 150 SP | velocity, fps: | 2799 | 2555 | 2323 | 2104 | |
| | energy, ft-lb: | 2610 | 2175 | 1798 | 1475 | |
| | arc, inches: | 0 | +1.9 | 0 | -8.3 | |

# Centerfire Rifle Ballistics

## .270 WINCHESTER TO .270 WEATHERBY MAGNUM

| CARTRIDGE BULLET | RANGE, YARDS: | 0 | 100 | 200 | 300 | 400 |
|---|---|---|---|---|---|---|
| PMC 130 Barnes X | velocity, fps: | 2910 | 2717 | 2533 | 2356 | 2186 |
| | energy, ft-lb: | 2444 | 2131 | 1852 | 1602 | 1379 |
| | arc, inches: | | +1.6 | 0 | -7.1 | -20.4 |
| PMC 130 SP boat-tail | velocity, fps: | 3050 | 2830 | 2620 | 2421 | 2229 |
| | energy, ft-lb: | 2685 | 2312 | 1982 | 1691 | 1435 |
| | arc, inches: | | +1.5 | 0 | -6.5 | -19.0 |
| PMC 130 Pointed Soft Point | velocity, fps: | 2816 | 2593 | 2381 | 2179 | 1987 |
| | energy, ft-lb: | 2288 | 1941 | 1636 | 1370 | 1139 |
| | arc, inches: | | +1.8 | 0 | -8.0 | -23.2 |
| PMC 150 Barnes X | velocity, fps: | 2700 | 2541 | 2387 | 2238 | 2095 |
| | energy, ft-lb: | 2428 | 2150 | 1897 | 1668 | 1461 |
| | arc, inches: | | +2.0 | 0 | -8.1 | -23.1 |
| PMC 150 SP boat-tail | velocity, fps: | 2850 | 2660 | 2477 | 2302 | 2134 |
| | energy, ft-lb: | 2705 | 2355 | 2043 | 1765 | 1516 |
| | arc, inches: | | +1.7 | 0 | -7.4 | -21.4 |
| PMC 150 Pointed Soft Point | velocity, fps: | 2547 | 2368 | 2197 | 2032 | 1875 |
| | energy, ft-lb: | 2160 | 1868 | 1607 | 1375 | 1171 |
| | arc, inches: | | +2.4 | 0 | -9.5 | -27.5 |
| Rem. 100 Pointed Soft Point | velocity, fps: | 3320 | 2924 | 2561 | 2225 | 1916 |
| | energy, ft-lb: | 2448 | 1898 | 1456 | 1099 | 815 |
| | arc, inches: | | +2.3 | +2.0 | -3.6 | -16.2 |
| Rem. 115 PSP Core-Lokt mr | velocity, fps: | 2710 | 2412 | 2133 | 1873 | 1636 |
| | energy, ft-lb: | 1875 | 1485 | 1161 | 896 | 683 |
| | arc, inches: | | +1.0 | -2.7 | -14.2 | -35.6 |
| Rem. 130 PSP Core-Lokt | velocity, fps: | 3060 | 2776 | 2510 | 2259 | 2022 |
| | energy, ft-lb: | 2702 | 2225 | 1818 | 1472 | 1180 |
| | arc, inches: | | +1.5 | 0 | -7.0 | -20.9 |
| Rem. 130 Bronze Point | velocity, fps: | 3060 | 2802 | 2559 | 2329 | 2110 |
| | energy, ft-lb: | 2702 | 2267 | 1890 | 1565 | 1285 |
| | arc, inches: | | +1.5 | 0 | -6.8 | -20.0 |
| Rem. 130 Swift Scirocco | velocity, fps: | 3060 | 2838 | 2677 | 2425 | 2232 |
| | energy, ft-lb: | 2702 | 2325 | 1991 | 1697 | 1438 |
| | arc, inches: | | +1.4 | 0 | -6.5 | -18.8 |
| Rem. 130 AccuTip BT | velocity, fps: | 3060 | 2845 | 2639 | 2442 | 2254 |
| | energy, ft-lb: | 2702 | 2336 | 2009 | 1721 | 1467 |
| | arc, inches: | | +1.4 | 0 | -6.4 | -18.6 |
| Rem. 140 Swift A-Frame | velocity, fps: | 2925 | 2652 | 2394 | 2152 | 1923 |
| | energy, ft-lb: | 2659 | 2186 | 1782 | 1439 | 1150 |
| | arc, inches: | | +1.7 | 0 | -7.8 | -23.2 |
| Rem. 140 PSP boat-tail | velocity, fps: | 2960 | 2749 | 2548 | 2355 | 2171 |
| | energy, ft-lb: | 2723 | 2349 | 2018 | 1724 | 1465 |
| | arc, inches: | | +1.6 | 0 | -6.9 | -20.1 |
| Rem. 140 Nosler Bal. Tip | velocity, fps: | 2960 | 2754 | 2557 | 2366 | 2187 |
| | energy, ft-lb: | 2724 | 2358 | 2032 | 1743 | 1487 |
| | arc, inches: | | +1.6 | 0 | -6.9 | -20.0 |
| Rem. 140 PSP C-L Ultra | velocity, fps: | 2925 | 2667 | 2424 | 2193 | 1975 |
| | energy, ft-lb: | 2659 | 2211 | 1826 | 1495 | 1212 |
| | arc, inches: | | +1.7 | 0 | -7.6 | -22.5 |
| Rem. 150 SP Core-Lokt | velocity, fps: | 2850 | 2504 | 2183 | 1886 | 1618 |
| | energy, ft-lb: | 2705 | 2087 | 1587 | 1185 | 872 |
| | arc, inches: | | +2.0 | 0 | -9.4 | -28.6 |
| Rem. 150 Nosler Partition | velocity, fps: | 2850 | 2652 | 2463 | 2282 | 2108 |
| | energy, ft-lb: | 2705 | 2343 | 2021 | 1734 | 1480 |
| | arc, inches: | | +1.7 | 0 | -7.5 | -21.6 |
| Speer 130 Grand Slam | velocity, fps: | 3050 | 2774 | 2514 | 2269 | |
| | energy, ft-lb: | 2685 | 2221 | 1824 | 1485 | |
| | arc, inches: | | +1.5 | 0 | -7.0 | -20.9 |
| Speer 150 Grand Slam | velocity, fps: | 2830 | 2594 | 2369 | 2156 | |
| | energy, ft-lb: | 2667 | 2240 | 1869 | 1548 | |
| | arc, inches: | | +1.8 | 0 | -8.1 | -23.6 |
| Win. 130 Power-Point | velocity, fps: | 3060 | 2802 | 2559 | 2329 | 2110 |
| | energy, ft-lb: | 2702 | 2267 | 1890 | 1565 | 1285 |
| | arc, inches: | | +1.8 | 0 | -7.1 | -20.6 |
| Win. 130 Power-Point Plus | velocity, fps: | 3150 | 2881 | 2628 | 2388 | 2161 |
| | energy, ft-lb: | 2865 | 2396 | 1993 | 1646 | 1348 |
| | arc, inches: | | +1.3 | 0 | -6.4 | -18.9 |
| Win. 130 Silvertip | velocity, fps: | 3060 | 2776 | 2510 | 2259 | 2022 |
| | energy, ft-lb: | 2702 | 2225 | 1818 | 1472 | 1180 |
| | arc, inches: | | +1.8 | 0 | -7.4 | -21.6 |
| Win. 130 Ballistic Silvertip | velocity, fps: | 3050 | 2828 | 2618 | 2416 | 2224 |
| | energy, ft-lb: | 2685 | 2309 | 1978 | 1685 | 1428 |
| | arc, inches: | | +1.4 | 0 | -6.5 | -18.9 |
| Win. 140 AccuBond | velocity, fps: | 2950 | 2751 | 2560 | 2378 | 2203 |
| | energy, ft-lb: | 2705 | 2352 | 2038 | 1757 | 1508 |
| | arc, inches: | | +1.6 | 0 | -6.9 | -19.9 |
| Win. 140 Fail Safe | velocity, fps: | 2920 | 2671 | 2435 | 2211 | 1999 |
| | energy, ft-lb: | 2651 | 2218 | 1843 | 1519 | 1242 |
| | arc, inches: | | +1.7 | 0 | -7.6 | -22.3 |
| Win. 150 Power-Point | velocity, fps: | 2850 | 2585 | 2336 | 2100 | 1879 |
| | energy, ft-lb: | 2705 | 2226 | 1817 | 1468 | 1175 |
| | arc, inches: | | +2.2 | 0 | -8.6 | -25.0 |
| Win. 150 Power-Point Plus | velocity, fps: | 2950 | 2679 | 2425 | 2184 | 1957 |
| | energy, ft-lb: | 2900 | 2391 | 1959 | 1589 | 1276 |
| | arc, inches: | | +1.7 | 0 | -7.6 | -22.6 |
| Win. 150 Partition Gold | velocity, fps: | 2930 | 2693 | 2468 | 2254 | 2051 |
| | energy, ft-lb: | 2860 | 2416 | 2030 | 1693 | 1402 |
| | arc, inches: | | +1.7 | 0 | -7.4 | -21.6 |

## .270 WINCHESTER SHORT MAGNUM

| CARTRIDGE BULLET | RANGE, YARDS: | 0 | 100 | 200 | 300 | 400 |
|---|---|---|---|---|---|---|
| Norma 150 Nosler Bal. Tip | velocity, fps: | 3280 | 3046 | 2824 | 2613 | |
| | energy, ft-lb: | 3106 | 2679 | 2303 | 1972 | |
| | arc, inches: | | +1.1 | 0 | -5.4 | |
| Win. 130 Bal. Silvertip | velocity, fps: | 3275 | 3041 | 2820 | 2609 | 2408 |
| | energy, ft-lb: | 3096 | 2669 | 2295 | 1964 | 1673 |
| | arc, inches: | | +1.1 | 0 | -5.5 | -16.1 |
| Win. 140 AccuBond | velocity, fps: | 3200 | 2989 | 2789 | 2597 | 2413 |
| | energy, ft-lb: | 3184 | 2779 | 2418 | 2097 | 1810 |
| | arc, inches: | | +1.2 | 0 | -5.7 | -16.5 |
| Win. 140 Fail Safe | velocity, fps: | 3125 | 2865 | 2619 | 2386 | 2165 |
| | energy, ft-lb: | 3035 | 2550 | 2132 | 1769 | 1457 |
| | arc, inches: | | +1.4 | 0 | -6.5 | -19.0 |
| Win. 150 Ballistic Silvertip | velocity, fps: | 3120 | 2923 | 2734 | 2554 | 2380 |
| | energy, ft-lb: | 3242 | 2845 | 2490 | 2172 | 1886 |
| | arc, inches: | | +1.3 | 0 | -5.9 | -17.2 |
| Win. 150 Power Point | velocity, fps: | 3150 | 2867 | 2601 | 2350 | 2113 |
| | energy, ft-lb: | 3304 | 2737 | 2252 | 1839 | 1487 |
| | arc, inches: | | +1.4 | 0 | -6.5 | -19.4 |

## .270 WEATHERBY MAGNUM

| CARTRIDGE BULLET | RANGE, YARDS: | 0 | 100 | 200 | 300 | 400 |
|---|---|---|---|---|---|---|
| Federal 130 Nosler Partition | velocity, fps: | 3200 | 2960 | 2740 | 2520 | 2320 |
| | energy, ft-lb: | 2955 | 2530 | 2160 | 1835 | 1550 |
| | arc, inches: | | +1.2 | 0 | -5.9 | -17.3 |
| Federal 130 Sierra GameKing BTSP | velocity, fps: | 3200 | 2980 | 2780 | 2580 | 2400 |
| | energy, ft-lb: | 2955 | 2570 | 2230 | 1925 | 1655 |
| | arc, inches: | | +1.2 | 0 | -5.7 | -16.6 |
| Federal 140 Trophy Bonded | velocity, fps: | 3100 | 2840 | 2600 | 2370 | 2150 |
| | energy, ft-lb: | 2990 | 2510 | 2100 | 1745 | 1440 |
| | arc, inches: | | +1.4 | 0 | -6.6 | -19.3 |
| Wby. 100 Pointed Expanding | velocity, fps: | 3760 | 3396 | 3061 | 2751 | 2462 |
| | energy, ft-lb: | 3139 | 2560 | 2081 | 1681 | 1346 |
| | arc, inches: | | +2.3 | +3.0 | 0 | -7.6 |

BALLISTICS

**BALLISTICS**

| CARTRIDGE BULLET | RANGE, YARDS: | 0 | 100 | 200 | 300 | 400 |
|---|---|---|---|---|---|---|
| Wby. 130 Pointed Expanding | velocity, fps: | 3375 | 3123 | 2885 | 2659 | 2444 |
|  | energy, ft-lb: | 3288 | 2815 | 2402 | 2041 | 1724 |
|  | arc, inches: |  | +2.8 | +3.5 | 0 | -8.4 |
| Wby. 130 Nosler Partition | velocity, fps: | 3375 | 3127 | 2892 | 2670 | 2458 |
|  | energy, ft-lb: | 3288 | 2822 | 2415 | 2058 | 1744 |
|  | arc, inches: |  | +2.8 | +3.5 | 0 | -8.3 |
| Wby. 140 Nosler Bal. Tip | velocity, fps: | 3300 | 3077 | 2865 | 2663 | 2470 |
|  | energy, ft-lb: | 3385 | 2943 | 2551 | 2204 | 1896 |
|  | arc, inches: |  | +2.9 | +3.6 | 0 | -8.4 |
| Wby. 140 Barnes X | velocity, fps: | 3250 | 3032 | 2825 | 2628 | 2438 |
|  | energy, ft-lb: | 3283 | 2858 | 2481 | 2146 | 1848 |
|  | arc, inches: |  | +3.0 | +3.7 | 0 | -8.7 |
| Wby. 150 Pointed Expanding | velocity, fps: | 3245 | 3028 | 2821 | 2623 | 2434 |
|  | energy, ft-lb: | 3507 | 3053 | 2650 | 2292 | 1973 |
|  | arc, inches: |  | +3.0 | +3.7 | 0 | -8.7 |
| Wby. 150 Nosler Partition | velocity, fps: | 3245 | 3029 | 2823 | 2627 | 2439 |
|  | energy, ft-lb: | 3507 | 3055 | 2655 | 2298 | 1981 |
|  | arc, inches: |  | +3.0 | +3.7 | 0 | -8. |

## 7-30 WATERS

| | | 0 | 100 | 200 | 300 | 400 |
|---|---|---|---|---|---|---|
| Federal 120 Sierra GameKing BTSP | velocity, fps: | 2700 | 2300 | 1930 | 1600 | 1330 |
|  | energy, ft-lb: | 1940 | 1405 | 990 | 685 | 470 |
|  | arc, inches: |  | +2.6 | 0 | -12.0 | -37.6 |

## 7MM MAUSER (7X57)

| | | 0 | 100 | 200 | 300 | 400 |
|---|---|---|---|---|---|---|
| Federal 140 Sierra Pro-Hunt. | velocity, fps: | 2660 | 2450 | 2260 | 2070 | 1890 |
|  | energy, ft-lb: | 2200 | 1865 | 1585 | 1330 | 1110 |
|  | arc, inches: |  | +2.1 | 0 | -9.0 | -26.1 |
| Federal 140 Nosler Partition | velocity, fps: | 2660 | 2450 | 2260 | 2070 | 1890 |
|  | energy, ft-lb: | 2200 | 1865 | 1585 | 1330 | 1110 |
|  | arc, inches: |  | +2.1 | 0 | -9.0 | -26.1 |
| Federal 175 Hi-Shok RN | velocity, fps: | 2440 | 2140 | 1860 | 1600 | 1380 |
|  | energy, ft-lb: | 2315 | 1775 | 1340 | 1000 | 740 |
|  | arc, inches: |  | +3.1 | 0 | -13.3 | -40.1 |
| Hornady 139 SP boat-tail | velocity, fps: | 2700 | 2504 | 2316 | 2137 | 1965 |
|  | energy, ft-lb: | 2251 | 1936 | 1656 | 1410 | 1192 |
|  | arc, inches: |  | +2.0 | 0 | -8.5 | -24.9 |
| Hornady 139 SP Interlock | velocity, fps: | 2680 | 2455 | 2241 | 2038 | 1846 |
|  | energy, ft-lb: | 2216 | 1860 | 1550 | 1282 | 1052 |
|  | arc, inches: | +2.1 | 0 | -9.1 | -26.6 | |
| Hornady 139 SP boat-tail LM | velocity, fps: | 2830 | 2620 | 2450 | 2250 | 2070 |
|  | energy, ft-lb: | 2475 | 2135 | 1835 | 1565 | 1330 |
|  | arc, inches: |  | +1.8 | 0 | -7.6 | -22.1 |
| Hornady 139 SP LM | velocity, fps: | 2950 | 2736 | 2532 | 2337 | 2152 |
|  | energy, ft-lb: | 2686 | 2310 | 1978 | 1686 | 1429 |
|  | arc, inches: |  | +2.0 | 0 | -7.6 | -21.5 |
| Norma 150 Soft Point | velocity, fps: | 2690 | 2479 | 2278 | 2087 |  |
|  | energy, ft-lb: | 2411 | 2048 | 1729 | 1450 |  |
|  | arc, inches: |  | +2.0 | 0 | -8.8 |  |
| PMC 140 Pointed Soft Point | velocity, fps: | 2660 | 2450 | 2260 | 2070 | 1890 |
|  | energy, ft-lb: | 2200 | 1865 | 1585 | 1330 | 1110 |
|  | arc, inches: |  | +2.4 | 0 | -9.6 | -27.3 |
| PMC 175 Soft Point | velocity, fps: | 2440 | 2140 | 1860 | 1600 | 1380 |
|  | energy, ft-lb: | 2315 | 1775 | 1340 | 1000 | 740 |
|  | arc, inches: |  | +1.5 | -3.6 | -18.6 | -46.8 |
| Rem. 140 PSP Core-Lokt | velocity, fps: | 2660 | 2435 | 2221 | 2018 | 1827 |
|  | energy, ft-lb: | 2199 | 1843 | 1533 | 1266 | 1037 |
|  | arc, inches: |  | +2.2 | 0 | -9.2 | -27.4 |
| Win. 145 Power-Point | velocity, fps: | 2660 | 2413 | 2180 | 1959 | 1754 |
|  | energy, ft-lb: | 2279 | 1875 | 1530 | 1236 | 990 |
|  | arc, inches: |  | +1.1 | -2.8 | -14.1 | -34.4 |

## 7X57 R

| | | 0 | 100 | 200 | 300 | 400 |
|---|---|---|---|---|---|---|
| Norma 150 FMJ | velocity, fps: | 2690 | 2489 | 2296 | 2112 |  |
|  | energy, ft-lb: | 2411 | 2063 | 1756 | 1486 |  |
|  | arc, inches: |  | +2.0 | 0 | -8.6 |  |
| Norma 154 Soft Point | velocity, fps: | 2625 | 2417 | 2219 | 2030 |  |
|  | energy, ft-lb: | 2357 | 1999 | 1684 | 1410 |  |
|  | arc, inches: |  | +2.2 | 0 | -9.3 |  |
| Norma 156 Oryx | velocity, fps: | 2608 | 2346 | 2099 | 1867 |  |
|  | energy, ft-lb: | 2357 | 1906 | 1526 | 1208 |  |
|  | arc, inches: |  | +2.4 | 0 | -10.3 |  |

## 7MM-08 REMINGTON

| | | 0 | 100 | 200 | 300 | 400 |
|---|---|---|---|---|---|---|
| Federal 140 Nosler Partition | velocity, fps: | 2800 | 2590 | 2390 | 2200 | 2020 |
|  | energy, ft-lb: | 2435 | 2085 | 1775 | 1500 | 1265 |
|  | arc, inches: |  | +1.8 | 0 | -8.0 | -23.1 |
| Federal 140 Nosler Bal. Tip | velocity, fps: | 2800 | 2610 | 2430 | 2260 | 2100 |
|  | energy, ft-lb: | 2440 | 2135 | 1840 | 1590 | 1360 |
|  | arc, inches: |  | +1.8 | 0 | -7.7 | -22.3 |
| Federal 140 Tr. Bonded HE | velocity, fps: | 2950 | 2660 | 2390 | 2140 | 1900 |
|  | energy, ft-lb: | 2705 | 2205 | 1780 | 1420 | 1120 |
|  | arc, inches: |  | +1.7 | 0 | -7.9 | -23.2 |
| Federal 150 Sierra Pro-Hunt. | velocity, fps: | 2650 | 2440 | 2230 | 2040 | 1860 |
|  | energy, ft-lb: | 2340 | 1980 | 1660 | 1390 | 1150 |
|  | arc, inches: |  | +2.2 | 0 | -9.2 | -26.7 |
| Hornady 139 SP boat-tail LM | velocity, fps: | 3000 | 2790 | 2590 | 2399 | 2216 |
|  | energy, ft-lb: | 2777 | 2403 | 2071 | 1776 | 1515 |
|  | arc, inches: |  | +1.5 | 0 | -6.7 | -19.4 |
| PMC 139 PSP | velocity, fps: | 2850 | 2610 | 2384 | 2170 | 1969 |
|  | energy, ft-lb: | 2507 | 2103 | 1754 | 1454 | 1197 |
|  | arc, inches: |  | +1.8 | 0 | -7.9 | -23.3 |
| Rem. 120 Hollow Point | velocity, fps: | 3000 | 2725 | 2467 | 2223 | 1992 |
|  | energy, ft-lb: | 2398 | 1979 | 1621 | 1316 | 1058 |
|  | arc, inches: |  | +1.6 | 0 | -7.3 | -21.7 |
| Rem. 140 PSP Core-Lokt | velocity, fps: | 2860 | 2625 | 2402 | 2189 | 1988 |
|  | energy, ft-lb: | 2542 | 2142 | 1793 | 1490 | 1228 |
|  | arc, inches: |  | +1.8 | 0 | -7.8 | -22.9 |
| Rem. 140 PSP boat-tail | velocity, fps: | 2860 | 2656 | 2460 | 2273 | 2094 |
|  | energy, ft-lb: | 2542 | 2192 | 1881 | 1606 | 1363 |
|  | arc, inches: |  | +1.7 | 0 | -7.5 | -21.7 |
| Rem. 140 AccuTip BT | velocity, fps: | 2860 | 2670 | 2488 | 2313 | 2145 |
|  | energy, ft-lb: | 2543 | 2217 | 1925 | 1663 | 1431 |
|  | arc, inches: |  | +1.7 | 0 | -7.3 | -21.2 |
| Rem. 140 Nosler Partition | velocity, fps: | 2860 | 2648 | 2446 | 2253 | 2068 |
|  | energy, ft-lb: | 2542 | 2180 | 1860 | 1577 | 1330 |
|  | arc, inches: |  | +1.7 | 0 | -7.6 | -22.0 |
| Speer 145 Grand Slam | velocity, fps: | 2845 | 2567 | 2305 | 2059 |  |
|  | energy, ft-lb: | 2606 | 2121 | 1711 | 1365 |  |
|  | arc, inches: |  | +1.9 | 0 | -8.4 | -25.5 |
| Win. 140 Power-Point | velocity, fps: | 2800 | 2523 | 2268 | 2027 | 1802 |
|  | energy, ft-lb: | 2429 | 1980 | 1599 | 1277 | 1010 |
|  | arc, inches: |  | +2.0 | 0 | -8.8 | -26.0 |
| Win. 140 Power-Point Plus | velocity, fps: | 2875 | 2597 | 2336 | 2090 | 1859 |
|  | energy, ft-lb: | 2570 | 1997 | 1697 | 1358 | 1075 |
|  | arc, inches: |  | +2.0 | 0 | -8.8 | 26.0 |
| Win. 140 Fail Safe | velocity, fps: | 2760 | 2506 | 2271 | 2048 | 1839 |
|  | energy, ft-lb: | 2360 | 1953 | 1603 | 1304 | 1051 |
|  | arc, inches: |  | +2.0 | 0 | -8.8 | -25.9 |
| Win. 140 Ballistic Silvertip | velocity, fps: | 2770 | 2572 | 2382 | 2200 | 2026 |
|  | energy, ft-lb: | 2386 | 2056 | 1764 | 1504 | 1276 |
|  | arc, inches: |  | +1.9 | 0 | -8.0 | -23.8 |

# Centerfire Rifle Ballistics

## 7x64 Brenneke to 7mm Remington Magnum

| CARTRIDGE BULLET | RANGE, YARDS: | 0 | 100 | 200 | 300 | 400 |
|---|---|---|---|---|---|---|
| **7x64 Brenneke** | | | | | | |
| Federal 160 Nosler Partition | velocity, fps: | 2650 | 2480 | 2310 | 2150 | 2000 |
| | energy, ft-lb: | 2495 | 2180 | 1895 | 1640 | 1415 |
| | arc, inches: | | +2.1 | 0 | -8.7 | -24.9 |
| Norma 154 Soft Point | velocity, fps: | 2821 | 2605 | 2399 | 2203 | |
| | energy, ft-lb: | 2722 | 2321 | 1969 | 1660 | |
| | arc, inches: | | +1.8 | 0 | -7.8 | |
| Norma 156 Oryx | velocity, fps: | 2789 | 2516 | 2259 | 2017 | |
| | energy, ft-lb: | 2695 | 2193 | 1768 | 1410 | |
| | arc, inches: | | +2.0 | 0 | -8.8 | |
| Norma 170 Vulkan | velocity, fps: | 2756 | 2501 | 2259 | 2031 | |
| | energy, ft-lb: | 2868 | 2361 | 1927 | 1558 | |
| | arc, inches: | | +2.0 | 0 | -8.8 | |
| Norma 170 Oryx | velocity, fps: | 2756 | 2481 | 2222 | 1979 | |
| | energy, ft-lb: | 2868 | 2324 | 1864 | 1478 | |
| | arc, inches: | | +2.1 | 0 | -9.2 | |
| Norma 170 Plastic Point | velocity, fps: | 2756 | 2519 | 2294 | 2081 | |
| | energy, ft-lb: | 2868 | 2396 | 1987 | 1635 | |
| | arc, inches: | | +2.0 | 0 | -8.6 | |
| PMC 170 Pointed Soft Point | velocity, fps: | 2625 | 2401 | 2189 | 1989 | 1801 |
| | energy, ft lb: | 2601 | 2175 | 1808 | 1493 | 1224 |
| | arc, inches: | | +2.3 | 0 | -9.6 | -27.9 |
| Rem. 175 PSP Core-Lokt | velocity, fps: | 2650 | 2445 | 2248 | 2061 | 1883 |
| | energy, ft-lb: | 2728 | 2322 | 1964 | 1650 | 1378 |
| | arc, inches: | | +2.2 | 0 | -9.1 | -26.4 |
| Speer 160 Grand Slam | velocity, fps: | 2600 | 2376 | 2164 | 1962 | |
| | energy, ft-lb: | 2401 | 2006 | 1663 | 1368 | |
| | arc, inches: | | +2.3 | 0 | -9.8 | -28.6 |
| Speer 175 Grand Slam | velocity, fps: | 2650 | 2461 | 2280 | 2106 | |
| | energy, ft-lb: | 2728 | 2353 | 2019 | 1723 | |
| | arc, inches: | | +2.4 | 0 | -9.2 | -26.2 |
| **7x65 R** | | | | | | |
| Norma 156 Oryx | velocity, fps: | 2723 | 2454 | 2200 | 1962 | |
| | energy, ft-lb: | 2569 | 2086 | 1678 | 1334 | |
| | arc, inches: | | +2.1 | 0 | -9.3 | |
| Norma 170 Plastic Point | velocity, fps: | 2625 | 2390 | 2167 | 1956 | |
| | energy, ft-lb: | 2602 | 2157 | 1773 | 1445 | |
| | arc, inches: | | +2.3 | 0 | -9.7 | |
| Norma 170 Vulkan | velocity, fps: | 2657 | 2392 | 2143 | 1909 | |
| | energy, ft-lb: | 2666 | 2161 | 1734 | 1377 | |
| | arc, inches: | | +2.3 | 0 | -9.9 | |
| Norma 170 Oryx | velocity, fps: | 2657 | 2378 | 2115 | 1871 | |
| | energy, ft-lb: | 2666 | 2135 | 1690 | 1321 | |
| | arc, inches: | | +2.3 | 0 | -10.1 | |
| **.284 Winchester** | | | | | | |
| Win. 150 Power-Point | velocity, fps: | 2860 | 2595 | 2344 | 2108 | 1886 |
| | energy, ft-lb: | 2724 | 2243 | 1830 | 1480 | 1185 |
| | arc, inches: | | +2.1 | 0 | -8.5 | -24.8 |
| **.280 Remington** | | | | | | |
| Federal 140 Sierra Pro-Hunt. | velocity, fps: | 2990 | 2740 | 2500 | 2270 | 2060 |
| | energy, ft-lb: | 2770 | 2325 | 1940 | 1605 | 1320 |
| | arc, inches: | | +1.6 | 0 | -7.0 | -20.8 |
| Federal 140 Trophy Bonded | velocity, fps: | 2990 | 2630 | 2310 | 2040 | 1730 |
| | energy, ft-lb: | 2770 | 2155 | 1655 | 1250 | 925 |
| | arc, inches: | | +1.6 | 0 | -8.4 | -25.4 |
| Federal 140 Tr. Bonded HE | velocity, fps: | 3150 | 2850 | 2570 | 2300 | 2050 |
| | energy, ft-lb: | 3085 | 2520 | 2050 | 1650 | 1310 |
| | arc, inches: | | +1.4 | 0 | -6.7 | -20.0 |
| Federal 150 Hi-Shok | velocity, fps: | 2890 | 2670 | 2460 | 2260 | 2060 |
| | energy, ft-lb: | 2780 | 2370 | 2015 | 1695 | 1420 |
| | arc, inches: | | +1.7 | 0 | -7.5 | -21.8 |
| Federal 150 Nosler Partition | velocity, fps: | 2890 | 2690 | 2490 | 2310 | 2130 |
| | energy, ft-lb: | 2780 | 2405 | 2070 | 1770 | 1510 |
| | arc, inches: | | +1.7 | 0 | -7.2 | -21.1 |
| Federal 160 Trophy Bonded | velocity, fps: | 2800 | 2570 | 2350 | 2140 | 1940 |
| | energy, ft-lb: | 2785 | 2345 | 1960 | 1625 | 1340 |
| | arc, inches: | | +1.9 | 0 | -8.3 | -24.0 |
| Hornady 139 SPBT LMmoly | velocity, fps: | 3110 | 2888 | 2675 | 2473 | 2280 |
| | energy, ft-lb: | 2985 | 2573 | 2209 | 1887 | 1604 |
| | arc, inches: | | +1.4 | 0 | -6.5 | -18.6 |
| Norma 156 Oryx | velocity, fps: | 2789 | 2516 | 2259 | 2017 | |
| | energy, ft-lb: | 2695 | 2193 | 1768 | 1410 | |
| | arc, inches: | | +2.0 | 0 | -8.8 | |
| Norma 170 Plastic Point | velocity, fps: | 2707 | 2468 | 2241 | 2026 | |
| | energy, ft-lb: | 2767 | 2299 | 1896 | 1550 | |
| | arc, inches: | | +2.1 | 0 | -9.1 | |
| Norma 170 Vulkan | velocity, fps: | 2592 | 2346 | 2113 | 1894 | |
| | energy, ft-lb: | 2537 | 2078 | 1686 | 1354 | |
| | arc, inches: | | +2.4 | 0 | -10.2 | |
| Norma 170 Oryx | velocity, fps: | 2690 | 2416 | 2159 | 1918 | |
| | energy, ft-lb: | 2732 | 2204 | 1760 | 1389 | |
| | arc, inches: | | +2.2 | 0 | -9.7 | |
| Rem. 140 PSP Core-Lokt | velocity, fps: | 3000 | 2758 | 2528 | 2309 | 2102 |
| | energy, ft-lb: | 2797 | 2363 | 1986 | 1657 | 1373 |
| | arc, inches: | | +1.5 | 0 | -7.0 | -20.5 |
| Rem. 140 PSP boat-tail | velocity, fps: | 2860 | 2656 | 2460 | 2273 | 2094 |
| | energy, ft-lb: | 2542 | 2192 | 1881 | 1606 | 1363 |
| | arc, inches: | | +1.7 | 0 | -7.5 | -21.7 |
| Rem. 140 Nosler Bal. Tip | velocity, fps: | 3000 | 2804 | 2616 | 2436 | 2263 |
| | energy, ft-lb: | 2799 | 2445 | 2128 | 1848 | 1593 |
| | arc, inches: | | +1.5 | 0 | -6.8 | -19.0 |
| Rem. 150 PSP Core-Lokt | velocity, fps: | 2890 | 2624 | 2373 | 2135 | 1912 |
| | energy, ft-lb: | 2781 | 2293 | 1875 | 1518 | 1217 |
| | arc, inches: | | +1.8 | 0 | -8.0 | -23.6 |
| Rem. 165 SP Core-Lokt | velocity, fps: | 2820 | 2510 | 2220 | 1950 | 1701 |
| | energy, ft-lb: | 2913 | 2308 | 1805 | 1393 | 1060 |
| | arc, inches: | | +2.0 | 0 | -9.1 | -27.4 |
| Speer 145 Grand Slam | velocity, fps: | 2900 | 2619 | 2354 | 2105 | |
| | energy, ft-lb: | 2707 | 2207 | 1784 | 1426 | |
| | arc, inches: | | +2.1 | 0 | -8.4 | -24.7 |
| Speer 160 Grand Slam | velocity, fps: | 2890 | 2652 | 2425 | 2210 | |
| | energy, ft-lb: | 2967 | 2497 | 2089 | 1735 | |
| | arc, inches: | | +1.7 | 0 | -7.7 | -22.4 |
| Win. 140 Fail Safe | velocity, fps: | 3050 | 2756 | 2480 | 2221 | 1977 |
| | energy, ft-lb: | 2893 | 2362 | 1913 | 1533 | 1216 |
| | arc, inches: | | +1.5 | 0 | -7.2 | -21.5 |
| Win. 140 Ballistic Silvertip | velocity, fps: | 3040 | 2842 | 2653 | 2471 | 2297 |
| | energy, ft-lb: | 2872 | 2511 | 2187 | 1898 | 1640 |
| | arc, inches: | | +1.4 | 0 | -6.3 | -18.4 |
| **7mm Remington Magnum** | | | | | | |
| A-Square 175 Monolithic Solid | velocity, fps: | 2860 | 2557 | 2273 | 2008 | 1771 |
| | energy, ft-lb: | 3178 | 2540 | 2008 | 1567 | 1219 |
| | arc, inches: | | +1.92 | 0 | -8.7 | -25.9 |
| Black Hills 140 Nos. Bal. Tip | velocity, fps: | 3150 | | | | |
| | energy, ft-lb: | 3084 | | | | |
| | arc, inches: | | | | | |

**BALLISTICS**

| CARTRIDGE BULLET | RANGE, YARDS: | 0 | 100 | 200 | 300 | 400 |
|---|---|---|---|---|---|---|
| Black Hills 140 Barnes X | velocity, fps | 3150 | | | | |
| | energy, ft-lb | 3084 | | | | |
| | arc, inches | | | | | |
| Federal 140 Nosler Partition | velocity, fps | 3150 | 2930 | 2710 | 2510 | 2320 |
| | energy, ft-lb | 3085 | 2660 | 2290 | 1960 | 1670 |
| | arc, inches | | +1.3 | 0 | -6.0 | -17.5 |
| Federal 140 Trophy Bonded | velocity, fps | 3150 | 2910 | 2680 | 2460 | 2250 |
| | energy, ft-lb | 3085 | 2630 | 2230 | 1880 | 1575 |
| | arc, inches | | +1.3 | 0 | -6.1 | -18.1 |
| Federal 150 Hi-Shok | velocity, fps | 3110 | 2830 | 2570 | 2320 | 2090 |
| | energy, ft-lb | 3220 | 2670 | 2200 | 1790 | 1450 |
| | arc, inches | | +1.4 | 0 | -6.7 | -19.9 |
| Federal 150 Sierra GameKing BTSP | velocity, fps | 3110 | 2920 | 2750 | 2580 | 2410 |
| | energy, ft-lb | 3220 | 2850 | 2510 | 2210 | 1930 |
| | arc, inches | | +1.3 | 0 | -5.9 | -17.0 |
| Federal 150 Nosler Bal. Tip | velocity, fps | 3110 | 2910 | 2720 | 2540 | 2370 |
| | energy, ft-lb | 3220 | 2825 | 2470 | 2150 | 1865 |
| | arc, inches | | +1.3 | 0 | -6.0 | -17.4 |
| Federal 160 Barnes XLC | velocity, fps | 2940 | 2760 | 2580 | 2410 | 2240 |
| | energy, ft-lb | 3070 | 2695 | 2360 | 2060 | 1785 |
| | arc, inches | | +1.5 | 0 | -6.8 | -19.6 |
| Federal 160 Sierra Pro-Hunt. | velocity, fps | 2940 | 2730 | 2520 | 2320 | 2140 |
| | energy, ft-lb | 3070 | 2640 | 2260 | 1920 | 1620 |
| | arc, inches | | +1.6 | 0 | -7.1 | -20.6 |
| Federal 160 Nosler Partition | velocity, fps | 2950 | 2770 | 2590 | 2420 | 2250 |
| | energy, ft-lb | 3090 | 2715 | 2375 | 2075 | 1800 |
| | arc, inches | | +1.5 | 0 | -6.7 | -19.4 |
| Federal 160 Trophy Bonded | velocity, fps | 2940 | 2660 | 2390 | 2140 | 1900 |
| | energy, ft-lb | 3070 | 2505 | 2025 | 1620 | 1280 |
| | arc, inches | | +1.7 | 0 | -7.9 | -23.3 |
| Federal 165 Sierra GameKing BTSP | velocity, fps | 2950 | 2800 | 2650 | 2510 | 2370 |
| | energy, ft-lb | 3190 | 2865 | 2570 | 2300 | 2050 |
| | arc, inches | | +1.5 | 0 | -6.4 | -18.4 |
| Federal 175 Hi-Shok | velocity, fps | 2860 | 2650 | 2440 | 2240 | 2060 |
| | energy, ft-lb | 3180 | 2720 | 2310 | 1960 | 1640 |
| | arc, inches | | +1.7 | 0 | -7.6 | -22.1 |
| Federal 175 Trophy Bonded | velocity, fps | 2860 | 2600 | 2350 | 2120 | 1900 |
| | energy, ft-lb | 3180 | 2625 | 2150 | 1745 | 1400 |
| | arc, inches | | +1.8 | 0 | -8.2 | -24.0 |
| Hornady 139 SPBT | velocity, fps | 3150 | 2933 | 2727 | 2530 | 2341 |
| | energy, ft-lb | 3063 | 2656 | 2296 | 1976 | 1692 |
| | arc, inches | | +1.2 | 0 | -6.1 | -17.7 |
| Hornady 139 SST (or Interbond) | velocity, fps | 3150 | 2948 | 2754 | 2569 | 2391 |
| | energy, ft-lb | 3062 | 2681 | 2341 | 2037 | 1764 |
| | arc, inches | | +1.1 | 0 | -5.7 | -16.7 |
| Hornady 139 SST LM (or Interbond) | velocity, fps | 3250 | 3044 | 2847 | 2657 | 2475 |
| | energy, ft-lb | 3259 | 2860 | 2501 | 2178 | 1890 |
| | arc, inches | | +1.1 | 0 | -5.5 | -16.2 |
| Hornady 139 SPBT HMmoly | velocity, fps | 3250 | 3041 | 2822 | 2613 | 2413 |
| | energy, ft-lb | 3300 | 2854 | 2458 | 2106 | 1797 |
| | arc, inches | | +1.1 | 0 | -5.7 | -16.6 |
| Hornady 154 Soft Point | velocity, fps | 3035 | 2814 | 2604 | 2404 | 2212 |
| | energy, ft-lb | 3151 | 2708 | 2319 | 1977 | 1674 |
| | arc, inches | | +1.3 | 0 | -6.7 | -19.3 |
| Hornady 154 SST (or Interbond) | velocity, fps | 3035 | 2850 | 2672 | 2501 | 2337 |
| | energy, ft-lb | 3149 | 2777 | 2441 | 2139 | 1867 |
| | arc, inches | | +1.4 | 0 | -6.5 | -18.7 |
| Hornady 162 SP boat-tail | velocity, fps | 2940 | 2757 | 2582 | 2413 | 2251 |
| | energy, ft-lb | 3110 | 2735 | 2399 | 2095 | 1823 |
| | arc, inches | | +1.6 | 0 | -6.7 | -19.7 |
| Hornady 175 SP | velocity, fps | 2860 | 2650 | 2440 | 2240 | 2060 |
| | energy, ft-lb | 3180 | 2720 | 2310 | 1960 | 1640 |
| | arc, inches | | +2.0 | 0 | -7.9 | -22.7 |
| Norma 140 Nosler Bal. Tip | velocity, fps | 3150 | 2936 | 2732 | 2537 | |
| | energy, ft-lb | 3085 | 2680 | 2320 | 2001 | |
| | arc, inches | | +1.2 | 0 | -5.9 | |
| Norma 150 Scirocco | velocity, fps | 3117 | 2934 | 2758 | 2589 | |
| | energy, ft-lb | 3237 | 2869 | 2535 | 2234 | |
| | arc, inches | | +1.2 | 0 | -5.8 | |
| Norma 156 Oryx | velocity, fps | 2953 | 2670 | 2404 | 2153 | |
| | energy, ft-lb | 3021 | 2470 | 2002 | 1607 | |
| | arc, inches | | +1.7 | 0 | -7.7 | |
| Norma 170 Vulkan | velocity, fps | 3018 | 2747 | 2493 | 2252 | |
| | energy, ft-lb | 3439 | 2850 | 2346 | 1914 | |
| | arc, inches | | +1.5 | 0 | -2.8 | |
| Norma 170 Oryx | velocity, fps | 2887 | 2601 | 2333 | 2080 | |
| | energy, ft-lb | 3147 | 2555 | 2055 | 1634 | |
| | arc, inches | | +1.8 | 0 | -8.2 | |
| Norma 170 Plastic Point | velocity, fps | 3018 | 2762 | 2519 | 2290 | |
| | energy, ft-lb | 3439 | 2880 | 2394 | 1980 | |
| | arc, inches | | +1.5 | 0 | -7.0 | |
| PMC 140 Barnes X | velocity, fps | 3000 | 2808 | 2624 | 2448 | 2279 |
| | energy, ft-lb | 2797 | 2451 | 2141 | 1863 | 1614 |
| | arc, inches | | +1.5 | 0 | -6.6 | 18.9 |
| PMC 140 Pointed Soft Point | velocity, fps | 3099 | 2878 | 2668 | 2469 | 2279 |
| | energy, ft-lb | 2984 | 2574 | 2212 | 1895 | 1614 |
| | arc, inches | | +1.4 | 0 | -6.2 | -18.1 |
| PMC 140 SP boat-tail | velocity, fps | 3125 | 2891 | 2669 | 2457 | 2255 |
| | energy, ft-lb | 3035 | 2597 | 2213 | 1877 | 1580 |
| | arc, inches | | +1.4 | 0 | -6.3 | -18.4 |
| PMC 160 Barnes X | velocity, fps | 2800 | 2639 | 2484 | 2334 | 2189 |
| | energy, ft-lb | 2785 | 2474 | 2192 | 1935 | 1703 |
| | arc, inches | | +1.8 | 0 | -7.4 | -21.2 |
| PMC 160 Pointed Soft Point | velocity, fps | 2914 | 2748 | 2586 | 2428 | 2276 |
| | energy, ft-lb | 3016 | 2682 | 2375 | 2095 | 1840 |
| | arc, inches | | +1.6 | 0 | -6.7 | -19.4 |
| PMC 160 SP boat-tail | velocity, fps | 2900 | 2696 | 2501 | 2314 | 2135 |
| | energy, ft-lb | 2987 | 2582 | 2222 | 1903 | 1620 |
| | arc, inches | | +1.7 | 0 | -7.2 | -21.0 |
| PMC 175 Pointed Soft Point | velocity, fps | 2860 | 2645 | 2442 | 2244 | 2957 |
| | energy, ft-lb | 3178 | 2718 | 2313 | 1956 | 1644 |
| | arc, inches | | +2.0 | 0 | -7.9 | -22.7 |
| Rem. 140 PSP Core-Lokt mr | velocity, fps | 2710 | 2482 | 2265 | 2059 | 1865 |
| | energy, ft-lb | 2283 | 1915 | 1595 | 1318 | 1081 |
| | arc, inches | | +1.0 | -2.5 | -12.8 | -31.3 |
| Rem. 140 PSP Core-Lokt | velocity, fps | 3175 | 2923 | 2684 | 2458 | 2243 |
| | energy, ft-lb | 3133 | 2655 | 2240 | 1878 | 1564 |
| | arc, inches | | +2.2 | +1.9 | -3.2 | -14.2 |
| Rem. 140 PSP boat-tail | velocity, fps | 3175 | 2956 | 2747 | 2547 | 2356 |
| | energy, ft-lb | 3133 | 2715 | 2345 | 2017 | 1726 |
| | arc, inches | | +2.2 | +1.6 | -3.1 | -13.4 |
| Rem. 150 AccuTip | velocity, fps | 3110 | 2926 | 2749 | 2579 | 2415 |
| | energy, ft-lb | 3221 | 2850 | 2516 | 2215 | 1943 |
| | arc, inches | | +1.3 | 0 | -5.9 | -17.0 |
| Rem. 150 PSP Core-Lokt | velocity, fps | 3110 | 2830 | 2568 | 2320 | 2085 |
| | energy, ft-lb | 3221 | 2667 | 2196 | 1792 | 1448 |
| | arc, inches | | +1.3 | 0 | -6.6 | -20.2 |
| Rem. 150 Nosler Bal. Tip | velocity, fps | 3110 | 2912 | 2723 | 2542 | 2367 |
| | energy, ft-lb | 3222 | 2825 | 2470 | 2152 | 1867 |
| | arc, inches | | +1.2 | 0 | -5.9 | -17.3 |

# Centerfire Rifle Ballistics

## 7MM REMINGTON MAGNUM TO 7MM DAKOTA

| CARTRIDGE BULLET | RANGE, YARDS: | 0 | 100 | 200 | 300 | 400 |
|---|---|---|---|---|---|---|
| Rem. 150 Swift Scirocco | velocity, fps: | 3110 | 2927 | 2751 | 2582 | 2419 |
| | energy, ft-lb: | 3221 | 2852 | 2520 | 2220 | 1948 |
| | arc, inches: | | +1.3 | 0 | -5.9 | -17.0 |
| Rem. 160 Swift A-Frame | velocity, fps: | 2900 | 2659 | 2430 | 2212 | 2006 |
| | energy, ft-lb: | 2987 | 2511 | 2097 | 1739 | 1430 |
| | arc, inches: | | +1.7 | 0 | -7.6 | -22.4 |
| Rem. 160 Nosler Partition | velocity, fps: | 2950 | 2752 | 2563 | 2381 | 2207 |
| | energy, ft-lb: | 3091 | 2690 | 2333 | 2014 | 1730 |
| | arc, inches: | | +0.6 | -1.9 | -9.6 | -23.6 |
| Rem. 175 PSP Core-Lokt | velocity, fps: | 2860 | 2645 | 2440 | 2244 | 2057 |
| | energy, ft-lb: | 3178 | 2718 | 2313 | 1956 | 1644 |
| | arc, inches: | | +1.7 | 0 | -7.6 | -22.1 |
| Speer 145 Grand Slam | velocity, fps: | 3140 | 2843 | 2565 | 2304 | |
| | energy, ft-lb: | 3174 | 2602 | 2118 | 1708 | |
| | arc, inches: | | +1.4 | 0 | -6.7 | |
| Speer 175 Grand Slam | velocity, fps: | 2850 | 2653 | 2463 | 2282 | |
| | energy, ft-lb: | 3156 | 2734 | 2358 | 2023 | |
| | arc, inches: | | +1.7 | 0 | -7.5 | -21.7 |
| Win. 140 Fail Safe | velocity, fps: | 3150 | 2861 | 2589 | 2333 | 2092 |
| | energy, ft-lb: | 3085 | 2544 | 2085 | 1693 | 1361 |
| | arc, inches: | | +1.4 | 0 | -6.6 | -19.5 |
| Win. 140 Ballistic Silvertip | velocity, fps: | 3100 | 2889 | 2687 | 2494 | 2310 |
| | energy, ft-lb: | 2988 | 2595 | 2245 | 1934 | 1659 |
| | arc, inches: | | +1.3 | 0 | -6.2 | -17.9 |
| Win. 150 Power-Point | velocity, fps: | 3090 | 2812 | 2551 | 2304 | 2071 |
| | energy, ft-lb: | 3181 | 2634 | 2167 | 1768 | 1429 |
| | arc, inches: | | +1.5 | 0 | -6.8 | -20.2 |
| Win. 150 Power-Point Plus | velocity, fps: | 3130 | 2849 | 2586 | 2337 | 2102 |
| | energy, ft-lb: | 3264 | 2705 | 2227 | 1819 | 1472 |
| | arc, inches: | | +1.4 | 0 | -6.6 | -19.6 |
| Win. 150 Ballistic Silvertip | velocity, fps: | 3100 | 2903 | 2714 | 2533 | 2359 |
| | energy, ft-lb: | 3200 | 2806 | 2453 | 2136 | 1853 |
| | arc, inches: | | +1.3 | 0 | -6.0 | -17.5 |
| Win. 160 AccuBond | velocity, fps: | 2950 | 2766 | 2590 | 2420 | 2257 |
| | energy, ft-lb: | 3091 | 2718 | 2382 | 2080 | 1809 |
| | arc, inches: | | +1.5 | 0 | -6.7 | -19.4 |
| Win. 160 Partition Gold | velocity, fps: | 2950 | 2743 | 2546 | 2357 | 2176 |
| | energy, ft-lb: | 3093 | 2674 | 2303 | 1974 | 1682 |
| | arc, inches: | | +1.6 | 0 | -6.9 | -20.1 |
| Win. 160 Fail Safe | velocity, fps: | 2920 | 2678 | 2449 | 2331 | 2025 |
| | energy, ft-lb: | 3030 | 2549 | 2131 | 1769 | 1457 |
| | arc, inches: | | +1.7 | 0 | -7.5 | -22.0 |
| Win. 175 Power-Point | velocity, fps: | 2860 | 2645 | 2440 | 2244 | 2057 |
| | energy, ft-lb: | 3178 | 2718 | 2313 | 1956 | 1644 |
| | arc, inches: | | +2.0 | 0 | -7.9 | -22.7 |

## 7MM REMINGTON SHORT ULTRA MAG

| CARTRIDGE BULLET | RANGE, YARDS: | 0 | 100 | 200 | 300 | 400 |
|---|---|---|---|---|---|---|
| Rem. 140 PSP C-L Ultra | velocity, fps: | 3175 | 2934 | 2707 | 2490 | 2283 |
| | energy, ft-lb: | 3133 | 2676 | 2277 | 1927 | 1620 |
| | arc, inches: | | +1.3 | 0 | -6.0 | -17.7 |
| Rem. 150 PSP Core-Lokt | velocity, fps: | 3110 | 2828 | 2563 | 2313 | 2077 |
| | energy, ft-lb: | 3221 | 2663 | 2188 | 1782 | 1437 |
| | arc, inches: | | +2.5 | +2.1 | -3.6 | -15.8 |
| Rem. 160 Partition | velocity, fps: | 2960 | 2762 | 2572 | 2390 | 2215 |
| | energy, ft-lb: | 3112 | 2709 | 2350 | 2029 | 1744 |
| | arc, inches: | | +2.6 | +2.2 | -3.6 | -15.4 |
| Rem. 160 PSP C-L Ultra | velocity, fps: | 2960 | 2733 | 2518 | 2313 | 2117 |
| | energy, ft-lb: | 3112 | 2654 | 2252 | 1900 | 1592 |
| | arc, inches: | | +2.7 | +2.2 | -3.7 | -16.2 |

## 7MM WINCHESTER SHORT MAGNUM

| CARTRIDGE BULLET | RANGE, YARDS: | 0 | 100 | 200 | 300 | 400 |
|---|---|---|---|---|---|---|
| Win. 140 Bal. Silvertip | velocity, fps: | 3225 | 3008 | 2801 | 2603 | 2414 |
| | energy, ft-lb: | 3233 | 2812 | 2438 | 2106 | 1812 |
| | arc, inches: | | +1.2 | 0 | -5.6 | -16.4 |
| Win. 150 Power Point | velocity, fps: | 3200 | 2915 | 2648 | 2396 | 2157 |
| | energy, ft-lb: | 3410 | 2830 | 2335 | 1911 | 1550 |
| | arc, inches: | | +1.3 | 0 | -6.3 | -18.6 |
| Win. 160 AccuBond | velocity, fps: | 3050 | 2862 | 2682 | 2509 | 2342 |
| | energy, ft-lb: | 3306 | 2911 | 2556 | 2237 | 1950 |
| | arc, inches: | | 1.4 | 0 | -6.2 | -17.9 |
| Win. 160 Fail Safe | velocity, fps: | 2990 | 2744 | 2512 | 2291 | 2081 |
| | energy, ft-lb: | 3176 | 2675 | 2241 | 1864 | 1538 |
| | arc, inches: | | +1.6 | 0 | -7.1 | -20.8 |

## 7MM WEATHERBY MAG.

| CARTRIDGE BULLET | RANGE, YARDS: | 0 | 100 | 200 | 300 | 400 |
|---|---|---|---|---|---|---|
| Federal 160 Nosler Partition | velocity, fps: | 3050 | 2850 | 2650 | 2470 | 2290 |
| | energy, ft-lb: | 3305 | 2880 | 2505 | 2165 | 1865 |
| | arc, inches: | | +1.4 | 0 | -6.3 | -18.4 |
| Federal 160 Sierra GameKing BTSP | velocity, fps: | 3050 | 2880 | 2710 | 2560 | 2400 |
| | energy, ft-lb: | 3305 | 2945 | 2615 | 2320 | 2050 |
| | arc, inches: | | +1.4 | 0 | -6.1 | -17.4 |
| Federal 160 Trophy Bonded | velocity, fps: | 3050 | 2730 | 2420 | 2140 | 1880 |
| | energy, ft-lb: | 3305 | 2640 | 2085 | 1630 | 1255 |
| | arc, inches: | | +1.6 | 0 | -7.6 | -22.7 |
| Hornady 154 Soft Point | velocity, fps: | 3200 | 2971 | 2753 | 2546 | 2348 |
| | energy, ft-lb: | 3501 | 3017 | 2592 | 2216 | 1885 |
| | arc, inches: | | +1.2 | 0 | -5.8 | -17.0 |
| Hornady 154 SST (or Interbond) | velocity, fps: | 3200 | 3009 | 2825 | 2648 | 2478 |
| | energy, ft-lb: | 3501 | 3096 | 2729 | 2398 | 2100 |
| | arc, inches: | | +1.2 | 0 | -5.7 | -16.5 |
| Hornady 175 Soft Point | velocity, fps: | 2910 | 2709 | 2516 | 2331 | 2154 |
| | energy, ft-lb: | 3290 | 2850 | 2459 | 2111 | 1803 |
| | arc, inches: | | +1.6 | 0 | -7.1 | -20.6 |
| Wby. 139 Pointed Expanding | velocity, fps: | 3340 | 3079 | 2834 | 2601 | 2380 |
| | energy, ft-lb: | 3443 | 2926 | 2478 | 2088 | 1748 |
| | arc, inches: | | +2.9 | +3.6 | 0 | -8.7 |
| Wby. 140 Nosler Partition | velocity, fps: | 3303 | 3069 | 2847 | 2636 | 2434 |
| | energy, ft-lb: | 3391 | 2927 | 2519 | 2159 | 1841 |
| | arc, inches: | | +2.9 | +3.6 | 0 | -8.5 |
| Wby. 150 Nosler Bal. Tip | velocity, fps: | 3300 | 3093 | 2896 | 2708 | 2527 |
| | energy, ft-lb: | 3627 | 3187 | 2793 | 2442 | 2127 |
| | arc, inches: | | +2.8 | +3.5 | 0 | -8.2 |
| Wby. 150 Barnes X | veloctiy, fps: | 3100 | 2901 | 2710 | 2527 | 2352 |
| | energy, ft-lb: | 3200 | 2802 | 2446 | 2127 | 1842 |
| | arc, inches: | | +3.3 | +4.0 | 0 | -9.4 |
| Wby. 154 Pointed Expanding | velocity, fps: | 3260 | 3028 | 2807 | 2597 | 2397 |
| | energy, ft-lb: | 3634 | 3134 | 2694 | 2307 | 1964 |
| | arc, inches: | | +3.0 | +3.7 | 0 | -8.8 |
| Wby. 160 Nosler Partition | velocity, fps: | 3200 | 2991 | 2791 | 2600 | 2417 |
| | energy, ft-lb: | 3638 | 3177 | 2767 | 2401 | 2075 |
| | arc, inches: | | +3.1 | +3.8 | 0 | -8.9 |
| Wby. 175 Pointed Expanding | velocity, fps: | 3070 | 2861 | 2662 | 2471 | 2288 |
| | energy, ft-lb: | 3662 | 3181 | 2753 | 2373 | 2034 |
| | arc, inches: | | +3.5 | +4.2 | 0 | -9.9 |

## 7MM DAKOTA

| CARTRIDGE BULLET | RANGE, YARDS: | 0 | 100 | 200 | 300 | 400 |
|---|---|---|---|---|---|---|
| Dakota 140 Barnes X | velocity, fps: | 3500 | 3253 | 3019 | 2798 | 2587 |
| | energy, ft-lb: | 3807 | 3288 | 2833 | 2433 | 2081 |
| | arc, inches: | | +2.0 | +2.1 | -1.5 | -9.6 |

BALLISTICS

**BALLISTICS**

| CARTRIDGE BULLET | RANGE, YARDS: | 0 | 100 | 200 | 300 | 400 |
|---|---|---|---|---|---|---|
| Dakota 160 Barnes X | velocity, fps: | 3200 | 3001 | 2811 | 2630 | 2455 |
| | energy, ft-lb: | 3637 | 3200 | 2808 | 2456 | 2140 |
| | arc, inches: | | +2.1 | +1.9 | -2.8 | -12.5 |

## 7MM STW

| | | | | | | |
|---|---|---|---|---|---|---|
| A-Square 140 Nos. Bal. Tip | velocity, fps: | 3450 | 3254 | 3067 | 2888 | 2715 |
| | energy, ft-lb: | 3700 | 3291 | 2924 | 2592 | 2292 |
| | arc, inches: | | +2.2 | +3.0 | 0 | -7.3 |
| A-Square 160 Nosler Part. | velocity, fps: | 3250 | 3071 | 2900 | 2735 | 2576 |
| | energy, ft-lb: | 3752 | 3351 | 2987 | 2657 | 2357 |
| | arc, inches: | | +2.8 | +3.5 | 0 | -8.2 |
| A-Square 160 SP boat-tail | velocity, fps: | 3250 | 3087 | 2930 | 2778 | 2631 |
| | energy, ft-lb: | 3752 | 3385 | 3049 | 2741 | 2460 |
| | arc, inches: | | +2.8 | +3.4 | 0 | -8.0 |
| Federal 140 Trophy Bonded | velocity, fps: | 3330 | 3080 | 2850 | 2630 | 2420 |
| | energy, ft-lb: | 3435 | 2950 | 2520 | 2145 | 1815 |
| | arc, inches: | | +1.1 | 0 | -5.4 | -15.8 |
| Federal 150 Trophy Bonded | velocity, fps: | 3250 | 3010 | 2770 | 2560 | 2350 |
| | energy, ft-lb: | 3520 | 3010 | 2565 | 2175 | 1830 |
| | arc, inches: | | +1.2 | 0 | -5.7 | -16.7 |
| Federal 160 Sierra GameKing BTSP | velocity, fps: | 3200 | 3020 | 2850 | 2670 | 2530 |
| | energy, ft-lb: | 3640 | 3245 | 2890 | 2570 | 2275 |
| | arc, inches: | | +1.1 | 0 | -5.5 | -15.7 |
| Rem. 140 PSP Core-Lokt | velocity, fps: | 3325 | 3064 | 2818 | 2585 | 2364 |
| | energy, ft-lb: | 3436 | 2918 | 2468 | 2077 | 1737 |
| | arc, inches: | | +2.0 | +1.7 | -2.9 | -12.8 |
| Rem. 140 Swift A-Frame | velocity, fps: | 3325 | 3020 | 2735 | 2467 | 2215 |
| | energy, ft-lb: | 3436 | 2834 | 2324 | 1892 | 1525 |
| | arc, inches: | | +2.1 | +1.8 | -3.1 | -13.8 |
| Speer 145 Grand Slam | velocity, fps: | 3300 | 2992 | 2075 | 2435 | |
| | energy, ft-lb: | 3506 | 2882 | 2355 | 1909 | |
| | arc, inches: | | +1.2 | 0 | -6.0 | -17.8 |
| Win. 140 Ballistic Silvertip | velocity, fps: | 3320 | 3100 | 2890 | 2690 | 2499 |
| | energy, ft-lb: | 3427 | 2982 | 2597 | 2250 | 1941 |
| | arc, inches: | | +1.1 | 0 | -5.2 | -15.2 |
| Win. 150 Power-Point | velocity, fps: | 3250 | 2957 | 2683 | 2424 | 2181 |
| | energy, ft-lb: | 3519 | 2913 | 2398 | 1958 | 1584 |
| | arc, inches: | | +1.2 | 0 | -6.1 | -18.1 |
| Win. 160 Fail Safe | velocity, fps: | 3150 | 2894 | 2652 | 2422 | 2204 |
| | energy, ft-lb: | 3526 | 2976 | 2499 | 2085 | 1727 |
| | arc, inches: | | +1.3 | 0 | -6.3 | -18.5 |

## 7MM REMINGTON ULTRA MAG

| | | | | | | |
|---|---|---|---|---|---|---|
| Rem. 140 PSP Core-Lokt | velocity, fps: | 3425 | 3158 | 2907 | 2669 | 2444 |
| | energy, ft-lb: | 3646 | 3099 | 2626 | 2214 | 1856 |
| | arc, inches: | | +1.8 | +1.6 | -2.7 | -11.9 |
| Rem. 140 Nosler Partition | velocity, fps: | 3425 | 3184 | 2956 | 2740 | 2534 |
| | energy, ft-lb: | 3646 | 3151 | 2715 | 2333 | 1995 |
| | arc, inches: | | +1.7 | +1.6 | -2.6 | -11.4 |
| Rem. 160 Nosler Partition | velocity, fps: | 3200 | 2991 | 2791 | 2600 | 2417 |
| | energy, ft-lb: | 3637 | 3177 | 2767 | 2401 | 2075 |
| | arc, inches: | | +2.1 | +1.8 | -3.0 | -12.9 |

## 7.21 (.284) FIREHAWK

| | | | | | | |
|---|---|---|---|---|---|---|
| Lazzeroni 140 Nosler Part. | velocity, fps: | 3580 | 3349 | 3130 | 2923 | 2724 |
| | energy, ft-lb: | 3985 | 3488 | 3048 | 2656 | 2308 |
| | arc, inches: | | +2.2 | +2.9 | 0 | -7.0 |
| Lazzeroni 160 Swift A-Fr. | velocity, fps: | 3385 | 3167 | 2961 | 2763 | 2574 |
| | energy, ft-lb: | 4072 | 3565 | 3115 | 2713 | 2354 |
| | arc, inches: | | +2.6 | +3.3 | 0 | -7.8 |

## 7.5x55 SWISS

| | | | | | | |
|---|---|---|---|---|---|---|
| Norma 180 Soft Point | velocity, fps: | 2651 | 2432 | 2223 | 2025 | |
| | energy, ft-lb: | 2810 | 2364 | 1976 | 1639 | |
| | arc, inches: | | +2.2 | 0 | -9.3 | |
| Norma 180 Oryx | velocity, fps: | 2493 | 2222 | 1968 | 1734 | |
| | energy, ft-lb: | 2485 | 1974 | 1549 | 1201 | |
| | arc, inches: | | +2.7 | 0 | -11.8 | |

## 7.62x39 RUSSIAN

| | | | | | | |
|---|---|---|---|---|---|---|
| Federal 123 Hi-Shok | velocity, fps: | 2300 | 2030 | 1780 | 1550 | 1350 |
| | energy, ft-lb: | 1445 | 1125 | 860 | 655 | 500 |
| | arc, inches: | | 0 | -7.0 | -25.1 | |
| Federal 124 FMJ | velocity, fps: | 2300 | 2030 | 1780 | 1560 | 1360 |
| | energy, ft-lb: | 1455 | 1135 | 875 | 670 | 510 |
| | arc, inches: | | +3.5 | 0 | -14.6 | -43.5 |
| PMC 123 FMJ | velocity, fps: | 2350 | 2072 | 1817 | 1583 | 1368 |
| | energy, ft-lb: | 1495 | 1162 | 894 | 678 | 507 |
| | arc, inches: | | 0 | -5.0 | -26.4 | -67.8 |
| PMC 125 Pointed Soft Point | velocity, fps: | 2320 | 2046 | 1794 | 1563 | 1350 |
| | energy, ft-lb: | 1493 | 1161 | 893 | 678 | 505 |
| | arc, inches: | | 0 | -5.2 | -27.5 | -70.6 |
| Rem. 125 Pointed Soft Point | velocity, fps: | 2365 | 2062 | 1783 | 1533 | 1320 |
| | energy, ft-lb: | 1552 | 1180 | 882 | 652 | 483 |
| | arc, inches: | | 0 | -6.7 | -24.5 | |
| Win. 123 Soft Point | velocity, fps: | 2365 | 2033 | 1731 | 1465 | 1248 |
| | energy, ft-lb: | 1527 | 1129 | 818 | 586 | 425 |
| | arc, inches: | | +3.8 | 0 | -15.4 | -46.3 |

## .30 CARBINE

| | | | | | | |
|---|---|---|---|---|---|---|
| Federal 110 Hi-Shok RN | velocity, fps: | 1990 | 1570 | 1240 | 1040 | 920 |
| | energy, ft-lb: | 965 | 600 | 375 | 260 | 210 |
| | arc, inches: | | 0 | -12.8 | -46.9 | |
| Federal 110 FMJ | velocity, fps: | 1990 | 1570 | 1240 | 1040 | 920 |
| | energy, ft-lb: | 965 | 600 | 375 | 260 | 210 |
| | arc, inches: | | 0 | -12.8 | -46.9 | |
| Magtech 110 FMC | velocity, fps: | 1990 | 1654 | | | |
| | energy, ft-lb: | 965 | 668 | | | |
| | arc, inches: | | 0 | | | |
| PMC 110 FMJ (and RNSP) | velocity, fps: | 1927 | 1548 | 1248 | | |
| | energy, ft-lb: | 906 | 585 | 380 | | |
| | arc, inches: | | 0 | -14.2 | | |
| Rem. 110 Soft Point | velocity, fps: | 1990 | 1567 | 1236 | 1035 | 923 |
| | energy, ft-lb: | 967 | 600 | 373 | 262 | 208 |
| | arc, inches: | | 0 | -12.9 | -48.6 | |
| Win. 110 Hollow Soft Point | velocity, fps: | 1990 | 1567 | 1236 | 1035 | 923 |
| | energy, ft-lb: | 967 | 600 | 373 | 262 | 208 |
| | arc, inches: | | 0 | -13.5 | -49.9 | |

## .30-30 WINCHESTER

| | | | | | | |
|---|---|---|---|---|---|---|
| Federal 125 Hi-Shok HP | velocity, fps: | 2570 | 2090 | 1660 | 1320 | 1080 |
| | energy, ft-lb: | 1830 | 1210 | 770 | 480 | 320 |
| | arc, inches: | | +3.3 | 0 | -16.0 | -50.9 |
| Federal 150 Hi-Shok FN | velocity, fps: | 2390 | 2020 | 1680 | 1400 | 1180 |
| | energy, ft-lb: | 1900 | 1355 | 945 | 650 | 460 |
| | arc, inches: | | +3.6 | 0 | -15.9 | -49.1 |
| Federal 170 Hi-Shok RN | velocity, fps: | 2200 | 1900 | 1620 | 1380 | 1190 |
| | energy, ft-lb: | 1830 | 1355 | 990 | 720 | 535 |
| | arc, inches: | | +4.1 | 0 | -17.4 | -52.4 |
| Federal 170 Sierra Pro-Hunt. | velocity, fps: | 2200 | 1820 | 1500 | 1240 | 1060 |
| | energy, ft-lb: | 1830 | 1255 | 845 | 575 | 425 |
| | arc, inches: | | +4.5 | 0 | -20.0 | -63.5 |

# Centerfire Rifle Ballistics

## .30-30 WINCHESTER TO .308 WINCHESTER

| CARTRIDGE BULLET | RANGE, YARDS | 0 | 100 | 200 | 300 | 400 |
|---|---|---|---|---|---|---|
| Federal 170 Nosler Partition | velocity, fps: | 2200 | 1900 | 1620 | 1380 | 1190 |
| | energy, ft-lb: | 1830 | 1355 | 990 | 720 | 535 |
| | arc, inches: | | +4.1 | 0 | -17.4 | -52.4 |
| Hornady 150 Round Nose | velocity, fps: | 2390 | 1973 | 1605 | 1303 | 1095 |
| | energy, ft-lb: | 1902 | 1296 | 858 | 565 | 399 |
| | arc, inches: | | 0 | -8.2 | -30.0 | |
| Hornady 170 Flat Point | velocity, fps: | 2200 | 1895 | 1619 | 1381 | 1191 |
| | energy, ft-lb: | 1827 | 1355 | 989 | 720 | 535 |
| | arc, inches: | | 0 | -8.9 | -31.1 | |
| Norma 150 Soft Point | velocity, fps: | 2329 | 2008 | 1716 | 1459 | |
| | energy, ft-lb: | 1807 | 1344 | 981 | 709 | |
| | arc, inches: | | +3.6 | 0 | -15.5 | |
| PMC 150 Starfire HP | velocity, fps: | 2100 | 1769 | 1478 | | |
| | energy, ft-lb: | 1469 | 1042 | 728 | | |
| | arc, inches: | | 0 | -10.8 | | |
| PMC 150 Flat Nose | velocity, fps: | 2159 | 1819 | 1554 | | |
| | energy, ft-lb: | 1552 | 1102 | 804 | | |
| | arc, inches: | | 0 | -9.0 | | |
| PMC 170 Flat Nose | velocity, fps: | 1965 | 1680 | 1480 | | |
| | energy, ft-lb: | 1457 | 1065 | 827 | | |
| | arc, inches: | | 0 | -10.7 | | |
| Rem. 55 PSP (sabot) "Accelerator" | velocity, fps: | 3400 | 2693 | 2085 | 1570 | 1187 |
| | energy, ft-lb: | 1412 | 886 | 521 | 301 | 172 |
| | arc, inches: | | +1.7 | 0 | -9.9 | -34.3 |
| Rem. 150 SP Core-Lokt | velocity, fps: | 2390 | 1973 | 1605 | 1303 | 1095 |
| | energy, ft-lb: | 1902 | 1296 | 858 | 565 | 399 |
| | arc, inches: | | 0 | -7.6 | -28.8 | |
| Rem. 170 SP Core-Lokt | velocity, fps: | 2200 | 1895 | 1619 | 1381 | 1191 |
| | energy, ft-lb: | 1827 | 1355 | 989 | 720 | 535 |
| | arc, inches: | | 0 | -8.3 | -29.9 | |
| Rem. 170 HP Core-Lokt | velocity, fps: | 2200 | 1895 | 1619 | 1381 | 1191 |
| | energy, ft-lb: | 1827 | 1355 | 989 | 720 | 535 |
| | arc, inches: | | 0 | -8.3 | -29.9 | |
| Speer 150 Flat Nose | velocity, fps: | 2370 | 2067 | 1788 | 1538 | |
| | energy, ft-lb: | 1870 | 1423 | 1065 | 788 | |
| | arc, inches: | | +3.3 | 0 | -14.4 | -43.7 |
| Win. 150 Hollow Point | velocity, fps: | 2390 | 2018 | 1684 | 1398 | 1177 |
| | energy, ft-lb: | 1902 | 1356 | 944 | 651 | 461 |
| | arc, inches: | | 0 | -7.7 | -27.9 | |
| Win. 150 Power-Point | velocity, fps: | 2390 | 2018 | 1684 | 1398 | 1177 |
| | energy, ft-lb: | 1902 | 1356 | 944 | 651 | 461 |
| | arc, inches: | | 0 | -7.7 | -27.9 | |
| Win. 150 Silvertip | velocity, fps: | 2390 | 2018 | 1684 | 1398 | 1177 |
| | energy, ft-lb: | 1902 | 1356 | 944 | 651 | 461 |
| | arc, inches: | | 0 | -7.7 | -27.9 | |
| Win. 150 Power-Point Plus | velocity, fps: | 2480 | 2095 | 1747 | 1446 | 1209 |
| | energy, ft-lb: | 2049 | 1462 | 1017 | 697 | 487 |
| | arc, inches: | | 0 | -6.5 | -24.5 | |
| Win. 170 Power-Point | velocity, fps: | 2200 | 1895 | 1619 | 1381 | 1191 |
| | energy, ft-lb: | 1827 | 1355 | 989 | 720 | 535 |
| | arc, inches: | | 0 | -8.9 | -31.1 | |
| Win. 170 Silvertip | velocity, fps: | 2200 | 1895 | 1619 | 1381 | 1191 |
| | energy, ft-lb: | 1827 | 1355 | 989 | 720 | 535 |
| | arc, inches: | | 0 | -8.9 | -31.1 | |

### .300 SAVAGE

| CARTRIDGE BULLET | RANGE, YARDS | 0 | 100 | 200 | 300 | 400 |
|---|---|---|---|---|---|---|
| Federal 150 Hi-Shok | velocity, fps: | 2630 | 2350 | 2100 | 1850 | 1630 |
| | energy, ft-lb: | 2305 | 1845 | 1460 | 1145 | 885 |
| | arc, inches: | | +2.4 | 0 | -10.4 | -30.9 |
| Federal 180 Hi-Shok | velocity, fps: | 2350 | 2140 | 1940 | 1750 | 1570 |
| | energy, ft-lb: | 2205 | 1825 | 1495 | 1215 | 985 |
| | arc, inches: | | +3.1 | 0 | -12.4 | -36.1 |
| Rem. 150 PSP Core-Lokt | velocity, fps: | 2630 | 2354 | 2095 | 1853 | 1631 |
| | energy, ft-lb: | 2303 | 1845 | 1462 | 1143 | 806 |
| | arc, inches: | | +2.4 | 0 | -10.4 | -30.9 |
| Rem. 180 SP Core-Lokt | velocity, fps: | 2350 | 2025 | 1728 | 1467 | 1252 |
| | energy, ft-lb: | 2207 | 1639 | 1193 | 860 | 626 |
| | arc, inches: | | +1.5 | -4.0 | -21.3 | -54.8 |
| Win. 150 Power-Point | velocity, fps: | 2630 | 2311 | 2015 | 1743 | 1500 |
| | energy, ft-lb: | 2303 | 1779 | 1352 | 1012 | 749 |
| | arc, inches: | | +2.8 | 0 | -11.5 | -34.4 |

### .307 WINCHESTER

| CARTRIDGE BULLET | RANGE, YARDS | 0 | 100 | 200 | 300 | 400 |
|---|---|---|---|---|---|---|
| Win. 180 Power-Point | velocity, fps: | 2510 | 2179 | 1874 | 1599 | 1362 |
| | energy, ft-lb: | 2519 | 1898 | 1404 | 1022 | 742 |
| | arc, inches: | | +1.5 | -3.6 | -18.6 | -47.1 |

### .30-40 KRAG

| CARTRIDGE BULLET | RANGE, YARDS | 0 | 100 | 200 | 300 | 400 |
|---|---|---|---|---|---|---|
| Rem. 180 PSP Core-Lokt | velocity, fps: | 2430 | 2213 | 2007 | 1813 | 1632 |
| | energy, ft-lb: | 2360 | 1957 | 1610 | 1314 | 1064 |
| | arc, inches, s: | | 0 | -5.6 | -18.6 | |
| Win. 180 Power-Point | velocity, fps: | 2430 | 2099 | 1795 | 1525 | 1298 |
| | energy, ft-lb: | 2360 | 1761 | 1288 | 929 | 673 |
| | arc, inches, s: | | 0 | -7.1 | -25.0 | |

### 7.62x54R RUSSIAN

| CARTRIDGE BULLET | RANGE, YARDS | 0 | 100 | 200 | 300 | 400 |
|---|---|---|---|---|---|---|
| Norma 150 Soft Point | velocity, fps: | 2953 | 2622 | 2314 | 2028 | |
| | energy, ft-lb: | 2905 | 2291 | 1784 | 1370 | |
| | arc, inches: | | +1.8 | 0 | -8.3 | |
| Norma 180 Alaska | velocity, fps: | 2575 | 2362 | 2159 | 1967 | |
| | energy, ft-lb: | 2651 | 2231 | 1864 | 1546 | |
| | arc, inches: | | +2.9 | 0 | -12.9 | |

### .308 WINCHESTER

| CARTRIDGE BULLET | RANGE, YARDS | 0 | 100 | 200 | 300 | 400 |
|---|---|---|---|---|---|---|
| Black Hills 150 Nosler B. Tip | velocity, fps: | 2800 | | | | |
| | energy, ft-lb: | 2611 | | | | |
| | arc, inches: | | | | | |
| Black Hills 165 Nosler B. Tip (and SP) | velocity, fps: | 2650 | | | | |
| | energy, ft-lb: | 2573 | | | | |
| | arc, inches: | | | | | |
| Black Hills 168 Barnes X (and Match) | velocity, fps: | 2650 | | | | |
| | energy, ft-lb: | 2620 | | | | |
| | arc, inches: | | | | | |
| Black Hills 175 Match | velocity, fps: | 2600 | | | | |
| | energy, ft-lb: | 2657 | | | | |
| | arc, inches: | | | | | |
| Federal 150 Hi-Shok | velocity, fps: | 2820 | 2530 | 2260 | 2010 | 1770 |
| | energy, ft-lb: | 2650 | 2140 | 1705 | 1345 | 1050 |
| | arc, inches: | | +2.0 | 0 | -8.8 | -26.3 |
| Federal 150 Nosler Bal. Tip. | velocity, fps: | 2820 | 2610 | 2410 | 2220 | 2040 |
| | energy, ft-lb: | 2650 | 2270 | 1935 | 1640 | 1380 |
| | arc, inches: | | +1.8 | 0 | -7.8 | -22.7 |
| Federal 150 FMJ boat-tail | velocity, fps: | 2820 | 2620 | 2430 | 2250 | 2070 |
| | energy, ft-lb: | 2650 | 2285 | 1965 | 1680 | 1430 |
| | arc, inches: | | +1.8 | 0 | -7.7 | -22.4 |
| Federal 150 Barnes XLC | velocity, fps: | 2820 | 2610 | 2400 | 2210 | 2030 |
| | energy, ft-lb: | 2650 | 2265 | 1925 | 1630 | 1370 |
| | arc, inches: | | +1.8 | 0 | -7.8 | -22.9 |
| Federal 155 Sierra MatchKg. BTHP | velocity, fps: | 2950 | 2740 | 2540 | 2350 | 2170 |
| | energy, ft-lb: | 2995 | 2585 | 2225 | 1905 | 1620 |
| | arc, inches: | | +13.2 | +23.3 | +28.1 | +26.5 |

BALLISTICS

| CARTRIDGE BULLET | RANGE, YARDS: | 0 | 100 | 200 | 300 | 400 |
|---|---|---|---|---|---|---|
| Federal 165 Sierra GameKing BTSP | velocity, fps: | 2700 | 2520 | 2330 | 2160 | 1990 |
| | energy, ft-lb: | 2670 | 2310 | 1990 | 1700 | 1450 |
| | arc, inches: | | +2.0 | 0 | -8.4 | -24.3 |
| Federal 165 Trophy Bonded | velocity, fps: | 2700 | 2440 | 2200 | 1970 | 1760 |
| | energy, ft-lb: | 2670 | 2185 | 1775 | 1425 | 1135 |
| | arc, inches: | | +2.2 | 0 | -9.4 | -27.7 |
| Federal 165 Tr. Bonded HE | velocity, fps: | 2870 | 2600 | 2350 | 2120 | 1890 |
| | energy, ft-lb: | 3020 | 2485 | 2030 | 1640 | 1310 |
| | arc, inches: | | +1.8 | 0 | -8.2 | -24.0 |
| Federal 168 Sierra MatchKg. BTHP | velocity, fps: | 2600 | 2410 | 2230 | 2060 | 1890 |
| | energy, ft-lb: | 2520 | 2170 | 1855 | 1580 | 1340 |
| | arc, inches: | | +17.7 | +31.0 | +37.2 | +35.4 |
| Federal 180 Hi-Shok | velocity, fps: | 2620 | 2390 | 2180 | 1970 | 1780 |
| | energy, ft-lb: | 2745 | 2290 | 1895 | 1555 | 1270 |
| | arc, inches: | | +2.3 | 0 | -9.7 | -28.3 |
| Federal 180 Sierra Pro-Hunt. | velocity, fps: | 2620 | 2410 | 2200 | 2010 | 1820 |
| | energy, ft-lb: | 2745 | 2315 | 1940 | 1610 | 1330 |
| | arc, inches: | | +2.3 | 0 | -9.3 | -27.1 |
| Federal 180 Nosler Partition | velocity, fps: | 2620 | 2430 | 2240 | 2060 | 1890 |
| | energy, ft-lb: | 2745 | 2355 | 2005 | 1700 | 1430 |
| | arc, inches: | | +2.2 | 0 | -9.2 | -26.5 |
| Federal 180 Nosler Part. HE | velocity, fps: | 2740 | 2550 | 2370 | 2200 | 2030 |
| | energy, ft-lb: | 3000 | 2600 | 2245 | 1925 | 1645 |
| | arc, inches: | | +1.9 | 0 | -8.2 | -23.5 |
| Hornady 110 Urban Tactical | velocity, fps: | 3170 | 2825 | 2504 | 2206 | 1937 |
| | energy, ft-lb: | 2454 | 1950 | 1532 | 1189 | 916 |
| | arc, inches: | | +1.5 | 0 | -7.2 | -21.2 |
| Hornady 150 SP boat-tail | velocity, fps: | 2820 | 2560 | 2315 | 2084 | 1866 |
| | energy, ft-lb: | 2648 | 2183 | 1785 | 1447 | 1160 |
| | arc, inches: | | +2.0 | 0 | -8.5 | -25.2 |
| Hornady 150 SST (or Interbond) | velocity, fps: | 2820 | 2593 | 2378 | 2174 | 1984 |
| | energy, ft-lb: | 2648 | 2240 | 1884 | 1574 | 1311 |
| | arc, inches: | | +1.9 | 0 | -8.1 | -22.9 |
| Hornady 150 SST LM (or Interbond) | velocity, fps: | 3000 | 2765 | 2541 | 2328 | 2127 |
| | energy, ft-lb: | 2997 | 2545 | 2150 | 1805 | 1506 |
| | arc, inches: | | +1.5 | 0 | -7.1 | -20.6 |
| Hornady 150 SP LM | velocity, fps: | 2980 | 2703 | 2442 | 2195 | 1964 |
| | energy, ft-lb: | 2959 | 2433 | 1986 | 1606 | 1285 |
| | arc, inches: | | +1.6 | 0 | -7.5 | -22.2 |
| Hornady 155 A-Max | velocity, fps: | 2815 | 2610 | 2415 | 2229 | 2051 |
| | energy, ft-lb: | 2727 | 2345 | 2007 | 1709 | 1448 |
| | arc, inches: | | +1.9 | 0 | -7.9 | -22.6 |
| Hornady 165 SP boat-tail | velocity, fps: | 2700 | 2496 | 2301 | 2115 | 1937 |
| | energy, ft-lb: | 2670 | 2283 | 1940 | 1639 | 1375 |
| | arc, inches: | | +2.0 | 0 | -8.7 | -25.2 |
| Hornady 165 SPBT LM | velocity, fps: | 2870 | 2658 | 2456 | 2283 | 2078 |
| | energy, ft-lb: | 3019 | 2589 | 2211 | 1877 | 1583 |
| | arc, inches: | | +1.7 | 0 | -7.5 | -21.8 |
| Hornady 165 SST LM (or Interbond) | velocity, fps: | 2880 | 2672 | 2474 | 2284 | 2103 |
| | energy, ft-lb: | 3038 | 2616 | 2242 | 1911 | 1620 |
| | arc, inches: | | +1.6 | 0 | -7.3 | -21.2 |
| Hornady 168 BTHP Match | velocity, fps: | 2700 | 2524 | 2354 | 2191 | 2035 |
| | energy, ft-lb: | 2720 | 2377 | 2068 | 1791 | 1545 |
| | arc, inches: | | +2.0 | 0 | -8.4 | -23.9 |
| Hornady 168 BTHP Match LM | velocity, fps: | 2640 | 2630 | 2429 | 2238 | 2056 |
| | energy, ft-lb: | 3008 | 2579 | 2201 | 1868 | 1577 |
| | arc, inches: | | +1.8 | 0 | -7.8 | -22.4 |
| Hornady 168 A-Max Match | velocity fps: | 2620 | 2446 | 2280 | 2120 | 1972 |
| | energy, ft-lb: | 2560 | 2232 | 1939 | 1677 | 1450 |
| | arc, inches: | | +2.6 | 0 | -9.2 | -25.6 |
| Hornady 168 A-Max | velocity, fps: | 2700 | 2491 | 2292 | 2102 | 1921 |
| | energy, ft-lb: | 2719 | 2315 | 1959 | 1648 | 1377 |
| | arc, inches: | | +2.4 | 0 | -9.0 | -25.9 |
| Hornady 178 A-Max | velocity, fps: | 2965 | 2778 | 2598 | 2425 | 2259 |
| | energy, ft-lb: | 3474 | 3049 | 2666 | 2323 | 2017 |
| | arc, inches: | | +1.6 | 0 | -6.9 | -19.8 |
| Hornady 180 A-Max Match | velocity, fps: | 2550 | 2397 | 2249 | 2106 | 1974 |
| | energy, ft-lb: | 2598 | 2295 | 2021 | 1773 | 1557 |
| | arc, inches: | | +2.7 | 0 | -9.5 | -26.2 |
| Norma 150 Nosler Bal. Tip | velocity, fps: | 2822 | 2588 | 2365 | 2154 | |
| | energy, ft-lb: | 2653 | 2231 | 1864 | 1545 | |
| | arc, inches: | | +1.6 | 0 | -7.1 | |
| Norma 150 Soft Point | velocity, fps: | 2861 | 2537 | 2235 | 1954 | |
| | energy, ft-lb: | 2727 | 2144 | 1664 | 1272 | |
| | arc, inches: | | +2.0 | 0 | -9.0 | |
| Norma 165 TXP Swift A-Fr. | velocity, fps: | 2700 | 2459 | 2231 | 2015 | |
| | energy, ft-lb: | 2672 | 2216 | 1824 | 1488 | |
| | arc, inches: | | +2.1 | 0 | -9.1 | |
| Norma 180 Plastic Point | velocity, fps: | 2612 | 2365 | 2131 | 1911 | |
| | energy, ft-lb: | 2728 | 2235 | 1815 | 1460 | |
| | arc, inches: | | +2.4 | 0 | -10.1 | |
| Norma 180 Nosler Partition | velocity, fps: | 2612 | 2414 | 2225 | 2044 | |
| | energy, ft-lb: | 2728 | 2330 | 1979 | 1670 | |
| | arc, inches: | | +2.2 | 0 | -9.3 | |
| Norma 180 Alaska | velocity, fps: | 2612 | 2269 | 1953 | 1667 | |
| | energy, ft-lb: | 2728 | 2059 | 1526 | 1111 | |
| | arc, inches: | | +2.7 | 0 | -11.9 | |
| Norma 180 Vulkan | velocity, fps: | 2612 | 2325 | 2056 | 1806 | |
| | energy, ft-lb: | 2728 | 2161 | 1690 | 1304 | |
| | arc, inches: | | +2.5 | 0 | -10.8 | |
| Norma 180 Oryx | velocity, fps: | 2612 | 2305 | 2019 | 1755 | |
| | energy, ft-lb: | 2728 | 2124 | 1629 | 1232 | |
| | arc, inches: | | +2.5 | 0 | -11.1 | |
| Norma 200 Vulkan | velocity, fps: | 2461 | 2215 | 1983 | 1767 | |
| | energy, ft-lb: | 2690 | 2179 | 1747 | 1387 | |
| | arc, inches: | | +2.8 | 0 | -11.7 | |
| PMC 147 FMJ boat-tail | velocity, fps: | 2751 | 2473 | 2257 | 2052 | 1859 |
| | energy, ft-lb: | 2428 | 2037 | 1697 | 1403 | 1150 |
| | arc, inches: | | +2.3 | 0 | -9.3 | -27.3 |
| PMC 150 Barnes X | velocity, fps: | 2700 | 2504 | 2316 | 2135 | 1964 |
| | energy, ft-lb: | 2428 | 2087 | 1786 | 1518 | 1284 |
| | arc, inches: | | +2.0 | 0 | -8.6 | -24.7 |
| PMC 150 Pointed Soft Point | velocity, fps: | 2643 | 2417 | 2203 | 1999 | 1807 |
| | energy, ft-lb: | 2326 | 1946 | 1615 | 1331 | 1088 |
| | arc, inches: | | +2.2 | 0 | -9.4 | -27.5 |
| PMC 150 SP boat-tail | velocity, fps: | 2820 | 2581 | 2354 | 2139 | 1935 |
| | energy, ft-lb: | 2648 | 2218 | 1846 | 1523 | 1247 |
| | arc, inches: | | +1.9 | 0 | -8.2 | -24.0 |
| PMC 168 Barnes X | velocity, fps: | 2600 | 2425 | 2256 | 2095 | 1940 |
| | energy, ft-lb: | 2476 | 2154 | 1865 | 1608 | 1379 |
| | arc, inches: | | +2.2 | 0 | -9.0 | -26.0 |
| PMC 168 HP boat-tail | velocity, fps: | 2650 | 2460 | 2278 | 2103 | 1936 |
| | energy, ft-lb: | 2619 | 2257 | 1935 | 1649 | 1399 |
| | arc, inches: | | +2.1 | 0 | --8.8 | -25.6 |
| PMC 168 Pointed Soft Point | velocity, fps: | 2559 | 2354 | 2160 | 1976 | 1803 |
| | energy, ft-lb: | 2443 | 2067 | 1740 | 1457 | 1212 |
| | arc, inches: | | +2.4 | 0 | -9.9 | -28.7 |
| PMC 180 Pointed Soft Point | velocity, fps: | 2410 | 2223 | 2044 | 1874 | 1714 |
| | energy, ft-lb: | 2320 | 1975 | 1670 | 1404 | 1174 |
| | arc, inches: | | +2.8 | 0 | -11.1 | -32.0 |

# Centerfire Rifle Ballistics

## .308 Winchester to .30-06 Springfield

| CARTRIDGE BULLET | RANGE, YARDS: | 0 | 100 | 200 | 300 | 400 |
|---|---|---|---|---|---|---|
| PMC 180 SP boat-tail | velocity, fps: | 2620 | 2446 | 2278 | 2117 | 1962 |
| | energy, ft-lb: | 2743 | 2391 | 2074 | 1790 | 1538 |
| | arc, inches: | | +2.2 | 0 | -8.9 | -25.4 |
| Rem. 150 PSP Core-Lokt | velocity, fps: | 2820 | 2533 | 2263 | 2009 | 1774 |
| | energy, ft-lb: | 2648 | 2137 | 1705 | 1344 | 1048 |
| | arc, inches: | | +2.0 | 0 | -8.8 | -26.2 |
| Rem. 150 PSP C-L Ultra | velocity, fps: | 2620 | 2404 | 2198 | 2002 | 1818 |
| | energy, ft-lb: | 2743 | 2309 | 1930 | 1601 | 1320 |
| | arc, inches: | | +2.3 | 0 | -9.5 | -26.4 |
| Rem. 150 Swift Scirocco | velocity, fps: | 2820 | 2611 | 2410 | 2219 | 2037 |
| | energy, ft-lb: | 2648 | 2269 | 1935 | 1640 | 1381 |
| | arc, inches: | | +1.8 | 0 | -7.8 | -22.7 |
| Rem. 165 AccuTip | velocity, fps: | 2700 | 2501 | 2311 | 2129 | 1958 |
| | energy, ft-lb: | 2670 | 2292 | 1957 | 1861 | 1401 |
| | arc, inches: | | +2.0 | 0 | -8.6 | -24.8 |
| Rem. 165 PSP boat-tail | velocity, fps: | 2700 | 2497 | 2303 | 2117 | 1941 |
| | energy, ft-lb: | 2670 | 2284 | 1942 | 1642 | 1379 |
| | arc, inches: | | +2.0 | 0 | -8.6 | -25.0 |
| Rem. 165 Nosler Bal. Tip | velocity, fps: | 2700 | 2613 | 2333 | 2161 | 1996 |
| | energy, ft-lb: | 2672 | 2314 | 1995 | 1711 | 1460 |
| | arc, inches: | | +2.0 | 0 | -8.4 | -24.3 |
| Rem. 165 Swift Scirocco | velocity, fps: | 2700 | 2513 | 2233 | 2161 | 1996 |
| | energy, fps: | 2670 | 2313 | 1994 | 1711 | 1459 |
| | arc, inches: | | +2.0 | 0 | -8.4 | -24.3 |
| Rem. 168 HPBT Match | velocity, fps: | 2680 | 2493 | 2314 | 2143 | 1979 |
| | energy, ft-lb: | 2678 | 2318 | 1998 | 1713 | 1460 |
| | arc, inches: | | +2.1 | 0 | -8.6 | -24.7 |
| Rem. 180 SP Core-Lokt | velocity, fps: | 2620 | 2274 | 1955 | 1666 | 1414 |
| | energy, ft-lb: | 2743 | 2066 | 1527 | 1109 | 799 |
| | arc, inches: | | +2.6 | 0 | -11.8 | -36.3 |
| Rem. 180 PSP Core-Lokt | velocity, fps: | 2620 | 2393 | 2178 | 1974 | 1782 |
| | energy, ft-lb: | 2743 | 2288 | 1896 | 1557 | 1269 |
| | arc, inches: | | +2.3 | 0 | -9.7 | -28.3 |
| Rem. 180 Nosler Partition | velocity, fps: | 2620 | 2436 | 2259 | 2089 | 1927 |
| | energy, ft-lb: | 2743 | 2371 | 2039 | 1774 | 1485 |
| | arc, inches: | | +2.2 | 0 | -9.0 | -26.0 |
| Speer 150 Grand Slam | velocity, fps: | 2900 | 2599 | 2317 | 2053 | |
| | energy, ft-lb: | 2800 | 2249 | 1788 | 1404 | |
| | arc, inches: | | +2.1 | 0 | -8.6 | -24.8 |
| Speer 165 Grand Slam | velocity, fps: | 2700 | 2475 | 2261 | 2057 | |
| | energy, ft-lb: | 2670 | 2243 | 1872 | 1550 | |
| | arc, inches: | | +2.1 | 0 | -8.9 | -25.9 |
| Speer 180 Grand Slam | velocity, fps: | 2620 | 2420 | 2229 | 2046 | |
| | energy, ft-lb: | 2743 | 2340 | 1985 | 1674 | |
| | arc, inches: | | +2.2 | 0 | -9.2 | -26.6 |
| Win. 150 Power-Point | velocity, fps: | 2820 | 2488 | 2179 | 1893 | 1633 |
| | energy, ft-lb: | 2648 | 2061 | 1581 | 1193 | 888 |
| | arc, inches: | | +2.4 | 0 | -9.8 | -29.3 |
| Win. 150 Power-Point Plus | velocity, fps: | 2900 | 2558 | 2241 | 1946 | 1678 |
| | energy, ft-lb: | 2802 | 2180 | 1672 | 1262 | 938 |
| | arc, inches: | | +1.9 | 0 | -8.9 | -27.0 |
| Win. 150 Partition Gold | velocity, fps: | 2900 | 2645 | 2405 | 2177 | 1962 |
| | energy, ft-lb: | 2802 | 2332 | 1927 | 1579 | 1282 |
| | arc, inches: | | +1.7 | 0 | -7.8 | -22.9 |
| Win. 150 Ballistic Silvertip | velocity, fps: | 2810 | 2601 | 2401 | 2211 | 2028 |
| | energy, ft-lb: | 2629 | 2253 | 1920 | 1627 | 1370 |
| | arc, inches: | | +1.8 | 0 | -7.8 | -22.8 |
| Win. 150 Fail Safe | velocity, fps: | 2820 | 2533 | 2263 | 2010 | 1775 |
| | energy, ft-lb: | 2649 | 2137 | 1706 | 1346 | 1049 |
| | arc, inches: | | +2.0 | 0 | -8.8 | -26.2 |
| Win. 168 Ballistic Silvertip | velocity, fps: | 2670 | 2484 | 2306 | 2134 | 1971 |
| | energy, ft-lb: | 2659 | 2301 | 1983 | 1699 | 1449 |
| | arc, inches: | | +2.1 | 0 | -8.6 | -24.8 |
| Win. 168 HP boat-tail Match | velocity, fps: | 2680 | 2485 | 2297 | 2118 | 1948 |
| | energy, ft-lb: | 2680 | 2303 | 1970 | 1674 | 1415 |
| | arc, inches: | | +2.1 | 0 | -8.7 | -25.1 |
| Win. 180 Power-Point | velocity, fps: | 2620 | 2274 | 1955 | 1666 | 1414 |
| | energy, ft-lb: | 2743 | 2066 | 1527 | 1109 | 799 |
| | arc, inches: | | +2.9 | 0 | -12.1 | -36.9 |
| Win. 180 Silvertip | velocity, fps: | 2620 | 2393 | 2178 | 1974 | 1782 |
| | energy, ft-lb: | 2743 | 2288 | 1896 | 1557 | 1269 |
| | arc, inches: | | +2.6 | 0 | -9.9 | -28.9 |

## .30-06 Springfield

| CARTRIDGE BULLET | RANGE, YARDS: | 0 | 100 | 200 | 300 | 400 |
|---|---|---|---|---|---|---|
| A-Square 180 M & D-T | velocity, fps: | 2700 | 2365 | 2054 | 1769 | 1524 |
| | energy, ft-lb: | 2913 | 2235 | 1687 | 1251 | 928 |
| | arc, inches: | | +2.4 | 0 | -10.6 | -32.4 |
| A-Square 220 Monolythic Solid | velocity, fps: | 2380 | 2108 | 1854 | 1623 | 1424 |
| | energy, ft-lb: | 2767 | 2171 | 1679 | 1287 | 990 |
| | arc, inches: | | +3.1 | 0 | -13.6 | -39.9 |
| Black Hills 150 Nosler B. Tip | velocity, fps: | 2900 | | | | |
| | energy, ft-lb: | 2770 | | | | |
| Black Hills 165 Nosler B. Tip | velocity, fps: | 2750 | | | | |
| | energy, ft-lb: | 2770 | | | | |
| Black Hills 168 Hor. Match | velocity, fps: | 2700 | | | | |
| | energy, ft-lb: | 2718 | | | | |
| Black Hills 180 Barnes X | velocity, fps: | 2650 | | | | |
| | energy, ft-lb: | 2806 | | | | |
| Federal 125 Sierra Pro-Hunt. | velocity, fps: | 3140 | 2780 | 2450 | 2140 | 1850 |
| | energy, ft-lb: | 2735 | 2145 | 1660 | 1270 | 955 |
| | arc, inches: | | +1.5 | 0 | -7.3 | -22.3 |
| Federal 150 Hi-Shok | velocity, fps: | 2910 | 2620 | 2340 | 2080 | 1840 |
| | energy, ft-lb: | 2820 | 2280 | 1825 | 1445 | 1130 |
| | arc, inches: | | +1.8 | 0 | -8.2 | -24.4 |
| Federal 150 Sierra Pro-Hunt. | velocity, fps: | 2910 | 2640 | 2380 | 2130 | 1900 |
| | energy, ft-lb: | 2820 | 2315 | 1880 | 1515 | 1205 |
| | arc, inches: | | +1.7 | 0 | -7.9 | -23.3 |
| Federal 150 Sierra GameKing BTSP | velocity, fps: | 2910 | 2690 | 2480 | 2270 | 2070 |
| | energy, ft-lb: | 2820 | 2420 | 2040 | 1710 | 1430 |
| | arc, inches: | | +1.7 | 0 | -7.4 | -21.5 |
| Federal 150 Nosler Bal. Tip | velocity, fps: | 2910 | 2700 | 2490 | 2300 | 2110 |
| | energy, ft-lb: | 2820 | 2420 | 2070 | 1760 | 1485 |
| | arc, inches: | | +1.6 | 0 | -7.3 | -21.1 |
| Federal 150 FMJ boat-tail | velocity, fps: | 2910 | 2710 | 2510 | 2320 | 2150 |
| | energy, ft-lb: | 2820 | 2440 | 2100 | 1800 | 1535 |
| | arc, inches: | | +1.6 | 0 | -7.1 | -20.8 |
| Federal 165 Sierra Pro-Hunt. | velocity, fps: | 2800 | 2560 | 2340 | 2130 | 1920 |
| | energy, ft-lb: | 2875 | 2410 | 2005 | 1655 | 1360 |
| | arc, inches: | | +1.9 | 0 | -8.3 | -24.3 |
| Federal 165 Sierra GameKing BTSP | velocity, fps: | 2800 | 2610 | 2420 | 2240 | 2070 |
| | energy, ft-lb: | 2870 | 2490 | 2150 | 1840 | 1580 |
| | arc, inches: | | +1.8 | 0 | -7.8 | -22.4 |
| Federal 165 Sierra GameKing HE | velocity, fps: | 3140 | 2900 | 2670 | 2450 | 2240 |
| | energy, ft-lb: | 3610 | 3075 | 2610 | 2200 | 1845 |
| | arc, inches: | | +1.5 | 0 | -6.9 | -20.4 |
| Federal 165 Nosler Bal. Tip | velocity, fps: | 2800 | 2610 | 2430 | 2250 | 2080 |
| | energy, ft-lb: | 2870 | 2495 | 2155 | 1855 | 1585 |
| | arc, inches: | | +1.8 | 0 | -7.7 | -22.3 |

## .30-06 SPRINGFIELD

| CARTRIDGE BULLET | RANGE, YARDS: | 0 | 100 | 200 | 300 | 400 |
|---|---|---|---|---|---|---|
| Federal 165 Trophy Bonded | velocity, fps: | 2800 | 2540 | 2290 | 2050 | 1830 |
| | energy, ft-lb: | 2870 | 2360 | 1915 | 1545 | 1230 |
| | arc, inches: | | +2.0 | 0 | -8.7 | -25.4 |
| Federal 165 Tr. Bonded HE | velocity, fps: | 3140 | 2860 | 2590 | 2340 | 2100 |
| | energy, ft-lb: | 3610 | 2990 | 2460 | 2010 | 1625 |
| | arc, inches: | | +1.6 | 0 | -7.4 | -21.9 |
| Federal 168 Sierra MatchKg. BTHP | velocity, fps: | 2700 | 2510 | 2320 | 2150 | 1980 |
| | energy, ft-lb: | 2720 | 2350 | 2010 | 1720 | 1460 |
| | arc, inches: | | +16.2 | +28.4 | +34.1 | +32.3 |
| Federal 180 Hi-Shok | velocity, fps: | 2700 | 2470 | 2250 | 2040 | 1850 |
| | energy, ft-lb: | 2915 | 2435 | 2025 | 1665 | 1360 |
| | arc, inches: | | +2.1 | 0 | -9.0 | -26.4 |
| Federal 180 Sierra Pro-Hunt. RN | velocity, fps: | 2700 | 2350 | 2020 | 1730 | 1470 |
| | energy, ft-lb: | 2915 | 2200 | 1630 | 1190 | 860 |
| | arc, inches: | | +2.4 | 0 | -11.0 | -33.6 |
| Federal 180 Nosler Partition | velocity, fps: | 2700 | 2500 | 2320 | 2140 | 1970 |
| | energy, ft-lb: | 2915 | 2510 | 2150 | 1830 | 1550 |
| | arc, inches: | | +2.0 | 0 | -8.6 | -24.6 |
| Federal 180 Nosler Part. HE | velocity, fps: | 2880 | 2690 | 2500 | 2320 | 2150 |
| | energy, ft-lb: | 3315 | 2880 | 2495 | 2150 | 1845 |
| | arc, inches: | | +1.7 | 0 | -7.2 | -21.0 |
| Federal 180 Sierra GameKing BTSP | velocity, fps: | 2700 | 2540 | 2380 | 2220 | 2080 |
| | energy, ft-lb: | 2915 | 2570 | 2260 | 1975 | 1720 |
| | arc, inches: | | +1.9 | 0 | -8.1 | -23.1 |
| Federal 180 Barnes XLC | velocity, fps: | 2700 | 2530 | 2360 | 2200 | 2040 |
| | energy, ft-lb: | 2915 | 2550 | 2220 | 1930 | 1670 |
| | arc, inches: | | +2.0 | 0 | -8.3 | -23.8 |
| Federal 180 Trophy Bonded | velocity, fps: | 2700 | 2460 | 2220 | 2000 | 1800 |
| | energy, ft-lb: | 2915 | 2410 | 1975 | 1605 | 1290 |
| | arc, inches: | | +2.2 | 0 | -9.2 | -27.0 |
| Federal 180 Tr. Bonded HE | velocity, fps: | 2880 | 2630 | 2380 | 2160 | 1940 |
| | energy, ft-lb: | 3315 | 2755 | 2270 | 1855 | 1505 |
| | arc, inches: | | +1.8 | 0 | -8.0 | -23.3 |
| Federal 220 Sierra Pro-Hunt. RN | velocity, fps: | 2410 | 2130 | 1870 | 1630 | 1420 |
| | energy, ft-lb: | 2835 | 2215 | 1705 | 1300 | 985 |
| | arc, inches: | | +3.1 | 0 | -13.1 | -39.3 |
| Hornady 150 SP | velocity, fps: | 2910 | 2617 | 2342 | 2083 | 1843 |
| | energy, ft-lb: | 2820 | 2281 | 1827 | 1445 | 1131 |
| | arc, inches: | | +2.1 | 0 | -8.5 | -25.0 |
| Hornady 150 SP LM | velocity, fps: | 3100 | 2815 | 2548 | 2295 | 2058 |
| | energy, ft-lb: | 3200 | 2639 | 2161 | 1755 | 1410 |
| | arc, inches: | | +1.4 | 0 | -6.8 | -20.3 |
| Hornady 150 SP boat-tail | velocity, fps: | 2910 | 2683 | 2467 | 2262 | 2066 |
| | energy, ft-lb: | 2820 | 2397 | 2027 | 1706 | 1421 |
| | arc, inches: | | +2.0 | 0 | -7.7 | -22.2 |
| Hornady 150 SST (or Interbond) | velocity, fps: | 2910 | 2802 | 2599 | 2405 | 2219 |
| | energy, ft-lb: | 3330 | 2876 | 2474 | 2118 | 1803 |
| | arc, inches: | | +1.5 | 0 | -6.6 | -19.3 |
| Hornady 150 SST LM | velocity, fps: | 3100 | 2860 | 2631 | 2414 | 2208 |
| | energy, ft-lb: | 3200 | 2724 | 2306 | 1941 | 1624 |
| | arc, inches: | | +1.4 | 0 | -6.6 | -19.2 |
| Hornady 165 SP boat-tail | velocity, fps: | 2800 | 2591 | 2392 | 2202 | 2020 |
| | energy, ft-lb: | 2873 | 2460 | 2097 | 1777 | 1495 |
| | arc, inches: | | +1.8 | 0 | -8.0 | -23.3 |
| Hornady 165 SPBT LM | velocity, fps: | 3015 | 2790 | 2575 | 2370 | 2176 |
| | energy, ft-lb: | 3330 | 2850 | 2428 | 2058 | 1734 |
| | arc, inches: | | +1.6 | 0 | -7.0 | -20.1 |
| Hornady 165 SST (or Interbond) | velocity, fps: | 2800 | 2598 | 2405 | 2221 | 2046 |
| | energy, ft-lb: | 2872 | 2473 | 2119 | 1808 | 1534 |
| | arc, inches: | | +1.9 | 0 | -8.0 | -22.8 |
| Hornady 165 SST LM | velocity, fps: | 3015 | 2802 | 2599 | 2405 | 2219 |
| | energy, ft-lb: | 3330 | 2878 | 2474 | 2118 | 1803 |
| | arc, inches: | | +1.5 | 0 | -6.5 | -19.3 |
| Hornady 168 HPBT Match | velocity, fps: | 2790 | 2620 | 2447 | 2280 | 2120 |
| | energy, ft-lb: | 2925 | 2561 | 2234 | 1940 | 1677 |
| | arc, inches: | | +1.7 | 0 | -7.7 | -22.2 |
| Hornady 180 SP | velocity, fps: | 2700 | 2469 | 2258 | 2042 | 1846 |
| | energy, ft-lb: | 2913 | 2436 | 2023 | 1666 | 1362 |
| | arc, inches: | | +2.4 | 0 | -9.3 | -27.0 |
| Hornady 180 SPBT LM | velocity, fps: | 2880 | 2676 | 2480 | 2293 | 2114 |
| | energy, ft-lb: | 3316 | 2862 | 2459 | 2102 | 1786 |
| | arc, inches: | | +1.7 | 0 | -7.3 | -21.3 |
| Norma 150 Nosler Bal. Tip | velocity, fps: | 2936 | 2713 | 2502 | 2300 | |
| | energy, ft-lb: | 2872 | 2453 | 2085 | 1762 | |
| | arc, inches: | | +1.6 | 0 | -7.1 | |
| Norma 150 Soft Point | velocity, fps: | 2972 | 2640 | 2331 | 2043 | |
| | energy, ft-lb: | 2943 | 2321 | 1810 | 1390 | |
| | arc, inches: | | +1.8 | 0 | -8.2 | |
| Norma 180 Alaska | velocity, fps: | 2700 | 2351 | 2028 | 1734 | |
| | energy, ft-lb: | 2914 | 2209 | 1645 | 1202 | |
| | arc, inches: | | +2.4 | 0 | -11.0 | |
| Norma 180 Nosler Partition | velocity, fps: | 2700 | 2494 | 2297 | 2108 | |
| | energy, ft-lb: | 2914 | 2486 | 2108 | 1777 | |
| | arc, inches: | | +2.1 | 0 | -8.7 | |
| Norma 180 Plastic Point | velocity, fps: | 2700 | 2455 | 2222 | 2003 | |
| | energy, ft-lb: | 2914 | 2409 | 1974 | 1603 | |
| | arc, inches: | | +2.1 | 0 | -9.2 | |
| Norma 180 Vulkan | velocity, fps: | 2700 | 2416 | 2150 | 1901 | |
| | energy, ft-lb: | 2914 | 2334 | 1848 | 1445 | |
| | arc, inches: | | +2.2 | 0 | -9.8 | |
| Norma 180 Oryx | velocity, fps: | 2700 | 2387 | 2095 | 1825 | |
| | energy, ft-lb: | 2914 | 2278 | 1755 | 1332 | |
| | arc, inches: | | +2.3 | 0 | -10.2 | |
| Norma 180 TXP Swift A-Fr. | velocity, fps: | 2700 | 2479 | 2268 | 2067 | |
| | energy, ft-lb: | 2914 | 2456 | 2056 | 1708 | |
| | arc, inches: | | +2.0 | 0 | -8.8 | |
| Norma 200 Vulkan | velocity, fps: | 2641 | 2385 | 2143 | 1916 | |
| | energy, ft-lb: | 3098 | 2527 | 2040 | 1631 | |
| | arc, inches: | | +2.3 | 0 | -9.9 | |
| Norma 200 Oryx | velocity, fps: | 2625 | 2362 | 2115 | 1883 | |
| | energy, ft-lb: | 3061 | 2479 | 1987 | 1575 | |
| | arc, inches: | | +2.3 | 0 | -10.1 | |
| PMC 150 X-Bullet | velocity, fps: | 2750 | 2552 | 2361 | 2179 | 2005 |
| | energy, ft-lb: | 2518 | 2168 | 1857 | 1582 | 1339 |
| | arc, inches: | | +2.0 | 0 | -8.2 | -23.7 |
| PMC 150 Pointed Soft Point | velocity, fps: | 2773 | 2542 | 2322 | 2113 | 1916 |
| | energy, ft-lb: | 2560 | 2152 | 1796 | 1487 | 1222 |
| | arc, inches: | | +1.9 | 0 | -8.4 | -24.6 |
| PMC 150 SP boat-tail | velocity, fps: | 2900 | 2657 | 2427 | 2208 | 2000 |
| | energy, ft-lb: | 2801 | 2351 | 1961 | 1623 | 1332 |
| | arc, inches: | | +1.7 | 0 | -7.7 | -22.5 |
| PMC 150 FMJ | velocity, fps: | 2773 | 2542 | 2322 | 2113 | 1916 |
| | energy, ft-lb: | 2560 | 2152 | 1796 | 1487 | 1222 |
| | arc, inches: | | +1.9 | 0 | -8.4 | -24.6 |
| PMC 165 Barnes X | velocity, fps: | 2750 | 2569 | 2395 | 2228 | 2067 |
| | energy, ft-lb: | 2770 | 2418 | 2101 | 1818 | 1565 |
| | arc, inches: | | +1.9 | 0 | -8.0 | -23.0 |
| PMC 180 Barnes X | velocity, fps: | 2650 | 2487 | 2331 | 2179 | 2034 |
| | energy, ft-lb: | 2806 | 2472 | 2171 | 1898 | 1652 |
| | arc, inches: | | +2.1 | 0 | -8.5 | -24.3 |

# Centerfire Rifle Ballistics

## .30-06 SPRINGFIELD

| CARTRIDGE BULLET | RANGE, YARDS: | 0 | 100 | 200 | 300 | 400 |
|---|---|---|---|---|---|---|
| PMC 180 Pointed Soft Point | velocity, fps: | 2550 | 2357 | 2172 | 1996 | 1829 |
| | energy, ft-lb: | 2598 | 2220 | 1886 | 1592 | 1336 |
| | arc, inches: | | +2.4 | 0 | -9.7 | -28.2 |
| PMC 180 SP boat-tail | velocity, fps: | 2700 | 2523 | 2352 | 2188 | 2030 |
| | energy, ft-lb: | 2913 | 2543 | 2210 | 1913 | 1646 |
| | arc, inches: | | +2.0 | 0 | -8.3 | -23.9 |
| Rem. 55 PSP (sabot) "Accelerator" | velocity, fps: | 4080 | 3484 | 2964 | 2499 | 2080 |
| | energy, ft-lb: | 2033 | 1482 | 1073 | 763 | 528 |
| | arc, inches: | | +1.4 | +1.4 | -2.6 | -12.2 |
| Rem. 125 PSP Core-Lokt mr | velocity, fps: | 2660 | 2335 | 2034 | 1757 | 1509 |
| | energy, ft-lb: | 1964 | 1513 | 1148 | 856 | 632 |
| | arc, inches: | | +1.1 | -3.0 | -15.5 | -37.4 |
| Rem. 125 Pointed Soft Point | velocity, fps: | 3140 | 2780 | 2447 | 2138 | 1853 |
| | energy, ft-lb: | 2736 | 2145 | 1662 | 1269 | 953 |
| | arc, inches: | | +1.5 | 0 | -7.4 | -22.4 |
| Rem. 150 AccuTip | velocity, fps: | 2910 | 2686 | 2473 | 2270 | 2077 |
| | energy, ft-lb: | 2820 | 2403 | 2037 | 1716 | 1436 |
| | arc, inches: | | +1.8 | 0 | -7.4 | -21.5 |
| Rem. 150 PSP Core-Lokt | velocity, fps: | 2910 | 2617 | 2342 | 2083 | 1843 |
| | energy, ft-lb: | 2820 | 2281 | 1827 | 1445 | 1131 |
| | arc, inches: | | +1.8 | 0 | -8.2 | -24.4 |
| Rem. 150 Bronze Point | velocity, fps: | 2910 | 2656 | 2416 | 2189 | 1974 |
| | energy, ft-lb: | 2820 | 2349 | 1944 | 1596 | 1298 |
| | arc, inches: | | +1.7 | 0 | -7.7 | -22.7 |
| Rem. 150 Nosler Bal. Tip | velocity, fps: | 2910 | 2696 | 2492 | 2298 | 2112 |
| | energy, ft-lb: | 2821 | 2422 | 2070 | 1769 | 1485 |
| | arc, inches: | | +1.6 | 0 | -7.3 | -21.1 |
| Rem. 150 Swift Scirocco | velocity, fps: | 2910 | 2696 | 2492 | 2298 | 2111 |
| | energy, ft-lb: | 2820 | 2421 | 2069 | 1758 | 1485 |
| | arc, inches: | | +1.6 | 0 | -7.3 | -21.1 |
| Rem. 165 AccuTip | velocity, fps: | 2800 | 2597 | 2403 | 2217 | 2039 |
| | energy, ft-lb: | 2872 | 2470 | 2115 | 1800 | 1523 |
| | arc, inches: | | +1.8 | 0 | -7.9 | -22.8 |
| Rem. 165 PSP Core-Lokt | velocity, fps: | 2800 | 2534 | 2283 | 2047 | 1825 |
| | energy, ft-lb: | 2872 | 2352 | 1909 | 1534 | 1220 |
| | arc, inches: | | +2.0 | 0 | -8.7 | -25.9 |
| Rem. 165 PSP boat-tail | velocity, fps: | 2800 | 2592 | 2394 | 2204 | 2023 |
| | energy, ft-lb: | 2872 | 2462 | 2100 | 1780 | 1500 |
| | arc, inches: | | +1.8 | 0 | -7.9 | -23.0 |
| Rem. 165 Nosler Bal. Tip | velocity, fps: | 2800 | 2609 | 2426 | 2249 | 2080 |
| | energy, ft-lb: | 2873 | 2494 | 2155 | 1854 | 1588 |
| | arc, inches: | | +1.8 | 0 | -7.7 | -22.3 |
| Rem. 168 PSP C-L Ultra | velocity, fps: | 2800 | 2546 | 2306 | 2079 | 1866 |
| | energy, ft-lb: | 2924 | 2418 | 1984 | 1613 | 1299 |
| | arc, inches: | | +1.9 | 0 | -8.5 | -25.1 |
| Rem. 180 SP Core-Lokt | velocity, fps: | 2700 | 2348 | 2023 | 1727 | 1466 |
| | energy, ft-lb: | 2913 | 2203 | 1635 | 1192 | 859 |
| | arc, inches: | | +2.4 | 0 | -11.0 | -33.8 |
| Rem. 180 PSP Core-Lokt | velocity, fps: | 2700 | 2469 | 2250 | 2042 | 1846 |
| | energy, ft-lb: | 2913 | 2436 | 2023 | 1666 | 1362 |
| | arc, inches: | | +2.1 | 0 | -9.0 | -26.3 |
| Rem. 180 PSP C-L Ultra | velocity, fps: | 2700 | 2480 | 2270 | 2070 | 1882 |
| | energy, ft-lb: | 2913 | 2457 | 2059 | 1713 | 1415 |
| | arc, inches: | | +2.1 | 0 | -8.9 | -25.8 |
| Rem. 180 Bronze Point | velocity, fps: | 2700 | 2485 | 2280 | 2084 | 1899 |
| | energy, ft-lb: | 2913 | 2468 | 2077 | 1736 | 1441 |
| | arc, inches: | | +2.1 | 0 | -8.8 | -25.5 |
| Rem. 180 Swift A-Frame | velocity, fps: | 2700 | 2465 | 2243 | 2032 | 1833 |
| | energy, ft-lb: | 2913 | 2429 | 2010 | 1650 | 1343 |
| | arc, inches: | | +2.1 | 0 | -9.1 | -26.6 |
| Rem. 180 Nosler Partition | velocity, fps: | 2700 | 2512 | 2332 | 2160 | 1995 |
| | energy, ft-lb: | 2913 | 2522 | 2174 | 1864 | 1590 |
| | arc, inches: | | +2.0 | 0 | -8.4 | -24.3 |
| Rem. 220 SP Core-Lokt | velocity, fps: | 2410 | 2130 | 1870 | 1632 | 1422 |
| | energy, ft-lb: | 2837 | 2216 | 1708 | 1301 | 988 |
| | arc, inches, s: | | 0 | -6.2 | -22.4 | |
| Speer 150 Grand Slam | velocity, fps: | 2975 | 2669 | 2383 | 2114 | |
| | energy, ft-lb: | 2947 | 2372 | 1891 | 1489 | |
| | arc, inches: | | +2.0 | 0 | -8.1 | -24.1 |
| Speer 165 Grand Slam | velocity, fps: | 2790 | 2560 | 2342 | 2134 | |
| | energy, ft-lb: | 2851 | 2401 | 2009 | 1669 | |
| | arc, inches: | | +1.9 | 0 | -8.3 | -24.1 |
| Speer 180 Grand Slam | velocity, fps: | 2690 | 2487 | 2293 | 2108 | |
| | energy, ft-lb: | 2892 | 2472 | 2101 | 1775 | |
| | arc, inches: | | +2.1 | 0 | -8.8 | -25.1 |
| Win. 125 Pointed Soft Point | velocity, fps: | 3140 | 2780 | 2447 | 2138 | 1853 |
| | energy, ft-lb: | 2736 | 2145 | 1662 | 1269 | 953 |
| | arc, inches: | | +1.8 | 0 | -7.7 | -23.0 |
| Win. 150 Power-Point | velocity, fps: | 2920 | 2580 | 2265 | 1972 | 1704 |
| | energy, ft-lb: | 2839 | 2217 | 1708 | 1295 | 967 |
| | arc, inches: | | +2.2 | 0 | -9.0 | -27.0 |
| Win. 150 Power-Point Plus | velocity, fps: | 3050 | 2685 | 2352 | 2043 | 1760 |
| | energy, ft-lb: | 3089 | 2402 | 1843 | 1391 | 1032 |
| | arc, inches: | | +1.7 | 0 | -8.0 | -24.3 |
| Win. 150 Silvertip | velocity, fps: | 2910 | 2617 | 2342 | 2083 | 1843 |
| | energy, ft-lb: | 2820 | 2281 | 1827 | 1445 | 1131 |
| | arc, inches: | | +2.1 | 0 | -8.5 | -25.0 |
| Win. 150 Partition Gold | velocity, fps: | 2960 | 2705 | 2464 | 2235 | 2019 |
| | energy, ft-lb: | 2919 | 2437 | 2022 | 1664 | 1358 |
| | arc, inches: | | +1.6 | 0 | -7.4 | -21.7 |
| Win. 150 Ballistic Silvertip | velocity, fps: | 2900 | 2687 | 2483 | 2289 | 2103 |
| | energy, ft-lb: | 2801 | 2404 | 2054 | 1745 | 1473 |
| | arc, inches: | | +1.7 | 0 | -7.3 | -21.2 |
| Win. 150 Fail Safe | velocity, fps: | 2920 | 2625 | 2349 | 2089 | 1848 |
| | energy, ft-lb: | 2841 | 2296 | 1838 | 1455 | 1137 |
| | arc, inches: | | +1.8 | 0 | -8.1 | -24.3 |
| Win. 165 Pointed Soft Point | velocity, fps: | 2800 | 2573 | 2357 | 2151 | 1956 |
| | energy, ft-lb: | 2873 | 2426 | 2036 | 1696 | 1402 |
| | arc, inches: | | +2.2 | 0 | -8.4 | -24.4 |
| Win. 165 Fail Safe | velocity, fps: | 2800 | 2540 | 2295 | 2063 | 1846 |
| | energy, ft-lb: | 2873 | 2365 | 1930 | 1560 | 1249 |
| | arc, inches: | | +2.0 | 0 | -8.6 | -25.3 |
| Win. 168 Ballistic Silvertip | velocity, fps: | 2790 | 2599 | 2416 | 2240 | 2072 |
| | energy, ft-lb: | 2903 | 2520 | 2177 | 1872 | 1601 |
| | arc, inches: | | +1.8 | 0 | -7.8 | -22.5 |
| Win. 180 Ballistic Silvertip | velocity, fps: | 2750 | 2572 | 2402 | 2237 | 2080 |
| | energy, ft-lb: | 3022 | 2644 | 2305 | 2001 | 1728 |
| | arc, inches: | | +1.9 | 0 | -7.9 | -22.8 |
| Win. 180 Power-Point | velocity, fps: | 2700 | 2348 | 2023 | 1727 | 1466 |
| | energy, ft-lb: | 2913 | 2203 | 1635 | 1192 | 859 |
| | arc, inches: | | +2.7 | 0 | -11.3 | -34.4 |
| Win. 180 Power-Point Plus | velocity, fps: | 2770 | 2563 | 2366 | 2177 | 1997 |
| | energy, ft-lb: | 3068 | 2627 | 2237 | 1894 | 1594 |
| | arc, inches: | | +1.9 | 0 | -8.1 | -23.6 |
| Win. 180 Silvertip | velocity, fps: | 2700 | 2469 | 2250 | 2042 | 1846 |
| | energy, ft-lb: | 2913 | 2436 | 2023 | 1666 | 1362 |
| | arc, inches: | | +2.4 | 0 | -9.3 | -27.0 |
| Win. 180 AccuBond | velocity, fps: | 2750 | 2573 | 2403 | 2239 | 2082 |
| | energy, ft-lb: | 3022 | 2646 | 2308 | 2004 | 1732 |
| | arc, inches: | | +1.9 | 0 | -7.9 | -22.8 |

# Centerfire Rifle Ballistics

## .30-06 SPRINGFIELD TO .300 WINCHESTER MAGNUM

| CARTRIDGE BULLET | RANGE, YARDS: | 0 | 100 | 200 | 300 | 400 |
|---|---|---|---|---|---|---|
| Win. 180 Partition Gold | velocity, fps: | 2790 | 2581 | 2382 | 2192 | 2010 |
| | energy, ft-lb: | 3112 | 2664 | 2269 | 1920 | 1615 |
| | arc, inches: | | +1.9 | 0 | -8.0 | -23.2 |
| Win. 180 Fail Safe | velocity, fps: | 2700 | 2486 | 2283 | 2089 | 1904 |
| | energy, ft-lb: | 2914 | 2472 | 2083 | 1744 | 1450 |
| | arc, inches: | | +2.1 | 0 | -8.7 | -25.5 |

### .300 H&H MAGNUM

| CARTRIDGE BULLET | RANGE, YARDS: | 0 | 100 | 200 | 300 | 400 |
|---|---|---|---|---|---|---|
| Federal 180 Nosler Partition | velocity, fps: | 2880 | 2620 | 2380 | 2150 | 1930 |
| | energy, ft-lb: | 3315 | 2750 | 2260 | 1840 | 1480 |
| | arc, inches: | | +1.8 | 0 | -8.0 | -23.4 |
| Win. 180 Fail Safe | velocity, fps: | 2880 | 2628 | 2390 | 2165 | 1952 |
| | energy, ft-lb: | 3316 | 2762 | 2284 | 1873 | 1523 |
| | arc, inches: | | +1.8 | 0 | -7.9 | -23.2 |

### .308 NORMA MAGNUM

| CARTRIDGE BULLET | RANGE, YARDS: | 0 | 100 | 200 | 300 | 400 |
|---|---|---|---|---|---|---|
| Norma 180 TXP Swift A-Fr. | velocity, fps: | 2953 | 2704 | 2469 | 2245 | |
| | energy, ft-lb: | 3486 | 2924 | 2437 | 2016 | |
| | arc, inches: | | +1.6 | 0 | -7.3 | |
| Norma 200 Vulkan | velocity, fps: | 2903 | 2624 | 2361 | 2114 | |
| | energy, ft-lb: | 3744 | 3058 | 2476 | 1985 | |
| | arc, inches: | 0 | +1.8 | 0 | -8.0 | |

### .300 WINCHESTER MAGNUM

| CARTRIDGE BULLET | RANGE, YARDS: | 0 | 100 | 200 | 300 | 400 |
|---|---|---|---|---|---|---|
| A-Square 180 Dead Tough | velocity, fps: | 3120 | 2756 | 2420 | 2108 | 1820 |
| | energy, ft-lb: | 3890 | 3035 | 2340 | 1776 | 1324 |
| | arc, inches: | | +1.6 | 0 | -7.6 | -22.9 |
| Black Hills 180 Nosler B. Tip | velocity, fps: | 3100 | | | | |
| | energy, ft-lb: | 3498 | | | | |
| | arc, inches: | | | | | |
| Black Hills 180 Barnes X | velocity, fps: | 2950 | | | | |
| | energy, ft-lb: | 3498 | | | | |
| | arc, inches: | | | | | |
| Black Hills 190 Match | velocity, fps: | 2950 | | | | |
| | energy, ft-lb: | 3672 | | | | |
| | arc, inches: | | | | | |
| Federal 150 Sierra Pro Hunt. | velocity, fps: | 3280 | 3030 | 2800 | 2570 | 2360 |
| | energy, ft-lb: | 3570 | 3055 | 2600 | 2205 | 1860 |
| | arc, inches: | | +1.1 | 0 | -5.6 | -16.4 |
| Federal 150 Trophy Bonded | velocity, fps: | 3280 | 2980 | 2700 | 2430 | 2190 |
| | energy, ft-lb: | 3570 | 2450 | 2420 | 1970 | 1590 |
| | arc, inches: | | +1.2 | 0 | -6.0 | -17.9 |
| Federal 180 Sierra Pro Hunt. | velocity, fps: | 2960 | 2750 | 2540 | 2340 | 2160 |
| | energy, ft-lb: | 3500 | 3010 | 2580 | 2195 | 1860 |
| | arc, inches: | | +1.6 | 0 | -7.0 | -20.3 |
| Federal 180 Barnes XLC | velocity, fps: | 2960 | 2780 | 2600 | 2430 | 2260 |
| | energy, ft-lb: | 3500 | 3080 | 2700 | 2355 | 2050 |
| | arc, inches: | | +1.5 | 0 | -6.6 | -19.2 |
| Federal 180 Trophy Bonded | velocity, fps: | 2960 | 2700 | 2460 | 2220 | 2000 |
| | energy, ft-lb: | 3500 | 2915 | 2410 | 1975 | 1605 |
| | arc, inches: | | +1.6 | 0 | -7.4 | -21.9 |
| Federal 180 Tr. Bonded HE | velocity, fps: | 3100 | 2830 | 2580 | 2340 | 2110 |
| | energy, ft-lb: | 3840 | 3205 | 2660 | 2190 | 1790 |
| | arc, inches: | | +1.4 | 0 | -6.6 | -19.7 |
| Federal 180 Nosler Partition | velocity, fps: | 2960 | 2700 | 2450 | 2210 | 1990 |
| | energy, ft-lb: | 3500 | 2905 | 2395 | 1955 | 1585 |
| | arc, inches: | | +1.6 | 0 | -7.5 | -22.1 |
| Federal 190 Sierra MatchKg. BTHP | velocity, fps: | 2900 | 2730 | 2560 | 2400 | 2240 |
| | energy, ft-lb: | 3550 | 3135 | 2760 | 2420 | 2115 |
| | arc, inches: | | +12.9 | +22.5 | +26.9 | +25.1 |

| CARTRIDGE BULLET | RANGE, YARDS: | 0 | 100 | 200 | 300 | 400 |
|---|---|---|---|---|---|---|
| Federal 200 Sierra GameKing BTSP | velocity, fps: | 2830 | 2680 | 2530 | 2380 | 2240 |
| | energy, ft-lb: | 3560 | 3180 | 2830 | 2520 | 2230 |
| | arc, inches: | | +1.7 | 0 | -7.1 | -20.4 |
| Federal 200 Nosler Part. HE | velocity, fps: | 2930 | 2740 | 2550 | 2370 | 2200 |
| | energy, ft-lb: | 3810 | 3325 | 2885 | 2495 | 2145 |
| | arc, inches: | | +1.6 | 0 | -6.9 | -20.1 |
| Federal 200 Trophy Bonded | velocity, fps: | 2800 | 2570 | 2350 | 2150 | 1950 |
| | energy, ft-lb: | 3480 | 2935 | 2460 | 2050 | 1690 |
| | arc, inches: | | +1.9 | 0 | -8.2 | -23.9 |
| Hornady 150 SP boat-tail | velocity, fps: | 3275 | 2988 | 2718 | 2464 | 2224 |
| | energy, ft-lb: | 3573 | 2974 | 2461 | 2023 | 1648 |
| | arc, inches: | | +1.2 | 0 | -6.0 | -17.8 |
| Hornady 150 SST (and Interbond) | velocity, fps: | 3275 | 3027 | 2791 | 2565 | 2352 |
| | energy, ft-lb: | 3572 | 3052 | 2593 | 2192 | 1842 |
| | arc, inches: | | +1.2 | 0 | -5.8 | -17.0 |
| Hornady 165 SP boat-tail | velocity, fps: | 3100 | 2877 | 2665 | 2462 | 2269 |
| | energy, ft-lb: | 3522 | 3033 | 2603 | 2221 | 1887 |
| | arc, inches: | | +1.3 | 0 | -6.5 | -18.5 |
| Hornady 165 SST | velocity, fps: | 3100 | 2885 | 2680 | 2483 | 2296 |
| | energy, ft-lb: | 3520 | 3049 | 2630 | 2259 | 1930 |
| | arc, inches: | | +1.4 | 0 | -6.4 | -18.6 |
| Hornady 180 SP boat-tail | velocity, fps: | 2960 | 2745 | 2540 | 2344 | 2157 |
| | energy, ft-lb: | 3501 | 3011 | 2578 | 2196 | 1859 |
| | arc, inches: | | +1.9 | 0 | -7.3 | -20.9 |
| Hornady 180 SST | velocity, fps: | 2960 | 2764 | 2575 | 2395 | 2222 |
| | energy, ft-lb: | 3501 | 3052 | 2650 | 2292 | 1974 |
| | arc, inches: | | +1.6 | 0 | -7.0 | -20.1 |
| Hornady 180 SPBT HM | velocity, fps: | 3100 | 2879 | 2668 | 2467 | 2275 |
| | energy, ft-lb: | 3840 | 3313 | 2845 | 2431 | 2068 |
| | arc, inches: | | +1.4 | 0 | -6.4 | -18.7 |
| Hornady 190 SP boat-tail | velocity, fps: | 2900 | 2711 | 2529 | 2355 | 2187 |
| | energy, ft-lb: | 3549 | 3101 | 2699 | 2340 | 2018 |
| | arc, inches: | | +1.6 | 0 | -7.1 | -20.4 |
| Norma 150 Nosler Bal. Tip | velocity, fps: | 3250 | 3014 | 2791 | 2578 | |
| | energy, ft-lb: | 3519 | 3027 | 2595 | 2215 | |
| | arc, inches: | | +1.1 | 0 | -5.6 | |
| Norma 165 Scirocco | velocity, fps: | 3117 | 2921 | 2734 | 2554 | |
| | energy, ft-lb: | 3561 | 3127 | 2738 | 2390 | |
| | arc, inches: | | +1.2 | 0 | -5.9 | |
| Norma 180 Soft Point | velocity, fps: | 3018 | 2780 | 2555 | 2341 | |
| | energy, ft-lb: | 3641 | 3091 | 2610 | 2190 | |
| | arc, inches: | | +1.5 | 0 | -7.0 | |
| Norma 180 Plastic Point | velocity, fps: | 3018 | 2755 | 2506 | 2271 | |
| | energy, ft-lb: | 3641 | 3034 | 2512 | 2062 | |
| | arc, inches: | | +1.6 | 0 | -7.1 | |
| Norma 180 TXP Swift A-Fr. | velocity, fps: | 2920 | 2688 | 2467 | 2256 | |
| | energy, ft-lb: | 3409 | 2888 | 2432 | 2035 | |
| | arc, inches: | | +1.7 | 0 | -7.4 | |
| Norma 200 Vulkan | velocity, fps: | 2887 | 2609 | 2347 | 2100 | |
| | energy, ft-lb: | 3702 | 3023 | 2447 | 1960 | |
| | arc, inches: | | +1.8 | 0 | -8.2 | |
| Norma 200 Oryx | velocity, fps: | 3018 | 2755 | 2506 | 2271 | |
| | energy, ft-lb: | 4046 | 3371 | 2791 | 2292 | |
| | arc, inches: | | +1.5 | 0 | -7.0 | |
| PMC 150 Barnes X | velocity, fps: | 3135 | 2918 | 2712 | 2515 | 2327 |
| | energy, ft-lb: | 3273 | 2836 | 2449 | 2107 | 1803 |
| | arc, inches: | | +1.3 | 0 | -6.1 | -17.7 |

# Centerfire Rifle Ballistics

## .300 Winchester Magnum to .300 Winchester Short Magnum

| CARTRIDGE BULLET | RANGE, YARDS: | 0 | 100 | 200 | 300 | 400 |
|---|---|---|---|---|---|---|
| PMC 150 Pointed Soft Point | velocity, fps: | 3150 | 2902 | 2665 | 2438 | 2222 |
| | energy, ft-lb: | 3304 | 2804 | 2364 | 1979 | 1644 |
| | arc, inches: | | +1.3 | 0 | -6.2 | -18.3 |
| PMC 150 SP boat-tail | velocity, fps: | 3250 | 2987 | 2739 | 2504 | 2281 |
| | energy, ft-lb: | 3517 | 2970 | 2498 | 2088 | 1733 |
| | arc, inches: | | +1.2 | 0 | -6.0 | -17.4 |
| PMC 180 Barnes X | velocity, fps: | 2910 | 2738 | 2572 | 2412 | 2258 |
| | energy, ft-lb: | 3384 | 2995 | 2644 | 2325 | 2037 |
| | arc, inches: | | +1.6 | 0 | -6.9 | -19.8 |
| PMC 180 Pointed Soft Point | velocity, fps: | 2853 | 2643 | 2446 | 2258 | 2077 |
| | energy, ft-lb: | 3252 | 2792 | 2391 | 2037 | 1724 |
| | arc, inches: | | +1.7 | 0 | -7.5 | -21.9 |
| PMC 180 SP boat-tail | velocity, fps: | 2900 | 2714 | 2536 | 2365 | 2200 |
| | energy, ft-lb: | 3361 | 2944 | 2571 | 2235 | 1935 |
| | arc, inches: | | +1.6 | 0 | -7.1 | -20.3 |
| Rem. 150 PSP Core-Lokt | velocity, fps: | 3290 | 2951 | 2636 | 2342 | 2068 |
| | energy, ft-lb: | 3605 | 2900 | 2314 | 1827 | 1859 |
| | arc, inches: | | +1.6 | 0 | -7.0 | -20.2 |
| Rem. 150 PSP C-L Ultra | velocity, fps: | 3290 | 2967 | 2666 | 2384 | 2120 |
| | energy, ft-lb: | 3065 | 2931 | 2366 | 1893 | 1496 |
| | arc, inches: | | +1.2 | 0 | -6.1 | -18.4 |
| Rem. 180 AccuTip | velocity, fps: | 2960 | 2764 | 2577 | 2397 | 2224 |
| | energy, ft-lb: | 3501 | 3053 | 2653 | 2295 | 1976 |
| | arc, inches: | | +1.5 | 0 | -6.8 | -19.6 |
| Rem. 180 PSP Core-Lokt | velocity, fps: | 2960 | 2745 | 2540 | 2344 | 2157 |
| | energy, ft-lb: | 3501 | 3011 | 2578 | 2196 | 1424 |
| | arc, inches: | | +2.2 | +1.9 | -3.4 | -15.0 |
| Rem. 180 PSP C-L Ultra | velocity, fps: | 2960 | 2727 | 2505 | 2294 | 2093 |
| | energy, ft-lb: | 3501 | 2971 | 2508 | 2103 | 1751 |
| | arc, inches: | | +2.7 | +2.2 | -3.8 | -16.4 |
| Rem. 180 Nosler Partition | velocity, fps: | 2960 | 2725 | 2503 | 2291 | 2089 |
| | energy, ft-lb: | 3501 | 2968 | 2503 | 2087 | 1744 |
| | arc, inches: | | +1.6 | 0 | -7.2 | -20.9 |
| Rem. 180 Nosler Bal. Tip | velocity, fps: | 2960 | 2774 | 2595 | 2424 | 2259 |
| | energy, ft-lb: | 3501 | 3075 | 2692 | 2348 | 2039 |
| | arc, inches: | | +1.5 | 0 | -6.7 | -19.3 |
| Rem. 180 Swift Scirocco | velocity, fps: | 2960 | 2774 | 2595 | 2424 | 2259 |
| | energy, ft-lb: | 3501 | 3075 | 2692 | 2348 | 2039 |
| | arc, inches: | | +1.5 | 0 | -6.7 | -19.3 |
| Rem. 190 PSP boat-tail | velocity, fps: | 2885 | 2691 | 2506 | 2327 | 2156 |
| | energy, ft-lb: | 3511 | 3055 | 2648 | 2285 | 1961 |
| | arc, inches: | | +1.6 | 0 | -7.2 | -20.8 |
| Rem. 190 HPBT Match | velocity, fps: | 2900 | 2725 | 2557 | 2395 | 2239 |
| | energy, ft-lb: | 3547 | 3133 | 2758 | 2420 | 2115 |
| | arc, inches: | | +1.6 | 0 | -6.9 | -19.9 |
| Rem. 200 Swift A-Frame | velocity, fps: | 2825 | 2595 | 2376 | 2167 | 1970 |
| | energy, ft-lb: | 3544 | 2989 | 2506 | 2086 | 1722 |
| | arc, inches: | | +1.8 | 0 | -8.0 | -23.5 |
| Speer 180 Grand Slam | velocity, fps: | 2950 | 2735 | 2530 | 2334 | |
| | energy, ft-lb: | 3478 | 2989 | 2558 | 2176 | |
| | arc, inches: | | +1.6 | 0 | -7.0 | -20.5 |
| Speer 200 Grand Slam | velocity, fps: | 2800 | 2597 | 2404 | 2218 | |
| | energy, ft-lb: | 3481 | 2996 | 2565 | 2185 | |
| | arc, inches: | | +1.8 | 0 | -7.9 | -22.9 |
| Win. 150 Power-Point | velocity, fps: | 3290 | 2951 | 2636 | 2342 | 2068 |
| | energy, ft-lb: | 3605 | 2900 | 2314 | 1827 | 1424 |
| | arc, inches: | | +2.6 | +2.1 | -3.5 | -15.4 |
| Win. 150 Fail Safe | velocity, fps: | 3260 | 2943 | 2647 | 2370 | 2110 |
| | energy, ft-lb: | 3539 | 2884 | 2334 | 1871 | 1483 |
| | arc, inches: | | +1.3 | 0 | -6.2 | -18.7 |
| Win. 165 Fail Safe | velocity, fps: | 3120 | 2807 | 2515 | 2242 | 1985 |
| | energy, ft-lb: | 3567 | 2888 | 2319 | 1842 | 1445 |
| | arc, inches: | | +1.5 | 0 | -7.0 | -20.0 |
| Win. 180 Power-Point | velocity, fps: | 2960 | 2745 | 2540 | 2344 | 2157 |
| | energy, ft-lb: | 3501 | 3011 | 2578 | 2196 | 1859 |
| | arc, inches: | | +1.9 | 0 | -7.3 | -20.9 |
| Win. 180 Power-Point Plus | velocity, fps: | 3070 | 2846 | 2633 | 2430 | 2236 |
| | energy, ft-lb: | 3768 | 3239 | 2772 | 2361 | 1999 |
| | arc, inches: | | +1.4 | 0 | -6.4 | -18.7 |
| Win. 180 Ballistic Silvertip | velocity, fps: | 2950 | 2764 | 2586 | 2415 | 2250 |
| | energy, ft-lb: | 3478 | 3054 | 2673 | 2331 | 2023 |
| | arc, inches: | | +1.5 | 0 | -6.7 | -19.4 |
| Win. 180 AccuBond | velocity, fps: | 2950 | 2765 | 2588 | 2417 | 2253 |
| | energy, ft-lb: | 3478 | 3055 | 2676 | 2334 | 2028 |
| | arc, inches: | | +1.5 | 0 | -6.7 | -19.4 |
| Win. 180 Fail Safe | velocity, fps: | 2960 | 2732 | 2514 | 2307 | 2110 |
| | energy, ft-lb: | 3503 | 2983 | 2528 | 2129 | 1780 |
| | arc, inches: | | +1.6 | 0 | -7.1 | -20.7 |
| Win. 180 Partition Gold | velocity, fps: | 3070 | 2859 | 2657 | 2464 | 2280 |
| | energy, ft-lb: | 3768 | 3267 | 2823 | 2428 | 2078 |
| | arc, inches: | | +1.4 | 0 | -6.3 | -18.3 |

## .300 Remington Short Ultra Mag

| CARTRIDGE BULLET | RANGE, YARDS: | 0 | 100 | 200 | 300 | 400 |
|---|---|---|---|---|---|---|
| Rem. 150 PSP C-L Ultra | velocity, fps: | 3200 | 2901 | 2672 | 2359 | 2112 |
| | energy, ft-lb: | 3410 | 2803 | 2290 | 1854 | 1485 |
| | arc, inches: | | +1.3 | 0 | -6.4 | -19.l |
| Rem. 165 PSP Core-Lokt | velocity, fps: | 3075 | 2792 | 2527 | 2276 | 2040 |
| | energy, ft-lb: | 3464 | 2856 | 2339 | 1828 | 1525 |
| | arc, inches: | | +1.5 | 0 | -7.0 | -20.7 |
| Rem. 180 Partition | velocity, fps: | 2960 | 2761 | 2571 | 2389 | 2214 |
| | energy, ft-lb: | 3501 | 3047 | 2642 | 2280 | 1959 |
| | arc, inches: | | +1.5 | 0 | -6.8 | -19.7 |
| Rem. 180 PSP C-L Ultra | velocity, fps: | 2960 | 2727 | 2506 | 2295 | 2094 |
| | energy, ft-lb: | 3501 | 2972 | 2509 | 2105 | 1753 |
| | arc, inches: | | +1.6 | 0 | -7.1 | -20.9 |
| Rem. 190 HPBT Match | velocity, fps: | 2900 | 2725 | 2557 | 2395 | 2239 |
| | energy, ft-lb: | 3547 | 3133 | 2758 | 2420 | 2115 |
| | arc, inches: | | +1.6 | 0 | -6.9 | -19.9 |

## .300 Winchester Short Magnum

| CARTRIDGE BULLET | RANGE, YARDS: | 0 | 100 | 200 | 300 | 400 |
|---|---|---|---|---|---|---|
| Federal 150 Nosler Bal. Tip | velocity, fps: | 3200 | 2970 | 2755 | 2545 | 2345 |
| | energy, ft-lb: | 3410 | 2940 | 2520 | 2155 | 1830 |
| | arc, inches: | | +1.2 | 0 | -5.8 | -17.0 |
| Federal 180 Grand Slam | velocity, fps: | 2970 | 2740 | 2530 | 2320 | 2130 |
| | energy, ft-lb: | 3525 | 3010 | 2555 | 2155 | 1810 |
| | arc, inches: | | +1.5 | 0 | -7.0 | -20.5 |
| Federal 180 Trophy Bonded | velocity, fps: | 2970 | 2730 | 2500 | 2280 | 2080 |
| | energy, ft-lb: | 3525 | 2975 | 2500 | 2085 | 1725 |
| | arc, inches: | | +1.5 | 0 | -7.2 | -21.0 |
| Federal 180 Nosler Partition | velocity, fps: | 2975 | 2750 | 2535 | 2290 | 2126 |
| | energy, ft-lb: | 3540 | 3025 | 2570 | 2175 | 1825 |
| | arc, inches: | | +1.5 | 0 | -7.0 | -20.3 |
| Federal 180 Hi-Shok SP | velocity, fps: | 2970 | 2520 | 2115 | 1750 | 1430 |
| | energy, ft-lb: | 3525 | 2540 | 1785 | 1220 | 820 |
| | arc, inches: | | +2.2 | 0 | -9.9 | -31.4 |
| Norma 180 Nosler Bal. Tip | velocity, fps: | 3215 | 2985 | 2767 | 2560 | |
| | energy, ft-lb: | 3437 | 2963 | 2547 | 2179 | |
| | arc, inches: | | +1.2 | 0 | -5.7 | |
| Norma 180 Oryx | velocity, fps: | 2936 | 2542 | 2180 | 1849 | |
| | energy, ft-lb: | 3446 | 2583 | 1900 | 1368 | |
| | arc, inches: | | +1.9 | 0 | -8.9 | |

**BALLISTICS**

| CARTRIDGE BULLET | RANGE, YARDS: | 0 | 100 | 200 | 300 | 400 |
|---|---|---|---|---|---|---|
| Win. 150 Ballistic Silvertip | velocity, fps: | 3300 | 3061 | 2834 | 2619 | 2414 |
| | energy, ft-lb: | 3628 | 3121 | 2676 | 2285 | 1941 |
| | arc, inches: | | +1.1 | 0 | -5.4 | -15.9 |
| Win. 180 Ballistic Silvertip | velocity, fps: | 3010 | 2822 | 2641 | 2468 | 2301 |
| | energy, ft-lb: | 3621 | 3182 | 2788 | 2434 | 2116 |
| | arc, inches: | | +1.4 | 0 | -6.4 | -18.6 |
| Win. 180 AccuBond | velocity, fps: | 3010 | 2822 | 2643 | 2470 | 2304 |
| | energy, ft-lb: | 3622 | 3185 | 2792 | 2439 | 2121 |
| | arc, inches: | | +1.4 | 0 | -6.4 | -18.5 |
| Win. 180 Fail Safe | velocity, fps: | 2970 | 2741 | 2524 | 2317 | 2120 |
| | energy, ft-lb: | 3526 | 3005 | 2547 | 2147 | 1797 |
| | arc, inches: | | +1.6 | 0 | -7.0 | -20.5 |
| Win. 180 Power Point | velocity, fps: | 2970 | 2755 | 2549 | 2353 | 2166 |
| | energy, ft-lb: | 3526 | 3034 | 2598 | 2214 | 1875 |
| | arc, inches: | | +1.5 | 0 | -6.9 | -20.1 |

## .300 WEATHERBY MAGNUM

| CARTRIDGE BULLET | RANGE, YARDS: | 0 | 100 | 200 | 300 | 400 |
|---|---|---|---|---|---|---|
| A-Square 180 Dead Tough | velocity, fps: | 3180 | 2811 | 2471 | 2155 | 1863 |
| | energy, ft-lb: | 4041 | 3158 | 2440 | 1856 | 1387 |
| | arc, inches: | | +1.5 | 0 | -7.2 | -21.8 |
| A-Square 220 Monolythic Solid | velocity, fps: | 2700 | 2407 | 2133 | 1877 | 1653 |
| | energy, ft-lb: | 3561 | 2830 | 2223 | 1721 | 1334 |
| | arc, inches: | | +2.3 | 0 | -9.8 | -29.7 |
| Federal 180 Sierra GameKing BTSP | velocity, fps: | 3190 | 3010 | 2830 | 2660 | 2490 |
| | energy, ft-lb: | 4065 | 3610 | 3195 | 2820 | 2480 |
| | arc, inches: | | +1.2 | 0 | -5.6 | -16.0 |
| Federal 180 Trophy Bonded | velocity, fps: | 3190 | 2950 | 2720 | 2500 | 2290 |
| | energy, ft-lb: | 4065 | 3475 | 2955 | 2500 | 2105 |
| | arc, inches: | | +1.3 | 0 | -5.9 | -17.5 |
| Federal 180 Tr. Bonded HE | velocity, fps: | 3330 | 3080 | 2850 | 2750 | 2410 |
| | energy, ft-lb: | 4430 | 3795 | 3235 | 2750 | 2320 |
| | arc, inches: | | +1.1 | 0 | -5.4 | -15.8 |
| Federal 180 Nosler Partition | velocity, fps: | 3190 | 2980 | 2780 | 2590 | 2400 |
| | energy, ft-lb: | 4055 | 3540 | 3080 | 2670 | 2305 |
| | arc, inches: | | +1.2 | 0 | -5.7 | -16.7 |
| Federal 180 Nosler Part. HE | velocity, fps: | 3330 | 3110 | 2810 | 2710 | 2520 |
| | energy, ft-lb: | 4430 | 3875 | 3375 | 2935 | 2540 |
| | arc, inches: | | +1.0 | 0 | -5.2 | -15.1 |
| Federal 200 Trophy Bonded | velocity, fps: | 2900 | 2670 | 2440 | 2230 | 2030 |
| | energy, ft-lb: | 3735 | 3150 | 2645 | 2200 | 1820 |
| | arc, inches: | | +1.7 | 0 | -7.6 | -22.2 |
| Hornady 150 SST (or Interbond) | velocity, fps: | 3375 | 3123 | 2882 | 2652 | 2434 |
| | energy, ft-lb: | 3793 | 3248 | 2766 | 2343 | 1973 |
| | arc, inches: | | +1.0 | 0 | -5.4 | -15.8 |
| Hornady 180 SP | velocity, fps: | 3120 | 2891 | 2673 | 2466 | 2268 |
| | energy, ft-lb: | 3890 | 3340 | 2856 | 2430 | 2055 |
| | arc, inches: | | +1.3 | 0 | -6.2 | -18.1 |
| Hornady 180 SST | velocity, fps: | 3120 | 2911 | 2711 | 2519 | 2335 |
| | energy, ft-lb: | 3890 | 3386 | 2936 | 2535 | 2180 |
| | arc, inches: | | +1.3 | 0 | -6.2 | -18.1 |
| Rem. 180 PSP Core-Lokt | velocity, fps: | 3120 | 2866 | 2627 | 2400 | 2184 |
| | energy, ft-lb: | 3890 | 3284 | 2758 | 2301 | 1905 |
| | arc, inches: | | +2.4 | +2.0 | -3.4 | -14.9 |
| Rem. 190 PSP boat-tail | velocity, fps: | 3030 | 2830 | 2638 | 2455 | 2279 |
| | energy, ft-lb: | 3873 | 3378 | 2936 | 2542 | 2190 |
| | arc, inches: | | +1.4 | 0 | -6.4 | -18.6 |
| Rem. 200 Swift A-Frame | velocity, fps: | 2925 | 2690 | 2467 | 2254 | 2052 |
| | energy, ft-lb: | 3799 | 3213 | 2701 | 2256 | 1870 |
| | arc, inches: | | +2.8 | +2.3 | -3.9 | -17.0 |

| CARTRIDGE BULLET | RANGE, YARDS: | 0 | 100 | 200 | 300 | 400 |
|---|---|---|---|---|---|---|
| Speer 180 Grand Slam | velocity, fps: | 3185 | 2948 | 2722 | 2508 | |
| | energy, ft-lb: | 4054 | 3472 | 2962 | 2514 | |
| | arc, inches: | | +1.3 | 0 | -5.9 | -17.4 |
| Wby. 150 Pointed Expanding | velocity, fps: | 3540 | 3225 | 2932 | 2657 | 2399 |
| | energy, ft-lb: | 4173 | 3462 | 2862 | 2351 | 1916 |
| | arc, inches: | | +2.6 | +3.3 | 0 | -8.2 |
| Wby. 150 Nosler Partition | velocity, fps: | 3540 | 3263 | 3004 | 2759 | 2528 |
| | energy, ft-lb: | 4173 | 3547 | 3005 | 2536 | 2128 |
| | arc, inches: | | +2.5 | +3.2 | 0 | -7.7 |
| Wby. 165 Pointed Expanding | velocity, fps: | 3390 | 3123 | 2872 | 2634 | 2409 |
| | energy, ft-lb: | 4210 | 3573 | 3021 | 2542 | 2126 |
| | arc, inches: | | +2.8 | +3.5 | 0 | -8.5 |
| Wby. 165 Nosler Bal. Tip | velocity, fps: | 3350 | 3133 | 2927 | 2730 | 2542 |
| | energy, ft-lb: | 4111 | 3596 | 3138 | 2730 | 2367 |
| | arc, inches: | | +2.7 | +3.4 | 0 | -8.1 |
| Wby. 180 Pointed Expanding | velocity, fps: | 3240 | 3004 | 2781 | 2569 | 2366 |
| | energy, ft-lb: | 4195 | 3607 | 3091 | 2637 | 2237 |
| | arc, inches: | | +3.1 | +3.8 | 0 | -9.0 |
| Wby. 180 Barnes X | velocity, fps: | 3190 | 2995 | 2809 | 2631 | 2459 |
| | energy, ft-lb: | 4067 | 3586 | 3154 | 2766 | 2417 |
| | arc, inches: | | +3.1 | +3.8 | 0 | -8.7 |
| Wby. 180 Bal. Tip | velocity, fps: | 3250 | 3051 | 2806 | 2676 | 2503 |
| | energy, ft-lb: | 4223 | 3721 | 3271 | 2867 | 2504 |
| | arc, inches: | | +2.8 | +3.6 | 0 | -8.4 |
| Wby. 180 Nosler Partition | velocity, fps: | 3240 | 3028 | 2826 | 2634 | 2449 |
| | energy, ft-lb: | 4195 | 3665 | 3193 | 2772 | 2396 |
| | arc, inches: | | +3.0 | +3.7 | 0 | -8.6 |
| Wby. 200 Nosler Partition | velocity, fps: | 3060 | 2860 | 2668 | 2485 | 2308 |
| | energy, ft-lb: | 4158 | 3631 | 3161 | 2741 | 2366 |
| | arc, inches: | | +3.5 | +4.2 | 0 | -9.8 |
| Wby. 220 RN Expanding | velocity, fps: | 2845 | 2543 | 2260 | 1996 | 1751 |
| | energy, ft-lb: | 3954 | 3158 | 2495 | 1946 | 1497 |
| | arc, inches: | | +4.9 | +5.9 | 0 | -14.6 |

## .300 DAKOTA

| CARTRIDGE BULLET | RANGE, YARDS: | 0 | 100 | 200 | 300 | 400 |
|---|---|---|---|---|---|---|
| Dakota 165 Barnes X | velocity, fps: | 3200 | 2979 | 2769 | 2569 | 2377 |
| | energy, ft-lb: | 3751 | 3251 | 2809 | 2417 | 2070 |
| | arc, inches: | | +2.1 | +1.8 | -3.0 | -13.2 |
| Dakota 200 Barnes X | velocity, fps: | 3000 | 2824 | 2656 | 2493 | 2336 |
| | energy, ft-lb: | 3996 | 3542 | 3131 | 2760 | 2423 |
| | arc, inches: | | +2.2 | +1.5 | -4.0 | -15.2 |

## .300 PEGASUS

| CARTRIDGE BULLET | RANGE, YARDS: | 0 | 100 | 200 | 300 | 400 |
|---|---|---|---|---|---|---|
| A-Square 180 SP boat-tail | velocity, fps: | 3500 | 3319 | 3145 | 2978 | 2817 |
| | energy, ft-lb: | 4896 | 4401 | 3953 | 3544 | 3172 |
| | arc, inches: | | +2.3 | +2.9 | 0 | -6.8 |
| A-Square 180 Nosler Part. | velocity, fps: | 3500 | 3295 | 3100 | 2913 | 2734 |
| | energy, ft-lb: | 4896 | 4339 | 3840 | 3392 | 2988 |
| | arc, inches: | | +2.3 | +3.0 | 0 | -7.1 |
| A-Square 180 Dead Tough | velocity, fps: | 3500 | 3103 | 2740 | 2405 | 2095 |
| | energy, ft-lb: | 4896 | 3848 | 3001 | 2312 | 1753 |
| | arc, inches: | | +1.1 | 0 | -5.7 | -17.5 |

## .300 REMINGTON ULTRA MAG

| CARTRIDGE BULLET | RANGE, YARDS: | 0 | 100 | 200 | 300 | 400 |
|---|---|---|---|---|---|---|
| Federal 180 Trophy Bonded | velocity, fps: | 3250 | 3000 | 2770 | 2550 | 2340 |
| | energy, ft-lb: | 4220 | 3605 | 3065 | 2590 | 2180 |
| | arc, inches: | | +1.2 | 0 | -5.7 | -16.8 |
| Rem. 150 Swift Scirocco | velocity, fps: | 3450 | 3208 | 2980 | 2762 | 2556 |
| | energy, ft-lb: | 3964 | 3427 | 2956 | 2541 | 2175 |
| | arc, inches: | | +1.7 | +1.5 | -2.6 | -11.2 |

# Centerfire Rifle Ballistics

## .300 REMINGTON ULTRA MAG TO 8MM MAUSER (8X57)

| CARTRIDGE BULLET | RANGE, YARDS: | 0 | 100 | 200 | 300 | 400 |
|---|---|---|---|---|---|---|
| Rem. 180 Nosler Partition | velocity, fps: | 3250 | 3037 | 2834 | 2640 | 2454 |
| | energy, ft-lb: | 4221 | 3686 | 3201 | 2786 | 2407 |
| | arc, inches: | | +2.4 | +1.8 | -3.0 | -12.7 |
| Rem. 180 Swift Scirocco | velocity, fps: | 3250 | 3048 | 2856 | 2672 | 2495 |
| | energy, ft-lb: | 4221 | 3714 | 3260 | 2853 | 2487 |
| | arc, inches: | | +2.0 | +1.7 | -2.8 | -12.3 |
| Rem. 180 PSP Core-Lokt | velocity, fps: | 3250 | 2988 | 2742 | 2508 | 2287 |
| | energy, ft-lb: | 3517 | 2974 | 2503 | 2095 | 1741 |
| | arc, inches: | | +2.1 | +1.8 | -3.1 | -13.6 |
| Rem. 200 Nosler Partition | velocity, fps: | 3025 | 2826 | 2636 | 2454 | 2279 |
| | energy, ft-lb: | 4063 | 3547 | 3086 | 2673 | 2308 |
| | arc, inches: | | +2.4 | +2.0 | -3.4 | -14.6 |

### .30-378 WEATHERBY MAGNUM

| CARTRIDGE BULLET | | 0 | 100 | 200 | 300 | 400 |
|---|---|---|---|---|---|---|
| Wby. 165 Nosler Bal. Tip | velocity, fps: | 3500 | 3275 | 3062 | 2859 | 2665 |
| | energy, ft-lb: | 4488 | 3930 | 3435 | 2995 | 2603 |
| | arc, inches: | | +2.4 | +3.0 | 0 | -7.4 |
| Wby. 180 Nosler Bal. Tip | velocity, fps: | 3420 | 3213 | 3015 | 2826 | 2645 |
| | energy, ft-lb: | 4676 | 4126 | 3634 | 3193 | 2797 |
| | arc, inches: | | +2.5 | +3.1 | 0 | -7.5 |
| Wby. 180 Barnes X | velocity, fps: | 3450 | 3243 | 3046 | 2858 | 2678 |
| | energy, ft-lb: | 4757 | 4204 | 3709 | 3264 | 2865 |
| | arc, inches: | | +2.4 | +3.1 | 0 | -7.4 |
| Wby. 200 Nosler Partition | velocity, fps: | 3160 | 2955 | 2759 | 2572 | 2392 |
| | energy, ft-lb: | 4434 | 3877 | 3381 | 2938 | 2541 |
| | arc, inches: | | +3.2 | +3.9 | 0 | -9.1 |

### 7.82 (.308) WARBIRD

| CARTRIDGE BULLET | | 0 | 100 | 200 | 300 | 400 |
|---|---|---|---|---|---|---|
| Lazzeroni 150 Nosler Part. | velocity, fps: | 3680 | 3432 | 3197 | 2975 | 2764 |
| | energy, ft-lb: | 4512 | 3923 | 3406 | 2949 | 2546 |
| | arc, inches: | | +2.1 | +2.7 | 0 | -6.6 |
| Lazzeroni 180 Nosler Part. | velocity, fps: | 3425 | 3220 | 3026 | 2839 | 2661 |
| | energy, ft-lb: | 4689 | 4147 | 3661 | 3224 | 2831 |
| | arc, inches: | | +2.5 | +3.2 | 0 | -7.5 |
| Lazzeroni 200 Swift A-Fr. | velocity, fps: | 3290 | 3105 | 2928 | 2758 | 2594 |
| | energy, ft-lb: | 4808 | 4283 | 3808 | 3378 | 2988 |
| | arc, inches: | | +2.7 | +3.4 | 0 | -7.9 |

### 7.65x53 ARGENTINE

| CARTRIDGE BULLET | | 0 | 100 | 200 | 300 | 400 |
|---|---|---|---|---|---|---|
| Norma 174 Soft Point | velocity, fps: | 2493 | 2173 | 1878 | 1611 | |
| | energy, ft-lb: | 2402 | 1825 | 1363 | 1003 | |
| | arc, inches: | | +2.0 | 0 | -9.5 | |
| Norma 180 Soft Point | velocity, fps: | 2592 | 2386 | 2189 | 2002 | |
| | energy, ft-lb: | 2686 | 2276 | 1916 | 1602 | |
| | arc, inches: | | +2.3 | 0 | -9.6 | |

### .303 BRITISH

| CARTRIDGE BULLET | | 0 | 100 | 200 | 300 | 400 |
|---|---|---|---|---|---|---|
| Federal 150 Hi-Shok | velocity, fps: | 2690 | 2440 | 2210 | 1980 | 1780 |
| | energy, ft-lb: | 2400 | 1980 | 1620 | 1310 | 1055 |
| | arc, inches: | | +2.2 | 0 | -9.4 | -27.6 |
| Federal 180 Sierra Pro-Hunt. | velocity, fps: | 2460 | 2230 | 2020 | 1820 | 1630 |
| | energy, ft-lb: | 2420 | 1995 | 1625 | 1315 | 1060 |
| | arc, inches: | | +2.8 | 0 | -11.3 | -33.2 |
| Federal 180 Tr. Bonded HE | velocity, fps: | 2590 | 2350 | 2120 | 1900 | 1700 |
| | energy, ft-lb: | 2680 | 2205 | 1795 | 1445 | 1160 |
| | arc, inches: | | +2.4 | 0 | -10.0 | -30.0 |
| Hornady 150 Soft Point | velocity, fps: | 2685 | 2441 | 2210 | 1992 | 1787 |
| | energy, ft-lb: | 2401 | 1984 | 1627 | 1321 | 1064 |
| | arc, inches: | | +2.2 | 0 | -9.3 | -27.4 |
| Hornady 150 SP LM | velocity, fps: | 2830 | 2570 | 2325 | 2094 | 1884 |
| | energy, ft-lb: | 2667 | 2199 | 1800 | 1461 | 1185 |
| | arc, inches: | | +2.0 | 0 | -8.4 | -24.6 |
| Norma 150 Soft Point | velocity, fps: | 2723 | 2438 | 2170 | 1920 | |
| | energy, ft-lb: | 2470 | 1980 | 1569 | 1228 | |
| | arc, inches: | | +2.2 | 0 | -9.6 | |
| PMC 174 FMJ (and HPBT) | velocity, fps: | 2400 | 2216 | 2042 | 1876 | 1720 |
| | energy, ft-lb: | 2225 | 1898 | 1611 | 1360 | 1143 |
| | arc, inches: | | +2.8 | 0 | -11.2 | -32.2 |
| PMC 180 SP boat-tail | velocity, fps: | 2450 | 2276 | 2110 | 1951 | 1799 |
| | energy, ft-lb: | 2399 | 2071 | 1779 | 1521 | 1294 |
| | arc, inches: | | +2.6 | 0 | -10.4 | -30.1 |
| Rem. 180 SP Core-Lokt | velocity, fps: | 2460 | 2124 | 1817 | 1542 | 1311 |
| | energy, ft-lb: | 2418 | 1803 | 1319 | 950 | 687 |
| | arc, inches, s: | | 0 | -5.8 | -23.3 | |
| Win. 180 Power-Point | velocity, fps: | 2460 | 2233 | 2018 | 1816 | 1629 |
| | energy, ft-lb: | 2418 | 1993 | 1627 | 1318 | 1060 |
| | arc, inches, s: | | 0 | -6.1 | -20.8 | |

### 7.7x58 JAPANESE ARISAKA

| CARTRIDGE BULLET | | 0 | 100 | 200 | 300 | 400 |
|---|---|---|---|---|---|---|
| Norma 174 Soft Point | velocity, fps: | 2493 | 2173 | 1878 | 1611 | |
| | energy, ft-lb: | 2402 | 1825 | 1363 | 1003 | |
| | arc, inches: | | +2.0 | 0 | -9.5 | |
| Norma 180 Soft Point | velocity, fps: | 2493 | 2291 | 2099 | 1916 | |
| | energy, ft-lb: | 2485 | 2099 | 1761 | 1468 | |
| | arc, inches: | | +2.6 | 0 | -10.5 | |

### .32-20 WINCHESTER

| CARTRIDGE BULLET | | 0 | 100 | 200 | 300 | 400 |
|---|---|---|---|---|---|---|
| Rem. 100 Lead | velocity, fps: | 1210 | 1021 | 913 | 834 | 769 |
| | energy, ft-lb: | 325 | 231 | 185 | 154 | 131 |
| | arc, inches: | | 0 | -31.6 | -104.7 | |
| Win. 100 Lead | velocity, fps: | 1210 | 1021 | 913 | 834 | 769 |
| | energy, ft-lb: | 325 | 231 | 185 | 154 | 131 |
| | arc, inches: | | 0 | -32.3 | -106.3 | |

### .32 WINCHESTER SPECIAL

| CARTRIDGE BULLET | | 0 | 100 | 200 | 300 | 400 |
|---|---|---|---|---|---|---|
| Federal 170 Hi-Shok | velocity, fps: | 2250 | 1920 | 1630 | 1370 | 1180 |
| | energy, ft-lb: | 1910 | 1395 | 1000 | 710 | 520 |
| | arc, inches: | | 0 | -8.0 | -29.2 | |
| Rem. 170 SP Core-Lokt | velocity, fps: | 2250 | 1921 | 1626 | 1372 | 1175 |
| | energy, ft-lb: | 1911 | 1393 | 998 | 710 | 521 |
| | arc, inches: | | 0 | -8.0 | -29.3 | |
| Win. 170 Power-Point | velocity, fps: | 2250 | 1870 | 1537 | 1267 | 1082 |
| | energy, ft-lb: | 1911 | 1320 | 892 | 606 | 442 |
| | arc, inches: | | 0 | -9.2 | -33.2 | |

### 8MM MAUSER (8X57)

| CARTRIDGE BULLET | | 0 | 100 | 200 | 300 | 400 |
|---|---|---|---|---|---|---|
| Federal 170 Hi-Shok | velocity, fps: | 2360 | 1970 | 1620 | 1330 | 1120 |
| | energy, ft-lb: | 2100 | 1465 | 995 | 670 | 475 |
| | arc, inches: | | 0 | -7.6 | -28.5 | |
| Hornady 195 SP | velocity, fps: | 2550 | 2343 | 2146 | 1959 | 1782 |
| | energy, ft-lb: | 2815 | 2377 | 1994 | 1861 | 1375 |
| | arc, inches: | +2.3 | 0 | -9.9 | -28.8 | -58.8 |
| Norma 196 Alaska | velocity, fps: | 2395 | 2112 | 1850 | 1611 | |
| | energy, ft-lb: | 2714 | 2190 | 1754 | 1399 | |
| | arc, inches: | | 0 | -6.3 | -22.9 | |
| Norma 196 Soft Point (JS) | velocity, fps: | 2526 | 2244 | 1981 | 1737 | |
| | energy, ft-lb: | 2778 | 2192 | 1708 | 1314 | |
| | arc, inches: | | +2.7 | 0 | -11.6 | |
| Norma 196 Vulkan (JS) | velocity, fps: | 2526 | 2276 | 2041 | 1821 | |
| | energy, ft-lb: | 2778 | 2256 | 1813 | 1443 | |
| | arc, inches: | | +2.6 | 0 | -11.0 | |
| Norma 196 Oryx (JS) | velocity, fps: | 2526 | 2269 | 2027 | 1802 | |
| | energy, ft-lb: | 2778 | 2241 | 1789 | 1413 | |
| | arc, inches: | | +2.6 | 0 | -11.1 | |

| CARTRIDGE BULLET | RANGE, YARDS: | 0 | 100 | 200 | 300 | 400 |
|---|---|---|---|---|---|---|
| PMC 170 Pointed Soft Point | velocity, fps: | 2360 | 1969 | 1622 | 1333 | 1123 |
| | energy, ft-lb: | 2102 | 1463 | 993 | 671 | 476 |
| | arc, inches: | +1.8 | 0 | -4.5 | -24.3 | -63.8 |
| Rem. 170 SP Core-Lokt | velocity, fps: | 2360 | 1969 | 1622 | 1333 | 1123 |
| | energy, ft-lb: | 2102 | 1463 | 993 | 671 | 476 |
| | arc, inches: | | 0 | -7.6 | -28.6 | |
| Win. 170 Power-Point | velocity, fps: | 2360 | 1969 | 1622 | 1333 | 1123 |
| | energy, ft-lb: | 2102 | 1463 | 993 | 671 | 476 |
| | arc, inches: | | 0 | -8.2 | -29.8 | |

## 8MM REMINGTON MAGNUM

| CARTRIDGE BULLET | RANGE, YARDS: | 0 | 100 | 200 | 300 | 400 |
|---|---|---|---|---|---|---|
| A-Square 220 Monolythic Solid | velocity, fps: | 2800 | 2501 | 2221 | 1959 | 1718 |
| | energy, ft-lb: | 3829 | 3055 | 2409 | 1875 | 1442 |
| | arc, inches: | | +2.1 | 0 | -9.1 | -27.6 |
| Rem. 200 Swift A-Frame | velocity, fps: | 2900 | 2623 | 2361 | 2115 | 1885 |
| | energy, ft-lb: | 3734 | 3054 | 2476 | 1987 | 1577 |
| | arc, inches: | | +1.8 | 0 | -8.0 | -23.9 |

## .338-06

| CARTRIDGE BULLET | RANGE, YARDS: | 0 | 100 | 200 | 300 | 400 |
|---|---|---|---|---|---|---|
| A-Square 200 Nos. Bal. Tip | velocity, fps: | 2750 | 2553 | 2364 | 2184 | 2011 |
| | energy, ft-lb: | 3358 | 2894 | 2482 | 2118 | 1796 |
| | arc, inches: | | +1.9 | 0 | -8.2 | -23.6 |
| A-Square 250 SP boat-tail | velocity, fps: | 2500 | 2374 | 2252 | 2134 | 2019 |
| | energy, ft-lb: | 3496 | 3129 | 2816 | 2528 | 2263 |
| | arc, inches: | | +2.4 | 0 | -9.3 | -26.0 |
| A-Square 250 Dead Tough | velocity, fps: | 2500 | 2222 | 1963 | 1724 | 1507 |
| | energy, ft-lb: | 3496 | 2742 | 2139 | 1649 | 1261 |
| | arc, inches: | | +2.8 | 0 | -11.9 | -35.5 |
| Wby. 210 Nosler Part. | velocity, fps: | 2750 | 2526 | 2312 | 2109 | 1916 |
| | energy, ft-lb: | 3527 | 2975 | 2403 | 2074 | 1712 |
| | arc, inches: | | +4.8 | +5.7 | 0 | -13.5 |

## .338 WINCHESTER MAGNUM

| CARTRIDGE BULLET | RANGE, YARDS: | 0 | 100 | 200 | 300 | 400 |
|---|---|---|---|---|---|---|
| A-Square 250 SP boat-tail | velocity, fps: | 2700 | 2568 | 2439 | 2314 | 2193 |
| | energy, ft-lb: | 4046 | 3659 | 3302 | 2972 | 2669 |
| | arc, inches: | | +4.4 | +5.2 | 0 | -11.7 |
| A-Square 250 Triad | velocity, fps: | 2700 | 2407 | 2133 | 1877 | 1653 |
| | energy, ft-lb: | 4046 | 3216 | 2526 | 1956 | 1516 |
| | arc, inches: | | +2.3 | 0 | -9.8 | -29.8 |
| Federal 210 Nosler Partition | velocity, fps: | 2830 | 2600 | 2390 | 2180 | 1980 |
| | energy, ft-lb: | 3735 | 3160 | 2655 | 2215 | 1835 |
| | arc, inches: | | +1.8 | 0 | -8.0 | -23.3 |
| Federal 225 Sierra Pro-Hunt. | velocity, fps: | 2780 | 2570 | 2360 | 2170 | 1980 |
| | energy, ft-lb: | 3860 | 3290 | 2780 | 2340 | 1960 |
| | arc, inches: | | +1.9 | 0 | -8.2 | -23.7 |
| Federal 225 Trophy Bonded | velocity, fps: | 2800 | 2560 | 2330 | 2110 | 1900 |
| | energy, ft-lb: | 3915 | 3265 | 2700 | 2220 | 1800 |
| | arc, inches: | | +1.9 | 0 | -8.4 | -24.5 |
| Federal 225 Tr. Bonded HE | velocity, fps: | 2940 | 2690 | 2450 | 2230 | 2010 |
| | energy, ft-lb: | 4320 | 3610 | 3000 | 2475 | 2025 |
| | arc, inches: | | +1.7 | 0 | -7.5 | -22.0 |
| Federal 225 Barnes XLC | velocity, fps: | 2800 | 2610 | 2430 | 2260 | 2090 |
| | energy, ft-lb: | 3915 | 3405 | 2950 | 2545 | 2190 |
| | arc, inches: | | +1.8 | 0 | -7.7 | -22.2 |
| Federal 250 Nosler Partition | velocity, fps: | 2660 | 2470 | 2300 | 2120 | 1960 |
| | energy, ft-lb: | 3925 | 3395 | 2925 | 2505 | 2130 |
| | arc, inches: | | +2.1 | 0 | -8.8 | -25.1 |
| Federal 250 Nosler Part HE | velocity, fps: | 2800 | 2610 | 2420 | 2250 | 2080 |
| | energy, ft-lb: | 4350 | 3775 | 3260 | 2805 | 2395 |
| | arc, inches: | | +1.8 | 0 | -7.8 | -22.5 |

| CARTRIDGE BULLET | RANGE, YARDS: | 0 | 100 | 200 | 300 | 400 |
|---|---|---|---|---|---|---|
| Hornady 225 Soft Point HM | velocity, fps: | 2920 | 2678 | 2449 | 2232 | 2027 |
| | energy, ft-lb: | 4259 | 3583 | 2996 | 2489 | 2053 |
| | arc, inches: | | +1.8 | 0 | -7.6 | -22.0 |
| Norma 225 TXP Swift A-Fr. | velocity, fps: | 2740 | 2507 | 2286 | 2075 | |
| | energy, ft-lb: | 3752 | 3141 | 2611 | 2153 | |
| | arc, inches: | | +2.0 | 0 | -8.7 | |
| Norma 250 Nosler Partition | velocity, fps: | 2657 | 2470 | 2290 | 2118 | |
| | energy, ft-lb: | 3920 | 3387 | 2912 | 2490 | |
| | arc, inches: | | +2.1 | 0 | -8.7 | |
| PMC 225 Barnes X | velocity, fps: | 2780 | 2619 | 2464 | 2313 | 2168 |
| | energy, ft-lb: | 3860 | 3426 | 3032 | 2673 | 2348 |
| | arc, inches: | | +1.8 | 0 | -7.6 | -21.6 |
| Rem. 200 Nosler Bal. Tip | velocity, fps: | 2950 | 2724 | 2509 | 2303 | 2108 |
| | energy, ft-lb: | 3866 | 3295 | 2795 | 2357 | 1973 |
| | arc, inches: | | +1.6 | 0 | -7.1 | -20.8 |
| Rem. 210 Nosler Partition | velocity, fps: | 2830 | 2602 | 2385 | 2179 | 1983 |
| | energy, ft-lb: | 3734 | 3157 | 2653 | 2214 | 1834 |
| | arc, inches: | | +1.8 | 0 | -7.9 | -23.2 |
| Rem. 225 PSP Core-Lokt | velocity, fps: | 2780 | 2572 | 2374 | 2184 | 2003 |
| | energy, ft-lb: | 3860 | 3305 | 2815 | 2383 | 2004 |
| | arc, inches: | | +1.9 | 0 | -8.1 | -23.4 |
| Rem. 225 PSP C-L Ultra | velocity, fps: | 2780 | 2582 | 2392 | 2210 | 2036 |
| | energy, ft-lb: | 3860 | 3329 | 2858 | 2440 | 2071 |
| | arc, inches: | | +1.9 | 0 | -7.9 | -23.0 |
| Rem. 225 Swift A-Frame | velocity, fps: | 2785 | 2517 | 2266 | 2029 | 1808 |
| | energy, ft-lb: | 3871 | 3165 | 2565 | 2057 | 1633 |
| | arc, inches: | | +2.0 | 0 | -8.8 | -25.2 |
| Rem. 250 PSP Core-Lokt | velocity, fps: | 2660 | 2456 | 2261 | 2075 | 1898 |
| | energy, ft-lb: | 3927 | 3348 | 2837 | 2389 | 1999 |
| | arc, inches: | | +2.1 | 0 | -8.9 | -26.0 |
| Speer 250 Grand Slam | velocity, fps: | 2645 | 2442 | 2247 | 2062 | |
| | energy, ft-lb: | 3883 | 3309 | 2803 | 2360 | |
| | arc, inches: | | +2.2 | 0 | -9.1 | -26.2 |
| Win. 200 Power-Point | velocity, fps: | 2960 | 2658 | 2375 | 2110 | 1862 |
| | energy, ft-lb: | 3890 | 3137 | 2505 | 1977 | 1539 |
| | arc, inches: | | +2.0 | 0 | -8.2 | -24.3 |
| Win. 200 Ballistic Silvertip | velocity, fps: | 2950 | 2724 | 2509 | 2303 | 2108 |
| | energy, ft-lb: | 3864 | 3294 | 2794 | 2355 | 1972 |
| | arc, inches: | | +1.6 | 0 | -7.1 | -20.8 |
| Win. 225 AccuBond | velocity, fps: | 2800 | 2634 | 2474 | 2319 | 2170 |
| | energy, ft-lb: | 3918 | 3467 | 3058 | 2688 | 2353 |
| | arc, inches: | | +1.8 | 0 | -7.4 | -21.3 |
| Win. 230 Fail Safe | velocity, fps: | 2780 | 2573 | 2375 | 2186 | 2005 |
| | energy, ft-lb: | 3948 | 3382 | 2881 | 2441 | 2054 |
| | arc, inches: | | +1.9 | 0 | -8.1 | -23.4 |
| Win. 250 Partition Gold | velocity, fps: | 2650 | 2467 | 2291 | 2122 | 1960 |
| | energy, ft-lb: | 3899 | 3378 | 2914 | 2520 | 2134 |
| | arc, inches: | | +2.1 | 0 | -8.7 | -25.2 |

## .340 WEATHERBY MAGNUM

| CARTRIDGE BULLET | RANGE, YARDS: | 0 | 100 | 200 | 300 | 400 |
|---|---|---|---|---|---|---|
| A-Square 250 SP boat-tail | velocity, fps: | 2820 | 2684 | 2552 | 2424 | 2299 |
| | energy, ft-lb: | 4414 | 3999 | 3615 | 3261 | 2935 |
| | arc, inches: | | +4.0 | +4.6 | 0 | -10.6 |
| A-Square 250 Triad | velocity, fps: | 2820 | 2520 | 2238 | 1976 | 1741 |
| | energy, ft-lb: | 4414 | 3524 | 2781 | 2166 | 1683 |
| | arc, inches: | | +2.0 | 0 | -9.0 | -26.8 |
| Federal 225 Trophy Bonded | velocity, fps: | 3100 | 2840 | 2600 | 2370 | 2150 |
| | energy, ft-lb: | 4800 | 4035 | 3375 | 2800 | 2310 |
| | arc, inches: | | +1.4 | 0 | -6.5 | -19.4 |

# Centerfire Rifle Ballistics

## .340 WEATHERBY MAGNUM TO .35 REMINGTON

| CARTRIDGE BULLET | RANGE, YARDS: | 0 | 100 | 200 | 300 | 400 |
|---|---|---|---|---|---|---|
| Wby. 200 Pointed Expanding | velocity, fps: | 3221 | 2946 | 2688 | 2444 | 2213 |
| | energy, ft-lb: | 4607 | 3854 | 3208 | 2652 | 2174 |
| | arc, inches: | | +3.3 | +4.0 | 0 | -9.9 |
| Wby. 200 Nosler Bal. Tip | velocity, fps: | 3221 | 2980 | 2753 | 2536 | 2329 |
| | energy, ft-lb: | 4607 | 3944 | 3364 | 2856 | 2409 |
| | arc, inches: | | +3.1 | +3.9 | 0 | -9.2 |
| Wby. 210 Nosler Partition | velocity, fps: | 3211 | 2963 | 2728 | 2505 | 2293 |
| | energy, ft-lb: | 4807 | 4093 | 3470 | 2927 | 2452 |
| | arc, inches: | | +3.2 | +3.9 | 0 | -9.5 |
| Wby. 225 Pointed Expanding | velocity, fps: | 3066 | 2824 | 2595 | 2377 | 2170 |
| | energy, ft-lb: | 4696 | 3984 | 3364 | 2822 | 2352 |
| | arc, inches: | | +3.6 | +4.4 | 0 | -10.7 |
| Wby. 225 Barnes X | velocity, fps: | 3001 | 2804 | 2615 | 2434 | 2260 |
| | energy, ft-lb: | 4499 | 3927 | 3416 | 2959 | 2551 |
| | arc, inches: | | +3.6 | +4.3 | 0 | -10.3 |
| Wby. 250 Pointed Expanding | velocity, fps: | 2963 | 2745 | 2537 | 2338 | 2149 |
| | energy, ft-lb: | 4873 | 4182 | 3572 | 3035 | 2563 |
| | arc, inches: | | +3.9 | +4.6 | 0 | -11.1 |
| Wby. 250 Nosler Partition | velocity, fps: | 2941 | 2743 | 2553 | 2371 | 2197 |
| | energy, ft-lb: | 4801 | 4176 | 3618 | 3120 | 2678 |
| | arc, inches: | | +3.9 | +4.6 | 0 | -10.9 |

### .330 DAKOTA

| CARTRIDGE BULLET | | 0 | 100 | 200 | 300 | 400 |
|---|---|---|---|---|---|---|
| Dakota 200 Barnes X | velocity, fps: | 3200 | 2971 | 2754 | 2548 | 2350 |
| | energy, ft-lb: | 4547 | 3920 | 3369 | 2882 | 2452 |
| | arc, inches: | | +2.1 | +1.8 | -3.1 | -13.4 |
| Dakota 250 Barnes X | velocity, fps: | 2900 | 2719 | 2545 | 2378 | 2217 |
| | energy, ft-lb: | 4668 | 4103 | 3595 | 3138 | 2727 |
| | arc, inches: | | +2.3 | +1.3 | -5.0 | -17.5 |

### .338 REMINGTON ULTRA MAG

| CARTRIDGE BULLET | | 0 | 100 | 200 | 300 | 400 |
|---|---|---|---|---|---|---|
| Federal 210 Nosler Partition | velocity, fps: | 3025 | 2800 | 2585 | 2385 | 2190 |
| | energy, ft-lb: | 4270 | 3655 | 3120 | 2645 | 2230 |
| | arc, inches: | | +1.5 | 0 | -6.7 | -19.5 |
| Federal 250 Trophy Bonded | velocity, fps: | 2860 | 2630 | 2420 | 2210 | 2020 |
| | energy, ft-lb: | 4540 | 3850 | 3245 | 2715 | 2260 |
| | arc, inches: | | +0.8 | 0 | -7.7 | -22.6 |
| Rem. 250 Swift A-Frame | velocity, fps: | 2860 | 2645 | 2440 | 2244 | 2057 |
| | energy, ft-lb: | 4540 | 3882 | 3303 | 2794 | 2347 |
| | arc, inches: | | +1.7 | 0 | -7.6 | -22.1 |
| Rem. 250 PSP Core-Lokt | velocity, fps: | 2860 | 2647 | 2443 | 2249 | 2064 |
| | energy, ft-lb: | 4540 | 3888 | 3314 | 2807 | 2363 |
| | arc, inches: | | +1.7 | 0 | -7.6 | -22.0 |

### .338 LAPUA

| CARTRIDGE BULLET | | 0 | 100 | 200 | 300 | 400 |
|---|---|---|---|---|---|---|
| Black Hills 250 Sierra MKing | velocity, fps: | 2950 | | | | |
| | energy, ft-lb: | 4831 | | | | |
| | arc, inches: | | | | | |
| Black Hills 300 Sierra MKing | velocity, fps: | 2800 | | | | |
| | energy, ft-lb: | 5223 | | | | |
| | arc, inches: | | | | | |

### .338-378 WEATHERBY MAGNUM

| CARTRIDGE BULLET | | 0 | 100 | 200 | 300 | 400 |
|---|---|---|---|---|---|---|
| Wby. 200 Nosler Bal. Tip | velocity, fps: | 3350 | 3102 | 2868 | 2646 | 2434 |
| | energy, ft-lb: | 4983 | 4273 | 3652 | 3109 | 2631 |
| | arc, inches: | 0 | +2.8 | +3.5 | 0 | -8.4 |
| Wby. 225 Barnes X | velocity, fps: | 3180 | 2974 | 2778 | 2591 | 2410 |
| | energy, ft-lb: | 5052 | 4420 | 3856 | 3353 | 2902 |
| | arc, inches: | 0 | +3.1 | +3.8 | 0 | -8.9 |
| Wby. 250 Nosler Partition | velocity, fps: | 3060 | 2856 | 2662 | 2475 | 2297 |
| | energy, ft-lb: | 5197 | 4528 | 3933 | 3401 | 2927 |
| | arc, inches: | 0 | +3.5 | +4.2 | 0 | -9.8 |

### 8.59 (.338) TITAN

| CARTRIDGE BULLET | | 0 | 100 | 200 | 300 | 400 |
|---|---|---|---|---|---|---|
| Lazzeroni 200 Nos. Bal. Tip | velocity, fps: | 3430 | 3211 | 3002 | 2803 | 2613 |
| | energy, ft-lb: | 5226 | 4579 | 4004 | 3491 | 3033 |
| | arc, inches: | | +2.5 | +3.2 | 0 | -7.6 |
| Lazzeroni 225 Nos. Partition | velocity, fps: | 3235 | 3031 | 2836 | 2650 | 2471 |
| | energy, ft-lb: | 5229 | 4591 | 4021 | 3510 | 3052 |
| | arc, inches: | | +3.0 | +3.6 | 0 | -8.6 |
| Lazzeroni 250 Swift A-Fr. | velocity, fps: | 3100 | 2908 | 2725 | 2549 | 2379 |
| | energy, ft-lb: | 5336 | 4697 | 4123 | 3607 | 3143 |
| | arc, inches: | | +3.3 | +4.0 | 0 | -9.3 |

### .338 A-SQUARE

| CARTRIDGE BULLET | | 0 | 100 | 200 | 300 | 400 |
|---|---|---|---|---|---|---|
| A-Square 200 Nos. Bal. Tip | velocity, fps: | 3500 | 3266 | 3045 | 2835 | 2634 |
| | energy, ft-lb: | 5440 | 4737 | 4117 | 3568 | 3081 |
| | arc, inches: | | +2.4 | +3.1 | 0 | -7.5 |
| A-Square 250 SP boat-tail | velocity, fps: | 3120 | 2974 | 2834 | 2697 | 2565 |
| | energy, ft-lb: | 5403 | 4911 | 4457 | 4038 | 3652 |
| | arc, inches: | | +3.1 | +3.7 | 0 | -8.5 |
| A-Square 250 Triad | velocity, fps: | 3120 | 2799 | 2500 | 2220 | 1958 |
| | energy, ft-lb: | 5403 | 4348 | 3469 | 2736 | 2128 |
| | arc, inches: | | +1.5 | 0 | -7.1 | -20.4 |

### .338 EXCALIBER

| CARTRIDGE BULLET | | 0 | 100 | 200 | 300 | 400 |
|---|---|---|---|---|---|---|
| A-Square 200 Nos. Bal. Tip | velocity, fps: | 3600 | 3361 | 3134 | 2920 | 2715 |
| | energy, ft-lb: | 5755 | 5015 | 4363 | 3785 | 3274 |
| | arc, inches: | | +2.2 | +2.9 | 0 | -6.7 |
| A-Square 250 SP boat-tail | velocity, fps: | 3250 | 3101 | 2958 | 2684 | 2553 |
| | energy, ft-lb: | 5863 | 5339 | 4855 | 4410 | 3998 |
| | arc, inches: | | +2.7 | +3.4 | 0 | -7.8 |
| A-Square 250 Triad | velocity, fps: | 3250 | 2922 | 2618 | 2333 | 2066 |
| | energy, ft-lb: | 5863 | 4740 | 3804 | 3021 | 2370 |
| | arc, inches: | | +1.3 | 0 | -6.4 | -19.2 |

### .348 WINCHESTER

| CARTRIDGE BULLET | | 0 | 100 | 200 | 300 | 400 |
|---|---|---|---|---|---|---|
| Win. 200 Silvertip | velocity, fps: | 2520 | 2215 | 1931 | 1672 | 1443 |
| | energy, ft-lb: | 2820 | 2178 | 1656 | 1241 | 925 |
| | arc, inches: | | 0 | -6.2 | -21.9 | |

### .357 MAGNUM

| CARTRIDGE BULLET | | 0 | 100 | 200 | 300 | 400 |
|---|---|---|---|---|---|---|
| Federal 180 Hi-Shok HP Hollow Point | velocity, fps: | 1550 | 1160 | 980 | 860 | 770 |
| | energy, ft-lb: | 960 | 535 | 385 | 295 | 235 |
| | arc, inches: | | 0 | -22.8 | -77.9 | -173.8 |
| Win. 158 Jacketed SP | velocity, fps: | 1830 | 1427 | 1138 | 980 | 883 |
| | energy, ft-lb: | 1175 | 715 | 454 | 337 | 274 |
| | arc, inches: | | 0 | -16.2 | -57.0 | -128.3 |

### .35 REMINGTON

| CARTRIDGE BULLET | | 0 | 100 | 200 | 300 | 400 |
|---|---|---|---|---|---|---|
| Federal 200 Hi-Shok | velocity, fps: | 2080 | 1700 | 1380 | 1140 | 1000 |
| | energy, ft-lb: | 1920 | 1280 | 840 | 575 | 445 |
| | arc, inches: | | 0 | -10.7 | -39.3 | |
| Rem. 150 PSP Core-Lokt | velocity, fps: | 2300 | 1874 | 1506 | 1218 | 1039 |
| | energy, ft-lb: | 1762 | 1169 | 755 | 494 | 359 |
| | arc, inches: | | 0 | -8.6 | -32.6 | |
| Rem. 200 SP Core-Lokt | velocity, fps: | 2080 | 1698 | 1376 | 1140 | 1001 |
| | energy, ft-lb: | 1921 | 1280 | 841 | 577 | 445 |
| | arc, inches: | | 0 | -10.7 | -40.1 | |
| Win. 200 Power-Point | velocity, fps: | 2020 | 1646 | 1335 | 1114 | 985 |
| | energy, ft-lb: | 1812 | 1203 | 791 | 551 | 431 |
| | arc, inches: | | 0 | -12.1 | -43.9 | |

BALLISTICS

| CARTRIDGE BULLET | RANGE, YARDS: | 0 | 100 | 200 | 300 | 400 |
|---|---|---|---|---|---|---|
| **.356 WINCHESTER** | | | | | | |
| Win. 200 Power-Point | velocity, fps: | 2460 | 2114 | 1797 | 1517 | 1284 |
| | energy, ft-lb: | 2688 | 1985 | 1434 | 1022 | 732 |
| | arc, inches: | | +1.6 | -3.8 | -20.1 | -51.2 |
| **.358 WINCHESTER** | | | | | | |
| Win. 200 Silvertip | velocity, fps: | 2490 | 2171 | 1876 | 1610 | 1379 |
| | energy, ft-lb: | 2753 | 2093 | 1563 | 1151 | 844 |
| | arc, inches: | | +1.5 | -3.6 | -18.6 | -47.2 |
| **.35 WHELEN** | | | | | | |
| Federal 225 Trophy Bonded | velocity, fps: | 2600 | 2400 | 2200 | 2020 | 1840 |
| | energy, ft-lb: | 3375 | 2865 | 2520 | 2030 | 1690 |
| | arc, inches: | | +2.3 | 0 | -9.4 | -27.3 |
| Rem. 200 Pointed Soft Point | velocity, fps: | 2675 | 2378 | 2100 | 1842 | 1606 |
| | energy, ft-lb: | 3177 | 2510 | 1958 | 1506 | 1145 |
| | arc, inches: | | +2.3 | 0 | -10.3 | -30.8 |
| Rem. 250 Pointed Soft Point | velocity, fps: | 2400 | 2197 | 2005 | 1823 | 1652 |
| | energy, ft-lb: | 3197 | 2680 | 2230 | 1844 | 1515 |
| | arc, inches: | | +1.3 | -3.2 | -16.6 | -40.0 |
| **.358 NORMA MAGNUM** | | | | | | |
| A-Square 275 Triad | velocity, fps: | 2700 | 2394 | 2108 | 1842 | 1653 |
| | energy, ft-lb: | 4451 | 3498 | 2713 | 2072 | 1668 |
| | arc, inches: | | +2.3 | 0 | -10.1 | -29.8 |
| Norma 250 TXP Swift A-Fr. | velocity, fps: | 2723 | 2467 | 2225 | 1996 | |
| | energy, ft-lb: | 4117 | 3379 | 2748 | 2213 | |
| | arc, inches: | | +2.1 | 0 | -9.1 | |
| Norma 250 Woodleigh | velocity, fps: | 2799 | 2442 | 2112 | 1810 | |
| | energy, ft-lb: | 4350 | 3312 | 2478 | 1819 | |
| | arc, inches: | | +2.2 | 0 | -10.0 | |
| **.358 STA** | | | | | | |
| A-Square 275 Triad | velocity, fps: | 2850 | 2562 | 2292 | 2039 | 1764 |
| | energy, ft-lb: | 4959 | 4009 | 3208 | 2539 | 1899 |
| | arc, inches: | | +1.9 | 0 | -8.6 | -26.1 |
| **9.3x57** | | | | | | |
| Norma 232 Vulkan | velocity, fps: | 2329 | 2031 | 1757 | 1512 | |
| | energy, ft-lb: | 2795 | 2126 | 1591 | 1178 | |
| | arc, inches: | | +3.5 | 0 | -14.9 | |
| Norma 285 Oryx | velocity, fps: | 2067 | 1859 | 1666 | 1490 | |
| | energy, ft-lb: | 2704 | 2188 | 1756 | 1404 | |
| | arc, inches: | | +4.3 | 0 | -16.8 | |
| Norma 286 Alaska | velocity, fps: | 2067 | 1857 | 1662 | 1484 | |
| | energy, ft-lb: | 2714 | 2190 | 1754 | 1399 | |
| | arc, inches: | | +4.3 | 0 | -17.0 | |
| **9.3x62** | | | | | | |
| A-Square 286 Triad | velocity, fps: | 2360 | 2089 | 1844 | 1623 | 1369 |
| | energy, ft-lb: | 3538 | 2771 | 2157 | 1670 | 1189 |
| | arc, inches: | | +3.0 | 0 | -13.1 | -42.2 |
| Norma 232 Vulkan | velocity, fps: | 2625 | 2327 | 2049 | 1792 | |
| | energy, ft-lb: | 3551 | 2791 | 2164 | 1655 | |
| | arc, inches: | | +2.5 | 0 | -10.8 | |
| Norma 232 Oryx | velocity, fps: | 2625 | 2294 | 1988 | 1708 | |
| | energy, ft-lb: | 3535 | 2700 | 2028 | 1497 | |
| | arc, inches: | | +2.5 | 0 | -11.4 | |
| Norma 286 Plastic Point | velocity, fps: | 2362 | 2141 | 1931 | 1736 | |
| | energy, ft-lb: | 3544 | 2911 | 2370 | 1914 | |
| | arc, inches: | | +3.1 | 0 | -12.4 | |

| CARTRIDGE BULLET | RANGE, YARDS: | 0 | 100 | 200 | 300 | 400 |
|---|---|---|---|---|---|---|
| Norma 286 Alaska | velocity, fps: | 2362 | 2135 | 1920 | 1720 | |
| | energy, ft-lb: | 3544 | 2894 | 2342 | 1879 | |
| | arc, inches: | | +3.1 | 0 | -12.5 | |
| **9.3x64** | | | | | | |
| A-Square 286 Triad | velocity, fps: | 2700 | 2391 | 2103 | 1835 | 1602 |
| | energy, ft-lb: | 4629 | 3630 | 2808 | 2139 | 1631 |
| | arc, inches: | | +2.3 | 0 | -10.1 | -30.8 |
| **9.3x74 R** | | | | | | |
| A-Square 286 Triad | velocity, fps: | 2360 | 2089 | 1844 | 1623 | |
| | energy, ft-lb: | 3538 | 2771 | 2157 | 1670 | |
| | arc, inches: | | +3.6 | 0 | -14.0 | |
| Norma 232 Vulkan | velocity, fps: | 2625 | 2327 | 2049 | 1792 | |
| | energy, ft-lb: | 3551 | 2791 | 2164 | 1655 | |
| | arc, inches: | | +2.5 | 0 | -10.8 | |
| Norma 232 Oryx | velocity, fps: | 2526 | 2191 | 1883 | 1605 | |
| | energy, ft-lb: | 3274 | 2463 | 1819 | 1322 | |
| | arc, inches: | | +2.9 | 0 | -12.8 | |
| Norma 285 Oryx | velocity, fps: | 2362 | 2114 | 1881 | 1667 | |
| | energy, ft-lb: | 3532 | 2829 | 2241 | 1758 | |
| | arc, inches: | | +3.1 | 0 | -13.0 | |
| Norma 286 Alaska | velocity, fps: | 2362 | 2135 | 1920 | 1720 | |
| | energy, ft-lb: | 3544 | 2894 | 2342 | 1879 | |
| | arc, inches: | | +3.1 | 0 | -12.5 | |
| Norma 286 Plastic Point | velocity, fps: | 2362 | 2135 | 1920 | 1720 | |
| | energy, ft-lb: | 3544 | 2894 | 2342 | 1879 | |
| | arc, inches: | | +3.1 | 0 | -12.5 | |
| **.375 WINCHESTER** | | | | | | |
| Win. 200 Power-Point | velocity, fps: | 2200 | 1841 | 1526 | 1268 | 1089 |
| | energy, ft-lb: | 2150 | 1506 | 1034 | 714 | |
| | arc, inches: | | 0 | -9.5 | -33.8 | |
| **.375 H&H MAGNUM** | | | | | | |
| A-Square 300 SP boat-tail | velocity, fps: | 2550 | 2415 | 2284 | 2157 | 2034 |
| | energy, ft-lb: | 4331 | 3884 | 3474 | 3098 | 2755 |
| | arc, inches: | | +5.2 | +6.0 | 0 | -13.3 |
| A-Square 300 Triad | velocity, fps: | 2550 | 2251 | 1973 | 1717 | 1496 |
| | energy, ft-lb: | 4331 | 3375 | 2592 | 1964 | 1491 |
| | arc, inches: | | +2.7 | 0 | -11.7 | -35.1 |
| Federal 250 Trophy Bonded | velocity, fps: | 2670 | 2360 | 2080 | 1820 | 1580 |
| | energy, ft-lb: | 3955 | 3100 | 2400 | 1830 | 1380 |
| | arc, inches: | | +2.4 | 0 | -10.4 | -31.7 |
| Federal 270 Hi-Shok | velocity, fps: | 2690 | 2420 | 2170 | 1920 | 1700 |
| | energy, ft-lb: | 4340 | 3510 | 2810 | 2220 | 1740 |
| | arc, inches: | | +2.4 | 0 | -10.9 | -33.3 |
| Federal 300 Hi-Shok | velocity, fps: | 2530 | 2270 | 2020 | 1790 | 1580 |
| | energy, ft-lb: | 4265 | 3425 | 2720 | 2135 | 1665 |
| | arc, inches: | | +2.6 | 0 | -11.2 | -33.3 |
| Federal 300 Nosler Partition | velocity, fps: | 2530 | 2320 | 2120 | 1930 | 1750 |
| | energy, ft-lb: | 4265 | 3585 | 2995 | 2475 | 2040 |
| | arc, inches: | | +2.5 | 0 | -10.3 | -29.9 |
| Federal 300 Trophy Bonded | velocity, fps: | 2530 | 2280 | 2040 | 1810 | 1610 |
| | energy, ft-lb: | 4265 | 3450 | 2765 | 2190 | 1725 |
| | arc, inches: | | +2.6 | 0 | -10.9 | -32.8 |
| Federal 300 Tr. Bonded HE | velocity, fps: | 2700 | 2440 | 2190 | 1960 | 1740 |
| | energy, ft-lb: | 4855 | 3960 | 3195 | 2550 | 2020 |
| | arc, inches: | | +2.2 | 0 | -9.4 | -28.0 |
| Federal 300 Trophy Bonded Sledgehammer Solid | velocity, fps: | 2530 | 2160 | 1820 | 1520 | 1280 |
| | energy, ft-lb: | 4265 | 3105 | 2210 | 1550 | 1090 |
| | arc, inches, s: | | 0 | -6.0 | -22.7 | -54.6 |

# Centerfire Rifle Ballistics

## .375 H&H Magnum to .41 Magnum

| CARTRIDGE BULLET | RANGE, YARDS: | 0 | 100 | 200 | 300 | 400 |
|---|---|---|---|---|---|---|
| Hornady 270 SP HM | velocity, fps: | 2870 | 2620 | 2385 | 2162 | 1957 |
| | energy, ft-lb: | 4937 | 4116 | 3408 | 2802 | 2296 |
| | arc, inches: | | +2.2 | 0 | -8.4 | -23.9 |
| Hornady 300 FMJ RN HM | velocity, fps: | 2705 | 2376 | 2072 | 1804 | 1560 |
| | energy, ft-lb: | 4873 | 3760 | 2861 | 2167 | 1621 |
| | arc, inches: | | +2.7 | 0 | -10.8 | -32.1 |
| Norma 300 Soft Point | velocity, fps: | 2549 | 2211 | 1900 | 1619 | |
| | energy, ft-lb: | 4329 | 3258 | 2406 | 1747 | |
| | arc, inches: | | +2.8 | 0 | -12.6 | |
| Norma 300 TXP Swift A-Fr. | velocity, fps: | 2559 | 2296 | 2049 | 1818 | |
| | energy, ft-lb: | 4363 | 3513 | 2798 | 2203 | |
| | arc, inches: | | +2.6 | 0 | -10.9 | |
| Norma 300 Barnes Solid | velocity, fps: | 2493 | 2061 | 1677 | 1356 | |
| | energy, ft-lb: | 4141 | 2829 | 1873 | 1234 | |
| | arc, inches: | | +3.4 | 0 | -16.0 | |
| PMC 270 PSP | velocity, fps: | | | | | |
| | energy, ft-lb: | | | | | |
| | arc, inches: | | | | | |
| PMC 270 Barnes X | velocity, fps: | 2690 | 2528 | 2372 | 2221 | 2076 |
| | energy, ft-lb: | 4337 | 3831 | 3371 | 2957 | 2582 |
| | arc, inches: | | +2.0 | 0 | -8.2 | -23.4 |
| PMC 300 Barnes X | velocity, fps: | 2530 | 2389 | 2252 | 2120 | 1993 |
| | energy, ft-lb: | 4263 | 3801 | 3378 | 2994 | 2644 |
| | arc, inches: | | +2.3 | 0 | -9.2 | -26.1 |
| Rem. 270 Soft Point | velocity, fps: | 2690 | 2420 | 2166 | 1928 | 1707 |
| | energy, ft-lb: | 4337 | 3510 | 2812 | 2228 | 1747 |
| | arc, inches: | | +2.2 | 0 | -9.7 | -28.7 |
| Rem. 300 Swift A-Frame | velocity, fps: | 2530 | 2245 | 1979 | 1733 | 1512 |
| | energy, ft-lb: | 4262 | 3357 | 2608 | 2001 | 1523 |
| | arc, inches: | | +2.7 | 0 | -11.7 | -35.0 |
| Speer 285 Grand Slam | velocity, fps: | 2610 | 2365 | 2134 | 1916 | |
| | energy, ft-lb: | 4310 | 3540 | 2883 | 2323 | |
| | arc, inches: | | +2.4 | 0 | -9.9 | |
| Speer 300 African GS Tungsten Solid | velocity, fps: | 2609 | 2277 | 1970 | 1690 | |
| | energy, ft-lb: | 4534 | 3453 | 2585 | 1903 | |
| | arc, inches: | | +2.6 | 0 | -11.7 | -35.6 |
| Win. 270 Fail Safe | velocity, fps: | 2670 | 2447 | 2234 | 2033 | 1842 |
| | energy, ft-lb: | 4275 | 3590 | 2994 | 2478 | 2035 |
| | arc, inches: | | +2.2 | 0 | -9.1 | -28.7 |
| Win. 300 Fail Safe | velocity, fps: | 2530 | 2336 | 2151 | 1974 | 1806 |
| | energy, ft-lb: | 4265 | 3636 | 3082 | 2596 | 2173 |
| | arc, inches: | | +2.4 | 0 | -10.0 | -26.9 |

### .375 Dakota

| CARTRIDGE BULLET | | 0 | 100 | 200 | 300 | 400 |
|---|---|---|---|---|---|---|
| Dakota 270 Barnes X | velocity, fps: | 2800 | 2617 | 2441 | 2272 | 2109 |
| | energy, ft-lb: | 4699 | 4104 | 3571 | 3093 | 2666 |
| | arc, inches: | | +2.3 | +1.0 | -6.1 | -19.9 |
| Dakota 300 Barnes X | velocity, fps: | 2600 | 2316 | 2051 | 1804 | 1579 |
| | energy, ft-lb: | 4502 | 3573 | 2800 | 2167 | 1661 |
| | arc, inches: | | +2.4 | -0.1 | -11.0 | -32.7 |

### .375 Weatherby

| CARTRIDGE BULLET | | 0 | 100 | 200 | 300 | 400 |
|---|---|---|---|---|---|---|
| A-Square 300 SP boat-tail | velocity, fps: | 2700 | 2560 | 2425 | 2293 | 2166 |
| | energy, ft-lb: | 4856 | 4366 | 3916 | 3503 | 3125 |
| | arc, inches: | | +4.5 | +5.2 | 0 | -11.9 |
| A-Square 300 Triad | velocity, fps: | 2700 | 2391 | 2103 | 1835 | 1602 |
| | energy, ft-lb: | 4856 | 3808 | 2946 | 2243 | 1710 |
| | arc, inches: | | +2.3 | 0 | -10.1 | -30.8 |
| Wby. 300 Nosler Part. | velocity, fps: | 2800 | 2572 | 2366 | 2140 | 1963 |
| | energy, ft-lb: | 5224 | 4408 | 3696 | 3076 | 2541 |
| | arc, inches: | | +1.9 | 0 | -8.2 | -23.9 |

### .375 JRS

| CARTRIDGE BULLET | | 0 | 100 | 200 | 300 | 400 |
|---|---|---|---|---|---|---|
| A-Square 300 SP boat-tail | velocity, fps: | 2700 | 2560 | 2425 | 2293 | 2166 |
| | energy, ft-lb: | 4856 | 4366 | 3916 | 3503 | 3125 |
| | arc, inches: | | +4.5 | +5.2 | 0 | -11.9 |
| A-Square 300 Triad | velocity, fps: | 2700 | 2391 | 2103 | 1835 | 1602 |
| | energy, ft-lb: | 4856 | 3808 | 2946 | 2243 | 1710 |
| | arc, inches: | | +2.3 | 0 | -10.1 | -30.8 |

### .375 Remington Ultra Mag

| CARTRIDGE BULLET | | 0 | 100 | 200 | 300 | 400 |
|---|---|---|---|---|---|---|
| Rem. 270 Soft Point | velocity, fps: | 2900 | 2558 | 2241 | 1947 | 1678 |
| | energy, fps: | 5041 | 3922 | 3010 | 2272 | 1689 |
| | arc, inches: | | +1.9 | 0 | -9.2 | -27.8 |
| Rem. 300 Swift A-Frame | velocity, fps: | 2760 | 2505 | 2263 | 2035 | 1822 |
| | energy, fps: | 5073 | 4178 | 3412 | 2759 | 2210 |
| | arc, inches: | | +2.0 | 0 | -8.8 | -26.1 |

### .375 A-Square

| CARTRIDGE BULLET | | 0 | 100 | 200 | 300 | 400 |
|---|---|---|---|---|---|---|
| A-Square 300 SP boat-tail | velocity, fps: | 2920 | 2773 | 2631 | 2494 | 2360 |
| | energy, ft-lb: | 5679 | 5123 | 4611 | 4142 | 3710 |
| | arc, inches: | | +3.7 | +4.4 | 0 | -9.8 |
| A-Square 300 Triad | velocity, fps: | 2920 | 2596 | 2294 | 2012 | 1762 |
| | energy, ft-lb: | 5679 | 4488 | 3505 | 2698 | 2068 |
| | arc, inches: | | +1.8 | 0 | -8.5 | -25.5 |

### .378 Weatherby

| CARTRIDGE BULLET | | 0 | 100 | 200 | 300 | 400 |
|---|---|---|---|---|---|---|
| A-Square 300 SP boat-tail | velocity, fps: | 2900 | 2754 | 2612 | 2475 | 2342 |
| | energy, ft-lb: | 5602 | 5051 | 4546 | 4081 | 3655 |
| | arc, inches: | | +3.8 | +4.4 | 0 | -10.0 |
| A-Square 300 Triad | velocity, fps: | 2900 | 2577 | 2276 | 1997 | 1747 |
| | energy, ft-lb: | 5602 | 4424 | 3452 | 2656 | 2034 |
| | arc, inches: | | +1.9 | 0 | -8.7 | -25.9 |
| Wby. 270 Pointed Expanding | velocity, fps: | 3180 | 2921 | 2677 | 2445 | 2225 |
| | energy, ft-lb: | 6062 | 5115 | 4295 | 3583 | 2968 |
| | arc, inches: | | +1.3 | 0 | -6.1 | -18.1 |
| Wby. 270 Barnes X | velocity, fps: | 3150 | 2954 | 2767 | 2587 | 2415 |
| | energy, ft-lb: | 5948 | 5232 | 4589 | 4013 | 3495 |
| | arc, inches: | | +1.2 | 0 | -5.8 | -16.7 |
| Wby. 300 RN Expanding | velocity, fps: | 2925 | 2558 | 2220 | 1908 | 1627 |
| | energy, ft-lb: | 5699 | 4360 | 3283 | 2424 | 1764 |
| | arc, inches: | | +1.9 | 0 | -9.0 | -27.8 |
| Wby. 300 FMJ | velocity, fps: | 2925 | 2591 | 2280 | 1991 | 1725 |
| | energy, ft-lb: | 5699 | 4470 | 3461 | 2640 | 1983 |
| | arc, inches: | | +1.8 | 0 | -8.6 | -26.1 |

### .38-40 Winchester

| CARTRIDGE BULLET | | 0 | 100 | 200 | 300 | 400 |
|---|---|---|---|---|---|---|
| Win. 180 Soft Point | velocity, fps: | 1160 | 999 | 901 | 827 | |
| | energy, ft-lb: | 538 | 399 | 324 | 273 | |
| | arc, inches: | | 0 | -23.4 | -75.2 | |

### .38-55 Winchester

| CARTRIDGE BULLET | | 0 | 100 | 200 | 300 | 400 |
|---|---|---|---|---|---|---|
| Black Hills 255 FN Lead | velocity, fps: | 1250 | | | | |
| | energy, ft-lb: | 925 | | | | |
| | arc, inches: | | | | | |
| Win. 255 Soft Point | velocity, fps: | 1320 | 1190 | 1091 | 1018 | |
| | energy, ft-lb: | 987 | 802 | 674 | 587 | |
| | arc, inches: | | 0 | -33.9 | -110.6 | |

### .41 Magnum

| CARTRIDGE BULLET | | 0 | 100 | 200 | 300 | 400 |
|---|---|---|---|---|---|---|
| Win. 240 Platinum Tip | velocity, fps: | 1830 | 1488 | 1220 | 1048 | |
| | energy, ft-lb: | 1784 | 1180 | 792 | 585 | |
| | arc inches: | | 0 | -15.0 | -53.4 | |

BALLISTICS

| CARTRIDGE BULLET | RANGE, YARDS: | 0 | 100 | 200 | 300 | 400 |
|---|---|---|---|---|---|---|
| **.450/.400 (3")** | | | | | | |
| A-Square 400 Triad | velocity, fps: | 2150 | 1910 | 1690 | 1490 | |
| | energy, ft-lb: | 4105 | 3241 | 2537 | 1972 | |
| | arc, inches: | | +4.4 | 0 | -16.5 | |
| **.450/.400 (3¼")** | | | | | | |
| A-Square 400 Triad | velocity, fps: | 2150 | 1910 | 1690 | 1490 | |
| | energy, ft-lb: | 4105 | 3241 | 2537 | 1972 | |
| | arc, inches: | | +4.4 | 0 | -16.5 | |
| **.404 JEFFERY** | | | | | | |
| A-Square 400 Triad | velocity, fps: | 2150 | 1901 | 1674 | 1468 | 1299 |
| | energy, ft-lb: | 4105 | 3211 | 2489 | 1915 | 1499 |
| | arc, inches: | | +4.1 | 0 | -16.4 | -49.1 |
| **.405 WINCHESTER** | | | | | | |
| Hornady 300 Flatpoint | velocity, fps: | 2200 | 1851 | 1545 | 1296 | |
| | energy, ft-lb: | 3224 | 2282 | 1589 | 1119 | |
| | arc, inches: | | +4.6 | 0 | -19.5 | |
| Hornady 300 SP Interlock | velocity, fps: | 2200 | 1890 | 1610 | 1370 | |
| | energy, ft-lb: | 3224 | 2379 | 1727 | 1250 | |
| | arc, inches: | | 0 | -8.3 | -30.2 | |
| **.416 TAYLOR** | | | | | | |
| A-Square 400 Triad | velocity, fps: | 2350 | 2093 | 1853 | 1634 | 1443 |
| | energy, ft-lb: | 4905 | 3892 | 3049 | 2371 | 1849 |
| | arc, inches: | | +3.2 | 0 | -13.6 | -39.8 |
| **.416 HOFFMAN** | | | | | | |
| A-Square 400 Triad | velocity, fps: | 2380 | 2122 | 1879 | 1658 | 1464 |
| | energy, ft-lb: | 5031 | 3998 | 3136 | 2440 | 1903 |
| | arc, inches: | | +3.1 | 0 | -13.1 | -38.7 |
| **.416 REMINGTON MAGNUM** | | | | | | |
| A-Square 400 Triad | velocity, fps: | 2380 | 2122 | 1879 | 1658 | 1464 |
| | energy, ft-lb: | 5031 | 3998 | 3136 | 2440 | 1903 |
| | arc, inches: | | +3.1 | 0 | -13.2 | -38.7 |
| Federal 400 Trophy Bonded Sledgehammer Solid | velocity, fps: | 2400 | 2150 | 1920 | 1700 | 1500 |
| | energy, ft-lb: | 5115 | 4110 | 3260 | 2565 | 2005 |
| | arc, inches: | | 0 | -6.0 | -21.6 | -49.2 |
| Federal 400 Trophy Bonded | velocity, fps: | 2400 | 2180 | 1970 | 1770 | 1590 |
| | energy, ft-lb: | 5115 | 4215 | 3440 | 2785 | 2245 |
| | arc, inches: | | 0 | -5.8 | -20.6 | -46.9 |
| Rem. 400 Swift A-Frame | velocity, fps: | 2400 | 2175 | 1962 | 1763 | 1579 |
| | energy, ft-lb: | 5115 | 4201 | 3419 | 2760 | 2214 |
| | arc, inches: | | +1.3 | -3.3 | -17.0 | -41.9 |
| **.416 RIGBY** | | | | | | |
| A-Square 400 Triad | velocity, fps: | 2400 | 2140 | 1897 | 1673 | 1478 |
| | energy, ft-lb: | 5115 | 4069 | 3194 | 2487 | 1940 |
| | arc, inches: | | +3.0 | 0 | -12.9 | -38.0 |
| Federal 400 Trophy Bonded | velocity, fps: | 2370 | 2150 | 1940 | 1750 | 1570 |
| | energy, ft-lb: | 4990 | 4110 | 3350 | 2715 | 2190 |
| | arc, inches: | | 0 | -6.0 | -21.3 | -48.1 |
| Federal 400 Trophy Bonded Sledgehammer Solid | velocity, fps: | 2370 | 2120 | 1890 | 1660 | 1460 |
| | energy, ft-lb: | 4990 | 3975 | 3130 | 2440 | 1895 |
| | arc, inches: | | 0 | -6.3 | -22.5 | -51.5 |
| Federal 410 Woodleigh Weldcore | velocity, fps: | 2370 | 2110 | 1870 | 1640 | 1440 |
| | energy, ft-lb: | 5115 | 4050 | 3165 | 2455 | 1895 |
| | arc, inches: | | 0 | -7.4 | -24.8 | -55.0 |
| Federal 410 Solid | velocity, fps: | 2370 | 2110 | 2870 | 1640 | 1440 |
| | energy, ft-lb: | 5115 | 4050 | 3165 | 2455 | 1895 |
| | arc, inches: | | 0 | -7.4 | -24.8 | -55.0 |
| Norma 400 TXP Swift A-Fr. | velocity, fps: | 2350 | 2127 | 1917 | 1721 | |
| | energy, ft-lb: | 4906 | 4021 | 3266 | 2632 | |
| | arc, inches: | | +3.1 | 0 | -12.5 | |
| Norma 400 Barnes Solid | velocity, fps: | 2297 | 1930 | 1604 | 1330 | |
| | energy, ft-lb: | 4687 | 3310 | 2284 | 1571 | |
| | arc, inches: | | +3.9 | 0 | -17.7 | |
| **.416 RIMMED** | | | | | | |
| A-Square 400 Triad | velocity, fps: | 2400 | 2140 | 1897 | 1673 | |
| | energy, ft-lb: | 5115 | 4069 | 3194 | 2487 | |
| | arc, inches: | | +3.3 | 0 | -13.2 | |
| **.416 DAKOTA** | | | | | | |
| Dakota 400 Barnes X | velocity, fps: | 2450 | 2294 | 2143 | 1998 | 1859 |
| | energy, ft-lb: | 5330 | 4671 | 4077 | 3544 | 3068 |
| | arc, inches: | | +2.5 | -0.2 | -10.5 | -29.4 |
| **.416 WEATHERBY** | | | | | | |
| A-Square 400 Triad | velocity, fps: | 2600 | 2328 | 2073 | 1834 | 1624 |
| | energy, ft-lb: | 6004 | 4813 | 3816 | 2986 | 2343 |
| | arc, inches: | | +2.5 | 0 | -10.5 | -31.6 |
| Wby. 350 Barnes X | velocity, fps: | 2850 | 2673 | 2503 | 2340 | 2182 |
| | energy, ft-lb: | 6312 | 5553 | 4870 | 4253 | 3700 |
| | arc, inches: | | +1.7 | 0 | -7.2 | -20.9 |
| Wby. 400 Swift A-Fr. | velocity, fps: | 2650 | 2426 | 2213 | 2011 | 1820 |
| | energy, ft-lb: | 6237 | 5227 | 4350 | 3592 | 2941 |
| | arc, inches: | | +2.2 | 0 | -9.3 | -27.1 |
| Wby. 400 RN Expanding | velocity, fps: | 2700 | 2417 | 2152 | 1903 | 1676 |
| | energy, ft-lb: | 6474 | 5189 | 4113 | 3216 | 2493 |
| | arc, inches: | | +2.3 | 0 | -9.7 | -29.3 |
| Wby. 400 Monolithic Solid | velocity, fps: | 2700 | 2411 | 2140 | 1887 | 1656 |
| | energy, ft-lb: | 6474 | 5162 | 4068 | 3161 | 2435 |
| | arc, inches: | | +2.3 | 0 | -9.8 | -29.7 |
| **10.57 (.416) METEOR** | | | | | | |
| Lazzeroni 400 Swift A-Fr. | velocity, fps: | 2730 | 2532 | 2342 | 2161 | 1987 |
| | energy, ft-lb: | 6621 | 5695 | 4874 | 4147 | 3508 |
| | arc, inches: | | +1.9 | 0 | -8.3 | -24.0 |
| **.425 EXPRESS** | | | | | | |
| A-Square 400 Triad | velocity, fps: | 2400 | 2136 | 1888 | 1662 | 1465 |
| | energy, ft-lb: | 5115 | 4052 | 3167 | 2454 | 1906 |
| | arc, inches: | | +3.0 | 0 | -13.1 | -38.3 |
| **.44-40 WINCHESTER** | | | | | | |
| Rem. 200 Soft Point | velocity, fps: | 1190 | 1006 | 900 | 822 | 756 |
| | energy, ft-lb: | 629 | 449 | 360 | 300 | 254 |
| | arc, inches: | | 0 | -33.1 | -108.7 | -235.2 |
| Win. 200 Soft Point | velocity, fps: | 1190 | 1006 | 900 | 822 | 756 |
| | energy, ft-lb: | 629 | 449 | 360 | 300 | 254 |
| | arc, inches: | | 0 | -33.3 | -109.5 | -237.4 |
| **.44 REMINGTON MAGNUM** | | | | | | |
| Federal 240 Hi-Shok HP | velocity, fps: | 1760 | 1380 | 1090 | 950 | 860 |
| | energy, ft-lb: | 1650 | 1015 | 640 | 485 | 395 |
| | arc, inches: | | 0 | -17.4 | -60.7 | -136.0 |
| Rem. 210 Semi-Jacketed HP | velocity, fps: | 1920 | 1477 | 1155 | 982 | 880 |
| | energy, ft-lb: | 1719 | 1017 | 622 | 450 | 361 |
| | arc, inches: | | 0 | -14.7 | -55.5 | -131.3 |
| Rem. 240 Soft Point | velocity, fps: | 1760 | 1380 | 1114 | 970 | 878 |
| | energy, ft-lb: | 1650 | 1015 | 661 | 501 | 411 |
| | arc, inches: | | 0 | -17.0 | -61.4 | -143.0 |

# Centerfire Rifle Ballistics

## .44 REMINGTON MAGNUM TO .450 DAKOTA

| CARTRIDGE BULLET | RANGE, YARDS: | 0 | 100 | 200 | 300 | 400 |
|---|---|---|---|---|---|---|
| Rem. 240 Semi-Jacketed | velocity, fps: | 1760 | 1380 | 1114 | 970 | 878 |
| Hollow Point | energy, ft-lb: | 1650 | 1015 | 661 | 501 | 411 |
| | arc, inches: | | 0 | -17.0 | -61.4 | -143.0 |
| Rem. 275 JHP Core-Lokt | velocity, fps: | 1580 | 1293 | 1093 | 976 | 896 |
| | energy, ft-lb: | 1524 | 1020 | 730 | 582 | 490 |
| | arc, inches: | | 0 | -19.4 | -67.5 | -210.8 |
| Win. 210 Silvertip HP | velocity, fps: | 1580 | 1198 | 993 | 879 | 795 |
| | energy, ft-lb: | 1164 | 670 | 460 | 361 | 295 |
| | arc, inches: | | 0 | -22.4 | -76.1 | -168.0 |
| Win. 240 Hollow Soft Point | velocity, fps: | 1760 | 1362 | 1094 | 953 | 861 |
| | energy, ft-lb: | 1650 | 988 | 638 | 484 | 395 |
| | arc, inches: | | 0 | -18.1 | -65.1 | -150.3 |
| Win. 250 Platinum Tip | velocity, fps: | 1830 | 1475 | 1201 | 1032 | 931 |
| | energy, ft-lb: | 1859 | 1208 | 801 | 591 | 481 |
| | arc, inches: | | 0 | -15.3 | -54.7 | -126.6 |

### .444 MARLIN

| | | 0 | 100 | 200 | 300 | 400 |
|---|---|---|---|---|---|---|
| Rem. 240 Soft Point | velocity, fps: | 2350 | 1815 | 1377 | 1087 | 941 |
| | energy, ft-lb: | 2942 | 1755 | 1010 | 630 | 472 |
| | arc, inches: | | +2.2 | -5.4 | -31.4 | -86.7 |
| Hornady 265 FP LM | velocity, fps: | 2335 | 1913 | 1551 | 1266 | |
| | energy, ft-lb: | 3208 | 2153 | 1415 | 943 | |
| | arc, inches: | | +2.0 | -4.9 | -26.5 | |

### .45-70 GOVERNMENT

| | | 0 | 100 | 200 | 300 | 400 |
|---|---|---|---|---|---|---|
| Black Hills 405 FPL | velocity, fps: | 1250 | | | | |
| Federal 300 Sierra Pro-Hunt. | velocity, fps: | 1880 | 1650 | 1430 | 1240 | 1110 |
| HP FN | energy, ft-lb: | 2355 | 1815 | 1355 | 1015 | 810 |
| | arc, inches: | | 0 | -11.5 | -39.7 | -89.1 |
| PMC 350 FNSP | velocity, fps: | | | | | |
| Rem. 300 Jacketed HP | velocity, fps: | 1810 | 1497 | 1244 | 1073 | 969 |
| | energy, ft-lb: | 2182 | 1492 | 1031 | 767 | 625 |
| | arc, inches: | | 0 | -13.8 | -50.1 | -115.7 |
| Rem. 405 Soft Point | velocity, fps: | 1330 | 1168 | 1055 | 977 | 918 |
| | energy, ft-lb: | 1590 | 1227 | 1001 | 858 | 758 |
| | arc, inches: | | 0 | -24.0 | -78.6 | -169.4 |
| Win. 300 Jacketed HP | velocity, fps: | 1880 | 1650 | 1425 | 1235 | 1105 |
| | energy, ft-lb: | 2355 | 1815 | 1355 | 1015 | 810 |
| | arc, inches: | | 0 | -12.8 | -44.3 | -95.5 |
| Win. 300 Partition Gold | velocity, fps: | 1880 | 1558 | 1292 | 1103 | 988 |
| | energy, ft-lb: | 2355 | 1616 | 1112 | 811 | 651 |
| | arc, inches: | | 0 | -12.9 | -46.0 | -104.9 |

### .450 NITRO EXPRESS (3¼")

| | | 0 | 100 | 200 | 300 | 400 |
|---|---|---|---|---|---|---|
| A-Square 465 Triad | velocity, fps: | 2190 | 1970 | 1765 | 1577 | |
| | energy, ft-lb: | 4952 | 4009 | 3216 | 2567 | |
| | arc, inches: | | +4.3 | 0 | -15.4 | |

### .450 #2

| | | 0 | 100 | 200 | 300 | 400 |
|---|---|---|---|---|---|---|
| A-Square 465 Triad | velocity, fps: | 2190 | 1970 | 1765 | 1577 | |
| | energy, ft-lb: | 4952 | 4009 | 3216 | 2567 | |
| | arc, inches: | | +4.3 | 0 | -15.4 | |

### .458 WINCHESTER MAGNUM

| | | 0 | 100 | 200 | 300 | 400 |
|---|---|---|---|---|---|---|
| A-Square 465 Triad | velocity, fps: | 2220 | 1999 | 1791 | 1601 | 1433 |
| | energy, ft-lb: | 5088 | 4127 | 3312 | 2646 | 2121 |
| | arc, inches: | | +3.6 | 0 | -14.7 | -42.5 |
| Federal 350 Soft Point | velocity, fps: | 2470 | 1990 | 1570 | 1250 | 1060 |
| | energy, ft-lb: | 4740 | 3065 | 1915 | 1205 | 870 |
| | arc, inches: | | 0 | -7.5 | -29.1 | -71.1 |

| | | 0 | 100 | 200 | 300 | 400 |
|---|---|---|---|---|---|---|
| Federal 400 Trophy Bonded | velocity, fps: | 2380 | 2170 | 1960 | 1770 | 1590 |
| | energy, ft-lb: | 5030 | 4165 | 3415 | 2785 | 2255 |
| | arc, inches: | | 0 | -5.9 | -20.9 | -47.1 |
| Federal 500 Solid | velocity, fps: | 2090 | 1870 | 1670 | 1480 | 1320 |
| | energy, ft-lb: | 4850 | 3880 | 3085 | 2440 | 1945 |
| | arc, inches: | | 0 | -8.5 | -29.5 | -66.2 |
| Federal 500 Trophy Bonded | velocity, fps: | 2090 | 1870 | 1660 | 1480 | 1310 |
| | energy, ft-lb: | 4850 | 3870 | 3065 | 2420 | 1915 |
| | arc, inches: | | 0 | -8.5 | -29.7 | -66.8 |
| Federal 500 Trophy Bonded | velocity, fps: | 2090 | 1860 | 1650 | 1460 | 1300 |
| Sledgehammer Solid | energy, ft-lb: | 4850 | 3845 | 3025 | 2365 | 1865 |
| | arc, inches: | | 0 | -8.6 | -30.0 | -67.8 |
| Federal 510 Soft Point | velocity, fps: | 2090 | 1820 | 1570 | 1360 | 1190 |
| | energy, ft-lb: | 4945 | 3730 | 2790 | 2080 | 1605 |
| | arc, inches: | | 0 | -9.1 | -32.3 | -73.9 |
| Hornady 500 FMJ-RN HM | velocity, fps: | 2260 | 1984 | 1735 | 1512 | |
| | energy, ft-lb: | 5670 | 4368 | 3341 | 2538 | |
| | arc, inches: | | 0 | -7.4 | -26.4 | |
| Norma 500 TXP Swift A-Fr. | velocity, fps: | 2116 | 1903 | 1705 | 1524 | |
| | energy, ft-lb: | 4972 | 4023 | 3228 | 2578 | |
| | arc, inches: | | +4.1 | 0 | -16.1 | |
| Norma 500 Barnes Solid | velocity, fps: | 2067 | 1750 | 1472 | 1245 | |
| | energy, ft-lb: | 4745 | 3401 | 2405 | 1721 | |
| | arc, inches: | | +4.9 | 0 | -21.2 | |
| Rem. 450 Swift A-Frame | velocity, fps: | 2150 | 1901 | 1671 | 1465 | 1289 |
| PSP | energy, ft-lb: | 4618 | 3609 | 2789 | 2144 | 1659 |
| | arc, inches: | | 0 | -8.2 | -28.9 | |
| Speer 500 African GS | velocity, fps: | 2120 | 1845 | 1596 | 1379 | |
| Tungsten Solid | energy, ft-lb: | 4989 | 3780 | 2828 | 2111 | |
| | arc, inches: | | 0 | -8.8 | -31.3 | |
| Speer African Grand Slam | velocity, fps: | 2120 | 1853 | 1609 | 1396 | |
| | energy, ft-lb: | 4989 | 3810 | 2875 | 2163 | |
| | arc, inches: | | 0 | -8.7 | -30.8 | |
| Win. 510 Soft Point | velocity, fps: | 2040 | 1770 | 1527 | 1319 | 1157 |
| | energy, ft-lb: | 4712 | 3547 | 2640 | 1970 | 1516 |
| | arc, inches: | | 0 | -10.3 | -35.6 | |

### .458 LOTT

| | | 0 | 100 | 200 | 300 | 400 |
|---|---|---|---|---|---|---|
| A-Square 465 Triad | velocity, fps: | 2380 | 2150 | 1932 | 1730 | 1551 |
| | energy, ft-lb: | 5848 | 4773 | 3855 | 3091 | 2485 |
| | arc, inches: | | +3.0 | 0 | -12.5 | -36.4 |
| Hornady 500 RNSP or solid | velocity, fps: | 2300 | 2022 | 1776 | 1551 | |
| | energy, ft-lb: | 5872 | 4537 | 3502 | 2671 | |
| | arc, inches: | | +3.4 | 0 | -1.43 | |

### .450 ACKLEY

| | | 0 | 100 | 200 | 300 | 400 |
|---|---|---|---|---|---|---|
| A-Square 465 Triad | velocity, fps: | 2400 | 2169 | 1950 | 1747 | 1567 |
| | energy, ft-lb: | 5947 | 4857 | 3927 | 3150 | 2534 |
| | arc, inches: | | +2.9 | 0 | -12.2 | -35.8 |

### .460 SHORT A-SQUARE

| | | 0 | 100 | 200 | 300 | 400 |
|---|---|---|---|---|---|---|
| A-Square 500 Triad | velocity, fps: | 2420 | 2198 | 1987 | 1789 | 1613 |
| | energy, ft-lb: | 6501 | 5362 | 4385 | 3553 | 2890 |
| | arc, inches: | | +2.9 | 0 | -11.6 | -34.2 |

### .450 DAKOTA

| | | 0 | 100 | 200 | 300 | 400 |
|---|---|---|---|---|---|---|
| Dakota 500 Barnes Solid | velocity, fps: | 2450 | 2235 | 2030 | 1838 | 1658 |
| | energy, ft-lb: | 6663 | 5544 | 4576 | 3748 | 3051 |
| | arc, inches: | | +2.5 | -0.6 | -12.0 | -33.8 |

| CARTRIDGE BULLET | RANGE, YARDS: | 0 | 100 | 200 | 300 | 400 |
|---|---|---|---|---|---|---|
| **.460 Weatherby Magnum** | | | | | | |
| A-Square 500 Triad | velocity, fps: | 2580 | 2349 | 2131 | 1923 | 1737 |
| | energy, ft-lb: | 7389 | 6126 | 5040 | 4107 | 3351 |
| | arc, inches: | | +2.4 | 0 | -10.0 | -29.4 |
| Wby. 450 Barnes X | velocity, fps: | 2700 | 2518 | 2343 | 2175 | 2013 |
| | energy, ft-lb: | 7284 | 6333 | 5482 | 4725 | 4050 |
| | arc, inches: | | +2.0 | 0 | -8.4 | -24.1 |
| Wby. 500 RN Expanding | velocity, fps: | 2600 | 2301 | 2022 | 1764 | 1533 |
| | energy, ft-lb: | 7504 | 5877 | 4539 | 3456 | 2608 |
| | arc, inches: | | +2.6 | 0 | -11.1 | -33.5 |
| Wby. 500 FMJ | velocity, fps: | 2600 | 2309 | 2037 | 1784 | 1557 |
| | energy, ft-lb: | 7504 | 5917 | 4605 | 3534 | 2690 |
| | arc, inches: | | +2.5 | 0 | -10.9 | -33.0 |
| **.500/.465** | | | | | | |
| A-Square 480 Triad | velocity, fps: | 2150 | 1928 | 1722 | 1533 | |
| | energy, ft-lb: | 4926 | 3960 | 3160 | 2505 | |
| | arc, inches: | | +4.3 | 0 | -16.0 | |
| **.470 Nitro Express** | | | | | | |
| A-Square 500 Triad | velocity, fps: | 2150 | 1912 | 1693 | 1494 | |
| | energy, ft-lb: | 5132 | 4058 | 3182 | 2478 | |
| | arc, inches: | | +4.4 | 0 | -16.5 | |
| Federal 500 Woodleigh Weldcore | velocity, fps: | 2150 | 1890 | 1650 | 1440 | 1270 |
| | energy, ft-lb: | 5130 | 3965 | 3040 | 2310 | 1790 |
| | arc, inches: | | 0 | -9.3 | -31.3 | -69.7 |
| Federal 500 Woodleigh Weldcore Solid | velocity, fps: | 2150 | 1890 | 1650 | 1440 | 1270 |
| | energy, ft-lb: | 5130 | 3965 | 3040 | 2310 | 1790 |
| | arc, inches: | | 0 | -9.3 | -31.3 | -69.7 |
| Federal 500 Trophy Bonded | velocity, fps: | 2150 | 1940 | 1740 | 1560 | 1400 |
| | energy, ft-lb: | 5130 | 4170 | 3360 | 2695 | 2160 |
| | arc, inches: | | 0 | -7.8 | -27.1 | -60.8 |
| Federal 500 Trophy Bonded Sledgehammer Solid | velocity, fps: | 2150 | 1940 | 1740 | 1560 | 1400 |
| | ft-lb: | 5130 | 4170 | 3360 | 2695 | 2160 |
| | arc, inches: | | 0 | -7.8 | -27.1 | -60.8 |
| **.470 Capstick** | | | | | | |
| A-Square 500 Triad | velocity, fps: | 2400 | 2172 | 1958 | 1761 | 1553 |
| | energy, ft-lb: | 6394 | 5236 | 4255 | 3445 | 2678 |
| | arc, inches: | | +2.9 | 0 | -11.9 | -36.1 |
| **475 #2** | | | | | | |
| A-Square 480 Triad | velocity, fps: | 2200 | 1964 | 1744 | 1544 | |
| | energy, ft-lb: | 5158 | 4109 | 3240 | 2539 | |
| | arc, inches: | | +4.1 | 0 | -15.6 | |
| **.475 #2 Jeffery** | | | | | | |
| A-Square 500 Triad | velocity, fps: | 2200 | 1966 | 1748 | 1550 | |
| | energy, ft-lb: | 5373 | 4291 | 3392 | 2666 | |
| | arc, inches: | | +4.1 | 0 | -15.6 | |
| **.495 A-Square** | | | | | | |
| A-Square 570 Triad | velocity, fps: | 2350 | 2117 | 1896 | 1693 | 1513 |
| | energy, ft-lb: | 6989 | 5671 | 4552 | 3629 | 2899 |
| | arc, inches: | | +3.1 | 0 | -13.0 | -37.8 |
| **.500 Nitro Express (3")** | | | | | | |
| A-Square 570 Triad | velocity, fps: | 2150 | 1928 | 1722 | 1533 | |
| | energy, ft-lb: | 5850 | 4703 | 3752 | 2975 | |
| | arc, inches: | | +4.3 | 0 | -16.1 | |
| **.500 A-Square** | | | | | | |
| A-Square 600 Triad | velocity, fps: | 2470 | 2235 | 2013 | 1804 | 1620 |
| | energy, ft-lb: | 8127 | 6654 | 5397 | 4336 | 3495 |
| | arc, inches: | | +2.7 | 0 | -11.3 | -33.5 |
| **.505 Gibbs** | | | | | | |
| A-Square 525 Triad | velocity, fps: | 2300 | 2063 | 1840 | 1637 | |
| | energy, ft-lb: | 6166 | 4962 | 3948 | 3122 | |
| | arc, inches: | | +3.6 | 0 | -14.2 | |
| **.577 Nitro Express** | | | | | | |
| A-Square 750 Triad | velocity, fps: | 2050 | 1811 | 1595 | 1401 | |
| | energy, ft-lb: | 6998 | 5463 | 4234 | 3267 | |
| | arc, inches: | | +4.9 | 0 | -18.5 | |
| **.577 Tyrannosaur** | | | | | | |
| A-Square 750 Triad | velocity, fps: | 2460 | 2197 | 1950 | 1723 | 1516 |
| | energy, ft-lb: | 10077 | 8039 | 6335 | 4941 | 3825 |
| | arc, inches: | | +2.8 | 0 | -12.1 | -36.0 |
| **.600 Nitro Express** | | | | | | |
| A-Square 900 Triad | velocity, fps: | 1950 | 1680 | 1452 | 1336 | |
| | energy, ft-lb: | 7596 | 5634 | 4212 | 3564 | |
| | arc, inches: | | +5.6 | 0 | -20.7 | |
| **.700 Nitro Express** | | | | | | |
| A-Square 1000 Monolithic Solid | velocity, fps: | 1900 | 1669 | 1461 | 1288 | |
| | energy, ft-lb: | 8015 | 6188 | 4740 | 3685 | |
| | arc, inches: | | +5.8 | 0 | -22.2 | |

# Centerfire Handgun Ballistics

## Centerfire Handgun Ballistics

Defense, targets, hunting - whatever you buy a handgun for, you'll find ballistics for the most useful factory loads in these tables. From the little .25 auto to the wrist-wrenching .475 Linebaugh you'll see just how modern handgun loads perform Data shown here is taken from manufacturers' charts; your chronograph readings may vary. Barrel lengths for pistol data vary, and depend in part on which pistols are typically chambered in a given cartridge. Velocity variations due to barrel length depend on the baseline bullet speed and the load. Velocity for the .30 Carbine, normally a rifle cartridge, was determined in a pistol barrel.

Listings are current as of February the year Shooter's Bible appears (not the cover year).

Listings are not intended as recommendations. For example, the data for the .25 Auto gives velocity and energy readings to 100 yards. Few handgunners would call the little .25 a 100-yard cartridge.

Abbreviations: Bullets are designated by loading company, weight (in grains) and type, with these abbreviations for shape and construction: BJHP=brass-jacketed hollowpoint; FN=Flat Nose; FMC=Full Metal Case; FMJ=Full Metal Jacket; HP=Hollowpoint; L=Lead; LF=Lead-Free; +P=a more powerful load than traditionally manufactured for that round; RN=Round Nose; SFHP=Starfire (PMC) Hollowpoint; SP=Softpoint; SWC=Semi Wadcutter; TMJ=Total Metal Jacket; WC=Wadcutter; CEPP, SXT and XTP are trademarked designations of Lapua, Winchester and Hornady, respectively.

### .25 AUTO TO .32 S&W LONG

| CARTRIDGE BULLET | RANGE, YARDS: | 0 | 25 | 50 | 75 | 100 |
|---|---|---|---|---|---|---|
| **.25 AUTO** | | | | | | |
| Federal 50 FMJ | velocity, fps: | 760 | 750 | 730 | 720 | 700 |
| | energy, ft-lb: | 65 | 60 | 60 | 55 | 55 |
| Hornady 35 JHP/XTP | velocity, fps: | 900 | | 813 | | 742 |
| | energy, ft-lb: | 63 | | 51 | | 43 |
| Magtech 50 FMC | velocity, fps: | 760 | | 707 | | 659 |
| | energy, ft-lb: | 64 | | 56 | | 48 |
| PMC 50 FMJ | velocity, fps: | 754 | 730 | 707 | 685 | 663 |
| | energy, ft-lb: | 62 | | | | |
| Rem. 50 Metal Case | velocity, fps: | 760 | | 707 | | 659 |
| | energy, ft-lb: | 64 | | 56 | | 48 |
| Speer 35 Gold Dot | velocity, fps: | 900 | | 816 | | 747 |
| | energy, ft-lb: | 63 | | 52 | | 43 |
| Speer 50 TMJ (and Blazer) | velocity, fps: | 760 | | 717 | | 677 |
| | energy, ft-lb: | 64 | | 57 | | 51 |
| Win. 45 Expanding Point | velocity, fps: | 815 | | 729 | | 655 |
| | energy, ft-lb | 66 | | 53 | | 42 |
| Win. 50 FMJ | velocity, fps: | 760 | | 707 | | |
| | energy, ft-lb | 64 | | 56 | | |
| **.30 LUGER** | | | | | | |
| Win. 93 FMJ | velocity, fps: | 1220 | | 1110 | | 1040 |
| | energy, ft-lb | 305 | | 255 | | 225 |
| **7.62x25 TOKAREV** | | | | | | |
| PMC 93 FMJ | velocity and energy figures not available | | | | | |
| **.30 CARBINE** | | | | | | |
| Win. 110 Hollow SP | velocity, fps: | 1790 | | 1601 | | 1430 |
| | energy, ft-lb | 783 | | 626 | | 500 |
| **.32 AUTO** | | | | | | |
| Federal 65 Hydra-Shok JHP | velocity, fps: | 950 | 920 | 890 | 860 | 830 |
| | energy, ft-lb: | 130 | 120 | 115 | 105 | 100 |
| Federal 71 FMJ | velocity, fps: | 910 | 880 | 860 | 830 | 810 |
| | energy, ft-lb: | 130 | 120 | 115 | 110 | 105 |
| Hornady 60 JHP/XTP | velocity, fps: | 1000 | | 917 | | 849 |
| | energy, ft-lb: | 133 | | 112 | | 96 |
| Hornady 71 FMJ-RN | velocity, fps: | 900 | | 845 | | 797 |

| CARTRIDGE BULLET | RANGE, YARDS: | 0 | 25 | 50 | 75 | 100 |
|---|---|---|---|---|---|---|
| | energy, ft-lb: | 128 | | 112 | | 100 |
| Magtech 71 FMC | velocity, fps: | 905 | | 855 | | 810 |
| | energy, ft-lb: | 129 | | 115 | | 103 |
| Magtech 71 JHP | velocity, fps: | 905 | | 855 | | 810 |
| | energy, ft-lb: | 129 | | 115 | | 103 |
| PMC 60 JHP | velocity, fps: | 980 | 849 | 820 | 791 | 763 |
| | energy, ft-lb: | 117 | | | | |
| PMC 71 FMJ | velocity, fps: | 870 | 841 | 814 | 791 | 763 |
| | energy, ft-lb: | 119 | | | | |
| Rem. 71 Metal Case | velocity, fps: | 905 | | 855 | | 810 |
| | energy, ft-lb: | 129 | | 115 | | 97 |
| Speer 60 Gold Dot | velocity, fps: | 960 | | 868 | | 796 |
| | energy, ft-lb: | 123 | | 100 | | 84 |
| Speer 71 TMJ (and Blazer) | velocity, fps: | 900 | | 855 | | 810 |
| | energy, ft-lb: | 129 | | 115 | | 97 |
| Win. 60 Silvertip HP | velocity, fps: | 970 | | 895 | | 835 |
| | energy, ft-lb | 125 | | 107 | | 93 |
| Win. 71 FMJ | velocity, fps: | 905 | | 855 | | |
| | energy, ft-lb | 129 | | 115 | | |
| **.32 S&W** | | | | | | |
| Rem. 88 LRN | velocity, fps: | 680 | | 645 | | 610 |
| | energy, ft-lb: | 90 | | 81 | | 73 |
| Win. 85 LRN | velocity, fps: | 680 | | 645 | | 610 |
| | energy, ft-lb | 90 | | 81 | | 73 |
| **.32 S&W LONG** | | | | | | |
| Federal 98 LWC | velocity, fps: | 780 | 700 | 630 | 560 | 500 |
| | energy, ft-lb: | 130 | 105 | 85 | 70 | 55 |
| Federal 98 LRN | velocity, fps: | 710 | 690 | 670 | 650 | 640 |
| | energy, ft-lb: | 115 | 105 | 100 | 95 | 90 |
| Lapua 83 LWC | velocity, fps: | 240 | | 189 | | 149 |
| | energy, ft-lb: | 154 | | 95 | | 59 |
| Lapua 98 LWC | velocity, fps: | 240 | | 202 | | 171 |
| | energy, ft-lb: | 183 | | 130 | | 93 |
| Magtech 98 LRN | velocity, fps: | 705 | | 670 | | 635 |
| | energy, ft-lb: | 108 | | 98 | | 88 |
| Magtech 98 LWC | velocity, fps: | 682 | | 579 | | 491 |

# Centerfire Handgun Ballistics

### .32 S&W Long to 9mm Luger

| CARTRIDGE BULLET | RANGE, YARDS: | 0 | 25 | 50 | 75 | 100 |
|---|---|---|---|---|---|---|
| | energy, ft-lb: | 102 | | 73 | | 52 |
| Norma 98 LWC | velocity, fps: | 787 | 759 | 732 | | 683 |
| | energy, ft-lb: | 136 | 126 | 118 | | 102 |
| PMC 98 LRN | velocity, fps: | 789 | 770 | 751 | 733 | 716 |
| | energy, ft-lb: | 135 | | | | |
| PMC 100 LWC | velocity, fps: | 683 | 652 | 623 | 595 | 569 |
| | energy, ft-lb: | 102 | | | | |
| Rem. 98 LRN | velocity, fps: | 705 | | 670 | | 635 |
| | energy, ft-lb: | 115 | | 98 | | 88 |
| Win. 98 LRN | velocity, fps: | 705 | | 670 | | 635 |
| | | 115 | | 98 | | 88 |

## .32 SHORT COLT

| CARTRIDGE BULLET | RANGE, YARDS: | 0 | 25 | 50 | 75 | 100 |
|---|---|---|---|---|---|---|
| Win. 80 LRN | velocity, fps: | 745 | | 665 | | 590 |
| | energy, ft-lb | 100 | | 79 | | 62 |

## .32-20

| CARTRIDGE BULLET | RANGE, YARDS: | 0 | 25 | 50 | 75 | 100 |
|---|---|---|---|---|---|---|
| Black Hills 115 FPL | velocity, fps: | 800 | | | | |
| | energy, ft-lb: | | | | | |

## .32 H&R MAGNUM

| CARTRIDGE BULLET | RANGE, YARDS: | 0 | 25 | 50 | 75 | 100 |
|---|---|---|---|---|---|---|
| Black Hills 85 JHP | velocity, fps | 1100 | | | | |
| | energy, ft-lb | 228 | | | | |
| Black Hills 90 FPL | velocity, fps | 750 | | | | |
| | energy, ft-lb | | | | | |
| Black Hills 115 FPL | velocity, fps | 800 | | | | |
| | energy, ft-lb | | | | | |
| Federal 85 Hi-Shok JHP | velocity, fps: | 1100 | 1050 | 1020 | 970 | 930 |
| | energy, ft-lb: | 230 | 210 | 195 | 175 | 165 |
| Federal 95 LSWC | velocity, fps: | 1030 | 1000 | 940 | 930 | 900 |
| | energy, ft-lb: | 225 | 210 | 195 | 185 | 170 |

## 9MM MAKAROV

| CARTRIDGE BULLET | RANGE, YARDS: | 0 | 25 | 50 | 75 | 100 |
|---|---|---|---|---|---|---|
| Federal 90 Hi-Shok JHP | velocity, fps: | 990 | 950 | 910 | 880 | 850 |
| | energy, ft-lb: | 195 | 180 | 165 | 155 | 145 |
| Federal 90 FMJ | velocity, fps: | 990 | 960 | 920 | 900 | 870 |
| | energy, ft-lb: | 205 | 190 | 180 | 170 | 160 |
| Hornady 95 JHP/XTP | velocity, fps: | 1000 | | 930 | | 874 |
| | energy, ft-lb: | 211 | | 182 | | 161 |
| PMC 100 FMJ-TC | velocity and energy figures not available | | | | | |
| Speer 95 TMJ Blazer | velocity, fps: | 1000 | | 928 | | 872 |
| | energy, ft-lb: | 211 | | 182 | | 161 |

## 9MM LUGER

| CARTRIDGE BULLET | RANGE, YARDS: | 0 | 25 | 50 | 75 | 100 |
|---|---|---|---|---|---|---|
| Black Hills 115 JHP +P | velocity, fps: | 1300 | | | | |
| | energy, ft-lb: | 431 | | | | |
| Black Hills 115 FMJ | velocity, fps: | 1150 | | | | |
| | energy, ft-lb: | 336 | | | | |
| Black Hills 115 EXP JHP | velocity, fps: | 1250 | | | | |
| | energy, ft-lb: | 400 | | | | |
| Black Hills 124 JHP +P | velocity, fps: | 1250 | | | | |
| | energy, ft-lb: | 430 | | | | |
| Black Hills 124 JHP | velocity, fps: | 1150 | | | | |
| | energy, ft-lb: | 363 | | | | |
| Black Hills 147 JHP subsonic | velocity, fps: | 975 | | | | |
| | energy, ft-lb: | 309 | | | | |
| Black Hills 147 FMJ subsonic | velocity, fps: | 975 | | | | |
| | energy, ft-lb: | 309 | | | | |
| Federal 105 EFMJ | velocity, fps: | 1225 | 1160 | 1105 | 1060 | 1025 |
| | energy, ft-lb: | 350 | 315 | 285 | 265 | 245 |

| CARTRIDGE BULLET | | 0 | 25 | 50 | 75 | 100 |
|---|---|---|---|---|---|---|
| Federal 115 Hi-Shok JHP | velocity, fps: | 1160 | 1100 | 1060 | 1020 | 990 |
| | energy, ft-lb: | 345 | 310 | 285 | 270 | 250 |
| Federal 115 FMJ | velocity, fps: | 1160 | 1100 | 1060 | 1020 | 990 |
| | energy, ft-lb: | 345 | 310 | 285 | 270 | 250 |
| Federal 124 FMJ | velocity, fps: | 1120 | 1070 | 1030 | 990 | 960 |
| | energy, ft-lb: | 345 | 315 | 290 | 270 | 255 |
| Federal 124 Hydra-Shok JHP | velocity, fps: | 1120 | 1070 | 1030 | 990 | 960 |
| | energy, ft-lb: | 345 | 315 | 290 | 270 | 255 |
| Federal 124 TMJ TMF Primer | velocity, fps: | 1120 | 1070 | 1030 | 990 | 960 |
| | energy, ft-lb: | 345 | 315 | 290 | 270 | 255 |
| Federal 124 Truncated FMJ Match | velocity, fps: | 1120 | 1070 | 1030 | 990 | 960 |
| | energy, ft-lb: | 345 | 315 | 290 | 270 | 255 |
| Federal 124 Nyclad HP | velocity, fps: | 1120 | 1070 | 1030 | 990 | 960 |
| | energy, ft-lb: | 345 | 315 | 290 | 270 | 255 |
| Federal 124 FMJ +P | velocity, fps: | 1120 | 1070 | 1030 | 990 | 960 |
| | energy, ft-lb: | 345 | 315 | 290 | 270 | 255 |
| Federal 135 Hydra-Shok JHP | velocity, fps: | 1050 | 1030 | 1010 | 980 | 970 |
| | energy, ft-lb: | 330 | 315 | 300 | 290 | 280 |
| Federal 147 Hydra-Shok JHP | velocity, fps: | 1000 | 960 | 920 | 890 | 860 |
| | energy, ft-lb: | 325 | 300 | 275 | 260 | 240 |
| Federal 147 Hi-Shok JHP | velocity, fps: | 980 | 950 | 930 | 900 | 880 |
| | energy, ft-lb: | 310 | 295 | 285 | 265 | 255 |
| Federal 147 FMJ FN | velocity, fps: | 960 | 930 | 910 | 890 | 870 |
| | energy, ft-lb: | 295 | 280 | 270 | 260 | 250 |
| Federal 147 TMJ TMF Primer | velocity, fps: | 960 | 940 | 910 | 890 | 870 |
| | energy, ft-lb: | 300 | 285 | 270 | 260 | 245 |
| Hornady 115 JHP/XTP | velocity, fps: | 1155 | | 1047 | | 971 |
| | energy, ft-lb: | 341 | | 280 | | 241 |
| Hornady 124 JHP/XTP | velocity, fps: | 1110 | | 1030 | | 971 |
| | energy, ft-lb: | 339 | | 292 | | 259 |
| Hornady 147 JHP/XTP | velocity, fps: | 975 | | 935 | | 899 |
| | energy, ft-lb: | 310 | | 285 | | 264 |
| Lapua 116 FMJ | velocity, fps: | 365 | | 319* | | 290* |
| | energy, ft-lb: | 500 | | 381* | | 315* |
| Lapua 120 FMJ CEPP Super | velocity, fps: | 360 | | 316* | | 288* |
| | energy, ft-lb: | 505 | | 390* | | 324* |
| Lapua 120 FMJ CEPP Extra | velocity, fps: | 360 | | 316* | | 288* |
| | energy, ft-lb: | 505 | | 390* | | 324* |
| Lapua 123 HP Megashock | velocity, fps: | 355 | | 311* | | 284* |
| | energy, ft-lb: | 504 | | 388* | | 322* |
| Lapua 123 FMJ | velocity, fps: | 320 | | 292* | | 272* |
| | energy, ft-lb: | 410 | | 342* | | 295* |
| Lapua 123 FMJ Combat | velocity, fps: | 55 | | 315* | | 289* |
| | energy, ft-lb: | 504 | | 397* | | 333* |
| Magtech 115 JHP +P | velocity, fps: | 1246 | | 1137 | | 1056 |
| | energy, ft-lb: | 397 | | 330 | | 285 |
| Magtech 115 FMC | velocity, fps: | 1135 | | 1027 | | 961 |
| | energy, ft-lb: | 330 | | 270 | | 235 |
| Magtech 115 JHP | velocity, fps: | 1155 | | 1047 | | 971 |
| | energy, ft-lb: | 340 | | 280 | | 240 |
| Magtech 124 FMC | velocity, fps: | 1109 | | 1030 | | 971 |
| | energy, ft-lb: | 339 | | 292 | | 259 |
| Norma 84 Lead Free Frangible (Geco brand) | velocity, fps: | 1411 | | | | |
| | energy, ft-lb: | 371 | | | | |
| Norma 124 FMJ (Geco brand) | velocity, fps: | 1120 | | | | |
| | energy, fps: | 341 | | | | |

# Centerfire Handgun Ballistics

## 9MM LUGER TO .380 AUTO

| CARTRIDGE BULLET | RANGE, YARDS: | 0 | 25 | 50 | 75 | 100 |
|---|---|---|---|---|---|---|
| Norma 123 FMJ | velocity, fps: | 1099 | 1032 | 980 | | 899 |
| | energy, ft-lb: | 331 | 292 | 263 | | 221 |
| Norma 123 FMJ | velocity, fps: | 1280 | 1170 | 1086 | | 972 |
| | energy, ft-lb: | 449 | 375 | 323 | | 259 |
| PMC 75 Non-Toxic Frangible | velocity, fps: | 1350 | 1240 | 1154 | 1088 | 1035 |
| | energy, ft-lb: | 303 | | | | |
| PMC 95 SFHP | velocity, fps: | 1250 | 1239 | 1228 | 1217 | 1207 |
| | energy, ft-lb: | 330 | | | | |
| PMC 115 FMJ | velocity, fps: | 1157 | 1100 | 1053 | 1013 | 979 |
| | energy, ft-lb: | 344 | | | | |
| PMC 115 JHP | velocity, fps: | 1167 | 1098 | 1044 | 999 | 961 |
| | energy, ft-lb: | 350 | | | | |
| PMC 124 SFHP | velocity, fps: | 1090 | 1043 | 1003 | 969 | 939 |
| | energy, ft-lb: | 327 | | | | |
| PMC 124 FMJ | velocity, fps: | 1110 | 1059 | 1017 | 980 | 949 |
| | energy, ft-lb: | 339 | | | | |
| Rem. 101 Lead Free Frangible | velocity, fps: | 1220 | | 1092 | | 1004 |
| | energy, ft-lb: | 334 | | 267 | | 226 |
| Rem. 115 FN Enclosed Base | velocity, fps: | 1135 | | 1041 | | 973 |
| | energy, ft-lb: | 329 | | 277 | | 242 |
| Rem. 115 Metal Case | velocity, fps: | 1135 | | 1041 | | 973 |
| | energy, ft-lb: | 329 | | 277 | | 242 |
| Rem. 115 JHP | velocity, fps: | 1155 | | 1047 | | 971 |
| | energy, ft-lb: | 341 | | 280 | | 241 |
| Rem. 115 JHP +P | velocity, fps: | 1250 | | 1113 | | 1019 |
| | energy, ft-lb: | 399 | | 316 | | 265 |
| Rem. 124 JHP | velocity, fps: | 1120 | | 1028 | | 960 |
| | energy, ft-lb: | 346 | | 291 | | 254 |
| Rem. 124 FNEB | velocity, fps: | 1100 | | 1030 | | 971 |
| | energy, ft-lb: | 339 | | 292 | | 252 |
| Rem. 124 BJHP | velocity, fps: | 1125 | | 1031 | | 963 |
| | energy, ft-lb: | 349 | | 293 | | 255 |
| Rem. 124 BJHP +P | velocity, fps: | 1180 | | 1089 | | 1021 |
| | energy, ft-lb: | 384 | | 327 | | 287 |
| Rem. 124 Metal Case | velocity, fps: | 1110 | | 1030 | | 971 |
| | energy, ft-lb: | 339 | | 292 | | 259 |
| Rem. 147 JHP subsonic | velocity, fps: | 990 | | 941 | | 900 |
| | energy, ft-lb: | 320 | | 289 | | 264 |
| Rem. 147 BJHP | velocity, fps: | 990 | | 941 | | 900 |
| | energy, ft-lb: | 320 | | 289 | | 264 |
| Speer 90 Frangible | velocity, fps: | 1350 | | 1132 | | 1001 |
| | energy, ft-lb: | 364 | | 256 | | 200 |
| Speer 115 JHP Blazer | velocity, fps: | 1145 | | 1024 | | 943 |
| | energy, ft-lb: | 335 | | 268 | | 227 |
| Speer 115 FMJ Blazer | velocity, fps: | 1145 | | 1047 | | 971 |
| | energy, ft-lb: | 341 | | 280 | | 241 |
| Speer 115 FMJ | velocity, fps: | 1200 | | 1060 | | 970 |
| | energy, ft-lb: | 368 | | 287 | | 240 |
| Speer 115 Gold Dot HP | velocity, fps: | 1200 | | 1047 | | 971 |
| | energy, ft-lb: | 341 | | 280 | | 241 |
| Speer 124 FMJ Blazer | velocity, fps: | 1090 | | 989 | | 917 |
| | energy, ft-lb: | 327 | | 269 | | 231 |
| Speer 124 FMJ | velocity, fps: | 1090 | | 987 | | 913 |
| | energy, ft-lb: | 327 | | 268 | | 230 |
| Speer 124 TMJ-CF (and Blazer) | velocity, fps: | 1090 | | 989 | | 917 |
| | energy, ft-lb: | 327 | | 269 | | 231 |
| Speer 124 Gold Dot HP | velocity, fps: | 1150 | | 1030 | | 948 |
| | energy, ft-lb: | 367 | | 292 | | 247 |
| Speer 124 Gold Dot HP+P | velocity, fps: | 1220 | | 1085 | | 996 |
| | energy, ft-lb: | 410 | | 324 | | 273 |
| Speer 147 TMJ Blazer | velocity, fps: | 950 | | 912 | | 879 |
| | energy, ft-lb: | 295 | | 272 | | 252 |
| Speer 147 TMJ | velocity, fps: | 985 | | 943 | | 906 |
| | energy, ft-lb: | 317 | | 290 | | 268 |
| Speer 147 TMJ-CF (and Blazer) | velocity, fps: | 985 | | 960 | | 924 |
| | energy, ft-lb: | 326 | | 300 | | 279 |
| Speer 147 Gold Dot | velocity, fps: | 985 | | 960 | | 924 |
| | energy, ft-lb: | 326 | | 300 | | 279 |
| Win. 105 Jacketed FP | velocity, fps: | 1200 | | 1074 | | 989 |
| | energy, ft-lb: | 336 | | 269 | | 228 |
| Win. 115 Silvertip HP | velocity, fps: | 1225 | | 1095 | | 1007 |
| | energy, ft-lb: | 383 | | 306 | | 259 |
| Win. 115 Jacketed HP | velocity, fps: | 1225 | | 1095 | | |
| | energy, ft-lb: | 383 | | 306 | | |
| Win. 115 FMJ | velocity, fps: | 1190 | | 1071 | | |
| | energy, ft-lb: | 362 | | 293 | | |
| Win. 115 EB WinClean | velocity, fps: | 1190 | | 1088 | | |
| | energy, ft-lb: | 362 | | 302 | | |
| Win. 124 FMJ | velocity, fps: | 1140 | | 1050 | | |
| | energy, ft-lb: | 358 | | 303 | | |
| Win. 124 EB WinClean | velocity, fps: | 1130 | | 1049 | | |
| | energy, ft-lb: | 352 | | 303 | | |
| Win. 147 FMJ FN | velocity, fps: | 990 | | 945 | | |
| | energy, ft-lb: | 320 | | 292 | | |
| Win. 147 SXT | velocity, fps: | 990 | | 947 | | 909 |
| | energy, ft-lb: | 320 | | 293 | | 270 |
| Win. 147 Silvertip HP | velocity, fps: | 1010 | | 962 | | 921 |
| | energy, ft-lb: | 333 | | 302 | | 277 |
| Win. 147 JHP | velocity, fps: | 990 | | 945 | | |
| | energy, ft-lb: | 320 | | 291 | | |
| Win. 147 EB WinClean | velocity, fps: | 990 | | 945 | | |
| | energy, ft-lb: | 320 | | 291 | | |

## 9 x 23 WINCHESTER

| CARTRIDGE BULLET | RANGE, YARDS: | 0 | 25 | 50 | 75 | 100 |
|---|---|---|---|---|---|---|
| Win. 124 Jacketed FP | velocity, fps: | 1460 | | 1308 | | |
| | energy, ft-lb: | 587 | | 471 | | |
| Win. 125 Silvertip HP | velocity, fps: | 1450 | | 1249 | | 1103 |
| | energy, ft-lb: | 583 | | 433 | | 338 |

## .38 S&W

| CARTRIDGE BULLET | RANGE, YARDS: | 0 | 25 | 50 | 75 | 100 |
|---|---|---|---|---|---|---|
| Rem. 146 LRN | velocity, fps: | 685 | | 650 | | 620 |
| | energy, ft-lb: | 150 | | 135 | | 125 |
| Win. 145 LRN | velocity, fps: | 685 | | 650 | | 620 |
| | energy, ft-lb: | 150 | | 135 | | 125 |

## .38 SHORT COLT

| CARTRIDGE BULLET | RANGE, YARDS: | 0 | 25 | 50 | 75 | 100 |
|---|---|---|---|---|---|---|
| Rem. 125 LRN | velocity, fps: | 730 | | 685 | | 645 |
| | energy, ft-lb: | 150 | | 130 | | 115 |

## .38 LONG COLT

| CARTRIDGE BULLET | RANGE, YARDS: | 0 | 25 | 50 | 75 | 100 |
|---|---|---|---|---|---|---|
| Black Hills 158 RNL | velocity, fps: | 650 | | | | |
| | energy, ft-lb: | | | | | |

## .380 AUTO

| CARTRIDGE BULLET | RANGE, YARDS: | 0 | 25 | 50 | 75 | 100 |
|---|---|---|---|---|---|---|
| Black Hills 90 JHP | velocity, fps: | 1000 | | | | |
| | energy, ft-lb: | 200 | | | | |
| Black Hills 95 FMJ | velocity, fps: | 950 | | | | |

| CARTRIDGE BULLET | RANGE, YARDS: | 0 | 25 | 50 | 75 | 100 |
|---|---|---|---|---|---|---|
|  | energy, ft-lb: | 190 |  |  |  |  |
| Federal 90 Hi-Shok JHP | velocity, fps: | 1000 | 940 | 890 | 840 | 800 |
|  | energy, ft-lb: | 200 | 175 | 160 | 140 | 130 |
| Federal 90 Hydra-Shok JHP | velocity, fps: | 1000 | 940 | 890 | 840 | 800 |
|  | energy, ft-lb: | 200 | 175 | 160 | 140 | 130 |
| Federal 95 FMJ | velocity, fps: | 960 | 910 | 870 | 830 | 790 |
|  | energy, ft-lb: | 190 | 175 | 160 | 145 | 130 |
| Hornady 90 JHP/XTP | velocity, fps: | 1000 |  | 902 |  | 823 |
|  | energy, ft-lb: | 200 |  | 163 |  | 135 |
| Magtech 85 JHP + P | velocity, fps: | 1082 |  | 999 |  | 936 |
|  | energy, ft-lb: | 221 |  | 188 |  | 166 |
| Magtech 95 FMC | velocity, fps: | 951 |  | 861 |  | 781 |
|  | energy, ft-lb: | 190 |  | 156 |  | 128 |
| Magtech 95 JHP | velocity, fps: | 951 |  | 861 |  | 781 |
|  | energy, ft-lb: | 190 |  | 156 |  | 128 |
| PMC 90 FMJ | velocity, fps: | 910 | 872 | 838 | 807 | 778 |
|  | energy, ft-lb: | 165 |  |  |  |  |
| PMC 90 JHP | velocity, fps: | 917 | 878 | 844 | 812 | 782 |
|  | energy, ft-lb: | 168 |  |  |  |  |
| PMC 95 SFHP | velocity, fps: | 925 | 884 | 847 | 813 | 783 |
|  | energy, ft-lb: | 180 |  |  |  |  |
| Rem. 88 JHP | velocity, fps: | 990 |  | 920 |  | 868 |
|  | energy, ft-lb: | 191 |  | 165 |  | 146 |
| Rem. 95 FNEB | velocity, fps: | 955 |  | 865 |  | 785 |
|  | energy, ft-lb: | 190 |  | 160 |  | 130 |
| Rem. 95 Metal Case | velocity, fps: | 955 |  | 865 |  | 785 |
|  | energy, ft-lb: | 190 |  | 160 |  | 130 |
| Rem. 102 BJHP | velocity, fps: | 940 |  | 901 |  | 866 |
|  | energy, ft-lb: | 200 |  | 184 |  | 170 |
| Speer 88 JHP Blazer | velocity, fps: | 950 |  | 920 |  | 870 |
|  | energy, ft-lb: | 195 |  | 164 |  | 148 |
| Speer 90 Gold Dot | velocity, fps: | 990 |  | 907 |  | 842 |
|  | energy, ft-lb: | 196 |  | 164 |  | 142 |
| Speer 95 TMJ Blazer | velocity, fps: | 945 |  | 865 |  | 785 |
|  | energy, ft-lb: | 190 |  | 160 |  | 130 |
| Speer 95 TMJ | velocity, fps: | 950 |  | 877 |  | 817 |
|  | energy, ft-lb: | 180 |  | 154 |  | 133 |
| Win. 85 Silvertip HP | velocity, fps: | 1000 |  | 921 |  | 860 |
|  | energy, ft-lb: | 189 |  | 160 |  | 140 |
| Win. 95 SXT | velocity, fps: | 955 |  | 889 |  | 835 |
|  | energy, ft-lb: | 192 |  | 167 |  | 147 |
| Win. 95 FMJ | velocity, fps: | 955 |  | 865 |  |  |
|  | energy, ft-lb: | 190 |  | 160 |  |  |
| Win. 95 EB WinClean | velocity, fps: | 955 |  | 881 |  |  |
|  | energy, ft-lb: | 192 |  | 164 |  |  |

## .38 Special

| CARTRIDGE BULLET | RANGE, YARDS: | 0 | 25 | 50 | 75 | 100 |
|---|---|---|---|---|---|---|
| Black Hills 125 JHP +P | velocity, fps: | 1050 |  |  |  |  |
|  | energy, ft-lb: | 306 |  |  |  |  |
| Black Hills 158 CNL | velocity, fps: | 800 |  |  |  |  |
|  | energy, ft-lb: |  |  |  |  |  |
| Federal 110 Hydra-Shok JHP | velocity, fps: | 1000 | 970 | 930 | 910 | 880 |
|  | energy, ft-lb: | 245 | 225 | 215 | 200 | 190 |
| Federal 110 Hi-Shok JHP +P | velocity, fps: | 1000 | 960 | 930 | 900 | 870 |
|  | energy, ft-lb: | 240 | 225 | 210 | 195 | 185 |
| Federal 125 Nyclad HP | velocity, fps: | 830 | 780 | 730 | 690 | 650 |
|  | energy, ft-lb: | 190 | 170 | 150 | 130 | 115 |
| Federal 125 Hi-Shok JSP +P | velocity, fps: | 950 | 920 | 900 | 880 | 860 |
|  | energy, ft-lb: | 250 | 235 | 225 | 215 | 205 |
| Federal 125 Hi-Shok JHP +P | velocity, fps: | 950 | 920 | 900 | 880 | 860 |
|  | energy, ft-lb: | 250 | 235 | 225 | 215 | 205 |
| Federal 125 Nyclad HP +P | velocity, fps: | 950 | 920 | 900 | 880 | 860 |
|  | energy, ft-lb: | 250 | 235 | 225 | 215 | 205 |
| Federal 129 Hydra-Shok JHP+P | velocity, fps: | 950 | 930 | 910 | 890 | 870 |
|  | energy, ft-lb: | 255 | 245 | 235 | 225 | 215 |
| Federal 130 FMJ | velocity, fps: | 950 | 920 | 890 | 870 | 840 |
|  | energy, ft-lb: | 260 | 245 | 230 | 215 | 205 |
| Federal 148 LWC Match | velocity, fps: | 710 | 670 | 630 | 600 | 560 |
|  | energy, ft-lb: | 165 | 150 | 130 | 115 | 105 |
| Federal 158 LRN | velocity, fps: | 760 | 740 | 720 | 710 | 690 |
|  | energy, ft-lb: | 200 | 190 | 185 | 175 | 170 |
| Federal 158 LSWC | velocity, fps: | 760 | 740 | 720 | 710 | 690 |
|  | energy, ft-lb: | 200 | 190 | 185 | 175 | 170 |
| Federal 158 Nyclad RN | velocity, fps: | 760 | 740 | 720 | 710 | 690 |
|  | energy, ft-lb: | 200 | 190 | 185 | 175 | 170 |
| Federal 158 SWC HP +P | velocity, fps: | 890 | 870 | 860 | 840 | 820 |
|  | energy, ft-lb: | 280 | 265 | 260 | 245 | 235 |
| Federal 158 LSWC +P | velocity, fps: | 890 | 870 | 860 | 840 | 820 |
|  | energy, ft-lb: | 270 | 265 | 260 | 245 | 235 |
| Federal 158 Nyclad SWC-HP+P | velocity, fps: | 890 | 870 | 860 | 840 | 820 |
|  | energy, ft-lb: | 270 | 265 | 260 | 245 | 235 |
| Hornady 125 JHP/XTP | velocity, fps: | 900 |  | 856 |  | 817 |
|  | energy, ft-lb: | 225 |  | 203 |  | 185 |
| Hornady 140 JHP/XTP | velocity, fps: | 825 |  | 790 |  | 757 |
|  | energy, ft-lb: | 212 |  | 194 |  | 178 |
| Hornady 140 Cowboy | velocity, fps: | 800 |  | 767 |  | 735 |
|  | energy, ft-lb: | 199 |  | 183 |  | 168 |
| Hornady 148 HBWC | velocity, fps: | 800 |  | 697 |  | 610 |
|  | energy, ft-lb: | 210 |  | 160 |  | 122 |
| Hornady 158 JHP/XPT | velocity, fps: | 800 |  | 765 |  | 731 |
|  | energy, ft-lb: | 225 |  | 205 |  | 188 |
| Lapua 123 HP Megashock | velocity, fps: | 355 |  | 311 |  | 284 |
|  | energy, ft-lb: | 504 |  | 388 |  | 322 |
| Lapua 148 LWC | velocity, fps: | 230 |  | 203 |  | 181 |
|  | energy, ft-lb: | 254 |  | 199 |  | 157 |
| Lapua 150 SJFN | velocity, fps: | 325 |  | 301 |  | 283 |
|  | energy, ft-lb: | 512 |  | 439 |  | 388 |
| Lapua 158 FMJLF | velocity, fps: | 255 |  | 243 |  | 232 |
|  | energy, ft-lb: | 332 |  | 301 |  | 275 |
| Lapua 158 LRN | velocity, fps: | 255 |  | 243 |  | 232 |
|  | energy, ft-lb: | 332 |  | 301 |  | 275 |
| Magtech 125 JHP +P | velocity, fps: | 1017 |  | 971 |  | 931 |
|  | energy, ft-lb: | 287 |  | 262 |  | 241 |
| Magtech 148 LWC | velocity, fps: | 710 |  | 634 |  | 566 |
|  | energy, ft-lb: | 166 |  | 132 |  | 105 |
| Magtech 158 LRN | velocity, fps: | 755 |  | 728 |  | 693 |
|  | energy, ft-lb: | 200 |  | 183 |  | 168 |
| Magtech 158 LFN | velocity, fps: | 800 |  | 776 |  | 753 |
|  | energy, ft-lb: | 225 |  | 211 |  | 199 |
| Magtech 158 SJHP | velocity, fps: | 807 |  | 779 |  | 753 |
|  | energy, ft-lb: | 230 |  | 213 |  | 199 |
| Magtech 158 LSWC | velocity, fps: | 755 |  | 721 |  | 689 |
|  | energy, ft-lb: | 200 |  | 182 |  | 167 |
| Magtech 158 FMC-Flat | velocity, fps: | 807 |  | 779 |  | 753 |
|  | energy, ft-lb: | 230 |  | 213 |  | 199 |

# Centerfire Handgun Ballistics

## .38 SPECIAL TO .357 SIG

BALLISTICS

| CARTRIDGE BULLET | RANGE, YARDS: | 0 | 25 | 50 | 75 | 100 |
|---|---|---|---|---|---|---|
| PMC 85 Non-Toxic Frangible | velocity, fps: | 1275 | 1181 | 1109 | 1052 | 1006 |
| | energy, ft-lb: | 307 | | | | |
| PMC 125 SFHP +P | velocity, fps: | 950 | 918 | 889 | 863 | 838 |
| | energy, ft-lb: | 251 | | | | |
| PMC 125 JHP +P | velocity, fps: | 974 | 938 | 906 | 878 | 851 |
| | energy, ft-lb: | 266 | | | | |
| PMC 132 FMJ | velocity, fps: | 841 | 820 | 799 | 780 | 761 |
| | energy, ft-lb: | 206 | | | | |
| PMC 148 LWC | velocity, fps: | 728 | 694 | 662 | 631 | 602 |
| | energy, ft-lb: | 175 | | | | |
| PMC 158 LRN | velocity, fps: | 820 | 801 | 783 | 765 | 749 |
| | energy, ft-lb: | 235 | | | | |
| PMC 158 JSP | velocity, fps: | 835 | 816 | 797 | 779 | 762 |
| | energy, ft-lb: | 245 | | | | |
| PMC 158 LFP | velocity, fps: | 800 | | 761 | | 725 |
| | energy, ft-lb: | 225 | | 203 | | 185 |
| Rem. 101 Lead Free Frangible | velocity, fps: | 950 | | 896 | | 850 |
| | energy, ft-lb: | 202 | | 180 | | 162 |
| Rem. 110 SJHP | velocity, fps: | 950 | | 890 | | 840 |
| | energy, ft-lb: | 220 | | 194 | | 172 |
| Rem. 110 SJHP +P | velocity, fps: | 995 | | 926 | | 871 |
| | energy, ft-lb: | 242 | | 210 | | 185 |
| Rem. 125 SJHP +P | velocity, ft-lb: | 945 | | 898 | | 858 |
| | energy, ft-lb: | 248 | | 224 | | 204 |
| Rem. 125 BJHP | velocity, fps: | 975 | | 929 | | 885 |
| | energy, ft-lb: | 264 | | 238 | | 218 |
| Rem. 125 FNEB | velocity, fps: | 850 | | 822 | | 796 |
| | energy, ft-lb: | 201 | | 188 | | 176 |
| Rem. 125 FNEB +P | velocity, fps: | 975 | | 935 | | 899 |
| | energy, ft-lb: | 264 | | 242 | | 224 |
| Rem. 130 Metal Case | velocity, fps: | 950 | | 913 | | 879 |
| | energy, ft-lb: | 261 | | 240 | | 223 |
| Rem. 148 LWC Match | velocity, fps: | 710 | | 634 | | 566 |
| | energy, ft-lb: | 166 | | 132 | | 105 |
| Rem. 158 LRN | velocity, fps: | 755 | | 723 | | 692 |
| | energy, ft-lb: | 200 | | 183 | | 168 |
| Rem. 158 SWC +P | velocity, fps: | 890 | | 855 | | 823 |
| | energy, ft-lb: | 278 | | 257 | | 238 |
| Rem. 158 SWC | velocity, fps: | 755 | | 723 | | 692 |
| | energy, ft-lb: | 200 | | 183 | | 168 |
| Rem. 158 LHP +P | velocity, fps: | 890 | | 855 | | 823 |
| | energy, ft-lb: | 278 | | 257 | | 238 |
| Speer 125 JHP +P Blazer | velocity, fps: | 945 | | 898 | | 858 |
| | energy, ft-lb: | 248 | | 224 | | 204 |
| Speer 125 Gold Dot +P | velocity, fps: | 945 | | 898 | | 858 |
| | energy, ft-lb: | 248 | | 224 | | 204 |
| Speer 158 TMJ +P (and Blazer) | velocity, fps: | 900 | | 852 | | 818 |
| | energy, ft-lb: | 278 | | 255 | | 235 |
| Speer 158 LRN Blazer | velocity, fps: | 755 | | 723 | | 692 |
| | energy, ft-lb: | 200 | | 183 | | 168 |
| Speer 158 Trail Blazer LFN | velocity, fps: | 800 | | 761 | | 725 |
| | energy, ft-lb: | 225 | | 203 | | 184 |
| Speer 158 TMJ-CF +P (and Blazer) | velocity, fps: | 900 | | 852 | | 818 |
| | energy, ft-lb: | 278 | | 255 | | 235 |
| Win. 110 Silvertip HP | velocity, fps: | 945 | | 894 | | 850 |
| | energy, ft-lb: | 218 | | 195 | | 176 |
| Win. 110 Jacketed FP | velocity, fps: | 975 | | 906 | | 849 |
| | energy, ft-lb: | 232 | | 201 | | 176 |
| Win. 125 Jacketed HP | velocity, fps: | 945 | | 898 | | |
| | energy, ft-lb: | 248 | | 224 | | |
| Win. 125 Jacketed HP +P | velocity, fps: | 945 | | 898 | | 858 |
| | energy, ft-lb: | 248 | | 224 | | 204 |
| Win. 125 Jacketed FP | velocity, fps: | 850 | | 804 | | |
| | energy, ft-lb: | 201 | | 179 | | |
| Win. 125 Silvertip HP + P | velocity, fps: | 945 | | 898 | | 858 |
| | energy, ft-lb: | 248 | | 224 | | 204 |
| Win. 125 JFP WinClean | velocity, fps: | 775 | | 742 | | |
| | energy, ft-lb: | 167 | | 153 | | |
| Win. 130 FMJ | velocity, fps: | 800 | | 765 | | |
| | energy, ft-lb: | 185 | | 169 | | |
| Win. 130 SXT +P | velocity, fps: | 925 | | 887 | | 852 |
| | energy, ft-lb: | 247 | | 227 | | 210 |
| Win. 148 LWC Super Match | velocity, fps: | 710 | | 634 | | 566 |
| | energy, ft-lb: | 166 | | 132 | | 105 |
| Win. 150 Lead | velocity, fps: | 845 | | 812 | | |
| | energy, ft-lb: | 238 | | 219 | | |
| Win. 158 Lead | velocity, fps: | 800 | | 761 | | 725 |
| | energy, ft-lb: | 225 | | 203 | | 185 |
| Win. 158 LRN | velocity, fps: | 755 | | 723 | | 693 |
| | energy, ft-lb: | 200 | | 183 | | 168 |
| Win. 158 LSWC | velocity, fps: | 755 | | 721 | | 689 |
| | energy, ft-lb: | 200 | | 182 | | 167 |
| Win. 158 LSWC HP +P | velocity, fps: | 890 | | 855 | | 823 |
| | energy, ft-lb: | 278 | | 257 | | 238 |

## .38-40

| | | 0 | 25 | 50 | 75 | 100 |
|---|---|---|---|---|---|---|
| Black Hills 180 FPL | velocity, fps: | 800 | | | | |
| | energy, ft-lb: | | | | | |

## .38 SUPER

| | | 0 | 25 | 50 | 75 | 100 |
|---|---|---|---|---|---|---|
| Federal 130 FMJ +P | velocity, fps: | 1200 | 1140 | 1100 | 1050 | 1020 |
| | energy, ft-lb: | 415 | 380 | 350 | 320 | 300 |
| PMC 115 JHP | velocity, fps: | 1116 | 1052 | 1001 | 959 | 923 |
| | energy, ft-lb: | 318 | | | | |
| PMC 130 FMJ | velocity, fps: | 1092 | 1038 | 994 | 957 | 924 |
| | energy, ft-lb: | 348 | | | | |
| Rem. 130 Metal Case | velocity, fps: | 1215 | | 1099 | | 1017 |
| | energy, ft-lb: | 426 | | 348 | | 298 |
| Win. 125 Silvertip HP +P | velocity, fps: | 1240 | | 1130 | | 1050 |
| | energy, ft-lb: | 427 | | 354 | | 306 |
| Win. 130 FMJ +P | velocity, fps: | 1215 | | 1099 | | |
| | energy, ft-lb: | 426 | | 348 | | |

## .357 SIG

| | | 0 | 25 | 50 | 75 | 100 |
|---|---|---|---|---|---|---|
| Federal 125 FMJ | velocity, fps: | 1350 | 1270 | 1190 | 1130 | 1080 |
| | energy, ft-lb: | 510 | 445 | 395 | 355 | 325 |
| Federal 125 JHP | velocity, fps: | 1350 | 1270 | 1190 | 1130 | 1080 |
| | energy, ft-lb: | 510 | 445 | 395 | 355 | 325 |
| Federal 150 JHP | velocity, fps: | 1130 | 1080 | 1030 | 1000 | 970 |
| | energy, ft-lb: | 420 | 385 | 355 | 330 | 310 |
| Hornady 124 JHP/XTP | velocity, fps: | 1350 | | 1208 | | 1108 |
| | energy, ft-lb: | 502 | | 405 | | 338 |
| Hornady 147 JHP/XTP | velocity, fps: | 1225 | | 1138 | | 1072 |
| | energy, ft-lb: | 490 | | 422 | | 375 |
| PMC 85 Non-Toxic Frangible | velocity, fps: | 1480 | 1356 | 1245 | 1158 | 1092 |
| | energy, ft-lb: | 413 | | | | |

**496** • 2005 Shooter's Bible

www.StoegerIndustries.com

| CARTRIDGE BULLET | | 0 | 25 | 50 | 75 | 100 |
|---|---|---|---|---|---|---|
| PMC 124 SFHP | velocity, fps: | 1350 | 1263 | 1190 | 1132 | 1083 |
| | energy, ft-lb: | 502 | | | | |
| PMC 124 FMJ/FP | velocity, fps: | 1350 | 1242 | 1158 | 1093 | 1040 |
| | energy, ft-lb: | 512 | | | | |
| Rem. 104 Lead Free Frangible | velocity, fps: | 1400 | | 1223 | | 1094 |
| | energy, ft-lb: | 453 | | 345 | | 276 |
| Rem. 125 Metal Case | velocity, fps: | 1350 | | 1146 | | 1018 |
| | energy, ft-lb: | 506 | | 422 | | 359 |
| Rem. 125 JHP | velocity, fps: | 1350 | | 1157 | | 1032 |
| | energy, ft-lb: | 506 | | 372 | | 296 |
| Speer 125 TMJ (and Blazer) | velocity, fps: | 1350 | | 1177 | | 1057 |
| | energy, ft-lb: | 502 | | 381 | | 307 |
| Speer 125 TMJ-CF | velocity, fps: | 1350 | | 1177 | | 1057 |
| | energy, ft-lb: | 502 | | 381 | | 307 |
| Speer 125 Gold Dot | velocity, fps: | 1375 | | 1203 | | 1079 |
| | energy, ft-lb: | 525 | | 402 | | 323 |
| Win. 105 JFP | velocity, fps: | 1370 | | 1179 | | 1050 |
| | energy, ft-lb | 438 | | 324 | | 257 |
| Win. 125 FMJ FN | velocity, fps: | 1350 | | 1185 | | |
| | energy, ft-lb | 506 | | 390 | | |

## .357 MAGNUM

| CARTRIDGE BULLET | | 0 | 25 | 50 | 75 | 100 |
|---|---|---|---|---|---|---|
| Black Hills 125 JHP | velocity, fps: | 1500 | | | | |
| | energy, ft-lb: | 625 | | | | |
| Black Hills 158 CNL | velocity, fps: | 800 | | | | |
| | energy, ft-lb: | | | | | |
| Federal 110 Hi-Shok JHP | velocity, fps: | 1300 | 1180 | 1090 | 1040 | 990 |
| | energy, ft-lb: | 410 | 340 | 290 | 260 | 235 |
| Federal 125 Hi-Shok JHP | velocity, fps: | 1450 | 1350 | 1240 | 1160 | 1100 |
| | energy, ft-lb: | 580 | 495 | 430 | 370 | 335 |
| Federal 130 Hydra-Shok JHP | velocity, fps: | 1300 | 1210 | 1130 | 1070 | 1020 |
| | energy, ft-lb: | 490 | 420 | 370 | 330 | 300 |
| Federal 158 Hi-Shok JSP | velocity, fps: | 1240 | 1160 | 1100 | 1060 | 1020 |
| | energy, ft-lb: | 535 | 475 | 430 | 395 | 365 |
| Federal 158 JSP | velocity, fps: | 1240 | 1160 | 1100 | 1060 | 1020 |
| | energy, ft-lb: | 535 | 475 | 430 | 395 | 365 |
| Federal 158 LSWC | velocity, fps: | 1240 | 1160 | 1100 | 1060 | 1020 |
| | energy, ft-lb: | 535 | 475 | 430 | 395 | 365 |
| Federal 158 Hi-Shok JHP | velocity, fps: | 1240 | 1160 | 1100 | 1060 | 1020 |
| | energy, ft-lb: | 535 | 475 | 430 | 395 | 365 |
| Federal 158 Hydra-Shok JHP | velocity, fps: | 1240 | 1160 | 1100 | 1060 | 1020 |
| | energy, ft-lb: | 535 | 475 | 430 | 395 | 365 |
| Federal 180 Hi-Shok JHP | velocity, fps: | 1090 | 1030 | 980 | 930 | 890 |
| | energy, ft-lb: | 475 | 425 | 385 | 350 | 320 |
| Federal 180 Castcore | velocity, fps: | 1250 | 1200 | 1160 | 1120 | 1080 |
| | energy, ft-lb: | 625 | 575 | 535 | 495 | 465 |
| Hornady 125 JHP/XTP | velocity, fps: | 1500 | | 1314 | | 1166 |
| | energy, ft-lb: | 624 | | 479 | | 377 |
| Hornady 125 JFP/XTP | velocity, fps: | 1500 | | 1311 | | 1161 |
| | energy, ft-lb: | 624 | | 477 | | 374 |
| Hornady 140 Cowboy | velocity, fps: | 800 | | 767 | | 735 |
| | energy, ft-lb: | 199 | | 183 | | 168 |
| Hornady 140 JHP/XTP | velocity, fps: | 1400 | | 1249 | | 1130 |
| | energy, ft-lb: | 609 | | 485 | | 397 |
| Hornady 158 JHP/XTP | velocity, fps: | 1250 | | 1150 | | 1073 |
| | energy, ft-lb: | 548 | | 464 | | 404 |
| Hornady 158 JFP/XTP | velocity, fps: | 1250 | | 1147 | | 1068 |
| | energy, ft-lb: | 548 | | 461 | | 400 |
| Lapua 150 FMJ CEPP Super | velocity, fps: | 370 | | 527 | | 303 |
| | energy, ft-lb: | 664 | | 527 | | 445 |
| Lapua 150 SJFN | velocity, fps: | 385 | | 342 | | 313 |
| | energy, ft-lb: | 719 | | 569 | | 476 |
| Lapua 158 SJHP | velocity, fps: | 470 | | 408 | | 359 |
| | energy, ft-lb: | 1127 | | 850 | | 657 |
| Magtech 158 SJSP | velocity, fps: | 1235 | | 1104 | | 1015 |
| | energy, ft-lb: | 535 | | 428 | | 361 |
| Magtech 158 SJHP | velocity, fps: | 1235 | | 1104 | | 1015 |
| | energy, ft-lb: | 535 | | 428 | | 361 |
| PMC 85 Non-Toxic Frangible | velocity, fps: | 1325 | 1219 | 1139 | 1076 | 1025 |
| | energy, ft-lb: | 331 | | | | |
| PMC 125 JHP | velocity, fps: | 1194 | 1117 | 1057 | 1008 | 967 |
| | energy, ft-lb: | 399 | | | | |
| PMC 150 JHP | velocity, fps: | 1234 | 1156 | 1093 | 1042 | 1000 |
| | energy, ft-lb: | 512 | | | | |
| PMC 150 SFHP | velocity, fps: | 1205 | 1129 | 1069 | 1020 | 980 |
| | energy, ft-lb: | 484 | | | | |
| PMC 158 JSP | velocity, fps: | 1194 | 1122 | 1063 | 1016 | 977 |
| | energy, ft-lb: | 504 | | | | |
| PMC 158 LFP | velocity, fps: | 800 | | 761 | | 725 |
| | energy, ft-lb: | 225 | | 203 | | 185 |
| Rem. 110 SJHP | velocity, fps: | 1295 | | 1094 | | 975 |
| | energy, ft-lb: | 410 | | 292 | | 232 |
| Rem. 125 SJHP | velocity, fps: | 1450 | | 1240 | | 1090 |
| | energy, ft-lb: | 583 | | 427 | | 330 |
| Rem. 125 BJHP | velocity, fps: | 1220 | | 1095 | | 1009 |
| | energy, ft-lb: | 413 | | 333 | | 283 |
| Rem. 125 FNEB | velocity, fps: | 1450 | | 1240 | | 1090 |
| | energy, ft-lb: | 583 | | 427 | | 330 |
| Rem. 158 SJHP | velocity, fps: | 1235 | | 1104 | | 1015 |
| | energy, ft-lb: | 535 | | 428 | | 361 |
| Rem. 158 SP | velocity, fps: | 1235 | | 1104 | | 1015 |
| | energy, ft-lb: | 535 | | 428 | | 361 |
| Rem. 158 SWC | velocity, fps: | 1235 | | 1104 | | 1015 |
| | energy, ft-lb: | 535 | | 428 | | 361 |
| Rem. 165 JHP Core-Lokt | velocity, fps: | 1290 | | 1189 | | 1108 |
| | energy, ft-lb: | 610 | | 518 | | 450 |
| Rem. 180 SJHP | velocity, fps: | 1145 | | 1053 | | 985 |
| | energy, ft-lb: | 542 | | 443 | | 388 |
| | energy, ft-lb: | 542 | | 443 | | 388 |
| Speer 125 Gold Dot | velocity, fps: | 1450 | | 1240 | | 1090 |
| | energy, ft-lb: | 583 | | 427 | | 330 |
| Speer 158 JHP Blazer | velocity, fps: | 1150 | | 1104 | | 1015 |
| | energy, ft-lb: | 535 | | 428 | | 361 |
| Speer 158 Gold Dot | velocity, fps: | 1235 | | 1104 | | 1015 |
| | energy, ft-lb: | 535 | | 428 | | 361 |
| Speer 170 Gold Dot SP | velocity, fps: | 1180 | | 1089 | | 1019 |
| | energy, ft-lb: | 525 | | 447 | | 392 |
| Win. 110 JFP | velocity, fps: | 1275 | | 1105 | | 998 |
| | energy, ft-lb: | 397 | | 298 | | 243 |
| Win. 110 JHP | velocity, fps: | 1295 | | 1095 | | |
| | energy, ft-lb: | 410 | | 292 | | |
| Win. 125 JFP WinClean | velocity, fps: | 1370 | | 1183 | | |
| | energy, ft-lb: | 521 | | 389 | | |
| Win. 145 Silvertip HP | velocity, fps: | 1290 | | 1155 | | 1060 |

# Centerfire Handgun Ballistics

| CARTRIDGE BULLET | RANGE, YARDS: | 0 | 25 | 50 | 75 | 100 |
|---|---|---|---|---|---|---|
| Win. 158 JHP | energy, ft-lb: | 535 | | 428 | | 361 |
| | velocity, fps: | 1235 | | 1104 | | 1015 |
| Win. 158 JSP | energy, ft-lb: | 535 | | 428 | | 361 |
| | velocity, fps: | 1235 | | 1104 | | 1015 |
| Win. 180 Partition Gold | velocity, fps: | 1180 | | 1088 | | 1020 |
| | energy, ft-lb: | 557 | | 473 | | 416 |

## .40 S&W

| CARTRIDGE BULLET | | 0 | 25 | 50 | 75 | 100 |
|---|---|---|---|---|---|---|
| Black Hills 155 JHP | velocity, fps: | 1150 | | | | |
| | energy, ft-lb: | 450 | | | | |
| Black Hills 165 EXP JHP | velocity, fps: | 1150 | | | | |
| | energy, ft-lb: | 483 | | | | |
| Black Hills 180 JHP | velocity, fps: | 1000 | | | | |
| | energy, ft-lb: | 400 | | | | |
| Federal 135 Hydra-Shok JHP | velocity, fps: | 1190 | 1050 | 970 | 900 | 850 |
| | energy, ft-lb: | 420 | 330 | 280 | 245 | 215 |
| Federal 155 FMJ Ball | velocity, fps: | 1140 | 1080 | 1030 | 990 | 960 |
| | energy, ft-lb: | 445 | 400 | 365 | 335 | 315 |
| Federal 155 Hi-Shok JHP | velocity, fps: | 1140 | 1080 | 1030 | 990 | 950 |
| | energy, ft-lb: | 445 | 400 | 365 | 335 | 315 |
| Federal 155 Hydra-Shok JHP | velocity, fps: | 1140 | 1080 | 1030 | 990 | 950 |
| | energy, ft-lb: | 445 | 400 | 365 | 335 | 315 |
| Federal 165 EFMJ | velocity, fps: | 1190 | 1060 | 970 | 905 | 850 |
| | energy, ft-lb: | 520 | 410 | 345 | 300 | 265 |
| Federal 165 FMJ | velocity, fps: | 1050 | 1020 | 990 | 960 | 935 |
| | energy, ft-lb: | 405 | 380 | 355 | 335 | 320 |
| Federal 165 FMJ Ball | velocity, fps: | 980 | 950 | 920 | 900 | 880 |
| | energy, ft-lb: | 350 | 330 | 310 | 295 | 280 |
| Federal 165 Hydra-Shok JHP | velocity, fps: | 980 | 950 | 930 | 910 | 890 |
| Federal 180 High Antim. Lead | velocity, fps: | 990 | 960 | 930 | 910 | 890 |
| | energy, ft-lb: | 390 | 365 | 345 | 330 | 315 |
| Federal 180 TMJ TMF Primer | velocity, fps: | 990 | 960 | 940 | 910 | 890 |
| | energy, ft-lb: | 390 | 370 | 350 | 330 | 315 |
| Federal 180 FMJ Ball | velocity, fps: | 990 | 960 | 940 | 910 | 890 |
| | energy, ft-lb: | 390 | 370 | 350 | 330 | 315 |
| Federal 180 Hi-Shok JHP | velocity, fps: | 990 | 960 | 930 | 910 | 890 |
| | energy, ft-lb: | 390 | 365 | 345 | 330 | 315 |
| Federal 180 Hydra-Shok JHP | velocity, fps: | 990 | 960 | 930 | 910 | 890 |
| | energy, ft-lb: | 390 | 365 | 345 | 330 | 315 |
| Hornady 155 JHP/XTP | velocity, fps: | 1180 | | 1061 | | 980 |
| | energy, ft-lb: | 479 | | 388 | | 331 |
| Hornady 180 JHP/XTP | velocity, fps: | 950 | | 903 | | 862 |
| | energy, ft-lb: | 361 | | 326 | | 297 |
| Magtech 155 JHP | velocity, fps: | 1025 | | 1118 | | 1052 |
| | energy, ft-lb: | 500 | | 430 | | 381 |
| Magtech 180 JHP | velocity, fps: | 990 | | 933 | | 886 |
| | energy, ft-lb: | 390 | | 348 | | 314 |
| Magtech 180 FMC | velocity, fps: | 990 | | 933 | | 886 |
| | energy, ft-lb: | 390 | | 348 | | 314 |
| PMC 115 Non-Toxic Frangible | velocity, fps: | 1350 | 1240 | 1154 | 1088 | 1035 |
| | energy, ft-lb: | 465 | | | | |
| PMC 155 SFHP | velocity, fps: | 1160 | 1092 | 1039 | 994 | 957 |
| | energy, ft-lb: | 463 | | | | |
| PMC 165 JHP | velocity, fps: | 1040 | 1002 | 970 | 941 | 915 |
| | energy, ft-lb: | 396 | | | | |
| PMC 165 FMJ | velocity, fps: | 1010 | 977 | 948 | 922 | 899 |

| CARTRIDGE BULLET | | 0 | 25 | 50 | 75 | 100 |
|---|---|---|---|---|---|---|
| PMC 180 FMJ/FP | energy, ft-lb: | 374 | | | | |
| | velocity, fps: | 985 | 957 | 931 | 908 | 885 |
| | energy, ft-lb: | 388 | | | | |
| PMC 180 SFHP | velocity, fps: | 985 | 958 | 933 | 910 | 889 |
| | energy, ft-lb: | 388 | | | | |
| Rem. 141 Lead Free Frangible | velocity, fps: | 1135 | | 1056 | | 996 |
| | energy, ft-lb: | | 403 | | 349 | 311 |
| Rem. 155 JHP | velocity, fps: | 1205 | | 1095 | | 1017 |
| | energy, ft-lb: | 499 | | 413 | | 356 |
| Rem. 165 BJHP | velocity, fps: | 1150 | | 1040 | | 964 |
| | energy, ft-lb: | 485 | | 396 | | 340 |
| Rem. 180 JHP | velocity, fps: | 1015 | | 960 | | 914 |
| | energy, ft-lb: | 412 | | 368 | | 334 |
| Rem. 180 FN Enclosed Base | velocity, fps: | 985 | | 936 | | 893 |
| | energy, ft-lb: | 388 | | 350 | | 319 |
| Rem. 180 Metal Case | velocity, fps: | 985 | | 936 | | 893 |
| | energy, ft-lb: | 388 | | 350 | | 319 |
| Rem. 180 BJHP | velocity, fps: | 1015 | | 960 | | 914 |
| | energy, ft-lb: | 412 | | 368 | | 334 |
| Speer 105 Frangible | velocity, fps: | 1380 | | 1128 | | 985 |
| | energy, ft-lb: | 444 | | 297 | | 226 |
| Speer 155 TMJ Blazer | velocity, fps: | 1175 | | 1047 | | 963 |
| | energy, ft-lb: | 475 | | 377 | | 319 |
| Speer 155 TMJ | velocity, fps: | 1200 | | 1065 | | 976 |
| | energy, ft-lb: | 496 | | 390 | | 328 |
| Speer 155 Gold Dot | velocity, fps: | 1200 | | 1063 | | 974 |
| | energy, ft-lb: | 496 | | 389 | | 326 |
| Speer 165 TMJ Blazer | velocity, fps: | 1100 | | 1006 | | 938 |
| | energy, ft-lb: | 443 | | 371 | | 321 |
| Speer 165 TMJ | velocity, fps: | 1150 | | 1040 | | 964 |
| | energy, ft-lb: | 484 | | 396 | | 340 |
| Speer 165 Gold Dot | velocity, fps: | 1150 | | 1043 | | 966 |
| | energy, ft-lb: | 485 | | 399 | | 342 |
| Speer 180 HP Blazer | velocity, fps: | 985 | | 951 | | 909 |
| | energy, ft-lb: | 400 | | 361 | | 330 |
| Speer 180 FMJ Blazer | velocity, fps: | 1000 | | 937 | | 886 |
| | energy, ft-lb: | 400 | | 351 | | 313 |
| Speer 180 FMJ | velocity, fps: | 1000 | | 951 | | 909 |
| | energy, ft-lb: | 400 | | 361 | | 330 |
| Speer 180 TMJ-CF (and Blazer) | velocity, fps: | 1000 | | 951 | | 909 |
| | energy, ft-lb: | 400 | | 361 | | 330 |
| Speer 180 Gold Dot | velocity, fps: | 1025 | | 957 | | 902 |
| | energy, ft-lb: | 420 | | 366 | | 325 |
| Win. 140 JFP | velocity, fps: | 1155 | | 1039 | | 960 |
| | energy, ft-lb: | 415 | | 336 | | 286 |
| Win. 155 Silvertip HP | velocity, fps: | 1205 | | 1096 | | 1018 |
| | energy, ft-lb | 500 | | 414 | | 357 |
| Win. 165 SXT | velocity, fps: | 1130 | | 1041 | | 977 |
| | energy, ft-lb: | 468 | | 397 | | 349 |
| Win. 165 FMJ FN | velocity, fps: | 1060 | | 1001 | | |
| | energy, ft-lb: | 412 | | 367 | | |
| Win. 165 EB WinClean | velocity, fps: | 1130 | | 1054 | | |
| | energy, ft-lb: | 468 | | 407 | | |
| Win. 180 JHP | velocity, fps: | 1010 | | 954 | | |
| | energy, ft-lb: | 408 | | 364 | | |
| Win. 180 FMJ | velocity, fps: | 990 | | 936 | | |

| CARTRIDGE BULLET | RANGE, YARDS: | 0 | 25 | 50 | 75 | 100 |
|---|---|---|---|---|---|---|
| | energy, ft-lb: | 390 | | 350 | | |
| Win. 180 SXT | velocity, fps: | 1010 | | 954 | | 909 |
| | energy, ft-lb: | 408 | | 364 | | 330 |
| Win. 180 EB WinClean | velocity, fps: | 990 | | 943 | | |
| | energy, ft-lb: | 392 | | 356 | | |

## 10 MM AUTO

| CARTRIDGE BULLET | RANGE, YARDS: | 0 | 25 | 50 | 75 | 100 |
|---|---|---|---|---|---|---|
| Federal 155 Hi-Shok JHP | velocity, fps: | 1330 | 1230 | 1140 | 1080 | 1030 |
| | energy, ft-lb: | 605 | 515 | 450 | 400 | 360 |
| Federal 180 Hi-Shok JHP | velocity, fps: | 1030 | 1000 | 970 | 950 | 920 |
| | energy, ft-lb: | 425 | 400 | 375 | 355 | 340 |
| Federal 180 Hydra-Shok JHP | velocity, fps: | 1030 | 1000 | 970 | 950 | 920 |
| | energy, ft-lb: | 425 | 400 | 375 | 355 | 340 |
| Federal 180 High Antim. Lead | velocity, fps: | 1030 | 1000 | 970 | 950 | 920 |
| | energy, ft-lb: | 425 | 400 | 375 | 355 | 340 |
| Federal 180 FMJ | velocity, fps: | 1060 | 1025 | 990 | 965 | 940 |
| | energy, ft-lb: | 400 | 370 | 350 | 330 | 310 |
| Hornady 155 JHP/XTP | velocity, fps: | 1265 | | 1119 | | 1020 |
| | energy, ft-lb: | 551 | | 431 | | 358 |
| Hornady 180 JHP/XTP | velocity, fps: | 1180 | | 1077 | | 1004 |
| | energy, ft-lb: | 556 | | 464 | | 403 |
| Hornady 200 JHP/XTP | velocity, fps: | 1050 | | 994 | | 948 |
| | energy, ft-lb: | 490 | | 439 | | 399 |
| PMC 115 Non-Toxic Frangible | velocity, fps: | 1350 | 1240 | 1154 | 1088 | 1035 |
| | energy, ft-lb: | 465 | | | | |
| PMC 170 JHP | velocity, fps: | 1200 | 1117 | 1052 | 1000 | 958 |
| | energy, ft-lb: | 543 | | | | |
| PMC 180 SFHP | velocity, fps: | 950 | 926 | 903 | 882 | 862 |
| | energy, ft-lb: | 361 | | | | |
| PMC 200 TC-FMJ | velocity, fps: | 1050 | 1008 | 972 | 941 | 912 |
| | energy, ft-lb: | 490 | | | | |
| Rem. 180 Metal Case | velocity, fps: | 1150 | | 1063 | | 998 |
| | energy, ft-lb: | 529 | | 452 | | 398 |
| Speer 200 TMJ Blazer | velocity, fps: | 1050 | | 966 | | 952 |
| | energy, ft-lb: | 490 | | 440 | | 402 |
| Win. 175 Silvertip HP | velocity, fps: | 1290 | | 1141 | | 1037 |
| | energy, ft-lb: | 649 | | 506 | | 418 |

## .41 REMINGTON MAGNUM

| CARTRIDGE BULLET | RANGE, YARDS: | 0 | 25 | 50 | 75 | 100 |
|---|---|---|---|---|---|---|
| Federal 210 Hi-Shok JHP | velocity, fps: | 1300 | 1210 | 1130 | 1070 | 1030 |
| | energy, ft-lb: | 790 | 680 | 595 | 540 | 495 |
| PMC 210 TCSP | velocity, fps: | 1290 | 1201 | 1128 | 1069 | 1021 |
| | energy, ft-lb: | 774 | | | | |
| PMC 210 JHP | velocity, fps: | 1289 | 1200 | 1127 | 1068 | 1020 |
| | energy, ft-lb: | 774 | | | | |
| Rem. 210 SP | velocity, fps: | 1300 | | 1162 | | 1062 |
| | energy, ft-lb: | 788 | | 630 | | 526 |
| Win. 175 Silvertip HP | velocity, fps: | 1250 | | 1120 | | 102 |
| | energy, ft-lb: | 607 | | 488 | | 412 |
| Win. 240 Platinum Tip | velocity, ft-lb: | 1250 | | 1151 | | 1075 |
| | energy, ft-lb: | 833 | | 706 | | 616 |

## .44 COLT

| CARTRIDGE BULLET | RANGE, YARDS: | 0 | 25 | 50 | 75 | 100 |
|---|---|---|---|---|---|---|
| Black Hills 230 FPL | velocity, fps: | 730 | | | | |
| | energy, ft-lb: | | | | | |

## .44 RUSSIAN

| CARTRIDGE BULLET | RANGE, YARDS: | 0 | 25 | 50 | 75 | 100 |
|---|---|---|---|---|---|---|
| Black Hills 210 FPL | velocity, fps: | 650 | | | | |
| | energy, ft-lb: | | | | | |

## .44 SPECIAL

| CARTRIDGE BULLET | RANGE, YARDS: | 0 | 25 | 50 | 75 | 100 |
|---|---|---|---|---|---|---|
| Black Hills 210 FPL | velocity, fps: | 700 | | | | |
| | energy, ft-lb: | | | | | |
| Federal 200 SWC HP | velocity, fps: | 900 | 860 | 830 | 800 | 770 |
| | energy, ft-lb: | 360 | 330 | 305 | 285 | 260 |
| Federal 250 CastCore | velocity, fps: | 1250 | 1200 | 1150 | 1110 | 1080 |
| | energy, ft-lb: | 865 | 795 | 735 | 685 | 645 |
| Hornady 180 JHP/XTP | velocity, fps: | 1000 | | 935 | | 882 |
| | energy, ft-lb: | 400 | | 350 | | 311 |
| Magtech 240 LFN | velocity, fps: | 750 | | 722 | | 696 |
| | energy, ft-lb: | 300 | | 278 | | 258 |
| PMC 180 JHP | velocity, fps: | 980 | 938 | 902 | 869 | 839 |
| | energy, ft-lb: | 383 | | | | |
| PMC 240 SWC-CP | velocity, fps: | 764 | 744 | 724 | 706 | 687 |
| | energy, ft-lb: | 311 | | | | |
| PMC 240 LFP | velocity, fps: | 750 | | 719 | | 690 |
| | energy, ft-lb: | 300 | | 275 | | 253 |
| Rem. 246 LRN | velocity, fps: | 755 | | 725 | | 695 |
| | energy, ft-lb: | 310 | | 285 | | 265 |
| Speer 200 HP Blazer | velocity, fps: | 875 | | 825 | | 780 |
| | energy, ft-lb: | 340 | | 302 | | 270 |
| Speer 200 Trail Blazer LFN | velocity, fps: | 750 | | 714 | | 680 |
| | energy, ft-lb: | 250 | | 226 | | 205 |
| Speer 200 Gold Dot | velocity, fps: | 875 | | 825 | | 780 |
| | energy, ft-lb: | 340 | | 302 | | 270 |
| Win. 200 Silvertip HP | velocity, fps: | 900 | | 860 | | 822 |
| | energy, ft-lb: | 360 | | 328 | | 300 |
| Win. 240 Lead | velocity, fps: | 750 | | 719 | | 690 |
| | energy, ft-lb | 300 | | 275 | | 253 |
| Win. 246 LRN | velocity, fps: | 755 | | 725 | | 695 |
| | energy, ft-lb: | 310 | | 285 | | 265 |

## .44 REMINGTON MAGNUM

| CARTRIDGE BULLET | RANGE, YARDS: | 0 | 25 | 50 | 75 | 100 |
|---|---|---|---|---|---|---|
| Black Hills 240 JHP | velocity, fps: | 1260 | | | | |
| | energy, ft-lb: | 848 | | | | |
| Black Hills 300 JHP | velocity, fps: | 1150 | | | | |
| | energy, ft-lb: | 879 | | | | |
| Federal 180 Hi-Shok JHP | velocity, fps: | 1610 | 1480 | 1370 | 1270 | 1180 |
| | energy, ft-lb: | 1035 | 875 | 750 | 640 | 555 |
| Federal 240 Hi-Shok JHP | velocity, fps: | 1180 | 1130 | 1080 | 1050 | 1010 |
| | energy, ft-lb: | 740 | 675 | 625 | 580 | 550 |
| Federal 240 Hydra-Shok JHP | velocity, fps: | 1180 | 1130 | 1080 | 1050 | 1010 |
| | energy, ft-lb: | 740 | 675 | 625 | 580 | 550 |
| Federal 240 JHP | velocity, fps: | 1180 | 1130 | 1080 | 1050 | 1010 |
| | energy, ft-lb: | 740 | 675 | 625 | 580 | 550 |
| Federal 300 CastCore | velocity, fps: | 1250 | 1200 | 1160 | 1120 | 1080 |
| | energy, ft-lb: | 1040 | 960 | 885 | 825 | 775 |
| Hornady 180 JHP/XTP | velocity, fps: | 1550 | | 1340 | | 1173 |
| | energy, ft-lb: | 960 | | 717 | | 550 |
| Hornady 200 JHP/XTP | velocity, fps: | 1500 | | 1284 | | 1128 |
| | energy, ft-lb: | 999 | | 732 | | 565 |
| Hornady 240 JHP/XTP | velocity, fps: | 1350 | | 1188 | | 1078 |
| | energy, ft-lb: | 971 | | 753 | | 619 |
| Hornady 300 JHP/XTP | velocity, fps: | 1150 | | 1084 | | 1031 |
| | energy, ft-lb: | 881 | | 782 | | 708 |

# Centerfire Handgun Ballistics

## .44 REMINGTON MAGNUM TO .45 AUTOMATIC (ACP)

| CARTRIDGE BULLET | RANGE, YARDS: | 0 | 25 | 50 | 75 | 100 |
|---|---|---|---|---|---|---|
| Magtech 240 SJSP | velocity, fps: | 1180 | | 1081 | | 1010 |
| | energy, ft-lb: | 741 | | 632 | | 623 |
| PMC 180 JHP | velocity, fps: | 1392 | 1263 | 1157 | 1076 | 1015 |
| | energy, ft-lb: | 772 | | | | |
| PMC 240 JHP | velocity, fps: | 1301 | 1218 | 1147 | 1088 | 1041 |
| | energy, ft-lb: | 900 | | | | |
| PMC 240 TC-SP | velocity, fps: | 1300 | 1216 | 1144 | 1086 | 1038 |
| | energy, ft-lb: | 900 | | | | |
| PMC 240 SFHP | velocity, fps: | 1300 | 1212 | 1138 | 1079 | 1030 |
| | energy, ft-lb: | 900 | | | | |
| PMC 240 LSWC-GCK | velocity, fps: | 1225 | 1143 | 1077 | 1025 | 982 |
| | energy, ft-lb: | 806 | | | | |
| Rem. 180 JSP | velocity, fps: | 1610 | | 1365 | | 1175 |
| | energy, ft-lb: | 1036 | | 745 | | 551 |
| Rem. 210 Gold Dot HP | velocity, fps: | 1450 | | 1276 | | 1140 |
| | energy, ft-lb: | 980 | | 759 | | 606 |
| Rem. 240 SP | velocity, fps: | 1180 | | 1081 | | 1010 |
| | energy, ft-lb: | 721 | | 623 | | 543 |
| Rem. 240 SJHP | velocity, fps: | 1180 | | 1081 | | 1010 |
| | energy, ft-lb: | 721 | | 623 | | 543 |
| Rem. 275 JHP Core-Lokt | velocity, fps: | 1235 | | 1142 | | 1070 |
| | energy, ft-lb: | 931 | | 797 | | 699 |
| Speer 240 JHP Blazer | velocity, fps: | 1200 | | 1092 | | 1015 |
| | energy, ft-lb: | 767 | | 636 | | 549 |
| Speer 240 Gold Dot HP | velocity, fps: | 1400 | | 1255 | | 1139 |
| | energy, ft-lb: | 1044 | | 839 | | 691 |
| Speer 270 Gold Dot SP | velocity, fps: | 1250 | | 1142 | | 1060 |
| | energy, ft-lb: | 937 | | 781 | | 674 |
| Win. 210 Silvertip HP | velocity, fps: | 1250 | | 1106 | | 1010 |
| | energy, ft-lb: | 729 | | 570 | | 475 |
| Win. 240 Hollow SP | velocity, fps: | 1180 | | 1081 | | 1010 |
| | energy, ft-lb: | 741 | | 623 | | 543 |
| Win. 240 JSP | velocity, fps: | 1180 | | 1081 | | |
| | energy, ft-lb: | 741 | | 623 | | |
| Win. 250 Partition Gold | velocity, fps: | 1230 | | 1132 | | 1057 |
| | energy, ft-lb: | 840 | | 711 | | 620 |
| Win. 250 Platinum Tip | velocity, fps: | 1250 | | 1148 | | 1070 |
| | energy, ft-lb: | 867 | | 732 | | 635 |

### .44-40

| CARTRIDGE BULLET | | 0 | 25 | 50 | 75 | 100 |
|---|---|---|---|---|---|---|
| Black Hills 200 RNFP | velocity, fps: | 800 | | | | |
| | energy, ft-lb: | | | | | |
| Hornady 205 Cowboy | velocity, fps: | 725 | | 697 | | 670 |
| | energy, ft-lb: | 239 | | 221 | | 204 |
| Magtech 225 LFN | velocity, fps: | 725 | | 703 | | 681 |
| | energy, ft-lb: | 281 | | 247 | | 232 |
| PMC 225 LFP | velocity, fps: | 725 | | 723 | | 695 |
| | energy, ft-lb: | 281 | | 261 | | 242 |
| Win. 225 Lead | velocity, fps: | 750 | | 723 | | 695 |
| | energy, ft-lb: | 281 | | 261 | | 242 |

### .45 AUTOMATIC (ACP)

| CARTRIDGE BULLET | | 0 | 25 | 50 | 75 | 100 |
|---|---|---|---|---|---|---|
| Black Hills 185 JHP | velocity, fps: | 1000 | | | | |
| | energy, ft-lb: | 411 | | | | |
| Black Hills 200 Match SWC | velocity, fps: | 875 | | | | |
| | energy, ft-lb: | 340 | | | | |
| Black Hills 230 FMJ | velocity, fps: | 850 | | | | |
| | energy, ft-lb: | 368 | | | | |
| Black Hills 230 JHP | velocity, fps: | 850 | | | | |
| | energy, ft-lb: | 368 | | | | |
| Black Hills 230 JHP +P | velocity, fps: | 950 | | | | |
| | energy, ft-lb: | 460 | | | | |
| Federal 165 Hydra-Shok JHP | velocity, fps: | 1060 | 1020 | 980 | 950 | 920 |
| | energy, ft-lb: | 410 | 375 | 350 | 330 | 310 |
| Federal 165 EFMJ | velocity, fps: | 1090 | 1045 | 1005 | 975 | 942 |
| | energy, ft-lb: | 435 | 400 | 370 | 345 | 325 |
| Federal 185 Hi-Shok JHP | velocity, fps: | 950 | 920 | 900 | 880 | 860 |
| | energy, ft-lb: | 370 | 350 | 335 | 315 | 300 |
| Federal 185 FMJ-SWC Match | velocity, fps: | 780 | 730 | 700 | 660 | 620 |
| | energy, ft-lb: | 245 | 220 | 200 | 175 | 160 |
| Federal 200 Exp. FMJ | velocity, fps: | 1030 | 1000 | 970 | 940 | 920 |
| | energy, ft-lb: | 470 | 440 | 415 | 395 | 375 |
| Federal 230 FMJ | velocity, fps: | 850 | 830 | 810 | 790 | 770 |
| | energy, ft-lb: | 370 | 350 | 335 | 320 | 305 |
| Federal 230 FMJ Match | velocity, fps: | 855 | 835 | 815 | 795 | 775 |
| | energy, ft-lb: | 375 | 355 | 340 | 325 | 305 |
| Federal 230 Hi-Shok JHP | velocity, fps: | 850 | 830 | 810 | 790 | 770 |
| | energy, ft-lb: | 370 | 350 | 335 | 320 | 300 |
| Federal 230 Hydra-Shok JHP | velocity, fps: | 850 | 830 | 810 | 790 | 770 |
| | energy, ft-lb: | 370 | 350 | 335 | 320 | 305 |
| Federal 230 FMJ | velocity, fps: | 850 | 830 | 810 | 790 | 770 |
| | energy, ft-lb: | 370 | 350 | 335 | 320 | 305 |
| Federal 230 TMJ TMF Primer | velocity, fps: | 850 | 830 | 810 | 790 | 770 |
| | energy, ft-lb: | 370 | 350 | 335 | 315 | 305 |
| Hornady 185 JHP/XTP | velocity, fps: | 950 | | 880 | | 819 |
| | energy, ft-lb: | 371 | | 318 | | 276 |
| Hornady 200 JHP/XTP | velocity, fps: | 900 | | 855 | | 815 |
| | energy, ft-lb: | 358 | | 325 | | 295 |
| Hornady 200 HP/XTP +P | velocity, fps: | 1055 | | 982 | | 925 |
| | energy, ft-lb: | 494 | | 428 | | 380 |
| Hornady 230 FMJ/RN | velocity, fps: | 850 | | 809 | | 771 |
| | energy, ft-lb: | 369 | | 334 | | 304 |
| Hornady 230 FMJ/FP | velocity, fps: | 850 | | 809 | | 771 |
| | energy, ft-lb: | 369 | | 334 | | 304 |
| Hornady 230 HP/XTP +P | velocity, fps: | 950 | | 904 | | 865 |
| | energy, ft-lb: | 462 | | 418 | | 382 |
| Magtech 185 JHP +P | velocity, fps: | 1148 | | 1066 | | 1055 |
| | energy, ft-lb: | 540 | | 467 | | 415 |
| Magtech 200 LSWC | velocity, fps: | 950 | | 910 | | 874 |
| | energy, ft-lb: | 401 | | 368 | | 339 |
| Magtech 230 FMC | velociy, fps: | 837 | | 800 | | 767 |
| | energy, ft-lb: | 356 | | 326 | | 300 |
| Magtech 230 FMC-SWC | velocity, fps: | 780 | | 720 | | 660 |
| | energy, ft-lb: | 310 | | 265 | | 222 |
| PMC 145 Non-Toxic Frangible | velocity, fps: | 1100 | 1045 | 999 | 961 | 928 |
| | energy, ft-lb: | 390 | | | | |
| PMC 185 JHP | velocity, fps: | 903 | 870 | 839 | 811 | 785 |
| | energy, ft-lb: | 339 | | | | |
| PMC 200 FMJ-SWC | velocity, fps: | 850 | 818 | 788 | 761 | 734 |
| | energy, ft-lb: | 321 | | | | |
| PMC 230 SFHP | velocity, fps: | 850 | 830 | 811 | 792 | 775 |
| | energy, ft-lb: | 369 | | | | |
| PMC 230 FMJ | velocity, fps: | 830 | 809 | 789 | 769 | 749 |
| | energy, ft-lb: | 352 | | | | |

| CARTRIDGE BULLET | RANGE, YARDS: | 0 | 25 | 50 | 75 | 100 |
|---|---|---|---|---|---|---|
| Rem. 175 Lead Free Frangible | velocity, fps: | 1020 | | 923 | | 851 |
| | energy, ft-lb: | 404 | | 331 | | 281 |
| Rem. 185 JHP | velocity, fps: | 1000 | | 939 | | 889 |
| | energy, ft-lb: | 411 | | 362 | | 324 |
| Rem. 185 BJHP | velocity, fps: | 1015 | | 951 | | 899 |
| | energy, ft-lb: | 423 | | 372 | | 332 |
| Rem. 185 BJHP +P | velocity, fps: | 1140 | | 1042 | | 971 |
| | energy, ft-lb: | 534 | | 446 | | 388 |
| Rem. 185 MC | velocity, fps: | 1015 | | 955 | | 907 |
| | energy, ft-lb: | 423 | | 375 | | 338 |
| Rem. 230 FN Enclosed Base | velocity, fps: | 835 | | 800 | | 767 |
| | energy, ft-lb: | 356 | | 326 | | 300 |
| Rem. 230 Metal Case | velocity, fps: | 835 | | 800 | | 767 |
| | energy, ft-lb: | 356 | | 326 | | 300 |
| Rem. 230 JHP | velocity, fps: | 835 | | 800 | | 767 |
| | energy, ft-lb: | 356 | | 326 | | 300 |
| Rem. 230 BJHP | velocity, fps: | 875 | | 833 | | 795 |
| | energy, ft-lb: | 391 | | 355 | | 323 |
| Speer 140 Frangible | velocity, fps: | 1200 | | 1029 | | 928 |
| | energy, ft-lb: | 448 | | 329 | | 268 |
| Speer 185 Gold Dot | velocity, fps: | 1050 | | 956 | | 886 |
| | energy, ft-lb: | 453 | | 375 | | 322 |
| Speer 185 TMJ/FN | velocity, fps: | 1000 | | 909 | | 839 |
| | energy, ft-lb: | 411 | | 339 | | 289 |
| Speer 200 JHP Blazer | velocity, fps: | 975 | | 917 | | 860 |
| | energy, ft-lb: | 421 | | 372 | | 328 |
| Speer 200 Gold Dot +P | velocity, fps: | 1080 | | 994 | | 930 |
| | energy, ft-lb: | 518 | | 439 | | 384 |
| Speer 200 TMJ/FN | velocity, fps: | 975 | | 897 | | 834 |
| | energy, ft-lb: | 422 | | 357 | | 309 |
| Speer 230 FMJ (and Blazer) | velocity, fps: | 845 | | 804 | | 775 |
| | energy, ft-lb: | 363 | | 329 | | 304 |
| Speer 230 TMJ-CF (and Blazer) | velocity, fps: | 845 | | 804 | | 775 |
| | energy, ft-lb: | 363 | | 329 | | 304 |
| Speer 230 Gold Dot | velocity, fps: | 890 | | 845 | | 805 |
| | energy, ft-lb: | 405 | | 365 | | 331 |
| Win. 170 JFP | velocity, fps: | 1050 | | 982 | | 928 |
| | energy, ft-lb: | 416 | | 364 | | 325 |
| Win. 185 Silvertip HP | velocity, fps: | 1000 | | 938 | | 888 |
| | energy, ft-lb: | 411 | | 362 | | 324 |
| Win. 185 FMJ FN | velocity, fps: | 910 | | 861 | | |
| | energy, ft-lb: | 340 | | 304 | | |
| Win. 185 EB WinClean | velocity, fps: | 910 | | 835 | | |
| | energy, ft-lb: | 340 | | 286 | | |
| Win. 230 JHP | velocity, fps: | 880 | | 842 | | |
| | energy, ft-lb: | 396 | | 363 | | |
| Win. 230 FMJ | velocity, fps: | 835 | | 800 | | |
| | energy, ft-lb: | 356 | | 326 | | |
| Win. 230 SXT | velocity, fps: | 880 | | 846 | | 816 |
| | energy, ft-lb: | 396 | | 366 | | 340 |
| Win. 230 JHP subsonic | velocity, fps: | 880 | | 842 | | 808 |
| | energy, ft-lb: | 396 | | 363 | | 334 |
| Win. 230 EB WinClean | velocity, fps: | 835 | | 802 | | |
| | energy, ft-lb: | 356 | | 329 | | |

## .45 GAP

| | | 0 | 25 | 50 | 75 | 100 |
|---|---|---|---|---|---|---|
| Federal 185 TMJ | velocity, fps: | 1090 | 1020 | 970 | 920 | 890 |
| | energy, ft-lb: | 490 | 430 | 385 | 350 | 320 |
| Federal 185 Hydra-Shok JHP | velocity, fps: | 1090 | 1020 | 970 | 920 | 890 |
| | energy, ft-lb: | 490 | 430 | 385 | 350 | 320 |
| Win. 185 STHP | velocity, fps: | 1000 | | 938 | | 887 |
| | energy, ft-lb: | 411 | | 361 | | 323 |
| Win. 230 JHP | velocity, fps: | 880 | | 842 | | |
| | Energy, ft-lb: | 396 | | 363 | | |
| Win. 230 EB WinClean | velocity, fps: | 875 | | 840 | | |
| | Energy, ft-lb: | 391 | | 360 | | |
| Win. 230 FMJ | velocity, fps: | 850 | | 814 | | |
| | Energy, ft-lb: | 369 | | 338 | | |

## .45 Winchester Magnum

| | | 0 | 25 | 50 | 75 | 100 |
|---|---|---|---|---|---|---|
| Win. 260 Partition Gold | velocity, fps: | 1200 | | 1105 | | 1033 |
| | energy, ft-lb: | 832 | | 705 | | 616 |
| Win. 260 JHP | velocity, fps: | 1200 | | 1099 | | 1026 |
| | energy, ft-lb: | 831 | | 698 | | 607 |

## .45 Schofield

| | | 0 | 25 | 50 | 75 | 100 |
|---|---|---|---|---|---|---|
| Black Hills 180 FNL | velocity, fps: | 730 | | | | |
| | energy, ft-lb: | | | | | |
| Black Hills 230 RNFP | velocity, fps: | 730 | | | | |
| | energy, ft-lb: | | | | | |

## .45 Colt

| | | 0 | 25 | 50 | 75 | 100 |
|---|---|---|---|---|---|---|
| Black Hills 250 RNFP | velocity, fps: | 725 | | | | |
| | energy, ft-lb: | | | | | |
| Federal 225 SWC HP | velocity, fps: | 900 | 880 | 860 | 840 | 820 |
| | energy, ft-lb: | 405 | 385 | 370 | 355 | 340 |
| Hornady 255 Cowboy | velocity, fps: | 725 | | 692 | | 660 |
| | energy, ft-lb: | 298 | | 271 | | 247 |
| Magtech 250 LFN | velocity, fps: | 750 | | 726 | | 702 |
| | energy, ft-lb: | 312 | | 293 | | 274 |
| PMC 250 LFP | velocity, fps: | 800 | | 767 | | 736 |
| | energy, ft-lb: | 355 | | 331 | | 309 |
| PMC 300 +P+ | velocity, fps: | 1250 | 1192 | 1144 | 1102 | 1066 |
| | energy, ft-lb: | 1041 | | | | |
| Rem. 225 SWC | velocity, fps: | 960 | | 890 | | 832 |
| | energy, ft-lb: | 460 | | 395 | | 346 |
| Rem. 250 RLN | velocity, fps: | 860 | | 820 | | 780 |
| | energy, ft-lb: | 410 | | 375 | | 340 |
| Speer 200 FMJ Blazer | velocity, fps: | 1000 | | 938 | | 889 |
| | energy, ft-lb: | 444 | | 391 | | 351 |
| Speer 230 Trail Blazer LFN | velocity, fps: | 750 | | 716 | | 684 |
| | energy, ft-lb: | 287 | | 262 | | 239 |
| Speer 250 Gold Dot | velocity, fps: | 900 | | 860 | | 823 |
| | energy, ft-lb: | 450 | | 410 | | 376 |
| Win. 225 Silvertip HP | velocity, fps: | 920 | | 877 | | 839 |
| | energy, ft-lb: | 423 | | 384 | | 352 |
| Win. 255 LRN | velocity, fps: | 860 | | 820 | | 780 |
| | energy, ft-lb: | 420 | | 380 | | 345 |
| Win. 250 Lead | velocity, fps: | 750 | | 720 | | 692 |
| | energy, ft-lb: | 312 | | 288 | | 266 |

## .454 Casull

| | | 0 | 25 | 50 | 75 | 100 |
|---|---|---|---|---|---|---|
| Federal 300 Trophy Bonded | velocity, fps: | 1630 | 1540 | 1450 | 1380 | 1300 |
| | energy, ft-lb: | 1760 | 1570 | 1405 | 1260 | 1130 |
| Federal 360 CastCore | velocity, fps: | 1500 | 1435 | 1370 | 1310 | 1255 |

# Centerfire Handgun Ballistics

## 454 CASUAL TO .50 ACTION EXPRESS

| CARTRIDGE BULLET | RANGE, YARDS: | 0 | 25 | 50 | 75 | 100 |
|---|---|---|---|---|---|---|
| | energy, ft-lb: | 1800 | 1640 | 1500 | 1310 | 1260 |
| Hornady 240 XTP-MAG | velocity, fps: | 1900 | | 1679 | | 1483 |
| | energy, ft-lb: | 1923 | | 1502 | | 1172 |
| Hornady 300 XTP-MAG | velocity, fps: | 1650 | | 1478 | | 1328 |
| | energy, ft-lb: | 1813 | | 1455 | | 1175 |
| Magtech 260 SJSP | velocity, fps: | 1800 | | 1577 | | 1383 |
| | energy, ft-lb: | 1871 | | 1437 | | 1104 |
| Rem. 300 Core-Lokt Ultra | velocity, fps: | 1625 | | 1472 | | 1335 |
| | energy, ft-lb: | 1759 | | 1442 | | 1187 |
| Speer 300 Gold Dot HP | velocity, fps: | 1625 | | 1477 | | 1343 |
| | energy, ft-lb: | 1758 | | 1452 | | 1201 |
| Win. 250 JHP | velocity, fps: | 1300 | | 1151 | | 1047 |
| | energy, ft-lb: | 938 | | 735 | | 608 |
| Win. 260 Partition Gold | velocity, fps: | 1800 | | 1605 | | 1427 |
| | energy, ft-lb: | 1871 | | 1485 | | 1176 |
| Win. 260 Platinum Tip | velocity, fps: | 1800 | | 1596 | | 1414 |
| | eneryg, ft-lb: | 1870 | | 1470 | | 1154 |
| Win. 300 JFP | velocity, fps: | 1625 | | 1451 | | 1308 |
| | energy, ft-lb: | 1759 | | 1413 | | 1141 |

## .475 LINEBAUGH

| CARTRIDGE BULLET | RANGE, YARDS: | 0 | 25 | 50 | 75 | 100 |
|---|---|---|---|---|---|---|
| Hornady 400 XTP-MAG | velocity, fps: | 1300 | | 1179 | | 1093 |
| | energy, ft-lb: | 1501 | | 1235 | | 1060 |

## .480 RUGER

| CARTRIDGE BULLET | RANGE, YARDS: | 0 | 25 | 50 | 75 | 100 |
|---|---|---|---|---|---|---|
| Hornady 325 XTP-MAG | velocity, fps: | 1350 | | 1191 | | 1076 |
| | energy, ft-lb: | 1315 | | 1023 | | 835 |
| Hornady 400 XTP-MAG | velocity, fps: | 1100 | | 1027 | | 971 |
| | Energy, ft-lb: | 1075 | | 937 | | 838 |
| Speer 275 Gold Dot HP | velocity, fps: | 1450 | | 1284 | | 1152 |
| | energy, ft-lb: | 1284 | | 1007 | | 810 |
| Speer 325 SP | velocity, fps: | 1350 | | 1224 | | 1124 |
| | energy, ft-lb: | 1315 | | 1082 | | 912 |

## .50 ACTION EXPRESS

| CARTRIDGE BULLET | RANGE, YARDS: | 0 | 25 | 50 | 75 | 100 |
|---|---|---|---|---|---|---|
| Speer 300 Gold Dot HP | velocity, fps: | 1550 | | 1361 | | 1207 |
| | energy, ft-lb: | 1600 | | 1234 | | 970 |
| Speer 325 UCHP | velocity, fps: | 1400 | | 1232 | | 1106 |
| | energy, ft-lb: | 1414 | | 1095 | | 883 |

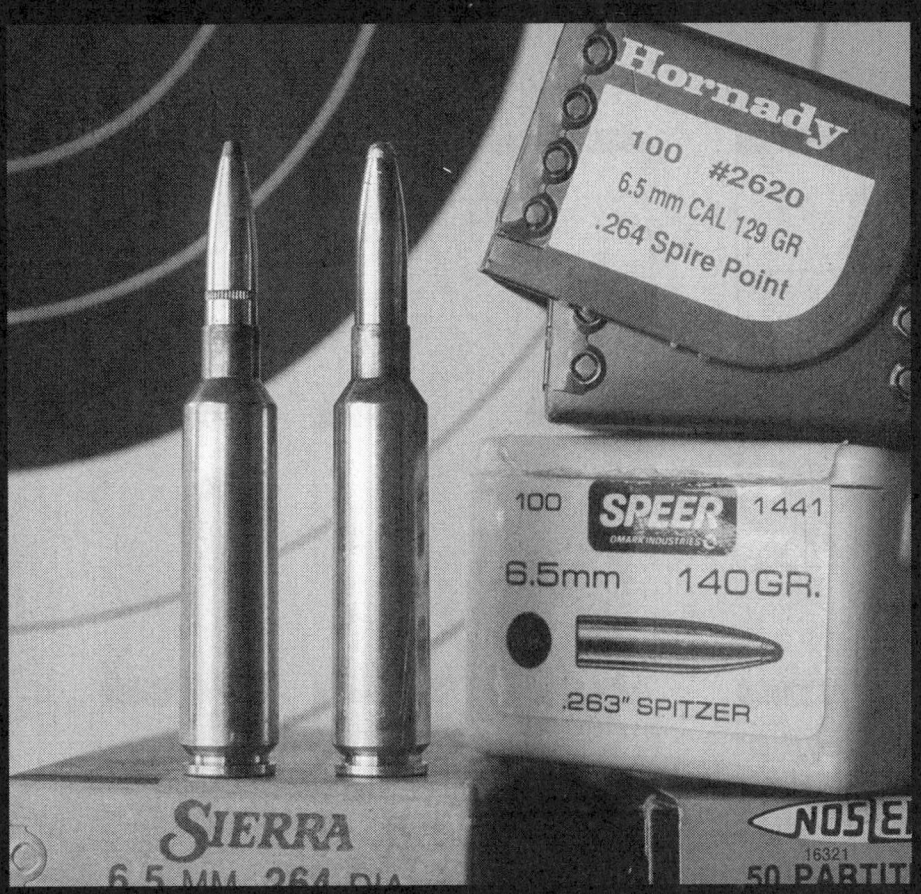

# Barnes Bullets
## The All Copper Barnes X-Bullet

| 22 CAL. | | |
|---|---|---|
| dia. | .224" | |
| wgt. | 50 gr | |
| type | "X" S | |
| dens. | .142 | |
| coef. | .220 | |
| cat. # | 22450 | |

| 22 CAL. | | |
|---|---|---|
| DIA. | .224" | |
| WGT. | 53 GR | |
| TYPE | "X" S | |
| DENS. | .151 | |
| COEF. | .231 | |
| CAT. # | 22453 | |

| 6MM | | |
|---|---|---|
| DIA. | .243" | |
| WGT. | 85 GR | |
| TYPE | "X" BT | |
| DENS. | .206 | |
| COEF. | .401 | |
| CAT. # | 24310 | |

| 6MM | | |
|---|---|---|
| DIA. | .243" | |
| WGT. | 90 GR | |
| TYPE | "X" S | |
| DENS. | .218 | |
| COEF. | .382 | |
| CAT. # | 24315 | |

| 25 CAL. | | |
|---|---|---|
| DIA. | .257" | |
| WGT. | 90 GR | |
| TYPE | "X" BT | |
| DENS. | .195 | |
| COEF. | .343 | |
| CAT. # | 25710 | |

| 25 CAL. | | |
|---|---|---|
| DIA. | .257" | |
| WGT. | 100 GR | |
| TYPE | "X" BT | |
| DENS. | .216 | |
| COEF. | .420 | |
| CAT. # | 25717 | |

| 6.5 CAL. | | |
|---|---|---|
| DIA. | .264" | |
| WGT. | 120 GR | |
| TYPE | "X" S | |
| DENS. | .246 | |
| COEF. | .441 | |
| CAT. # | 26402 | |

| 270 CAL. | | |
|---|---|---|
| DIA. | .277" | |
| WGT. | 130 GR | |
| TYPE | "X" S | |
| DENS. | .242 | |
| COEF. | .428 | |
| CAT. # | 7715 | |

| 270 CAL. | | |
|---|---|---|
| DIA. | .277" | |
| WGT. | 130 GR | |
| TYPE | "X" BT | |
| DENS. | .242 | |
| COEF. | .466 | |
| CAT. # | 27717 | |

| 270 CAL. | | |
|---|---|---|
| DIA. | .277" | |
| WGT. | 140 GR | |
| TYPE | "X" BT | |
| DENS. | .261 | |
| COEF. | .497 | |
| CAT. # | 27727 | |

| 270 CAL. | | |
|---|---|---|
| DIA. | .277" | |
| WGT. | 150 GR | |
| TYPE | "X" S | |
| DENS. | .279 | |
| COEF. | .491 | |
| CAT. # | 27735 | |

| 7MM | | |
|---|---|---|
| DIA. | .284" | |
| WGT. | 120 GR | |
| TYPE | "X" BT | |
| DENS. | .213 | |
| COEF. | .411 | |
| CAT. # | 28417 | |

| 7MM | | |
|---|---|---|
| DIA. | .284" | |
| WGT. | 130 GR | |
| TYPE | "X" BT | |
| DENS. | .230 | |
| COEF. | .444 | |
| CAT. # | 28420 | |

| 7MM | | |
|---|---|---|
| DIA. | .284" | |
| WGT. | 140 GR | |
| TYPE | "X" S | |
| DENS. | .248 | |
| COEF. | .436 | |
| CAT. # | 28425 | |

| 7MM | | |
|---|---|---|
| DIA. | .284" | |
| WGT. | 140 GR | |
| TYPE | "X" BT | |
| DENS. | .248 | |
| COEF. | .477 | |
| CAT. # | 28426 | |

| 7MM | | |
|---|---|---|
| DIA. | .284" | |
| WGT. | 150 GR | |
| TYPE | "X" BT | |
| DENS. | .266 | |
| COEF. | .529 | |
| CAT. # | 28428 | |

| 7MM | | |
|---|---|---|
| DIA. | .284" | |
| WGT. | 160 GR | |
| TYPE | "X" S | |
| DENS. | .283 | |
| COEF. | .508 | |
| CAT. # | 28435 | |

| 7MM | | |
|---|---|---|
| DIA. | .284" | |
| WGT. | 175 GR | |
| TYPE | "X" S | |
| DENS. | .310 | |
| COEF. | .530 | |
| CAT. # | 28445 | |

| 30 CAL. | | |
|---|---|---|
| DIA. | .308" | |
| WGT. | 130 GR | |
| TYPE | "X" BT | |
| DENS. | .196 | |
| COEF. | .374 | |
| CAT. # | 30808 | |

| 30 CAL. | | |
|---|---|---|
| DIA. | .308" | |
| WGT. | 140 GR | |
| TYPE | "X" BT | |
| DENS. | .211 | |
| COEF. | .398 | |
| CAT. # | 30810 | |

| 30 CAL. | | |
|---|---|---|
| DIA. | .308" | |
| WGT. | 150 GR | |
| TYPE | "X" S | |
| DENS. | .226 | |
| COEF. | .386 | |
| CAT. # | 30815 | |

| 30 CAL. | | |
|---|---|---|
| DIA. | .308" | |
| WGT. | 150 GR | |
| TYPE | "X" BT | |
| DENS. | .226 | |
| COEF. | .428 | |
| CAT. # | 30817 | |

| 30 CAL. | | |
|---|---|---|
| DIA. | .308" | |
| WGT. | 165 GR | |
| TYPE | "X" S | |
| DENS. | .247 | |
| COEF. | .456 | |
| CAT. # | 30825 | |

| 30 CAL. | | |
|---|---|---|
| DIA. | .308" | |
| WGT. | 165 GR | |
| TYPE | "X" BT | |
| DENS. | .247 | |
| COEF. | .505 | |
| CAT. # | 30827 | |

| 30 CAL. | | |
|---|---|---|
| DIA. | .308" | |
| WGT. | 180 GR | |
| TYPE | "X" S | |
| DENS. | .271 | |
| COEF. | .511 | |
| CAT. # | 30835 | |

| 30 CAL. | | |
|---|---|---|
| DIA. | .308" | |
| WGT. | 180 GR | |
| TYPE | "X" BT | |
| DENS. | .271 | |
| COEF. | .552 | |
| CAT. # | 30840 | |

| 30 CAL. | | |
|---|---|---|
| DIA. | .308" | |
| WGT. | 200 GR | |
| TYPE | "X" S | |
| DENS. | .301 | |
| COEF. | .550 | |
| CAT. # | 30845 | |

| 30/30 CAL. | | |
|---|---|---|
| DIA. | .308" | |
| WGT. | 150 GR | |
| TYPE | "X" FN | |
| DENS. | .226 | |
| COEF. | .269 | |
| CAT. # | 30819 | |

| 8MM | | |
|---|---|---|
| DIA. | .323" | |
| WGT. | 180 GR | |
| TYPE | "X" S | |
| DENS. | .246 | |
| COEF. | .382 | |
| CAT. # | 32305 | |

# Barnes Bullets
## The All Copper Barnes X-Bullet

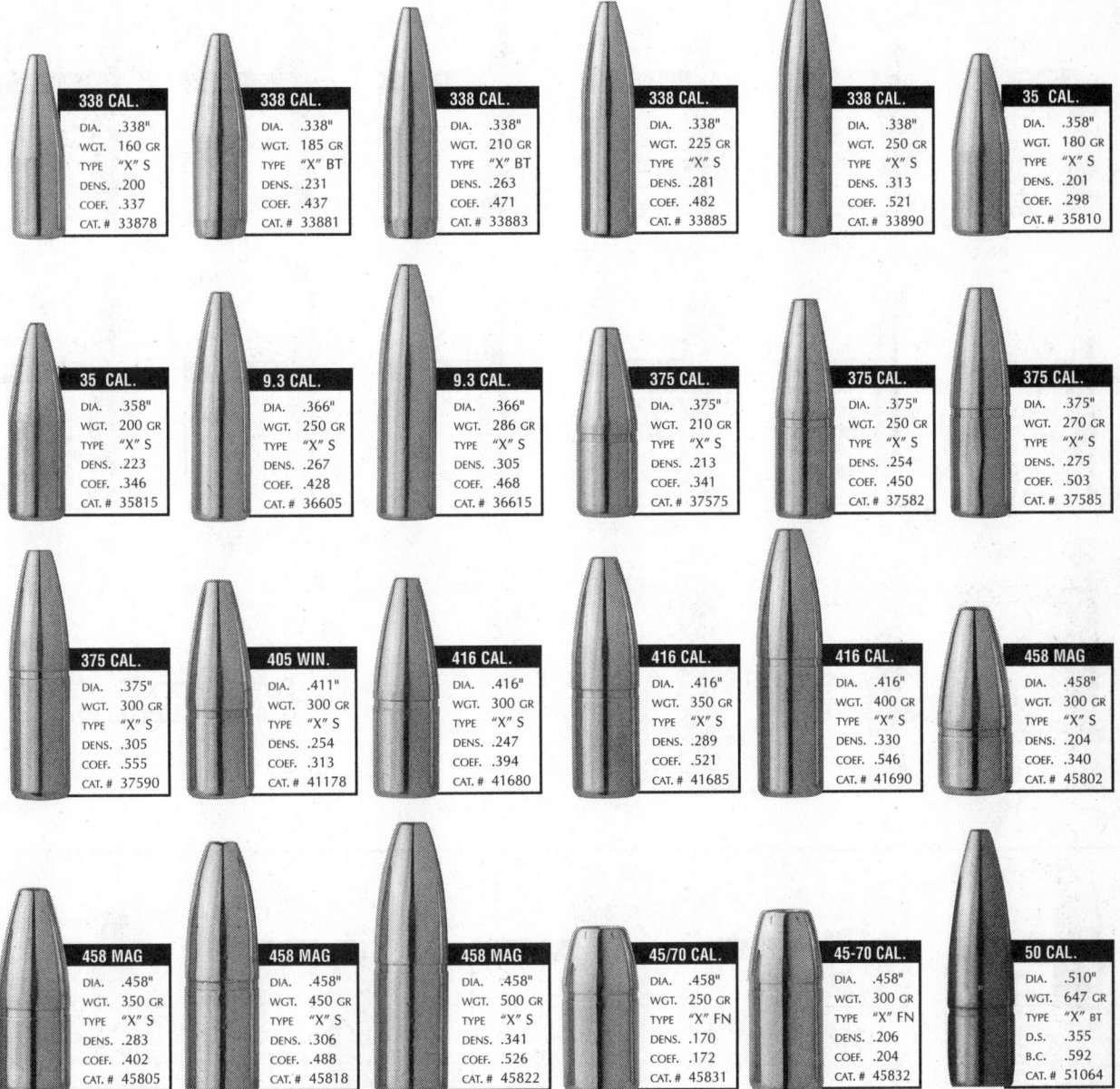

| 338 CAL. | |
|---|---|
| DIA. | .338" |
| WGT. | 160 GR |
| TYPE | "X" S |
| DENS. | .200 |
| COEF. | .337 |
| CAT. # | 33878 |

| 338 CAL. | |
|---|---|
| DIA. | .338" |
| WGT. | 185 GR |
| TYPE | "X" BT |
| DENS. | .231 |
| COEF. | .437 |
| CAT. # | 33881 |

| 338 CAL. | |
|---|---|
| DIA. | .338" |
| WGT. | 210 GR |
| TYPE | "X" BT |
| DENS. | .263 |
| COEF. | .471 |
| CAT. # | 33883 |

| 338 CAL. | |
|---|---|
| DIA. | .338" |
| WGT. | 225 GR |
| TYPE | "X" S |
| DENS. | .281 |
| COEF. | .482 |
| CAT. # | 33885 |

| 338 CAL. | |
|---|---|
| DIA. | .338" |
| WGT. | 250 GR |
| TYPE | "X" S |
| DENS. | .313 |
| COEF. | .521 |
| CAT. # | 33890 |

| 35 CAL. | |
|---|---|
| DIA. | .358" |
| WGT. | 180 GR |
| TYPE | "X" S |
| DENS. | .201 |
| COEF. | .298 |
| CAT. # | 35810 |

| 35 CAL. | |
|---|---|
| DIA. | .358" |
| WGT. | 200 GR |
| TYPE | "X" S |
| DENS. | .223 |
| COEF. | .346 |
| CAT. # | 35815 |

| 9.3 CAL. | |
|---|---|
| DIA. | .366" |
| WGT. | 250 GR |
| TYPE | "X" S |
| DENS. | .267 |
| COEF. | .428 |
| CAT. # | 36605 |

| 9.3 CAL. | |
|---|---|
| DIA. | .366" |
| WGT. | 286 GR |
| TYPE | "X" S |
| DENS. | .305 |
| COEF. | .468 |
| CAT. # | 36615 |

| 375 CAL. | |
|---|---|
| DIA. | .375" |
| WGT. | 210 GR |
| TYPE | "X" S |
| DENS. | .213 |
| COEF. | .341 |
| CAT. # | 37575 |

| 375 CAL. | |
|---|---|
| DIA. | .375" |
| WGT. | 250 GR |
| TYPE | "X" S |
| DENS. | .254 |
| COEF. | .450 |
| CAT. # | 37582 |

| 375 CAL. | |
|---|---|
| DIA. | .375" |
| WGT. | 270 GR |
| TYPE | "X" S |
| DENS. | .275 |
| COEF. | .503 |
| CAT. # | 37585 |

| 375 CAL. | |
|---|---|
| DIA. | .375" |
| WGT. | 300 GR |
| TYPE | "X" S |
| DENS. | .305 |
| COEF. | .555 |
| CAT. # | 37590 |

| 405 WIN. | |
|---|---|
| DIA. | .411" |
| WGT. | 300 GR |
| TYPE | "X" S |
| DENS. | .254 |
| COEF. | .313 |
| CAT. # | 41178 |

| 416 CAL. | |
|---|---|
| DIA. | .416" |
| WGT. | 300 GR |
| TYPE | "X" S |
| DENS. | .247 |
| COEF. | .394 |
| CAT. # | 41680 |

| 416 CAL. | |
|---|---|
| DIA. | .416" |
| WGT. | 350 GR |
| TYPE | "X" S |
| DENS. | .289 |
| COEF. | .521 |
| CAT. # | 41685 |

| 416 CAL. | |
|---|---|
| DIA. | .416" |
| WGT. | 400 GR |
| TYPE | "X" S |
| DENS. | .330 |
| COEF. | .546 |
| CAT. # | 41690 |

| 458 MAG | |
|---|---|
| DIA. | .458" |
| WGT. | 300 GR |
| TYPE | "X" S |
| DENS. | .204 |
| COEF. | .340 |
| CAT. # | 45802 |

| 458 MAG | |
|---|---|
| DIA. | .458" |
| WGT. | 350 GR |
| TYPE | "X" S |
| DENS. | .283 |
| COEF. | .402 |
| CAT. # | 45805 |

| 458 MAG | |
|---|---|
| DIA. | .458" |
| WGT. | 450 GR |
| TYPE | "X" S |
| DENS. | .306 |
| COEF. | .488 |
| CAT. # | 45818 |

| 458 MAG | |
|---|---|
| DIA. | .458" |
| WGT. | 500 GR |
| TYPE | "X" S |
| DENS. | .341 |
| COEF. | .526 |
| CAT. # | 45822 |

| 45/70 CAL. | |
|---|---|
| DIA. | .458" |
| WGT. | 250 GR |
| TYPE | "X" FN |
| DENS. | .170 |
| COEF. | .172 |
| CAT. # | 45831 |

| 45-70 CAL. | |
|---|---|
| DIA. | .458" |
| WGT. | 300 GR |
| TYPE | "X" FN |
| DENS. | .206 |
| COEF. | .204 |
| CAT. # | 45832 |

| 50 CAL. | |
|---|---|
| DIA. | .510" |
| WGT. | 647 GR |
| TYPE | "X" BT |
| D.S. | .355 |
| B.C. | .592 |
| CAT. # | 51064 |

# Barnes Bullets
## Triple-Shock and Expander MZ Muzzleloader Bullets

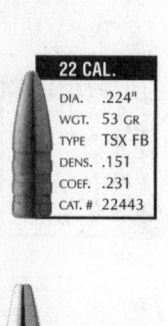

**22 CAL.**
DIA. .224"
WGT. 53 GR
TYPE TSX FB
DENS. .151
COEF. .231
CAT. # 22443

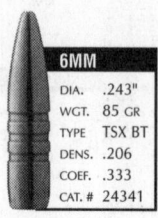

**6MM**
DIA. .243"
WGT. 85 GR
TYPE TSX FB
DENS. .206
COEF. .333
CAT. # 24341

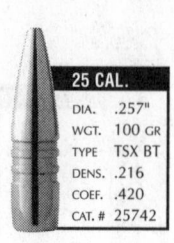

**25 CAL.**
DIA. .257"
WGT. 100 GR
TYPE TSX BT
DENS. .216
COEF. .420
CAT. # 25742

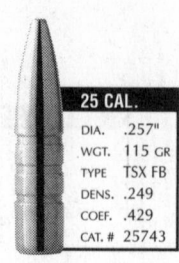

**25 CAL.**
DIA. .257"
WGT. 115 GR
TYPE TSX FB
DENS. .249
COEF. .429
CAT. # 25743

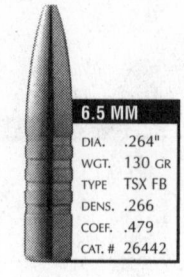

**6.5 MM**
DIA. .264"
WGT. 130 GR
TYPE TSX FB
DENS. .266
COEF. .479
CAT. # 26442

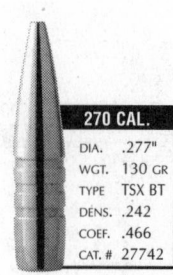

**270 CAL.**
DIA. .277"
WGT. 130 GR
TYPE TSX BT
DENS. .242
COEF. .466
CAT. # 27742

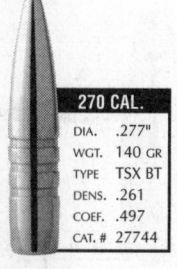

**270 CAL.**
DIA. .277"
WGT. 140 GR
TYPE TSX BT
DENS. .261
COEF. .497
CAT. # 27744

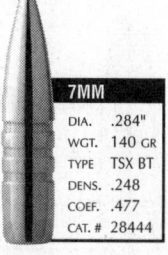

**7MM**
DIA. .284"
WGT. 140 GR
TYPE TSX BT
DENS. .248
COEF. .477
CAT. # 28444

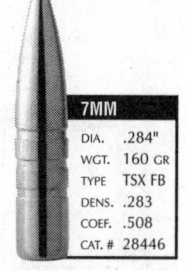

**7MM**
DIA. .284"
WGT. 160 GR
TYPE TSX FB
DENS. .283
COEF. .508
CAT. # 28446

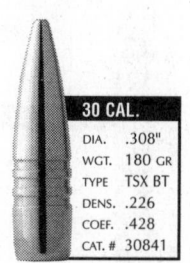

**30 CAL.**
DIA. .308"
WGT. 180 GR
TYPE TSX BT
DENS. .226
COEF. .428
CAT. # 30841

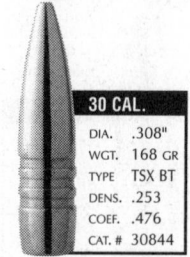

**30 CAL.**
DIA. .308"
WGT. 168 GR
TYPE TSX BT
DENS. .253
COEF. .476
CAT. # 30844

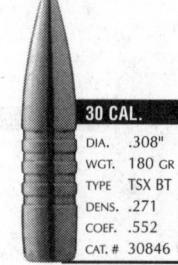

**30 CAL.**
DIA. .308"
WGT. 180 GR
TYPE TSX BT
DENS. .271
COEF. .552
CAT. # 30846

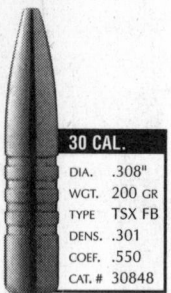

**30 CAL.**
DIA. .308"
WGT. 200 GR
TYPE TSX FB
DENS. .301
COEF. .550
CAT. # 30848

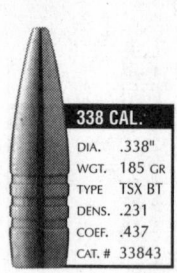

**338 CAL.**
DIA. .338"
WGT. 185 GR
TYPE TSX BT
DENS. .231
COEF. .437
CAT. # 33843

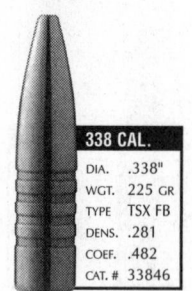

**338 CAL.**
DIA. .338"
WGT. 225 GR
TYPE TSX FB
DENS. .281
COEF. .482
CAT. # 33846

## TRIPLE-SHOCK™ BARNES X-BULLET™
Greater velocity, lower pressure, and less fouling.

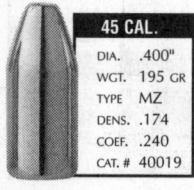

**45 CAL.**
DIA. .400"
WGT. 195 GR
TYPE MZ
DENS. .174
COEF. .240
CAT. # 40019

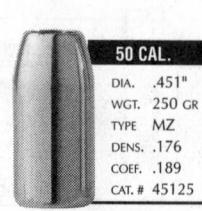

**50 CAL.**
DIA. .451"
WGT. 250 GR
TYPE MZ
DENS. .176
COEF. .189
CAT. # 45125

**50 CAL.**
DIA. .451"
WGT. 300 GR
TYPE MZ
DENS. .211
COEF. .207
CAT. # 45130

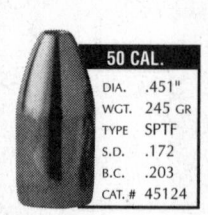

**50 CAL.**
DIA. .451"
WGT. 245 GR
TYPE SPTF
S.D. .172
B.C. .203
CAT. # 45124

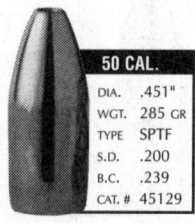

**50 CAL.**
DIA. .451"
WGT. 285 GR
TYPE SPTF
S.D. .200
B.C. .239
CAT. # 45129

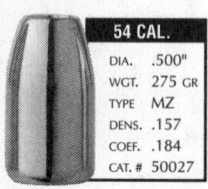

**54 CAL.**
DIA. .500"
WGT. 275 GR
TYPE MZ
DENS. .157
COEF. .184
CAT. # 50027

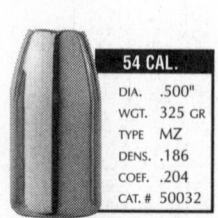

**54 CAL.**
DIA. .500"
WGT. 325 GR
TYPE MZ
DENS. .186
COEF. .204
CAT. # 50032

**45 CAL. ALIGNER**
CAT. # 04500

**50 CAL. ALIGNER**
CAT. # 05000

**54 CAL. ALIGNER**
CAT. # 05400

## EXPANDER MZ™ MUZZLELOADER BULLETS
With only one shot available, it better be with the best.

# Barnes Bullets
## XLC Coated X-Bullets

**6.5 CAL.**
| | |
|---|---|
| DIA. | .264" |
| WGT. | 140 GR |
| TYPE | "XLC" S |
| DENS. | .287 |
| COEF. | .522 |
| CAT. # | 26453 |

**270 CAL.**
| | |
|---|---|
| DIA. | .277" |
| WGT. | 130 GR |
| TYPE | "XLC" BT |
| DENS. | .242 |
| COEF. | .466 |
| CAT. # | 27754 |

**7MM**
| | |
|---|---|
| DIA. | .284" |
| WGT. | 140 GR |
| TYPE | "XLC" BT |
| DENS. | .248 |
| COEF. | .477 |
| CAT. # | 28455 |

**7MM**
| | |
|---|---|
| DIA. | .284" |
| WGT. | 160 GR |
| TYPE | "XLC" S |
| DENS. | .283 |
| COEF. | .508 |
| CAT. # | 28458 |

**30 CAL.**
| | |
|---|---|
| DIA. | .308" |
| WGT. | 130 GR |
| TYPE | "XLC" BT |
| DENS. | .196 |
| COEF. | .374 |
| CAT. # | 30851 |

**30 CAL.**
| | |
|---|---|
| DIA. | .308" |
| WGT. | 150 GR |
| TYPE | "XLC" BT |
| DENS. | .226 |
| COEF. | .428 |
| CAT. # | 30854 |

**30 CAL.**
| | |
|---|---|
| DIA. | .308" |
| WGT. | 165 GR |
| TYPE | "XLC" BT |
| DENS. | .247 |
| COEF. | .505 |
| CAT. # | 30857 |

**30 CAL.**
| | |
|---|---|
| DIA. | .308" |
| WGT. | 168 GR |
| TYPE | "XLC" BT |
| DENS. | .253 |
| COEF. | .476 |
| CAT. # | 30856 |

**30 CAL.**
| | |
|---|---|
| DIA. | .308" |
| WGT. | 180 GR |
| TYPE | "XLC" S |
| DENS. | .271 |
| COEF. | .511 |
| CAT. # | 30858 |

**30 CAL.**
| | |
|---|---|
| DIA. | .308" |
| WGT. | 180 GR |
| TYPE | "XLC" S |
| DENS. | .271 |
| COEF. | .552 |
| CAT. # | 30859 |

**8MM**
| | |
|---|---|
| DIA. | .323" |
| WGT. | 200 GR |
| TYPE | "XLC" S |
| DENS. | .274 |
| COEF. | .429 |
| CAT. # | 32312 |

**338 CAL.**
| | |
|---|---|
| DIA. | .338" |
| WGT. | 185 GR |
| TYPE | "XLC" BT |
| DENS. | .231 |
| COEF. | .437 |
| CAT. # | 33854 |

**338 CAL.**
| | |
|---|---|
| DIA. | .338" |
| WGT. | 210 GR |
| TYPE | "XLC" BT |
| DENS. | .263 |
| COEF. | .471 |
| CAT. # | 33856 |

**338 CAL.**
| | |
|---|---|
| DIA. | .338" |
| WGT. | 225 GR |
| TYPE | "XLC" S |
| DENS. | .281 |
| COEF. | .482 |
| CAT. # | 33855 |

**35 CAL.**
| | |
|---|---|
| DIA. | .358" |
| WGT. | 225 GR |
| TYPE | "XLC" S |
| DENS. | .250 |
| COEF. | .405 |
| CAT. # | 35826 |

**375 CAL.**
| | |
|---|---|
| DIA. | .375" |
| WGT. | 235 GR |
| TYPE | "XLC" S |
| DENS. | .239 |
| COEF. | .400 |
| CAT. # | 37553 |

**375 CAL.**
| | |
|---|---|
| DIA. | .375" |
| WGT. | 270 GR |
| TYPE | "XLC" S |
| DENS. | .275 |
| COEF. | .503 |
| CAT. # | 37557 |

**416 CAL.**
| | |
|---|---|
| DIA. | .416" |
| WGT. | 400 GR |
| TYPE | "XLC" S |
| DENS. | .330 |
| COEF. | .546 |
| CAT. # | 41658 |

**470 NITRO**
| | |
|---|---|
| DIA. | .474" |
| WGT. | 500 GR |
| TYPE | "XLC" S |
| DENS. | .326 |
| COEF. | .318 |
| CAT. # | 47550 |

**50 CAL.**
| | |
|---|---|
| DIA. | .509" |
| WGT. | 570 GR |
| TYPE | "XLC" S |
| DENS. | .335 |
| COEF. | .316 |
| CAT. # | 50957 |

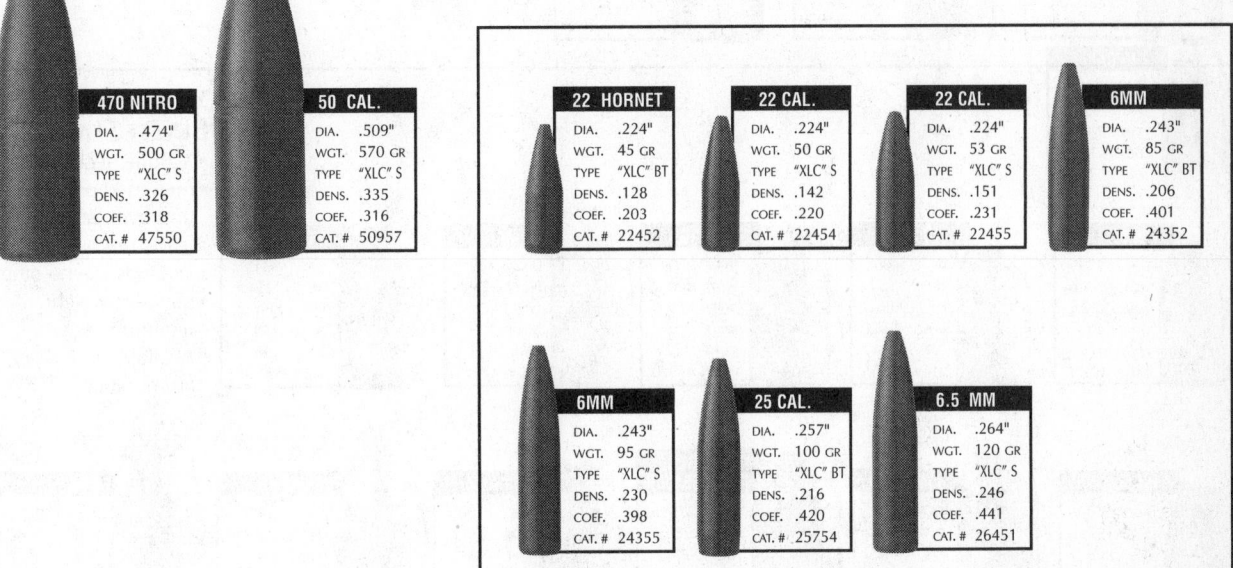

**22 HORNET**
| | |
|---|---|
| DIA. | .224" |
| WGT. | 45 GR |
| TYPE | "XLC" BT |
| DENS. | .128 |
| COEF. | .203 |
| CAT. # | 22452 |

**22 CAL.**
| | |
|---|---|
| DIA. | .224" |
| WGT. | 50 GR |
| TYPE | "XLC" S |
| DENS. | .142 |
| COEF. | .220 |
| CAT. # | 22454 |

**22 CAL.**
| | |
|---|---|
| DIA. | .224" |
| WGT. | 53 GR |
| TYPE | "XLC" S |
| DENS. | .151 |
| COEF. | .231 |
| CAT. # | 22455 |

**6MM**
| | |
|---|---|
| DIA. | .243" |
| WGT. | 85 GR |
| TYPE | "XLC" BT |
| DENS. | .206 |
| COEF. | .401 |
| CAT. # | 24352 |

**6MM**
| | |
|---|---|
| DIA. | .243" |
| WGT. | 95 GR |
| TYPE | "XLC" S |
| DENS. | .230 |
| COEF. | .398 |
| CAT. # | 24355 |

**25 CAL.**
| | |
|---|---|
| DIA. | .257" |
| WGT. | 100 GR |
| TYPE | "XLC" BT |
| DENS. | .216 |
| COEF. | .420 |
| CAT. # | 25754 |

**6.5 MM**
| | |
|---|---|
| DIA. | .264" |
| WGT. | 120 GR |
| TYPE | "XLC" S |
| DENS. | .246 |
| COEF. | .441 |
| CAT. # | 26451 |

# Barnes Bullets

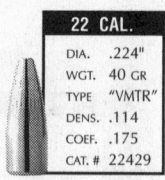

**22 CAL.**
| | |
|---|---|
| DIA. | .224" |
| WGT. | 40 GR |
| TYPE | "VMTR" |
| DENS. | .114 |
| COEF. | .175 |
| CAT. # | 22429 |

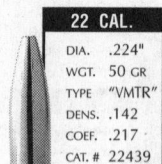

**22 CAL.**
| | |
|---|---|
| DIA. | .224" |
| WGT. | 50 GR |
| TYPE | "VMTR" |
| DENS. | .142 |
| COEF. | .217 |
| CAT. # | 22439 |

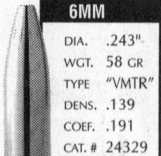

**6MM**
| | |
|---|---|
| DIA. | .243" |
| WGT. | 58 GR |
| TYPE | "VMTR" |
| DENS. | .139 |
| COEF. | .191 |
| CAT. # | 24329 |

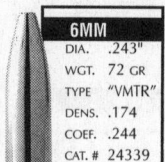

**6MM**
| | |
|---|---|
| DIA. | .243" |
| WGT. | 72 GR |
| TYPE | "VMTR" |
| DENS. | .174 |
| COEF. | .244 |
| CAT. # | 24339 |

## BARNES BURNER™ VARMIN-A-TOR™ BULLET

Taking varmint hunting to new extremes in explosive accuracy.

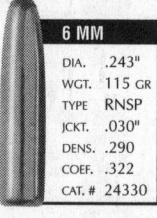

**6 MM**
| | |
|---|---|
| DIA. | .243" |
| WGT. | 115 GR |
| TYPE | RNSP |
| JCKT. | .030" |
| DENS. | .290 |
| COEF. | .322 |
| CAT. # | 24330 |

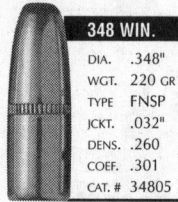

**348 WIN.**
| | |
|---|---|
| DIA. | .348" |
| WGT. | 220 GR |
| TYPE | FNSP |
| JCKT. | .032" |
| DENS. | .260 |
| COEF. | .301 |
| CAT. # | 34805 |

**348 WIN.**
| | |
|---|---|
| DIA. | .348" |
| WGT. | 250 GR |
| TYPE | FNSP |
| JCKT. | .032" |
| DENS. | .295 |
| COEF. | .327 |
| CAT. # | 34810 |

**375 WIN.**
| | |
|---|---|
| DIA. | .375" |
| WGT. | 255 GR |
| TYPE | FNSP |
| JCKT. | .032" |
| DENS. | .259 |
| COEF. | .290 |
| CAT. # | 375W20 |

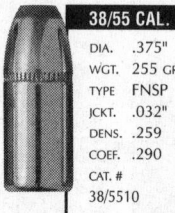

**38/55 CAL.**
| | |
|---|---|
| DIA. | .375" |
| WGT. | 255 GR |
| TYPE | FNSP |
| JCKT. | .032" |
| DENS. | .259 |
| COEF. | .290 |
| CAT. # | 38/5510 |

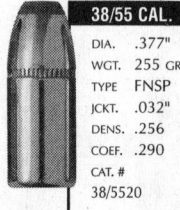

**38/55 CAL.**
| | |
|---|---|
| DIA. | .377" |
| WGT. | 255 GR |
| TYPE | FNSP |
| JCKT. | .032" |
| DENS. | .256 |
| COEF. | .290 |
| CAT. # | 38/5520 |

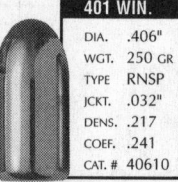

**401 WIN.**
| | |
|---|---|
| DIA. | .406" |
| WGT. | 250 GR |
| TYPE | RNSP |
| JCKT. | .032" |
| DENS. | .217 |
| COEF. | .241 |
| CAT. # | 40610 |

**40/65 WIN.**
| | |
|---|---|
| DIA. | .406" |
| WGT. | 250 GR |
| TYPE | FNSP |
| JCKT. | .032" |
| DENS. | .217 |
| COEF. | .231 |
| CAT. # | 40611 |

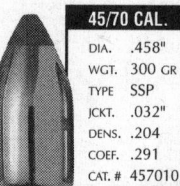

**45/70 CAL.**
| | |
|---|---|
| DIA. | .458" |
| WGT. | 300 GR |
| TYPE | SSP |
| JCKT. | .032" |
| DENS. | .204 |
| COEF. | .291 |
| CAT. # | 457010 |

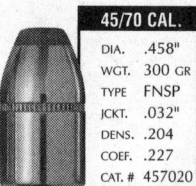

**45/70 CAL.**
| | |
|---|---|
| DIA. | .458" |
| WGT. | 300 GR |
| TYPE | FNSP |
| JCKT. | .032" |
| DENS. | .204 |
| COEF. | .227 |
| CAT. # | 457020 |

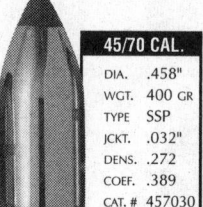

**45/70 CAL.**
| | |
|---|---|
| DIA. | .458" |
| WGT. | 400 GR |
| TYPE | SSP |
| JCKT. | .032" |
| DENS. | .272 |
| COEF. | .389 |
| CAT. # | 457030 |

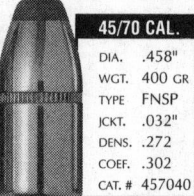

**45/70 CAL.**
| | |
|---|---|
| DIA. | .458" |
| WGT. | 400 GR |
| TYPE | FNSP |
| JCKT. | .032" |
| DENS. | .272 |
| COEF. | .302 |
| CAT. # | 457040 |

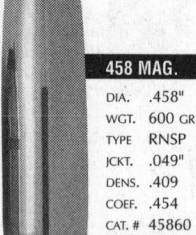

**458 MAG.**
| | |
|---|---|
| DIA. | .458" |
| WGT. | 600 GR |
| TYPE | RNSP |
| JCKT. | .049" |
| DENS. | .409 |
| COEF. | .454 |
| CAT. # | 45860 |

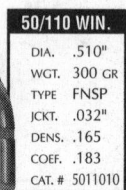

**50/110 WIN.**
| | |
|---|---|
| DIA. | .510" |
| WGT. | 300 GR |
| TYPE | FNSP |
| JCKT. | .032" |
| DENS. | .165 |
| COEF. | .183 |
| CAT. # | 5011010 |

**50/110 WIN.**
| | |
|---|---|
| DIA. | .510" |
| WGT. | 450 GR |
| TYPE | FNSP |
| JCKT. | .032" |
| DENS. | .247 |
| COEF. | .274 |
| CAT. # | 5011020 |

## COPPER-JACKET/LEAD CORE BARNES ORIGINAL

The preferred bullet of discriminating hunters for more than 65 years.

## XPB™ PISTOL BULLET FEATURES

- X-Bullet technology
- Increased penetration over jacketed lead-core bullets
- Expands like no other
- Superior weight retention
- Available in factory ammunition

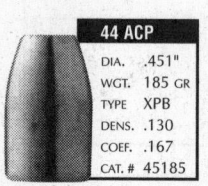

**9MM**
| | |
|---|---|
| DIA. | .355" |
| WGT. | 115 GR |
| TYPE | XPB |
| DENS. | .130 |
| COEF. | .167 |
| CAT. # | 35515 |

**40 S&W**
| | |
|---|---|
| DIA. | .400" |
| WGT. | 155 GR |
| TYPE | XPB |
| DENS. | .138 |
| COEF. | .189 |
| CAT. # | 40055 |

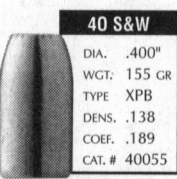

**44 MAG.**
| | |
|---|---|
| DIA. | .429" |
| WGT. | 200 GR |
| TYPE | XPB |
| DENS. | .155 |
| COEF. | .172 |
| CAT. # | 42920 |

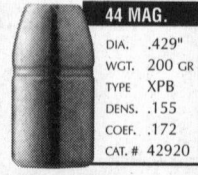

**44 MAG.**
| | |
|---|---|
| DIA. | .429" |
| WGT. | 225 GR |
| TYPE | XPB |
| DENS. | .175 |
| COEF. | .195 |
| CAT. # | 42922 |

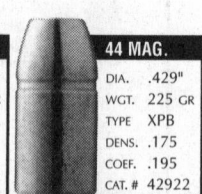

**45 LONG COLT**
| | |
|---|---|
| DIA. | .451" |
| WGT. | 225 GR |
| TYPE | XPB |
| DENS. | .158 |
| COEF. | .146 |
| CAT. # | 45120 |

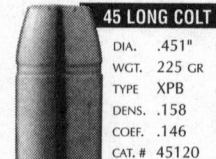

**44 ACP**
| | |
|---|---|
| DIA. | .451" |
| WGT. | 185 GR |
| TYPE | XPB |
| DENS. | .130 |
| COEF. | .167 |
| CAT. # | 45185 |

**454 CASULL**
| | |
|---|---|
| DIA. | .451" |
| WGT. | 250 GR |
| TYPE | XPB |
| DENS. | .176 |
| COEF. | .141 |
| CAT. # | 45123 |

**480 RUGER 475 LINEBAUGH**
| | |
|---|---|
| DIA. | .475" |
| WGT. | 275 GR |
| TYPE | XPB |
| DENS. | .174 |
| COEF. | .155 |
| CAT. # | 48010 |

**50 CAL.**
| | |
|---|---|
| DIA. | .500" |
| WGT. | 275 GR |
| TYPE | XPB |
| DENS. | .157 |
| COEF. | .141 |
| CAT. # | 50025 |

**50 CAL.**
| | |
|---|---|
| DIA. | .500" |
| WGT. | 325 GR |
| TYPE | XPB |
| DENS. | .186 |
| COEF. | .228 |
| CAT. # | 50026 |

**50 CAL.**
| | |
|---|---|
| DIA. | .500" |
| WGT. | 375 GR |
| TYPE | XPB |
| DENS. | .214 |
| COEF. | .261 |
| CAT. # | 50028 |

# Barnes Bullets
## Barnes Solids

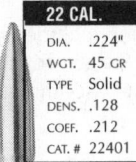

**22 CAL.**
| | |
|---|---|
| DIA. | .224" |
| WGT. | 45 GR |
| TYPE | Solid |
| DENS. | .128 |
| COEF. | .212 |
| CAT. # | 22401 |

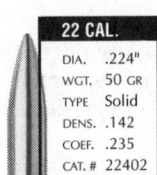

**22 CAL.**
| | |
|---|---|
| DIA. | .224" |
| WGT. | 50 GR |
| TYPE | Solid |
| DENS. | .142 |
| COEF. | .235 |
| CAT. # | 22402 |

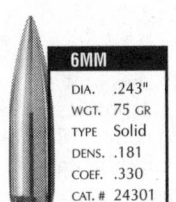

**6MM**
| | |
|---|---|
| DIA. | .243" |
| WGT. | 75 GR |
| TYPE | Solid |
| DENS. | .181 |
| COEF. | .330 |
| CAT. # | 24301 |

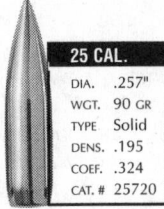

**25 CAL.**
| | |
|---|---|
| DIA. | .257" |
| WGT. | 90 GR |
| TYPE | Solid |
| DENS. | .195 |
| COEF. | .324 |
| CAT. # | 25720 |

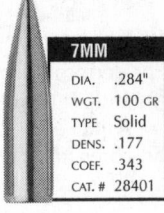

**7MM**
| | |
|---|---|
| DIA. | .284" |
| WGT. | 100 GR |
| TYPE | Solid |
| DENS. | .177 |
| COEF. | .343 |
| CAT. # | 28401 |

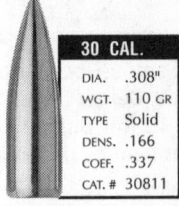

**30 CAL.**
| | |
|---|---|
| DIA. | .308" |
| WGT. | 110 GR |
| TYPE | Solid |
| DENS. | .166 |
| COEF. | .337 |
| CAT. # | 30811 |

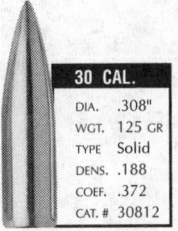

**30 CAL.**
| | |
|---|---|
| DIA. | .308" |
| WGT. | 125 GR |
| TYPE | Solid |
| DENS. | .188 |
| COEF. | .372 |
| CAT. # | 30812 |

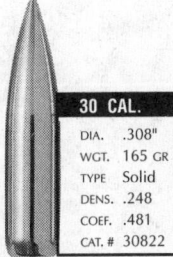

**30 CAL.**
| | |
|---|---|
| DIA. | .308" |
| WGT. | 165 GR |
| TYPE | Solid |
| DENS. | .248 |
| COEF. | .481 |
| CAT. # | 30822 |

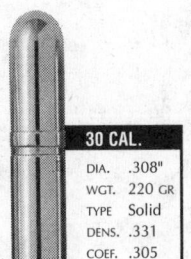

**30 CAL.**
| | |
|---|---|
| DIA. | .308" |
| WGT. | 220 GR |
| TYPE | Solid |
| DENS. | .331 |
| COEF. | .305 |
| CAT. # | 30842 |

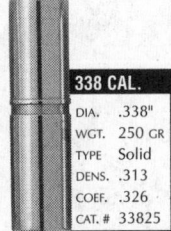

**338 CAL.**
| | |
|---|---|
| DIA. | .338" |
| WGT. | 250 GR |
| TYPE | Solid |
| DENS. | .313 |
| COEF. | .326 |
| CAT. # | 33825 |

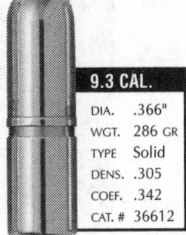

**9.3 CAL.**
| | |
|---|---|
| DIA. | .366" |
| WGT. | 286 GR |
| TYPE | Solid |
| DENS. | .305 |
| COEF. | .342 |
| CAT. # | 36612 |

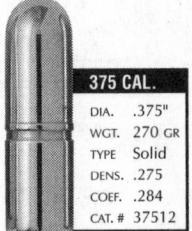

**375 CAL.**
| | |
|---|---|
| DIA. | .375" |
| WGT. | 270 GR |
| TYPE | Solid |
| DENS. | .275 |
| COEF. | .284 |
| CAT. # | 37512 |

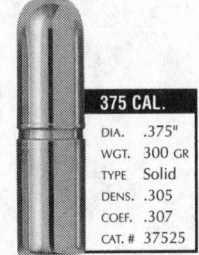

**375 CAL.**
| | |
|---|---|
| DIA. | .375" |
| WGT. | 300 GR |
| TYPE | Solid |
| DENS. | .305 |
| COEF. | .307 |
| CAT. # | 37525 |

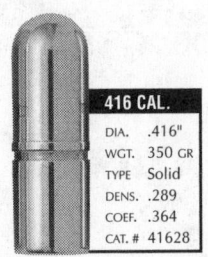

**416 CAL.**
| | |
|---|---|
| DIA. | .416" |
| WGT. | 350 GR |
| TYPE | Solid |
| DENS. | .289 |
| COEF. | .364 |
| CAT. # | 41628 |

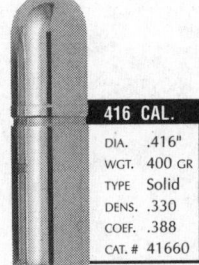

**416 CAL.**
| | |
|---|---|
| DIA. | .416" |
| WGT. | 400 GR |
| TYPE | Solid |
| DENS. | .330 |
| COEF. | .388 |
| CAT. # | 41660 |

**458 MAG.**
| | |
|---|---|
| DIA. | .458" |
| WGT. | 400 GR |
| TYPE | Solid |
| DENS. | .272 |
| COEF. | .321 |
| CAT. # | 45825 |

**458 MAG.**
| | |
|---|---|
| DIA. | .458" |
| WGT. | 500 GR |
| TYPE | Solid |
| DENS. | .341 |
| COEF. | .394 |
| CAT. # | 45855 |

**577 NITRO**
| | |
|---|---|
| DIA. | .585" |
| WGT. | 750 GR |
| TYPE | Solid |
| DENS. | .313 |
| COEF. | .351 |
| CAT. # | 58520 |

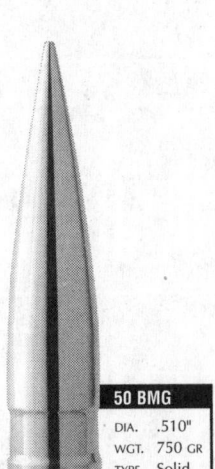

**50 BMG**
| | |
|---|---|
| DIA. | .510" |
| WGT. | 750 GR |
| TYPE | Solid |
| DENS. | .412 |
| COEF. | 1.070 |
| CAT. # | 510750A |

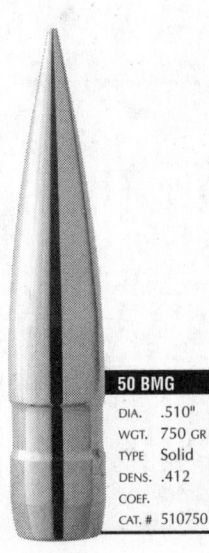

**50 BMG**
| | |
|---|---|
| DIA. | .510" |
| WGT. | 750 GR |
| TYPE | Solid |
| DENS. | .412 |
| COEF. | |
| CAT. # | 510750 |

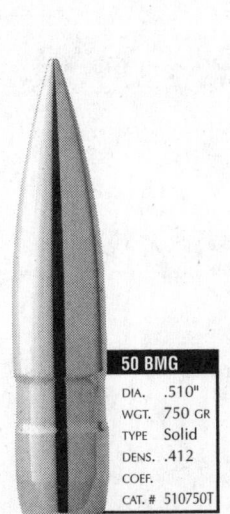

**50 BMG**
| | |
|---|---|
| DIA. | .510" |
| WGT. | 750 GR |
| TYPE | Solid |
| DENS. | .412 |
| COEF. | |
| CAT. # | 510750T |

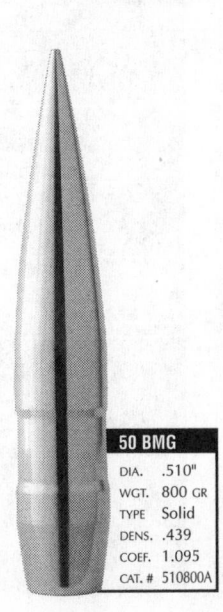

**50 BMG**
| | |
|---|---|
| DIA. | .510" |
| WGT. | 800 GR |
| TYPE | Solid |
| DENS. | .439 |
| COEF. | 1.095 |
| CAT. # | 510800A |

**600 NITRO**
| | |
|---|---|
| DIA. | .620" |
| WGT. | 900 GR |
| TYPE | Solid |
| DENS. | .334 |
| COEF. | .380 |
| CAT. # | 62020 |

# Berger Bullets

Famous for their superior performance in benchrest matches, Berger bullets now include hunting designs. From .17 to .30, all Bergers feature 14 jackets with wall concentricity tolerance of .0003. Lead cores are 99.9% pure and swaged in dies to within .0001 of round. Berger's line includes several profiles: Low Drag, Very Low Drag, Length Tolerant, Maximum-Expansion, besides standard flat-base and standard boat-tail.

| ITEM | WEIGHT | TWIST |
|------|--------|-------|
| .172 17 Cal. | 15 Gr. MEF | 12 |
| .172 17 Cal. | 18 Gr. MEF | 12 |
| .172 17 Cal. | 20 Gr. | 12 |
| .172 17 Cal. | 22 Gr. | 11 |
| .172 17 Cal. | 25 Gr. | 10 |
| .172 17 Cal. | 30 Gr. | 9 |
| .172 17 Cal. | 37 Gr. VLD | 6 |
| .204 20 Cal. | 36 Gr. MEF | 12 |
| .224 22 Cal. | 30 Gr MEF | 15 |
| .224 22 Cal. | 35 Gr. MEF | 15 |
| .224 22 Cal. | 40 Gr. MEF | 15 |
| .224 22 Cal. | 45 Gr. | 15 |
| .224 22 Cal. | 50 Gr. | 14 |
| .224 22 Cal. | 52 Gr. | 14 |
| .224 22 Cal. | 55 Gr. | 14 |
| .224 22 Cal. | 60 Gr. | 12 |
| .224 22 Cal. | 62 Gr. | 12 |
| .224 22 Cal. | 64 Gr. | 12 |
| .224 22 Cal. | 70 Gr. VLD | 9 |
| .224 22 Cal. | 70 Gr. LTB | 10 |
| .224 22 Cal. | 73 Gr. LTB | 9 |
| .224 22 Cal. | 75 Gr. VLD | 9 |
| .224 22 Cal. | 80 Gr. VLD | 8 |
| .243 (6mm) Cal. | 60 Gr. | 14 |
| .243 (6mm) Cal. | 62 Gr | 14 |
| .243 (6mm) Cal. | 65 Gr | 13 |
| .243 (6mm) Cal. | 65 Gr. Short | 14 |
| .243 (6mm) Cal. | 65 Gr. BT | 13 |
| .243 (6mm) Cal. | 66 Gr. LD | 13 |
| .243 (6mm) Cal. | 68 Gr. | 13 |
| .243 (6mm) Cal. | 69 Gr. LD | 12 |
| .243 (6mm) Cal. | 70 Gr. | 13 |
| .243 (6mm) Cal. | 71 Gr. BT | 12 |
| .243 (6mm) Cal. | 74 Gr. | 13 |
| .243 (6mm) Cal. | 80 Gr. | 12 |
| .243 (6mm) Cal. | 88 Gr. LD | 10 |
| .243 (6mm) Cal. | 90 Gr. BT | 10 |
| .243 (6mm) Cal. | 95 Gr. VLD | 9 |
| .243 (6mm) Cal. | 105 Gr. LTB | 9 |
| .243 (6mm) Cal. | 105 Gr. VLD | 8 |
| .243 (6mm) Cal. | 115 Gr. VLD | 7 |
| .257 25 Cal. | 72 Gr. | 15 |
| .257 25 Cal. | 78 Gr. | 13 |
| .257 25 Cal. | 82 Gr. | 14 |
| .257 25 Cal. | 87 Gr. | 13 |
| .257 25 Cal. | 95 Gr. | 12 |
| .257 25 Cal. | 110 Gr. | 12 |
| .257 25 Cal. | 115 Gr. VLD | 10 |
| .264 (6.5mm) Cal. | 140 Gr. VLD | 9 |
| .284 (7mm) Cal. | 168 Gr. VLD | 10 |
| .284 (7mm) Cal. | 180 Gr. VLD | 9 |
| .308 30 Cal. | 110 Gr. | 19 |
| .308 30 Cal. | 125 Gr. | 19 |
| .308 30 Cal. | 135 Gr. | 16 |
| .308 30 Cal. | 150 Gr. | 15 |
| .308 30 Cal. | 155 Gr. LTB | 14 |
| .308 30 Cal. | 155 Gr. VLD | 14 |
| .308 30 Cal. | 168 Gr. LTB | 13 |
| .308 30 Cal. | 168 Gr. VLD | 13 |
| .308 30 Cal. | 175 Gr. VLD | 13 |
| .308 30 Cal. | 185 Gr. VLD | 12 |
| .308 30 Cal. | 190 Gr. VLD | 12 |
| .308 30 Cal. | 210 Gr. VLD | 11 |

# Cor-Bon Handloading

Specializing in high-performance handgun ammo, Cor-Bon collaborated with Smith & Wesson to develop the .500 S&W cartridge. From the S&W X-Frame revolver, it easily outperforms the .454 Casull. A 275-grain Barnes X-Bullet clocks 1665 fps – about the same speed as a 400-grain Hawk Softpoint, which turns up 2500 foot-pounds of energy. The 440 lead bullet from Cast Performance leaves at 1625 fps, to generate 2580 foot-pounds. The newest in Cor-Bon's line is ammunition loaded with Pow'Rball, a controlled expansion bullet with a polymer ball in the nose. It's designed to penetrate glass and light sheet metal but expand readily in flesh.

# Lapua Handloading

Naturalis is Lapua's copper expanding bullet with a hollow, polymer-capped nose. Factory loads include 130-grain 6.5x55, 180-grain .308 Winchester, 180-grain .30-06 and 270-grain 9.3x62. Lapua Aficionado centerfire target loads are available in .223 and .308 with 69-grain and 167-grain match bullets. A line of .22 rim fire rounds carries the Lapua Signum bullet, whose tiny lube grooves on the front of a diving band minimize gumming in bore and chamber. The bullet's design reduces pressure by 15 percent, say the people who've tested them. Lapua offers 13 kinds of .22 ammo, including specialty rounds for pistol and biathlon competition.

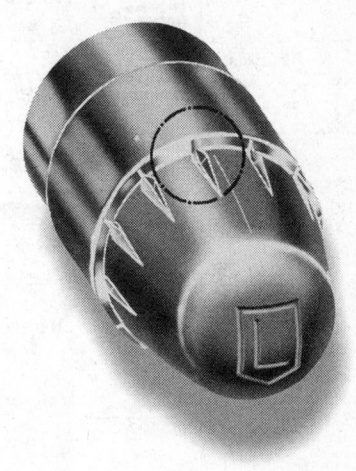

# Hornady Rifle Bullets

The Hornady SST bullet is now available for black powder shooters. The 200-grain .40 and 250- and 300-grain .45 bullets are meant for use in sabot sleeves. They feature a jacketed lead core with the signature red polymer tip. The SST has lead also to Hornady's newest big game bullet, the Interbond. Essentially, it's an SST with a thicker jacket that has an inner "expansion control ring" near the front of the shank. Jacket and core are also bonded to ensure deep penetration and high weight retention. Though it typically opens to double its initial diameter, the Interbond bullet can be expected to hold 90 percent of its weight in the animal.

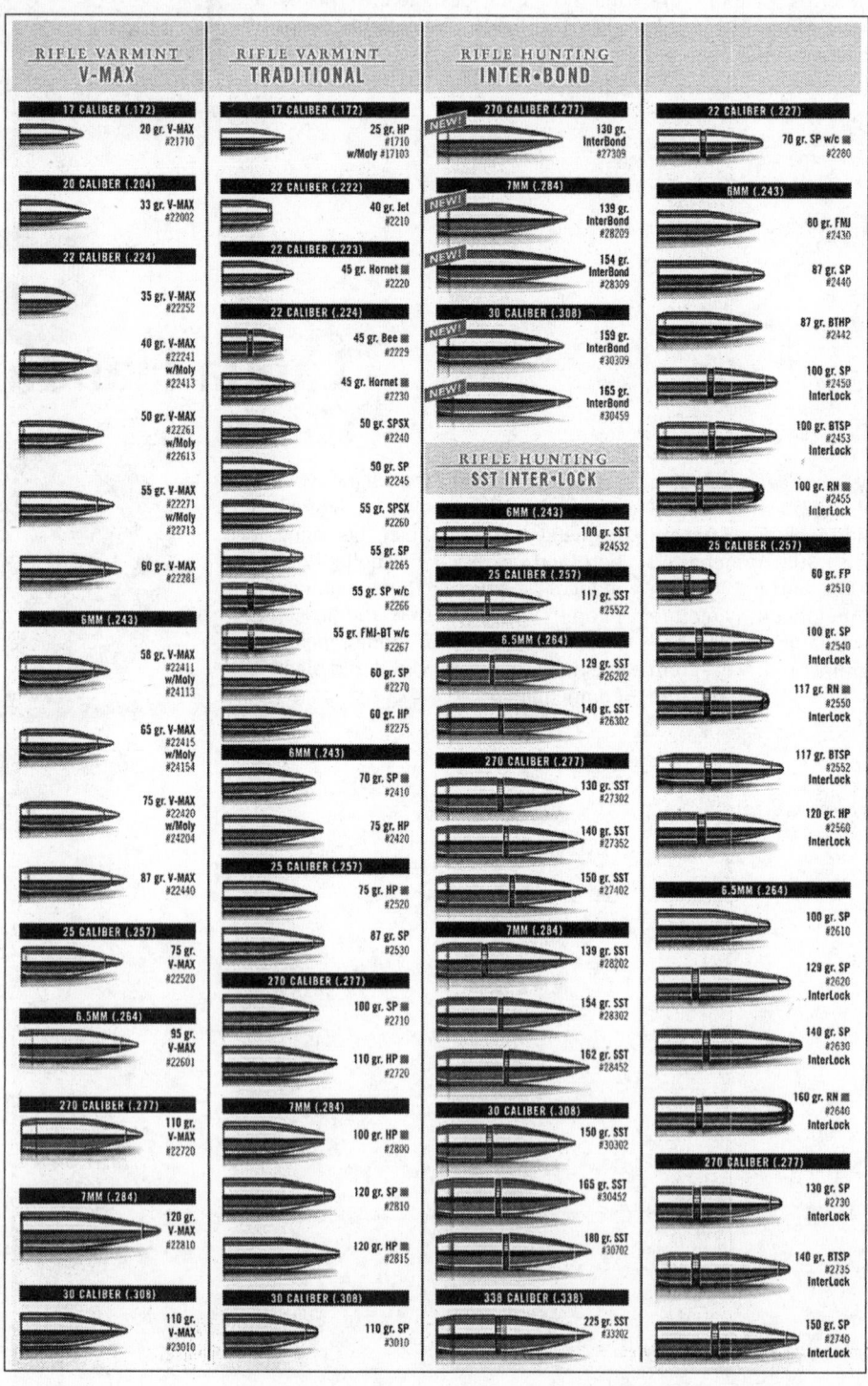

# Hornady Rifle Bullets

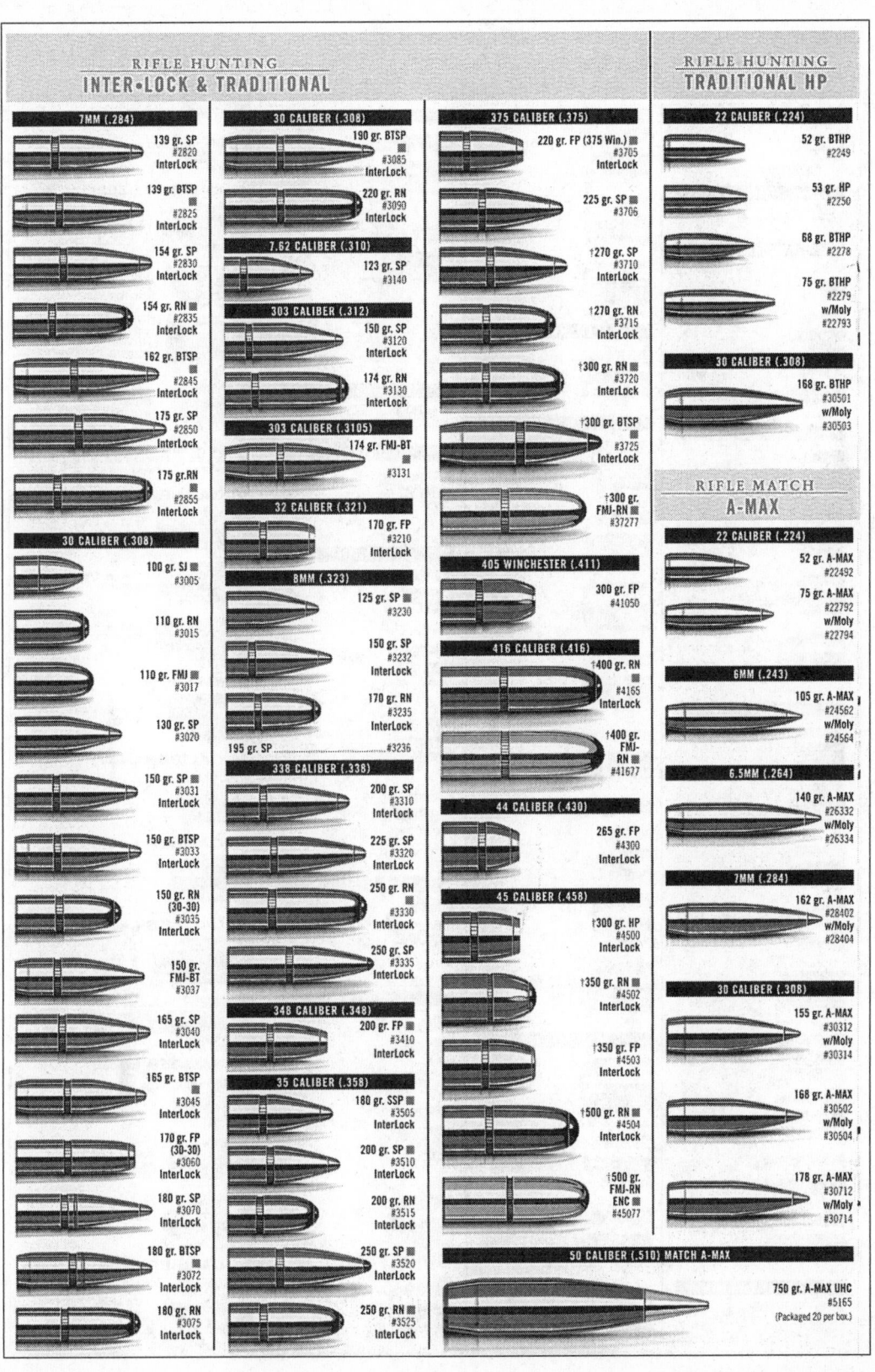

## RIFLE HUNTING
### INTER·LOCK & TRADITIONAL

**7MM (.284)**

- 139 gr. SP #2820 InterLock
- 139 gr. BTSP #2825 InterLock
- 154 gr. SP #2830 InterLock
- 154 gr. RN #2835 InterLock
- 162 gr. BTSP #2845 InterLock
- 175 gr. SP #2850 InterLock
- 175 gr. RN #2855 InterLock

**30 CALIBER (.308)**

- 100 gr. SJ #3005
- 110 gr. RN #3015
- 110 gr. FMJ #3017
- 130 gr. SP #3020
- 150 gr. SP #3031 InterLock
- 150 gr. BTSP #3033 InterLock
- 150 gr. RN (30-30) #3035 InterLock
- 150 gr. FMJ-BT #3037
- 165 gr. SP #3040 InterLock
- 165 gr. BTSP #3045 InterLock
- 170 gr. FP (30-30) #3060 InterLock
- 180 gr. SP #3070 InterLock
- 180 gr. BTSP #3072 InterLock
- 180 gr. RN #3075 InterLock

**30 CALIBER (.308)**

- 190 gr. BTSP #3085 InterLock
- 220 gr. RN #3090 InterLock

**7.62 CALIBER (.310)**

- 123 gr. SP #3140

**303 CALIBER (.312)**

- 150 gr. SP #3120 InterLock
- 174 gr. RN #3130 InterLock

**303 CALIBER (.3105)**

- 174 gr. FMJ-BT #3131

**32 CALIBER (.321)**

- 170 gr. FP #3210 InterLock

**8MM (.323)**

- 125 gr. SP #3230
- 150 gr. SP #3232 InterLock
- 170 gr. RN #3235 InterLock
- 195 gr. SP .........#3236

**338 CALIBER (.338)**

- 200 gr. SP #3310 InterLock
- 225 gr. SP #3320 InterLock
- 250 gr. RN #3330 InterLock
- 250 gr. SP #3335 InterLock

**348 CALIBER (.348)**

- 200 gr. FP #3410 InterLock

**35 CALIBER (.358)**

- 180 gr. SSP #3505 InterLock
- 200 gr. SP #3510 InterLock
- 200 gr. RN #3515 InterLock
- 250 gr. SP #3520 InterLock
- 250 gr. RN #3525 InterLock

**375 CALIBER (.375)**

- 220 gr. FP (375 Win.) #3705 InterLock
- 225 gr. SP #3706
- †270 gr. SP #3710 InterLock
- †270 gr. RN #3715 InterLock
- †300 gr. RN #3720 InterLock
- †300 gr. BTSP #3725 InterLock
- †300 gr. FMJ-RN #37277

**405 WINCHESTER (.411)**

- 300 gr. FP #41050

**416 CALIBER (.416)**

- †400 gr. RN #4165 InterLock
- †400 gr. FMJ-RN #41677

**44 CALIBER (.430)**

- 265 gr. FP #4300 InterLock

**45 CALIBER (.458)**

- †300 gr. HP #4500 InterLock
- †350 gr. RN #4502 InterLock
- †350 gr. FP #4503 InterLock
- †500 gr. RN #4504 InterLock
- †500 gr. FMJ-RN ENC #45077

## RIFLE HUNTING
### TRADITIONAL HP

**22 CALIBER (.224)**

- 52 gr. BTHP #2249
- 53 gr. HP #2250
- 68 gr. BTHP #2278
- 75 gr. BTHP #2279 w/Moly #22793

**30 CALIBER (.308)**

- 168 gr. BTHP #30501 w/Moly #30503

### RIFLE MATCH
### A-MAX

**22 CALIBER (.224)**

- 52 gr. A-MAX #22492
- 75 gr. A-MAX #22792 w/Moly #22794

**6MM (.243)**

- 105 gr. A-MAX #24562 w/Moly #24564

**6.5MM (.264)**

- 140 gr. A-MAX #26332 w/Moly #26334

**7MM (.284)**

- 162 gr. A-MAX #28402 w/Moly #28404

**30 CALIBER (.308)**

- 155 gr. A-MAX #30312 w/Moly #30314
- 168 gr. A-MAX #30502 w/Moly #30504
- 178 gr. A-MAX #30712 w/Moly #30714

**50 CALIBER (.510) MATCH A-MAX**

- 750 gr. A-MAX UHC #5165 (Packaged 20 per box.)

# Hornady Handguns Bullets

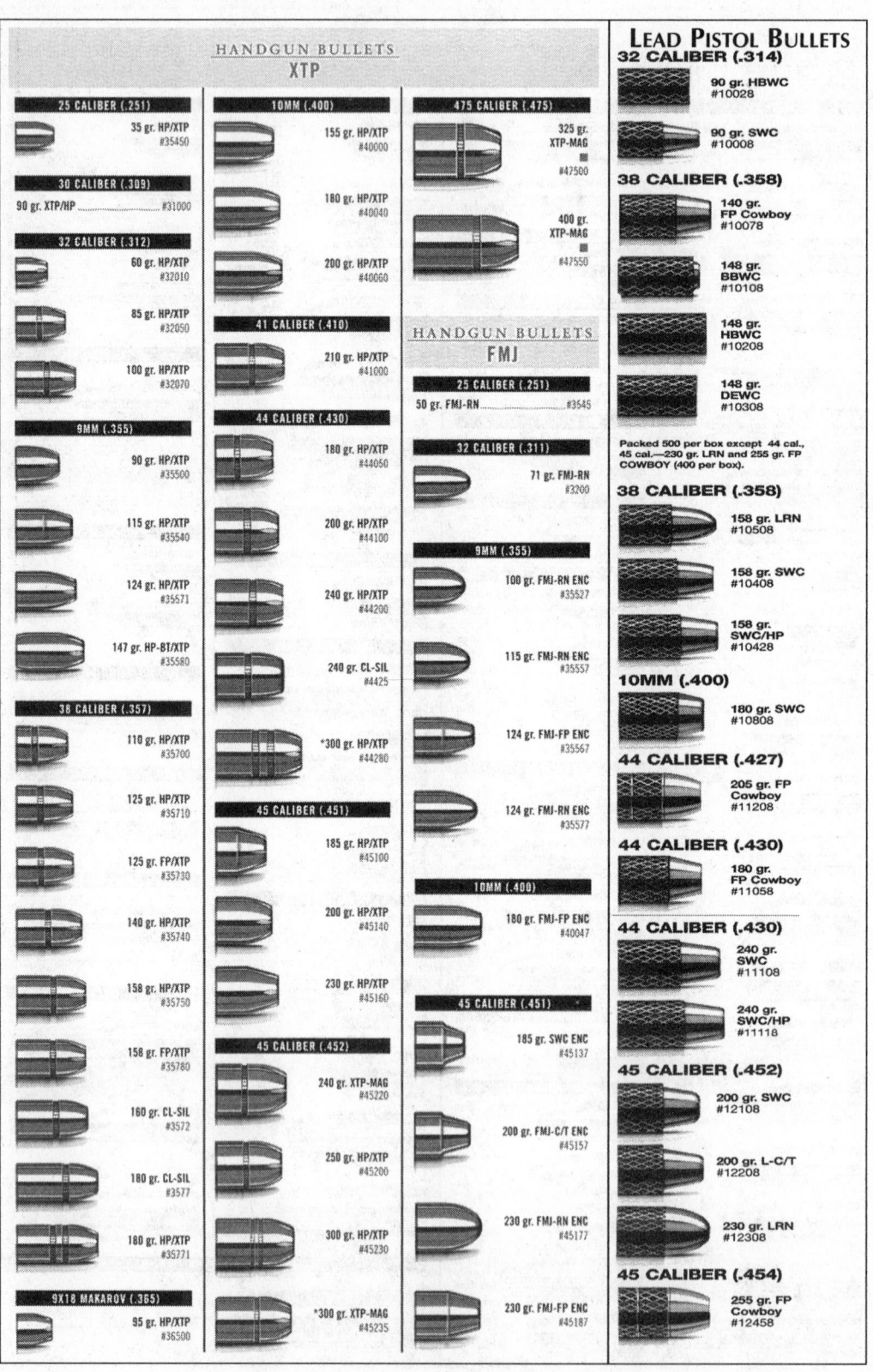

## HANDGUN BULLETS
### XTP

**25 CALIBER (.251)**
35 gr. HP/XTP #35450

**30 CALIBER (.309)**
90 gr. XTP/HP ........................ #31000

**32 CALIBER (.312)**
60 gr. HP/XTP #32010
85 gr. HP/XTP #32050
100 gr. HP/XTP #32070

**9MM (.355)**
90 gr. HP/XTP #35500
115 gr. HP/XTP #35540
124 gr. HP/XTP #35571
147 gr. HP-BT/XTP #35580

**38 CALIBER (.357)**
110 gr. HP/XTP #35700
125 gr. HP/XTP #35710
125 gr. FP/XTP #35730
140 gr. HP/XTP #35740
158 gr. HP/XTP #35750
158 gr. FP/XTP #35780
160 gr. CL-SIL #3572
180 gr. CL-SIL #3577
180 gr. HP/XTP #35771

**9X18 MAKAROV (.365)**
95 gr. HP/XTP #36500

**10MM (.400)**
155 gr. HP/XTP #40000
180 gr. HP/XTP #40040
200 gr. HP/XTP #40060

**41 CALIBER (.410)**
210 gr. HP/XTP #41000

**44 CALIBER (.430)**
180 gr. HP/XTP #44050
200 gr. HP/XTP #44100
240 gr. HP/XTP #44200
240 gr. CL-SIL #4425
*300 gr. HP/XTP #44280

**45 CALIBER (.451)**
185 gr. HP/XTP #45100
200 gr. HP/XTP #45140
230 gr. HP/XTP #45160

**45 CALIBER (.452)**
240 gr. XTP-MAG #45220
250 gr. HP/XTP #45200
300 gr. HP/XTP #45230
*300 gr. XTP-MAG #45235

**475 CALIBER (.475)**
325 gr. XTP-MAG #47500
400 gr. XTP-MAG #47550

## HANDGUN BULLETS
### FMJ

**25 CALIBER (.251)**
50 gr. FMJ-RN ........................ #3545

**32 CALIBER (.311)**
71 gr. FMJ-RN #3260

**9MM (.355)**
100 gr. FMJ-RN ENC #35527
115 gr. FMJ-RN ENC #35557
124 gr. FMJ-FP ENC #35567
124 gr. FMJ-RN ENC #35577

**10MM (.400)**
180 gr. FMJ-FP ENC #40047

**45 CALIBER (.451)**
185 gr. SWC ENC #45137
200 gr. FMJ-C/T ENC #45157
230 gr. FMJ-RN ENC #45177
230 gr. FMJ-FP ENC #45187

## LEAD PISTOL BULLETS

**32 CALIBER (.314)**
90 gr. HBWC #10028
90 gr. SWC #10008

**38 CALIBER (.358)**
140 gr. FP Cowboy #10078
148 gr. BBWC #10108
148 gr. HBWC #10208
148 gr. DEWC #10308

Packed 500 per box except 44 cal., 45 cal.—230 gr. LRN and 255 gr. FP COWBOY (400 per box).

**38 CALIBER (.358)**
158 gr. LRN #10508
158 gr. SWC #10408
158 gr. SWC/HP #10428

**10MM (.400)**
180 gr. SWC #10808

**44 CALIBER (.427)**
205 gr. FP Cowboy #11208

**44 CALIBER (.430)**
180 gr. FP Cowboy #11058

**44 CALIBER (.430)**
240 gr. SWC #11108
240 gr. SWC/HP #11118

**45 CALIBER (.452)**
200 gr. SWC #12108
200 gr. L-C/T #12208
230 gr. LRN #12308

**45 CALIBER (.454)**
255 gr. FP Cowboy #12458

# Nosler Bullets

## NOSLER CUSTOM COMPETITION

Nosler has blended the renowned accuracy of the J4 bullet jacket with its own ultra-precise lead alloy cores to create a new performance standard for the popular .30 caliber match bullets.

| Cal. Dia. | BULLET WEIGHT AND STYLE | SECT. DENS. | BAL. COEF. | PART# |
|---|---|---|---|---|
| 22 .224" | 69 GR. HPBT 250 QUANTITY BULK PACK | .196 | .359 | 53065 |
| | 80 GR. HPBT 250 QUANTITY BULK PACK | .228 | .440 | 53080 |
| 30 .308" | 155 GR. HPBT 250 QUANTITY BULK PACK | .233 | .450 | 53155 53169 |
| | 168 GR. HPBT 250 QUANTITY BULK PACK | .253 | .462 | 53164 53168 |

## Custom Competition™ formerly J4™ Competition

| Cal. Dia. | BULLET WEIGHT AND STYLE | SECT. DENS. | BAL. COEF. | PART# |
|---|---|---|---|---|
| 22 .224" | 69 GR. HPBT 250 QUANTITY BULK PACK | .196 | .359 | 17101 53065 |
| | 77 GR. HPBT 250 QUANTITY BULK PACK | .219 | .340 | 22421 53064 |
| | 80 GR. HPBT 250 QUANTITY BULK PACK | .228 | .440 | 25116 53080 |
| 30 .308" | 155 GR. HPBT 250 QUANTITY BULK PACK | .233 | .450 | 53155 53169 |
| | 168 GR. HPBT 250 QUANTITY BULK PACK | .253 | .462 | 53164 53168 |

## Bullets for Pistols

| Cal. Dia. | BULLET WEIGHT AND STYLE | SECT. DENS. | BAL. COEF. | PART# |
|---|---|---|---|---|
| 9mm .355" | 115 GR. HOLLOW POINT 250 QUANTITY BULK PACK | .130 | .110 | 44848 |
| 38 .357" | 115 GR. HOLLOW POINT PRACTICAL PISTOL™ 250 QUANTITY BULK PACK | .129 | .110 | 44835 |
| | 135 GR. PRACTICAL PISTOL™ 250 QUANTITY BULK PACK | .151 | .149 | 44836 |
| 10mm .400" | 135 GR. HOLLOW POINT 250 QUANTITY BULK PACK | .121 | .093 | 44852 |
| | 150 GR. HOLLOW POINT 250 QUANTITY BULK PACK | .134 | .106 | 44860 |
| 45 .451" | 185 GR. HOLLOW POINT 250 QUANTITY BULK PACK | .130 | .142 | 44847 |
| | 230 GR. FULL METAL JACKET | .162 | .183 | 42064 |

## Bullets for Revolvers

| Cal. Dia. | BULLET WEIGHT AND STYLE | SECT. DENS. | BAL. COEF. | PART# |
|---|---|---|---|---|
| 38 .357" | 125 GR. HOLLOW POINT 250 QUANTITY BULK PACK | .140 | .143 | 44840 |
| | 158 GR. HOLLOW POINT 250 QUANTITY BULK PACK | .177 | .182 | 44841 |
| | 180 GR. SILHOUETTE 250 QUANTITY BULK PACK | .202 | .210 | 44851 |
| 41 .410" | 210 GR. HOLLOW POINT | .178 | .170 | 43012 |
| | 200 GR. HOLLOW POINT 250 QUANTITY BULK PACK | .155 | .151 | 44846 |
| 44 .429" | 240 GR. HOLLOW POINT 250 QUANTITY BULK PACK | .186 | .173 | 44842 |
| | 240 GR. SOFT POINT 250 QUANTITY BULK PACK | .186 | .177 | 44868 |
| | 300 GR. HOLLOW POINT | .233 | .206 | 42069 |
| 45 Colt .451" | 250 GR. HOLLOW POINT | .176 | .177 | 43013 |

## Partition-HG™

| | | |
|---|---|---|
| 50 cal/250 GR. JHP | .429" | 50441 |
| 50 cal/260 GR. JHP | .451" | 50260 |
| 54 cal/260 GR. JHP | .451" | 54261 |
| 50 cal/300 GR. JPP | .451" | 50281 |
| 54 cal/300 GR. JPP | .451" | 54281 |

## S.H.O.T.S.™

| | | |
|---|---|---|
| 50 cal/250 grain JHP | .451" | 50251 |
| 50 cal/300 grain JHP | .429" | 50301 |
| 54 cal/250 grain JHP | .451" | 54251 |

*High volume shooters can now get Nosler's specially designed plastic muzzleloading sabots in 50-count Bulk Packs:*

| | |
|---|---|
| 50 cal. sabots for 44 cal. bullets | 50095 |
| 50 cal. sabots for 45 cal. bullets | 50096 |
| 54 cal. sabots for 45 cal. bullets | 50097 |

HANDLOADING

# Nosler Bullets

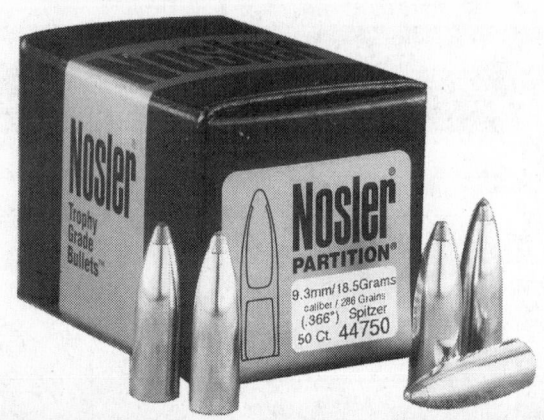

## NOSLER PARTITION® BULLETS

The Nosler Partition® bullet earned its reputation among professional guides and serious hunters for one reason: it doesn't fail. The patented Partition® design offers a dual core that is unequalled in mushrooming, weight retention and hydrostatic shock.

| Cal. Dia. | BULLET WEIGHT AND STYLE | SECT. DENS. | BAL. COEF. | PART# |
|---|---|---|---|---|
| 22 .224" | 60 GR. SPITZER | .171 | .228 | 16316 |
| 6mm .243" | 85 GR. SPITZER | .206 | .315 | 16314 |
| | 95 GR. SPITZER | .230 | .365 | 16315 |
| | 100 GR. SPITZER | .242 | .384 | 35642 |
| 25 .257" | 100 GR. SPITZER | .216 | .377 | 16317 |
| | 115 GR. SPITZER | .249 | .389 | 16318 |
| | 120 GR. SPITZER | .260 | .391 | 35643 |
| 6.5mm .264" | 100 GR. SPITZER | .205 | .326 | 16319 |
| | 125 GR. SPITZER | .256 | .449 | 16320 |
| | 140 GR. SPITZER | .287 | .490 | 16321 |
| 270 .277" | 130 GR. SPITZER | .242 | .416 | 16322 |
| | 140 GR. SPITZER **NEW!** | .261 | .432 | 35200 |
| | 150 GR. SPITZER | .279 | .465 | 16323 |
| | 160 GR. SEMI SPITZER | .298 | .434 | 16324 |
| 7mm .284" | 140 GR. SPITZER | .248 | .434 | 16325 |
| | 150 GR. SPITZER | .266 | .456 | 16326 |
| | 160 GR. SPITZER | .283 | .475 | 16327 |
| | 175 GR. SPITZER | .310 | .519 | 35645 |
| 30 .308" | 150 GR. SPITZER | .226 | .387 | 16329 |
| | 165 GR. SPITZER | .248 | .410 | 16330 |
| | 170 GR. ROUND NOSE | .256 | .252 | 16333 |
| | 180 GR. PROTECTED POINT | .271 | .361 | 25396 |

| Cal. Dia. | BULLET WEIGHT AND STYLE | SECT. DENS. | BAL. COEF. | PART# |
|---|---|---|---|---|
| | 180 GR. SPITZER | .271 | .474 | 16331 |
| | 200 GR. SPITZER | .301 | .481 | 35626 |
| | 220 GR. SEMI SPITZER | .331 | .351 | 16332 |
| 8mm .323" | 200 GR. SPITZER | .274 | .426 | 35277 |
| 338 .338" | 210 GR. SPITZER | .263 | .400 | 16337 |
| | 225 GR. SPITZER | .281 | .454 | 16336 |
| | 250 GR. SPITZER | .313 | .473 | 35644 |
| 35 .358" | 225 GR. SPITZER | .251 | .430 | 44800 |
| | 250 GR. SPITZER | .279 | .446 | 44801 |
| 9.3mm .366" | 286 GR. SPITZER (18.5 GRAM) | .307 | .482 | 44750 |
| 375 .375" | 260 GR. SPITZER | .264 | .314 | 44850 |
| | 300 GR. SPITZER | .305 | .398 | 44845 |
| 416 .416" | 400 GR. SPITZER | .330 | .390 | 45200 |
| 45-70 .458" | 300 GR. PROTECTED POINT | .204 | .199 | 45325 |
| PARTITION-HG™ 38 .357" | 180 GR. HOLLOW POINT | .202 | .201 | 35180 |
| PARTITION-HG™ 44 .429" | 250 GR. HOLLOW POINT | .194 | .200 | 44250 |
| PARTITION-HG™ 45 .451" | 260 GR. HOLLOW POINT | .182 | .174 | 45260 |
| PARTITION-HG™ 45 .451" | 300 GR. PROTECTED POINT | .211 | .199 | 45350 |

## NOSLER BALLISTIC TIP® HUNTING BULLETS

Nosler has replaced the familiar lead point of the Spitzer with a tough polycarbonate tip. The purpose of this new Ballistic Tip® is to resist deforming in the magazine and feed ramp of many rifles. The Solid Base® design produces controlled expansion for excellent mushrooming and exceptional accuracy.

### Varmint Bullets

| Cal. Dia. | BULLET WEIGHT AND STYLE | SECT. DENS. | BAL. COEF. | PART# |
|---|---|---|---|---|
| 22 .224" | 40 GR. SPITZER (ORANGE TIP) 250 CT. VARMINT PAK™ | .114 | .221 | 39510 39555 |
| | 45 GR. HORNET (SOFT LEAD TIP) | .128 | .144 | 35487 |
| | 50 GR. SPITZER (ORANGE TIP) 250 CT. VARMINT PAK™ | .142 | .238 | 39522 39557 |
| | 55 GR. SPITZER (ORANGE TIP) 250 CT. VARMINT PAK™ | .157 | .267 | 39526 39560 |
| 6mm .243" | 55 GR. SPITZER (PURPLE TIP) 250 CT. VARMINT PAK™ | .133 | .276 | 24055 39565 |
| | 70 GR. SPITZER (PURPLE TIP) 250 CT. VARMINT PAK™ | .169 | .310 | 39532 39570 |
| | 80 GR. SPITZER (PURPLE TIP) | .194 | .339 | 24080 |
| 25 .257" | 85 GR. SPITZER (BLUE TIP) | .183 | .331 | 43004 |

### Hunting Bullets

| Cal. Dia. | BULLET WEIGHT AND STYLE | SECT. DENS. | BAL. COEF. | PART# |
|---|---|---|---|---|
| 6mm .243" | 90 GR. SPITZER (PURPLE TIP) | .218 | .365 | 24090 |
| | 95 GR. SPITZER (PURPLE TIP) | .230 | .379 | 24095 |
| 25 .257" | 100 GR. SPITZER (BLUE TIP) | .216 | .393 | 25100 |
| | 115 GR. SPITZER (BLUE TIP) | .249 | .453 | 25115 |
| 6.5mm .264" | 100 GR. SPITZER (BROWN TIP) | .205 | .350 | 26100 |
| | 120 GR. SPITZER (BROWN TIP) | .246 | .458 | 26120 |

| Cal. Dia. | BULLET WEIGHT AND STYLE | SECT. DENS. | BAL. COEF. | PART# |
|---|---|---|---|---|
| 270 .277" | 130 GR. SPITZER (YELLOW TIP) | .242 | .433 | 27130 |
| | 140 GR. SPITZER (YELLOW TIP) | .261 | .456 | 27140 |
| | 150 GR. SPITZER (YELLOW TIP) | .279 | .496 | 27150 |
| 7mm .284" | 120 GR. FLAT POINT (SOFT LEAD TIP) | .213 | .195 | 28121 |
| | 120 GR. SPITZER (RED TIP) | .213 | .417 | 28120 |
| | 140 GR. SPITZER (RED TIP) | .248 | .485 | 28140 |
| | 150 GR. SPITZER (RED TIP) | .266 | .493 | 28150 |
| 30 .308" | 125 GR. SPITZER (GREEN TIP) | .188 | .366 | 30125 |
| | 150 GR. SPITZER (GREEN TIP) | .226 | .435 | 30150 |
| | 165 GR. SPITZER (GREEN TIP) | .248 | .475 | 30165 |
| | 180 GR. SPITZER (GREEN TIP) | .271 | .507 | 30180 |
| 8mm .323" | 180 GR. SPITZER (GUNMETAL TIP) | .247 | .394 | 32180 |
| 338 .338" | 180 GR. SPITZER (MAROON TIP) | .225 | .372 | 33180 |
| | 200 GR. SPITZER (MAROON TIP) | .250 | .414 | 33200 |
| 35 .358" | 225 GR. WHELEN (BUCKSKIN TIP) | .251 | .421 | 35225 |
| 9.3mm .366" | 250 GR. SPITZER (OLIVE TIP) *Available Mid-year* | .267 | .494 | 36250 |

# Nosler Bullets

## BALLISTIC SILVERTIP

| | CAL. | DIA. | BULLET WEIGHT | SECT. DENS. | BAL. COEF. | PART # |
|---|---|---|---|---|---|---|
| | 22 | .224" | 40 grain | .114 | .221 | 51005 |
| | 22 | .224" | 50 grain | .142 | .238 | 51010 |
| | 22 | .224" | 55 grain | .157 | .267 | 51031 |
| | 6mm | .243" | 55 grain | .133 | .276 | 51030 |
| | 6mm | .243" | 95 grain | .230 | .379 | 51040 |
| | 25 | .257" | 85 grain | .183 | .331 | 51045 |
| | 25 | .257" | 115 grain | .249 | .453 | 51050 |

## BALLISTIC SILVERTIP

| | CAL. | DIA. | BULLET WEIGHT | SECT. DENS. | BAL. COEF. | PART # |
|---|---|---|---|---|---|---|
| | 270 | .277" | 130 grain | .242 | .433 | 51075 |
| | 270 | .277" | 150 grain | .279 | .496 | 51100 |
| | 270 | .277" | 130 grain | .242 | .433 | 51075 |
| | 7mm | .284" | 140 grain | .248 | .485 | 51105 |
| | 7mm | .284" | 150 grain | .266 | .493 | 51110 |
| | 30 | .308" | 150 grain | .226 | .435 | 51150 |
| | 30 | .308" | 168 grain | .253 | .490 | 51160 |
| | 30 | .308" | 180 grain | .271 | .507 | 51170 |
| | 338 | .338" | 200 grain | .250 | .414 | 51200 |

## ACCUBOND

| | CAL. DIA. | BULLET WEIGHT | SECT. DENS. | BAL. COEF. | PART # |
|---|---|---|---|---|---|
| | 270/ .277" | 140 Gr. Spitzer | 0.261 | 0.496 | 54765 |
| | 7mm/ .284" | 140 Gr. Spitzer | 0.248 | 0.485 | 59992 |
| | | 160 Gr. Spitzer | 0.283 | 0.531 | 54932 |
| | 30/ .308" | 180 Gr. Spitzer | 0.271 | 0.507 | 54825 |
| | | 200 Gr. Spitzer | 0.301 | 0.588 | 54618 |
| | 338/ .338" | 225 Gr. Spitzer | 0.281 | 0.550 | 54357 |
| | 375/ .375" | 260 Gr. Spitzer | 0.264 | 0.473 | 54413 |

## FAIL SAFE

| | CAL. | DIA. | BULLET WEIGHT | SECT. DENS. | BAL. COEF. | PART # |
|---|---|---|---|---|---|---|
| | 270 | .277" | 140 grain | .261 | .322 | 53140 |
| | 7mm | .284" | 140 grain | .248 | .323 | 53150 |
| | 7mm | .284" | 160 grain | .283 | .382 | 53160 |
| | 30 | .308" | 150 grain | .226 | .308 | 53170 |
| | 30 | .308" | 165 grain | .248 | .314 | 53175 |
| | 30 | .308" | 180 grain | .271 | .391 | 53180 |
| | 338 | .338" | 230 grain | .288 | .436 | 53230 |
| | 375 | .375" | 270 grain | .274 | .393 | 53350 |
| | 375 | .375" | 300 grain | .305 | .441 | 53360 |

## PARTITION GOLD MOLY-FREE

| | CAL. | DIA. | BULLET WEIGHT | SECT. DENS. | BAL. COEF. | PART # |
|---|---|---|---|---|---|---|
| | 270 | .277" | 150 grain | .279 | .465 | 52101 |
| | 7mm | .284" | 160 grain | .283 | .475 | 52151 |
| | 30 | .308" | 150 grain | .226 | .387 | 52201 |
| | 30 | .308" | 180 grain | .271 | .474 | 52231 |
| | 338 | .338" | 250 grain | .313 | .473 | 52281 |

Ballistic Silvertip, Fail Safe and Partition Gold bullets are made by Nosler for loading in Winchester ammunition in a project known as Combined Technology.

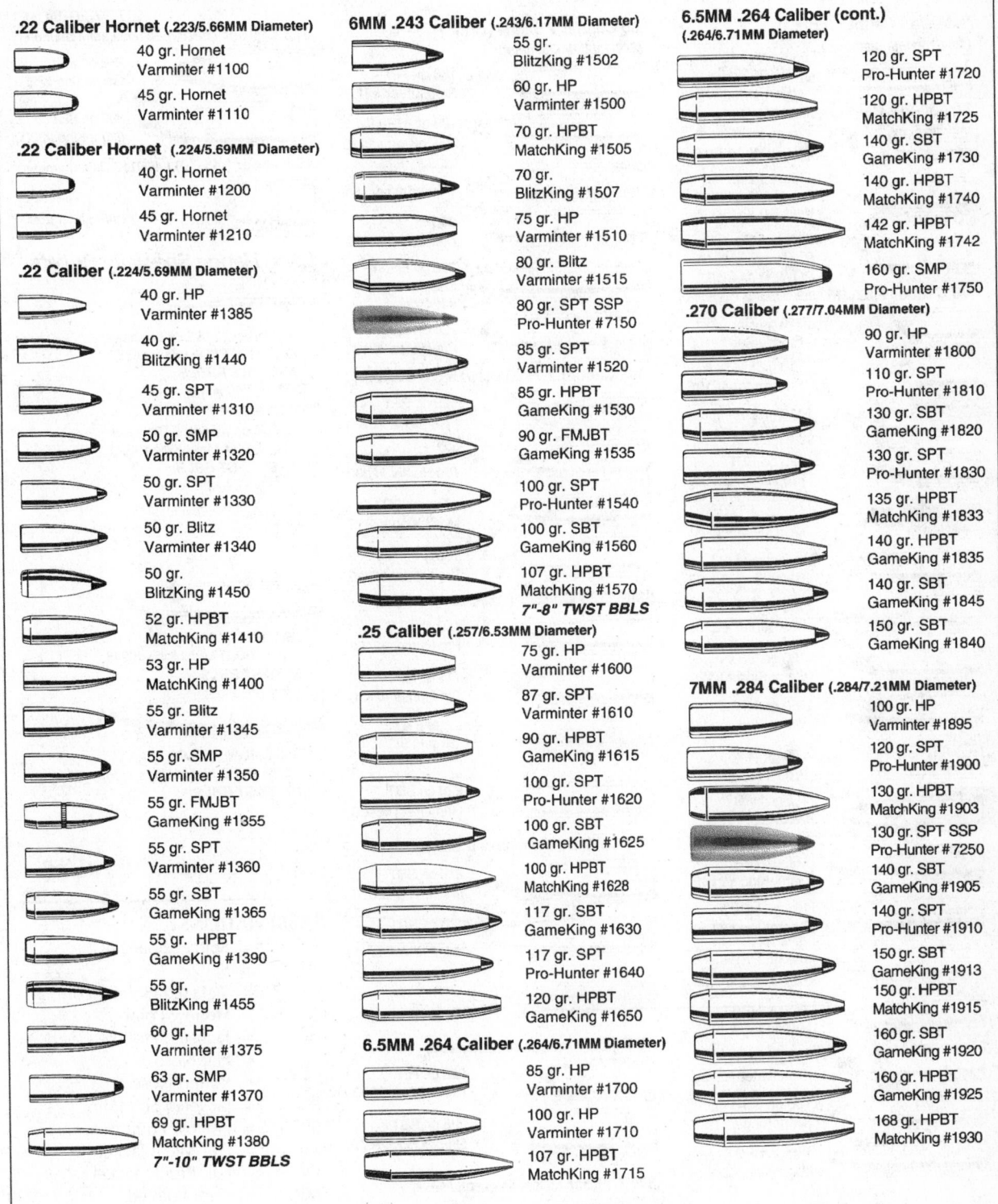

**.22 Caliber Hornet** (.223/5.66MM Diameter)

40 gr. Hornet
Varminter #1100

45 gr. Hornet
Varminter #1110

**.22 Caliber Hornet** (.224/5.69MM Diameter)

40 gr. Hornet
Varminter #1200

45 gr. Hornet
Varminter #1210

**.22 Caliber** (.224/5.69MM Diameter)

40 gr. HP
Varminter #1385

40 gr.
BlitzKing #1440

45 gr. SPT
Varminter #1310

50 gr. SMP
Varminter #1320

50 gr. SPT
Varminter #1330

50 gr. Blitz
Varminter #1340

50 gr.
BlitzKing #1450

52 gr. HPBT
MatchKing #1410

53 gr. HP
MatchKing #1400

55 gr. Blitz
Varminter #1345

55 gr. SMP
Varminter #1350

55 gr. FMJBT
GameKing #1355

55 gr. SPT
Varminter #1360

55 gr. SBT
GameKing #1365

55 gr. HPBT
GameKing #1390

55 gr.
BlitzKing #1455

60 gr. HP
Varminter #1375

63 gr. SMP
Varminter #1370

69 gr. HPBT
MatchKing #1380
***7"-10" TWST BBLS***

**6MM .243 Caliber** (.243/6.17MM Diameter)

55 gr.
BlitzKing #1502

60 gr. HP
Varminter #1500

70 gr. HPBT
MatchKing #1505

70 gr.
BlitzKing #1507

75 gr. HP
Varminter #1510

80 gr. Blitz
Varminter #1515

80 gr. SPT SSP
Pro-Hunter #7150

85 gr. SPT
Varminter #1520

85 gr. HPBT
GameKing #1530

90 gr. FMJBT
GameKing #1535

100 gr. SPT
Pro-Hunter #1540

100 gr. SBT
GameKing #1560

107 gr. HPBT
MatchKing #1570
***7"-8" TWST BBLS***

**.25 Caliber** (.257/6.53MM Diameter)

75 gr. HP
Varminter #1600

87 gr. SPT
Varminter #1610

90 gr. HPBT
GameKing #1615

100 gr. SPT
Pro-Hunter #1620

100 gr. SBT
GameKing #1625

100 gr. HPBT
MatchKing #1628

117 gr. SBT
GameKing #1630

117 gr. SPT
Pro-Hunter #1640

120 gr. HPBT
GameKing #1650

**6.5MM .264 Caliber** (.264/6.71MM Diameter)

85 gr. HP
Varminter #1700

100 gr. HP
Varminter #1710

107 gr. HPBT
MatchKing #1715

**6.5MM .264 Caliber (cont.)**
(.264/6.71MM Diameter)

120 gr. SPT
Pro-Hunter #1720

120 gr. HPBT
MatchKing #1725

140 gr. SBT
GameKing #1730

140 gr. HPBT
MatchKing #1740

142 gr. HPBT
MatchKing #1742

160 gr. SMP
Pro-Hunter #1750

**.270 Caliber** (.277/7.04MM Diameter)

90 gr. HP
Varminter #1800

110 gr. SPT
Pro-Hunter #1810

130 gr. SBT
GameKing #1820

130 gr. SPT
Pro-Hunter #1830

135 gr. HPBT
MatchKing #1833

140 gr. HPBT
GameKing #1835

140 gr. SBT
GameKing #1845

150 gr. SBT
GameKing #1840

**7MM .284 Caliber** (.284/7.21MM Diameter)

100 gr. HP
Varminter #1895

120 gr. SPT
Pro-Hunter #1900

130 gr. HPBT
MatchKing #1903

130 gr. SPT SSP
Pro-Hunter #7250

140 gr. SBT
GameKing #1905

140 gr. SPT
Pro-Hunter #1910

150 gr. SBT
GameKing #1913

150 gr. HPBT
MatchKing #1915

160 gr. SBT
GameKing #1920

160 gr. HPBT
GameKing #1925

168 gr. HPBT
MatchKing #1930

**HANDLOADING**

# Sierra Bullets

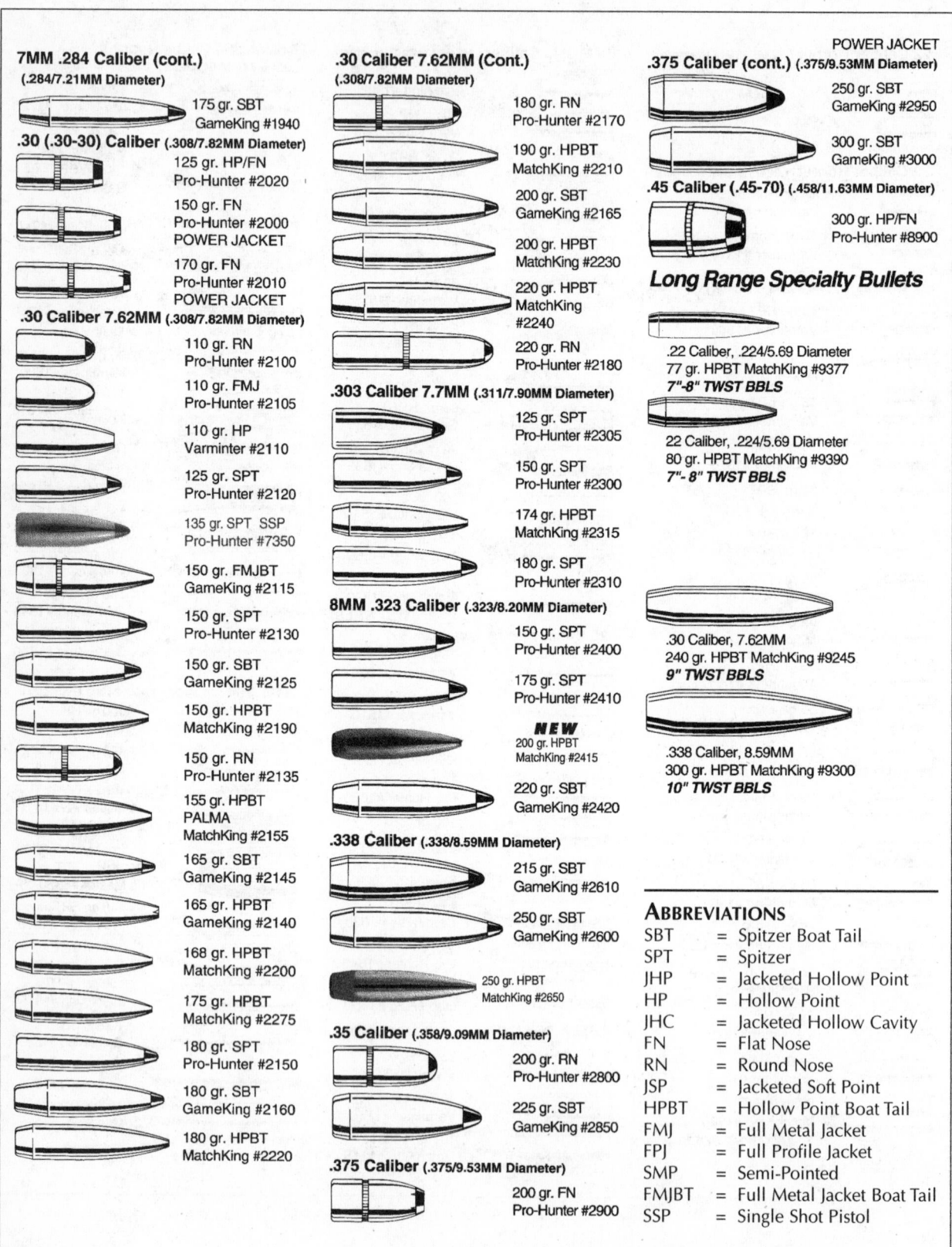

**7MM .284 Caliber (cont.)**
(.284/7.21MM Diameter)

175 gr. SBT
GameKing #1940

**.30 (.30-30) Caliber** (.308/7.82MM Diameter)

125 gr. HP/FN
Pro-Hunter #2020

150 gr. FN
Pro-Hunter #2000
POWER JACKET

170 gr. FN
Pro-Hunter #2010
POWER JACKET

**.30 Caliber 7.62MM** (.308/7.82MM Diameter)

110 gr. RN
Pro-Hunter #2100

110 gr. FMJ
Pro-Hunter #2105

110 gr. HP
Varminter #2110

125 gr. SPT
Pro-Hunter #2120

135 gr. SPT  SSP
Pro-Hunter #7350

150 gr. FMJBT
GameKing #2115

150 gr. SPT
Pro-Hunter #2130

150 gr. SBT
GameKing #2125

150 gr. HPBT
MatchKing #2190

150 gr. RN
Pro-Hunter #2135

155 gr. HPBT
PALMA
MatchKing #2155

165 gr. SBT
GameKing #2145

165 gr. HPBT
GameKing #2140

168 gr. HPBT
MatchKing #2200

175 gr. HPBT
MatchKing #2275

180 gr. SPT
Pro-Hunter #2150

180 gr. SBT
GameKing #2160

180 gr. HPBT
MatchKing #2220

**.30 Caliber 7.62MM (Cont.)**
(.308/7.82MM Diameter)

180 gr. RN
Pro-Hunter #2170

190 gr. HPBT
MatchKing #2210

200 gr. SBT
GameKing #2165

200 gr. HPBT
MatchKing #2230

220 gr. HPBT
MatchKing
#2240

220 gr. RN
Pro-Hunter #2180

**.303 Caliber 7.7MM** (.311/7.90MM Diameter)

125 gr. SPT
Pro-Hunter #2305

150 gr. SPT
Pro-Hunter #2300

174 gr. HPBT
MatchKing #2315

180 gr. SPT
Pro-Hunter #2310

**8MM .323 Caliber** (.323/8.20MM Diameter)

150 gr. SPT
Pro-Hunter #2400

175 gr. SPT
Pro-Hunter #2410

**NEW**
200 gr. HPBT
MatchKing #2415

220 gr. SBT
GameKing #2420

**.338 Caliber** (.338/8.59MM Diameter)

215 gr. SBT
GameKing #2610

250 gr. SBT
GameKing #2600

250 gr. HPBT
MatchKing #2650

**.35 Caliber** (.358/9.09MM Diameter)

200 gr. RN
Pro-Hunter #2800

225 gr. SBT
GameKing #2850

**.375 Caliber** (.375/9.53MM Diameter)

200 gr. FN
Pro-Hunter #2900

POWER JACKET

**.375 Caliber (cont.)** (.375/9.53MM Diameter)

250 gr. SBT
GameKing #2950

300 gr. SBT
GameKing #3000

**.45 Caliber (.45-70)** (.458/11.63MM Diameter)

300 gr. HP/FN
Pro-Hunter #8900

## *Long Range Specialty Bullets*

.22 Caliber, .224/5.69 Diameter
77 gr. HPBT MatchKing #9377
*7"-8" TWST BBLS*

22 Caliber, .224/5.69 Diameter
80 gr. HPBT MatchKing #9390
*7"- 8" TWST BBLS*

.30 Caliber, 7.62MM
240 gr. HPBT MatchKing #9245
*9" TWST BBLS*

.338 Caliber, 8.59MM
300 gr. HPBT MatchKing #9300
*10" TWST BBLS*

## ABBREVIATIONS

| | | |
|---|---|---|
| SBT | = | Spitzer Boat Tail |
| SPT | = | Spitzer |
| JHP | = | Jacketed Hollow Point |
| HP | = | Hollow Point |
| JHC | = | Jacketed Hollow Cavity |
| FN | = | Flat Nose |
| RN | = | Round Nose |
| JSP | = | Jacketed Soft Point |
| HPBT | = | Hollow Point Boat Tail |
| FMJ | = | Full Metal Jacket |
| FPJ | = | Full Profile Jacket |
| SMP | = | Semi-Pointed |
| FMJBT | = | Full Metal Jacket Boat Tail |
| SSP | = | Single Shot Pistol |

# Sierra Bullets
## Handgun Bullets

**.25 Caliber** (.251/6.38MM Diameter)

50 gr. FMJ
Tournament Master #8000

**.30 Caliber** (.308/7.82MM Diameter)

85 gr. RN
Sports Master #8005

**.32 Caliber 7.65MM** (.312/7.92MM Diameter)

71 gr. FMJ
Tournament Master #8010

**.32 Mag.** (.312/7.92MM Diameter)

90 gr. JHC
Sports Master #8030
POWER JACKET

**9MM .355 Caliber** (.355/9.02MM Diameter)

90 gr. JHP
Sports Master #8100
POWER JACKET

95 gr. FMJ
Tournament Master #8105

115 gr. JHP
Sports Master #8110
POWER JACKET

115 gr. FMJ
Tournament Master #8115

125 gr. JHP Sports Master
#8125 POWER JACKET

125 gr. FMJ
Tournament Master #8120

130 gr. FMJ
Tournament Master #8345

**.38 Caliber** (.357/9.07MM Diameter)

110 gr. JHC Blitz
Sports Master #8300
POWER JACKET

125 gr. JSP
Sports Master #8310

125 gr. JHC
Sports Master #8320
POWER JACKET

**.38 Caliber (cont.)** (.357/9.07MM Diameter)

140 gr. JHC
Sports Master #8325
POWER JACKET

158 gr. JSP
Sports Master #8340

158 gr. JHC
Sports Master #8360
POWER JACKET

170 gr. JHC
Sports Master #8365
POWER JACKET

170 gr. FMJ Match
Tournament Master #8350

180 gr. FPJ Match
Tournament Master #8370

**9MM Makarov** (.363/9.22MM Diameter)

100 gr. FPJ
Tournament Master #8210

**10MM .400 Caliber** (.400/10.16MM Diameter)

135 gr. JHP
Sports Master #8425
POWER JACKET

150 gr. JHP
Sports Master #8430
POWER JACKET

165 gr. JHP
Sports Master #8445
POWER JACKET

180 gr. JHP
Sports Master #8460
POWER JACKET

190 gr. FPJ
Tournament Master #8480

**.41 Caliber** (.410/10.41MM Diameter)

170 gr. JHC
Sports Master #8500
POWER JACKET

210 gr. JHC
Sports Master #8520
POWER JACKET

**.44 Caliber** (.4295/10.91MM Diameter)

180 gr. JHC
Sports Master #8600
POWER JACKET

**.44 Caliber (cont.)** (.4295/10.91MM Diameter)

210 gr. JHC
Sports Master #8620
POWER JACKET

220 gr. FPJ Match
Tournament Master #8605

240 gr. JHC
Sports Master #8610
POWER JACKET

250 gr. FPJ Match
Tournament Master #8615

300 gr. JSP
Sports Master #8630

**.45 Caliber** (.4515/11.47MM Diameter)

185 gr. JHP
Sports Master #8800
POWER JACKET

185 gr. FPJ Match
Tournament Master #8810

200 gr. FPJ Match
Tournament Master #8825

230 gr. JHP
Sports Master #8805
POWER JACKET

230 gr. FMJ Match
Tournament Master #8815

240 gr. JHC
Sports Master #8820
POWER JACKET

300 gr. JSP
Sports Master #8830

## ABBREVIATIONS

| | | |
|---|---|---|
| SBT | = | Spitzer Boat Tail |
| SPT | = | Spitzer |
| JHP | = | Jacketed Hollow Point |
| HP | = | Hollow Point |
| JHC | = | Jacketed Hollow Cavity |
| FN | = | Flat Nose |
| RN | = | Round Nose |
| JSP | = | Jacketed Soft Point |
| HPBT | = | Hollow Point Boat Tail |
| FMJ | = | Full Metal Jacket |
| FPJ | = | Full Profile Jacket |
| SMP | = | Semi-Pointed |
| FMJBT | = | Full Metal Jacket Boat Tail |
| SSP | = | Single Shot Pistol |

HANDLOADING

# Speer Handgun Bullets

## Gold Dot Handgun Bullets

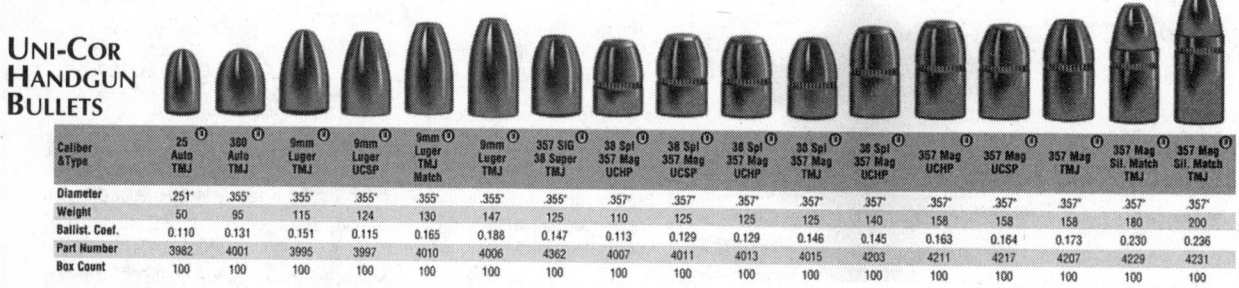

| Caliber & Type | 25 Auto Gold Dot HP | 32 Auto Gold Dot HP | 380 Auto Gold Dot HP | 9mm Luger Gold Dot HP | 9mm Luger Gold Dot HP | 9mm Luger Gold Dot HP | 357 SIG 38 Super Gold Dot HP | 38 Special Gold Dot HP | 38 Special Gold Dot HP | 38 Special Gold Dot HP | 357 Mag Gold Dot HP | 357 Mag Gold Dot HP | 357 Mag Gold Dot SP | 9x18mm Makarov Gold Dot HP | 40/10mm Gold Dot HP | 40/10mm Gold Dot HP | 40/10mm Gold Dot HP |
|---|---|---|---|---|---|---|---|---|---|---|---|---|---|---|---|---|---|
| Diameter | .251" | .312" | .355" | .355" | .355" | .355" | .355" | .357" | .357" | .357" | .357" | .357" | .357" | .364" | .400" | .400" | .400" |
| Weight | 35 | 60 | 90 | 115 | 124 | 147 | 125 | 135 | 147 | 125 | 158 | 170 | | 90 | 155 | 165 | 180 |
| Ballist. Coef. | 0.091 | 0.118 | 0.101 | 0.125 | 0.134 | 0.164 | 0.141 | 0.117 | 0.141 | 0.153 | 0.140 | 0.168 | 0.185 | 0.107 | 0.123 | 0.138 | 0.143 |
| Part Number | 3985 | 3986 | 3992 | 3994 | 3998 | 4002 | 4360 | 4009 | 4014 | 4016 | 4012 | 4215 | 4230 | 3999 | 4400 | 4397 | 4408 |
| Box Count | 100 | 100 | 100 | 100 | 100 | 100 | 100 | 100 | 100 | 100 | 100 | 100 | 100 | 100 | 100 | 100 | 100 |

| Caliber & Type | 41 Mag Gold Dot HP | 44 Special Gold Dot HP | 44 Mag Gold Dot HP | 44 Mag Gold Dot HP | 44 Mag Gold Dot SP | 44 Mag Gold Dot SP | 45 Auto Gold Dot HP | 45 Auto Gold Dot HP | 45 Auto Gold Dot HP | 45 Colt Gold Dot HP | 454 Casull Gold Dot HP | 475 Linebaugh† Gold Dot SP | 480 Ruger Gold Dot HP | 480 Ruger Gold Dot HP | 50 Action Express Gold Dot HP |
|---|---|---|---|---|---|---|---|---|---|---|---|---|---|---|---|
| Diameter | .410" | .429" | .429" | .429" | .429" | .429" | .451" | .451" | .451" | .452" | .452" | .475" | .475" | .475" | .500" |
| Weight | 210 | 200 | 210 | 240 | 240 | 270 | 185 | 200 | 230 | 250 | 300 | 400 | 325 | 275 | 300 |
| Ballist. Coef. | 0.183 | 0.145 | 0.154 | 0.175 | 0.175 | 0.193 | 0.109 | 0.138 | 0.143 | 0.165 | 0.233 | 0.242 | 0.191 | 0.162 | 0.155 |
| Part Number | 4430 | 4427 | 4428 | 4455 | 4456 | 4461 | 4470 | 4478 | 4483 | 4484 | 3974 | 3976 | 3978 | 3973 | 4493 |
| Box Count | 100 | 100 | 100 | 100 | 100 | 50 | 100 | 100 | 100 | 100 | 100 | 50 | 50 | 50 | 50 |

†=475 linebaugh is a registered trademark of Timothy B. Sundles

## Uni-Cor Handgun Bullets

| Caliber & Type | 25 Auto TMJ | 380 Auto TMJ | 9mm Luger TMJ | 9mm Luger UCSP | 9mm Luger TMJ Match | 9mm Luger TMJ | 357 SIG 38 Super TMJ | 38 Spl UCHP | 38 Spl 357 Mag UCSP | 38 Spl 357 Mag UCHP | 38 Spl 357 Mag TMJ | 38 Spl 357 Mag UCHP | 357 Mag UCHP | 357 Mag UCSP | 357 Mag TMJ | 357 Mag Sil. Match TMJ | 357 Mag Sil. Match TMJ |
|---|---|---|---|---|---|---|---|---|---|---|---|---|---|---|---|---|---|
| Diameter | .251" | .355" | .355" | .355" | .355" | .355" | .355" | .357" | .357" | .357" | .357" | .357" | .357" | .357" | .357" | .357" | .357" |
| Weight | 50 | 95 | 115 | 124 | 130 | 147 | 125 | 110 | 125 | 125 | 125 | 140 | 158 | 158 | 158 | 180 | 200 |
| Ballist. Coef. | 0.110 | 0.131 | 0.151 | 0.115 | 0.165 | 0.188 | 0.147 | 0.113 | 0.129 | 0.129 | 0.146 | 0.145 | 0.163 | 0.164 | 0.173 | 0.230 | 0.236 |
| Part Number | 3982 | 4001 | 3995 | 3997 | 4010 | 4006 | 4362 | 4007 | 4011 | 4013 | 4015 | 4203 | 4211 | 4217 | 4207 | 4229 | 4231 |
| Box Count | 100 | 100 | 100 | 100 | 100 | 100 | 100 | 100 | 100 | 100 | 100 | 100 | 100 | 100 | 100 | 100 | 100 |

| Caliber & Type | 9x18mm Makarov TMJ | 40/10mm TMJ | 40/10mm TMJ | 40/10mm TMJ | 40/10mm TMJ | 44 Mag Sil. Match TMJ | 44 Mag UCSP | 45 Auto Match TMJ SWC | 45 Auto Match TMJ SWC | 45 Auto TMJ FN | 45 Auto TMJ FN | 45 Auto TMJ RN | 45 Colt UCSP | 50 Action Express FN TMJ | 50 Action Express UCHP |
|---|---|---|---|---|---|---|---|---|---|---|---|---|---|---|---|
| Diameter | .364" | .400" | .400" | .400" | .400" | .429" | .429" | .451" | .451" | .451" | .451" | .451" | .451" | .500" | .500" |
| Weight | 95 | 155 | 165 | 180 | 200 | 240 | 300 | 185 | 200 | 185 | 200 | 230 | 300 | 300 | 325 |
| Ballist. Coef. | 0.127 | 0.125 | 0.135 | 0.143 | 0.168 | 0.206 | 0.213 | 0.090 | 0.128 | 0.094 | 0.102 | 0.153 | 0.199 | 0.157 | 0.169 |
| Part Number | 4375 | 4399 | 4410 | 4402 | 4403 | 4459 | 4463 | 4473 | 4475 | 4476 | 4471 | 4480 | 4485 | 4490 | 4495 |
| Box Count | 100 | 100 | 100 | 100 | 100 | 50 | 100 | 100 | 100 | 100 | 100 | 100 | 100 | 50 | 50 |

# Speer Handgun Bullets

## JACKETED HANDGUN BULLETS

| Caliber &Type | 32 JHP | 32 JHP |
|---|---|---|
| Diameter | .312" | .312" |
| Weight | 85 | 100 |
| Ballist. Coef. | 0.121 | 0.167 |
| Part Number | 3987 | 3981 |
| Box Count | 100 | 100 |

| Caliber &Type | 38/357 JSP | 41 Mag JSP-SWC | 44 Mag JHP | 44 Mag JHP-SWC | 44 Mag JSP-SWC | 44 Mag JHP | 44 Mag JSP | 45 JHP | 45 JHP |
|---|---|---|---|---|---|---|---|---|---|
| Diameter | .357" | .410" | .429" | .429" | .429" | .429" | .429" | .451" | .451" |
| Weight | 158 | 220 | 200 | 225 | 240 | 240 | 240 | 225 | 260 |
| Ballist. Coef. | 0.158 | 0.137 | 0.122 | 0.146 | 0.157 | 0.165 | 0.164 | 0.169 | 0.183 |
| Part Number | 4217 | 4417 | 4425 | 4435 | 4447 | 4453 | 4457 | 4479 | 4481 |
| Box Count | 100 | 100 | 100 | 100 | 100 | 100 | 100 | 100 | 100 |

## LEAD HANDGUN BULLETS

All Speer lead bullets feature our hi-tech, multilayer lube system first introduced in our Idaho Territory lead bullets. This great lube is, simplet stated, the best thing in lead bullets. It stays with the bullet instead of burning off, virtually eliminating the gas cutting that causes most leading problems. It won't melt-off in storage or transport, and is clean and dry to the touch.

For target shooting or plinking, Speer lead bullets are now even a better value. Available in calibers from 32 through 45.

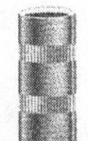

| Caliber & Type | 32 HB-WC | 9mm RN | 38 BB-WC | 38 DE-WC | 38 HB-WC | 38 SWC | 38 HP-SWC | 38 RN | 44 SWC | 45 SWC | 45 RN | 45 SWC |
|---|---|---|---|---|---|---|---|---|---|---|---|---|
| Diameter | .314" | .356" | .358" | .358" | .358" | .358" | .358" | .358" | .430" | .452" | .452" | .452" |
| Weight (grs.) | 98 | 125 | 148 | 148 | 148 | 158 | 158 | 158 | 240 | 200 | 230 | 250 |
| Part Number | -- | 4601 | 4605 | -- | 4617 | 4623 | 4627 | 4647 | 4660 | 4677 | 4690 | 4683 |
| Bulk Part No. | 4600 | 4602 | 4606 | 4611 | 4618 | 4624 | 4628 | 4648 | 4661 | 4678 | 4691 | 4684 |

# Speer Rifle Bullets

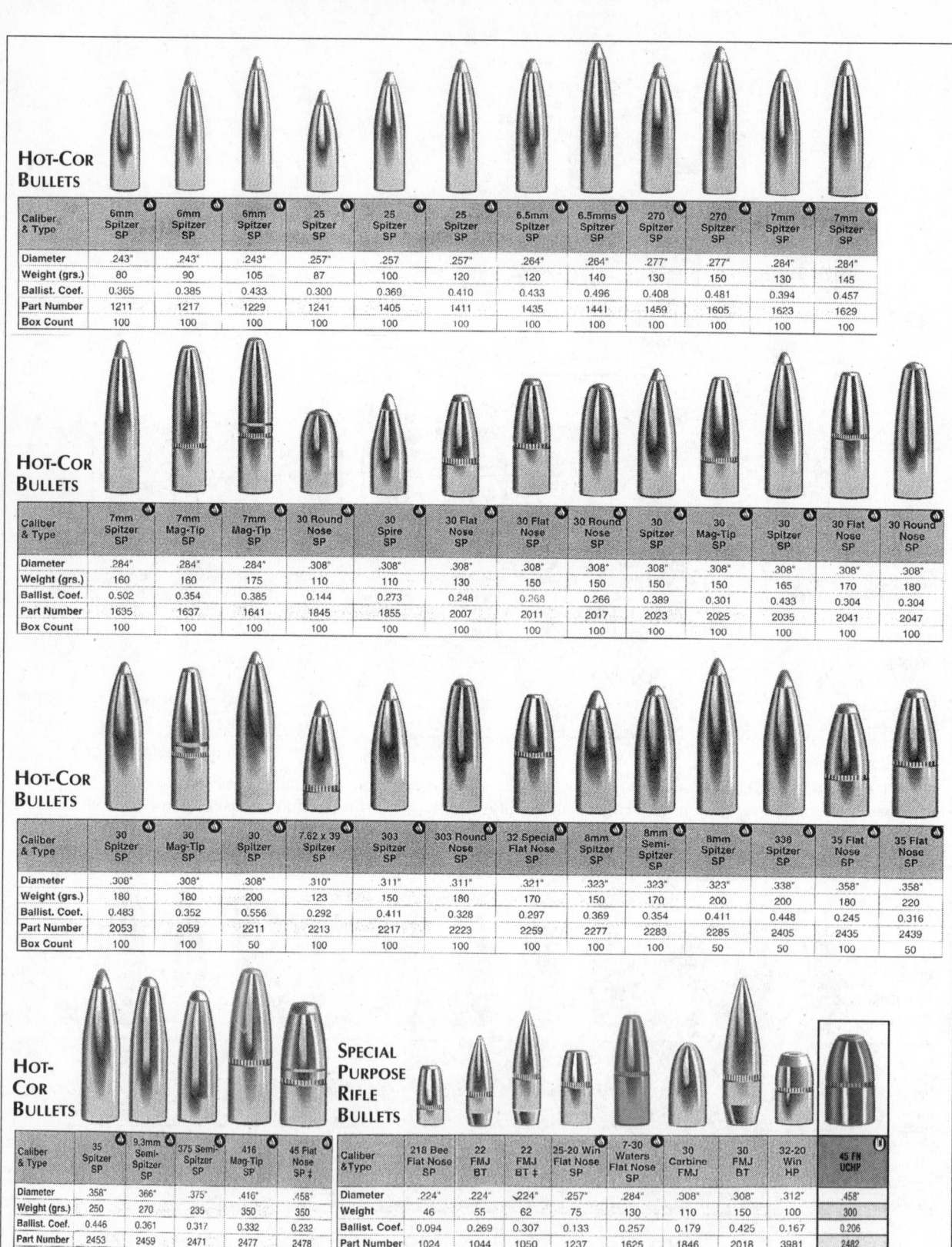

## Hot-Cor Bullets

| Caliber & Type | 6mm Spitzer SP | 6mm Spitzer SP | 6mm Spitzer SP | 25 Spitzer SP | 25 Spitzer SP | 25 Spitzer SP | 6.5mm Spitzer SP | 6.5mms Spitzer SP | 270 Spitzer SP | 270 Spitzer SP | 7mm Spitzer SP | 7mm Spitzer SP |
|---|---|---|---|---|---|---|---|---|---|---|---|---|
| Diameter | .243" | .243" | .243" | .257" | .257 | .257" | .264" | .264" | .277" | .277" | .284" | .284" |
| Weight (grs.) | 80 | 90 | 105 | 87 | 100 | 120 | 120 | 140 | 130 | 150 | 130 | 145 |
| Ballist. Coef. | 0.365 | 0.385 | 0.433 | 0.300 | 0.369 | 0.410 | 0.433 | 0.496 | 0.408 | 0.481 | 0.394 | 0.457 |
| Part Number | 1211 | 1217 | 1229 | 1241 | 1405 | 1411 | 1435 | 1441 | 1459 | 1605 | 1623 | 1629 |
| Box Count | 100 | 100 | 100 | 100 | 100 | 100 | 100 | 100 | 100 | 100 | 100 | 100 |

## Hot-Cor Bullets

| Caliber & Type | 7mm Spitzer SP | 7mm Mag-Tip SP | 7mm Mag-Tip SP | 30 Round Nose SP | 30 Spire SP | 30 Flat Nose SP | 30 Flat Nose SP | 30 Round Nose SP | 30 Spitzer SP | 30 Mag-Tip SP | 30 Spitzer SP | 30 Flat Nose SP | 30 Round Nose SP |
|---|---|---|---|---|---|---|---|---|---|---|---|---|---|
| Diameter | .284" | .284" | .284" | .308" | .308" | .308" | .308" | .308" | .308" | .308" | .308" | .308" | .308" |
| Weight (grs.) | 160 | 160 | 175 | 110 | 110 | 130 | 150 | 150 | 150 | 150 | 165 | 170 | 180 |
| Ballist. Coef. | 0.502 | 0.354 | 0.385 | 0.144 | 0.273 | 0.248 | 0.268 | 0.266 | 0.389 | 0.301 | 0.433 | 0.304 | 0.304 |
| Part Number | 1635 | 1637 | 1641 | 1845 | 1855 | 2007 | 2011 | 2017 | 2023 | 2025 | 2035 | 2041 | 2047 |
| Box Count | 100 | 100 | 100 | 100 | 100 | 100 | 100 | 100 | 100 | 100 | 100 | 100 | 100 |

## Hot-Cor Bullets

| Caliber & Type | 30 Spitzer SP | 30 Mag-Tip SP | 30 Spitzer SP | 7.62 x 39 Spitzer SP | 303 Spitzer SP | 303 Round Nose SP | 32 Special Flat Nose SP | 8mm Spitzer SP | 8mm Semi-Spitzer SP | 8mm Spitzer SP | 338 Spitzer SP | 35 Flat Nose SP | 35 Flat Nose SP |
|---|---|---|---|---|---|---|---|---|---|---|---|---|---|
| Diameter | .308" | .308" | .308" | .310" | .311" | .311" | .321" | .323" | .323" | 323" | 338" | .358" | .358" |
| Weight (grs.) | 180 | 180 | 200 | 123 | 150 | 180 | 170 | 150 | 170 | 200 | 200 | 180 | 220 |
| Ballist. Coef. | 0.483 | 0.352 | 0.556 | 0.292 | 0.411 | 0.328 | 0.297 | 0.369 | 0.354 | 0.411 | 0.448 | 0.245 | 0.316 |
| Part Number | 2053 | 2059 | 2211 | 2213 | 2217 | 2223 | 2259 | 2277 | 2283 | 2285 | 2405 | 2435 | 2439 |
| Box Count | 100 | 100 | 50 | 100 | 100 | 100 | 100 | 100 | 100 | 100 | 50 | 50 | 50 |

## Hot-Cor Bullets

| Caliber & Type | 35 Spitzer SP | 9.3mm Semi-Spitzer SP | 375 Semi-Spitzer SP | 416 Mag-Tip SP | 45 Flat Nose SP ‡ |
|---|---|---|---|---|---|
| Diameter | .358" | .366" | .375" | .416" | .458" |
| Weight (grs.) | 250 | 270 | 235 | 350 | 350 |
| Ballist. Coef. | 0.446 | 0.361 | 0.317 | 0.332 | 0.232 |
| Part Number | 2453 | 2459 | 2471 | 2477 | 2478 |
| Box Count | 50 | 50 | 50 | 50 | 50 |

‡ Not recommended for lever-action rifles.

## Special Purpose Rifle Bullets

| Caliber & Type | 218 Bee Flat Nose SP | 22 FMJ BT | 22 FMJ BT ‡ | 25-20 Win Flat Nose SP | 7-30 Waters Flat Nose SP | 30 Carbine FMJ | 30 FMJ BT | 32-20 Win HP | 45 FN UCHP |
|---|---|---|---|---|---|---|---|---|---|
| Diameter | .224" | .224" | .224" | .257" | .284" | .308" | .308" | .312" | .458" |
| Weight | 46 | 55 | 62 | 75 | 130 | 110 | 150 | 100 | 300 |
| Ballist. Coef. | 0.094 | 0.269 | 0.307 | 0.133 | 0.257 | 0.179 | 0.425 | 0.167 | 0.206 |
| Part Number | 1024 | 1044 | 1050 | 1237 | 1625 | 1846 | 2018 | 3981 | 2482 |
| Box Count | 100 | 100 | 100 | 100 | 100 | 100 | 100 | 100 | 50 |

‡ Recommended for twist rates of 1 in 10" or faster.

# Speer Rifle Bullets

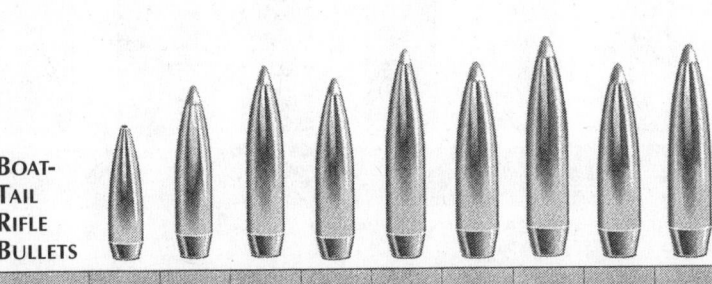

## BOAT-TAIL RIFLE BULLETS

| Bullet Caliber & Type | 22* Match HPBT | 6mm Spitzer SPBT | 6mm Spitzer SPBT | 25 Spitzer SPBT | 25 Spitzer SPBT | 270 Spitzer SPBT | 270 Spitzer SPBT | 7mm Spitzer SPBT | 7mm Spitzer SPBT |
|---|---|---|---|---|---|---|---|---|---|
| Diameter | .224" | .243" | .243" | .257" | .257" | .277" | .277" | .284" | .284" |
| Weight (grs.) | 52 | 85 | 100 | 100 | 120 | 130 | 150 | 130 | 145 |
| Ballist. Coef. | 0.253 | 0.404 | 0.430 | 0.393 | 0.435 | 0.449 | 0.496 | 0.411 | 0.502 |
| Part Number | 1036 | 1213 | 1220 | 1408 | 1410 | 1458 | 1604 | 1624 | 1628 |
| Box Count | 100 | 100 | 100 | 100 | 100 | 100 | 100 | 100 | 100 |

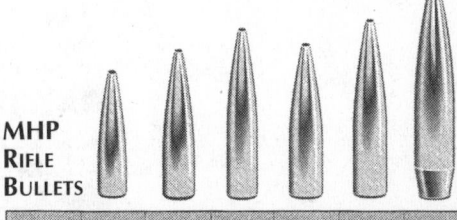

## MHP RIFLE BULLETS

| Caliber & Type | 22 MHP HP | 6mm MHP HP | 25 MHP HP | 270 MHP HP | 7mm MHP HP | 30 MHP Match HPBT |
|---|---|---|---|---|---|---|
| Diameter | .224" | .243" | .257" | .277" | .284" | .308" |
| Weight | 50 | 70 | 87 | 90 | 110 | 168 |
| Ballist. Coef. | 0.234 | 0.296 | 0.325 | 0.289 | 0.355 | 0.504 |
| Part Number | 1031 | 1207 | 1247 | 1457 | 1615 | 2039 |
| Box Count | 100 | 100 | 100 | 100 | 100 | 100 |

## BOAT-TAIL RIFLE BULLETS

| Bullet Caliber & Type | 7mm* Match HPBT | 7mm Spitzer SPBT | 30 Spitzer SPBT | 30 Spitzer SPBT | 30* Match HPBT | 30 Spitzer SPBT | 338 Spitzer SPBT | 375 Spitzer SPBT |
|---|---|---|---|---|---|---|---|---|
| Diameter | .284" | .284" | .308" | .308" | .308" | .308" | .338" | .375" |
| Weight (grs.) | 145 | 160 | 150 | 165 | 168 | 180 | 225 | 270 |
| Ballist. Coef. | 0.465 | 0.556 | 0.423 | 0.477 | 0.480 | 0.540 | 0.484 | 0.429 |
| Part Number | 1631 | 1634 | 2022 | 2034 | 2040 | 2052 | 2406 | 2472 |
| Box Count | 100 | 100 | 100 | 100 | 100 | 100 | 50 | 50 |

*Match bullets are not recommended for use on game animals.

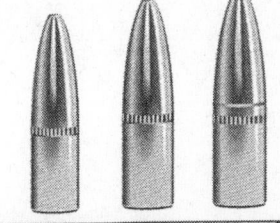

## GRAND SLAM

| Bullet Caliber & Type | 6mm GS SP | 25 GS SP | 6.5mm GS SP |
|---|---|---|---|
| Diameter | .243" | .257" | .264" |
| Weight (grs.) | 100 | 120 | 140 |
| Ballist. Coef. | 0.351 | 0.328 | 0.385 |
| Part Number | 1222 | 1415 | 1444 |
| Box Count | 50 | 50 | 50 |

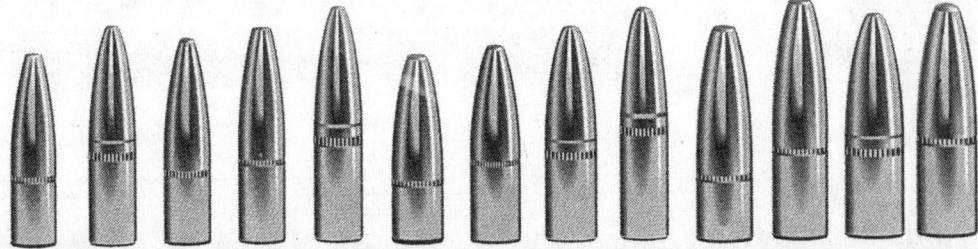

## GRAND SLAM

| Bullet Caliber & Type | 270 Grand Slam SP | 270 Grand Slam SP | 7mm Grand Slam SP | 7mm Grand Slam SP | 7mm Grand Slam SP | 30 Grand Slam SP | 30 Grand Slam SP | 30 Grand Slam SP | 30 Grand Slam SP | 338 Grand Slam SP | 338 Grand Slam SP | 35 Grand Slam SP | 375 Grand Slam SP |
|---|---|---|---|---|---|---|---|---|---|---|---|---|---|
| Diameter | .277" | .277" | .284" | .284" | .284" | .308" | .308" | .308" | .308" | .338" | .338" | .358" | .375" |
| Weight (grs.) | 130 | 150 | 145 | 160 | 175 | 150 | 165 | 180 | 200 | 225 | 250 | 250 | 285 |
| Ballist. Coef. | 0.345 | 0.385 | 0.327 | 0.387 | 0.465 | 0.305 | 0.393 | 0.416 | 0.448 | .0382 | 0.431 | 0.335 | 0.354 |
| Part Number | 1465 | 1608 | 1632 | 1638 | 1643 | 2026 | 2038 | 2063 | 2212 | 2407 | 2408 | 2455 | 2473 |
| Box Count | 50 | 50 | 50 | 50 | 50 | 50 | 50 | 50 | 50 | 50 | 50 | 50 | 50 |

# Speer Rifle Bullets

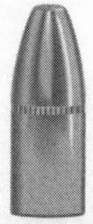

**AFRICAN GRAND SLAM**

| Bullet Caliber & Type | 375 AGS SP | 375 AGS Tungsten Solid | 416 AGS SP | 416 AGS Tungsten Solid | 45 AGS SP | 45 AGS Tungsten Solid |
|---|---|---|---|---|---|---|
| Diameter | .375" | .375" | .416" | .416" | .458" | .458" |
| Weight (grs.) | 300 | 300 | 400 | 400 | 500 | 500 |
| Ballist. Coef. | 0.323 | 0.258 | 0.318 | 0.262 | 0.285 | 0.277 |
| Part Number | 2470 | 2474 | 2475 | 2476 | 2485 | 2486 |
| Box Count | 25 | 25 | 25 | 25 | 25 | 25 |

**JACKETED RIFLE BULLETS**

| Caliber & Type | 22 Spire SP | 22 Spitzer SP | 22 Spitzer SP | 22 HP | 22 Spitzer SP | 22 Semi-Spitzer SP | 6mm HP |
|---|---|---|---|---|---|---|---|
| Diameter | .224" | .224" | .224" | .224" | .224" | .224" | .243" |
| Weight | 40 | 45 | 50 | 52 | 55 | 70 | 75 |
| Ballist. Coef. | 0.144 | 0.167 | 0.231 | 0.225 | 0.255 | 0.214 | 0.234 |
| Part Number | 1017 | 1023 | 1029 | 1035 | 1047 | 1053 | 1205 |
| Box Count | 100 | 100 | 100 | 100 | 100 | 100 | 100 |

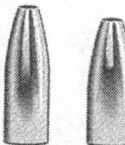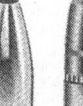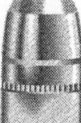

**JACKETED RIFLE BULLETS**

| Caliber & Type | 25 HP | 270 HP | 7mm HP | 30 Plinker RN SP | 30 HP | 30 HP | 45 Flat Nose SP |
|---|---|---|---|---|---|---|---|
| Diameter | .257" | .277" | .284" | .308" | .308" | .308" | .458" |
| Weight | 100 | 100 | 115 | 100 | 110 | 130 | 400 |
| Ballist. Coef. | 0.255 | 0.225 | 0.257 | 0.124 | 0.136 | 0.263 | 0.214 |
| Part Number | 1407 | 1447 | 1617 | 1805 | 1835 | 2005 | 2479 |
| Box Count | 100 | 100 | 100 | 100 | 100 | 100 | 50 |

**TROPHY BONDED BEAR CLAW**

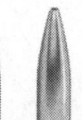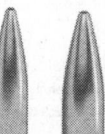

**TNT RIFLE BULLETS**

| Caliber & Type | 22 Hornet TNT HP | 22 TNT HP | 22 TNT HP (HV) | 6mm TNT HP | 25 TNT HP | 6.5mm TNT HP | 270 TNT HP | 7mm TNT HP | 30 TNT HP |
|---|---|---|---|---|---|---|---|---|---|
| Diameter | .224" | .224" | .224" | .243" | .257" | .264" | .277" | .284" | .308" |
| Weight | 33 | 50 | 55 | 70 | 87 | 90 | 90 | 110 | 125 |
| Ballist. Coef. | 0.112 | 0.223 | 0.233 | 0.282 | 0.310 | 0.261 | 0.275 | 0.338 | 0.326 |
| Part Number | 1014 | 1030 | 1032 | 1206 | 1246 | 1445 | 1446 | 1616 | 1986 |
| Box Count | 100 | 100 | 100 | 100 | 100 | 100 | 100 | 100 | 100 |

## TROPHY BONDED® BEAR CLAW® RIFLE BULLETSZ

- Fusion-bonded core Fusion bonding ensures retained weights in excess of 95 percent.
- Solid copper shank ensures deep penetration
- Protected soft point Long jacket p rotects lead tip against recoil damage
- Available from .224 55 gr. to .458 500 gr.

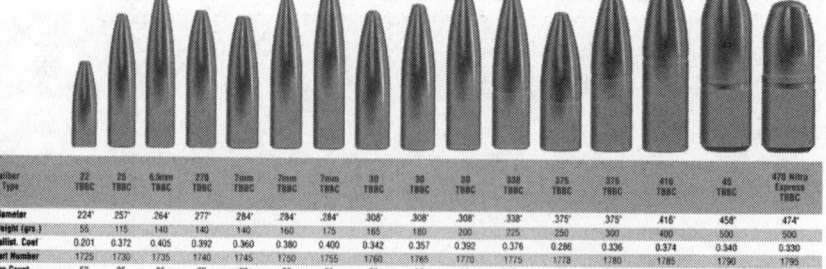

| Caliber & Type | 22 TBBC | 25 TBBC | 6.5mm TBBC | 270 TBBC | 7mm TBBC | 7mm TBBC | 7mm TBBC | 30 TBBC | 30 TBBC | 30 TBBC | 338 TBBC | 375 TBBC | 375 TBBC | 416 TBBC | 45 TBBC | 470 Nitro Express TBBC |
|---|---|---|---|---|---|---|---|---|---|---|---|---|---|---|---|---|
| Diameter | .224" | .257" | .264" | .277" | .284" | .284" | .284" | .308" | .308" | .308" | .338" | .375" | .375" | .416" | .458" | .474" |
| Weight (grs.) | 55 | 115 | 140 | 140 | 140 | 160 | 175 | 165 | 180 | 200 | 225 | 250 | 300 | 400 | 500 | 500 |
| Ballist. Coef | 0.201 | 0.372 | 0.405 | 0.392 | 0.360 | 0.380 | 0.400 | 0.342 | 0.357 | 0.376 | 0.392 | 0.286 | 0.336 | 0.374 | 0.340 | 0.330 |
| Part Number | 1725 | 1730 | 1735 | 1740 | 1745 | 1750 | 1755 | 1760 | 1765 | 1770 | 1775 | 1778 | 1780 | 1785 | 1790 | 1795 |
| Box Count | 50 | 25 | 25 | 25 | 25 | 25 | 25 | 25 | 25 | 25 | 25 | 25 | 25 | 25 | 25 | 25 |

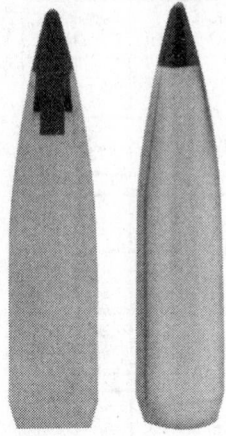

**SWIFT SCIROCCO BONDED 30 CAL. (.308") 180-GR. POLYMER TIP/BOAT TAIL SPITZER**
Tapered jacket and proprietary bonding process produce controlled mushrooming with high weight retention. Ideally suited to fast, flat-shooting calibers.

### SCIROCCO™ RIFLE BULLETS

| Cal. | Scirocco™ Bullet | Dia. | Wt. (gr.) | Profile | Sect. Den. | Ball. Coef. |
|------|-------------------|-------|-----------|---------|------------|-------------|
| 270  |                   | .277" | 130       | BTS     | .242       | .450        |
| 7mm  |                   | .284" | 150       | BTS     | .266       | .515        |
| 30   |                   | .308" | 150       | BTS     | .226       | .430        |
|      |                   | .308" | 165       | BTS     | .248       | .470        |
|      |                   | .308" | 180       | BTS     | .271       | .520        |

## THE SWIFT BULLET COMPANY

The Scirocco rifle bullet starts with a tough, pointed polymer tip that reduces air resistance, prevents tip deformation, and blends into the radius of its secant ogive nose section. A moderate 15-degree boat-tail base reduces drag and eases seating. The thick base prevents bullet deformation during launch. Scirocco's shape creates two other significant advantages. One is an extremely high ballistic coefficient. The other, derived from the secant ogive nose, is a comparatively long bearing surface for a sharply pointed bullet, a feature that improves rotational stability.

Inside, the Scirocco has a bonded-core construction with a pure lead core encased in a tapered, progressively thickening jacket of pure copper. Pure copper was selected because it is more malleable and less brittle than less expensive gilding metal. Both jacket and core are bonded by Swift's proprietary process so that the bullet expands without break-up as if the two parts were the same metal. In tests, the new bullet mushroomed effectively at velocities as low as 1440 fps, yet stayed together at velocities in excess of 3,000 fps, with over 70 percent weight retention.

Swift A-Frame bullet, with its mid-section wall of copper, is still earning praise for its deep-driving dependability in tough game. Less aerodynamic than the Scirocco, it produces a broad mushroom while carrying almost all its weight through muscle and bone. Available in a wide range of weights and diameters, it is also a bonded-core bullet.

**A-Frame Bullet**

The Swift A-Frame, noted for deep penetration in tough game, is loaded in Remington Premier ammunition.

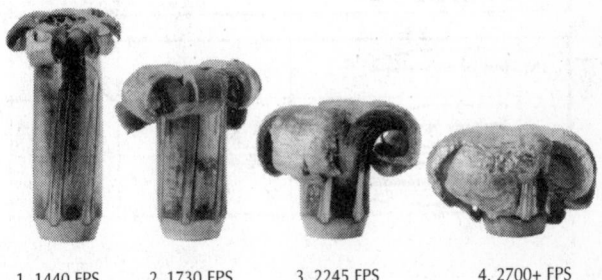

1. 1440 FPS    2. 1730 FPS    3. 2245 FPS    4. 2700+ FPS

**Swift Scirocco™ Expands dependably over a wide range of velocities, and maintains high jacket/core integrity.**

HANDLOADING

# Swift
## A-Frame Rifle Bullet Specifications

| Cal. | A-Frame Bullet | Dia. | Wt. (gr.) | Profile | Sect. Den. | Ball. Coef. |
|---|---|---|---|---|---|---|
| .25 | | .257" | 100 | AF/SS | .216 | .318 |
| | | .257" | 120 | AF/SS | .260 | .382 |
| 6.5 mm | | .264" | 120 | AF/SS | .246 | .344 |
| | | .264" | 140 | AF/SS | .287 | .401 |
| .270 | | .277" | 130 | AF/SS | .242 | .323 |
| | | .277" | 140 | AF/SS | .261 | .414 |
| | | .277" | 150 | AF/SS | .279 | .444 |
| 7mm | | .284" | 140 | AF/SS | .248 | .335 |
| | | .284" | 160 | AF/SS | .283 | .450 |
| | | .284" | 175 | AF/SS | .310 | .493 |
| .30 | | .308" | 165 | AF/SS | .249 | .367 |
| | | .308" | 180 | AF/SS | .271 | .400 |
| | | .308" | 200 | AF/SS | .301 | .444 |
| 8mm | | .323" | 200 | AF/SS | .274 | .357 |
| | | .323" | 220 | AF/SS | .301 | .393 |
| .338 | | .338" | 225 | AF/SS | .281 | .384 |
| | | .338" | 250 | AF/SS | .313 | .427 |
| | | .338" | 275 | AF/SS | .344 | .469 |
| .35 | | .358" | 225 | AF/SS | .251 | .312 |
| | | .358" | 250 | AF/SS | .279 | .347 |
| | | .358" | 280 | AF/SS | .312 | .388 |

| Cal. | A-Frame Bullet | Dia. | Wt. (gr.) | Profile | Sect. Den. | Ball. Coef. |
|---|---|---|---|---|---|---|
| 9.3 mm | | .366" | 250 | AF/SS | .267 | .285 |
| | | .366" | 300 | AF/SS | .320 | .342 |
| .375 | | .375" | 250 | AF/SS | .254 | .271 |
| | | .375" | 270 | AF | | |
| | | .375" | 300 | AF/SS | .305 | .325 |
| .416 | | .416" | 350 | AF/SS | .289 | .321 |
| | | .416" | 400 | AF/SS | .330 | .367 |
| .458 | | .458" | 400 | AF/FN | .272 | .258 |
| | | .458" | 450 | AF/SS | .307 | .325 |
| | | .458" | 500 | AF/SS | .341 | .361 |
| .470 | | .475" | 500 | AF/RN | .329 | .364 |

## Handgun Bullet Specifications

| Cal. | A-Frame Bullet | Dia. | Wt. (gr.) | Profile | Sect. Den. | Ball. Coef. |
|---|---|---|---|---|---|---|
| .44 | * | .430" | 240 | AF/HP | .185 | .119 |
| | | .430" | 280 | AF/HP | .216 | .139 |
| | * | .430" | 300 | AF/HP | .232 | .147 |
| .45 | * | .452" | 265 | AF | .210 | .135 |
| | | .452" | 300 | AF/HP | .210 | .135 |
| | * | .452" | 325 | AF | .210 | .135 |

\* also available with Sabots for Muzzleloaders

HANDLOADING

# Woodleigh Premium Bullets

## WELDCORE SOFT NOSE

A product of Australia, Woodleigh weldcore Soft Nose bullets are made from 90/100 gilding metal (90% copper; 10% zinc) 1.6 mm thick. Maximum retained weight is obtained by fusing the pure lead to the gilding metal jacket, hence the name "Weldcore."

## FULL METAL JACKET

Fashioned from gilding metal-clad steel 2mm thick, jackets on FMJ bullets are heavy at the nose for extra impact resistance. The jacket then tapers towards the base to assist rifling engraving.

| Calibre Diameter | Type | Weight Grain | SD | BC |
|---|---|---|---|---|
| 700 Nitro .700" | SN | 1000 | .292 | .340 |
| | FMJ | 1000 | .292 | .340 |
| 600 Nitro .620" | SN | 900 | .334 | .371 |
| | FMJ | 900 | .334 | .334 |
| 577 Nitro .585" | SN | 750 | .313 | .346 |
| | FMJ | 750 | .313 | .351 |
| | SN | 650 | .271 | .292 |
| | FMJ | 650 | .271 | .292 |
| 577 B.P. .585" | SN | 650 | .271 | .320 |
| 500 Nitro .510" | SN | 570 | .313 | .474 |
| | FMJ | 570 | .313 | .434 |
| 500 B.P. .510" | SN | 440 | .242 | .336 |
| 500 Jeffery .510" | PP | 535 | .304 | .460 |
| | SN | 535 | .304 | .460 |
| | FMJ | 535 | .304 | .422 |
| | PP | 600 | .330 | .423 |
| | FMJ | 600 | .330 | .330 |
| 505 Gibbs .505" | PP | 600 | .336 | .450 |
| | SN | 525 | .294 | .445 |
| | FMJ | 525 | .294 | .408 |
| | FMJ | 600 | .366 | .450 |
| 475 No2 Jeffery .488" | SN | 500 | .300 | .420 |
| | FMJ | 500 | .300 | .416 |
| 475 No2 .483" | SN | 480 | .303 | .400 |
| | FMJ | 480 | .303 | .410 |
| 476 W.R. .476" | SN | 520 | .328 | .420 |
| | FMJ | 520 | .328 | .455 |
| 475 Nitro .476" | SN | 480 | .227 | .307 |
| | FMJ | 480 | .227 | .257 |
| 470 Nitro .474" | SN | 500 | .318 | .411 |
| | FMJ | 500 | .318 | .410 |
| 465 Nitro .468" | SN | 480 | .318 | .410 |
| | FMJ | 480 | .318 | .407 |
| 450 Nitro .458" | SN | 480 | .327 | .419 |
| | FMJ | 480 | .327 | .410 |
| 458 Mag. .458" | SN | 500 | .341 | .430 |
| | SN | 550 | .375 | .480 |
| | FMJ | 500 | .341 | .405 |
| | FMJ | 550 | .375 | .426 |
| | PP | 400 | .272 | .420 |
| | RN | 350 | .238 | .305 |
| 45/70 .458" | FN | 405 | .276 | .250 |
| 11.3x62 Schuler .440" | SN | 401 | .296 | .411 |
| 425 W.R. .435" | SN | 410 | .310 | .344 |
| | FMJ | 410 | .310 | .336 |
| 404 Jeffery .423" | SN | 400 | .319 | .354 |
| | FMJ | 400 | .319 | .358 |
| | SN | 350 | .279 | .357 |
| 10.75x68mm .423" | SN | 347 | .277 | .355 |
| | FMJ | 347 | .277 | .307 |
| 416 Rigby .416" | SN | 410 | .338 | .375 |
| | FMJ | 410 | .338 | .341 |
| | PP | 340 | .281 | .425 |
| | SN | 450 | .372 | .402 |
| 450/400 Nitro .411" or .408" | SN | 400 | .338 | .384 |
| | FMJ | 400 | .338 | .433 |

| Calibre Diameter | Type | Weight Grain | SD | BC |
|---|---|---|---|---|
| .408 | SN | 400 | .338 | .384 |
| | FMJ | 400 | .338 | .433 |
| 375 Mag. .375" | PP | 235 | .239 | .331 |
| | RN | 270 | .275 | .305 |
| | SP | 270 | .275 | .380 |
| | PP | 270 | .275 | .352 |
| | RN | 300 | .305 | .340 |
| | SP | 300 | .305 | .425 |
| | PP | 300 | .305 | .420 |
| | FMJ | 300 | .305 | .307 |
| | RN | 350 | .354 | .354 |
| | PP | 350 | .354 | .440 |
| | FMJ | 350 | .354 | .372 |
| 405 Win., .411" | SN | 300 | .254 | .194 |
| 9.3mm .366" | SN | 286 | .305 | .331 |
| | PP | 286 | .305 | .381 |
| | FMJ | 286 | .305 | .324 |
| | SN | 250 | .267 | .296 |
| 360 No2 .366" | SN | 320 | .341 | .378 |
| | FMJ | 320 | .341 | .362 |
| | PP | 320 | .343 | .428 |
| 358 Cal .358" | SN | 225 | .250 | .277 |
| | FMJ | 225 | .250 | .298 |
| | SN | 250 | .285 | .365 |
| | SN | 310 | .346 | .400 |
| | FMJ | 310 | .346 | .378 |
| 338 Mag .338" | PP | 225 | .281 | .425 |
| | SN | 250 | .313 | .332 |
| | PP | 250 | .313 | .470 |
| | FMJ | 250 | .313 | .326 |
| | SN | 300 | .375 | .416 |
| | FMJ | 300 | .375 | .398 |
| 333 Jeffery .333" | SN | 250 | .328 | .400 |
| | SN | 300 | .386 | .428 |
| | FMJ | 300 | .386 | .419 |
| 318 W.R. .330" | SN | 250 | .328 | .420 |
| | FMJ | 250 | .328 | .364 |
| 8mm .323" | SN | 196 | .268 | .370 |
| | SN | 220 | .302 | .363 |
| | SN | 250 | .343 | .389 |
| 8X57 | SN | 200 | .282 | .370 |
| 303 British .312 | SN | 174 | .257 | .342 |
| | PP | 215 | .316 | .359 |
| 308 Cal .308" | FMJ | 220 | .331 | .359 |
| | RN | 220 | .331 | .367 |
| | PP | 180 | .273 | .376 |
| | PP | 165 | .250 | .320 |
| | PP | 150 | .226 | .301 |
| Win Mag. | PP | 180 | .273 | .435 |
| | PP | 200 | .301 | .450 |
| 275 H&H .287" | PP | 160 | .275 | .474 |
| | PP | 175 | .301 | .518 |
| 7mm .284" | PP | 140 | .247 | .436 |
| | PP | 160 | .282 | .486 |
| | PP | 175 | .312 | .530 |
| 270 Win .277" | PP | 130 | .241 | .409 |
| | PP | 150 | .278 | .463 |

*SP = Semi-point • PP = Protected Point • FN = Flat Nose • RN = Round Nose • FMJ = Full Metal Jacket. All PP, FN, RN, SP, SN bullets are Weldcore Softnose*

98% & 95% RETAINED WEIGHT 300 WIN MAG 180GR PP

458 X 500GN SN RECOVERED FROM BUFFALO

270 WIN 150GN PP 86% RETAINED WEIGHT

94% RETAINED WEIGHT 300 WIN MAG 180GR PP

500/465 RECOVERED FROM BUFFALO

HANDLOADING

# Accurate Powder

## ACCURATE POWDER SPECIFICATIONS

| | NG* | AVG. LENGTH/THICKNESS | | AVG. DIAMETER | | BULK DENSITY | VMD | COMPARATIVE POWDERS*** | |
|---|---|---|---|---|---|---|---|---|---|
| | | INCHES | MM | INCHES | MM | GRAM/CC | CC/GRAIN | BALL | EXTRUDED |
| **BALL PROPELLANTS** | | | | | | | | | |
| Handguns/Shotshell | | | | | | | | | |
| No.2 Imp. | 14.0 | | | 0.018 | 0.457 | 0.650 | 0.100 | WIN 231 | Bullseye |
| No. 5 | 18.0 | | | 0.027 | 0.686 | 0.950 | 0.068 | WIN 540 | |
| No. 7 | 12.0 | | | 0.012 | 0.305 | 0.985 | 0.066 | WIN 630 | |
| No. 9 | 10.0 | | | 1.015 | 0.381 | 0.935 | 0.069 | WIN 296 | |
| 1680 | 10.0 | | | 0.014 | 0.356 | 0.950 | 0.068 | WIN 680 | |
| Solo 4100 | 10.0 | | | 0.011 | 0.279 | 0.960 | 0.068 | WIN 296 | |
| Rifle | | | | | | | | | |
| 2230 | 10.0 | | | 0.022 | 0.559 | 0.980 | 0.066 | BL C2, WIN 748 | |
| 2460 | 10.0 | | | 0.022 | 0.559 | 0.990 | 0.065 | BL C2, WIN 748 | |
| 2520 | 10.0 | | | 0.022 | 0.559 | 0.970 | 0.067 | | |
| 2700 | 10.0 | | | 0.022 | 0.559 | 0.960 | 0.068 | WIN 760 | |
| MAGPRO | 9.0 | | | 0.030 | 0.762 | 0.970 | 0.067 | | |
| 8700 | 10.0 | | | 0.030 | 0.762 | 0.960 | 0.068 | H870 | |
| **EXTRUDED PROPELLANTS** | | | | | | | | | |
| Shotshell/Handguns | | | | | | | | | |
| Nirto 100 | 21.0 | 0.010 | 0.254 | 0.058 | 1.473 | 0.505 | 0.128 | | 700X, Red Dot |
| Solo 1000 | | 0.010 | 0.254 | 0.052 | 1.321 | 0.510 | 0.127 | | Green Dot |
| Solo 1250 | | 0.013 | 0.033 | 0.051 | 1.295 | 0.550 | 0.118 | | PB |
| Rifle/handgun | | | | | | | | | |
| 5744 | 20.00 | 0.048 | 1.219 | 0.033 | 0.838 | 0.880 | 0.074 | | |
| Rifle | | | | | | | | | |
| 2015 | | 0.039 | 0.991 | 0.031 | 0.787 | 0.880 | 0.074 | | H322,N201 IMR 4198 |
| 2495 | | 0.068 | 1.727 | 0.029 | 0.737 | 0.880 | 0.074 | | IMR 4895 |
| 4064 | | 0.050 | 1.270 | 0.035 | 0.889 | 0.890 | 0.072 | | IMR 4064 |
| 4350 | | 0.083 | 0.038 | 0.038 | 0.965 | 0.890 | 0.072 | | IMR 4350 |
| 3100 | | 0.083 | 0.038 | 0.038 | 0.965 | 0.920 | 0.070 | | IMR 4831 |

*NG-NItroglycerin   ***For comparison only, not a loading recommendation

# Alliant Smokeless Powders

### BULLSEYE®
America's best known pistol powder. Unsurpassed for .45 ACP target loads. *Available in 8-lb., 4-lb., and 1-lb. canisters.*

### POWER PISTOL®
Designed for high performance in semi-automatic pistols and is the powder of choice for 9mm, .40 S&W and .357 SIG. *Available in 4-lb. and 1-lb. canisters.*

### 2400®
Legendary for its performance in .44 magnum and other magnum pistol loads. Originally developed for the .22 Hornet, it's also the shooter's choice for .410 bore. *Available in 8-lb., 4-lb., and 1-lb. canisters.*

### UNIQUE®
The most versatile shotgun/handgun powder made. Great for 12, 16, 20 and 28 gauge. loads. Use with most hulls, primers and wads. *Available in 8- lb., 4-lb., and 1- lb. canisters.*

### RELODER 7®
Designed for small caliber varmint loads, it meters consistently, and meets the needs of the most demanding bench rest shooter. Great in .45-70 and .450 Marlin. *Available in 5-lb. and 1-lb. canisters.*

### RELODER 10X®
Best choice for light bullet applications in .222 Rem, .223 Rem, .22-250 Rem and key bench rest calibers. Also great in light bullet .308 Win loads. *Available in 5 lb. and 1 lb. containers.*

### RELODER 15®
The best all-around medium speed rifle powder. It provides excellent .223 and .308 cal. performance. Selected as the powder for U.S. Military's M118 Special Ball Long Range Sniper Round. *Available in 5-lb. and 1-lb. canisters.*

### RELODER 19®
Provides superb accuracy in most medium and heavy rifle loads and is the powder of choice for 30-06 and .338 calibers. *Available in 5-lb. and 1-lb. canisters.*

### RELODER 22®
This top performing powder for big game loads provides excellent metering, and is the powder of choice for .270, 7mm magnum and .300 Win. magnum. *Available in 5-lb. and 1-lb. canisters.*

### RELODER 25®
This new, advanced powder for big game hunting features improved slower burning, and delivers the high ener-gy that heavy magnum loads need. *Available in 5-lb. and 1-lb. canisters.*

HANDLOADING

# Alliant Shotshell Powders

HANDLOADING

### RED DOT®
America's #1 choice for clay target loads, now 50% cleaner. Since 1932, more 100 straights than any other powder. *Available in 8-lb., 4-lb., and 1-lb. canisters.*

### e³®
The first of a new generation of high performance powders.

### GREEN DOT®
NOW CLEANER BURNING! It delivers precise burn rates for uniformly tight patterns, and you'll appreciate the lower felt recoil. Versatile for target and field. *Available in 8-lb., 4-lb., and 1-lb. canisters.*

### AMERICAN SELECT®
Our "ultra clean" burning premium powder makes a versatile target load and superior 1-oz. load for improved clay target scores. Great for Cowboy Action handgun loading too! *Available in 8-lb., 4-lb., and 1-lb. canisters.*

### 410®
Cleanest .410 bore powder on the market.

### STEEL®
Designed for waterfowl shotshell. Gives steel shot high velocity within safe pressure limits for 10 and 12 gauge loads. *Available in 4-lb. and 1-lb. canisters.*

### BLUE DOT®
The powder of choice for magnum lead shotshell loads. 10, 12, 16, and 20 gauge. Consistent and accurate. Doubles as magnum handgun powder. *Available in 5-lb., and 1-lb. canisters.*

### HERCO®
Since 1920, a proven powder for heavy shotshell loads, including 10, 12, 16, 20 and 28 gauge target loads. The ultimate in 12 gauge, 1-1/4 oz. upland game loads. *Available in 8-lb., 4-lb., and 1-lb. canisters.*

# Hodgdon Smokeless Powder

Hodgdon Powder Company offers its popular sulfur-free Triple Seven powder in 50-grain pellets. Formulated for use with 209 shotshell primers, Triple Seven leaves no rotten egg smell, and the residue is easy to clean from the bore with water only. The pellets are sized for 50-caliber muzzleloaders and can be used singly (for target shooting or small game) as well as two at a time (for a 100-grain big game charge). Also available in .45 caliber/50 grain and .50 caliber/30 grain sizes.

### PYRODEX PELLETS
Both rifle and pistol pellets eliminate powder measures, speeds shooting for black powder enthusiasts.

### EXTREME H4198
H4198 was developed especially for small and medium capacity cartridges.

### EXTREME H322
This powder fills the gap between H4198 and BL-C9(2). Performs best in small to medium capacity cases.

### EXTREME BENCHMARK
A fine choice for small rifle cases like the .223 Rem and PPC competition rounds. Appropriate also for the 300-30 and 7x57.

### SPHERICAL BL-C2
Best performance is in the 222, .308 other cases smaller than 30/06.

### SPHERICAL H335®
Similar to BL-C(2), H335 is popular for its performance in medium capacity cases, especially in 222 and 308 Winchester.

### EXTREME VARGET
Features small extruded grain powder for uniform metering, plus higher velocities/normal pressures in such calibers as .223, 22-250, 306, 30-06, 375 H&H

### EXTREME H4895®
4895 gives desirable performance in almost all cases from 222 Rem. to 458 Win. Reduced loads, to as low as 3/5 maximum, still give target accuracy.

### SPHERICAL H380®
This number fills a gap between 4320 and 4350. It is excellent in 22/250, 220 Swift, the 6mm's, 257 and 30/06.

### SPHERICAL H414®
In many popular medium to medium-large calibers, pressure velocity relationship is better.

### EXTREME H4350
This powder gives superb accuracy at optimum velocity for many large capacity metallic rifle cartridges.

### EXTREME H4831®
Outstanding performance with medium and heavy bullets in the 6mm's, 25/06, 270 and Magnum calibers. Also available with shortened grains (H4831SC) for easy metering.

### EXTREME H1000 EXTRUDED POWDER
Fills the gap between H4831 and H870. Works especially well in overbore capacity cartridges (1,000-yard shooters take note).

### EXTREME H50 BMG
Designed for the 50 Browning Machine Gun cartridge.

### RETUMBO
A true magnum rifle powder, designed for such cartridges as the 300 Rem. Ultra Mag., 30-378 Weatherby, the 7mm STW and other cases with large capacities and small bores. Shooters can expect up to 40-100 feet per second more velocity than other magnum powders.

### TRIPLE SEVEN
A muzzleloading propellant that does not use sulfur, keeping shooter's hand clean. No offensive odor and cleaning is as easy as running a water soaked patch down the barrel followed by 3 or 4 dry patches!

Highly insensitive to extreme temperature changes.

### CLAYS
Tailored for use in 12 ga., ⅞, 1-oz. and 1⅛-oz. loads. Also performs well in many handgun applications, including .38 Special, .40 S&W and 45 ACP. Perfect for 1⅛ and 1 oz. loads.

### UNIVERSAL CLAYS
Loads nearly all of the straight-wall pistol cartridges as well as 12 ga. 1.25 oz. thru 28 ga. ¾ oz. target loads.

### INTERNATIONAL CLAYS
Ideal for 12 and 20 ga. autoloaders who want reduced recoil.

### TITEWAD
This 12 ga. flattened spherical shotgun powder is ideal for ⅞, 1 and 1⅛ oz. loads, with minimum recoil and mild muzzle report. The fastest fuel in Hodgdon's line.

### HS-6 AND HS-7
HS-6 and HS-7 for Magnum field loads are unsurpassed, since they do not pack in the measure. They deliver uniform charges and are dense to allow sufficient wad column for best patterns.

### LONGSHOT
A spherical powder for heavy shotgun loads.

### HP38
A fast pistol powder for most pistol loading. Especially recommended for mid-range 38 specials.

### TITEGROUP
Excellent for most straight-walled pistol cartridges, incl. 38 Spec., 44 Spec., 45 ACP. Low charge weights, clean burning; position insensitive and flawless ignition.

### H110
A spherical powder made especially for the 30 M1 carbine. H110 also does very well in 357, 44 spec., 44 Mag. or 410 ga. shotshell. Magnum primers are recommended for consistent ignition.

### H4227
An extruded powder similar to H110, it is recommended for the 22 Hornet and some specialized loading in the 45-70 caliber. Also excellent in magnum pistol and .410 shotgun.

### LIL' GUN
This powder was developed specifically for the .410 shotgun but works very well in rifle cartridges like the .22 Hornet and in the .44 magnum.

# IMR Powders

E.I. DuPont de Nemours began its corporate life in 1802, on Delaware's Brandywine River. The varied product line that evolved over the next couple of centuries could hardly have been imagined by its founder, French immigrant Eleuthere Irenee DuPont.

"I can make better black powder than what your country has in its magazines," DuPont told Alexander Hamilton. The enterprising engineer got the help he needed to build a plant in Wilmington. The new propellant satisfied U.S. ordnance officers, and DuPont put down roots. Gunpowder was the firm's primary product for most of the 19th century. In the 1880s, DuPont built a plant at Carney's Point to boost capacity. During World War I, 25,000 people went to work at this facility on the Brandywine, providing more than 80 percent of the military powders used by the Allies (the British, French, Danes, and Russians as well as U.S. troops.

Soon after the transition from black to smokeless powders at the close of the 19th century, "MR" began appearing on canisters of DuPont powders. It meant "military rifle." The IMR line of "improved military rifle" powders came along in the 1920s, when four-digit numbers replaced two-digit numbers in DuPont designations. MR 10 and the like died out. IMR fuels, beginning with 4198, supplanted them. The first had relatively fast burn rates, because in those days, rifle cartridges were small. In 1934, DuPont introduced IMR 4227. In the early 1940s, IMR 4895 came along, specifically for the .30-06 in the M1 Garand service rifle. About that time the first slow IMR propellant made its debut. Developed for 20mm cannons, IMR 4831 would become one of the most popular powders for high-capacity rifle cartridges developed by wildcatters like Roy Weatherby and P.O. Ackley. Incidentally, label numbers have nothing to do with burning rate. According to long-time DuPont engineer Larry Werner, powder is labeled chronologically. The highest numbers indicate the most recent propellants.

You'll find differences in charts ranking the burn rates of IMR and other smokeless powders. The reason: powders can behave differently as you change case shape and bore diameter, fuel charge and bullet weight. IMR gives all its powders a Relative Quickness value, assigning IMR 4350 an arbitrary value of 100. According to Larry Werner, quick-burning IMR 4227 has an RQ of 180; IMR 4198 comes in at 165 and IMR 3031 at 135. IMR 4064, 4320 and 4895 are listed at 120, 115 and 110 respectively, though some loading manuals suggest a different order. IMR 4831 and 7828 burn more slowly. "Closed bomb" tests are used to gauge burn rate. A unit charge of powder ignited in a chamber of known volume produces a pressure curve that's then compared to the curves from other propellants.

DuPont's MR line included single-base (nitrocellulose) and double-base (nitrocellulose with nitroglycerine) powders. "The nitro gives you more energy per grain," explains Larry, "and it reduces the tendency for the grains to pick up moisture. Its drawback is more residue. Double-base powders generally don't burn as clean. To get the full effect of nitroglycerine, you really need 8 to 12 percent in the mix, but some powders claimed to be double-base contain less." All commercial ball powders are double-base, he says. The current IMR line includes only single-base propellants.

IMR powders are no longer made by DuPont. The IMR trademark belongs to EXPRO, another chemical firm. The transfer has its roots in the Depression, which DuPont weathered. But scathing political attacks from certain U.S. senators accused the company of war-mongering. As Hitler tuned his war machine and the U.S. prepared to re-arm, DuPont boosted its production capacity. "But the company was fed up with the treatment it had received from Congress," Larry remembers. Rather than build new plants, it contracted to operate government facilities for one dollar a year. That way, it could not be said to have had a stake in the hostilities. Of course, the government had no powder works that could match DuPont's, so the firm supervised construction of seven factories modeled on the Carney's Point plant. Another was built in Canada. At the height of the Second World War, these facilities shipped a million pounds of powder a day.

In the summer of 1978, DuPont contracted with Valleyfield Chemical Products in Quebec to produce its commercial smokeless propellants. (The Valleyfield plant was the Canadian factory built during World War II. It had been operated by CIL, or Canadian Industries, Ltd., a branch of the government.) In 1982, Valleyfield Chemical sold to Welland Chemical, which became EXPRO.

In December, 1986, DuPont sold its smokeless powder business to EXPRO. The IMR Powder Company became a testing and marketing firm for EXPRO propellants. IMR's laboratory and offices in Plattsburg, New York, developed ballistics data for IMR powders and packaged and distributed them to dealers. EXPRO, with an annual manufacturing capacity of more than 10 million pounds, also made other powders, including Alliant. Though DuPont owned 70 percent of Remington for decades, it has from time to time provided powder for competing ammunition firms.

In October 2003, Hodgdon Powder Company purchased IMR and retains it as a division. IMR powders are still available under their familiar product names. The phone number for IMR is now 913-362-9455. Learn more at www.imrpowder.com

Ramshot (Western Powders, Inc.) powders are all double-base propellants, meaning they contain nitrocellulose and nitroglycerine. While some spherical or ball powders are known for leaving plenty of residue in barrels, Ramshots people say these new fuels burn very clean. They meter easily, as do all ball powders. Plastic cannisters are designed for spill-proof use and include basic loading data on the labels.

**RAMSHOT COMPETITION** is for the clay target shooter. A fast-burning powder comparable to 700-X or Red Dot it performs well in a variety of 12-gauge target loads, offering low recoil, consistent pressures and clean combustion.

**RAMSHOT TRUE BLUE** was designed for small to medium-size handgun cartridges. Similar to Winchester 231 and Hodgdon HP-38, it has enough bulk to nearly fill most cases, thereby better positioning the powder for ignition.

**RAMSHOT ZIP,** a fast-burning target powder for cartridges like the .38 Special and .45 ACP, gives competitors uniform velocities.

**RAMSHOT SILHOUETTE** is ideal for the 9mm handgun cartridge, from light to heavy loads. It also works well in the .40 Smith & Wesson and combat loads for the .45 Auto.

**RAMSHOT ENFORCER** is a match for high-performance handgun hulls like the .40 Smith & Wesson. It is designed for full-power loading and high velocities.Ramshot X-Terminator, a fast-burning rifle powder, excels in small-caliber, medium-capacity cartridges. It has the versatility to serve in both target and high-performance varmint loads.

**RAMSHOT TAC** was formulated for tactical rifle cartridges, specifically the .223 and .308. It has produced exceptional accuracy with a variety of bullets and charge weights.

**RAMSHOT BIG GAME** is a versatile propellant for cartridges as diverse as the .30-06 and the .338 Winchester, and for light-bullet loads in small-bore magnums.

**RAMSHOT MAGNUM** is the slowest powder of the Western line, and does its best work in cartridges with lots of case volume and small to medium bullet diameter. It is the powder of choice in 7mm and .30 Magnums.

**RAMSHOT X-TERMINATOR** is a clean burning powder designed for the .222 Rem., 223 Rem., and .22 Benchrest calibers.

www.ramshot.com

# Vihtavuori

Kaltron-Pettibone imports Vihtavuori propellants (and Lapua ammunition in the U.S.) The powders, only recently available Stateside, have become popular with American shooters, who applaud their consistency. Their burning rates complement those of powders from IMR, Accurate, Hodgdon and Alliant (the ReLoder series). Here's a synopsis. Note that "similar" in these descriptions does NOT connote interchangeability!

**N110:** very fast, for rifle cartridges like the .22 Hornet and .25-20, and for powerful handgun rounds like the .357 and .44 Magnums; similar powders include H110, Winchester 296, Alliant 2400.

**N120:** a fast powder that requires high pressure for complete and efficient burn; similar to IMR 4227 and best used in small-capacity .22 centerfires.

**N130:** a bit slower than 4227 but still quick; a standard propellant in the .22 and 6mm PPC.

**N133:** slow enough for use in medium-capacity .22 cartridges like the .223; also useful in the .45-70 and similar cartridges with little or no neck restriction; similar to IMR 4198.

**N135:** a versatile powder of medium burn rate, ideal in the .308 and close derivatives, as well as the .30-06; applications from the various 17-calibers to the .458 Winchester; similar to RL-12.

**N140:** . . slightly slower than N135, but useful in the same cartridges and any that would be served with RL-15 or IMR 4320; a fine choice for the .30-06 and .375 H&H.

**N150:** a medium-slow powder for light-bullet loads in the .270 and the 30-caliber magnums; an excellent alternative to Winchester 760, Hodgdon H414, IMR 4350.

**N160:** a workhorse powder for magnum cases and high-velocity rounds on the .308 and .30-06 hulls; similar to RL-19, IMR 4831, Accurate 3100; useful in the .243, .270, 7mm Remington and .300 and .338 Winchester Magnums.

**N165:** a slow powder for "overbore" magnum cases and for heavy-bullet loads in the medium-bore magnums; ideal for high-performance .300s with all bullet weights; similar to H4831 and RL-22.

**N170:** the slowest-burning of Vihtavuori's propellants, for small-bore magnums like the .257 Weatherby and .264 Winchester; similar to H1000 and RL-25.

Unlike the single-base (nitrocellulose) N100 series, the N500 series of Vihtavuori powders has a nitroglycerol component (up to 25 percent, by impregnation). There's also a special stabilizer, a flame reducing agent, a wear-reducing agent and coating agents that ensure progressive burning in the case to provide uniform and efficient pressure curves. These high-energy double-base powders are available in three burning rates, equivalent to the 100-series powders with the same last digits. N540 is applicable in the same cartridges as N140. N550 is a match for N150. N560 is the slowest, an ideal propellant for the .270 Winchester and 6.5x55 Swedish Mauser.

Vihtavuori also makes single-base powders for the .50 BMG. The 24N41 is slightly faster than the 20N29. Eight Vihtavuori pistol powders complete the 2003 line:

**N310:** as fast as Bullseye, for small-capacity cartridges like the .25 ACP up to the 9mm Luger.

**N320:** slightly faster than Winchester 231, a versatile powder for the most popular of pistol rounds, including the .38 Special, .357 Magnum, .45 ACP, .44 Magnum and .45 Long Colt.

**N330:** useful in medium- to large-capacity cases from the .38 Special to the various .44s and .45s; similar to Green Dot.

**N340:** slow enough for high-performance loads in the .357 and .44 Magnums, also useful in the .38 Super and .30 Luger; similar to Winchester 540.

**N350:** a slow powder for magnum and heavy-bullet handgun loads; burning rate like that of Blue Dot or Hi-Skor 800-X.

**3N37:** between N340 and N350 in burn rate; recommended for competitive shooters.

**3N38:** a competition powder specifically for high-speed loads in the .38 Super and 9mm Luger.

**N105 Super Magnum:** a very slow pistol powder for heavy-bullet loads in magnum cases; almost as slow as N110.

# Dillon Precision Reloaders

Besides manufacturing high-speed metallic cartridge reloading machines, Dillon Precision is a leader in the shotshell reloading market with its SL 900 progressive press. Based on Dillon's proven XL 650 O-frame design, it incorporates the same powerful compound linkage. The automatic case insert system, fed by an electric case collator, ranks high among the new features of this reloader. Adjustable shot and powder bars come as standard equipment. Both the powder and shot bars are case-activated, so no powder or shot can spill when no shell is at that station. Should the operator forget to insert a wad during the reloading process, the SL 900 will not dispense shot into the powder-charged hull. Both powder and shot systems are based on Dillon's adjustable powder bar design, which is accurate to within a few tenths of a grain. These systems also eliminate the need for fixed-volume bushings. Simply adjust the measures to dispense the exact charges required.

The Dillon SL 900 is the first progressive shotshell loader on which it is practical to change gauges. An interchangeable toolhead makes it quick and easy to change from one gauge to another. The SL 900 also has an extra large, remote shot hopper that holds an entire 25-pound bag of shot, making it easy to fill with a funnel. The unique shot reservoir/dispenser helps ensure that a consistent volume of shot is delivered to each shell.

For shotgunners who shoot and load for multiple gauges or different kinds of shooting, the SL 900's interchangeable toolhead feature makes quick work of changing from one gauge to another. It uses a collet-type sizing die that re-forms the base of the shotshell to factory specifications—a feature that ensures reliable feeding in all shotguns. The heat-treated steel crimp die forms and folds the hull before the final taper crimp die radiuses and blends the end of the hull and locks the crimp into place.

## MODEL RL550B PROGRESSIVE LOADER

- Accommodates over 120 calibers
- Interchangeable toolhead assembly
- Auto/Powder priming systems
- Uses standard 7/8" by 14 dies
- Loading rate: 500-600 rounds per hour

**Price:** . . . . . . . . . . . . . . . . . . . . . . . . . . . . . . . $330

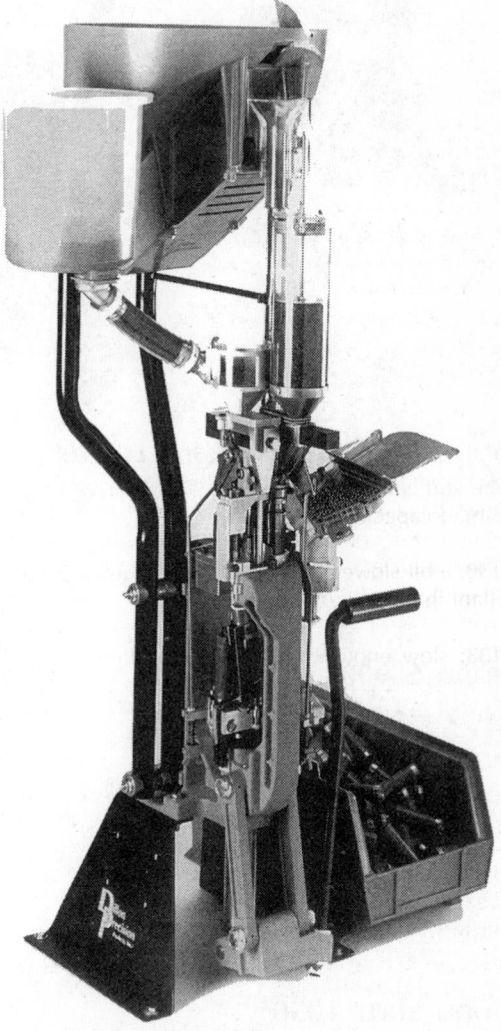

## MODEL SL900
**Price:** $820

# Dillon Precision Reloaders

MODEL SQUARE DEAL B

MODEL XL 650

MODEL AT-500

MODEL SUPER 1050 AND RL 1050

### MODEL RL550B PROGRESSIVE LOADER
- Accommodates over 120 calibers
- Interchangeable toolhead assembly
- Auto/Powder priming systems
- Uses standard ⅞" by 14 dies
- Loading rate: 500-600 rounds per hour

Price:.....................................$330

### MODEL SL900
Price:.....................................$820

### MODEL SQUARE DEAL B
- Automatic indexing
- Auto Powder/Priming Systems
- Available in 14 handgun calibers
- Loading rate: 400-500 rounds per hour
- Loading dies standard
- factory adjusted, ready-to-use

Price .....................................$278

### MODEL SUPER 1050
- Automatic indexing
- Auto powder/priming systems
- Automatic casefeeder

- Commercial grade machine
- Swages military primer pockets
- Loading rate: 1000-1200 rounds per hour
- Weighs 54 lbs.
- Eight stations

Price .....................................$1400

### MODEL XL 650
- Rotary indexing plate for primers
- Automatic indexing
- Uses standard ⅞" x 14 dies
- Loading rate: 800-1000 rounds per hour
- Five-station interchangeable toolhead

Price .....................................$444

### MODEL AT-500
- Loads over 40 calibers
- Uses standard ⅞" by 14 dies
- Upgradeable to Model RL 550B
- Interchangeable toolhead
- Switch from one caliber to another in 30 seconds
- Universal shellplate

Price .....................................$194

# Forster Reloading

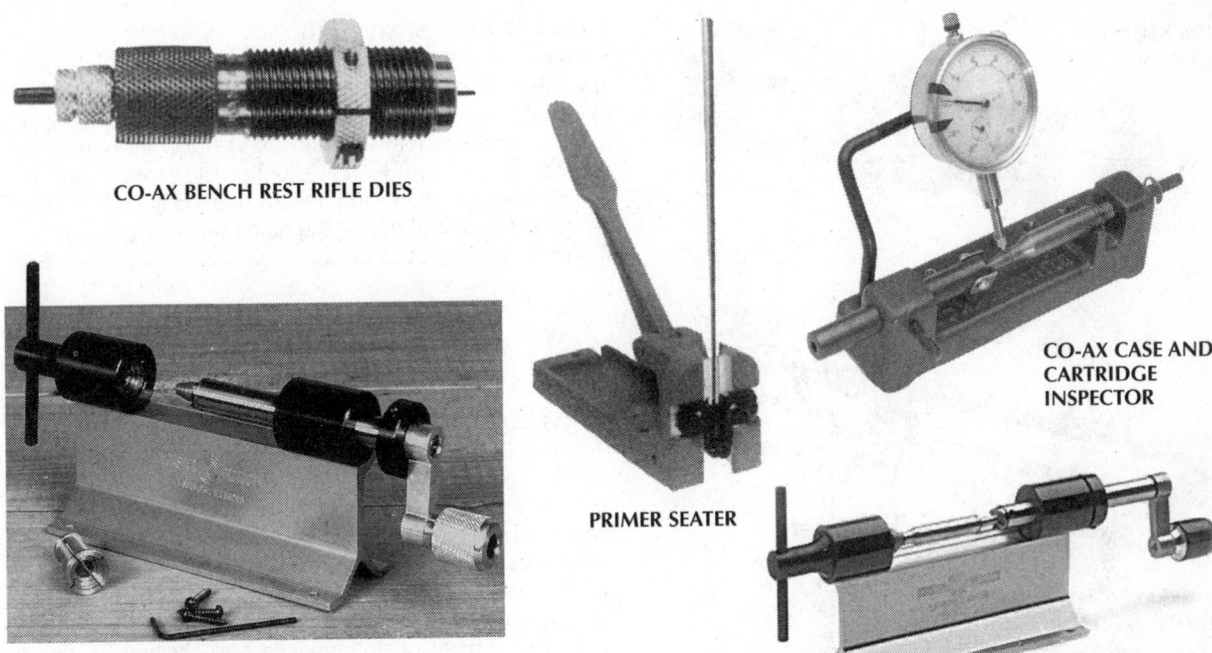

**CO-AX BENCH REST RIFLE DIES**

**HAND CASE TRIMMER**

**PRIMER SEATER**

**CO-AX CASE AND CARTRIDGE INSPECTOR**

**PRIMER POCKET CLEANER**

**HANDLOADING**

## CO-AX® BENCH REST® RIFLE DIES

Bench Rest Rifle Dies are glass-hard and polished mirror-smooth with special attention given to headspace, tapers and diameters. Sizing die has an elevated expander button to ensure better alignment of case and neck.

Bench Rest® Die Set . . . . . . . . . . . . . . . . . . . . . . . $79
Ultra Bench Rest Die Set . . . . . . . . . . . . . . . . . . . . 104
Full Length Sizer . . . . . . . . . . . . . . . . . . . . . . . . . . 37
Bench Rest Seating Die . . . . . . . . . . . . . . . . . . . . . 44

## HAND CASE TRIMMER

Shell holder is a Brown & Sharpe-type collet. Case and cartridge conditioning accessories include inside neck reamer, outside neck turner, deburring tool, hollow pointer and primer pocket cleaners. The case trimmer trims all cases, ranging from 17 to 458 Winchester caliber.
Price:. . . . . . . . . . . . . . . . . . . . . . . . . . . . . . . . . . . $66

## PRIMER SEATER WITH "E-Z-JUST" SHELLHOLDER

The Bonanza Primer Seater is designed so that primers are seated co-axially (primer in line with primer pocket). Mechanical leverage allows primers to be seated fully without crushing. With the addition of one extra set of disc shell holders and one extra Primer Unit, all modern cases, rim or rimless, from 222 up to 458 Magnum, can be primed. Shell holders are easily adjusted to any case by rotating to contact rim or cannelure of the case.
Primer Seater . . . . . . . . . . . . . . . . . . . . . . . . . . . $77

## "CLASSIC 50" CASE TRIMMER (NOT SHOWN)

Handles more than 100 different big bore calibers–500 Nitro Express, 416 Rigby, 50 Sharps, 475 H&H, etc. Also available: .50 BMG Case Trimmer, designed specifically for reloading needs of .50 Cal. BMG shooters.
Price: "Classic 50" Case Trimmer . . . . . . . . . . . . . . $94
.50 BMG Case Trimmer . . . . . . . . . . . . . . . . . . . . . . $99

## CO-AX® CASE AND CARTRIDGE INSPECTOR

One tool to perform three vital measurements. Accurate performance from ammunition is absolutely dependent on uniformity of both the bullet and the case. Forster's exclusive Co-Ax® Case & Cartridge Inspector provides the ability to ensure uniformity by measuring three critical dimensions: • Neck wall thickness • Case neck concentricity • Bullet runout.

Measurements are in increments of one-thousandth of an inch. The Inspector is unique because it checks both the bullet and case alignment in relation to the centerline (axis) of the entire cartridge or case.
Price:. . . . . . . . . . . . . . . . . . . . . . . . . . . . . . . . . . . $89

## PRIMER POCKET CLEANER

The Primer Pocket Cleaner helps ensure consistent ignition and reduce the incidence of misfires by removing powder and primer residue frm the primer pockets of your cases. This simple took is easy to use: Just hold the case mouth over the Primer Pocket Center with one hand while you quickly and easily clean the primer pockets by turning the Case Trimmer Handle.
Price:. . . . . . . . . . . . . . . . . . . . . . . . . . . . . . . . . . . $8

Handloading • 539

# Forster Reloading

**ULTRA BULLET
SEATER DIE**

## ULTRA BULLET SEATER DIE

Forster's new Ultra Die is available in 56 calibers, more than any other brand of micrometer-style seater. Adjustment is identical to that of a precision micrometer—the head is graduated to .001" increments with .025" bullet movement per revolution. The cartridge case, bullet and seating stem are completely supported and perfectly aligned in a close-fitting chamber before and during the bullet seating operation.
**Price:. . . . . . . . . . . . . . . . . . . . . . . . . . . . . . . . . . . . . \$70**

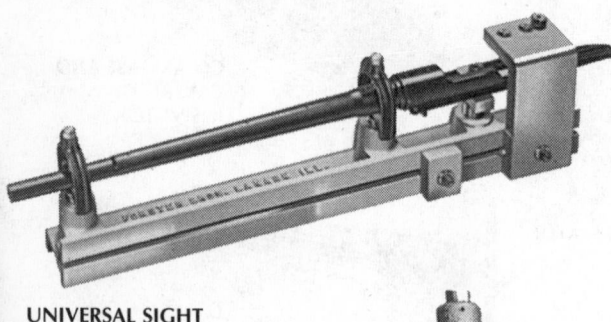

**UNIVERSAL SIGHT
MOUNTING FIXTURE**

## UNIVERSAL SIGHT MOUNTING FIXTURE

This product fills the exacting requirements needed for drilling and tapping holes for the mounting of scopes, receiver sights, shotgun beads, etc. The fixture handles any single-barrel gun—bolt-action, lever-action or pump-action—as long as the barrel can be laid into the "V" blocks of the fixture. Rifles with tube magazines are drilled in the same manner by removing the magazine tube. The fixture's main body is made of aluminum casting. The two "V" blocks are adjustable for height and are made of hardened steel ground accurately on the "V" as well as the shaft.
**Price:. . . . . . . . . . . . . . . . . . . . . . . . . . . . . . . . . . . . \$391**

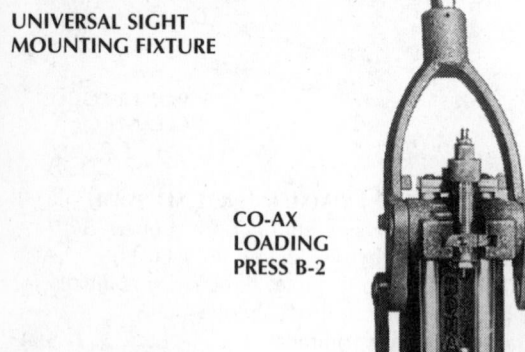

**CO-AX
LOADING
PRESS B-2**

## CO-AX® LOADING PRESS MODEL B-2

Designed to make reloading easier and more accurate, this press offers the following features: Snap-in and snap-out die change • Positive spent primer catcher • Automatic self-acting shell holder • Floating guide rods • Working room for right- or left-hand operators • Top priming device seats primers to factory specifications • Uses any standard $7/_8$" x 14 dies • No torque on the head • Perfect alignment of die and case • Three times the mechanical advantage of a "C" press
**Price:. . . . . . . . . . . . . . . . . . . . . . . . . . . . . . . . . . . . \$318**

**BENCH REST
POWDER MEASURE**

## BENCH REST POWDER MEASURE

When operated uniformly, this measure will throw uniform charges from 2½ grains Bullseye to 95 grains #4320. No extra drums are needed. Powder is metered from the charge arm, allowing a flow of powder without extremes in variation while minimizing powder shearing. Powder flows through its own built-in baffle, entering the charge arm uniformly.
**Price:. . . . . . . . . . . . . . . . . . . . . . . . . . . . . . . . . . . . \$117**

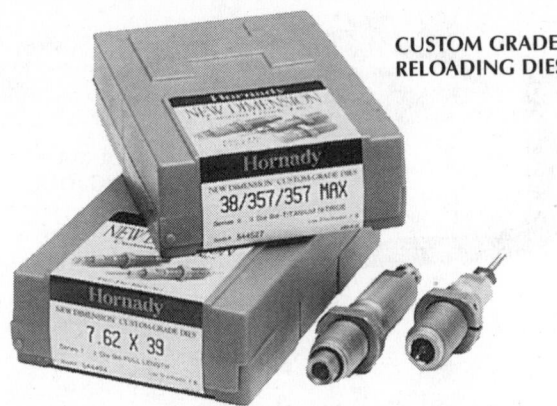

CUSTOM GRADE
RELOADING DIES

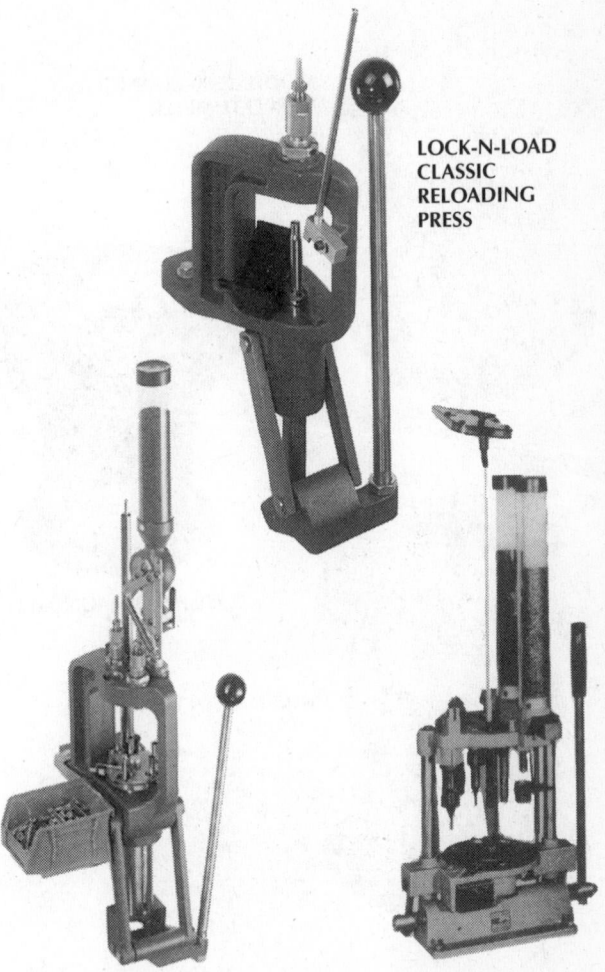

LOCK-N-LOAD
CLASSIC
RELOADING
PRESS

LOCK-N-LOAD          MODEL 366

## CUSTOM GRADE RELOADING DIES

An Elliptical Expander in new Hornady dies minimizes friction and reduces case neck stretch. (No need for a tapered expander for "necking up" to the next larger caliber.) Other recent design changes include a hardened steel decap pin that will not break, bend or crack even when depriming stubborn military cases. A bullet seater alignment sleeve guides the bullet and case neck into the die for in-line benchrest alignment. All New Dimension Reloading Dies include: collar and collar lock to center expander precisely; one-piece expander spindle with tapered bottom for easy cartridge insertion; wrench flats on die body, Sure-Loc™ lock rings and collar lock for easy tightening; and built-in crimper.

**Prices:**
**New Dimension Custom Grade Reloading Dies:**
Series II Three-die Rifle Set . . . . . . . . . . . . . . . . . $32
Series III . . . . . . . . . . . . . . . . . . . . . . . . . . . . 40
Match Grade . . . . . . . . . . . . . . . . . . . . . . . . . . 39

## LOCK-N-LOAD CLASSIC PRESS

Lock-N-Load is available on Hornady's single stage and progressive reloader models. This bushing system locks the die into the press like a rifle bolt. Instead of threading dies in and out of the press, you simply lock and unlock them with a slight twist. Dies are held firmly in a die bushing that stays with the die and retains the die setting. The Lock-N-Load Classic Press features an easy-grip handle, an O-style frame made of high-strength alloy, and a positive priming system that feeds, aligns and seats the primer smoothly and automatically.

Prices: Lock-N-Load Press. . . . . . . . . . . . . . . . . . $123
Lock-N-Load Classic Press Kit . . . . . . . . . . . . . . 292
Also Available: Lock-N-Load
50 BMG Press. . . . . . . . . . . . . . . . . . . . . . . . 353
50 BMG Press Kit . . . . . . . . . . . . . . . . . . . . . . 575

## LOCK-N-LOAD AUTO PROGRESSIVE PRESS

The Lock-N-Load Automatic Progressive reloading press featuring the Lock-N-Load bushing system offers the flexibility to add a roll or taper crimp die. Dies and powder measure are inserted into Lock-N-Load die bushings, which lock securely into the press. The bushings remain with the die and powder measure and can be removed in seconds. They also fit on other presses. Other features include: deluxe powder measure, automatic indexing, off-set handle, power-pac linkage, case ejector.

**Price:**
Lock-N-Load Auto Progressive Press (includes five die bushings, shellplate, primer catcher, Positive Priming System, powder drop, Deluxe Powder Measure, automatic primer feed) . . . . . . . . . . . . . . . . . . . $397

## MODEL 366 AUTO SHOTSHELL RELOADER

The 366 Auto features full-length resizing with each stroke, automatic primer feed, swing-out wad guide, three-state crimping featuring Taper-Loc for factory tapered crimp, automatic advance to the next station and automatic ejection. The turntable holds 8 shells for 8 operations with each stroke. Automatic charge bar loads shot and powder, dies and crimp starters for 6 point, 8 point and paper crimps.

**Price:**
Model 366 Auto Shotshell Reloader:
12, 20, 28 gauge or .410 bore . . . . . . . . . . . . . . . 523

HANDLOADING

# Lyman Reloading Tools

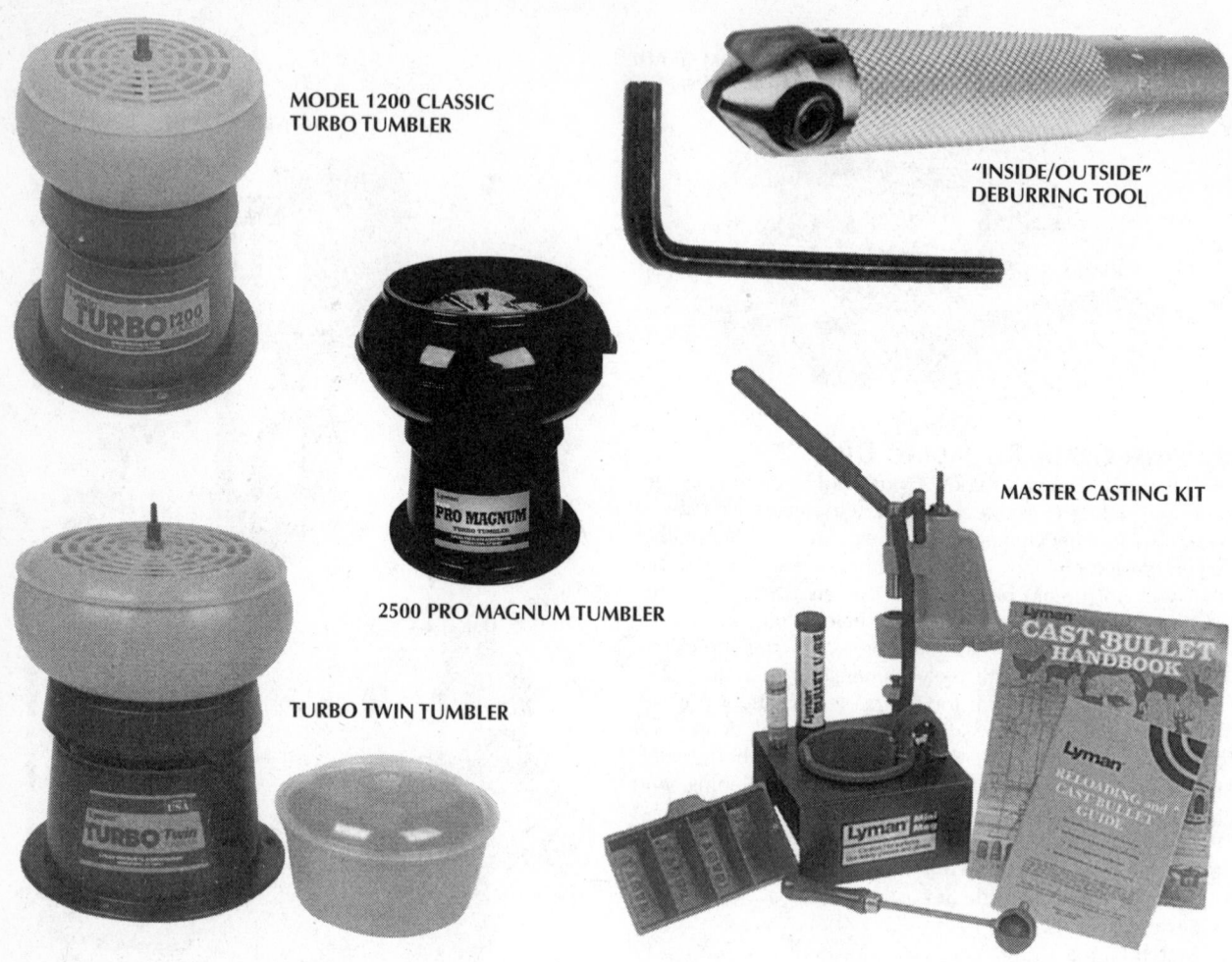

MODEL 1200 CLASSIC
TURBO TUMBLER

"INSIDE/OUTSIDE"
DEBURRING TOOL

MASTER CASTING KIT

2500 PRO MAGNUM TUMBLER

TURBO TWIN TUMBLER

## MODEL 1200 CLASSIC TURBO TUMBLER

This sturdy case tumbler features a redesigned base and drive system, plus a stronger suspension system and built-in exciters for better tumbling action and faster cleaning

| | |
|---|---|
| Model 1200 Classic | $100 |
| Model 1200 Auto-Flo | 100 |

**Also available:**

| | |
|---|---|
| Model 600 | 70 |
| Model 2200 Auto-Flo | 129 |
| Model 3200 Auto-Flo | 185 |

## 2500 PRO MAGNUM TUMBLER

Prep your cases with a new Lyman 2500 Pro Magnum tumbler. The bin handles up to 900 .38 Special cartridges at once.

| | |
|---|---|
| 2500 Pro Magnum Tumbler | $102 |
| with Auto Flow feature | 125 |

## "INSIDE/OUTSIDE" DEBURRING TOOL

This tool features an adjustable cutting blade that adapts easily to the mouth of any rifle or pistol case from 22 caliber to 45 caliber with a simple hex wrench adjustment. Inside deburring is completed by a conical internal section with slotted cutting edges, thus providing uniform inside and outside deburring in one simple operation. The deburring tool is mounted on an anodized aluminum handle that is machine-knurled for a sure grip.

| | |
|---|---|
| Deburring Tool | $14 |

## TURBO TWIN TUMBLER

The Twin features Lyman 1200 Pro Tumbler with an extra, 600 bowl system. Reloaders may use each bowl interchangeably for small or large capacity loads. 1200 Pro Bowl System has a built-in sifter lid for easy sifting of cases and media at the end of the polishing cycle. The Twin Tumbler features the Lyman Hi-Profile base design with built-in exciters and anti-rotation pads for faster, more consistent tumbling action.

| | |
|---|---|
| Turbo Twin Tumbler 110V | $80 |

## MASTER CASTING KIT

Designed especially to meet the needs of blackpowder shooters, this kit features Lyman's combination round ball and maxi ball mould blocks. It also contains a combination double cavity mould, mould handle, mini-mag furnace, lead dipper, bullet lube, a user's manual and a cast bullet guide. Kits are available in 45, 50 and 54 caliber.

| | |
|---|---|
| Master Casting Kit | $175 |

# Lyman Reloading Tools

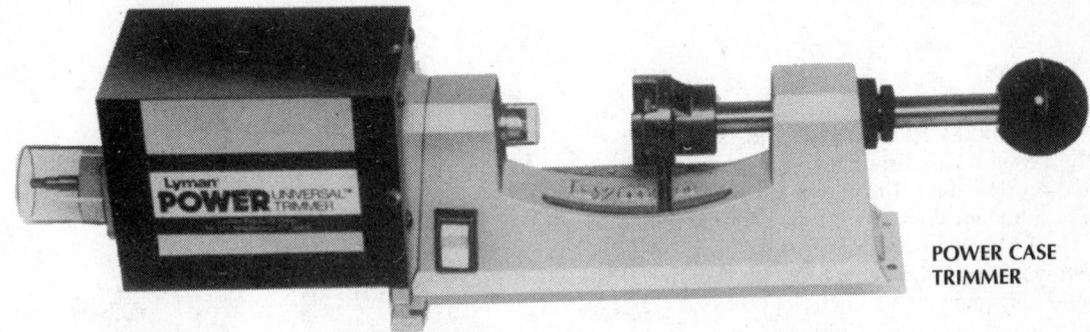

**POWER CASE TRIMMER**

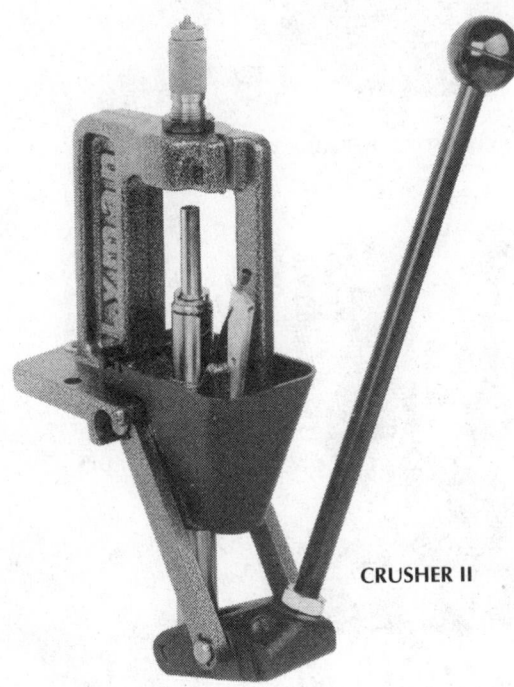

CRUSHER II

## ACCULINE OUTSIDE NECK TURNER (NOT SHOWN)

To obtain perfectly concentric case necks, Lyman's Outside Neck Turner assures reloaders of uniform neck wall thickness and outside neck diameter. The unit fits Lyman's Universal Trimmer and AccuTrimmer. In use, each case is run over a mandrel, which centers the case for the turning operation. The cutter is carefully adjusted to remove a minimum amount of brass. Rate of feed is adjustable and a mechanical stop controls length of cut. Mandrels are available for calibers from .17 to .375; cutter blade can be adjusted for any diameter from .195" to .405".

**Outside Neck Turner w/extra blade, 6 mandrels . . . . $30**
**Individual Mandrels . . . . . . . . . . . . . . . . . . . . . . . . . . . . 4**

## CRUSHER II PRO KIT

Includes press, loading block, case lube kit, primer tray, Model 500 Pro scale, powder funnel and Lyman Reloading Handbook.
**Starter Kit . . . . . . . . . . . . . . . . . . . . . . . . . . . . . . . $175**

## LYMAN CRUSHER II RELOADING PRESS

The only press for rifle or pistol cartridges that offers the advantage of powerful compound leverage combined with a true Magnum press opening. A unique handle design transfers power easily to the center of the ram. A 4½-inch press opening accommodates even the largest cartridges.

## CRUSHER II PRESS
**With Priming Arm and Catcher . . . . . . . . . . . . . . . . $125**

## POWER CASE TRIMMER

The Lyman Power Trimmer is powered by a fan-cooled electric motor designed to withstand the severe demands of case trimming. The unit, which features the Universal™ Chuckhead, allows cases to be positioned for trimming or removed with fingertip ease. The Power Trimmer package includes Nine-Pilot Multi-Pack. Two cutter heads and a pair of wire end brushes for cleaning primer pockets are included. Other features include safety guards, on-off rocker switch, heavy cast base with receptacles for nine pilots, and bolt holes for mounting on a work bench. Available for 110 V or 220 V systems.

**Prices: 110 V Model . . . . . . . . . . . . . . . . . . . . . . . . . $219**
**220 V Model . . . . . . . . . . . . . . . . . . . . . . . . . . . . . . . 222**

# Lyman Reloading Tools

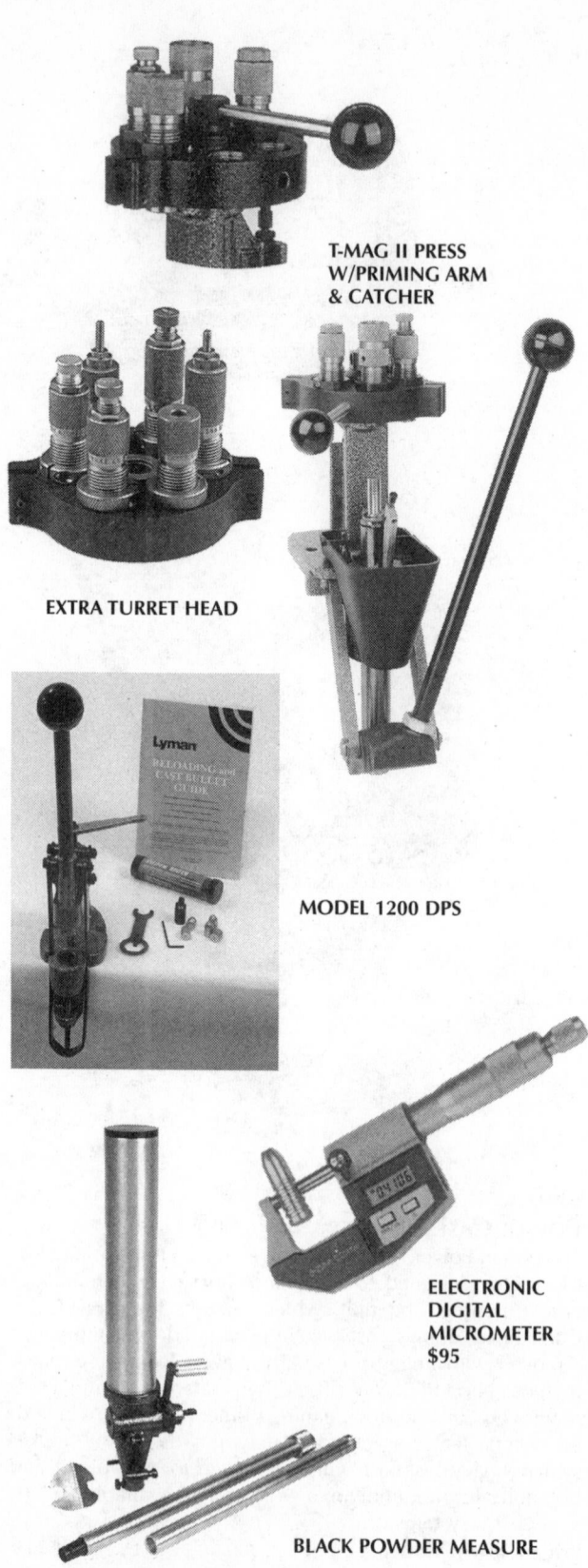

### T-Mag II Turret Reloading Press

With the T-Mag II, up to six different reloading dies can be mounted on one turret. This means all dies can be set up, precisely mounted, locked in and ready to reload at all times. The T-Mag works with all $^7/_8$ x 14 dies. The T-Mag II turret with its quick-disconnect release system is held in rock-solid alignment by a $^3/_4$-inch steel stud.

Also featured is Lyman's Crusher II compound leverage system. It has a longer handle with a ball-type knob that mounts easily for right- or left-handed operation.

**T-Mag II Press w/Priming Arm & Catcher** . . . . . . . . **$175**
    **Extra Turret Head** . . . . . . . . . . . . . . . . . . . . . . . . **38**
**Also available:**
Expert Kit that includes T-MAG II Press, Universal Case Trimmer and pilot Multi-Pak, Model 500 powder scale and Model 50 powder measure, plus accessories and Reloading Manual. Available in calibers 30-06,270 and 308
**Price:** . . . . . . . . . . . . . . . . . . . . . . . . . . . . . . . . . . **$379**

**T-MAG II PRESS W/PRIMING ARM & CATCHER**

**EXTRA TURRET HEAD**

**MODEL 1200 DPS**

### Model 1200 DPS (Digital Powder System)

The 1200 DPS dispenses powder quickly, with .1-grain precision. The 4500 Lube sizer, with a one-piece base casting and a built-in heating element (choose 110- or 220-volt). The long ball-knob handle offers the leverage for sizing and lubricating big bullets. It comes with a gas check seater.

**1200 DPS.** . . . . . . . . . . . . . . . . . . . . . . . . . . . . . . **$333**
**4500 Lube sizer** . . . . . . . . . . . . . . . . . . . . . . . . . . **167**

**ELECTRONIC DIGITAL MICROMETER $95**

### 55 Classic Black Powder Measure

Lyman's 55 Classic Powder Measure is ideal for the Cowboy Action Competition or the growing number of black powder cartridge shooters. The one-pound-capacity aluminum reservoir and brass powder meter eliminate static. The internal powder baffel assures highly accurate and consistent charges. The 24" powder compacting drop tube allows the maximum charge in each cartridge. Drop tube works on calibers 38 through 50 and mounts easily to the bottom of the measure. Clamp on back allows easy mounting of the measure at a convenient height, when using long drop tubes.

**55 Classic Powder Measure (std model-no tubes)** . . . **$115**
**55 Classic Powder Measure (with drop tubes)** . . . . . . **133**
**Powder Drop Tubes Only** . . . . . . . . . . . . . . . . . . . . . **35**

**BLACK POWDER MEASURE**

# Lyman Reloading Tools

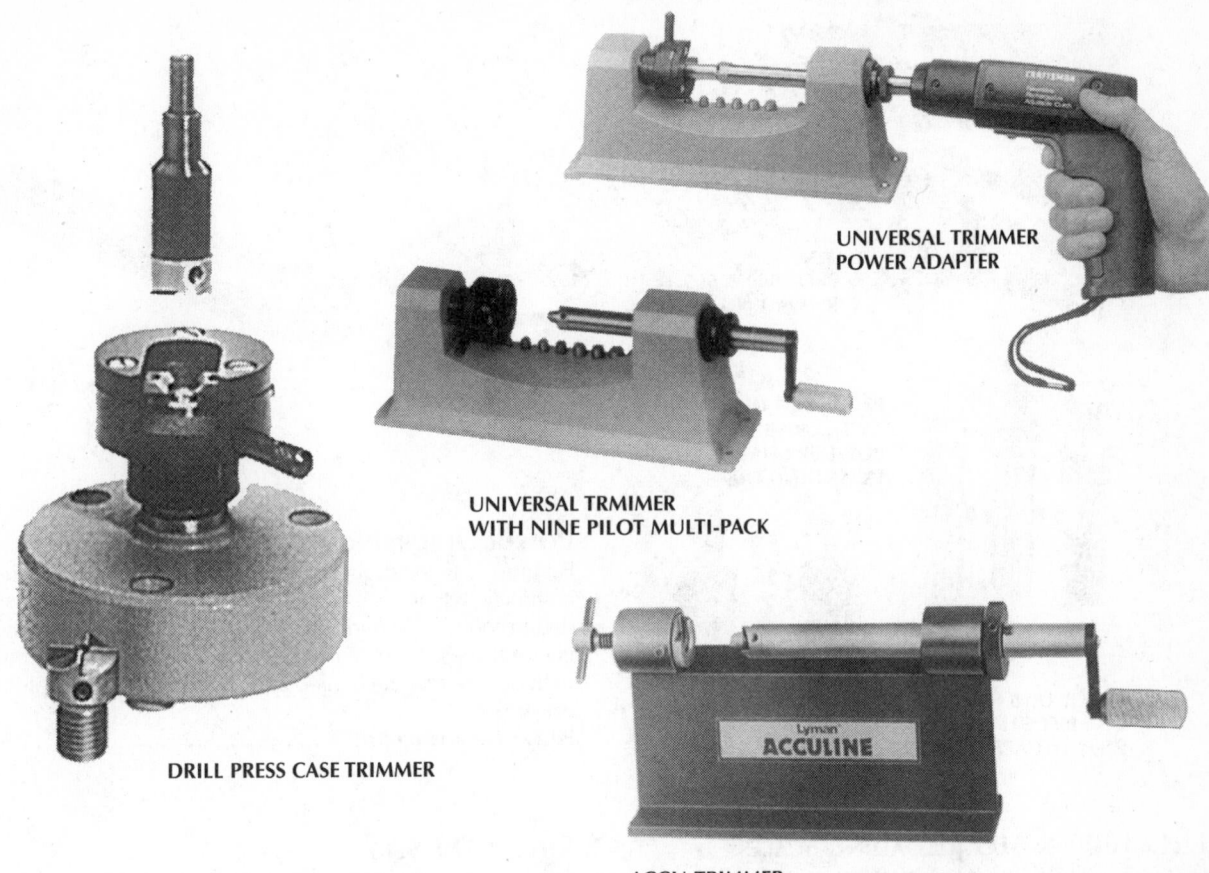

UNIVERSAL TRIMMER
POWER ADAPTER

UNIVERSAL TRMIMER
WITH NINE PILOT MULTI-PACK

DRILL PRESS CASE TRIMMER

ACCU-TRIMMER

## DRILL PRESS CASE TRIMMER

Intended for competitive shooters, varmint hunters, and other sportsmen who use large quantities of reloaded ammunition, this drill press case trimmer consists of the Universal™ Chuckhead, a cutter shaft adapted for use in a drill press, and two quick-change cutter heads. Its two major advantages are speed and accuracy. An experienced operator can trim several hundred cases an hour, and each will be trimmed to a precise length.

**Drill Press Case Trimmer** . . . . . . . . . . . . . . . . . . . . . $54

## ACCU-TRIMMER

Lyman's Accu Trimmer can be used for all rifle and pistol cases from 22 to 458 Winchester Magnum. Standard shellholders are used to position the case, and the trimmer incorporates standard Lyman cutter heads and pilots. Mounting options include bolting to a bench, C-clamp or vise.

**Accu Trimmer w/9-pilot multi-pak** . . . . . . . . . . . . . . $45

## UNIVERSAL TRMIMER
## WITH NINE PILOT MULTI-PACK

This trimmer with patented chuckhead accepts all metallic rifle or pistol cases, regardless of rim thickness. To change calibers, simply change the case head pilot. Other features include coarse and fine cutter adjustments, an oil-impregnated bronze bearing, and a rugged cast base to assure precision alignment and years of service. Optional carbide cutter available. Trimmer Stop Ring includes 20 indicators as reference marks.

**Trimmer Multi-Pack (incl. 9 pilots: 22, 24, 27,**
    **28/7mm, 30, 9mm, 35, 44 and 4A**. . . . . . . . . . . . $80
**Nine Pilot Multi-Pack** . . . . . . . . . . . . . . . . . . . . . . . . . 13
**Power Pack Trimmer**. . . . . . . . . . . . . . . . . . . . . . . . . . 78
**Universal Trimmer Power Adapter**. . . . . . . . . . . . . . . . 20

## ELECTRONIC DIGITAL CALIPER (NOT SHOWN)

Lyman's 6" electronic caliper gives a direct digital readout for both inches and millimeters and can perform both inside and outside depth measurements. Its zeroing function allows the user to select zeroing dimensions and sort parts or cases by their plus or minus variation. The caliper works on a single, standard 1.5 volt silver oxide battery and comes with a fitted wooden storage case.

**Electronic Caliper**. . . . . . . . . . . . . . . . . . . . . . . . . . . $100
**Also Available:**
    **4" Pocket Electronic Caliper** . . . . . . . . . . . . . . . . . . 83

# Lyman Reloading Tools

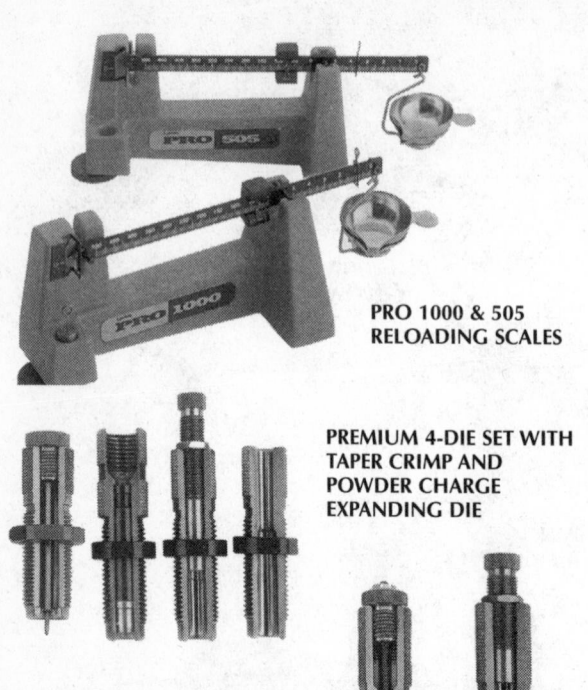

PRO 1000 & 505
RELOADING SCALES

PREMIUM 4-DIE SET WITH
TAPER CRIMP AND
POWDER CHARGE
EXPANDING DIE

PISTOL DIES FEATURE
ONE PIECE HARDENED
STEEL DECAPPING ROD

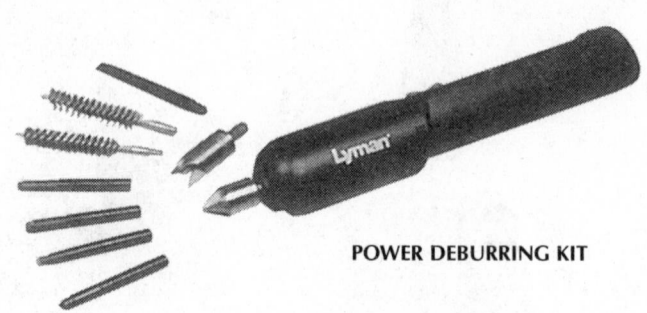

POWER DEBURRING KIT

## POWER DEBURRING KIT

Features a high torque, rechargeable power driver plus a complete set of accessories, including inside and outside deburr tools, large and small reamers and cleaners and case neck brushes. No threading or chucking required. Set also includes battery recharger and standard flat and phillips driver bits.

**Power Deburring Kit**. . . . . . . . . . . . . . . . . . . . . . . . $55

## PRO 1000 & 505 RELOADING SCALES

Features include improved platform system; hi-tech base design of high-impact styrene; extra-large, smooth leveling wheel; dual agate bearings; larger damper for fast zeroing; built-in counter weight compartment; easy-to-read beam.

**Pro 1000 Scale**. . . . . . . . . . . . . . . . . . . . . . . . . . $68
**Pro 500 Scale**. . . . . . . . . . . . . . . . . . . . . . . . . . . 48

## RIFLE DIE SETS

Lyman precision rifle dies are manufactured on computer controlled equipment ensuring th extra smoothness. Fine adjustment threads on the bullet seating stem allow for precision adjustments of bullet seating depth. Lyman dies fit all popular presses using industry standard ⅞ x 14 threads, including RCBS, Lee, Hornady, Dillon, Redding and others.at each die is chambered perfectly and has a smooth finish. Each sizing die for bottle-necked rifle cartridges is then carefully vented. This vent hole is precisely placed to prevent air traps that can damage cartridge cases. Each sizing die is polished, then heat treated for toughness. It receives a final hand polish for

## RIFLE 2-DIE SETS

Set consists of a full length resizing die with decapping stem and neck expanding button and a bullet seating die for loading jacketed bullets in bottlenecked rifle cases. For those who load cast bullets, use a neck expanding die, available separately.

**Price:**. . . . . . . . . . . . . . . . . . . . . . . . . . . . . . . . $30

## RIFLE 3-DIE SETS

Straight wall rifle cases require these three die sets consisting of a full length resizing die with decapping stem, a two step neck expanding (M) die and a bullet seating die. These sets are ideal for loading cast bullets due to the inclusion of the neck expanding die.

**Price:**. . . . . . . . . . . . . . . . . . . . . . . . . . . . . . . . $40
   **Classic Calibers** . . . . . . . . . . . . . . . . . . . . . . . . 50
   **Classic Neck Size Dies** . . . . . . . . . . . . . . . . . . . . 32

## PREMIUM CARBIDE 4-DIE SETS FOR PISTOLS

Lyman 4-Die Sets feature a separate taper crimp die and powder charge/expanding die. The powder charge/expand die has a special hollow 2-step neck expanding plug which allows powder to flow through the die from a powder measure directly into the case. The powder charge/expanding die has a standard ⅞ x 14 thread and will accept Lyman's 55 Powder Measure, or most other powder measures.

**Price:**. . . . . . . . . . . . . . . . . . . . . . . . . . . . . . . . $57

## 3-DIE CARBIDE PISTOL DIE SETS

Lyman originated the Tungsten Carbide (T-C) sizing die and the addition of extra seating screws for pistol die sets and the two step neck expanding die. Multi-Deluxe Die sets offer these features; a one-piece hardened steel decapping rod and extra seating screws for all popular bullet nose shapes; all-steel construction.

**Price:**. . . . . . . . . . . . . . . . . . . . . . . . . . . . . . . . $44

# MEC Shotshell Reloaders

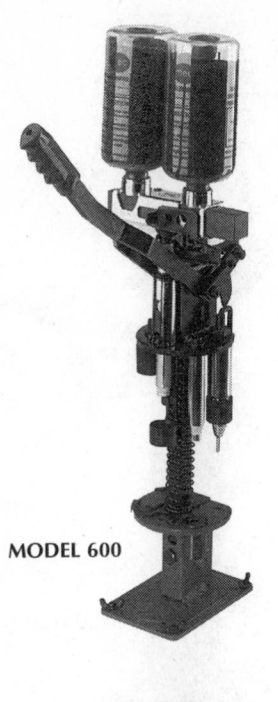

**MODEL 600**

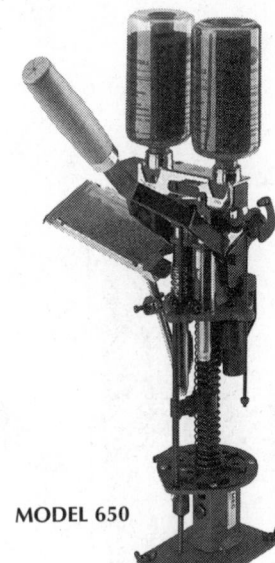

**MODEL 650**

**MODEL 8567**

**MODEL 8120**

### MODEL 600 JR. MARK V

This single-stage reloader features a cam-action crimp die to ensure that each shell returns to its original condition. MEC's 600 Jr. Mark 5 can load 6 to 8 boxes per hour and can be updated with the 285 CA primer feed. Press is adjustable for 3" shells.
**Price:** . . . . . . . . . . . . . . . . . . . . . . . . . . . . . . . . . . **$118**

### MODEL 650

This reloader works on 6 shells at once. A reloaded shell is completed with every stroke. The MEC 650 does not resize except as a separate operation. Automatic Primer feed is standard. Simply fill it with a full box of primers and it will do the rest. Reloader has 3 crimping stations: the first one starts the crimp, the second closes the crimp, and the third places a taper on the shell. Available in 12, 16, 20 and 28 gauge and .410 bore. No die sets are available.
**Price:** . . . . . . . . . . . . . . . . . . . . . . . . . . . . . . . . . . **$224**

### MODEL 8567 GRABBER

This reloader features 12 different operations at all 6 stations, producing finished shells with each stroke of the handle. It includes a fully automatic primer feed and Auto-Cycle charging, plus MEC's exclusive 3-stage crimp. The "Power Ring" resizer ensures consistent, accurately sized shells without interrupting the reloading sequence. Simply put in the wads and shell casings, then remove the loaded shells with each pull of the handle. Optional kits to load 3" shells and steel shot make this reloader tops in its field. Resizes high and low base shells. Available in 12, 16, 20, 28 gauge and .410 bore. No die sets are available.
**Price:** . . . . . . . . . . . . . . . . . . . . . . . . . . . . . . . . . . **$321**

### MODEL 8120 SIZEMASTER

Sizemaster's "Power Ring" collet resizer returns each base to factory specifications. This generation resizing station handles brass or steel heads, both high and low base. An 8-fingered collet squeezes the base back to original dimensions, then opens up to release the shell easily. The E-Z Prime auto primer feed is standard equipment (not offered in .410 bore). Press is adjustable for 3" shells and is available in 10, 12, 16, 20, 28 gauge and .410 bore. Die sets are available at: $88.67 ($104.06 in 10 ga.)
**Price:** . . . . . . . . . . . . . . . . . . . . . . . . . . . . . . . . . . **$179**

HANDLOADING

# MEC Reloading

### STEELMASTER SINGLE STATE

The only shotshell reloader equipped to load steel shot-shells as well as lead ones. Every base is resized to factory specs by a precision "power ring" collet. Handles brass or steel heads in high or low base. The E-Z prime auto primer feed dispenses primers automatically and is standard equipment. Separate presses are available for 12 gauge 2¾", 3", 12 gauge 3½" and 10 gauge.

**8639 Steelmaster 10 &12 ga** . . . . . . . . . . . . . . . . . $193
**8755 Steelmaster 12 ga. 31/2" only**. . . . . . . . . . . . . 216

### MEC 9000 SERIES SHOTSHELL RELOADER

MEC's 9000 Series features automatic indexing and finished shell ejection for quicker and easier reloading. The factory set speed provides uniform movement through every reloading stage. Dropping the primer into the reprime station no longer requires operator "feel." The reloader requires only a minimal adjustment from low to high brass domestic shells, any one of which can be removed for inspection from any station. Can be set up for automatic or manual indexing. Available in 12, 16, 20 and 28 gauge and .410 bore. No die sets are available.

**MEC 9000H**. . . . . . . . . . . . . . . . . . . . . . . . . . . . . . $942
**MEC 9000H without pump**. . . . . . . . . . . . . . . . . . . 509
**MEC 9000G Series** . . . . . . . . . . . . . . . . . . . . . . . . . 390
Also Available: MEC Super Sizer
Resize shotgun shells back to factory specs!
**Price:**. . . . . . . . . . . . . . . . . . . . . . . . . . . . . . . . . . . 67

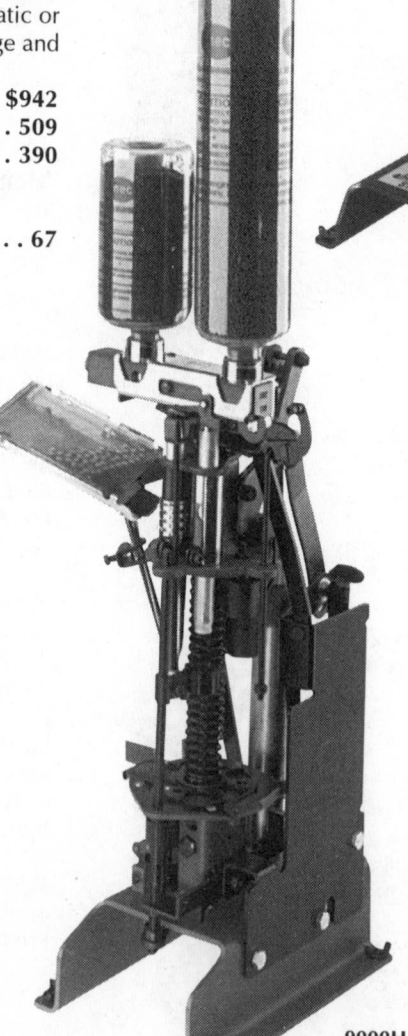

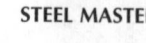

**STEEL MASTER**

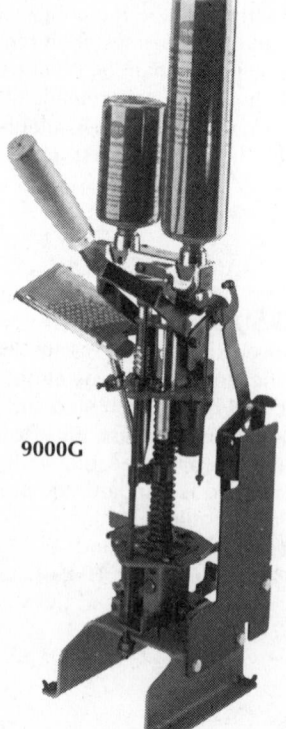

**9000G**

**9000H**

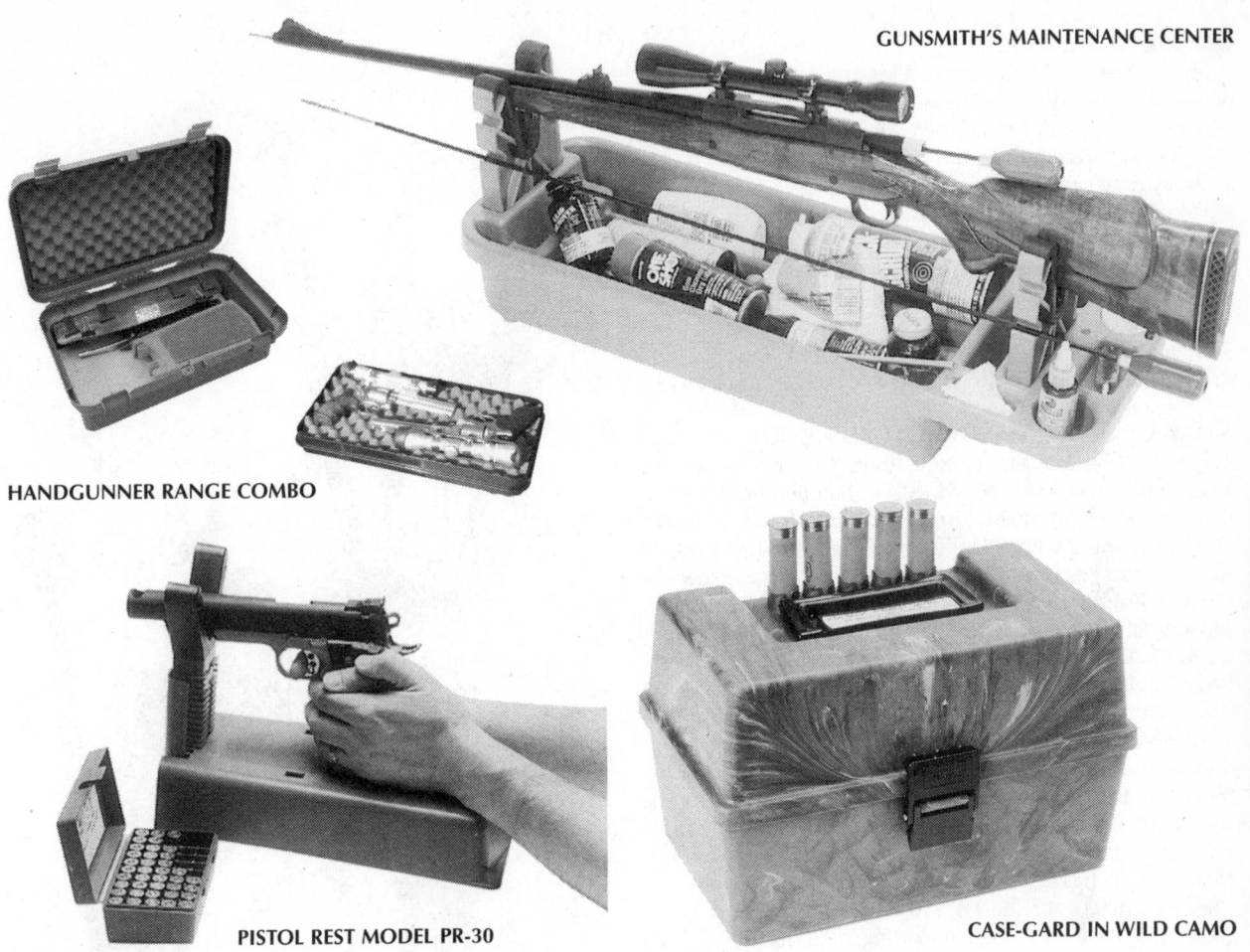

GUNSMITH'S MAINTENANCE CENTER

HANDGUNNER RANGE COMBO

PISTOL REST MODEL PR-30

CASE-GARD IN WILD CAMO

## GUNSMITH'S MAINTENANCE CENTER

MTM's Gunsmiths Maintenance Center (RMC-5) is designed for mounting scopes and swivels, bedding actions or for cleaning rifles and shotguns. Multi-positional forks allow for eight holding combinations, making it possible to service firearm level, upright or upside down. The large middle section keeps tools and cleaning supplies in one area. Individual solvent compartments help to eliminate accidental spills. Cleaning rods stay where they are needed with the two built-in holders provided. Both forks (covered with a soft molded-on rubber pad) grip and protect the firearm. The RMC-5 is made of engineering- grade plastic for years of rugged use. Not Shown: Extensive line of plastic ammo boxes, reloading trays, pistol cases, target holders, clay target throwers, arrow and tackle boxes.

**Dimensions:** 29.5" X 9.5"
**Model RMC-5-30** . . . . . . . . . . . . . . . . . . . . . . . . . . . . **$31**

## PISTOL REST MODEL PR-30

MTM's PR-30 Pistol Rest will accommodate any size handgun, from a Derringer to a 14" Contender. A locking front support leg adjusts up or down, allowing 20 different positions. Rubber padding molded to the tough polypropylene fork protects firearms from scratches. Fork clips into the base when not in use for compact storage.

**Dimensions:** 6" x 11" x 2.5
**Pistol Rest Model PR-30** . . . . . . . . . . . . . . . . . . . . . . **$17**

## HANDGUNNER RANGE COMBO

Known for molded plastic handloading trays and ammo boxes, MTM now offers a kit for the handgunner to take to the range. A hard-sided, foam-padded utility case holds pistols or revolvers in a top tray, a "jammit" compact target stand and a 20-position pistol rest in the well below. There's also an all-weather target backer. The Handgunner Range Combo will accommodate long-barreled magnums.

**Price** . . . . . . . . . . . . . . . . . . . . . . . . . . . . . . . . . . . **$54**

## CASE-GARD IN WILD CAMO

The CASE-GARD SF-100 holds 100 shotshells in two removable trays. Designed primarily for hunters, this dust and moisture resistant carrier features a heavy-duty latch, fold-down handle, integral hinge and textured finish.

**Price: SF-100 12 or 20 ga.**
**Wild Camo Shotshell Box** . . . . . . . . . . . . . . . . . . . . . **17**

# RCBS Reloading Tools

### ROCK CHUCKER PRESS

With its easy operation, outstanding strength and versatility, a Rock Chucker press serves beginner and pro alike. It can also be upgraded to a progressive press with an optional Piggyback conversion unit.
- Heavy-duty cast iron for easy case-resizing
- 1" ram held in place by 12.5 sq. in. of rambearing surface
- Toggle blocks of ductile iron
- Compound leverage system
- 7/8"-14 thread for all standard reloading dies and accessories
- Milled slot and set screws accept optional RCBS automatic primer feed

Price:. . . . . . . . . . . . . . . . . . . . . . . . . . . . . . $156

### ROCK CHUCKER MASTER RELOADING KIT

The Rock Chucker Master Reloading Kit includes all the tools and accessories needed to start handloading: • Rock Chucker Press • RCBS 505 Reloading Scale • Speer TrimPro Manual #12 • Uniflow Powder Measure • RCBS Rotary Case Trimmer-2 • deburring tool • case loading block • Primer Tray-2 • Automatic Primer Feed Combo • powder funnel • case lube pad • case neck brushes • fold-up hex key set • Trim Pro Manual Case Trimmer Kit

Price:. . . . . . . . . . . . . . . . . . . . . . . . . . . . . . $394

### .50 BMG PACK

Shooters who favor the .50 BMG have all they need in the .50 BMG Pack from RCBS®. The Pack includes the press, dies, and accessory items needed, all in one box. The press is the powerful Ammo Master® Single Stage rigged for 1.5-inch dies. It has a massive 1.5-inch solid steel ram and plenty of height for the big .50. The kit also has a set of RCBS .50 BMG, 1.5-inch reloading dies, including both full-length sizer and seater. Other items are a shell holder, ram priming unit, and a trim die.

Price:. . . . . . . . . . . . . . . . . . . . . . . . . . . . . . $599

### AMMOMASTER RELOADING SYSTEM

The AmmoMaster offers any handloader the freedom to configure a press to his particular needs and preferences. It covers the complete spectrum of reloading, from single stage through fully automatic pro-gressive reloading, from .25 Auto to .50 caliber. The AmmoMaster Auto has all the features of a five-station press.

Single Stage . . . . . . . . . . . . . . . . . . . . . . . . . . $227

### RELOADER SPECIAL-5

The Reloader Special press features a comfortable ball handle and a primer arm so that cases can be primed and resized at the same time.
- Compound leverage system
- Solid aluminum black "O" frame offset for unobstructed access
- Corrosion-resistant baked-powder finish
- Can be upgraded to progressive reloading with an optional Piggyback II conversion unit
- 7/8" - 14 thread for all standard reloading dies and accessories

Price:. . . . . . . . . . . . . . . . . . . . . . . . . . . . . . $124
Reloading Starter Kit . . . . . . . . . . . . . . . . . . . . 290

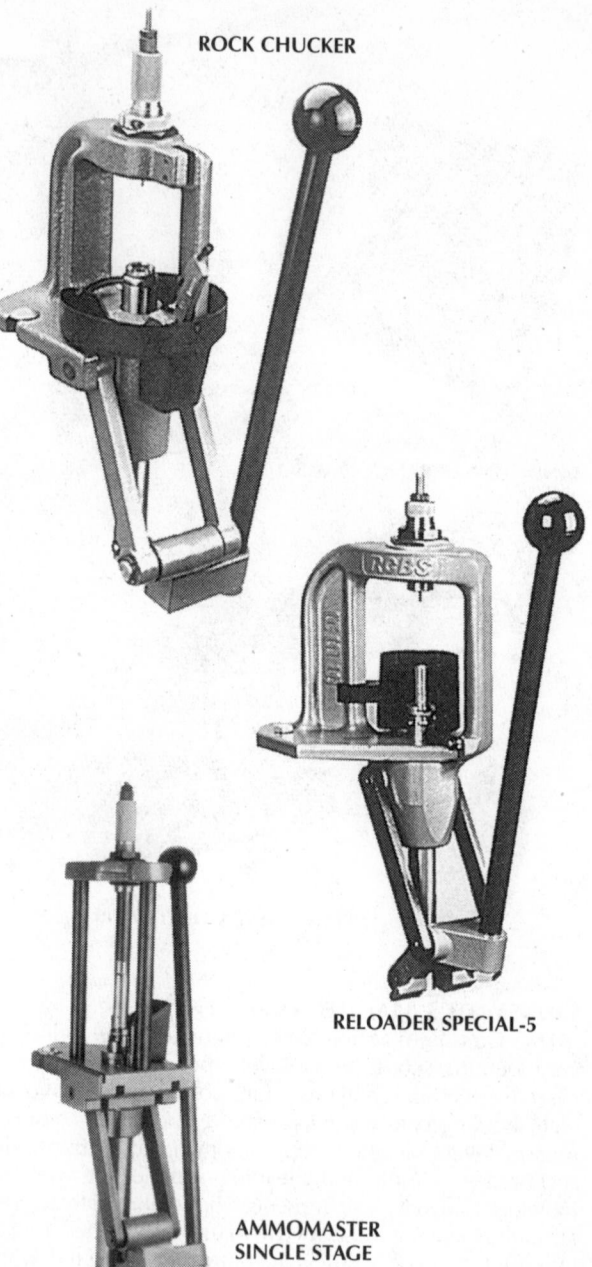

ROCK CHUCKER

RELOADER SPECIAL-5

AMMOMASTER
SINGLE STAGE

### PIGGYBACK III CONVERSION KIT
(NOT SHOWN)

- The Piggyback III conversion unit moves from single-stage reloading to 5-station, manual-indexing, progressive reloading in one step
- Increases output from 50 rounds an hour to well over 400

The Piggyback III will work with the RCBS Rock Chucker, Reloader Special-3, and Reloader Special-5.

Price:. . . . . . . . . . . . . . . . . . . . . . . . . . . . . . 4313

# RCBS Reloading Tools

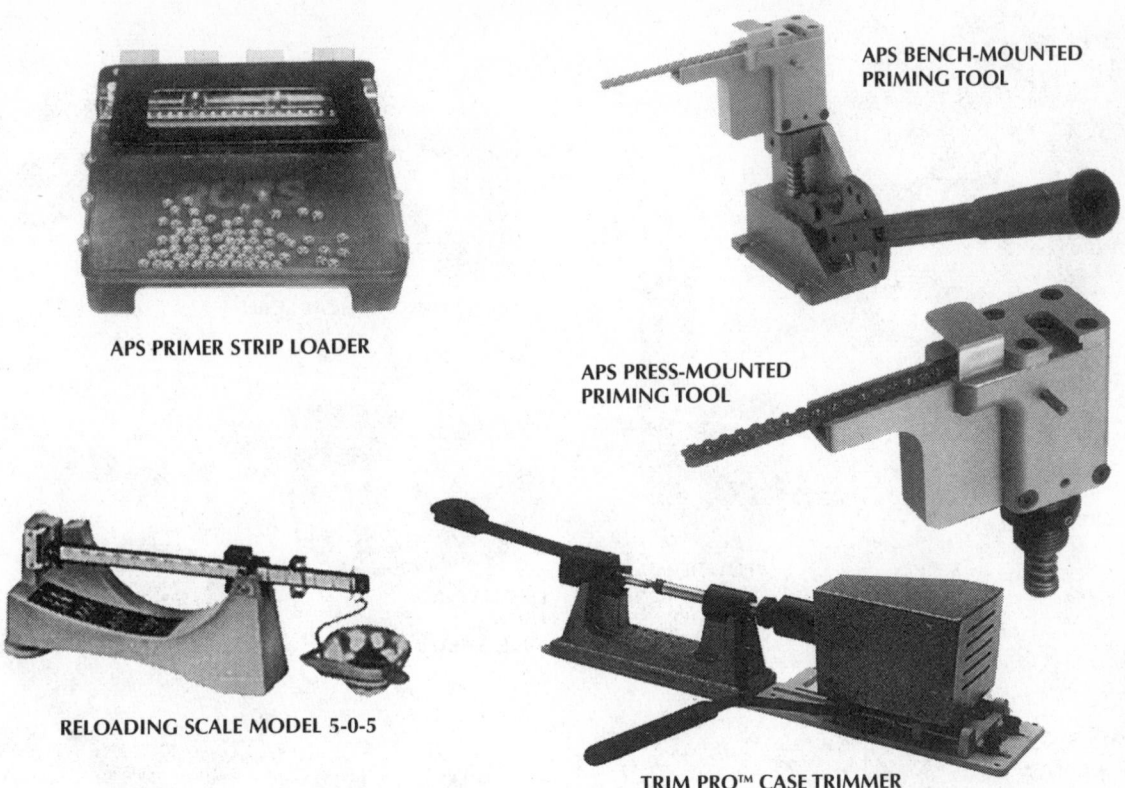

APS BENCH-MOUNTED PRIMING TOOL

APS PRIMER STRIP LOADER

APS PRESS-MOUNTED PRIMING TOOL

RELOADING SCALE MODEL 5-0-5

TRIM PRO™ CASE TRIMMER

## APS BENCH-MOUNTED PRIMING TOOL
The APS Bench-Mounted Priming Tool was created for reloaders who prefer a separate, specialized tool dedicated to priming only. The handle of the bench-mounted tool is designed to provide hours of comfortable loading. Handle position can be adjusted for bench height.
Price:. . . . . . . . . . . . . . . . . . . . . . . . . . . . . . . . . . $102

## APS PRIMER STRIP LOADER
For those who keep a supply of CCI primers in conventional packaging, the APS primer strip loader allows quick filling of empty strips. Each push of the handle seats 25 primers.
Price:. . . . . . . . . . . . . . . . . . . . . . . . . . . . . . . . . . . $30

## POW'R PULL BULLET PULLER (NOT SHOWN)
The RCBS Pow'r Pull bullet puller features a three-jaw chuck that grips the case rim—just rap it on any solid surface like a hammer, and powder and bullet drop into the main chamber for re-use. A soft cushion protects bullets from damage. Works with most centerfire cartridges from .22 to .45 (not for use with rimfire cartridges).
Price:. . . . . . . . . . . . . . . . . . . . . . . . . . . . . . . . . . . $16

## RELOADING SCALE MODEL 5-0-5
This 511-grain capacity scale has a three-poise system with widely spaced, deep beam notches to keep them in place. Two smaller poises on right side adjust from 0.1 to 10 grains, larger one on left side adjusts in full 10-grain steps.

The first scale to use magnetic dampening to eliminate beam oscillation, the 5-0-5 also has a sturdy die-cast base with large leveling legs for stability. Self-aligning agate bearings support the hardened steel beam pivots for a guaranteed sensitivity to 0.1 grains.
Price:. . . . . . . . . . . . . . . . . . . . . . . . . . . . . . . . . . . $91

## APS PRESS-MOUNTED PRIMING TOOL
This APS press-mounted priming tool provides the same features as the bench-mounted tool, except it attaches to any single-stage press that accepts standard ⅞" x 14 dies.
Price:. . . . . . . . . . . . . . . . . . . . . . . . . . . . . . . . . . . $65

## TRIM PROTM CASE TRIMMER
Cartridge cases are trimmed quickly and easily with a few turns of the RCBS Trim Pro case trimmer. The lever-type handle is more accurate to use than draw collet systems. A flat plate shell holder keeps cases locked in place and aligned. A micrometer fine adjustment bushing offers trimming accuracy to within .001". Made of die-cast metal with hardened cutting blades. The power model is like having a personal lathe, delivering plenty of torque. Positive locking handle and in-line power switch make it simple and safe.
Price: Power 120 Vac Kit. . . . . . . . . . . . . . . . . . . . $270
      Manual Kit . . . . . . . . . . . . . . . . . . . . . . . . . . . 101
Also available:
**Trim Pro Case Trimmer Stand** . . . . . . . . . . . . . . . . . . 20
      **Case Holder Accessory** . . . . . . . . . . . . . . . . . . . 42
Price:. . . . . . . . . . . . . . . . . . . . . . . . . . . . . . . . . . . 298

# RCBS Reloading Tools

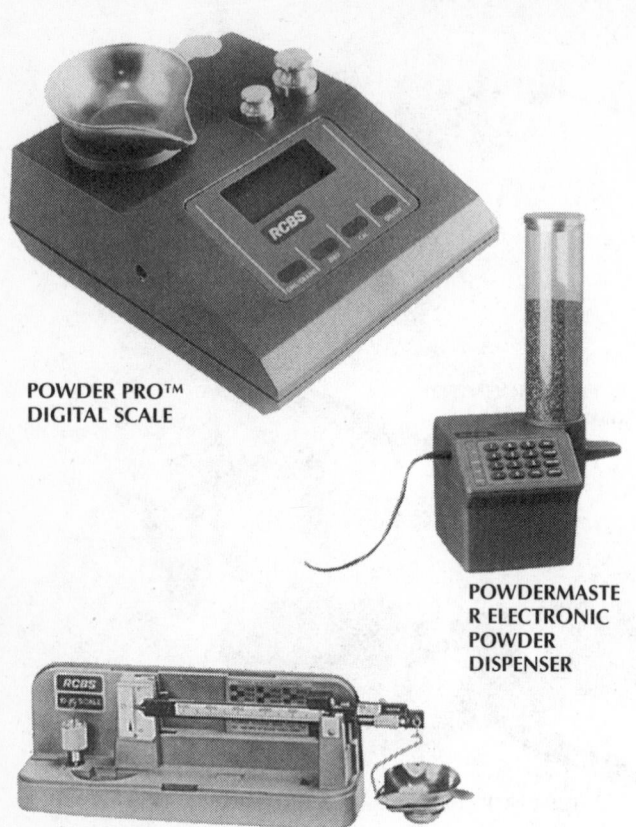

**POWDER PRO™ DIGITAL SCALE**

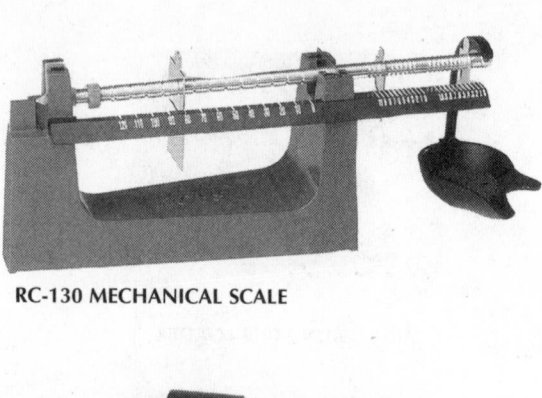

RC-130 MECHANICAL SCALE

**POWDERMASTER ELECTRONIC POWDER DISPENSER**

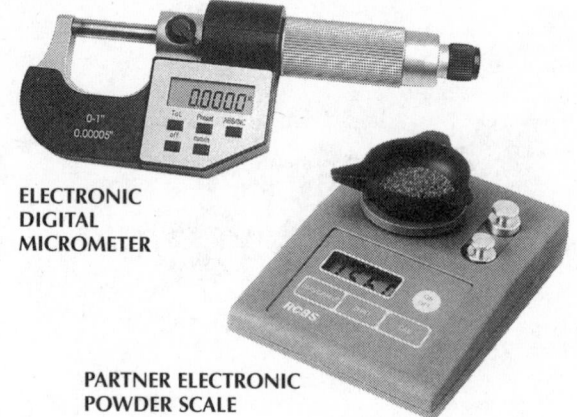

**ELECTRONIC DIGITAL MICROMETER**

**PARTNER ELECTRONIC POWDER SCALE**

**RELOADING SCALE MODEL 10-10 UP TO 1010 GRAIN CAPACITY**

HANDLOADING

## POWDER PRO™ DIGITAL SCALE

The RCBS Powder Pro Digital Scale has a 1500-grain capacity. Powder, bullets, even cases can be weighed with accuracy of 0.1 grain. Includes infra-red data port for transferring information to the Powdermaster Electronic Powder Dispenser and electronic powder trickler.
**Price: 110 VAC . . . . . . . . . . . . . . . . . . . . . . . . . $247**

## POWDERMASTER ELECTRONIC POWDER DISPENSER

Works in combination with the RCBS Powder Pro Digital Scale and with all types of smokeless powder. Can be used as a power trickler as well as a powder dispenser. Accurate to one-tenth of a grain.
**Price: . . . . . . . . . . . . . . . . . . . . . . . . . . . . . . . $265**

## RELOADING SCALE MODEL 1010 UP TO 1010 GRAIN CAPACITY

Normal capacity is 510 grains, which can be increased without loss of sensitivity by attaching the included extra weight. Features include micrometer poise for quick, precise weighing, special approach-to-weight indicator, easy-to-read graduation, magnetic dampener, agate bearings, anti-tip pan, and dustproof lid snaps on to cover scale for storage. Sensitivity is guaranteed to 0.1 grains.
**Price: . . . . . . . . . . . . . . . . . . . . . . . . . . . . . . . $150**

## RC-130 MECHANICAL SCALE

The RC130 features a 130 grain capacity and maintenance-free movement, plus a magnetic dampening system for fast readings. A 3-poise design incorporates easy adjustments with a beam that is graduated in increments of 10 grains and one grain. A micrometer poise measures in 0.1 grain increments with acuracy to ±0.1 grain.
**Price: . . . . . . . . . . . . . . . . . . . . . . . . . . . . . . . $44**

## ELECTRONIC DIGITAL MICROMETER

• Instant reading • Large, easy to read numbers for error reduction with instant inch/millimeter conversion • Zero adjust at any position • thimble lock for measuring like objects • replaceable silver oxide cell – 1.55 Volt • auto off after 5 minutes for longer battery life • adjustment wrench included • fitted wooden storage cases
**Price: . . . . . . . . . . . . . . . . . . . . . . . . . . . . . . . $110**

## PARTNER ELECTRONIC POWDER SCALE

Accurate for +/- one-tenth of a grain up to 350 grains and +/- two-tenths from 350 to 750 grains. Large LCD display is angled for easy reading over a wide range of positions. Pow-ered by 9-volt battery.
**Price: . . . . . . . . . . . . . . . . . . . . . . . . . . . . . . . $178**

# RCBS Reloading Tools

### RCBS TURRET PRESS

Handloaders who want to speed up the loading process without giving up the level of control offered by a single-stage press can boost their output fourfold with the RCBS Turret Press. With pre-set dies in the six-station turret head, the Turret Press can increase production from 50 to 200 rounds per hour with a simple manual operation.

The frame, links, and toggle block of the press are constructed of strong, reliable, cast iron. The handle offers compound leverage for full-length sizing of any caliber from .25 ACP to .460 Wea-therby Magnum. Priming is accomplished with a reliable tube feed priming system.

Six stations allow the handloader to customize his set-up with the options of using a lube die in station one and seating and crimping bullets in separate operations. The quick-change turret head makes caliber changes fast and easy. Dies can be left in the turret head to eliminate set-up and tear-down time. This press accepts all standard $7/8$ - 14 dies and shell holders and comes with the RCBS lifetime warranty.

**Price: RCBS Turret Press** . . . . . . . . . . . . . . . . . . . . . **$215**
**Turret Deluxe Reloading Kit** . . . . . . . . . . . . . . . . . . **415**

### RCBS PRO 2000
#### PROGRESSIVE PRESS

Constructed of strong and reliable cast iron, the Pro 2000 features five reloading stations. It can be set up with a lube die in station one, sizing dies in station two and three, a Powder Checker or Lock Out Die in station four and seating die in station five. Bullet seating and crimping can also be done in separate operations in station four and five.

The case-actuated powder measure assures repeatability of dispensing powder and eliminates spillage. A Micrometer Adjustment Screw allows precise return to previously recorded powder charges. All dies are standard $7/8$-14, including the Expander Die.

The press incorporates RCBS's exclusive APS Priming System. Using preloaded plastic priming strips, it eliminates handling of primers and loading tube priming. Compound leverage in the press allows effortless full-length sizing in any caliber, from .32 Auto to the .460 Weatherby Magnum. The press is covered by the RCBS Lifetime Warranty.

**Prices:**
**RCBS Pro 2000 Progressive Press** . . . . . . . . . . . . . **$543**
**Pro 2000 Deluxe Reloading Kit** . . . . . . . . . . . . . . . . **931**

### RCBS GRAND
#### SHOTSHELL PRESS

Features: The combination of the Powder system and shot system and Case Holders allows the user to reload shells without fear of spillage. The powder system is case-actuated: no hull, no powder. Cases are easily removed with universal 12 and 20 gauge case holders allowing cases to be sized down to the rim. Priming system: Only one primer feeds at a time. Steel size ring: Provides complete resizing of high and low base hulls. Holds 25 lbs of shot and $1\frac{1}{2}$ lbs. of powder. Lifetime warranty.

**Price** . . . . . . . . . . . . . . . . . . . . . . . . . . . . . . . . . . . . **$724**
**Grand Conversion kit** . . . . . . . . . . . . . . . . . . . . . . . . **336**

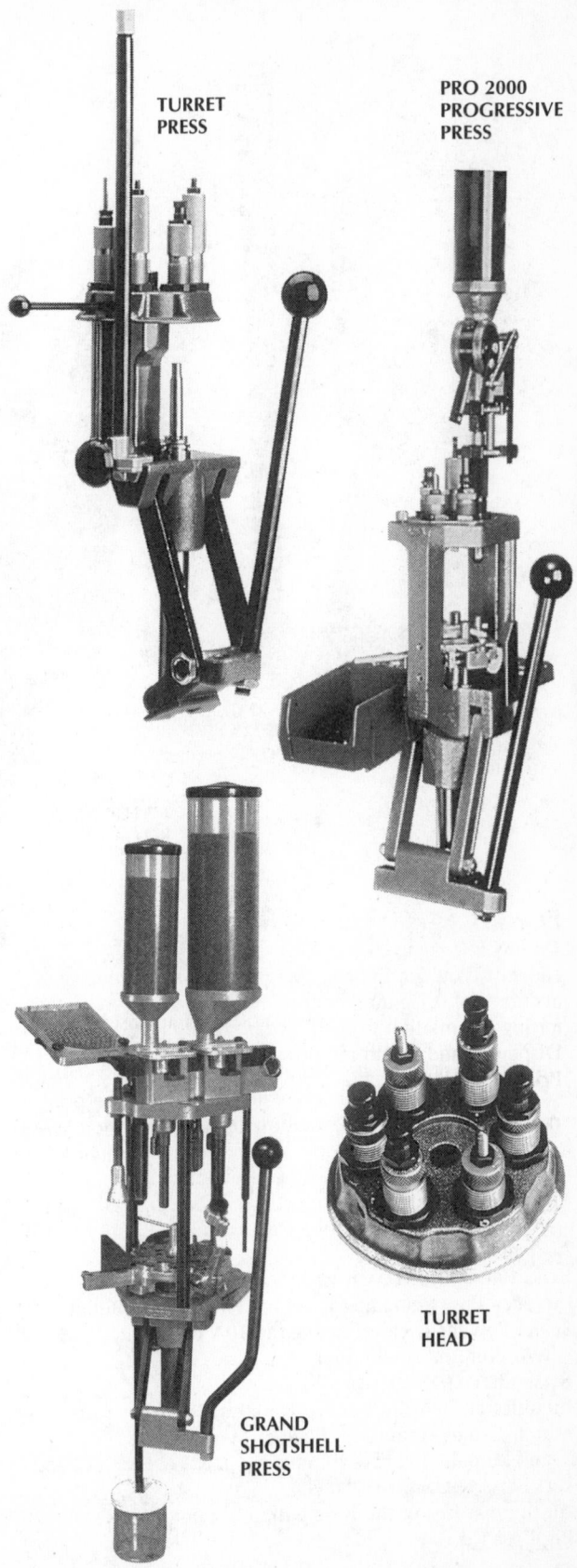

TURRET
PRESS

PRO 2000
PROGRESSIVE
PRESS

GRAND
SHOTSHELL
PRESS

TURRET
HEAD

HANDLOADING

# Redding Reloading Tools

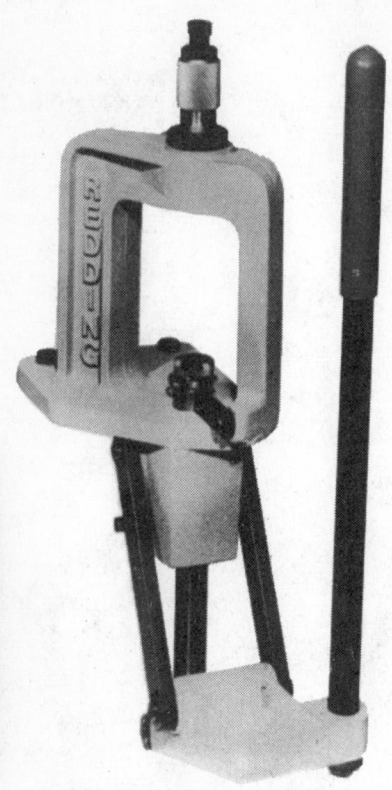

MODEL 721

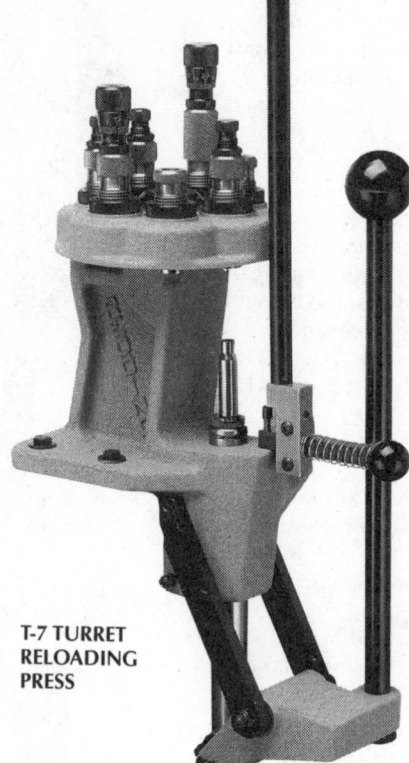

T-7 TURRET
RELOADING
PRESS

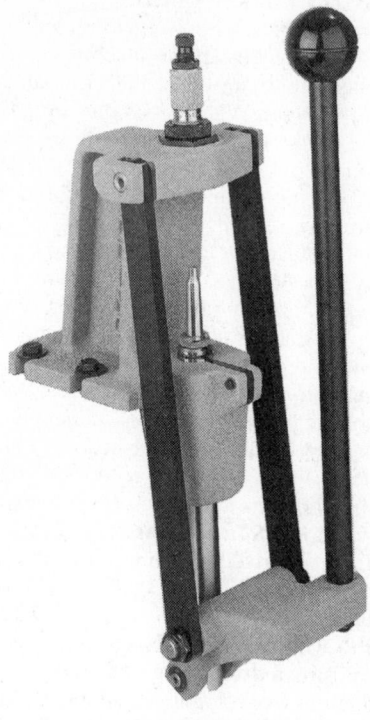

MODEL 7000

## MODEL 721 "THE BOSS" PRESS

This "O" type reloading press features a rigid cast iron frame whose 36° offset provides the best visibility and access of comparable presses. Its "Smart" primer arm moves in and out of position automatically with ram travel. The priming arm is positioned at the bottom of ram travel for lowest leverage and best feel. Model 721 accepts all standard ⅞-14 threaded dies and universal shell holders.

Model 721 "The Boss" . . . . . . . . . . . . . . . . . . . . . . $143
   With Shellholder and 10A Dies . . . . . . . . . . . . . 189
Also available:
**BOSS PRO-PAK RELOADING KIT.**
**Includes Boss Reloading Press, #2 Powder and Bullet Scale, Powder Trickler, Reloading 10A Dies** . . . . . . . $387
   w/o dies and shellholder . . . . . . . . . . . . . . . . . . . 333
**BOSS DELUXE RELOADING KIT.**
**Includes all items in the Pro-Pak plus:**
**Match-Grade Model 3BR Powder Measure
   and Model 1400 case trimmer** . . . . . . . . . . . . . . . $621
**BIG BOSS RELOADING PRESS.**
**All the features of the Boss with a heavier frame.** . . . 178
**Big Boss Kit** . . . . . . . . . . . . . . . . . . . . . . . . . . . . . . 224

## ULTRAMAG MODEL 7000

Unlike other reloading presses that connect the linkage to the lower half of the press, the Ultramag's compound leverage system is connected at the top of the press frame. This allows the reloader to develop tons of pressure without the usual concern about press frame deflection. Huge frame opening will handle 50 x 3¼-inch Sharps with ease.

No. 700 Press, complete . . . . . . . . . . . . . . . . . . . . . . $321
No. 700K Kit, includes shell holder and
   one set of 10A dies . . . . . . . . . . . . . . . . . . . . . . . 363

## T-7 TURRET RELOADING PRESS

Features: 7 station turret head, heavy duty cast iron frame, 1" diameter ram, optional "Slide Bar Automatic Primer Feeder System". This feeder eliminates handling of primers during sizing and speeds up reloading operations.

T-7 Turret Press. . . . . . . . . . . . . . . . . . . . . . . . . . . . . $306
Kit, including press, shellholder and 10A dies . . . . . . 348
Slide Bar Automatic Primer Feeder System . . . . . . . . . 45

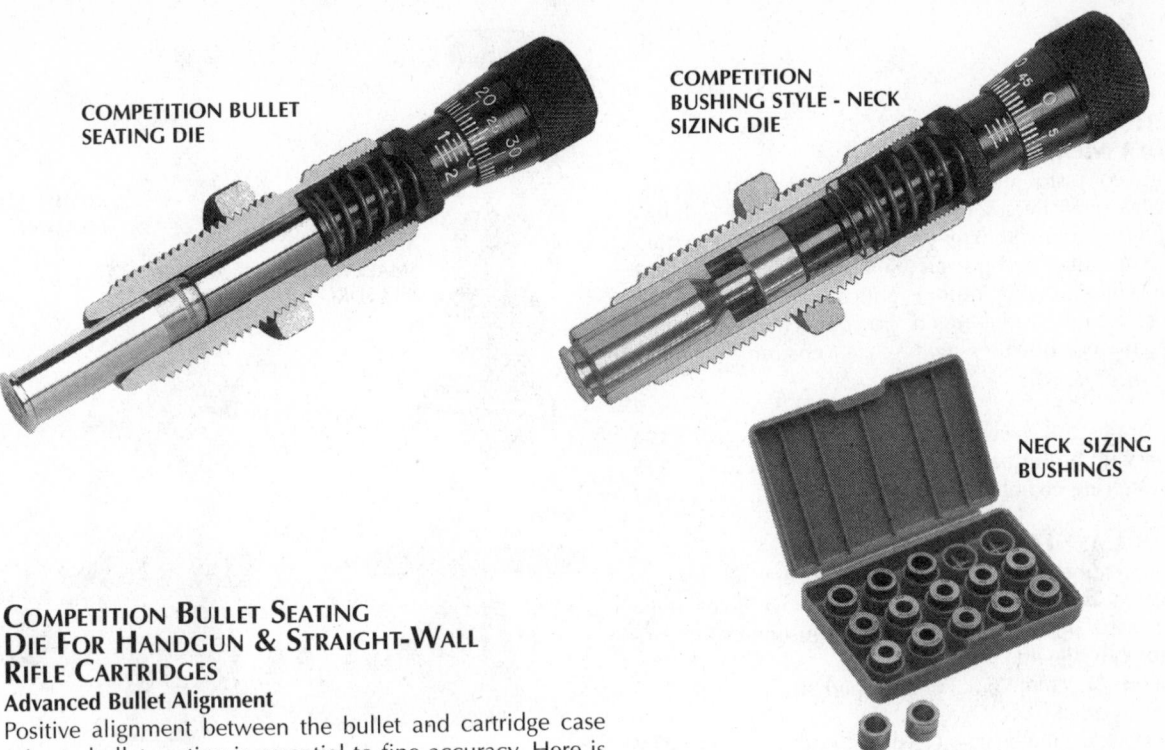

**COMPETITION BULLET SEATING DIE**

**COMPETITION BUSHING STYLE - NECK SIZING DIE**

**NECK SIZING BUSHINGS**

## COMPETITION BULLET SEATING DIE FOR HANDGUN & STRAIGHT-WALL RIFLE CARTRIDGES

### Advanced Bullet Alignment

Positive alignment between the bullet and cartridge case prior to bullet seating is essential to fine accuracy. Here is how this die works:

The precision fitting seating stem is allowed to move well down into the chamber of the die to accomplish early bullet contact. The spring loading of the seating stem provides the positive alignment bias between its tapered nose and the bullet ogive. Thus spring loading and bullet alignment are maintained as the bullet and cartridge case move upward until the actual seating of the bullet begins.

### Micrometer Adjustment

The micrometer adjustment simplifies setting and recording bullet seating depth. By recording the micrometer setting of reloads one can return to that same overall length by simply "dialing it in." The micrometer is calibrated in .001" increments, is infinitely adjustable and has a "zero" set feature that allows setting desired load to zero if desired.

### Separate Crimp

Competition shooters generally prefer bullet crimping as a separate operation from bullet seating. A superior crimp will be acomplished by using a Redding "Profile Crimp" or "Taper Crimp" die.

### Progressive Press Compatible

The Competition Seating Die for straight-wall cartridges has been made compatible with all popular progressive reloading presses. The industry standard ⅞ x 14 threaded die bodies have been slightly extended to allow full thread engagement of the lock ring. An oversize bell-mouth chamfer with smooth radius has been added to the bottom of the die to ease case and bullet entry in progressive presses.

**Price:.......................................$84**

## COMPETITION BUSHING STYLE - NECK SIZING DIE

This die allows you to fit the neck of your case perfectly in the chamber. As in the Competition Seating Die, the cartridge case is completely supported and aligned with the sizing bushing and remains supported in the sliding sleeve as it moves upward while the resizing bushing self-centers on the case neck.

The micrometer adjustment of the bushing position delivers precise control to the desired neck length. All dies are supplied without bushings.

**Category I** . . . . . . . . . . . . . . . . . . . . . . . . . . . . . . **$111**
**Category II.** . . . . . . . . . . . . . . . . . . . . . . . . . . . . . 135
**Category III** . . . . . . . . . . . . . . . . . . . . . . . . . . . . . 165

## REDDING NECK SIZING BUSHINGS

Redding Neck Sizing Bushings are available in two styles. Both share the same external dimensions (1/2" O.D. x 3/8" long) and freely interchange in all Redding Bushing style Neck Sizing Dies.

They are available in .001" size increments throughout the range of .185" thru .365", covering all calibers from .17 to .338.

By selecting the correct bushing, the right amount of neck tension is provided to properly hold the bullet.

**Part No. 73185 thru 73365.** . . . . . . . . . . . . . . . . . . . **$14**
Heat treated steel. The sizing diameters are hand-polished with a surface hardness of Rc 60-62 to reduce sizing effort.

**Part No. 76185 thru 76365** . . . . . . . . . . . . . . . . . . . . 25
Heat treated steel as above but with the addition of a Titanium Nitride surface treatment to further increase the effective surface hardness and reduce sizing friction.

**HANDLOADING**

# Redding Reloading Tools

## MATCH-GRADE POWDER MEASURE MODEL 3BR

Universal- or pistol-metering chambers interchange in seconds. Measures charges 100 grains. Unit is fitted with lock ring for fast dump with large "clear" plastic reservoir. "See-thru" drop tube accepts all calibers from 22 to 600. Precision-fitted rotating drum is critically honed to prevent powder escape. Knife-edged powder chamber shears coarse-grained powders with ease, ensuring accurate charges.

**Prices:**

Match Grade 3BR measure . . . . . . . . . . . . . . . . . . $174
3BR Kit, with both Chambers . . . . . . . . . . . . . . . . 215
Pistol Metering chamber (0-10 grains). . . . . . . . . . . 52

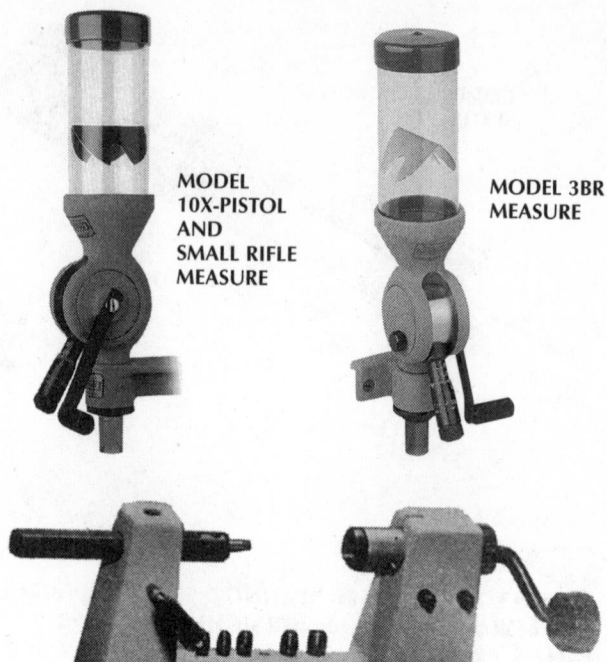

MODEL 10X-PISTOL AND SMALL RIFLE MEASURE

MODEL 3BR MEASURE

## MASTER CASE TRIMMER MODEL 1400

This unit features a universal collet that accepts all rifle and pistol cases. The frame is cast iron with storage holes in the base for extra pilots. Coarse and fine adjustments are provided for case length.

- Six pilots (22, 6mm, 25, 270, 7mm and 30 cal.)
- Universal collet
- Two neck cleaning brushes (22 thru 30 cal.)
- Two primer pocket cleaners (large and small)
- Tin coated replaceable cutter
- Accessory power screwdriver adaptor

**Prices:**

No. 1400 Master Case Trimmer complete . . . . . . . . $99
No. 1500 Pilots . . . . . . . . . . . . . . . . . . . . . . . . . . . 5

**MODEL 1400 TRIMMER**

## COMPETITION MODEL BR-30 POWDER MEASURE (NOT SHOWN)

This powder measure features a drum and micrometer that limit the overall charging range from a low of 10 grains to a maximum of 50 grains. The diameter of Model 3BR's metering cavity has been reduced, and the metering plunger has a unique hemispherical shape, creating a powder cavity that resembles the bottom of a test tube. The result: irregular powder settling is alleviated and charge-to-charge uniformity is enhanced.

**Price:**

Competition Model BR-30 Powder Measure . . . . . . $208

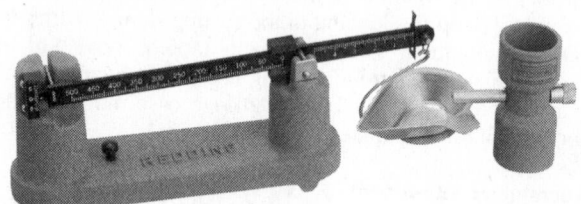

**MODEL NO. 2SCALE**

## MODEL NO. 2 MASTER POWDER AND BULLET SCALE

- 505-grain capacity
- dampened beam
- 1/10-grain accuracy
- hardened knife edges and milled stainless bearing seats for smooth, consistent operation and a high level of durability

## COMPETITION MODEL 10X-PISTOL AND SMALL RIFLE POWDER MEASURE

This powder measure uses all of the special features of Competition Model BR-30, combined with new drum and metering unit designed to provide the most uniform meter-ing of small charge weights. To achieve the best metering possible at the targeted charge weight of approximately 10 grains, the diameter of the metering cavity is reduced and the metering plunger is given a unique hemispherical shape. Charge range: 1 to 25 grains.

To provide increased versatility, the 10X-Pistol Powder Measure has a drum assembly that can be easily changed from right to left-handed operation. In addition to offering left-handed reloaders increased ease of operation, this feature adapts the 10X-Pistol Powder Measure to progressive reloading presses.

**No. 03400 COMPETITION MODEL 10X-PISTOL**

Price: Powder Measure. . . . . . . . . . . . . . . . . . . . . . $208

# Redding Reloading Accessories

### "INSTANT INDICATOR" HEADSPACE AND BULLET COMPARATOR

The Instant Indicator checks the head-space from the case shoulder to the base. Bullet seating depths can be compared and bullets can be sorted by checking the base of bullet to give dimension. Case length can be measured. Available for 33 cartridges from .222 Rem to .338 Win. Mag., including new WSSM cartridges.

Price: w/Dial Indicator . . . . . . . . . . . . . . . . . . . . . . $124
     w/o Dial Indicator . . . . . . . . . . . . . . . . . . . . . . . 94

### "EZ FEED" SHELLHOLDERS

Redding shellholders are of a Universal "snap-in" design recommended for use with all Redding dies and presses, as well as all other popular brands. They are pre-cision mach-ined to very close tolerances and heat treated to fit cases and eliminate potential resizing problems. The outside knurling makes them easier to handle and change.

Price: . . . . . . . . . . . . . . . . . . . . . . . . . . . . . . . . . $9

### FORM & TRIM DIES

Redding trim dies file trim cases without unnecessary resizing because they are-made to chamber dimensions. For case forming and necking brass down from another caliber, Redding trim dies can be the perfect intermediate step before full length resizing.

Prices:
Series A . . . . . . . . . . . . . . . . . . . . . . . . . . . . . . . $29
Series B . . . . . . . . . . . . . . . . . . . . . . . . . . . . . . . . 40
Series C . . . . . . . . . . . . . . . . . . . . . . . . . . . . . . . . 47
Series D . . . . . . . . . . . . . . . . . . . . . . . . . . . . . . . . 55

### NECK SIZING DIES

These dies size only the necks of bottle-neck cases to prolong brass life and improve accuracy. These dies size only the neck and not the shoulder or body, fired cases should not be interchanged between rifles of the same caliber. Available indi-vidually or in Deluxe Die Sets.

Prices:
Series A . . . . . . . . . . . . . . . . . . . . . . . . . . . . . . . $34
Series B . . . . . . . . . . . . . . . . . . . . . . . . . . . . . . . . 46
Series C . . . . . . . . . . . . . . . . . . . . . . . . . . . . . . . . 57
Series D . . . . . . . . . . . . . . . . . . . . . . . . . . . . . . . . 64

### PISTOL TRIM DIES

Redding trim dies for pistol calibers allow trimming cases without excessive resizing. Pistol trim dies require extended shell-holders.

Series A . . . . . . . . . . . . . . . . . . . . . . . . . . . . . . . $29
Series B . . . . . . . . . . . . . . . . . . . . . . . . . . . . . . . . 40
Series C . . . . . . . . . . . . . . . . . . . . . . . . . . . . . . . . 47
Series D . . . . . . . . . . . . . . . . . . . . . . . . . . . . . . . . 55

### PROFILE CRIMP DIES

For handgun cartridges which do not head-space on the case mouth. These dies were designed for those who want the best possi-ble crimp. Profile crimp dies provide a tighter, more uniform roll type crimp, and require the bullet to be seated to the correct depth in a previous operation.

Series A . . . . . . . . . . . . . . . . . . . . . . . . . . . . . . . $28
Series B . . . . . . . . . . . . . . . . . . . . . . . . . . . . . . . . 34
Series C . . . . . . . . . . . . . . . . . . . . . . . . . . . . . . . . 38
Series D . . . . . . . . . . . . . . . . . . . . . . . . . . . . . . . . 43

### CARBIDE SIZE BUTTON KITS

Make inside neck sizing smoother and easier without lubrication. Now die sets can be upgraded with a car-bide size button kit. Available for bottleneck cartridges 22 thru 338 cal. The carbide size button is free-floating on the decap rod, allowing it to self-center in the case neck. Kits contain: car-bide size button, retainer and spare decapping pin. These kits also fit all Type-S dies

Price: . . . . . . . . . . . . . . . . . . . . . . . . . . . . . . . . . $25

### EXTENDED SHELL HOLDERS

Extended shellholders are required when trimming short cases under 1½" O.A.L. They are machined to the same tolerances as standard shellholders except they're longer.

Price: . . . . . . . . . . . . . . . . . . . . . . . . . . . . . . . . . $15

### TAPER AND CRIMP DIES

Designed for handgun cartridges which headspace on the case mouth where con-ventional roll crimping is undesirable. Also available for some revolver cartridges, for those who prefer the uniformity of a taper crimp. Now available in the following rifle calibers: 223 Rem., 7.62MM x 39, 30-30, 308 Win, 30-06, 300, Win Mag

Prices:
Series A . . . . . . . . . . . . . . . . . . . . . . . . . . . . . . . $28
Series B . . . . . . . . . . . . . . . . . . . . . . . . . . . . . . . . 34
Series C . . . . . . . . . . . . . . . . . . . . . . . . . . . . . . . . 38
Series D . . . . . . . . . . . . . . . . . . . . . . . . . . . . . . . . 43

HANDLOADING

# Directory of Manufacturers & Suppliers

The following manufacturers, suppliers and distributors of firearms, reloading equipment, sights, scopes, ammo and accessories all appear with their products in the "Specifications" and/or "Manufacturers' Showcase" sections of this edition of Shooter's Bible.

ACCURATE ARMS CO., INC.
(gunpowder, reloading)
5891 Hwy. 230 W
McEwen TN 37101
Tel: 931-729-4207; 800-416-3006
Fax: 931-729-4211
Web Site: www.accuratepowder.com

AIMPOINT INC.
(sights, scopes, mounts)
3989 HWY 62 West
Berryville AR 72616
Tel: 870-423-3398 Fax: 870-423-2960
Web Site: www.aimpoint.com
E-mail: info@aimpoint.com

ALLIANT POWDER
(gunpowder)
Route 114, P.O. Box 6 Bldg. 229
Radford VA 24143-0096
Tel: 540-639-7805; 800-276-9337
Fax: 540-639-8496
E-mail: peter_jackson@atk.com
Web site: www.alliantpowder.com

AMERICAN DERRINGER CORP.
(handguns)
127 North Lacy Drive
Waco TX 76705
Tel: 817-799-9111 Fax: 817-799-7935
Web site: www.amderringer.com

AMERICAN HUNTING RIFLES, INC.
(AHR rifles)
P.O. Box 300
Hamilton MT 59840
Tel: 406-961-1410
Web site: www.hunting-rifles.com

A.G. ANSCHUTZ GmbH
(rifles, pistols)
Web site: www.anschutz-sporters.com
Available through Tristar Sporting Arms

ARMSCO
(shotguns)
1247 Rand Road
Des Plaines IL 60016
Tel: 847-768-1000
Fax: 847-768-1001
Website: www.armsco.net

AUSTIN & HALLECK
2150 South 950 East
Provo UT 84606-6285
Tel: 801-371-0412
Fax: 801-374-9998
Website: www.austinhalleck.com

AUTO-ORDNANCE CORP.
Available through Kahr Arms

AXTELL RIFLE CO.
The Riflesmith
353 Mill Creek Rd.
Sheridan MT 59749
Tel: 406-842-5814
Website: www.riflesmith.com

AYA
(shotguns)
Available through New England
Custom Gun Service

LES BAER CUSTOM, INC.
29601 34th St.
Hillsdale IL 61257
Tel: 309-658-2716 Fax: 309-658-2610

BANSNER'S ULTIMATE RIFLES L.L.C.
Mark Bansner (custom guns)
P.O. Box 839
261 East Main St.
Adamstown PA 19501
Tel: 717-484-2370 Fax: 717-484-0523
Website: www.bansnersrifle.com

BATTENFELD TECHNOLOGIES, INC.
(reloading equipment)
5875 West Van Horn Tavern Rd.
Columbia MO 65203

BARNES BULLETS
P.O. Box 215
750 N. 2600 W.
Lindon UT 84042
Tel: 385-756-4222; 800-574-9200
Fax: 385-756-2465
E-mail: email@barnesbullets.com
Website: www.barnesbullets.com

BARRETT FIREARMS MFG.
P.O. Box 1077
Murfreesboro TN 37133-1077
Tel: 615-896-2938 Fax: 615-896-7313
Website: www.barrettrifles.com

BATTENFIELD TECHNOLOGIES, INC.
(reloading equipment)
5885 West Van Horn Tavery Rd.
Columbia MO 65203
Tel:877-509-9160 Fax: 573-446-6606
Website: www.midwayusa.com

B.C. OUTDOORS
(Eldorado Cartridge Co.)
(PMC ammo, Docter scopes and
Verona shotguns)
PO Box 61497
Boulder City NV 89006
Tel: 702-294-3056 Fax: 702-294-0413
Website: ww.pmcammo.com

BENELLI U.S.A. CORP.
(shotguns)
17603 Indian Head Hwy, Suite 200
Accokeek MD 20607-2501
Tel: 301-283-6981 Fax: 301-283-6988
Website: www.benelliusa.com
E-mail benusa1@aol.com

BERETTA U.S.A. CORP.
(handguns, rifles, shotguns;
Sako,Tikka)
17601 Beretta Drive
Accokeek MD 20607
Tel: 301-283-2191 Fax: 301-283-0189
Website: www.berettausa.com
E-mail: cwilliams@berettausa.com

BERGER BULLETS, INC.
4275 N. Palm St.
Fullerton CA 92835
Tel: 714-447-5456 Fax: 714-447-5407
www.bergerbullets.com
Website: www.bergerbullets.com

BERNARDELLI
(handguns, shotguns)
Available through Armsport

BERSA
(handguns)
Available through Eagle Imports Inc.

ROGER BIESEN
(custom guns)
10323 N. Woodridge Dr.
Spokane WA 99208-8644
Tel: 509-328-9340

MANUFACTURERS

# Directory of Manufacturers & Suppliers

BLACK HILLS AMMUNITION
P.O. Box 3090
3050 Eglin
Rapid City SD 57709-3090
Tel: 605-348-5150 Fax: 605-348-9827
Website www.black-hills.com
E-mail: black-hills.com

BLACKPOWDER PRODUCTS, INC.
(CVA & Winchester Blackpowder)
5988 Peachtree Corners East
Norcross GA 30071
Tel: 770-449-4687 Fax: 770-242-8546
Website: www.bpiguns.com

BLASER USA, INC.
(rifles)   Available through Sig Arms

BONANZA
(reloading tools)
See Forster Products

BOND ARMS INC.
(handguns)
204 Alpha Lane
P.O. Box 1296
Granbury TX 76048
Tel: 817-573-4445 Fax: 817-573-5636

KENT BOWERLY
(custom guns)
710 Golden Pheasant Drive
Redmond OR 97756
Tel: 541-923-3501

BRENNEKE OF AMERICA LTD.
(ammunition)
P.O. Box 1481
Clinton IA 52733-1481
Tel.: 800-753-9733 Fax: 563-244 7421
Website: www.brennekeusa.com

ED BROWN PRODUCTS, INC.
(rifles, handguns)
P.O. Box 492
Perry MO 63462
Tel: 573-565-3261 Fax: 573-565-2791
Website: www.edbrown.com

BROWNING
(handguns, rifles, shotguns,
blackpowder guns)
One Browning Place
Morgan UT 84050
Tel: 801-876-2711 Fax: 801-876-3331
Website: www.browning.com

BROWN PRECISION, INC.
(custom rifles)
7786 Molinos Avenue
P.O. Box 270 W.
Los Molinos CA 96055
Tel: 530-384-2506 Fax: 530-384-1638

BSA OPTICS, INC.
3911 SW 47th Ave., Ste 914
Ft. Lauderdale FL 33314
Tel: 954-581-2144
Fax: 954-581-3165
Website: www.bsa.optic.com
E-mail: bsaoptic@bellsouth.net

BURRIS COMPANY, INC.
(scopes)
331 East Eighth Street
P.O. Box 1899
Greeley CO 806321-1899
Tel:  970-356-1670; 888-228-7747
Fax: 970-356-8702
Website: www.burrisoptics.com

BUSHNELL
(scopes, Tasco scopes)
Performance Optics
9200 Cody
Overland Park KS 66214
Tel: 913-752-3400 Fax: 913-752-3550
Website: www.bushnell.com

CABELA'S INC.
(blackpowder rifles)
One Cabella Drive
Sidney NE 69160
Tel: 308-254-5505 Fax: 308-254-6669

CCI/SPEER-BLOUNT, INC.
(ammunition, bullets)
2299 Snake River Ave., P.O. Box 856
Lewiston ID 83501
Tel: 208-746-2351 Fax: 208-746-3904
Website: www.cci-ammunition.com
www.speer-bullets.com

CHRISTENSEN ARMS
(rifles)
192 E. 100 N.
Fayette UT 84630
Tel: 801-528-7199
Website: www.christensenarms.com

DAVID CHRISTMAN, JR.
(custom gunmaker)
216 Rundell Loop Rd.
Delhi LA 71232
Tel: 318-878-1395

CIMARRON FIREARMS CO.
(revolvers, rifles)
Wedsite: www.cimarron-firearms.com
E-mail:cimarron@fbg.net

CLARK CUSTOM GUNS INC.
Jim Clark, Jr.
336 Shootout Lane
Princeton LA 71067
Tel: 888-458-4126
Website: www.clarkcustomguns.com

COLT BLACKPOWDER ARMS CO.
(handguns)
110 8th street
Brooklyn NY 11215
Tel: 718-499-4678 Fax: 718-768-8056

COLT'S MANUFACTURING CO., INC.
(handguns, rifles)
P.O. Box 1868
Hartford CT 06144-1868
Tel: 800-962-COLT
Fax: 860-244-1467
Website: www.colt.com

COMANCHE
Available through Eagle Imports

CONNECTICUT SHOTGUN
MFG. CO.
(A.H. Fox shotguns)
35 Woodland Street, P.O. Box 1692
New Britain CT 06051-1692
Tel: 860-225-6581 Fax: 860-832-8707

COOPER FIREARMS of Montana, Inc.
P.O. Box 114
Stevensville MT 59870
Tel: 406-777-5534
Website: www.cooperfirearms.com

COR-BON/Glaser
(reloading)
1311 Industry Rd.
P.O. Box 369
Sturgis SD 57785
Tel: 605-347-4544 Fax: 605-347-5055
Website: www.corbon.com

CVA
(blackpowder arms)
5988 Peachtree Corners East
Norcross GA 30071
Tel: 800-320-8767 Fax: 770-242-8546
Website: www.cva.com
E-mail: sales@cva.com

# Directory of Manufacturers & Suppliers

CZ-USA
(pistols, rifles)
P.O. Box 171073
Kansas City KS 66117-0073
Tel: 913-321-1811; 800-955-4486
Fax: 913-321-2251
Website: www.cz-usa.com
E-mail: cz-usa@qvl.net

DAKOTA ARMS
(rifles, shotguns)
1310 Industry Road
Sturgis SD 57785
Tel:605-347-4686
Fax: 605-347-4459; 508-302-4784
Website: www.dakotarms.com
E-mail: dakarms@sturgis.com

CHARLES DALY (pistols, shotguns)
Available through K.B.I., Inc.

DAYTONA
(shotguns)
Available through Renato Gamba
U.S.A.

DESERT EAGLE
(handguns)
Available through Magnum
Research Inc.

DGS, INC.
(Dale A. Storey custom guns)
1117 E. 12th Street
Casper WY 82601
Tel: 307-237-2414

DILLON PRECISION PRODUCTS,
INC. (reloading equipment)
8009 East Dillon's Way
Scottsdale AZ 85260-9865
Tel: 800-223-4570; 602-948-8009
Fax: 602-998-2786
Website: www.dillonprecision.com

DIXIE GUN WORKS
(blackpowder guns)
P.O. Box 130
Union City TN 38281
Tel: 800-238-6785
Fax: 901-885-0440
info: 901-885-0700
Website: www.dixiegun.com

DOCTER SCOPES
Available through B.C. Outdoors

DOWNSIZER CORPORATION
(handguns)
P.O. Box 710316
Santee CA 92072-0316
Tel: 619-448-5510 Fax: 619-448-5780
Website: www.downsizer.com

DYNAMIT NOBEL/RWS
(Rottweil shotguns and ammunition,
Steyr Mannlicher)
81 Ruckman Road
Closter NJ 07624
Tel: 201-767-1995
Fax: 201-767-1589

EAGLE IMPORTS, INC.
(Bersa, Comanche, Llama and
Firestorm handguns)
1750 Brielle Avenue, Unit B1
Wanamassa NJ 07712
Tel: 732-493-0302 Fax: 732-493-0301

D'ARCY ECHOLS
(custom rifles)
98 West 300 South, P.O. Box 421
Millville UT 84326
Tel: 435-755-6842

E.M.F. COMPANY, INC.
(Dakota handguns; Uberti
handguns,
blackpower arms, rifles)
1900 East Warner Avenue,
Suite 1-D
Santa Ana CA 92705
Tel: 714-261-6611 Fax: 714-756-0133
Website: www.emf-company.com

ENTRÉPRISE ARMS
(handguns)
15861 Busines Center Drive
Irwindale CA 91706-2062
Tel: 626-962-8712 Fax: 626-962-4692
Website: www.entreprise.com

ESCORT
(shotguns)
Available through Legacy Sports Intl.

EUROARMS OF AMERICA INC.
(blackpowder arms)
P.O. Box 3277
Winchester VA 22604
Tel: 540-662-1863

EUROPEAN AMERICAN
ARMORY CORP.
(E.A.A. handguns, rifles)

P.O. Box 1299
Sharpes FL 32959
Tel: 800-536-4442 Tel: 321-639-4842
Fax: 321-639-7006
Website: www.eaacorp.com

FABARMS
(shotguns)
Available through Heckler & Koch

FEDERAL CARTRIDGE CO.
(ammunition, ballistics)
900 Ehlen Drive
Anoka MN 55303-7503
Tel: 800-322-2342; 763-323-2300
Fax: 763-323-2506
Website: www.federalcartridge.com

KENT "BUZZ" FLETCHER
(custom gunmaker)
121 Sunset Dr.
Espanola NM 87532
Tel: 505-753-5434

FLODMAN GUNS SWEDEN
640 60 Akers styckebruk
Jarsta, Sweden
Tel: 46 159308 61 Fax: 46 159300 61
Website: www.flodman.com

FIRESTORM PISTOLS
Available through Eagle Imports

FIOCCHI OF AMERICA
(ammunition)
6930 Fremont Rd.
Ozark MO 65721
Tel: 800-721-AMMO; 417-725-4118
Fax: 417-725-1039
Website: www.fiocchiusa.com

FLINTLOCKS, ETC.
(Pedersoli replica rifles)
160 Rossiter Road, P.O. Box 181
Richmond MA 01254
Tel: 413-698-3822
Fax: 1-888-GUNCLIP
Website: www.GUNMAGS.com

FORSTER PRODUCTS
(reloading)
310 East Lanark Avenue
Lanark IL 61046
Tel: 815-493-6360 Fax: 815-493-2371
Website: forsterproducts.com
E-mail: infor@forsterproducts.com

# Directory of Manufacturers & Suppliers

A.H. FOX (shotguns)
Available through Connecticut
Shotgun Mfg. Co.

FRANCHI
(shotguns)
Available through Beretta

FREEDOM ARMS
(handguns)
314 Hyw. 239, P.O. Box 150
Freedom WY 83120-0150
Tel: 307-883-2468 Fax: 307-883-2005
Website: www.freedomarms.com
E-mail: freedom@freedomarms.com

GIBBS RIFLE COMPANY
211 Lawn Street
Martinsburg WV 25401
Tel: 304-262-1651 Fax: 304-262-1658
E-mail: support@gibbsrifle.com

GLOCK, INC.
(pistols)
6000 Highland Parkway
Smyrna GA 30082
Tel: 770-432-1202 Fax: 770-433-8719

GONIC ARMS
134 Flagg Rd.
Gonic NH 03839

GARY GOUDY
(custom gunmaker)
1512 S. 5th St.
Dayton WA 99328
Tel: 509-382-2726

CHARLES GRACE
(custom gunmaker)
1006 Western Avenue
Trinidad CO 81081
Tel: 719-846-9435

GSI (GUN SOUTH INC.)
(Mauser rifles; Merkel shotguns)
7661 Commerce Lane, P.O. Box 129
Trussville AL 35173
Tel: 800-821-3021; 205-655-8299
Fax: 205-655-7078
Website: www.gsifirearms.com
E-mail: infor@gsifirearms.com

H&R 1871 INC.
Available through New England
Firearms
Website: www.hr1871.com

H-S PRECISION
(rifles, pistols)
1301 Turbine Drive
Rapid City SD 57703
Tel: 605-341-3006 Fax: 605-342-8964
Website: www.hsprecision.com

HAMMERLI U.S.A.
(handguns)
19296 Oak Grove Circle
Groveland CA 95321
Tel: 209-962-5311 Fax: 209-962-5931

HECKLER & KOCH
(handguns, rifles; and Fabarms
shotguns)
21480 Pacific Blvd.
Sterling VA 20166
Tel: 703-450-1900
Fax: 703-450-8160
Website: www.hecklerkoch-usa.com

HENRY REPEATING ARMS CO.
(rifles)
110 8th Street
Brooklyn NY 11215
Tel: 718-499-5600 Fax: 718-768-8056
Website: www.henryrepeatingcom

DARWIN HENSLEY
(custom rifles)
63133 E. Barlow Trail Rd.
Brightwood OR 97011
Tel: 503-622-5411

HERITAGE MANUFACTURING
(handguns)
4600 NW 135 St.
Opa Locka FL 33054
Tel: 305-685-5966
Fax: 305-687-6721
Website: www.heritagemfg.com

HI-POINT FIREARMS
(handguns)
MKS Supply, Inc.
8611-A North Dixie Drive
Dayton OH 45414
Tel/Fax: 877-425-48671
Website: www.hi-pointfirearms.com

HIGH STANDARD MFG. CO., INC.
5200 Mitchelldale Suite E-17
Houston TX 77092
Tel: 800-272-7816; 713-462-4200
Fax: 713-681-5665

HILL COUNTRY RIFLE CO.
5726 Morningside Dr.
New Braunfels TX 78132
Tel: 830-609-3139
Website: www.hillcountryrifle.com

BOB HISSERICH
(custom gunmaker)
StockWorks Rifles
1843 S. Los Alamos
Mesa AZ 85204
Tel: 480-545-2994
Fax: 480-507-7560
Website: www.stockworks.net

HODGDON POWDER CO., INC.
(gunpowder, IMR)
6231 Robinson, P.O. Box 2932
Shawnee Mission KS 66201
Tel: 913-362-9455
Fax: 913-362-1307
Website: www.hodgdon.com
E-mail: info@hodgdon.com

PATRICK HOLEHAN
(custom rifles)
5758 E. 34th St.
Tucson AZ 85711
Tel: 520-745-0622
E-mail: plholehan@juno.com

HORNADY MFG. CO.
(ammunition, reloading)
P.O. Box 1848; 3625 Old Potash Hwy.
Grand Island NE 68803
Tel: 308-382-1390 Fax: 308-382-5761
Website: www.hornady.com

HOWA
(rifles)
Available through Legacy Sports Intl.

STEVEN DODD HUGHES
(custom rifles)
P.O. Box 545
Livingston MT 59047
Tel: 406-222-9377

IMR POWDER CO. INC.
See Hodgdon Powder
Website: www.imrpowder.com

ITHACA GUN CO.
(shotguns)
901 Route 34-B
Kings Ferry NY 13081
Tel: 315-364-7171 Fax: 315-364-5134
Website: www.ithacagun.com

MANUFACTURERS

# Directory of Manufacturers & Suppliers

JARRETT RIFLES INC.
(custom rifles)
383 Brown Road
Jackson SC 29831
Tel: 803-471-3616 Fax: 803-471-9246
Website: www.jarrettrifles.com

JOHANNSEN EXPRESS RIFLE
(available through New England
Custom Guns)

KAHLES
(scopes)
2 Slater Rd.
Cranston RI 02920
Tel: 800-426-3089 Fax: 401-734-5888
Website: www.kahlesoptik.com

KAHR ARMS
(handguns, Auto-Ordnance)
630 Route 303, POB 220
Blauvelt NY 10913
Tel: 508-795-3919 Fax: 508-795-7046
Website: www.kahr.com

KAPS OPTICS
Karl Kaps Gmbh
Europastrasse
35614 Asslar/Wetzlar
Germany
Tel: 49-6441-80704
Fax: 49-6441-85985

K.B.I., INC.
(rifles, handguns, shotguns; Charles
Daly rifles, shotguns; FEG handguns)
P.O. box 6625
Harrisburg PA 17112-0625
Tel: 717-540-8518 Fax: 717-540-8567
Website: www.kbi-inc.com or
www.charlesdaly.com
E-mail: sales @kbi-inc.com

KEL-TEC CNC IND INC.
(handguns)
P.O. Box 236009
Cocoa FL 32926
Tel: 321-631-0068 Fax: 231-631-1169
Website: www.kel-tec.com
E-mail: aimkeltec@aol.com

KIMBER MANUFACTURING, INC.
(handguns, rifles)
1 Lawton Street
Yonkers NY 10705
Tel: 914-964-0771; 888-243-4522
E-mail: info@kimberamerica.com

KNIGHT RIFLES
(blackpowder rifles)
P.O. Box 130, 21852 Hwy. J46
Centerville IA 52544-0130
Tel: 515-856-2626 Fax: 515-856-2628
Website: www.knightrifles.com
E-mail: knightrifles@lisco.net

KRIEGHOFF INTERNATIONAL INC.
(rifles, shotguns)
337A Route 611, P.O. Box 549
Ottsville PA 18942
Tel: 610-847-5173 Fax: 610-847-8691

KYNOCH AMMUNITION
Kynamco Limited -
The Old Railway Station
Mildenhall, IP28 7DT England
Tel: +44 (0) 1638 711999
Fax: +44 (0) 1638 515251

LAPUA
(ammunition)
Available through Vihtavuori
Website: www.lapua.com

L.A.R. MANUFACTURING, INC.
(Grizzly rifles)
4133 West Farm Rd.
West Jordan UT 84088-4997
Tel: 801-280-3505
Fax: 801-280-1972
Website: www.largrizzly.com
E-mail: guns@largrizzly.com

LASERAIM TECHNOLOGIES INC.
(sights)
721 Main St., P.O. Box 3548
Little Rock AR 72203-3548
Tel: 501-375-2227 Fax: 501-372-1445

LAZZERONI ARMS CO.
1415 South Cherry Ave.
Tucson AZ 85713
Tel: 888-4-WAR-BIRD
Fax: 520-624-4250
Website: www.lazzeroni.com

LEGACY SPORTS INTL.
(Howa & Mauser rifles,
Escort shotguns)
206 S. Union St.
Alexandria VA 22314
Tel: 703-548-4837 Fax: 703-549-7826
Website: www.legacysports.com

LENARTZ MUZZLOADING
(blackpowder guns)
8001 Whitneyville Rd.

Alto MI 49302
LEUPOLD & STEVENS, INC.
(scopes, mounts)
14400 N.W. Greenbriar Parkway,
P.O. Box 688
Beaverton OR 97075
Tel: 503-646-9171 Fax: 503-526-1475
Website: www.leupold.com

LLAMA
(handguns)
Available through Eagle Imports

LONE STAR RIFLE CO., INC.
11231 Rose Road
Conroe TX 77303
Tel: 409-856-3363
Website: www.lonstarrifle.com

LYMAN PRODUCTS CORP.
(blackpowder guns, reloading tools)
475 Smith Street
Middletown CT 06457
Tel: 800-225-9626; 860-632-2020
Fax: 860-632-1699
Website: ww.lymanproducts.com
E-mail: lymansales@cshore.com

MAGNUM RESEARCH INC.
(handguns, rifles, Desert Eagle)
7110 University Avenue N.E.
Minneapolis MN 55432
Tel: 612-574-1868 Fax: 612-574-0109
Website: www.magnumresearch.com

MAGTECH AMMUNITION CO.INC
6845 20th Ave. South
Suite 120
Centerville MN 55038
Tel: 800-466-7191 Fax: 651-429-9485

MARKESBERY MUZZLELOADERS,
INC. (blackpowder guns)
7785 Foundation Drive, Suite 6
Florence KY 41042
Tel: 606-342-5553 Fax: 606-342-2380
Website: www.markesbery.com

MARLIN FIREARMS COMPANY
(rifles, shotguns, blackpowder)
100 Kenna Drive, P.O. Box 248
North Haven CT 06473
Tel: 203-239-5621 Fax: 203-234-7991
Website: www.marlinfirearms.com

MAROCCHI
(Conquista shotguns)
Available through Precision Sales Int'l.

# Directory of Manufacturers & Suppliers

MEC INC.
(reloading tools)
c/o Mayville Engineering Co.
715 South Street
Mayville WI 53050
Tel: 800-797-4MEC; 920-387-4500
Fax: 920-387-5802
Website: www.mecreloaders.com
E-mail: reloaders@mayvl.com

MERKEL
(shotguns, rifles)
Available through GSI
(Gun South Inc.)
Website: www.gsifirearms.com

DAVID MILLER
(custom rifles)
3131 E. Greenlee Rd.
Tucson AZ 85716

M.O.A. CORP.
(handguns)
2451 Old Camden Pike
Eaton OH 45302
Tel: 937-456-3669 Fax: 937-456-9331
Website: moaguns.com

O.F. MOSSBERG & SONS, INC.
(shotguns, rifles)
7 Grasso Avenue, P.O. Box 497
North Haven CT 06473
Tel: 203-230-5300 Fax: 203-230-5420
Website: www.mossberg.com

MTM MOLDED PRODUCTS
(cases, reloading accessories)
P.O. Box 13117
Dayton OH 45413
Tel: 937-890-7461 Fax: 937-890-1747
Website: www.mtmcase-gard.com

NAVY ARMS COMPANY, INC.
(handguns, rifles,
blackpowder guns)
219 Lawn St.
Martinsburg WV 25401
Tel: 800-669-6289 Fax: 304-262-1658
Website: www.navyarms.com

NELSON'S CUSTOM GUNS, INC.
Stephen Nelson
7430 NW Valley View Dr.
Corvallis OR 97330
Tel: 541-745-5232

NEW ENGLAND ARMS CORP./FAIR
TECHNI MEC
6 Lawrence Lane,
P.O. Box 278
Kittery Point ME 03905
Tel: 207-439-0593 Fax: 207-439-6726

NEW ENGLAND CUSTOM GUN LTD.
(AYA shotguns and Schmidt-Bender
Scopes)
438 Willow Brook Rd.
Plainfield NH 03781
Tel: 603-469-3450  Fax 603-469-3471

NEW ENGLAND FIREARMS CO. INC.
(handguns, rifles, shotguns,
H&R 1871)
60 Industrial Rowe
Gardner MA 01440
Tel: 978-632-9393
Fax: 978-632-2300

NEW ULTRA LIGHT ARMS, LLC
1024 Grafton Road
Morgantown WV 26508
Tel: 304-292-0600 Fax: 304-292-9662
E-mail: newultralightarm@cs.com

NIKON INC.
(scopes)
1300 Walt Whitman Road
Melville NY 11747-3064
Tel: 631-547-4200
Fax: 631-547-4040
Website: www.nikonusa.com

DAVE NORIN
(custom gunmaker)
2010 Washington St.
Waukegan IL 60085
Tel: 847-662-4034

NORTH AMERICAN ARMS
(handguns)
2150 South 950 East
Provo UT 84606-6285
Tel: 800-821-5783; 801-374-9990
Fax: 801-374-9998
Website: www.naaminis.com

NOSLER BULLETS, INC.
(bullets)
P.O. Box 671, 107 SW Columbia
Bend OR 97709
Tel: 541-382-3921 Fax: 541-388-4667
Website: www.nosler.com

OLIN/WINCHESTER
(ammunition, primers, cases)
427 No. Shamrock St.
East Alton IL 62024-1174
Tel: 618-258-3692 Fax: 618-258-3609
Website: www.winchester.com

PARA-ORDNANCE MFG, INC.
(handguns)
PO Box 1
Oakhurst CA 93644
Tel: 559-683-3060Fax: 559-683-3061
Website: www.paraord.com
E-mail: info@paraord.com

PEDERSOLI, DAVIDE
(replica arms)
Available through Flintlocks Etc.
Website: www.davide-pedersoli.com

PENTAX
(scopes)
P.O. Box 6509 (80155)
35 Inverness Drive East
Englewood CO 80112
Tel: 303-799-8000 Fax: 303-790-1131
Website: www.pentax.com

PERAZZI U.S.A.
1010 W. 10th St.
Azusa CA 91702
Tel: 626-334-1234 Fax: 626-334-0344
PerazziUSA@aol.com

PMC CARTRIDGES
Available through B.C. Outdoors
Website: www.pmcammo.com

PRAIRIE GUN WORKS
(rifles)
1-761 Marion St.
Winnipeg, Manitoba,
Canada R2J0K6
Tel: 204-231-2976 Fax: 204-231-8566
Website: www.prairiegunworks.com

PRECISION SALES INTERNATIONAL
(Marocchi shotguns)
P.O. Box 1776
Westfield MA 01086
Tel: 413-562-5055 Fax: 413-562-5056
Website: www.precision-sales.com

RAMSHOT PROPELLANT
(gunpowder)
Available through Western Powders

# Directory of Manufacturers & Suppliers

RCBS
(reloading equipment)
605 Oro Dam Blvd.
Oroville CA 95965
Tel: 916-533-5191 Fax: 916-533-1647
Website: www.rcbs.com

REDDING RELOADING EQUIPMENT
(reloading tools)
1089 Starr Road
Cortland NY 13045
Tel: 607-753-3331 Fax: 607-756-8445
Website: www.redding-reloading.com
E-mail:
techline@redding-reloading.com

REDFIELD
Available through Simmons
(scopes)
P.O. Box 38
Onalaska WI 54650
Tel: 608-781-5800 Fax: 608-781-0368
Website: www.redfieldoptics.com

REMINGTON ARMS COMPANY, INC.
(rifles, shotguns, blackpowder arms,
ammunition)
870 Remington Drive, P.O. Box 700
Madison NC 27025-0700
Tel: 800-243-9700 Fax: 336-548-7741
Website: www.remington.com

RENATO GAMBA U.S.A. INC.
(Daytona shotguns)
375 Park Ave.
New York NY 10152
Tel: 212-618-1391
RIFLES, INC.
3580 Leal Rd.
Pleasanton TX 78064
Tel: 830-569-2055 Fax: 830-569-2297

RAY RIGANIAN
(custom gunmaker)
324 N. Central Ave., Unit B
Glendale CA 91203
Tel: 818-502-2678

RIZZINI
(shotguns)
Available through Traditions Firearms
Website: www.rizzini.it

ROGUE RIFLE CO.
1140 36th St. North, Suite B
Lewiston ID 83501
Tel: 208-743-4355 Fax: 208-743-4163
Website: www.roguerifle.com

ROSSI FIREARMS
(handguns, rifles, shotguns)
BrazTech Intl.
16175 NW 49th Ave.
Miami FL 33014
Tel: 305-624-1115 Fax: 305-623-7506
Website: www.rossiusa.com

ROTTWEIL BRENNEKE
(see Brenneke)

RUGER
(handguns, rifles, shotguns,
blackpowder guns)
See Sturm, Ruger & Co., Inc.

RWS
Available through
Dynamit Nobel

SAFARI ARMS
(handguns)
c/o Olympic Arms, Inc.
624 Old Pacific Hwy SE
Olympia WA 98513
Tel: 360-459-7940, 800-228-3471
Fax: 360-491-3447
Website: www.olyarms.com

SAKO
(rifles, actions, scope mounts, ammo)
Available through
Beretta U.S.A. Corp.

SAUER
(rifles)
c/o Paul Company, Inc.
27385 Pressonville Road
Wellsville KS 66092
Tel: 913-883-4444 Fax: 913-883-1515

SAVAGE ARMS
(handguns, rifles, shotguns)
Savage Arms, Inc.
100 Springdale Road
Westfield MA 01085
Tel: 413-568-7001
Fax: 413-562-7764
Website: www.savagearms.com

SCHMIDT AND BENDER INC.
(scopes)
Schmidt & Bender U.S.A.
P.O. Box 134
Meriden NH 03770
Tel: 800-468-3450 Fax: 603-469-3471
Website: www.schmidt-bender.de

ANTHONY SCHUELKE
(custom guns)
1606 N. Baxter Ave.
Glencoe MN 55336
Tel: 320-864-3905

SHILOH RIFLE MANUFACTURING
(Blackpowder guns)
PO Box 279
Big Timber MT 59011
Tel: 406-932-4454 Fax: 406-932-5627
Website: www.Shilohrifle.com

SIERRA BULLETS
(bullets)
P.O. Box 818
1400 West Henry Steet
Sedalia MO 65301
Tel: 888-223-3006; 660-827-6300
Fax: 660-827-4999
Website: www.sierrabullets.com
E-mail: sierra@sierrabullets.com

SIGARMS INC.
(Sig-Sauer shotguns, handguns,
Blaser rifles)
18 Industrial Dr.
Exeter NH 03833
Tel: 603-772-2302 Fax: 603-772-1481
Website: www.sigarms.com

SIGHTRON, INC.
(scopes)
100 Jeffrey Way, Suite A
Youngville NC 27596
Tel: 919-562-3000 Fax: 919-556-0157
Website: www.sightron.com

GENE SIMILLION
(custom guns)
220 S. Wisconsin
Gunnison CO 81230
Tel: 970-641-1126

SIMMONS Outdoor corp.
(scopes, Weaver, Redfield)
201 Plantation Oak Drive
Thomasville GA 31792
Tel: 229-227-9053 Fax: 229-227-6454
Website: www.simmonsoptics.com

SISK RIFLES
(cusom rifles)
Charlie Sisk
400 County Road
Dayton TX 77535-3294
Tel: 936-258-4984

# Directory of Manufacturers & Suppliers

SKB SHOTGUNS
(shotguns)
4325 S. 120th Street
Omaha NE 68137-1253
Tel: 800-752-2767 Fax: 402-330-8040
Website: www.skbshotguns.com
E-mail: SKB@radiks.net

SMITH & WESSON
(handguns)
2100 Roosevelt Avenue, P.O. Box 2208
Springfield MA 01102-2208
Tel: 413-781-8300; 800-331-0852
Fax: 413-747-3317
Website: www.smith-wesson.com

SPEER
(bullets)
Available through CCI/Speer-Blount, Inc.

SPRINGFIELD INC.
(handguns, rifles, Aimpoint scopes, & sights)
420 West Main Street
Geneseo IL 61254
Tel: 800-680-6866; 309-944-5631
Fax: 309-944-3676
Website: www.springfield-armory.com

STEVENS
(a Savage Arms Co.)
118 Mountain Rd.
Suffield CT 06078

STEYR-MANNLICHER
(rifles)
Available through Dynamit/Nobel
Website: www.dnrws.com

STOEGER INDUSTRIES
(shotguns)
17603 Indian Head Hwy., Suite 200
Accokeek MD 20607
Tel: 301-283-6300 Fax: 301-283-6586
email: jtroiani@stoegerindustries.com
DALE STOREY
(custom gunmaker) (See DGS, Inc.)

MARK STRATTON
(custom gunmaker)
Mukilteo WA 98037
Tel: 425-745-8309
Website: www.gunmaker.net
E-mail: octbarrel@aol.com

STURM, RUGER AND COMPANY, INC.
(Ruger handguns, rifles, shotguns, blackpowder, revolvers)
200 Ruger Road
Prescott AZ 86301
Tel: 203-259-7843 Fax: 203-256-3367
Website: www.ruger-firearms.com

SWAROVSKI OPTIK NORTH AMERICA
(scopes)
2 Slater Road
Cranston RI 02920
Tel: 800-426-3089; 401-734-1800
Fax: 401-734-5888; 877-287-8517
Website: www.swarovskioptik.com

SWIFT BULLET CO.
(bullets)
201 Main Street
P.O. Box 27
Quinter KS 67752
Tel: 785-754-3959 Fax: 785-754-2359

SWIFT INSTRUMENTS, INC.
(scopes, mounts)
952 Dorchester Avenue
Boston MA 02125
Tel: 800-446-1116 Fax: 617-436-3232
Website: www.swift-optics.com

SZECSEI & FUCHS
(custom rifles)
450 Charles Street
Windsor, Ontario N8X 371 Canada
Tel: 001 519 966 1234

TASCO WORLDWIDE, INC.
See Bushnell
(scopes, mounts)
Website: www.tasco.com

TAURUS INT'L, INC.
(handguns)
16175 N.W. 49th Avenue
Miami FL 33014-6314
Tel: 800-327-3776; 305-624-1115
Fax: 305-623-7506
Website: www.taurususa.com

TAYLOR'S & CO. INC.
(rifles, carbines)
304 Lenoir Drive
Winchester VA 22603
Tel: 540-722-2017 Fax: 540-722-2018
Website: ww.taylorsfirearms.com
E-mail: info@taylorsfirearms.com

THOMPSON & CAMPBELL
(custom rifles)
Cromarty – The Black Isle
Ross-Shire IV11 8YB Scotland
Tel: +44 (0) 1381 600 536
Fax: +44 (0) 1381 600 767

THOMPSON/CENTER ARMS
(handguns, rifles, reloading, blackpowder arms)
Farmington Road, P.O. Box 5002
Rochester NH 03867
Tel: 603-332-2394 Fax: 603-332-5133
Website: www.tcarms.com

TIKKA
(rifles, shotguns))
Available through Beretta U.S.A.

TRADITIONS PERFORMANCE-FIREARMS
(blackpowder arms, Rizzini Shotguns)
1375 Boston Post Road
P.O. Box 776
Old Saybrook CT 06475-0776
Tel: 860-388-4656 Fax: 860-388-4657
Website: www.traditionfirearms.com
E-mail: info@traditionsfirearms.com

TRIJICON
(rifle scopes)
49385 Shafer Ave. P.O. Box 930059
Wixom MI 48393
Tel: 248-960-7700; 800-338-0563
Fax: 248-960-7725
Website: www.trijikon-inc.com

TRISTAR SPORTING ARMS, LTD.
1814-16 Linn St.
North Kansas City MO 64116
Tel: 816-421-1400
Fax: 816-421-4182
Website: www.tristarsportingarms.com

UBERTI USA, INC.
(handguns, rifles, blackpowder guns)
Stoeger Industries
17603 Indian Head Hwy, Suite 200
Accokeek MD 20607
Tel: 301-283-6300

U.S. REPEATING ARMS CO.
(Winchester rifles, shotguns)
275 Winchester Ave.
Morgan UT 84050-9326
Tel: 801-876-3440 Fax: 801-876-3737
Website: www.winchesterguns.com

# Directory of Manufacturers & Suppliers

VERONA SHOTGUNS
Available through B.C. Outdoors

VIHTAVUORI
(powder and Lapua ammunition)
1241 Ellis St.
Bensenville IL 60106
Tel: 630-350-1116 Fax: 630-350-1606

VIRGIN VALLEY GUNS
(custom guns)
Steve Stratton
2410 West 350 North
Hurricane UT 84737

WALTHER U.S.A.
(handguns)
2100 Roosevelt Ave.
Springfield MA 01104
Tel: 800-372-6454 Fax: 413-747-3592
Website: www.walther-usa.com

WEATHERBY, INC.
(rifles, shotguns, ammunition)
3100 El Camino Real
Atascadero CA 93422
Tel: 800-227-2016; 805-466-1767
Fax: 805-466-2527
Website: www.weatherby.com

WEAVER
(scopes)
Available through
Simmons
Website: www.weaveroptics.com

WESTERN POWDER
(Ramshot ppowder)
P.O. Box 158
Miles City MT 59301
Tel: 406-232-0422 Fax: 406-232-0430
Website: www.westernpowders.com

WHITE RIFLES
(blackpowder)
P.O. Box 1044
Orem UT 84059-1044
Tel: 877-684-4867
Fax: 801-932-7959
Website: www.whiterifles.com

WILDEY F.A. INC.
(handguns)
45 Angevine Road
Warren CT 06754
Tel: 860-355-9000 Fax: 860-354-7759
Website: www.wildeyguns.com

WILD WEST GUNS, INC.
(Summit rifles)
7521 Old Seward Hwy., Unit A
Anchorage AK 99518
Tel: 800-992-4570 Fax: 907-344-4005
Website: www.wildwestguns.com
E-mail: wwguns@ak.net

WILLIAMS GUN SIGHT CO.
7389 Lapeer Road
P.O. Box 329
Davison MI 48423
Tel: 800-530-9028; 810-653-2131
Fax: 810-658-2140
Website: www.williamsgunsight.com

WINCHESTER
(ammunition, primers,
cases, ballistics)
Available through Olin/Winchester
Website: www.winchester.com

WINCHESTER FIREARMS
(rifles, shotguns)
Available through U.S. Repeating
Arms Co.
Website: www.winchester-guns.com

WINCHESTER MUZZLELOADING
Available through Blackpowder Prods.

WOODLEIGH BULLETS
Huntingtons
POB 991
601 Oro Dam Blvd.
Oroville CA 95965
Fax: 530-534-1212

XS SIGHT SYSTEMS
2401 Ludelle St.
Forth Worth TX 76105
Tel: 817-536-0136; 888-744-4880
Fax: 817-536-3517
Website: www.xssights.com

CARL ZEISS OPTICAL, INC.
13017 N. Kingston Ave.
Chester VA 23836
Tel: 804-530-8300
Fax: 804-530-8325

Z-HAT CUSTOM DIES
(reloading)
4010A S. Poplar, Suite 72
Casper WY 82601
Tel: 307-577-7443
Website: www.z-hat.com
E-mail: RifleBuilder@z-hat.com

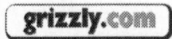
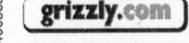
MANUFACTURER'S SHOWCASE

# Manufacturer's Showcase

**MANUFACTURER'S
SHOWCASE**

# Gunfinder Index

To help you find the model of your choice, the following index includes every firearm found in the Shooter's Bible 2004, listed by type of gun.

## RIFLES

### Centerfire Bolt Action

**BLASER**
| | |
|---|---|
| Model R93 | 176 |
| Model R93 | |
|    Long Range Sporter 2 | 176 |
| Model R93 | |
|    Long Range Tactical | 176 |

**BROWN PRECISION**
| | |
|---|---|
| High Country | 177 |
| High Country Youth | 177 |
| Pro Hunter | 178 |
| Pro Varminter | 178 |
| Tactical Elite | 178 |

**BROWNING**
| | |
|---|---|
| A-Bolt Hunter | 180 |
| A-Bolt Medallion | 180 |
| A-Bolt Hunter Magnum | 180 |
| A-Bolt Stalker | 180 |

**CHRISTENSEN ARMS**
| | |
|---|---|
| Carbon One Custom | 182 |
| Carbon One Hunter | 182 |
| Carbon Ranger | 182 |
| Carbon Tactical | 182 |

**COOPER ARMS**
| | |
|---|---|
| Custom Classic | 186 |
| Montana Varminter | 186 |
| Varminter | 186 |
| Varminter Extreme | 186 |
| Western Classic | 186 |

**CZ**
| | |
|---|---|
| Model 527 Lux | 187 |
| Model 550 FS | 187 |
| Model 550 Lux | 188 |
| Model 550 Safari magnum | 188 |
| Model 550 Varmint | 188 |
| Model 700 Sniper M1 | 188 |

**DAKOTA ARMS**
| | |
|---|---|
| Model 76 African | 189 |
| Model 76 Classic | 189 |
| Model 76 Safari | 189 |
| Model 97 Hunter | 189 |
| Long Bow Tactical | 190 |
| Traveler Classic | 190 |
| Traveler Safari | 190 |
| Traveler African | 190 |

**ED BROWN**
| | |
|---|---|
| Bushveld | 192 |
| Denali | 192 |
| Model M40A2 Marine Sniper | 192 |
| Ozark | 192 |
| Savannah | 193 |
| Tactical | 193 |
| Varmint | 193 |

**GIBBS RIFLE COMPANY**
| | |
|---|---|
| Model 71/84 Mauser | 195 |
| Quest II Extreme Carbine | 195 |

**H-S PRECISION**
| | |
|---|---|
| Model PHR | |
|    (Professional Hunter Rifle) | 200 |
| Model SPR (Lightweight) | 200 |
| Take-Down Rifle | 200 |
| VAR (Varmint ) | 200 |

**JARRETT**
| | |
|---|---|
| .50 Caliber | 201 |
| Professional Hunter | 201 |
| Standard Hunting Rifle | 201 |
| Walk About | 201 |
| Wind Walker | 201 |

**JOHANNSEN EXPRESS RIFLES**
| | |
|---|---|
| Classic Safari | 202 |
| Safari | 202 |
| Tradition | 202 |

**KBI/CHARLES DALY**
| | |
|---|---|
| Field Grade Mauser | 203 |
| Superior grade | 203 |
| Superior magnum | 203 |
| Superior safari | 203 |

**KIMBER**
| | |
|---|---|
| Model 84M Classic | |
| Model 84M | |
|    Long Master Classic | 204 |
| Model 84M Long Master VT | 204 |
| Model 84M Long Master Pro | 204 |
| Model 84M Super America | 204 |
| Model 84M Varmint | 204 |
| Classic | 205 |
| Classic Hunter | 205 |
| Classic Super America | 205 |
| HS (Hunter Silhouette) | 205 |
| SVT (Short Varmint Target) | 205 |

**L.A.R**
| | |
|---|---|
| Grizzly Big Bore | 206 |

**LAZZERONI**
| | |
|---|---|
| Model L2000DG | 207 |
| Model L2000SA | 207 |
| Model L2000SP | 207 |
| Model L2000ST | 207 |

**LEGACY SPORTS**
| | |
|---|---|
| Howa Model 1500 Lightning | 208 |
| Howa Model 1500 Hunter | 208 |
| Howa Model 1500 Varmint | 208 |
| Howa Model 1500 Ultralight | 208 |
| Mauser M98 Rifle | 208 |

**MAGNUM RESEARCH**
| | |
|---|---|
| Mountain Eagle | 209 |
| Mountain Eagle | |
|    Varmint Model | 209 |
| Tactical Rifle | 209 |

**NEW ULTRA LIGHT ARMS**
| | |
|---|---|
| Model 20 Mountain Rifle | 219 |
| Model 24 | 219 |

**PRAIRIE GUN WORKS**
| | |
|---|---|
| Model 15Ti Ultra Light | 221 |
| Model 18Ti Ultra Light | 221 |

**REMINGTON ARMS**
| | |
|---|---|
| Model 40-XB Target Rifle | 223 |
| Model 700 ADL | 224 |
| Model 700 African | 224 |
| Model 700 African | |
|    Plains Rifle | 225 |
| Model 700 Classic | 225 |
| Model 700 DBL | 225 |
| Model 700 Etronix | 227 |
| Model 700 KS Mountain Rifle | 225 |
| Model 700 Mountain | |
|    Rifle DM | 225 |
| Model 700 Sendero SF | 226 |
| Model 700 Titanium | 226 |
| Model 700 VS | 226 |
| Model 710 | 226 |
| Model Seven AWR | 228 |
| Model Seven LS | 228 |
| Model Seven Magnum | 228 |

**RIFLES INC.**
| | |
|---|---|
| Classic | 229 |
| Lightweight Strata Stainless | 229 |
| Master Series | 229 |
| Safari Model | 229 |

**RUGER**
| | |
|---|---|
| Model 77R Mark II | 233 |
| Model 77RL Mark II | |
|    Ultra Light | 233 |
| Model 77 RFP Mark II | 231 |
| Model 77 RSM | 232 |
| Model 77 VT Mark II | 232 |
| Model 77/22 RH Hornet | 232 |
| Model 77/44RS | 233 |

**SAKO**
| | |
|---|---|
| Model 75 Deluxe | 235 |
| Model 75 Finnlight | 235 |
| Model 75 Hunter | 235 |
| Model 75 Varmint | 236 |
| Model TRG-22 | 236 |
| Model TRGS M995 | 236 |

**SAUER**
| | |
|---|---|
| Model 202 | 237 |
| Model 202 Lightweight | 237 |
| Model 202 Varmint | 237 |
| Model 202 SSG 3000 Tactical | 237 |

**SAVAGE**
| | |
|---|---|
| Model 10FM Sierra | 238 |
| Model 11F | 239 |
| Model 12FV (Short Action) | 238 |
| Model 112 FVSS | |
|    (Long-Action) | 238 |

# Gunfinder Index

GUNFINDER INDEX

# Gunfinder Index

GUNFINDER INDEX

# Gunfinder Index

# Gunfinder Index